AutoCAD® 2009 in 3D

A Modern Perspective

Frank E. Puerta

Upper Saddle River, New Jersey
Columbus, Ohio

Library of Congress Control Number: 2007943931

Editor in Chief: Vernon Anthony
Acquisitions Editor: Jill Jones-Renger
Editorial Assistant: Doug Greive
Production Coordination: Karen Fortgang, bookworks publishing services
Project Manager: Louise Sette
AV Project Manager: Janet Portisch
Operations Supervisor: Deidra Schwartz
Art Director: Diane Ernsberger
Cover Designer: Jason Moore
Cover Image: Super Stock
Director of Marketing: David Gesell
Senior Marketing Coordinator: Alicia Dysert
Copyeditor: Marianne L'Abbate

This book was set in Times New Roman by Aptara, Inc. and was printed and bound by Bind-Rite Graphics. The cover was printed by Coral Graphic Services.

Disclaimer:
This publication is designed to provide tutorial information about AutoCAD® and/or other Autodesk computer programs. Every effort has been made to make this publication complete and as accurate as possible. The reader is expressly cautioned to use any and all precautions necessary, and to take appropriate steps to avoid hazards, when engaging in the activities described herein. Neither the author nor the publisher makes any representations or warranties of any kind, with respect to the materials set forth in this publication, express or implied, including without limitation any warranties of fitness for a particular purpose or merchantability. Nor shall the author or the publisher be liable for any special, consequential or exemplary damages resulting, in whole or in part, directly or indirectly, from the reader's use of, or reliance upon, this material or subsequent revisions of this material.

Pearson Education Ltd., London
Pearson Education Singapore Pte. Ltd.
Pearson Education Canada, Inc.
Pearson Education—Japan
Pearson Education Australia Pty. Limited
Pearson Education North Asia Ltd., Hong Kong
Pearson Educación de Mexico, S.A. de C.V.
Pearson Education Malaysia Pte. Ltd.

10 9 8 7 6 5 4 3 2 1
ISBN-13: 978-0-13-813540-9
ISBN-10: 0-13-813540-1

To my two sons, Frank and Daniel,
who inspire me every day

The New Autodesk Design Institute Press Series

Pearson/Prentice Hall has formed an alliance with Autodesk® to develop textbooks and other course materials that address the skills, methodology, and learning pedagogy for the industries that are supported by the Autodesk® Design Institute (ADI) software products. The Autodesk Design Institute is a comprehensive software program that assists educators in teaching technological design.

Features of the Autodesk Design Institute Press Series

JOB SKILLS—Coverage of computer-aided drafting job skills, compiled through research of industry associations, job websites, college course descriptions, and The Occupational Information Network database, has been integrated throughout the ADI Press books.

PROFESSIONAL AND INDUSTRY ASSOCIATION INVOLVEMENT—These books are written in consultation with and reviewed by professional associations to ensure that they meet the needs of industry employers.

AUTODESK LEARNING LICENSES AVAILABLE—Many students ask how they can get a copy of the AutoCAD® software for their home computer. Through a recent agreement with Autodesk®, Prentice Hall now offers the option of purchasing textbooks with either a 180-day or a 1-year student software license agreement for AutoCAD. This provides adequate time for a student to complete all the activities in the book. The software is functionally identical to the professional license, but is intended for student personal use only. It is not for professional use.

Learning licenses may only be purchased by ordering a special textbook package ISBN. Instructors should contact their local Pearson Professional and Career sales representative. For the name and number of your sales representative, please contact Pearson Faculty Services at 1-800-526-0485.

FEATURES OF *AUTOCAD®* *2009 IN 3D*

AutoCAD 2009 in 3D: A Modern Perspective represents a complete reference and practice guide to 3D modeling. Based on a modern approach, this text utilizes the modeling drawing capabilities of AutoCAD to allow the reader to master the creation and modification of 3D models. The numerous practice sections found in this text provide a unique source of tips and ideas that will demonstrate how to use the knowledge acquired in many practical ways.

The design and development of this textbook include the special features discussed below. They have been carefully created to provide the reader with a fresh, enhanced look at the material and facilitate the reader's understanding of the content effectively.

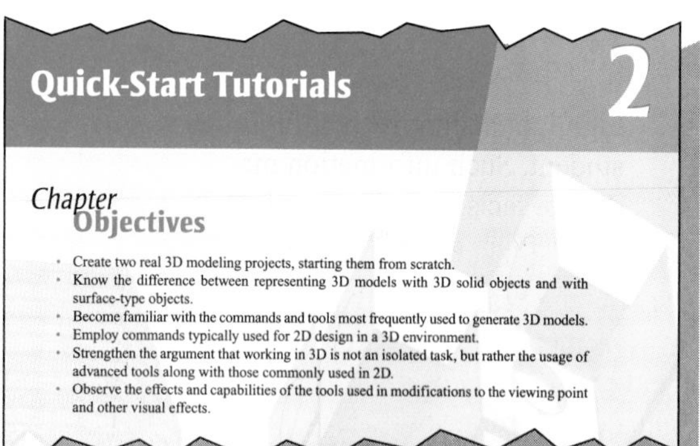

Quick-Start Tutorials 2

Chapter Objectives

- Create two real 3D modeling projects, starting them from scratch.
- Know the difference between representing 3D models with 3D solid objects and with surface-type objects.
- Become familiar with the commands and tools most frequently used to generate 3D models.
- Employ commands typically used for 2D design in a 3D environment.
- Strengthen the argument that working in 3D is not an isolated task, but rather the usage of advanced tools along with those commonly used in 2D.
- Observe the effects and capabilities of the tools used in modifications to the viewing point and other visual effects.

Because users need lots of practice, a **Quick-Start Tutorials** chapter (provided right after the introductory chapter) challenges the user to create two 3D models prior to learning the theory behind the operations used. These tutorials are designed with special step-by-step instructions that will walk the reader through the entire development process while raising interest in mastering the content to come in the rest of the chapters.

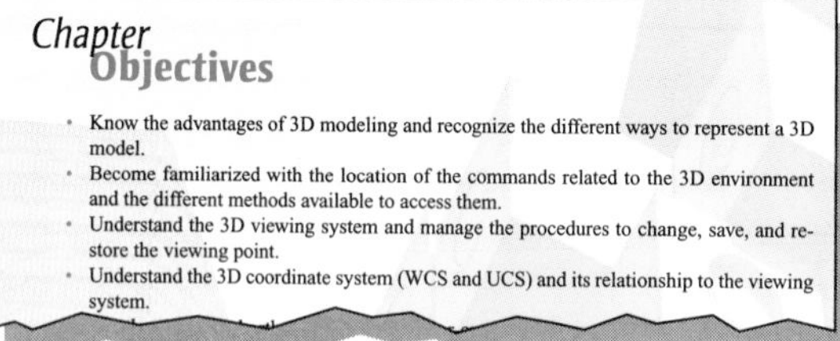

Chapter Objectives

- Know the advantages of 3D modeling and recognize the different ways to represent a 3D model.
- Become familiarized with the location of the commands related to the 3D environment and the different methods available to access them.
- Understand the 3D viewing system and manage the procedures to change, save, and restore the viewing point.
- Understand the 3D coordinate system (WCS and UCS) and its relationship to the viewing system.

Chapter objectives appear at the beginning of each chapter, providing users with a roadmap to the elements, concepts, and practices to be introduced.

copy you must define a mirror plane.

imaginary axis of rotation: An imaginary vector defined by specifying two points, or a direction vector and a point, about which the objects are rotated.

rotate grip tool: Editing tool that enables you to choose among three directions of rotation that are aligned with the axes of the current UCS.

The 3DROTATE Command

This command allows you to rotate the selected object about an ***imagin***… is parallel to one of the three axes of the current UCS (*X*, *Y*, and *Z*). The … nary axis of rotation is parallel is defined by picking one of the axis ha… ***tool***. The display switches to the **3D Wireframe** visual style while this c… the current visual style is **2D Wireframe** (Figure 3-2).

The first appearance of each ***key term*** is bold and italic within the running text and accompanied by a brief definition in the margin. The glossary at the end of the book contains a complete list of the key terms and a more detailed definition to help students understand and use the language of the computer-aided drafting (CAD) world.

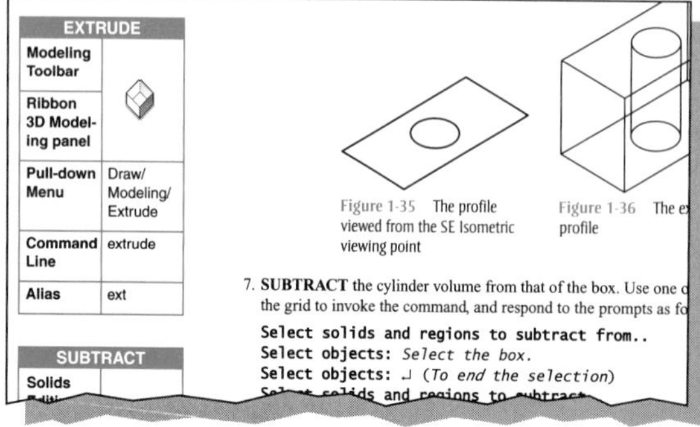

EXTRUDE	
Modeling Toolbar	
Ribbon 3D Modeling panel	
Pull-down Menu	Draw/ Modeling/ Extrude
Command Line	extrude
Alias	ext

SUBTRACT	
Solids	

Figure 1-35 The profile viewed from the SE Isometric viewing point

Figure 1-36 The e… profile

7. **SUBTRACT** the cylinder volume from that of the box. Use one … the grid to invoke the command, and respond to the prompts as f…

```
Select solids and regions to subtract from..
Select objects: Select the box.
Select objects: ↵ (To end the selection)
```

Command grids appear in the margin alongside the discussion of the command or the particular exercise in which it is demonstrated. These grids provide specific information about the ways of invoking each command, including any of the following:

- Toolbar icon
- Control panel of the **Ribbon**
- Pull-down menu
- Command line
- Command alias

6. Repeat the process for the next 3D face. Its edge should be aligned with the corresponding edge of the 3D face that was previously placed.

Project 4-3: Community Recreational Hall

Architectural prototypes are easily achieved by using surface objects. One of the key elements is to try to keep the design as simple as possible. You can use any type of object to represent each surface according to its shape. You should keep in mind, however, that the simpler the objects, the smaller your file will be. Why use a polygon mesh or a 3D face to represent a rectangular face when a polyline with a certain thickness or a region would work as well?

In this project you will use the knowledge that you have acquired in this chapter. Here only basic information will be given, along with some hints. The recreational hall you will develop does not have to be exactly like the one shown in Figure 4-117. You can be as creative as you want.

Discipline icons appear in the margin alongside each exercise, tutorial, and project. These icons identify the discipline to which the practice section applies, allowing instructors to quickly select discipline-specific assignments for in-class and homework activities that will appeal to the interests of their students. This allows students to work on projects that have the most relevance to their course of study and to get practical tips on how the commands and tools can be used in a particular application.

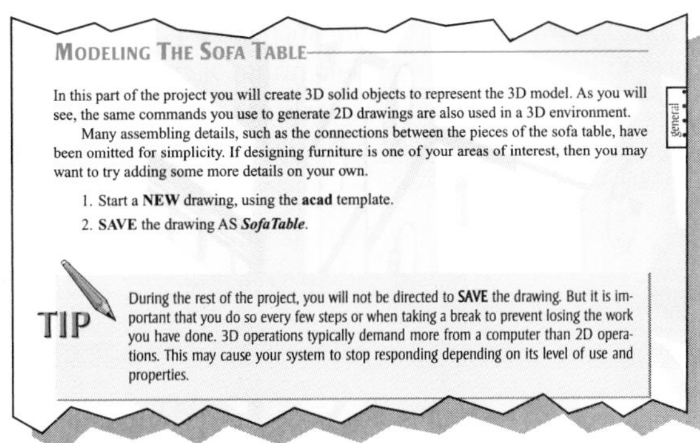

MODELING THE SOFA TABLE

In this part of the project you will create 3D solid objects to represent the 3D model. As you will see, the same commands you use to generate 2D drawings are also used in a 3D environment.

Many assembling details, such as the connections between the pieces of the sofa table, have been omitted for simplicity. If designing furniture is one of your areas of interest, then you may want to try adding some more details on your own.

1. Start a **NEW** drawing, using the **acad** template.
2. **SAVE** the drawing AS ***SofaTable***.

TIP During the rest of the project, you will not be directed to **SAVE** the drawing. But it is important that you do so every few steps or when taking a break to prevent losing the work you have done. 3D operations typically demand more from a computer than 2D operations. This may cause your system to stop responding depending on its level of use and properties.

Tip, Notes, and For More Details boxes highlight additional helpful information for the student. Such information may contain dos and don'ts, facts, warnings, and alternative ways of proceeding, as well as cross-references to other chapters and topics.

between them. This prevents the screen from filling up with toolbars and windows t necessary for a particular task.

The AutoCAD program comes with three predefined workspaces: **3D Modeling, Classic,** and **2D Drafting & Annotation.** To switch between these workspaces, you c drop-down lists located in the **Workspaces** toolbars, the **Tools** drop-do **(Tools/Workspaces),** or the Workspace icon located at the right end of the status bar (F

You can create a new workspace or modify an existing one. The easiest way to cr workspace is by selecting **Save Current As. . .** from the drop-down list in the **Worksp** bars after arranging the toolbars and dockable windows. You can overwrite a workspa ply reselecting it in the **Save Workspace** dialog box (Figure 1-7).

New to AutoCAD 2009 icons indicate the commands and tools that are new to the program. This feature allows instructors and other users to quickly identify topics that are completely new, saving them a good amount of research time. It also demonstrates to students the recent improvements to the AutoCAD software, as well as the valuable updated information contained in this textbook.

The different operations used to create faceted surfaces, in particular the **EDGESURF** comma portant tools in the development of complex shapes. The flexibility of polygon meshes and th transformations can be helpful in achieving complex designs. Understanding these tools is be the design process because they can assist users in the development of complex 3D models engineering documentation.

Job Skills boxes provide information on how specific book content relates to particular job skills needed in the workplace.

SUMMARY

Throughout this chapter you have learned the different operations used to develop 3D models that are represented by faceted surfaces and other similar objects. You have also been introduced to the considerations involved in determining whether surface modeling is the appropriate method to use. By following the tutorials, you should realize how important it is to develop the necessary curves throughout the 3D space prior to creating faceted surfaces.

You have studied in depth the different operations used to generate polygon meshes. These are the most important and complex objects used in this t 3D objects.

Other types of objects such as r and thickened 2D objects have als chapter. Because of their characterist for use with polygon meshes in achi covering all the surfaces of the 3D m be shaded and that can hide other obj

You have also learned that by p tions with regions, you can easily obtai

CHAPTER TEST QUESTIONS

The End-of-Chapter material can easily be located by the shading on the page edges. This material will help students evaluate and practice the knowledge they've acquired about the most important concepts explained in the chapter. This material's content includes:

- Summary
- Chapter Test Questions
- Chapter Tutorials
- Chapter Projects

Exercise 4-3: Creating an Apex Pyramid Using the 3D Command

1. Start a **NEW** drawing using the **acad** template.
2. **SAVE** the drawing **AS** ***Exercise 4-3.***
3. Select the **SE Isometric** viewing point.
4. Invoke the **Pyramid** option of the **3D** command. Respond to the prompts as follows:

```
Specify first corner point for base of pyramid: 0,0 ↵
Specify second corner point for base of pyramid: 3,0 ↵
Specify third corner point for base of pyramid: 3,4 ↵
Specify fourth corner point for base of pyramid or [Tetrahedron]:
0,4 ↵
Specify apex point of pyramid or [Ridge/Top]: 1.5,3,4 ↵
```

5. Invoke the **HIDE** command. The 3D model should look like Figure 4-13.
6. Practice creating other types of pyramids and tetrahedrons.
7. **SAVE** the drawing.

Many **Exercises** are contained within the chapters. They provide step-by-step walk-through activities for the student, allowing immediate practice to reinforce the content previously discussed.

Tutorial 8-3: A 3D Exploded View of the Bench Vise

1. **OPEN** the ***Bench-Vise*** drawing file as it was finished in Chapter 7.
2. **SAVE** the drawing **AS** ***Tutorial 8-3***.
3. Select the **Isometric SE** viewing point.
4. Select the **Front** UCS.
5. With ORTHO mode on, **MOVE** the following nine components **3.5″** along the positive *X*-axis (Figure 8-154).
   - the two *Guides*
   - the *Moving Jaw*
   - the *Aluminum Block* located on the *Moving Jaw*
   - the two *Screws* located on the *Moving Jaw*

Chapter Tutorials are activities for the students that appear at the end of each chapter (with the exception of Chapters 2 and 7). Longer than exercises, each step-by-step tutorial walks the student through the completion of a particular discipline-specific project, reinforcing the understanding of the chapter's content from a practical viewpoint.

CHAPTER PROJECTS

Project 8-1: Isometric Drawing of a Valve with Dimensions in the 3D Space

OPEN the drawing ***Tutorial 5-4*** that you developed in Chapter 5 and **SAVE** it **AS** ***Project 8-1***. With the **FLATSHOT** command, obtain the top, front, and side orthographic views. Use a section object to generate the 3D section shown in Figure 8-165.

Chapter Projects are additional assignments located at the end of each chapter in which students are directed to solve particular discipline-specific tasks on their own. To do so, the students will use the knowledge acquired throughout the chapter as well as previous chapters.

Exercise 8-3: Placing Dimensions in the 3D Space and Setting up the Page in Paper Space

1. **OPEN** the file ***Exercise 8-3*** you saved in **Exercise 8-1** by creating a 3D section also open this file from the CD in case you did not complete the exercise.
2. **SAVE** the drawing **AS** ***Exercise 8-3 solved***.
3. Select the **SE Isometric** viewing point.
4. Open the **Visual Styles Manager** palette. Select the **2D Wireframe** visual style ing on its sample image and make the following changes (Figure 8-65):
   - Set **Contour lines** to **0**
   - Set **Draw true silhouettes** to **Yes**
   - Set **Solid smoothness** to **8**
5. Close the **Visual Styles Manager** palette and invoke the **REGEN** command.

CD icons appear in the margin alongside exercises, tutorials, and projects whenever students are directed to open a file from the CD included with the textbook.

Instructor Resources

The Online Instructor's Manual provides answers to unit exercises and tests and solutions to end-of-chapter problems; drawing files to get learners started; and lecture-supporting PowerPoint® slides.

To access supplementary materials online, instructors need to request an instructor access code. Go to **www.pearsonhighered.com/irc,** where you can register for an instructor access code. Within 48 hours after registering, you will receive a confirming e-mail, including an instructor access code. Once you have received your code, go to the site and log on for full instructions on downloading the materials you wish to use.

Instructor Resource Center

Register today at www.prenhall.com to access instructor resources digitally.

Student Resources

Companion Website—This text is accompanied by a Companion Website at **www.prenhall.com/puerta,** which includes an interactive study guide.

Preface

We live in a 3D world, where the trend in technology is to duplicate reality as much as possible. As time goes on, more and more processes require the input of a 3D CAD file. AutoCAD has long been, and will remain, the most popular CAD software; its 3D capabilities are more than sufficient to generate excellent 3D work.

AutoCAD® 2009 in 3D: A Modern Perspective offers a complete guide for students and professionals who want to enter the interesting world of 3D modeling using AutoCAD. This book covers all aspects related to the AutoCAD program's 3D work, from the basic concepts to the most powerful tools used in design and engineering.

In this book, readers will find an interesting combination of theory and many complex projects and exercises, as well as many clear and descriptive illustrations. Real design problems starting from scratch will be solved throughout the projects. In addition, many other short exercise sections are included to ensure full comprehension of the commands.

Concepts are explained clearly in simple language and are accompanied by descriptive illustrations, an approach that helps the reader understand each topic and speeds up the learning process. By following the project's steps, readers will immediately see results and will understand the development process as they go along, rather than simply entering instructions at the command line.

After reading this book, the reader will realize that the AutoCAD software was made for much more than simply generating 2D drawings. Actually, it will be a better idea to leave this task to the AutoCAD program itself.

About This Book

This book can serve as a reference for designers, draftspersons, or anyone with a basic knowledge of the AutoCAD program to learn about the most advanced techniques of the program. Through this book users will be able to enter the interesting world of 3D modeling. The projects as well as the exercise sections are designed to enhance and help the reader retain the content learned in each chapter.

It is not necessary to be an expert in traditional 2D usage to understand the book's content; however, explaining the use of the AutoCAD software from the beginning is not the purpose of this book, so you should know the basic commands used for 2D drafting prior to reading this text. Concepts such as paper space and tracking methods, however, as well as commands related to 3D work, such as **SPLINE, FILLET,** and **CHAMFER,** are explained herein. This text will give you the basic tools and theory you need to start creating some objects in 3D. Its main purpose is to make you understand that 3D modeling is, above all else, the combination of the way you look at the objects and the way the working plane is set.

Besides learning the basic tools, you will also learn to recognize and use these tools to achieve specific goals. Each chapter of the book contains a specific project that walks you through the process of building or using a complex model. Brief definitions of the commands involved, as well as notes containing tips and warnings, will give you extra help in understanding the commands.

Chapter Organization

The book is written to stimulate the reader, making the journey into 3D as smooth as possible. ***Chapter 1: Introduction to 3D in the AutoCAD® Program*** introduces the theory needed to begin your journey into the 3D modeling world, equipping you with a solid background. Here you will be given the most important tools for success, such as controlling the point from where you look at the 3D model, managing the User Coordinate System (UCS), and many more.

Chapter 2: Quick-Start Tutorials challenges you to create two different 3D models by following step-by-step instructions, without going through the theory behind it beforehand. The commands introduced in this chapter will be further discussed in subsequent chapters. This chapter has been intentionally designed to stimulate your interest in 3D modeling with AutoCAD, walking you through the entire process of creating 3D objects that are common to you.

Even though the modeling techniques used in the AutoCAD program have much in common, this chapter treats the three methods separately for better organization as well as understanding. In everyday real usage, different disciplines tend to use one of these methods specifically.

Chapter 3: Wireframe Modeling describes the curves used in the AutoCAD program, including the most complex ones (splines and spline-fit polylines), as well as other wireframe-type objects. You will also learn the importance of using such objects for 3D work and how to control them properly.

Chapter 4: Creating and Modifying Faceted Surfaces allows you to discover and practice specific tools used to create and modify meshes or faceted surfaces. You will also learn how to use these tools on other objects that are suitable for this particular method of representing 3D models.

Faceted surfaces are the oldest type of 3D object used in the AutoCAD program. In fact, no tools are available that make this particular type of object interact with any other object. The use of faceted surfaces in the AutoCAD program persists, however, due to their very specific uses.

Chapter 5: Creating 3D Solids and Surfaces introduces you to the two most important objects in the creation of 3D models: surfaces and 3D solids. In this chapter you will learn aspects of the AutoCAD software that are particularly related to the creation of these two types of objects.

An AutoCAD file or drawing file (DWG) can contain any kind of object. You can actually create a 3D model that is a combination of meshes, 3D solids, and surfaces. The AutoCAD program, however, provides specific tools that allow 3D solids and surfaces to interact, so studying these two objects separately will deepen your understanding of them.

Surfaces and 3D solids are the most useful objects in the development of 3D models. In fact, short courses could use only this chapter along with specific material selected from Chapter 1. Such content will provide you with the knowledge needed to start generating 3D models and to understand the construction process.

Unlike with faceted surfaces or meshes, a wide set of tools allows you to edit surfaces and 3D solids after they have been created. All these tools, as well as their practical uses, are presented in ***Chapter 6: Editing 3D Solids and Surfaces***.

Chapter 7: Advanced Tutorials walks you from scratch through the complete design process of a bench vise. This 3D project allows you to review and put into practice most of the knowledge you have acquired in Chapters 5 and 6.

Chapter 8: Generating Drawings and DWF Files instructs you on some of the advantages of creating 3D models. Here you will learn different procedures to generate drawings and other documents from existing 3D models and to create DWF files. This knowledge will allow you to generate high-quality technical documentation.

Chapter 9: Rendering and Other Presentations demonstrates more of the many advantages of generating 3D models. This chapter provides you with sufficient knowledge to generate artistic presentations from your 3D models. Here you will learn how to control the effect of light, shadows, and materials on 3D objects, and use these objects to generate rendered images and animations.

Acknowledgments

We want to thank the following individuals, whose contributions helped to shape the final text:

Joel Robert Brodeur
Montana State University—Northern

George Gibson
Athens Technical College

Dimitrios Karamanlidis
University of Rhode Island

Mohd Fairuz Shiratuddin
The University of Southern Mississippi

John Smith
Southwestern College

Style Conventions in AutoCAD® 2009 in 3D: A Modern Perspective

Text Element	Example
Key terms—Bold and italic on first mention (first letter lowercase) in the body of the text. Brief glossary definition in margin following first mention.	Views are created by placing ***viewport*** objects in the paper space layout.
AutoCAD commands—Bold and uppercase.	Start the **LINE** command.
Toolbar names, menu items and dialog box names—Bold and follow capitalization convention in AutoCAD toolbar or pull-down menu (generally first letter capitalized).	The **Layer Manager** dialog box The **File** pull-down menu
Toolbar buttons and dialog box controls/buttons/input items—Bold and follow capitalization convention of the name of the item or the name shown in the AutoCAD tooltip.	Choose the **Line** tool from the **Draw** toolbar. Choose the **Symbols and Arrows** tab in the **Modify Dimension Style** dialog box. Choose the **New Layer** button in the **Layer Properties Manager** dialog box. In the **Lines and Arrows** tab, set the **Arrow size:** to **.125.**
AutoCAD prompts—Dynamic input prompts are italic. Command window prompts use a different font (Courier New) and are boldface. This makes them look like the text in the command window. Prompts follow capitalization convention in AutoCAD prompt (generally first letter capitalized).	AutoCAD prompts you to *Specify first point:* **Specify center point for circle or [3P/2P/Ttr (tan_tan radius)]:**
Keyboard input—Bold with special keys in brackets.	Type **3.5 <Enter>.** In the **Lines and Arrows** tab, set the **Arrow size:** to **.125.**

Contents

Chapter 4 Creating and Modifying Faceted Surfaces

Chapter 5 Creating 3D Solids and Surfaces

Chapter 6 Editing 3D Solids and Surfaces

Chapter 7 Advanced Tutorials

Chapter 8 Generating Drawings and DWF Files

Chapter 9 Rendering and Other Presentations

Introduction to 3D in the AutoCAD® Program

1

Chapter Objectives

- Know the advantages of 3D modeling and recognize the different ways to represent a 3D model.
- Become familiarized with the location of the commands related to the 3D environment and the different methods available to access them.
- Understand the 3D viewing system and manage the procedures to change, save, and restore the viewing point.
- Understand the 3D coordinate system (WCS and UCS) and its relationship to the viewing system.
- Use the predefined orthogonal UCS and user-created UCS.
- Learn the different systems to express the 3D coordinates of a point.
- Use the **3DORBIT** command and other navigation tools related to it.
- Learn to use the mouse wheel efficiently to navigate the 3D space.
- Understand and use the predefined visual styles.
- Learn advanced drafting aids to find points in the 3D space.

INTRODUCTION

2D Drawing vs. 3D Model

Drawings have long been regarded as the universal technical language. They are used to represent any object's shape, dimensions, and specifications on a piece of paper.

With the development of the computer in the 1980s, programmers began to focus on Computer Aided Design (CAD), which led to the development of pioneering software to perform important drawing tasks. This marked the beginning of a new era for designers and drafters, allowing them to greatly increase their accuracy and productivity with less work strain.

As the speed and power of computers increased, the concept of three-dimensional (3D) modeling started to develop as well. This new capability gave designers the most efficient tool they had ever had, substituting for costly prototypes in many cases.

Most two-dimensional (2D) drawings simply show an object's projections, and in many cases they tend to confuse personnel in charge of interpreting them. 3D models, however, give an exact understanding of what the real object looks like. With some experience, you will look at 2D work the same way you looked at hand drafting when you first started to work with AutoCAD.

Ways of Representing a 3D Model

Regardless of specific conventions used in particular disciplines, the main purpose of generating electronic drawings is to represent objects as accurately as possible. Using the AutoCAD software, you can represent objects electronically in either two or three dimensions.

The two-dimensional ways of representing objects are:

- 2D drawings
- Isometric drawings using the Isometric snap style

The three-dimensional ways of representing 3D objects are:

- Wireframe models
- Surface models
- Solid models

In all the three-dimensional ways of representing objects, the entities or elements that are used are actually placed throughout the 3D space. Creating 3D models with AutoCAD is not limited to a particular method or set of tools. You can use as many tools and objects as you wish in conjunction with representing a 3D object.

A 3D object is represented as a *wireframe* model simply by placing lines, polylines, arcs, splines, and 3D polylines in the 3D space where the edges of the object are located. For example, to represent a box by modeling its wires you will need 12 *lines* or *polylines* to represent its 12 edges. A cylinder would be represented less clearly because it has no physical vertical edge, but rather a single continuous surface (Figure 1-1).

Representing a box with a hole, therefore, would require the same 12 straight lines and the two circles (Figure 1-2).

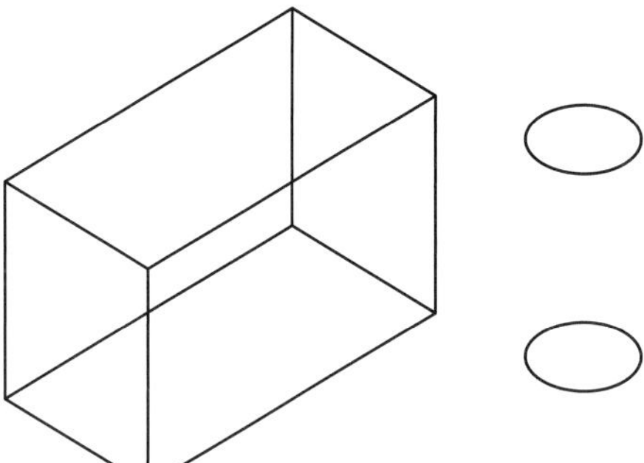

Figure 1-1 Wireframe representation of a box and a cylinder

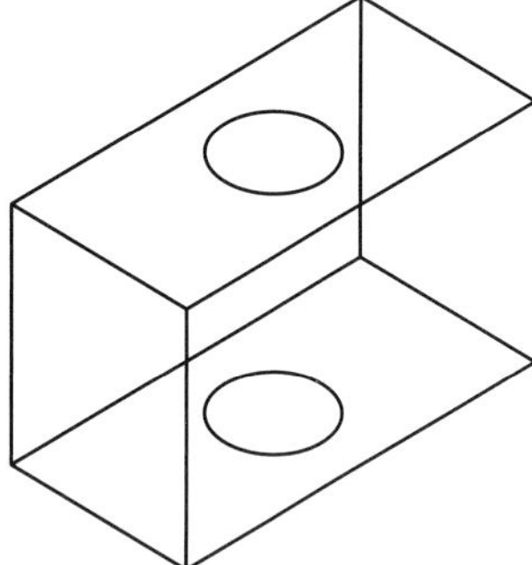

Figure 1-2 Wireframe representation of a box with a cylindrical hole

A wireframe or skeleton model is the simplest way to represent objects three-dimensionally; however, it is more difficult to achieve. A wireframe model does not allow you to perform an operation in which the supposedly occulted lines of the represented 3D object are actually hidden. Thus, this procedure is rarely used as a final representation of 3D objects. In most cases, a wireframe model is merely used to find points in the 3D space, or to create objects that will be used in the creation of other 3D entities.

A *surface model* is the representation of a 3D object's skin. Any type of surface entity can hide objects located behind it when tools related to this operation are invoked. Representing the box as a surface model would require placing six planar surfaces. The cylinder would be composed of three surfaces: two planar surfaces for the top and bottom, and a nonplanar surface to represent the cylindrical face (Figure 1-3).

Regions are the most suitable entity to represent planar surfaces. Nonplanar surfaces are commonly represented by faceted surfaces or true surfaces; however, faceted surfaces or meshes offer very few tools for further modifications. Figure 1-4 shows a box with a hole. The top and bottom planar surfaces of the box are represented by two regions, whereas the cylindrical surface of the hole is represented by a polygon mesh. This is one of many approaches that can be used to represent this particular object as a surface model.

Using a solid model is the easiest way of representing a 3D object three-dimensionally, and the most realistic one. Unlike wireframe and surface models, a single 3D solid can be used to

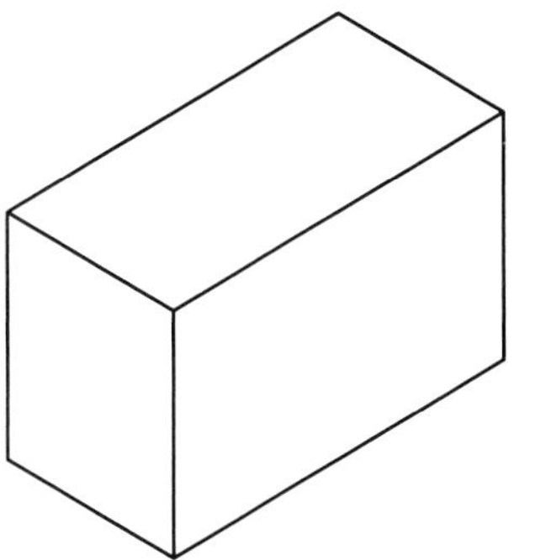

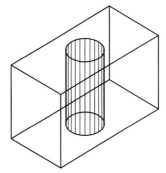

Figure 1-3 Surface representation of a box and a cylinder

Figure 1-4 Surface representation of a box with a cylindrical hole

represent the entire 3D model of an object. 3D solids can also hide objects located behind them and hide occulted edges.

The process of creating the box with a hole is as simple as subtracting a solid cylinder from a solid box. Figure 1-5 shows the 3D solid model of the box in a wireframe mode on the left, and with the hidden lines removed on the right.

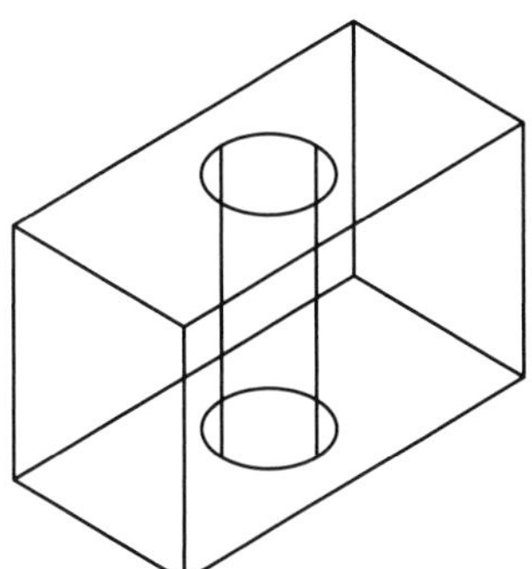
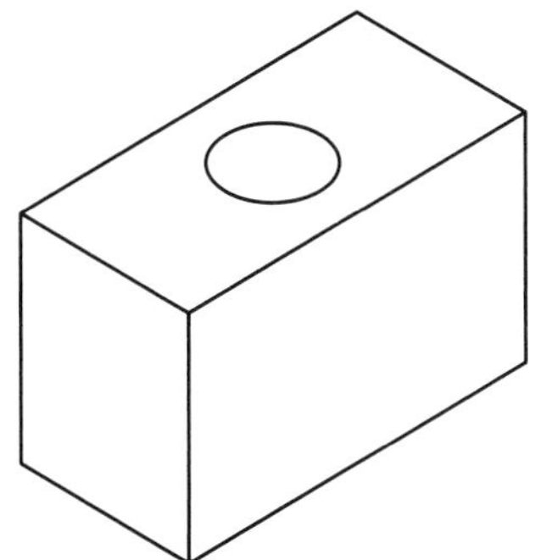

Figure 1-5 Box with a cylindrical hole represented with a 3D solid

Valuable mathematical information such as volume, center of gravity, moments of inertia, and other data can be obtained from 3D solid entities. A 3D solid can be edited using many 3D operations.

Preparing clear, concise, and accurate conceptual 3D models based on engineering information received electronically or by other means is part of the activity of designers and drafters. In order to properly visualize, conceive, and provide solutions to design problems and prepare appropriate engineering documentation, 3D users must be able to properly identify the different techniques used to represent 3D models. A complete understanding of these methods will assure a better comprehension and analysis of any information received. It will also ensure that data is properly generated according to the process and the use for which it is intended.

CUSTOMIZATION FOR 3D

Access to 3D Commands and Other Settings

Using Workspaces

workspaces: Specific arrangements of user interface elements, including their contents, properties, display status, and locations.

Due to the number of toolbars, menus, and dockable windows available in the AutoCAD program, it is necessary to switch back and forth between different screen arrangements. The ***Workspaces*** customization tools allow you to save these arrangements and quickly switch

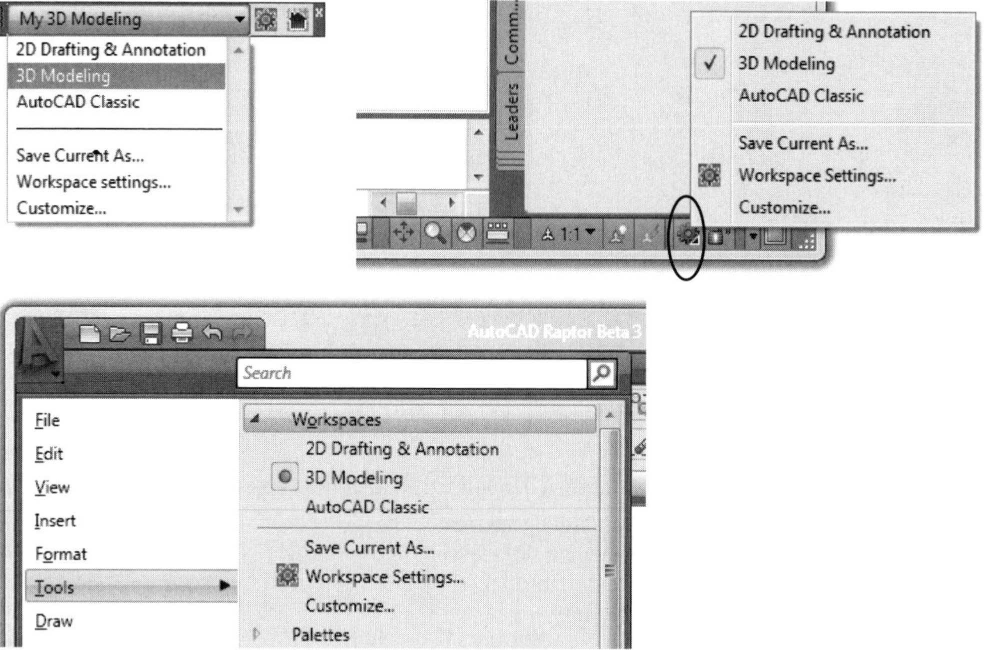

Figure 1-6 Workspaces can be selected from the toolbars' drop-down lists, the enhanced AutoCAD menu, and the menu that shows on the status bar when clicking the Workspace icon

between them. This prevents the screen from filling up with toolbars and windows that are not necessary for a particular task.

The AutoCAD program comes with three predefined workspaces: **3D Modeling, AutoCAD Classic,** and **2D Drafting & Annotation.** To switch between these workspaces, you can use the drop-down lists located in the **Workspaces** toolbars, the **Tools** drop-down menu **(Tools/Workspaces),** or the Workspace icon located at the right end of the status bar (Figure 1-6).

You can create a new workspace or modify an existing one. The easiest way to create a new workspace is by selecting **Save Current As. . .** from the drop-down list in the **Workspaces** toolbars after arranging the toolbars and dockable windows. You can overwrite a workspace by simply reselecting it in the **Save Workspace** dialog box (Figure 1-7).

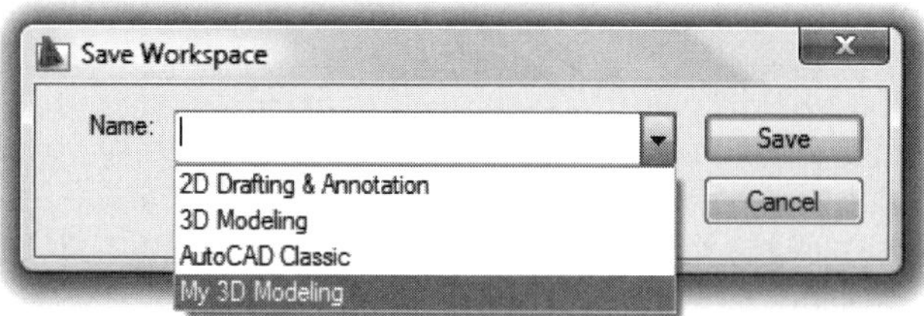

Figure 1-7 The Save Workspace dialog box

The Command Line Window

Just as in 2D work, the *command line* can be used to access 3D command tools and settings. Due to the occasionally large amount of information that you must read at one time, three text lines should be opened above the bottom line in the command line window when working in a 3D environment (Figure 1-8). This can be achieved by moving the mouse pointer slowly toward the command line window's top border. When the pointer changes its appearance, pick, drag, and drop the window. If needed, the command line window can be undocked or closed, and its transparency can be changed. To do such operations, you will have to pick it from the left ribbon and drag it to the drawing area, then you can right-click on its ribbon to display the controls. You can open or close the command line window by clicking on Tools > Command Line.

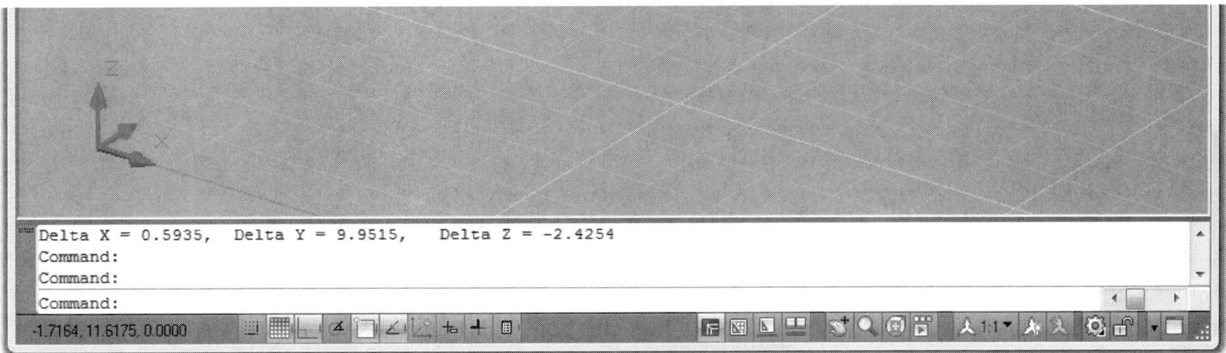

Figure 1-8 The command line window

Reading the command line window frequently can make the difference between learning to use the AutoCAD program faster, or slower.

The Ribbon and Tool Palettes

The ***Ribbon*** is a special palette that contains the commands and controls most frequently used to create, view, and render 3D models. The commands and controls contained in the Ribbon palette are organized by ***Ribbon Panels,*** which at the same time are organized into ***Ribbon Tabs.*** Each one of the Ribbon Panels that is prebuilt in AutoCAD contains tools that are organized by category to help you find a particular tool more easily. In the Ribbon palette (Figure 1-9), practically everything can be customized: the Ribbon Tabs that will be available, the Ribbon Panels that will be displayed within each Ribbon Tab, and the tools that will be available in each Ribbon Panel. Furthermore, you can define a different Ribbon palette for each saved Workspace. The Ribbon palette can be closed or opened by invoking the **RIBBONCLOSE** or the **RIBBON** commands, respectively. The Ribbon Tabs in particular allow you to quickly display a complete set of categorized tools by themselves. This is extremely helpful in the 3D work, where the screen gets crowded occasionally with so many toolbars that you can hardly find a place to draw.

Ribbon: A totally customizable palette where you can organize the tools and controls most frequently used to create, view, and render 3D models.

Ribbon Tab: The most general grouping element in the *Ribbon palette*; each *Ribbon Tab* can contain several *Ribbon Panels*.

Ribbon Panel: The panels contained in each *Ribbon Tab*; each *Ribbon Panel* can contain different commands and controls.

The customization of Workspaces and Ribbon palettes is made in the Customize User Interface, and it will be discussed further in this chapter.

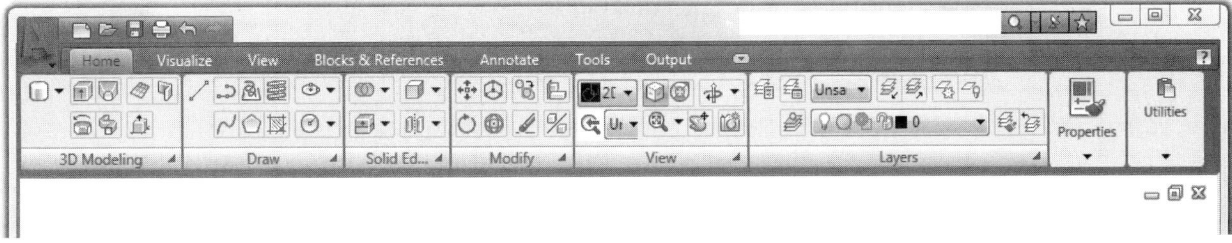

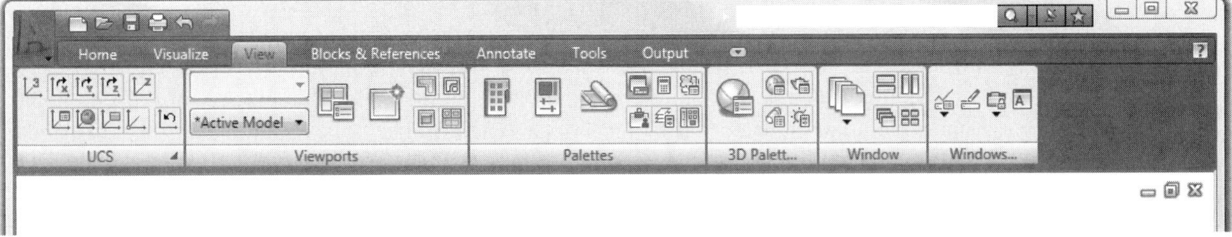

Figure 1-9 The **Home** tab (above) and the **View** tab (below) showing the different panels contained in each one according to the predefined **3D Modeling** Workspace

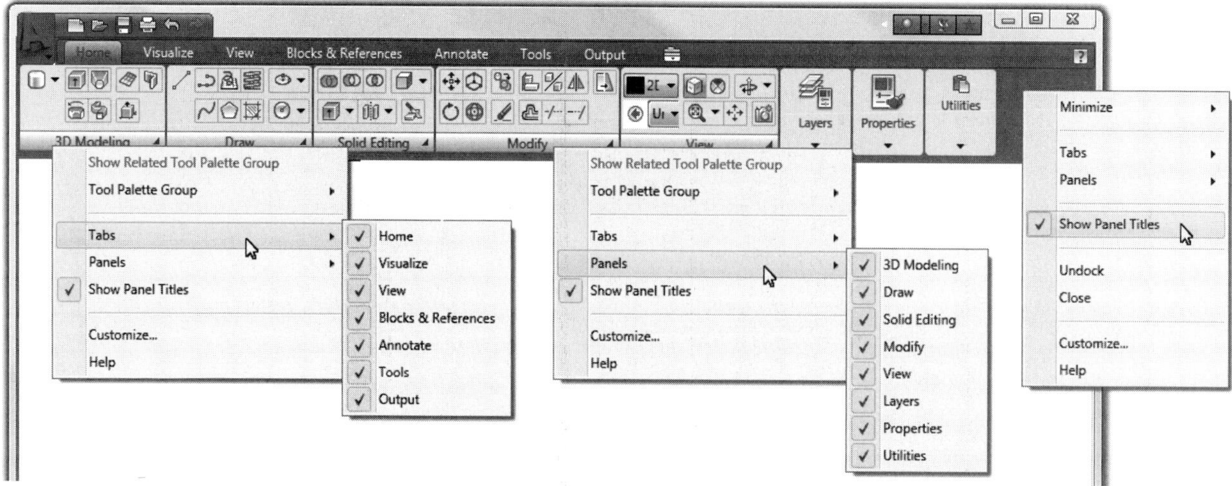

Figure 1-10 Different shortcut menus on the Ribbon to access the list of **Tabs** available on the current Workspace and the list of Panels available on the current Tab. The shortcut on the right shows the **Undock** operation.

In any particular Ribbon palette displayed, you can choose to hide or to show any of the Ribbon Tabs available; this is done by unchecking or checking the Tab from the list displayed in the shortcut menu. Right-clicking the top ribbon on the Ribbon palette or inside an empty area will show this shortcut menu (Figure 1-10); in the same way, you can hide or show Panels individually from the currently selected Tab. In a different shortcut menu, displayed by right-clicking the side ribbon on the Ribbon palette, you can specify whether the Ribbon palette will **Allow Docking,** so it can be anchored to the top right or left of the drawing area; to do so, you must grab it from its side ribbon, or the top one when is it docked at one of the sides. Other settings such as **Auto-hide** or **Transparency** can be controlled as well. You should turn the **Allow Docking** property off if you intend to use the **Auto-hide** feature. This will allow you to move the Ribbon palette to one of the ends of the drawing area without docking it.

Many of the panels of the Ribbon palette expand to show additional tools. Take a look at the **Navigation** panel located in the **View** tab in Figure 1-11 as an example.

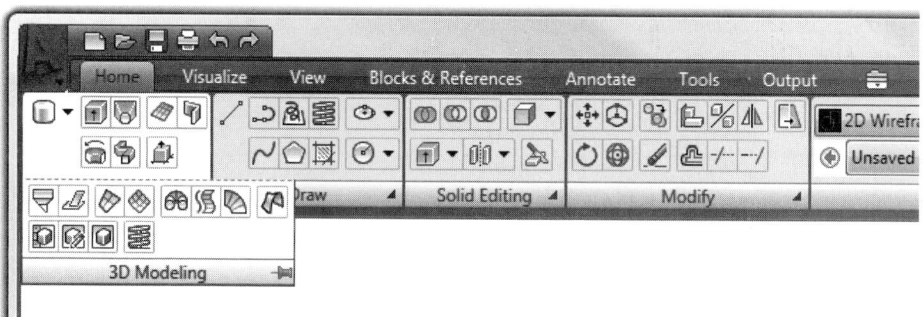

Figure 1-11 The 3D Modeling panel on the Ribbon shown in an expanded mode

To expand a control panel you can click on the small triangle located at the bottom (when it is docked at the top) or the side of the panel. You can choose to keep the panel expanded by clicking on the pushpin located at the bottom corner.

Flyout buttons for tools that do not fit in a particular row, as well as frequently used drop-down lists (i.e., the predefined view), can also be accessed from the Ribbon palette (Figure 1-12).

Tool Palettes: Customizable AutoCAD window that allows the user to organize tools and many other settings by palettes. You can add a tool by dragging objects into a palette.

The **Tool Palettes** window, on the other hand, allows you to organize commands, materials, visual styles, blocks, hatches, and many other customizable tools. Right-clicking the title ribbon of this window shows its shortcut menu (Figure 1-13).

The ***Tool Palettes*** window is basically a group of palettes organized as a stack of pages. Clicking on a tab will bring a specific palette up; just like the tabs on any dialog box, it allows you to see the tools contained in it. You can create and customize palettes, as well as groups of palettes.

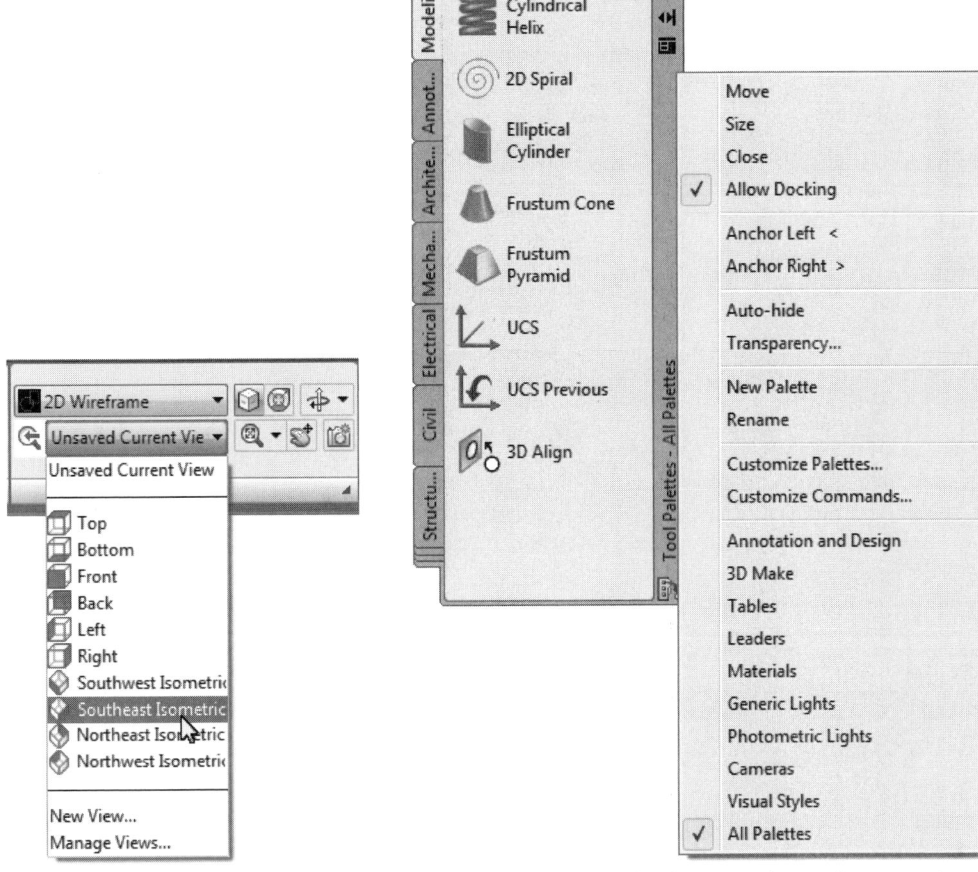

Figure 1-12 The predefined view drop-down lists on the View panel

Figure 1-13 The Tool Palettes window and its main shortcut menu

When customizing the palettes, you can add your most-used tools inside them. You add each tool by dropping it inside the palette. You can add commands as well as objects such as blocks, hatches, dimensions, polylines, raster images, materials, visual styles, and so on. Commands must be dragged from the **Command List:** section of the **Customize User Interface** window and dropped into the palette.

FOR MORE DETAILS

See the Customize User Interface (CUI) in this chapter for details about accessing the **Customize User Interface** window.

The groups of palettes are customized in the **Customize** window, which can be accessed by clicking on **Customize Palettes...** from the shortcut menu (Figure 1-14). In the **Customize** window you can drag and drop palettes from the list of **Palettes** into specific **Palette Groups.**

The control panels on the Ribbon palette can be linked to one of the existing **Palette Groups.** To do so you must right-click on the specific panel and select a **Tool Palette Group** in the shortcut menu (Figure 1-15). Now you can slide down a Ribbon panel that contains your most frequently used tools, settings, and drop-down lists while selecting the palette group that you previously specified and associated to it in one single action.

Using the panels on the Ribbon palette along with the palette group associated with them is an effective way of accessing the AutoCAD tools and settings used in 3D modeling. The Ribbon and the Tool palettes can be placed one below the other to make effective use of the workspace

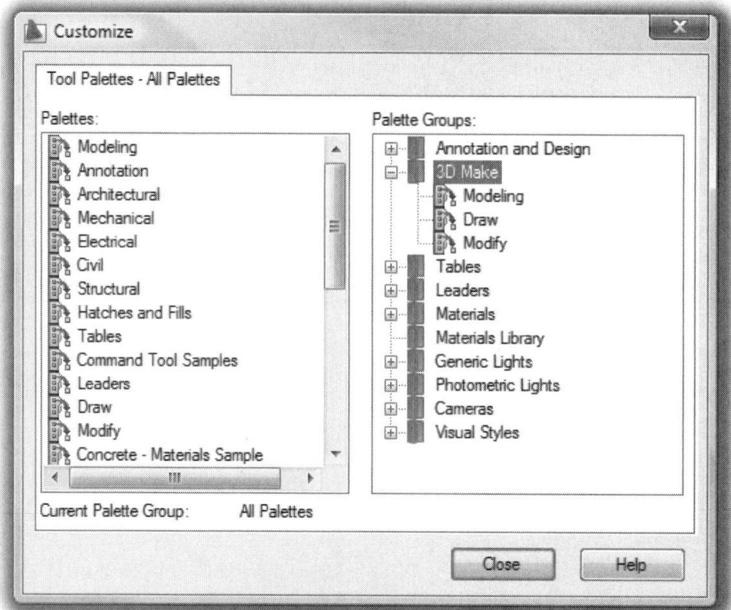

Figure 1-14 The Customize window

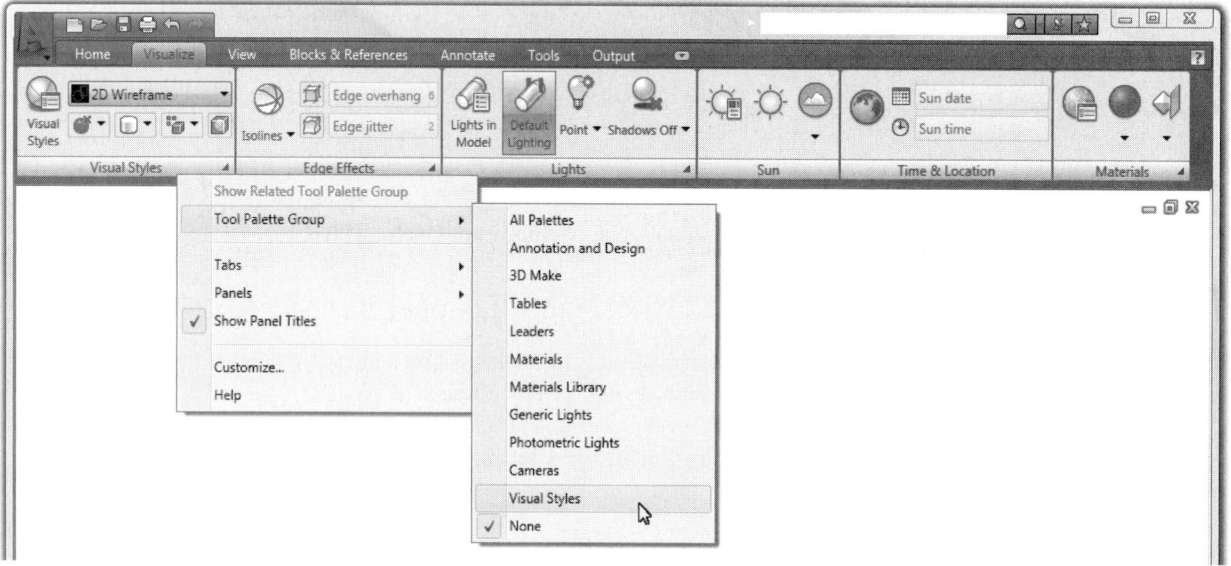

Figure 1-15 Linking a Ribbon panel to a palette group. The **Show Related Tool Palette Group** becomes available after the Tool palette group is defined.

(Figure 1-16). If you have a widescreen display, this particular arrangement could benefit your working space; however, there is a tendency to dock the Ribbon panel on the top side of the drawing area, especially if you plan not to display any toolbar at all.

Toolbars and Menus

With the use of the completely customizable Ribbon palette, there is not much need to display the Toolbars; some of the predefined Workspaces do not even show any Toolbar by default. However, you can choose to display them if you prefer to. The displaying of any Toolbar is easy if there is any toolbar already shown; just right-click on the toolbar to display a complete list of toolbars and check one by one those you need. Then you can drag the toolbars to your preferred location. Such arrangement is only temporary because it is not saved with any Workspace in particular, which means that recalling the current Workspace will hide them.

If you want to show a Toolbar in a Workspace that has no Toolbars displayed, then you need to redefine the customization of this particular Workspace. Choosing to display Toolbars in this

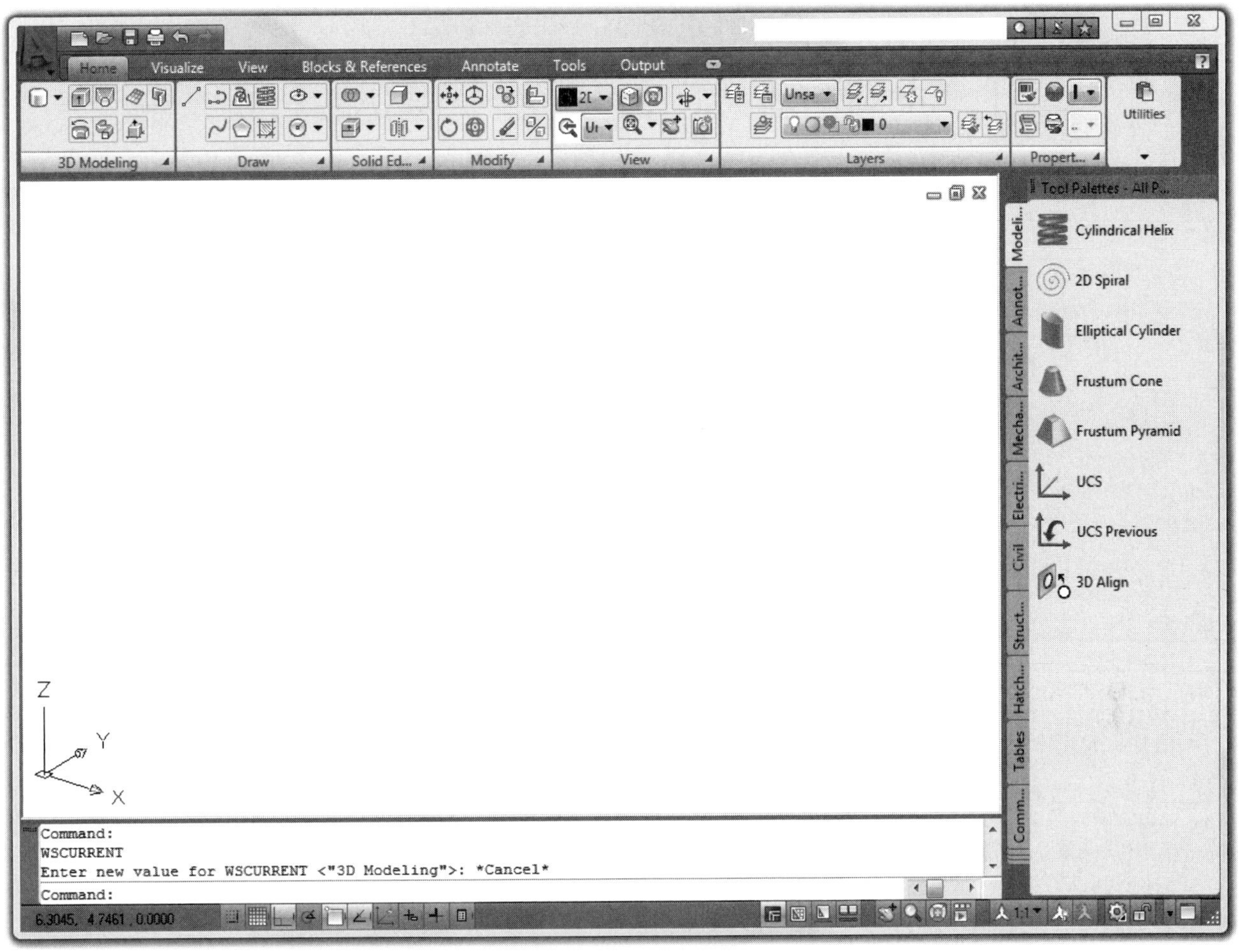

Figure 1-16 Using the Ribbon and the Tool Palettes jointly

way will become part of the definition of the Workspace; therefore, they will be shown every time the Workspace is recalled.

FOR MORE DETAILS You will learn more about customizing Workspaces and Ribbon palettes later in this chapter.

Many of the tools that are used to generate 2D work are also used to generate 3D work, and there are other toolbars that contain commands and settings specifically related to 3D work. These toolbars are shown in Figure 1-17 for your reference. When docking the **View, UCS II, Viewports,** and **3D Navigation** toolbars, make sure they are placed horizontally; otherwise, the drop-down list won't show up.

The **Menus** or drop-down menus also can be used to access commands. There are now two different ways of displaying the Menus: the traditional drop-down Menus, as in previous AutoCAD versions, and a new enhanced Menu, which is displayed by simply clicking on the AutoCAD logo (Figure 1-18). Showing the traditional Menus might not be practical now because the space is much better used with the new enhanced Menus. The **MENUBAR** system variable allows you to quickly show or hide the traditional menus.

The **Modeling** tools, used to create surfaces, 3D solids, and meshes, are found in the **Draw/Modeling** enhanced menu (Figure 1-19).

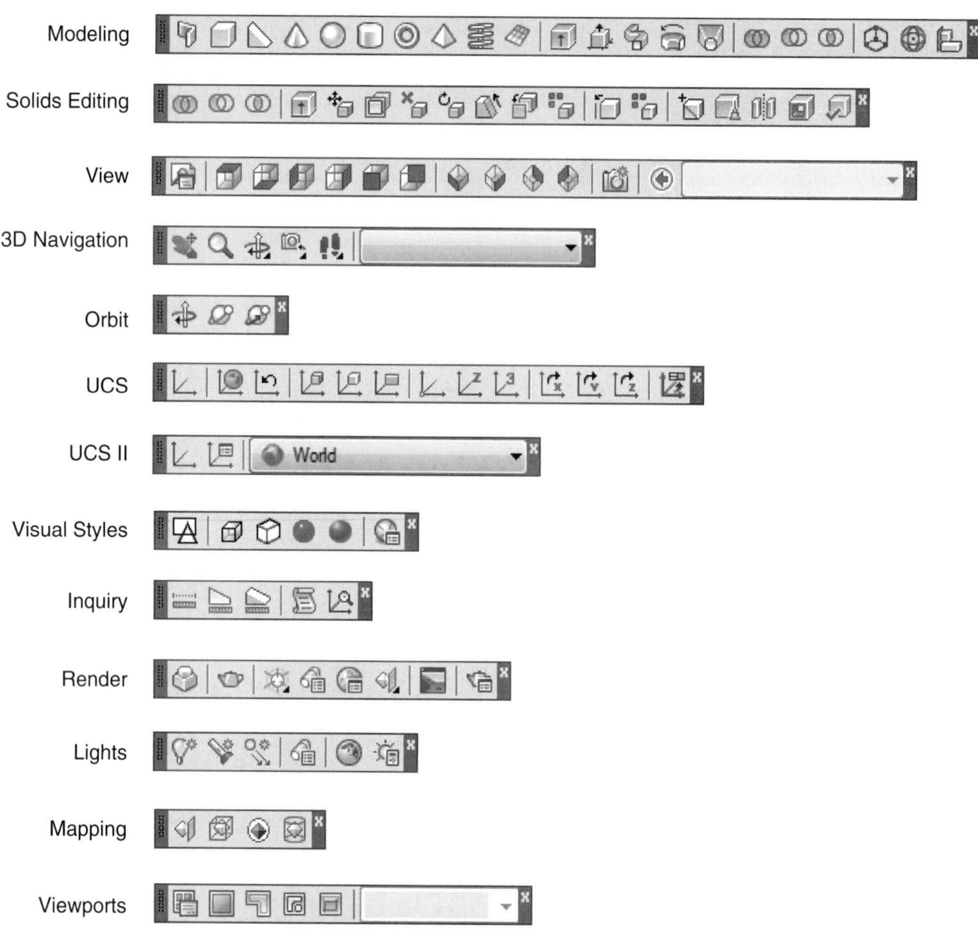

Figure 1-17 Toolbars containing commands and settings specifically related to 3D work

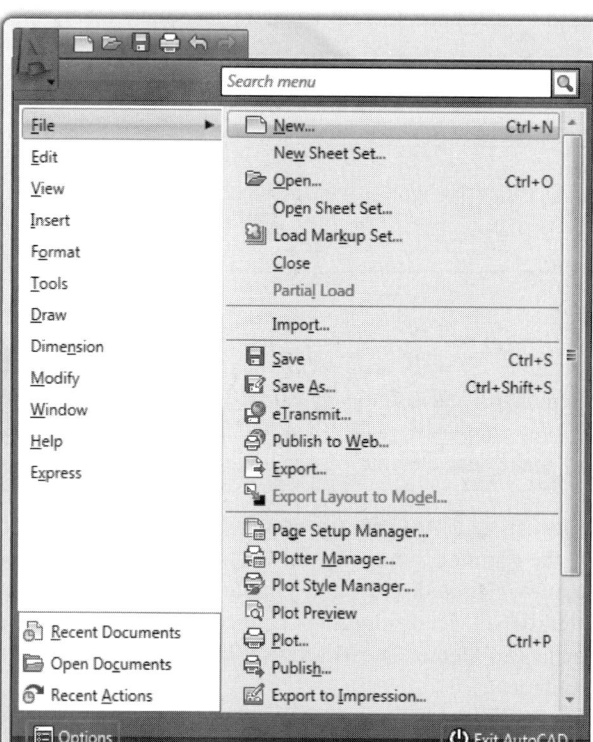

Figure 1-18 The new AutoCAD enhanced menu

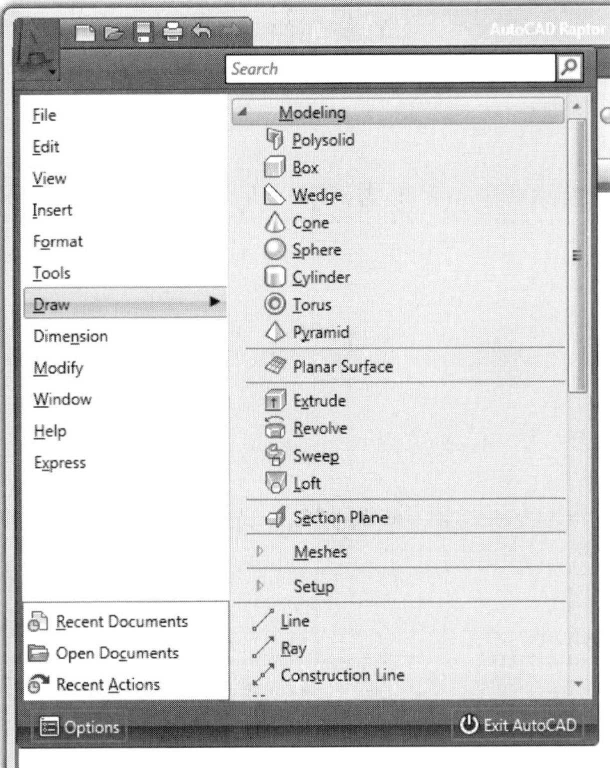

Figure 1-19 The Modeling tools in the Draw enhanced menu

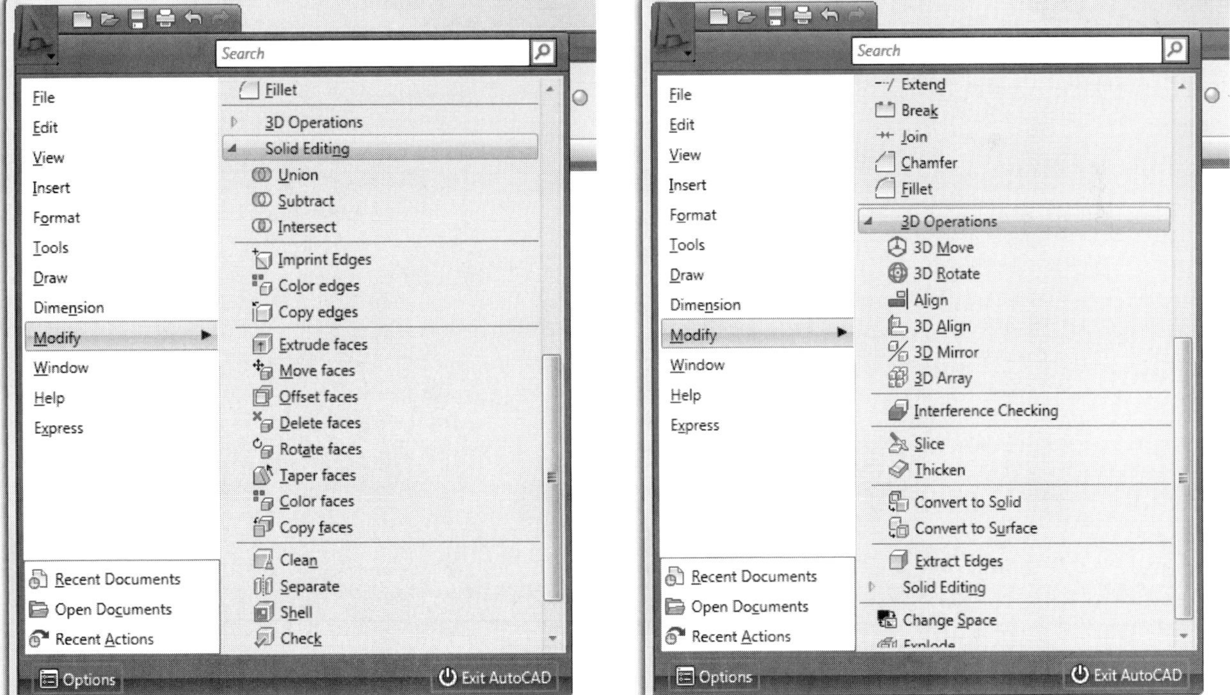

Figure 1-20 The Solids Editing tools and other 3D operation tools located in the Modify enhanced menu

The **Solids Editing** tools, as well as the **3D operations** tools, are found in the **Modify** enhanced menu (Figure 1-20).

The **View** enhanced menu contains the tools related to 3D navigation, visualization, and rendering (Figure 1-21).

The **Inquiry** group of commands as well as the tools to create a **New UCS** are both found in the **Tools** enhanced menu (Figure 1-22).

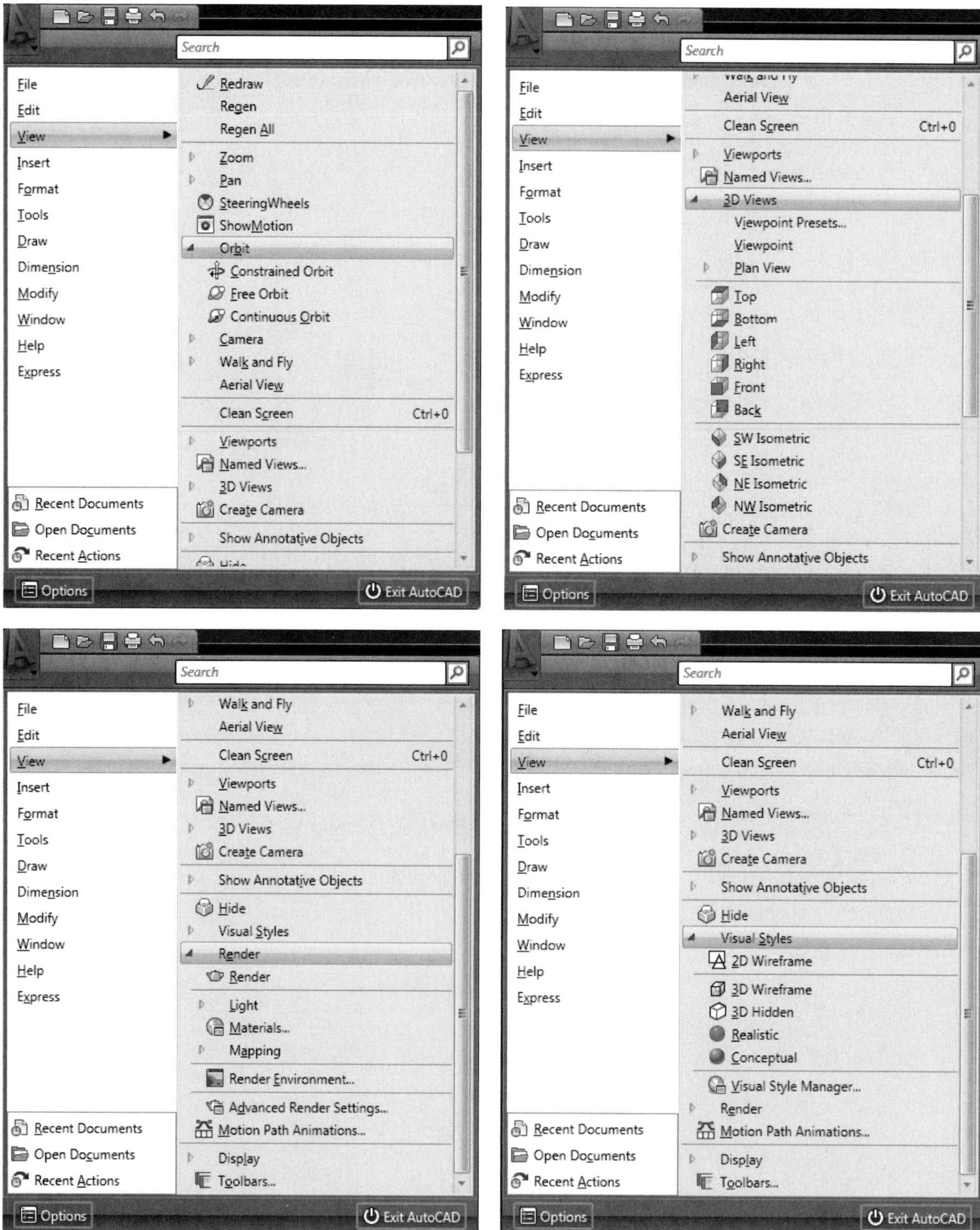

Figure 1-21 The View drop-down enhanced AutoCAD menu

Shortcut Menus Customization

When working in 3D, it is very important to speed up access to the command options and suboptions. Shortcut menus can save a good amount of time if they are used correctly.

By default, the AutoCAD shortcut menus are enabled. But if you ever need to change this setting, you can do so through the **Options** dialog box. Clicking on the **Right-click Customization. . .** button located under the **User Preferences** tab (Figure 1-23) will open the **Right-Click Customization** dialog box. You must enable **Shortcut Menu** for each mode (Figure 1-24).

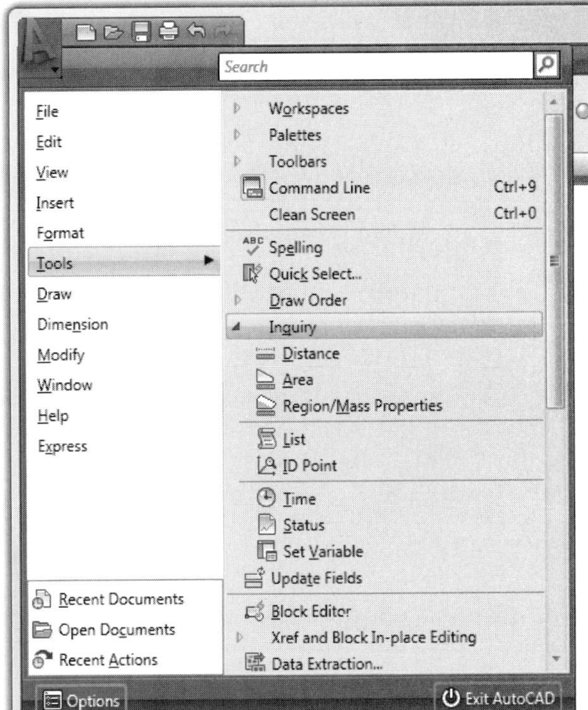

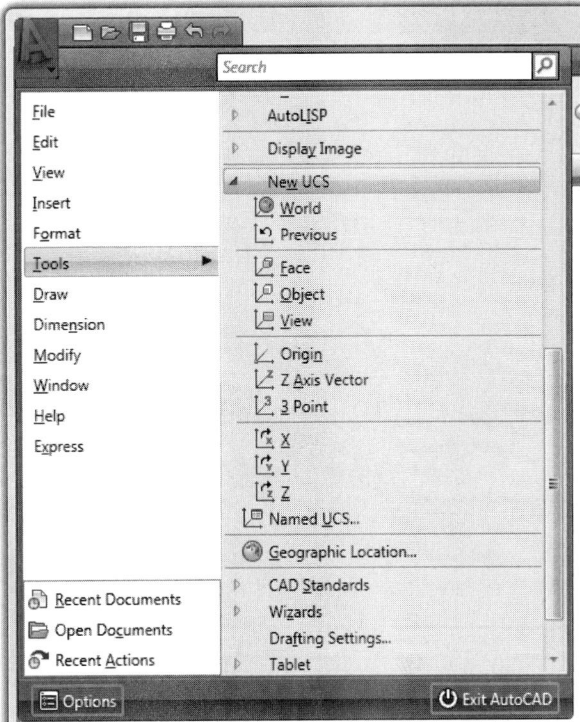

Figure 1-22 The Inquiry commands and the UCS tools located in the Tools enhanced menu

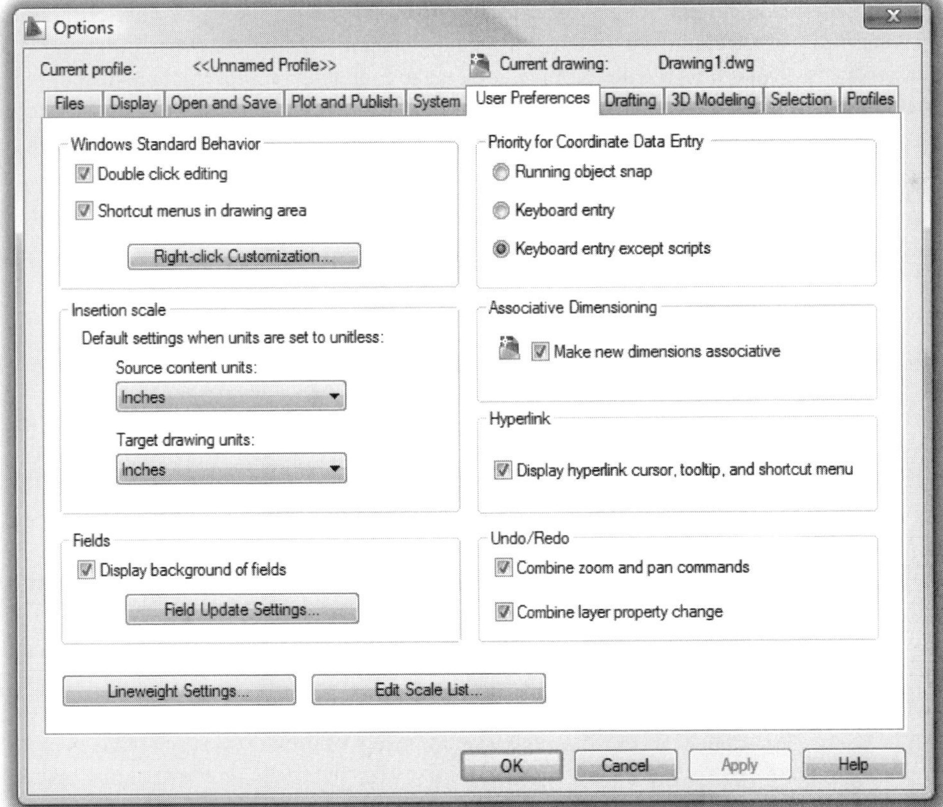

Figure 1-23 Location of the Right-click Customization. . . button

Options	
Pull-down Menu	Tools/ Options. . .
Command Line	options
Alias	op

To invoke the **OPTIONS** command, you can use one of the methods shown in the grid located at the margin of the page.

After enabling shortcut menus, which is the default setting, right-clicking in the drawing area will bring up a general shortcut menu if no command is in progress. This is where the **Options** dialog box can also be accessed, along with the **Edit** tools (Figure 1-25).

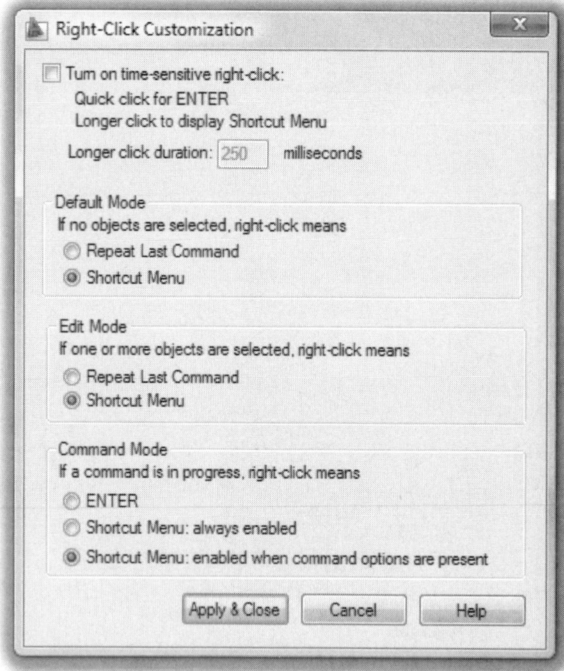

Figure 1-24 The Right-Click Customization dialog box

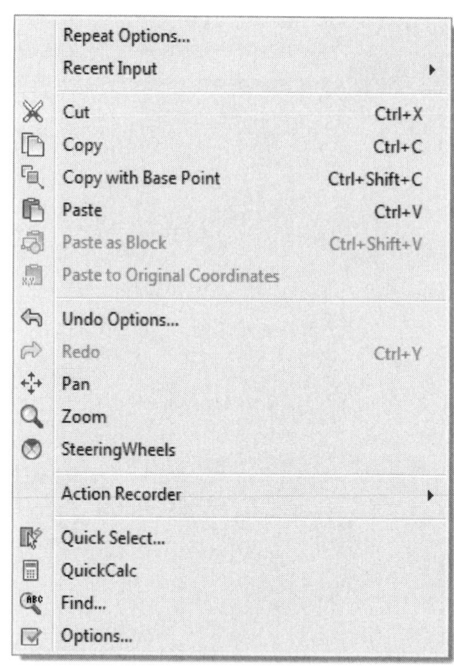

Figure 1-25 The standard shortcut menu when no command is in progress

When a command is in progress, you can make a shortcut menu pop up by right-clicking in the drawing. A list of the command's options will be included in the shortcut menu, providing you with easier access than typing. As an example, look at the following prompts that are displayed in the command line window when the **CIRCLE** command is invoked. These same options are displayed in the shortcut menu shown in Figure 1-26, allowing easier access with the mouse pointer.

```
Command:_circle Specify center point for circle or [3P/2P/Ttr
(tan tan radius)]:
```

The Customize User Interface (CUI)

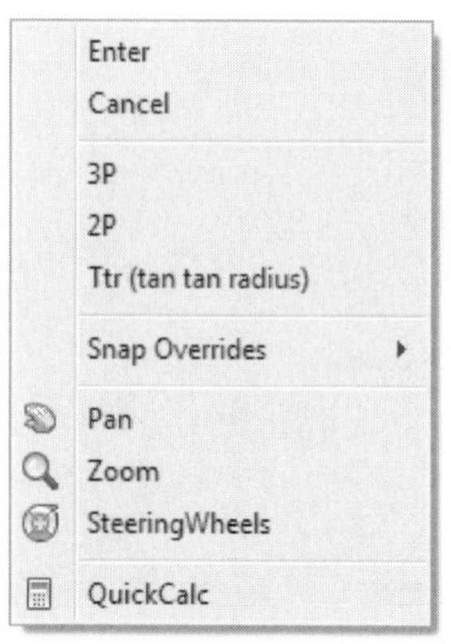

Figure 1-26 The CIRCLE command shortcut menu

The **Workspace** is the most general element in terms of customization. In the **Customize User Interface** window (Figure 1-27), you can create, customize, set as default, and delete workspaces. For each selected workspace, you can then customize which toolbars, menus, and other palettes in general will show up; you can also customize which Tabs will be available for the Ribbon palette corresponding to the selected Workspace, as well as the Panels that will be available for each Tab.

To add or remove Ribbon Tabs, you must enter the customize mode; this is achieved by selecting **Customize Workspace** from the shortcut menu, displayed after right-clicking on the selected Workspace (Figure 1-27); you can also click on the **Customize Workspace** button on the **Workspace Contents** pane. One in the customization mode, you can add Tabs to the Workspace's Ribbon by checking them in the **Customization in ALL CUI files** pane (Figure 1-28). You can exit the customization mode by clicking on the **Done** button in the **Workspace Contents** pane. To add or remove panels to a particular tab, you can drag them from the **Ribbon Panels** list into the desired tab from the **Ribbon Tabs** list. This operation must be performed while not in the customize mode. You can also set other default properties of a selected workspace (e.g., showing or not showing the Model/Layout tabs). The Customize User Interface window can be opened through the drop-down menus by selecting **Tools/Customize/Interface....** It is also possible to create new workspaces, toolbars, Ribbon Tabs, Ribbon Panels, and many other elements by using the options on the shortcut menus.

In the Customize User Interface, you can use drag and drop actions to remove commands and tools from toolbars, menus, Ribbon Panels, and so on. In the **Customization in All CUI Files** pane, you can also customize which elements will show up inside the default shortcut menus and also for specific objects selected (Figure 1-30). Another important task you can

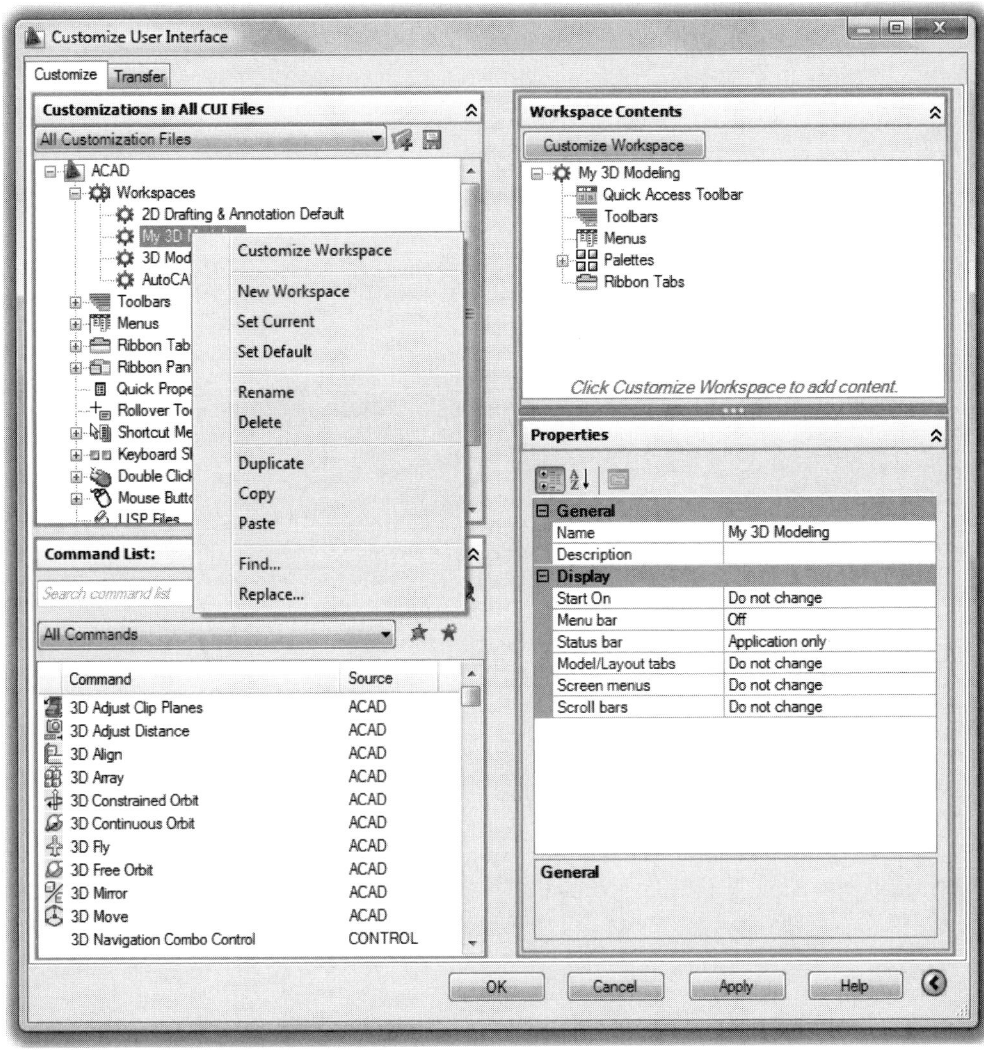

Figure 1-27 The Customize User Interface window

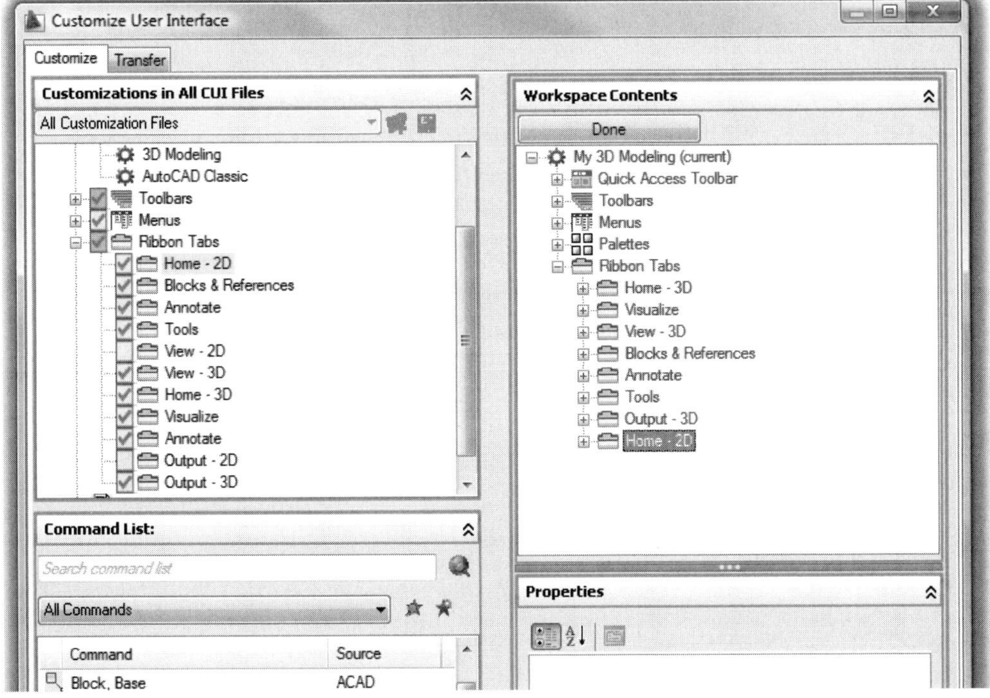

Figure 1-28 The **Home-2D** Tab is added to the list of Ribbon Tabs by checking its box on the left while in customization mode

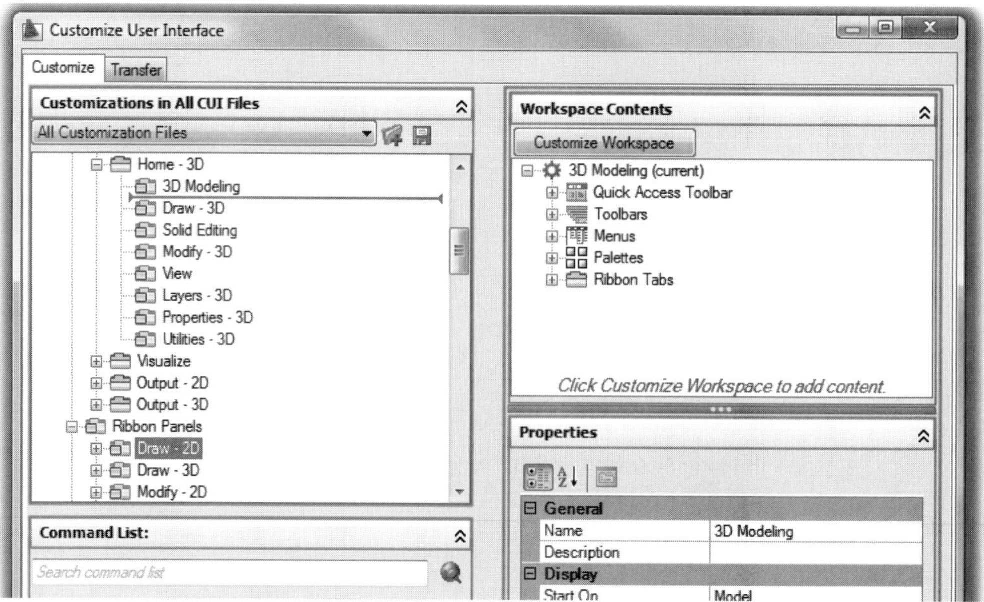

Figure 1-29 The **Draw-2D** panel is added to the list of panels included in the **Output-3D** Tab when not in the customization mode

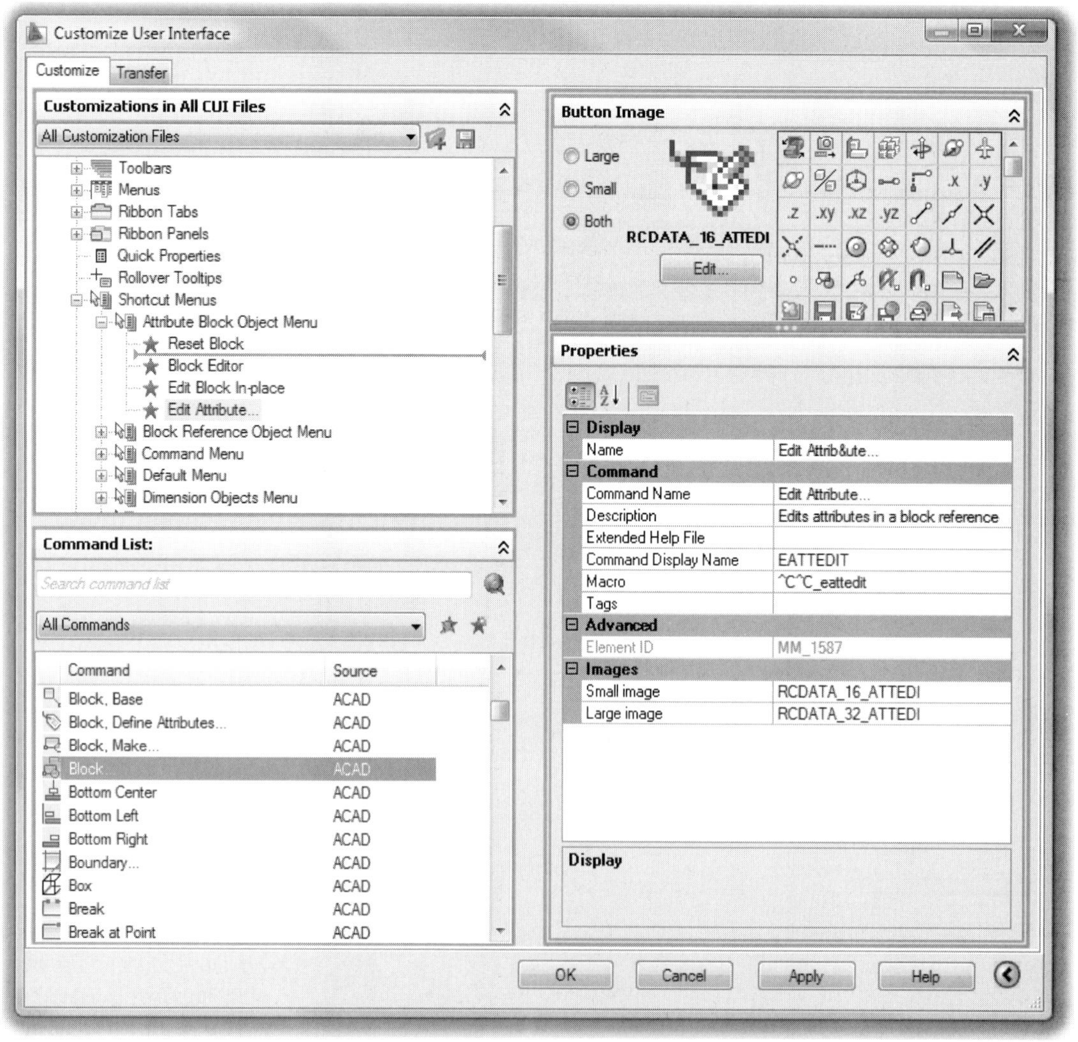

Figure 1-30 Customizing a shortcut menu in the CUI window

perform while in the customize mode is the selection of the commands that will show on the **Quick Access Toolbar**, located at the top left corner on the AutoCAD display.

The **Customize User Interface** window shows the **Command List** pane only when accessed through the shortcut menu that appears by right-clicking on any of the toolbar's icons.

Exercise 1-1: Creating a Custom Workspace

In this exercise you will create a new workspace containing the toolbars, windows, and settings that you will use in other exercises, tutorials, and projects.

1. Start a **NEW** drawing by selecting **File/New** in the drop-down menu or using any method. In the **Select template** dialog box (Figure 1-31), select **acad** from the list of template files and click on the **Open** button.

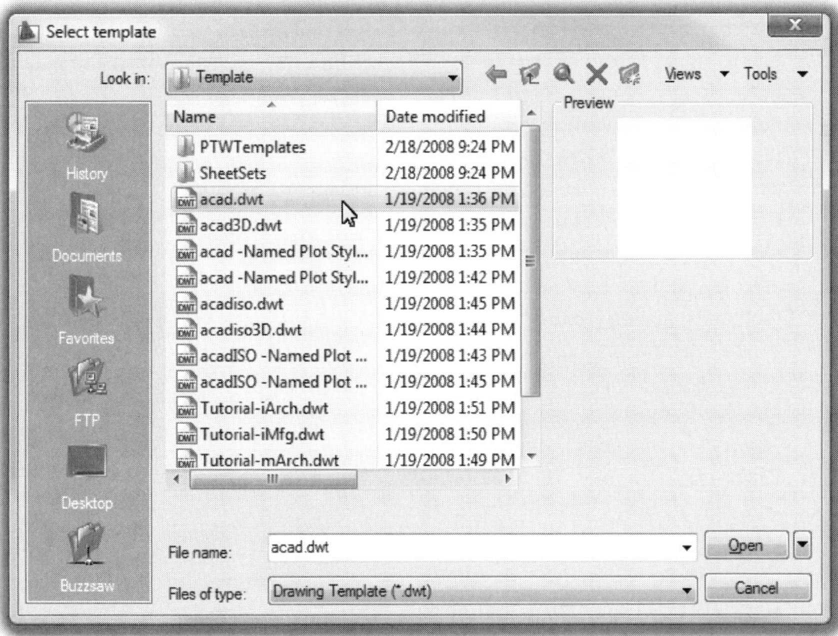

Figure 1-31 The Select template window

2. Open the **Customize User Interface** window through the enhanced drop-down menus by clicking on the AutoCAD logo and then selecting Tools/Workspaces/Customize . . . In the **Customization in All CUI Files** pane, open the list of Workspaces and select the **3D Modeling** workspace. Right-click on it and select **Duplicate** from the shortcut menu. When the copy is created, rename it as **My 3D Workspace** also from its shortcut menu.
3. In the **Customization in All CUI Files** pane, right-click on **Ribbon Tabs** and select **New Tab.** Rename the new Tab to ***Modeling 1***. Repeat the same operation to add a new tab named ***Modeling 2.***
4. Now you will add some panels to the Tabs you just created. Click the plus icon next to **Ribbon Panels** to show the complete list

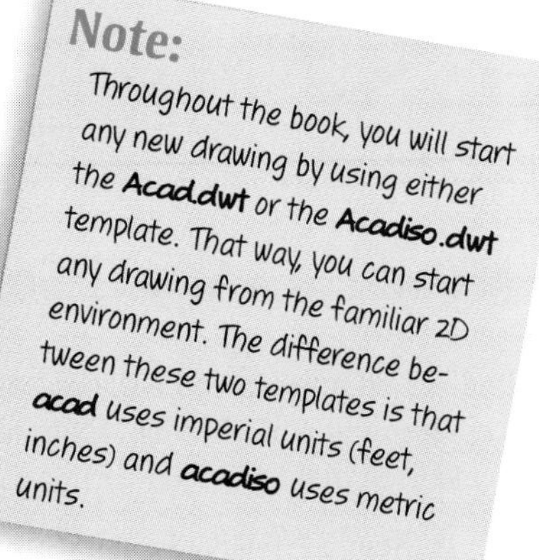

of panels. Holding the control key down, drag one by one the panels listed under ***Modeling 1***, and drop them into the **Modeling 1** Tab. If needed, reorder the panels so they are shown in the same order as below. Repeat the same procedure for ***Modeling 2***.

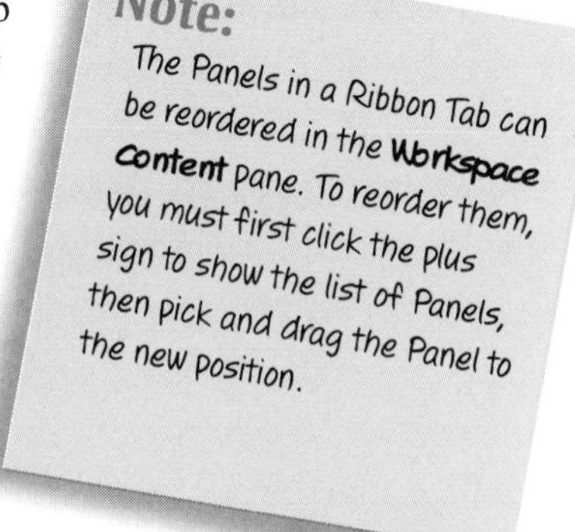
Note:
The Panels in a Ribbon Tab can be reordered in the Workspace Content pane. To reorder them, you must first click the plus sign to show the list of Panels, then pick and drag the Panel to the new position.

Modeling 1:	***Modeling 2:***
Draw—3D	Layers 3D
Modify—3D	Render
3D Modeling	Light
Solid Editing	Materials
View	Properties—3D
UCS—3D	Visual Styles
3D Palettes	Edge Effects

5. Click on **My 3D Modeling** workspace to display the content on the right pane. Drag the **Modeling 1** tab and drop it into the Ribbon Tabs on the right pane (**Workspace Content**). Do the same with the **Modeling 2** tab.
6. On the right pane, click the plus sign to show the list of Tabs and delete all the Tabs except the ones you just created: ***Modeling 1*** and ***Modeling 2***. You can delete Tabs by right-clicking on it and selecting **Remove from Workspace,** or by pressing the Delete key.
7. On the right pane, click the plus sign next to **Palettes** to display the list of palettes; select **Tool Palettes** and change its **Show** property to **No**.
8. Select **My 3D Modeling** workspace and click the **Customize Workspace** button; make sure the Menus checkbox located in the **Customization in All CUI Files** pane is checked, as well as all of the menus available. If you would like, check some of the toolbars that you would like to display. When you are finished, click on the **Done** button to exit the customize mode.
9. On the **Properties** pane, make sure **Model/Layout tabs** is set to on.
10. Right-click on **My 3D Workspace** and select **Set Current** from the shortcut menu.
11. Click **OK** to close the **Customize User Interface** window and save the settings. Your AutoCAD screen should lock similar to the one shown in Figure 1-32.

Note:

My 3D Modeling workspace is not set to be your default workspace; it is just for practicing. If you leave the AutoCAD program and open it again, the default workspace will show up again. You are encouraged, however, to keep adding tools, palettes, and other elements as you move forward with the book. This way you can create, little by little, a workspace you are familiar with, one that contains the tools and settings more related to your particular work.

TIP Selecting **My 3D Workspace** will bring up all the toolbars and windows arranged as they were when you saved the workspace. You should use this workspace for every exercise, tutorial, or project in this book.

Modeling a Simple Solid: A Quick Tutorial

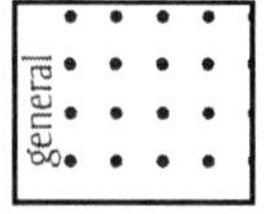
general

In this first tutorial, you will create the simple 3D solid model that was discussed in the "Ways of Representing a 3D Model" section. The dimensions are shown in Figure 1-33. (Any new command used in this tutorial will be explained later in this book.)

1. Start a **NEW** drawing, using the **acad** template.
2. **SAVE** the drawing **AS *SimpleSolid.***
3. Select the workspace named **My 3D Workspace** to set it as current.

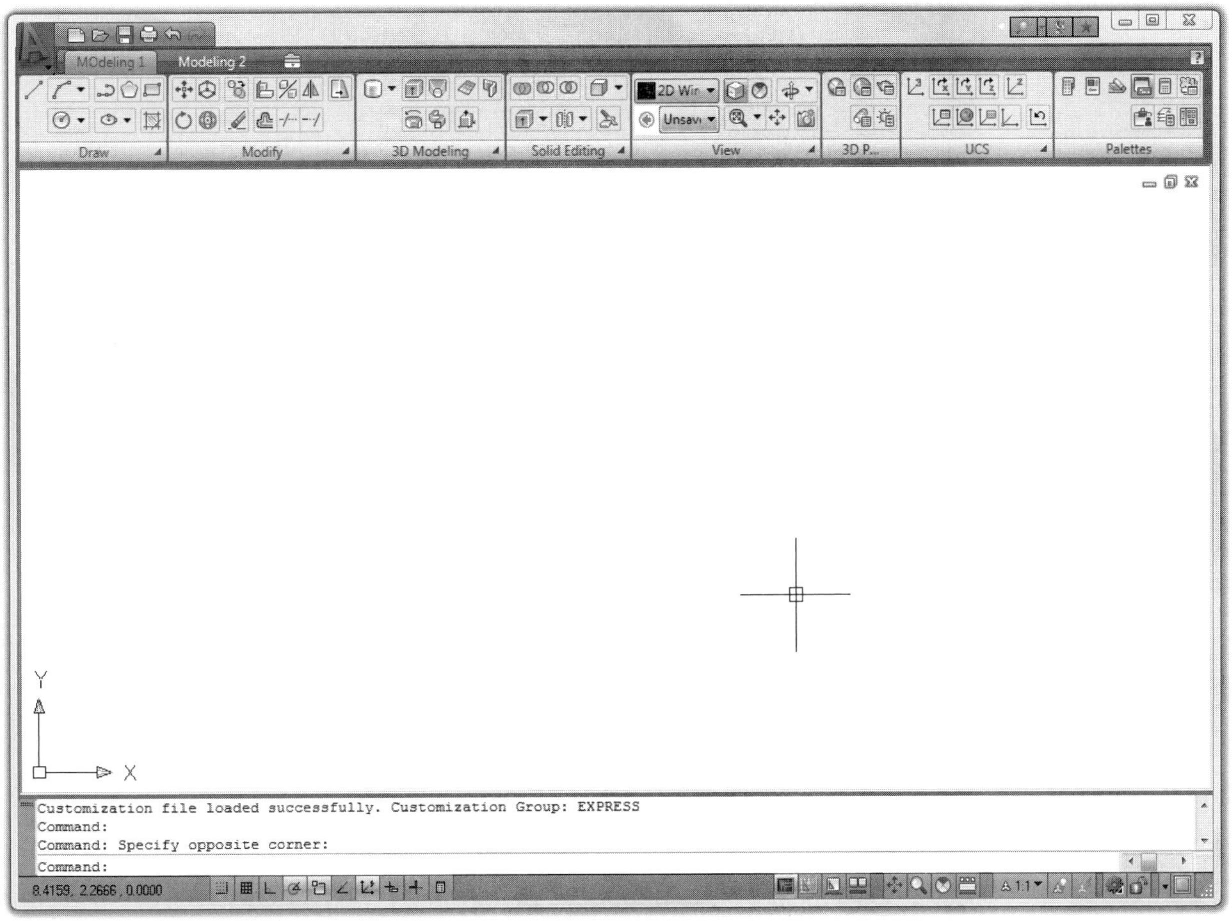

Figure 1-32 A custom work environment

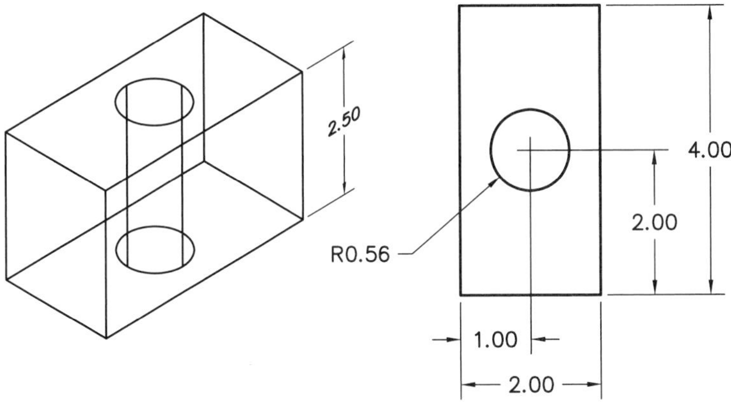

Figure 1-33 Dimensions for the simple 3D solid model

4. Draw the objects shown in Figure 1-34, using the **RECTANGLE** and the **CIRCLE** commands. Enter 1, 0.5 when prompted to specify the first corner point.

As a general rule, you should not place dimensions when creating 3D models. Rather, you can use the **DIST** command to find distances between points in your 3D objects.

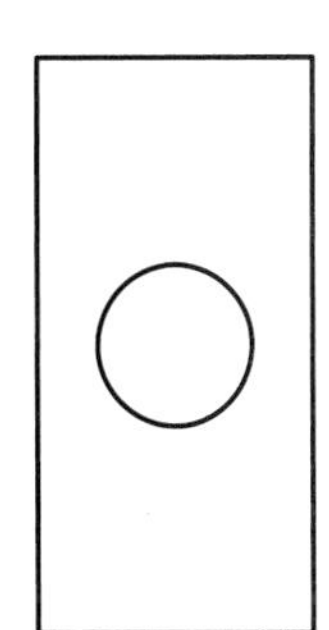

Figure 1-34 Drawing the profile

SE ISOMETRIC	
View Toolbar	[icon]
Ribbon 3D Navigate panel	Drop-down list
Pull-down Menu	View/3D Views/SE Isometric

EXTRUDE	
Modeling Toolbar	[icon]
Ribbon 3D Modeling panel	
Pull-down Menu	Draw/ Modeling/ Extrude
Command Line	extrude
Alias	ext

SUBTRACT	
Solids Editing Toolbar	[icon]
Ribbon 3D Modeling panel	
Pull-down Menu	Modify/ Solids Editing/ Subtract
Command Line	subtract
Alias	su

HIDE	
Render Toolbar	[icon]
Pull-down Menu	View/Hide
Command Line	hide
Alias	hi

5. Change the viewing point to look at the model from **SE Isometric** view (Figure 1-35). Use one of the methods shown in the grid in the margin.
6. **EXTRUDE** the two profiles to create the box and the cylinder, as shown in Figure 1-36. Use one of the methods shown in the grid to invoke the **EXTRUDE** command, and respond to the prompts as follows:

```
Select objects to extrude: Select the rectangle and the circle in any order.
Select objects to extrude: ↵ (To end the selection)
Specify height of extrusion or [Direction/Path/Taper angle]: 2.5 ↵
```

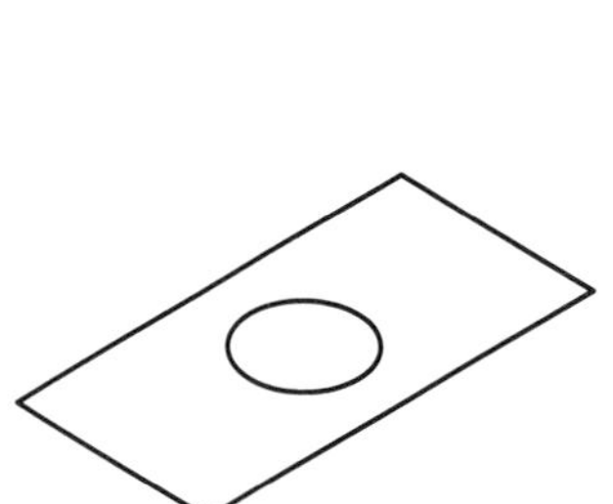

Figure 1-35 The profile viewed from the SE Isometric viewing point

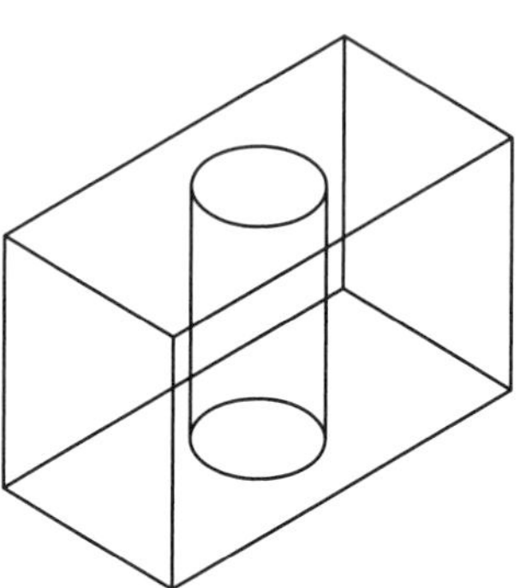

Figure 1-36 The extruded profile

7. **SUBTRACT** the cylinder volume from that of the box. Use one of the methods shown in the grid to invoke the command, and respond to the prompts as follows:

```
Select solids and regions to subtract from..
Select objects: Select the box.
Select objects: ↵ (To end the selection)
Select solids and regions to subtract..
Select objects: Select the cylinder.
Select objects: ↵ (To end the selection)
```

FOR MORE DETAILS

SUBTRACT is one of the Boolean commands. It is performed on regions and 3D solids, and will be discussed in Chapters 4 and 5.

8. Invoke the **HIDE** command. Use one of the methods shown in the grid. The 3D solid should now look as shown in Figure 1-37.

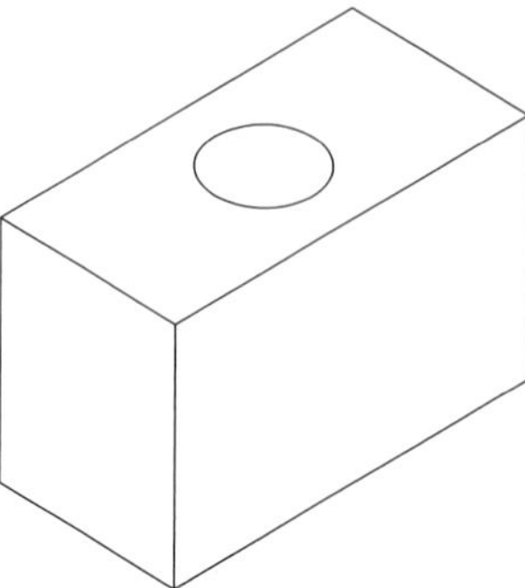

Figure 1-37 The 3D solid model with the occulted lines hidden

Note:

An alternative solution to this model is to convert the Rectangle and the Circle into two Regions, and then subtract one Region from the other to create a composite Region that would simply have to be extruded. You will learn more about this choice in later chapters.

TIP

The **ZOOM Realtime** and **PAN** commands cannot be used immediately after the **HIDE** command has been invoked, unless the display is regenerated.

9. Invoke the **REGEN** command to revoke the effects of the **HIDE** command. Use one of the methods shown in the grid to access the command.
10. **SAVE** the drawing.

REGEN	
Pull-down Menu	View/ Regen
Command Line	regen
Alias	re

WORKING IN THE 3D ENVIRONMENT

THE 3D VIEWING SYSTEM

The 3D space is always present within the model space in the AutoCAD program. The 3D viewing system allows you to control the viewing point from where you look at objects in the 3D space. It is based on three infinite imaginary planes (typically called *TOP, RIGHT,* and *FRONT*), each of which is perpendicular to the others (Figure 1-38). The TOP plane is the plane where all the objects are normally placed when working in 2D.

The planes divide the entire 3D space into eight spaces because of their relative location. An object can be located anywhere inside these eight spaces or between them. Let's focus our attention on one of these eight spaces and locate an object inside it (Figure 1-39).

Note:
The viewing system is not limited to looking at the objects perpendicularly to the imaginary planes. You can actually look at the object from any point in the 3D space, just as you can when holding an object in your hand.

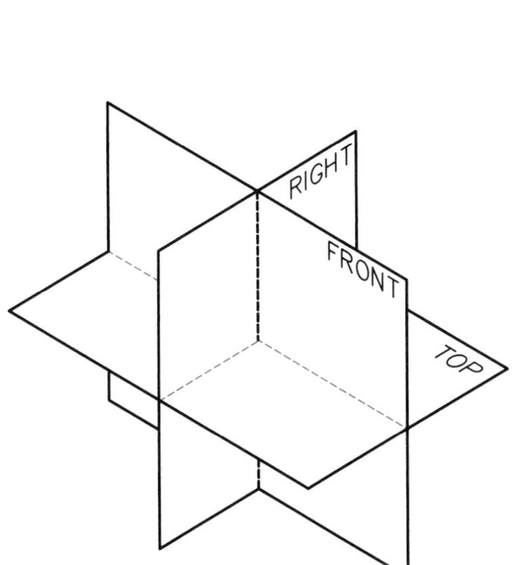

Figure 1-38 The TOP, RIGHT, and FRONT imaginary planes

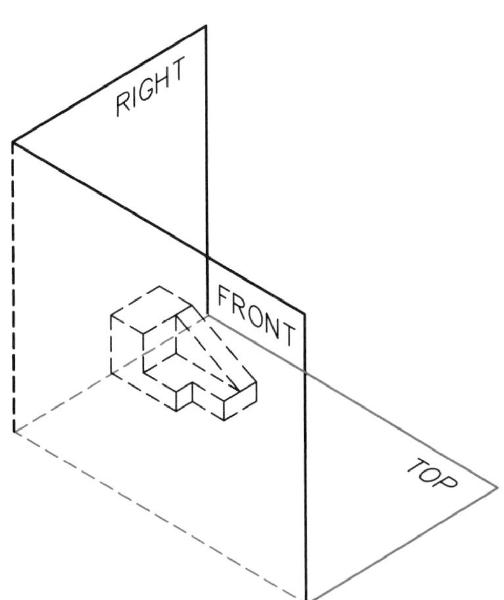

Figure 1-39 An object inside the positive octant

viewing point: The point in the 3D space that establishes the viewing direction of the user.

The location from where you look at an object determines the face(s) of the object that you see. This location is known as the ***viewing point.***

A person looking at an object from a viewing point that is perpendicular to the TOP plane will see the **Top** view of the object, which is the same as the projection of the object onto the TOP plane. The same will happen if a person looks from a direction perpendicular to the FRONT and the RIGHT imaginary planes (Figure 1-40).

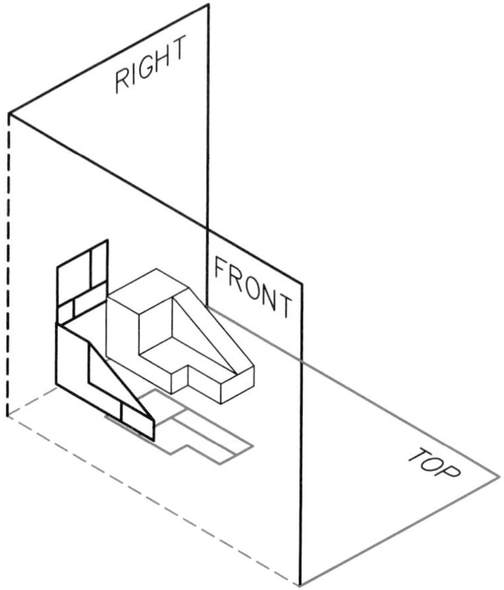

Figure 1-40 The object is seen from the TOP, FRONT, and RIGHT imaginary planes as it projects onto the planes

Orthographic Views

orthographic view: View in which objects are seen from a viewing point perpendicular to one of the orthographic imaginary planes.

The projection of an object onto an imaginary plane is known as an ***orthographic view.*** AutoCAD stores the six possible orthographic views, allowing you to quickly switch between them. Three of the orthographic views are **Top, Right,** and **Front,** just like the three imaginary planes. The other three orthographic views are **Bottom, Left,** and **Back,** the opposite sides of the three imaginary planes.

Selecting one of the orthographic views makes AutoCAD rotate the entire viewing system to align the selected plane parallel to your display.

TIP

Most 3D operations are better performed from a viewing point that is different from the orthogonal views.

Exercise 1-2: Selecting Orthographic Views

1. **OPEN *SimpleSolid.***
2. Change the viewing point to the **Top** view. Access this tool through the View toolbar or through the drop-down menus by selecting View/3D Views/. . .
3. **ZOOM** out as needed! Your drawing should look like Figure 1-41.
4. Select the **Front** view (Figure 1-42).
5. Select the **Right** view (Figure 1-43).

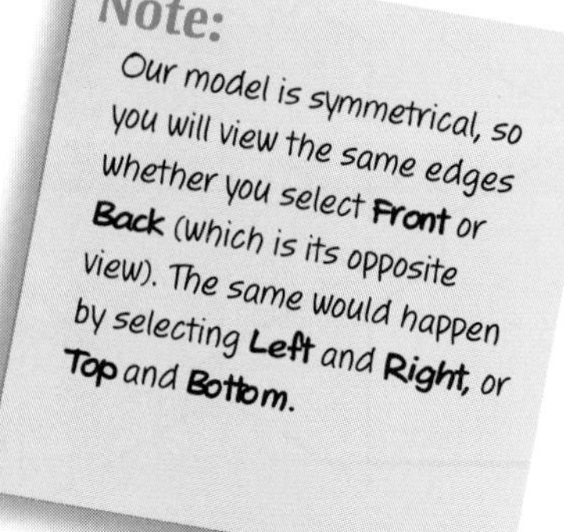

Note:
Our model is symmetrical, so you will view the same edges whether you select Front or Back (which is its opposite view). The same would happen by selecting Left and Right, or Top and Bottom.

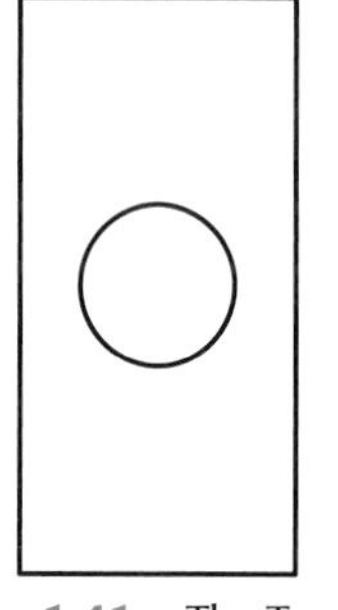

Figure 1-41 The Top view of the Simple Solid model

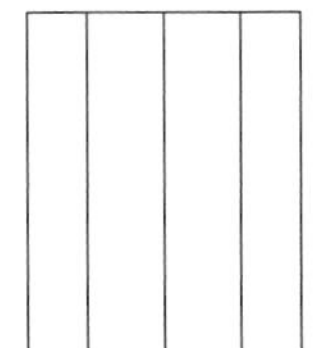

Figure 1-42 The Front view of the Simple Solid model

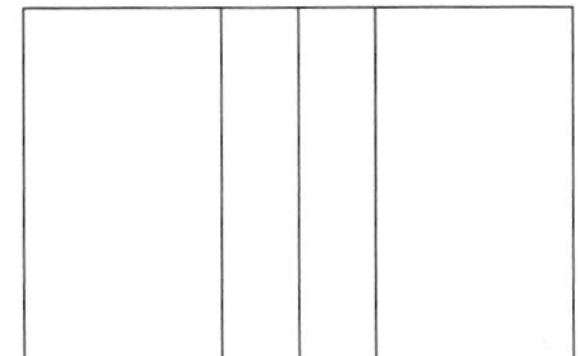

Figure 1-43 The Right view of the Simple Solid model

6. Practice selecting the rest of the orthographic views.
7. Select the **SE Isometric** viewing point.
8. **SAVE** the drawing.

Isometric Viewing Points

Other predefined viewing points in AutoCAD are the four Isometric viewing points:

- **SW Isometric**
- **SE Isometric**
- **NE Isometric**
- **NW Isometric**

An Isometric viewing point is the computer version of the ***isometric view*** used in manual drafting. An isometric view was a quick way of creating 3D views of objects in the days of manual drafting. It was based on the thesis that the projection of the three axes onto the drawing paper would have the same angle (120°) between them.

isometric view: A 3D drawing view in which the three principal dimensions of the objects are aligned with three axes 120° apart as they project onto the viewing plane.

Isometric views remain the standard 3D view in drawing documents. The AutoCAD program still allows you to use this technique of 2D drafting by enabling the **Isometric** snap type in the **Drafting Settings** dialog box; however, creating actual 3D models is easier, faster, and more accurate.

Figure 1-44 shows the four different Isometric viewing directions from which objects can be seen. Because the current viewing point is **SE Isometric,** its arrow is viewed as a circle, which is the projection of the arrow onto the viewing plane or display. From the **SE Isometric** viewing point you can see the TOP, FRONT, and RIGHT faces of the model.

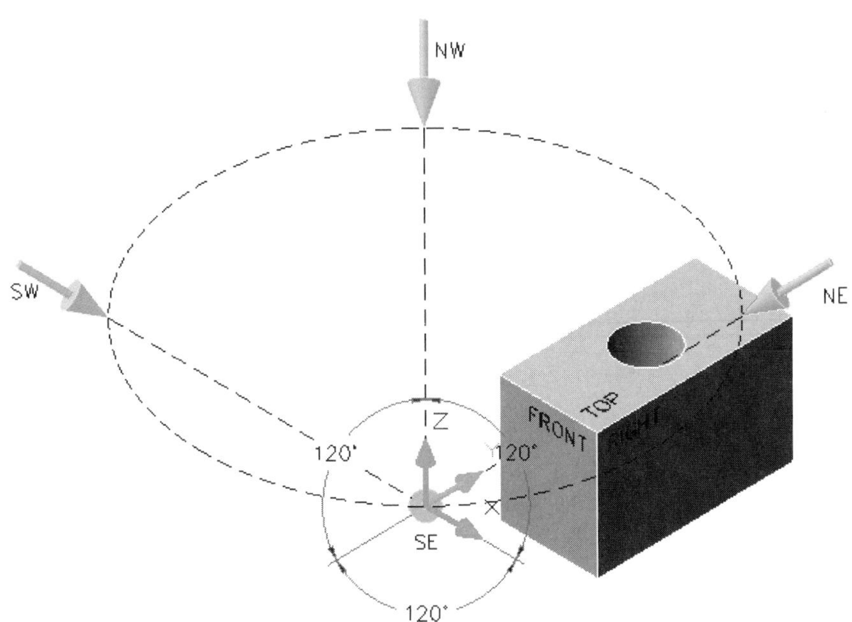

Figure 1-44 The four predefined Isometric viewing directions

Exercise 1-3: Selecting the Isometric Views

1. **OPEN** ***SimpleSolid.***
2. Select each of the four Isometric viewing points. Access these tools through the **View** toolbar, or through the drop-down menus by selecting **View/ 3D Views/. . .**
3. Invoke the **HIDE** command after changing the viewing point.
4. Select the **SE Isometric** viewing point.
5. **SAVE** the drawing.

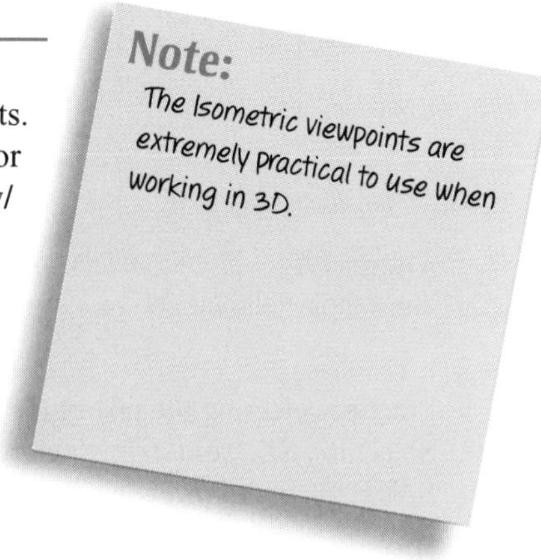

Note:
The Isometric viewpoints are extremely practical to use when working in 3D.

TIP

The **REGEN** command need not be invoked if you select a different viewing point; this operation also regenerates the display.

THE 3D COORDINATE SYSTEM

Mathematically, the 3D space is represented by three imaginary planes: *XY*, *YZ*, and *ZX*. Similar to the three viewing planes, the *XY*, *YZ*, and *ZX* planes are perpendicular to each other. The intersecting lines between these planes are the three axes *X*, *Y*, and *Z* (Figure 1-45). AutoCAD shows you the axes of its coordinate system through the UCS icon.

The *X*-axis is the intersecting line between the *XY* and *ZX* planes, whereas the *Y*-axis is the intersecting line between the *XY* and *YZ* planes. Analogously, the *XY* plane goes through the *X*- and *Y*-axes. The point where the three axes meet is called the *origin.*

From the **Top** view, which is the default view of a new drawing, the *Z*-axis is not shown in the UCS icon. The reason is that from this viewing point, you can look at the *Z*-axis only perpendicular to it (Figure 1-46). The hatched area is the default area of the *XY* plane where you typically perform 2D work every time you start a new drawing from scratch.

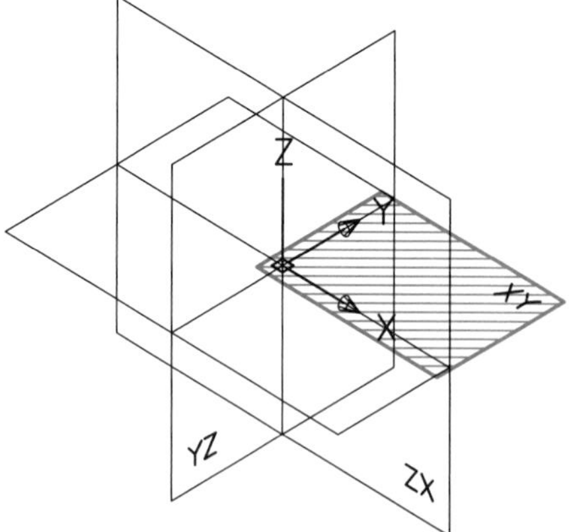

Figure 1-45 The XYZ coordinate system with the positive portion of the XY plane highlighted

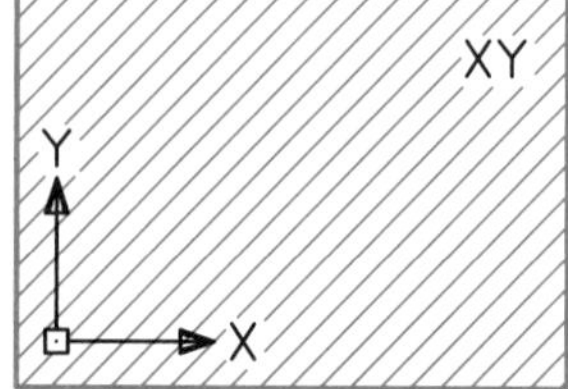

Figure 1-46 The positive portion of the XY plane as seen when starting a new drawing from scratch, where 2D work is typically done

Changing the viewing point allows you to look at the same imaginary *XY* plane in such a way that the *Z*-axis is not perpendicular to the display, as it is by default. By simply doing so, you can be said to be working in a 3D environment (Figure 1-47).

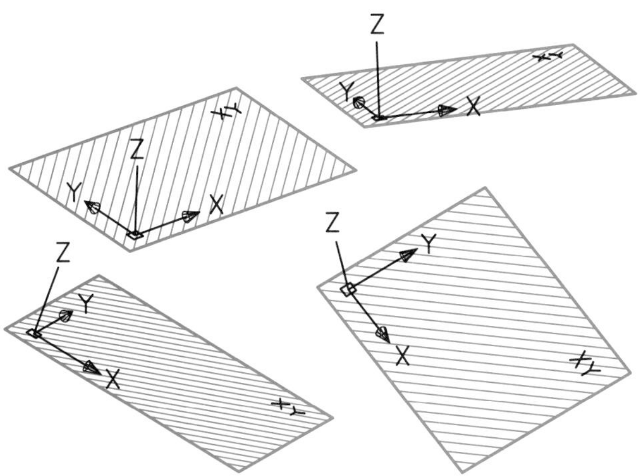

Figure 1-47 Looking at the positive portion of the XY plane from different viewing points in which the Z-axis is not perpendicular to the display

The WCS and the UCS

By default, the *XY*, *YZ*, and *ZX* planes of the coordinate system are located exactly where the three imaginary viewing planes (TOP, RIGHT, and FRONT) are, respectively (Figure 1-48). The coordinate system that has this characteristic is known as the ***World Coordinate System (WCS).*** The WCS icon is always shown with a little square in its origin.

World Coordinate System (WCS): The AutoCAD program's reference coordinate system. It serves as a reference for any user coordinate system.

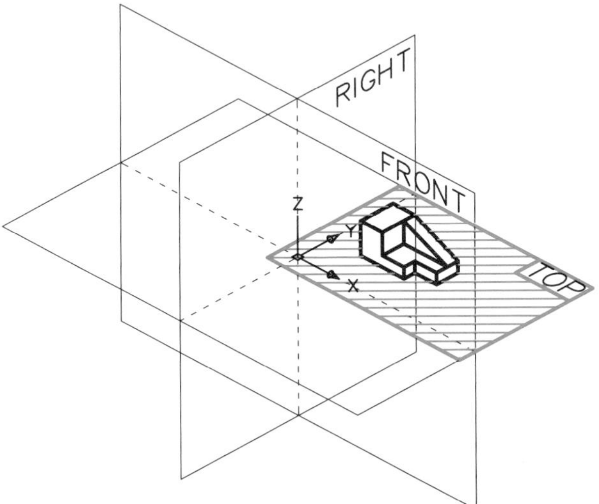

Figure 1-48 The XY plane of the World Coordinate System (WCS) is coincident with the imaginary Top plane

As you will learn later, the user can modify the coordinate system. A coordinate system that has been modified to reflect any arrangement of the viewing planes that is different from the WCS is known as the ***User Coordinate System (UCS)***. Figure 1-49 shows the **Front** UCS. Notice that the square in the UCS icon has disappeared.

User Coordinate System (UCS): The WCS after it has been reoriented using one of many possible methods.

Orthographic UCS

AutoCAD has six predefined ***orthographic UCSs*** **(Top, Right, Front, Bottom, Left,** and **Back)**. Selecting any orthographic UCS rotates the entire coordinate system so that its *XY* plane aligns with the corresponding orthographic view. The origin for any orthographic UCS is the same.

orthographic UCS: A reorientation of the WCS in which the *XY* plane aligns parallel to the corresponding imaginary orthographic viewing planes.

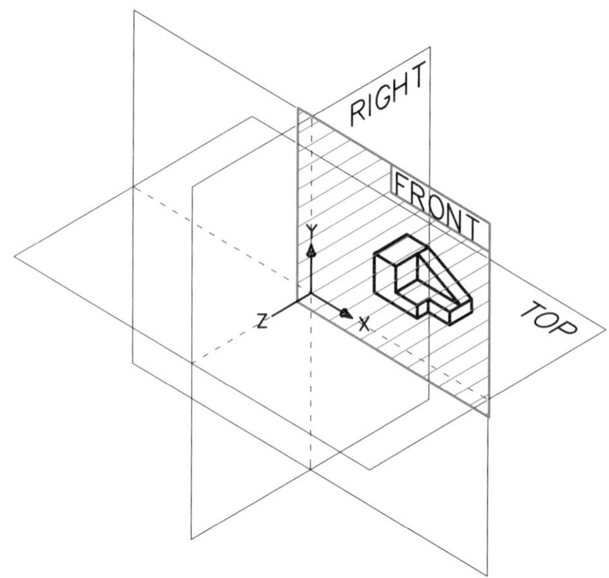

Figure 1-49 The XY plane of the Front UCS is coincident with the imaginary Front plane

Exercise 1-4: Using the Orthographic UCS

1. **OPEN *SimpleSolid.***
2. Select each of the orthographic UCSs. Use the drop-down list located in the **UCS II** toolbar (Figure 1-50).

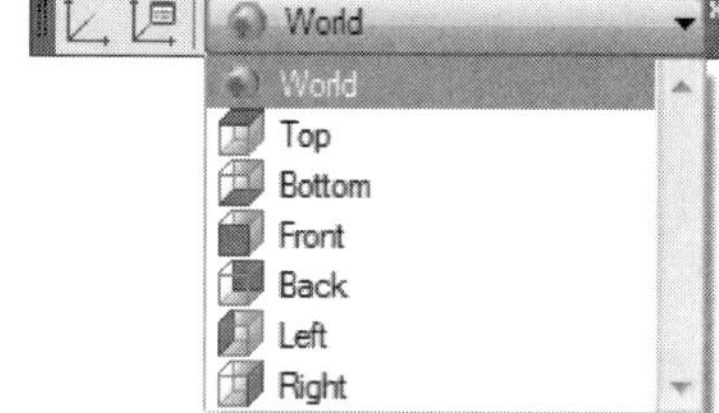

Figure 1-50 The UCS drop-down list located in the UCS II toolbar

3. Select the **SE Isometric** viewing point.
4. Select the **World** UCS.
5. **SAVE** the drawing.

Figure 1-51 shows all the orthographic UCSs viewed from the same viewing point. The **Bottom, Back,** and **Right** orthographic UCS icons show the *Z*-axis in hidden lines. This means that the positive portion of the *Z*-axis is behind the imaginary *XY* plane.

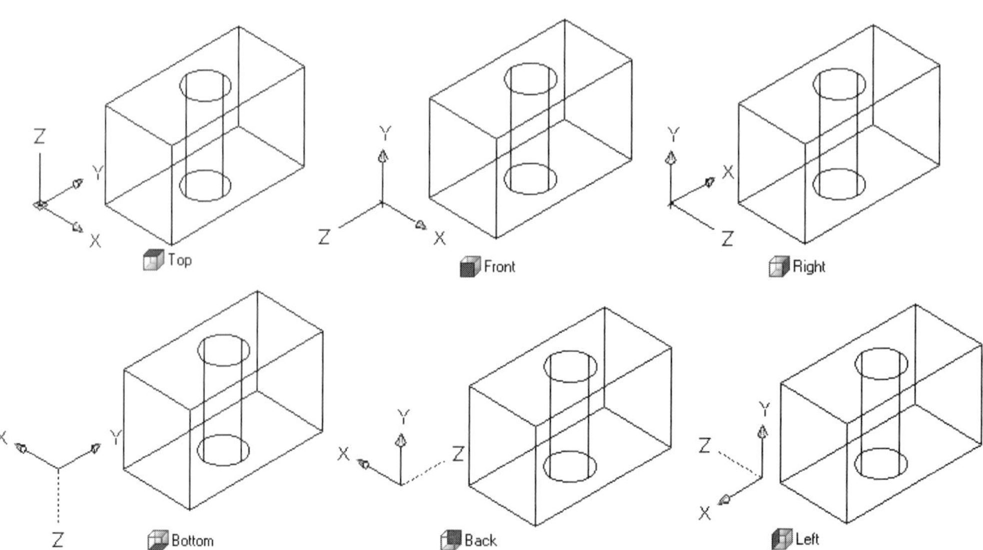

Figure 1-51 All the orthographic UCSs viewed from the same viewing point

An orthographic UCS can be activated from any viewing point, including the orthographic views. When using one of the orthographic views, however, you must not select an orthographic UCS other than the one corresponding to the orthographic view. But if you do so, either the *X*- or the *Y*-axis will not be seen and, therefore, the *XY* plane will be perpendicular to the viewing plane. Such a situation is almost impossible to work with. Figure 1-52 shows the **Top** orthographic view on the left, with the **Top** orthographic UCS selected; on the right, the *Y*-axis disappears after the **Right** UCS is selected.

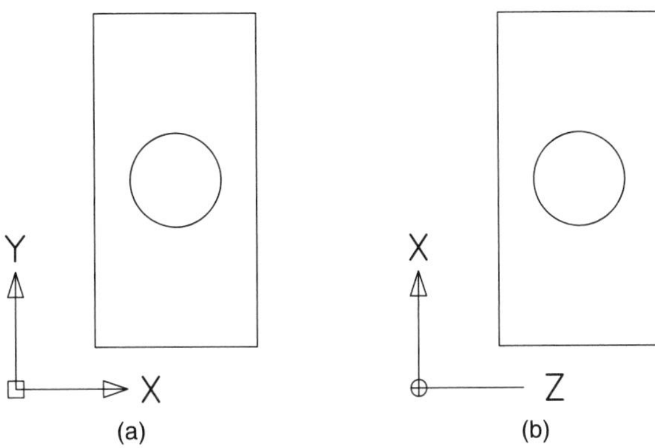

Figure 1-52 (a) The Top view and the Top UCS (b) The Y-axis disappears after you select the Right UCS

The UCSORTHO and UCSFOLLOW System Variables

The orthographic views of the viewing system are closely related to the orthographic UCSs of the coordinate system. The settings of the **UCSORTHO** and the **UCSFOLLOW** system variables determine the way each affects the other.

The **UCSORTHO** system variable determines whether or not selecting an orthographic view automatically sets its corresponding orthographic UCS. When this variable is turned on (**1**), which is the default value, selecting the **Front** view, for example, will automatically set the **Front** UCS.

The **UCSFOLLOW** system variable, on the other hand, determines whether or not selecting an orthographic UCS automatically displays its corresponding orthographic view. When it is turned on (**1**), selecting the **Front** UCS, for example, will automatically display the **Front** view. This system variable is turned off (**0**) by default. It is more convenient to work with the **UCSFOLLOW** system variable turned off. The **PLAN** command can be invoked to align the view with any current UCS.

The PLAN Command

PLAN	
Pull-down Menu	3D Views/ Plan View/ Current UCS
Command Line	plan

The **PLAN** command can change the viewing point so that the view is aligned with the *XY* plane of the current UCS.

Modifying the UCS

Many tools are available in the AutoCAD program to make specific modifications to the current UCS. You can use these tools to align the UCS at your convenience throughout the 3D space. Occasionally, you must perform two or more of these operations in order to achieve the desired result.

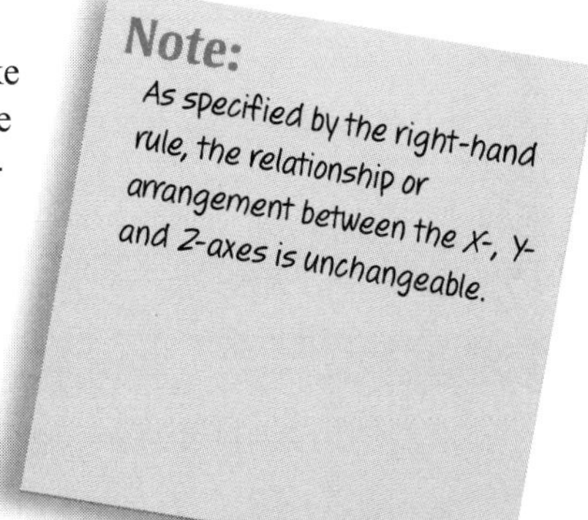

Note:
As specified by the right-hand rule, the relationship or arrangement between the X-, Y- and Z-axes is unchangeable.

UCS ORIGIN	
UCS Toolbar	
Ribbon UCS panel	
Pull-down Menu	Tools/ New UCS/ Origin
Command Line	ucs ↵ o

FOR MORE DETAILS See the information regarding the use of the right-hand rule later in this chapter.

The following is a list of the operations that can be made to the UCS in order to modify it. These are all options of the **UCS** command.

1. Relocate the **Origin** of the UCS.

   With the **Origin UCS** command, you can move the UCS origin to a different location. Its orientation will remain the same.

   ```
   Specify new origin point <0,0,0>:
   ```

2. Specify a **Z Axis Vector**.

   The first point defines the UCS origin. The second point defines the positive direction of the *Z*-axis (Figure 1-53).

   ```
   Specify new origin point or [Object] <0,0,0>:
   Specify point on positive portion of Z-axis <-1.2598,
   -4.7789,5.1736>:
   ```

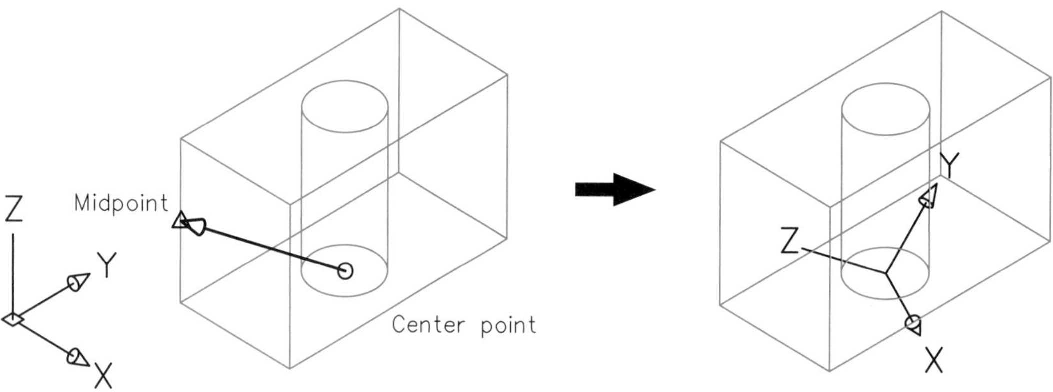

Figure 1-53 Modifying the UCS by specifying a Z-Axis Vector

UCS Z-AXIS	
UCS Toolbar	
Ribbon UCS panel	
Pull-down Menu	Tools/ New UCS/ Z Axis Vector
Command Line	ucs ↵ za

The **Object** option of this method aligns the *XY* plane normal to an open curve, locating the origin at the endpoint closest to the point where the selection was made. The *Z*-axis will be aligned in the opposite direction of the curve (Figure 1-54). This type of alignment is very useful when specifying the path for the **EXTRUSION** or the **SWEEP** commands.

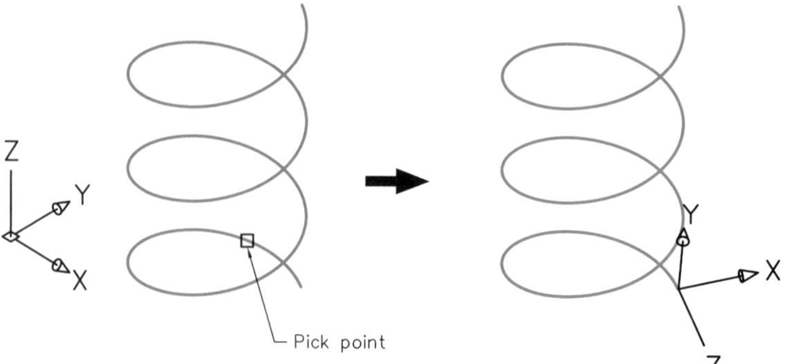

Figure 1-54 Modifying the UCS by using an object to specify a Z-Axis Vector

FOR MORE DETAILS See Chapter 5 to learn more about the EXTRUSION and SWEEP commands.

3. Specify three points (**3 Point**).

   The first point defines the UCS origin. The second point defines the positive direction of the *X*-axis. The third point defines the location and orientation of the UCS (Figure 1-55).

UCS 3 POINTS	
UCS Toolbar	
Ribbon UCS panel	
Pull-down Menu	Tools/ New UCS/ 3 Point
Command Line	ucs ↵ 3

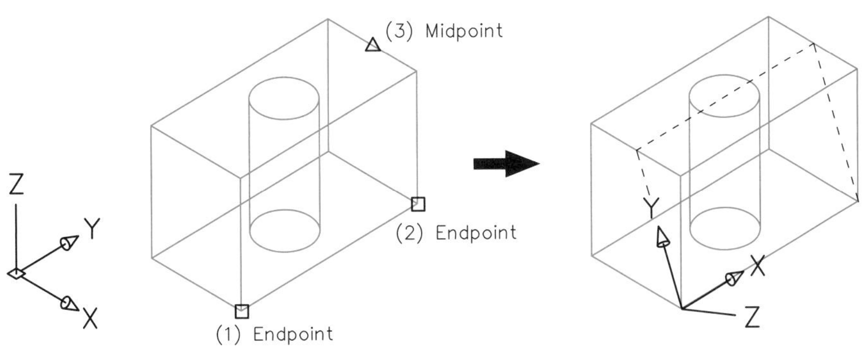

Figure 1-55 Modifying the UCS by specifying three points (3 Point)

4. Rotate about the **X**-, **Y**-, or **Z**-axis.

   This option simply rotates the UCS about the axis specified. The positive rotational direction can be determined by the right-hand rule.

   `Specify rotation angle about X axis <90>:`

UCS X-ROTATE	
UCS Toolbar	
Ribbon UCS panel	
Pull-down Menu	Tools/ New UCS/ X
Command Line	ucs ↵ 3

FOR MORE DETAILS

See the information regarding the use of the right-hand rule later in this chapter.

If you make a mistake when entering a positive or negative angle value, just **UNDO** the operation and enter its opposite value.

UCS Y-ROTATE	
UCS Toolbar	
Ribbon UCS panel	
Pull-down Menu	Tools/ New UCS/ Y
Command Line	ucs ↵ y

5. Align the UCS with the **View**.

   The UCS is aligned with the current viewing plane or display. This modification is very useful when you have saved views, or when placing text aligned with the current viewing plane.

6. Align the UCS with an **Object**.

   The resulting UCS depends on the object selected. For instance, if a circle is selected, the origin will relocate on its center, the *XY* plane will align with the plane in which the circle lies, and the *X*-axis will go through the point where you picked the circle.

   Selecting an arc will relocate the UCS origin in its centerpoint as well. The *X*-axis, however, will pass through one of the endpoints of the arc.

   `Select object to align UCS:`

UCS Z-ROTATE	
UCS Toolbar	
Ribbon UCS panel	
Pull-down Menu	Tools/ New UCS/ Z
Command Line	ucs ↵ z

7. Align the UCS with a 3D solid's **Face**.

   This method can be used only with a planar face of a 3D solid. To select a 3D solid's face you can either click within the boundary of the face or on one of its edges. If you click within the boundary of the face, the origin will relocate on the corner of the face closest to the point where it is selected, and the *X*-axis will align with the closest edge (Figure 1-56).

UCS VIEW	
UCS Toolbar	
Ribbon UCS panel	
Pull-down Menu	Tools/New UCS/View
Command Line	ucs ↵ v

UCS OBJECT	
UCS Toolbar	
Ribbon UCS panel	
Pull-down Menu	Tools/ New UCS/ Object
Command Line	ucs ↵ ob

UCS FACE	
UCS Toolbar	
Ribbon UCS panel	
Pull-down Menu	Tools/New UCS/Face
Command Line	ucs ↵ fa

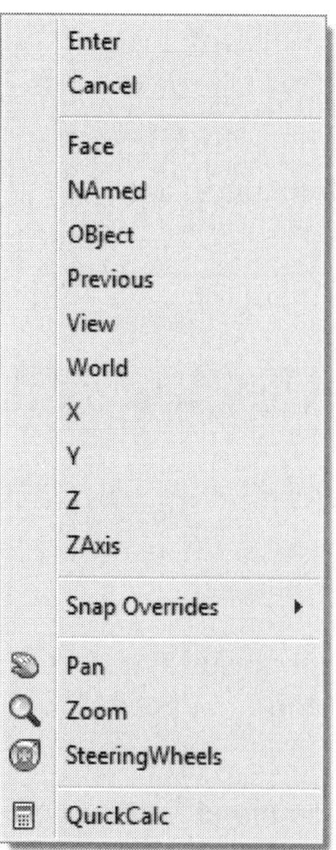

Figure 1-57 The UCS shortcut menu

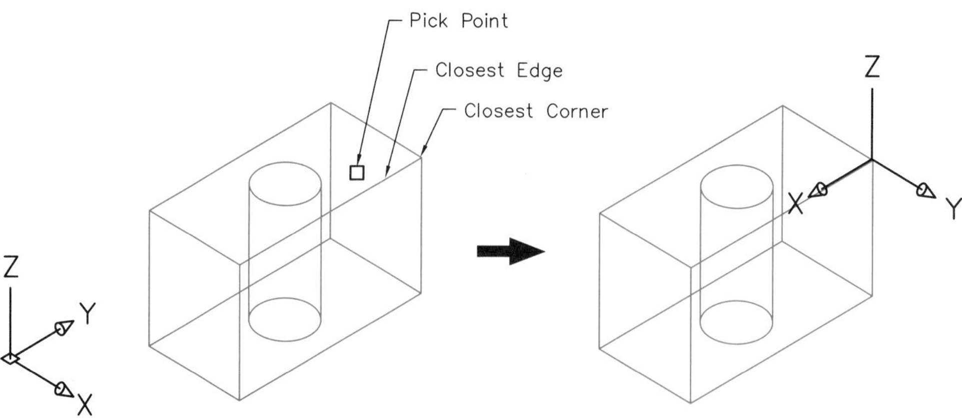

Figure 1-56 Modifying the UCS by aligning it with a 3D solid's face

Because an edge is always shared by two adjacent faces, when selecting an edge you will most likely have to refine your selection. You can do this by using the **Next** option. You can also flip the UCS around the *X*- and *Y*-axes, if necessary.

`Enter an option [Next/Xflip/Yflip] <accept>:`

FOR MORE DETAILS See Chapter 6 to learn more about face selection techniques on 3D solids.

8. Go back to a **Previous** UCS.

   This option allows you to go back to a UCS that you previously defined in the drawing, regardless of whether it has been saved or not. You can go back up to the last ten UCSs used.

9. Restore the **World** UCS.

   The **UCS** shortcut menu, shown in Figure 1-57, provides easy access to the different options used to modify the UCS. You can display this menu by right-clicking in the drawing area while the **UCS** command is in progress.

Exercise 1-5: Modifying the UCS by Specifying 3 Points

1. **OPEN** ***SimpleSolid*** from the location where you saved it.
2. Invoke the **3 Point** option of the **UCS** command. Respond to the prompts as follows:

   `Specify new origin point <0,0,0>:` *`Snap to the top center point of the cylinder`* `[Figure 1-58(a)].`

   `Specify point on positive portion of X-axis <Current X,Y,Z>:` *`Snap to the top-right edge's midpoint.`*

   `Specify point on positive-Y portion of the UCS XY plane <Current X,Y,Z>:` *`Snap to the endpoint shown in`* `Figure 1-58(b).`
3. Select the **SE Isometric** viewing point.
4. Select the **World** UCS.
5. **SAVE** the drawing.

Note

The X-axis is defined by the first two points. The third point defines the XY plane and the rest of the UCS. The Y-axis is then defined as contained in that plane. The third point is on the same side of the X-axis as the Y-axis. A point along the previously defined X-axis is not a valid entry.

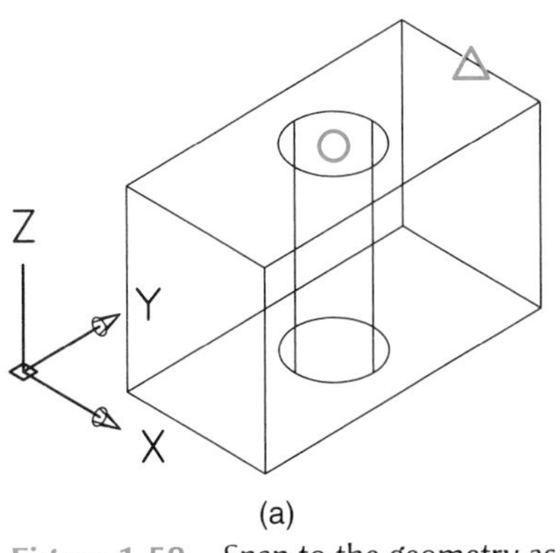

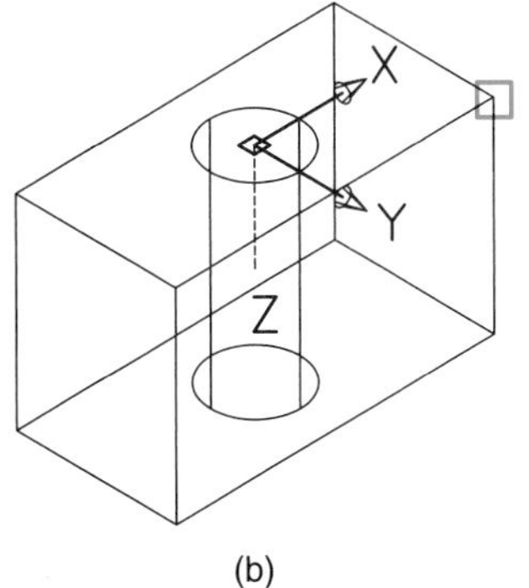

Figure 1-58 Snap to the geometry as shown

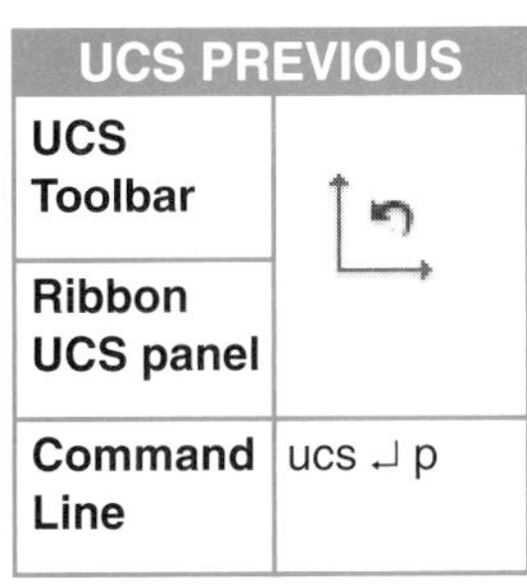

UCS PREVIOUS	
UCS Toolbar	
Ribbon UCS panel	
Command Line	ucs ↵ p

UCS WORLD	
UCS Toolbar	
Ribbon UCS panel	
Command Line	ucs ↵
Drop-down List	UCS II Toolbar

Saving a UCS

After the UCS has been modified, you can save it in order to access it later. By using a saved UCS, you can even modify the location of the planes for the viewing system (Top, Front, Right, etc.) by changing the UCS that these planes are relative to. You will learn more about the procedure to save a UCS in the following exercise.

Exercise 1-6: Working with the UCS Manager

1. **OPEN** ***SimpleSolid.***
2. Rotate the **UCS** 30° around the *X*-axis.

```
Specify rotation angle about X axis <90>: 30 ↵
```

3. Open the **UCS** dialog box to save the UCS you just created.
4. In the **UCS** dialog box (Figure 1-59), click in the **Named UCSs** tab, right-click on the **Unnamed** UCS, and select **Rename** from the list. Type in the new name **MyUCS.** Click on the white area and then click the **OK** button. The new name will appear in the drop-down dialog box on the **UCS II** toolbar (Figure 1-60).
6. Select the **SE Isometric** viewing point.
7. Select the **World** UCS.
8. **SAVE** the drawing.

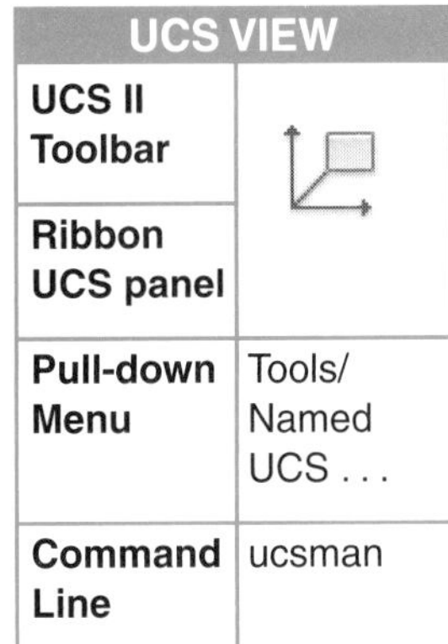

UCS VIEW	
UCS II Toolbar	
Ribbon UCS panel	
Pull-down Menu	Tools/ Named UCS . . .
Command Line	ucsman

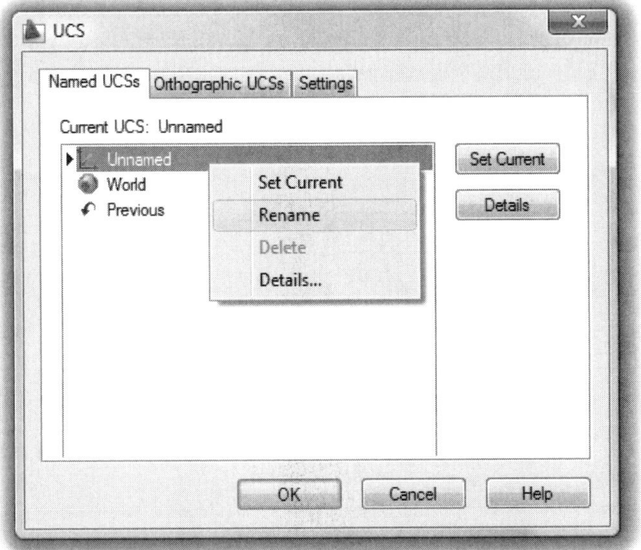

Figure 1-59 Saving a UCS in the UCS dialog box by giving it a name

Figure 1-60 The new named UCS appears in the drop-down dialog box in the UCS II toolbar

Deleting a UCS

To delete a previously saved UCS, open the **UCS** dialog box. In the **Named UCSs** tab, right-click on the saved UCS and click **Delete** (Figure 1-61).

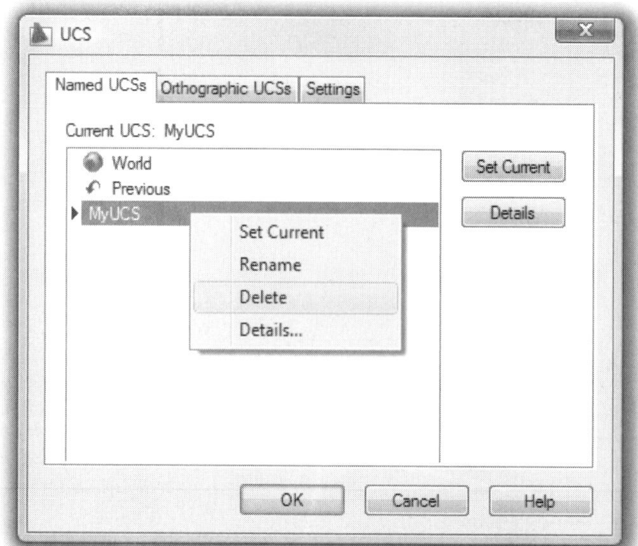

Figure 1-61 Deleting a Saved UCS in the UCS dialog box

Concluding Remarks on the 2D and 3D Environments

As mentioned earlier, the 3D space is always present in AutoCAD. The **2D environment,** however, is the one in which the geometry is placed on a single plane parallel to the current viewing plane, such as the default working condition that is used to generate 2D drawings. This type of work is normally performed on the *XY* plane of the WCS, using the **Top** orthographic view.

An operation that either uses or generates geometry that is not contained in the *XY* plane of the current UCS is considered to be performed in a **3D environment.** This environment requires you to view the model from different viewing points and use different techniques, regardless of how simple the 3D model is.

The UCS Icon

In the **UCS Icon** dialog box (Figure 1-62), you can change the default appearance of the UCS icon by choosing **2D** under the **UCS icon style** setting. You can also change the UCS icon size and modify other settings. The **UCS Icon** dialog box can be accessed by selecting **Properties** from the **View** drop-down menu (Figure 1-63).

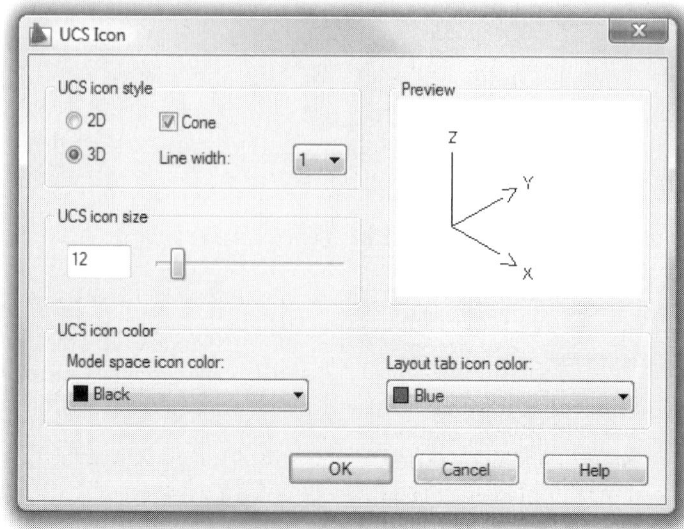

Figure 1-62 The UCS Icon dialog box

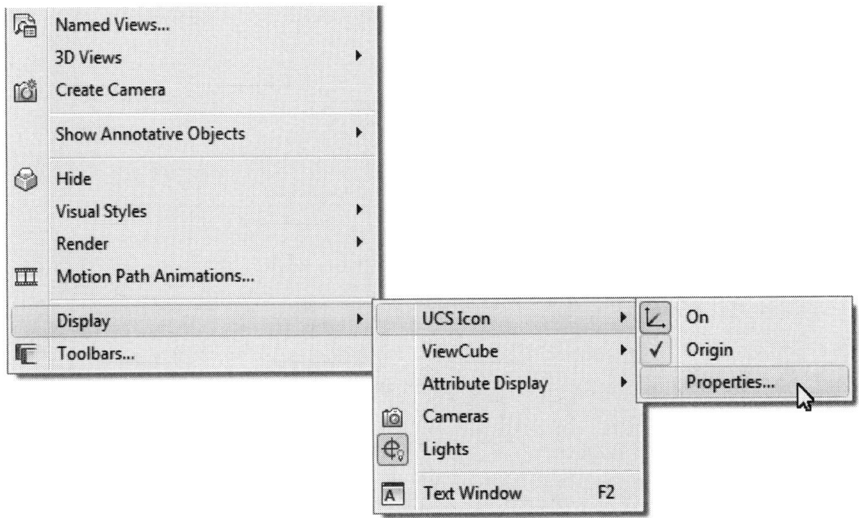

Figure 1-63 Accessing the UCS Icon dialog box from the View drop-down menu

In the same drop-down menu, you can turn the UCS icon either on or off. You can also choose whether the UCS icon will display at the origin or in the lower-left corner on the drawing area.

The 3D Crosshairs Cursor

When working in a 3D environment, you can choose one of the two following looks for the crosshairs cursor:

- The traditional look, showing only two hairs aligned with the *X*- and *Y*-axes [Figure 1-64(a)].
- The 3D look, which shows all three axes aligned with the current UCS. The longer portions of the hairs show the positive direction of each axis [Figure 1-64(b)].

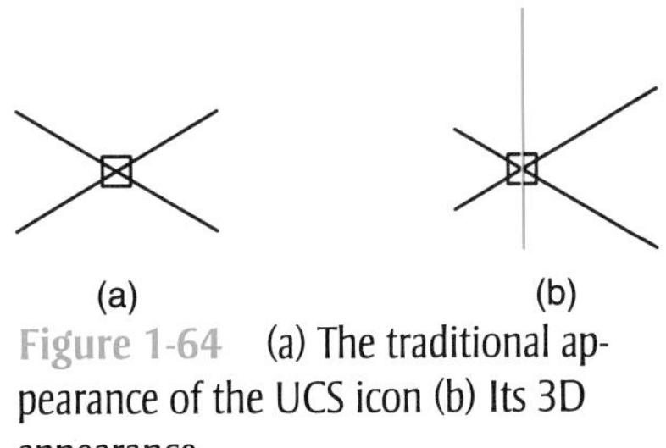

Figure 1-64 (a) The traditional appearance of the UCS icon (b) Its 3D appearance

You can control this setting in the **3D Modeling** tab of the **Options** dialog box (Figure 1-65) by selecting **Show Z axis in crosshairs** under **3D Crosshairs.** The 3D look will not show if you switch to a 2D environment (i.e., select an orthogonal view, align the UCS to the viewing plane, or align the viewing plane with the *XY* plane of the current UCS). You can also control where the 3D crosshairs will show the labels for the *X*-, *Y*-, and *Z*-axes, or any other customized labels.

You can display the crosshairs either in different colors (red, green, and blue) or in a single color. You can change this setting in the **Drawing Window Colors** dialog box (Figure 1-66). This window is accessed by clicking the **Colors . . .** button on the **Display** tab of the **Options** dialog box.

In the **Drawing Window Colors** dialog box, you select **3D parallel projection** from the **Context:** window, which is the preferred working context for 3D modeling. Then you select **Crosshairs** from the **Interface element:** window and, finally, check the **Tint for X, Y, Z** checkbox. You cannot change the color of the three hairs; you can, however, change the tint of the three colors used from lighter to darker by selecting a different **Color.**

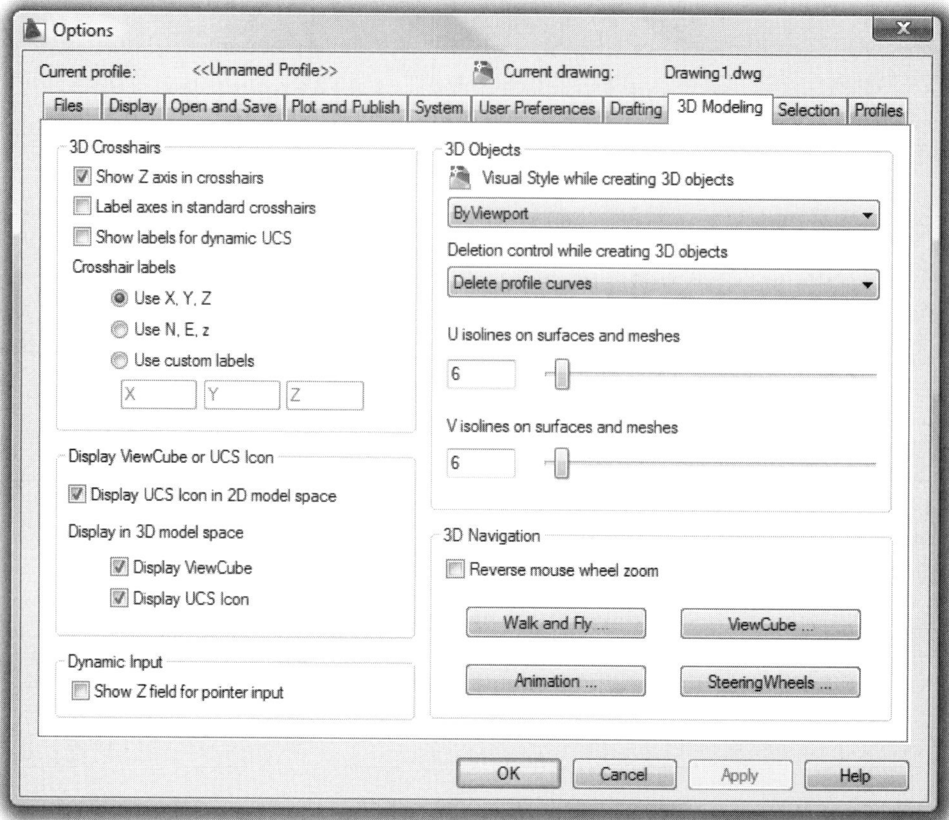

Figure 1-65 Controlling the UCS icon's appearance in the 3D Modeling tab of the Options dialog box

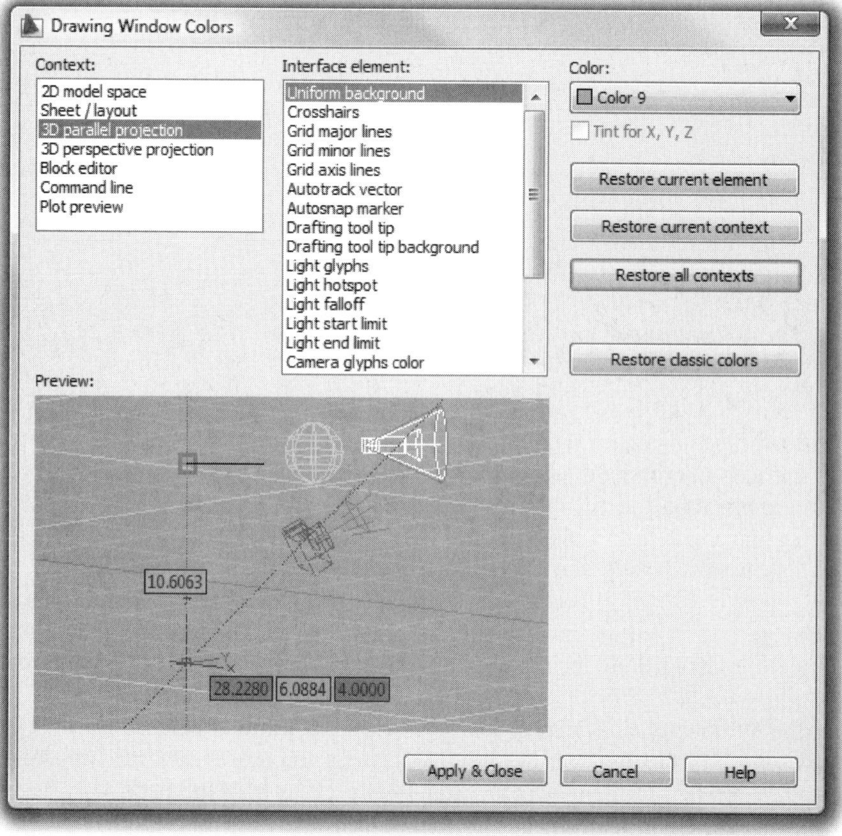

Figure 1-66 Changing the UCS icon's colors in the Drawing Window Colors dialog box

USING THE DYNAMIC UCS

When the **Dynamic UCS** is on, you can easily create objects on the faces of 3D solids, regardless of the UCS currently in use. This feature temporarily auto-aligns the UCS with one of the faces of the 3D solid as you place the crosshairs close to it in a situation in which the progress of a command requires you to specify a point. The faces will highlight and the crosshairs change their orientation as you hover over the different faces. Clicking or snapping to geometry while a face is highlighted concludes the definition of the UCS with which the object will be aligned.

The **Dynamic UCS** feature is controlled by the **DUCS** button on the status bar. You can also change its setting by pressing the <**F6**> key or by invoking the **UCSDETECT** system variable. This feature should be turned on only at the precise moment of placing objects on a face of a 3D solid to avoid affecting other 3D operations.

Exercise 1-7: Using the Dynamic UCS

1. **OPEN** ***SimpleSolid.***
2. **SAVE** the drawing **AS** ***Exercise 1-7.***
3. Turn **DUCS** mode on.
4. Invoke the **BOX** command by typing it in the command line, and respond to the prompts as follows:

   Specify first corner or [Center]: *Move the crosshairs over the right face of the 3D solid. Once the face is highlighted, snap to the top rightmost endpoint.*

   Specify other corner or [Cube/Length]: *Snap to the midpoint of the bottom edge.*

   Specify height or [2Point] <1.0000>: *1* ↵
5. The 3D model should look like Figure 1-67. Invoke the **CIRCLE** command, and respond to the prompts as follow:

   Specify center point for circle or [3P/2P/Ttr (tan tan radius)]: *m2p* ↵

   First point of mid: *Snap to the midpoint of any of the four edges of the front face.*

   Second point of mid: *Snap to the midpoint of its opposite parallel edge.*

   Specify radius of circle or [Diameter]: *.5* ↵
6. Invoke the **HIDE** command. The 3D model should look like Figure 1-68.
7. **SAVE** the drawing.

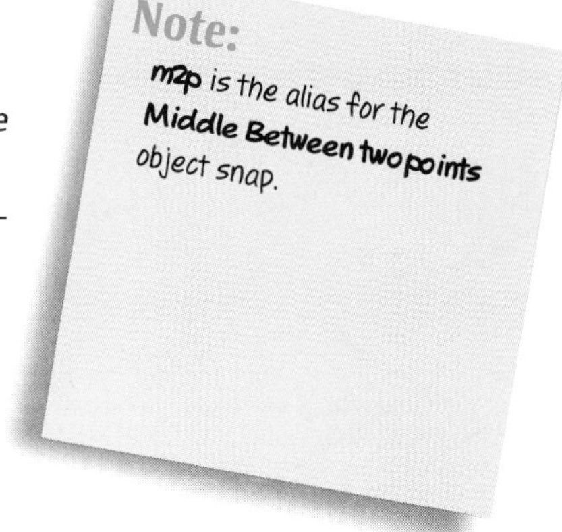

Note:
m2p is the alias for the Middle Between two points object snap.

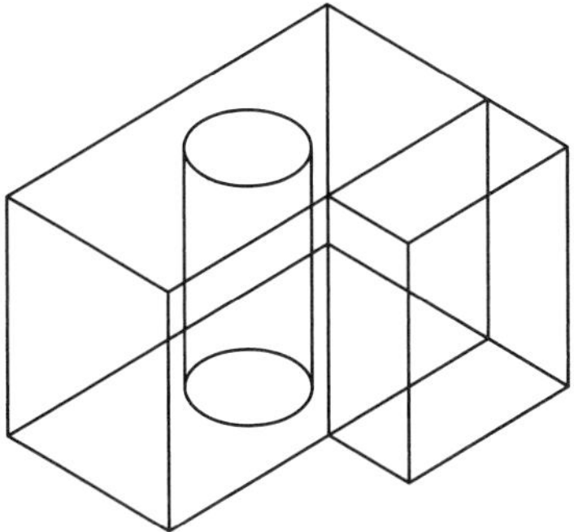

Figure 1-67 The 3D model after adding a box using the Dynamic UCS

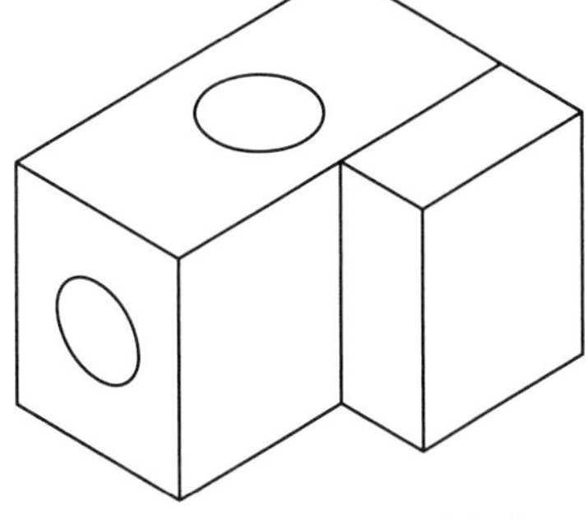

Figure 1-68 The 3D model after invoking the HIDE command

Entering Point Coordinates in 3D

Rectangular Coordinates

In a 2D coordinate system, the rectangular coordinates of a point are expressed as *X,Y*, where *X* is the distance from the origin 0,0 to the point parallel to the *X*-axis, and *Y* is the distance from the origin 0,0 to the point parallel to the *Y*-axis. Figure 1-69 shows the point 1.25, 0.75 located on the *XY* plane.

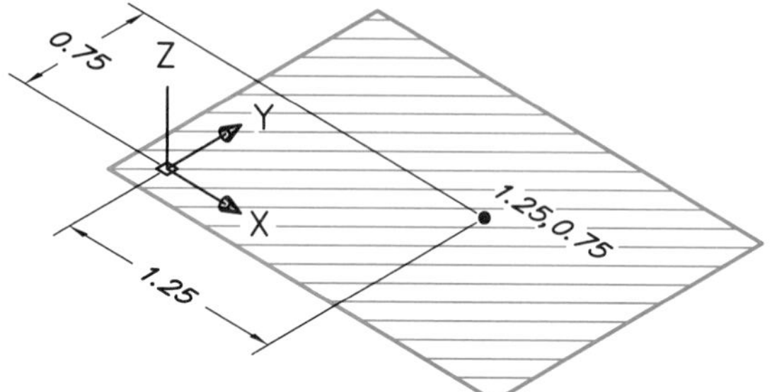

Figure 1-69 The 2D rectangular coordinates of the point 1.25, 0.75

Working in 2D does not require a specified *Z* value. All objects are placed on the *XY* plane, where the *Z* value for any given point is 0. This operation simulates drawing on a piece of paper.

In a 3D coordinate system, the rectangular coordinates of a point are expressed as *X,Y, Z*. Here *Z* is the distance from the origin 0,0,0 to the point parallel to the *Z*-axis. Figure 1-70 shows the point 1.25, 0.75, 1.00.

Note:

Any point in the AutoCAD display has 3D coordinates. The Z coordinate is simply assumed to be 0 when its value is not specified.

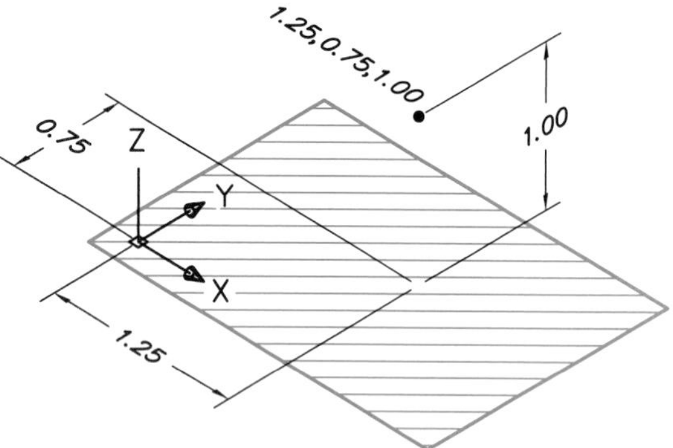

Figure 1-70 The 3D rectangular coordinates of the point 1.25, 0.75, 1.00

Polar Coordinates

In a 2D coordinate system, the polar coordinates of a point are expressed as $r < \theta$, where *r* is the distance of a straight line measured from the origin 0,0 to the point (or the radius of an imaginary circle whose center is located at 0,0) and θ is the angle, measured counterclockwise, between the *X*-axis and the straight line between the origin and the point. Figure 1-71 shows the point 1.46<31.

In a 3D coordinate system, the polar coordinates of a point can be expressed in one of the following ways:

- Cylindrical coordinates
- Spherical coordinates

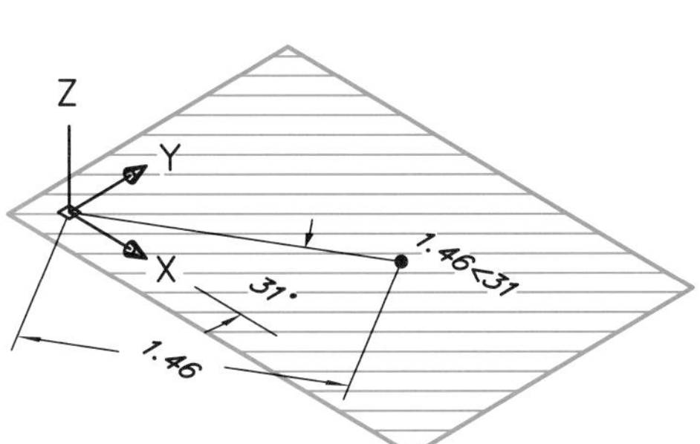

Figure 1-71 The 2D polar coordinates of the point 1.46<31

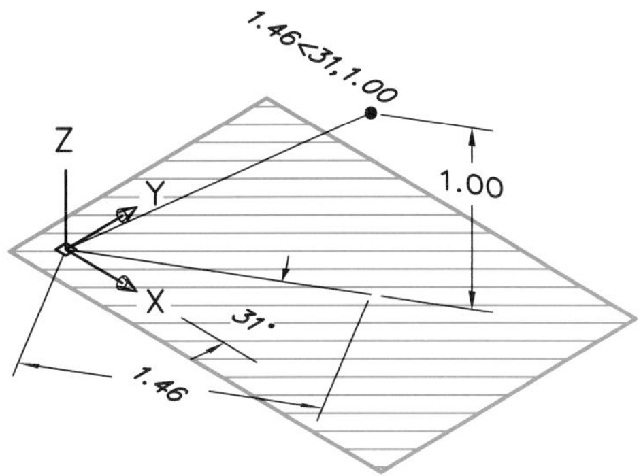

Figure 1-72 The cylindrical coordinates of the point 1.46<31, 1.00

The polar cylindrical coordinates of a point are expressed as $r < \theta, Z$. This expression is just an extension of the 2D polar coordinates. $r < \theta$ are the 2D polar coordinates of the projection of the point onto the *XY* plane. *Z* is the distance from the *XY* plane to the point. Figure 1-72 shows the cylindrical coordinates of the point 1.46<31,1.00.

The polar spherical coordinates of a point are expressed as $r < \theta < \varphi$. These are not as close to the 2D polar coordinates, because *r* now is the 3D distance of an imaginary line that extends from the origin 0,0,0 to the point itself, θ is still the angle between the *X*-axis and a line between the origin and the point projected onto the *XY* plane, and φ is the angle between the imaginary line representing the 3D distance and the *XY* plane. Figure 1-73 shows the spherical coordinates of the point 1.77<31<34 (the same point as 1.46<31,1.00, but expressed in a different manner).

Unless necessary, entering 3D points in either rectangular or polar coordinates is impractical, and may result in extensive work. In many 3D operations, AutoCAD generates geometry whose points can be specified later in any command. Figure 1-74 shows a 3D solid box after it has been sliced and moved away. This operation generates new geometry, which you can snap to when specifying a point, such as the midpoint shown.

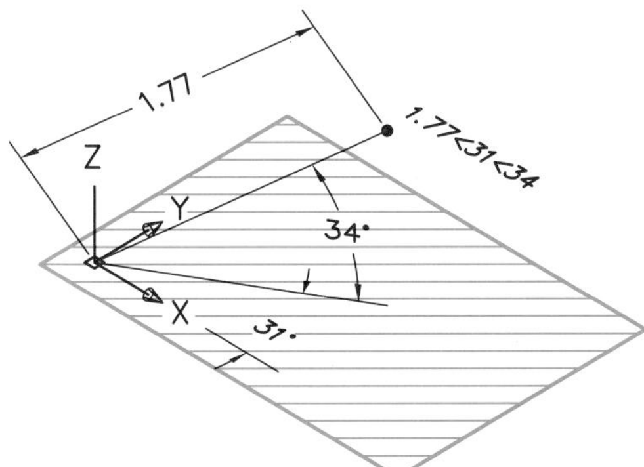

Figure 1-73 The spherical coordinates of the point 1.77<31<34

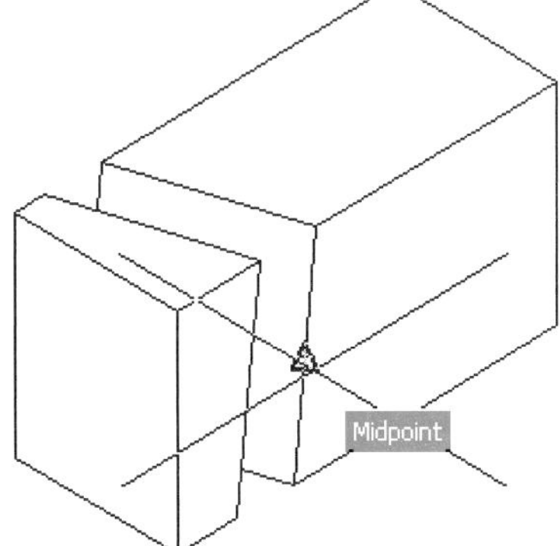

Figure 1-74 New geometry generated after slicing a 3D solid box

Exercise 1-8: Specifying Points in Cylindrical Coordinates

1. Start a **NEW** drawing using the **acad** template.
2. **SAVE** the drawing **AS** ***Exercise 1-8.***
3. Select the **Isometric SE** viewing point.
4. Using the **PAN** command, displace the drawing area so that the UCS icon appears more or less centered on the screen.

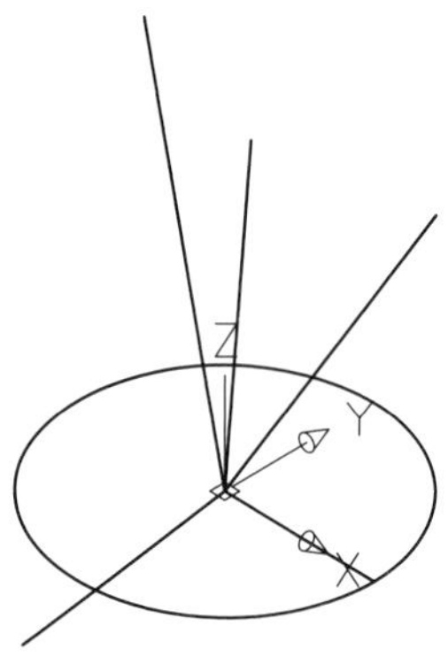

Figure 1-75 The 3D model after drawing the circle

5. Invoke the **LINE** command five times to draw five lines. Each line will start on the point 0,0,0 and will end on each of the following points:
   - 1.5<158,3
   - 1.5<45,2.32
   - 1.5<0,0
   - 1.5<–38, 4
   - 1.5<214.2,–1
6. Invoke the **CIRCLE** command and draw a circle with the center on 0,0,0 and a radius of **1.5** (Figure 1-75).
7. Select the **Top** orthographic view. The drawing should look like Figure 1-76.
8. **SAVE** the drawing.

Note:
All the endpoints of the lines were specified using the same *r* value. Therefore all the points are located on the surface of an imaginary cylinder, which projects on the Top plane as a circle of equal radius.

Exercise 1-9: Specifying Points in Spherical Coordinates

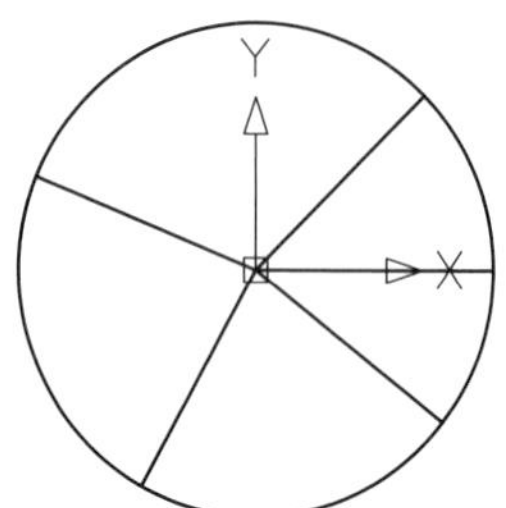

Figure 1-76 The 3D model as seen from the Top view

1. Start a **NEW** drawing using the **acad** template.
2. **SAVE** the drawing **AS *Exercise 1-9.***
3. Select the **Isometric SE** viewing point.
4. Using the **PAN** command, displace the drawing area so that the UCS icon appears more or less centered on the screen.
5. Invoke the **LINE** command five times to draw five lines. Each line will start on the point 0,0,0 and will end on each of the following points:
   - 1.5<158<31
   - 1.5<45<–91.5
   - 1.5<0<0
   - 1.5<–38<47
   - 1.5<214.2<–31
6. Invoke the **SPHERE** command by typing it in the command line. When prompted, specify **0,0,0** for the center and **1.4** for the radius.
7. Change the color of the 3D solid sphere to yellow.
8. Set the **FACETRES** system variable value to **6.**
9. Select the **Realistic** visual style from the drop-down menus, located at **View/Visual Styles.**
10. Invoke the **3DORBIT** command by typing its name in the command line window. In the drawing area, hold the click button of the mouse and drag it to interactively change the viewing point (Figure 1-77).
11. **SAVE** the drawing.

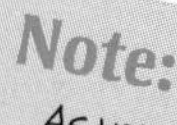
Note:
As you can see, all the lines stick out the same distance from the sphere (0.1 unit). In spherical coordinates, the *r* value determines the imaginary sphere in which the point is located in the 3D space.

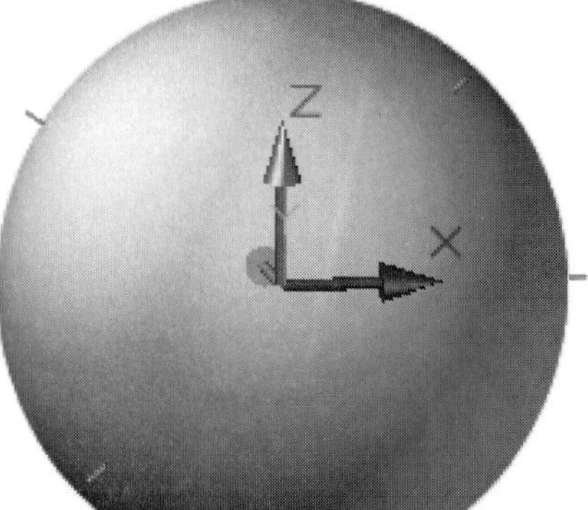

Figure 1-77 The 3D model after rotating the viewing point

THE RIGHT-HAND RULE

When working in a 3D environment you can use your right hand as a mnemonic tool to easily orient yourself in the 3D space. Two different uses of the ***right-hand rule*** can be given:

right-hand rule: A method used to remember the unchangeable relationship between the three axes of the coordinate system and the positive rotation about them.

1. Determining the positive direction of the *X*-, *Y*-, and *Z*-axes.

The relationship between the positive directions of the three axes is unchangeable. By knowing the positive direction of any two axes you can determine the positive direction of the third one.

Close all your right-hand fingers, open the thumb and index finger until they make a square, then open the middle finger halfway. The thumb represents the *X*-axis, the index finger represents the *Y*-axis, and the middle finger the *Z*-axis (Figure 1-78). Rotating your hand so that any two fingers align with the positive direction of their corresponding axes determines the positive direction of the third one.

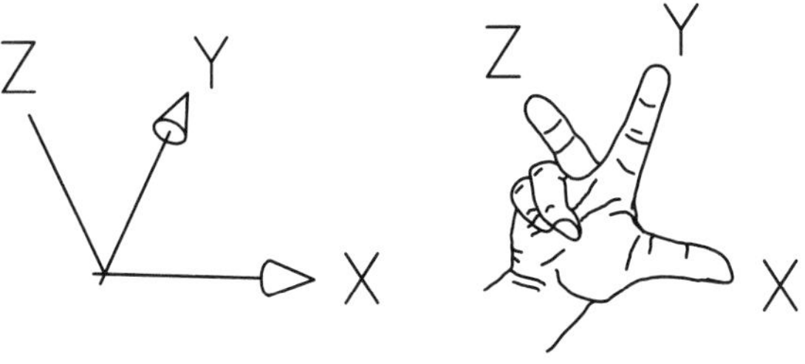

Figure 1-78 Using the right-hand rule to determine the relationship between the three axes

This rule was very useful in AutoCAD 2000 or earlier versions for determining the positive direction of the *Z*-axis because no 3D UCS icon was available. You can still use it as an aid to visualize the 3D coordinate system.

2. Determining the positive rotation about an axis.

Curling the fingers of your right hand while pointing the thumb in the positive direction of any axis shows you the positive direction of rotation about the axis (Figure 1-79).

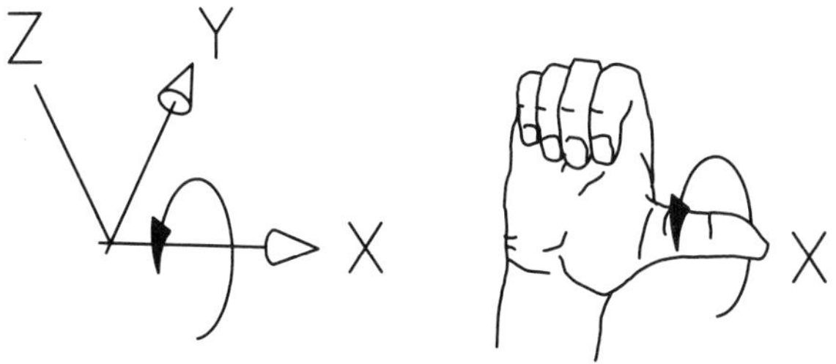

Figure 1-79 Using the right-hand rule to determine the positive rotation about any axis

TIP

You should use the right-hand rule to find the positive direction within any tool where rotation is involved.

THE 3D ORBIT TOOL

Besides the six orthographic views and the four Isometric viewing points, you can use the ***3D Orbit*** viewing tool to dynamically change the viewing point. The **3DORBIT** command launches this viewing tool. After it is invoked, all you need to do is to click and drag the cursor in the drawing area to interactively rotate the entire viewing system. This operation does not affect the UCS; it

3D Orbit: The most useful viewing tool for quickly selecting any viewing point.

just follows whatever rotation is made to the viewing system. The UCS icon changes to shaded 3D look while the 3D Orbit is active because the AutoCAD program automatically changes to the **3D Wireframe** visual style in case the **2D Wireframe** visual style is being used.

FOR MORE DETAILS To learn more about the different visual styles, see the "Using the Predefined Visual Styles" section in this chapter.

3D Orbit must be used when an Isometric viewing point does not provide a clear picture due to the location of the object's edges in the 3D space. Figure 1-80(a) is a clear example of such a situation. Slightly changing the viewing point [Figure 1-80(b)] shows the edges of the same 3D model more clearly.

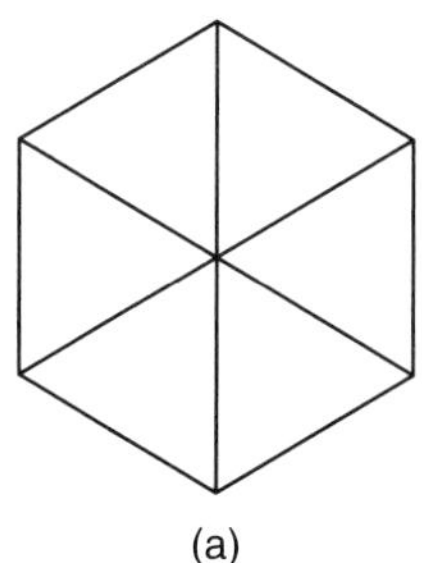
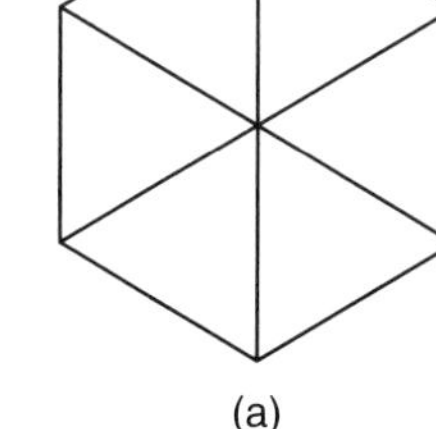

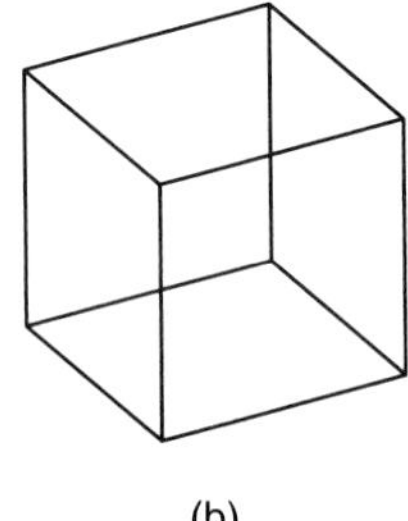

Figure 1-80 Slightly changing the viewing point shows the edges of the 3D model more clearly

3DORBIT	
3D Navigation Toolbar	
Ribbon Navigation panel	
Pull-down Menu	View/ Orbit/ Cons-trained Orbit
Command Line	3dorbit

The **3D Orbit** viewing tool can be used in two different modes. Each mode is activated by a different command:

- **Constrained Orbit,** invoked with the **3DORBIT** command
- **Free Orbit,** invoked with the **3DFORBIT** command

The **Constrained Orbit** mode constrains orbiting so that the *Z*-axis maintains its verticality at all times, as well as any edges parallel to it. The Arcball is not shown while this command is active. The **Free Orbit** mode, on the other hand, allows orbiting in any direction, and it shows the Arcball.

You can invoke the **3DFORBIT** command by pressing the <**Shift**> key and the wheel button of the mouse simultaneously. The **3DORBIT** command can be invoked by pressing the <**Shift**> + <**Ctrl**> keys and the wheel button of the mouse simultaneously, too. While using these methods all you have to do is drag the mouse while the wheel button and the specific key(s) are pressed.

Note: Regardless of which command you invoke, you can switch between these two modes within the same operation by using the **3D Orbit** shortcut menu. You will see more details about this in the next topic.

3DFORBIT	
3D Navigation Toolbar	
Ribbon Navigation panel	
Pull-down Menu	View/ 3D Orbit
Command Line	3dforbit

TIP Both the **3DORBIT** and **3DFORBIT** commands can be used transparently while other commands are in progress.

When invoking the **3DFORBIT** command, you will see the Arcball, which is represented as a big circle with four smaller ones on its quadrants (Figure 1-81). The UCS icon changes its appearance, and the cursor changes to an orbit-like type.

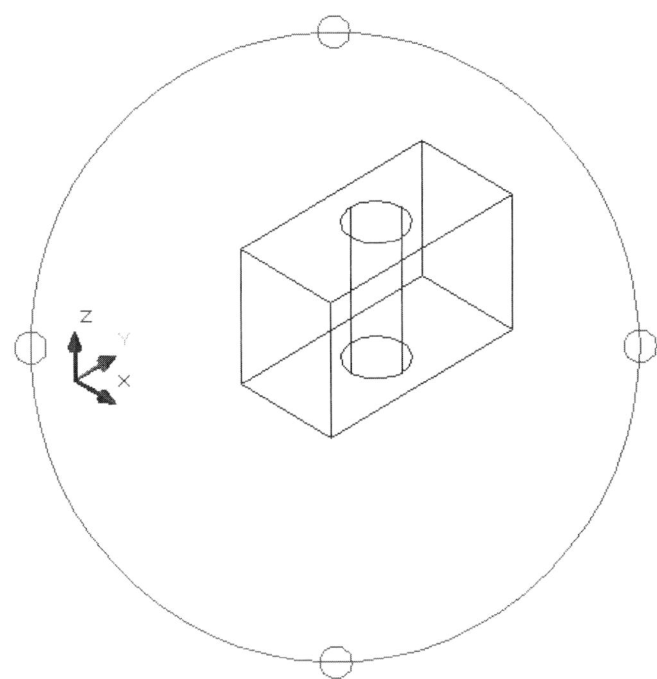

Figure 1-81 The Arcball after invoking the 3DFORBIT command

The pointer changes its appearance as you move it from one location to another. Clicking and dragging the mouse in each particular location causes a different effect (Table 1-1). If the command is invoked by pressing the <**Shift**> + <**Ctrl**> keys along with the wheel button, such effects will not be available.

Table 1-1 Figures, to Obtain Pointers

Pointer	Location where it shows up	Effect
	Inside the Arcball	Spins your model around an imaginary axis that is perpendicular to the direction you are moving your pointer to
	Outside the Arcball	Spins your model around an imaginary axis that is perpendicular to the display
	Inside the left or right small circles	Spins your model around an imaginary vertical axis
	Inside the top or bottom small circles	Spins your model around an imaginary horizontal axis

Exercise 1-10: The 3D Orbit

1. **OPEN** ***SimpleSolid.***
2. Select the **SW Isometric** view and invoke the **ZOOM Realtime** command to zoom into your drawing.
3. Invoke the **3DORBIT** command and spin the object around to inspect all its faces.
4. Select the **SE Isometric** viewing point.
5. Select the **World** UCS.
6. **SAVE** the drawing.

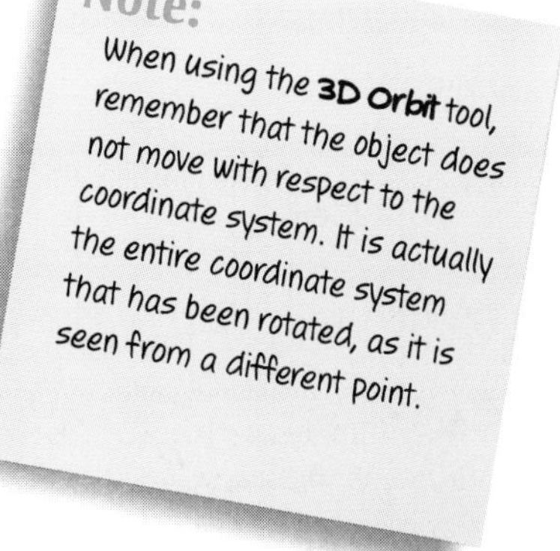

Note:
When using the 3D Orbit tool, remember that the object does not move with respect to the coordinate system. It is actually the entire coordinate system that has been rotated, as it is seen from a different point.

The 3D Orbit Shortcut Menu: Other 3D Navigation Tools

Right-clicking in the drawing area while the **3D Orbit** tool is activated displays the **3D Orbit** shortcut menu (Figure 1-82). Through this shortcut menu you can perform the following operations:

- Select different visual styles
- Select preset and named views
- Use other visual aids: compass, grid, and UCS icon

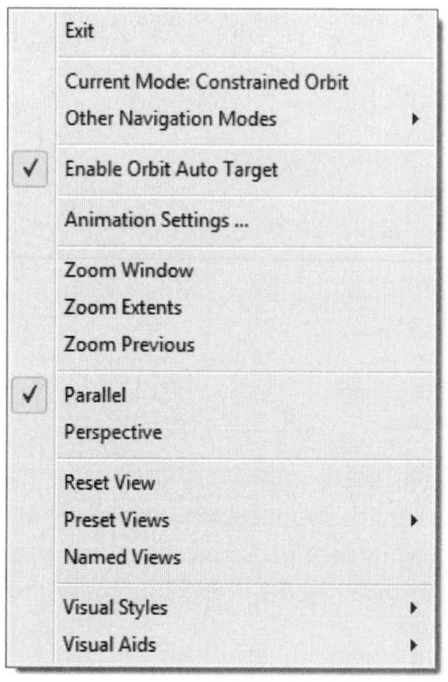

Figure 1-82 The 3D Orbit shortcut menu

- Switch between parallel and perspective views
- Enable Orbit Auto Target
- Use other navigation modes

FOR MORE DETAILS	The **Visual Styles** and **Named Views** options are explained later in this chapter.

Other Visual Aids. Deactivating the **UCS Icon** turns this element off, even after exiting the 3D Orbit tool. Activating the **Grid** displays this element, which is the same as pressing the <**F7**> key outside the **3D Orbit** tool. Activating the **Compass** enhances the **3D Orbit** appearance by showing a scale around the axes and their rotations.

perspective view: View in which the 3D objects represented give the impression not only of height, width, and depth, but also of relative distance from the viewing point to the viewing target.

Parallel and Perspective Views. You can switch between these two viewing modes by selecting them from the shortcut menu while in the **3DORBIT** command. You can also change this setting outside the **3DORBIT** command through the **PERSPECTIVE** system variable. The parallel view and ***perspective view*** are compared in Figure 1-83.

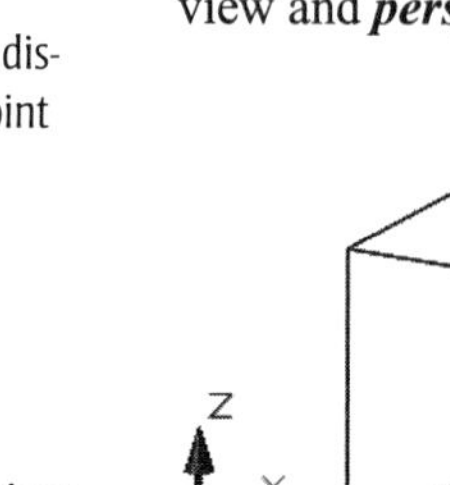
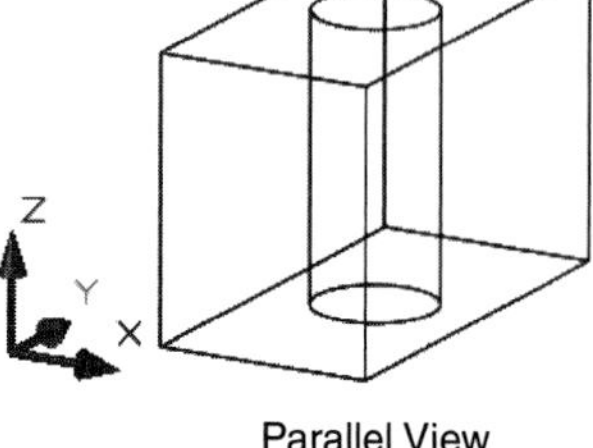

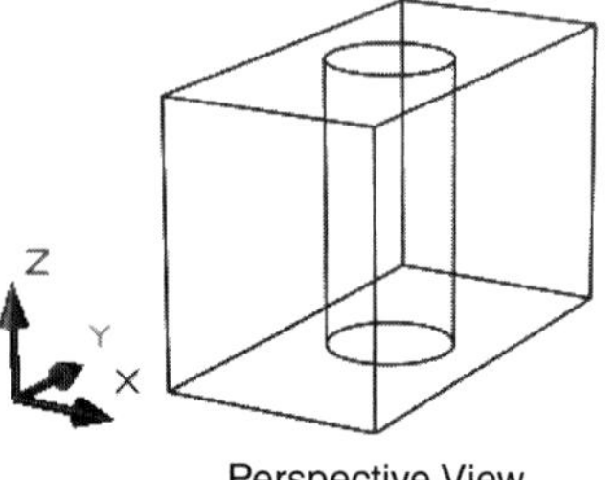

Figure 1-83 Comparison between the parallel and perspective views

Orbit Auto Target. This feature keeps the target point on the objects you are viewing rather than on the center of the viewport. It is turned on by default. Besides this feature, you can also use the **3DORBITCTR** command, which allows you to specify the exact center of the orbiting operation.

Other Navigation Modes. Inside the **Other Navigation Modes** submenu (Figure 1-84) you will find tools associated with the viewing system:

- **Continuous Orbit** causes the 3D model to spin continuously in a direction specified by briefly clicking and dragging the left mouse button in the drawing area.
- **Swivel** simulates the effect of swiveling the camera.

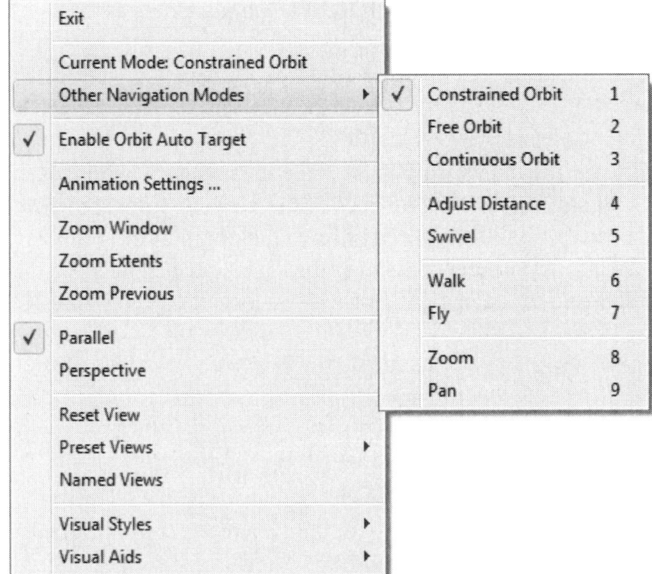

Figure 1-84 The Other Navigation Modes submenu

- **Walk** allows you to move the viewing point as if you were walking through the 3D model at a fixed height above the *XY* plane. This operation is available only in a perspective view.
- **Fly** allows you to move the viewing point to simulate flying through the 3D model without being restricted to a fixed height above the *XY* plane. This operation is available only in a perspective view.
- **Zoom** and **Pan** allow you to use the **3DZOOM** and **3DPAN** commands inside the **3D Orbit** tool.

FOR MORE DETAILS See Chapter 9 for more details about the **Walk** and **Fly** operations, using the **3DWALK** and **3DFLY** commands.

Visualizing objects three-dimensionally requires special imaginative and abstract skills. The 3D viewing system of the AutoCAD program, along with the **3D Orbit** tool, allow users to observe 3D models from virtually anywhere, regardless of whether 3D abstract visualization is present or not.

Therefore, achieving a complete understanding of the 3D viewing system is a key factor for success in 3D modeling. Recognizing the different operations of the 3D viewing system and becoming proficient in their use will automatically improve the user's 3D visualization, which is an asset for the workplace.

The 3DZOOM and 3DPAN Commands

Using the **ZOOM** and **PAN** commands provides effects similar to those of the **3DZOOM** and **3DPAN** commands. The two last commands, however, are much better tools for a 3D environment.

The regular **ZOOM** and **PAN** commands sometimes require invoking the **REGEN** command intermediately to be able to proceed. With the **3DZOOM** and **3DPAN** commands, however, this is not necessary.

The **3DZOOM** and **3DPAN** commands can be invoked in the following ways:

- From the icons located in the **3DORBIT** toolbar
- Entering **3dzoom** or **3dpan** in the command line
- Activating the standard **ZOOM** and **PAN** commands while any visual style is active (except the default **2D Wireframe** visual style)
- Through the **3DORBIT** command's shortcut menu
- By manipulating the mouse wheel while inside the **3DORBIT** command

The VPOINT Command

The **VPOINT** command allows you to define the viewing point more accurately. When invoked through the command line, it allows you to enter the coordinates of the viewing point anywhere in the 3D space. This point defines a vector from the viewing point to the origin of the WCS.

The viewing plane on your screen is aligned perpendicular to the vector defined between the viewing point and the origin. This establishes the direction in which you look at objects in the 3D space.

The **Rotate** option specifies a new viewing vector using two angles:

```
Enter angle in XY plane from X axis <315>:
Enter angle from XY plane <35>:
```

The first angle is the angle between the projection of the viewing vector on the *XY* plane of the WCS and its *X*-axis. The second angle is measured between the viewing vector and the *XY* plane of the **World** UCS.

For example, the two angles corresponding to the **SE Isometric** viewing point are **315°** and **35°;** and the angles corresponding to the **Right** view are **0°** and **0°.**

Pressing <**Enter**> displays a compass and axis tripod, allowing you also to define a viewing direction.

Exercise 1-11: Using the VPOINT Command

1. **OPEN** ***SimpleSolid.***
2. **SAVE** the drawing **AS** ***Exercise 1-11.***
3. Invoke the **VPOINT** command by typing its name in the command line. When prompted to specify a viewing point, enter **1,0.5,2.5.**
4. **ZOOM** out. The display reflects the new viewing direction (Figure 1-85).
5. Draw a line from the point **0,0,0** to the point **1,0.5,2.5.**

Note:
The line cannot be seen before the **SE Isometric** viewing point is selected because it is located in the same direction as the viewing vector.

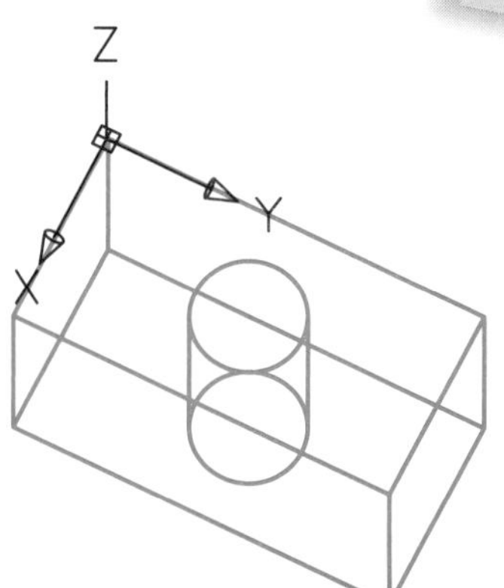

Figure 1-85 The viewing point modified with the VPOINT command

6. Select the **SE Isometric** viewing point to see the location of the line.
7. **SAVE** the drawing.

The CAMERA Command

The **CAMERA** command allows you to specify and save different viewing directions by specifying the camera location, or viewing point, and the target location. The **VPOINT** command, on the other hand, allows you to specify only the viewing point because the viewing target is always the origin of the WCS.

The **CAMERA** command creates a special object or entity called a ***camera.*** The **CAMERADISPLAY** system variable controls whether or not the cameras are shown. Its value, however, is automatically set to **1** (on) whenever a camera is created. Selecting a camera object will display a pyramid representing its viewing field (Figure 1-86). It will also display the **Camera Preview** window, containing a perspective preview of the 3D model as seen by the selected camera (Figure 1-87). You can use the grips of the viewing field to manipulate the camera lens length as well as the camera and target locations.

camera: An object that encapsulates the geometric definitions of a particular view.

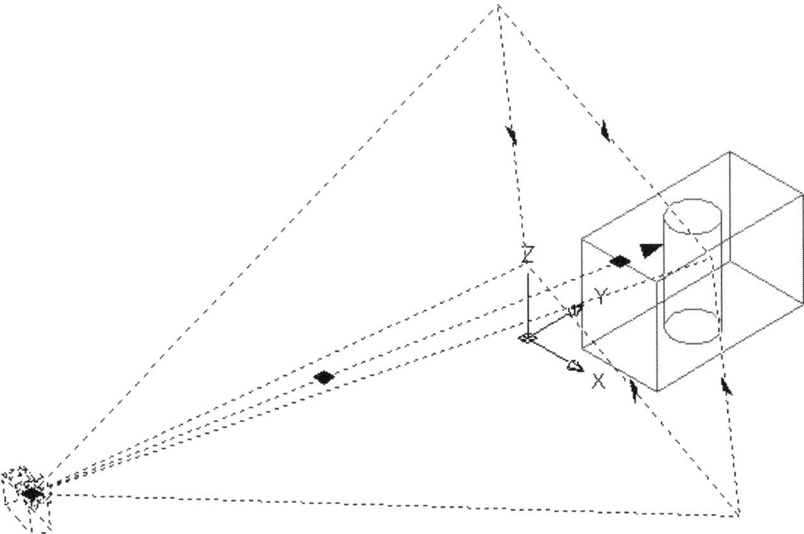

Figure 1-86 A camera object selected

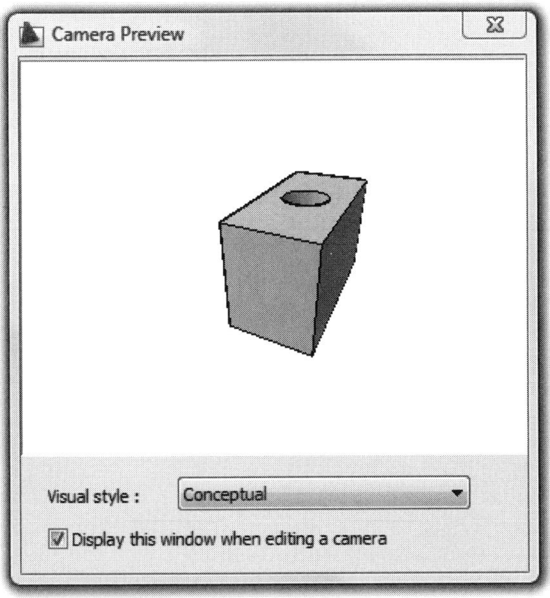

Figure 1-87 The Camera Preview window

Each camera creates a new model view, which allows you to quickly change between previously defined viewing points. Model views are displayed in the drop-down list of the **View** toolbar (Figure 1-88). Selecting a model view changes the display to a perspective view according to the camera geometric definitions (Figure 1-89).

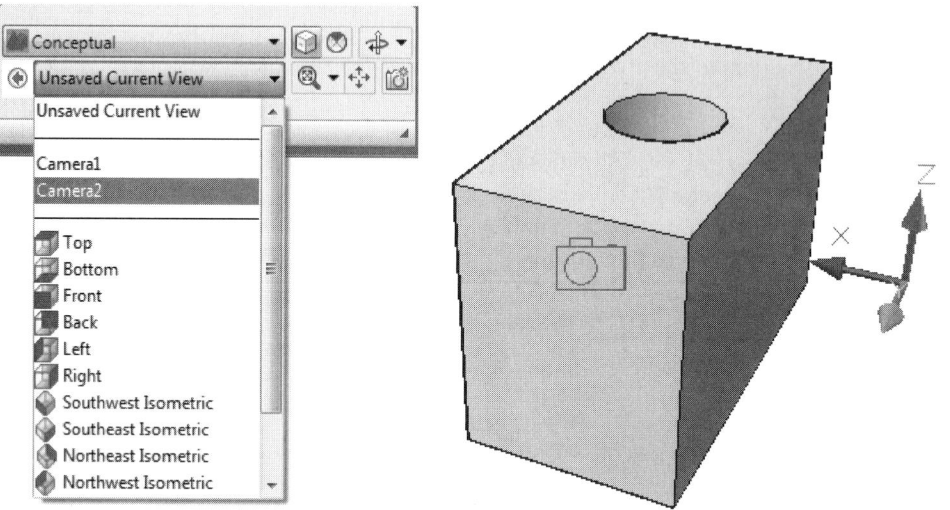

Figure 1-88 The drop-down list of the View panel on the Ribbon

Figure 1-89 A perspective view displayed according to the camera definitions

When specifying the camera location, you can specify only the *X* and *Y* coordinates of the point. The *Z* coordinate is controlled by the **CAMERAHEIGHT** system variable. The *Z* coordinate can also be changed within the **CAMERA** command by selecting the **Height** option, which automatically updates the **CAMERAHEIGHT** system variable. This and other properties or definitions of the camera object, such as its name, can also be changed through the **Properties** window (Figure 1-90).

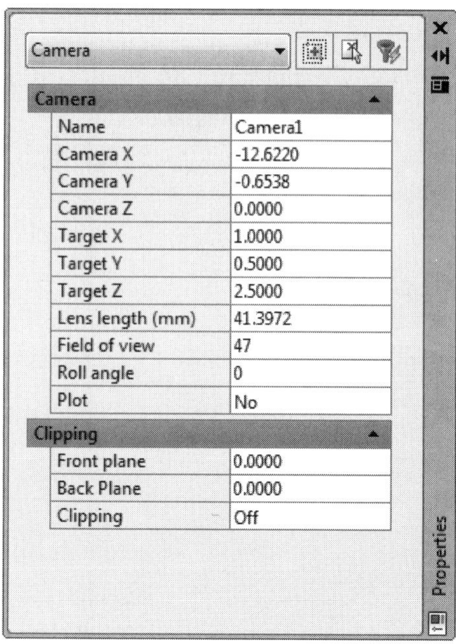

Figure 1-90 The camera properties shown in the Properties palette

Exercise 1-12: Working with the Camera

CAMERA	
View Toolbar	
Ribbon Navigation panel	
Pull-down Menu	View/ Create Camera
Command Line	camera
Alias	cam

1. **OPEN** ***SimpleSolid.***
2. **ZOOM** out as needed and **SAVE** the drawing **AS** ***Exercise 1-12.***
3. Invoke the **CAMERA** command using one of the methods shown in the grid, and respond to the prompts as follows:

   Specify camera location: *-9,-6* ↵

   Specify target location: *1,0.5,2.5* ↵

   Enter an option

   [?/Name/LOcation/Height/Target/LEns/Clipping/View/eXit]: ↵*(To exit the command)*
4. Invoke the **CAMERA** command again to create a second camera. Specify the camera and target locations as **–7,3** and **1,4.5,2.5.**
5. The 3D model should look like Figure 1-91. Select the second camera you created. Right-click in the drawing area and select **Properties** from the shortcut menu.

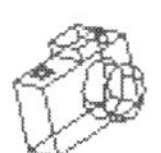

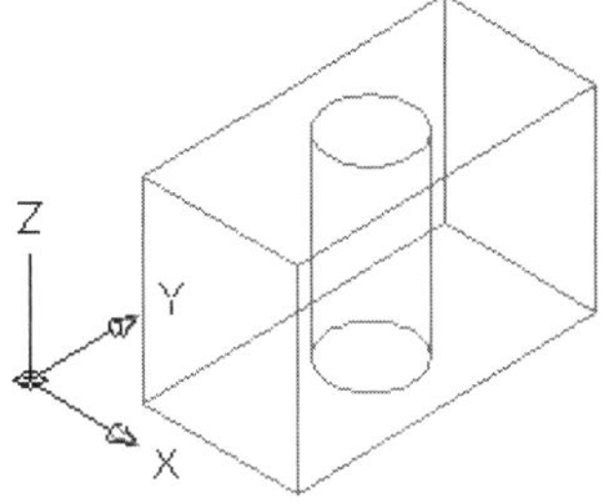

Figure 1-91 The 3D model with the two cameras shown

6. In the **Properties** window, change the **Name** to **High Camera,** and change the camera *Z* value to **6.** Close the **Properties** window and press the <**Esc**> key to close the **Camera Preview** window and hide the camera viewing field pyramid.
7. Click on the drop-down list of views located on the **View** panel of the Ribbon (Figure 1-92). Select **High Camera** from the list.

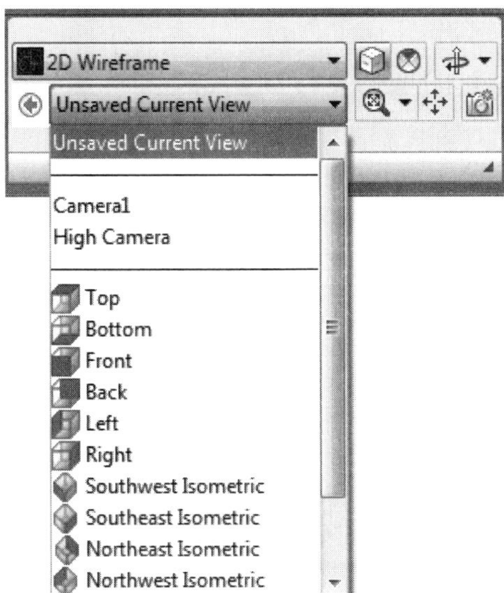

Figure 1-92 The views drop-down list located on the View panel of the Ribbon

8. Invoke the **ZOOM Realtime** command and zoom out to obtain a smaller view of the 3D model.
9. Invoke the **CAMERADISPLAY** system variable to hide the cameras. The 3D model should look like Figure 1-93.
10. **SAVE** the drawing.

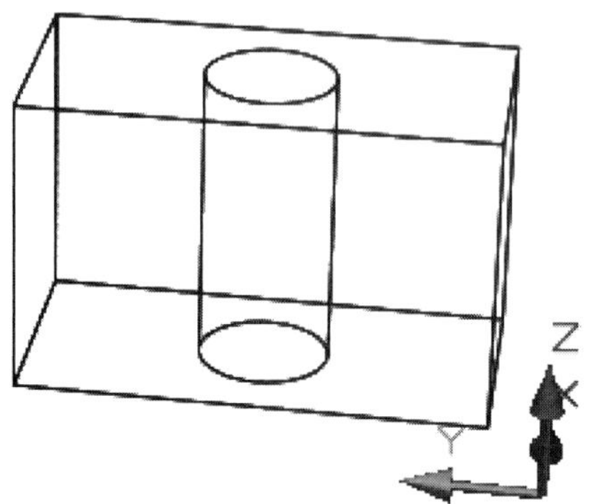

Figure 1-93 The 3D model as seen by the camera

SAVING AND USING MODEL VIEWS

model view: A combination of geometric specifications that define a view plus additional elements such as UCS, layer snapshot, and visual style.

AutoCAD uses ***model views*** to store viewing points and other parameters associated with them. You can create or save a model view either by using the **CAMERA** command or through the **View Manager** dialog box (Figure 1-94).

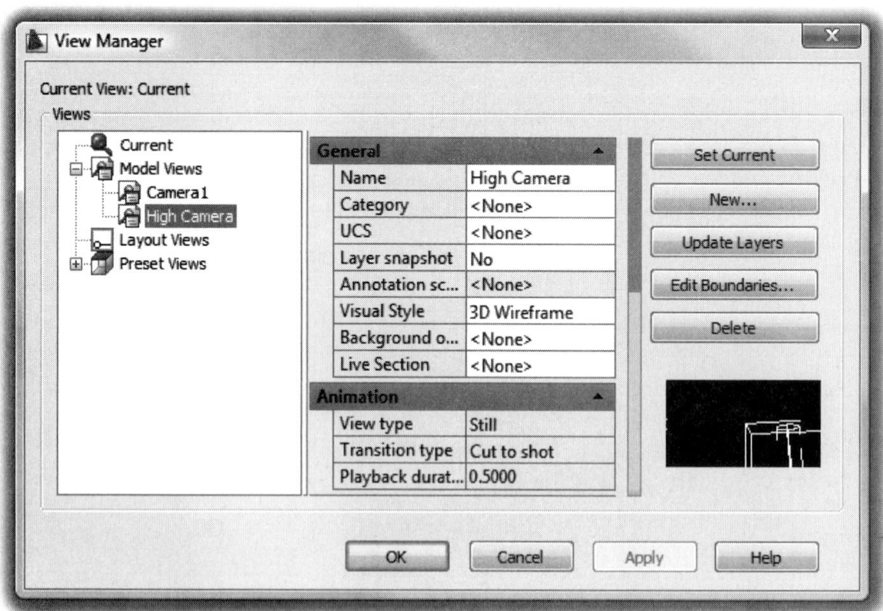

Figure 1-94 The View Manager dialog box

In the **View Manager** dialog box you can see the coordinates of any camera and target points. Through this dialog box you can also specify certain details for any saved model view such as linking a previously saved UCS or visual styles to it. You can also rename a model view and specify whether the view will show in parallel or perspective mode.

The procedure to save a model view though the **View Manager** dialog box is explained in the next exercise.

Exercise 1-13: Using the View Manager

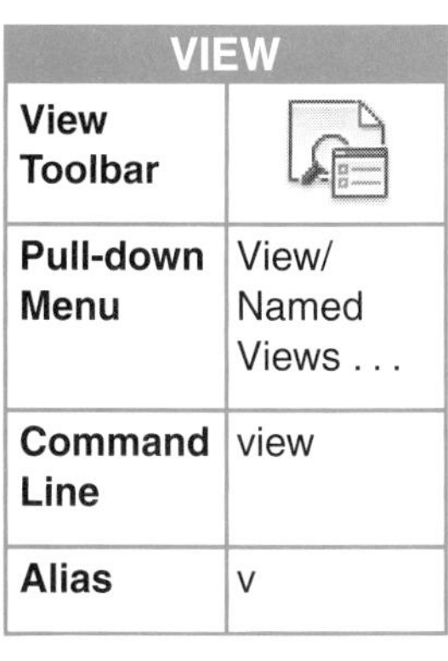

VIEW	
View Toolbar	
Pull-down Menu	View/ Named Views . . .
Command Line	view
Alias	v

1. **OPEN** ***Exercise 1-12.***
2. **SAVE** the drawing **AS** ***Exercise 1-13.***
3. Select the **SE Isometric** viewing point.
4. Invoke the **Rotate** option of the **VPOINT** command. Specify **300** and **15** when prompted for the first and second angles.
5. Change the **PERSPECTIVE** system variable to **0.** Invoke this setting by entering its name in the command line.
6. **ZOOM** the view out to make the 3D model smaller. The 3D model should look like Figure 1-95.

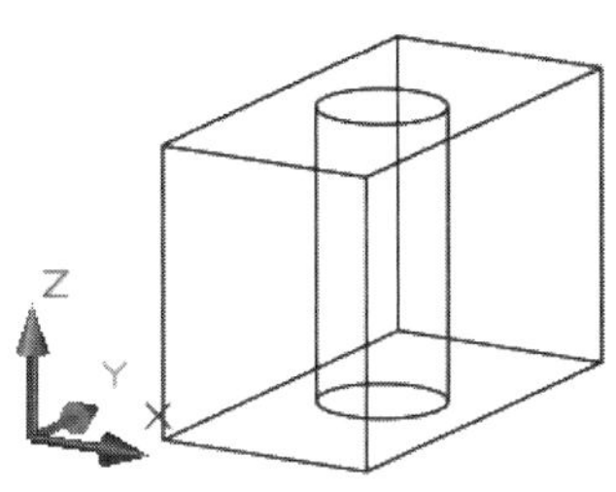

Figure 1-95 The 3D model shows the new viewing point after zooming out

7. Invoke the **VIEW** command by using one of the methods from the grid. In the **View Manager** dialog box, click on the **New . . .** button to open the **New View** dialog box (Figure 1-96). In this dialog box, type **My3Dview** in the **View Name:** field and click **OK** to return to the **View Manager.**

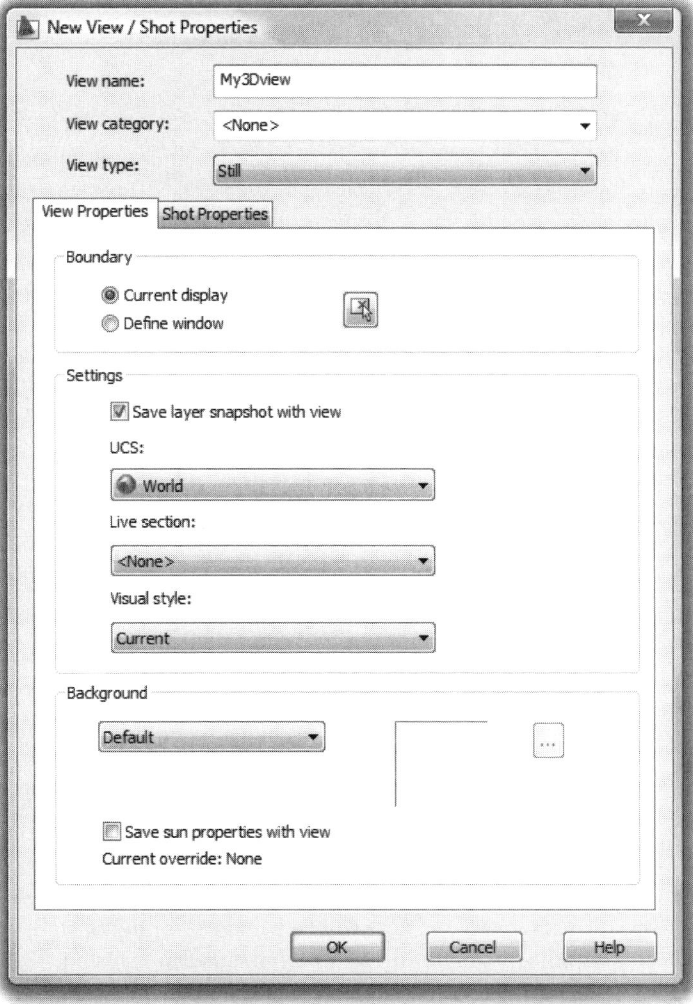

Figure 1-96 The New View dialog box

8. The new model view is added to the list. Under the **General** category of properties, select the **Conceptual** visual style. Under the **View** category, set **Perspective** as **On.** Click **OK** to close the **View Manager** dialog box.
9. Select **My3Dview** from the drop-down list on the **View** toolbar. The 3D model should look like Figure 1-97.
10. **SAVE** the drawing.

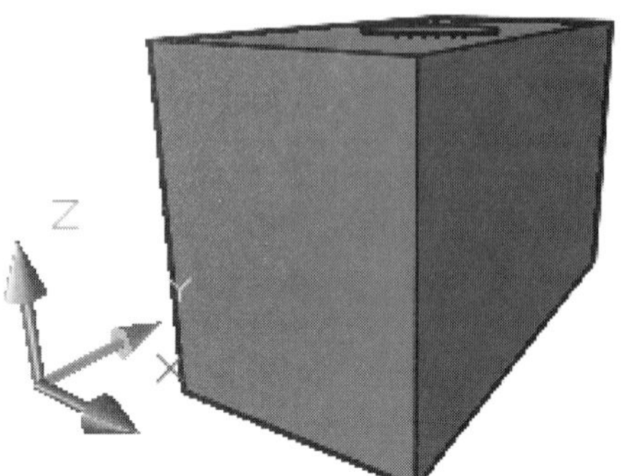

Figure 1-97 The 3D model after selecting My3Dview from the drop-down list on the View toolbar

Using the Mouse Wheel in the AutoCAD Program

In AutoCAD the mouse wheel can be used to perform the following four **3D Navigation** operations:

- **ZOOM Realtime**
- **PAN**
- **ZOOM Extents**
- **Transparent 3D Orbit**

ZOOM Realtime enables you to zoom in or zoom out by rotating the mouse wheel forward and backward. This feature allows you to keep a specific area of the display stationary by simply positioning the pointer there. With the standard **ZOOM Realtime** command, you cannot control this because this command always zooms from the center of the screen.

One complete turn of the wheel is divided into small steps. Each step tells the AutoCAD program to zoom in or out by a certain factor. The **ZOOMFACTOR** system variable allows you to set a value ranging from 3 to 100.

PAN allows you to perform a panning operation in the drawing area. Just click and drag the mouse wheel in the drawing area. You must set the **MBUTTONPAN** system variable to **1** (the default value) in order to use the wheel button for this purpose. Otherwise, AutoCAD displays the **Object Snap** shortcut menu.

ZOOM Extents works just like the **Extents** option of the **ZOOM** command. It zooms in or out automatically to the factor where all the existing objects in the model fit in the screen. This operation is performed simply by double-clicking the mouse wheel.

The **3D Swivel** navigation mode is activated by pressing the <**Ctrl**> key and the wheel button together while dragging the mouse.

Transparent 3D Orbit activates the constrained mode of the **3D Orbit** tool. It is activated by pressing the <**Shift**> key and the wheel button at the same time, and then dragging in the drawing area. Releasing either key or the wheel button will cancel the function.

You can use the **3DORBIT** command transparently inside other commands. But using this feature is more convenient because you save the time needed to invoke and exit the command.

In most cases, all these operations can be performed without any problems. Sometimes, however, the AutoCAD program might not respond properly to one or more of these operations. The cause is probably an incompatibility between the mouse settings and the AutoCAD software. To solve these issues, you can first try changing some mouse settings regarding the wheel. Second, you can download your mouse's driver from the manufacturer's website and install it in your computer. If none of the above work, you can purchase a different wheel mouse.

TIP Using the mouse wheel increases productivity, especially when working in a 3D environment. Its main advantage is that it can be used at any stage of a command without having to invoke other commands.

THE STEERINGWHEELS

NEW to AutoCAD 2009

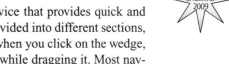

The **SteeringWheels**, or wheel to simplify, is a new navigation device that provides quick and easy access to the different navigation tools. The steering wheel is divided into different sections, known as Wedges; each wedge activates a different navigation tool when you click on the wedge, or when you click on the wedge and hold the pointing down device while dragging it. Most navigation tools, however, need to be activated by clicking on their corresponding wedge and holding the pointing down device while dragging it.

Wheels can be shown in seven different modes; the mode is controlled by the **NAVSWHEELMODE** system variable, which can be set from 0 to 6. Figure 1-98 shows the different types of wheels, and the corresponding mode for the **NAVSWHEELMODE** system variable. Each of the wheel modes contains a particular set of navigation tools. Beside the **NAVSWHEELMODE** system variable, you can also switch between the different modes through the shortcut menu that is displayed by right-clicking the drawing area while the wheel is in use (Figure 1-99), or by clicking the arrow located in the lower right corner of the wheel.

One important aspect common to any of the SteeringWheels is that they travel along with your cursor wherever it goes throughout the en-

Notes:

1. The arrow used to bring up the SteeringWheels shortcut menu is available only in the Big SteeringWheels.
2. When the 2D Navigation wheel mode is active, you cannot switch to any other mode through the shortcut menu; it can be changed only through the **NAVSWHEELMODE** system variable.

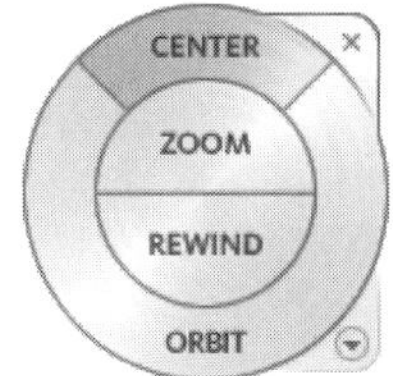

0 Big View Object wheel

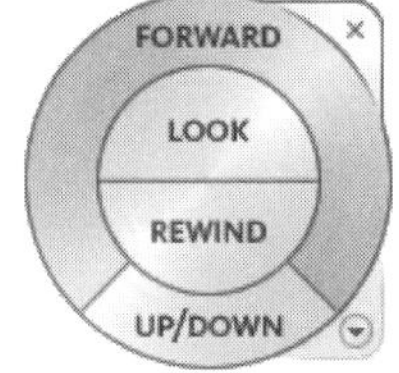

1 Big Tour Building wheel

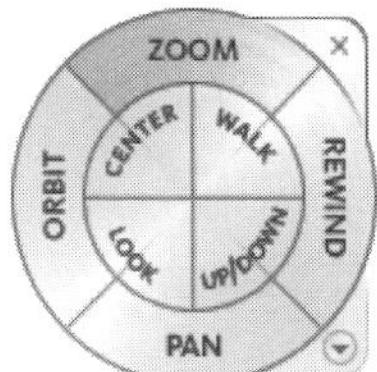

2 Big Full Navigation wheel

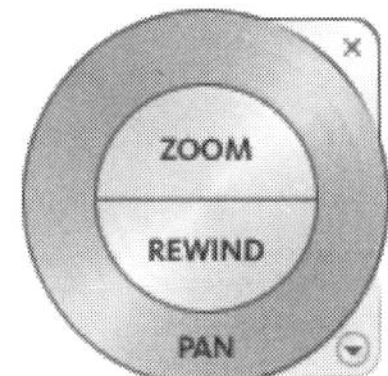

3 2D Navigation wheel

4 Mini View Object wheel

5 Mini Tour Building wheel

6 Mini Full Navigation wheel

Figure 1-98 The different types of SteeringWheels, the value of the **NAVSWHEELMODE** system variable associated with each one, and a brief description

Figure 1-99 The SteeringWheels shortcut menu

tire drawing area. This can save you a great amount of time because it shortens by much the distance that the pointing device has to be moved to reach the navigation tool. Different properties on the SteeringWheels, such as the transparency and the size, among others, can be adjusted in the **SteeringWheels Setting** dialog box (Figure 1-100). You can access this dialog box through the shortcut menu as well.

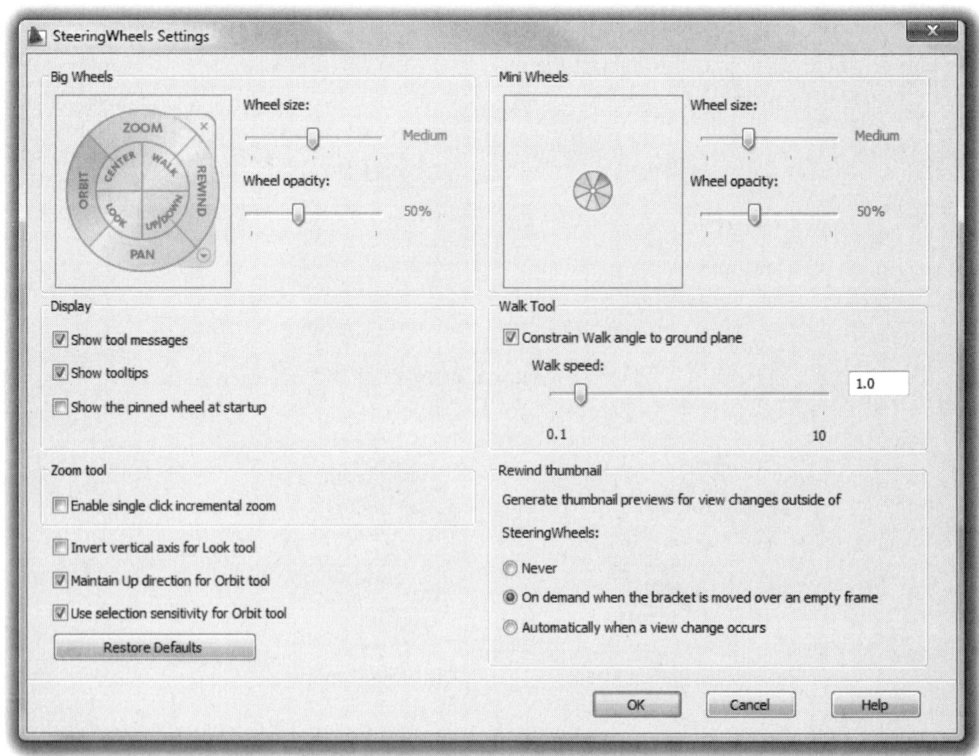

Figure 1-100 The Steering Wheels Settings dialog box

SteeringWheels: Navigation tool that provides quick and easy access to the different navigation tools. Each tool is activated though its corresponding Wedge.

Most of the navigation tools contained in the **SteeringWheels** work just as discussed in previous topics. For example, the Center wedge works similar to the **3DORBITCTR** command, allowing you to define the orbiting center. A tool that is unique to this group is **Rewind**. This tool allows you to go back and forth through the most recent views you have used. The view stages you can go through can even be previewed in a thumbnail picture, that is, if the **CAPTURETHUMBNAILS** system variable is set to **1** or **2**, which you can also control in the **SteeringWheels Settings** dialog box.

Wedge: When talking about SteeringWheels, refers to the different areas that these tools are divided into; each Wedge activates a different navigation tool.

THE VIEWCUBE

The **ViewCube,** or simply the cube (Figure 1-101), is another new navigation device that provides quick and easy access to displaying the different predefined viewing points, including the standard and isometric views. The **ViewCube** is displayed whenever you switch to a visual style other than the 2D Wireframe visual style. The **NAVVCUBE** command serves two purposes in the displaying of the ViewCube:

Figure 1-101 The **ViewCube**

1. To turn the ViewCube on and off while you are in an appropriate visual style.
2. To determine whether the ViewCube will show up the next time you leave the 2D Wireframe visual style to go to another one. Figure 1-102 shows the options of this command in its shortcut menu.

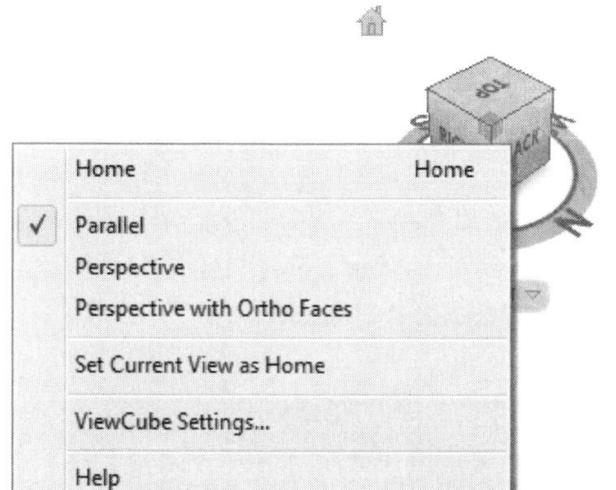

Figure 1-102 The ViewCube shortcut menu

FOR MORE DETAILS See "Using the Predefined Visual Styles" to learn about Visual Styles.

By hovering the mouse pointer over each element, the different elements of the **ViewCube** are highlighted. Clicking on a highlighted geometrical element, which could be a face, an edge, or a vertex, the viewing point is changed accordingly. The four top vertices of the box, for instance, will bring the four predefined Isometric viewing points. You can also spin around the 3D model by spinning the compass below the cube. Right-clicking on the cube will bring up its shortcut menu, where you can change between parallel and perspective views and access the ViewCube settings. The orientation of the views can be made with respect to the WCS or to any UCS stored or currently in use.

ViewCube: 3D navigation tool that appears when a Visual style other than the 2D Wireframe is selected. This tool allows you to switch quickly between the different predefined viewing points, including the standard and isometric views.

VIEWPORTS IN MODEL SPACE

In general, two types of ***viewports*** are available in AutoCAD:

viewports: Areas into which the model space is divided.

- Model space viewports
- Paper space viewports, also called *floating viewports*

When you start a new drawing from scratch, the entire model space consists of a single viewport. Working with multiple viewports splits the model space into smaller drawing areas or viewports (Figure 1-103). In each viewport you can select the viewing point and the UCS independently.

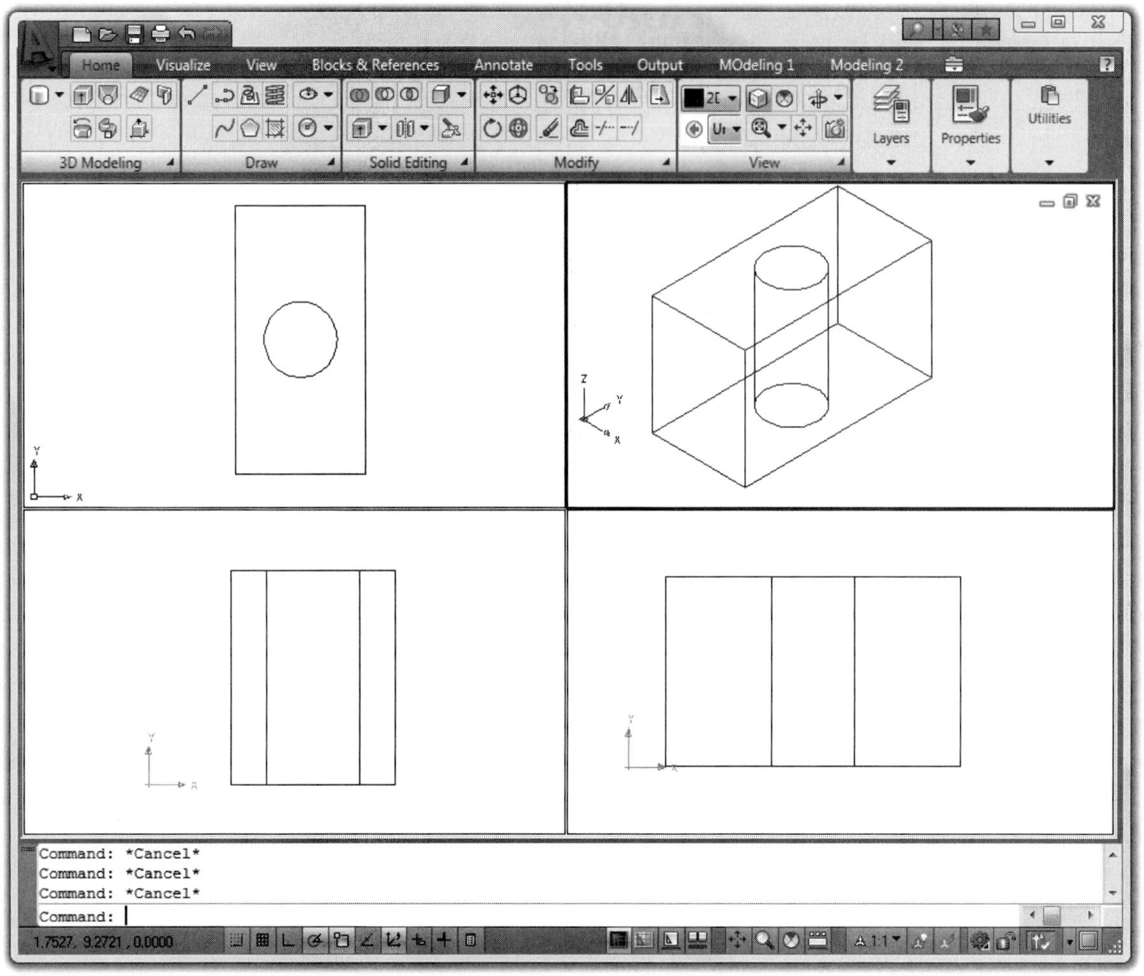

Figure 1-103 The drawing areas split into smaller areas or viewports

The viewports cannot overlap each other, and only one can be active at a time. To make a viewport active you just click inside it.

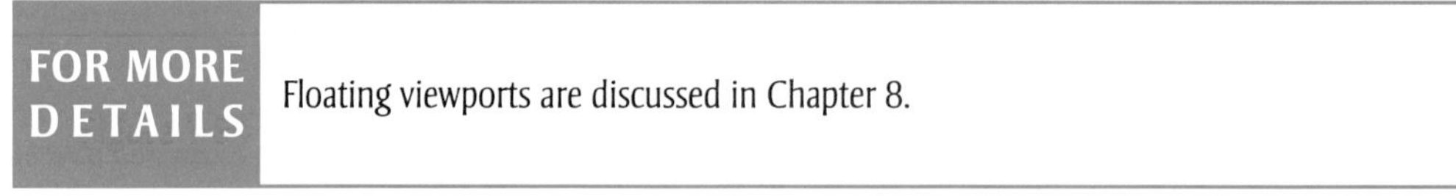

FOR MORE DETAILS
Floating viewports are discussed in Chapter 8.

Using more than one viewport enables you to look at the 3D model from different viewing points at the same time. You can invoke a command while a viewport is active and then switch to another viewport within the command. Because you can **ZOOM** in each viewport independently, you can make a detailed modification through a specific viewport while seeing the changes in another one, without having to **ZOOM** back and forth.

Splitting the display into multiple viewports also reduces the work area, so you might want to use multiple viewports only when they are really needed. A 3D model can always be created in a single viewport.

With the **UCSVP** system variable you can specify whether or not the UCS on a specific viewport is free to update its UCS, so it reflects the same UCS as that of the current viewport. The UCS is free or unlocked when the value of the **UCSVP** variable is **0;** and when its value is **1** (the default value), the UCS is locked, remaining unchanged.

Different configurations are preestablished by the AutoCAD software, but you are not limited to them. If you have divided the default single viewport into four equal viewports, you can keep dividing each of these four viewports into any other configuration.

The **VPORTS** command is used to perform operations on viewport configurations. It can be invoked in two different ways through the command line:

1. **VPORTS:** Opens up the **Viewports** dialog box.
2. **–VPORTS:** Prompts you to enter one of the following options in the command line.

```
Enter an option [Save/Restore/Delete/Join/SIngle/?/2/3/4] <3>:
```

You can join two viewports into one as long as the two viewports together form a rectangle. For example, in Figure 1-105, you could join only the two viewports at the bottom of the screen. The UCS and the viewing point of the resulting viewport will be the same as those of the first viewport selected. You can also save, retrieve, and delete your own viewport configurations. When you save a configuration, the UCS and the **UCSVP** system variable information contained in each viewport are saved together with it.

Exercise 1-14: Creating Viewports in Model Space

1. **OPEN** ***SimpleSolid.***
2. **SAVE** the drawing **AS** ***Exercise 1-14.***
3. Make sure the **SW Isometric** view and the **World** UCS are selected.
4. Set the **UCSFOLLOW** system variable to **0.** Set the **UCSORTHO** and **UCSVP** system variables to **1.**
5. Split the display into three viewports with the biggest one on top. To do this, open the **Viewports** dialog box. In the **New Viewports** tab, click on the **Three: Above** Standard viewport configuration.
6. Select **3D** from the **Setup** drop-down list (Figure 1-104). Click on the **OK** button to close the **Viewports** dialog box.

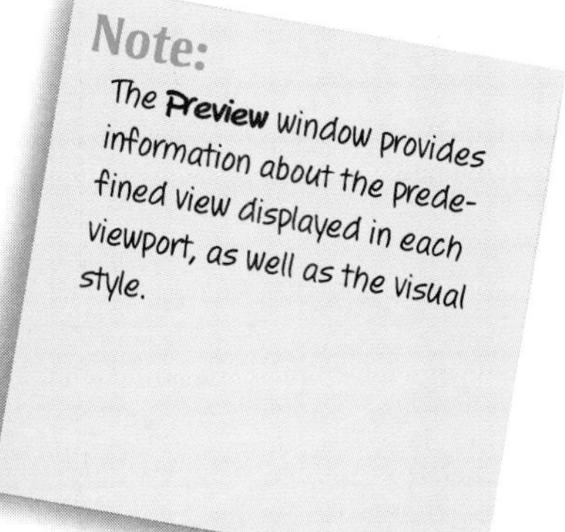

Note:
The Preview window provides information about the predefined view displayed in each viewport, as well as the visual style.

VIEWPORTS	
Viewports Toolbar	
Pull-down Menu	View/ Viewports/ New Viewports . . .
Command Line	viewports
Alias	vports

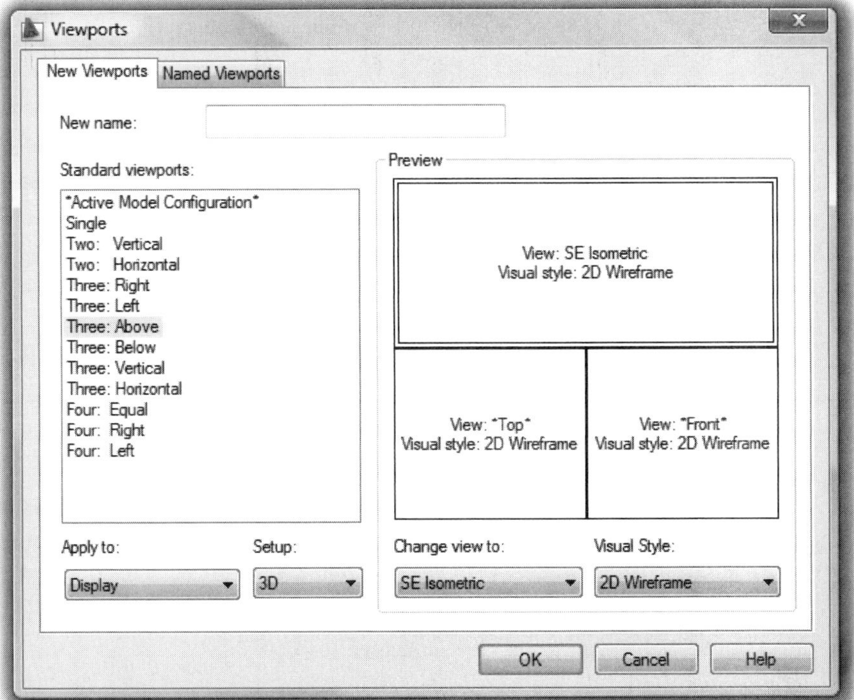

Figure 1-104 The Viewports dialog box with a 3D setup configuration

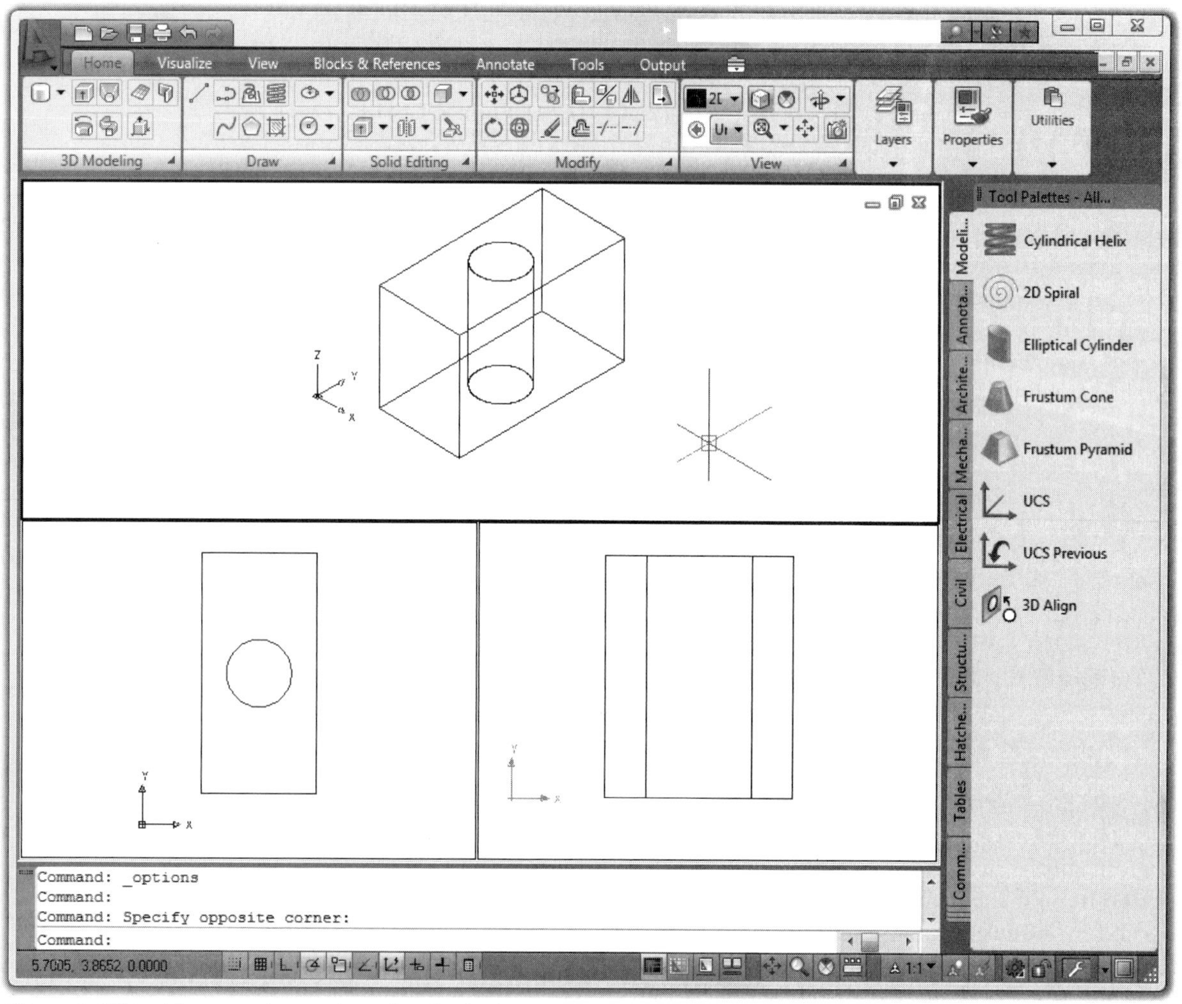

Figure 1-105 After zooming out in each individual viewport

7. In the drawing area, **ZOOM** out in each viewport until the UCS icon can be seen at its origin. Your drawing should look like Figure 1-105.

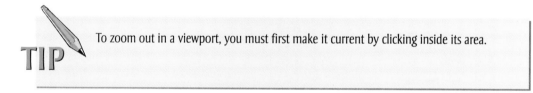

TIP: To zoom out in a viewport, you must first make it current by clicking inside its area.

8. Click inside the viewport on top to make it current and change the **UCSVP** system variable value to **0.**
9. Click inside the bottom-left and the bottom-right viewports, in that order. Observe how the UCS in the top viewport is automatically updated when you make the other viewport current.
10. **SAVE** the drawing.

Exercise 1-15: More Operations with Viewports in Model Space

In this exercise, you will change the viewport configuration by splitting the top viewport into four equal areas. Then you will save the configuration.

1. **OPEN** ***Exercise 1-14.***
2. **SAVE** the drawing **AS** ***Exercise 1-15.***
3. Make the top viewport current, and open the **Viewports** dialog box.

4. In the **New Viewports** tab, click on the **Two: Vertical** Standard viewport configuration. In the **Apply to:** drop-down dialog box, choose **Current Viewport.** Click the **OK** button.
5. Repeat the same process to subdivide the new top-right and top-left viewports into **Two: Vertical** viewports each. By doing so, you will end up splitting the initial top viewport into four viewports.
6. Select the **SW Isometric, SE Isometric, NE Isometric,** and **NW Isometric** viewing points from left to right on each viewport. Your display should look like Figure 1-106.

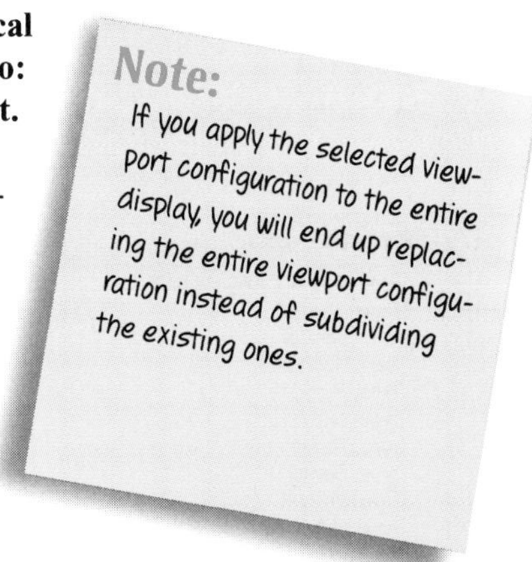

Note:
If you apply the selected viewport configuration to the entire display, you will end up replacing the entire viewport configuration instead of subdividing the existing ones.

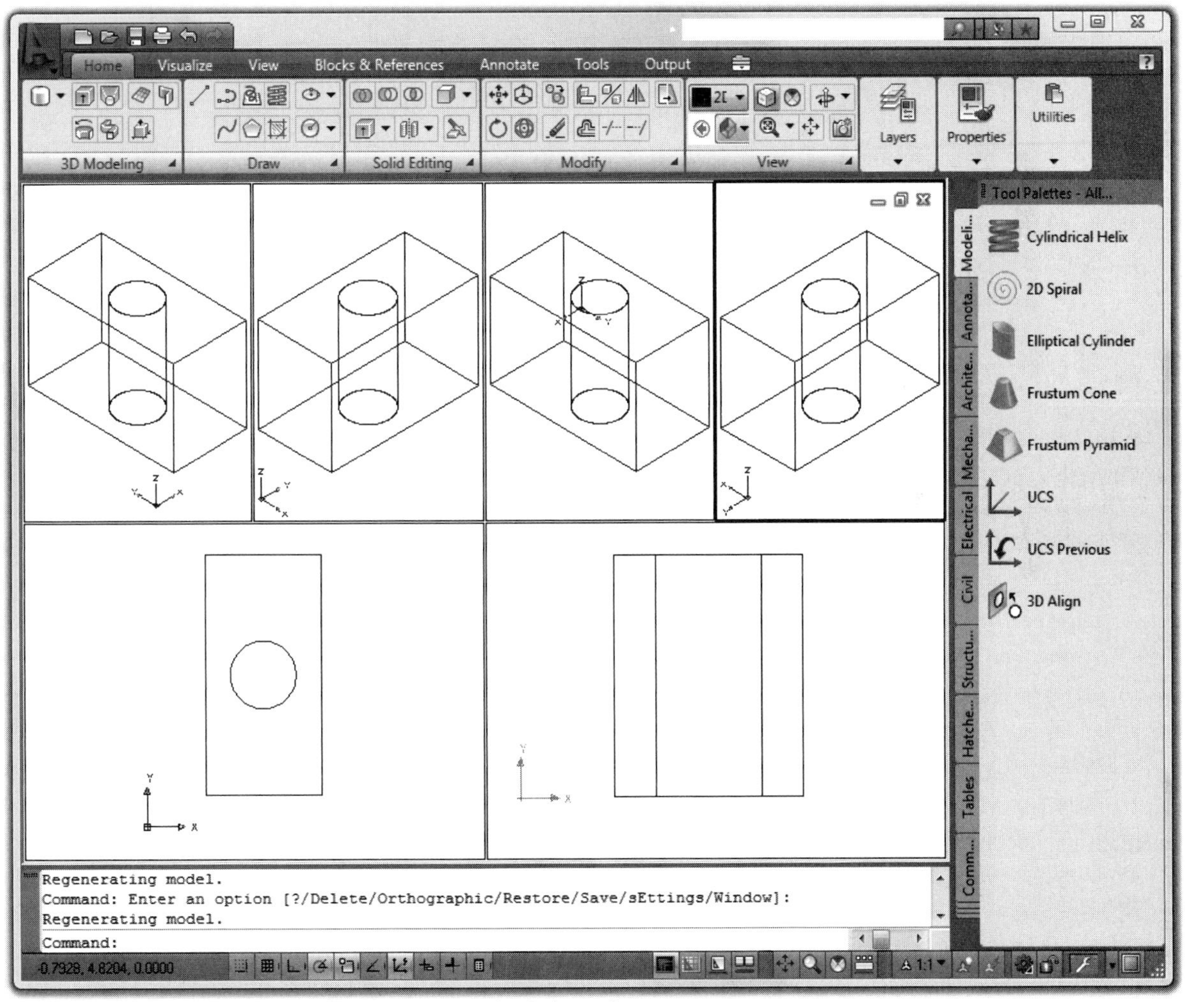

Figure 1-106 In three steps, the top viewport is divided into four viewports

7. Save the viewport configuration you just created. To do so, open the **Viewports** dialog box again. In the **New Viewports** tab, type **Six-Two below** in the **New Name:** field (Figure 1-107). Click the **OK** button.
8. Change the viewport configuration to **Three: Vertical.** Open the **Viewports** dialog box again. In the **New Viewports** tab of the **Viewports** dialog box, select the **Three: Vertical** Standard viewport configuration. This time, leave the **Apply to:** drop-down dialog box as its default **Display** so you can change the entire display. Then, click the **OK** button.

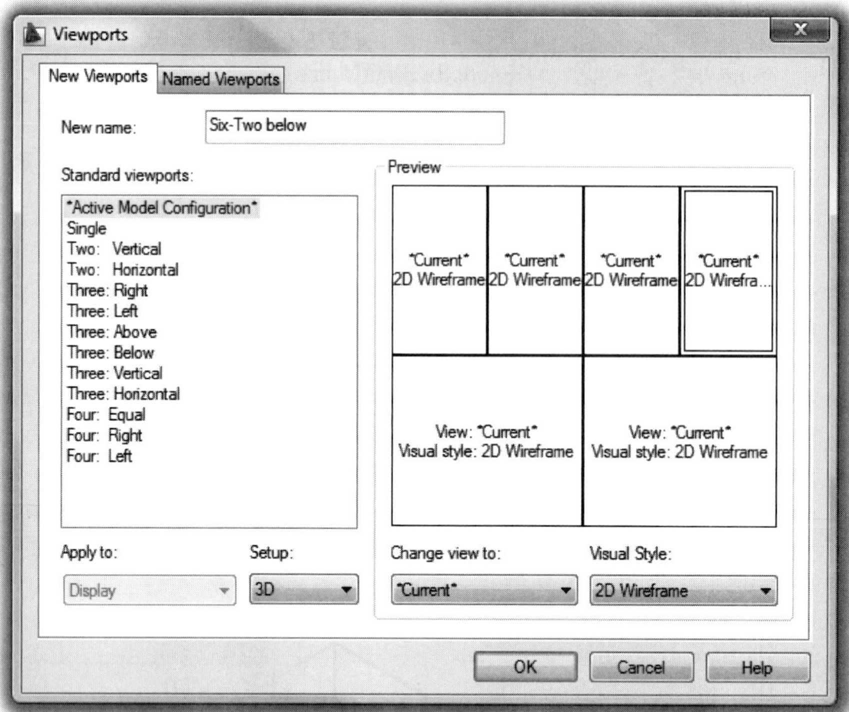

Figure 1-107 Saving the Six-Two below viewport configuration

9. Open the **Viewports** dialog box again to retrieve your saved configuration. In the **Named Viewports** tab, click on the **Six-Two below** viewport to make it current. Click the **OK** button.
10. Invoke the **–VPORTS** command by typing its entire name in the command line. Respond to the prompts as follows.

    Enter an option [Save/Restore/Delete/Join/SIngle/?/2/3/4] <3>: *j* ↵

    Select dominant viewport <current viewport>: *Click inside one of the viewports you want to join.*

    Select viewport to join: *Click inside the other viewport you want to join.*
11. **SAVE** the drawing.

Using the Predefined Visual Styles

visual style: A collection of settings or modifiers that control the display of edges and faces of 3D objects.

predefined visual styles: Predefined collections of settings, saved as visual styles, that control the display of edges and faces of 3D objects.

3D models are always displayed in a particular ***visual style.*** The default visual style is **2D Wireframe.** By selecting a different visual style you can create different shaded displays of the 3D objects in each viewport.

AutoCAD supplies five ***predefined visual styles.*** These styles combine the most useful display styles for 3D models:

- **2D Wireframe**
- **3D Hidden**
- **3D Wireframe**
- **Conceptual**
- **Realistic**

Note:
Visual styles are the modern version of the shademodes used in previous versions of AutoCAD.

The **2D Wireframe** visual style shows all the edges of the 3D model and displays the standard UCS icon (Figure 1-108). The **DISPSILH** system variable controls whether or not the silhouette lines are shown.

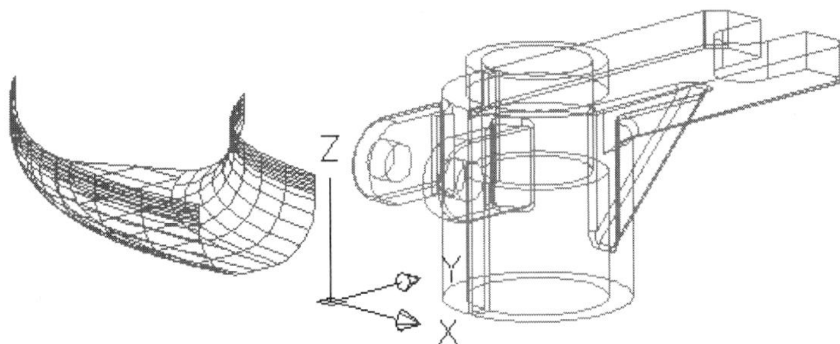

Figure 1-108 The 2D Wireframe visual style

The **3D Wireframe** visual style shows all the edges of the 3D model and displays the 3D UCS icon (Figure 1-109). The **DISPSILH** system variable controls whether or not the silhouette lines are shown.

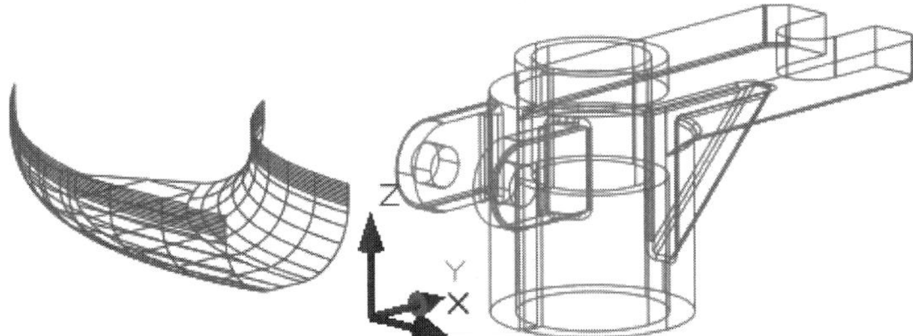

Figure 1-109 The 3D Wireframe visual style

The **3D Hidden** visual style removes the obscured edges and objects from the view (Figure 1-110).

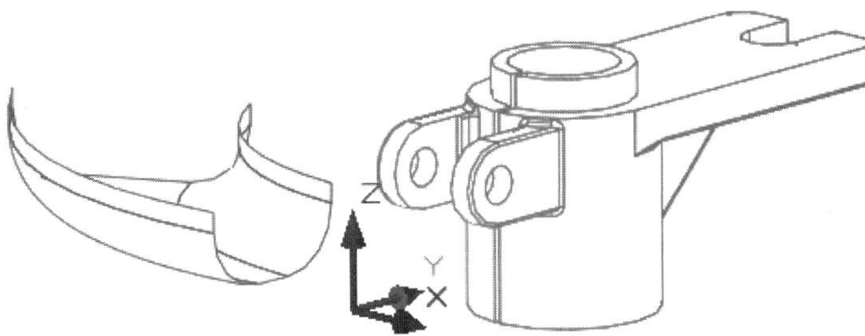

Figure 1-110 The 3D Hidden visual style

The **Conceptual** visual style provides a shaded display of the 3D model, using the color of the object in a warm-cool face style (Figure 1-111).

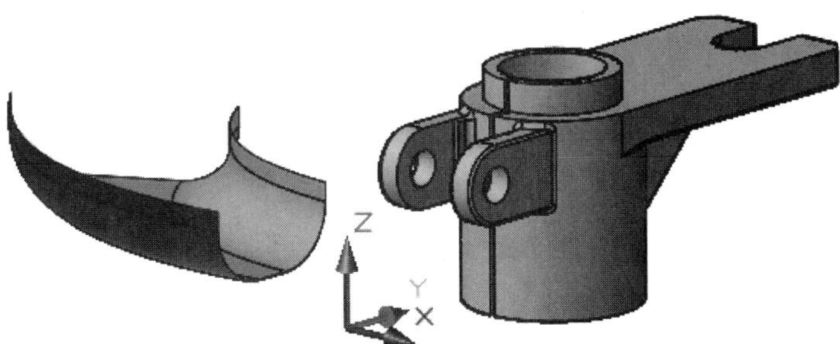

Figure 1-111 The Conceptual visual style

The **Realistic** visual style provides a shaded display of the 3D model using the color and texture of the material applied to the object, or the color of the objects in its defect. Faces are shown in a real style (Figure 1-112).

Figure 1-112 The Realistic visual style

You can quickly apply a predefined visual style in the following ways:

- Clicking the visual style icon directly on the **Visual Style** toolbar
- Through the **View** panel in the **Ribbon palette** (Figure 1-113)
- Using the **Visual Styles Manager** palette (Figure 1-114)

Figure 1-113 The predefined visual styles can be selected from the Visual Styles panel in the Ribbon

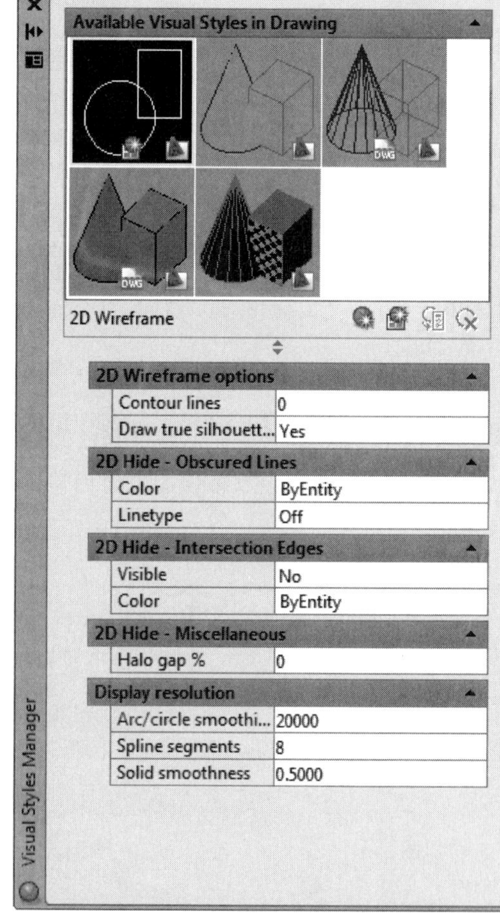

Figure 1-114 Selecting the predefined visual styles from the Visual Styles Manager palette

VISUALSTYLES	
Visual Styles Toolbar	
Ribbon: Visual Styles panel	
Pull-down Menu	View/ Visual Styles/ Visual Styles Manager. . .
Command Line	visualstyles

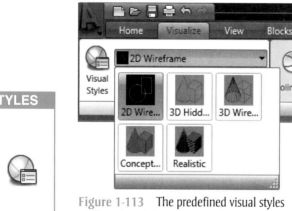

You can display the **Visual Styles Manager** palette by invoking the **VISUALSTYLES** command or by selecting it from the **Tools** drop-down menu under **Palettes.** To apply a visual style from the **Visual Styles Manager** palette specifically, you can perform one of the following operations:

- Drag and drop one of the sample images into the drawing area or a specific viewport.
- Double-click the sample image to apply the visual style on the current viewport.
- Click the **Apply Selected Visual Style to Current Viewport** button.

You can modify a visual style in two different ways:

- Using the controls on the **Visual Style** panel in the **Ribbon**
- Using the categorized settings in the **Visual Styles Manager** palette

Changes made using the controls located in the **Visual Style** panel of the **Ribbon** (Figure 1-115) are not saved to the visual style.

On the other hand, changes made to the settings in the **Visual Styles Manager** palette are permanently stored in the visual styles for the current drawing.

You can always **Reset to default** any of the AutoCAD program's predefined visual styles by right-clicking on its sample image. These visual styles cannot be deleted.

By simply changing some of visual style modifiers, you can obtain a pictorial result similar to Figure 1-116.

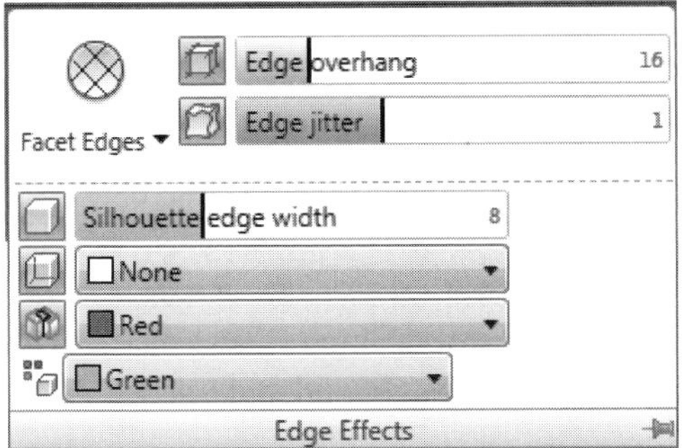

Figure 1-115 The display of the objects can be temporarily modified through the Edge Effects panel of the Ribbon

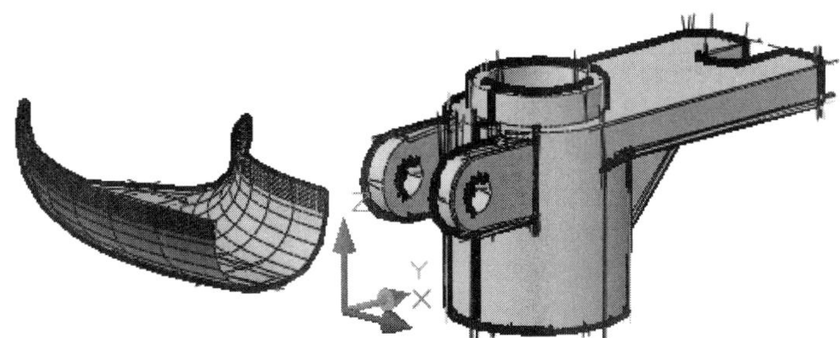

Figure 1-116 You can obtain pictorial illustrations by modifying the predefined Visual Style

FOR MORE DETAILS To learn specific details about creating and modifying visual styles, see Chapter 9.

The Hide Command

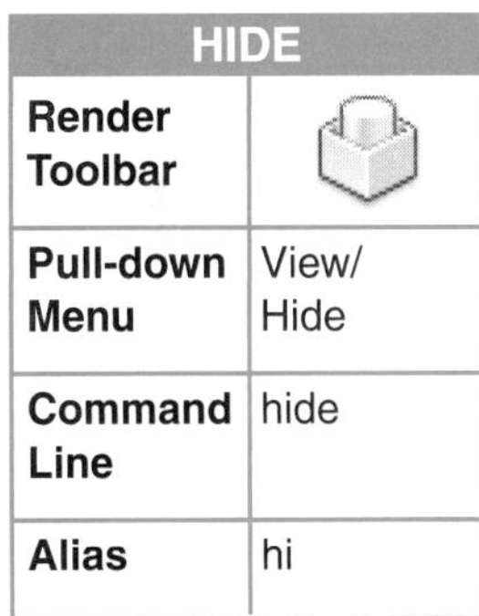

HIDE	
Render Toolbar	
Pull-down Menu	View/ Hide
Command Line	hide
Alias	hi

The **HIDE** command is the traditional tool used to quickly inspect the 3D model when using the **2D Wireframe** visual style. This command hides the ***obscured lines*** by default; however, you can customize or fine-tune this effect in the **Visual Styles Manager** window. The **HIDE** command can be invoked by using one of the methods shown in the grid. To access the hidden line settings, the **2D Wireframe** sample image must be selected (Figure 1-117).

obscured lines: Edges or other objects that cannot be seen from the current viewing point because of their position relative to other objects.

TIP Invoking the **HIDE** command while a visual style other than the **2D Wireframe** is current will simply apply the **3D Hidden** visual style.

Under **2D Hide – Obscured Lines,** you can change the default settings for the **Linetype** and **Color** of the obscured lines. When the linetype is off, the obscured lines are completely removed. Figure 1-118(a) shows all of the objects' edges. Figure 1-118(b) shows the obscured lines removed, and Figure 1-118(c) shows the obscured lines in a different linetype and color.

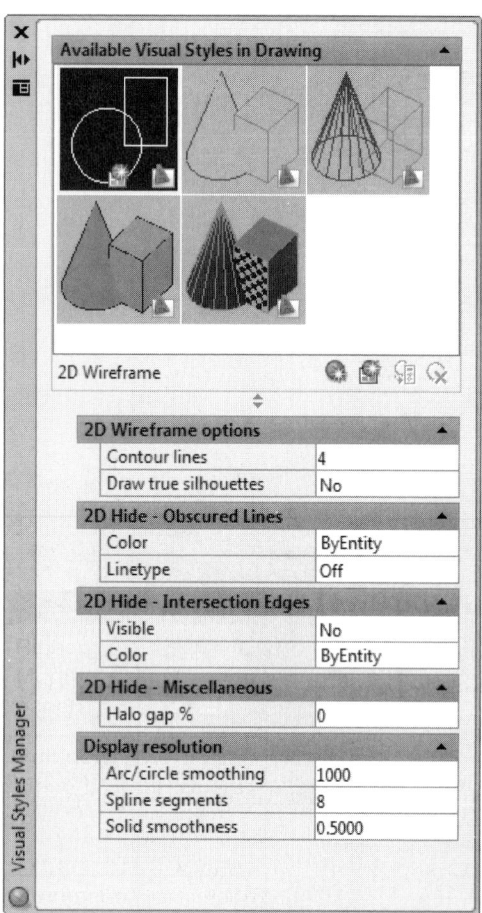

Figure 1-117 The 2D Wireframe visual style settings

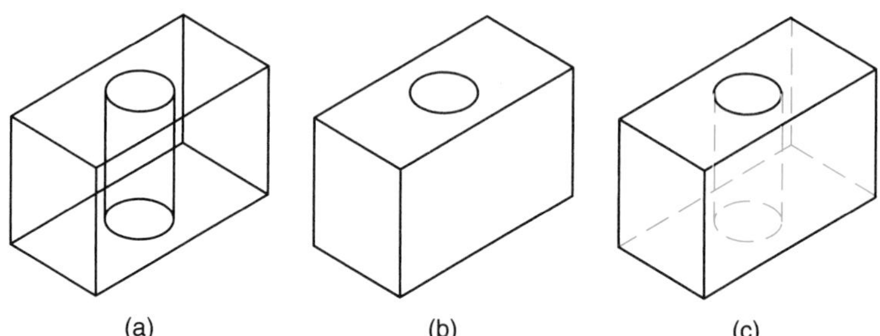

Figure 1-118 (a) Before invoking the HIDE command (b) After invoking the HIDE command with linetype off (c) With the Dashed linetype

Under **2D Hide – Intersection Edges,** you can change the settings for the **Linetype** and **Color** of the intersecting curves between 3D objects. Figure 1-119 compares the effects after the **HIDE** operation with and without enabling this setting. The color of the intersecting lines can also be changed.

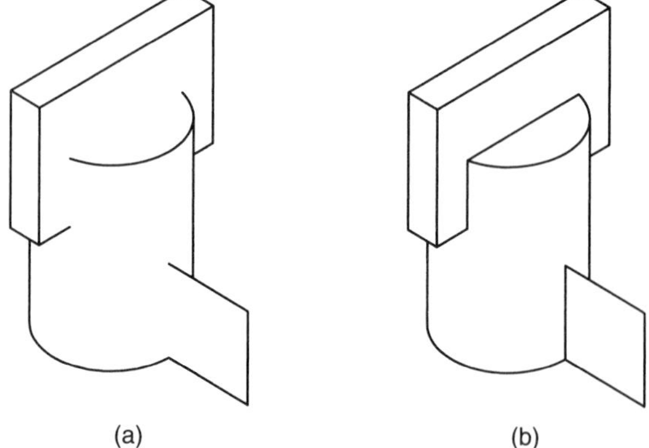

Figure 1-119 After invoking the HIDE command; with Intersection Edges disabled (a) and enabled (b)

Other settings that can be controlled in the **Visual Styles Manager** palette for the **2D Wireframe** visual style are:

- **Contour lines:** Controls the number of isolines displayed per curved face. This setting is also controlled by the **ISOLINES** system variable.
- **Draw true silhouettes:** Controls the display of silhouettes. This setting is also controlled by the **DISPSILH** system variable.

- **Halo gap %:** Controls the gap displayed where an object is hidden by another object.
- **Arc/circle smoothing:** This value controls the appearance of curves. Increasing its value will cause arc, circles, ellipses, and splines to look smoother. It is also controlled by the **VIEWRES** command.
- **Spline segments:** Sets the number of line segments to be generated for each spline-fit polyline generated by the **Spline** option of the **PEDIT** command. This value is also set by the **SPLINESEGS** system variable.
- **Solid smoothness:** Controls the smoothness of 3D solids by increasing or reducing the number of facets on curved faces. This setting is also controlled by the **FACETRES** system variable.

After invoking the **HIDE** command, you can revoke its effect by invoking the **REGEN** command. This operation is necessary prior to performing **ZOOM Realtime** or **PAN** operations.

Using Point Filters and Tracking Methods

When working in a 3D environment, finding points throughout the 3D space is essential. Because there are sometimes no physical objects to snap to, you will place objects temporarily in order to find these points. Or you can use methods such as point filters and tracking tools.

Point Filters

When you enter a point by either clicking or typing it, you enter all three coordinates (*X*, *Y*, and *Z*) at the same time. Using ***point filters,*** on the other hand, allows you to subdivide the process of entering the coordinates of a point into two or three steps. For example, you can specify the *Y* coordinate, and then the *X* and *Z* coordinates as the AutoCAD program prompts you to do so.

point filters: A method of entering a point by which the *X*, *Y*, and *Z* coordinates are given in separate stages using any combination.

Point filters can be accessed whenever you are prompted to specify a point (Figure 1-120). There are two ways of specifying point filters:

- Shortcut menu: <**Shift**> + Right-click or <**Ctrl**> + Right-click (Figure 1-120)
- Keyboard entry: [.X .Y .Z .XY .YZ .ZX] ↵

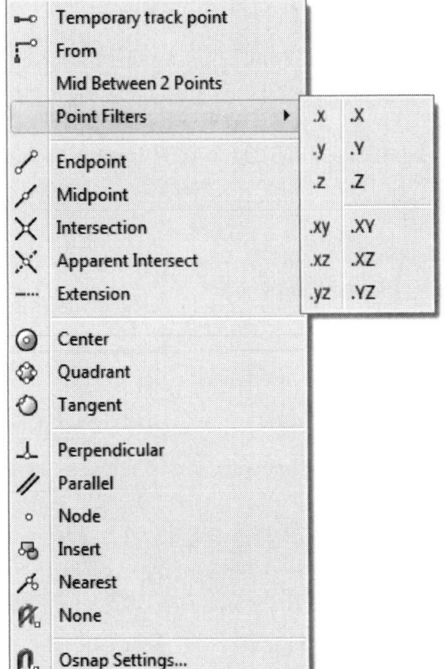

Figure 1-120 The Point Filters shortcut menu

SPHERE	
Solids Toolbar	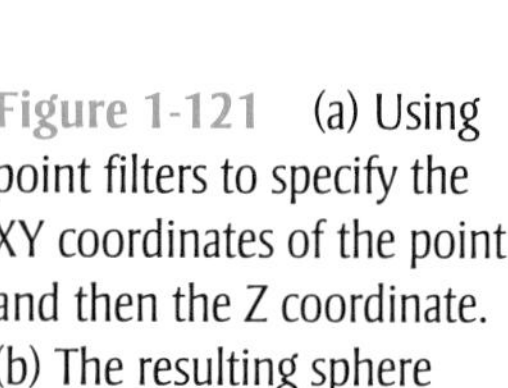
Ribbon 3D Modeling panel	
Pull-down Menu	Draw/ Solids/ Sphere
Command Line	sphere

Exercise 1-16: Using Point Filters to Place Geometry

In this exercise, you will create a sphere in the center of the model by using point filters.

1. **OPEN** ***SimpleSolid.***
2. **SAVE** the drawing **AS** ***Exercise 1-16.***
3. Make sure the **DUCS** (Dynamic UCS) mode in the status bar is turned off.
4. Set the **ISOLINES** system variable to **4.**
5. Invoke the **SPHERE** command by using one of the methods in the grid. Respond to the prompts as follows:

   Specify center of sphere <0,0,0>: *.xy* ↵

   Of: *Click on the center 1 of the top circle* [Figure 1-121(a)].

   Of (need Z): *Click on the midpoint 2 of the edge.*

   Specify radius of sphere or [Diameter]: *0.5* ↵

6. The model should look like Figure 1-121(b). **SAVE** the drawing.

Note: You could also have drawn a line temporarily from the bottom circle to the top circle of the cylindrical hole. When prompted for the center of sphere, you then could have just clicked on the line's midpoint and then erased the line (if you did not plan to use it anymore).

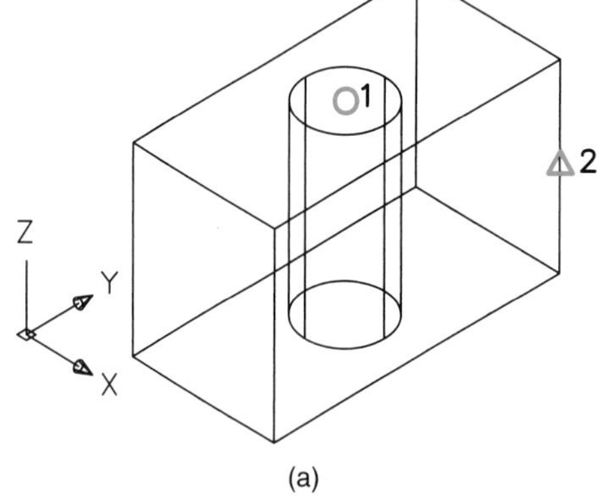

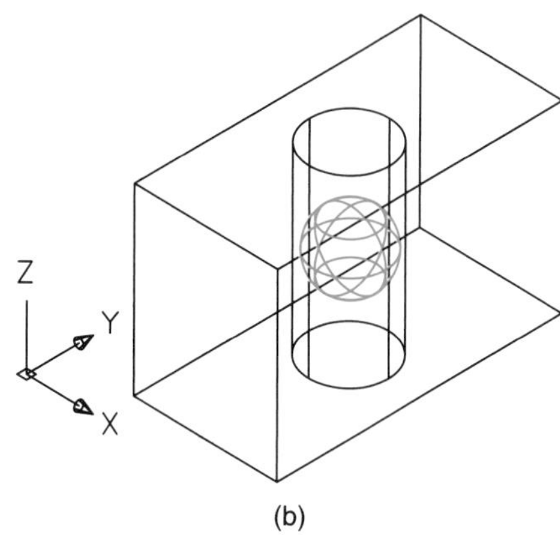

Figure 1-121 (a) Using point filters to specify the XY coordinates of the point and then the Z coordinate. (b) The resulting sphere

AutoTrack

AutoTrack: A powerful drafting tool that allows you to find points or to align objects along specified directions named *traces*, instead of snapping directly to the objects.

AutoTrack is a useful drafting aid to specify points in both 2D and 3D work. Using this tool, you can achieve the same results as those obtained by using the point filters, only in a more efficient way (especially when working with orthogonal views).

To turn **AutoTrack** mode on, you can press <**F11**> or click on the **OTRACK** button in the status bar.

Exercise 1-17: Using the Tracking Tools

In this exercise, you will create the same sphere in the same place as in the previous exercise. This time you will use a different method to find its center point.

1. **OPEN** ***SimpleSolid.***
2. **SAVE** the drawing **AS** ***Exercise 1-17.***
3. Turn **AutoTrack** mode on.
4. Open the **Drafting Settings** dialog box (Figure 1-122) and make sure that **Center** is one of the **Object Snap modes** checked.

TIP You must enable a particular object snap before using it for tracking.

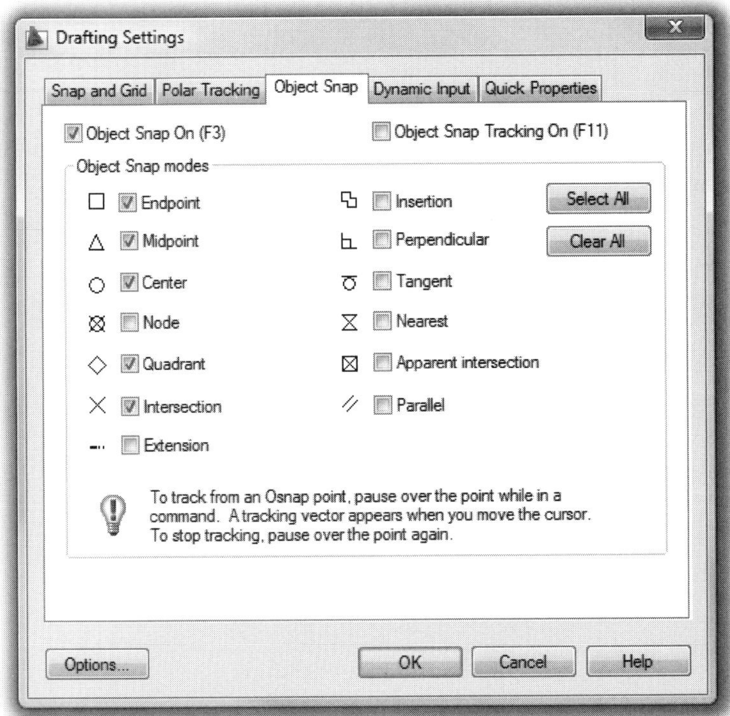

Figure 1-122 The Center object snap enabled in the Drafting Settings dialog box

5. Click on the **Polar Tracking** tab. Make sure that the **Track orthogonally only** choice is selected (Figure 1-123).
6. Turn **DUCS** (Dynamic UCS) off on the status bar.
7. Set the **ISOLINES** system variable to **2.**
8. Invoke the **SPHERE** command. When prompted for the *center point*, place the crosshairs cursor at the *center point* of the bottom circular edge for about a second to place a mark. Then move your pointer up.
9. While the vector is still showing, type **1.25** and press <**Enter**>.

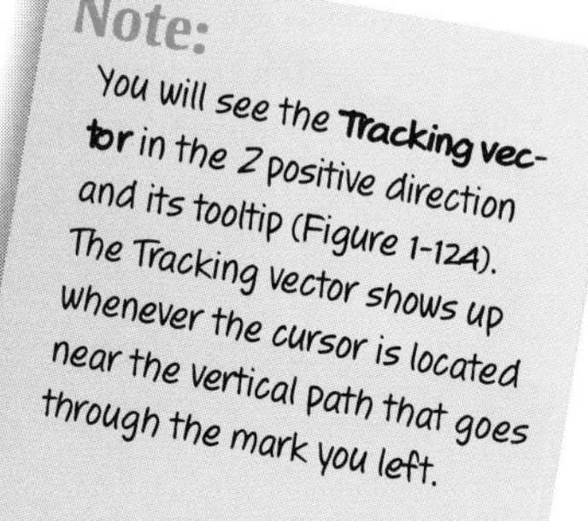

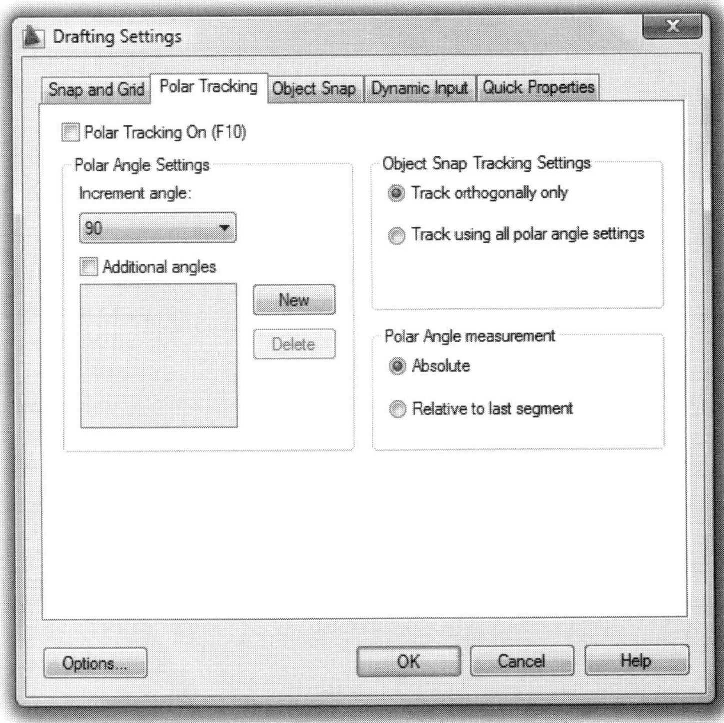

Figure 1-123 Selecting the Track orthogonally only option allows tracking in four directions only

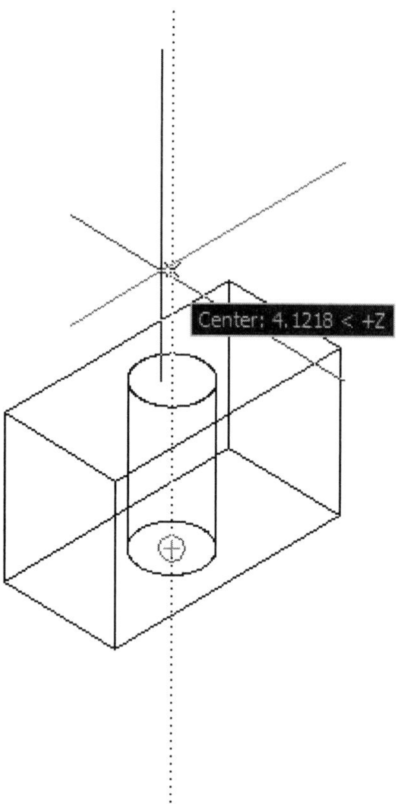

Figure 1-124 The Tracking vector in the Z positive direction and its tooltip

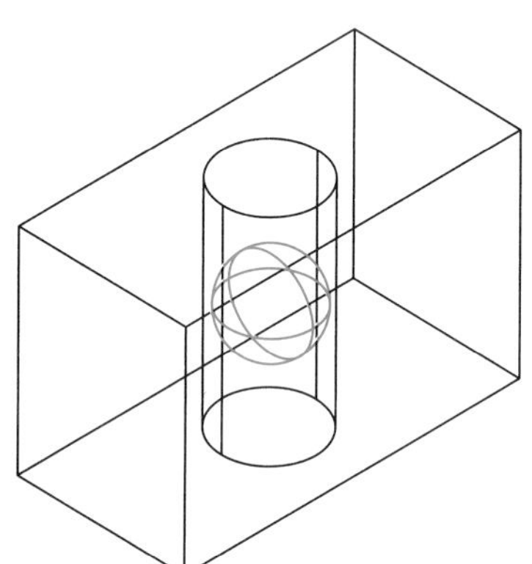

Figure 1-125 After placing the sphere

TIP Placing the crosshairs back on a mark for about a second will eliminate the mark. Zoom operations will eliminate the mark as well.

10. Finish the command by specifying the sphere radius as **0.5.** The sphere should be placed as in Figure 1-125.
11. **SAVE** the drawing.

In the **Polar Tracking** tab of the **Drafting Settings** dialog box (Figure 1-123) you can select the **Track orthogonally only** option. This will allow you to restrain the tracking along the axes, including the *Z*-axis. You can also choose to **Track using all polar angle settings.** In this option, the tracking is made according to the established polar angle settings. You can use any angle increment plus any other additional angles and along the *Z*-axis. Tracking along *Z* is not possible if one of the angle increments is coincident with the direction of the *Z*-axis in the current view. For example, you cannot track along *Z* in the **SE Isometric** viewing point if the angle increments are set to **45°.**

You can change **AutoTrack Settings** in the **Drafting** tab of the **Options** dialog box (Figure 1-126). Clicking the **Drafting Tooltip Settings. . .** button will allow you to modify the **Tooltip Appearance** as well, as long as **Override OS settings for all drafting tooltips** is selected in the **Tooltip Appearance** dialog box (Figure 1-127).

The tracking of a point occurs in a plane that is parallel to the *XY* plane of the current UCS. The plane goes through the point you are tracking and along the *Z*-axis.

Leaving tracking marks on two points will enable you to find the intersection of two tracking vectors. You should use this method only if the two points and the intersection point are located on a common plane parallel to any of the major planes of the current UCS (*XY*, *YZ*, or ZX).

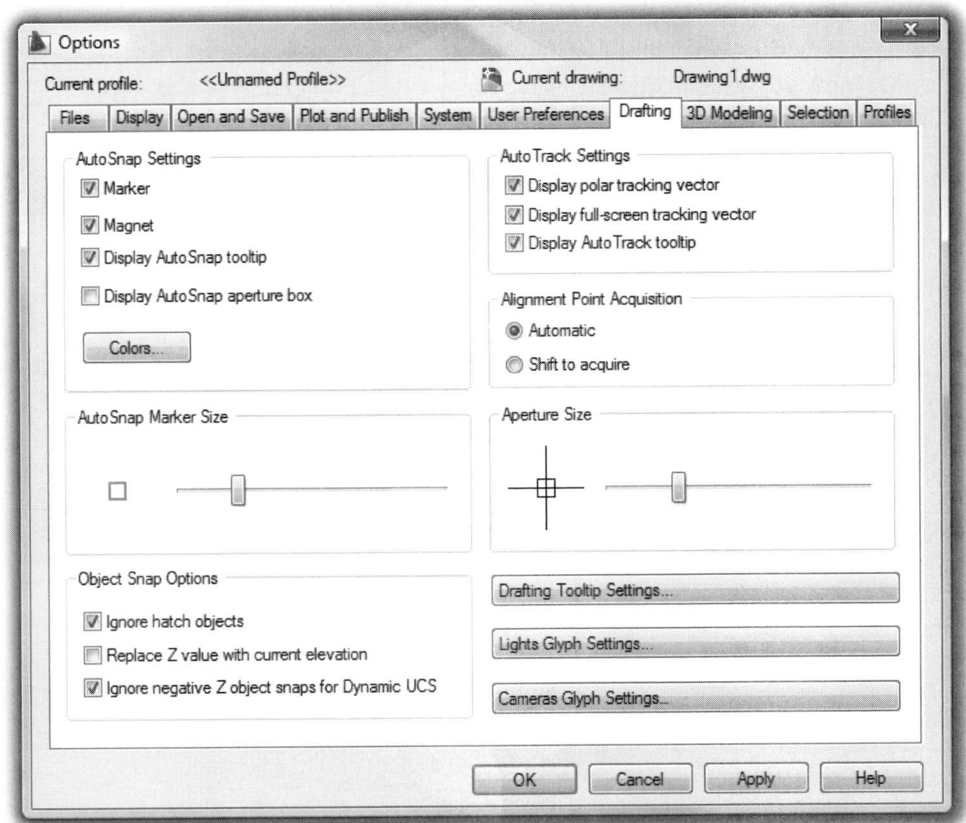

Figure 1-126 The Drafting Tooltip Settings . . . button in the Drafting tab of the Options dialog box opens the Tooltip Appearance dialog box

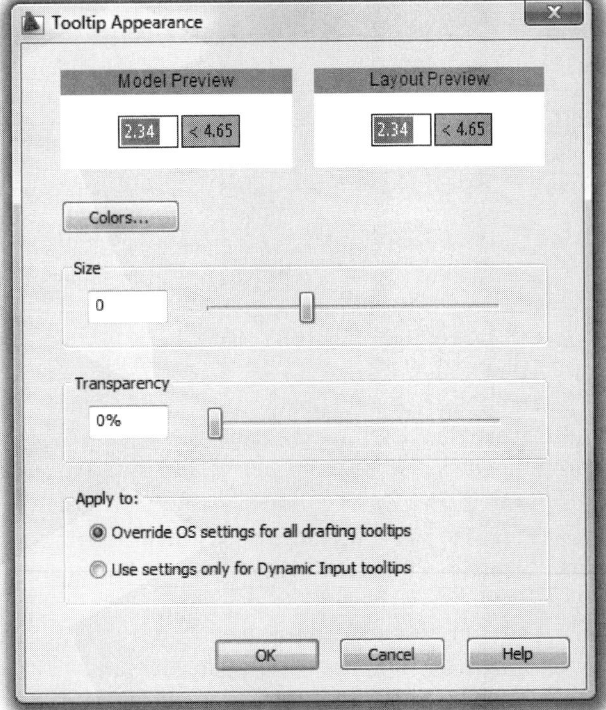

Figure 1-127 The Tooltip Appearance dialog box

Exercise 1-18: Copying Objects Using Tracking Techniques

In this exercise you will create a copy of the sphere using the tracking tool. You will locate the center of the new sphere in the middle of the left face of the box.

1. **OPEN** ***Exercise 1-17.***
2. **SAVE** the drawing **AS** ***Exercise 1-18.***

3. Turn **ORTHO** mode off, and select the **Front** UCS.
4. Invoke the **COPY** command, and respond to the prompts as follows:

Select objects: *Select the sphere.*

Select objects: ↵ *(To end the selection)*

Specify base point or [Displacement] <Displacement>: *Snap to the center point of the sphere.*

Specify second point or

<use first point as displacement>: *Leave a mark in the midpoint of the two edges shown in* Figure 1-128 *and move the pointer near the center of the front face. Slightly move the pointer until you see the two tracking vectors. Click to specify the point.*

Specify second point or [Exit/Undo] <Exit>: ↵ *(To end the command)*

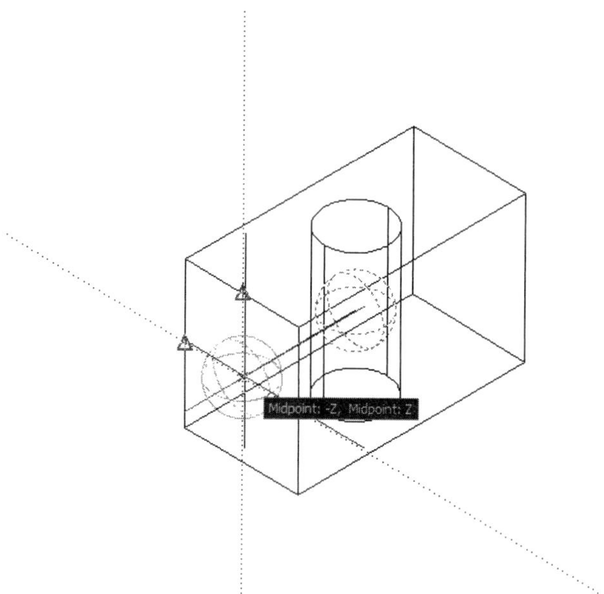

Figure 1-128 The Tracking vectors for the two midpoints show up when near the intersection

5. A second sphere should be placed in the middle of the left face. **SAVE** the drawing.
6. Select the **Right** view and **ZOOM** out to make the 3D model view smaller.
7. Turn **ORTHO** mode on.
8. Invoke the **COPY** command again and, when prompted, select the sphere. Respond to the remaining prompts as follows:

Specify base point or [Displacement] <Displacement>: *Snap to the center point of the sphere.*

Specify second point or

<use first point as displacement>: *Leave a mark in the lower-right endpoint of the 3D solid* (Figure 1-129). *Then move the pointer up to find the intersection between the vertical tracking vector and the Ortho alignment of the center point.*

Specify second point or [Exit/Undo] <Exit>: ↵ *(To end the command)*

9. Select the **SE Isometric** viewpoint. The 3D model should look like Figure 1-130.
10. **Save** the drawing.

Note:
The copied sphere maintains the Z coordinate of the original object. This occurs even though the point used for tracking does not have the same Z coordinate as the first point.

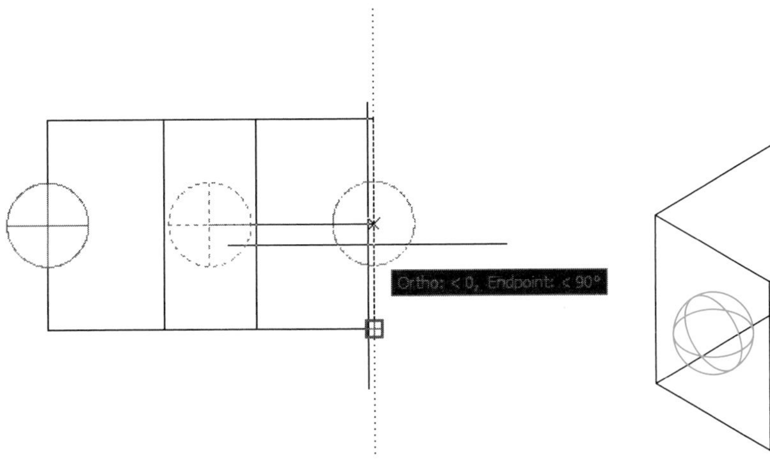

Figure 1-129 Leaving a mark in the lower-right endpoint allows you to use a vector that tracks this point

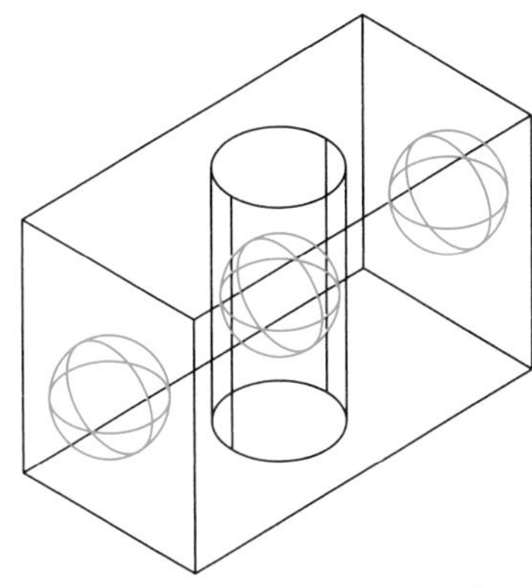

Figure 1-130 The original sphere and two other spheres copied using different tracking techniques

Polar Tracking

Activating the **POLAR** mode automatically deactivates the **ORTHO** mode, and vice versa. This tool allows you to use an angle increment and the additional angles specified in the **Drafting Settings** dialog box (Figure 1-131). This tool also allows you to find the polar coordinates of the points.

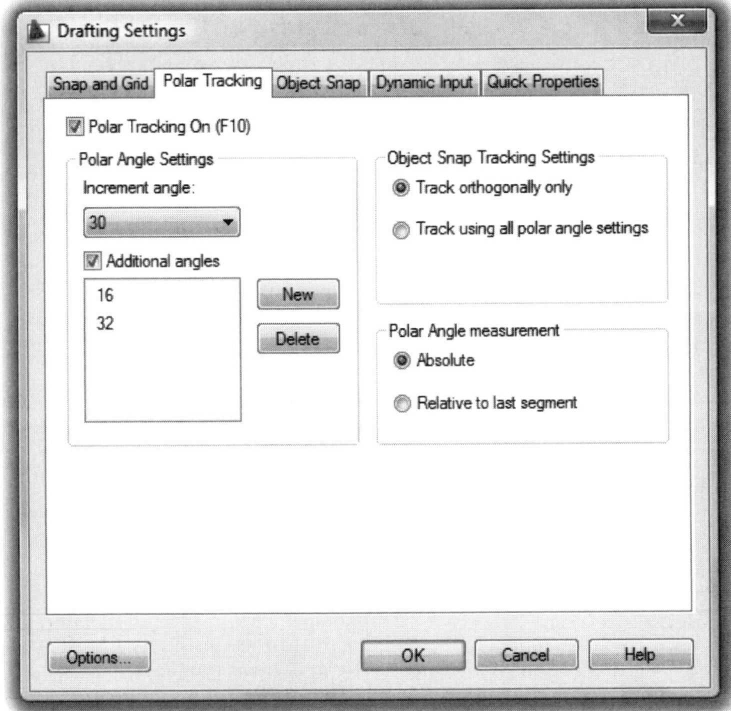

Figure 1-131 POLAR tracking mode uses an angle increment and the additional angles, as specified in the Drafting Settings dialog box

When using the **POLAR** mode, you can specify points by first finding the direction predefined in the angle settings. You just move the mouse around until you see a path, like the one in Figure 1-132, that indicates the specific preset angle you want. Then you release the mouse and enter the distance from the tracking point to finish specifying the polar coordinate.

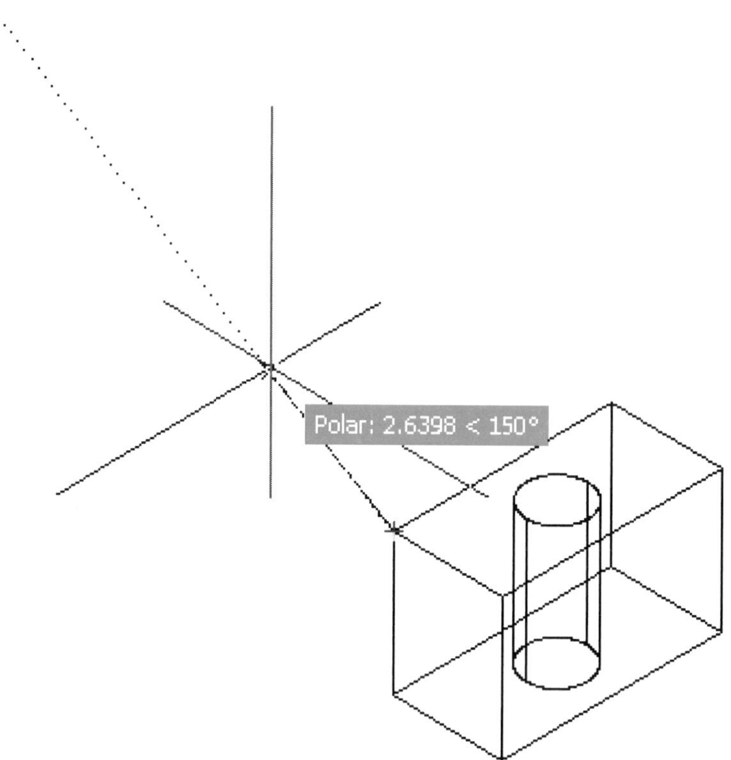

Figure 1-132 A polar coordinate on a plane parallel to the current XY plane in the direction of 150°

TIP

You can use **POLAR** tracking and **AutoTrack** jointly to find points by the intersection of the tracking paths generated by both tools.

Direct Distance Entry

direct distance entry: A practical method of specifying the coordinates of the next point by entering a distance while the cursor indicates a specific known direction.

Direct distance entry can be used with either the **ORTHO** or **POLAR** mode. In this method you release the mouse while the pointer indicates a known direction. You then enter the distance directly in the command line.

Now you can also use the direct distance entry method in the direction of the *Z*-axis.

Dynamic Input

Dynamic input consists of a group of elements that allow you to interface with the AutoCAD software near the cursor. It is not intended to completely replace the command line window. The three dynamic input features are **Pointer Input, Dimension Input,** and **Dynamic Prompts.** These features can be turned on and off individually according to your needs, level of usage, and preferences (Figure 1-133). You can also turn the entire **Dynamic Input** mode on and off by clicking the **DYN** button in the status bar, or by pressing the <**F12**> key.

Pointer Input allows you to see the current coordinates of the cursor and enter them in the tooltip boxes. You move to the next box by typing one of the coordinate separators (, or <), or by pressing the <**Tab**> key (Figure 1-134).

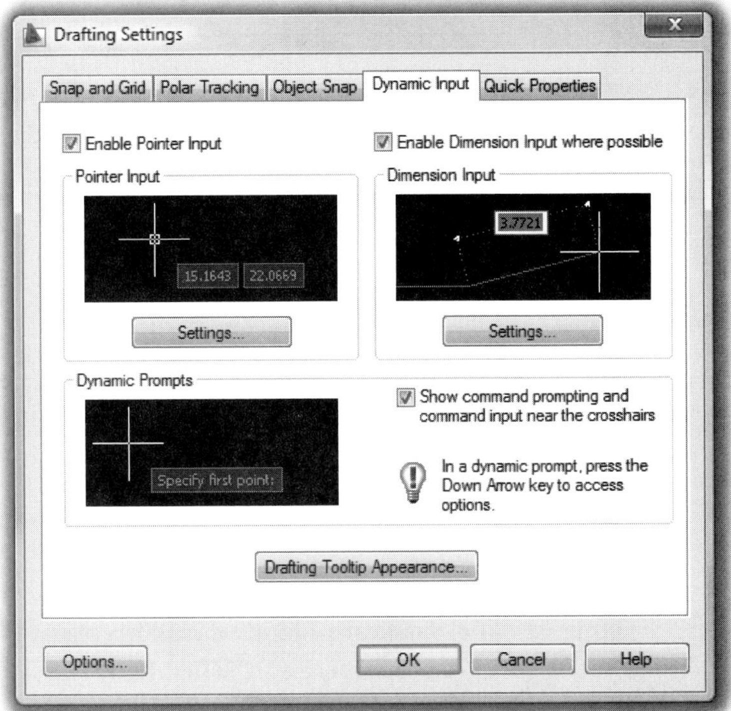

Figure 1-133 The Pointer Input, Dimension Input, and Dynamic Prompts features can be turned on and off in the Dynamic Input tab of the Drafting Settings dialog box

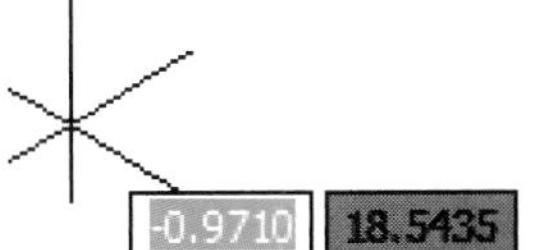

Figure 1-134 The Pointer Input feature of Dynamic Input

The **Dimension Input** element is activated by specifying the first point on most of the commands that require the specification of more than one point or distances (i.e., **LINE, CIRCLE, CYLINDER, BOX,** and **CONE**). Instead of coordinates, the tooltip boxes display current distances and angle, depending on the particular command invoked. Pressing the <**Tab**> key allows you to move from one tooltip box to the next (Figure 1-135).

The **Dynamic Prompts** element allows you to read the command prompts in a tooltip near the cursor. In case other options are available in a command, they can be selected from the dynamic prompt list after pressing the <**Down Arrow**> key, similarly to the shortcut menu (Figure 1-136).

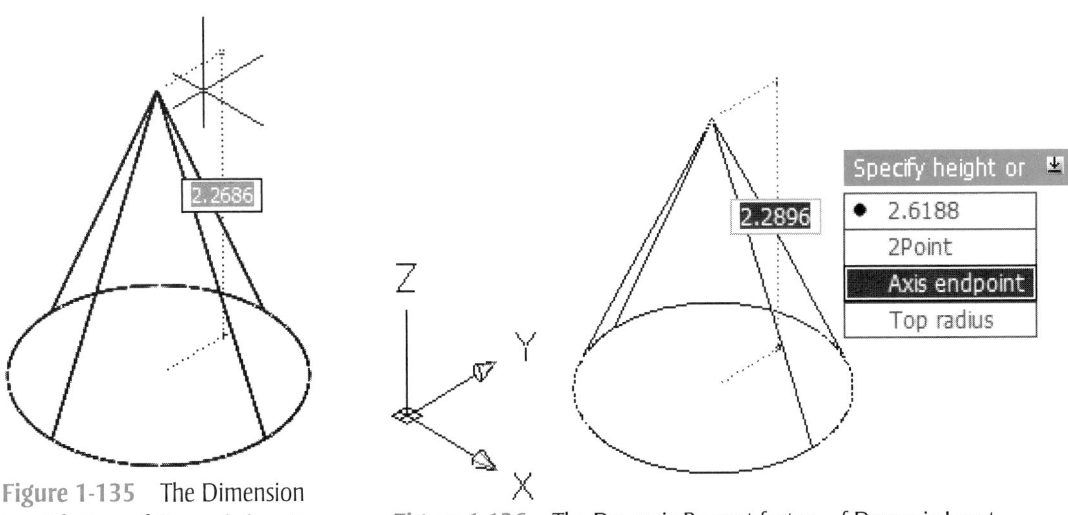

Figure 1-135 The Dimension Input feature of Dynamic Input

Figure 1-136 The Dynamic Prompt feature of Dynamic Input

SUMMARY

After going though this chapter, you should have clarified your idea about what working in 3D space means. You should also have become familiar with some of the main tools involved. Many important topics have been discussed here, although isolated in some cases. These will be very useful in your future 3D work, so you can consult this particular chapter as a reference from time to time.

The key point of the entire chapter is that you must understand how important is the relationship between the way you look at the 3D space, and the location of the current working plane. That is, you must clearly grasp the relationship between the 3D viewing system and the 3D coordinate system. The mathematics of the coordinate system, along with the introduction to the third coordinate (*Z*), will allow you to understand more clearly what the computer 3D space is.

Many 3D modeling aids and tools, such as the visual styles, the 3D Orbit, and the tracking tools in 3D, among others, have been presented in this chapter. These are some of the tools that will be essential for your future success.

CHAPTER TEST QUESTIONS

Multiple Choice

1. The AutoCAD program's 3D space:
   a. Is always present
   b. Needs to be activated
   c. Interferes with 2D work
   d. Requires additional software
2. Which of the following can be linked to specific Tool palette groups?
   a. **Design Center**
   b. **Properties**
   c. **Ribbon Panels**
   d. **Visual Styles Manager**
3. The number of viewing points you can use in the AutoCAD program:
   a. Is ten (six Orthographic and four Isometric)
   b. Depends on whether you are working in 3D or 2D
   c. Is infinite
   d. Depends on the current UCS
4. The UCS can be modified by:
   a. Selecting an object
   b. Specifying a *Z*-axis vector
   c. Rotating it around the *Y*-axis
   d. All of the above
5. The **3D Orbit** tool is used mainly to:
   a. Rotate objects in the 3D space
   b. Change the viewing point
   c. Place some objects closer to others
   d. Relocate the UCS
6. Which of the following methods cannot be used to create a new UCS in the AutoCAD program?
   a. Specify two points to align the *Z*-axis
   b. Rotate counterclockwise about the *Y*-axis
   c. Align with a selected face
   d. Locate the *XY* plane normal to a selected line
7. Turning on (**1**) the **UCSORTHO** system variable causes:
   a. A change in the viewing point when an orthographic UCS is selected
   b. A change in the UCS when an orthographic view is selected
   c. A viewport to update its UCS to agree with the current one
   d. None of the above
8. Which of the following is not one of the AutoCAD program's predefined visual styles?
   a. **3D Hidden**
   b. **Gouraud Shaded**
   c. **Conceptual**
   d. **Realistic**
9. Which of the following actions does not change the viewing point?
   a. Using the **3D Orbit** tool
   b. Selecting a new Isometric viewing point
   c. Invoking the **PLAN** command
   d. Zooming into the drawing area
10. Which of the following is a method used to find points in the 3D space?
    a. Point filters
    b. AutoTrack
    c. Direct entry method
    d. All of the above

Matching

a. NW Isometric View
b. 3D Orbit

1. Shows the object's silhouettes
2. Changes the viewpoint when the UCS is changed

c. Top imaginary plane
d. Cylindrical coordinates
e. UCS
f. Conceptual
g. DISPSILH
h. Shortcut menu
i. REGEN
j. UCSFOLLOW

3. Provides easy access to many command options
4. AutoCAD's default viewing point
5. A predefined viewing point
6. A tool to change the viewing point freely
7. A method of entering the 3D coordinates of a point
8. Revokes the effect of the **HIDE** command
9. Gives the object an artistic shaded appearance
10. The World Coordinate System, modified by the user

True or False

1. True or False: The default location of the *YZ* plane of the coordinate system is on the Right imaginary plane of the viewing system.
2. True or False: You can modify the UCS and obtain an infinite number of other possible UCSs.
3. True or False: The only way you can specify the 3D coordinates of a point is by using one of the following formats:

   X,Y,Z $r<\theta, Z$ $r<\theta<\varphi$
4. True or False: If the value of the **UCSORTHO** system variable is **1,** then selecting the **Right** view will automatically update the UCS so that the *XY* plane is in the **Right** imaginary viewing plane.
5. True or False: The right-hand rule can help you determine the positive direction of the rotation about any axis.
6. True or False: You can create a new workspace only through the **Customize User Interface** dialog box.
7. True or False: In the presence of the 2D Wireframe visual style, the effect of the **HIDE** command is automatically revoked if the **SE Isometric** viewing point is selected.
8. True or False: Scrolling the mouse wheel forward will zoom into the 3D model at the current location of the cursor the moment the operation is performed.
9. True or False: When splitting the display into several viewports, you cannot modify the UCS in each one independently.
10. True or False: Using AutoTrack is an efficient way to find points in both 2D and 3D work.

Chapter Tutorials

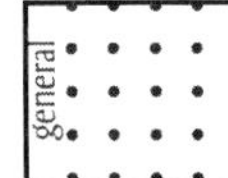

Tutorial 1-1: UCS Manipulation

In this tutorial you will practice the different procedures used to manipulate the UCS. Mastering this aspect of 3D work is a key factor for successful future learning. Figure 1-137 shows how the final 3D model will look after we add the different texts throughout the 3D space.

1. **OPEN** the finished *SimpleSolid* drawing you created earlier in this chapter.
2. **SAVE** it **AS** ***Tutorial 1-1***.

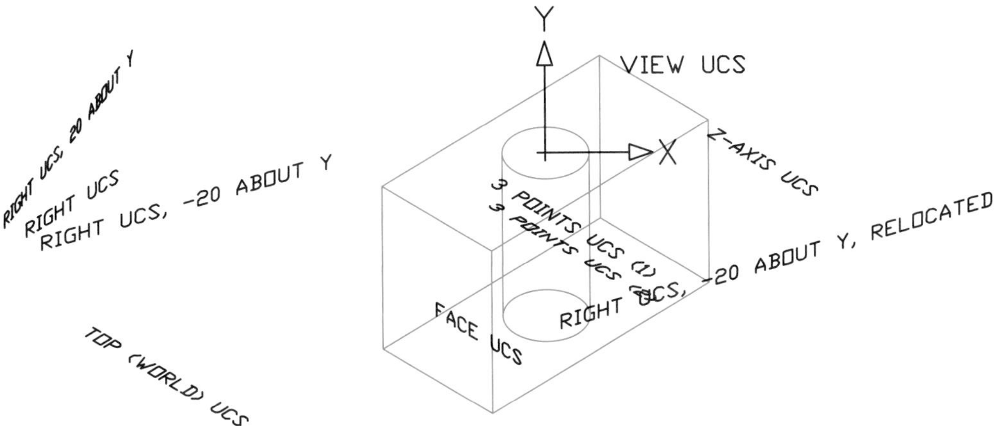

Figure 1-137 Preview of the final model after adding the texts throughout the 3D space

3. Make sure the **UCSORTHO** system variable is set to **1**.
4. Select the **Top** view.
5. **MOVE** the 3D solid **3″** orthogonally to the right (along the positive X-axis).
6. **MOVE** the 3D solid **3″** orthogonally up (along the positive Y-axis) (Figure 1-138).

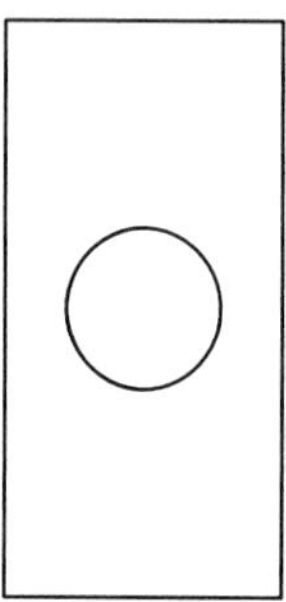

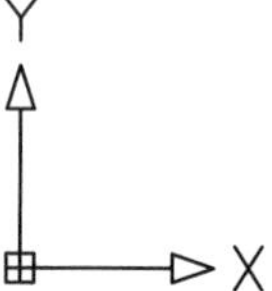

Figure 1-138 A Top view of the moved 3D solid

7. Invoke the **TEXT** command through the command line, and respond to the prompts as follows:

   Specify start point of text or [Justify/Style]: *1,1* ↵

   Specify height <0.2000>: ↵ *(To accept the height value)*

   Specify rotation angle of text <0>: ↵*(To accept the height value)*

8. When the simplified text editor opens, type **TOP (WORLD)** UCS and press <**Enter**> twice to exit the **TEXT** command (Figure 1-139).

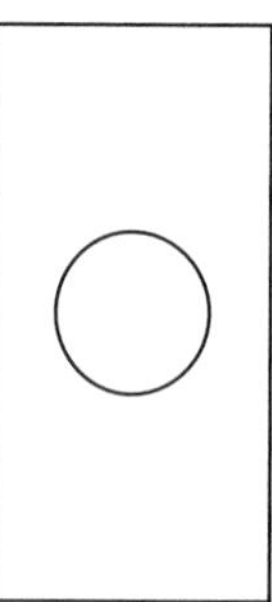

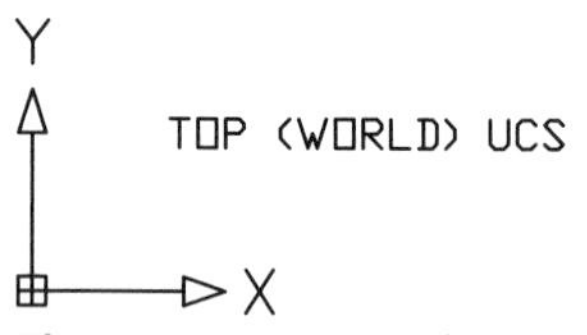

Figure 1-139 Text placed in the WCS

9. Invoke the **COPYBASE** command through the drop-down menu: **Edit/Copy with Base Point.** When prompted for the base point, enter 0,0,0. Select the text when prompted to select the objects, and press <**Enter**> to exit the command.
10. Select the **SE Isometric** viewing point (Figure 1-140).

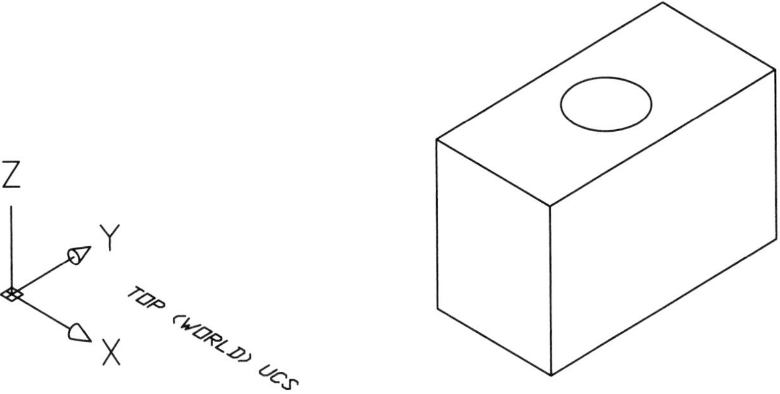

Figure 1-140 The SE Isometric view of the 3D model

11. Select the **Right** UCS.
12. Invoke the **PASTECLIP** command through the drop-down menu: **Edit/Paste.** When prompted for the insertion point, enter **0,0,0.**
13. Double-click the text to open the simplified text editor (**DDEDIT**) and edit it to read **RIGHT UCS** (Figure 1-141). Press <**Enter**> twice to exit the **DDEDIT** command.

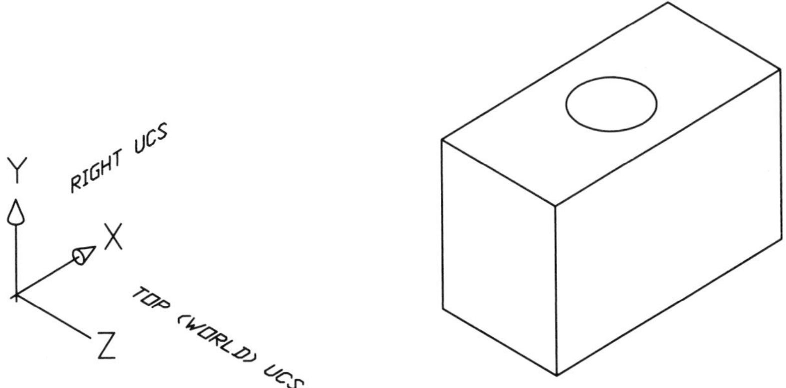

Figure 1-141 New text placed in the Right UCS

14. Rotate the UCS **20**° about the *Y*-axis, using the icon on the UCS toolbar.
15. Double-click the text and edit it to read **RIGHT UCS, 20 ABOUT Y** (Figure 1-142).
16. Select the **Right** UCS again.
17. Rotate the UCS **−20**° about the *Y*-axis.
18. Invoke the **PASTECLIP** command, and enter **0,0,0** for the insertion point.
19. Double-click the text and edit it to read **RIGHT UCS, -20 ABOUT Y** (Figure 1-143).

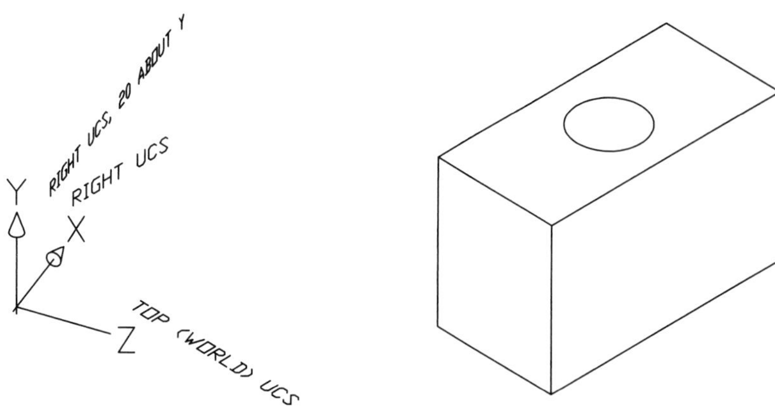

Figure 1-142 New text placed in a user-defined UCS, 20° about the Y-axis with respect to the previous UCS

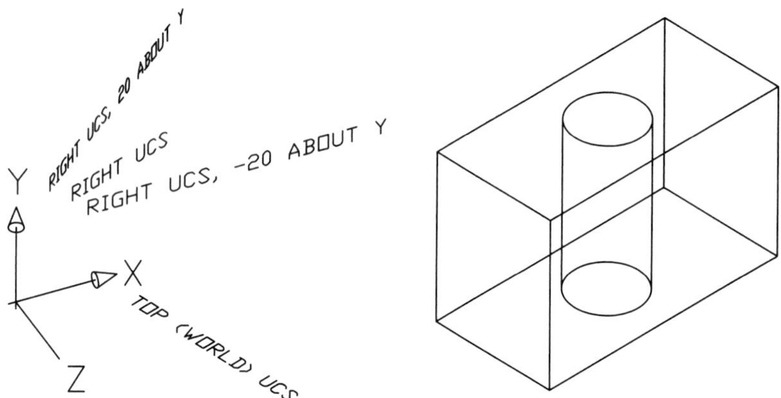

Figure 1-143 New text placed in a user-defined UCS,–20° about the Y-axis with respect to the previous UCS

20. Relocate the origin of the UCS, using the icon on the **UCS** toolbar. When prompted to specify the new origin point, snap on the endpoint of the 3D solid indicated in Figure 1-144.

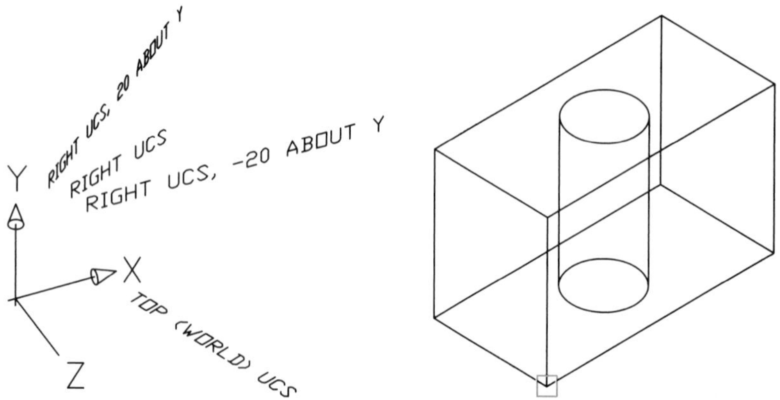

Figure 1-144 Specifying a point to relocate the origin of the UCS

21. Invoke the **PASTECLIP** command, and enter **0,0,0** for the insertion point.
22. Double-click the text and edit it to read **RIGHT UCS, -20 ABOUT Y, RELOCATED** (Figure 1-145).

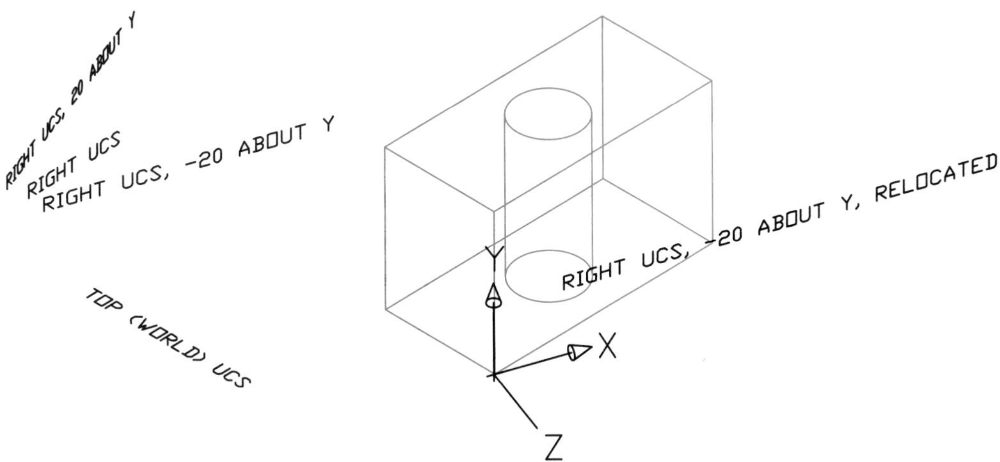

Figure 1-145 New text placed in a user-defined UCS, in a different location with respect to the previous UCS

23. Define the next orientation of the UCS by specifying three points. Use the icon on the **UCS** toolbar. To specify the three points, snap to the 3D solid's points in the order indicated in Figure 1-146.

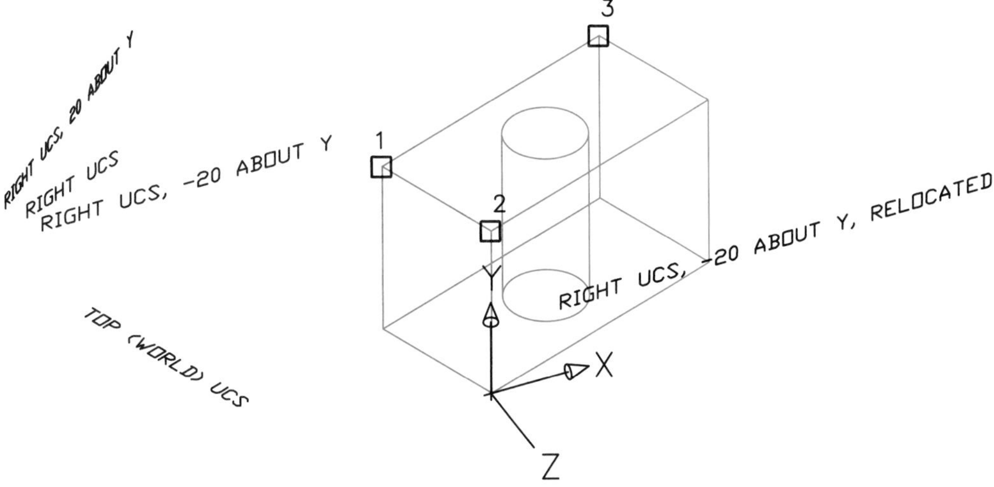

Figure 1-146 The three points used to specify the new user-defined UCS

24. Invoke the **PASTECLIP** command, and enter **0,0,0** for the insertion point.
25. Double-click the text and edit it to read **3 POINTS UCS (1)** (Figure 1-147).

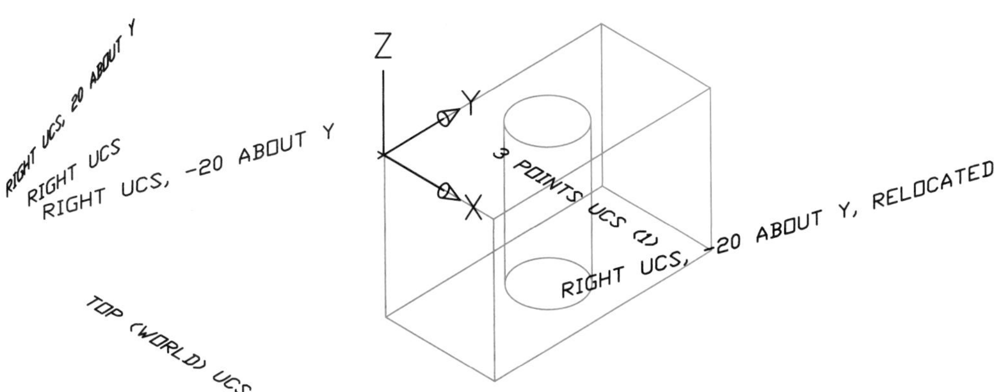

Figure 1-147 New text placed in the new user-defined UCS

26. Define the orientation of the UCS by specifying three points again. Use the icon on the **UCS** toolbar. Snap to the 3D solid's points in the order indicated in Figure 1-148.

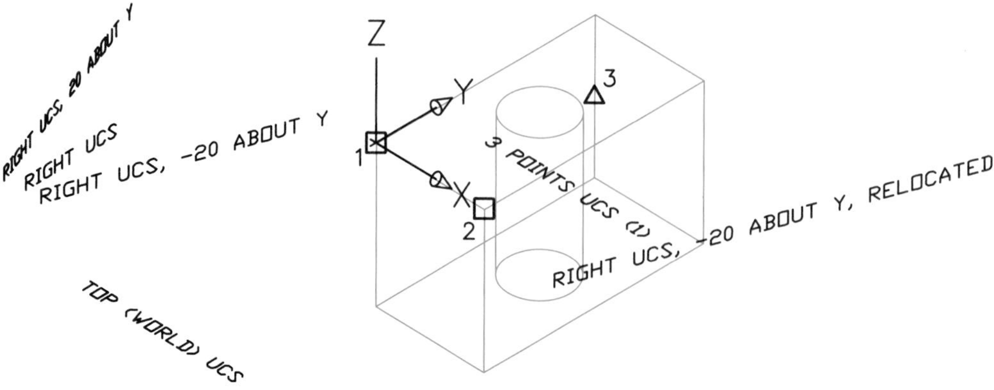

Figure 1-148 The three points used to specify the new user-defined UCS

27. Invoke the **PASTECLIP** command, and enter **0,0,0** for the insertion point.
28. Double-click the text and edit it to read **3 POINTS UCS (2)** (Figure 1-149).

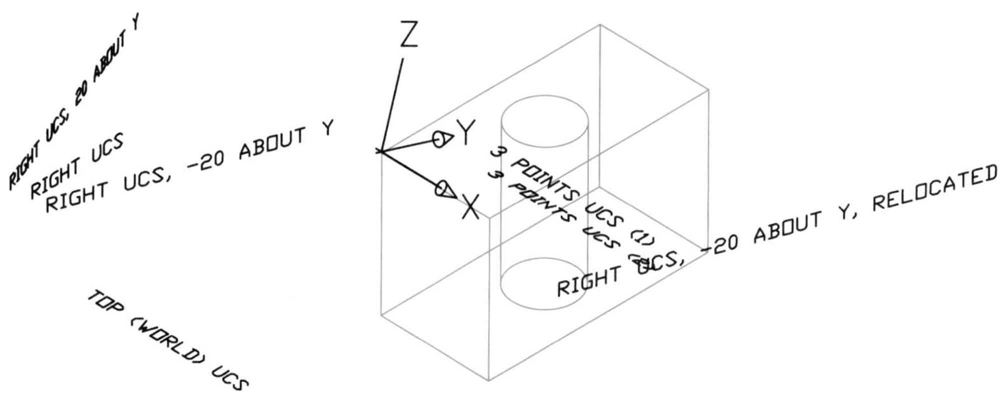

Figure 1-149 New text placed in the new user-defined UCS

29. Define the orientation of the UCS by selecting the face of a 3D solid. Use the corresponding icon on the **UCS** toolbar. When prompted to select the face of the 3D solid object, click as close as possible to the area indicated in Figure 1-150. Press <**Enter**> to accept the selected face.

Note:
Selecting the face of the 3D solid in a particular area, when defining the UCS, is interpreted by the AutoCAD program in the following way:
- The closest corner locates the origin.
- The closest edge locates the X-axis.

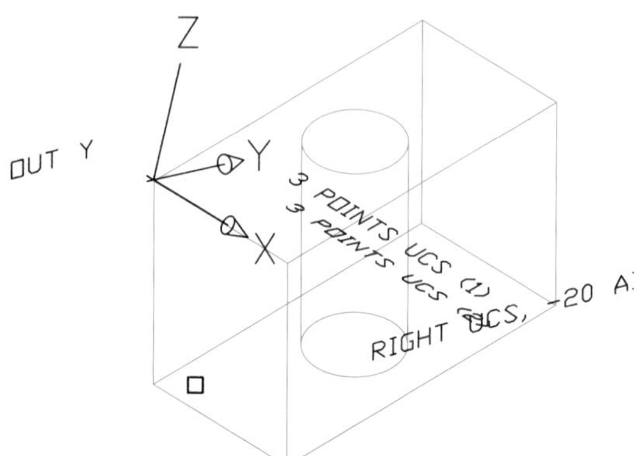

Figure 1-150 The selected face of the 3D solid used to define the new UCS

30. Invoke the **PASTECLIP** command, and enter 0,0,0 for the insertion point.
31. Double-click the text and edit it to read **FACE UCS** (Figure 1-151).

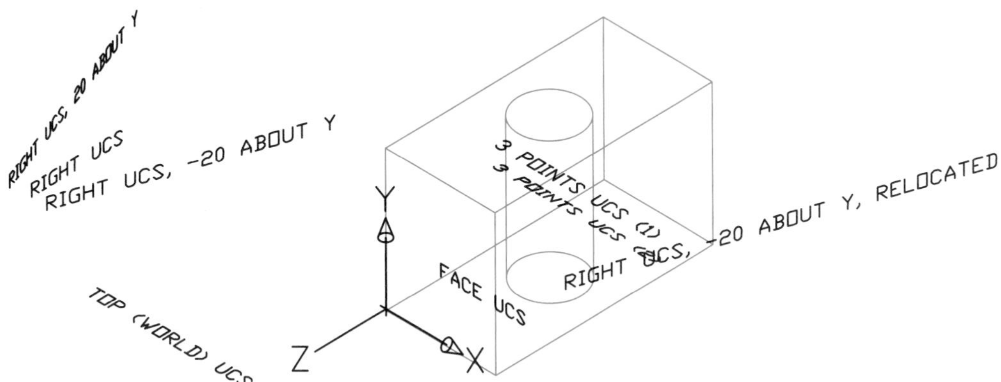

Figure 1-151 New text placed in the new user-defined UCS

32. Define the orientation of the UCS by specifying a **Z axis Vector,** using the corresponding icon on the **UCS** toolbar. To specify the new origin point and a point on the positive portion of the *Z*-axis, snap to the 3D solid's points in the order indicated in Figure 1-152.

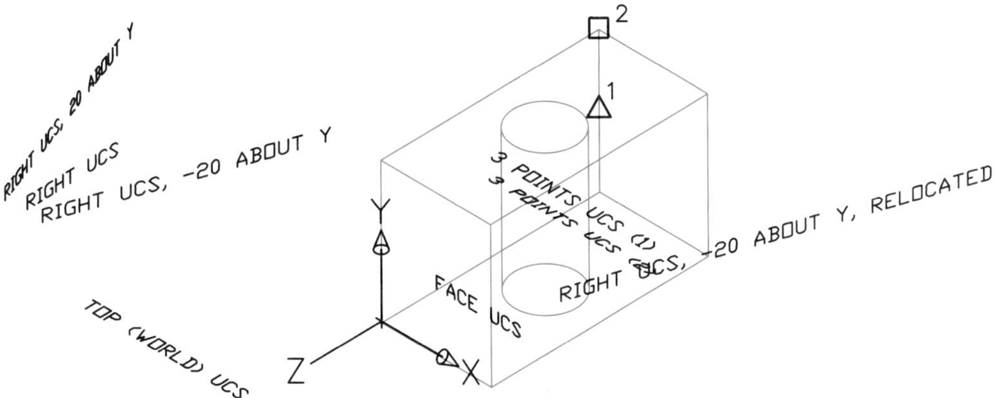

Figure 1-152 Points used to define a new UCS using the Z Axis Vector option

33. Invoke the **PASTECLIP** command, and enter **0,0,0** for the insertion point.
34. Double-click the text and edit it to read **Z-AXIS UCS** (Figure 1-153).
35. Relocate the origin of the UCS. When prompted to specify the new origin point, snap to the center point on the top circular edge of the 3D solid.
36. Relocate the UCS again to align it with the current view. Use the corresponding icon on the **UCS** toolbar.

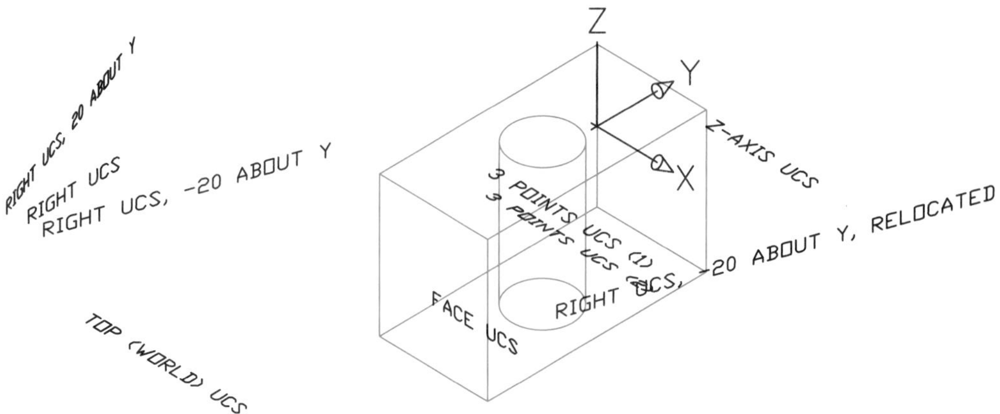

Figure 1-153 New text placed in the new user-defined UCS

Note:
When the UCS is aligned with the current viewing plane, the Z-axis letter disappears, indicating that this axis is perpendicular to the display at this moment.

37. Invoke the **PASTECLIP** command, and enter **0,0,0** for the insertion point.
38. Double-click the text and edit it to read **VIEW UCS** (Figure 1-154).

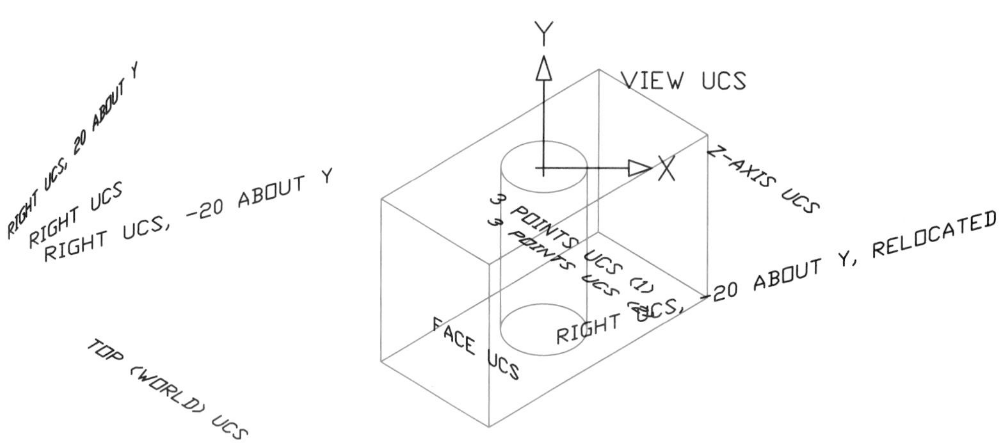

Figure 1-154 New text placed in a UCS coincident with the viewing plane

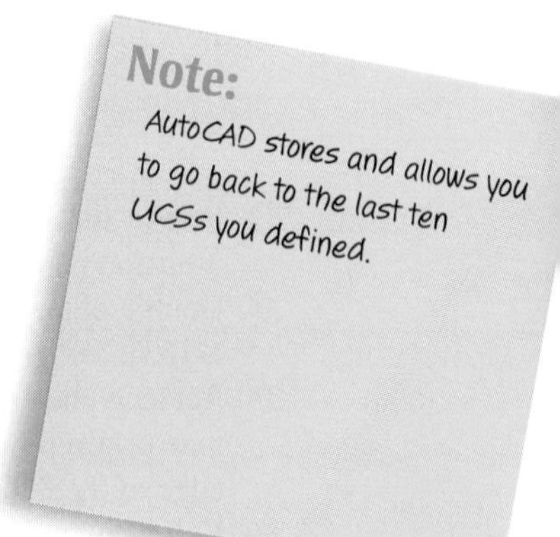

Note:
AutoCAD stores and allows you to go back to the last ten UCSs you defined.

39. Relocate the UCS by selecting the **Previous** one. Use the corresponding icon on the **UCS** toolbar.
40. Repeat the **Previous** operation until the UCS no longer changes.
41. Relocate the UCS by selecting an **Object.** Use the corresponding icon on the **UCS** toolbar. When prompted to select the object, select any of the text objects you edited.

42. Repeat the **Object** operation for each of the text objects.
43. Invoke the **3DORBIT** command to explore in greater depth the alignments of the text objects and the planes that they define in the 3D space.
44. **SAVE** the drawing.

Note:

The AutoCAD program stores the information of the UCS when each object is created, allowing you to go back to its particular UCS. The origin of the UCS relocates on the insertion point of the text. What is more difficult to achieve is not precisely relocating the origin of the UCS, but aligning the UCS in the 3D space.

Quick-Start Tutorials 2

Chapter Objectives

- Create two real 3D modeling projects, starting them from scratch.
- Know the difference between representing 3D models with 3D solid objects and with surface-type objects.
- Become familiar with the commands and tools most frequently used to generate 3D models.
- Employ commands typically used for 2D design in a 3D environment.
- Strengthen the argument that working in 3D is not an isolated task, but rather the usage of advanced tools along with those commonly used in 2D.
- Observe the effects and capabilities of the tools used in modifications to the viewing point and other visual effects.

INTRODUCTION

These introductory tutorials will provide you with the opportunity to get a better idea about what 3D modeling is. Hands-on practice will help you better comprehend the further detailed explanation of these concepts.

Before you start the projects, make sure all the toolbars and dockable windows used in 3D modeling are available. You can do so by simply recalling the workspace you created in the previous chapter.

MODELING THE SOFA TABLE

In this part of the project you will create 3D solid objects to represent the 3D model. As you will see, the same commands you use to generate 2D drawings are also used in a 3D environment.

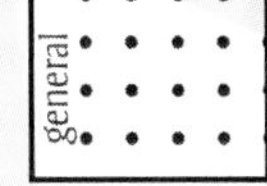

Many assembling details, such as the connections between the pieces of the sofa table, have been omitted for simplicity. If designing furniture is one of your areas of interest, then you may want to try adding some more details on your own.

1. Start a **NEW** drawing, using the **acad** template.
2. **SAVE** the drawing AS ***SofaTable***.

TIP

During the rest of the project, you will not be directed to **SAVE** the drawing. But it is important that you do so every few steps or when taking a break to prevent losing the work you have done. 3D operations typically demand more from a computer than 2D operations. This may cause your system to stop responding depending on its level of use and properties.

3. Open the **Visual Styles Manager** palette and click on the **2D Wireframe** sample image.
4. Under **2D Hide – Obscured Lines**, set the **Linetype** to **Dashed** and the **Color** to **Green** or any other color you like. Close the **Visual Styles Manager** palette.
5. Select the **SE Isometric** viewing point.
6. Invoke the **BOX** command using one of the methods in the grid. Respond to the prompts as follows:

   Specify first corner or [Center]: *Click anywhere in the drawing area.*

   Specify other corner or [Cube/Length]: *Move the mouse to open a rectangle and click anywhere in the drawing area.*

   Specify height or [2Point]: *Move the mouse up and click anywhere in the drawing area.*

7. Select the **3D Solid** box and right-click in the drawing area. Select **Properties** from the shortcut menu.
8. In the **Properties** palette, under **Geometry**, change the values of the following elements as shown:
   - Position X=12
   - Position Y=12
   - Length=24
   - Width=24
   - Height=1
9. **ZOOM** to extents and invoke the **HIDE** command. The 3D model should look now like Figure 2-2.

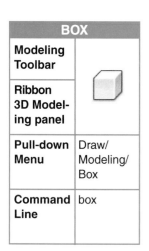

BOX	
Modeling Toolbar	
Ribbon 3D Modeling panel	
Pull-down Menu	Draw/ Modeling/ Box
Command Line	box

Note:
The 3D solid box is interactively created as you specify the points.

Note:
The AutoCAD® program now allows you to modify geometrical parameters related to dimensions and location of objects in 3D space through the **Properties** palette (Figure 2-1).

3D Solid	
General	
Color	ByLayer
Layer	0
Linetype	ByLayer
Linetype scale	1.0000
Plot style	ByColor
Lineweight	ByLayer
Hyperlink	
3D Visualization	
Material	ByLayer
Shadow display	Casts and Rece...
Geometry	
Solid type	Box
Position X	-3.3409
Position Y	8.3629
Position Z	0.0000
Length	0.8387
Width	0.6447
Height	0.4338
Rotation	180
Solid History	
History	Record
Show History	No

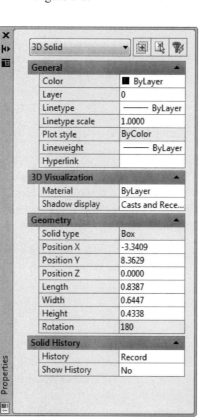

Figure 2-1 Using the Properties palette to modify the 3D solid box

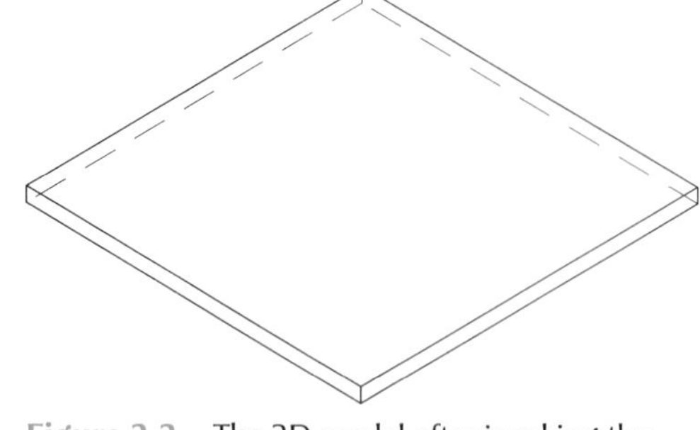

Figure 2-2 The 3D model after invoking the HIDE command

TIP In order to **ZOOM** and **PAN** in the drawing right after using the **HIDE** command, you must always regenerate the display by invoking the **REGEN** command.

10. Using the **RECTANGLE** command, draw a square as shown in Figure 2-3. When prompted for the first corner, snap to the top endpoint of the table top and enter **@8,8** for the second corner.
11. **MOVE** the square away from the table top corner, as shown in Figure 2-4.

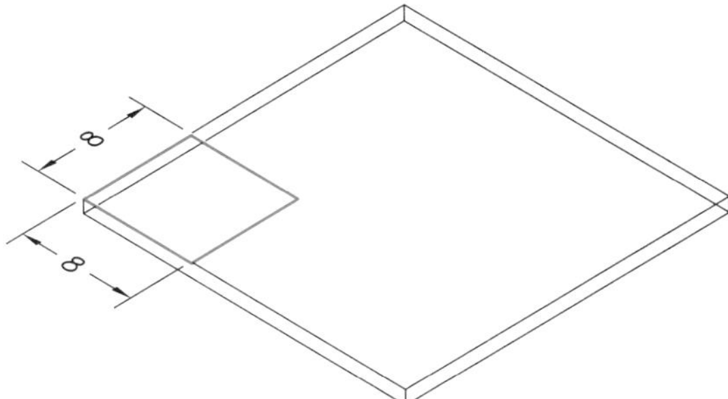

Figure 2-3 An 8 × 8 square is placed on the top face

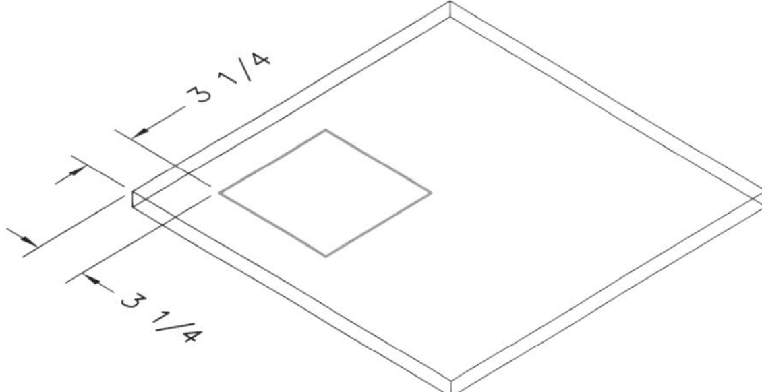

Figure 2-4 The square is moved to the proper place

12. Select the **Top** view.
13. Using the **MIRROR** command, obtain the other three squares shown in Figure 2-5.
14. Select the **SE Isometric** viewing point. Invoke the **EXTRUDE** command and respond to the prompts as follows:

    Select objects to extrude: *Select the four squares.*

    Select objects to extrude: ↵ *(To end the selection process)*

    Specify height of extrusion or [Direction/Path/Taper angle]: *-6* ↵ *(The minus sign causes the extrusion to be made downward.)*

15. The 3D model should look like Figure 2-6. Invoke the **SUBTRACT** command, and respond to the prompts as follows:

    Select solids and regions to subtract from ..

    Select objects: *Select the table top.*

    Select objects: ↵ *(To end the selection)*

    Select solids and regions to subtract ..

    Select objects: *Select the four new solid blocks.*

    Select objects: ↵ *(To end the selection)*

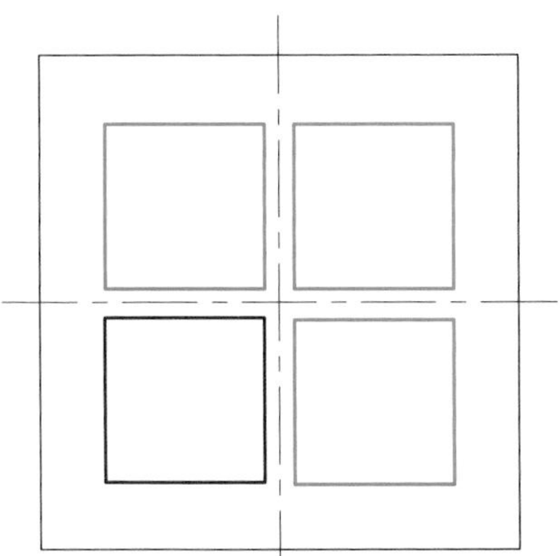

Figure 2-5 The other three squares are created

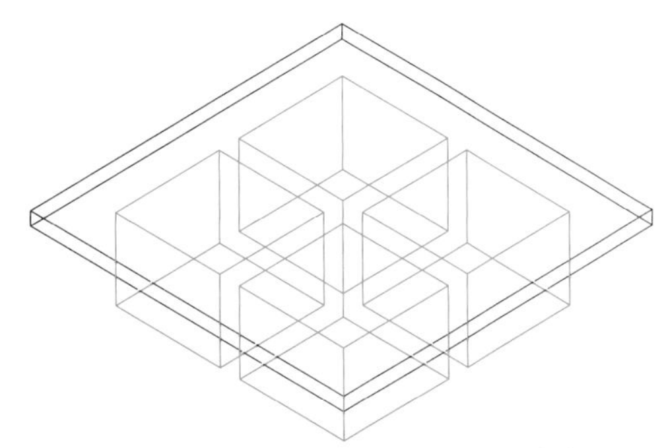

Figure 2-6 The four squares are extruded downward

16. Select the **Realistic** visual style. The 3D model now should look like Figure 2-7.
17. Select the **2D Wireframe** visual style.
18. Make sure either the **Top** or the **World** UCS is shown as current. Otherwise, select one of them.
19. With the **RECTANGLE** command, draw the square highlighted in Figure 2-8, using the endpoints for the square hole on the board. Using a different color will help you visualize the new object.

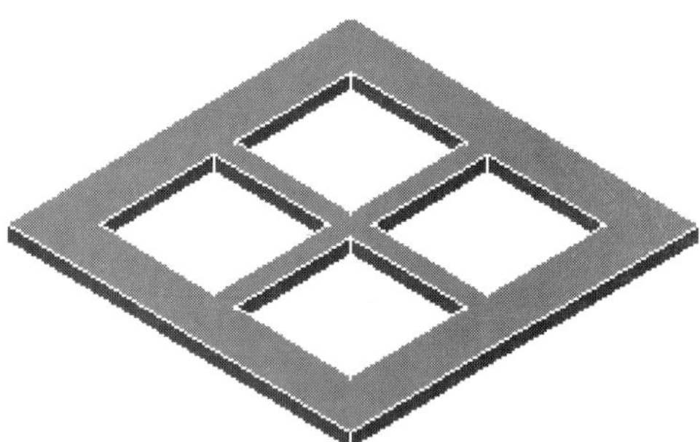

Figure 2-7 The four holes are created by subtracting the four 3D solids from the board

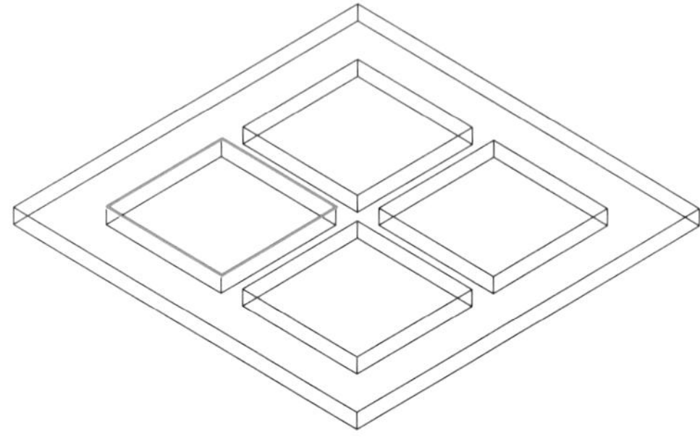

Figure 2-8 A new square using the geometry originated

20. **OFFSET** the square **3/8″** outward. **ERASE** the original rectangle (Figure 2-9).
21. **EXTRUDE** the new rectangle **–1/4″** (down).
22. **COPY** the new 3D solid from any endpoint on the square hole where it is located to the same point in the rest of the holes (Figure 2-10).

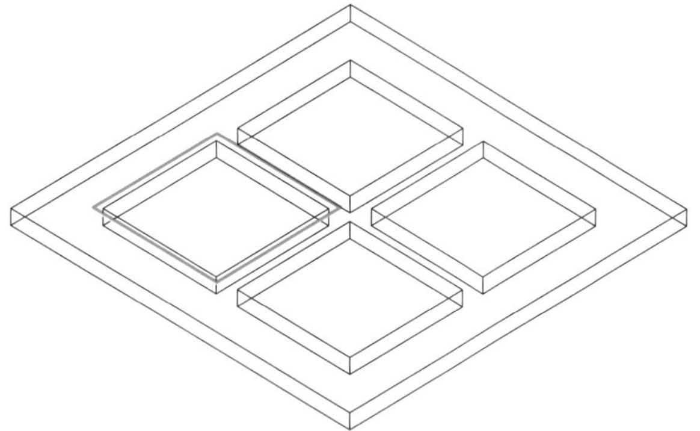

Figure 2-9 The offset square

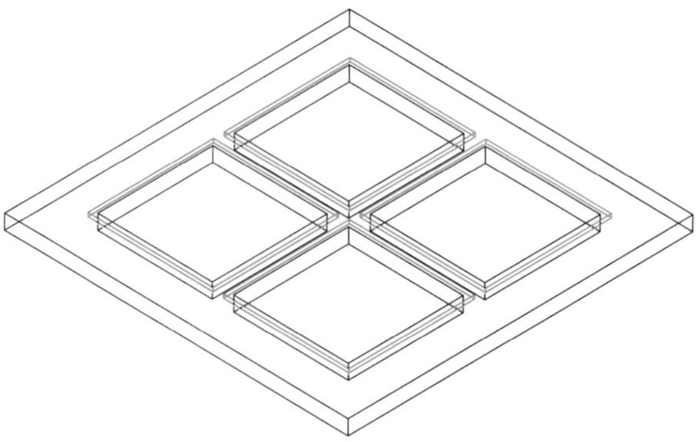

Figure 2-10 The four thin 3D solids are placed in the right locations

PLANESURF	
Modeling Toolbar	
Ribbon Modeling panel	
Pull-down Menu	Draw/ Modeling/ Planesurf
Command Line	planesurf

23. **SUBTRACT** the four new 3D solids from the table top to create a recessed surface where the glass pieces will sit.
24. Select the **Realistic** visual style. The 3D model should look like Figure 2-11.
25. Select the **2D Wireframe** visual style again.
26. Next, you will create the four 3D solids representing the glass pieces of the table. Invoke the **PLANESURF** command. When prompted, snap to the endpoints of one of the recessed holes on the board (Figure 2-12).

Note:
If you used 3D solids with different colors for the **SUBTRACT** operation, the resulting 3D faces of the solid will show both colors. By changing the color property of the resulting 3D solid, you can give it a uniform color.

Figure 2-11 The four recesses are created by subtracting the four thin 3D solids

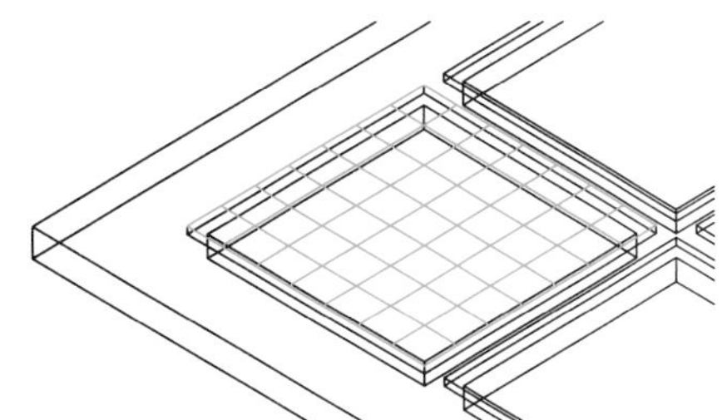

Figure 2-12 A surface is created with the PLANESURF command

27. Invoke the **THICKEN** command. When prompted, select the surface and specify **–1/4″** for the thickness. The 3D model should look like Figure 2-13.
28. **COPY** the first 3D solid representing the piece of glass from any point on the square hole to the same point in the rest of the holes.
29. Open the **Layer Properties Manager** dialog box and create a new layer. Name it **Glass** and change its color to **cyan** (**4**) (Figure 2-14).
30. Select the four glass pieces and change their **Layer** to **Glass.**

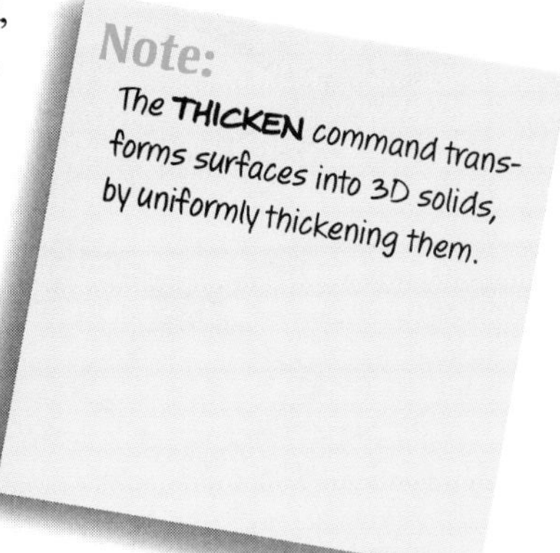

THICKEN	
Ribbon Solid Editing panel	
Pull-down Menu	Modify/ 3D Operation/ Thicken
Command Line	thicken

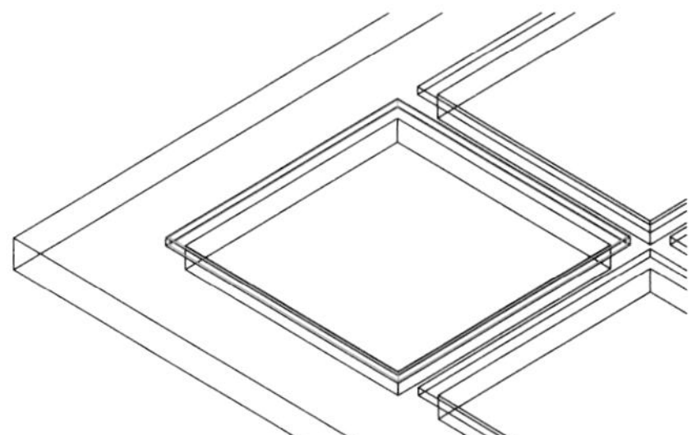

Figure 2-13 The surface is turned into a 3D solid using the THICKEN command

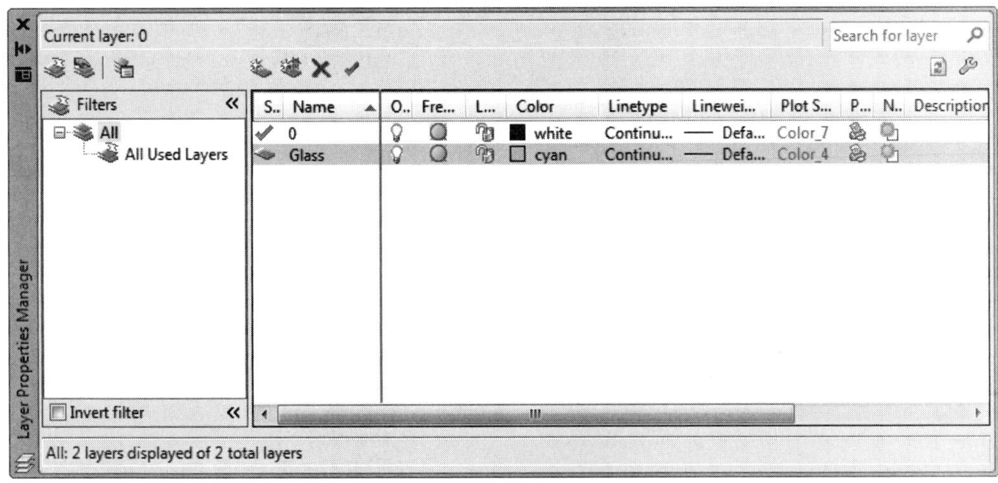

Figure 2-14 The Layer Properties Manager dialog box

31. Invoke the **HIDE** command. The 3D model should look now like Figure 2-15.
32. Turn the **Glass** layer OFF to hide all 3D solids representing the pieces of glass.
33. Invoke the **REGEN** command.
34. Next, you will create the table legs. Using the **RECTANGLE** command, draw a 2½ × 2½ rectangle anywhere in the drawing area. **MOVE** the rectangle to the endpoint of the rectangular hole, as shown in Figure 2-16.

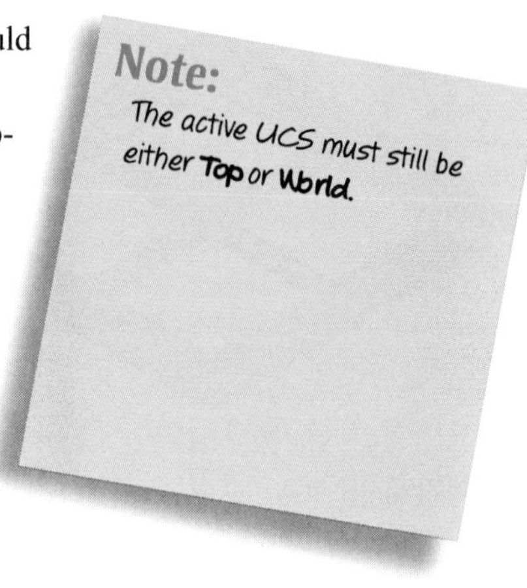

Note:
The active UCS must still be either Top or World.

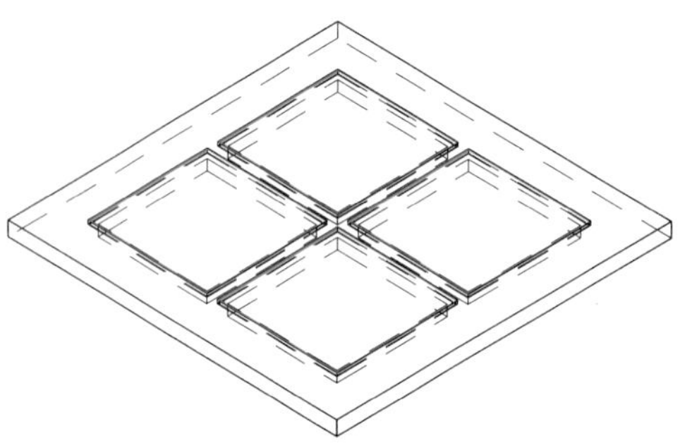

Figure 2-15 After invoking the HIDE command

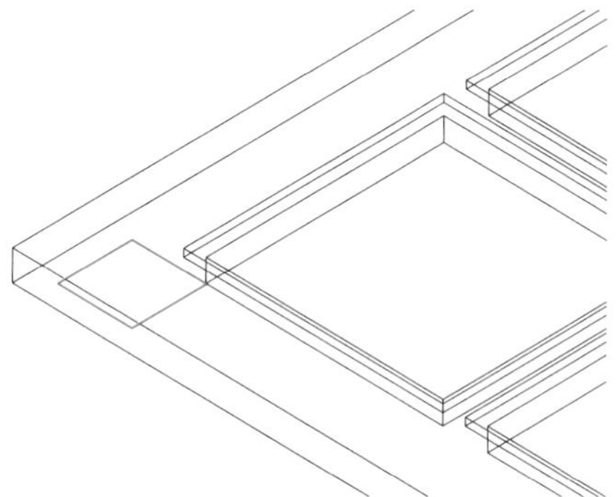

Figure 2-16 A 3 × 3 square in the bottom face

35. **EXTRUDE** the rectangle **–22″** (down).
36. Select the **Realistic** visual style. The 3D model should look like Figure 2-17.
37. Select the **2D Wireframe** visual style.
38. Using the **3DORBIT** command slightly change the viewing point to have a clearer picture. **ZOOM** into the bottom part of the leg.
39. Draw the polyline shown in Figure 2-18.

Figure 2-17 The extruded leg displayed in the Realistic visual style

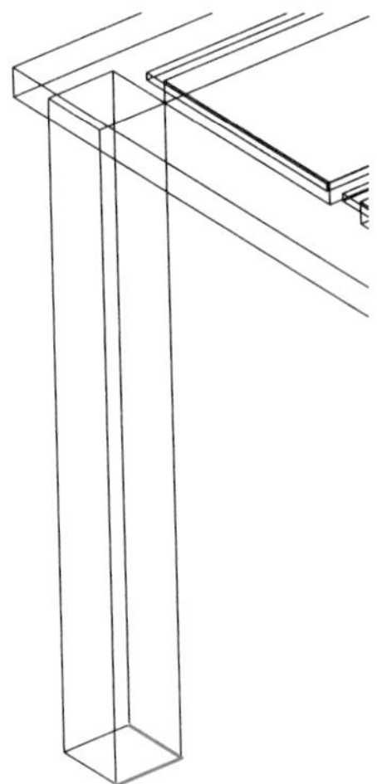

Figure 2-18 The polyline is created at the bottom of the leg

40. Select the **Front** UCS.
41. **MOVE** the polyline up **7″** (Figure 2-19).
42. Invoke the **IMPRINT** tool, and respond to the prompts as follows:

    Select a 3D solid: *Select the table leg 3D solid.*

    Select an object to imprint: *Select the polyline.*

    Delete the source object [Yes/No] <N>: *y* ↵

    Select an object to imprint: ↵ *(To end the selection and end the command)*

> **Note:**
> When you extrude a single profile, the extrusion height is interactively displayed as you move the crosshair cursor. This allows you to simply specify a distance or another point for the extrusion height.

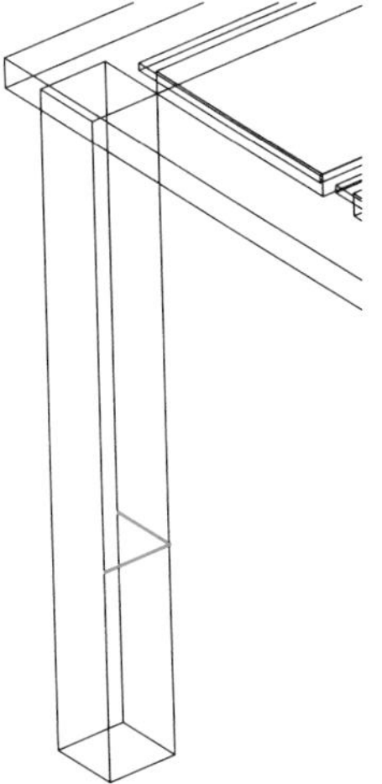

Figure 2-19 The polyline is moved up

43. Invoke the **Taper faces** tool of the **SOLIDEDIT** Command. Use Figure 2-20 as a reference and respond to the prompts as follows:

    Select faces or [Undo/Remove]: *Pick edge 1.*

    Select faces or [Undo/Remove/ALL]: ↵ *(To end the selection)*

    Specify the base point: *Snap to endpoint 2.*

    Specify another point along the axis of tapering: *Snap to endpoint 3.*

    Specify the taper angle: *7* ↵

    Enter a face editing option [Extrude/Move/Rotate/Offset/Taper/Delete/Copy/coLor/Undo/eXit] <eXit>: *Press the <Esc> key to exit the SOLIDEDIT command.*

44. After the operation, the lower end of the leg should look like Figure 2-21. Invoke the **MIRROR3D** command to obtain the second leg. Respond to the prompts as follows:

    Select objects: *Select the table leg 3D solid.*

    Select objects: ↵ *(To end the selection)*

IMPRINT	
Solid Editing Toolbar	
Ribbon Solid Editing panel	
Pull-down Menu	Modify/ Solid Editing/ Imprint
Command Line	imprint

TAPER FACES	
Solid Editing Toolbar	
Ribbon Solid Editing panel	
Pull-down Menu	Modify/ Solid Editing/Taper Faces
Command Line	solidedit ↵ f ↵ t

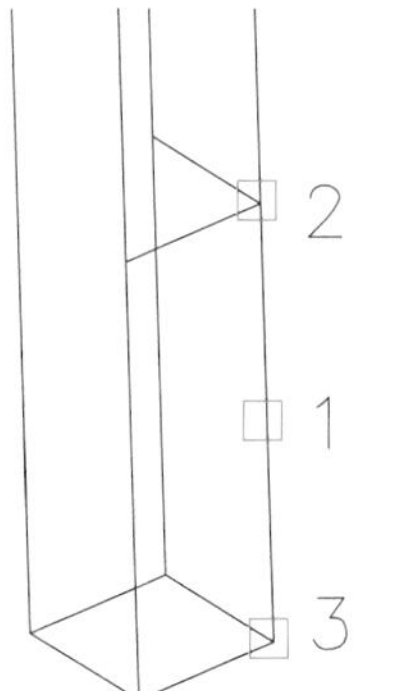

Figure 2-20 Points are specified for the Taper faces operation

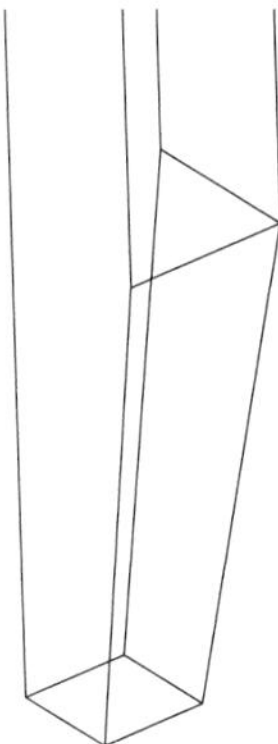

Figure 2-21 The split faces after tapering

Specify first point of mirror plane (3 points) or [Object/Last/Zaxis/View/XY/YZ/ZX/3points] <3points>: *Specify any of the midpoints indicated* in Figure 2-22.

Specify second point on mirror plane: *Specify another midpoint indicated.*

Specify third point on mirror plane: *Specify a third midpoint indicated.*

Delete source objects? [Yes/No] <N>: ↵ *(To keep the source object)*

45. The 3D model should look like Figure 2-23. Invoke the **MIRROR3D** command again and repeat the process of the previous step to obtain the two remaining legs. This time, the three midpoints must be specified perpendicularly to the ones specified previously.

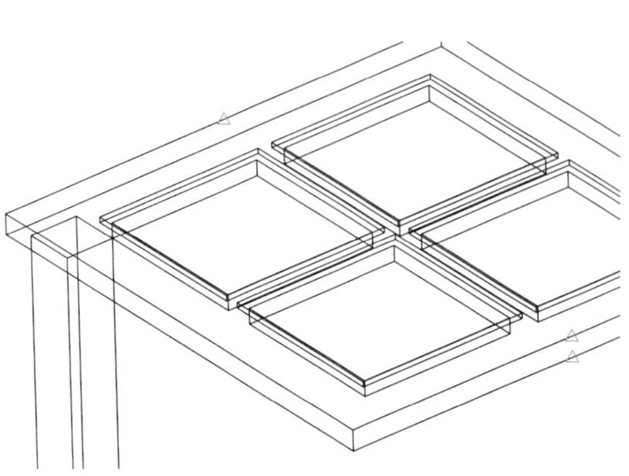

Figure 2-22 Points specified in the MIRROR3D command

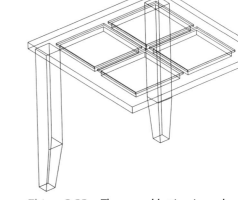

Figure 2-23 The second leg is mirrored

MIRROR3D	
Ribbon Modify panel	
Pull-down Menu	Modify/ 3D Operation/3D Mirror
Command Line	3dmirror

46. Select the **Realistic** visual style. The 3D model should look like Figure 2-24.
47. Select the **Right** UCS. Then, using the **3D ORBIT** command, change the viewing point so that you can see the bottom face of the table top (Figure 2-25).

Figure 2-24 After obtaining the four legs

Figure 2-25 After changing the viewing point

48. Select the **2D Wireframe** visual style.
49. Draw a **1 × 3** rectangle anywhere in the drawing area.
50. Select the **3D Hidden** visual style and **MOVE** the rectangle to the endpoint of the leg, as shown in Figure 2-26.
51. Invoke the **EXTRUDE** command, and respond to the prompts as follows:

    Select objects: *Select the table rectangle.*

    Select objects: ↵ *(To end the selection)*

    Specify height of extrusion or [Direction/Path/Taper angle]: *Snap to the endpoint indicated* in Figure 2-27.
52. Turn off the **Linetype** generation of the **Obscured Lines.**

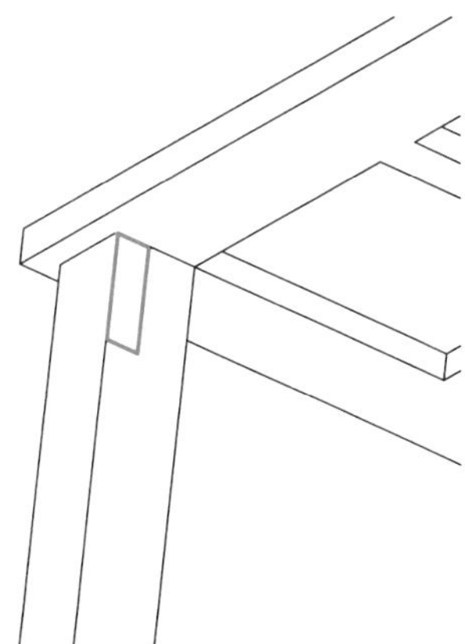

Figure 2-26 The 1 × 3 rectangle in the correct place

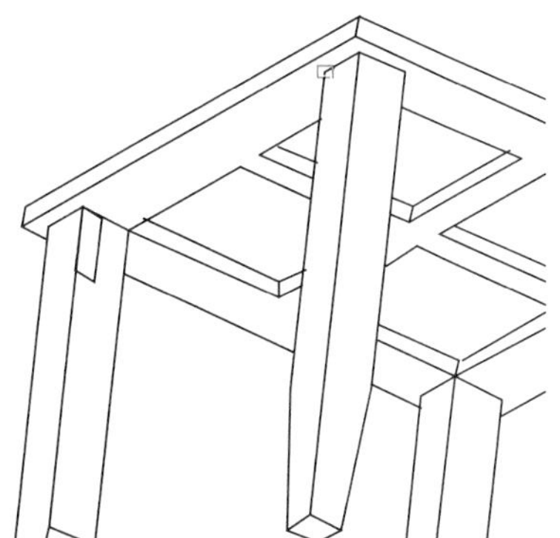

Figure 2-27 Point to indicate the height of extrusion

FOR MORE DETAILS Refer to Steps 3 and 4 for more details about changing this setting.

53. Select the **2D Wireframe** visual style and invoke the **HIDE** command. The first reinforcement 3D solid should look like Figure 2-28.
54. Select the **Top** view.
55. Draw a diagonal polyline, snapping to endpoints, as shown in Figure 2-29.

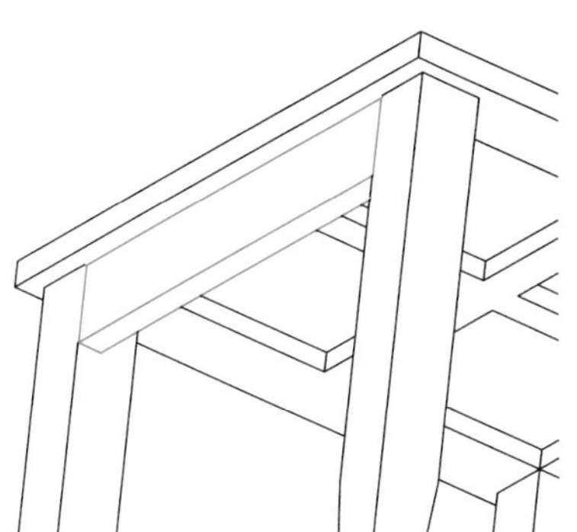

Figure 2-28 After invoking the HIDE command

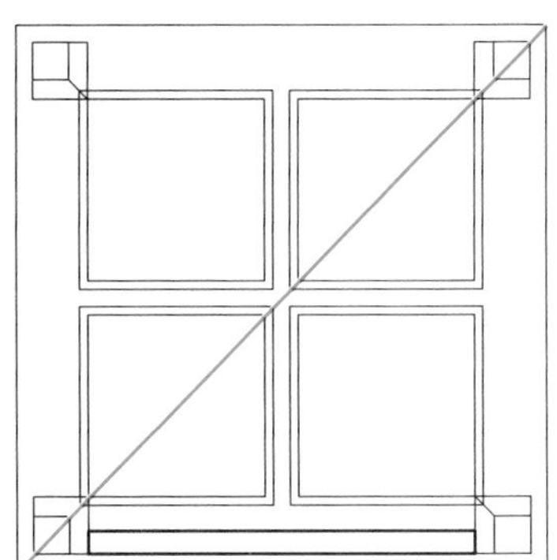

Figure 2-29 A diagonal polyline to locate the center point of the table

56. Invoke the **ARRAY** command. In the **Array** dialog box (Figure 2-30), select **Polar Array.** Click the **Select objects** button to select the reinforcement 3D solid. Click the **Center point:** button and snap to the midpoint of the polyline you just drew. Click the **OK** button to close the dialog box.
57. **ERASE** the diagonal polyline.
58. Select the **SE Isometric** viewing point.
59. Select the **Realistic** visual style. The model should look like Figure 2-31.
60. Select the **2D Wireframe** visual style.
61. Select the **Bottom** view.
62. Invoke the **HIDE** command.

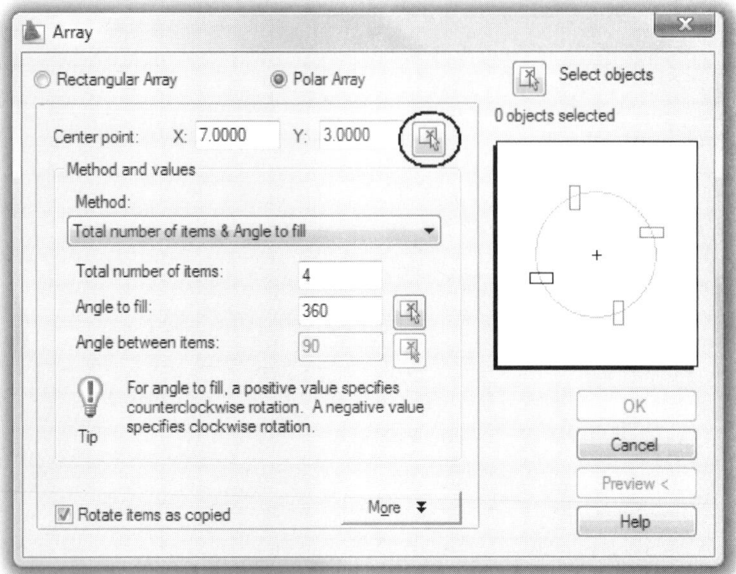

Figure 2-30 The Array dialog box

Figure 2-31 The resulting reinforcements after the ARRAY operation

63. Invoke the **PLINE** command. With **ORTHO** activated, draw the polyline highlighted in Figure 2-32. You should snap only to endpoints. Try using a different color to distinguish the object better.
64. Select the **SE Isometric** viewing point.
65. Select the **Front** UCS.
66. If necessary, **MOVE** the polyline to where the straight section of the legs begins. Use endpoints to snap to (Figure 2-33).
67. **EXTRUDE** the polyline **1″** up.

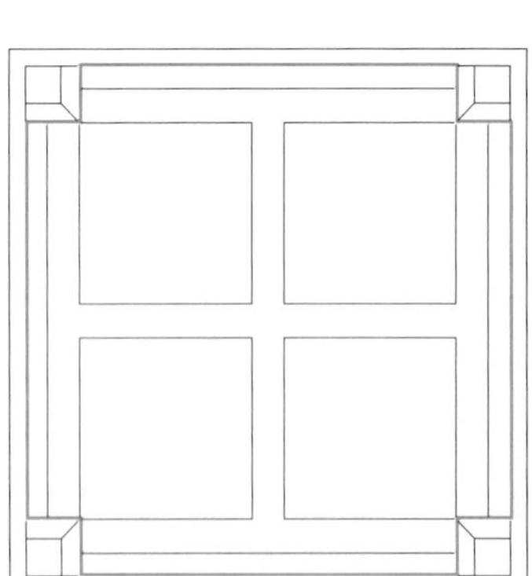

Figure 2-32 A profile created from the Top view

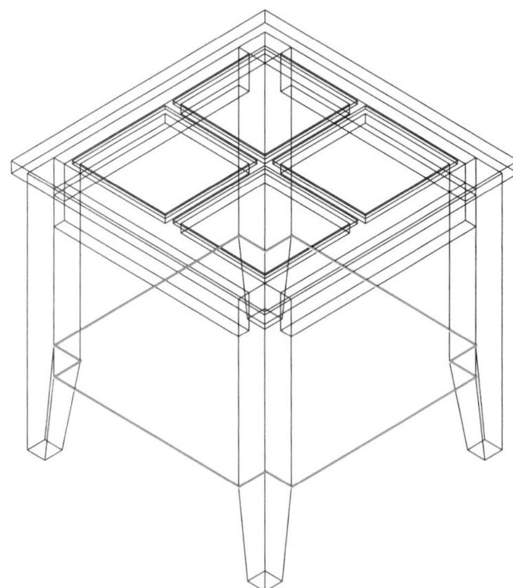

Figure 2-33 The profile is moved to its final location

68. Turn on the **Glass** layer.
69. Select the **Conceptual** visual style.
70. In the **Visual Style** panel of the **Ribbon,** click on the **Edge jitter** button and move the slide bar to the third position from left to right (Figure 2-34).

71. Invoke the **3DORBIT** command to inspect the 3D model of the sofa table. It should look like Figure 2-35.
72. **SAVE** the drawing.

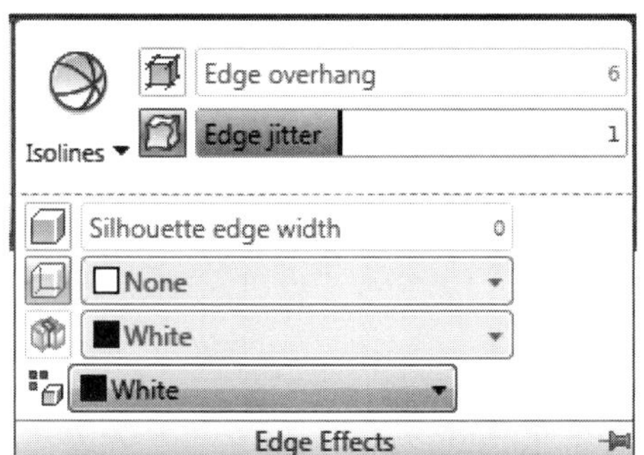

Figure 2-34 The Edge Jitter control on the Edge Effects panels of the Ribbon

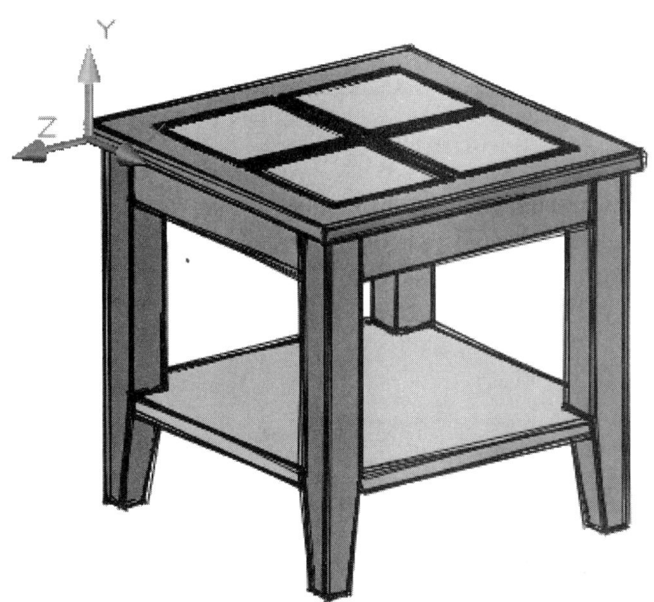

Figure 2-35 The 3D model shown in a modified Conceptual visual style

The 3D models created with the AutoCAD program have many uses. As demonstrated in this tutorial, this versatile program can create 3D models of objects for interior design and space planning projects. The 3D representation of objects can provide different levels of complexity. Unlike 3D models prepared for manufacturing processes according to a company's specifications and standards, the construction of 3D models used for other purposes, such as interior design and space planning, can be simplified. Recognizing the procedures and techniques that enable the development of different levels of complexity of 3D models and systems is an important skill for the workplace. Organizations recognize this skill as efficiency and productiveness.

Modeling the Lamp

In this tutorial, you will use surfaces, faceted surfaces, and regions jointly to create a 3D model of a lamp. As in the previous tutorial, many details have been avoided. As a general rule, you can create different levels of detail according to the purpose of the 3D model.

1. Start a **NEW** drawing, using the **acad** template.
2. **SAVE** the drawing AS ***TableLamp***.
3. Set the **VIEWRES** system variable to **3000.** When prompted about fast zooms, respond **Yes** by pressing **<Enter>**.
4. Set the **DISPSILH** system variable to **1.**
5. By default, the **Top** view and the **WCS** should be current. Do not change these settings yet.
6. You will start by creating the lamp base. To do so, first draw the profile shown in Figure 2-36. The next few steps will assist you in creating the polyline that will be used as the profile.

When using the **Tan tan radius** option of the **CIRCLE** command, try to select the circles in a location close to where the tangent point will be, so you prevent AutoCAD from finding a second solution.

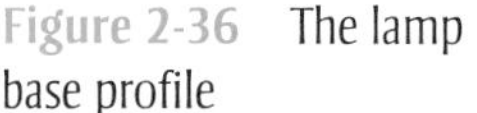

Figure 2-36 The lamp base profile

7. Start the curve or wire by drawing the objects shown in Figure 2-37.
8. **TRIM** the existing objects as necessary. Add the other highlighted objects as shown in Figure 2-38.

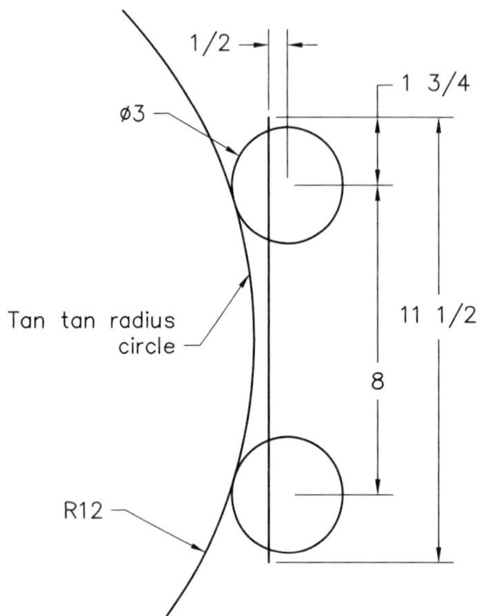

Figure 2-37 Instructions to create the profile

ø3/8
TYP.
Circles Are Tangent
at Quadrants
1/2
R1

Figure 2-38 Instructions to create the profile, continued

PEDIT	
Modify II Toolbar	
Ribbon Modify panel	
Pull-down Menu	Modify/ Object/ Polyline
Command Line	pedit
Alias	pe

9. Perform the final **TRIM** operations. Add an extra line as shown in Figure 2-39. Align its endpoints horizontally with the endpoints of the first and last objects.
10. Invoke the **PEDIT** command in order to join all the continuously drawn objects into a single polyline. Respond to the prompts as follows:

Select polyline or [Multiple]: *Select any of the objects.*

Object selected is not a polyline

Do you want to turn it into one? <Y> ↵ *(To turn the selected object into a polyline)*

Enter an option [Close/Join/Width/Edit vertex/Fit/Spline/Decurve/Ltype gen/Undo]: *j* ↵

Select objects: *Using a selection window, select all the objects.*

Select objects: ↵ *(To end the selection)*

Enter an option [Close/Join/Width/Edit vertex/Fit/Spline/Decurve/Ltype gen/Undo]: ↵ *(To exit the command)*

Note: Two or more wire-type objects can be joined as a single polyline object. As a requirement, all objects must lie in the same plane and the endpoints of two continuous objects must be located in the same place.

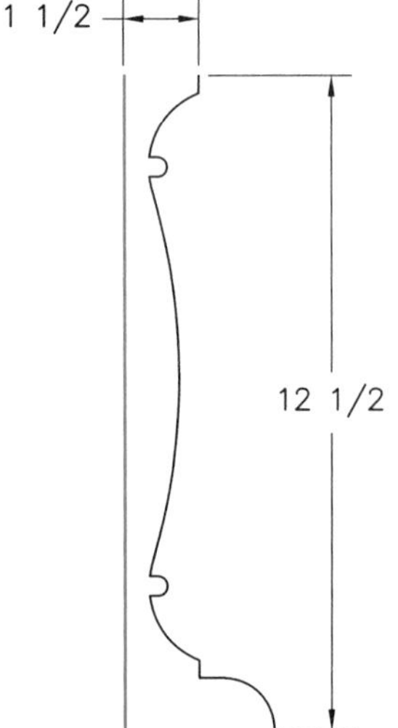

Figure 2-39 Placing the lamp base axis

TIP You can check whether all the objects were joined by simply hovering the cursor above the polyline, or by selecting it.

11. Select the two objects by picking them directly. With the objects selected, invoke the **CUTCLIP** command to move them to the clipboard.

12. Select the **Front** View.
13. Invoke the **PASTECLIP** command. When prompted to specify the insertion point, click anywhere in the drawing area.
14. Select the **SE Isometric** viewing point and zoom as needed.
15. Select the **Top** UCS, and draw the two circles shown in Figure 2-40. Snap to the endpoints of the objects to specify the center and radius of both circles.
16. Invoke the **REGION** command. When prompted, select the two circles. This operation will turn the circles into regions.
17. Invoke the **REVOLVE** command. Respond to the command prompts as follows:

    `Select object to revolve:` *`Select the polyline.`*

    `Select object to revolve:` ↵ *`(To end the selection)`*

    `Specify axis start point or define axis by [Object/X/Y/Z] <Object>:` *`o`* ↵

    `Select an object:` *`Select the line.`*

    `Specify angle of revolution or [STart angle] <360>:` ↵ *`(To accept the default angle)`*

18. **ERASE** the line.
19. Set the **FACETRES** system variable to **8** to enhance the visual effects.
20. Invoke the **HIDE** command. The 3D model should look like Figure 2-41.
21. Invoke the **REGEN** command.
22. With the **Top** UCS still active, invoke the **CYLINDER** command. When prompted, specify the center point of the base in the center point of the top circular region. Specify **0.5** for the radius and **3** for the height (Figure 2-42).
23. Now you will create the 3D model of the lightbulb as a polygon mesh. Select the **Front** UCS and draw the three objects shown in Figure 2-43.
24. Invoke the **PEDIT** and join the arc with the small line as a single polyline.
25. Set the **SURFTAB1** and **SURFTAB2** system variables to **15.** To access these settings, enter their names in the command line.
26. Invoke the **REVSURF** command and create a revolved faceted surface. Respond to the prompts as follows:

    `Select object to revolve:` *`Select the polyline.`*

    `Select object that defines the axis of revolution:` *`Select the line.`*

    `Specify start angle <0>:` ↵ *`(To accept the default)`*

    `Specify included angle (+=ccw, -=cw) <360>:` ↵ *`(To accept the default)`*

27. **ERASE** the polyline and the line. The result, after invoking the **HIDE** command, is shown in Figure 2-44.

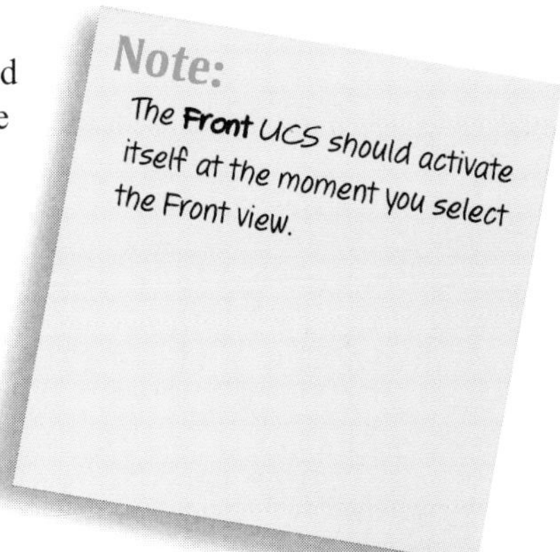

Note:
The objects inserted from the clipboard were simply moved from the **Top** plane to the **Front** plane, where the XY plane or the current UCS now lies. Cutting and pasting objects from one plane to another is equivalent to rotating the objects in the 3D space.

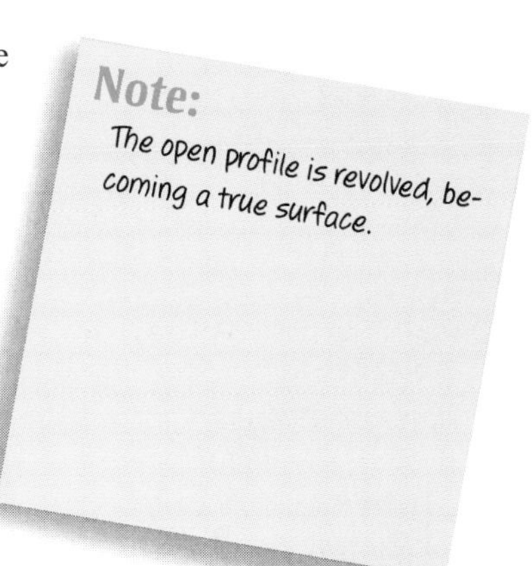

Note:
The open profile is revolved, becoming a true surface.

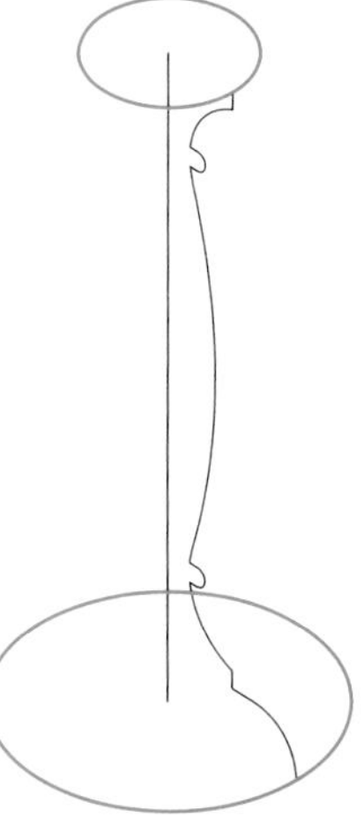

Figure 2-40 The top and bottom circles are drawn in place

REGION	
Draw Toolbar	
Ribbon Draw panel	
Pull-down Menu	Draw/ Region
Command Line	region

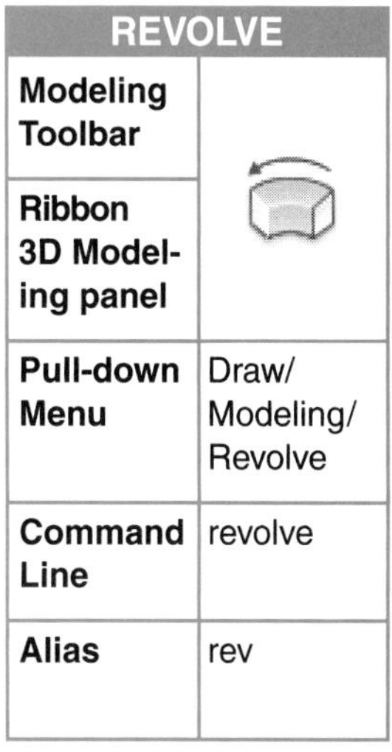

REVOLVE	
Modeling Toolbar	
Ribbon 3D Modeling panel	
Pull-down Menu	Draw/ Modeling/ Revolve
Command Line	revolve
Alias	rev

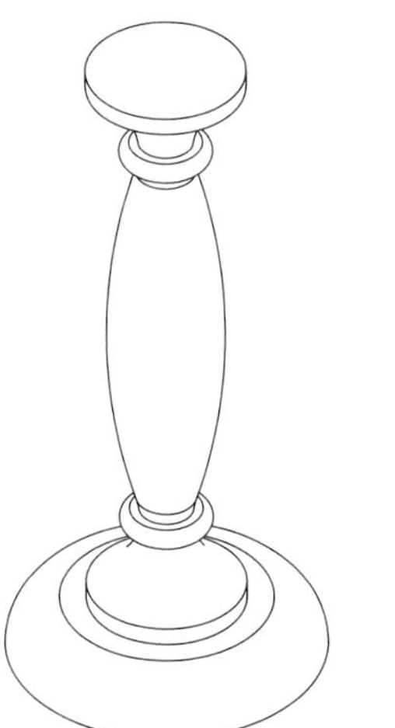
Figure 2-41 The lamp base surface is generated with the REVOLVE command

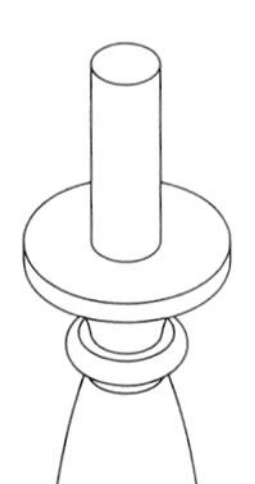
Figure 2-42 A 3D solid cylinder is placed on top of the lamp base

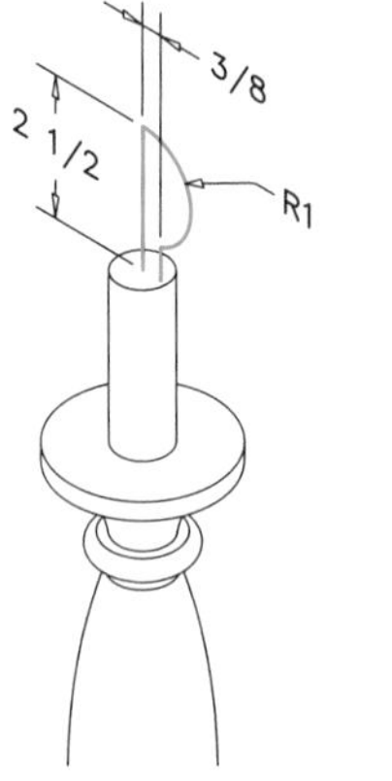

Figure 2-43 Draw the three objects shown

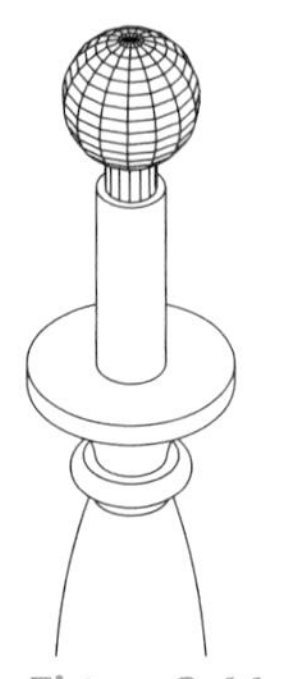
Figure 2-44 After invoking the HIDE command

CYLINDER	
Modeling Toolbar	
Ribbon 3D Modeling panel	
Pull-down Menu	Draw/ Modeling/ Cylinder
Command Line	cylinder
Alias	cyl

REVSURF	
Ribbon 3D Modeling panel	
Pull-down Menu	Draw/ Modeling/ Meshes/ Revolved Mesh
Command Line	revsurf

28. Select the **Front** view and draw the two highlighted objects in an empty spot, as shown in Figure 2-45.
29. Select the **SE Isometric** viewing point.
30. **MOVE** the objects so that the lower endpoint of the line is placed at the bottom center point of the cylinder (Figure 2-46).

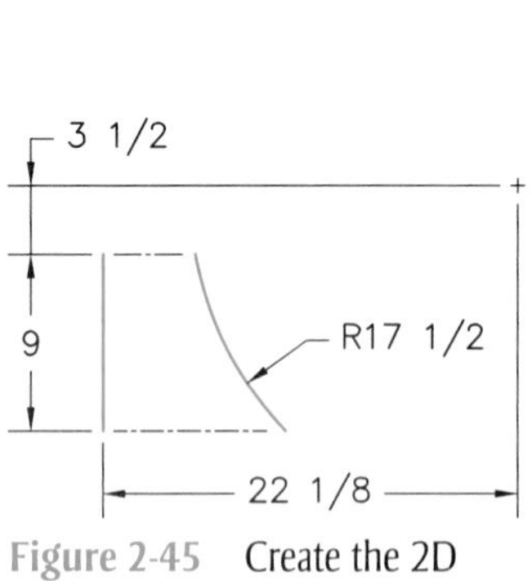

Figure 2-45 Create the 2D objects as shown

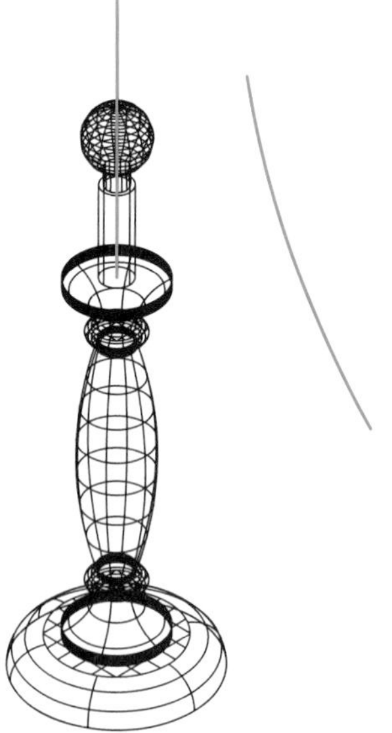
Figure 2-46 The 2D objects after they are moved to the proper location

31. Select the **World** UCS.
32. Select the arc and invoke the **ARRAY** command. In the **Array** dialog box (Figure 2-47), select **Polar Array,** click the **Center point:** button, and snap to the top endpoint of the line. In the **Total number of items:** field, specify **8.** After clicking on the **OK** button, the array should look like Figure 2-48.
33. Invoke the **3DORBIT** command to slightly change the viewing point.
34. Draw two lines between any two arcs as shown in Figure 2-49.

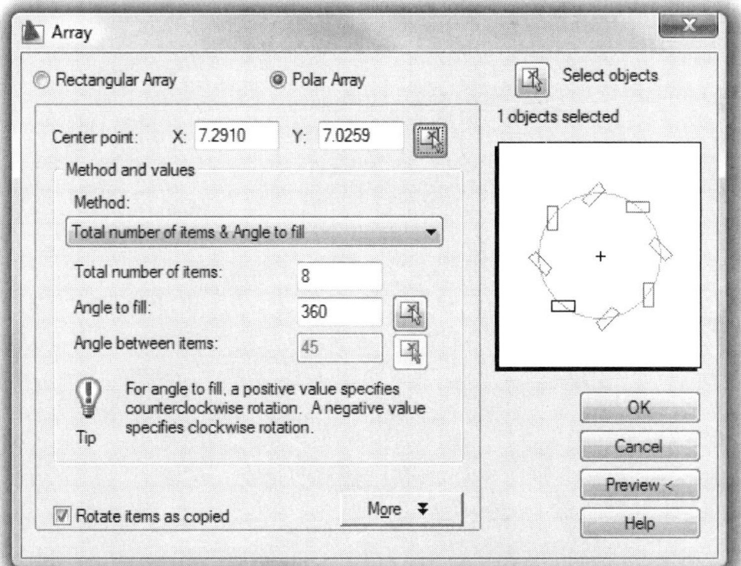

Figure 2-47 The Array dialog box

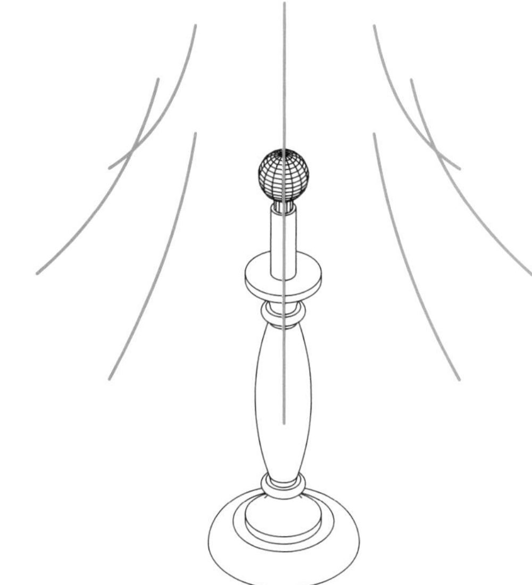

Figure 2-48 The arrayed copies of the arc

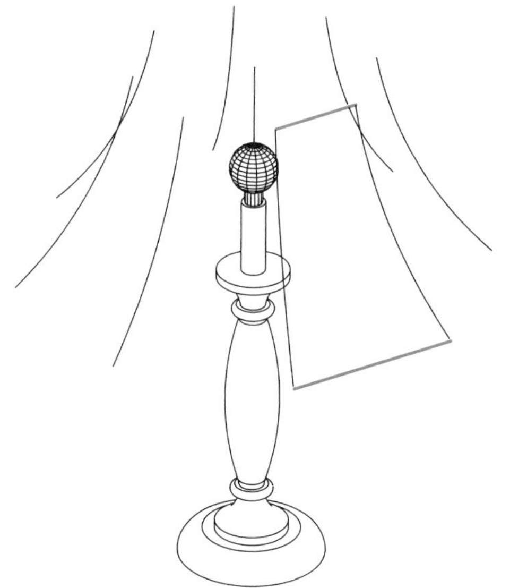

Figure 2-49 Draw the two lines shown

35. Change the values of the **SURFTAB1** and **SURFTAB2** system variables to **8.**
36. Invoke the **EDGESURF** command and, when prompted, select the two lines and the two arcs connecting them in any order.
37. Change the **Color** property of the polygon mesh you just created to any color you like.
38. Invoke the **DRAWORDER** command by entering its name in the command line and respond to the prompts as follows:

    Select objects: *Select the polygon mesh.*

    Select objects: ↵ *(To end the selection)*

    Enter object ordering option [Above objects/Under objects/Front/Back] <Back>: ↵ *(To accept the default, which is sending it to the back)*

EDGESURF	
Ribbon 3D Modeling panel	
Pull-down Menu	Draw/ Modeling/ Meshes/ Edge Mesh
Command Line	edgesurf

Alternating the order in which overlapping objects are displayed facilitates the selection of the objects on top.

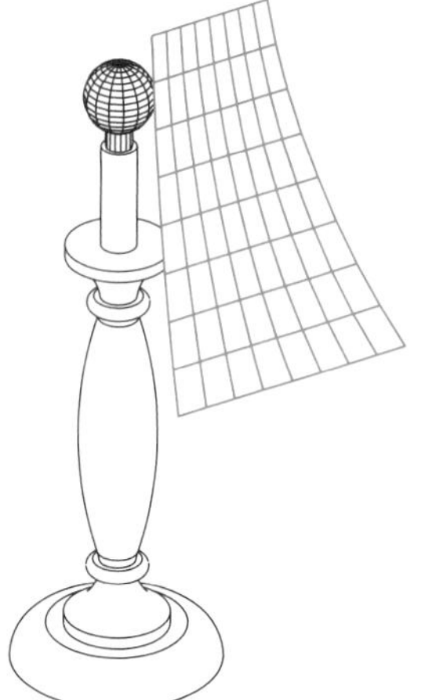

Figure 2-50 After erasing the lines and arcs

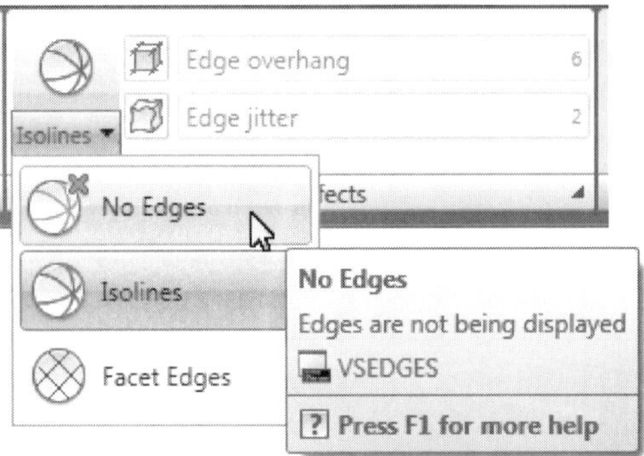

Figure 2-51 Modifying the edge display in the Edge Effects panel of the Ribbon

39. **ERASE** all the lines and arcs, except the vertical line in the middle of the lamp (Figure 2-50).
40. With the **World** or **Top** UCS still active, select the polygon mesh and invoke the **ARRAY** command. Use the same parameters as in the previous **ARRAY** operation. Use the endpoint of the vertical line in the middle to specify the **Center point:.**
41. **ERASE** the vertical line.
42. Change the **Color** property of the lamp base to color 42, the cylinder to color 251, and the lightbulb to yellow.
43. Select the **Realistic** visual style.
44. Invoke the **3DORBIT** command to inspect the 3D model from underneath.
45. Select **No edges** from the **Edges** flyout buttons located in the **Edge Effects** panel of the **Ribbon** (Figure 2-51).
46. Select **Desaturate Mode** from the **Face color mode** flyout buttons located in the same panel of the Ribbon (Figure 2-52).
47. The 3D model should look like Figure 2-53. **SAVE** the drawing.

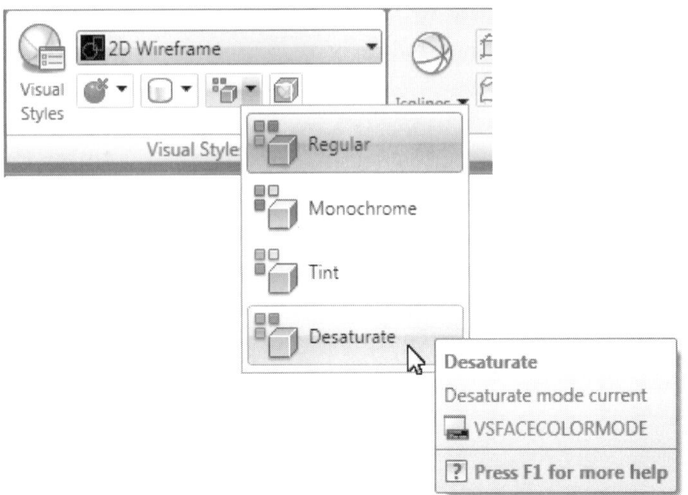

Figure 2-52 Modifying the face display in the Visual Style panel of the Ribbon

Figure 2-53 A modified Realistic visual style to display the 3D model

SUMMARY

You have just walked though two different projects. In the first project, you were able to use operations related to the creation of 3D solid objects. In the second project, you mixed other types of objects used to generate 3D models.

You should now have a better idea of what 3D modeling is about. Throughout the remaining chapters, you will find the answers to the many questions you might have gathered from these projects.

Wireframe Modeling

3

Chapter Objectives

- Learn to create and modify simple objects throughout the 3D space.
- Explore the behavior of common objects in the 3D environment.
- Learn the differences between modifying objects in 2D and 3D environments.
- Know other commands specifically used to modify objects in a 3D environment.
- Explore in depth polylines, 3D polylines, splines, and helixes.
- Learn to create 3D models represented as wireframes.
- Know the uses of 3D wireframes.
- Learn about editing with grips and using the grip tools.
- Use the wireframe modeling method in preparatory work to create more complex 3D models using other objects.

INTRODUCTION

About Wireframes

As its name implies, a **wireframe** represents a 3D model by placing its edges, or *wires,* in the 3D space using the most common AutoCAD® objects (lines, arcs, circles, ellipses, polylines, 3D polylines, splines, and helixes). To create a wireframe, you simply invoke the same commands used in 2D work to create and modify the objects. The difference between this type of work and 2D drafting is that the objects are placed in the 3D space, which requires you to modify the UCS and use other techniques to properly place the objects.

Wireframe representation is the simplest type because there are no surfaces where the light rays can hit. Thus, no shading or hiding effect can be obtained from this type of 3D model. In most cases, however, constructing a wireframe object is not a simple task. Imagine how laborious it would be to find the intersecting curve between a cone and an inclined cylinder throughout the 3D space using only wires. With other types of objects, however, such as 3D solids, this curve can be obtained by simply making the cone and cylinder intersect each other.

In practice, there are very few applications in which representing a 3D model as a simple wireframe is the final goal. (A pipeline diagram is an example, where substituting the traditional isometric drawing for a 3D wire can lead to better results.) But despite the difficulty involved in using wires, placing wires is usually a necessary task prior to using the commands and tools needed to create meshes, surfaces, and 3D solid objects.

Types of Objects Used to Represent Wires or Edges

Any wire or edge of an object that is being modeled can be classified into one of the following categories:

- Straight edges
- Planar curve
- ***Nonplanar curve***

nonplanar curve: A curve placed throughout the 3D space that is not completely contained in a plane.

AutoCAD wireframe objects or curves can also be classified into two different groups according to their behavior:

- Curves that belong to a particular plane and can be placed only on a plane parallel to the *XY* plane of the current UCS:
  - Circle
  - Ellipse
  - Arc
  - Polyline
- Curves that do not belong to a particular plane and can be placed anywhere in the 3D space, regardless of the current UCS:
  - Line
  - 3D polyline
  - Spline

Straight edges are represented using lines and polylines. Wires that have the characteristics of planar curves can be represented by almost any type of objects. Wires that are nonplanar curves, however, can be represented only by splines, 3D polylines transformed into splines, and helixes.

When creating objects that belong to a particular plane, the first point defines the location of the imaginary plane parallel to the current *XY* plane to which the object belongs. In the case of polylines, including those created with the **RECTANGLE** and **POLYGON** commands, any subsequent point specified that is not contained in such a plane is perpendicularly projected onto it.

When you create a circle in the default mode, for example, the plane is defined when you specify the circle's center. If you specify the circle's radius by specifying a second point, AutoCAD considers the radius to be the 3D distance from the center to the second point.

Despite certain peculiarities, you will use all these objects to create 3D models exactly the same way you use them to create 2D drawings.

MODIFYING OBJECTS IN 3D

Using Standard Commands in the 3D Environment

The following commands used to modify the objects in a 2D environment have special particularities or considerations when used in a 3D environment.

OFFSET: Works only for planar objects. The parallel offset copies are created on the same *XY* plane that the objects belong to.

TRIM/EXTEND: If the cutting edge and the object to be trimmed are contained in the same plane, the command works as a 2D operation. If the cutting edge and the object to be trimmed are not contained in the same plane, you can control its result by changing the **Projection** option after selecting the cutting edge(s).

```
Current settings: Projection=UCS, Edge=None
Select cutting edges...
Select objects: Select the objects.
```

Select objects: ↵ *(To end the selection)*

Select object to trim or shift-select to extend or [Fence/Crossing/Project/Edge/eRase/Undo]: *p* ↵

Enter a projection option [None/Ucs/View] <Ucs>: *Enter an option.* ↵

Ucs: When using this option, the objects are trimmed as if both the object and the cutting edge were projected onto the current *XY* plane. You can also visualize this operation as if the cutting edge were a surface perpendicular to the *XY* plane extending to infinity in both directions (Figure 3-1).

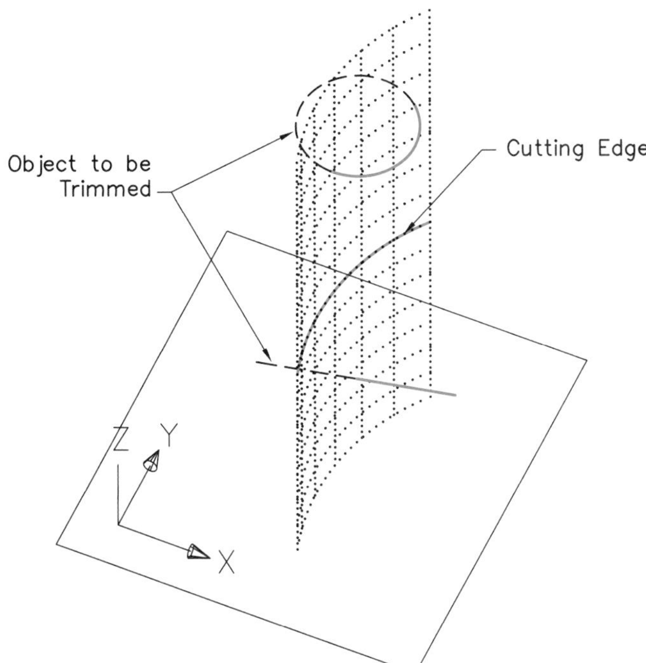

Figure 3-1 When the Projection option of the TRIM/EXTEND command is used, the objects interrelate as if placed on the same plane

None: With this option, you cannot trim any objects unless they really meet in the space. Because no projecting method is used, the current UCS does not affect the result.

View: Will project both the object and the cutting edge onto the viewing plane instead of the current *XY* plane.

Additionally, the **Edge** option can be changed to establish whether or not the cutting edge or the imaginary cutting surface resulting from its projection actually needs to intersect the object to be trimmed.

Select object to trim or shift-select to extend or [Fence/Crossing/Project/Edge/eRase/Undo]: *e* ↵

Enter an implied edge extension mode [Extend/No extend] <No extend>: *Enter a choice.* ↵

By choosing the **Extend** option, the cutting edge or the imaginary cutting surface will behave as if it were infinite.

MIRROR: Any object can mirrored in the 3D space. When specifying the two points of the mirror line, however, AutoCAD accepts only points that belong to the *XY* plane of the current UCS. Specifying a point that is not contained in the *XY* plane causes the AutoCAD program to snap not to the point itself, but to its projection on the *XY* plane. It is always more comfortable to use this command in an orthogonal view, in which both the point and its projection appear to be the same.

SCALE: Its behavior is completely 3D. It will scale objects proportionally in all directions regardless of the current UCS.

STRETCH: For objects that can be drawn freely in the 3D space, you can stretch points freely as well. For objects that can be placed only on a plane parallel to the *XY* plane, the vertices can only be stretched, so they continue to pertain to the same plane.

FILLET and CHAMFER: Work only for objects that pertain to the same plane, regardless of the current UCS. By setting the radius value to **0**, in case of the **FILLET** command, you can make the two lines meet without generating an arc.

ROTATE: The 2D rotation of an object is produced around a point. This command, in a 3D environment, requires you to specify a point as well, but to better understand the rotation, you can think of that point as if it were an axis parallel to the *Z*-axis, so you do not necessarily have to specify a point on the current *XY* plane. The result of the rotation depends on the UCS you are currently using. The objects, however, can belong to any plane.

ARRAY: The arrayed copies of objects are generated relative to the *XY* plane of the UCS. You can, however, select objects that are placed in any plane.

COPY and MOVE: Any object can be freely moved or copied from any point to any other point, regardless of the current UCS.

Most of the standard commands used to modify objects work in a 2D way. Consequently, their results depend on the location of the working plane (the *XY* plane of the UCS).

Commands Specially Designed to Modify Objects in 3D

Another group of commands is used to modify objects in a 3D environment: **3DROTATE**, **ROTATE3D**, **3DMOVE**, **MIRROR3D**, **3DARRAY**, **3DALIGN**, and **ALIGN**. In general, these operations can be compared with 2D operations based on the following two rules:

- 2D rotations are made around a point, whereas 3D rotations are made around an axis.
- To create a 2D mirrored copy you define a mirror line, whereas to create a 3D mirrored copy you must define a mirror plane.

The 3DROTATE Command

imaginary axis of rotation:
An imaginary vector defined by specifying two points, or a direction vector and a point, about which the objects are rotated.

rotate grip tool:
Editing tool that enables you to choose among three directions of rotation that are aligned with the axes of the current UCS.

3DROTATE	
Modeling Toolbar	
Ribbon Modify panel	
Pull-down Menu	Modify/ 3D Operation/3D Rotate
Command Line	3drotate

This command allows you to rotate the selected object about an ***imaginary axis of rotation*** that is parallel to one of the three axes of the current UCS (*X*, *Y*, and *Z*). The axis to which the imaginary axis of rotation is parallel is defined by picking one of the axis handles of the ***rotate grip tool***. The display switches to the **3D Wireframe** visual style while this command is in progress if the current visual style is **2D Wireframe** (Figure 3-2).

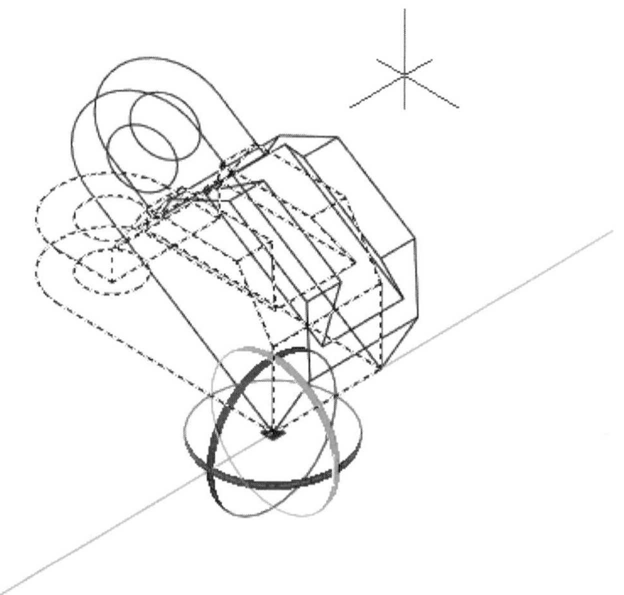

Figure 3-2 The 3DROTATE command in action

The command prompts are as follows:

Select objects: Specify opposite corner: *Select the objects.*

Select objects: ↵ *(To end the selection)*

Specify base point: *Specify a base point to locate the rotate grip tool.*

Pick a rotation axis: *Specify which of the three axes the objects will be rotated around. You do so by clicking on the axis handle of the rotate grip tool.*

Specify angle start point: *Enter the angle of rotation and end the command, or specify the angle start point.*

Specify angle end point: *Specify the angle end point (this prompt appears only if you specify the angle start point).*

TIP You can interactively view the rotation by specifying the angle start and endpoint by clicking in the drawing area. This is useful when you intend to approximate the alignment of an object.

Figure 3-3 The ROTATE3D command's shortcut menu

The ROTATE3D Command

The **ROTATE3D** command allows you to rotate selected objects about an imaginary axis of rotation that can be defined anywhere in the 3D space by using different options, some of which depend on the UCS currently in use. Figure 3-3 shows the shortcut menu containing these options. The **ROTATE3D** command can be invoked only through the command line.

2points: Is the default option; by specifying a first point, you are prompted to specify the second one. The two points can be specified anywhere independently of the current UCS. The right-hand rule can be used to determine the positive direction of rotation, by knowing that the vector goes from the first point to the second one (Figure 3-4).

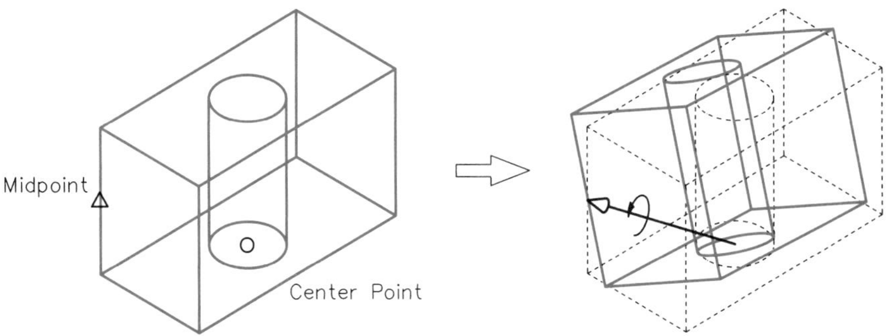

Figure 3-4 The imaginary axis of rotation defined with the 2points option of the ROTATE3D command

Object: Allows you to select an object to define the imaginary axis of rotation; however, only lines, circles, arcs, and 2D polyline segments are valid selections. Lines and straight 2D polyline segments are used directly as the imaginary axis of rotation. Circles and arcs, on the other hand, define the imaginary axis of rotation perpendicular to the object's plane and through its center point.

View: The imaginary axis of rotation is defined normal to the viewing plane (monitor display) and through a point that you specify (Figure 3-5).

Xaxis/Yaxis/Zaxis: These options work similar to the **3DROTATE** command in that they define the imaginary axis of rotation parallel to one of the three major axes of the current UCS (*X*, *Y*, and *Z*), and a point that you specify. In Figure 3-6, the objects are rotated about the endpoint specified using the **Xaxis** option.

Last: In this option, the AutoCAD program uses the imaginary axis of rotation you defined in the previous operation.

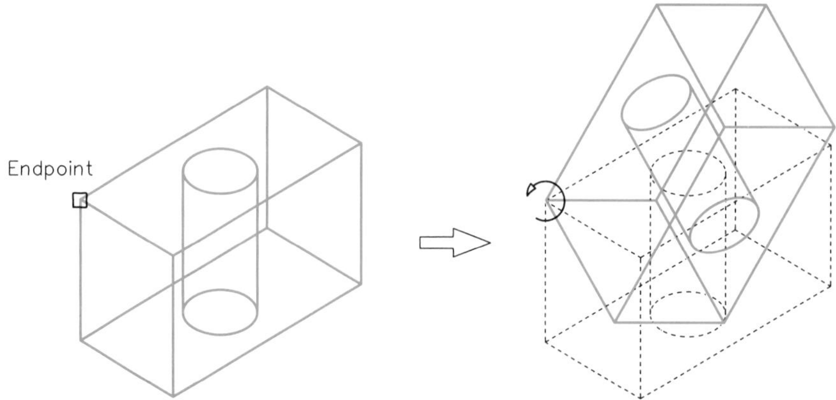

Figure 3-5 The imaginary axis of rotation defined with the View option of the ROTATE3D command

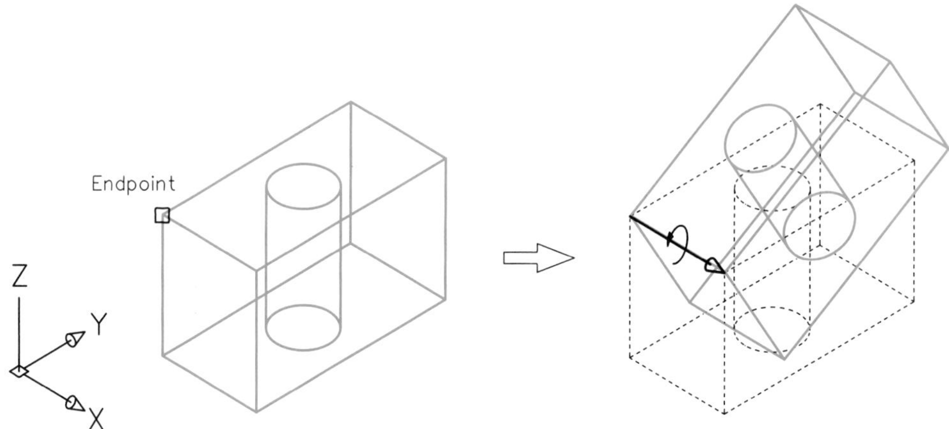

Figure 3-6 The imaginary axis of rotation of the ROTATE3D command defined parallel to the Xaxis

Exercise 3-1: Using the ROTATE3D Command

1. **OPEN** the drawing named ***Exercise 3-00-A*** from the CD.
2. **SAVE** the drawing **AS *Exercise 3-1***.
3. Invoke the **ROTATE3D** command by typing its name in the command line. Respond to the prompts as follows:

   Select objects: *Using a selection window, select all the objects.*

   Select objects: ↵ *(To end the selection)*

   Specify first point on axis or define axis by

   [Object/Last/View/Xaxis/Yaxis/Zaxis/2points]: *y* ↵

   Specify a point on the Y axis <0,0,0>: *-1,20,-1* ↵

   Specify rotation angle or [Reference]: *30* ↵

Note:

Because the imaginary axis is defined as an infinite axis parallel to the Y-axis, the Y coordinate of the point is not significant. Only the X and Z coordinates of the point define the imaginary axis.

4. Your drawing should look like Figure 3-7. Invoke the **ROTATE3D** command again and respond to the prompts as follows:

   Select objects: p ↵ *(To use the previous selection)*

   Select objects: ↵ *(To end the selection)*

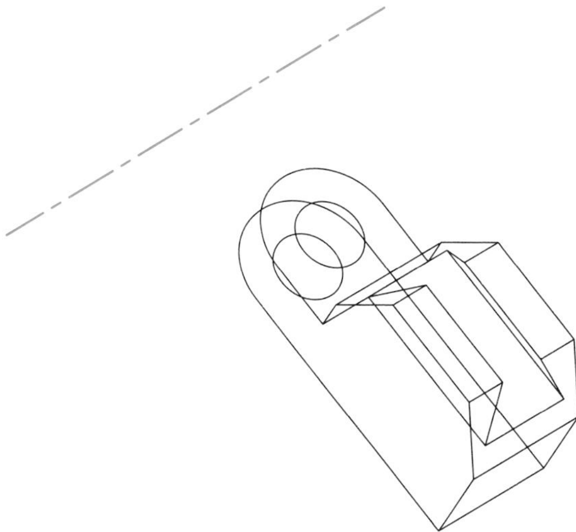

Figure 3-7 The 3D model rotated 30° about an imaginary axis parallel to the Y-axis

```
Specify first point on axis or define axis by
[Object/Last/View/Xaxis/Yaxis/Zaxis/2points]: 1 ↵
Specify rotation angle or [Reference]: -30 ↵
```

5. This will take the model back to its original position. **SAVE** the drawing.

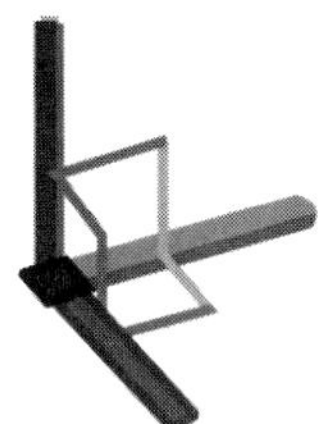

Figure 3-8 The move grip tool

The 3DMOVE Command

This command allows you to move selected objects throughout the 3D space. By using the elements of the ***move grip tool***, you can change the movement behavior as follows:

- Freely, when no element of the move grip tool is selected.
- Constrained along the direction of one of the axes of the current UCS. This direction is specified by clicking one of the three handles of the move grip tool (Figure 3-8).
- Constrained to a plane that is parallel to one of the three planes of the current UCS. You specify this behavior by clicking one of the squares on the move grip tool, which automatically selects two handles.

move grip tool: Editing tool that allows you to choose among six movements along one of the three axes or parallel to one of the three planes.

As with **3DROTATE**, the display switches to the **3D Wireframe** visual style while this command is in progress if the current visual style is **2D Wireframe**. Figure 3-9 shows the **3DMOVE** command in action.

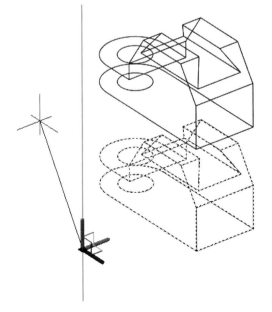

3DMOVE	
Modeling Toolbar	
Ribbon Modify control panel	
Pull-down Menu	Modify/ 3D Operation/3D Move
Command Line	3dmove

Figure 3-9 The 3DMOVE command in action

3DARRAY	
Ribbon Modify panel	
Pull-down Menu	Modify/ 3D Operation/3D Array
Command Line	3darray

The 3DARRAY Command

The **3DARRAY** command is a 3D version of the standard **ARRAY** command. With this command you can create both rectangular and polar 3D arrays.

With the rectangular 3D array you are allowed to create multiple objects arranged not only in rows and columns but also in levels. In the event you enter **1** as the number of levels, the array will behave just like a standard 2D array.

The result of a rectangular 3D array depends on the current UCS. The rows are created in the *Y*-axis direction, the columns in the *X*-axis direction, and the levels in the *Z*-axis direction. For example, a 2 × 2 × 2 array of the highlighted circle with the dimensions rows, columns, levels = 6,10,5.5 will be as shown in Figure 3-10.

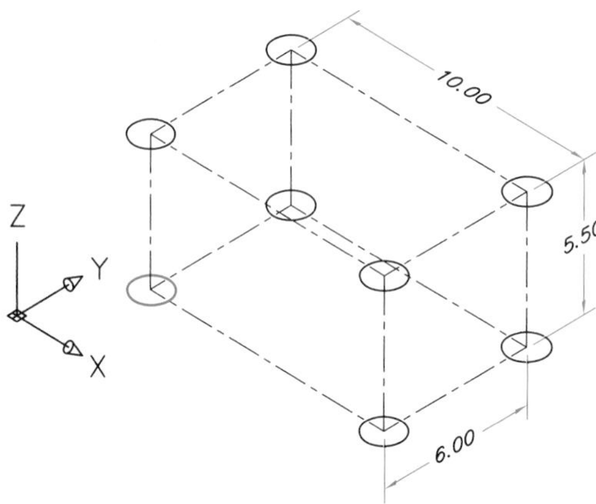

Figure 3-10 A 3D array of the highlighted circle

With the polar 3D array, you can create multiple objects that are uniformly distributed around an imaginary axis of rotation. Unlike the rectangular 3D array, the results do not depend on the current UCS, but on the two points you specify to establish the axis of rotation.

Exercise 3-2: A 3D Rectangular Array Operation

1. **OPEN** the drawing named ***Exercise 3-00-A*** from the CD.
2. **SAVE** the drawing **AS** ***Exercise 3-2***.
3. Invoke the **3DARRAY** command and respond to the prompts as follows:

   Select objects: *Select the two circles representing the hole on the 3D model.*

   Select objects: ↵ *(To end the selection)*

   Enter the type of array [Rectangular/Polar] <R>: ↵ *(To accept the default)*

   Enter the number of rows (---) <1>: *2* ↵

   Enter the number of columns (|||) <1>: *2* ↵

   Enter the number of levels (...) <1>: *2* ↵

   Specify the distance between rows (---): *6* ↵

   Specify the distance between columns (|||): *10* ↵

   Specify the distance between levels (...): *5.5* ↵
4. Invoke the **3DORBIT** command to inspect the 3D model.
5. The drawing should look like Figure 3-11.
6. **SAVE** the drawing.

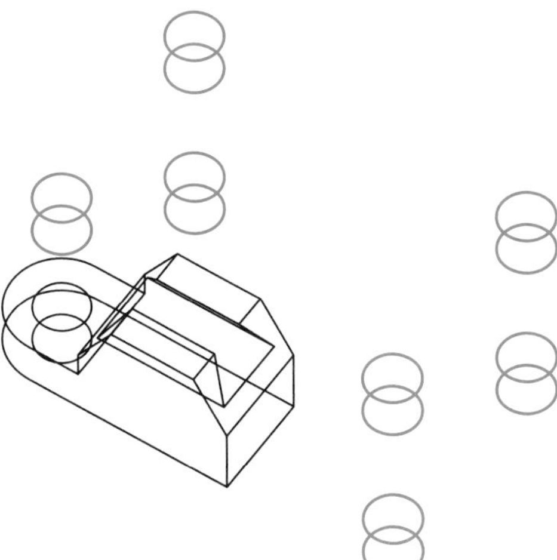

Figure 3-11 The 3D model after the 3DARRAY operation

Exercise 3-3: A 3D Polar Array Operation

1. **OPEN** the drawing named ***Exercise 3-00-A*** from the CD.
2. **SAVE** the drawing **AS *Exercise 3-3***.
3. Select the **Front** UCS.
4. Draw a line from the center point of the top circle to the center point of the bottom circle (Figure 3-12).
5. With ORTHO activated, **MOVE** the line **3″** along the negative *X*-axis direction.
6. **ROTATE** the line **15°** using the lower endpoint as the rotation base point (Figure 3-13).

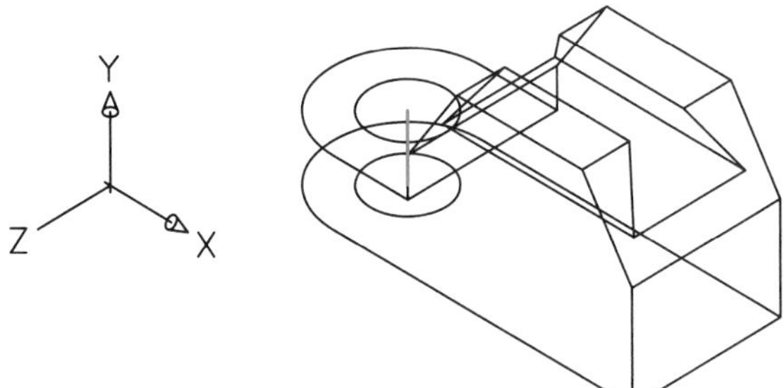

Figure 3-12 A line is drawn between the center points

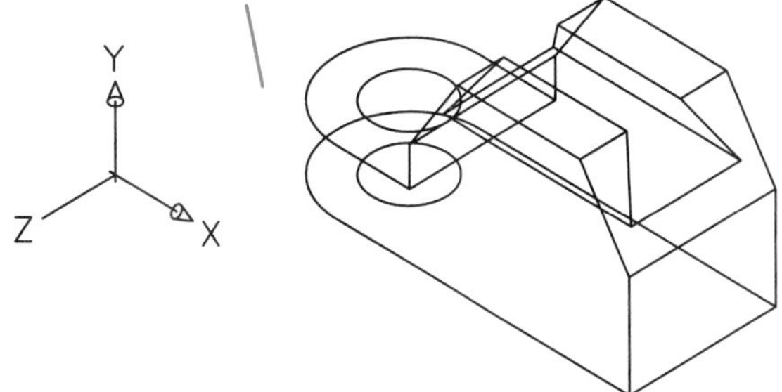

Figure 3-13 After the line is moved and rotated

7. Invoke the **3DARRAY** command and respond to the prompts as follows:

   Select objects: *all* ↵ *(To select all the objects)*

   Select objects: ↵ *(To end the selection)*

   Enter the type of array [Rectangular/Polar] <R>: *p* ↵

   Enter the number of items in the array: *4* ↵

   Specify the angle to fill (+=ccw, -=cw) <360>: ↵ *(To accept the default)*

   Rotate arrayed objects? [Yes/No] <Y>: ↵ *(To accept the default)*

   Specify center point of array: *Select one of the endpoints of the line you drew.*

   Specify second point on axis of rotation: *Select the other endpoint of the line.*
8. The drawing should look like Figure 3-14.
9. Invoke the **3DORBIT** command to inspect the operation you just performed.
10. **SAVE** the drawing.

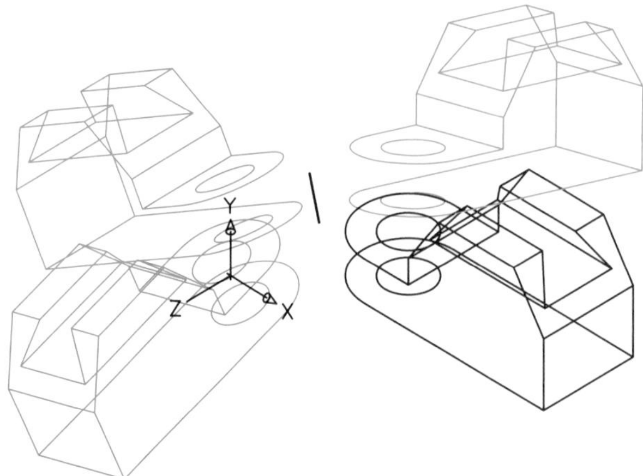

Figure 3-14 The resulting 3D array about the line

MIRROR3D	
Ribbon Modify panel	
Pull-down Menu	Modify/ 3D Operation/3D Mirror
Command Line	mirror3d

imaginary mirror plane: Imaginary plane about which the selected object is copied to the opposite side as a mirror image.

The MIRROR3D Command

This command is the 3D version of the standard **MIRROR** command. It allows you to create mirror copies of objects in 3D by specifying an ***imaginary mirror plane***. With the standard **MIRROR** command, you simply define an imaginary mirror line.

After selecting the object, you can choose one of the options to define the imaginary mirror plane. At this stage, right-clicking in the drawing area will display the shortcut menu (Figure 3-15). Or, if **DYN** (Dynamic Input) is on, you can also see the options by using the **<Down Arrow>** key.

TIP Regardless of whether a plane is to be used in the **MIRROR3D** command or any other, knowing how to define planes in the 3D space is a key aspect of 3D modeling in general.

Figure 3-15 The MIRROR3D command shortcut menu

3points: This is the default option. If you enter a point instead of specifying another option, you are automatically asked for two more points. The mirror plane is defined by specifying any three noncollinear points. The UCS currently in use does not affect the result.

Object: If you select this option, AutoCAD will ask you to select an object in order to use the plane it defines as the imaginary mirror plane. Only circles, arcs, and polylines can be selected. Selecting any other type of object will cause AutoCAD to prompt the following message:

```
Improper type of object picked.
```

Zaxis: With this option you define a plane by specifying two points (Figure 3-16). The first point (1) defines a point on the imaginary mirror plane. The second point (2) defines the direction of a vector to which the imaginary plane is normal.

View: In this option the imaginary mirror plane is defined parallel to the viewing plane (your monitor display). Because the orientation of the plane is already known with this option, all you are required to do is to specify the point that defines its location.

XY/YZ/ZX: By selecting one of the planes of the current UCS, you define the imaginary mirror plane parallel to it. As with the **View** option, the plane requires an additional point

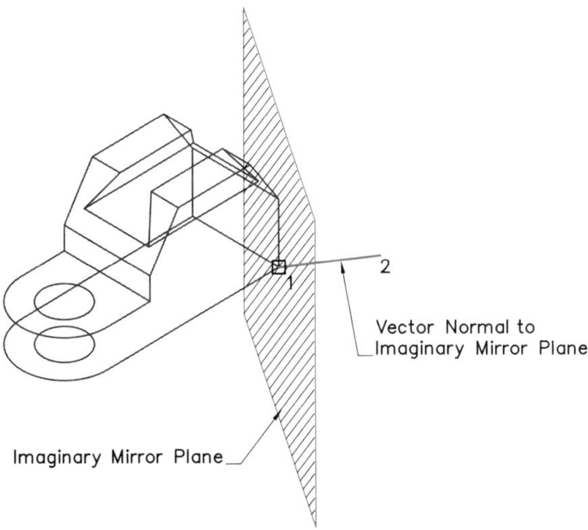

Figure 3-16 The imaginary mirror plane defined with the Zaxis option of the MIRROR3D command

to fully define its location. These three options and the **3points** option are the most frequently used in practice.

Last: Reuses the last imaginary mirror plane you defined.

Exercise 3-4: A 3D Mirror Operation by Specifying Three Points

1. **OPEN** the drawing named ***Exercise 3-00-A*** from the CD.
2. **SAVE** the drawing **AS** *Exercise 3-4*.
3. Invoke the **MIRROR3D** command and respond to the prompts as follows:

   Select objects: *all ↵ (To select all the objects)*

   Select objects: *↵ (To end the selection)*

   Specify first point of mirror plane (3 points) or [Object/Last/Zaxis/View/XY/YZ/ZX/3points] <3points>: *Specify any point on the wires of the face highlighted in* Figure 3-17.

   Specify second point on mirror plane: *Specify a second point on the same face.*

   Specify third point on mirror plane: *Specify a third point on the same face.*

   Delete source objects? [Yes/No] <N>: *↵ (To accept the default)*
4. The 3D model should look like Figure 3-18. Invoke the **3DORBIT** command and inspect the mirror image you just created.
5. **SAVE** the drawing.

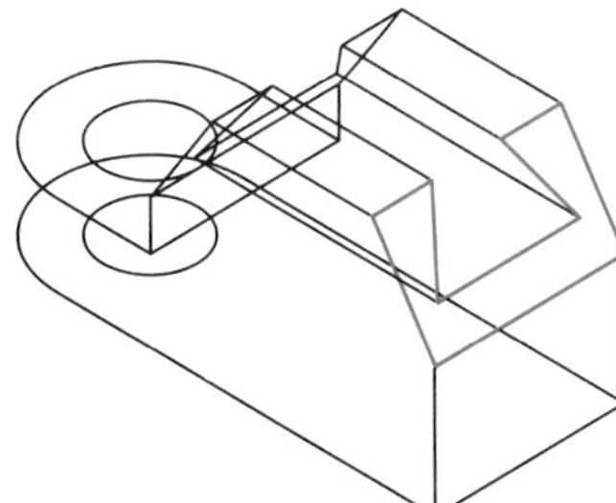

Figure 3-17 Reference face to specify the three points for the MIRROR3D operation

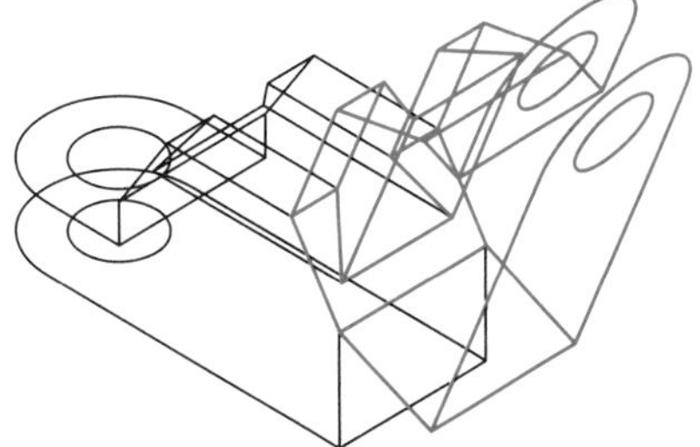

Figure 3-18 The 3D model after the MIRROR3D operation

Exercise 3-5: A 3D Mirror Operation by Using an Object

You will create a mirrored copy of the model using the bottom circle that represents the hole in the model.

1. **OPEN** the drawing named ***Exercise 3-00-A*** from the CD.
2. **SAVE** the drawing **AS** ***Exercise 3-5***.
3. Invoke the **MIRROR3D** command and respond to the prompts as follows:

   Select objects: *all ↵ (To select all the objects)*

   Select objects: *↵ (To end the selection)*

   Specify first point of mirror plane (3 points) or

   [Object/Last/Zaxis/View/XY/YZ/ZX/3points] <3points>: *o ↵*

   Select a circle, arc, or 2D-polyline segment: *Select the bottom circle.*

   Delete source objects? [Yes/No] <N>: *y ↵ (To flip the model without creating a copy)*

4. The 3D model should look like Figure 3-19. Explore the model with the **3DORBIT** command.
5. **SAVE** the drawing.

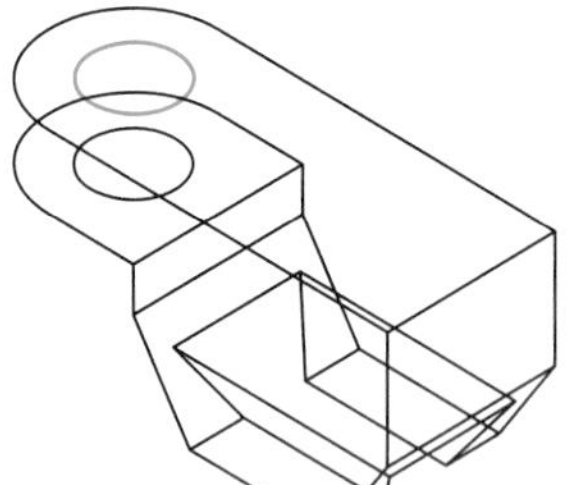

Figure 3-19 The 3D model is turned over using a MIRROR3D operation

Exercise 3-6: A 3D Mirror Operation Using a *Z*-Axis Vector

You will mirror the objects of the 3D model by specifying a vector perpendicular to the mirroring plane.

1. **OPEN** the drawing named ***Exercise 3-00-A*** from the CD.
2. **SAVE** the drawing **AS** ***Exercise 3-6***.
3. Select the **SW Isometric** viewing point.
4. Invoke the **MIRROR3D** command and respond to the prompts as follows:

   Select objects: *all ↵ (To select all the objects)*

   Select objects: *↵ (To end the selection)*

   Specify first point of mirror plane (3 points) or

   [Object/Last/Zaxis/View/XY/YZ/ZX/3points] <3points>: ***z*** *↵*

   Specify point on mirror plane: *Specify the endpoint shown in* Figure 3-20.

   Specify point on Z-axis (normal) of mirror plane: *@2,-1,0 ↵*

   Delete source objects? [Yes/No] <N>: *↵ (To accept the default)*

5. Select a **Top** view. Your drawing should look like Figure 3-21.
6. **SAVE** the drawing.

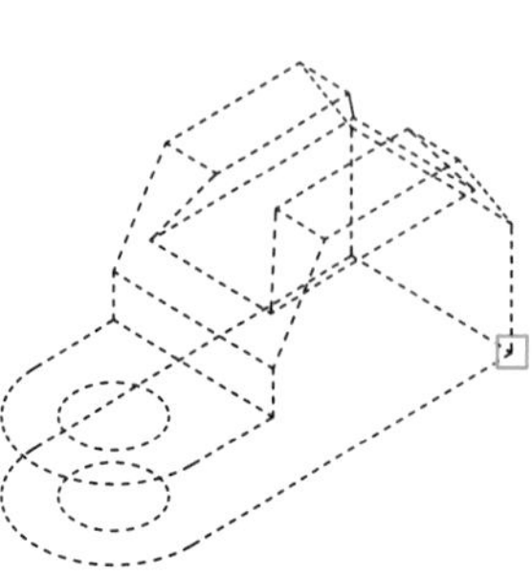

Figure 3-20 Point to specify the imaginary mirror plane for the Zaxis option of the MIRROR3D command

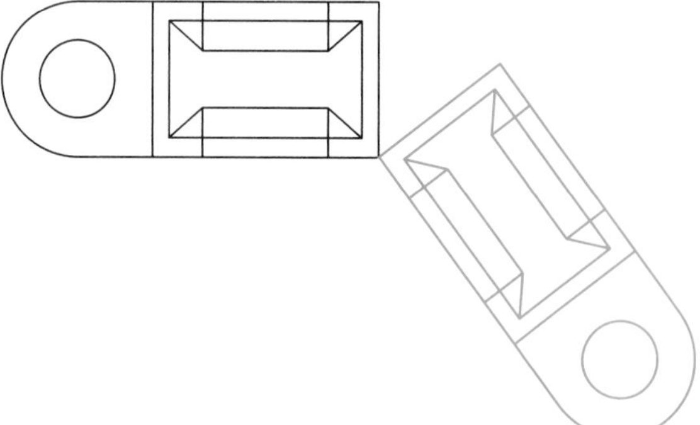

Figure 3-21 The 3D model after the MIRROR3D operation

Exercise 3-7: A 3D Mirror Operation Using the View Option

In this exercise you will create a mirror image of the model by specifying a mirroring plane that is parallel to the viewing plane.

Note:
Because the mirroring plane is specified parallel to the viewing plane, you will not be able to see the mirrored copy until you change the viewing point.

Student Files

1. **OPEN** the drawing named ***Exercise 3-00-A*** from the CD.
2. **SAVE** the drawing **AS *Exercise 3-7***.
3. Select the **Top** view.
4. Invoke the **MIRROR3D** command and respond to the prompts as follows:

   Select objects: *Use a selection window to select all the objects.*

   Select objects: ↵ *(To end the selection)*

   Specify first point of mirror plane (3 points) or [Object/Last/Zaxis/ View/XY/YZ/ZX/3points]<3points>: *v* ↵

   Specify point on view plane: *0,0,6* ↵

   Delete source objects? [Yes/No] <N>: ↵ *(To accept the default)*

4. Select the **SE Isometric** view. Your drawing should look like Figure 3-22.
5. **SAVE** the drawing.

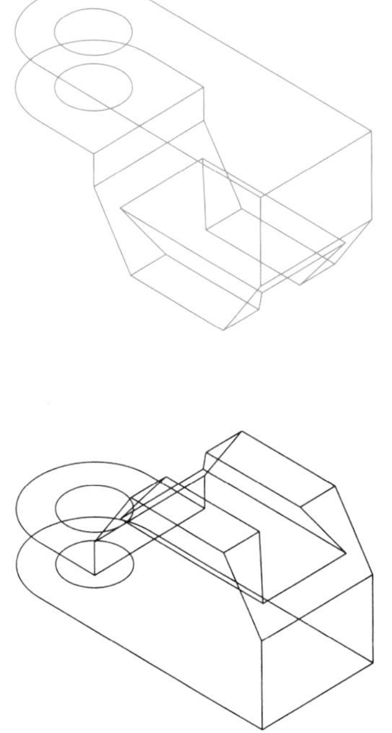

Figure 3-22 The 3D model after the MIRROR3D operation using the View option

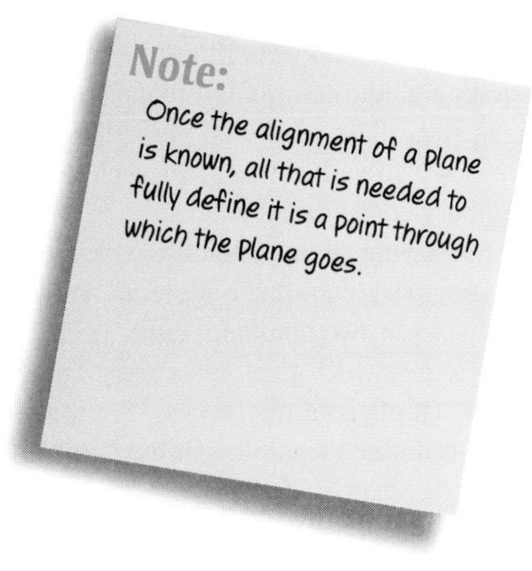

Note:
Once the alignment of a plane is known, all that is needed to fully define it is a point through which the plane goes.

Exercise 3-8: A 3DMIRROR Operation Using One of the Planes of the Current UCS

You will now create a mirror image of the same model by specifying the mirroring plane oriented parallel to the *ZX* plane.

1. **OPEN** the drawing named ***Exercise 3-00-A*** from the CD.
2. **SAVE** the drawing **AS *Exercise 3-8***.

3. Invoke the **MIRROR3D** command and respond to the prompts as follows:

   Select objects: *Use a selection window to select all the wires.*

   Select objects: ↵ *(To end the selection)*

   Specify first point of mirror plane (3 points) or [Object/Last/Zaxis/View/XY/YZ/ZX/3points] <3points>: *Right-click in the drawing area to open the shortcut menu and click on **ZX**.*

   Specify point on ZX plane <0,0,0>: *15,-1,15* ↵

   Delete source objects? [Yes/No] <N>: ↵ *(To accept the default)*
4. Your drawing should look like Figure 3-23.
5. **SAVE** the drawing.

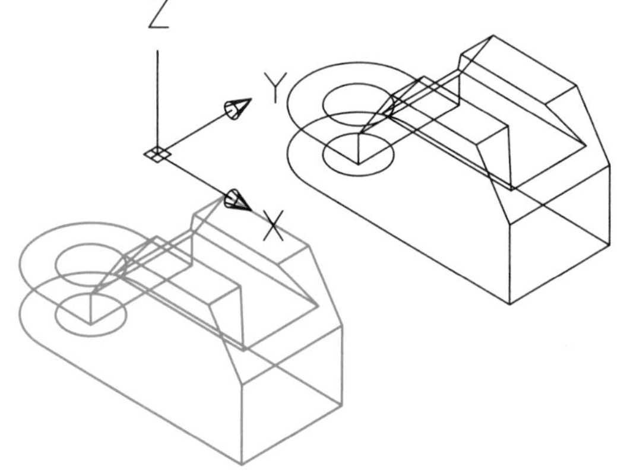

Figure 3-23 The 3D model after the MIRROR3D operation using one of the current UCS planes

The 3DALIGN Command

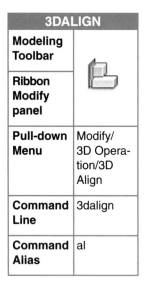

3DALIGN	
Modeling Toolbar	
Ribbon Modify panel	
Pull-down Menu	Modify/ 3D Operation/3D Align
Command Line	3dalign
Command Alias	al

This is probably the most complex and useful command in this group. In general, this command allows you to align objects by matching a source-oriented plane to the destination-oriented plane, regardless of the combinations of displacements and rotations involved. Both oriented planes can be visualized as imaginary coordinate systems.

Specifying all three points enables you to fully define the two imaginary coordinate systems. However, you can also specify one or two points for either of the imaginary coordinate systems, which gives you a total of nine different combinations. Throughout the process, the imaginary coordinate system is defined regardless of the number of points specified. The current UCS provides the missing alignment information in case fewer than three points are specified.

The example in Figure 3-24 shows two 3D solids before and after one of them is aligned with the other 3D solid, using fully defined imaginary coordinate systems.

After selecting the object(s), you start by defining the source imaginary coordinate system. The first point simply locates its origin. Choosing to specify only this point would define the imaginary coordinate system as shown in Figure 3-25. If you specified only one point to define the destination imaginary coordinate system, it would simply become a **MOVE** operation.

The second point defines the X'-axis of the imaginary coordinate system (Figure 3-26). Using two points will enable you to align the object so that its edge is flush with the destination imaginary coordinate system.

Note:
Because the mirroring plane is parallel with the ZX plane, only the Y coordinate of the point is read.

Note:
The imaginary coordinate system will not show up in the program. It is just an illustrative element to show you the object's current location and orientation. Because the coordinate system is not real, its axes are named X', Y', and Z' for the source imaginary coordinate system and X'', Y'', and Z''; for the destination imaginary coordinate system.

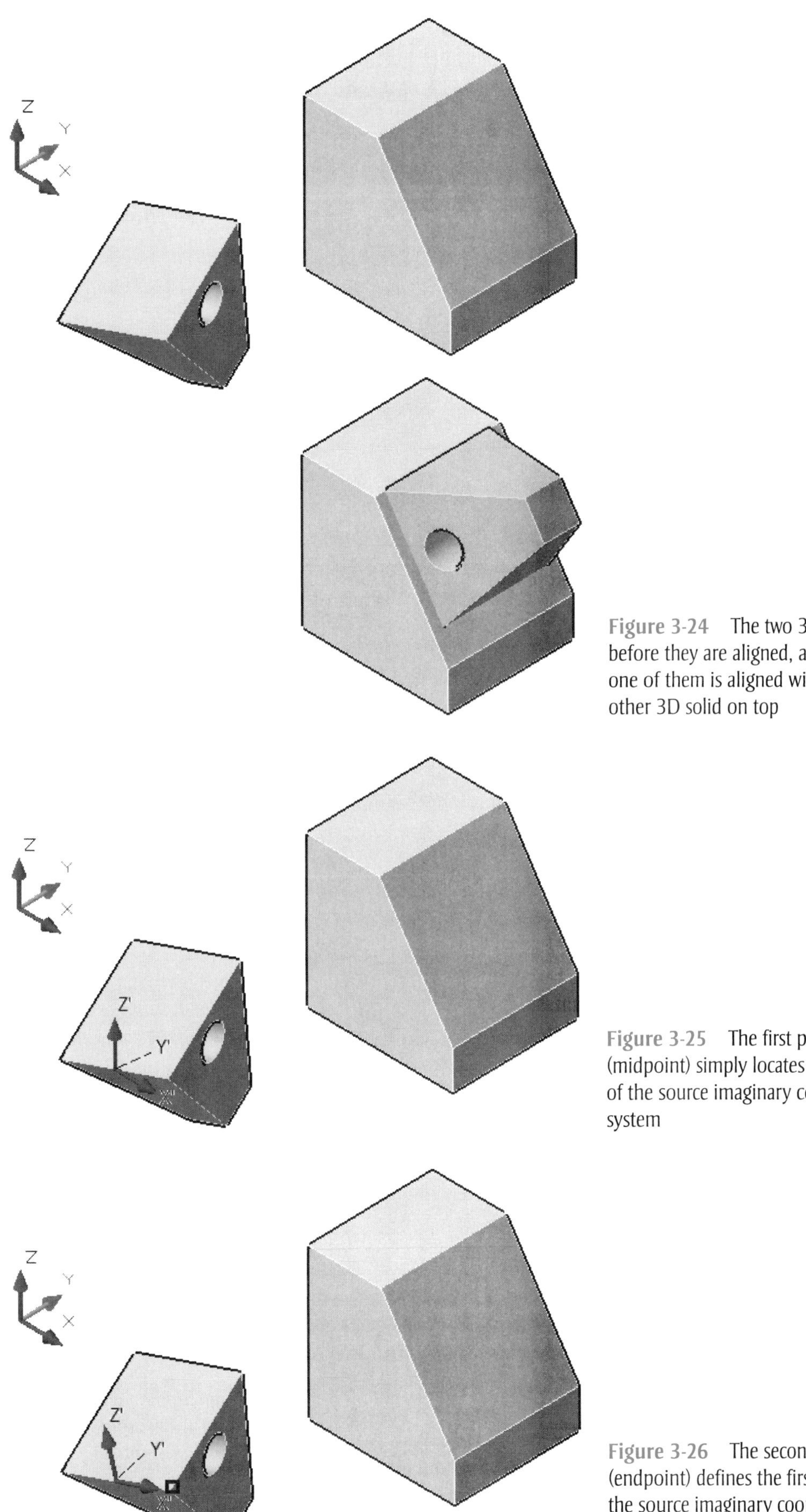

Figure 3-24 The two 3D solids before they are aligned, and after one of them is aligned with the other 3D solid on top

Figure 3-25 The first point (midpoint) simply locates the origin of the source imaginary coordinate system

Figure 3-26 The second point (endpoint) defines the first axis of the source imaginary coordinate system

The third point finally aligns the $X'Y'$ plane to the face that we want to mate with the other 3D solid (Figure 3-27).

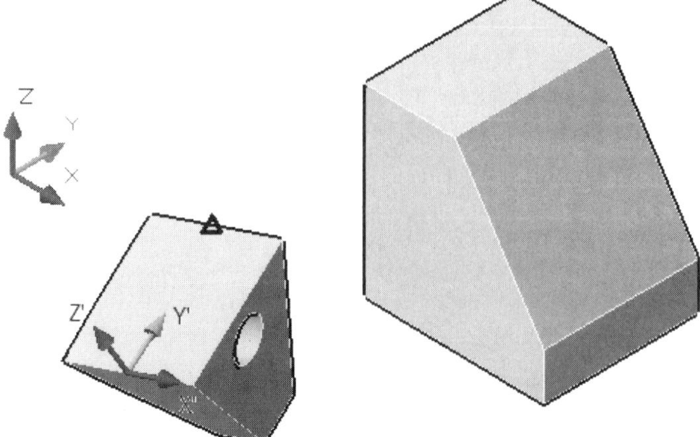

Figure 3-27 The third point (midpoint) fully aligns the source imaginary coordinate system

As with the source imaginary coordinate system, the first point of the destination imaginary coordinate system locates its origin (Figure 3-28). Using only this point will align the source object so that its imaginary coordinate system matches the destination imaginary coordinate system as defined so far.

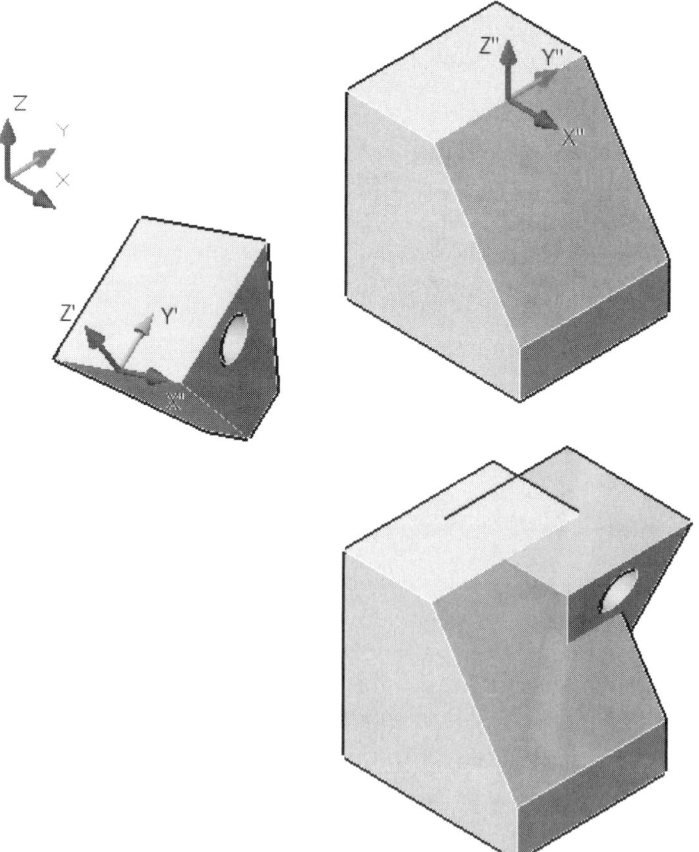

Figure 3-28 The first point (midpoint) of the destination imaginary coordinate system simply defines its origin. Ending the command at this stage will align the selected object so that both imaginary coordinate systems match

The second point continues aligning the destination imaginary coordinate system so that the X''-axis aligns with the specified point. Choosing not to specify the third point will also align the objects based on the current orientation of the two imaginary coordinate systems (Figure 3-29).

Specifying the third point fully defines the destination imaginary coordinate system. The object is now placed in the face we planned for (Figure 3-30).

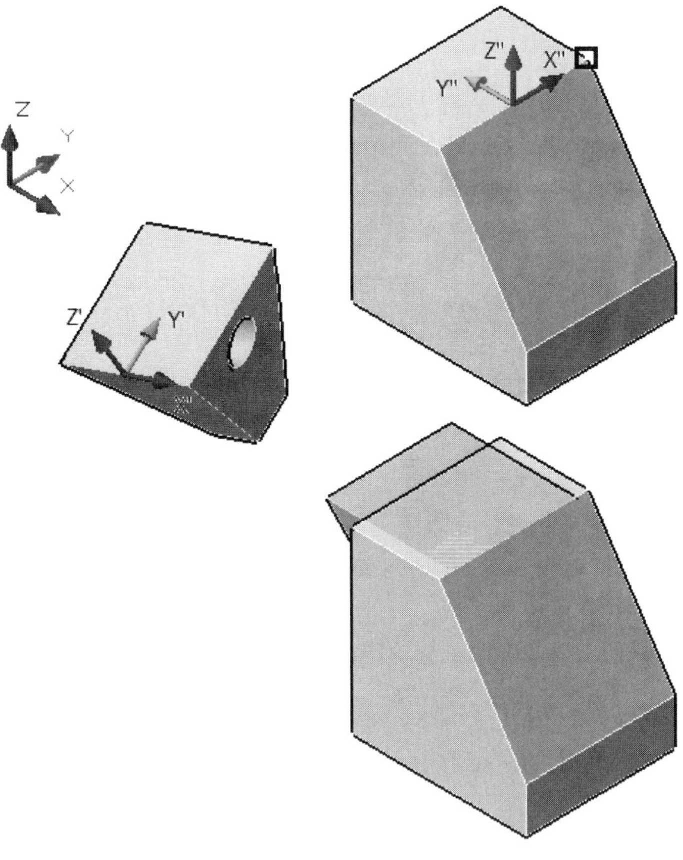

Figure 3-29 The second point (endpoint) of the destination imaginary coordinate system defines its first axis. Alignment is achieved if the command ends at this stage

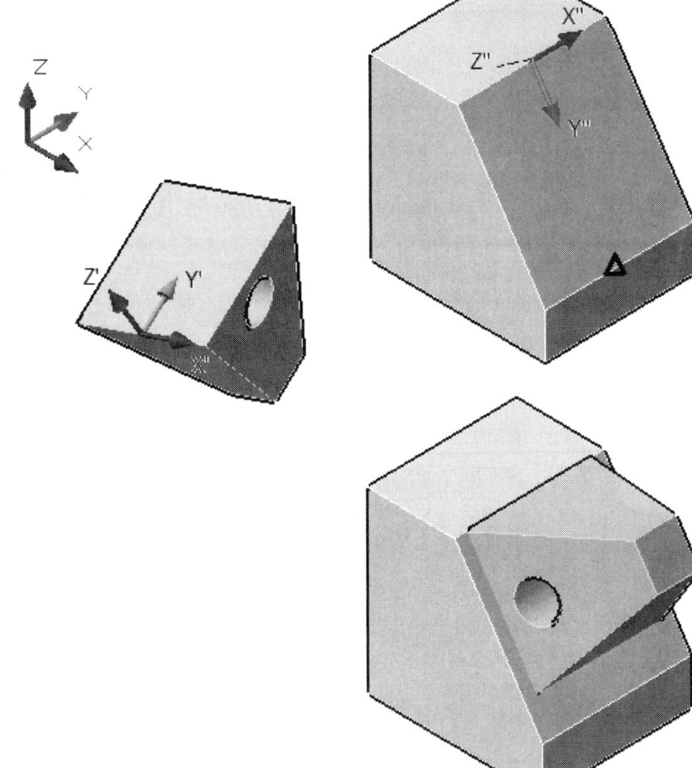

Figure 3-30 The third point (midpoint) of the destination imaginary coordinate system fully defines it. By matching the two imaginary coordinate systems, the selected object is aligned exactly as expected

TIP With the 3DALIGN command, you can create a rotated copy of selected objects by using the **COPY** option.

TIP You should turn **DUCS** (Dynamic UCS) mode off when using the **3DALIGN** command.

Exercise 3-9: Using the 3DALIGN Command as a 2D Operation

In this exercise you will align a 2D shape contained in the current UCS with another object that is also contained in the current UCS. This is how this command is normally used when working in 2D.

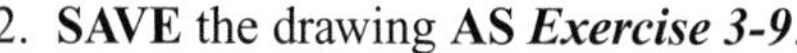

Student Files

1. **OPEN** the drawing named ***Exercise 3-00-A*** from the CD.
2. **SAVE** the drawing **AS *Exercise 3-9***.
3. Draw the shape shown near the 3D model in Figure 3-31.

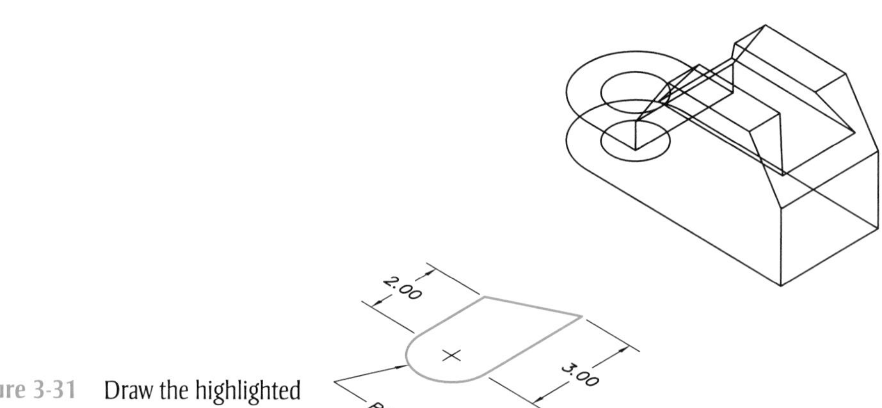

Figure 3-31 Draw the highlighted objects

4. Invoke the **3DALIGN** command and respond to the prompts as follows:
   Select objects: *Select the entire shape you just drew.*
   Select objects: ↵ *(To end the selection)*
   Specify source plane and orientation ...
   Specify base point or [Copy]: *Snap to endpoint 1* (Figure 3-32).
   Specify second point or [Continue] <C>: *Snap to endpoint 2.*
   Specify third point or [Continue] <C>: ↵ *(To continue with the other stage of the command)*
   Specify destination plane and orientation ...
   Specify first destination point: *Snap to endpoint 3.*
   Specify second destination point or [eXit] <X>: *Snap to endpoint 4.*
   Specify third destination point or [eXit] <X>: ↵ *(To exit the command)*
5. Your drawing should look like Figure 3-33. **SAVE** the drawing.

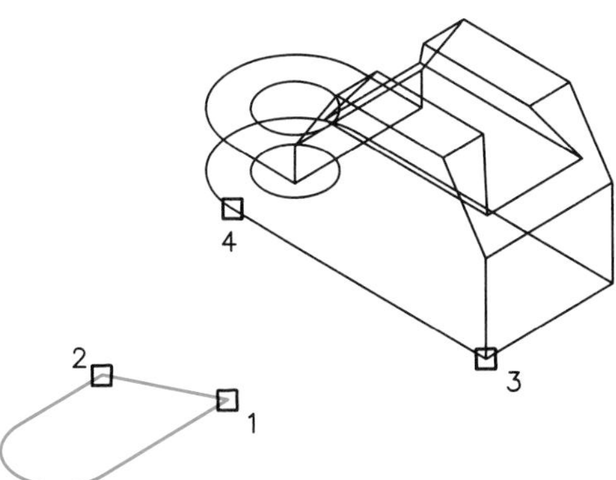

Figure 3-32 Follow this order to specify the points for the 3DALIGN operation

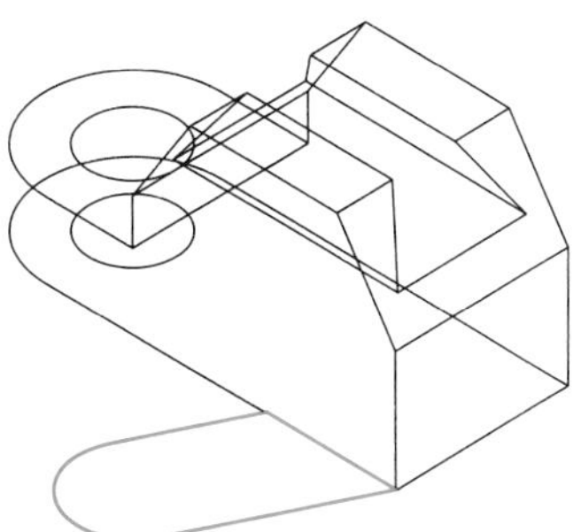

Figure 3-33 The objects are aligned using two points to define both the source and the destination imaginary coordinate systems

Exercise 3-10: Using the 3DALIGN Command to Align a Cylinder in a Hole

1. **OPEN** the drawing named ***Exercise 3-00-A*** from the CD.
2. **SAVE** the drawing **AS** ***Exercise 3-10***.
3. Select the **Right** UCS.
4. Use the **CYLINDER** command to create a 3D solid cylinder near the model. When prompted, specify **0.7** as the radius and **3** for the height.
5. Invoke the **3DALIGN** command and respond to the prompts as follows:

   Select objects: *Select the cylinder.*

   Select objects: ↵ *(To end the selection)*

   Specify source plane and orientation ...

   Specify base point or [Copy]: *Snap to center point 1* (Figure 3-34).

   Specify second point or [Continue] <C>: *Snap to center point 2.*

   Specify third point or [Continue] <C>: ↵ *(To continue with the other stage of the command)*

   Specify destination plane and orientation ...

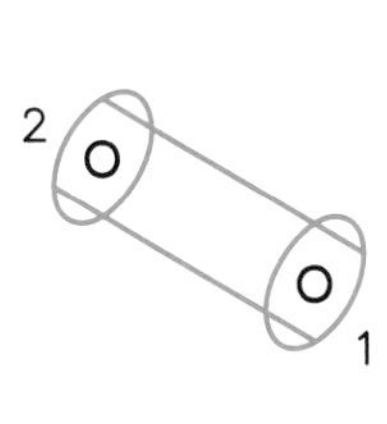

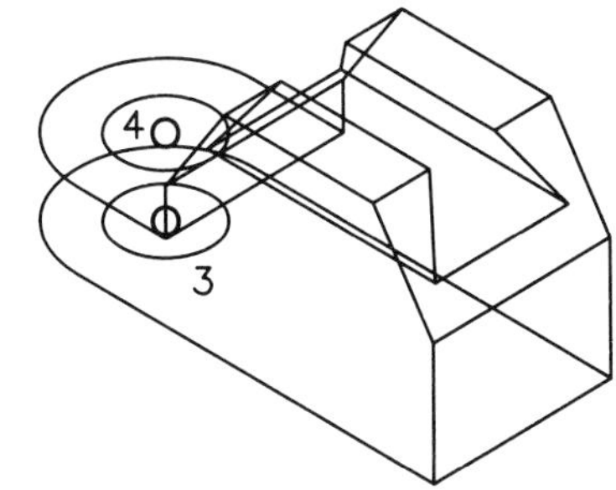

Figure 3-34 Follow this order to specify the points for the 3DALIGN operation

   Specify first destination point: *Snap to center point 3.*

   Specify second destination point or [eXit] <X>: *Snap to center point 4.*

   Specify third destination point or [eXit] <X>: ↵ *(To exit the command)*

6. Select the **Realistic** visual style. Your drawing should look like Figure 3-35.
7. **SAVE** the drawing.

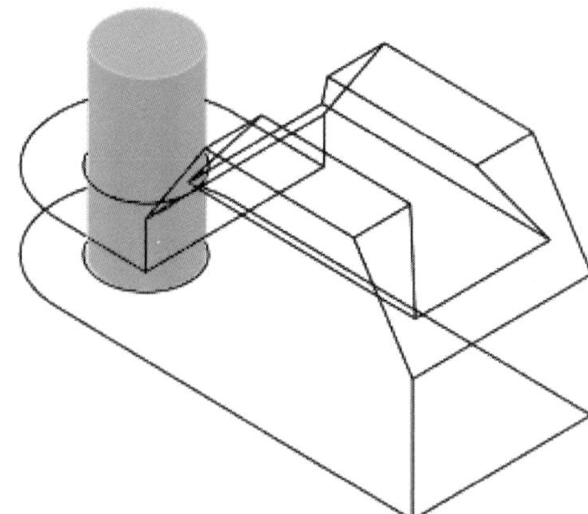

Figure 3-35 The cylinder is aligned, using two points to define both the source and the destination imaginary coordinate systems

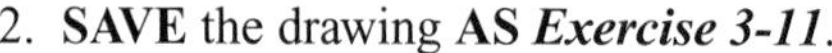

Exercise 3-11: The 3DALIGN Command Using All Points to Specify the Source and Destination Imaginary Coordinate Systems

1. **OPEN** the drawing named ***Exercise 3-00-A*** from the CD.
2. **SAVE** the drawing **AS** ***Exercise 3-11***.
3. Re-create the 2D shape you drew in ***Exercise 3-9***.
4. Invoke the **3DALIGN** command and respond to the prompts as follows:

   Select objects: *Select the shape's objects.*
   Select objects: ↵ *(To end the selection)*
   Specify source plane and orientation ...
   Specify base point or [Copy]: *Snap to endpoint 1* (Figure 3-36).
   Specify second point or [Continue] <C>: *Snap to endpoint 2.*
   Specify third point or [Continue] <C>: *Snap to endpoint 3.*
   Specify destination plane and orientation ...
   Specify first destination point: *Snap to endpoint 4.*
   Specify second destination point or [eXit] <X>: *Snap to endpoint 5.*
   Specify third destination point or [eXit] <X>: *Snap to midpoint 6.*
5. Your drawing should look like Figure 3-37. **SAVE** the drawing.

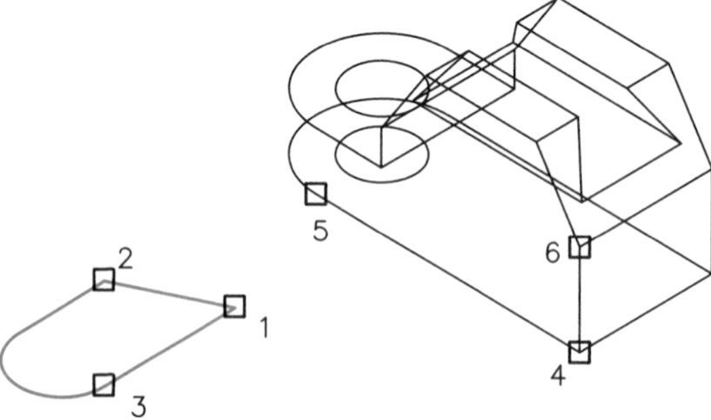

Figure 3-36 Follow this order to specify the points for the 3DALIGN operation

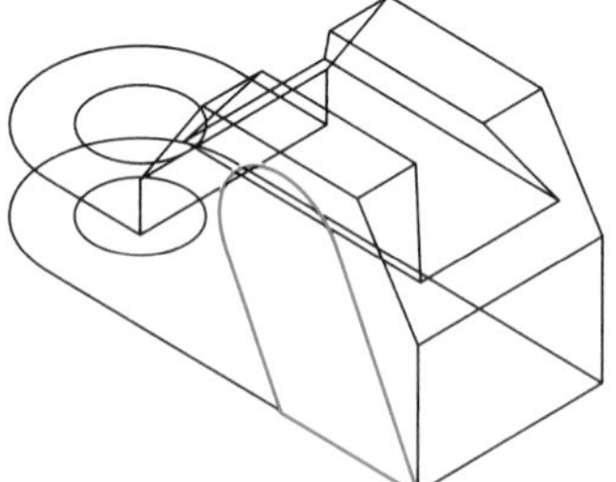

Figure 3-37 The objects are aligned using fully defined source and destination imaginary coordinate systems

Exercise 3-12: Using the 3DALIGN Command to Align a Cylinder in a Hole in a Specified Position

1. **OPEN** the drawing named ***Exercise 3-00-B*** from the CD.
2. **SAVE** the drawing **AS** ***Exercise 3-12***.
3. Select the **Right** UCS.

4. Invoke the **3DALIGN** command and respond to the prompts as follows:

Select objects: *Select the shape's objects.*

Select objects: ↵ *(To end the selection)*

Specify source plane and orientation ...

Specify base point or [Copy]: *Snap to center point 1* (Figure 3-38).

Specify second point or [Continue] <C>: *Snap to center point 2.*

Specify third point or [Continue] <C>: *Snap to midpoint 3.*

Specify destination plane and orientation ...

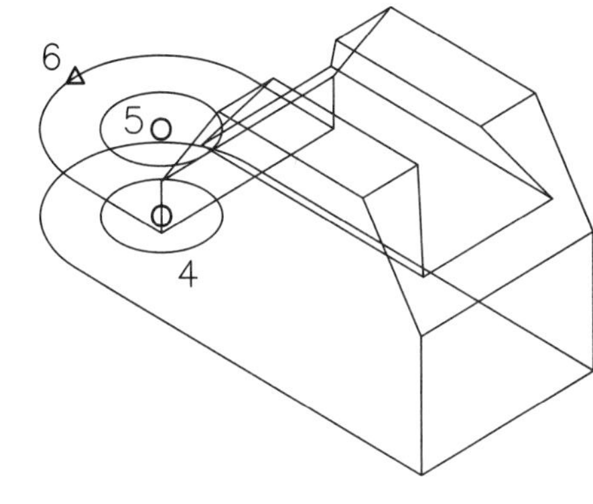

Figure 3-38 Follow this order to specify the points for the 3DALIGN operation

Specify first destination point: *Snap to center point 4.*

Specify second destination point or [eXit] <X>: *Snap to center point 5.*

Specify third destination point or [eXit] <X>: *Snap to midpoint 6.*

5. Select the **Realistic** visual style. Your 3D model should look like Figure 3-39.
6. **SAVE** the drawing.

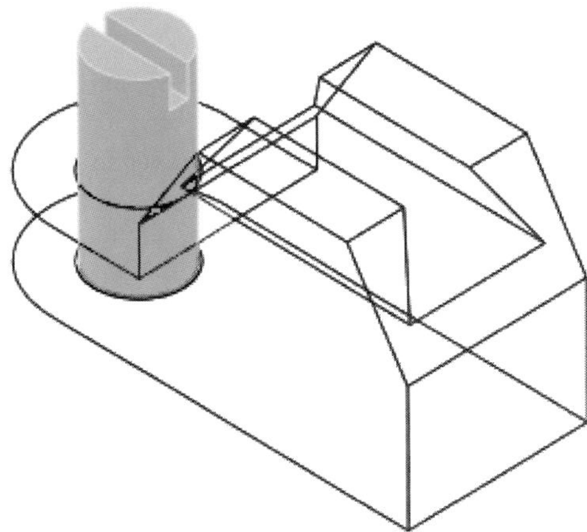

Figure 3-39 The cylinder and its slot are aligned using fully defined source and destination imaginary coordinate systems

The ALIGN Command

ALIGN	
Pull-down Menu	Modify/3D Operation/ Align
Command Line	align
Command Alias	al

The **ALIGN** command is very similar to the **3DALIGN** command. The only difference is the order in which it collects the source and destination points.

The **3DALIGN** command collects the source points first and then the destination points. By doing so, the command tries to define a 2D source imaginary coordinate system, or aligned plane, and match it with a 2D destination imaginary coordinate system, which is also an aligned plane.

The **ALIGN** command, on the other hand, performs the alignment by defining each pair of source-destination points one by one.

As with the **3DALIGN** command, the AutoCAD software determines all the necessary operations (move, rotate, and scale) needed to align the source points with the destination points. The command temporarily draws traces from each source point to its corresponding destination while it is still in process to help you preview the results.

Because you must enter complete pairs, the number of combinations you can obtain is smaller than you get with the **3DALIGN** command. Depending on the number of pairs entered, the **ALIGN** command can perform different operations in both the 2D and 3D environments. Pressing **<Enter>** after you enter a complete pair of points will end the command, resulting in one of the following operations:

1 pair results in a **MOVE** operation. In practice, the **ALIGN** command is seldom used for this purpose.

2 pairs allows you to align the objects in two straight lines, where the first pair of points establishes the origin and the second pair the alignment. This operation is very useful when you are aligning objects by an imaginary axis (e.g., a bolt in a hole).

When you press **<Enter>** after entering the second pair, the command will prompt for the scaling option. This is the only event in which the **Scale** operation can be performed.

Using the **ALIGN** command with two pairs of points is useful only in a 2D environment. This enables you to move, rotate, and scale objects at the same time.

Both the **ALIGN** and the **3DALIGN** commands guarantee that objects can be repositioned throughout 3D space regardless of their relative location. Such reliability and versatility make these commands key operations in the development of 3D models for mechanical assemblies. A complete understanding of 3D modeling operations performed with these two commands constitutes a valuable skill for individuals involved in the creation of complex mechanical assemblies.

CREATING AND MODIFYING 3D CURVES

NONPLANAR CURVES

3DPOLYLINE	
Ribbon Draw panel	
Pull-down Menu	Draw/3D Polyline
Command Line	3dpoly

3D Polylines

A ***3D polyline*** is a single continuous object made of straight segments whose points can be located anywhere in the 3D space. This object is created with the **3DPOLY** command.

A polyline can be made of line and arc segments, whereas a 3D polyline can contain only line segments. The use of the 3D polyline is so limited that it cannot even be filleted. You can draw a 3D polyline on a plane; however, its characteristics will still be different from those of a regular polyline.

3D polyline: A curve made of straight segments that are placed in 3D space that does not belong to a plane.

spline: A nonplanar continuous curve that goes through a set of points specified anywhere in the 3D space.

Splines

A ***spline*** is a smooth curve that goes through a set of points located anywhere in the 3D space, turning and twisting so that it is *continuously curved* at any point. This object is created with the **SPLINE** command.

In Figure 3-40, the two-segment polyline is continuous in all its points. If you were to modify it by performing a **FILLET** operation, you would add a new arc segment and it would become a three-segment polyline. Then besides being continuous, it would also be *continuously tangent* at any point; however, there would still be an abrupt transition at the points where the lines and the arc segments met.

A spline, on the other hand, is a more complex object that is not only continuous and continuously tangent, but also *continuously curved* at any point. The AutoCAD program uses a larger number of segments, which are not physically seen, to achieve this effect.

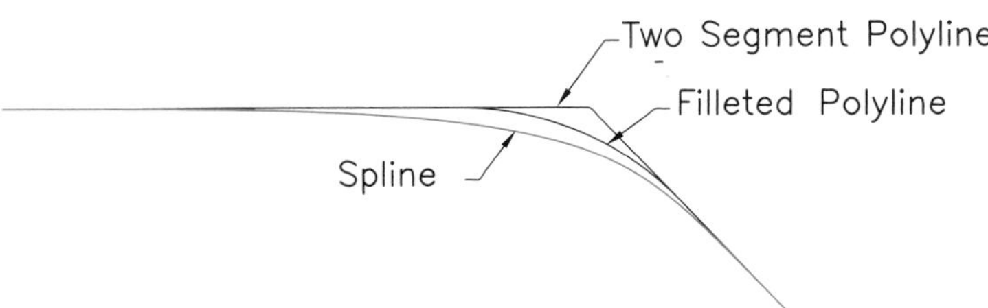

Figure 3-40 The spline is not only continuously tangent at any point, but also continuously curved

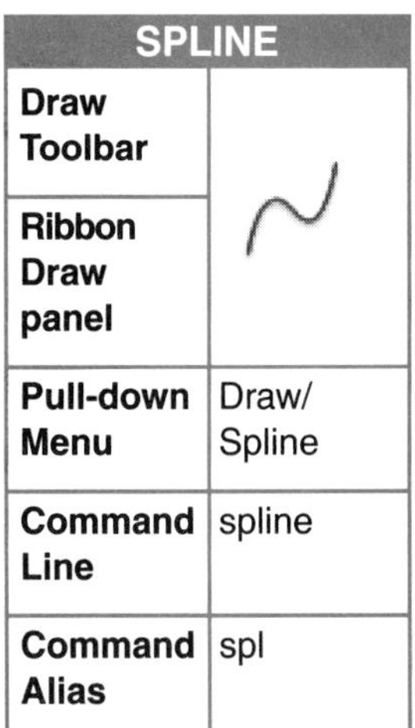

SPLINE	
Draw Toolbar	
Ribbon Draw panel	
Pull-down Menu	Draw/ Spline
Command Line	spline
Command Alias	spl

There are many types of splines: Bezier curves, B-splines, uniform nonrational B-splines, nonuniform nonrational B-splines, Beta splines, V-splines, and so on. The AutoCAD program uses a particular type of spline known as a nonuniform rational B-spline (NURBS) curve. "Nonuniform" refers to the difference in segment lengths into which these curves are divided and "rational" to the fact that its control points can be given different weight values individually to change the curve path. "B-spline" stands for "Basis spline."

NURBS curves are the industry standard for the representation of complex geometry. They are very useful when creating irregular-shaped or free-form curves, for example, geographic contour curves, automobile design lines, and boat hull design lines.

The **SPLINE** command prompt is structured as follows:

Specify first point or [Object]: *Here you have two choices:*

- If you specify a first point, you will be prompted for the next one.
- When selecting **Object** as the initial option, the only type of object you can select to convert to a spline is a spline-fit polyline. This will be covered in the next topic.

Specify next point: *At least a second point has to be selected in order to enter the spline options.*

Specify next point or [Close/Fit tolerance] <start tangent>: *Here you have four choices:*

- Specify another point.
- Select the **Close** option to create a closed spline. You will be asked for a point tangent to the spline at the closing point.
- Change the **Fit tolerance**. By changing this option you allow AutoCAD to calculate a spline curve of a smaller degree of complexity. The curve will then go through different points than the ones you specified, but never farther than the fit tolerance value specified. A fit tolerance of 0, which is the default value, will make the spline go through each point exactly. These settings apply for all the points except the start and end ones.
- Hit the <**Enter**> key to let the AutoCAD program know that this is the last point. You will be then asked for the tangencies. An open spline has two tangencies; a closed spline has only one.

Specify start tangent: *Here you have two choices:*

- Press the <**Enter**> key to accept the default natural tangency of the start point.
- Specify a point to establish a different tangency.

Specify end tangent: *The same as with the start point*

In practice, when you specify the last point of the spline, and you do not want to specify any tangent, just remember to press <**Enter**> three times consecutively.

Exercise 3-13: Creating Splines Using 3D Geometry

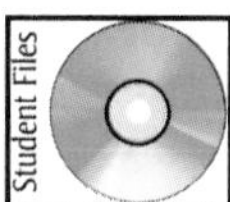

1. **OPEN** the drawing named ***Exercise 3-00-A*** from the CD.
2. **SAVE** the drawing **AS *Exercise 3-13***.
3. Invoke the **SPLINE** command and respond to the prompts as follows:

   Specify first point or [Object]: *Snap to the endpoint 1* (Figure 3-41).

   Specify next point: *Snap to the endpoint 2.*

   Specify next point or [Close/Fit tolerance] <start tangent>: *Snap to the endpoint 3. (Repeat until endpoint 6.)*

   Specify next point or [Close/Fit tolerance] <start tangent>: ↵

   Specify start tangent: ↵

   Specify end tangent: ↵

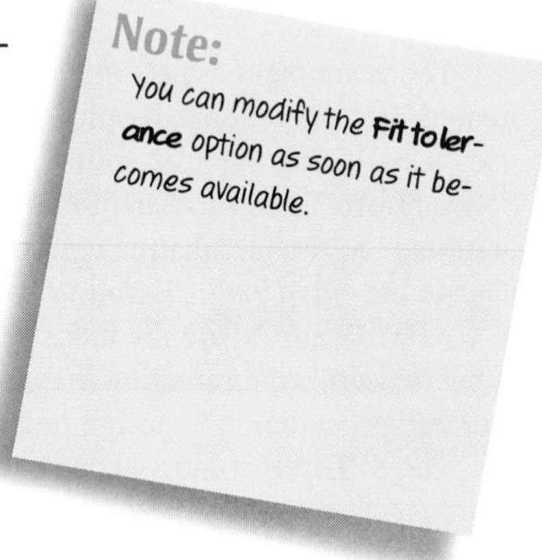

Note:
You can modify the Fit tolerance option as soon as it becomes available.

4. The drawing should look like Figure 3-42. Create another two splines. Specify the same points as the one before, but this time specify a **Fit tolerance** of **1.25** for the first one and **2.50** for the second one.

   Specify next point or [Close/Fit tolerance] <start tangent>: *f* ↵

   Specify fit tolerance <0.0000>: *1.25* ↵ *(2.50 ↵ for the second spline)*

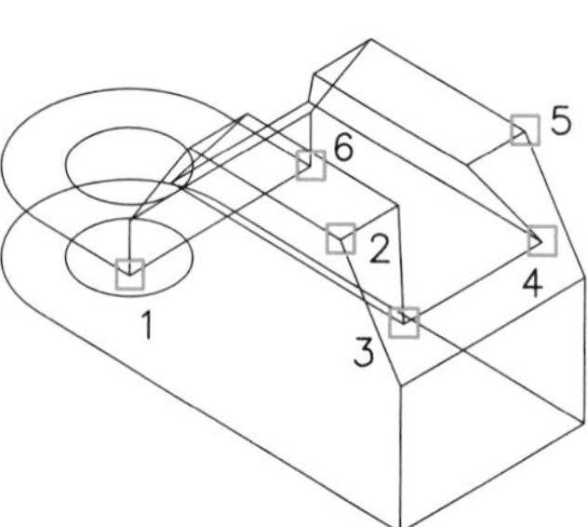

Figure 3-41 Create a spline through the specified points

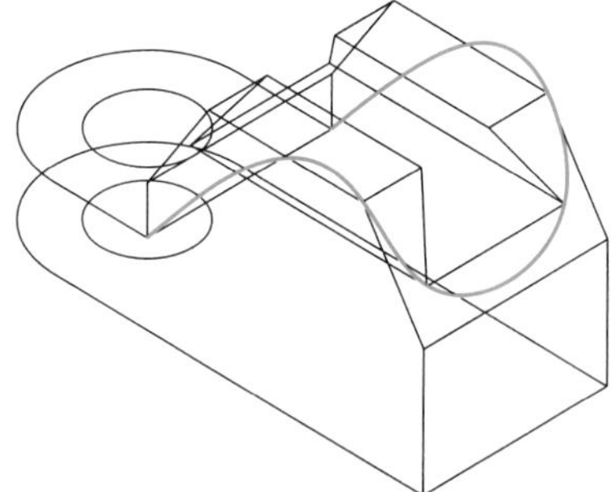

Figure 3-42 Resulting spline curve throughout the 3D space

5. Select the **3DWireframe** visual style.
6. Invoke the **3DORBIT** command to inspect the splines you just created (Figure 3-43).
7. **SAVE** the drawing.

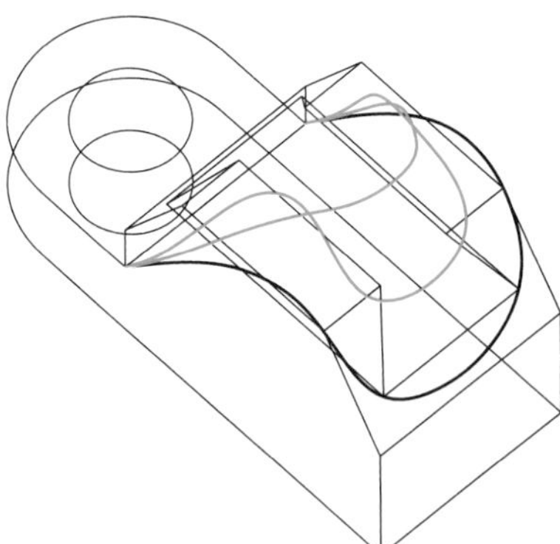

Figure 3-43 A second spline curve through the same points using a different Fit tolerance value

Helixes

A ***helix*** is a continuous open spiral curve that smoothly grows horizontally, vertically, or in both directions. The **HELIX** command creates this type of object, allowing you to specify the six elements that define its geometric characteristics (Figure 3-44).

helix: 2D or 3D spiral curve that coils around an axis, gradually growing horizontally, vertically, or in both directions. 2D spiral curves grow only horizontally.

HELIX	
Modeling Toolbar	
Ribbon Draw panel	
Pull-down Menu	Draw/ Helix
Command Line	helix

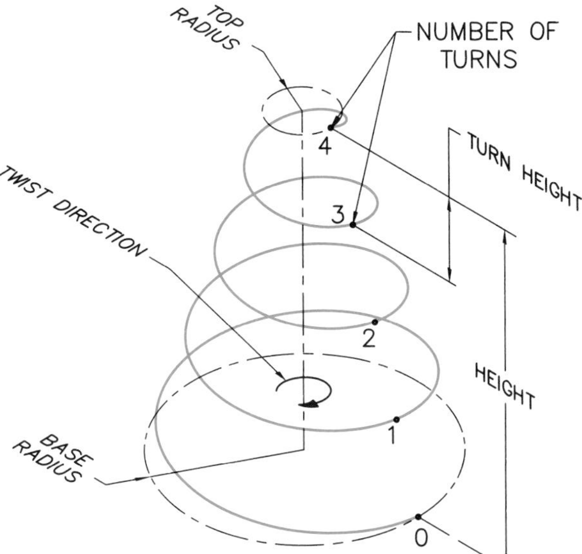

Figure 3-44 The six geometric elements that define a helix's shape

According to the values of the parameters specified, you can create one of the three types of helixes (Figure 3-45):

- 2D spiral
- Cylindrical 3D spiral
- Conical 3D spiral

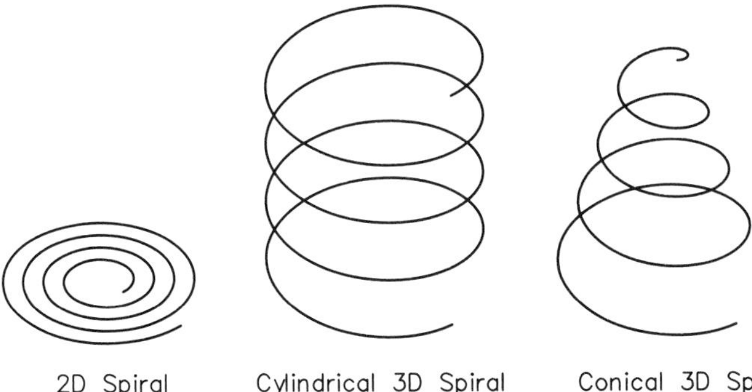

Figure 3-45 From left to right: 2D spiral, cylindrical 3D spiral, and conical 3D spiral

2D SPIRAL: Simply known as a *spiral,* this is a helix that grows only horizontally. This curve is obtained as the result of specifying the height as **0**, and the base and top radius as different values.

CYLINDRICAL 3D SPIRAL: Also known as a *cylindrical helix,* this curve is a helix that grows only vertically. It is obtained as the result of specifying the base and top radius as the same value, and the height as a value different from **0**.

CONICAL 3D SPIRAL: Also known as a *conical helix,* this is a helix that grows in both directions, vertically and horizontally. This curve is obtained as the result of specifying the base and top radius as different values, and the height as a value different from **0**.

The six geometric elements of the helix can be modified in the **Properties** palette after it is created (Figure 3-46). The **Turn Height**, **Height**, and **Turns** parameters are related to each other by the expression:

Height = Turn Height × Turns

In the **Properties** palette, you can constrain one of the three values so that it is not affected when modifying the two others. For example, constraining the **Turn Height** will cause the number of **Turns** to change if the **Height** value is changed (Figure 3-47).

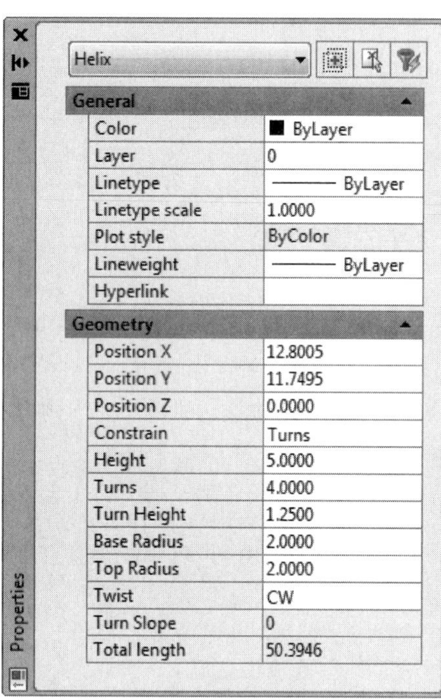

Figure 3-46 A helix's geometry can be modified through the Properties palette

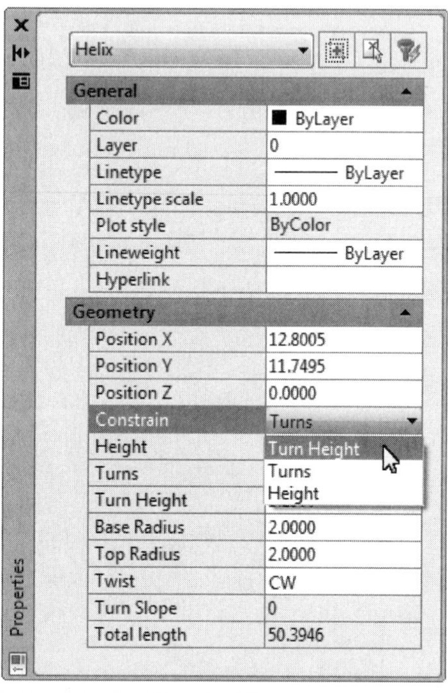

Figure 3-47 Changing the constrained parameter through the Properties palette

Exercise 3-14: Creating a Spiral and a Helix with the HELIX Command

1. Start a **NEW** drawing using the **acad** template.
2. **SAVE** it **AS** ***Exercise 3-14***.
3. Select the **SE Isometric** viewing point.
4. Select the **Front** UCS.
5. Invoke the **HELIX** command and respond to the prompts as follows:

   Specify center point of base: *Click anywhere in the drawing area.*

   Specify base radius or [Diameter] <1.0000>: *2 ↵*

   Specify top radius or [Diameter] <2.0000>: *6 ↵*

   Specify helix height or [Axis endpoint/Turns/turn Height/tWist] 0.2727: *t ↵ (To specify the number of turns)*

   Enter number of turns <3.0000>: *5 ↵*

   Specify helix height or [Axis endpoint/Turns/turn Height/tWist] <1.000>: *0 ↵*

6. **ZOOM** as needed. The spiral should look like Figure 3-48.
7. Invoke the **HELIX** command again and respond to the prompts as follows:

   Specify center point of base: ***Click anywhere in the drawing area.***

   Specify base radius or [Diameter] <2.0000>: *3.5 ↵*

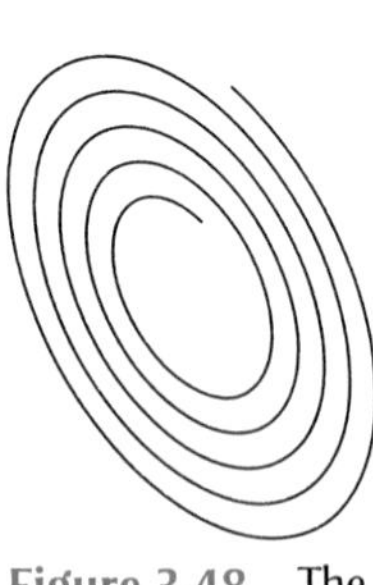
Figure 3-48 The resulting 2D spiral

Specify top radius or [Diameter] <3.5000>: ↵ *(To accept the same value as the base radius)*

Specify helix height or [Axis endpoint/Turns/turn Height/tWist] <0.2727>: *15* ↵

8. **ZOOM** as needed. The two spirals should look like Figure 3-49.
8. **SAVE** the drawing.

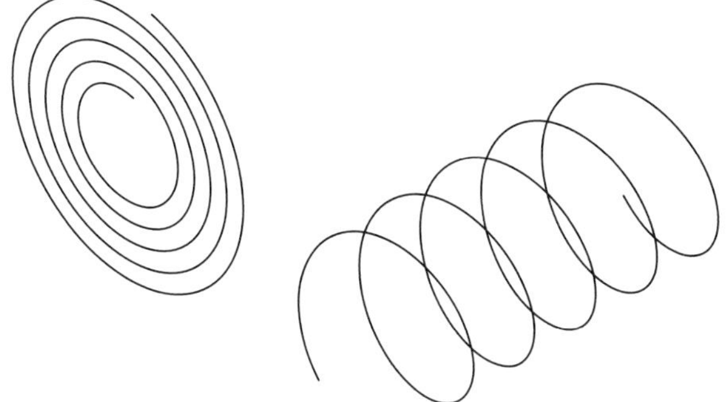

Figure 3-49 The resulting 3D cylindrical spiral next to the 2D spiral

Figure 3-50 The 3D cylindrical spiral with three turns

Exercise 3-15: Modifying Helixes Through the Properties Palette

1. Open *Exercise 3-14*.
2. **SAVE** it **AS** *Exercise 3-15*.
3. Select the **Cylindrical Helix**, and right-click to select **Properties** from the shortcut menu.
4. In the **Properties** palette, constrain the **Turn Height** and change the value of the **Height** to **9**.
5. The number of **Turns** changes to **3.** Press the **<Esc>** key. The modified helix should look like Figure 3-50.
6. Select the **Cylindrical Helix** again. In the **Properties** palette, change the value of the top radius to **1.5**.
7. The cylindrical helix transforms into a conical helix. Press the **<Esc>** key. The modified helix should look like Figure 3-51.
8. Close the **Properties** palette.
9. **SAVE** the drawing.

Figure 3-51 You make the 3D spiral conical by changing its top radius value

Helixes are very complex objects. They are used by engineers, architects, and designers to prepare clear, concise, and accurate 3D models whose geometry is described by this type of curve. Identification of this type of geometry and its subsequent use, based on a complete understanding of its principles, will allow users to develop accurate 3D models of known elements such as threads, spiral stairs, and cams. Helixes can also be applied to perform research tasks and to find enhanced solutions to conceptual design problems in the development of new products and systems.

PEDIT	
Modify II Toolbar	
Ribbon Modify panel	
Pull-down Menu	Modify/ Object/ Polyline
Command Line	pedit
Command Alias	pe

EDITING POLYLINES: THE PEDIT COMMAND

With the **PEDIT** command you can edit both polylines and 3D polylines. There are different options available for these two types of objects. Figure 3-52 shows the shortcut menus for these two objects once the command is in progress. The shortcut menu of options available for polylines is the one on the left. To invoke the **PEDIT** command, you can use one of the methods shown in the grid.

For a polyline, the following options are the ones you will more frequently use when working in the 3D environment:

- **Close** adds a new segment from the starting point of the first segment to the last point on the end segment.

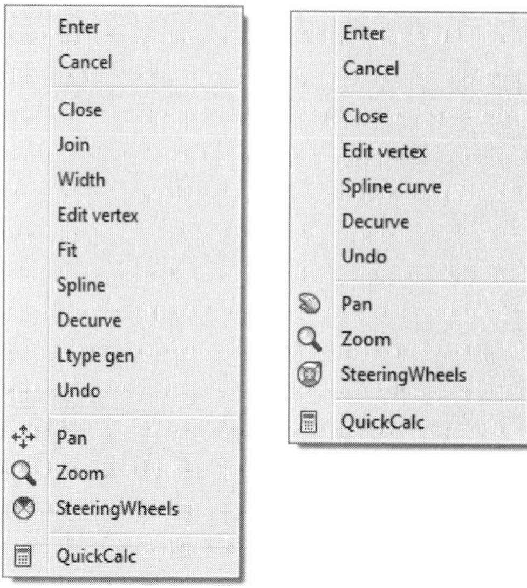

Figure 3-52 The PEDIT command's shortcut menu shows the options available for a polyline (to the left) and a 3D polyline (to the right)

- **Join** adds lines, arcs, or opened polylines to the selected line, arc, or polyline. In the event that the object is not a polyline, but a line or an arc, the AutoCAD program will ask you if you want to convert it into one.
- **Fit** converts the polyline to a continuously tangent curve called a *fit polyline,* which is made of arc segments only. For every segment, AutoCAD creates two new arc segments.
- **Spline** converts the polyline into a ***spline-fit polyline***. The endpoints of the original polyline segments become the control points of the spline-fit polyline.
- **Decurve** converts polylines, fit polylines, and spline-fit polylines to the simplest polyline made of straight segments only, eliminating all extra segments.

spline-fit polyline: Polylines and 3D polylines after they have been transformed by the **Spline** option of the **PEDIT** command.

When converting polylines to fit polylines or spline-fit polylines, the arc segments are considered to be straight. This is why you obtain the same result from a polyline regardless of whether the **Decurve** operation was previously performed or not (Figure 3-53).

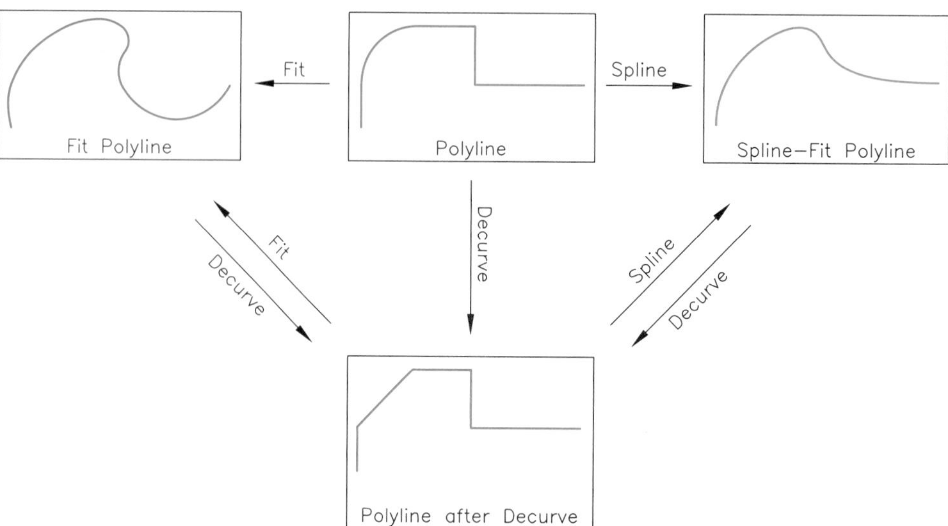

Figure 3-53 Polyline transformations

The **PEDIT** command has fewer options when used with 3D polylines. These are the most useful options:

- **Close** performs the same function as with polylines.
- **Spline curve** converts the 3D polyline to a 3D curve that is continuously curved at any point, called a *spline-fit polyline*. As with polylines, the endpoints of the polyline segments become the control points of the resulting spline-fit polyline.
- **Decurve** converts spline-fit polylines to their original 3D polylines.

Spline-Fit Polylines

The **Spline** and **Spline curve** options of the **PEDIT** command smooth polylines and 3D polylines by subdividing them into many straight segments that approximate a spline curve. This type of object is known as a spline-fit polyline.

If a spline-fit polyline is exploded, all the segments are separated. Two system variables control how polylines and 3D polylines are transformed into spline-fit polylines: **SPLINESEGS** and **SPLINETYPE**.

The **SPLINESEGS** variable controls the number of segments that polylines and 3D polylines will be divided into. The default value of this variable is **8**, but it can be set from **–32768** to **32767**. For polylines only, negative values tell AutoCAD to change the straight segments into arc segments, which are much better spline approximations.

You can change the **SPLINESEGS** value by typing the string entirely in the command line. You can also change it by changing the **Segments in a polyline curve** value on the **Display** tab of the **Options** dialog box (Figure 3-54).

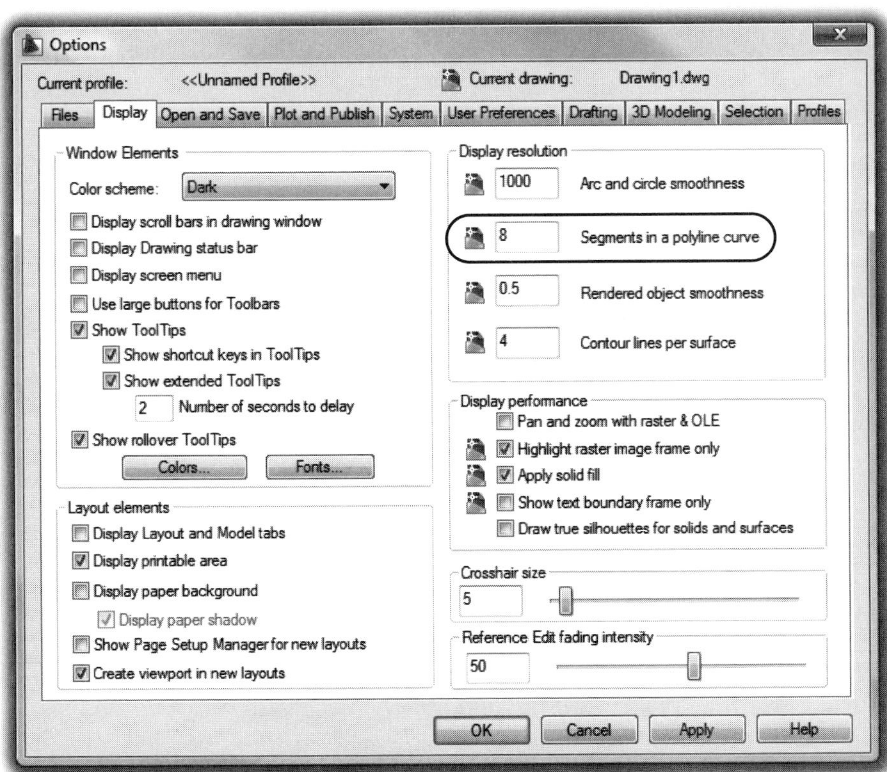

Figure 3-54 The SPLINESEGS system variable can be specified as Segments in a polyline curve value on the Display tab of the Options dialog box

The **SPLINETYPE** variable controls the type of curve (cubic or quadratic) into which the **Spline-fit Polylines** operation will transform the original polyline. To change the value of the **SPLINETYPE** variable, enter its name in the command line.

There are two values for this system variable:

- **6** for cubic spline-fit polylines (default value)
- **5** for quadratic spline-fit polylines

The quadratic spline curves are less complex mathematically because they are third-order equations, whereas the cubic splines are fourth-order equations. Figure 3-55 shows the highlighted cubic splines, together with the highlighted quadratic splines in hidden line and the original polylines.

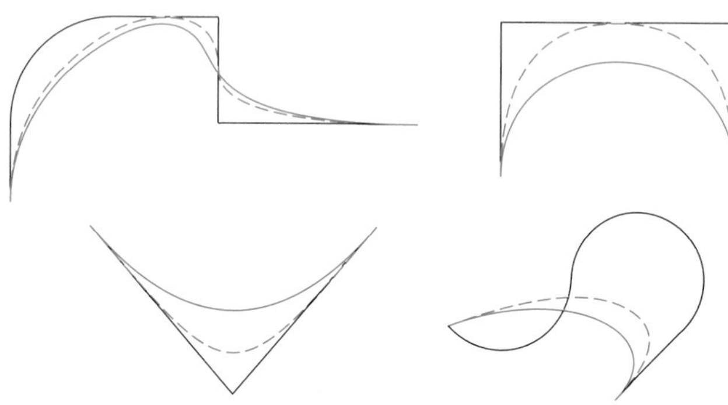

Figure 3-55 Cubic and quadratic spline-fit polyline transformations

SPLINEDIT	
Modify II Toolbar	
Ribbon Modify panel	
Pull-down Menu	Modify/ Object/ Spline
Command Line	splinedit

EDITING SPLINES: THE SPLINEDIT COMMAND

The **SPLINEDIT** command offers many editing operations that can be performed to modify splines. No operations are available, however, for splines without Fit data and spline-fit polylines. Figure 3-56 shows the **SPLINEDIT** command shortcut menu and submenus.

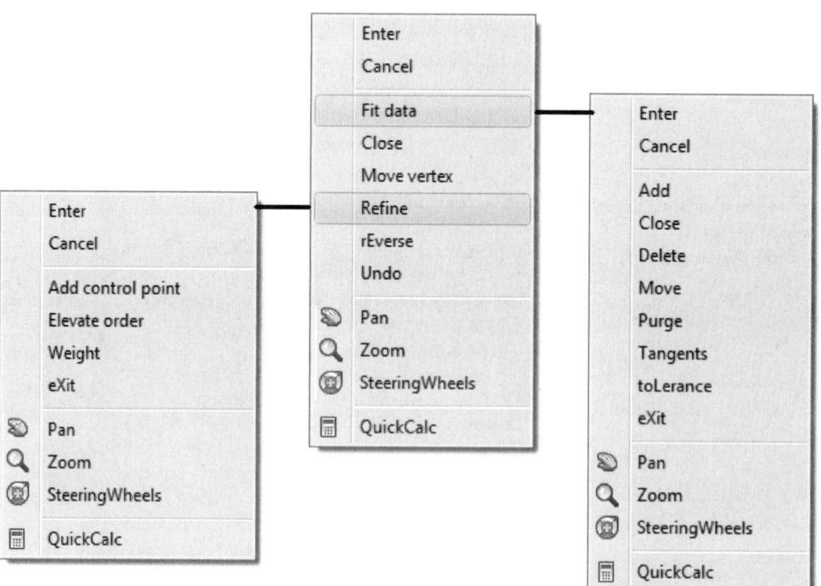

Figure 3-56 The SPLINEDIT command's shortcut menu and submenus

When you enter the **Fit data** submenu, you can **Add**, **Delete**, or **Move** the fit points. AutoCAD places an additional point in between the two highlighted points (the one you select and the one after it). The **Object Snap** needs to be turned off so you can select the desired fit point.

Other operations you can perform while in the **Fit data** submenu are: **Purge** the **Fit data** information and, together with it, its fit points; change the **Tangents** of the start and end points;

change the fit **toLerance**; and **Close** or **Open** splines, depending on the current status, without losing the **Fit data**. These operations are similar to the operations found in the **SPLINE** command menu. The fit points can be moved easily by selecting the grips, without entering the **SPLINEDIT** command.

By entering the **Refine** submenu you basically have three operations available: **Add control point**; **Elevate** the **order** of the spline to a maximum of 26; and change the **Weight** of the control points individually. This last option pulls the spline closer to the control points; the higher the **Weight** value, the closer the spline will be to the control points. All these operations will eliminate the **Fit data** at once.

In the main menu you have three other options: the **Close/Open** operation, which leads to a slightly different result; **Move** the **vertex** (control points); and **rEverse** the spline direction to switch the start and end points. The first two operations eliminate the **Fit data**.

The AutoCAD program allows you to either create a spline from scratch or transform a spline-fit polyline. In general, there are three methods you can use to obtain splines:

1. Invoking the **SPLINE** command and specifying a set of points.
2. Invoking the **SPLINE** command and selecting the **Object** option to select a spline-fit polyline, which is the only type of object that can be converted. The conversion is irreversible.
3. Invoking the **SPLINEDIT** command and selecting a spline-fit polyline.

The difference between creating a spline using the first method and using the other two methods is the **Fit data**. The information contained in a spline's **Fit data** is the fit points, the tangents of the start and end points, and the fit tolerance.

The fit points are the set of points you specified when you created the spline. All splines have control points, regardless of whether or not they have fit points.

The control points are not specified by you, but are the endpoints of the control polygon that controls the spline. The control polygon can be displayed, or not, on a spline with **Fit data** depending on the value of the **SPLFRAME** system variable.

The **SPLFRAME** system variable controls the visibility of the control polygon for splines and spline-fit polylines. When the value of this variable is **0** (default), the control polygon is not visible; when the value is **1**, it will be visible. As with many other display-related commands, a **REGEN** operation is needed after changing the value so you can see the result. The **SPLFRAME** system variable is invoked by entering its name in the command line.

Exercise 3-16: Transforming the Splines

1. Open a **NEW** drawing using the **acad** template.
2. **SAVE** it **AS** ***Exercise 3-16***.
3. Invoke the **SPLINE** command. When prompted, specify five points following more or less the order shown in Figure 3-57. After completing the spline, it should look close to the one shown in Figure 3-58.

Remember to press <**Enter**> three times to accept the default tangent directions.

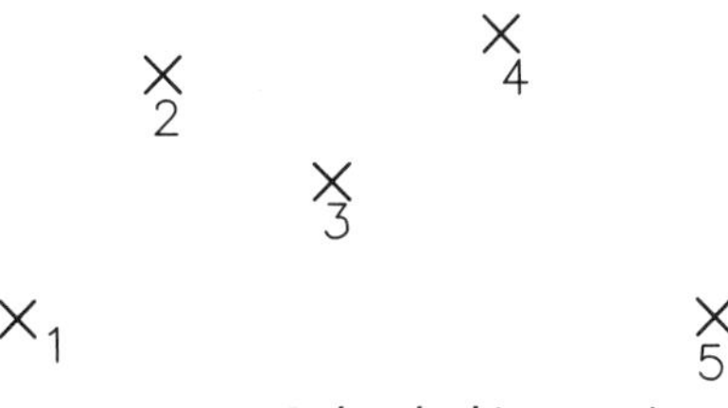

Figure 3-57 Ordered arbitrary points through which the spline will go

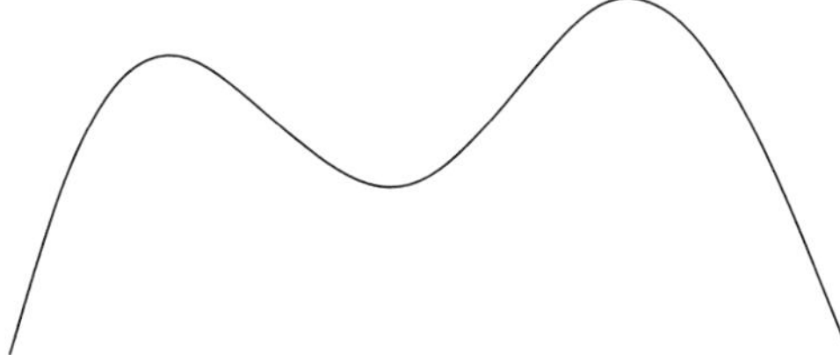

Figure 3-58 After completing the spline

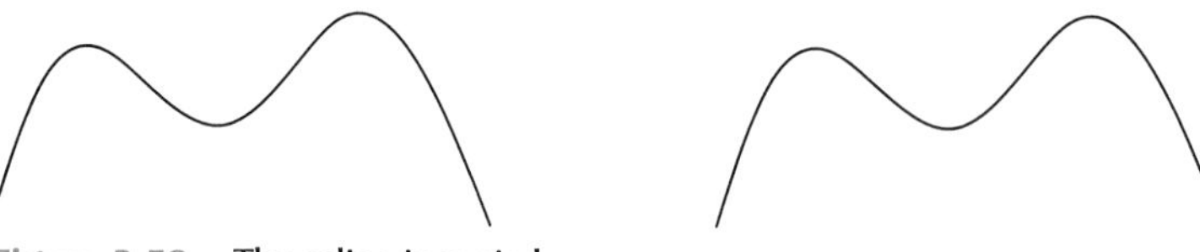

Figure 3-59 The spline is copied

4. With **ORTHO** activated, **COPY** the spline to the right (Figure 3-59).
5. Invoke the **SPLINEDIT** command and respond to the prompts as follows:

```
Select spline: Select the spline on the left.
Enter an option [Fit data/Close/Move vertex/Refine/rEverse/Undo]: f ↵
Enter a fit data option
[Add/Close/Delete/Move/Purge/Tangents/toLerance/eXit] <eXit>: p ↵
Enter an option [Close/Move vertex/Refine/rEverse/Undo/eXit] <eXit>: x ↵
```

6. Without having any command in progress, select the two splines in order to reveal their grips (Figure 3-60).
7. Press the **<Esc>** key to unselect the objects.

Note:
After the **Fit data** of the left spline have been purged, its grips appear at the control points when the left spline is selected instead of appearing at the fit points, the default location.

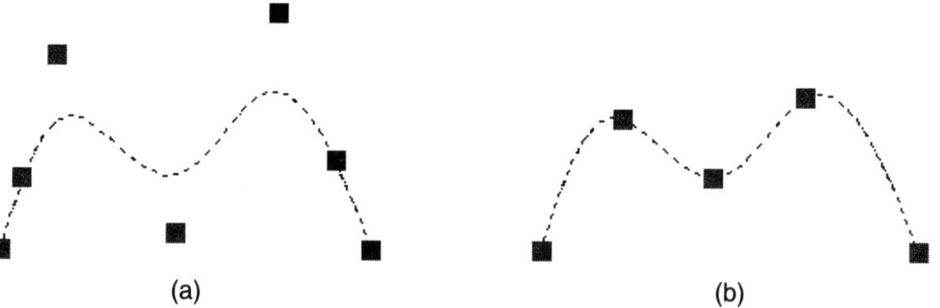

Figure 3-60 Splines selected, without (A) and with (B) Fit data information

8. Invoke the **SPLFRAME** command to turn on the display of the control polygon.

```
Enter new value for SPLFRAME <0>: 1 ↵
```

9. Invoke the **REGEN** command. The drawing should now look like Figure 3-61.
10. Select the two splines again to reveal their grips (Figure 3-62).

Note:
Now the right spline shows both the fit points and the control points.

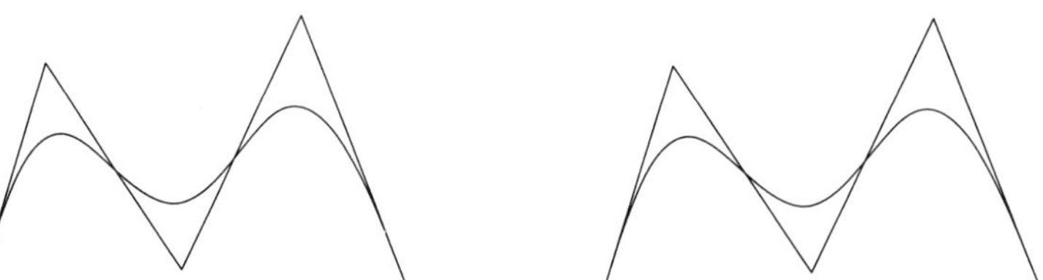

Figure 3-61 Splines displayed after the SPLFRAME system variable is turned on

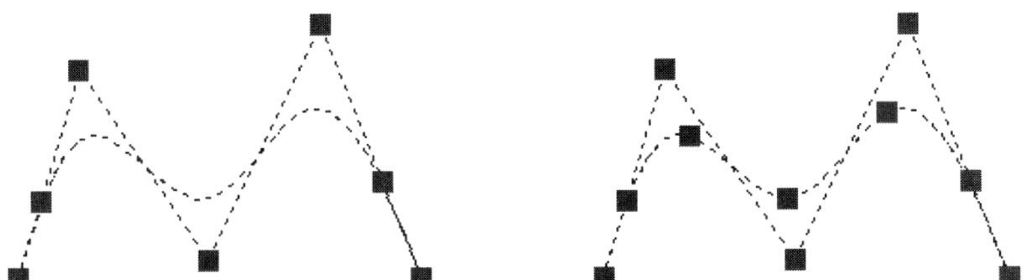

Figure 3-62 Selecting the splines reveals that the one on the left has lost its Fit data

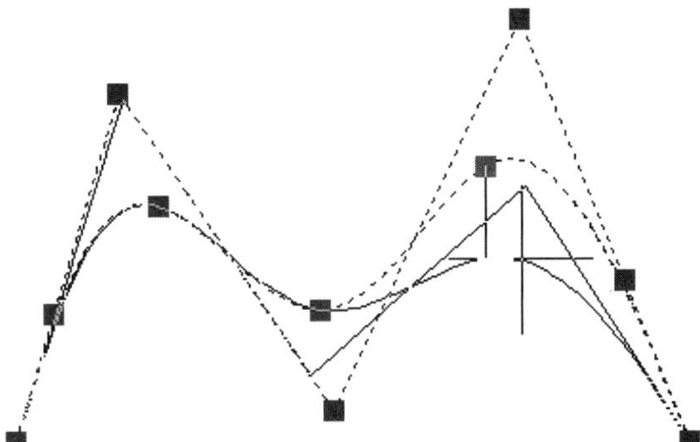

Figure 3-63 Moving a fit points grip

11. Select the fit points grip shown in the right spline and stretch it downward, as shown in Figure 3-63.
12. Select the control points grip and move it upward, as shown in Figure 3-65.
13. **SAVE** the drawing.

> **Note:**
> The spline is readjusted, without losing the fit points (Figure 3-64).

The splines created can lose the **Fit data** after any of these editing operations.

- **Purge**
- **Refine**
- **Move** a control point or control vertex
- **Add** control points

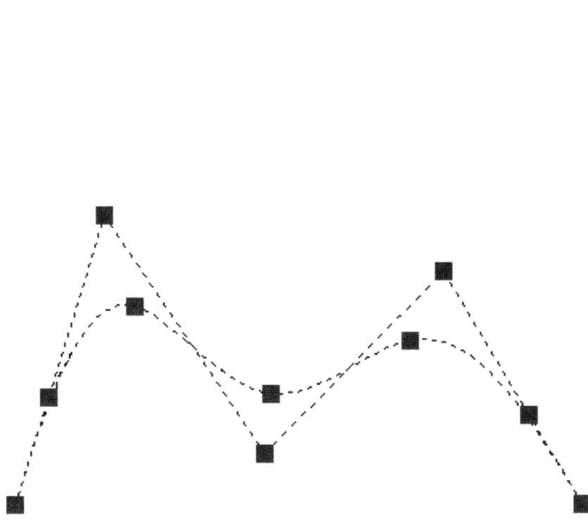

Figure 3-64 The spline maintains its fit points

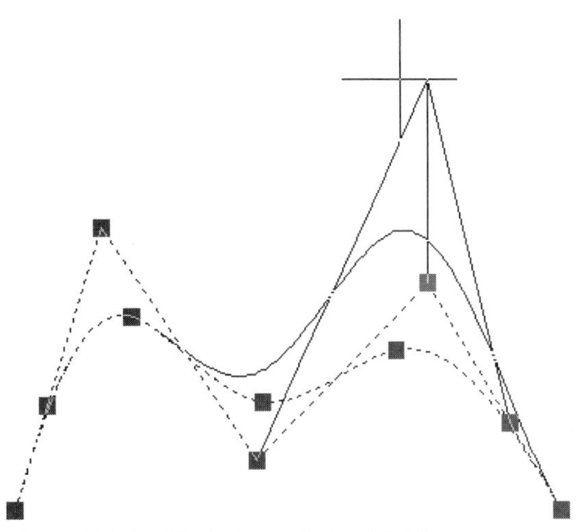

Figure 3-65 Moving a control point grip

- **Open** or **Close** with the option of the main menu
- **Elevate** the **order**
- Change the **Weight** of a control point.

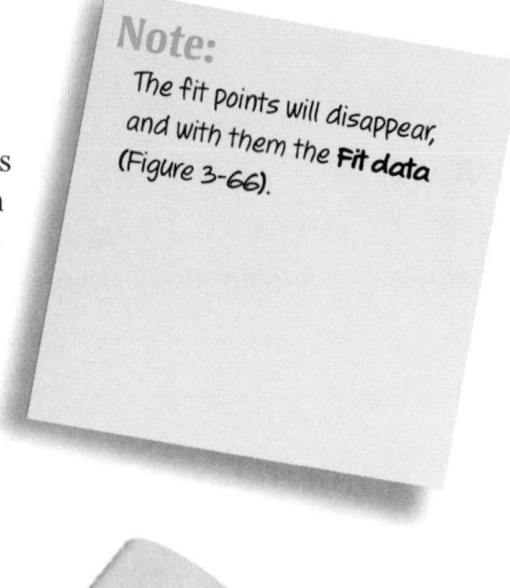

Note:
The fit points will disappear, and with them the **Fit data** (Figure 3-66).

In practice, splines are not exactly the type of objects most used to create 3D models. Using more common geometry, such as straight segments and arcs, can lead to excellent results in most cases without necessarily creating a much simpler 3D model.

Most of the time, splines are not intentionally created but are obtained as the result of extracting them from existing geometry (e.g., the edge formed by the intersection of two faces (Figure 3-67).

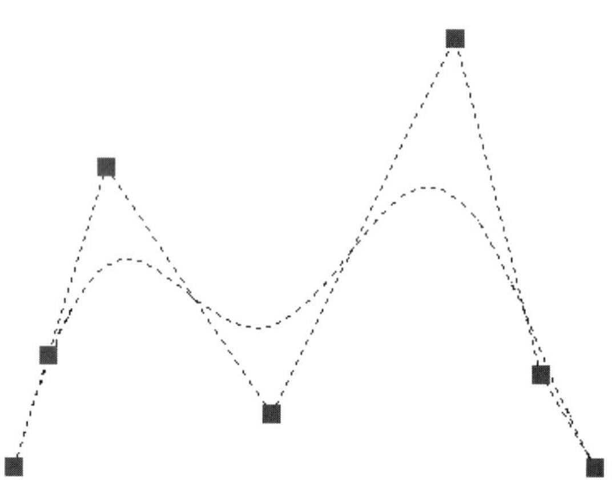

Figure 3-66 The spline does not maintain its Fit data

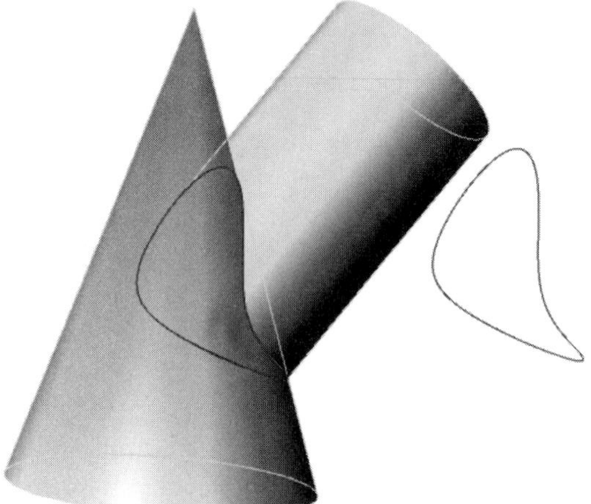

Figure 3-67 A spline edge formed by the intersection of two faces

Using Grips to Edit Wires

When selecting a wire without any command in progress, the object not only changes its appearance, indicating that it has been selected, but also shows its grips. This operation is known as "revealing the object's grips." Figure 3-68 shows a group of different wire objects on top, and the same objects after their grips have been revealed at the bottom.

Figure 3-68 Objects before and after revealing their grips

The grips must be turned on so they show up when selecting an object. You turn the grips on in the **Selection** tab of the **Options** dialog box by checking the **Enable grips** option (Figure 3-69). You can also change the size and color of the grips.

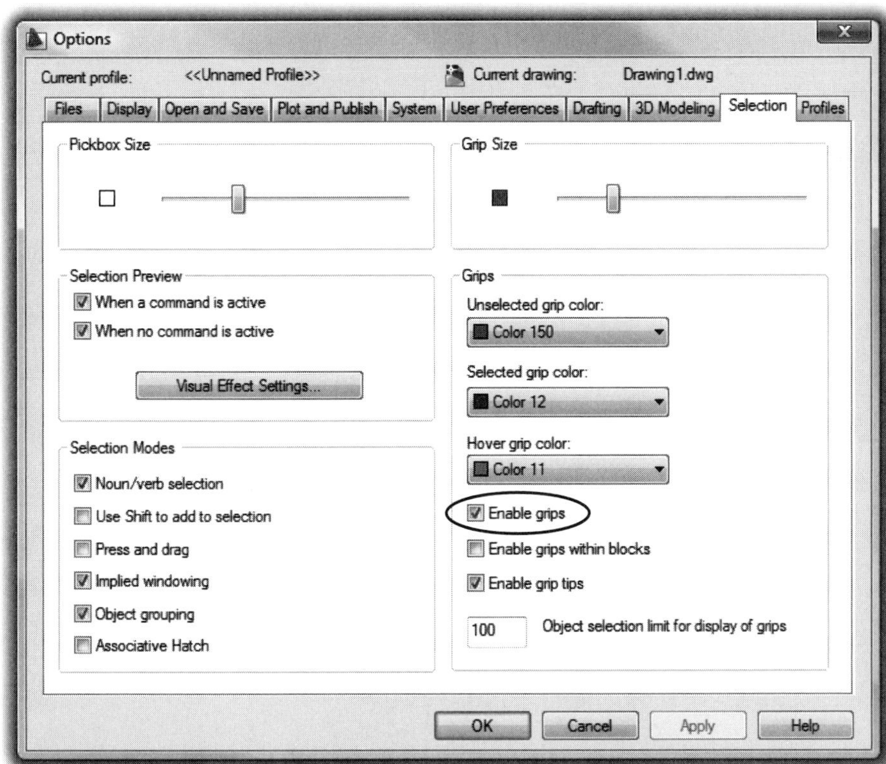

Figure 3-69 The grips can be turned on in the Selection tab of the Options dialog box by checking the Enable grips

The grips are located at strategic places on the object. For example, a line will reveal a grip at each endpoint, and another one at the midpoint; a circle will reveal a grip on each quadrant, and another one in its center point. A polyline shows grips at each endpoint of the line segments, and at the endpoints and midpoints of the arc segments.

An originally blue grip changes its color to green when it is hovered, and to red when it is selected. Selecting any grip activates the grip editing routine, allowing you to perform one of the five following operations: **STRETCH**, **MOVE**, **ROTATE**, **SCALE**, and **MIRROR**.

To move on to the next operation, you must press the **<Space>** key.

```
** STRETCH **
Specify stretch point or [Base point/Copy/Undo/eXit]:
** MOVE **
Specify move point or [Base point/Copy/Undo/eXit]:
** ROTATE **
Specify rotation angle or [Base point/Copy/Undo/Reference/eXit]:
** SCALE **
Specify scale factor or [Base point/Copy/Undo/Reference/eXit]:
** MIRROR **
Specify second point or [Base point/Copy/Undo/eXit]:
```

The **STRETCH** command is the default and the most frequently used operation of this group. Stretching a selected grip modifies the geometry of the object so that the selected grip is placed in another location. You can select multiple grips by holding down the **<Shift>** key before selecting them. You can also create copies of the selected objects by selecting the **Copy** option within any operation.

Besides the standard grips, arcs and helixes also reveal special triangular grips, which allow you to perform other operations in a specific direction. For example, you can lengthen an arc by grabbing one of its triangular grips at the endpoints. Pulling one of the triangular grips along the axis of a helix modifies its **Height** value and the value of another parameter, depending on which one is constrained.

Grips and Their Relation to the UCS

The behavior of the grips is affected by the current UCS. Figure 3-70(a) shows the grips revealed when the current UCS is parallel to the object's UCS. Figure 3-70(b) shows the same objects selected when the current UCS is not parallel to the object's UCS.

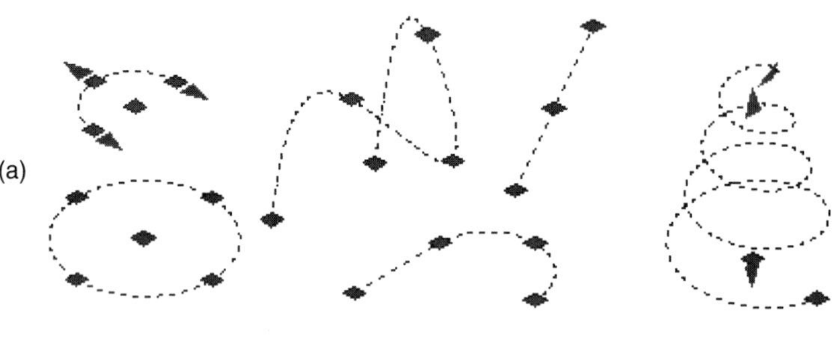

Figure 3-70 The grips of a planar object can be pulled only within its UCS, whereas the grips of a nonplanar object can be pulled in any direction

The grips of a planar object are always aligned with the *XY* plane of the UCS that it belongs to. When stretching the grips of planar objects, the UCS temporarily changes to the object's UCS, allowing you to edit the object only in its plane.

The grips of nonplanar objects, on the other hand, can be stretched in any direction, and the UCS maintains its current orientation. The grips of nonplanar objects are aligned with the *XY* plane of the current UCS.

The Move Grip Tool

When the current visual style is not **2D Wireframe**, the move grip tool, in addition to the object's grips, also appears when selecting the objects. You can choose to use the standard grips selection by selecting a grip directly. However, placing the mouse for more than a second over a particular grip without selecting it will relocate the move grip tool to this grip, which changes its color to yellow (Figure 3-71).

To relocate a grip using the move grip tool, you must click one of the grip's elements instead of clicking on the grip itself (Figure 3-72).

FOR MORE DETAILS See the **3DMOVE** command section for more information regarding the use of the move grip tool.

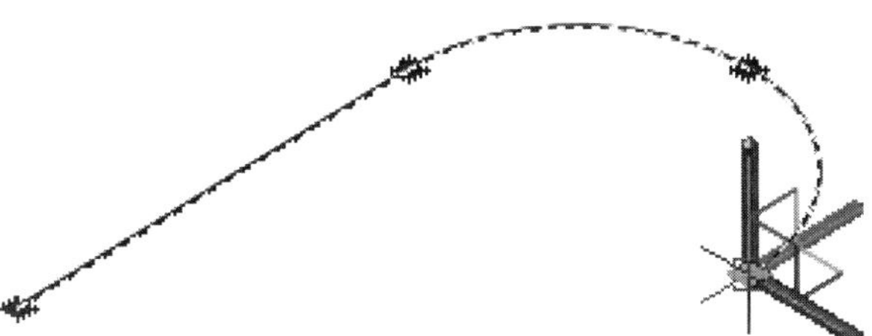

Figure 3-71 The move grip tool

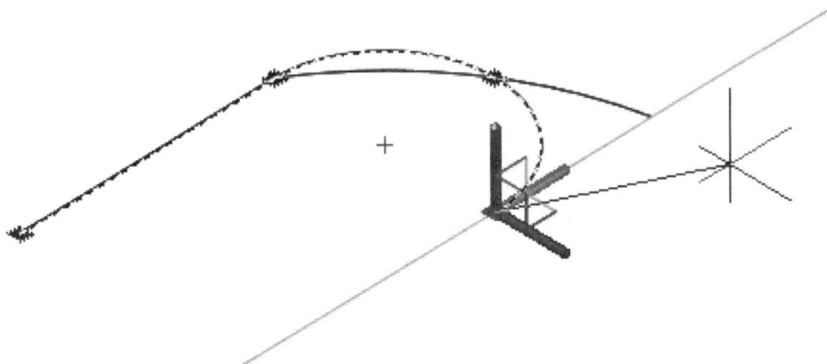

Figure 3-72 Clicking the Y-axis of the move grip tool constrains the movement of the selected grip along the Y-axis

SUMMARY

Rather than showing you an isolated way of representing 3D models, this chapter has focused on how objects commonly used in 2D work behave in a 3D environment, and demonstrated the way they relate to the UCS. It has also given you key aspects to consider when using the standard 2D commands to modify objects in a 3D environment, allowing you to compare them with other commands that focus particularly on 3D modifications. You also learned about creating and editing complex objects with special uses in 3D, such as splines, polylines, 3D polylines, and helixes.

Understanding the behavior of wire objects or curves in 3D space is essential for success in 3D modeling. Always remember that regardless of which final objects you use to represent a 3D model, wire objects will always be involved.

CHAPTER TEST QUESTIONS

Multiple Choice

1. Which of the following objects can be drawn in the 3D space, without necessarily being parallel to the *XY* plane of the current UCS?
   a. Circle
   b. Line
   c. Arc
   d. Polyline
2. Which of the following can you perform using the move grip tool?
   a. Move the objects constrained to one of the three planes of the current UCS
   b. Move objects along one of the three axes of the current UCS
   c. Move an object to any point in the 3D space
   d. All of the above
3. Which of the following commands allow you to rotate objects around any specified imaginary axis, regardless of the current UCS?
   a. **ROTATE**
   b. **3DMIRROR**
   c. **3DROTATE**
   d. None of the above
4. Which of the following is not one of the options that define the imaginary mirror plane in the **3DMIRROR** command?
   a. **Xaxis**
   b. **XY**
   c. **Zaxis**
   d. **3points**

5. Which of the following characteristics best describes a spline curve?
   a. Continuous
   b. Continuously tangent
   c. Continuously curved
   d. Continuously tangent and curved
6. Which of the following objects can be edited by using the **PEDIT** command?
   a. Circle
   b. Polyline
   c. Spline
   d. None of the above
7. From a 3D viewing point, a circle appears to be an ellipse. Under what conditions can a circle appear completely round?
   a. When it is parallel to the *XY* plane
   b. When it is created using the **Ttr** (tan tan radius) option
   c. When it is located on a plane parallel to the viewing plane
   d. All of the above
8. When using the **MIRROR** command from a 3D viewing point, which of the following may cause you not to see the object snap when the command is certainly recognizing a snap point?
   a. The current *XY* plane is not parallel to the viewing plane.
   b. The projection of the point onto the current *XY* plane is out of the display.
   c. None of the above
   d. All of the above
9. Which of the following is not one of the options you could use to define the axis of rotation with the **ROTATE3D** command?
   a. **Xaxis**
   b. **XY**
   c. **Zaxis**
   d. **2points**
10. Which of the following is not one of the elements that define the geometric characteristics of helixes?
   a. **Turn Height**
   b. **Bottom Radius**
   c. **Start Angle**
   d. **Turns**

Matching

Column A	Column B
a. SPLINESEGS	1. 2D or 3D spiral curve that coils around an axis
b. ROTATE3D	2. Planar object made of straight and arc segments
c. SPLINETYPE	3. Sets the number of segments for the spline fit process
d. Spline-fit polyline	4. Point requested by the **ALIGN** command
e. 3D polyline	5. A smooth 3D curve tangent and continuous at any point
f. Source point	6. Versatile command useful for 3D operations
g. Polyline	7. Polylines and 3D polylines smoothed by adding segments
h. Helix	8. Command that allows you to rotate objects about any axis
i. Spline	9. Sets the type of curve for the spline fit process
j. ALIGN	10. 3D object made of straight segments only

True or False

1. True or False: A 3D solid object can also be considered to be a wire object if any of the wireframe visual styles is active.
2. True or False: Both the **RECTANGLE** and the **POLYGON** commands generate polylines.
3. True or False: With the UCS projection option of the **TRIM** command, you can trim wire objects even though the object used as a cutting edge does not intersect the object to be trimmed in the 3D space.
4. True or False: By properly specifying the source and destination points, you can use the **ALIGN** command to rotate a cylinder around its axis.
5. True or False: The **Zaxis** option defines a plane normal to a vector in both the **MIRROR3D** and the **ROTATE3D** commands.
6. True or False: Circles and arcs are always created parallel to the *XY* plane of the current UCS.
7. True or False: A 3D polyline is a single continuous object made of lines and arc segments.
8. True or False: The parallel copies of planar curves created with the **OFFSET** command are placed on the *XY* plane of the current UCS.
9. True or False: You can **COPY** and **MOVE** an object throughout the 3D space, regardless of which UCS was current when the object was created and which UCS is current at the moment of the operation.
10. True or False: You can stretch a polyline by selecting one of the revealed grips and move it to any point in the 3D space.

CHAPTER TUTORIALS

Tutorial 3-1: The Bracket Wireframe

This tutorial will show you how to develop the 3D model that you have used in some of the exercises. It will also help you practice using common commands in a 3D environment. Bear in mind that when working in 3D, the most important aspect is controlling the UCS. Figure 3-73 shows the dimensions of the object, the edges of which you will represent three-dimensionally using wire objects.

1. Start a **NEW** drawing using the **acad** template.
2. **SAVE** it **AS** ***Tutorial 3-1***.
3. Draw the shape shown in Figure 3-74.

TIP You can start by creating two concentric circles and the three straight lines, and then trim the bigger circle.

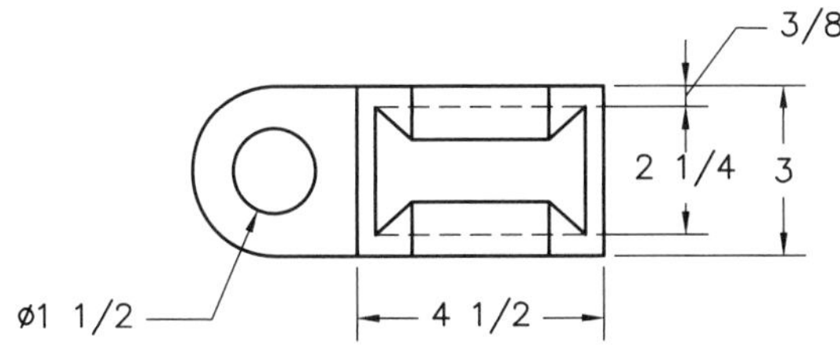

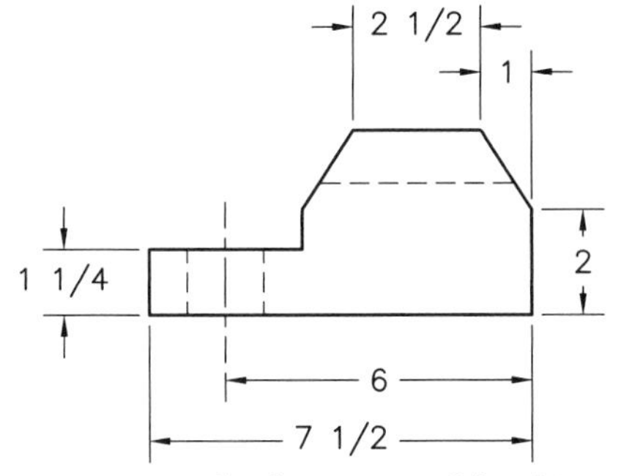

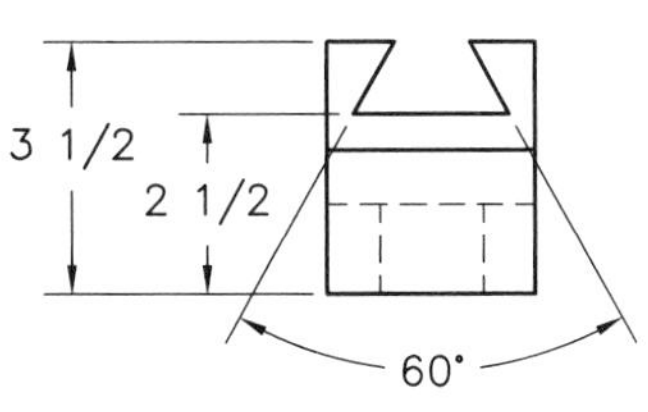

Figure 3-73 The dimensions of the object

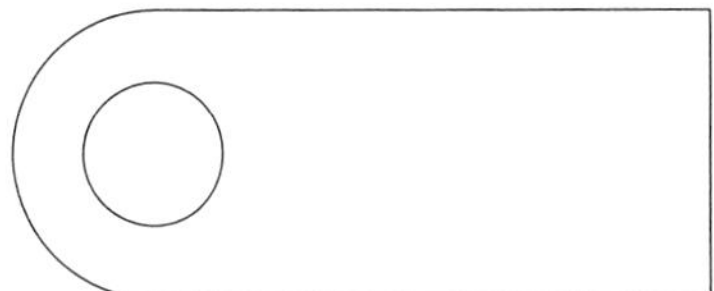

Figure 3-74 Drawing the first objects

4. Select the **SW Isometric** viewing point, using any of the methods you studied before.
5. Select the **Front** orthographic UCS from the **UCS II** toolbar drop-down window.

6. **COPY** all the objects 1¼″ up along the *Y*-axis (Figure 3-75).
7. Select the **Top** orthographic UCS. **MOVE** the small vertical line **4½″** to the left and **TRIM** the rest of the two horizontal lines.
8. Select the **Left** orthographic UCS. Draw the two **3/4″**-long vertical polylines shown in Figure 3-76.

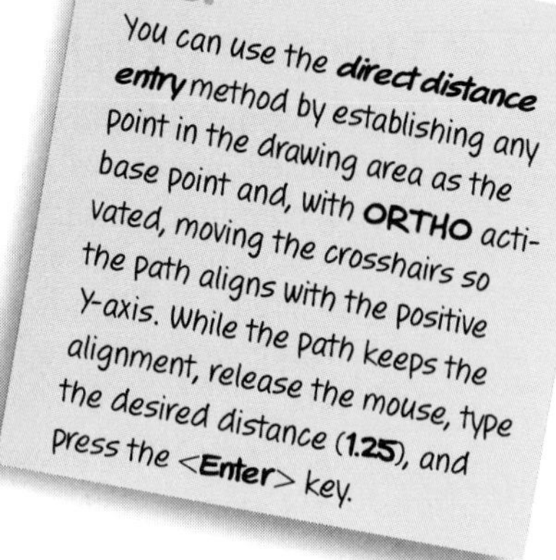
Note:
You can use the ***direct distance entry*** method by establishing any point in the drawing area as the base point and, with **ORTHO** activated, moving the crosshairs so the path aligns with the positive Y-axis. While the path keeps the alignment, release the mouse, type the desired distance (**1.25**), and press the <**Enter**> key.

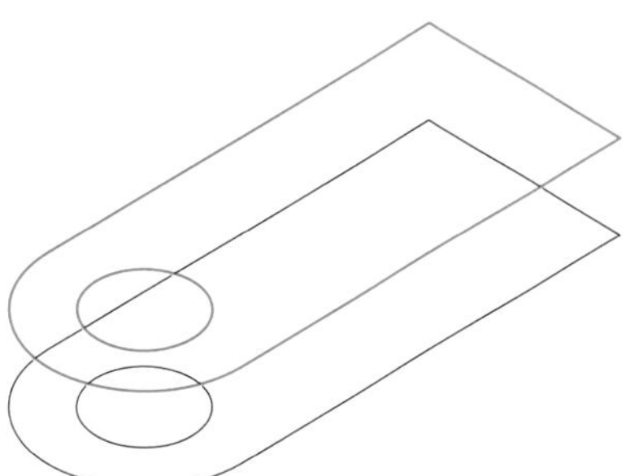

Figure 3-75 The objects are copied up

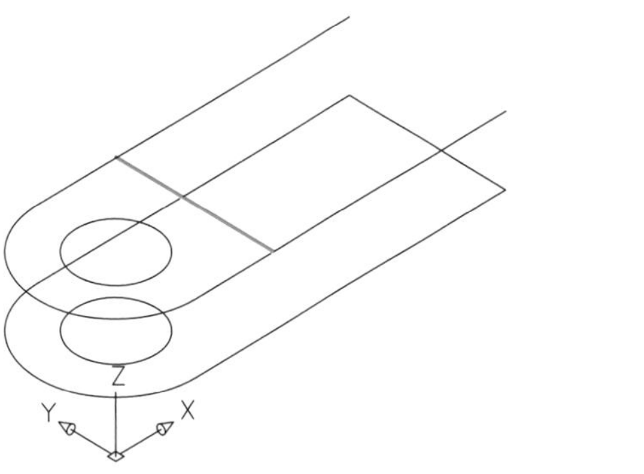

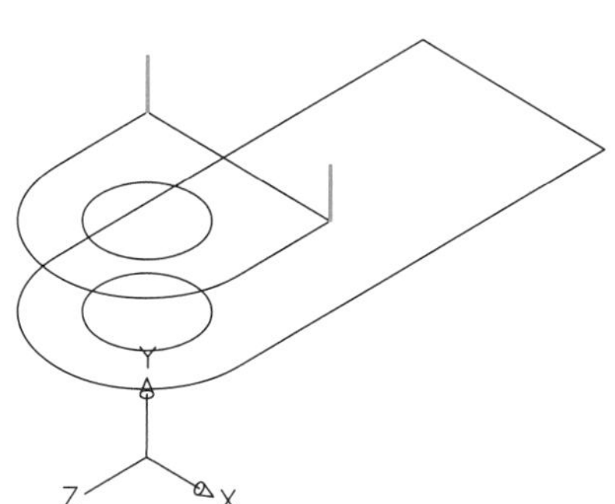

Figure 3-76 After placing the two vertical lines

9. With **Ortho** mode on, draw a polyline from point 1 to point 2 (Figure 3-77(a)). When you are close to the second endpoint, you will notice that the snap symbol is projected automatically onto a plane parallel to the *XY* plane where the first point was specified (Figure 3-77(b)).

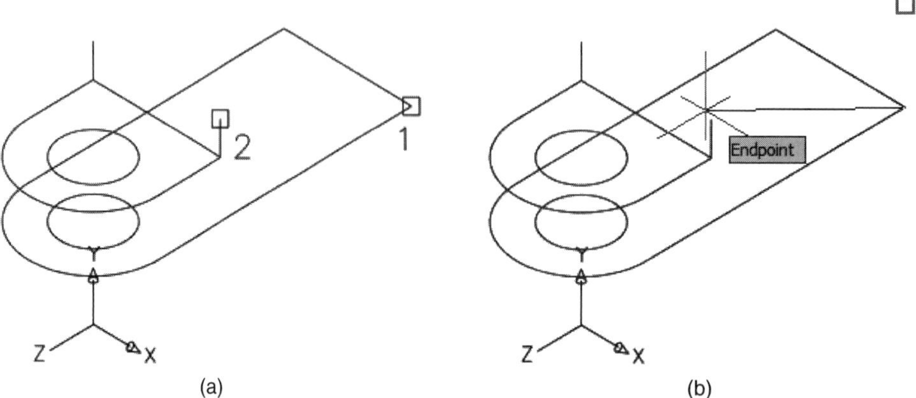

Figure 3-77 When specifying the second point for the polyline, the snap symbol is projected onto a plane parallel to the XY plane of the first point

10. **COPY** the polyline from endpoint to endpoint as shown in Figure 3-78.
11. Select the **Front** orthographic UCS.

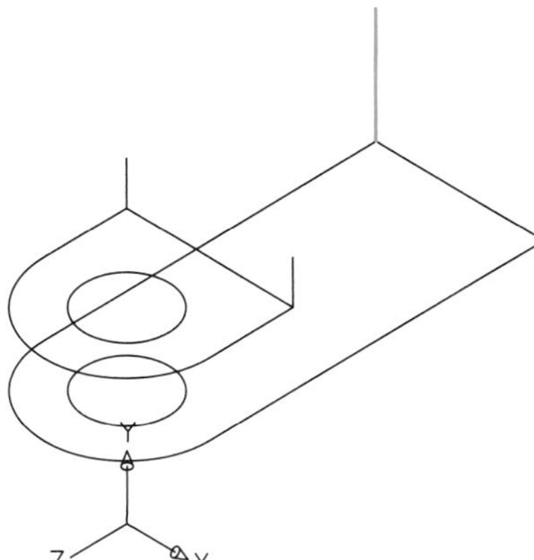

Figure 3-78 The polyline is copied

12. Draw a line from the endpoint of one of the short vertical lines to the point **@1.00,1.50** (Figure 3-79).
13. Draw a horizontal line from the endpoint of one of the short vertical lines to the endpoint of the longer vertical line.
14. **MIRROR** the inclined line using the geometry of the horizontal line (Figure 3-80).

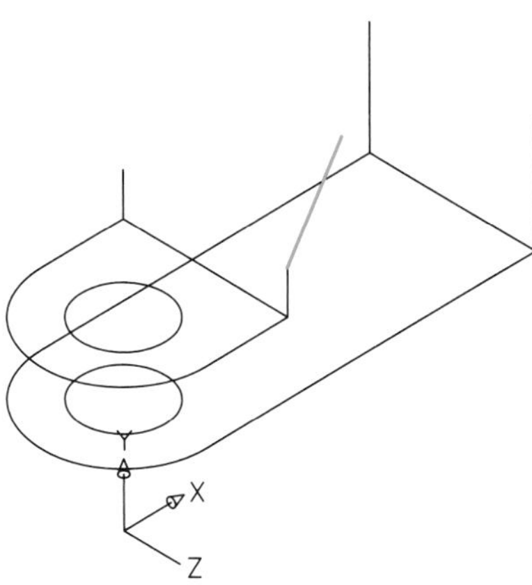

Figure 3-79 After placing the inclined line

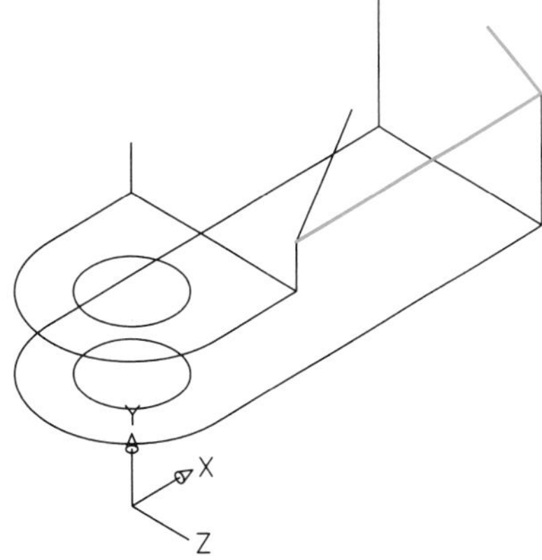

Figure 3-80 The inclined line is mirrored

TIP

When asked for the first point of the mirror line, place the cursor close to the midpoint of the horizontal line. AutoCAD projects the midpoint onto the *XY* plane. With **Ortho** mode on, specify the second point anywhere above or below the first one.

15. **ERASE** the horizontal line.
16. **COPY** the two inclined lines, from any endpoint on the front face of the model to the same point on the back face.
17. Select the **Top** orthographic UCS.
18. Relocate its origin to the top endpoint of any inclined line.
19. Using the **RECTANGLE** command, draw a rectangle by selecting any two top diagonal endpoints. The model should now look like Figure 3-81(a).
20. Draw the two lines that represent the edges between the vertical faces and the inclined faces (Figure 3-81b).

Note:
These lines could have been mirrored as well, if the **Top** UCS had been selected previously.

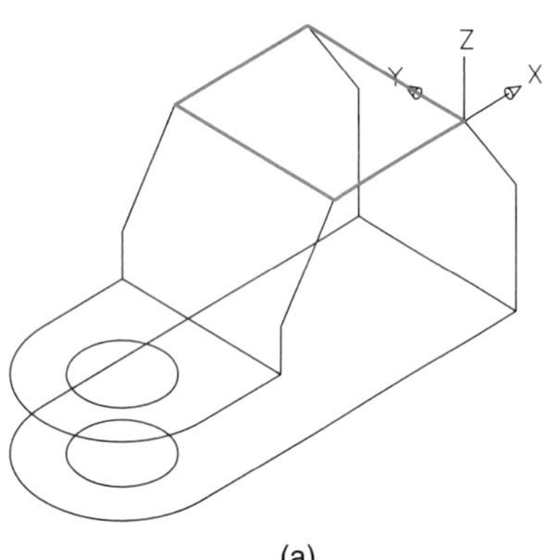

(a)

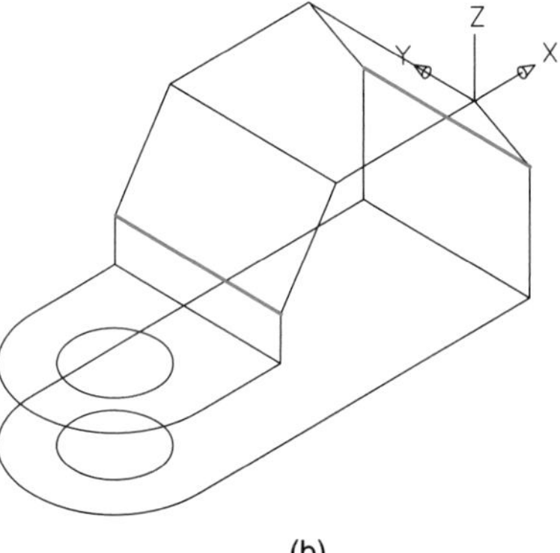

(b)

Figure 3-81 Placing the top rectangle, and then the two highlighted lines

Note:
Your model is almost finished. All you need to do is add the geometry that represents the slot on the top. Our purpose now is to find points 1 and 2, which are the vertices of the edge of the intersection of one of the slot faces with the inclined face (Figure 3-82). The rest is simple; it can be done using the **MIRROR** command.

21. Select the **Front** orthographic UCS.
22. **EXPLODE** the rectangle.
23. **COPY** the top edge of the back face **1.00″** down (Figure 3-83).
24. **EXTEND** the new line to the two inclined edges of the same face (Figure 3-84).

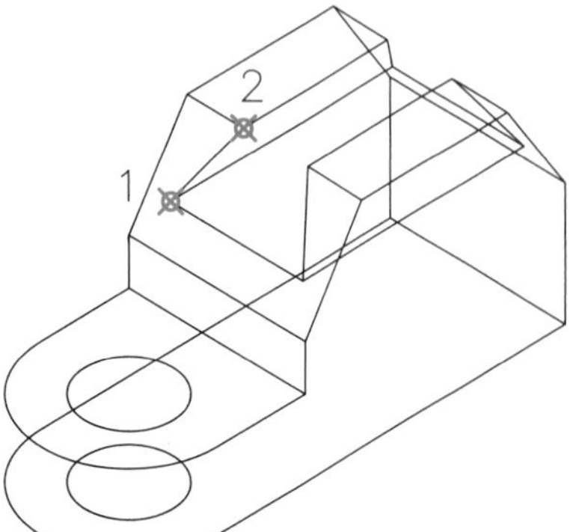

Figure 3-82 The next task is to find points 1 and 2

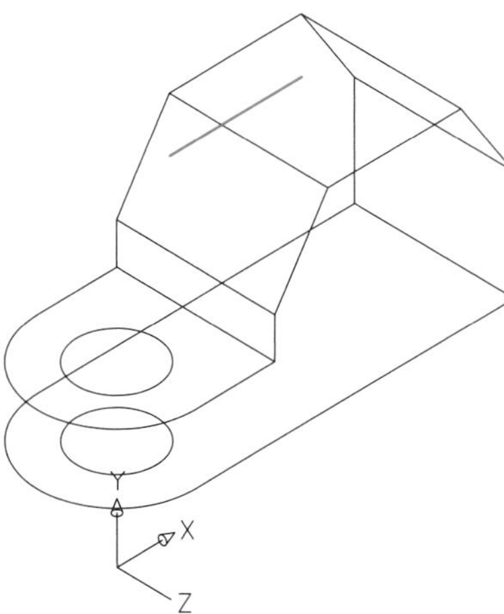

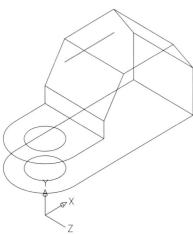

Figure 3-83 The top line is copied

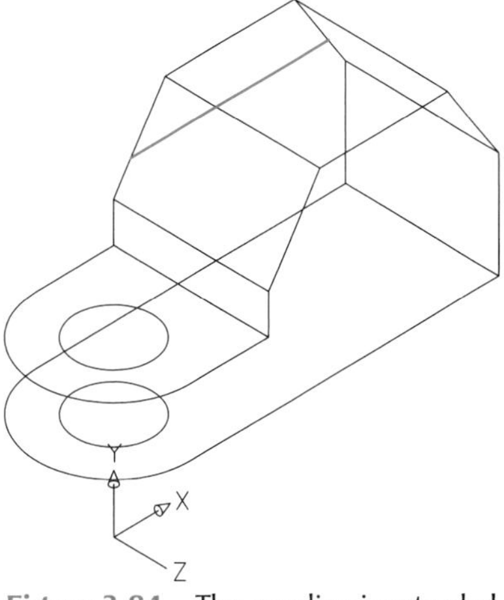

Figure 3-84 The new line is extended

Note:
Remember that both entries (fractional or decimal) are accepted the same way by the AutoCAD program. Because the distance from the back or front face to point 2 is not known, finding point 2 is probably the most difficult part. You do know, however, that the inside walls of the slot are symmetrically inclined 60°.

25. Select the **Top** orthographic UCS.
26. **MOVE** the new line **3/8″** (0.375″) along the *Y*-axis inside the model (Figure 3-85). By doing this you have found point 1.

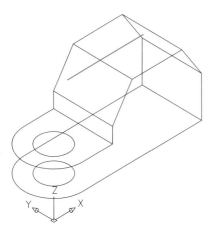

Figure 3-85 The extended line is moved in to find point 2

Note:
The line is trimmed by projecting the cutting edge toward the XY plane of the current UCS.

27. Select the **Left** orthographic UCS.
28. Draw a **2.50″** vertical line from point 1 [Figure 3-86(a)].
29. **ROTATE** the line **−30**° using point 1 as the base point [Figure 3-86(b)].
30. **TRIM** line **2**, using the top-left wire 1 as the cutting edge [Figure 3-87(a)]. The result is shown in Figure 3-87(b).
31. Select the **Top** UCS.
32. Draw a line from the endpoint of the trimmed line perpendicular to the top-right edge [Figure 3-88(a)].
33. **TRIM** the new line using the top-left edge [Figure 3-88(b)].

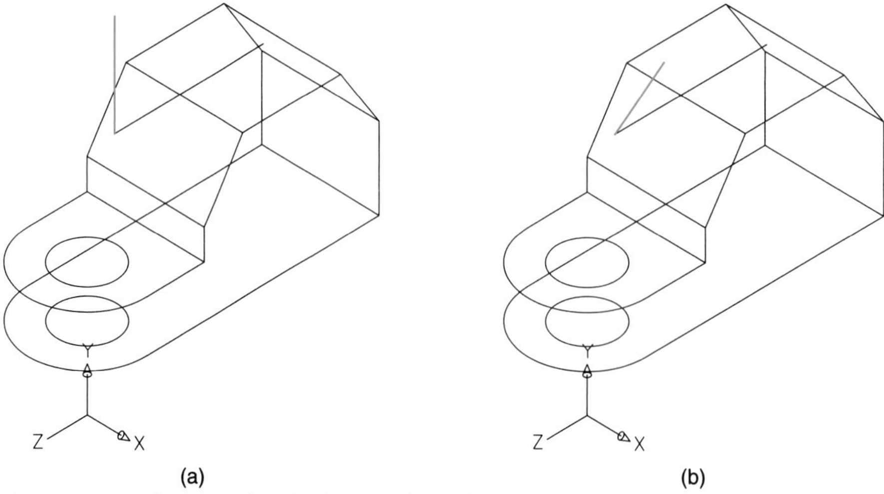

Figure 3-86 A new vertical line is created and then rotated

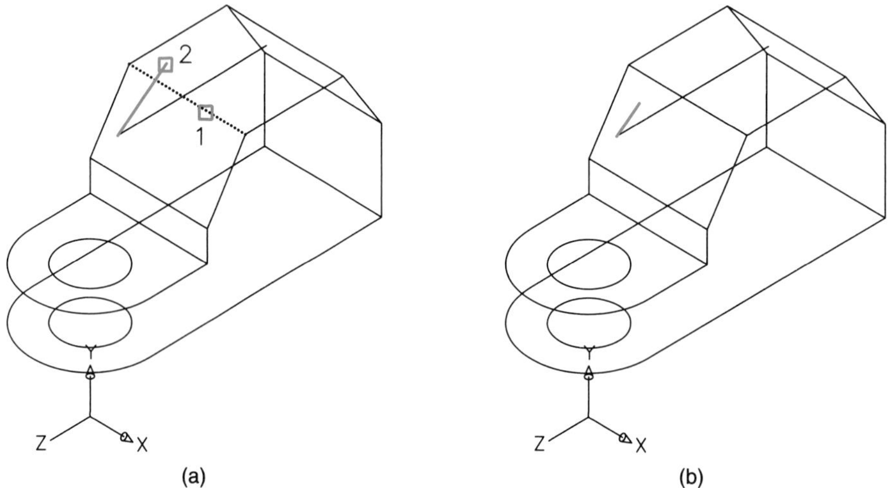

Figure 3-87 The line is trimmed using the UCS projection method

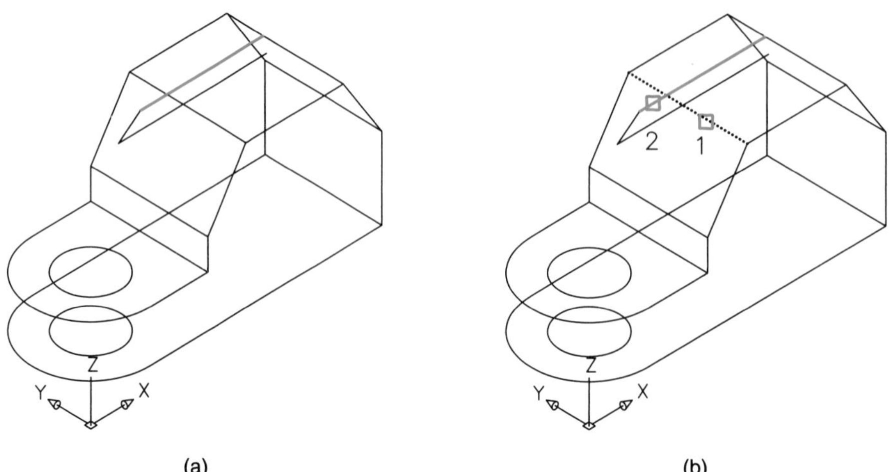

Figure 3-88 A new horizontal line is created and then trimmed

34. You have already found the two points needed (1 and 2). **ERASE** the small line 1 (Figure 3-89).
35. **MIRROR** the top and bottom edges of the slot face. Select the midpoint of any edge aligned with the *Y*-axis as the first point of the mirror line (Figure 3-90).

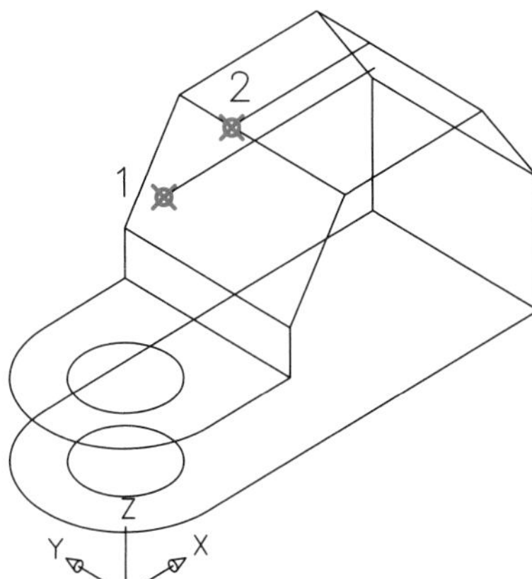

Figure 3-89 Points 1 and 2 are found

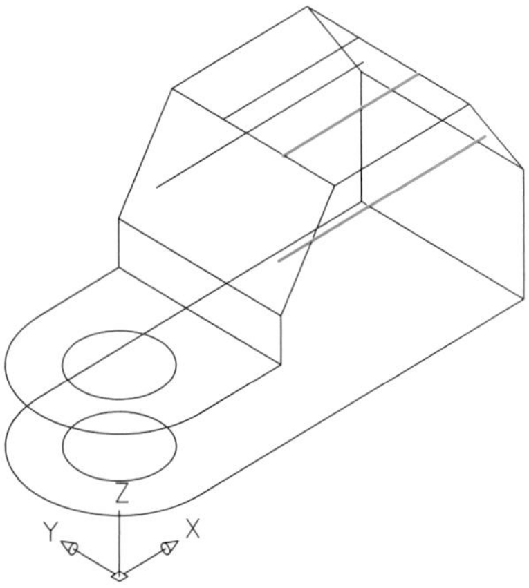

Figure 3-90 The two lines are mirrored

36. **TRIM** the top edges as shown in Figure 3-91. Select the two highlighted lines as cutting edges.
37. Invoke the **3DPOLY** command and draw the two highlighted 3D polylines as shown in Figure 3-92. Zoom in and out as needed.
38. Invoke the **3DORBIT** command to inspect the 3D model.
39. **SAVE** the drawing.

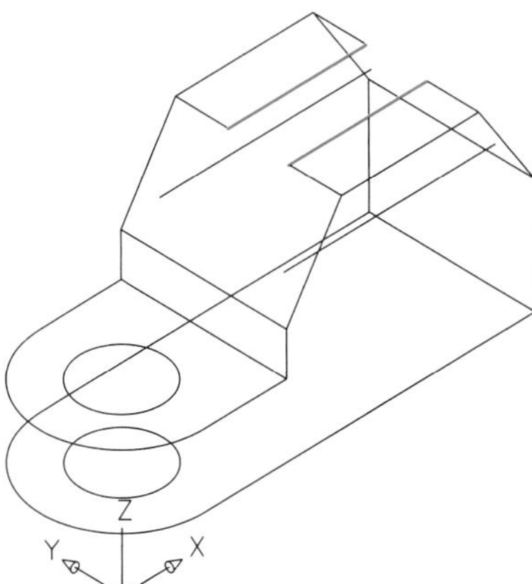

Figure 3-91 The two horizontal lines are trimmed

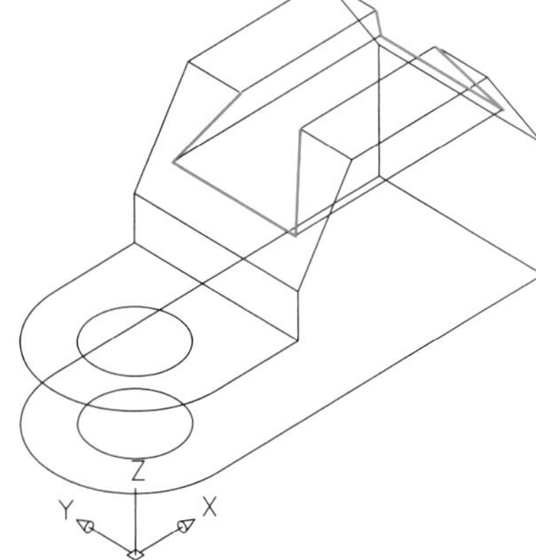

Figure 3-92 The two 3D polylines complete the 3D model

As you probably have noticed, building a wireframe model is certainly a laborious task. The main reason is that you have to place each of the wires one by one. Besides, the use of 3D models represented by wire objects is very limited; visual aids, such as the **HIDE** operation or applying the different visual styles, do not have any effect on them.

Tutorial 3-2: The Mouse Wireframe

The faceted surface representation of a 3D model requires creating a wire skeleton of the model first. The wire skeleton must be placed in such a way that it can be used for this particular type of representation of 3D models. The following tutorial will walk you through this first stage of creating a faceted surface 3D model.

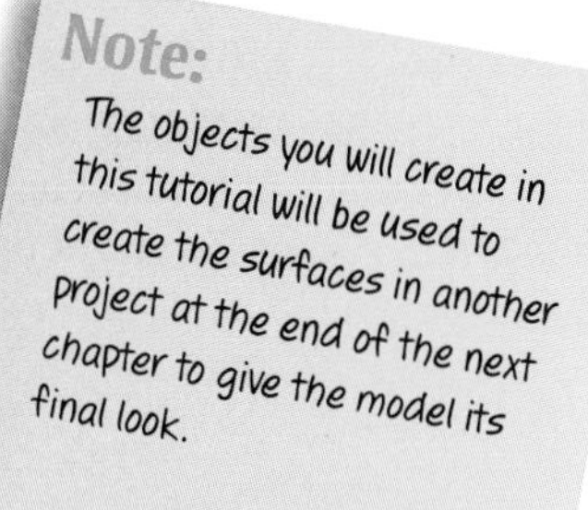

Note:
The objects you will create in this tutorial will be used to create the surfaces in another project at the end of the next chapter to give the model its final look.

1. Start a **NEW** drawing using the **acad** template.
2. **SAVE** the drawing **AS** ***Tutorial 3-2***.
3. Draw the shape shown in Figure 3-93.
4. Select the **SE Isometric** viewing point.

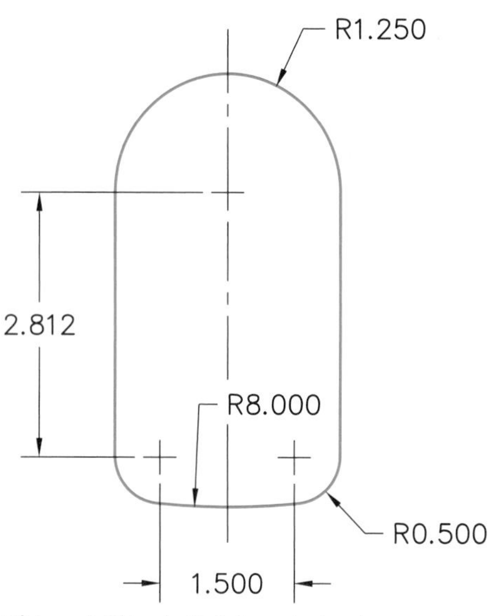

Figure 3-93 Initial shape to be drawn on the XY plane

Remember not to place any dimensions or centerlines. These are not necessary unless you are generating a drawing document.

If you need additional help, Figure 3-94 will give you additional hints on how to start.

Because the model is symmetric, you can consider using the **MIRROR** command in order to save time.

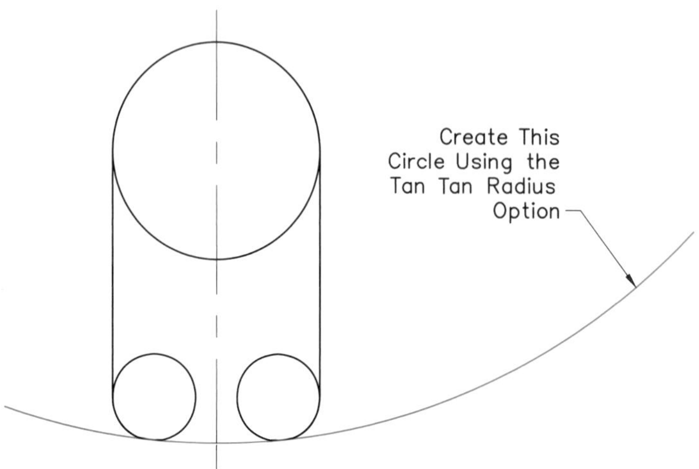

Figure 3-94 Instructions to create the shape

5. Join all the objects into a single polyline. Use the **Join** option of the **PEDIT** command.
6. Select the **Right** UCS.

TIP

It is always a good practice to **SAVE** your file every two or three steps. Another good practice is to **SAVE AS** the drawing under a different name every certain number of steps in case you need to go back to a previous stage for any reason. Drawings could be named Tutorial 3-2a, Tutorial 3-2b, and so on.

7. **COPY** the polyline two times: **0.188** and **0.313** orthogonally upward (Figure 3-95).
8. Draw a **1″** polyline orthogonally from the endpoint of the arc.
9. **COPY** the polyline to the midpoint of the arc, as shown in Figure 3-96.

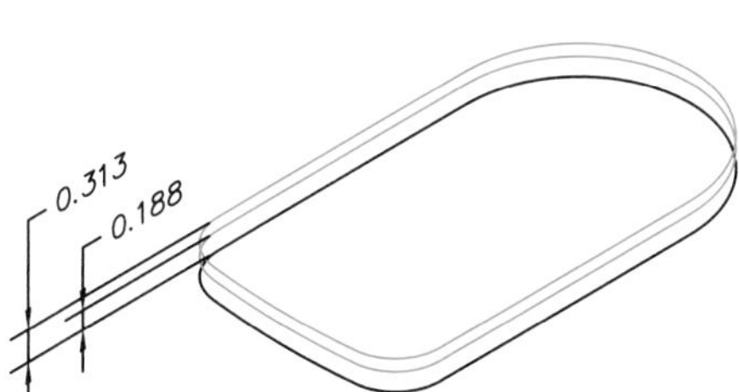

Figure 3-95 Two copies of the polyline are placed above the original one

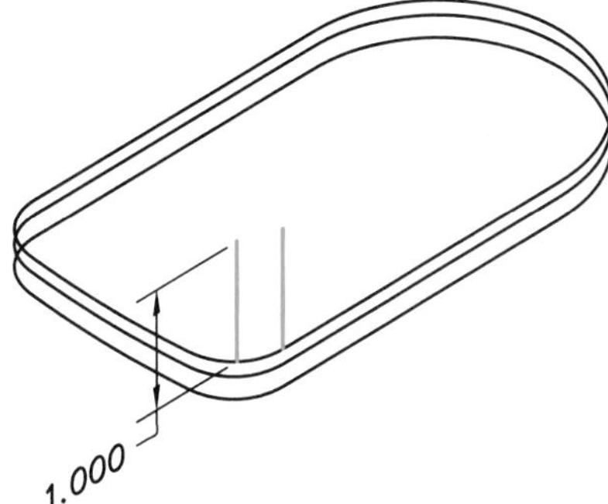

Figure 3-96 Two polylines are added

10. Draw a new polyline **4″** long inclined at **20°** off the *X*-axis from the other endpoint of the arc segment (Figure 3-97).

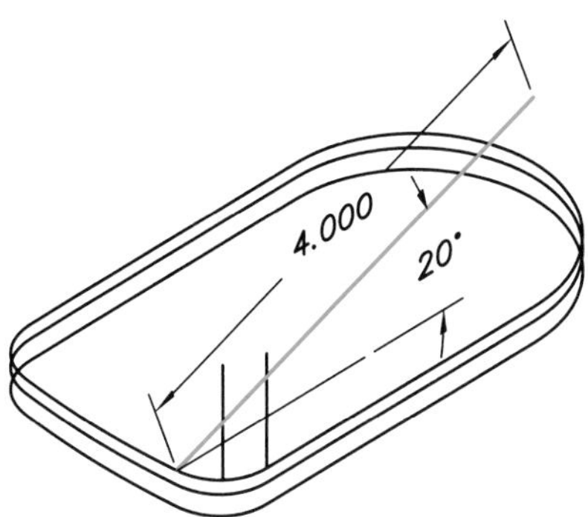

Figure 3-97 Another inclined polyline is added

TIP

You could also create a horizontal polyline and then **ROTATE** it around its endpoint.

11. Select the **UCS Projection** option of the **TRIM** command and trim the two small polylines, using the 4″ polyline as the cutting edge. Respond to the prompts as follows:

```
Select cutting edges...
Select objects: Select the 4" polyline.
Select objects: ↵ (To end the selection)
Select object to trim or shift-select to
extend or
[Fence/Crossing/Project/Edge/
eRase/Undo]: p ↵
Enter a projection option [None/Ucs/View]
<View>: u ↵
```

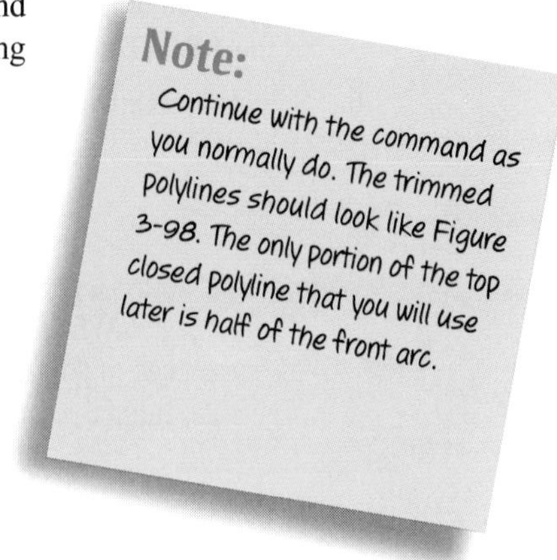

Note:
Continue with the command as you normally do. The trimmed polylines should look like Figure 3-98. The only portion of the top closed polyline that you will use later is half of the front arc.

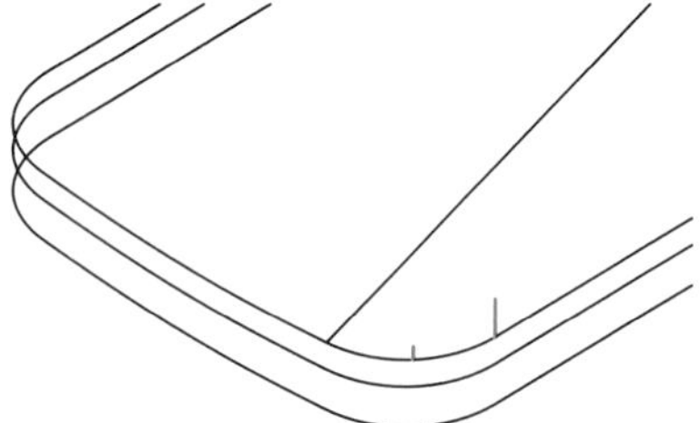

Figure 3-98 The first two polylines are trimmed as they project onto the inclined polyline

12. Select the **World** UCS. Create two short polylines, as shown in Figure 3-99(a) and then **TRIM** the closed polyline using the two short polylines.
13. **DELETE** the two short polylines. The 3D model should look like Figure 3-99(b).
14. **MOVE** the polyline from its endpoint to the endpoint of the small vertical polyline, as shown in Figure 3-100.

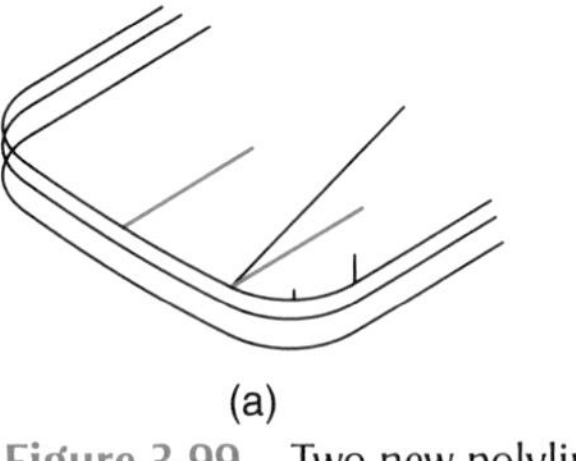

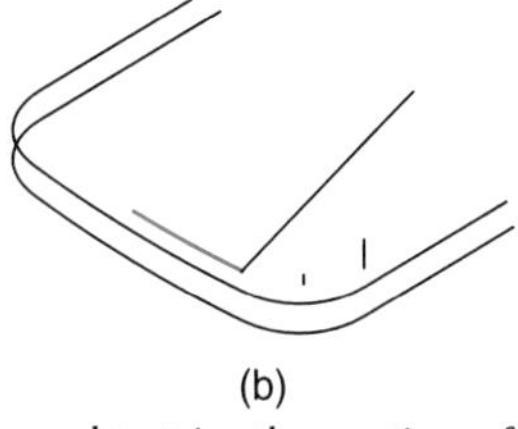

Figure 3-99 Two new polylines are used to trim the portion of the top polyline that is not desired, and are then erased

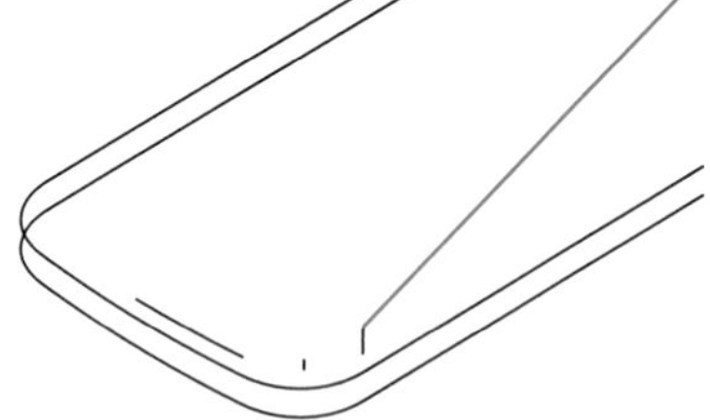

Figure 3-100 Another inclined polyline is added

15. While the **World** UCS is still current, rotate the UCS **20°** about the *X*-axis. This will align the UCS with the 4″ polyline.
16. Create an arc using the default **3Points** option. Snap to the three endpoints, as shown in Figure 3-101.
17. **ERASE** the two small vertical polylines.
18. Select the **Right** UCS.
19. Draw a **2″** polyline at a **20°** angle from a vertical line. Start from the right endpoint of the arc on the back (Figure 3-102).

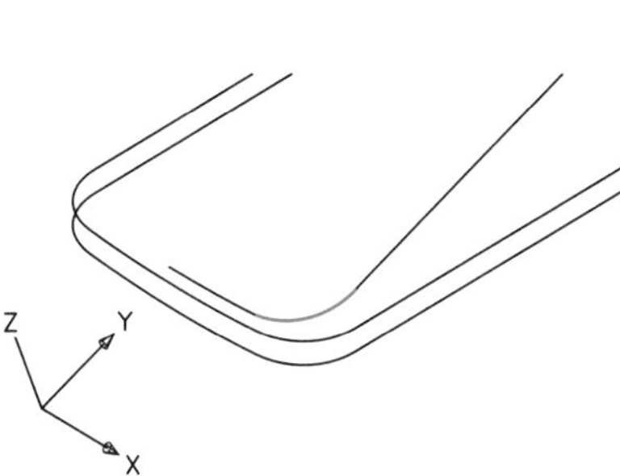

Figure 3-101 An arc is created in a previously defined UCS

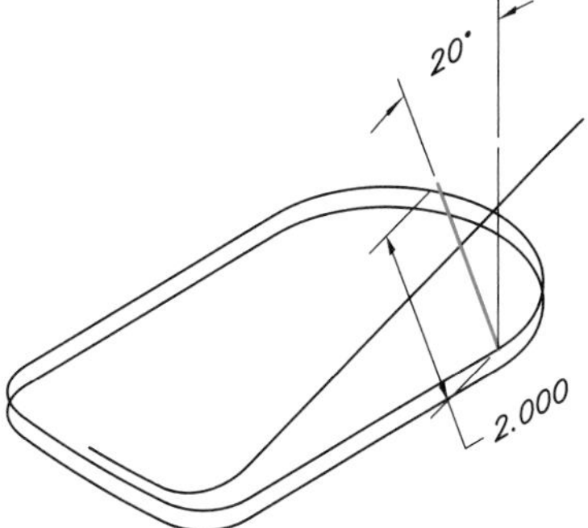

Figure 3-102 A second inclined polyline is added

20. **FILLET** the two polylines using **1.125″** as the radius value (Figure 3-103).
21. Select the **World** UCS and rotate the UCS again **20°** around the *X*-axis.
22. Draw a **2.5″**-long polyline from the endpoint of the arc as shown in Figure 3-104.

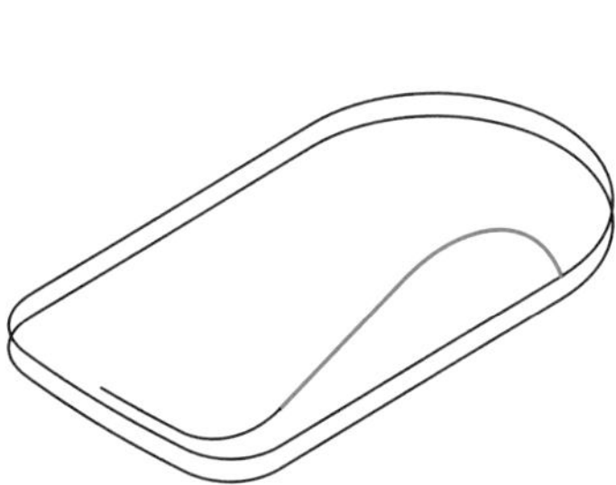
Figure 3-103 The two inclined polylines are filleted

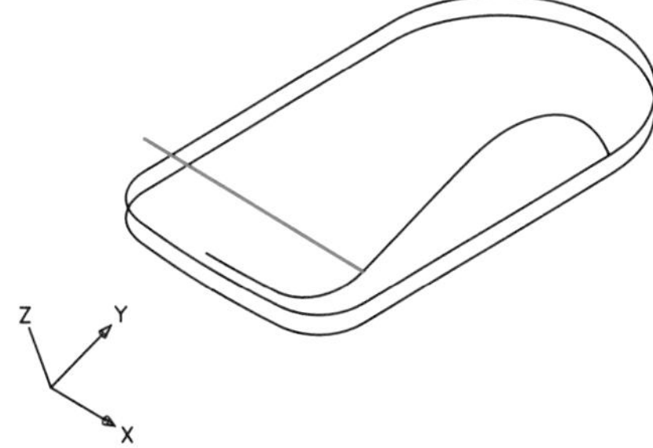

Figure 3-104 A polyline is placed across the 3D model

23. **MOVE** the polyline **1″** along the positive direction of the *X*-axis (Figure 3-105).
24. Rotate the **UCS 40°** around the *X*-axis.
25. **COPY** the last polyline **0.25″** orthogonally along the positive direction of the *Y*-axis (Figure 3-106).

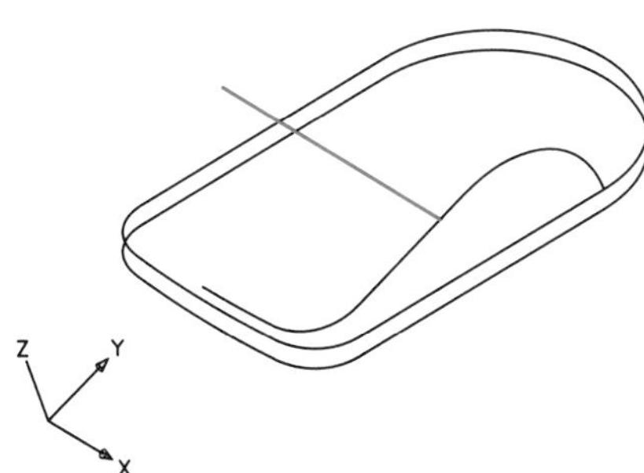

Figure 3-105 The polyline is moved

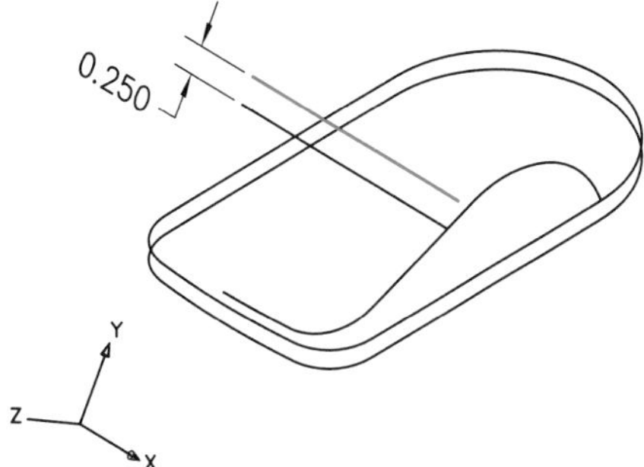

Figure 3-106 A **COPY** operation creates a new polyline placed in the XY plane of the new UCS

26. Create an arc using the two endpoints of the lower polyline, and the midpoint of the top polyline (Figure 3-107).
27. **TRIM** the arc, using the top polyline as the cutting edge.
28. **ERASE** the two straight polylines (Figure 3-108).

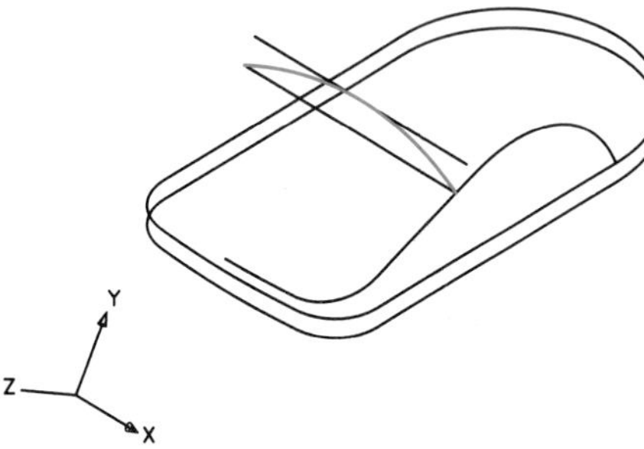

Figure 3-107 An arc is created between the two polylines

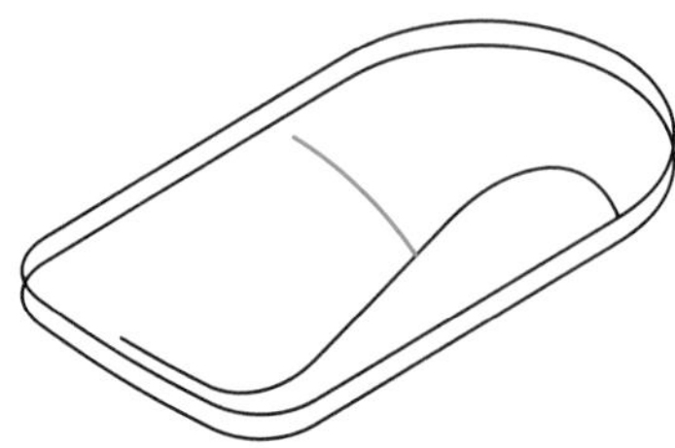

Figure 3-108 The arc is trimmed and the polylines are erased

29. Select the **Right** UCS.
30. Draw a **3″** polyline from the endpoint of the arc you just drew and a second **2″** polyline from the back midpoint of the top closed polyline. Place the polylines at the angles shown in Figure 3-109.

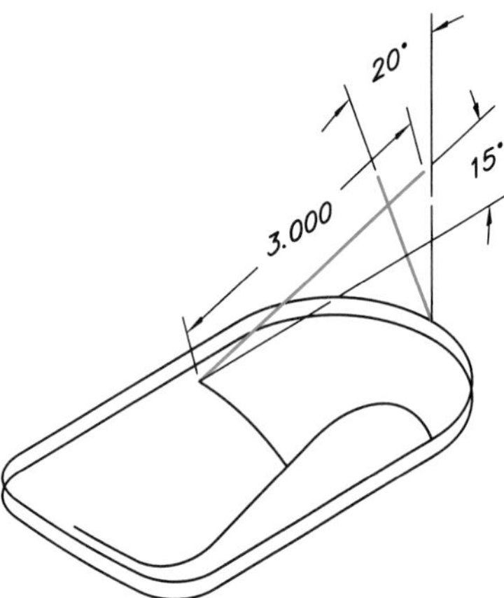

Figure 3-109 Two new inclined polylines are added

31. Construct the arc by using a **FILLET** operation between the two new polylines with a radius of **1.50″** (Figure 3-110).
32. Make sure the two highlighted curves in Figure 3-111 are each a single polyline by either selecting them or hovering over them. If either of these two objects is not a polyline, you will need to join them with the **PEDIT** command.

Note:
When you perform **FILLET** operations between two different polylines, the polylines are joined into a single one.

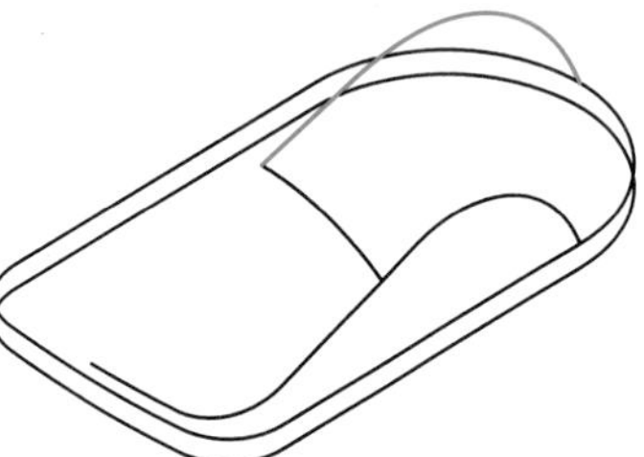

Figure 3-110 The inclined polylines are filleted

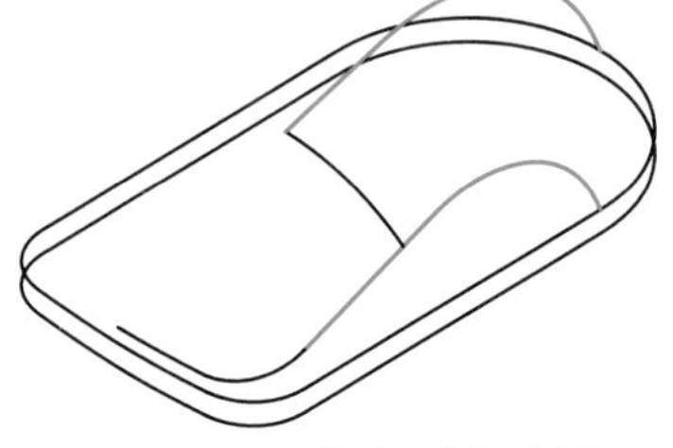

Figure 3-111 Each of the highlighted polylines is a single polyline

33. The polyline located at the side of the mouse model needs to be split at the intersection with the arc (Figure 3-112). Invoke the **BREAK AT POINT** command, and respond to the prompts as follows:

    Select object: *Select the polyline.*

    Specify second break point or [First point]: *_f*

    Specify first break point: *Select the intersection with the arc.*

    Specify second break point: @

> **Note:**
> The **BREAK AT POINT** command is a version of the standard **BREAK** command. This version makes simple the splitting of a wire object into two pieces without eliminating a portion, as happens with the standard **BREAK** command. You can invoke this command by clicking the icon located above the icon of the **BREAK** command.

34. The left half of the top closed polyline is not needed (Figure 3-113). Eliminate this portion by using the **BREAK** command. Respond to the prompts as follows:

    Select object: *Select the polyline.*

    Specify second break point or [First point]: *f* ↵

    Specify first break point: ***Select the midpoint of the front arc.***

    Specify second break point: *Select the midpoint of the arc located at the back.*

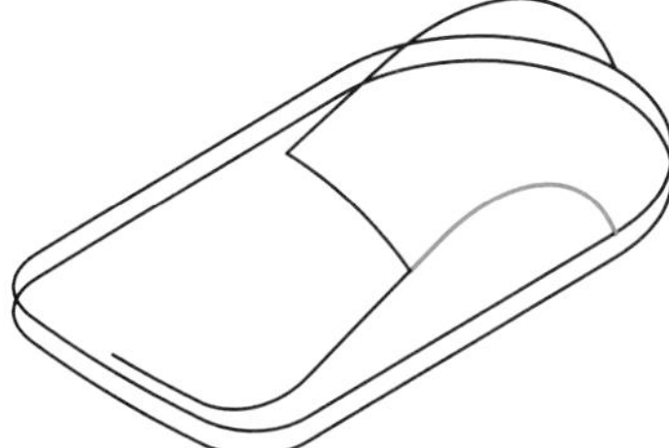

Figure 3-112 One of the polylines is split at the intersection

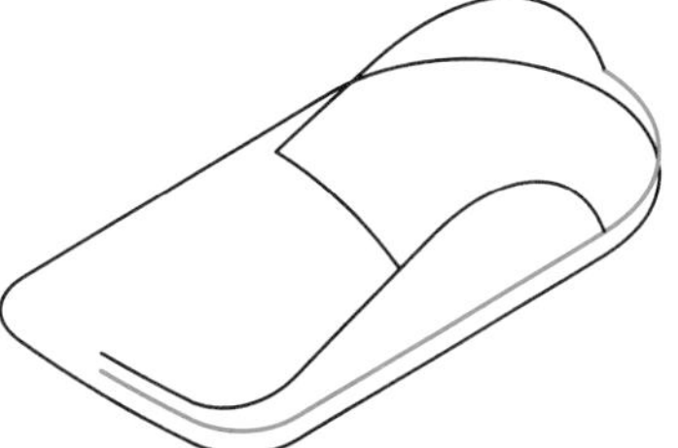

Figure 3-113 The other half of the closed, highlighted polyline is eliminated

TIP If the eliminated portion of the polyline is not the correct one, you can use the **MIRROR** command to correct the mistake.

35. Draw a line from the endpoint of the arc to the perpendicular point of the polyline below it (Figure 3-114).
36. **BREAK** the polyline into four portions, as shown in Figure 3-115.
37. **ERASE** the vertical line afterward.

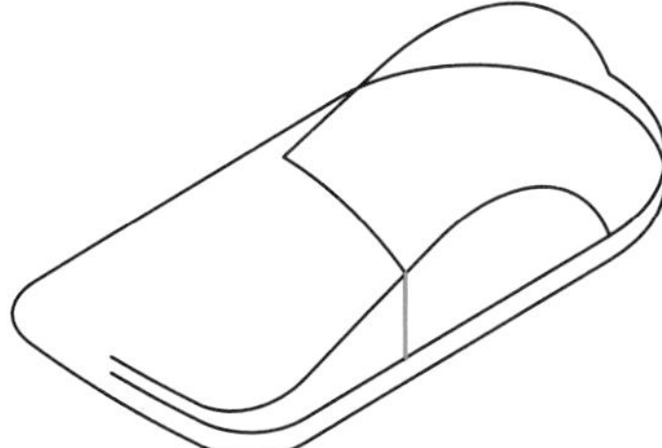

Figure 3-114 A line is added

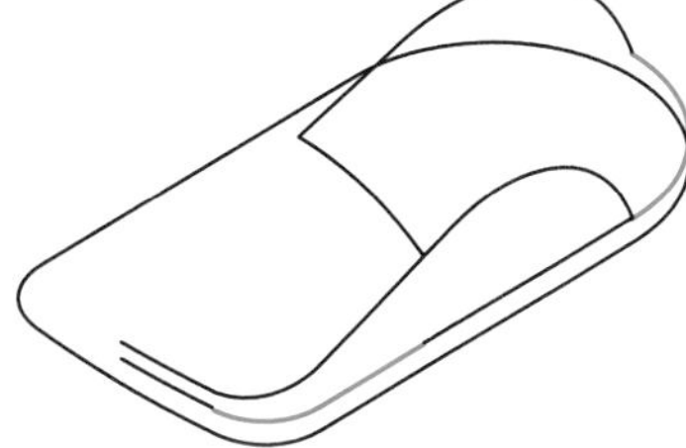

Figure 3-115 The polyline is split, as shown by the highlighted segments

38. Select the **World** UCS and then rotate the UCS **20°** around the *X*-axis.
39. **EXPLODE** the inclined polyline shown in Figure 3-116(a) to turn it into a line.
40. Invoke the **PEDIT** command to join the line with the arc, as shown in Figure 3-116(b).
41. Draw the two lines as shown in Figure 3-117.
42. Invoke the **3DORBIT** command to inspect the 3D model.
43. Select the **Isometric SE** viewpoint and the **World** UCS.
44. **SAVE** the drawing.

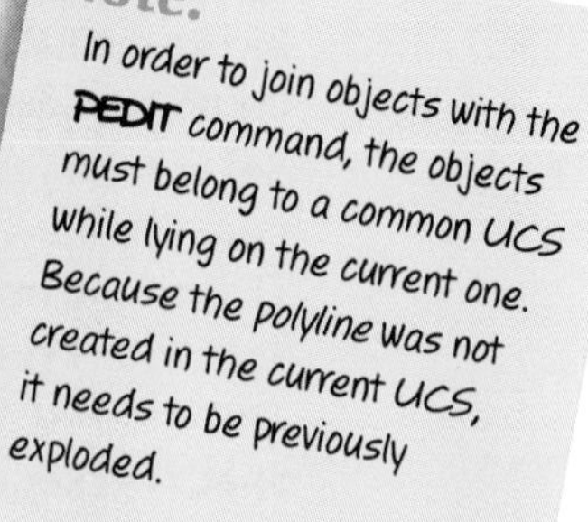

Note:
In order to join objects with the PEDIT command, the objects must belong to a common UCS while lying on the current one. Because the polyline was not created in the current UCS, it needs to be previously exploded.

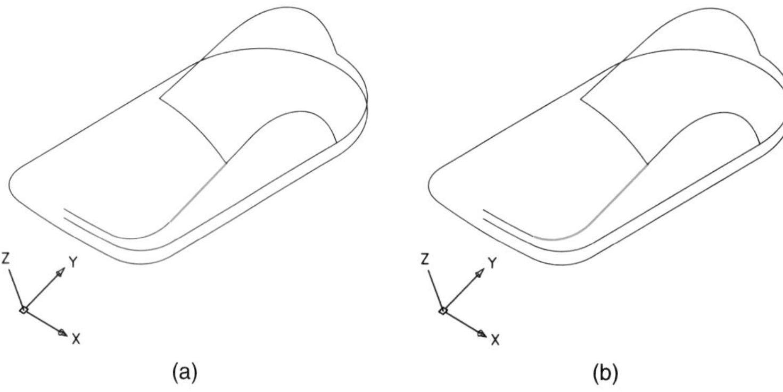

Figure 3-116 The polyline is separated and the highlighted segments are joined into a single polyline

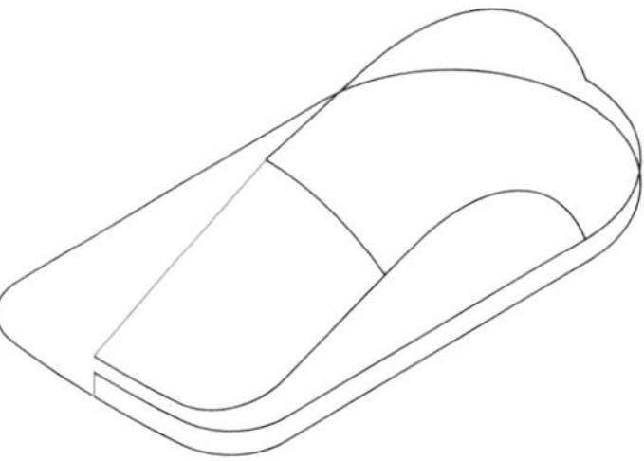

Figure 3-117 Two lines complete the desired 3D wireframe model

You have successfully completed this tutorial. The curves will be used in another tutorial at the end of Chapter 4, where you will add the polygon meshes.

Tutorial 3-3: The Boat Hull

A hull is the main part of a boat. Typically made of fiberglass, its geometry is very complex since its shape is determined by hydrodynamic concepts. Designers prefer to represent 3D models of hulls using surface objects, which requires placing a wire skeleton first.

First, you will create several cross sections of the boat hull. Then, you will place the sections at the proper location aided by a main curve, which represents the side view of the boat. Finally, you will use the resulting locations of the points throughout the 3D space to generate the final curves defining the edges of the surface object.

1. Start a **NEW** drawing using the **acad** template.
2. **SAVE** the drawing **AS *Tutorial 3-3***.

3. Select the **Front** view. The UCS should automatically change to **Front** as well, if the **UCSORTHO** system variable is set to **1**. Draw the 2D curve as shown in Figure 3-118. Locate the leftmost point on the UCS's origin **(0,0,0)**.

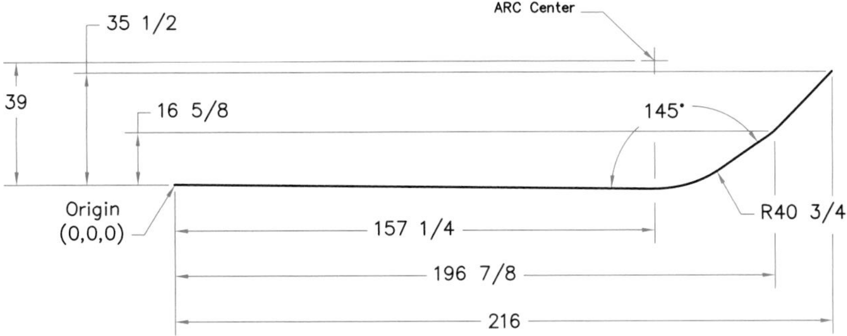

Figure 3-118 The main curve of the hull

4. Invoke the **PEDIT** command and use the **Join** option to turn all the objects into a single polyline.
5. Draw a **48″**-long vertical line anywhere. **MOVE** the line so its midpoint is located at the left endpoint of the curve.
6. Invoke the **ARRAY** command to create an arrayed set of copies of the line, as shown in Figure 3-119. Specify the array parameters as shown in Figure 3-120.

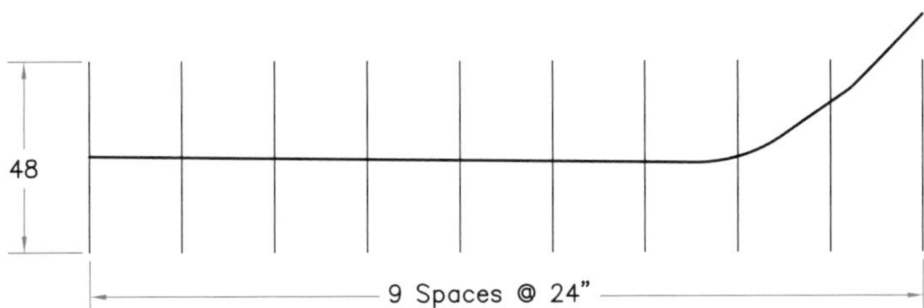

Figure 3-119 An arrayed copy of the line

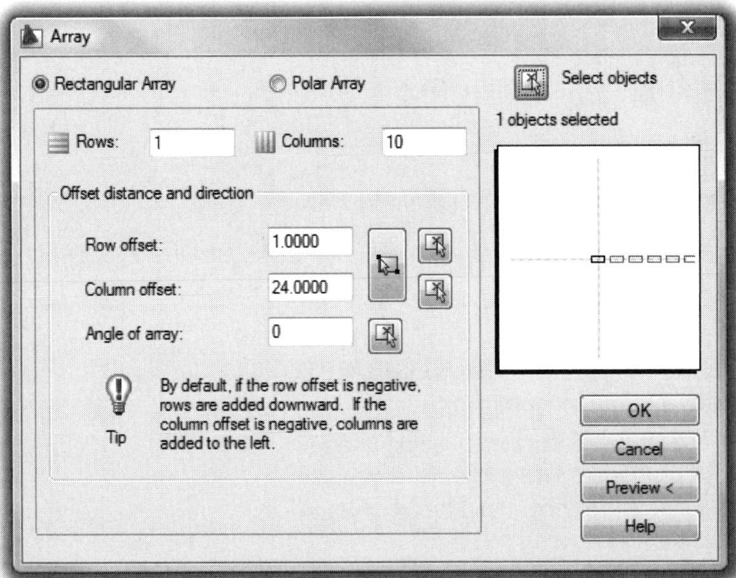

Figure 3-120 The Array dialog box

7. Select the **Right** view.
8. Draw the 2D curve shown in Figure 3-121.
9. Select the **Isometric SE** viewpoint and **MOVE** all the objects belonging to the curve you just drew, placing its lower corner at the first intersection (or endpoint) (Figure 3-122). Any UCS may be used for this operation.

Note:
Do not be concerned about placing the objects in a specific place; they will be moved later. This curve does not need to be turned into a polyline.

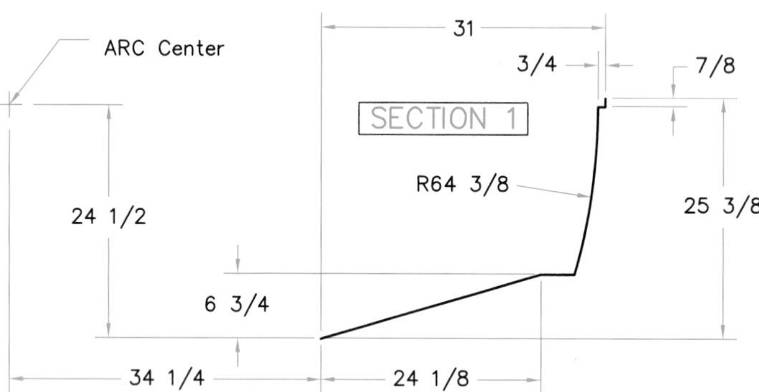

Figure 3-121 The first half section of the hull

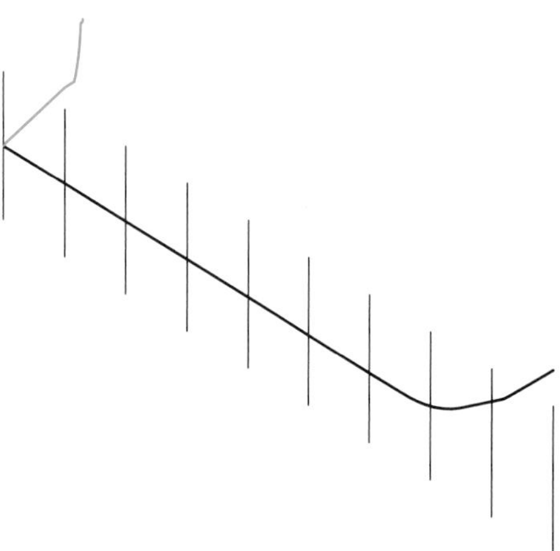
Figure 3-122 The first half section in place

10. Select the **Right** view again and draw the rest of the section's 2D curves, as shown in Figure 3-123. You can place them anywhere, but try to place them in order so that you don't get confused later. If possible, give them names such as *Section 2*, *Section 3,* and so on.
11. Select the **Isometric SE** viewpoint, or use the **3DORBIT** command to achieve an appropriate view.
12. **MOVE** each section one by one to its corresponding location. The results should look like Figure 3-124. Make sure you snap to the intersection when specifying the second point of displacement in each move operation.
13. **ERASE** all the vertical lines that were used to locate the hull's sections (Figure 3-125).

SECTION 2
7/8 3/4 18 3/4 7 3/8 24 1/2 3 5/8 31 1/4

SECTION 3
3 3/8 1 3/4 19 1/4 8 1/8 24 7/8 3 1/2 31 7/8

SECTION 4
4 1/8 1 3/4 19 3/4 8 3/4 25 3 3/8 32 1/4

SECTION 5
4 1/2 1 1/8 3/4 20 9 5/8 24 7/8 3 1/8 32

SECTION 6
4 1/2 1 5/8 3/4 19 3/4 10 3/4 23 7/8 2 7/8 30 7/8

SECTION 7
4 1/2 2 5/8 3/4 18 7/8 12 1/2 2 1/8 20 7/8 28 5/8

SECTION 8
4 5/8 4 1/8 3/4 16 7/8 13 1/2 1 1/8 14 24 7/8

SECTION 9
4 3/4 6 7/8 14 3/8 7/8 2 3/4 1/4 3 1/4 15 3/8

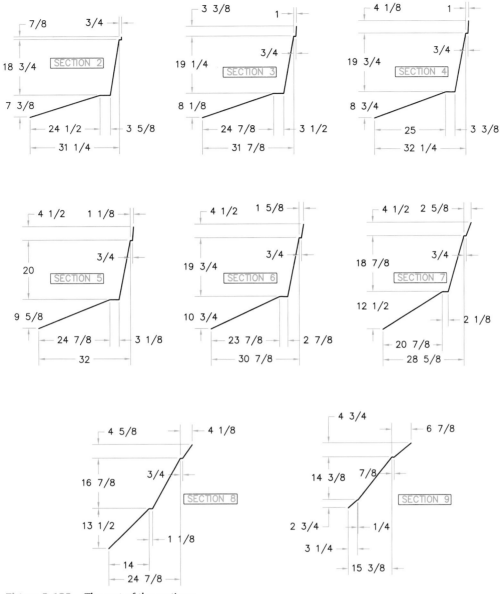

Figure 3-123 The rest of the sections

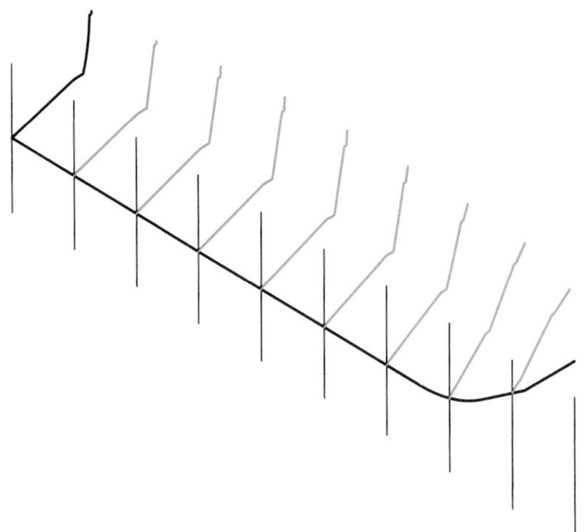

Figure 3-124 The sections are placed in their corresponding locations

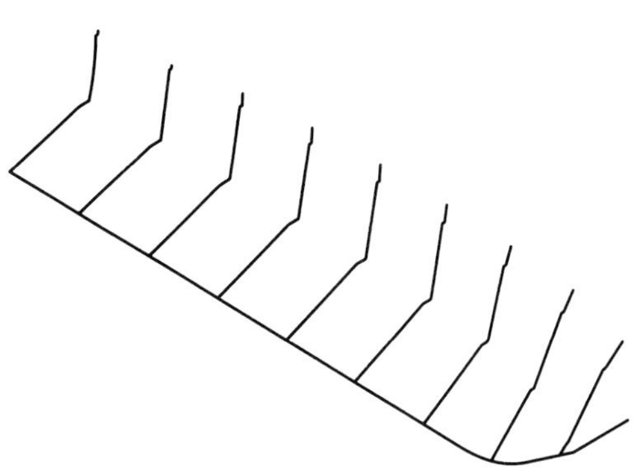

Figure 3-125 The arrayed lines are erased

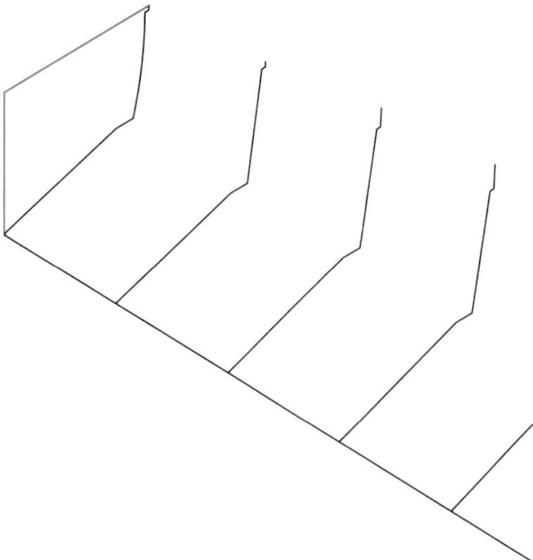

Figure 3-126 Two lines are placed at the first section

Note:

In step 14, one of the lines is parallel to the X-axis and the other one is parallel to the Y-axis. In this case, Autotrack can be helpful.

14. Select the **Right** UCS and draw the two lines shown in Figure 3-126.
15. Invoke the **SPLINE** command and create the first two splines going through the two sets of points that are closer to the main curve on each section, as shown in Figure 3-127.

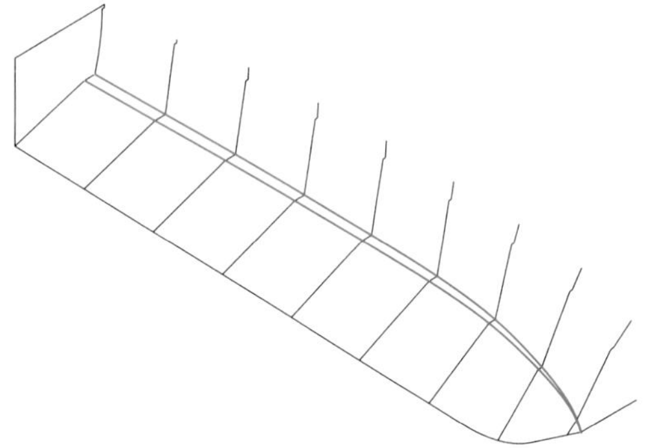

Figure 3-127 Two splines are created through a common set of points in the sections

Note:

An additional vertical line needs to be placed at the nose. It will locate the point where the next set of splines will meet.

TIP When specifying the last point of the splines, you will need to press the <**Enter**> key three times to accept the default tangency conditions.

16. Select the **Front** UCS and create the line shown in Figure 3-128. Do not be concerned about its length.

TIP A line of sufficient length can be created on the rightmost endpoint, then moved toward the left 5 3/8″ and trimmed.

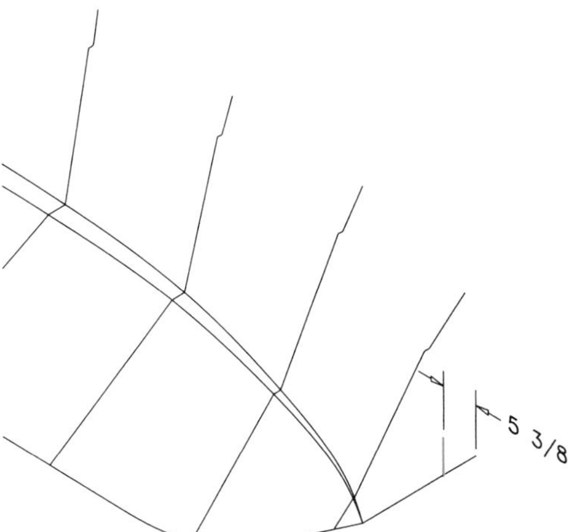

Figure 3-128 A new short line is created

17. Invoke the **SPLINE** command and place the last three splines through the remaining set of points.
18. **ERASE** the line you drew in the previous step (Figure 3-129).

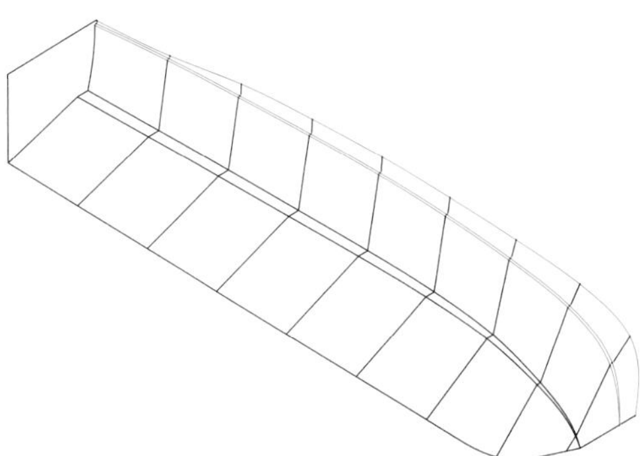

Figure 3-129 Three more splines are created through a common set of points in the sections

19. **ERASE** all the intermediate sections (Figure 3-130).
20. Select the **Isometric SE** viewpoint. Double-click the mouse wheel to **ZOOM** to extents.
21. **SAVE** the drawing.

This project will continue at the end of Chapter 4, where you will add the polygon meshes.

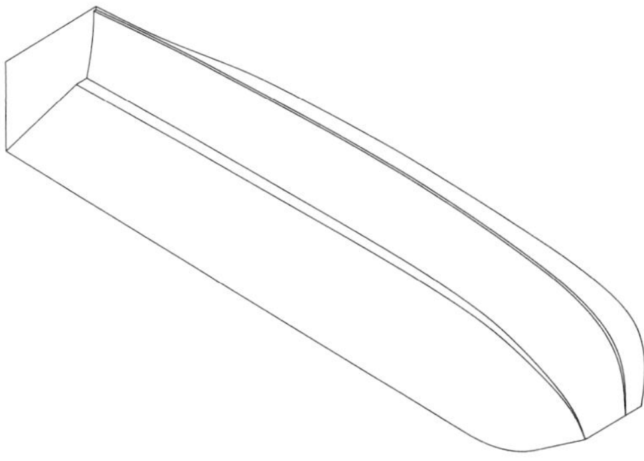

Figure 3-130 The hull sections are erased and the desired wireframe is obtained

Chapter Projects

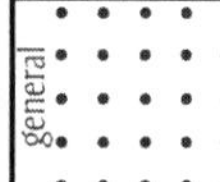

Project 3-1: Objects: Part 1

Using the same objects that you use to generate 2D work, develop the wireframe 3D model of the object shown in Figure 3-131. Do not place any dimensions or use any linetypes other than **Continuous**. Their only purpose in the figure is to clarify your task.

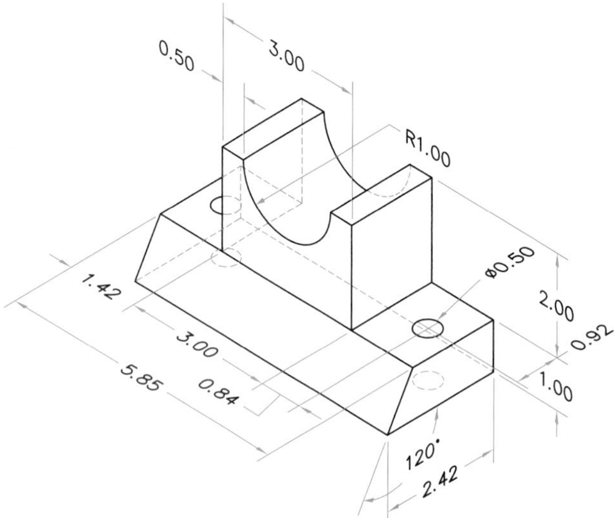

Figure 3-131 Dimensions for Objects: Part 1

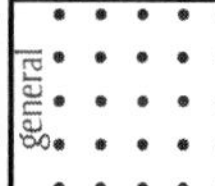

Project 3-2: Objects: Part 2

Using the same objects that you use to generate 2D work, develop the wireframe 3D model of the object shown in Figure 3-132. Do not place any dimensions or use any linetypes other than **Continuous**. Their only purpose in the figure is to clarify your task.

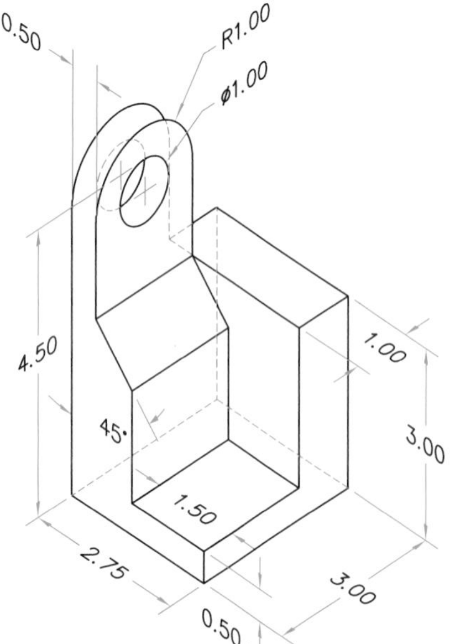

Figure 3-132 Dimensions for Objects: Part 2

general

Project 3-3: Objects: Part 3

Using the same objects that you use to generate 2D work, develop the wireframe 3D model of the object shown in Figure 3-133. Do not place any dimensions or use any linetypes other than **Continuous**. Their only purpose in the figure is to clarify your task.

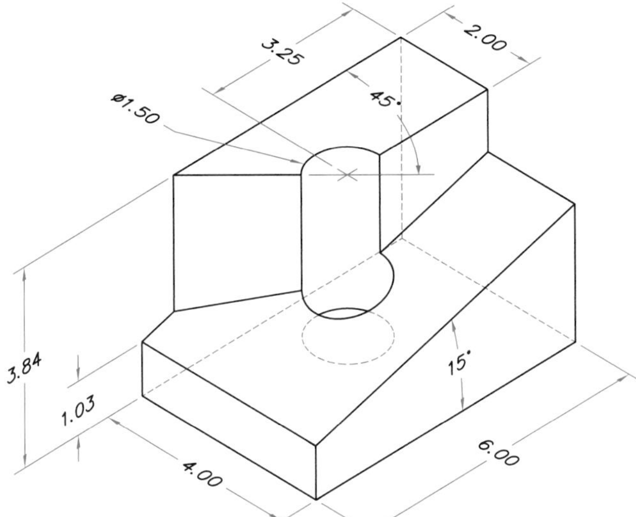

Figure 3-133 Dimensions for Objects: Part 3

Creating and Modifying Faceted Surfaces

4

Chapter Objectives

- Explore the advantages and disadvantages of using meshes or faceted surfaces to represent 3D models.
- Study other objects that can be used along with faceted surfaces to represent 3D models.
- Learn to create 3D primitives with faceted surfaces.
- Know the system variable that controls the smoothness of polygon meshes.
- Learn how to create complex polygon meshes.
- Learn the different procedures to modify polygon meshes.
- Combine meshes with other objects to create the final 3D model.
- Know specific uses of grips with faceted meshes.
- Learn how to transform polygon meshes into smoother faceted surfaces.
- Learn and practice the uses of 2D solids and 3D faces.
- Change the system variable settings to control the quality of shaded faceted surfaces.
- Explore and create other objects used in surface modeling.
- Learn the details about Boolean operations with regions.
- Create 3D models of real objects using faceted surfaces.

INTRODUCTION

Classification of Surfaces in 3D Models

When 3D models are represented with faceted surfaces, only the outer skin is placed throughout the 3D space. In most cases, several faceted surfaces or meshes are placed next to each other to represent the delimited object's surfaces or faces. The surfaces of any object can be classified into three general types (Figure 4-1):

- Planar surfaces
- Surfaces with a single curvature (i.e., cylindrical and conical surfaces)
- Surfaces with curvature in both directions (i.e., a spherical surface)

Unlike wires, faceted surfaces or meshes, along with other entities that are used to represent the surfaces of objects, can hide objects located behind them. They can also be used to obtain shaded and rendered images.

Types of Objects Used to Represent Faceted Surfaces

Several types of objects or entities can be used to represent individual surfaces of a 3D model depending on the type of surface that is being modeled, as well as its geometric complexity. In some cases, a single object or entity can represent more than one surface.

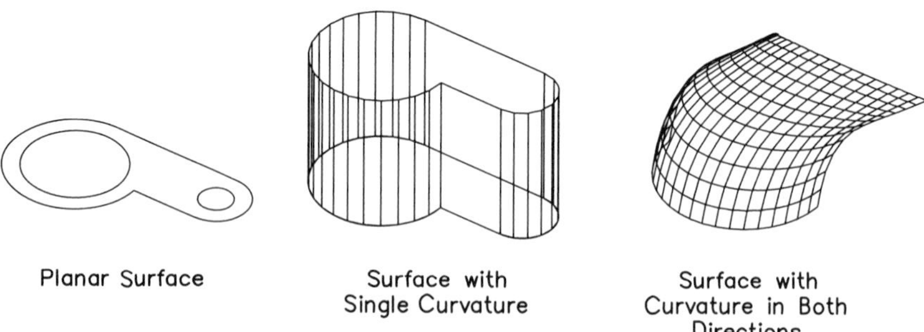

Figure 4-1 Examples of an object's surfaces and how they are represented using faceted surfaces and similar entities

Planar surfaces can be represented with the following objects:

- Thickened objects (lines, circles, arcs, etc.)
- Regions
- 2D solids
- 3D faces
- Polygon meshes

Surfaces with a single curvature are represented with the following objects:

- Thickened objects (lines, circles, arcs, etc.)
- Polygon meshes

Surfaces with curvature in both directions can be represented only with polygon meshes.

Polygon Meshes

polygon mesh: Surface object composed of individual three- or four-sided polygons joined together.

A ***polygon mesh*** is a surface object composed of individual three- or four-sided polygons joined together (Figure 4-2). The set of polygons is organized by an N × M set of vertices or matrices. A polygon mesh can be either *open* or *closed* in either of the two directions M or N (Figure 4-3). When a mesh is closed in a certain direction, the first or last row or column of vertices is shared.

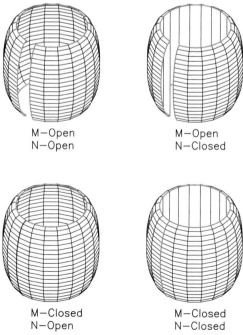

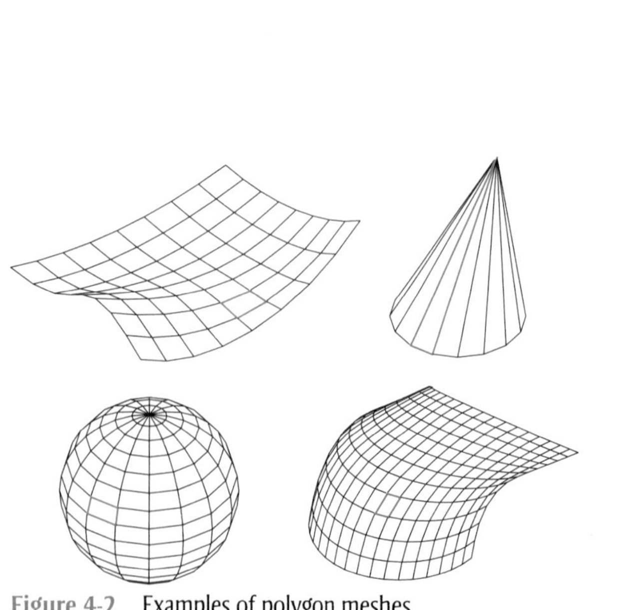

Figure 4-2 Examples of polygon meshes

M–Open
N–Open

M–Open
N–Closed

M–Closed
N–Open

M–Closed
N–Closed

Figure 4-3 Examples of open and closed polygon meshes in the M and N directions

Polygon meshes are the primary objects used to create 3D models with faceted surfaces because they can represent any type of surface, and can be edited to generate more complex surfaces. Sometimes, however, it is much easier to use another type of object to achieve the same result.

Polyface meshes are another type of object used to represent faceted surfaces. Like polygon meshes, polyface meshes are made of smaller faces joined together. This type of object is typically created by applications rather than by the user. For example, 3D primitives such as boxes, wedges, and pyramids are created as polyface meshes by AutoCAD (Figure 4-4).

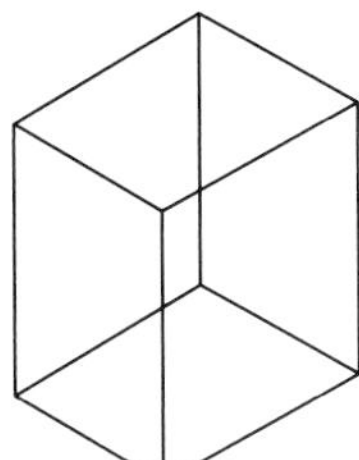
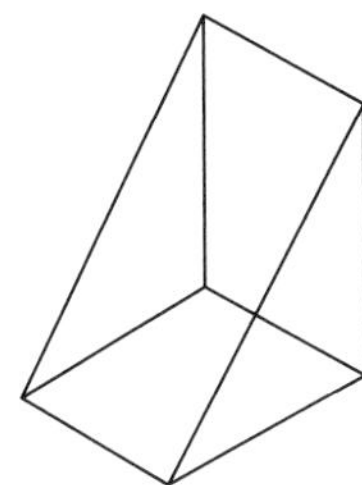
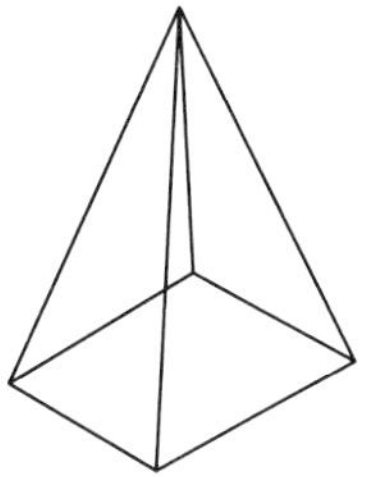

Figure 4-4 Examples of polyface meshes created by specific applications

The polygon mesh is an old type of object used to represent the surfaces of 3D models. Now, with the AutoCAD software, you can also use true surfaces for such purposes. Generally, true surfaces are more easily edited than are faceted surfaces. Unlike faceted surfaces, true surfaces can interact with 3D solids.

FOR MORE DETAILS See Chapters 5 and 6 to learn more about true surfaces.

Using faceted surfaces to represent 3D models, however, still has two remarkable advantages over using surfaces and 3D solids:

1. They can be transformed and smoothed into more complex surface shapes.
2. They are highly flexible. Their grips can be stretched in any direction in order to create free-form shapes.

Deciding When to Use Faceted Surfaces

The thickness of a real object is never 0. For certain objects, however, the thickness is not relevant to the design process. For those objects it is necessary to model only the outer or inner surfaces.

A molded fiberglass part such as a boat hull is an example in which the surfaces of an object are the only geometrically relevant aspect for the concept design. The design of an automobile body can also be considered conceptually as involving only surfaces.

Using meshes and other related objects can also be considered when the only purpose of the 3D model is to create a rendered image. An example is a drawing of the exterior walls of a building.

You can combine meshes, surfaces, and 3D solids in your 3D model. For instance, when creating 3D models for interior design, the inside face of walls can be represented with surfaces, whereas furniture and other objects can be created as 3D solids.

If the purpose of a model is totally artistic, a faceted surface may be the best choice because of its flexibility. For topographical and landscape representations of terrains, polygon meshes are also a good choice.

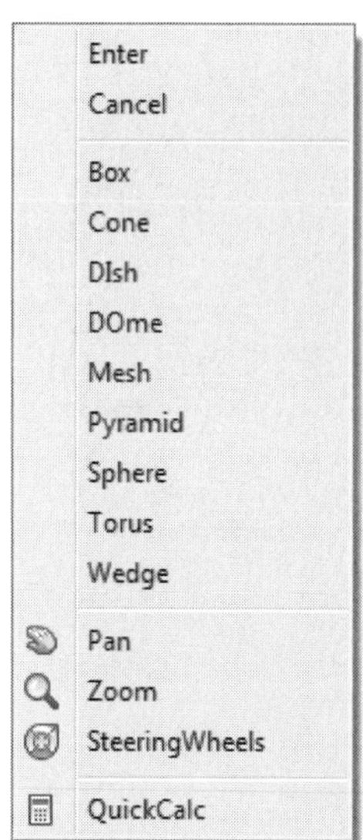

Figure 4-5 The 3D command's shortcut menu

CREATING 3D PRIMITIVES AS FACETED SURFACES

THE 3D COMMAND

The **3D** command is used to create polygon meshes and polyface meshes that look like 3D primitives such as boxes, cones, and spheres. Each of these is created by specifying one of the options of the **3D** command. This command can be invoked only through the command line window. Figure 4-5 shows the command's shortcut menu with the available options.

The Box Option

The **Box** option creates a polyface mesh with the shape of a box. You need to specify the five geometric elements shown in Figure 4-6. The base of the box will be constructed parallel to the current UCS.

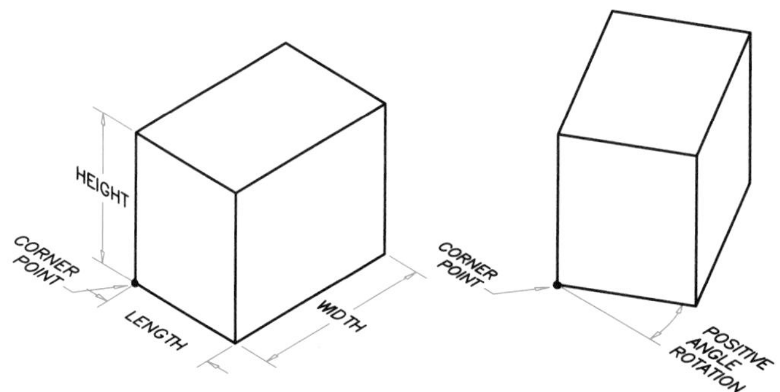

Figure 4-6 Geometric elements specified when creating a box-shaped polyface mesh using the Box option of the 3D command

Exercise 4-1: Creating a Box Surface with the 3D Command

1. Start a **NEW** drawing using the **acad** template.
2. **SAVE** the drawing **AS *Exercise 4-1.***
3. Select the **SE Isometric** viewing point.
4. Invoke the **Box** option of the **3D** command to create the box shown in Figure 4-7. Respond to the prompts as follows:

`Specify corner point of box:` *`Click anywhere in the drawing area.`*

`Specify length of box:` *`2 ↵`*

`Specify width of box or [Cube]:` *`3 ↵`*

`Specify height of box:` *`2.5 ↵`*

`Specify rotation angle of box about the Z axis or [Reference]:` `↵` *`(To accept the default value 0)`*

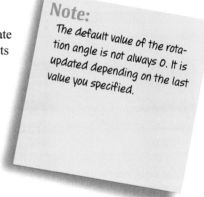

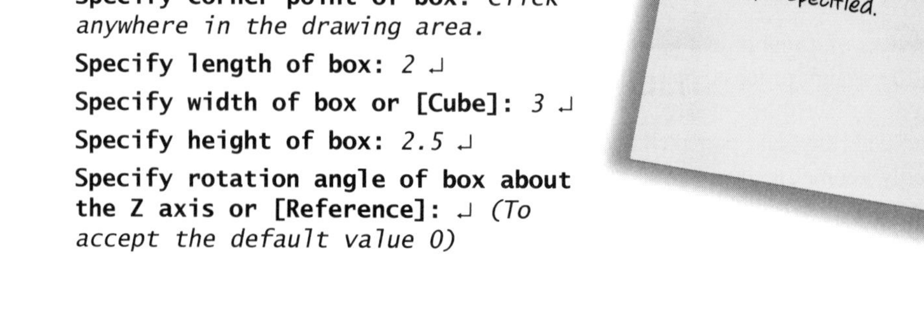

Note:
The default value of the rotation angle is not always 0. It is updated depending on the last value you specified.

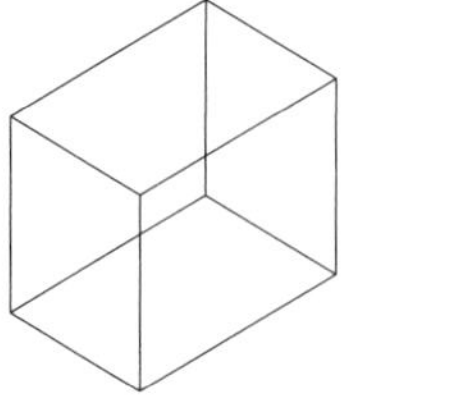

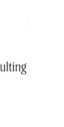

Figure 4-7 The resulting box

After entering the width dimension, you can use the **Cube** option to create a cube surface.

5. Invoke the **Box** option of the **3D** command again and respond to the prompts as follows:

   Specify corner point of box: *Specify endpoint 1 as shown in Figure 4-8.*

   Specify length of box: *4 ↵*

   Specify width of box or [Cube]: *c ↵*

   Specify rotation angle of box about the Z axis or [Reference]: *Snap to midpoint 2.*
6. Invoke the **HIDE** command. The 3D model should look like Figure 4-9.
7. **SAVE** the drawing.

Note:

The object snaps are temporarily turned off when any of the objects of the **3D** command is invoked. To snap to a point, you can click on the specific object snap icon directly.

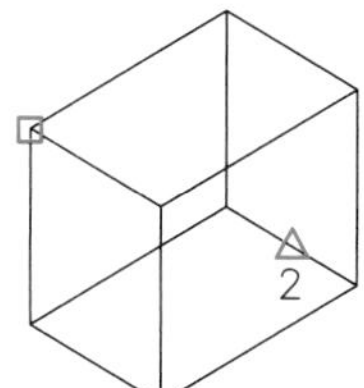

Figure 4-8 Points to be specified with the operation

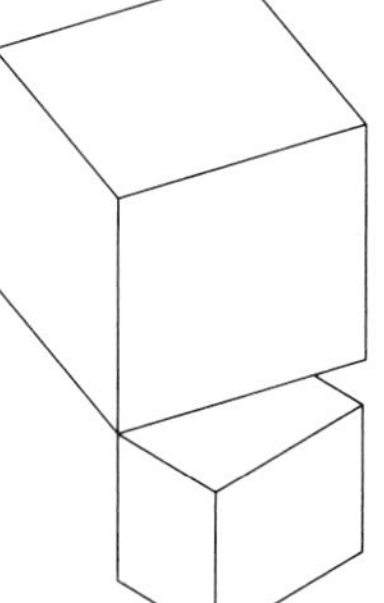

Figure 4-9 The resulting second box

The Wedge Option

The **Wedge** option creates a polyface mesh in the shape of a wedge (Figure 4-10). This command proceeds exactly like the **Box** option of the **3D** command. Again, the base of the wedge will be constructed parallel to the current UCS.

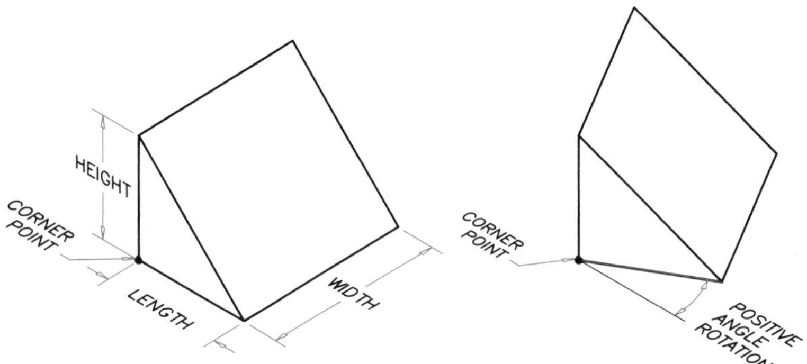

Figure 4-10 Geometric elements specified when creating a wedge-shaped polyface mesh using the Wedge option of the 3D command

Exercise 4-2: Creating a Wedge Surface with the 3D Command

1. Start a **NEW** drawing using the **acad** template.
2. **SAVE** the drawing **AS *Exercise 4-2.***
3. Select the **SE Isometric** viewing point.
4. Invoke the **Wedge** option of the **3D** command.
5. Create two wedges, specifying the exact same values and snap points as in ***Exercise 4-1.*** After you invoke the **HIDE** command, the 3D model should look like Figure 4-11.
6. **SAVE** the drawing.

Note:

Because a wedge object cannot be a cube, this option will not be available for this type of object. You will need to specify the width and height using the same value as for the length.

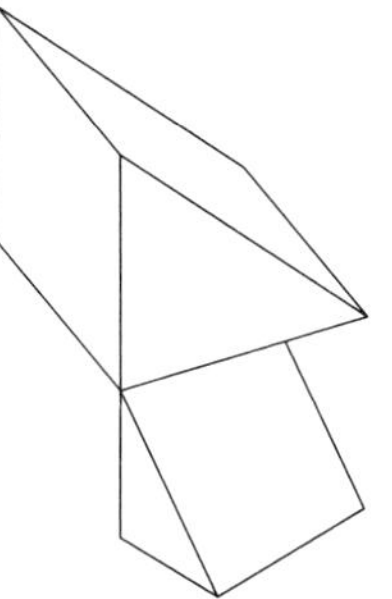

Figure 4-11 The two resulting wedges

The Pyramid Option

The **Pyramid** option creates a polyface mesh in the shape of a pyramid or a tetrahedron, depending on whether the base has four or three vertices. Basically, you can combine these two types of bases with three different types of roof to achieve the desired final shape of the polygon mesh. Figure 4-12 shows the order in which the points will need to be specified according to the options you use.

In this type of object, neither the base nor the roof has to lie in the current UCS in which the object is created. Therefore, you do not need to change the UCS before invoking the **3D** command.

When creating pyramids, you must pay special attention to the relative location of the points to avoid an undesired twisting of the object.

	APEX	RIDGE	TOP
PYRAMIDS			
TETRAHEDRONS			

Figure 4-12 Different types of pyramids and tetrahedrons that can be created using the Pyramid option of the 3D command, and the order in which the points must be specified

Exercise 4-3: Creating an Apex Pyramid Using the 3D Command

1. Start a **NEW** drawing using the **acad** template.
2. **SAVE** the drawing **AS *Exercise 4-3.***
3. Select the **SE Isometric** viewing point.
4. Invoke the **Pyramid** option of the **3D** command. Respond to the prompts as follows:

```
Specify first corner point for base of pyramid: 0,0 ↵
Specify second corner point for base of pyramid: 3,0 ↵
Specify third corner point for base of pyramid: 3,4 ↵
Specify fourth corner point for base of pyramid or [Tetrahedron]:
0,4 ↵
Specify apex point of pyramid or [Ridge/Top]: 1.5,3,4 ↵
```

5. Invoke the **HIDE** command. The 3D model should look like Figure 4-13.
6. Practice creating other types of pyramids and tetrahedrons.
7. **SAVE** the drawing.

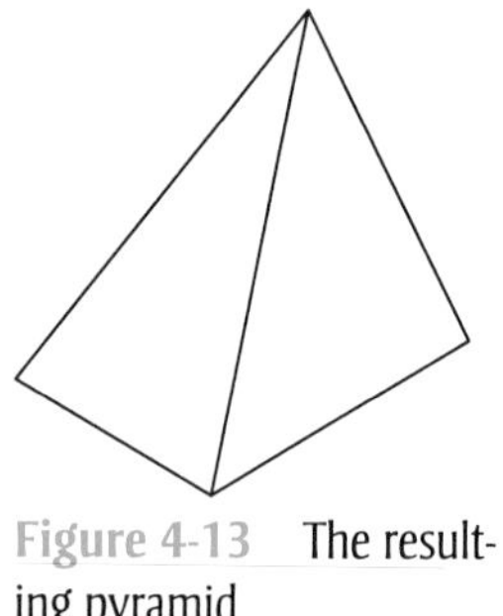

Figure 4-13 The resulting pyramid

The Cone Option

The **Cone** option creates M-open, N-closed polygon meshes in the shape of a cone or a cylinder. The command prompts you to specify points and distances to define the geometric figure. In the event the radius for the top and bottom is specified as the same, the surface obtained will be a cylinder. The base of the cone is placed on a plane parallel to the UCS; its axis is parallel to the current *Z*-axis (Figure 4-14).

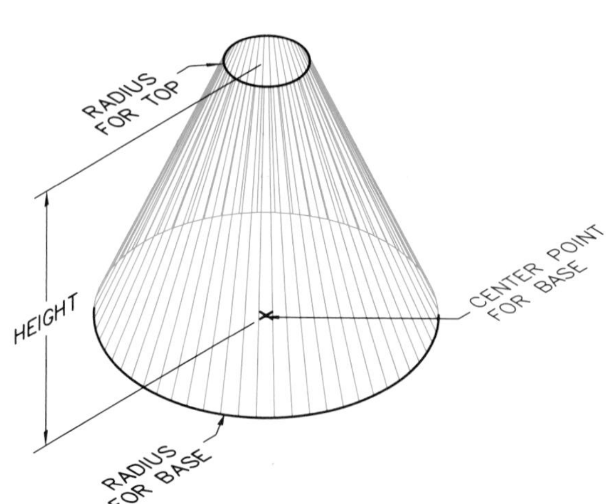

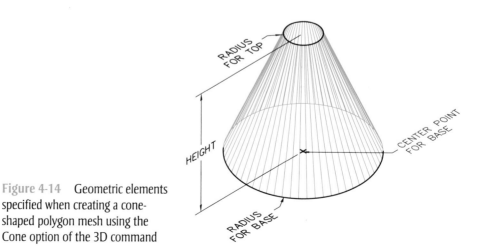

Figure 4-14 Geometric elements specified when creating a cone-shaped polygon mesh using the Cone option of the 3D command

Exercise 4-4: Creating Cones with the 3D Command

1. Start a **NEW** drawing using the **acad** template.
2. **SAVE** the drawing **AS *Exercise 4-4.***
3. Select the **SE Isometric** viewing point.
4. Invoke the **Cone** option of the **3D** command. Respond to the prompts as follows:

   Specify center point for base of cone: *Click anywhere in the drawing area.*

   Specify radius for base of cone or [Diameter]: *3* ↵

   Specify radius for top of cone or [Diameter] <0>: *1* ↵

   Specify height of cone: *5* ↵

   Enter number of segments for surface of cone <16>: *25* ↵

5. Invoke the **Cone** option of the **3D** command again. Respond to the prompts as follows:

   Specify center point for base of cone: *Click in the drawing area, next to the other cone.*

   Specify radius for base of cone or [Diameter]: *3* ↵

   Specify radius for top of cone or [Diameter] <0>: ↵ *(To accept the default 0)*

   Specify height of cone: *5* ↵

   Enter number of segments for surface of cone <16>: *4* ↵

6. Invoke the **HIDE** command. The two objects should look like Figure 4-15.
7. **SAVE** the drawing.

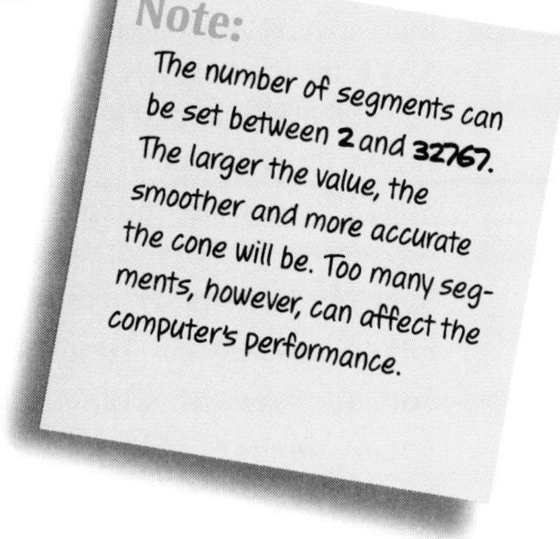

Note:
The number of segments can be set between 2 and 32767. The larger the value, the smoother and more accurate the cone will be. Too many segments, however, can affect the computer's performance.

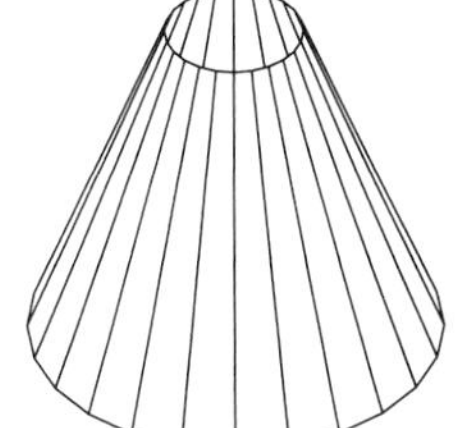

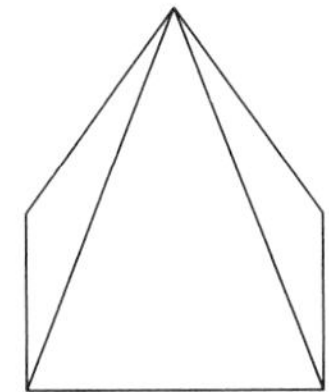

Figure 4-15 Two resulting objects created with the Cone option of the 3D command

By simply specifying a small number of segments, you can create a polygon mesh shaped like a pyramid. Using the **Cone** option, you can also create a cylinder by specifying the same value for the top and base radii.

The Sphere, Dome, and Dish Options

The **Sphere, Dome,** and **Dish** options create M-closed, N-open polygon meshes in the shape of a sphere and the top and bottom halves of a sphere, respectively. For these options you must specify the center point and the radius, as well as the longitudinal and latitudinal number of segments. The imaginary line joining the two poles, or a pole with the center point, will be parallel to the *Z*-axis of the current UCS (Figure 4-16).

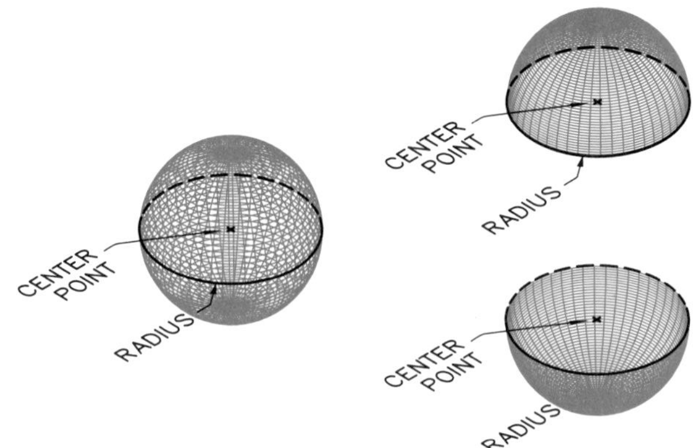

Figure 4-16 Geometric elements specified when using the Sphere, Dome, and Dish options of the 3D command to create polygon meshes

Exercise 4-5: Creating a Dish with the 3D Command

1. Start a **NEW** drawing using the **acad** template.
2. **SAVE** the drawing **AS *Exercise 4-5.***
3. Select the **SE Isometric** viewing point.
4. Invoke the **Dish** option of the **3D** command. Respond to the prompts as follows:

   Specify center point of dish: *Click anywhere in the drawing area.*

   Specify radius of dish or [Diameter]: *3* ↵

   Enter number of longitudinal segments for surface of dish, <16>: *30* ↵

   Enter number of latitudinal segments for surface of dish <8>: *15* ↵
5. Invoke the **HIDE** command. The dish should look like Figure 4-17.
6. Practice creating a sphere and a dome.
7. **SAVE** the drawing.

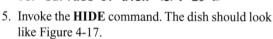

Note:
As with the **Cone** option, the number of segments for a dish can be set between **2** and **32767**.

Figure 4-17 The resulting dish

The Torus Option

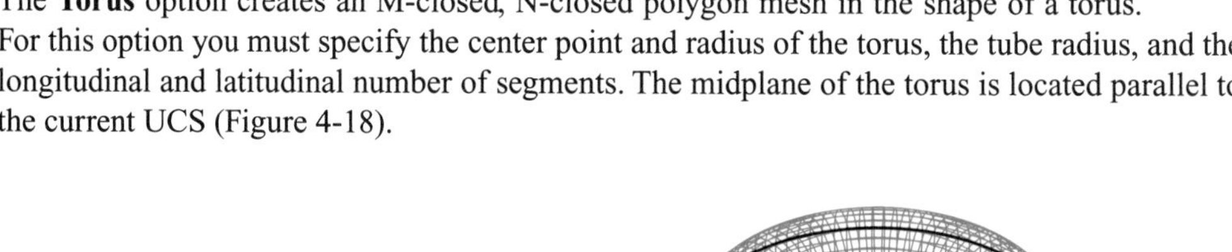

The **Torus** option creates an M-closed, N-closed polygon mesh in the shape of a torus. For this option you must specify the center point and radius of the torus, the tube radius, and the longitudinal and latitudinal number of segments. The midplane of the torus is located parallel to the current UCS (Figure 4-18).

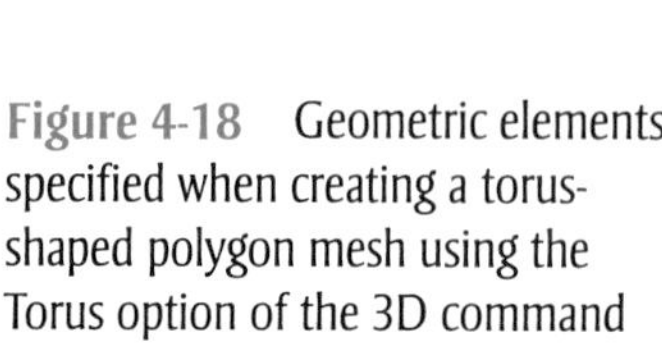

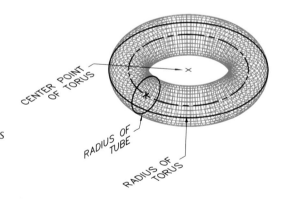

Figure 4-18 Geometric elements specified when creating a torus-shaped polygon mesh using the Torus option of the 3D command

Exercise 4-6: Creating a Torus with the 3D Command

1. Start a **NEW** drawing using the **acad** template.
2. **SAVE** the drawing **AS *Exercise 4-6.***
3. Select the **SE Isometric** viewing point.

4. Invoke the **Torus** option of the **3D** command. Respond to the prompts as follows:

   Specify center point of torus: *Click anywhere in the drawing area.*

   Specify radius of torus or [Diameter]: *3* ↵

   Specify radius of tube or [Diameter]: *.75* ↵

   Enter number of segments around tube circumference <16>: *60* ↵

   Enter number of segments around torus circumference <16>: *20* ↵

5. Invoke the **HIDE** command. The torus should look like Figure 4-19.
6. **SAVE** the drawing.

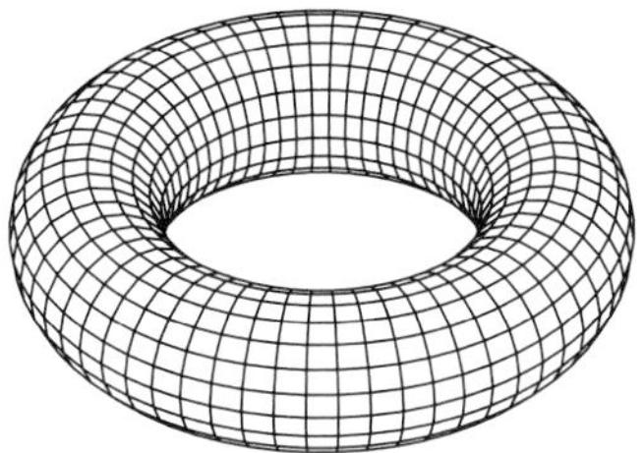

Figure 4-19 The resulting torus

The Mesh Option

The **Mesh** option creates an M-open, N-open polygon mesh by specifying its four corner points. The points must be entered in the form of a loop to avoid creating self-intersecting surfaces. If the four points are specified on the same plane, the result will be a planar polygon mesh. If one of the points does not belong to a common plane, the result will be a nonplanar polygon mesh (Figure 4-20).

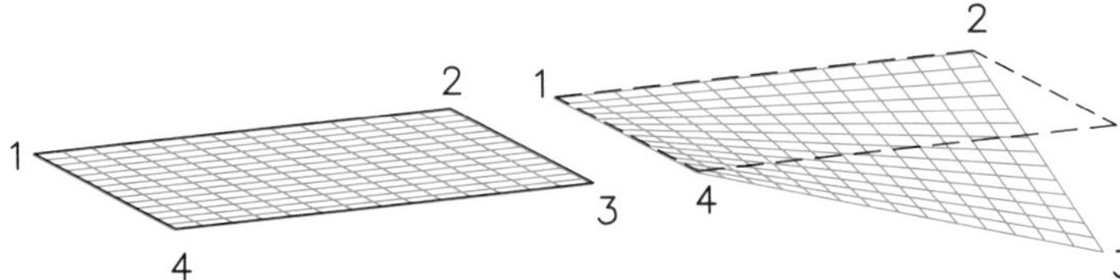

Figure 4-20 Depending on the points specified, the resulting mesh can be either planar or nonplanar

In practice, it is more useful to create planar polygon mesh with this option. Its grips can then be edited to produce other shapes. Figure 4-21 shows a planar polygon mesh after stretching some of its grips and smoothing it.

FOR MORE DETAILS You can find more information about deforming meshes with grips later in this chapter.

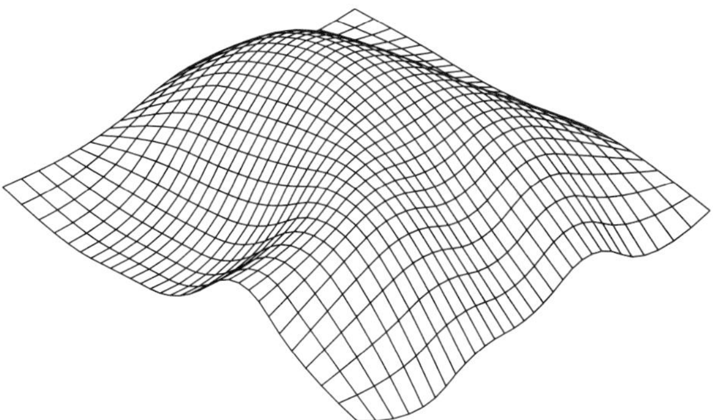

Figure 4-21 A mesh created with this command can be deformed by pulling its grips

The 3DMESH Command

The **3DMESH** command creates an M-open, N-open polygon mesh by specifying first the number of vertices in terms of the *M* and *N* values, and then the location of every individual vertex. You can create a planar polygon mesh by specifying all the points on the same plane, or you can create a mesh in any 3D shape by specifying the locations of the vertices throughout the 3D space.

When using the **3DMESH** command, pay special attention to the order in which the points are entered to avoid creating self-intersecting meshes. You should try to enter the points in such a way that they form a zigzag relative to a particular plane, so that for each M number of vertices you will enter an N number of vertices. Figure 4-22 shows the approximate order in which you would enter the location of the vertices for a **5 × 4** mesh (Figure 4-23).

> **Note:**
> You will have to enter the number of points given by the result of the multiplication M × N. Specifying a large number of vertex locations is a laborious task. Therefore, most of the time programmers have this command activated inside other applications rather than by the user directly. With the **Mesh** option of the **3D** command, you can easily create an M × N mesh and then change the location of each specific vertex individually.

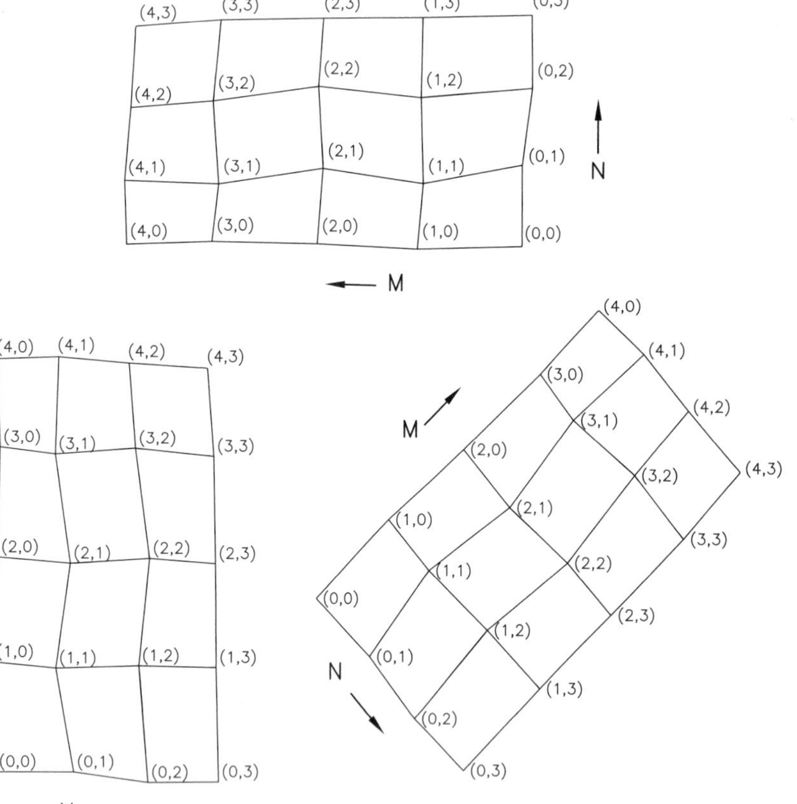

Figure 4-22 The zigzag order in which the points of the mesh must be entered

	N_1	N_2	N_3	N_4
M_1	(0,0)	(0,1)	(0,2)	(0,3)
M_2	(1,0)	(1,1)	(1,2)	(1,3)
M_3	(2,0)	(2,1)	(2,2)	(2,3)
M_4	(3,0)	(0,1)	(3,2)	(3,3)
M_5	(4,0)	(4,1)	(4,2)	(4,3)

Figure 4-23 Examples of meshes and the order in which to enter the points

CREATING COMPLEX POLYGON MESHES

Commands Used to Create Complex Polygon Meshes

The following group of commands is used to create complex polygon meshes:

- **REVSURF** (Revolved Surfaces)
- **TABSURF** (Tabulated Surfaces)

- **RULESURF** (Ruled Surfaces)
- **EDGESURF** (Edge Surfaces)

These commands are similar in that they all require other wire objects to be selected. Also, the current UCS does not affect the result for any of these commands.

Unlike the **3D** command, the commands in this group cannot control the density of the polygon meshes internally. The density of the polygon meshes created by these commands has to be set prior to invoking the command.

The SURFTAB1 and SURFTAB2 System Variables

The **SURFTAB1** and **SURFTAB2** system variables control the number of vertices that the polygon meshes created with the **REVSURF, TABSURF, RULESURF,** and **EDGESURF** commands will have. The **SURFTAB1** variable affects the number of vertices in the N direction of meshes that are created with the **RULESURF** and **TABSURF** commands, and the number of vertices in the M direction of meshes created with the **REVSURF** and **EDGESURF** commands. The **SURFTAB2** variable, on the other hand, affects the number of vertices in the N direction of meshes created with the **REVSURF** and **EDGESURF** commands (Table 4-1).

Table 4-1 Resulting number of M and N tabulations according to the specific command

		RULESURF	TABSURF	REVSURF	EDGESURF
OPEN	M	2	2	SURFTAB1 + 1	SURFTAB1 + 1
	N	SURFTAB1 + 1	SURFTAB1 + 1	SURFTAB2 + 1	SURFTAB2 + 1
CLOSED	M			SURFTAB1	
	N	SURFTAB1	SURFTAB1	SURFTAB2	

The values of the **SURFTAB1** and **SURFTAB2** variables can be set to any integer number between **2** and **32766.** The default value of both variables is **6.** Higher values generate denser, smoother polygon meshes, but they also affect computer performance.

When creating polygon meshes using polylines and 3D polylines that have not been transformed into fitted polylines or into spline-fit polylines using the **REVSURF** and **TABSURF** commands, the M and N values can be determined as shown in Table 4-2. This consideration is based on the fact that polyline straight segments and arc segments are treated differently. Arc segments are tabulated individually, whereas straight segments always have a tabulation of 1.

Table 4-2 The resulting number of M and N tabulations when using polylines and 3D polylines with the REVSURF and TABSURF commands

		TABSURF	REVSURF
OPEN	M	2	SURFTAB1 + 1
	N	SURFTAB1 × No. Arc Segments + No. Straight Segments + 1	SURFTAB2 × No. Arc Segments + No. Straight Segments + 1
CLOSED	M		SURFTAB1
	N	SURFTAB1 × No. Arc Segments + No. Straight Segments	SURFTAB2 × No. Arc Segments + No. Straight Segments

The REVSURF Command

The **REVSURF** command creates a polygon mesh that looks like a revolved faceted surface by rotating a planar or nonplanar curve around a selected axis (Figure 4-24).

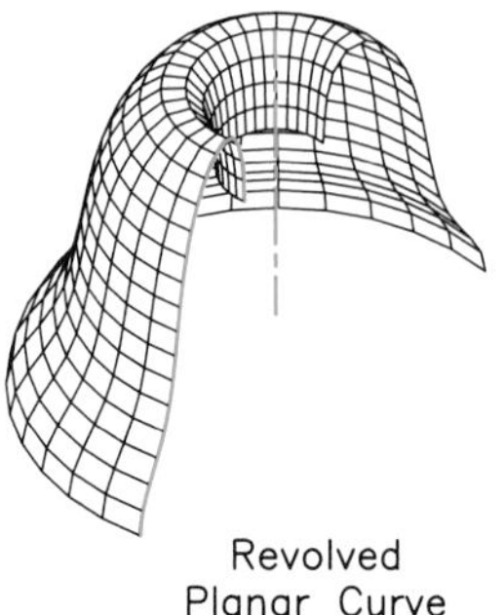

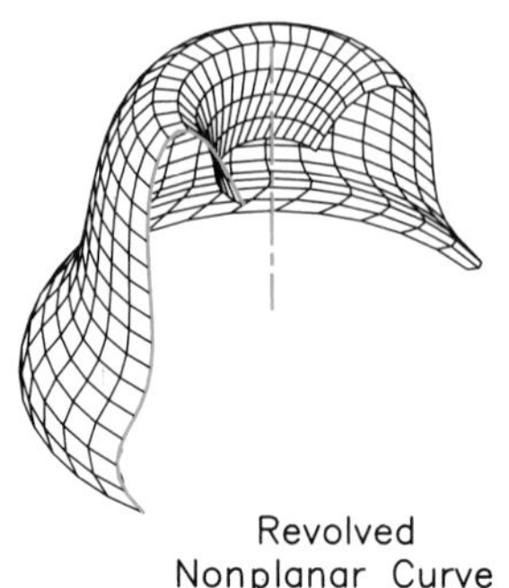

Figure 4-24 Both planar and nonplanar curves can be used to generate polygon meshes by rotating them about a selected axis with the REVSURF command

The axis of revolution is defined by selecting a line, an open polyline, or an open 3D polyline. In the event that a polyline or a 3D polyline is selected, the axis will be considered to be a straight line that goes from the start point of the first segment to the endpoint of the last segment.

The curve defines the type and N size of the mesh. If the curve is closed, the mesh will be N-closed. The mesh will be M-closed only if the angle of revolution is specified as an entire turn (**360°**).

Exercise 4-7: Using the REVSURF Command

1. Start a **NEW** drawing using the **acad** template.
2. **SAVE** the drawing **AS *Exercise 4-7.***
3. Select the **Front** viewing point.
4. Draw the two polylines shown in Figure 4-25.
5. Select the **SE Isometric** viewing point and **ZOOM** in as needed.
6. Set the **SURFTAB1** variable to **4** and the **SURFTAB2** variable to **20.**
7. Invoke the **REVSURF** command, using any of the methods shown in the grid. Respond to the prompts as follows:

Note: Make sure the UCS has updated to **Front** as well. If not, select it manually.

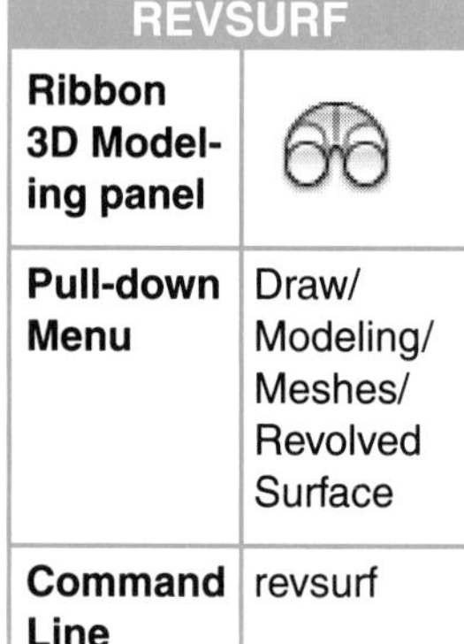

REVSURF	
Ribbon 3D Modeling panel	
Pull-down Menu	Draw/ Modeling/ Meshes/ Revolved Surface
Command Line	revsurf

Select object to revolve: *Select polyline 1* (Figure 4-26).

Select object that defines the axis of revolution: *Select polyline 2.*

Specify start angle <0>: ↵ *(To accept the default value)*

Specify included angle (+=ccw, -=cw) <360>: ↵ *(To accept the default value)*

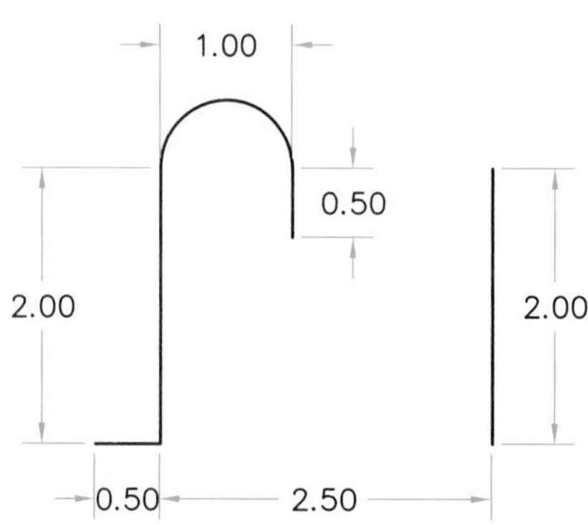

Figure 4-25 Profile and axis to be created

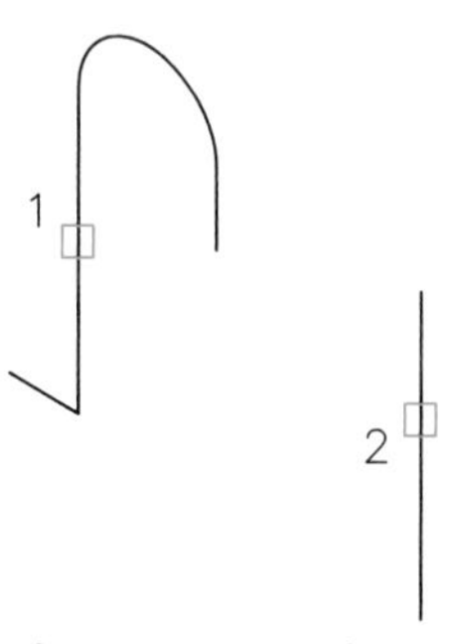

Figure 4-26 Selection procedure

You can use different colors to differentiate a surface from a curve.

8. Invoke the **3DORBIT** command to inspect your model.
9. Invoke the **HIDE** command. The 3D model should look like Figure 4-27.
10. **SAVE** the drawing.

Exercise 4-8: Using the REVSURF Command with Different SURFTAB Values

1. **OPEN** the drawing ***Exercise 4-7.***
2. **SAVE** the drawing **AS *Exercise 4-8.***
3. Select the **SW Isometric** viewing point.
4. **ERASE** the polygon mesh you just created, leaving only the two *polylines*.
5. Change the **SURFTAB1** variable to **20** and invoke the **REVSURF** command again. Respond to the prompts as follows:

   Select object to revolve: *Select the same polyline as in the previous exercise.*

   Select object that defines the axis of revolution: *Select the same polyline as in the previous exercise.*

   Specify start angle <0>: ↵ *(To accept the default)*

   Specify included angle (+=ccw, -=cw)<360>: *-180* ↵
6. **HIDE** the objects. The 3D model should look like Figure 4-28.
7. **SAVE** the drawing.

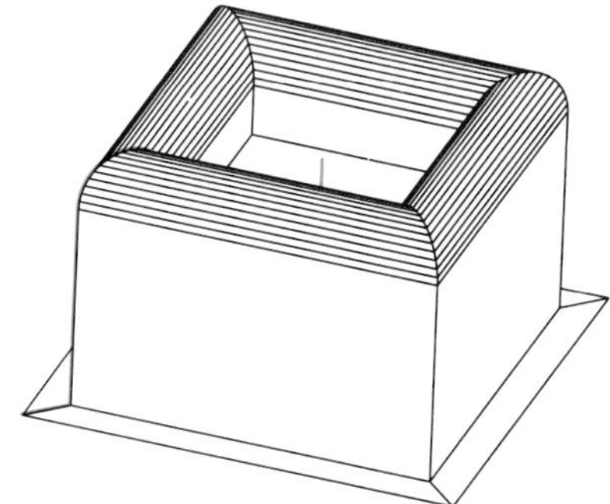

Figure 4-27 The resulting faceted surface model

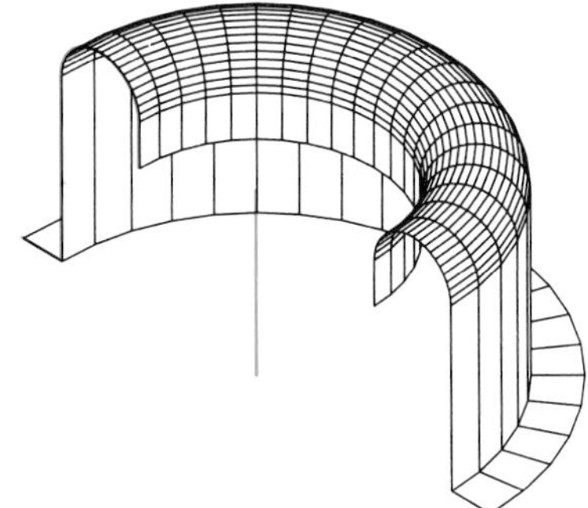

Figure 4-28 The resulting faceted surface model

The TABSURF Command

The **TABSURF** command creates a polygon mesh that looks like an extruded faceted surface. With this command, you can extrude a planar or nonplanar curve along the direction of a selected vector (Figure 4-29).

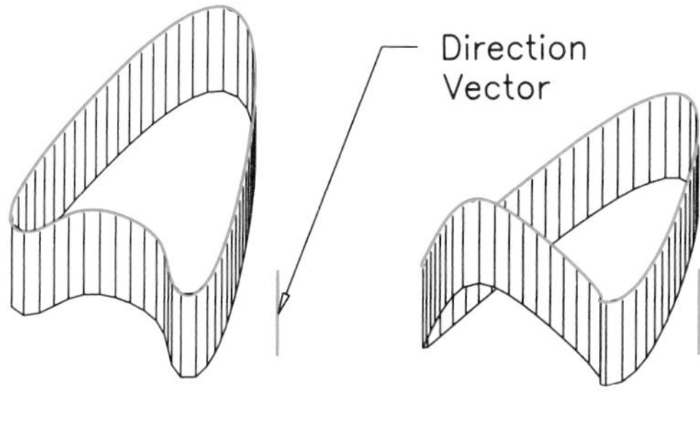

Figure 4-29 Both planar and nonplanar curves can be used to generate polygon meshes by extruding them along a selected vector with the TABSURF command

Lines, open polylines, and open 3D polylines are the only types of objects that can be selected to define the vector. As with the **REVSURF** command, if a polyline or a 3D polyline is selected, the vector will be considered to be a straight line that goes from the start point of the first segment to the endpoint of the last segment. The extrusion can be made toward one side or the other, depending on which of the two halves of the vector you click on when selecting it.

The curve defines whether the polygon mesh is open or closed in the N direction. You cannot create an M-closed mesh with this command. For this reason, the M size of meshes created with this command is always **2**.

Exercise 4-9: Using the TABSURF Command

TABSURF	
Ribbon 3D Modeling panel	
Pull-down Menu	Draw/ Modeling/ Meshes/ Tabulated Surface
Command Line	tabsurf

1. **OPEN** ***Exercise 4-8.***
2. **SAVE** the drawing **AS** ***Exercise 4-9.***
3. Select the **Top** UCS.
4. **ERASE** the vertical polyline that served as the axis of revolution in the previous exercise.
5. Draw a **3″**-long polyline from the endpoint shown in Figure 4-30 and parallel to the *Y*-axis.
6. Change the color of the polygon mesh.
7. Invoke the **DRAWORDER** command and select the polygon mesh to send it to the back. This allows the polyline to stand out, so it can be easily selected.
8. Invoke the **TABSURF** command, using any of the methods shown in the grid. Respond to the prompts as follows:

   Select object for path curve: *Select polyline 1* (Figure 4-31).

   Select object for direction vector: *Select polyline 2.*

> **TIP** When selecting line 2, make sure to do it on its right half. Picking the opposite portion will change the direction in which the polygon mesh is created.

9. **HIDE** the objects. The 3D model should look like Figure 4-32.
10. **SAVE** the drawing.

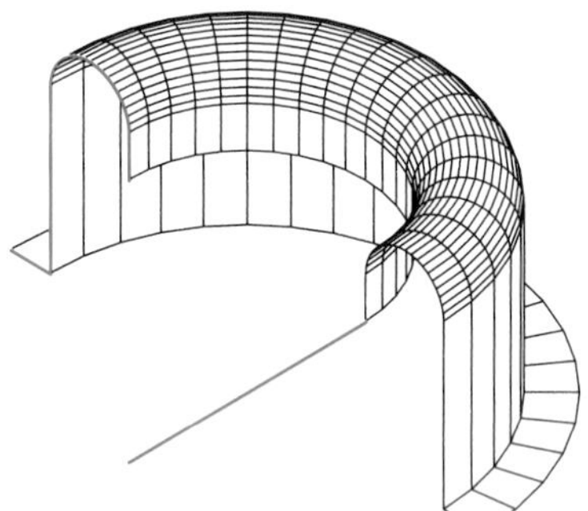

Figure 4-30 The 3D model after adding a polyline

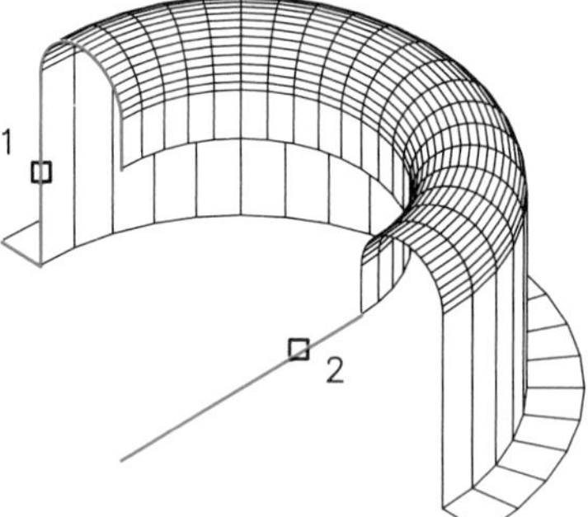

Figure 4-31 Selection order

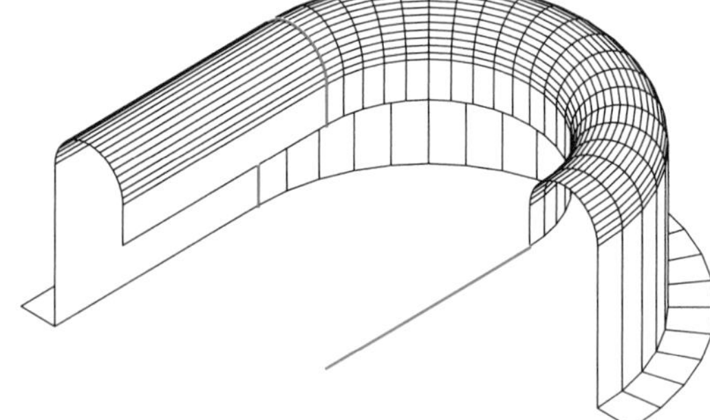

Figure 4-32 The resulting tabulated faceted surface

The RULESURF Command

The **RULESURF** command creates polygon meshes that look like ruled faceted surfaces by specifying two curves, or a curve and a point. A cone is an example of a ruled faceted surface obtained by selecting a circle and a point.

Depending on the situation of the curves, you can create polygon meshes that have two, three, or four edges (Figure 4-33).

You can place planar and nonplanar curves anywhere in the 3D space to define the ruled faceted surface. It is important to pick the curve at the same half portion to avoid producing self-intersecting meshes (Figure 4-34).

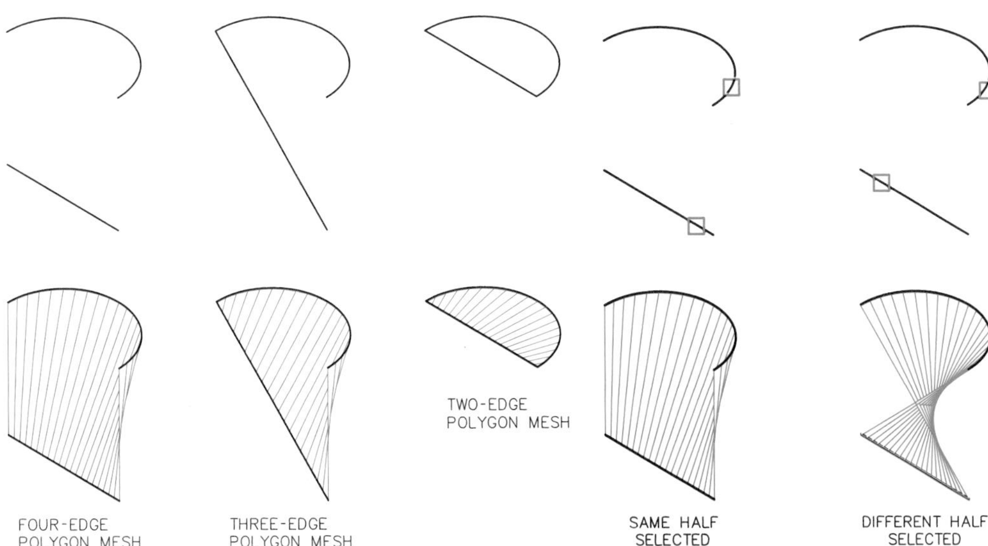

Figure 4-33 You can use the RULESURF command to create different polygon meshes according to the relative location of the curves

Figure 4-34 The two curves must be selected at the same half to avoid self-intersecting polygon meshes

Both the selected edges must be either open or closed. The AutoCAD program cannot create a polygon mesh between a closed and an open curve. Two closed curves will generate an N-closed mesh. The 3D model of the hood shown in Figure 4-35 can be represented by four ruled faceted surfaces.

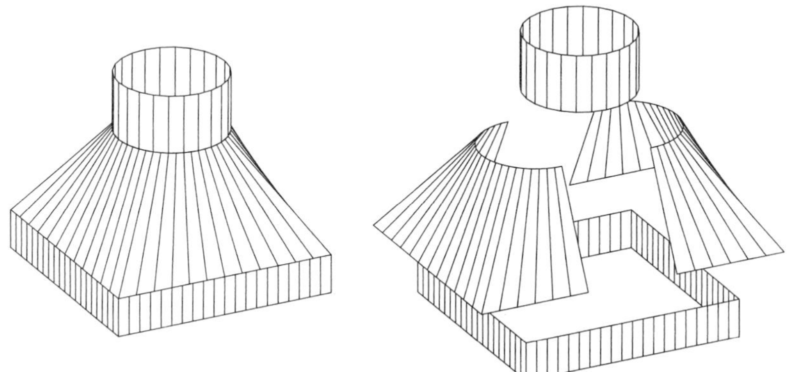

Figure 4-35 The hood shown is an example of the use of ruled faceted surfaces

Exercise 4-10: Using the RULESURF Command

1. **OPEN** ***Exercise 4-9.***
2. **SAVE** the drawing **AS** ***Exercise 4-10.***
3. Select the **Top** view.
4. Invoke the **MIRROR** command. Respond to the prompts as follows:

   Select objects: Specify opposite corner: *Using a selection window, select the polyline located between the two polygon meshes.*

   Select objects: ↵ *(To end the selection)*

   Specify first point of mirror line: *Snap to endpoint 1* (Figure 4-36).

   Specify second point of mirror line: *With Ortho mode activated, specify a second point 2, vertically above endpoint 1.*

   Erase source objects? [Yes/No] <N>: ↵ *(To accept the default value and keep the selected polyline)*

5. Select the **SE Isometric** viewing point.

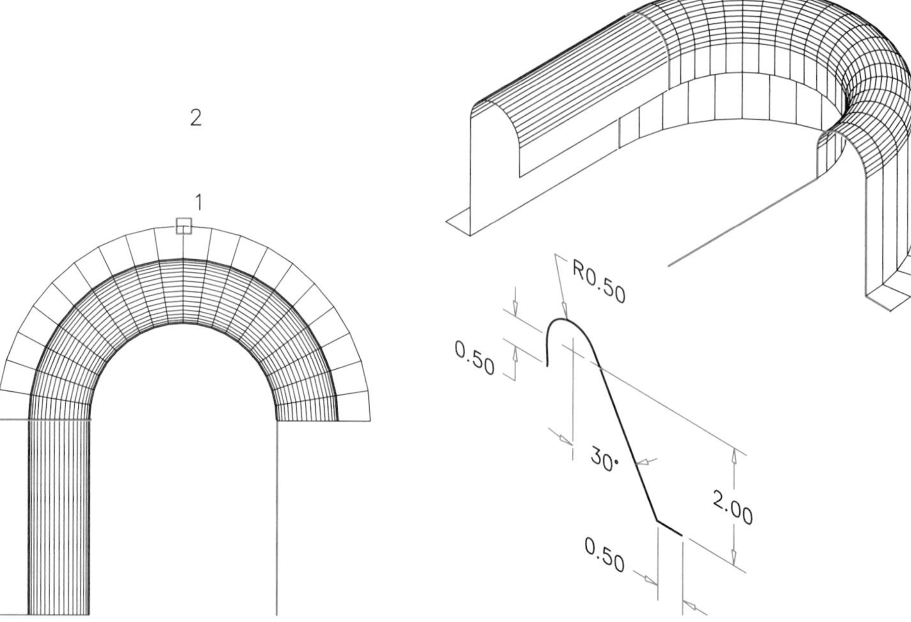

Figure 4-36 Selection order

Figure 4-37 Dimensions to draw the profile

6. Select the **Front** UCS.
7. Draw the object shown in Figure 4-37 anywhere in an empty space. It will be created on the *XY* plane of the UCS automatically.

TIP You can start by creating a circle, and then add other objects.

RULESURF	
Ribbon 3D Modeling panel	
Pull-down Menu	Draw/ Modeling/ Meshes/ Ruled Surface
Command Line	rulesurf

8. Using the **PEDIT** command, join the objects into a single polyline.
9. **MOVE** the polyline to the endpoint of the **30**-long polyline (Figure 4-38).
10. **ERASE** the **30″**-long polyline.
11. Set the **SURFTAB1** variable to **40.**
12. Invoke the **RULESURF** command, using any of the methods shown in the grid. Respond to the prompts as follows:

    `Select first defining curve:` *`Select polyline 1`* **`(Figure 4-39).`**
    `Select second defining curve:` *`Select polyline 2.`*

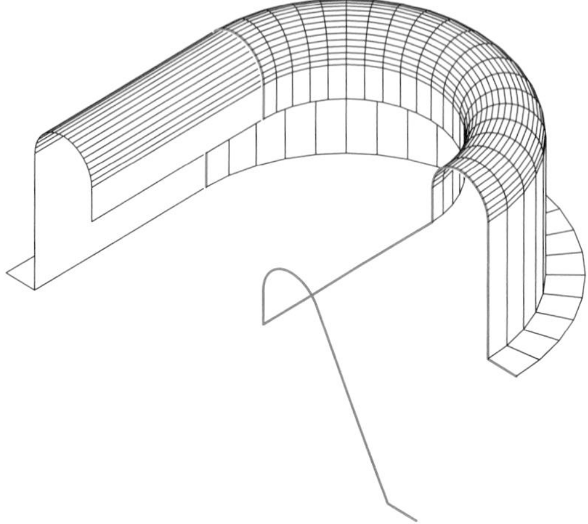

Figure 4-38 The profile after it has been moved

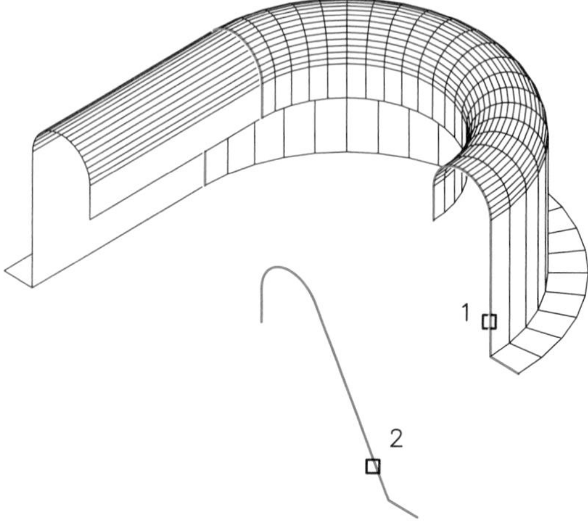

Figure 4-39 Selection order

TIP

Be careful to select both polylines in the same half. Otherwise, the result will be a twisted polygon mesh.

13. Invoke the **HIDE** command. The 3D model with the polygon mesh added should look like Figure 4-40.
14. **SAVE** the drawing.

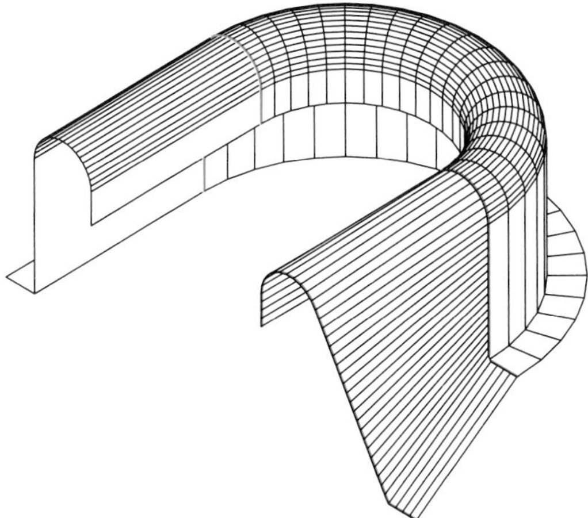

Figure 4-40 The resulting ruled faceted surface

The EDGESURF Command

The **EDGESURF** command creates a polygon mesh that looks like a Coons patch faceted surface by specifying four edges. A *Coons patch* is a bicubic surface resulting from interpolating two curves, one controlling the curvature in the M direction and the other one controlling the curvature in the N direction. Examples of this type of surface can be observed in Figure 4-41.

The four edges required can be selected in any order, but all must be open and placed end to end, forming a closed path. The side and back of a boat hull are examples of a faceted surface created with the **EDGESURF** command (Figure 4-42).

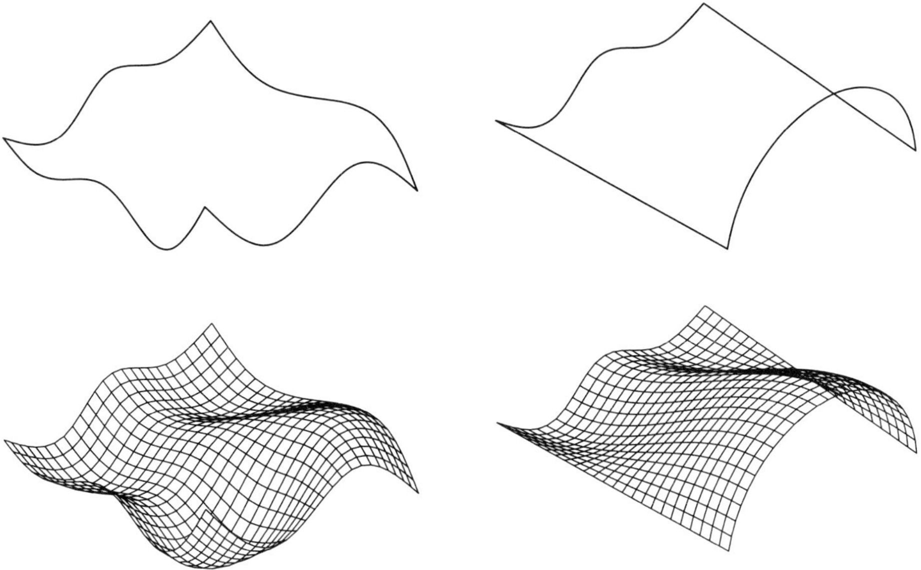

Figure 4-41 Wireframe models and their corresponding Coons patch faceted surfaces

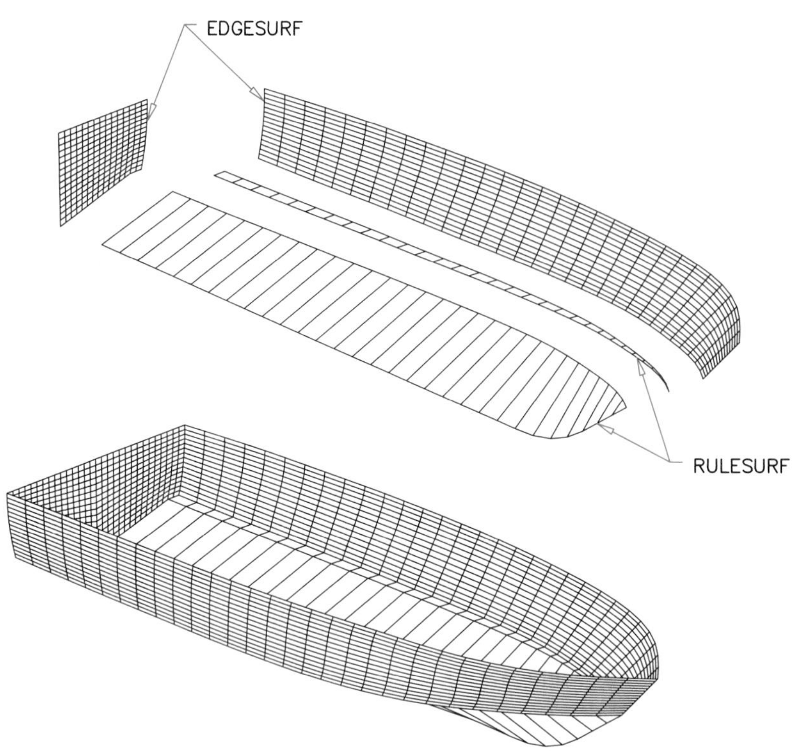

Figure 4-42 Some of the surfaces of a boat hull can be created using the EDGESURF command

Exercise 4-11: Using the EDGESURF Command

1. **OPEN** ***Exercise 4-10.***
2. **SAVE** the drawing **AS** ***Exercise 4-11.***
3. Select the **SE Isometric** viewing point.
4. Your 3D model should still contain three polylines. **MOVE** the leftmost polyline to the other end of the tabulated faceted surface, snapping to any of the endpoints (Figure 4-43).
5. Select the **Top** UCS.
6. **MOVE** the three polygon meshes **4″** toward the positive direction of the *Y*-axis. This will separate the polylines so you can select them more easily.
7. **ERASE** the rightmost polyline.
8. Using the **2Points** option of the **CIRCLE** command and snapping to endpoints only, draw the three highlighted circles. Then with the **LINE** command, draw the two highlighted lines shown in Figure 4-44.

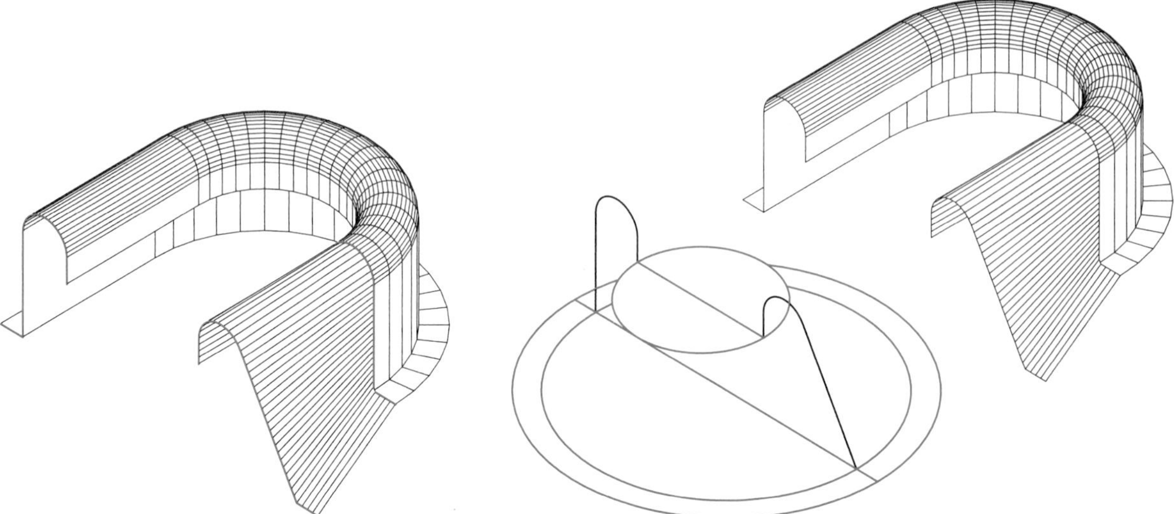

Figure 4-43 Polylines to be moved

Figure 4-44 Other objects to be added

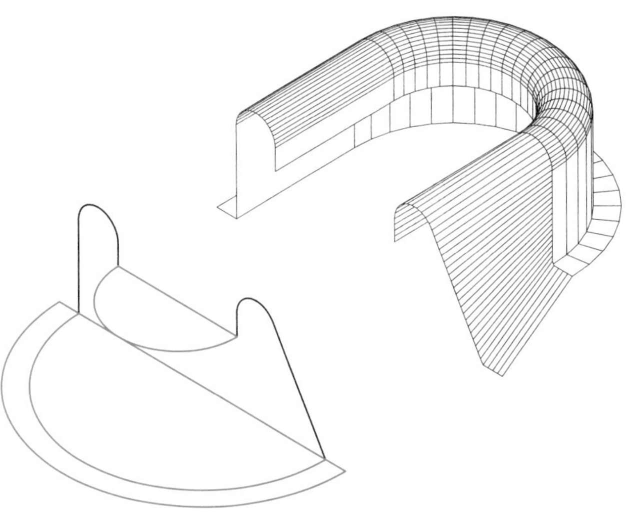

Figure 4-45 After trimming the objects

9. Using the two lines as the cutting edges, **TRIM** the portions of the circles as shown in Figure 4-45. Make sure the projection option of the **TRIM** command is set to UCS after you select the objects.
10. **ERASE** the two lines and select the **Front** UCS.
11. Using the polylines as the cutting edges, **TRIM** each of its end straight segments. The result is shown in Figure 4-46.

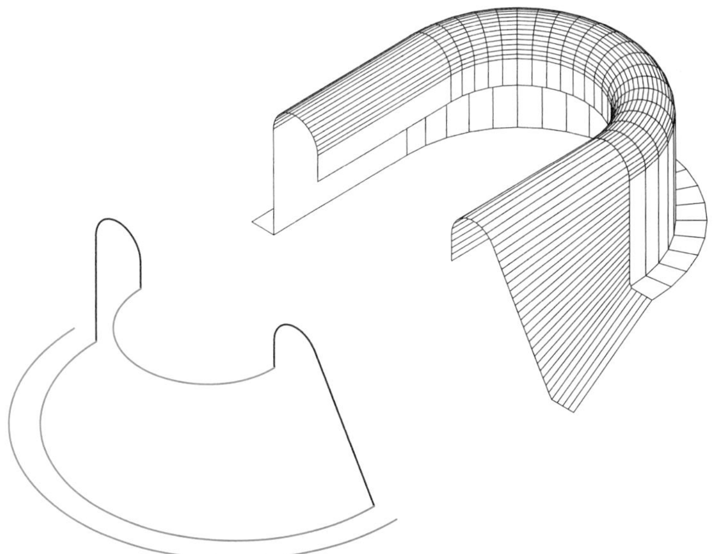

Figure 4-46 After performing the final trims

12. Invoke the **EDGESURF** command, using any of the methods shown in the grid. When prompted, select in any order the four edges that form a closed contour.
13. Select the **Top** UCS and **MOVE** the polygon mesh just created **4″** toward the positive direction of the *Y*-axis (Figure 4-47).
14. **ERASE** all the curves, leaving only the two arcs at the bottom.
15. Draw two small lines between the endpoints of the arcs, as shown in Figure 4-48.
16. Set the **SURFTAB2** variable to **4.**
17. Invoke the **EDGESURF** command again. When prompted, first select any of the arcs to make this the M direction of the mesh; then select the other three objects in any order.
18. **MOVE** the new polygon mesh 4″ toward the positive direction of the *Y*-axis.
19. **ERASE** the remaining arcs and lines.
20. Explore your 3D model using the **3DORBIT** command.
21. Invoke the **HIDE** command. The **3D** model should look like Figure 4-49.
22. **SAVE** the drawing.

EDGESURF	
Ribbon 3D Modeling panel	
Pull-down Menu	Draw/ Modeling/ Meshes/ Edge Surface
Command Line	edgesurf

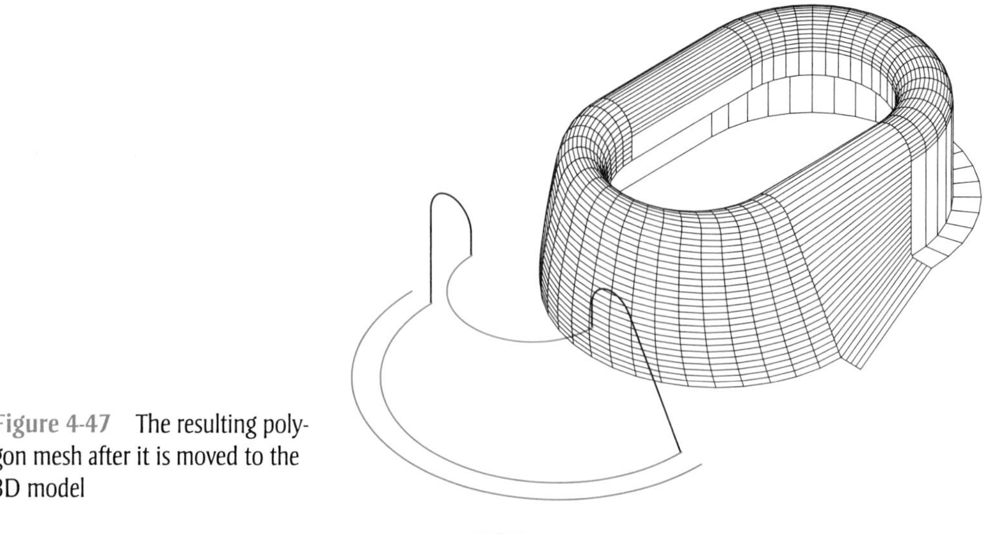

Figure 4-47 The resulting polygon mesh after it is moved to the 3D model

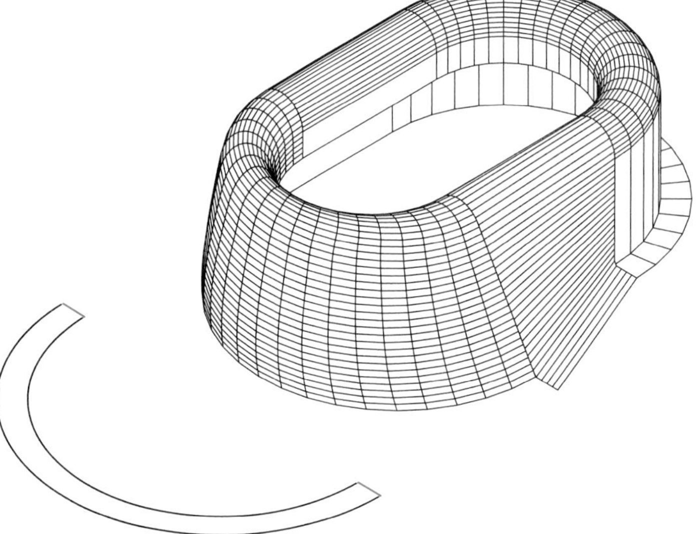

Figure 4-48 Preparing the last four edges

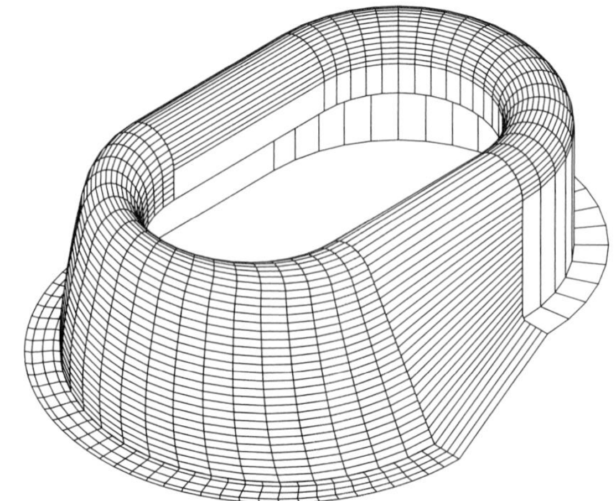

Figure 4-49 Final look of the 3D model

The different operations used to create faceted surfaces, in particular the **EDGESURF** command, are important tools in the development of complex shapes. The flexibility of polygon meshes and their possible transformations can be helpful in achieving complex designs. Understanding these tools is beneficial for the design process because they can assist users in the development of complex 3D models to support engineering documentation.

EDITING POLYGON MESHES

METHODS USED TO EDIT POLYGON MESHES

A polygon mesh can be easily transformed by stretching its grips. It is precisely its flexibility that makes this particular object useful for creating artistic and other free-form shapes. The following operations can be used to deform the vertices of a polygon mesh:

- Pulling the grips
- Using the **STRETCH** command
- Editing the polygon mesh with the **PEDIT** command
- Modifying the properties of the polygon mesh in the **Properties** palette

Deforming by Pulling the Grips

Pulling the selected grips of a polygon mesh will deform its original shape. The jar spout model shown in Figure 4-50 is a typical example. The procedure is simple. The grips first must be revealed by selecting the polygon mesh. Then specific grips must be selected and pulled a certain distance toward the desired direction. You can use the move grip tool to move the grips only in the direction of one of the three axes or within one of the three planes. You can select more than one grip by holding the **<Shift>** key down.

FOR MORE DETAILS See Chapter 3 for more information about using the move grip tool.

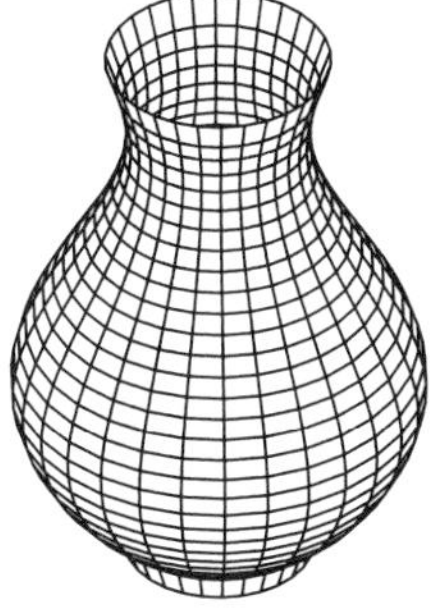

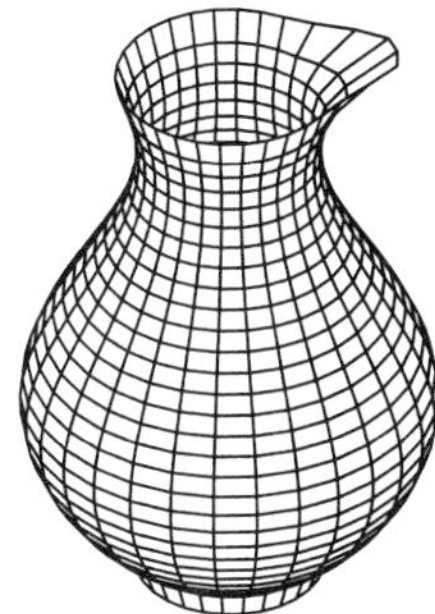

Figure 4-50 A jar spout is a typical example of how a shape can be produced by deforming the polygon mesh grips

If a grip is moved to the location of another grip, both grips will share the same location. You can move as many grips to the same location as you want. For example, by deforming the grips of a polyface mesh created with the **Box** option of the **3D** command, you can create another object such as a ridged pyramid (Figure 4-51).

Editing with the STRETCH Command

The **STRETCH** command also can be used to pull the vertices of a polygon mesh. All vertices enclosed with the crossing window are automatically deleted.

Editing with the PEDIT Command

The **PEDIT** command is used to edit not only polylines and 3D polylines, but also polygon meshes. Objects created as polyface meshes (boxes, wedges, and pyramids), however, cannot be edited with the **PEDIT** command.

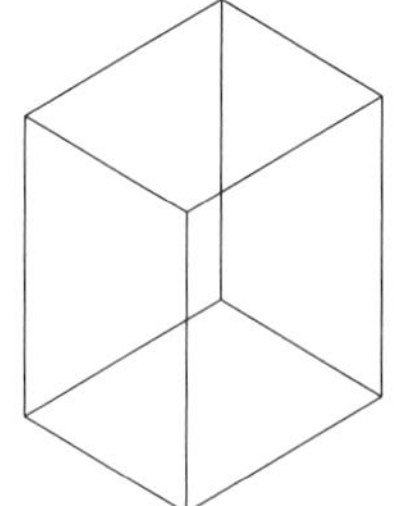
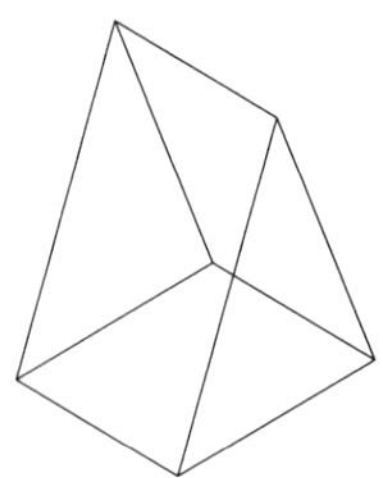

Figure 4-51 A ridge pyramid obtained by moving two grips of a box

When the **PEDIT** command is invoked, and the object selected is a polygon mesh, the options available are different from those for a polyline or a 3D polyline. Figure 4-52 compares the shortcut menus for these three types of objects.

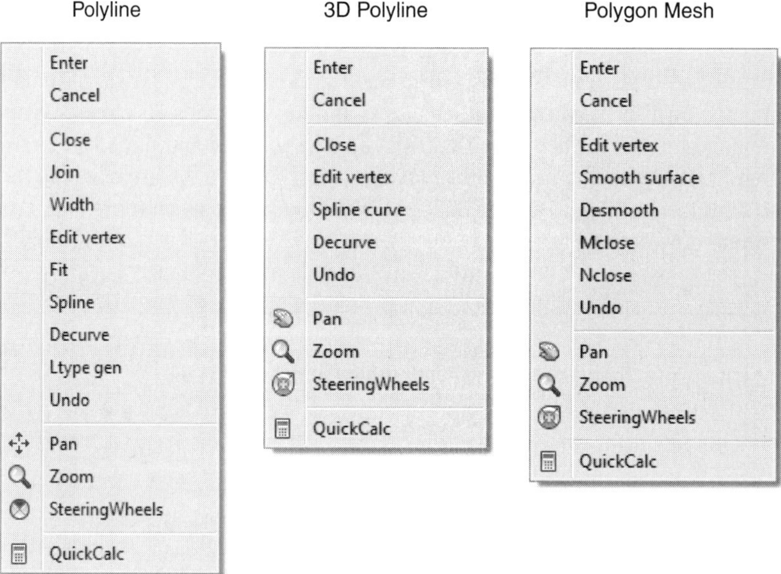

Figure 4-52 Comparison among the different PEDIT command shortcut menus displayed, depending on the type of object selected

The **Edit Vertex** option is used to move a specific vertex to a new location. You first specify the vertex by the submenu options (**Left, Right, Up, Down**), and then specify the **Move** option within this submenu. You will have to repeat the operation for the next vertex, or select the **eXit** option to return to the main menu.

[Next/Previous/Left/Right/Up/Down/Move/REgen/eXit]<N>:

It is easier to move a vertex by using the grips than with the **PEDIT** command. But if two vertices are in the same location, their common grip will move both vertices at the same time (Figure 4-53). The **PEDIT** command, on the other hand, allows you to select one specific vertex whether or not it shares the same location with another vertex.

The **Smooth surface** option smoothes the polygon mesh by fitting it into another type of surface generated by higher-degree mathematical equations.

Polygon meshes can be smoothed into three different types of surfaces (Figure 4-54). The value of the **SURFTYPE** system variable determines the type of surface that the original polygon mesh will be transformed to when smoothed.

- **5** will smooth the polygon mesh to a quadratic B-spline surface.
- **6** will smooth the polygon mesh to a cubic B-spline surface.
- **8** will smooth the polygon mesh to a Bezier surface.

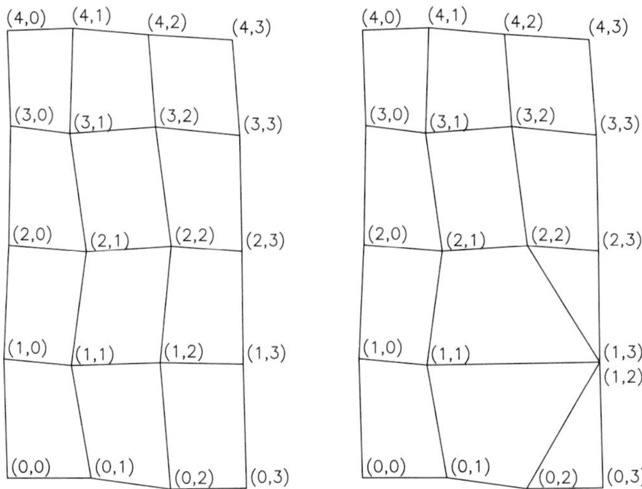

Figure 4-53 Two vertices located in the same place

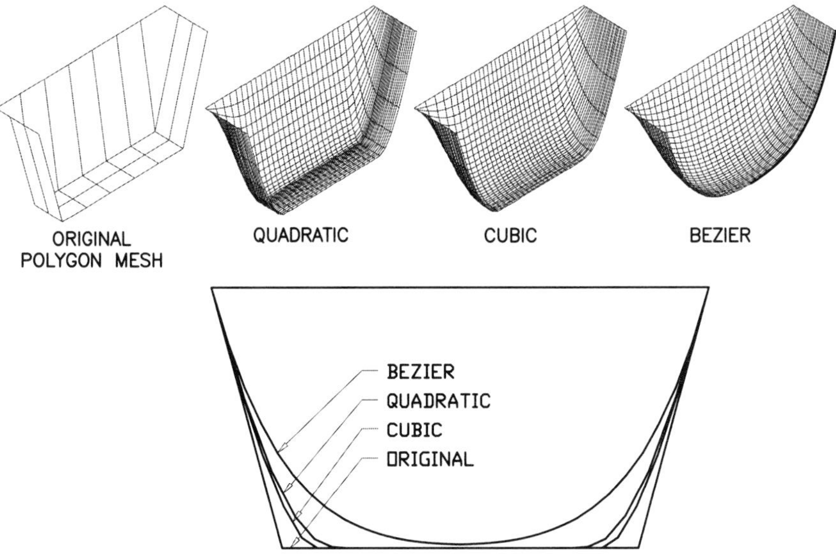

Figure 4-54 Polygon meshes can be transformed into three other smooth types of surfaces

The SURFU and SURFV System Variables

The **SURFU** and **SURFV** system variables control the density of the smoothed polygon mesh in the M and N directions, respectively. This is similar to the effect that the **SURFTAB1** and **SURFTAB2** system variables have on the number of vertices of the polygon meshes generated with the **REVSURF, TABSURF, RULESURF,** and **EDGESURF** commands.

The **SURFU** and **SURFV** variables can be set from **2** to **200, 6** being the default value. After you have established what type of surface the polygon mesh will be fitted into, and the density that it will have, you can proceed with the **Smooth surface** option.

The new smoothed faceted surface will have a different number of vertices placed in new locations, depending on the **SURFU** and **SURFV** values. The new M size will be **SURFU** + 1, and the new N size **SURFV** + 1.

The **Desmooth** option restores the smoothed mesh to the original polygon mesh. When a polygon mesh is in its smoothed state, its grips cannot be deformed, so this option will reset the polygon mesh back into its deformable stage.

The **Mclose** and **Nclose** options close or open a polygon mesh in the M or N direction by adding or removing the last set of polygons in the specified direction. The options change to **Mopen** and **Nopen** when the selected polygon mesh is closed in both directions (Figure 4-55).

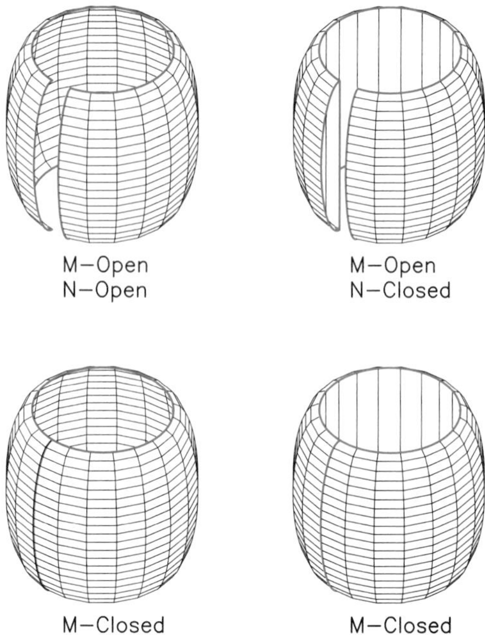

Figure 4-55 Polygon meshes can be transformed by closing or opening them in the N and M directions

Exercise 4-12: Deforming the Grips of a Polygon Mesh

1. Start a **NEW** drawing using the **acad** template.
2. **SAVE** the drawing **AS *Exercise 4–12.***
3. Select the **SW Isometric** viewing point.
4. Select the **Front** UCS.
5. Using the **3D** command, create a 4 × 8 mesh as shown in Figure 4-56. Respond to the command prompts as follows:

   Specify first corner point of mesh: *Specify point 1.*

   Specify second corner point of mesh: *Specify point 2.*

   Specify third corner point of mesh: *Specify point 3.*

   Specify fourth corner point of mesh: *Specify point 4.*

   Enter mesh size in the M direction: *4* ↵

   Enter mesh size in the N direction: *8* ↵

6. Select the **Right** UCS.
7. Select the polygon mesh to reveal its grips. Stretch all the highlighted grips in Figure 4-57 **6″** orthogonally in the positive direction of the *X*-axis. If needed, you can stretch the grips in several stages. When you are finished, the mesh should look like Figure 4-58.

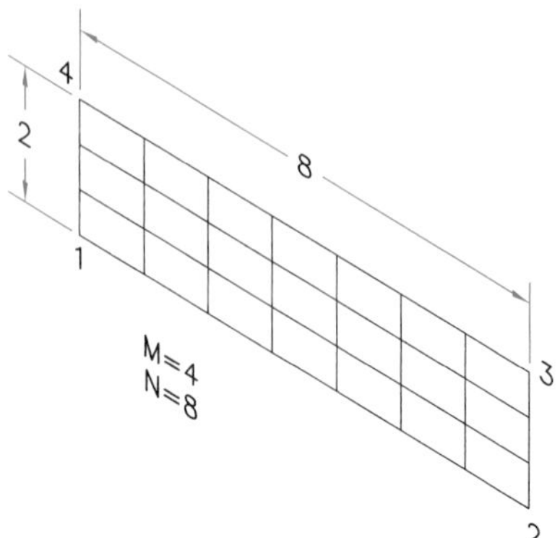

Figure 4-56 Mesh created with the 3D command

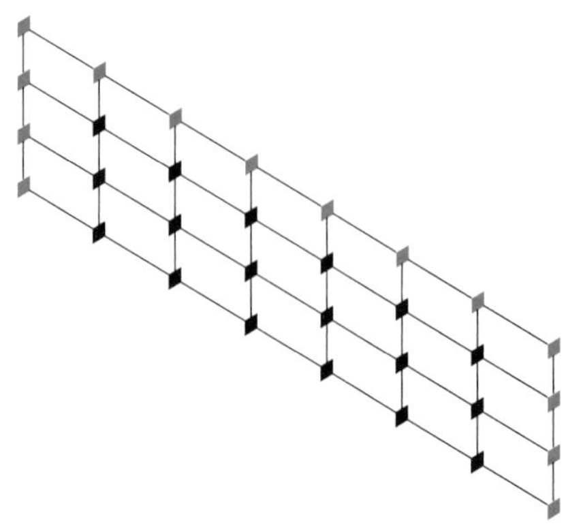

Figure 4-57 Grips to be selected

8. Select the polygon mesh to reveal its grips again. Stretch the two grips in the top rightmost edge **1″** up, orthogonally. The polygon mesh should look like Figure 4-59.
9. Set both system variables, **SURFU** and **SURFV**, to **30.**
10. Invoke the **PEDIT** command and respond to the prompts as follows:

Select polyline or [Multiple]:
Select the mesh.
Enter an option [Edit vertex/ Smooth surface/Desmooth/Mclose/ Nclose/Undo]: *s* ↵
Enter an option [Edit vertex/Smooth surface/Desmooth/Mclose/Nclose/Undo]:
↵ *(To exit the command)*

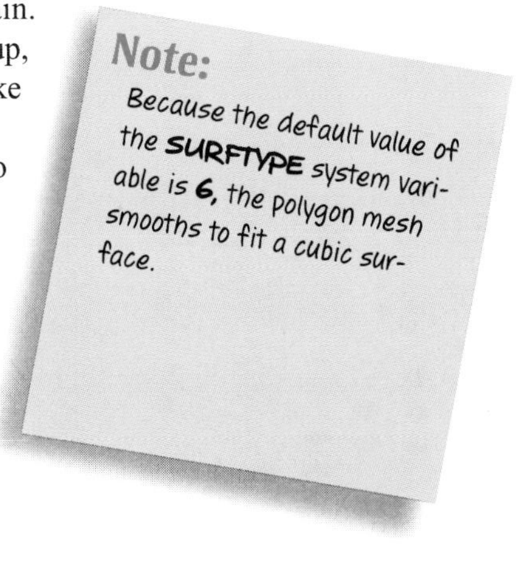

Note:
Because the default value of the SURFTYPE system variable is 6, the polygon mesh smooths to fit a cubic surface.

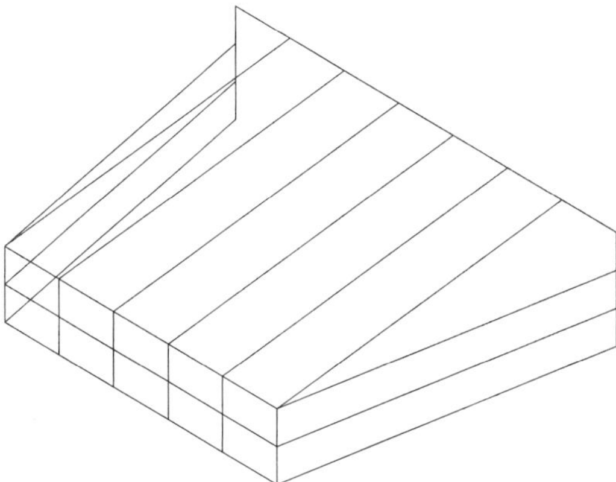

Figure 4-58 After the grips have been moved

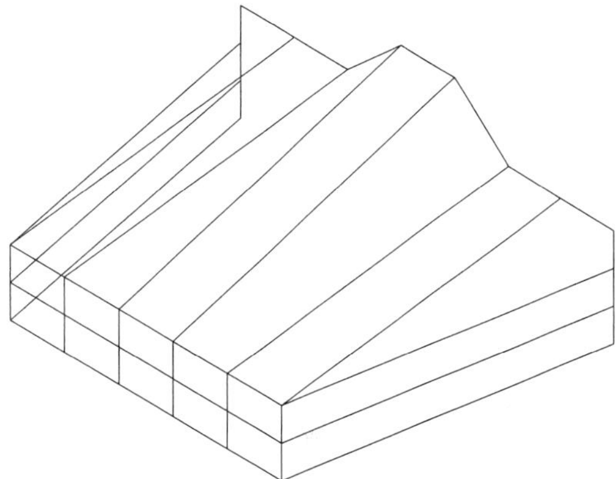

Figure 4-59 After the top grips have been moved

11. Invoke the **HIDE** command. The smoothed polygon mesh should look like Figure 4-60.
12. Select the **Realistic** visual style and use the **3DORBIT** command to check the other side of the 3D model.
13. Practice changing the **SURFTYPE** system variable to **5** and then **8** to smooth the polygon mesh into the quadratic and the Bezier types, respectively.
14. **SAVE** the drawing.

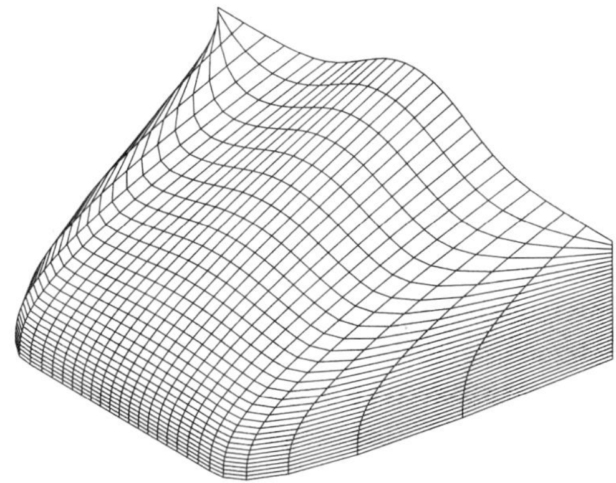

Figure 4-60 Polygon mesh smoothed into a cubic surface

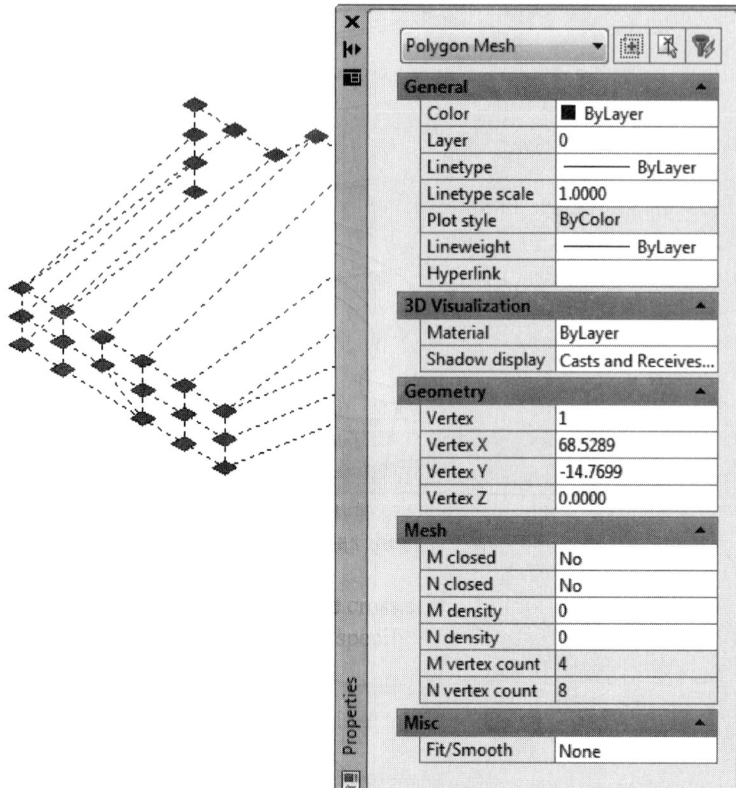

Figure 4-61 The Properties palette can be used to see and modify a polygon mesh's properties

Editing Polygon Meshes Through the Properties Palette

The **Properties** palette is a very useful tool for editing operations with almost every object. When the selection is a polygon mesh, this palette allows you to access the same editing tools as with the **PEDIT** command. Selecting the vertices is easy when using the **Properties** palette, especially when more than one vertex shares the same place (Figure 4-61).

You can smooth meshes by fitting them to any type of surface through the **Properties** window, without having to change the **SURFTYPE** system variable beforehand.

ADDITIONAL OBJECTS USED ALONG WITH POLYGON MESHES

Solids

As mentioned before, other simpler objects can be used along with polygon meshes to simplify the creation of planar surfaces and surfaces that curve in one direction.

A solid (also known as a 2D solid) is a planar object with four vertices, whose shape depends on the location of the vertices. Usually, a solid has a tetragonal shape, but it can also be triangular if two of its four edges are located in the same place. This type of object is created with the **SOLID** command. It allows you to specify either three or four points. Pressing the <**Enter**> key after specifying the third point will create a triangular solid. After you have drawn the first solid, the command will continue by asking for the points of the following solid.

A solid is always created in a plane parallel to the current *XY* plane of the current UCS. Its vertices can be moved individually to any other location within the *XY* plane of its UCS either by pulling its grips, or through the **Properties** palette (Figure 4-62).

Solids are better to use when working in a 2D environment because they can be turned into filled objects only when the viewing direction is perpendicular to the *XY* plane of the current UCS. Both the **FILL** and **FILLMODE** system variables control this setting.

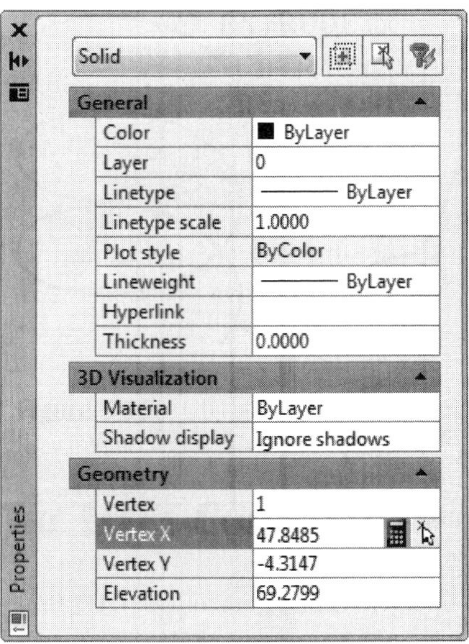

Figure 4-62 The Properties palette allows you to move the vertices of a 2D solid

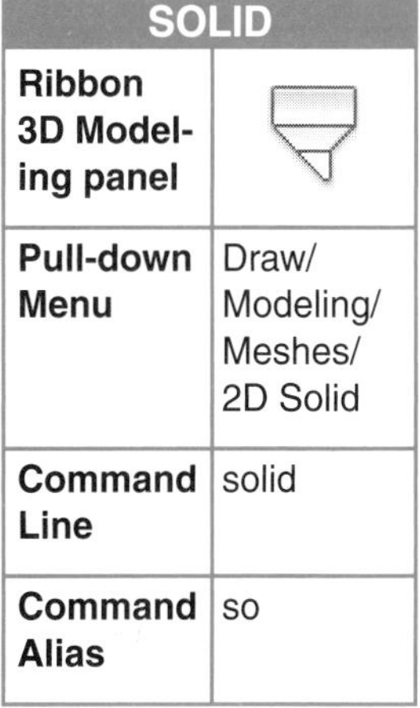

SOLID	
Ribbon 3D Modeling panel	
Pull-down Menu	Draw/ Modeling/ Meshes/ 2D Solid
Command Line	solid
Command Alias	so

Exercise 4-13: Creating and Modifying 2D Solid Objects

1. Start a **NEW** drawing.
2. **SAVE** the drawing **AS *Exercise 4-13.***
3. Set the **FILL** system variable to **0.**
4. Invoke the **SOLID** command. Draw, as closely as possible, the shape shown in Figure 4-63. Respond to the prompts as follows:

```
Specify first point: Specify point 1.
Specify second point: Specify point 2.
Specify third point: Specify point 3.
Specify fourth point or <exit>: Specify point 4.
Specify third point: Specify point 5.
Specify fourth point or <exit>: Specify point 6.
Specify third point: Specify point 7.
Specify fourth point or <exit>: Specify point 8.
Specify third point: ↵
```

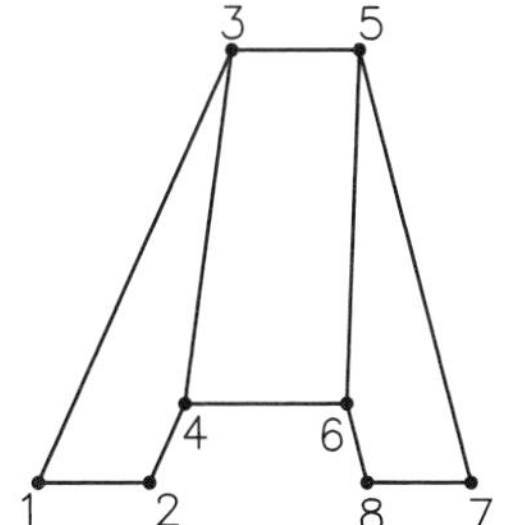

Figure 4-63 Shape to be drawn and the order in which the points should be specified

The AutoCAD® program uses the last two points entered on the first solid as the first two points for the next solid. That's why you are asked for only the third and fourth points. It is difficult to enter so many points at the same time without making mistakes, and the only advantage of doing so is to save time. If you prefer, you can stop the command right after the fourth point and start over. This way, you will simply create an individual solid in each operation, obtaining the same result.

5. Change the **FILL** system variable to **1.**
6. Invoke the **REGEN** command. The drawing should look like Figure 4-64.
7. Select the three 2D solids and practice stretching their grips while they are filled.
8. Select the **SE Isometric** viewing point. The fill should not show up from this viewing point.
9. Select the **Realistic** visual style to see the effects of shading this type of object.
10. Select the **2D Wireframe** visual style again.
11. Select the **Top** view again to see the fill.
12. **SAVE** the drawing.

Figure 4-64 The resulting 2D solid with the FILL mode on

3D Faces

A 3D face is an object with four vertices that is similar to a 2D solid. A 3D face, however, does not necessarily need to be planar; its four vertices can be located anywhere in the space. This type of object is created with the **3DFACE** command.

When two of the four vertices of a 3D face share the same location, the result will be a triangular 3D face. When all four vertices are located at different points, the resulting object will have either a tetragonal planar shape (if all the vertices belong to a common plane) or two adjoined triangular planar faces (Figure 4-65). AutoCAD divides the 3D face into two triangles, with the sole purpose of reflecting the light when using a shaded visual style or creating a rendered image.

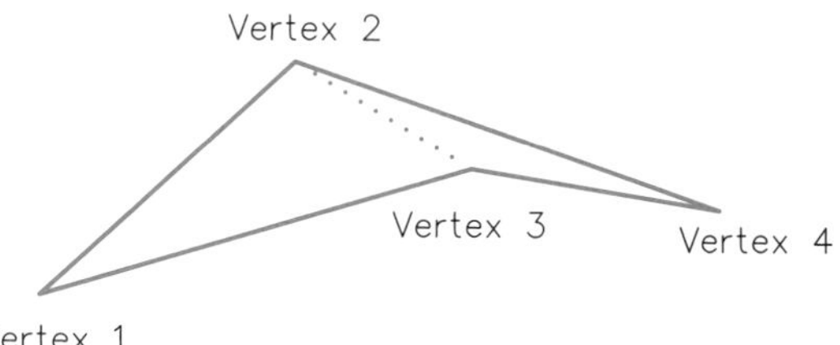

Figure 4-65 A nonplanar 3D face is shown by the AutoCAD program as two adjoined triangular planar faces

3D faces are also obtained by exploding polygon meshes. Depending on the shape of the mesh, some of the 3D faces can be planar and some nonplanar. But all of them can be used to represent a portion of any surface by stretching their vertices, just as if they were created with the **3DFACE** command.

Exercise 4-14: Using 3D Faces

1. Start a **NEW** drawing using the **acad** template.
2. **SAVE** the drawing **AS *Exercise 4-14.***
3. Set the **Drawing Units** to **Architectural,** by going to **Format/Units...**
4. Without placing any dimensions, draw the perimeter and the two centerlines shown in Figure 4-66.

TIP You must use a zoom factor big enough to fit the perimeter into the display. To do so, you can simply create a line 80′ long or so without worrying about seeing it in its entirety. Then you can invoke the **ZOOM Extents** command. The line can be erased afterward.

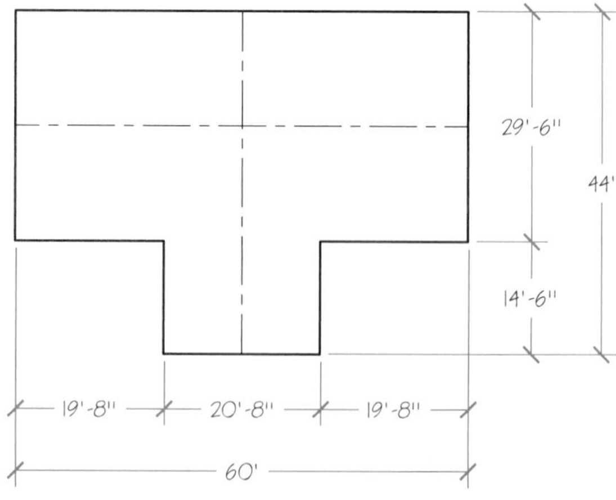

Figure 4-66 Contour shape to be drawn

5. Select the **SE Isometric** viewing point and the **2D Wireframe** visual style.
6. Select the **Front** UCS.
7. Place vertical lines as shown in Figure 4-67. Their endpoints will be used to create the roof using 3D faces. Two different linetypes show the two heights needed.
8. **ERASE** the two centerlines.

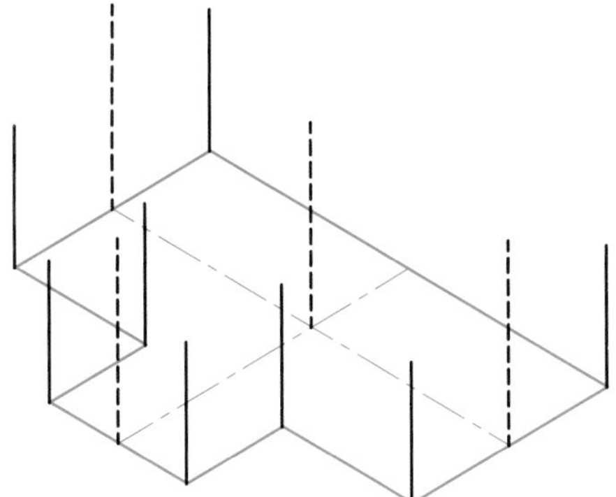

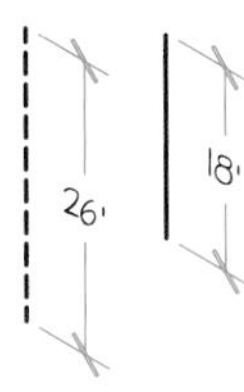

Figure 4-67 After the vertical lines are placed

3DFACE	
Ribbon 3D Modeling panel	
Pull-down Menu	Draw/ Modeling/ Meshes/ 3D Face
Command Line	3dface

9. Invoke the **3DFACE** command. Use one of the methods shown in the grid. Respond to the prompts as follows:

   Specify first point or [Invisible]: *Specify endpoint 1* (Figure 4-68).

   Specify second point or [Invisible]: *Specify endpoint 2.*

   Specify third point or [Invisible] <exit>: *Specify endpoint 3.*

   Specify fourth point or [Invisible] <create three-sided face>: *Specify endpoint 4.*

   Specify third point or [Invisible] <exit>: ↵ *(To end the command)*

Note:
After you specify the first point, you enter the rest of the points in a continuous order, either clockwise or counterclockwise, instead of in zigzag as with the **SOLID** command. Right after the third point is entered, you can specify the fourth one, or you can press the <**Enter**> key to create a triangular 3D face.

10. Invoke the **3DFACE** command again. Within the same operation, create two new 3D faces, one next to the other. Respond to the prompts as follows:

    Specify first point or [Invisible]: *Specify endpoint 1* (Figure 4-69).

    Specify second point or [Invisible]: *Specify endpoint 2.*

    Specify third point or [Invisible] <exit>: *Specify endpoint 3.*

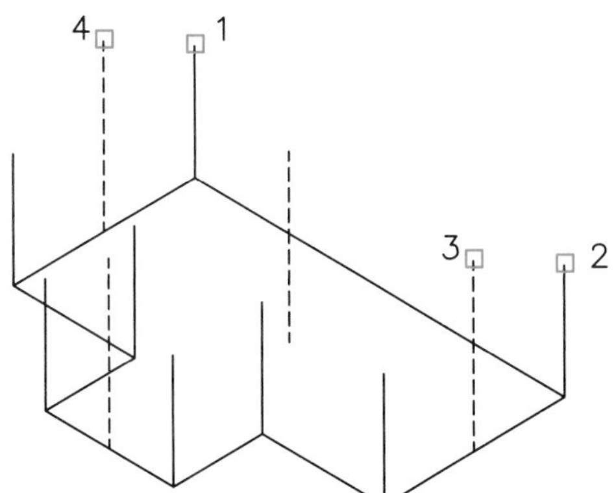

Figure 4-68 Order to specify the points for the 3DFACE operation

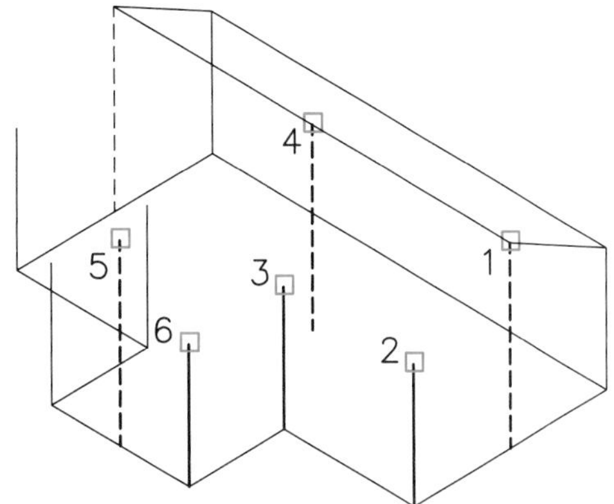

Figure 4-69 Order to specify the points for the 3DFACE operation

Specify fourth point or [Invisible] <create three-sided face>: *Specify endpoint 4.*

Specify third point or [Invisible]<exit>: *Specify endpoint 5.*

Specify fourth point or [Invisible] <create three-sided face>: *Specify endpoint 6.*

Specify third point or [Invisible] <exit>: ↵ *(To end the command)*

11. Select the **SW Isometric** viewing point.
12. Invoke the **HIDE** command.
13. Create the two 3D faces on the other side. Repeat the procedure you performed in step 10, using Figure 4-70 as a reference on how to specify the points.

Note:
You can create as many 3D faces within the same command as you want, as long as you carefully study the order in which the points should be entered. If you prefer, you can also stop the command and create the faces one by one. Regardless of which way you do it, the result will always be individual 3D faces.

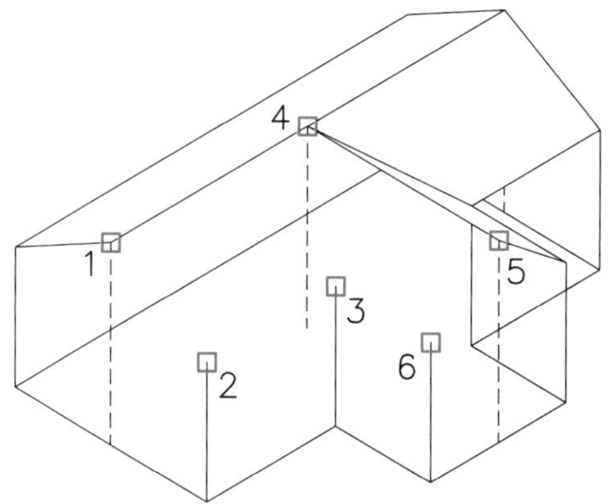

Figure 4-70 Order to specify the points for the 3DFACE operation

TIP Remember that to **ZOOM** or **PAN** after the **HIDE** command has been invoked, you must first invoke the **REGEN** command.

TIP Because the last 3D faces created are symmetrical to the previous ones, you could also have obtained them with the **MIRROR** or the **MIRROR3D** command.

14. **ERASE** all the vertical lines.
15. Add two 3D faces to create the left side of the house. This time, use the **Invisible** option so that the common edge for both faces is not shown.

Specify first point or [Invisible]: *Specify endpoint 1* (Figure 4-71).

Specify second point or [Invisible]: *Specify endpoint 2.*

Specify third point or [Invisible] <exit>: *i* ↵

Specify third point or [Invisible] <exit>: *Specify endpoint 3.*

Specify fourth point or [Invisible] <create three-sided face>: *Specify midpoint 4.*

Specify third point or [Invisible] <exit>: *Specify endpoint 5.*

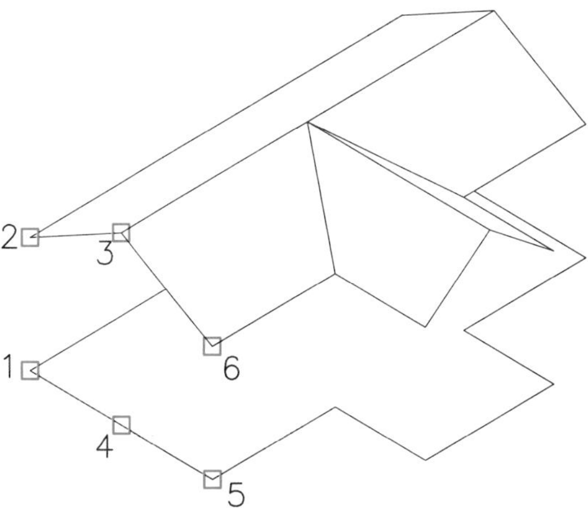

Figure 4-71 Order to specify the points for the 3DFACE operation

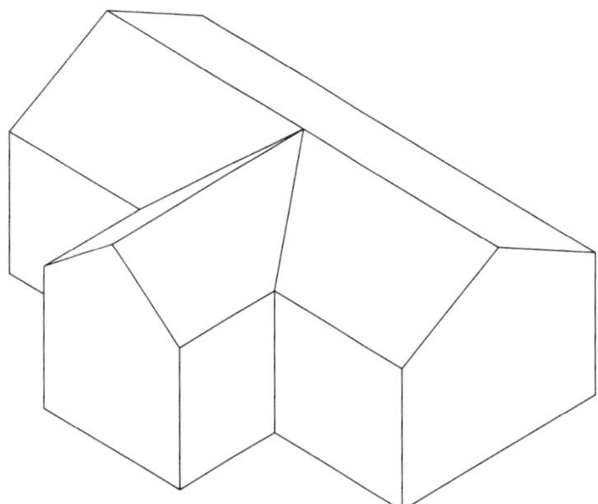

Figure 4-72 3D model completed using 3D faces

Specify fourth point or [Invisible] <create three-sided face>: *Specify endpoint 6.*

Specify third point or [Invisible] <exit>:↵ *(To end the command)*

16. Create the rest of the walls to complete the 3D model. When you are finished, the model should look like Figure 4-72 from the **SE Isometric** viewing point.
17. Select the **Realistic** visual style and invoke the **3DORBIT** command to inspect the 3D model.
18. **SAVE** the drawing.

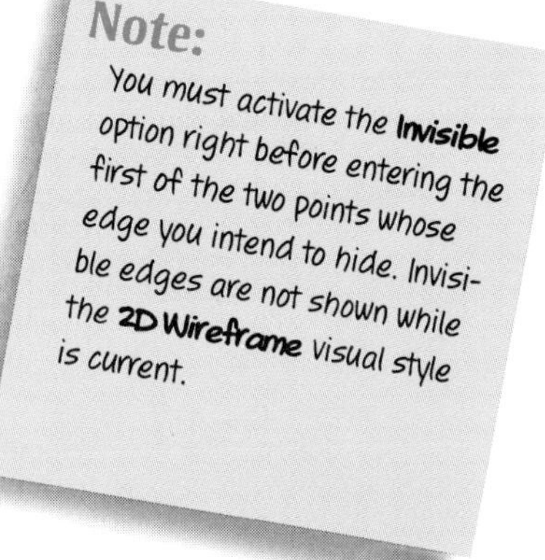

EDGE	
Ribbon 3D Modeling panel	
Pull-down Menu	Draw/ Modeling/ Meshes/ Edge
Command Line	edge

By using several 3D faces next to one another, and hiding some of the edges by using the **Invisible** option, you can create many different surface models. Sometimes, however, it is difficult to make the correct edge invisible. To solve this problem, you can use one of two different methods:

1. Use the **Properties** palette (Figure 4-73) to change the visibility of each individual edge.
2. Use the **EDGE** command. It can be invoked by using any of the methods shown in the grid.

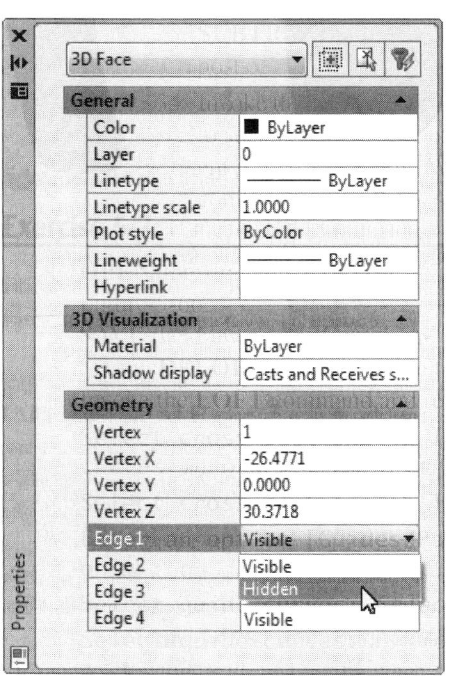

Figure 4-73 Using the Properties palette to hide edges

With the **EDGE** command, you can select as many edges as you need on multiple 3D faces. You then press the <**Enter**> key to finish the selection and exit the command, toggling the display of selected edges.

The **Display All** option of the **EDGE** command can be used to temporarily show the hidden edges of all the 3D faces in the drawing.

THICKENED OBJECTS

This is the simplest type of 3D object. Simply changing the **Thickness** property of certain objects extrudes them perpendicularly to the *XY* plane of the object's UCS. An object can be thickened by a positive value, or by a negative value (to reverse the direction of the operation).

Objects whose thickness value can be changed are arcs, circles, lines, polylines, donuts, single-line texts, and 2D solids (Figure 4-74). Some of the objects whose thickness value cannot be changed include regions, ellipses, multiline texts, 3D polylines, splines, 3D faces, and polygon meshes.

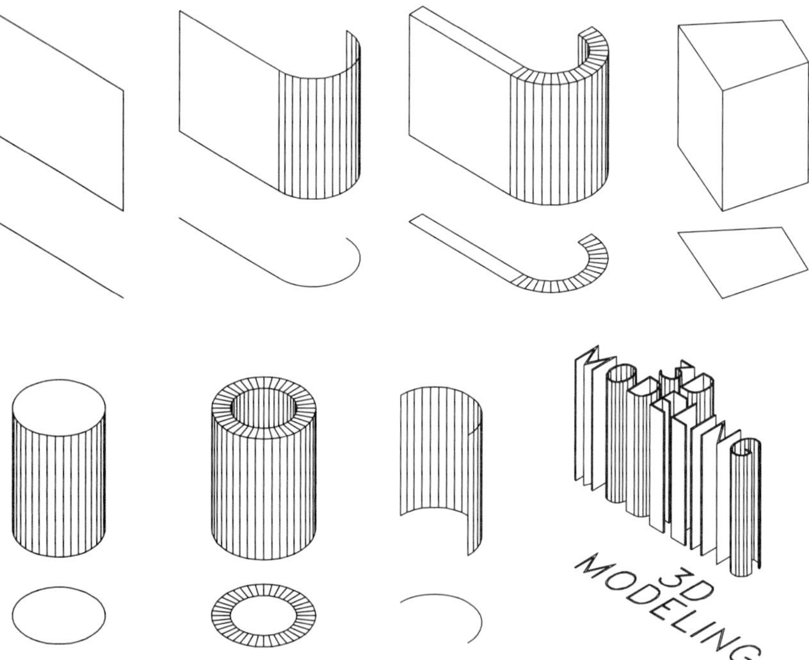

Figure 4-74 Different objects shown with and without a thickness value

The **Thickness** property can be easily changed in the **Properties** palette (Figure 4-75).

The following is a description of some of the characteristics that are added to the objects if the thickness property is different from the default value of 0.00.

Arcs and circles: When these objects are thickened, the number of points that you can snap to, as well as the number of grips, is doubled (Figure 4-76).

Lines and polylines: The number of grips is doubled. The snap points, besides being doubled, have an additional midpoint to snap to in each vertical element. The **Width** property in polylines does not give this type of object any extra grips or snap points (Figure 4-77).

When the default **2D Wireframe** visual style is active, the **VIEWRES** system variable controls the number of segments of thickened arcs and circles.

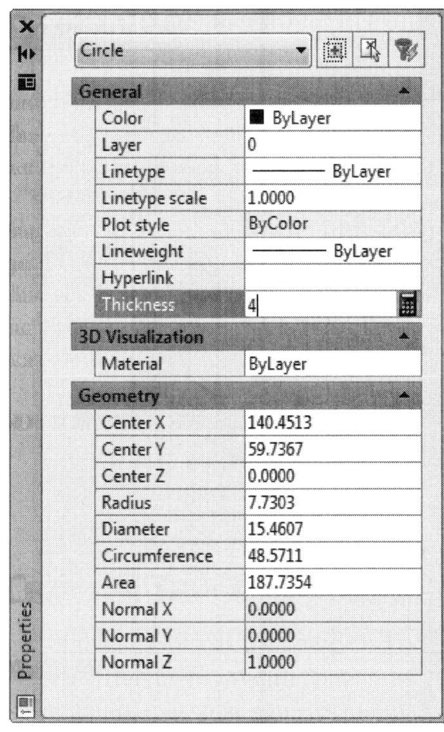

Figure 4-75 The Thickness property in the Properties palette

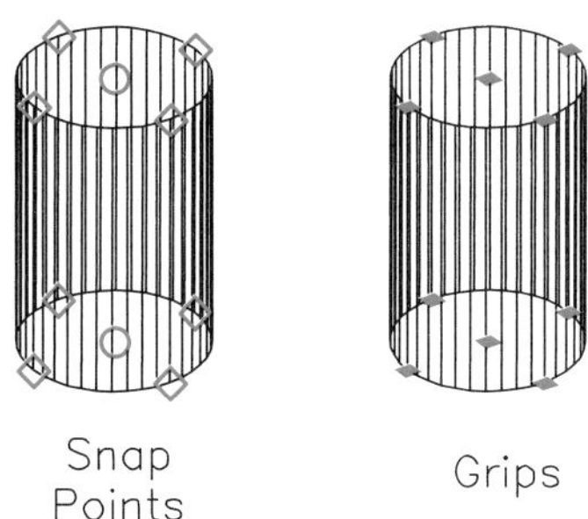

Figure 4-76 Points to snap to and grips are doubled for arcs and circles with a thickness value

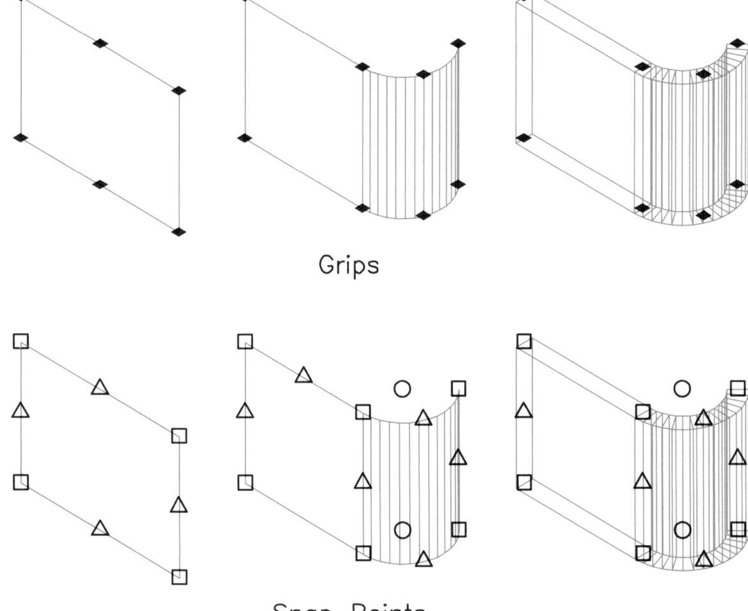

Figure 4-77 Points to snap to and grips on thickened lines and polylines

Regions

A *region* is a bounded 2D area that can more easily be used to represent any planar surface than can polygon meshes, 2D solids, and 3D faces. Regions can be obtained from a group of planar curves, using either the **REGION** or the **BOUNDARY** commands; or by performing 3D operations, such as sectioning a 3D solid with the **SECTION** command; or by copying planar faces with the **SOLIDEDIT** command.

FOR MORE DETAILS See Chapter 5 for more information about the **SECTION** command. See Chapter 6 for more information about the **SOLIDEDIT** command.

REGION	
Draw Toolbar **Ribbon Draw panel**	
Pull-down Menu	Draw/ Region
Command Line	region

The **REGION** command is really simple to use. It simply prompts you to select the objects that will be turned into regions. Creating the objects is the part you must pay the most attention to because all the objects that will be turned into a region must meet the following conditions:

- They must all be either planar curves or straight lines.
- They must all be placed in the same plane.
- They must all be placed in contact with each other (their endpoints must meet).
- They must form a closed loop.
- No object can intersect another one.

Even though regions are infinitely thin objects, they accept the same ***Boolean operations*** that are used to modify 3D solids. Their mass property information, such as area, moment of inertia, and centroid, can be obtained with the **MASSPROP** command.

Boolean operations: Union, subtract, and intersect operations that are performed on regions and 3D solids.

Another advantage of regions is that splines can also be used to create this type of object, allowing you to create more complex shapes.

Boolean Operations with Regions: UNION, SUBTRACT, and INTERSECT

You can combine regions that coexist in the same plane by using one of the following Boolean operation commands:

- **UNION**
- **SUBTRACT**
- **INTERSECT**

UNION	
Solids Editing Toolbar **Ribbon Solid Editing panel**	
Pull-down Menu	Modify/ Solids Editing/ Union
Command Line	union
Command Alias	uni

UNION creates a region by joining any number of regions that belong to the same plane. The resulting area will be the sum of all the areas that are not common.

The **SUBTRACT** command creates a region by subtracting a region or group of regions from another region or group of regions. When subtracting regions, you must consider the selection of regions to be divided into two groups:

- First group: Region(s) to subtract from
- Second group: Region(s) to subtract

If more than one region is selected in the first group, this part of the operation will automatically be considered to be a **UNION.**

INTERSECT creates a region from the unique common area among a group of regions.

The region resulting from a Boolean operation depends on the relative location of the two regions or groups of regions selected. Figure 4-78 shows the three possible situations for each particular operation:

- The two regions have no area in common.
- One of the regions is completely contained inside the other region.
- One of the regions is partially contained inside the other region.

Note: In Figure 4-78, the region shown in hidden lines in the **SUBTRACT** operation is the one to be subtracted.

Regions are no longer rigid objects that can be edited only by performing Boolean operations. When you use the **MOVE, ROTATE,** or **SCALE** command, rather than selecting the entire region, you can now hold the <**Ctrl**> key down and select edges instead. Performing such operations on the edges of the region will readjust its geometry and location, as well as modify adjacent edges accordingly. The grips of the region, however, cannot be used to stretch the region.

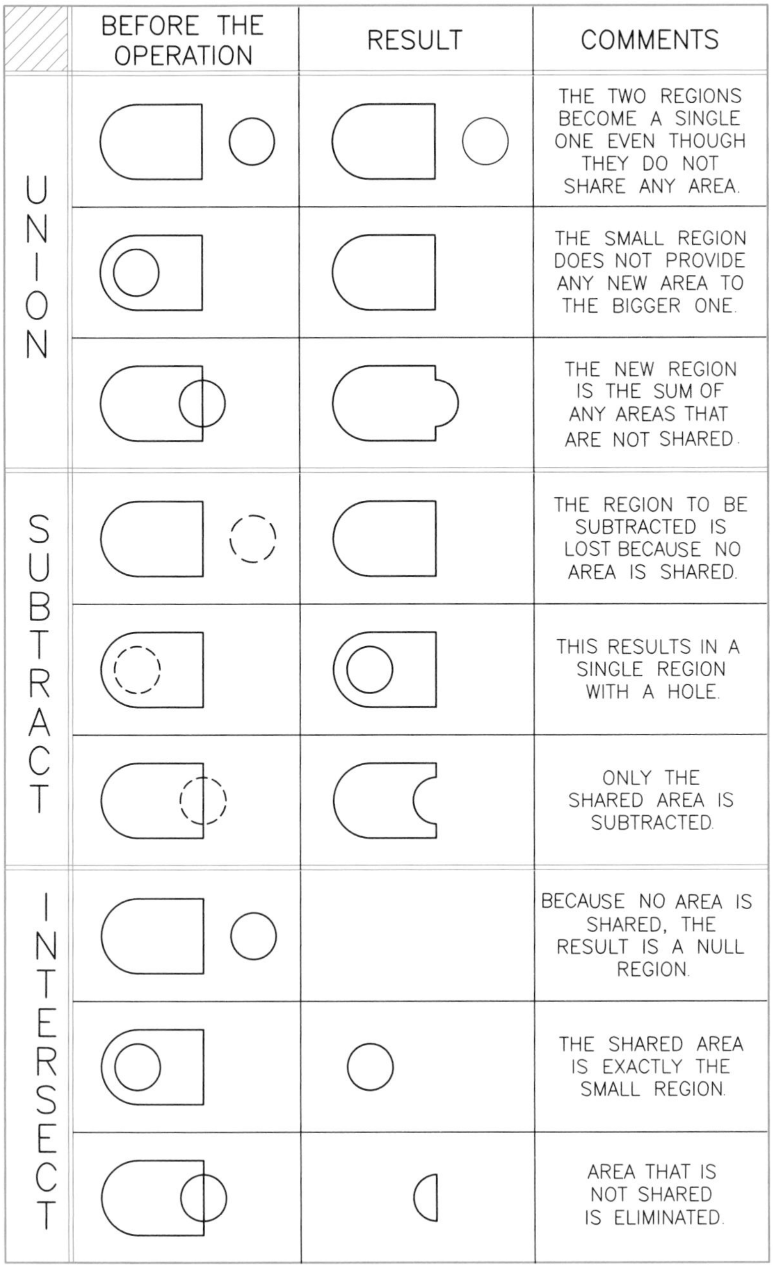

	BEFORE THE OPERATION	RESULT	COMMENTS
UNION			THE TWO REGIONS BECOME A SINGLE ONE EVEN THOUGH THEY DO NOT SHARE ANY AREA.
			THE SMALL REGION DOES NOT PROVIDE ANY NEW AREA TO THE BIGGER ONE.
			THE NEW REGION IS THE SUM OF ANY AREAS THAT ARE NOT SHARED.
SUBTRACT			THE REGION TO BE SUBTRACTED IS LOST BECAUSE NO AREA IS SHARED.
			THIS RESULTS IN A SINGLE REGION WITH A HOLE.
			ONLY THE SHARED AREA IS SUBTRACTED.
INTERSECT			BECAUSE NO AREA IS SHARED, THE RESULT IS A NULL REGION.
			THE SHARED AREA IS EXACTLY THE SMALL REGION.
			AREA THAT IS NOT SHARED IS ELIMINATED.

Figure 4-78 The three possible situations and results for each Boolean operation with regions

SUBTRACT	
Solids Editing Toolbar	
Ribbon Solid Editing panel	
Pull-down Menu	Modify/ Solids Editing/ Subtract
Command Line	subtract
Alias	su

INTERSECT	
Solids Editing Toolbar	
Ribbon Solid Editing panel	
Pull-down Menu	Modify/ Solids Editing/ Intersect
Command Line	intersect
Command Alias	in

REGION	
Draw Toolbar	
Ribbon Solid Editing panel	
Pull-down Menu	Draw/ Region
Command Line	region

Exercise 4-15: Combining Different Types of Objects to Generate Surface Models

In this exercise you will create a simple 3D model in which you will combine regions and thickened objects to represent the surfaces.

1. Start a **NEW** drawing using the **acad** template.
2. **SAVE** the drawing **AS *Exercise 4-15.***
3. Using only lines and arcs, draw the objects shown in Figure 4-79 anywhere in the drawing area. Instead of circles place two mirrored arcs. That way, you will create the effect of a cylindrical hole when changing their thickness.
4. With **Ortho** mode activated, **COPY** all the objects **5″** orthogonally to the right.
5. Invoke the **REGION** command, using one of the methods shown in the grid. When prompted, select the group of objects on the left. In the command line window, the AutoCAD program should advise you about the creation of three regions:

   `3 loops extracted.`

   `3 Regions created.`

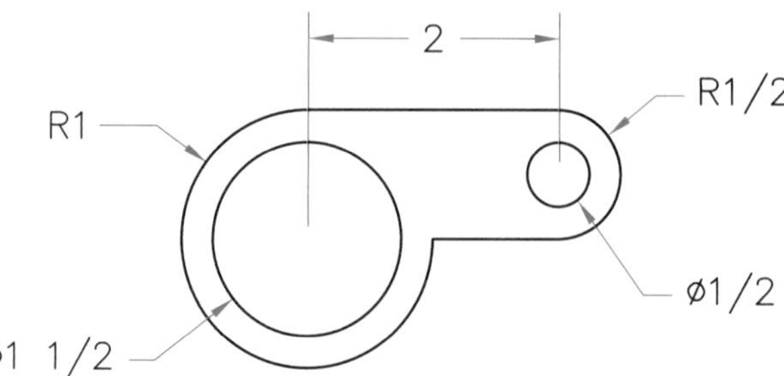

Figure 4-79 Dimensions for the objects to be drawn

6. Select the **SE Isometric** viewing point.
7. **ZOOM** in as needed.
8. Assign a **Color** to the two circular regions that is different from the color used for the bigger region.
9. Select the **Conceptual** visual style.
10. Invoke the **SUBTRACT** command. You will subtract the two circular regions from the main region. Respond to the prompts as follows:

    `Select solids and regions to subtract from...`

    `Select objects:` *`Select the main region by picking on its border, not inside the shaded area.`*

    `Select objects:` ↵ *`(To end the selection)`*

    `Select solids and regions to subtract...`

    `Select objects:` *`Select the two circular regions using selection windows.`*

    `Select objects:` ↵ *`(To end the selection)`*

11. Make sure no command is in progress and select the group of objects on the right. Right-click in the drawing area and select **Properties** from the shortcut menu. In the **Properties** palette, change the **Thickness** value of the selected objects to **2**.
12. Select the **2D Wireframe** visual style.
13. Invoke the **HIDE** command. The model should look like Figure 4-80.
14. **MOVE** the region from the center point of the bigger hole to the corresponding center point on the top of the thickened objects.
15. **COPY** the region from any endpoint on the thickened objects to the endpoint located vertically below it.
16. Invoke the **HIDE** command again. The 3D model should look now like Figure 4-81.
17. **SAVE** the drawing.

Note:

When copying the region, you might have some difficulty selecting it because it shares all its edges with the thickened objects. One way to make the selection easier is to use the **DRAWORDER** command. This command places selected objects under the other objects, changing the order in which they will be picked.

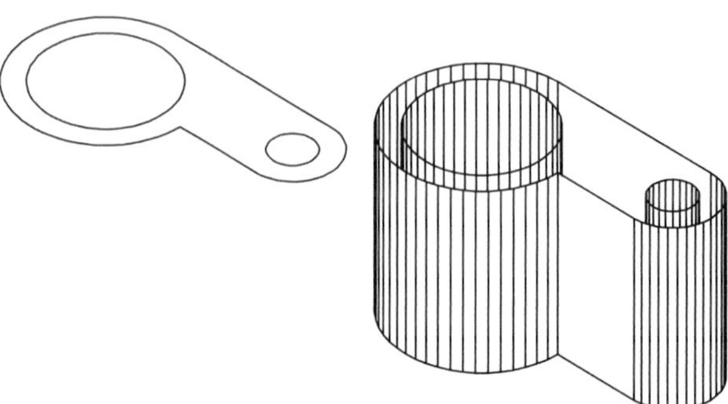

Figure 4-80 After hiding the occulted lines of the thickened objects

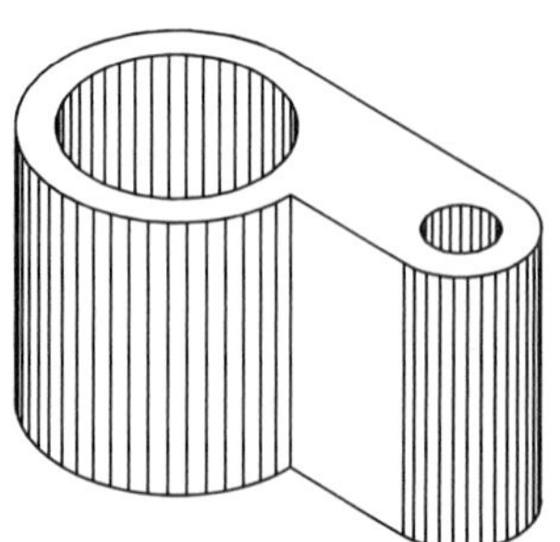

Figure 4-81 The 3D model after placing the regions

Exploding Faceted Surfaces

The **EXPLODE** command can be useful when working with faceted surfaces. When a polygon mesh or a polyface mesh is exploded, all the adjacent faces of the mesh are separated into 3D faces, which you studied previously.

On the other hand, solids and 3D faces cannot be exploded any further. If you need to explode a 3D face or a solid, the procedure requires converting it into regions first, which then can be exploded into lines. Just keep in mind that regions are planar objects, so only planar 3D faces can be converted to regions.

Summary

Throughout this chapter you have learned the different operations used to develop 3D models that are represented by faceted surfaces and other similar objects. You have also been introduced to the considerations involved in determining whether surface modeling is the appropriate method to use. By following the tutorials, you should realize how important it is to develop the necessary curves throughout the 3D space prior to creating faceted surfaces.

You have studied in depth the different operations used to generate polygon meshes. These are the most important and complex objects used in this type of representation of 3D objects.

Other types of objects such as regions, 3D faces, solids, and thickened 2D objects have also been discussed in this chapter. Because of their characteristics, they are also suitable for use with polygon meshes in achieving the main purpose: covering all the surfaces of the 3D model with objects that can be shaded and that can hide other objects.

You have also learned that by performing Boolean operations with regions, you can easily obtain complex planar surfaces.

Chapter Test Questions

Multiple Choice

1. Which of the following objects can represent any type of faceted surface?
   a. Region
   b. 3D face
   c. Polygon mesh
   d. 2D solid
2. Which primitive 3D model can be created with the 3D command?
   a. Cylinder
   b. Torus
   c. Sphere
   d. All of the above
3. Which of the following methods cannot be used to edit polygon meshes?
   a. The **STRETCH** command
   b. Pulling the grips
   c. The **PEDIT** command
   d. The **TRIM** command
4. Which of the following commands requires selecting four curves, one next to the other, forming a closed path?
   a. **REVSURF**
   b. **TABSURF**
   c. **EDGESURF**
   d. **RULESURF**
5. Which of the following can be used to perform Boolean operations?
   a. Polygon meshes
   b. 3D faces
   c. Regions
   d. Thickened objects
6. If you had to represent a flat piece of sheet metal with a slotted hole on it, which single object would you use to achieve your purpose?
   a. 3D face
   b. Region
   c. 2D solid
   d. Polygon mesh
7. For which of the following can the thickness value **not** be changed?
   a. 2D solids
   b. Regions
   c. Arcs
   d. Single-line texts
8. Which of the following is not a Boolean operation command?
   a. **INTERSECT**
   b. **UNION**
   c. **COMBINE**
   d. **SUBTRACT**

9. When converting objects into regions, the objects should meet which of the following conditions?
   a. All should be planar curves.
   b. All must coexist in the same plane.
   c. They must form a closed loop.
   d. All of the above
10. If you perform a **SUBTRACT** operation between two concentric circles of different diameters and select the bigger circle as the object to subtract, the result of the operation will be:
   a. The bigger circle
   b. The bigger circle, with a hole
   c. No object
   d. None of the above

Matching

a. REVSURF
b. TABSURF
c. UNION
d. SURFTAB1
e. SURFTYPE
f. EDGESURF
g. INTERSECT
h. RULESURF
i. 2D Solid
j. SURFU

1. Creates faceted surfaces that look like Coons patches
2. Controls the density of smoothed meshes
3. Creates surfaces between two curves
4. Returns the sum of all unshared areas of the regions selected
5. Planar surface having four vertices
6. Sets the type of surface to smooth the mesh
7. Creates faceted surfaces that look like extrusions
8. Creates faceted surfaces of revolution
9. Returns the unique area of selected regions
10. Controls the number of vertices for the M direction

True or False

1. True or False: Surfaces with a single curvature (with curvature in only one direction) can be represented only with polygon meshes.
2. True or False: When one of the objects of the **3D** command is invoked, the object snap is temporarily turned off.
3. True or False: The M × N mesh of a polygon mesh can be closed in only one direction, either M or N, but not in both directions.
4. True or False: The **SURFTAB1** and **SURFTAB2** system variables control the density of the meshes created with the **3D** command.
5. True or False: The **REVSURF** command will proceed if the curve to be revolved forms a closed contour.
6. True or False: Just like regions, the grips of 3D faces cannot be stretched to deform the object.
7. True or False: When a polygon mesh is exploded, all the joined polygons are separated into 3D faces. These 3D faces are completely different from the ones created with the **3DFACE** command.
8. True or False: The command that can be more appropriately used to create the faceted surface of a truncated cone is the **RULESURF** command.
9. True or False: A thickened object is obtained by simply changing its thickness property. This type of object, however, does not hide the lines of the objects located behind it when the **HIDE** command is invoked.
10. True or False: An equilateral triangle is drawn on the *XY* plane. One of its sides is constructed by placing two overlapping lines, each shorter than the triangle's side length. Regardless of the condition of the four lines, a region can be created from these objects.

Chapter Tutorials

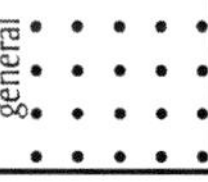

Tutorial 4-1: The Mouse Surfaces

This tutorial is a continuation of **Tutorial 3-2.** Here, you will create the polygon meshes that cover the entire mouse, using the knowledge you have acquired from this chapter.

1. **OPEN** the drawing ***Tutorial 3-2*** you created in Chapter 3.
2. **SAVE** the drawing **AS *Tutorial 4-1.***
3. Create a layer named **Surfaces** in the **Layer Properties Manager** window (Figure 4-82) and assign a color to it.

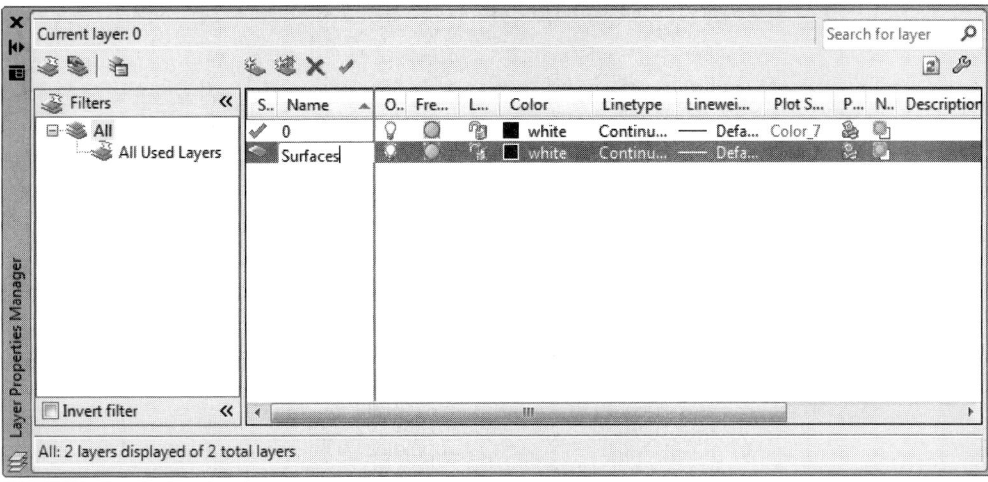

Figure 4-82 The Layer Properties Manager dialog box

4. Make sure the **Surfaces** layer is not set as current, and turn it off from the drop-down list located in the **Layers** panel of the Ribbon (Figure 4-83).
5. Change both the **SURFTAB1** and **SURFTAB2** system variable values to **20**.

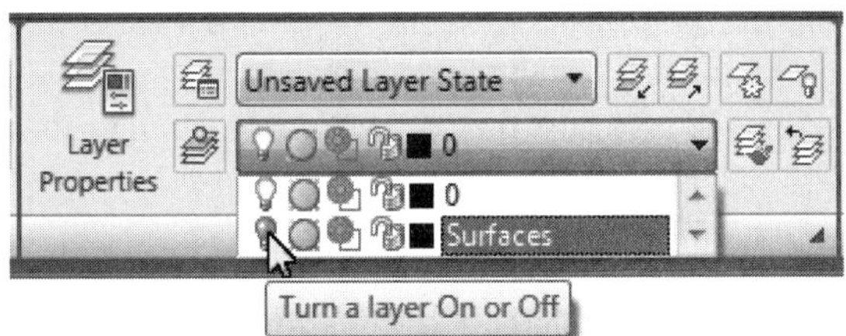

Figure 4-83 The drop-down list located in the Layers panel of the Ribbon

6. Invoke the **EDGESURF** command and, when prompted, select the four curves or wires that are required to create the polygon mesh shown highlighted in Figure 4-84.
7. Change the layer of the polygon mesh to the **Surfaces** layer. This will hide the object, facilitating the selection of the wires below in case it is required.

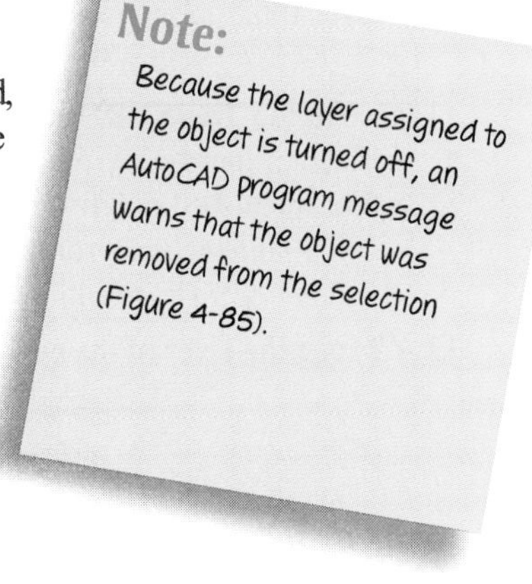

Note:
Because the layer assigned to the object is turned off, an AutoCAD program message warns that the object was removed from the selection (Figure 4-85).

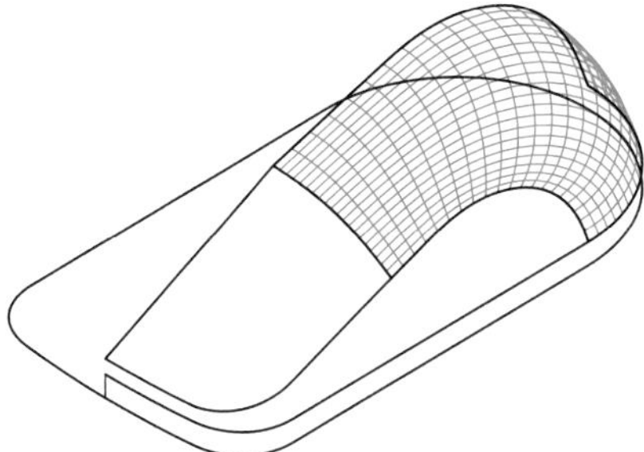

Figure 4-84 Polygon mesh generated with the EDGESURF command

8. Create another polygon mesh using the **EDGESURF** command. Select the four wires required to create the highlighted polygon mesh shown in Figure 4-86.

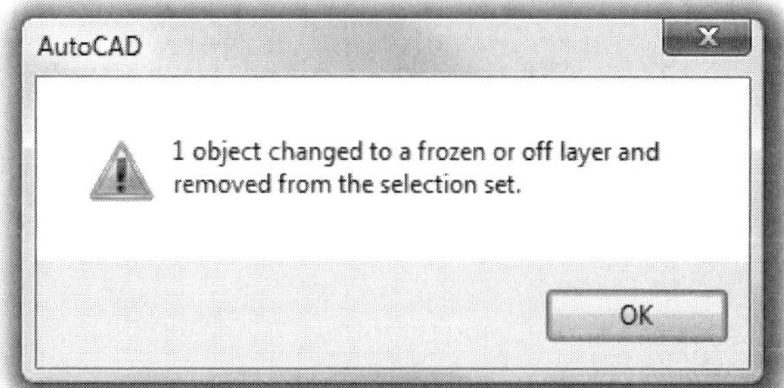

Figure 4-85 Warning from the AutoCAD program

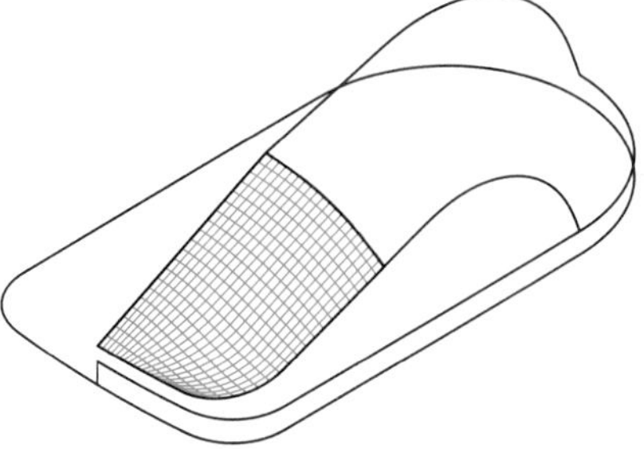

Figure 4-86 New polygon mesh generated with the EDGESURF command

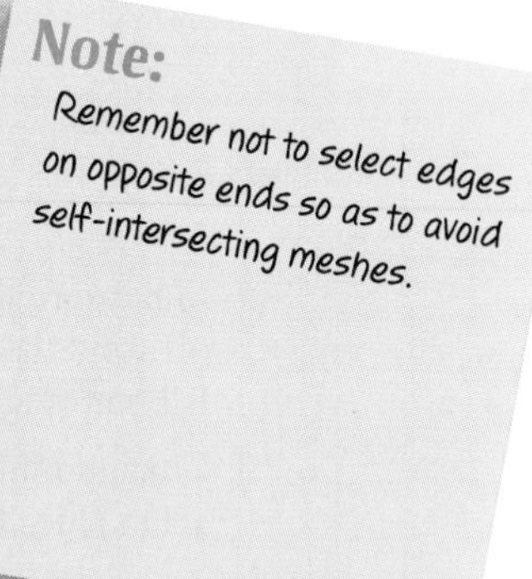

Note:
Remember not to select edges on opposite ends so as to avoid self-intersecting meshes.

9. Change its layer to the **Surfaces** layer. This will remove the object from the display.
10. Because of the way in which the wires are prepared, the side and the front surfaces will be made of three ruled surfaces. Invoke the **RULESURF** command for each case, and select the proper curves in order to create the three polygon meshes shown in Figure 4-87. After each mesh is created, change its layer to **Surfaces.**

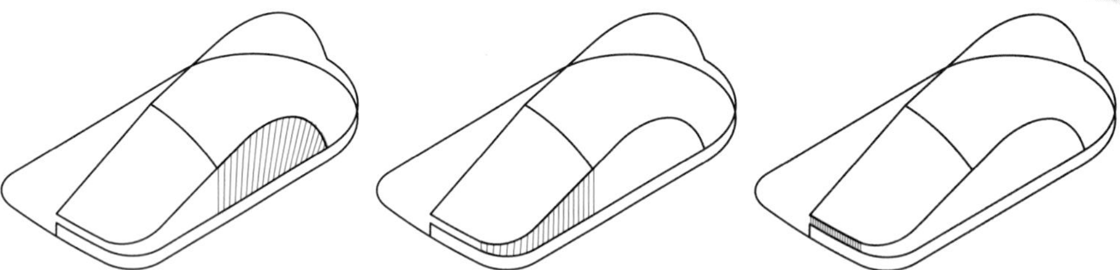

Figure 4-87 Three polygon meshes generated with the RULESURF command

11. Invoke the **TABSURF** command to create the base side surface of the model. When prompted for the path curve, select the closed polyline at the bottom. Select the small vertical line when prompted for the direction vector (Figure 4-88). The resulting mesh is shown in Figure 4-89.
12. Change the layer of the new polygon mesh to **Surfaces.**

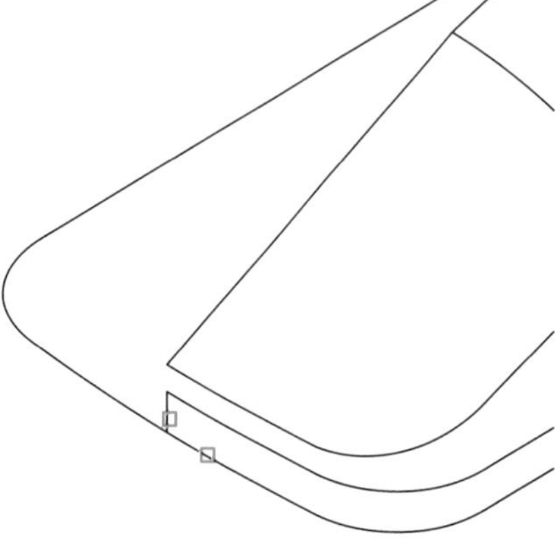

Figure 4-88 Objects to be selected

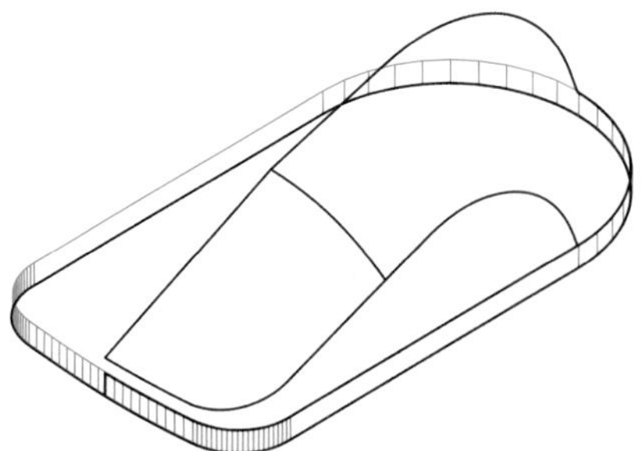

Figure 4-89 Resulting polygon mesh generated with the TABSURF command

When selecting the line, you must pick on the half closer to the bottom to ensure that the extrusion does not go in the opposite direction.

13. Now you can turn off all the wireframes. In the **Layers** drop-down list, turn on the **Surfaces** layer and set it current. Then turn layer **0** off.
14. Invoke the **HIDE** command. The 3D model should look like Figure 4-90.

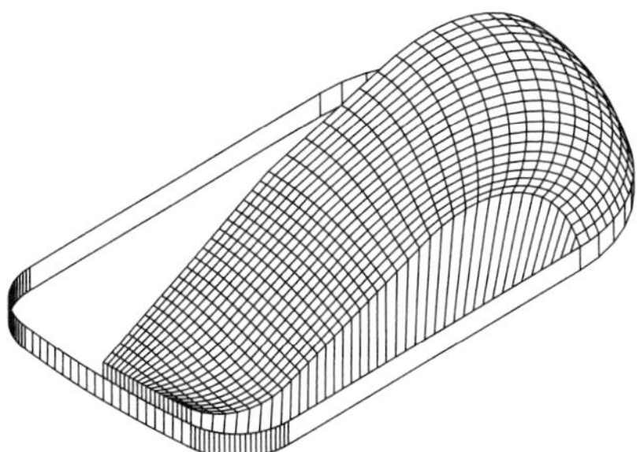

Figure 4-90 The entire polygon mesh is shown after you invoke the HIDE command

15. Invoke the **REGEN** command.
16. Invoke the **MIRROR3D** command to create the other half of the 3D model. When prompted, select every polygon mesh, except the base closed surface. Accept the default **3points** method and specify any three noncollinear endpoints on the meshes, locating them on the imaginary symmetry plane. The result is shown in Figure 4-91.

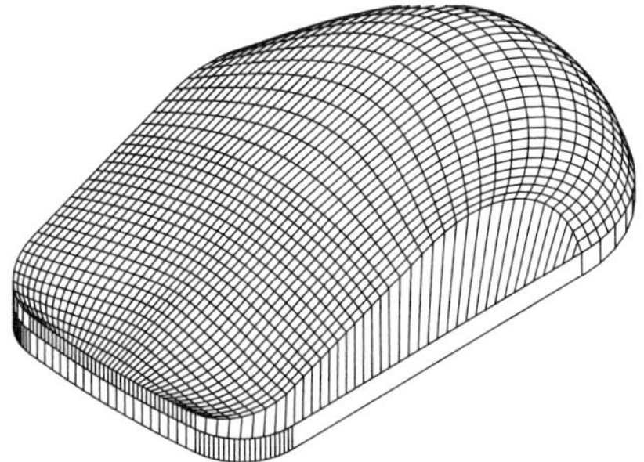

Figure 4-91 After the MIRROR3D operation

17. Next you will change the type of surface on some of the meshes to transform them into smoother surfaces. Set the **SURFU** and the **SURFV** system variables value to **30.**
18. Select the four polygon meshes created with the **EDGESURF** command. Then right-click in the drawing area and select **Properties.** In the **Properties** palette, set the **Fit/Smooth** value to **Cubic** (Figure 4-92).

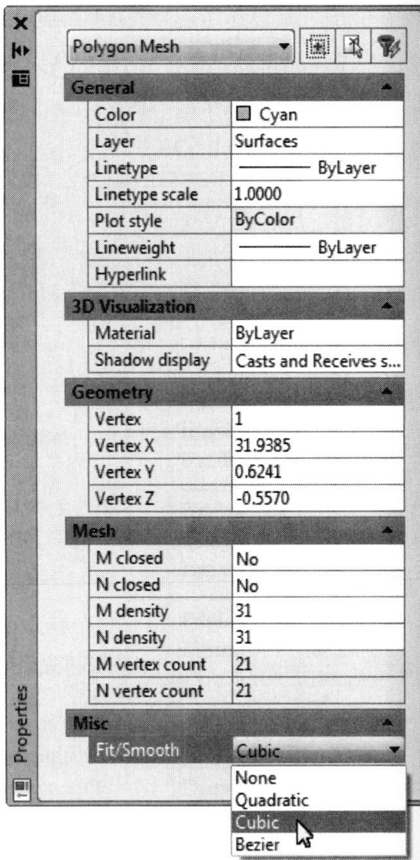

Figure 4-92 Setting the Fit/Smooth value to Cubic in the Properties palette

19. Select the **Realistic** visual style.
20. In the **Edge Effects** panel of the **Ribbon**, set the **Edges** control to **No Edges.**
21. The model should look like Figure 4-93. Invoke the **3DORBIT** command to inspect the 3D model.
22. **SAVE** the drawing.

Figure 4-93 A shaded view of the final 3D model represented by faceted surfaces

Many other details (e.g., the buttons) would need to be added to obtain the final product; however, so far you *have* obtained the concept design of the product.

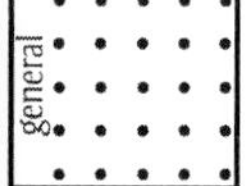

Tutorial 4-2: The Boat Hull

Continuing with **Tutorial 3-3** from Chapter 3, you will give the boat hull its final touch. The task will consist of creating the polygon meshes needed to fill the entire surface of the object.

1. **OPEN** ***Tutorial 3-3*** created in Chapter 3.
2. **SAVE** it **AS** ***Tutorial 4-2.***
3. Open the **Layer Manager** dialog box and create a new layer. Name it **Surfaces**, change its color to one you prefer, and turn it off. Close the **Layer Manager** dialog box by clicking on the **OK** button.
4. Set both system variables **SURFTAB1** and **SURFTAB2** to **15**.
5. You need to prepare the wireframes so they are suitable for the requirements of the commands used to create polygon meshes. **ZOOM** in to the back of the boat hull and select the **Right** UCS.
6. **COPY** the top line from its rightmost endpoint, as shown in Figure 4-94.
7. **TRIM** the portion of the copied line that extends beyond the boat's centerline. **TRIM** also the top portion of the vertical line (Figure 4-95).

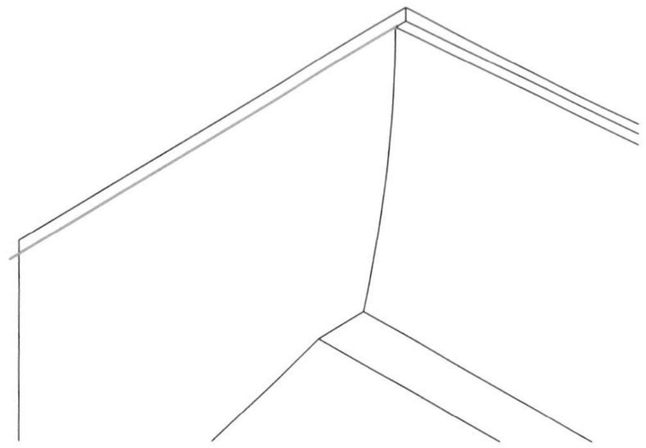

Figure 4-94 After copying the top line

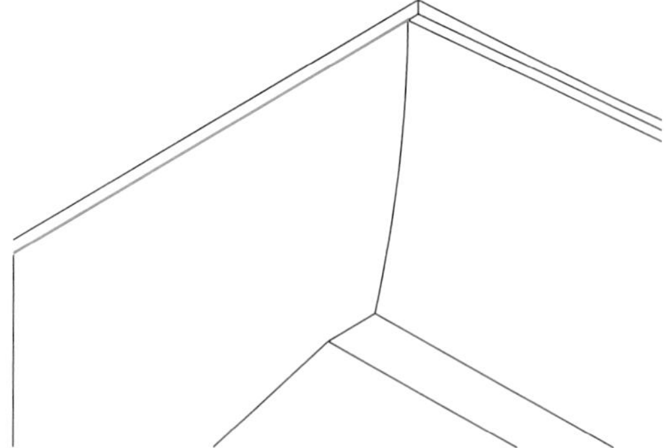

Figure 4-95 After trimming the lines

8. With the **Right** UCS still current, turn the second group of highlighted objects in Figure 4-96 into a single polyline, using the **Join** option of the **PEDIT** command.

FOR MORE DETAILS To find information about using the **PEDIT** command, refer to Chapter 3.

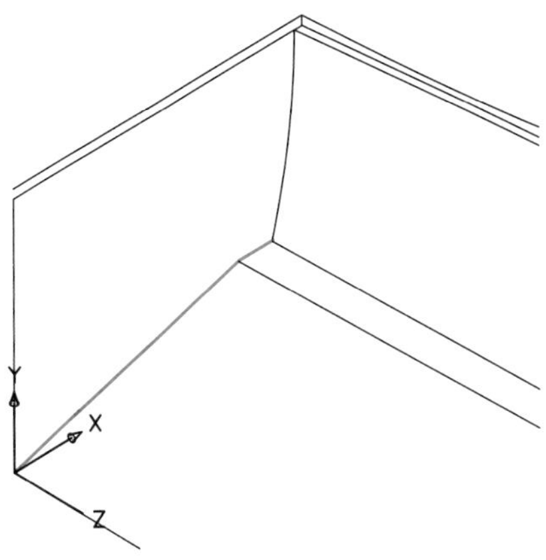

Figure 4-96 The highlighted objects must be joined into a single polyline

9. Select the **Front** UCS, and **ZOOM** into the front part of the boat hull.
10. **BREAK** the polyline along the hull into three portions. The polyline shown highlighted in Figure 4-97 should be independent from the other two segments.
11. Invoke the **EDGESURF** command. When prompted, select the four objects that define the outline of the polygon mesh shown highlighted in Figure 4-98.
12. Select the polygon mesh and change its layer to **Surfaces.** You can perform this operation either in the **Properties** palette or in the drop-down list on the **Layers** panel of the Ribbon (Figure 4-99).

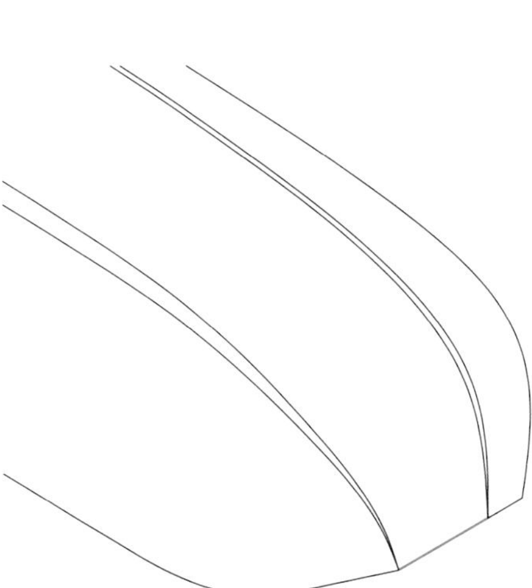

Figure 4-97 The 2D polyline along the hull must be split into three portions so the highlighted segment is independent

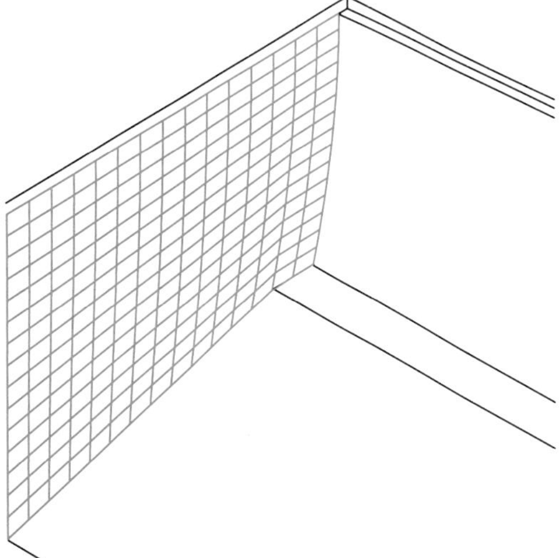

Figure 4-98 Polygon mesh generated with the EDGESURF command

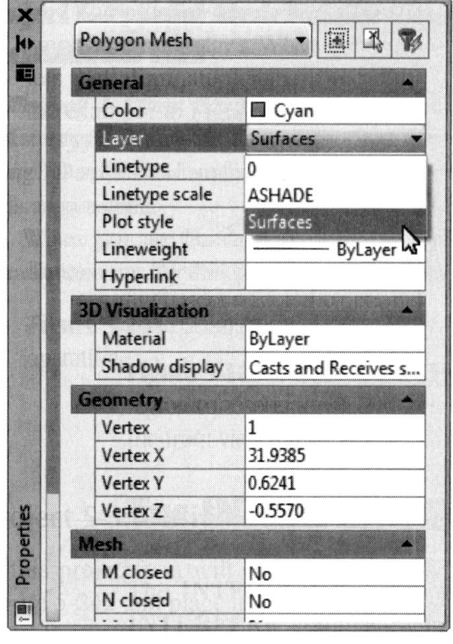

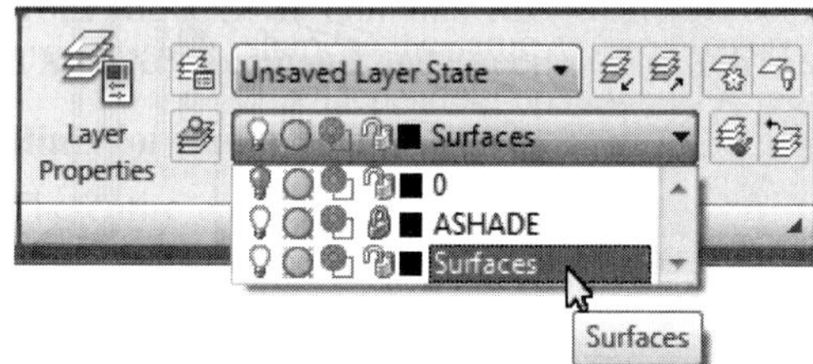

Figure 4-99 Your choices for changing the layer of the polygon mesh

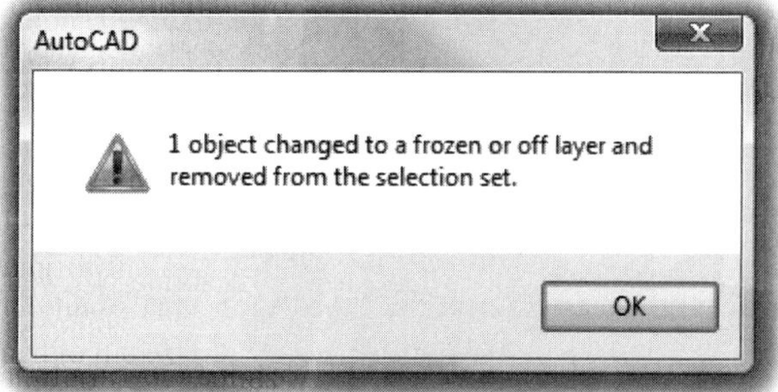

Figure 4-100 Warning from the AutoCAD program

Because the new layer is turned off, the mesh will turn off as well. The message shown in Figure 4-100 will warn you.

13. Set the **SURFTAB1** systzem variable to **30.**
14. Invoke the **EDGESURF** command again. Select the four objects that define the outline of the highlighted polygon mesh (Figure 4-101).
15. Select the new polygon mesh and change its layer to **Surfaces** to hide the object shown.
16. Invoke the **RULESURF** command. When prompted, select the two highlighted curves in Figure 4-102.

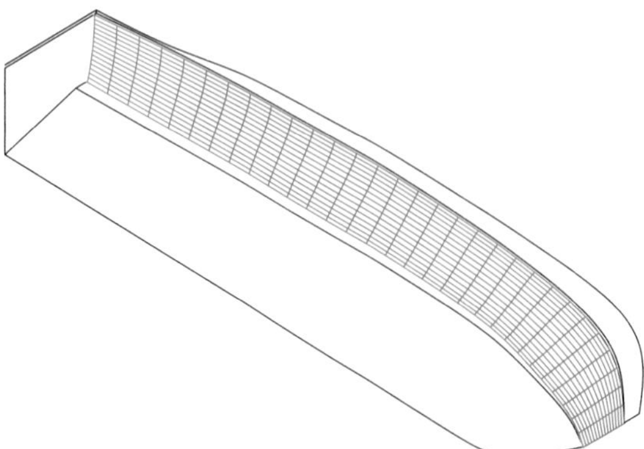

Figure 4-101 New polygon mesh generated with the EDGESURF command

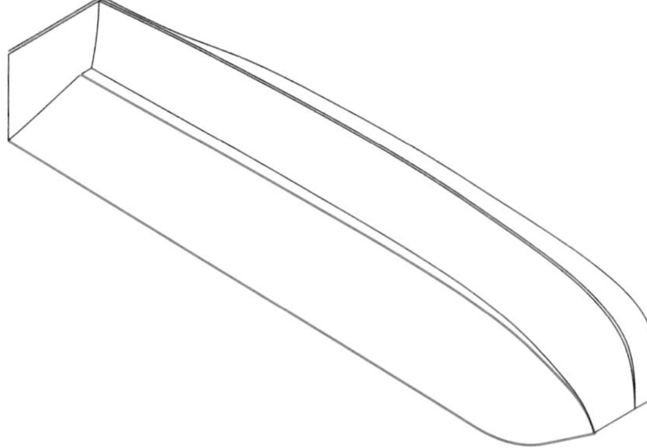

Figure 4-102 Curves to be selected for the RULESURF operation

17. Invoke the **RULESURF** command again and select the two curves highlighted in Figure 4-103.
18. Select the two polygon meshes and assign them the **Surfaces** layer.
19. Create the two remaining polygon meshes (Figure 4-104).

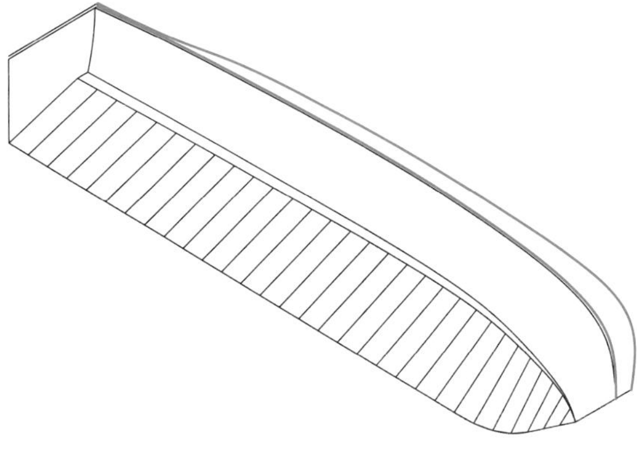

Figure 4-103 Curves to be selected for the new RULESURF operation

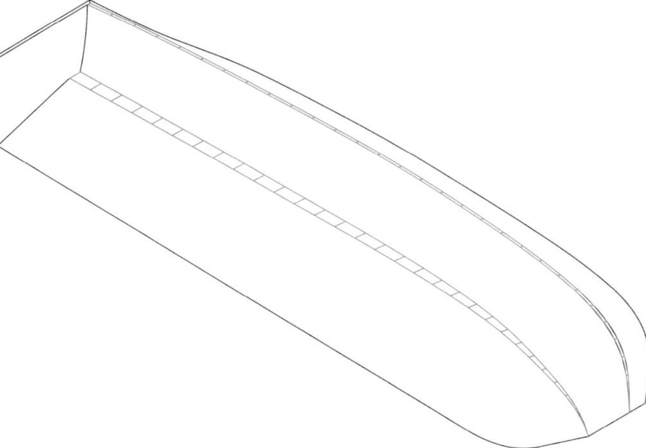

Figure 4-104 Creating two more polygon meshes

20. Set the **SURFTAB1** system variables to **15.**
21. **ZOOM** into the back of the boat. Invoke the **TABSURF** command. Respond to the prompts as follow:

Select object for path curve: *Select the horizontal line* (Figure 4-105).

Select object for direction vector: *Select the small vertical line.*

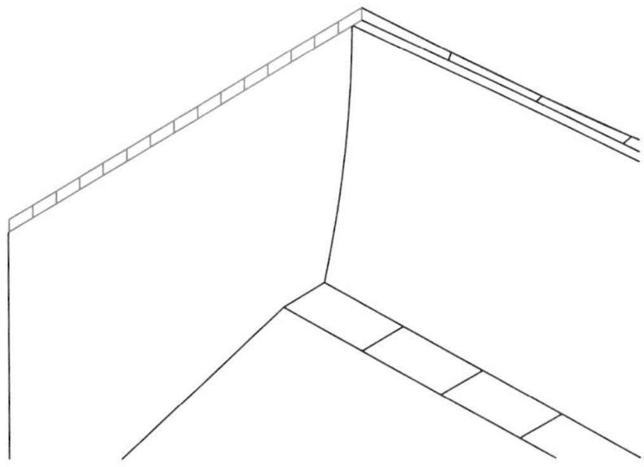

Figure 4-105 Polygon meshes created with the TABSURF command

22. Change the layer of the three polygon meshes to **Surfaces.**
23. You no longer need the wireframe objects. Make sure no polygon mesh is displayed and **ERASE** all the remaining objects in the screen.
24. Turn the **Surfaces** layer on.
25. Select the **Top** view and **MIRROR** all the polygon meshes to create a symmetrical copy (Figure 4-106).

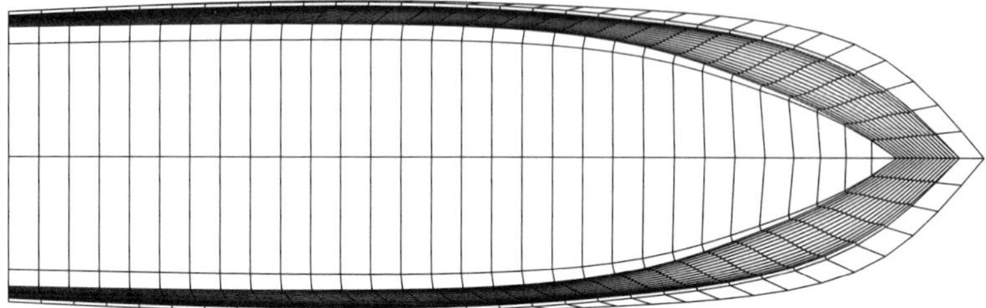

Figure 4-106 After mirroring the polygon meshes

26. Select the **Realistic** visual style.
27. In the **Visual Style** panel of the **Ribbon,** change the **Edge** setting to show **No edges** (Figure 4-107).
28. Invoke the **3DORBIT** command to inspect the faceted surface 3D model. It should look much like Figure 4-108.
29. **SAVE** the drawing.

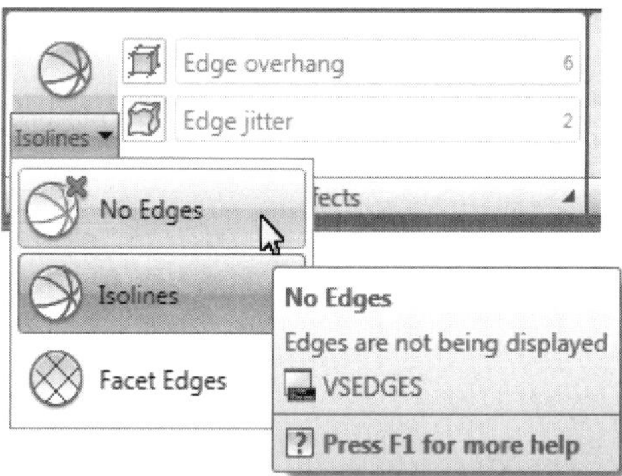

Figure 4-107 The Edge Effects panel of the Ribbon

Figure 4-108 A shaded view of the final 3D model represented by faceted surfaces

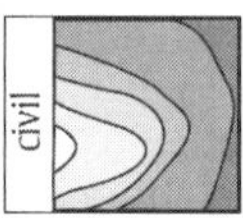

Tutorial 4-3: A 3D Landscape Surface

The topographical elevations of a 36 × 36–mile landscape terrain have been measured on each point of a 6 × 6–mile grid. The *X* and *Y* coordinates of each point measured are located according to the grid; the *Z* coordinate of the point is the terrain elevation. Figure 4-109 shows the respective elevations for each of the grid's points. You will represent the actual 3D shape of the terrain as a faceted surface.

1. Start a **NEW** drawing.
2. **SAVE** the drawing **AS Tutorial 4-3.**
3. Set the **Units** format to **Decimal** and **Miles.**

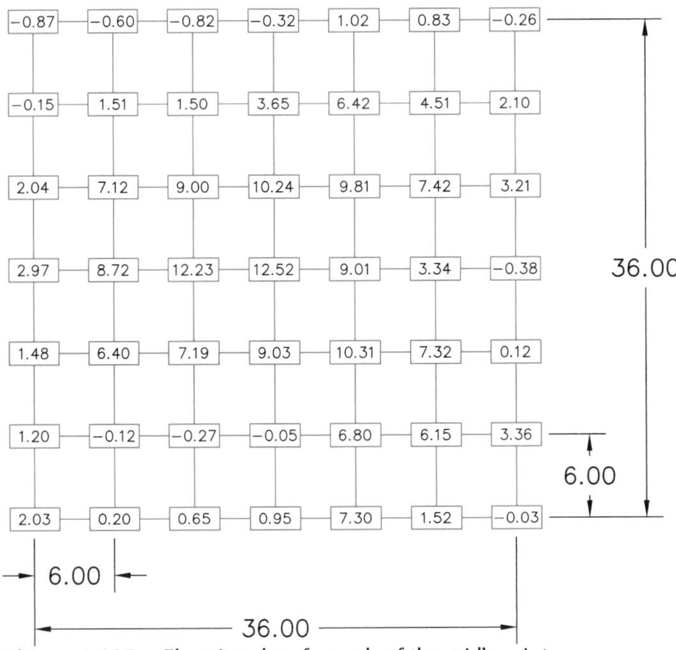

Figure 4-109 Elevation data for each of the grid's points

4. Invoke the **LIMITS** command and set the drawing limits between **0,0** and **60,50.**
5. Invoke the **ZOOM Extents** command to display the entire drawing limits.
6. Without changing the UCS or the viewing point, invoke the **3D** command and select the **Mesh** option to create an M × N mesh. Respond to the prompts as follows:

   Specify first corner point of mesh: *Click any point on the drawing area.*

   Specify second corner point of mesh: *Specify a point 36 miles orthogonally toward the right of the first point.*

   Specify third corner point of mesh: *Specify a point 36 miles orthogonally above the second point.*

   Specify fourth corner point of mesh: *Specify a point 36 miles orthogonally toward the left of the third point.*

   Enter mesh size in the M direction: *7↵*

   Enter mesh size in the N direction: *7↵*

7. Select the **SE Isometric** viewpoint. Select either the **Right** or the **Front** UCS.
8. Select the polygon mesh and start modifying the grids one by one. Figure 4-110 shows the mesh after the first grid has been stretched. Grids with negative values must be stretched downward.
9. After all the grips have been stretched to the proper elevation, the polygon mesh should look like Figure 4-111.
10. Set the **SURFU** and **SURFV** system variables to **30.**
11. Select the deformed polygon mesh and open up the **Properties** dialog box. Under **Misc,** change the **Fit/Smooth** property to **Quadratic.**

Note:

Remember that you do not need to specify "miles" or any other type of unit when entering points and distances. The only time you ever need to specify the type of unit is when using architectural units, to differentiate between inches and feet.

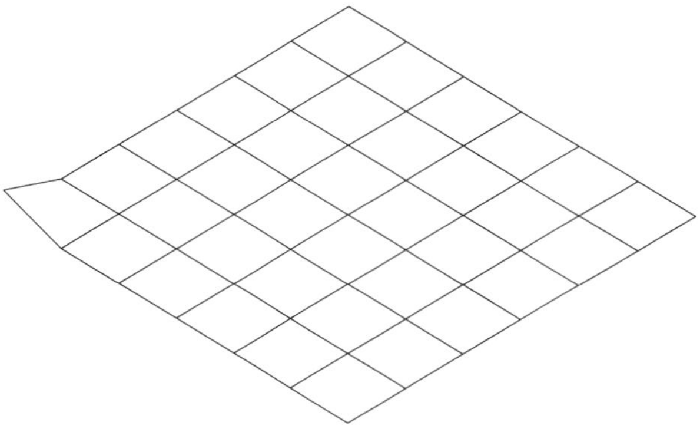

Figure 4-110 The mesh after the first grid has been pulled up

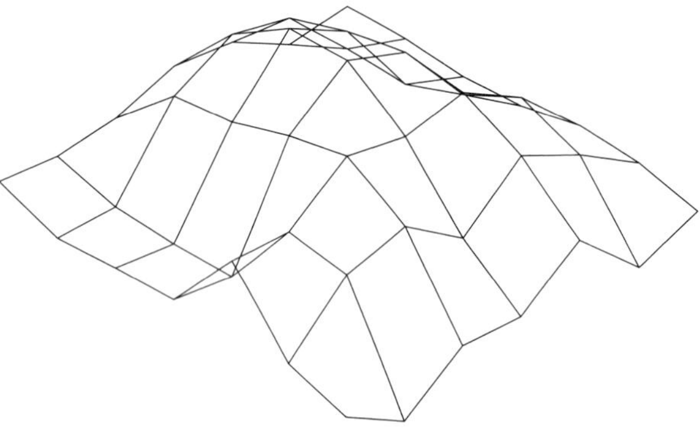

Figure 4-111 After all the grips have been moved either up or down

12. Select the **Realistic** visual style. The 3D landscape surface should look like Figure 4-112.
13. Invoke the **3DORBIT** command to examine the 3D model.
14. **SAVE** the drawing.

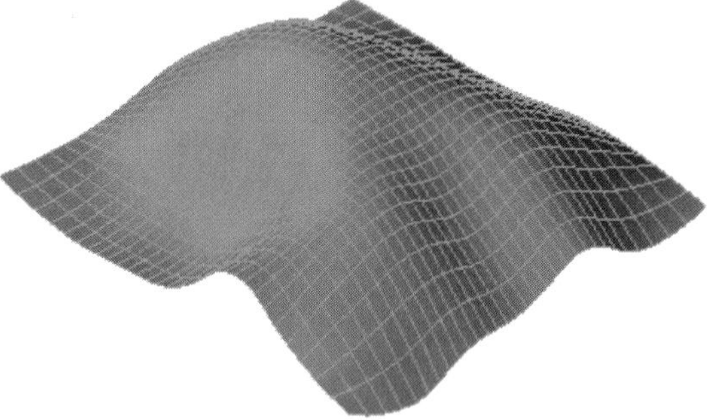

Figure 4-112 A shaded view of the final 3D terrain represented by faceted surfaces

Chapter Projects

Project 4-1: Industrial Hood

Using faceted surface objects, create the 3D surface model shown in Figure 4-113. The dimensions for this model can be found in Figure 4-114.

Hints for the Project

The four curved surfaces that represent the transition of the hood can be produced by creating a ruled surface between a quarter of the top circle and any other temporary object such as a line. Subsequently, the grips along the temporary line can be stretched in order to be gathered

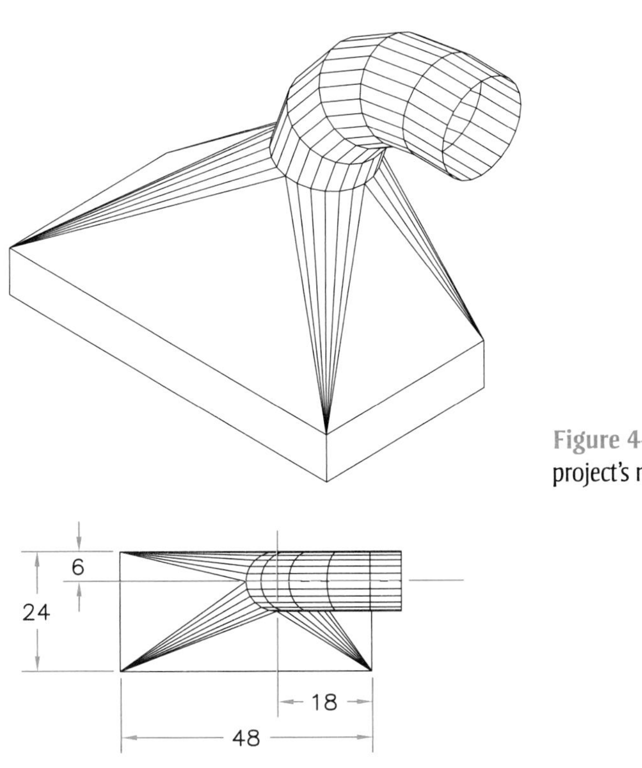

Figure 4-113 A 3D view of the project's model

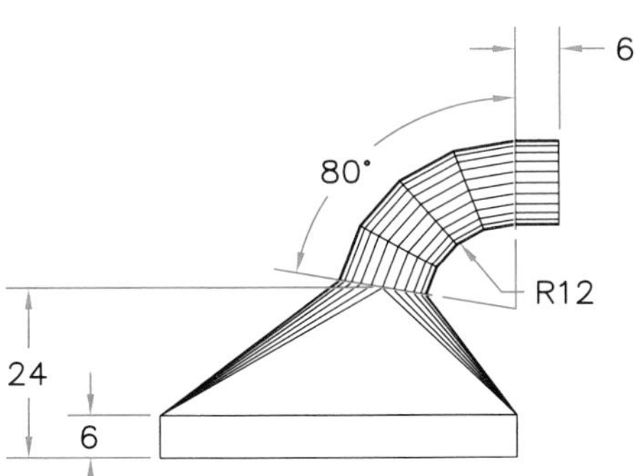

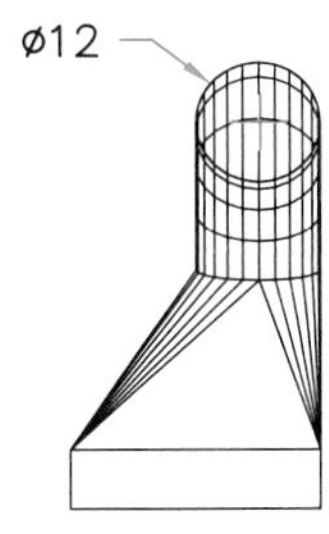

Figure 4-114 Dimensions for the project

at the same point, and the line can be erased. Figure 4-115 shows the steps just described. The same polygon mesh can also be created in an easier way between the same arc and a point.

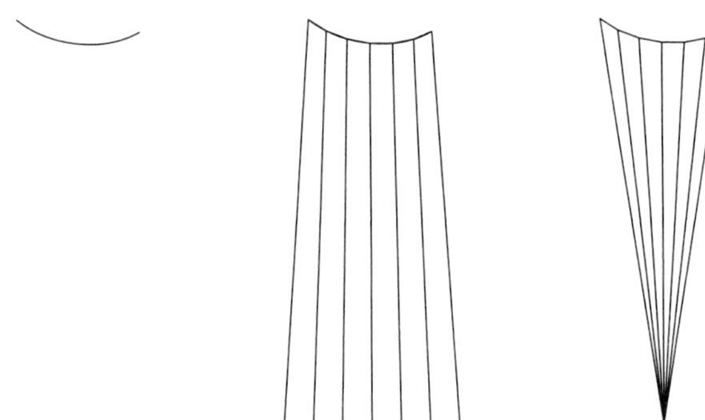

Figure 4-115 Hints about how to create specific geometry

Project 4-2: Industrial Hood: The Flat Pattern

When only 2D capability exists, sheet metal work can get very complicated for designers and engineers, especially if the piece to be developed is an uncommon one. If carefully handled, the AutoCAD software can assist you with the task of generating an accurate flat pattern.

Open the drawing containing the 3D model you created in Project 4-1 and develop a 2D drawing that represents the flat pattern or development of the hood. When you finish, the drawing should look like Figure 4-116.

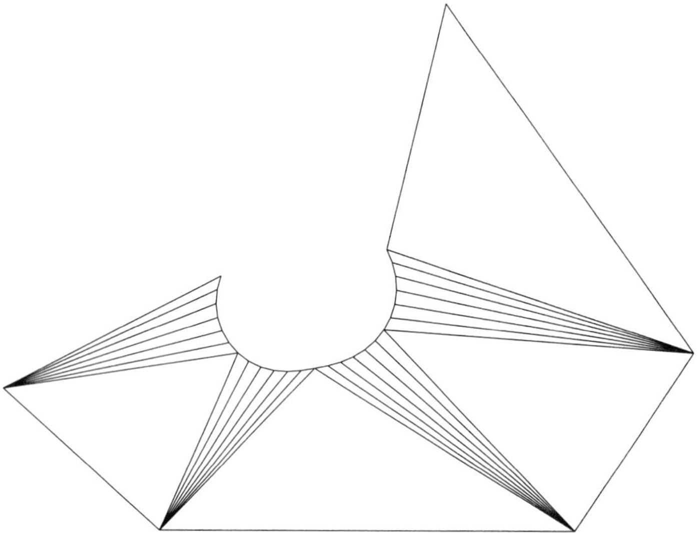

Figure 4-116 The resulting flat pattern

Hints for the Project

As you learned previously, when a polygon mesh is exploded, it disintegrates into individual 3D faces. Such objects can be moved and rotated throughout the 3D space one by one until all are placed in a common plane.

One sequence of operations that can be used is as follows:

1. Modify the UCS by three given points so that its *XY* plane is coincident with the 3D face object.
2. **CUT** the 3D face to remove it from its location.
3. Change the UCS to a common one that you will use over and over to **PASTE** all the 3D faces.
4. **PASTE** the 3D face.
5. Use the **ALIGN, MIRROR,** or **ROTATE** commands as necessary.
6. Repeat the process for the next 3D face. Its edge should be aligned with the corresponding edge of the 3D face that was previously placed.

Project 4-3: Community Recreational Hall

Architectural prototypes are easily achieved by using surface objects. One of the key elements is to try to keep the design as simple as possible. You can use any type of object to represent each surface according to its shape. You should keep in mind, however, that the simpler the objects, the smaller your file will be. Why use a polygon mesh or a 3D face to represent a rectangular face when a polyline with a certain thickness or a region would work as well?

In this project you will use the knowledge that you have acquired in this chapter. Here only basic information will be given, along with some hints. The recreational hall you will develop does not have to be exactly like the one shown in Figure 4-117. You can be as creative as you want.

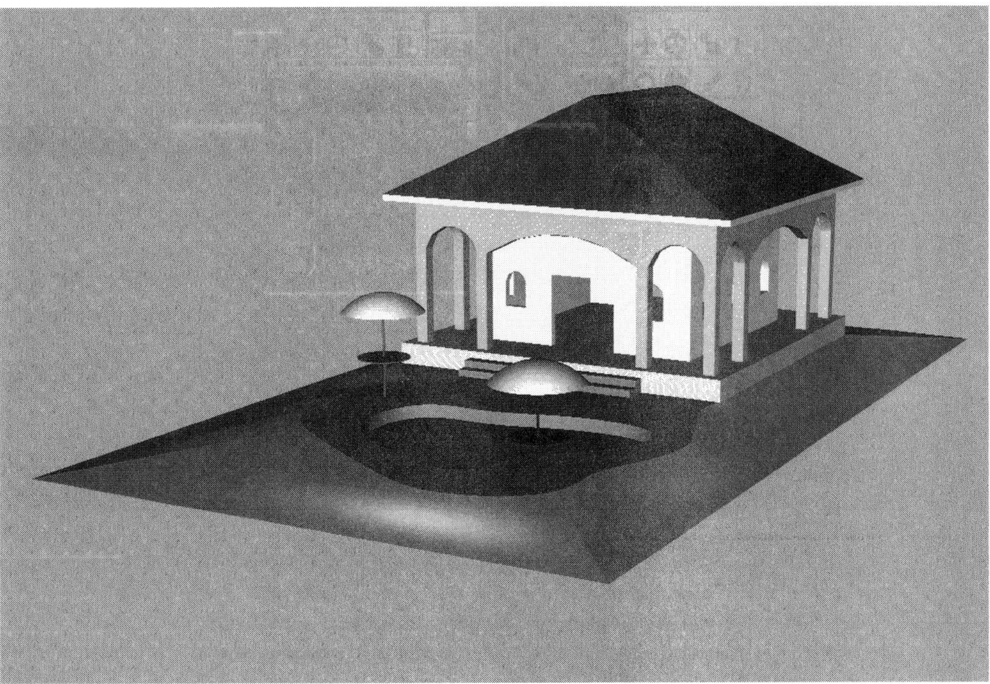

Figure 4-117 A shaded 3D view of the recreational hall's 3D model

Hints for the Project

When constructing walls with arcs, you can create the front and back surfaces with regions and use thickened polylines for the surfaces representing the width (Figure 4-118).

To represent the green area of the 3D model, you can use five surfaces created with the **EDGESURF** command (Figure 4-119).

The umbrellas are easily made with the **REVSURF** command. The roof can be made of either 3D faces or regions. To create the pool

Figure 4-118 Hints for the walls with arcs

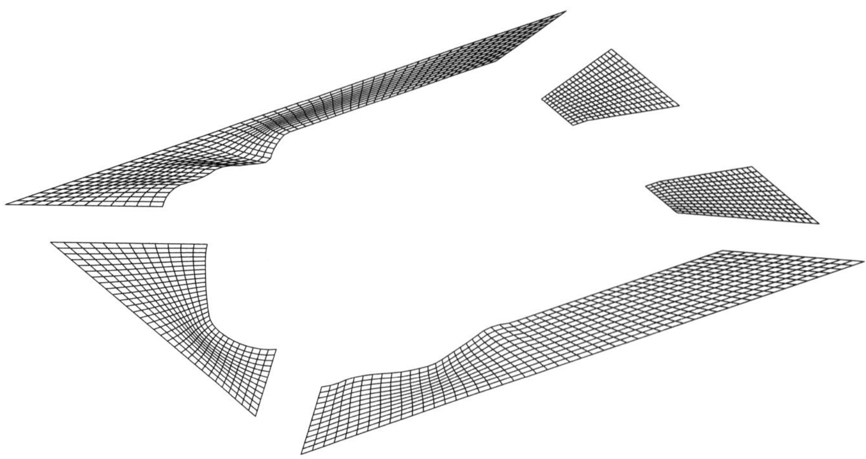

Figure 4-119 Hints to represent the green area

area, you can use the **SPLINES** command to create the shape and turn it into regions. If needed, you can always perform Boolean operations to give the regions their final shape. The main dimensions of the 3D model are shown in Figure 4-120.

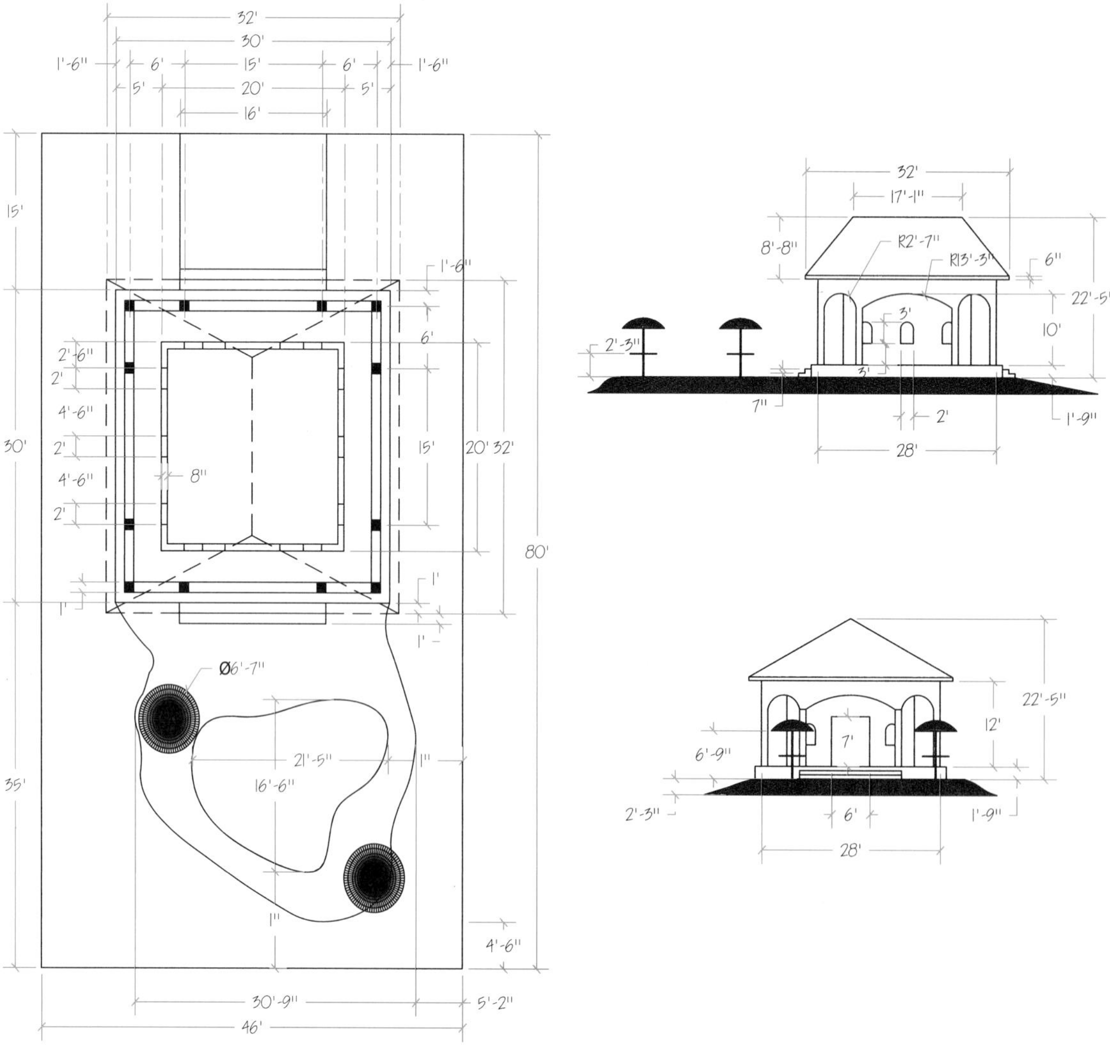

Figure 4-120 The main dimensions of the 3D model

Creating 3D Solids and Surfaces

5

Chapter Objectives

- Control the system variables to improve the visualization of 3D solids and surfaces.
- Understand the differences between surfaces and faceted surfaces.
- Learn the use of commands to create 3D primitives with 3D solids.
- Learn the use of commands to create complex surfaces and 3D solids.
- Learn other commands and operations to create surfaces and 3D solids.
- Use Boolean operations to create composite 3D solids.
- Learn an efficient way to convert 2D drawings into 3D models.
- Learn the practical usage of the **INTERFERE** command.
- Learn the operations to slice 3D solids and extract regions from their cross sections.
- Learn the specifics of using the **FILLET** and **CHAMFER** commands on 3D solids.
- Learn and practice how to generate 3D assemblies with the AutoCAD® program.

INTRODUCTION

ABOUT 3D SOLIDS

Without any doubt, the use of 3D solids is the easiest and most realistic way to generate a 3D model. Instead of simply representing the object's skeleton, or its outer skin, 3D solids represent the 3D model of real objects as a whole volumetric shape. 3D solids, along with the new true surfaces and their interaction possibilities, offer a complete set of tools to create excellent 3D models, which allow designers to develop better designs and innovations in less time.

The AutoCAD software's 3D solids can also be used to obtain important mathematical information such as volume, area, and moment of inertia. Data obtained from 3D solids can be exported into specific file formats and used by other applications to generate CNC (computer numeric control) programs, for FEA (finite element analysis), to produce rapid prototypes, and so on.

SURFACES VS. FACETED SURFACES

Faceted surfaces or meshes are only approximations of surfaces because they are made of smaller planar faces placed one next to the other. Faceted surfaces can be created through several operations, allowing you to obtain many different shapes. They can be shaded by the incidence of light, have materials applied, and be used to hide objects located behind them. Editing or post operations with faceted surfaces, however, are limited to simply deforming the vertices and smoothing the mesh.

Surfaces, on the other hand, are created with the same commands used to create 3D solids, and they are as smooth as the faces of 3D solids. Besides their capabilities of being shaded, having materials applied, and hiding objects, surfaces can be used in other post operations, such as slicing 3D solids, or be transformed into 3D solids by thickening them.

When 3D solids are exploded, regions and surfaces are obtained from the operation. Regions are created from the planar faces, and surfaces from the nonplanar faces of the 3D solids.

Depending on their type, surfaces can be edited by using their grips. Unlike 3D solids, however, surfaces cannot be used to generate 2D drawing views.

Controlling the Displaying of Surfaces and 3D Solids

When creating a 3D model, it is important to know how to improve the display of the objects in order to ensure a clearer visualization. Depending on the visual style selected, specific system variables or settings concerning the visual style can drastically affect the way that 3D solids are displayed, particularly the nonplanar faces.

The **2D Wireframe** is the visual style you will most likely use to develop 3D model objects. For this reason, we will focus on this particular visual style. Other visual styles are used at the development stage of the 3D modeling process simply to temporarily visualize the result of the operations performed.

When the **2D Wireframe** is the current visual style, the **DISPSILH** system variable controls two important visual effects on surfaces and 3D solids:

silhouette: Outline that defines the limit or profile of the curved faces of an object in the 3D space, causing it to look more real. Silhouettes are not physical edges.

facets: Edges or subdivisions of a 3D solid's nonplanar faces and nonplanar surfaces, produced by internal calculations of the AutoCAD program.

1. Display of the ***silhouettes*** before hiding occulted lines with the **HIDE** command
2. Displaying of the edges of ***facets*** after hiding occulted lines with the **HIDE** command

The default value of the **DISPSILH** variable is **0** (off) and can be turned on by setting it to **1**. This setting affects only the current drawing. Figure 5-1 shows how the **DISPSILH** variable affects the display of a 3D solid's nonplanar faces and nonplanar surfaces before and after the **HIDE** command is invoked.

The **ISOLINES** system variable controls the number of contour lines that the AutoCAD program uses to represent nonplanar faces of 3D solids. Its default value is **4**. Faces with double curvature, such as spherical faces, generate contour lines in both directions.

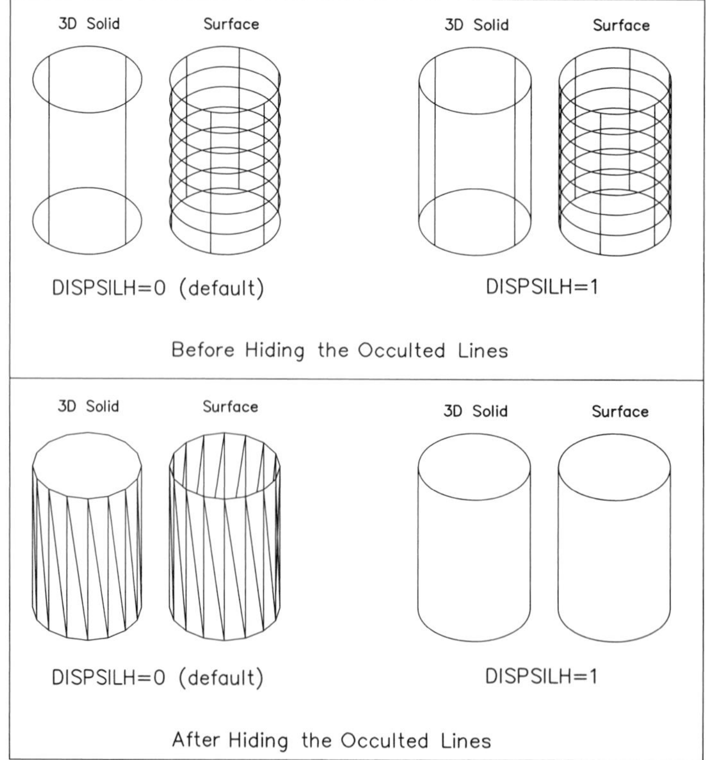

Figure 5-1 Effect of the DISPSILH system variable in the display of the 3D solids and surfaces

Figure 5-2 shows the effects of changing the **ISOLINES** variable on the display of 3D solids when the **DISPSILH** variable is **0**.

As you can see, setting both the **DISPSILH** and the **ISOLINES** system variables as **0** does not provide a clear display of 3D solids. Using **DISPSILH=1** and **ISOLINES=0** provides a good visualization of 3D solids when the occulted lines are not hidden (Figure 5-3).

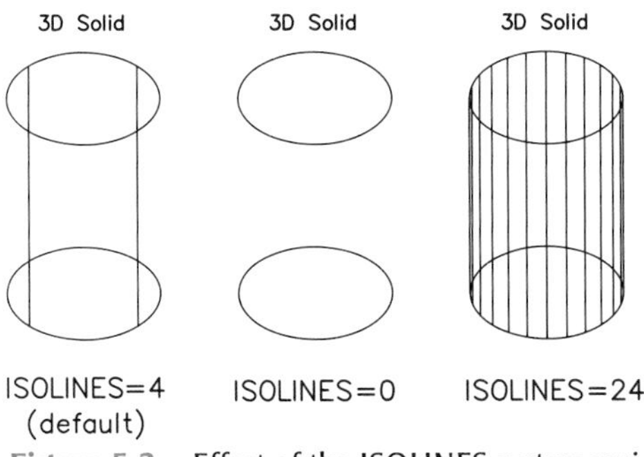

Figure 5-2 Effect of the ISOLINES system variable in the display of the 3D solids

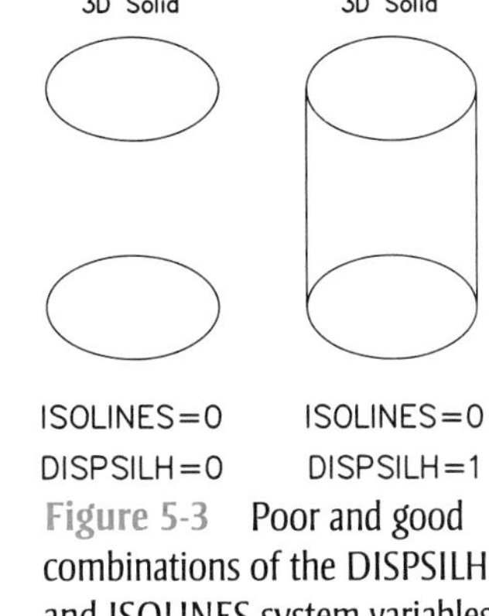

Figure 5-3 Poor and good combinations of the DISPSILH and ISOLINES system variables on 3D solids

For surfaces, the number of lines displayed in each direction is controlled by the **SURFU** and **SURFV** system variables, respectively. These variables also control the M and N density of smoothed meshes. Figure 5-4 shows how changing these two variables affects the display of surfaces when the **DISPSILH** system variable is **0**.

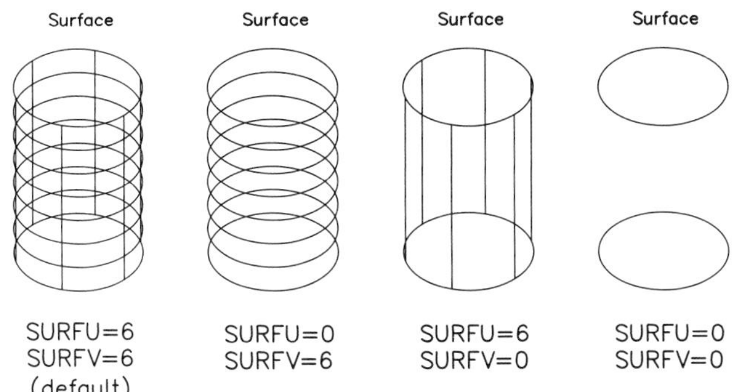

Figure 5-4 Effect of the SURFU and SURFV system variables on the display of the surfaces

As you can see, setting the **DISPSILH** system variable to **0** when the **SURFU** and **SURFV** values are both **0** does not provide a clear display of surfaces.

Using **DISPSILH=1** when the **SURFU** and **SURFV** values are both **0** provides a clear visualization of surfaces when the occulted lines are not hidden (Figure 5-5).

The **FACETRES** system variable improves the visualization of surfaces and 3D solids by increasing the number of facets used to represent nonplanar faces of 3D solids. Increasing its value will make the faces look smoother after hiding the occulted lines. Its default value is **0.50**, and it can be set between **0.01** and **10.00**. Figure 5-6 shows the comparison between high and low **FACETRES** values when the **DISPSILH** system variable is set to **1**.

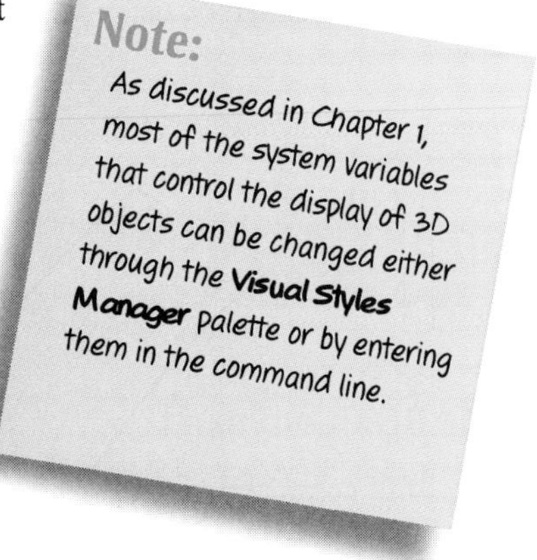

Note:
As discussed in Chapter 1, most of the system variables that control the display of 3D objects can be changed either through the **Visual Styles Manager** palette or by entering them in the command line.

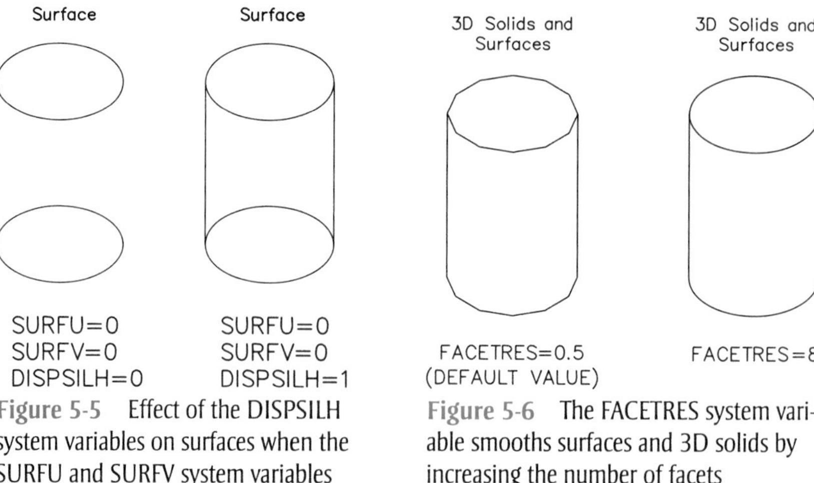

Figure 5-5 Effect of the DISPSILH system variables on surfaces when the SURFU and SURFV system variables are set to 0

Figure 5-6 The FACETRES system variable smooths surfaces and 3D solids by increasing the number of facets

CREATING 3D SOLID PRIMITIVES

COMMANDS USED TO CREATE 3D SOLID PRIMITIVES

Typically, the creation of a 3D model represented by 3D solids starts with the creation of several simple 3D solids, such as 3D solid primitives. Then these simple 3D solids are combined, edited, and modified by using other operations until the final shape is achieved. The **BOX, WEDGE, CONE, SPHERE, CYLINDER, TORUS,** and **PYRAMID** commands are used to create 3D solid primitives. Figure 5-7(b) shows the location of these commands in the **3D Modeling** panel of the Ribbon. To display the list you must click on the down arrow [Figure 5-7(a)]; the last command you invoked from the list is displayed by default. Two different tooltips are displayed according to the delay time that you keep the mouse pointer over a particular commands [Figures 5-7(b) and (c)]. Longer times will display a more detailed tooltip.

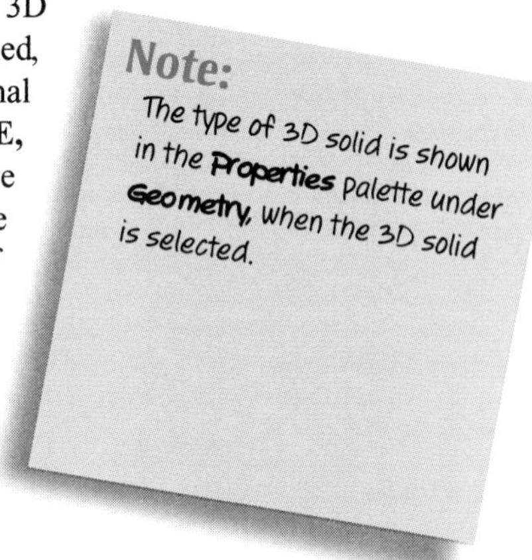

Note:
The type of 3D solid is shown in the Properties palette under Geometry, when the 3D solid is selected.

With the newly redesigned 3D solid primitives commands, you can create objects more easily while seeing their development process interactively as you move the cursor when specifying the points. Each command in this group generates its own type of 3D solid, which can be edited by using its unique grips or through the **Properties** palette.

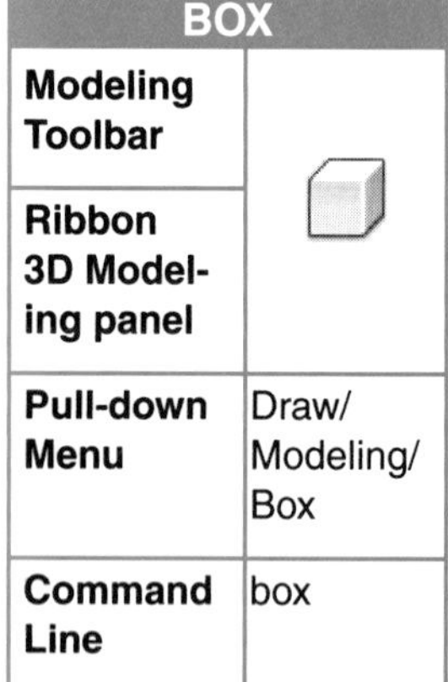

BOX	
Modeling Toolbar	
Ribbon 3D Modeling panel	
Pull-down Menu	Draw/ Modeling/ Box
Command Line	box

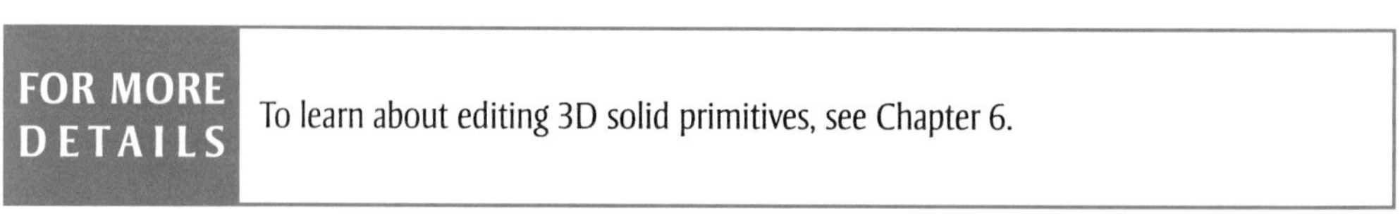

FOR MORE DETAILS To learn about editing 3D solid primitives, see Chapter 6.

The BOX Command

The **BOX** command creates a box-shaped 3D solid, with the base located parallel to the current *XY* plane.

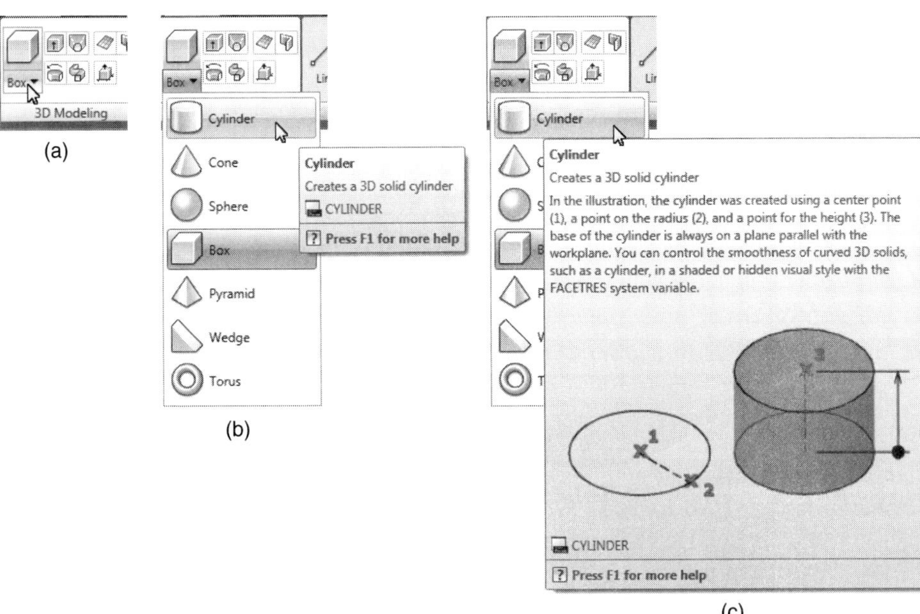

Figure 5-7 The commands used to create 3D solid primitives

You can combine the command's options to create boxes by using different procedures. The following, also shown in Figure 5-8, are most typically used to create a solid box:

- Specify a corner point, another corner in the same plane, and the height.
- Specify two corner points.
- Specify a corner point and a distance (length) using the **Cube** option.
- Specify the center point and one of the corner points.
- Specify a corner and three distances (length, width, and height).
- Specify the center and three distances (length, width, and height).

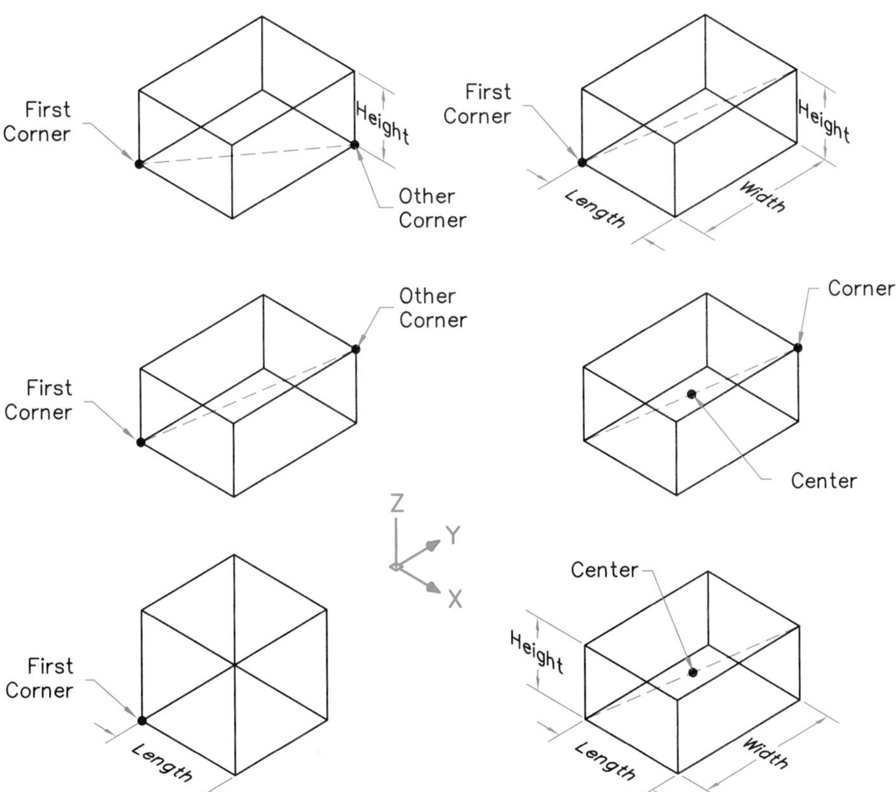

Figure 5-8 Different procedures used to create a box-shaped 3D solid

For procedures in which you specify a second corner point, AutoCAD uses the relative distances *X*, *Y*, and *Z* from the first point as the length, width, and height, respectively.

With any of the procedures in which you are required to specify the length, you automatically specify the alignment of the box as well, regardless of whether you enter a distance or specify a second point. The **ORTHO** mode must be turned on in order to align the faces of the box with the planes of the current UCS.

Regardless of which procedure you use, you must always enter the length, width, and height of the box. If either length or width information is missing from the points specified, the AutoCAD program will prompt you with one of the following messages:

Box of zero length not permitted.

Box of zero width not permitted.

Exercise 5-1: Creating 3D Solid Primitives with the BOX Command

1. Start a **NEW** drawing using the acad3D.dwt template.
2. **SAVE** the drawing **AS** ***Exercise 5-1.***
3. Select the **SE Isometric** viewing point.
4. Select the **Conceptual** visual style.
5. Turn on the **GRID** by pressing the **<F7>** key, in case it is not turned on.
6. Turn off the **SNAP** mode by pressing the **<F9>** key.
7. Invoke the **BOX** command and respond to the prompts as follows:

   Specify first corner or [Center]: *Move the mouse pointer to the coordinates 1.0000, 1.0000, 0.0000 and click to specify this point.(Zoom in as needed.)*

   Specify other corner or [Cube/Length]: *Move the mouse pointer to the coordinates 2.0000, 3.0000, 0.0000 and click to specify this point.*

   Specify height or [2Point]: *Move the mouse pointer up and enter 1.5 as the height value.*

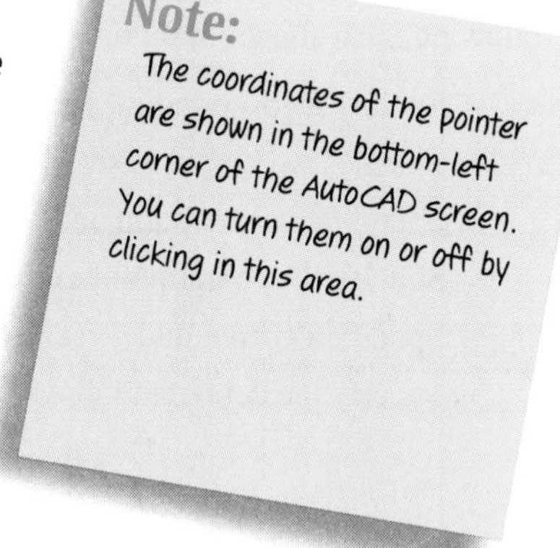

Note:
The coordinates of the pointer are shown in the bottom-left corner of the AutoCAD screen. You can turn them on or off by clicking in this area.

8. Invoke the **BOX** command again. Respond to the prompts as follows:

   Specify first corner or [Center]: *c* ↵

   Specify center: *Click on the coordinates 2.5000, 2.0000, 0.0000.*

   Specify other corner or [Cube/Length]: *L* ↵

   Specify length: *With ORTHO mode on, place the pointer so as to align the trace with the positive direction of the X-axis, and enter 1.*

   Specify width: *2* ↵

   Specify height or [2Point]: *1.5* ↵

Note:
When using the **Length** option, you use the **Length** value to specify this distance as well as the rotation in the *XY*-axis. In this exercise you also could have specified **@1 <0**. Specifying an angle different from 0 will not align the length side parallel to the *X*-axis.

9. The 3D model should look like Figure 5-9. Turn off the **GRID** and the **SNAP** modes.
10. Invoke the **3DORBIT** command to inspect the 3D model.
11. **SAVE** the drawing.

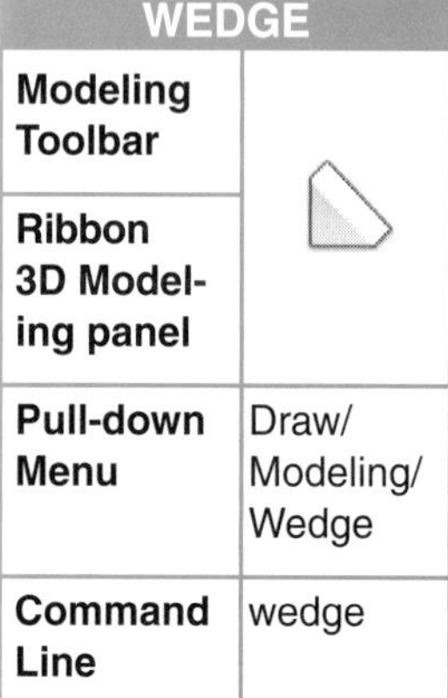

WEDGE	
Modeling Toolbar	
Ribbon 3D Modeling panel	
Pull-down Menu	Draw/ Modeling/ Wedge
Command Line	wedge

The WEDGE Command

The **WEDGE** command creates a wedge-shaped 3D solid with the base located parallel to the current *XY* plane.

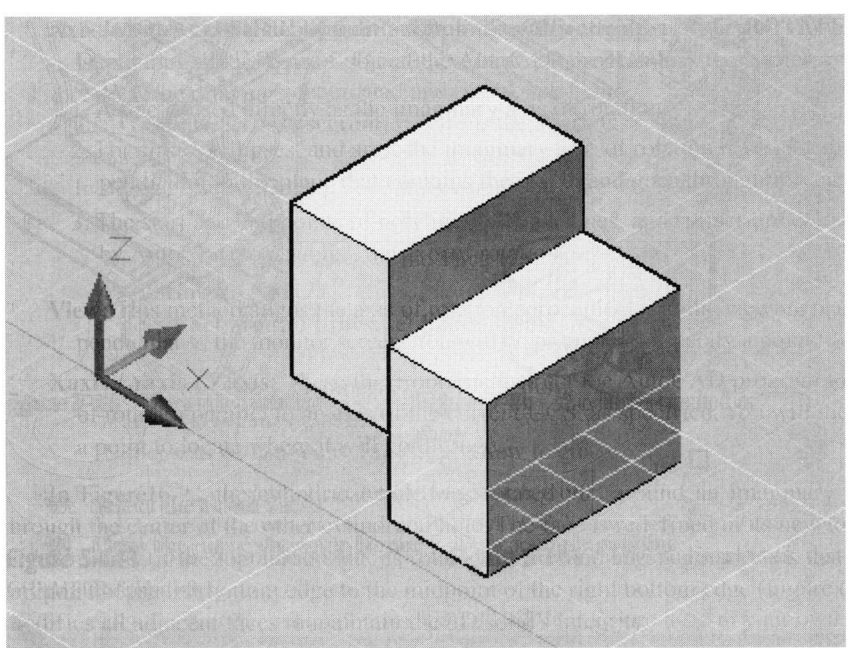

Figure 5-9 The two boxes created

The same procedures used to create a box can be used to create a wedge. You can easily visualize a wedge by thinking of a box diagonally sliced by a plane that is perpendicular to the *ZX* plane (Figure 5-10).

The CONE Command

The **CONE** command creates a cone-shaped 3D solid with a circular or elliptical base (Figure 5-11). Similar to the construction of the circle, the circular base of the cone can be specified by the **2 points, 3 points,** or **Tangent-tangent-radius** options. Elliptical bases are specified by entering three

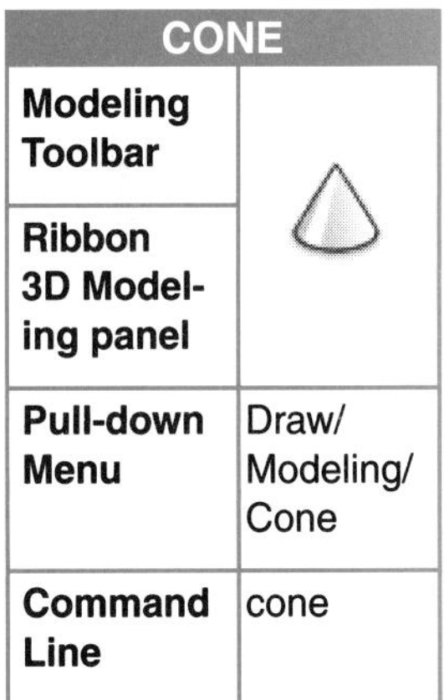

CONE	
Modeling Toolbar	
Ribbon 3D Modeling panel	
Pull-down Menu	Draw/ Modeling/ Cone
Command Line	cone

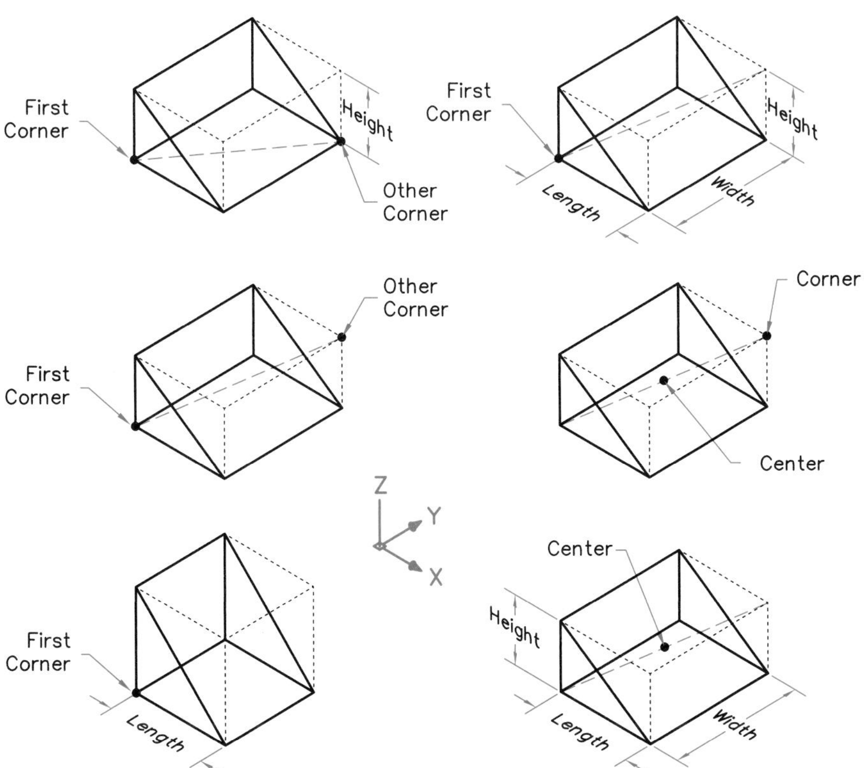

Figure 5-10 Different procedures used to create a wedge-shaped 3D solid

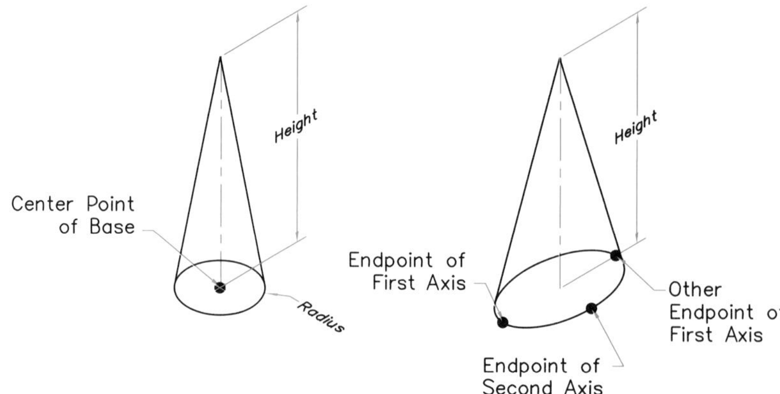

Figure 5-11 The parameters to specify both types of 3D solid cone (with a circular or elliptical base)

endpoints of the axis, or by entering the center point, the distance to the first axis, and the endpoint of the second axis.

If the height of the cone is specified, its base is located parallel to the current *XY* plane. Specifying a point with the **Axis endpoint** option, on the other hand, will align the base normal to the axis of the cone (Figure 5-12).

You can also create a cone that does not end in an apex point by specifying a value in the **Top radius** option (Figure 5-13). In cones with an elliptical base, the top radius value is the distance from the center to the major axis.

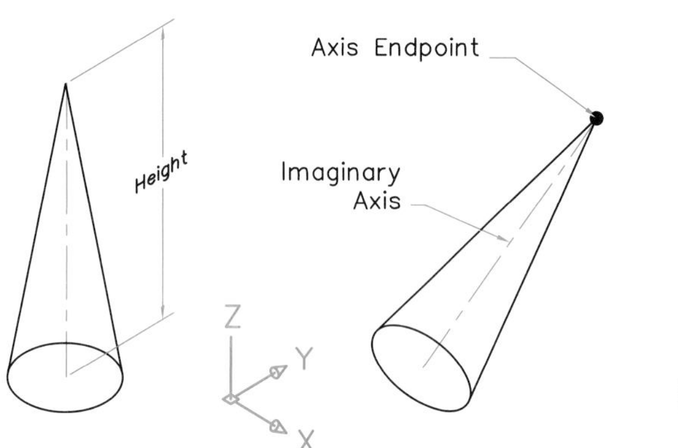

Figure 5-12 Specifying an Axis endpoint aligns the imaginary axis of the cone differently

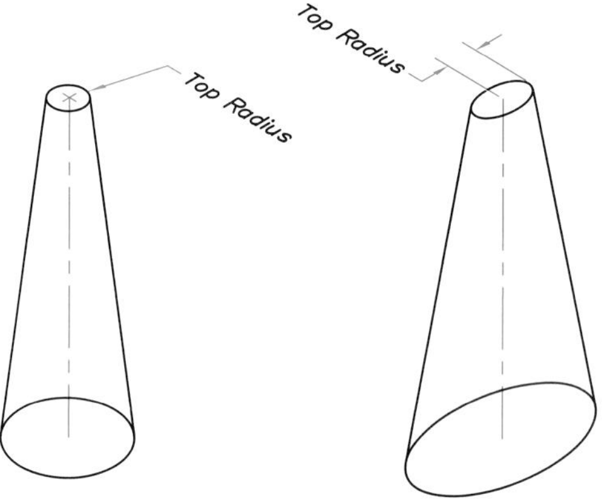

Figure 5-13 If you specify a Top radius value, the cone does not end in an apex point

By specifying the radius and the top radius as the same value, you can create a 3D solid in the shape of a cylinder, even though it would still be a cone.

Exercise 5-2: Creating 3D Solid Primitives with the CONE Command

1. Start a **NEW** drawing using the acad3D.dwf template.
2. **SAVE** the drawing **AS** ***Exercise 5-2.***
3. Select the **SE Isometric** viewing point.
4. Select the **Conceptual** visual style.
5. Turn on the **GRID** by pressing the **<F7>** key, in case it is not turned on
6. Turn off the **SNAP** mode by pressing the **<F9>** key.
7. Invoke the **CONE** command and respond to the prompts as follows:

   Specify center point of base or [3P/2P/Ttr/Elliptical]: *Click on the coordinates 2.0000, 2.0000, 0.0000. (Zoom in as needed.)*

   Specify base radius or [Diameter]: 1 ↵

   Specify height or [2Point/Axis endpoint/Top radius]: *3* ↵

8. Invoke the **CONE** command again. Respond to the prompts as follows:
   `Specify center point of base or [3P/2P/Ttr/Elliptical]:` *`Click on the coordinates 4.0000, 4.0000, 0.0000. (Zoom in as needed.)`*
   `Specify base radius or [Diameter]:` `1 ↵`
   `Specify height or [2Point/Axis endpoint/Top radius]:` *`t`* `↵`
   `Specify top radius:` *`0.5`* `↵`
   `Specify height or [2Point/Axis endpoint]:` *`a`* `↵`
   `Specify axis endpoint:` *`Click on the coordinates 4.0000, 2.0000, 0.0000.`*
9. The 3D model should look like Figure 5-14. Turn off the **GRID** and the **SNAP** modes.
10. Invoke the **3DORBIT** command to inspect the 3D model.
11. **SAVE** the drawing.

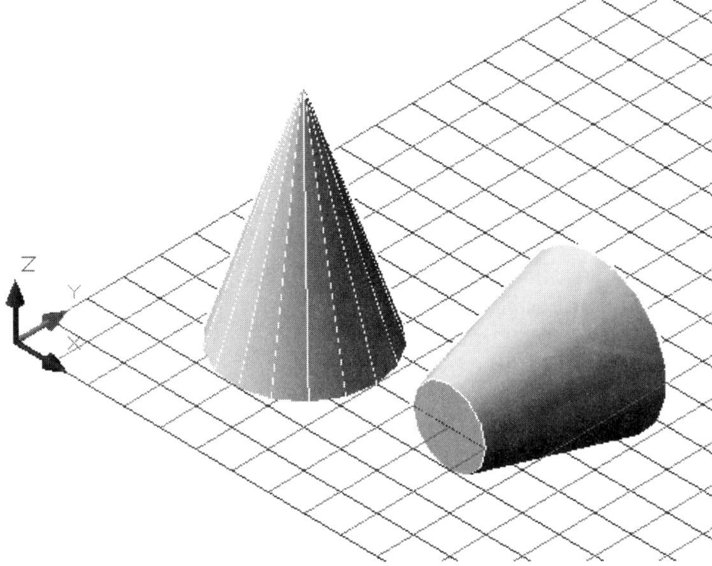

Figure 5-14 The two cylinders created

The SPHERE Command

SPHERE	
Modeling Toolbar **Ribbon 3D Modeling panel**	
Pull-down Menu	Draw/ Modeling/ Sphere
Command Line	sphere

The **SPHERE** command creates a sphere-shaped 3D solid with its midplane located parallel to the current *XY* plane. The default procedure for creating the sphere is by specifying its center and its radius or diameter (Figure 5-15). A 3D solid sphere can also be created by using the **3 points, 2 points,** and **Tangent-tangent-radius** options:

`Specify center point or [3P/2P/Ttr]:`

Using the other options allows you to have further control over the location and dimension of the sphere:

- **2P Option:** Locates the center of the sphere on the midpoint between the two points specified. Its diameter is the distance between the two points [Figure 5-16(a)].

Figure 5-15 Parameters defined in the default procedure for creating the sphere

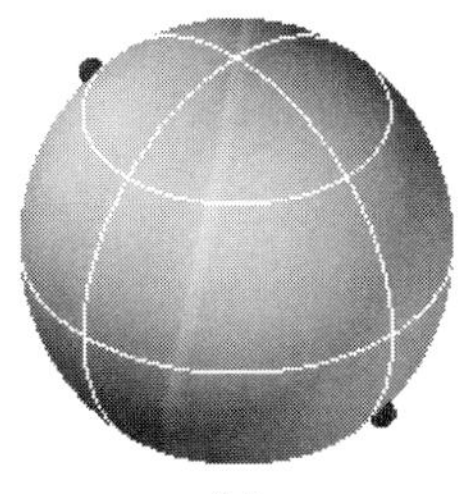

(a)

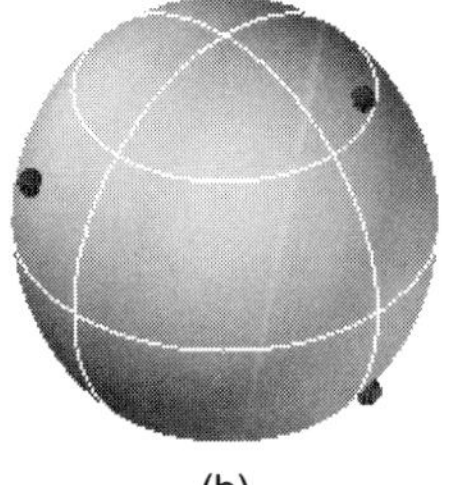

(b)

Figure 5-16 2P (a) and 3P (b) options for creating the sphere

- **3P Option:** Calculates the center point and the radius of the sphere, so that all three points are located exactly on its surface [Figure (5-16(b)].
- **Ttr Option:** Creates a sphere that is tangent to two lines, arcs, circles, or similar edges of any other object.

CYLINDER	
Modeling Toolbar	
Ribbon 3D Modeling panel	
Pull-down Menu	Draw/ Modeling/ Cylinder
Command Line	cylinder
Command Alias	cyl

The CYLINDER Command

The **CYLINDER** command creates a cylinder-shaped 3D solid with a circular or elliptical base. This command works similarly to the **CONE** command. Because the top and bottom faces of a cylinder are identical, however, there is not an option to specify the top radius (Figure 5-17).

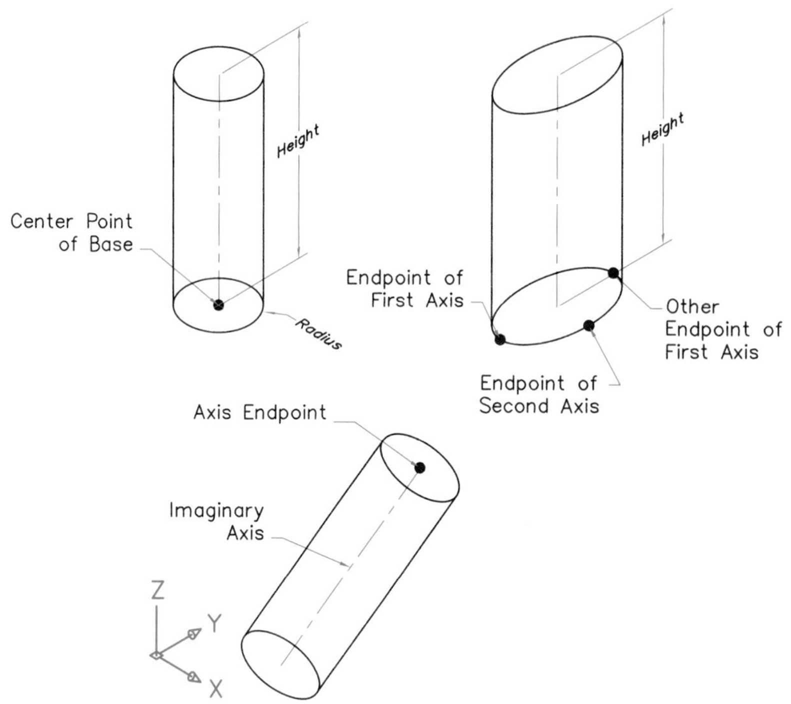

Figure 5-17 The parameters used to specify both types of 3D solid cylinder (with a circular or elliptical base); specifying an Axis endpoint aligns the axis of the cylinder differently

TORUS	
Modeling Toolbar	
Ribbon 3D Modeling panel	
Pull-down Menu	Draw/ Modeling/ Torus
Command Line	torus

The TORUS Command

The **TORUS** command creates a torus-shaped 3D solid, defined by the torus radius and a tube radius (Figure 5-18). Depending on the values specified, three different toroidal shapes can be obtained with this command (Figure 5-19).

- **Donut** The torus and tube radii are both positive. The torus radius is greater than the tube radius.

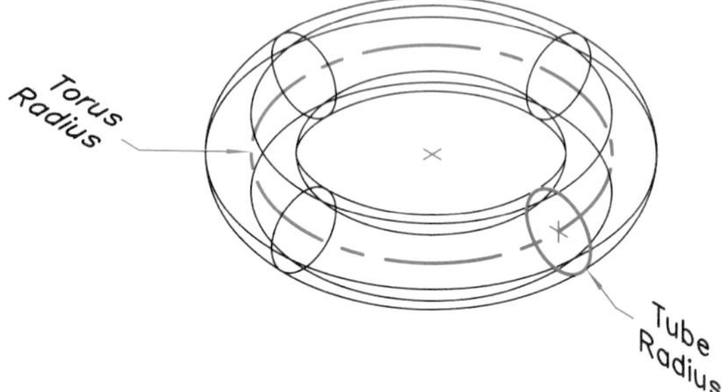

Figure 5-18 The parameters specified to create a torus-shaped 3D solid

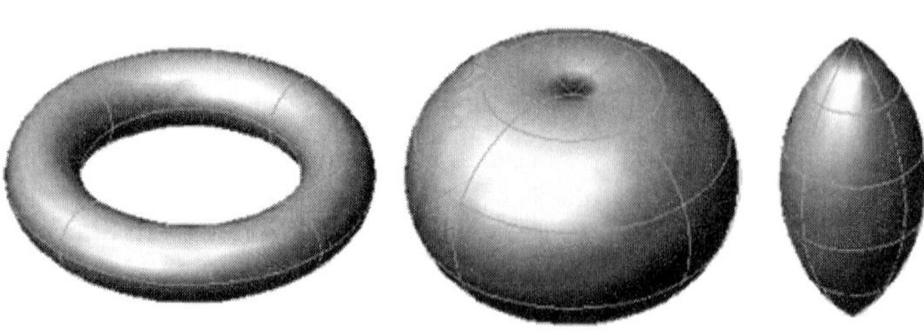

Figure 5-19 Different 3D objects obtained according to the sign and relation of the values specified

- **Tangerine** The torus and tube radii are both positive. The torus radius is smaller than the tube radius.
- **Football** The torus radius is negative and the tube radius is positive. The tube radius must be positive and greater than the absolute value of the torus radius.

The imaginary circle defining the torus radius or centerline can be defined by its center point and a radius, or by the **3 points, 2 points,** and **Tangent-tangent-radius** options, similar to the construction of a circle. By using the **3 points** option, you can specify three points anywhere in the 3D space, which enables you to create a torus whose midplane is not parallel to the current *XY* plane.

The PYRAMID Command

PYRAMID	
Modeling Toolbar	
Ribbon 3D Modeling panel	
Pull-down Menu	Draw/ Modeling/ Pyramid
Command Line	pyramid

The **PYRAMID** command creates a pyramid-shaped 3D solid. The polygonal base can have between 2 and 32 sides. If the polygonal base of the pyramid is created by specifying a center point then, similar to the **POLYGON** command, it can be created circumscribed or inscribed on a circle. You can also determine the geometry of the base by specifying the first and second points of the leading edge. The default settings of the base are four sides circumscribed on a circle (Figure 5-20).

The rest of the geometry is determined very similarly to the **CONE** command. By specifying the height of the pyramid, you can locate its base parallel to the current *XY* plane. Specifying a point with the **Axis endpoint** option will align the base normal to the axis of the cone (Figure 5-21).

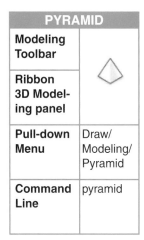

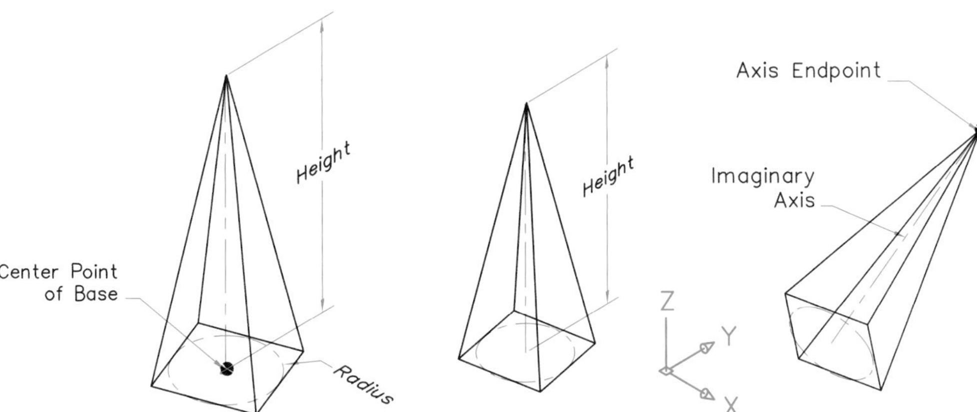

Figure 5-20 The parameters specified to create a pyramid-shaped 3D solid

Figure 5-21 Specifying an Axis endpoint aligns the axis of the pyramid differently

As with the cone, you can create a pyramid that does not end in an apex point by specifying a value in the **Top radius** option (Figure 5-22).

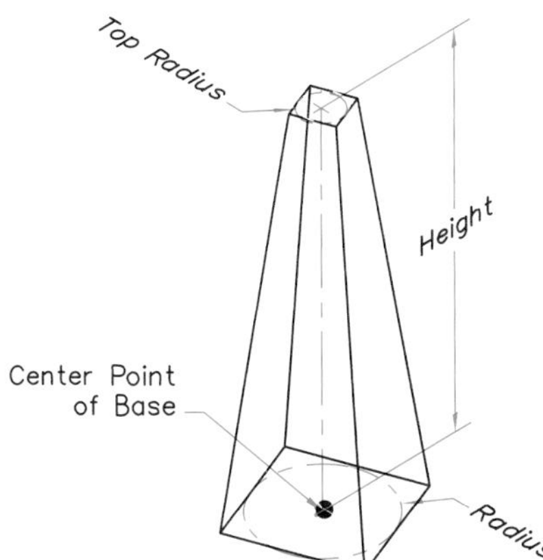

Figure 5-22 If you specify a Top radius value, the pyramid does not end in an apex point

CREATING COMPLEX 3D SOLIDS AND SURFACES

DIFFERENT APPROACHES TO CREATING 3D SOLID OBJECTS

The commands that are used to create 3D solid primitives enable you to create the most common 3D objects. As you will learn later, you can combine 3D solid primitives through Boolean operations to create more complex 3D models. More complex commands (**EXTRUDE, REVOLVE, SWEEP,** and **LOFT**), however, can also be used to obtain the same 3D solids with less effort. Figure 5-23 shows two alternative ways of developing the same 3D solid model.

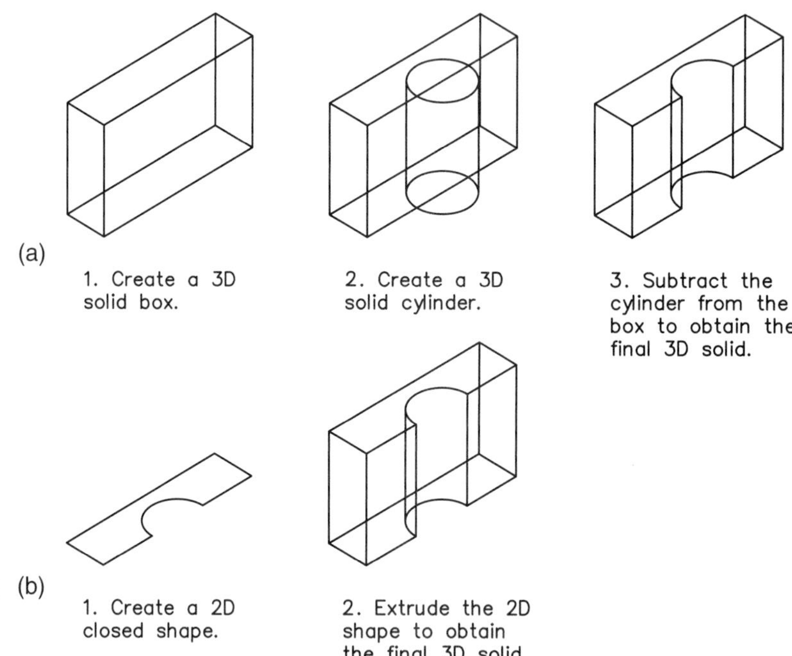
(a)
1. Create a 3D solid box.
2. Create a 3D solid cylinder.
3. Subtract the cylinder from the box to obtain the final 3D solid.
(b)
1. Create a 2D closed shape.
2. Extrude the 2D shape to obtain the final 3D solid.

Figure 5-23 Two approaches to creating a 3D solid model: (a) using and combining primitives and (b) using the EXTRUDE command

The **EXTRUDE, REVOLVE, SWEEP,** and **LOFT** commands also allow you to create 3D solids and surfaces of very complex shapes. All these commands require you to select certain types of objects depending on the operation performed. As a general rule, 3D solids are created from closed objects such as circles, regions, and closed polylines, whereas surfaces are created from open objects such as arcs, lines, and open polylines.

Each of these commands generates its own type of 3D solid and surface. Each particular type of 3D object contains properties unique to it. You can then use these properties to perform further editing.

FOR MORE DETAILS

To learn about editing different types of 3D solids and surfaces, see Chapter 6.

By default, the selected objects are deleted after the 3D solid or surface is created through the different operations. This setting is controlled by the **DELOBJ** system variable. You can change its value to **1** to keep the selected objects.

THE EXTRUDE COMMAND

The name **EXTRUDE** comes from a manufacturing process called *extrusion,* in which heat-softened metal or plastic is pushed under high pressure through a mold opening, producing bars with constant cross sections. Figure 5-24 shows a 3D solid model of an aluminum bar extrusion created with the **EXTRUDE** command.

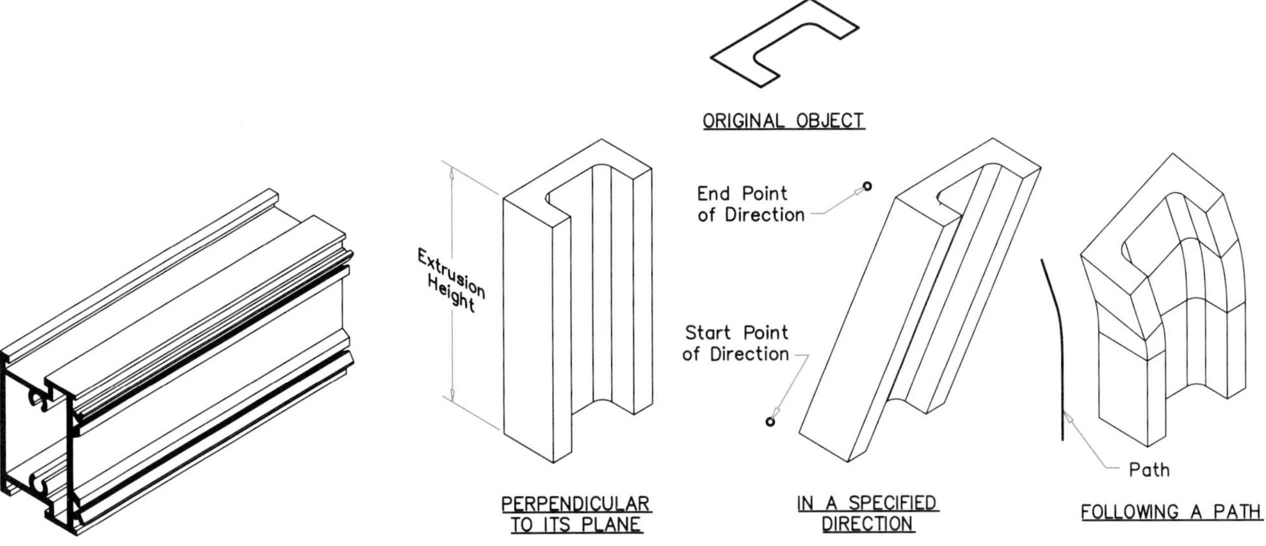

Figure 5-24 Extruded aluminum bars can be created using the EXTRUDE command

Figure 5-25 Different ways of creating extrusions

The **EXTRUDE** command creates 3D solids and surfaces of the **Extrusion** type by protruding planar objects. Depending on the options you use, the extrusion can be performed in one of the following ways (Figure 5-25):

- Perpendicular to its plane (default)
- In a specified direction
- Following a path

By specifying the height of extrusion, the object is automatically extruded perpendicular to the plane where it exists. You can change this course by selecting either the **Direction** or the **Path** option.

Defining a **Direction** by specifying the start and end points creates the same 3D solid or surface shape as does selecting a line between these two points using the **Path** option. The types of 3D solids and surfaces created with the **Path** option, however, are not the same as those created with the **Direction** option. The **Path** option creates 3D solids and surfaces of the **Sweep** type, whereas using the **Direction** option or simply extruding the object perpendicular to its plane both create 3D solids and surfaces of the **Extrusion** type. These different types of 3D solids and surfaces offer different editing capabilities.

FOR MORE DETAILS See Chapter 6 to find more information about procedures to edit the different types of 3D solids and surfaces.

You can also specify a **Taper angle** for any of the operations to create both 3D solids and surfaces (Figure 5-26).

The following AutoCAD objects or entities can be extruded into either 3D solids or surfaces:

- Lines
- Arcs
- Circles
- Regions
- Ellipses and elliptical arcs
- Non-self-intersecting polylines
- Non-self-intersecting, planar 3D polylines

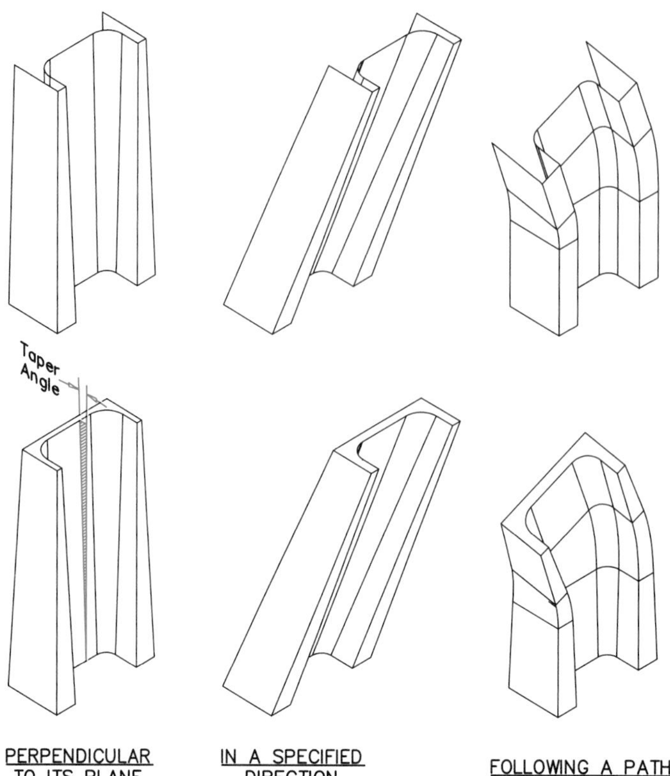

Figure 5-26 A Taper angle can also be specified for both 3D solids and surfaces

- Planar splines
- Planar 3D faces
- Non-self-intersecting 2D solids
- Planar surfaces
- Planar faces on 3D solids (see below)

You can create extruded 3D solids from planar faces of other 3D solids by holding down the **<Ctrl>** key while selecting objects. The 3D solids created from the selected faces will be independent of the original 3D solids whose faces were selected. You can select different faces on the same 3D solid or on different 3D solids. You can also select faces along with any other object.

Almost any object can be used as a path as well, as long as it is not placed in the same plane as the extruded object. The following list contains the objects allowed in the selection:

- Lines
- Arcs
- Circles
- Ellipses and elliptical arcs
- Non-self-intersecting polylines
- Non-self-intersecting 3D polylines
- Splines
- Edges of 3D solids and surfaces (see below)
- Helixes

You can create extruded 3D solids and surfaces using the edges of other 3D solids and surfaces by holding down the **<Ctrl>** key while selecting the object that defines the path.

Polylines are very useful for defining the path of extrusions. Two applications in which extruding objects by using this path can be helpful are the pipe and duct lines shown in Figure 5-27. If two continuous segments of the polyline path are not tangent, the resulting 3D solid will look as if it were mitered by the midplane between the two segments (Figure 5-28).

Extruding a circle along a helix path allows you to create springs (Figure 5-29).

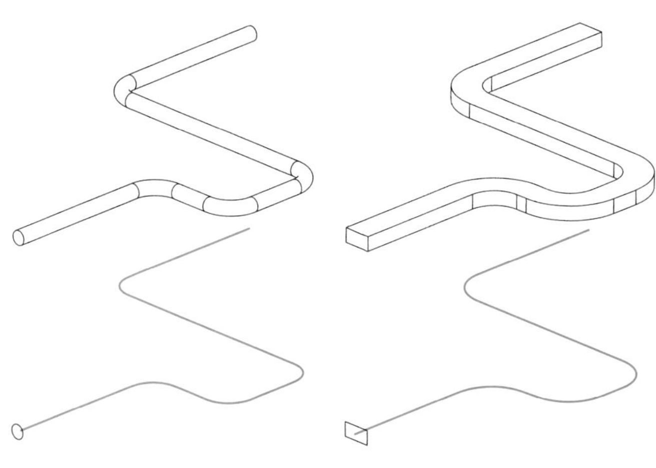

Figure 5-27 Pipe and duct lines are easily created by extruding the profile through a path

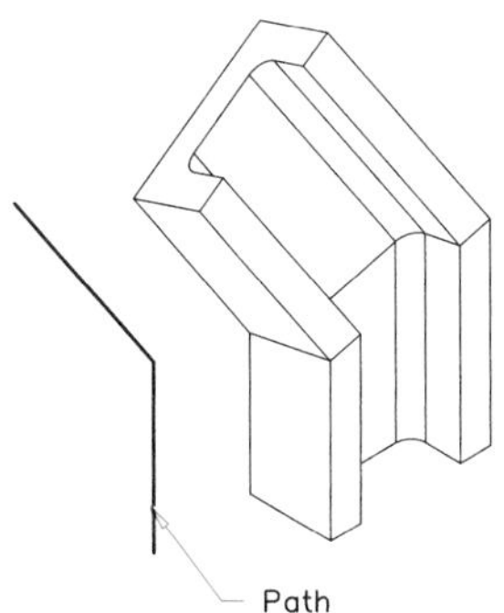

Figure 5-28 Mitered transitions can be obtained by using a path with two continuous straight segments

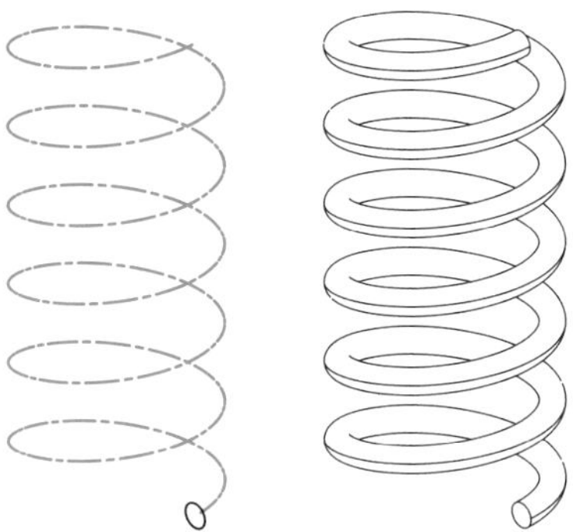

Figure 5-29 Extruding along a helix path allows you to create springs

It is a good practice to place the object to be extruded on the starting point of the path in a plane perpendicular to the path curve. This helps to avoid unpredicted results. You can find the plane that is perpendicular to a curve by using the **Object** option of the **Z axis** method of modifying the UCS.

Exercise 5-3: Using the EXTRUDE Command

1. **OPEN** the drawing ***Exercise 5-3*** from the CD.
2. **SAVE** the drawing **AS *Exercise 5-3 solved*** on your computer.
3. Select the **SE Isometric** viewing point.
4. Invoke the **EXTRUDE** command. Respond to the prompts as follows:

   Select objects to extrude: *Select the region.*

   Select objects to extrude: ↵ *(To end the selection)*

   Specify height of extrusion or [Direction/Path/Taper angle]: *t* ↵

   Specify angle of taper for extrusion: *−30* ↵

   Specify height of extrusion or [Direction/Path/Taper angle]: *−1.5* ↵

Note:

The extrusion is performed 1.5 units toward the negative direction of the Z-axis. Due to the negative taper angle, the cross section of the 3D solid gets bigger toward the extrusion end (Figure 5-30, with the hidden lines removed).

EXTRUDE	
Modeling Toolbar	
Ribbon 3D Modeling panel	
Pull-down Menu	Draw/ Modeling/ Extrude
Command Line	extrude
Command Alias	ext

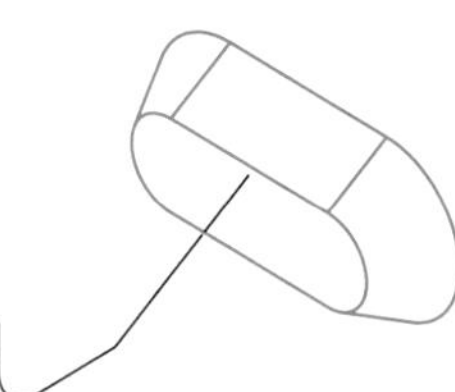

Figure 5-30 After extruding the profile as specified

5. Invoke the **EXTRUDE** command again and respond to the prompts as follows:

   Select objects to extrude: *Hold down the <Ctrl> and <Alt> keys, and click on the front face once it is highlighted.*

   Select objects to extrude: *Holding down the <Ctrl> key, click inside the front face.*

   Specify height of extrusion or [Direction/Path/Taper angle]: *p* ↵

   Select extrusion path or [Taper angle]: *Select the open polyline.*

TIP

Now you can select the objects before invoking the **EXTRUDE** command. This enables you to avoid the selection process.

6. Invoke the **HIDE** command. The objects should look like Figure 5-31.
7. Invoke the **REGEN** command.
8. With **ORTHO** mode on, **COPY** the first extruded 3D solid and the polyline **12″** along the positive direction of the *X*-axis (Figure 5-32).

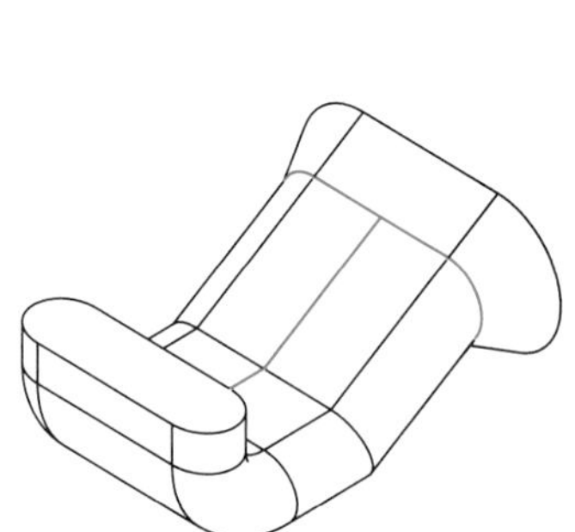

Figure 5-31 The resulting 3D model with occulted lines removed

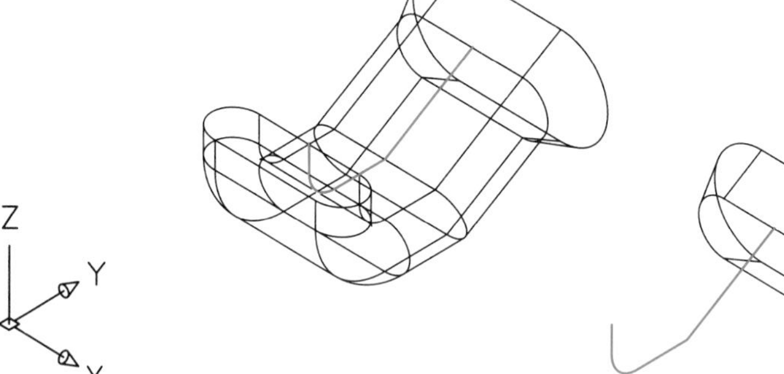
Z
Y
X

Figure 5-32 After copying the objects

9. **EXTRUDE** the front face of the copied 3D solid. Use a **Taper** angle of **5°**, and a **Direction** specified between the two endpoints of the open polyline's first segment. The result should look like Figure 5-33 with the hidden lines removed.
10. With **ORTHO** mode on, **MOVE** the two open polylines **12″** along the negative direction of the Z-axis (Figure 5-34).
11. Select the leftmost polyline and invoke the **EXTRUDE** command to create an extruded surface. Enter **–8** when prompted to specify the height of extrusion.
12. **EXPLODE** the remaining polyline.
13. Select the longest of the separated segments and invoke the **EXTRUDE** command again. Respond to the prompts as follows:

    Specify height of extrusion or [Direction/Path/Taper angle] <3.3500>: *p* ↵

    Select extrusion path or [Taper angle]: *Holding down the <Ctrl> key, select the edge highlighted in* Figure 5-35.

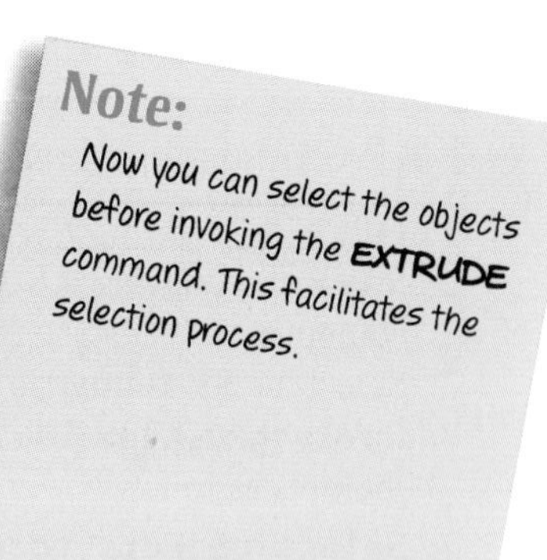
Note:
Now you can select the objects before invoking the EXTRUDE command. This facilitates the selection process.

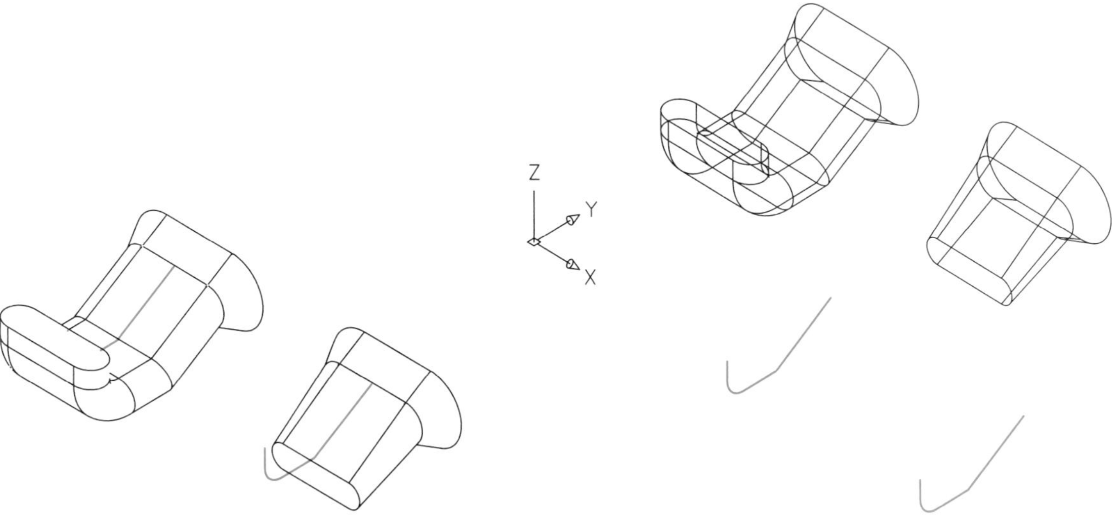

Figure 5-33 After extruding the profile using a taper angle

Figure 5-34 The polylines are moved

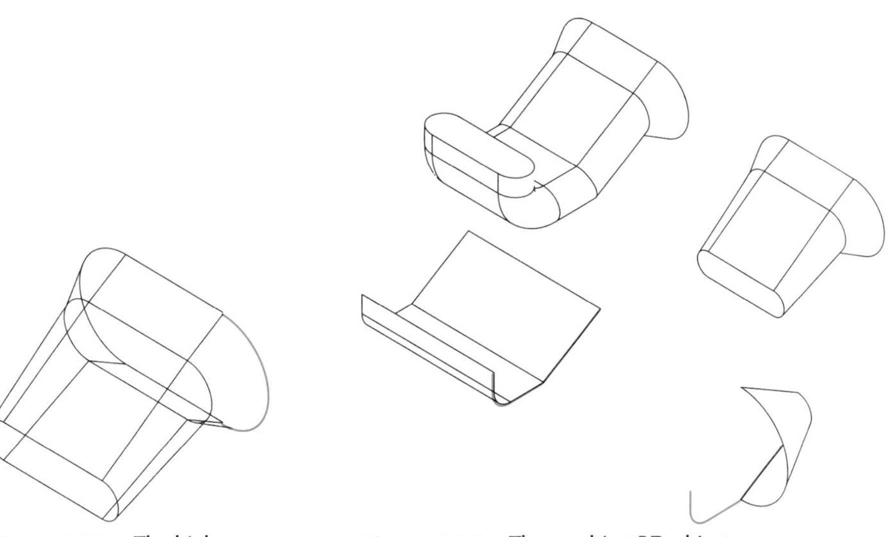

Figure 5-35 The highlighted edge is selected as the extrusion path

Figure 5-36 The resulting 3D objects

14. After invoking the **HIDE** command, the 3D objects should look like Figure 5-36.
15. **SAVE** the drawing.

Extruding Implied Faces: The PRESSPULL Command

EXTRUDE is the command most widely used in 3D modeling. You can also create 3D solids by extruding a bounded area perpendicular to its plane without even invoking the **EXTRUDE** command. This operation is known as **Extrude Implied Faces**.

PRESSPULL	
Modeling Toolbar	
Ribbon 3D Modeling	
Command Line	presspull

The **Extrude Implied Faces** detection process is initiated automatically by holding down the **<Ctrl>** and **<Alt>** keys together, or by invoking the **PRESSPULL** command. Then you just click inside the bounded planar area or contour detected to extrude it in one of two directions by either entering a value or clicking on another point. For example, the rectangle and the line shown in Figure 5-37, which are placed on a common plane, contain two bounded planar areas that are recognized by this operation. Clicking on one of the detected implied faces and specifying a height creates the 3D solid.

Besides bounded planar areas, delimited by crossing coplanar objects, implied faces can also be detected from any single closed planar object, such as a closed polyline or a region. Moreover,

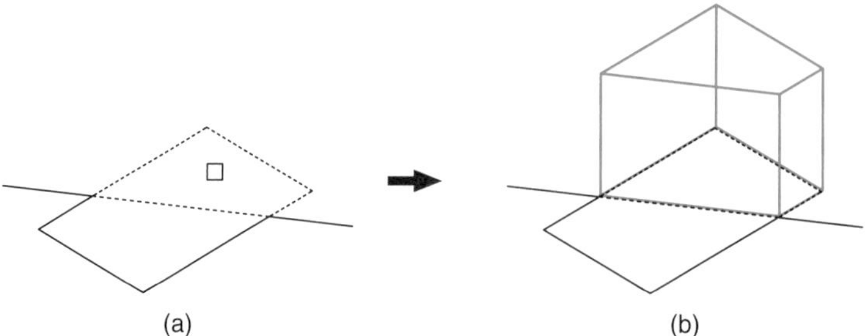

Figure 5-37 (a) Selecting one of the implied faces; (b) the extruded implied faces

the faces of existing 3D solids can also become part of the implied face boundary along with other coplanar curves. Figure 5-38 shows the creation of a 3D solid by extruding an implied face between the bottom face of the 3D solid and a circle.

The **IMPLIEDFACE** system variable controls whether or not the implied faces are detected.

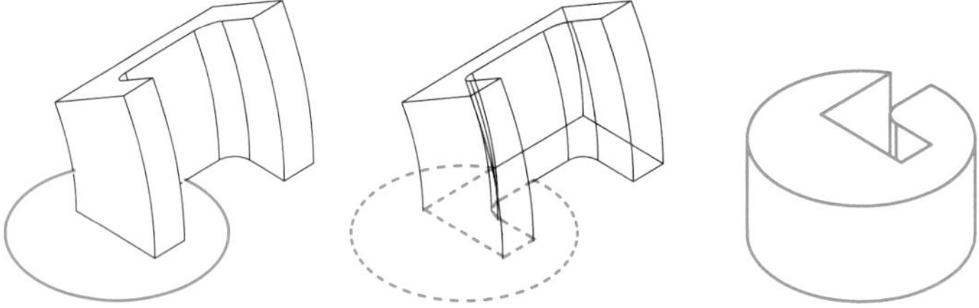

Figure 5-38 The faces of 3D solids are included in the implied face boundary selection

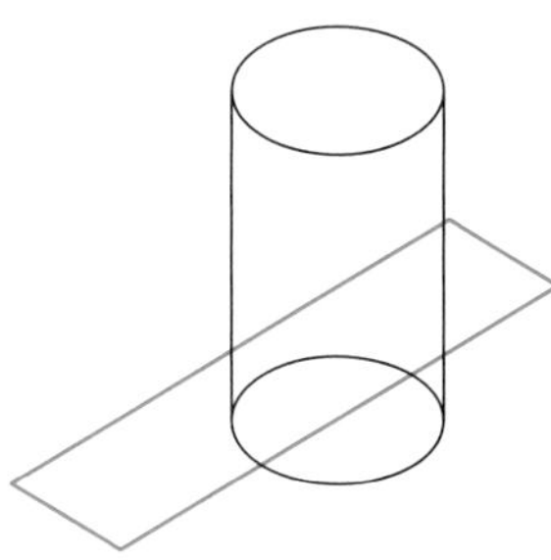

Figure 5-39 The rectangle is moved toward the cylinder

Exercise 5-4: Extruding Implied Faces

1. Start a **NEW** drawing using **Imperial** units.
2. **SAVE** the drawing **AS *Exercise 5-4.***
3. Set the **DISPSILH** system variable to **1**.
4. Set the **ISOLINES** system variable to **0**.
5. Select the **SE Isometric** viewing point.
6. Invoke the **CYLINDER** command and create a cylinder anywhere in the drawing area. Specify **11/16″** for the radius, and **2½″** for the height.
7. **ZOOM** in as needed and create a **4 × 1** rectangle using the **RECTANGLE** command. Then **MOVE** the rectangle so the midpoint of its long side is located on the center point of the bottom face of the cylinder (Figure 5-39).
8. Press and hold down the **<Ctrl>** and **<Alt>** keys to initiate the **Extrude Implied Faces** process. Once recognized, click inside the area that is bounded by the rectangle and the circular edge of the cylinder.
9. Release the **<Ctrl>** and **<Alt>** keys. Move the pointer upward and type **4** in the command line. Press **<Enter>** to finish the operation.
10. After invoking the **HIDE** command, the two 3D solids should look like Figure 5-40.
11. **SAVE** the drawing.

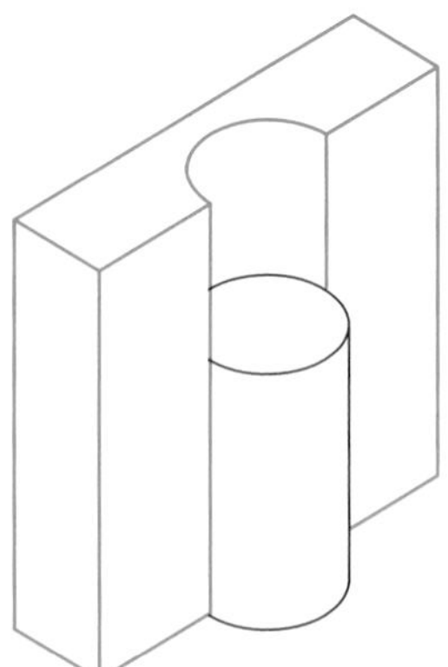

Figure 5-40 A new 3D solid created by extruding an implied face

THE REVOLVE COMMAND

imaginary axis of revolution: The vector, defined by specifying any two points, about which the objects are revolved. Its direction is defined from the first point to the second point.

The **REVOLVE** command creates revolved 3D solids and surfaces by turning closed and open objects in a circular direction around an ***imaginary axis of revolution*** at a specified angle. Objects machined in a lathe, such as the pulley shown in Figure 5-41, are good examples of 3D objects that can be easily created using this command.

Basically, the same type of objects that can be extruded can be revolved as well, including planar faces on 3D solids. As with the **EXTRUDE** command, holding down the **<Ctrl>** key while selecting objects allows you to select faces from one or more 3D solids, which you can combine with any other valid selection. The new revolved 3D solids and surfaces created by selecting the faces of 3D solids will be independent of the original 3D solid from which the faces were selected.

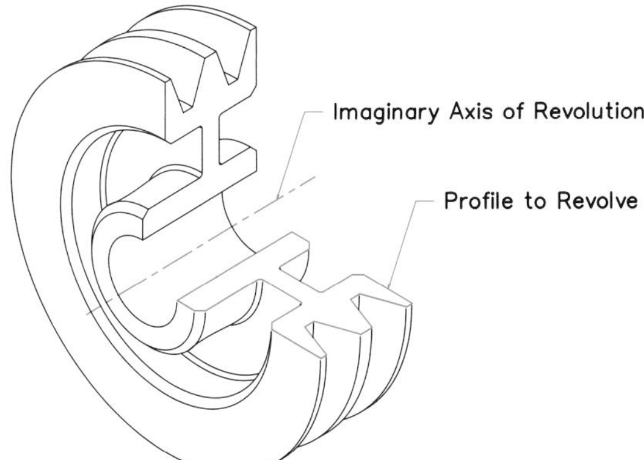

Figure 5-41 A pulley can easily be created as a revolved 3D solid

The imaginary axis of revolution can be defined anywhere in the 3D space, as long as it is not perpendicular to the plane of the object to be revolved. Depending on the option selected, you can define the imaginary axis of revolution using one of the following methods:

- Two points
- The *X*-axis of the current UCS
- The *Y*-axis of the current UCS
- The *Z*-axis of the current UCS
- Using an existing object (lines, open polylines, and straight edges on 3D solids)

When using the **Object** option, you can select a straight edge of other 3D solids or surfaces by holding down the **<Ctrl>** key. If you select a polyline with more than one segment, the axis of revolution will be considered to be a vector between the start and end points of the polyline.

Exercise 5-5: Using the REVOLVE Command

1. **OPEN** the drawing ***Exercise 5-5*** from the CD. It contains the objects shown in Figure 5-42.
2. **SAVE** the drawing **AS *Exercise 5-5 solved*.**
3. Invoke the **REVOLVE** command, and respond to the prompts as follows:

   Select objects to revolve: *Select the region on the right.*

   Select objects to revolve: ↵ *(To end the selection)*

   Specify axis start point or define axis by [Object/X/Y/Z] <Object>: *Specify the leftmost endpoint of the line next to it.*

   Specify axis endpoint: *Specify the other endpoint of the line.*

   Specify angle of revolution or [STart angle] <360>: *225* ↵
4. Invoke the **HIDE** command. The 3D solid should look like Figure 5-43.

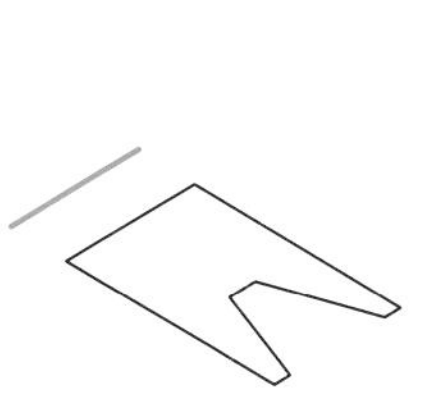

Figure 5-42 Objects contained in the CD file

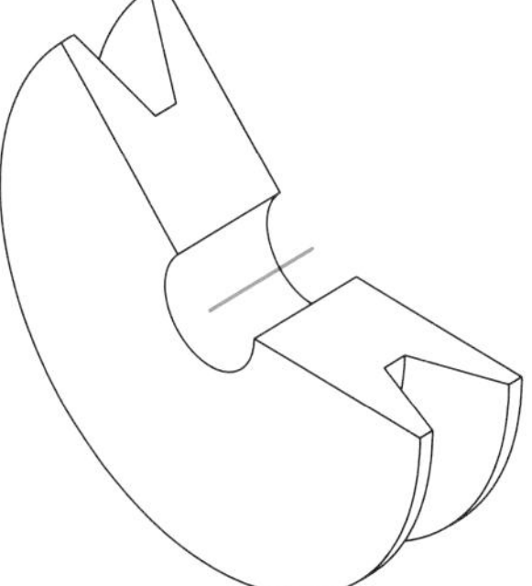

Figure 5-43 The revolved 3D solid with the obscured lines removed

REVOLVE	
Modeling Toolbar	
Ribbon 3D Modeling panel	
Pull-down Menu	Draw/ Modeling/ Revolve
Command Line	revolve
Command Alias	rev

FOR MORE DETAILS In a rotation, the positive angle direction is determined by the right-hand rule. See Chapter 1 for more information on this topic.

5. Invoke the **REGEN** command.
6. Invoke the **REVOLVE** command, and respond to the prompts as follows:

   Select objects to revolve: *Select the region on the left.*

   Select objects to revolve: ↵ *(To end the selection)*

   Specify start point for axis of revolution or

   Specify axis start point or define axis by [Object/X/Y/Z] <Object>: *o* ↵

   Select an object: *Select the line by picking it on the top half portion.*

   Specify angle of revolution or [STart angle] <360>: *180* ↵

7. **ERASE** the line you used to define the axis of revolution.
8. Invoke the **HIDE** command. The new revolved 3D solid should look like Figure 5-44.
9. Invoke the **REGEN** command and select the **Right** UCS.
10. Draw the two lines shown in Figure 5-45. Using AutoTrack might be helpful for this operation.
11. Invoke the **REVOLVE** command, and respond to the prompts as follows:

Note: When using an object to specify the axis of revolution, the portion of the object at which it is picked determines the positive angle for the **REVOLVE** operation.

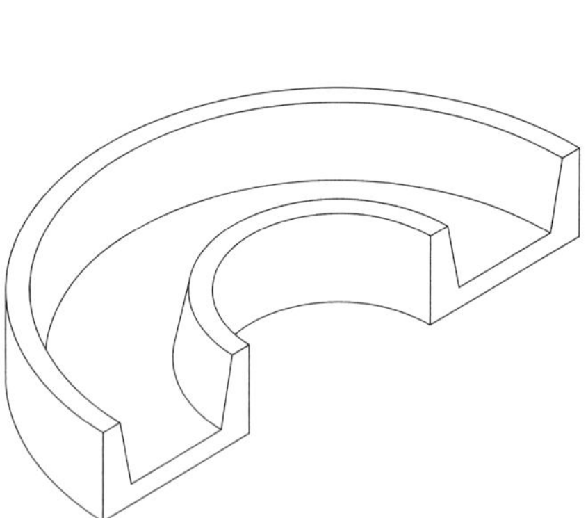
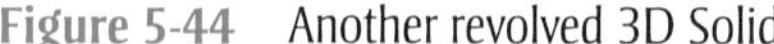

Figure 5-44 Another revolved 3D Solid

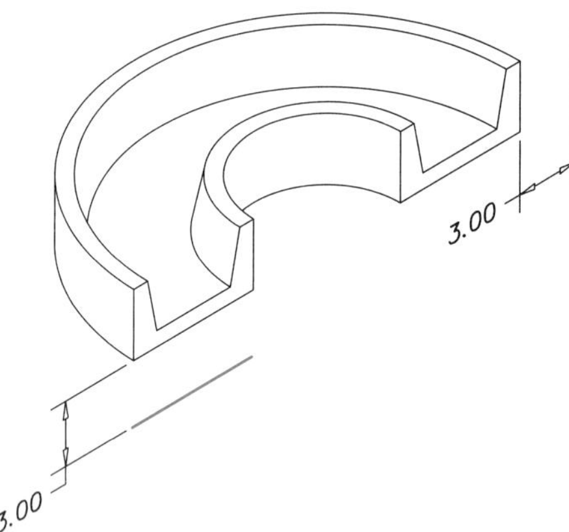

Figure 5-45 Dimensions of lines to be created

Select objects to revolve: *Holding down the* **<Ctrl>** *key, click on the face shown highlighted in* Figure 5-46.

Select objects to revolve: ↵ *(To end the selection)*

Specify start point for axis of revolution or

Specify axis start point or define axis by [Object/X/Y/Z] Object: *o* ↵

Select an object: *Select the line by picking it on the left half portion.*

Specify angle of revolution or [STart angle] <360>: *60* ↵

12. **ERASE** the line you used to define the axis of revolution.
13. Create a third revolved 3D solid by revolving the other planar face 60° as well. Define the axis of revolution by selecting the line on its lower half portion.
14. **ERASE** the line and invoke the **UNION** command. When prompted, select the three 3D solids.
15. Select the **Conceptual** visual style.

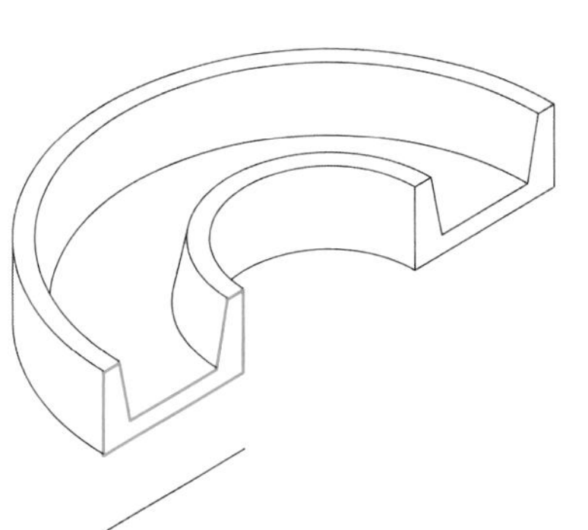

Figure 5-46 Face to be selected for the REVOLVE operation

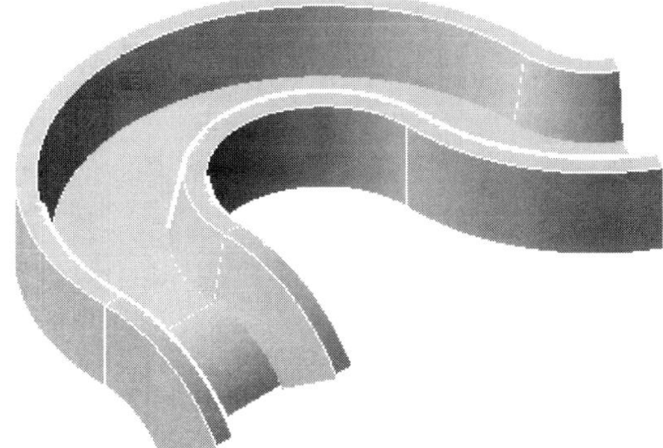

Figure 5-47 A shaded view of the resulting 3D model

16. In the **Edge Effects** panel of the **Ribbon,** make sure the **Obscured edges** button is turned off. The 3D model should look like Figure 5-47.
17. Invoke the **3DORBIT** command to inspect the geometry of the 3D model.
18. **SAVE** the drawing.

THE SWEEP COMMAND

The **SWEEP** command creates 3D solids of the **Sweep** type and surfaces by sweeping closed planar and open planar objects along a sweep path. Figure 5-48 shows a rectangular polyline and a line that have both been swept along a helical path. The operation aligns itself with the cross section normal to the path at any point.

sweep: Operation in which open or closed planar objects are passed through a curve, creating 3D solids and surfaces.

The different options you can use to fine-tune the sweep operation once the objects are selected are shown in the **SWEEP** shortcut menu (Figure 5-49).

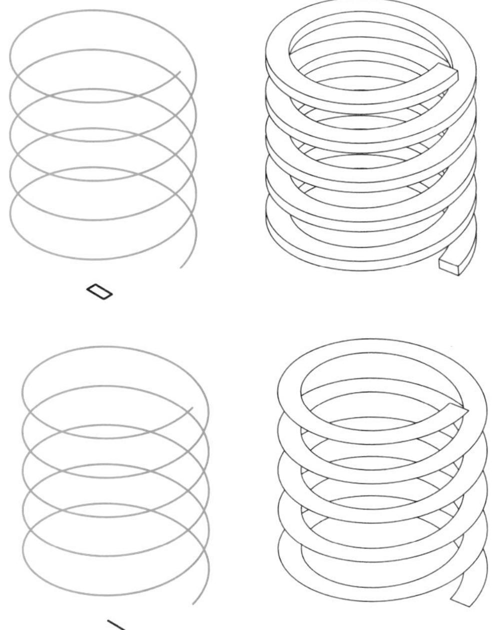

Figure 5-48 Objects swept along a helical path

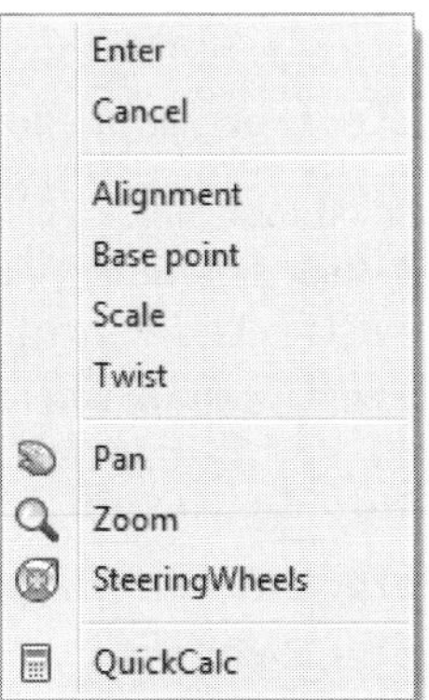

Figure 5-49 The SWEEP command shortcut menu

The **Alignment** option determines whether the planar objects are aligned normal to the sweep path before the sweep operation or swept with their current alignment.

By default, the location of the selected objects with respect to the swept path is in the middle of all the objects selected. This setting can be changed through the **Base point** option, or by manually locating the objects at the desired location (Figure 5-50).

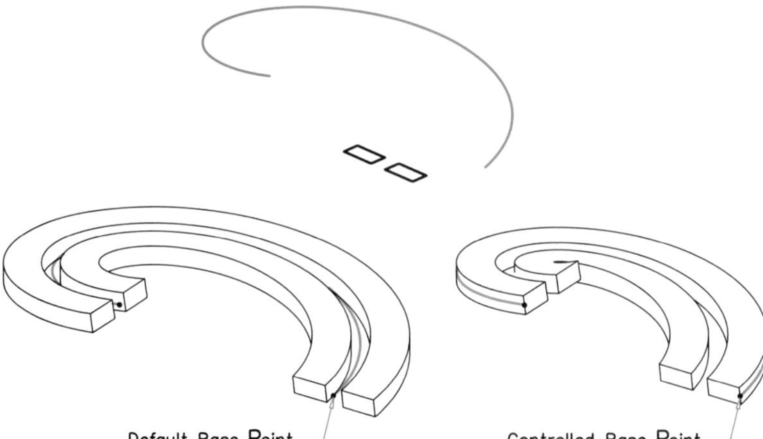

Figure 5-50 The Base point option controls the relative location of the cross section with respect to the path's start point

The **Scale** option allows you to create 3D solids and surfaces for which the cross section increases or decreases uniformly as they are swept along the path, depending on the scale factor you specify (Figure 5-51).

The **Twist** option rotates the cross section uniformly as the object is swept along the path, depending on the angle value you specify (Figure 5-52).

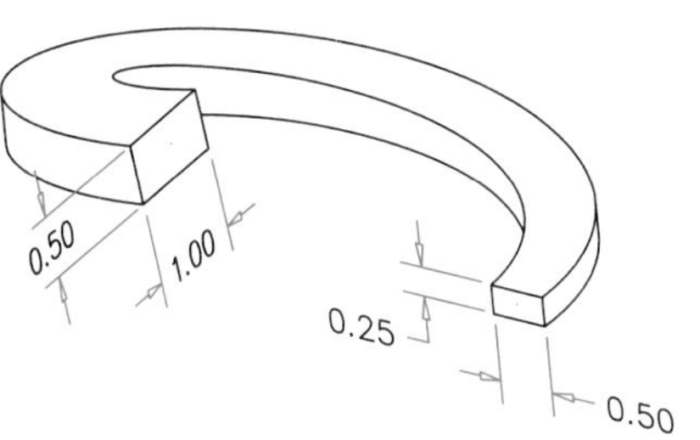

Figure 5-51 Using the Scale option creates swept 3D objects with cross sections that increase or decrease uniformly

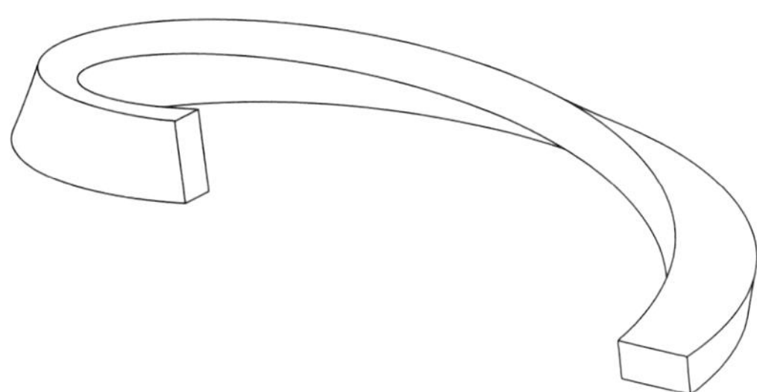

Figure 5-52 The Twist option rotates the cross section uniformly

Exercise 5-6: Using the SWEEP Command

1. **OPEN** the drawing ***Exercise 5-6*** from the CD. It contains the objects shown in Figure 5-53.
2. **SAVE** the drawing **AS *Exercise 5-6 solved.***
3. Invoke the **SWEEP** command, and respond to the prompts as follows:

   Select objects to sweep: *Select the small polyline.*

   Select objects to sweep: ↵ *(To end the selection)*

   Select sweep path or [Alignment/Base point/Scale/Twist]: *b* ↵

   Specify base point: *Snap to the rightmost endpoint on the polyline.*

   Select sweep path or [Alignment/Base point/Scale/Twist]: *Select the helix close to its bottom portion.*
4. Invoke the **SWEEP** command again, and respond to the prompts as follows:

   Select objects to sweep: *Select the small line.*

   Select objects to sweep: ↵ *(To end the selection)*

   Select sweep path or [Alignment/Base point/Scale/Twist]: *s* ↵

   Enter scale factor or [Reference] <1.0000>: *3* ↵

   Select sweep path or [Alignment/Base point/Scale/Twist]: *Select the spline on the topmost portion of the current view.*
5. Invoke the **HIDE** command. The 3D model should look like Figure 5-54.
6. Select the **Realistic** visual style and invoke the **3DORBIT** command to inspect the 3D model.
7. **SAVE** the drawing.

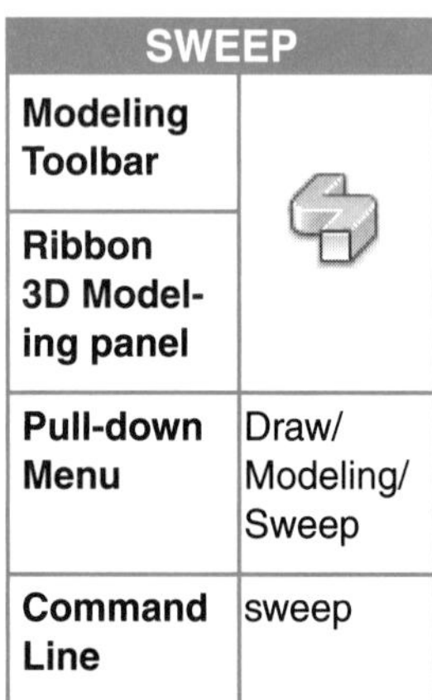

SWEEP	
Modeling Toolbar	
Ribbon 3D Modeling panel	
Pull-down Menu	Draw/ Modeling/ Sweep
Command Line	sweep

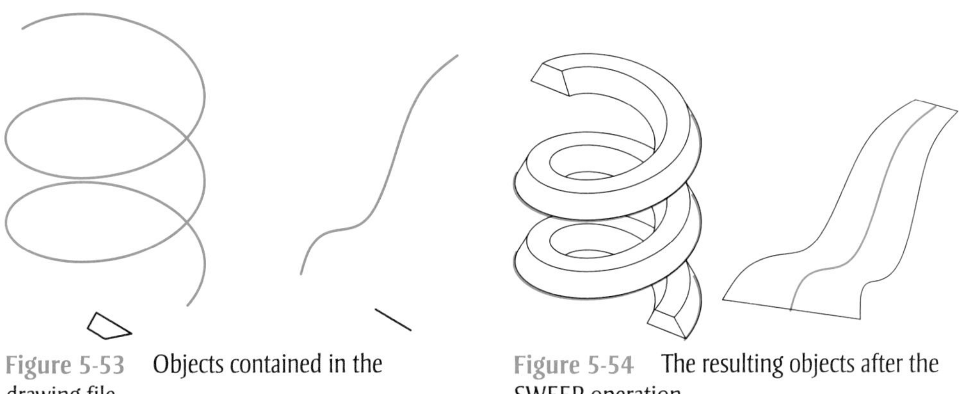

Figure 5-53 Objects contained in the drawing file

Figure 5-54 The resulting objects after the SWEEP operation

THE LOFT COMMAND

LOFT	
Modeling Toolbar	
Ribbon 3D Modeling panel	
Pull-down Menu	Draw/ Modeling/ Loft
Command Line	loft

The **LOFT** command creates 3D solids or surfaces of the **Loft** type by lofting a set of two or more cross sections. This operation can alternatively be assisted by a path or a set of guides. Unlike other commands, **LOFT** generates three different types of 3D solids and surfaces depending on which option you use:

- Loft with cross sections only
- Loft with path
- Loft with guide curves

Each of these types of 3D solids or surfaces contains properties that are unique to them, which you can then use to perform further editing. You can see the type of 3D solid or surface in the **Geometry** section of the **Properties** palette.

FOR MORE DETAILS To learn about editing different types of 3D solids and surfaces, see Chapter 6.

Each type of 3D solid or surface is created by using one of the options available. Figure 5-55 shows the **LOFT** command shortcut menu with the three options available.

loft: Operation in which a set of open or closed objects are connected through a blended smooth transition, creating 3D solids and surfaces.

The **Cross sections only** option is the default. It simply requires you to select a set of two noncoplanar curves. Sets of closed curves generate a 3D solid, whereas sets of open curves generate a surface (Figure 5-56). Closed and open curves cannot be combined in the same set of cross sections. Nonplanar curves can be used as cross sections, as long as they are not the first and last ones.

The following objects can be used as cross sections:

- Lines
- Arcs

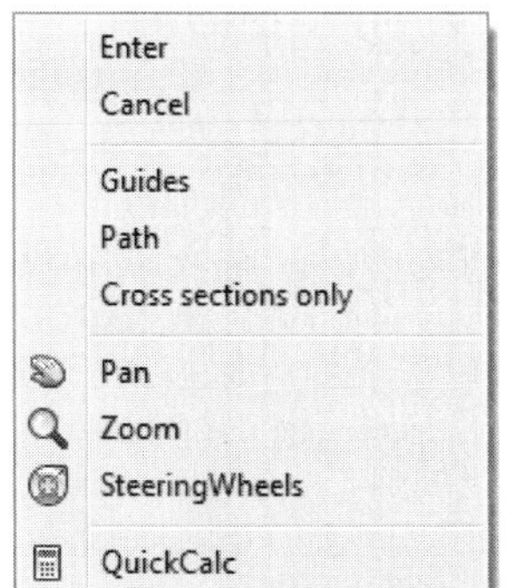

Figure 5-55 The LOFT command shortcut menu

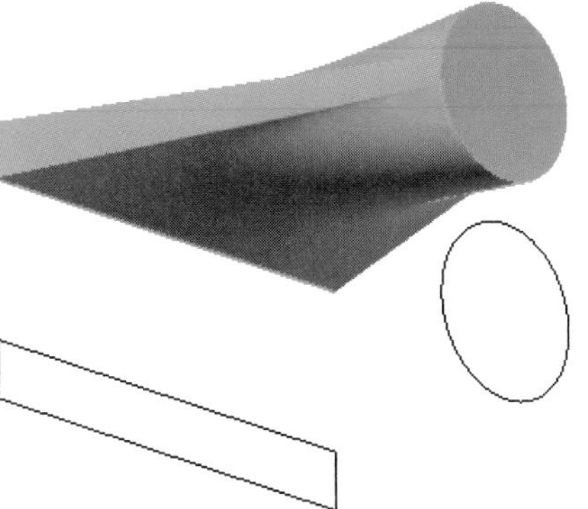

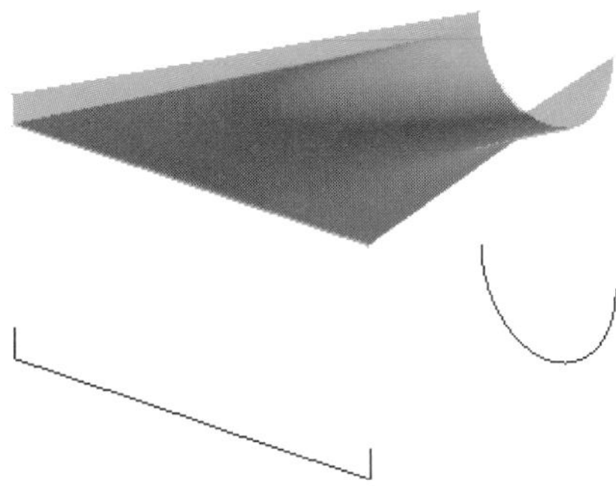

Figure 5-56 A simple LOFT operation using the Cross-section only option simply requires selecting two open or closed noncoplanar curves

- Circles
- Ellipses and elliptical arcs
- Non-self-intersecting polylines
- Non-self-intersecting 3D polylines
- Splines
- Points (only the start and end cross sections)

In the world of design, loft operations are known as *free-form generation tools.* They connect the cross section through a blended smooth transition, from which many different shapes can be obtained, depending on the options used (Figure 5-57). Many shampoo and liquid soap bottles, among other items, are designed using this operation.

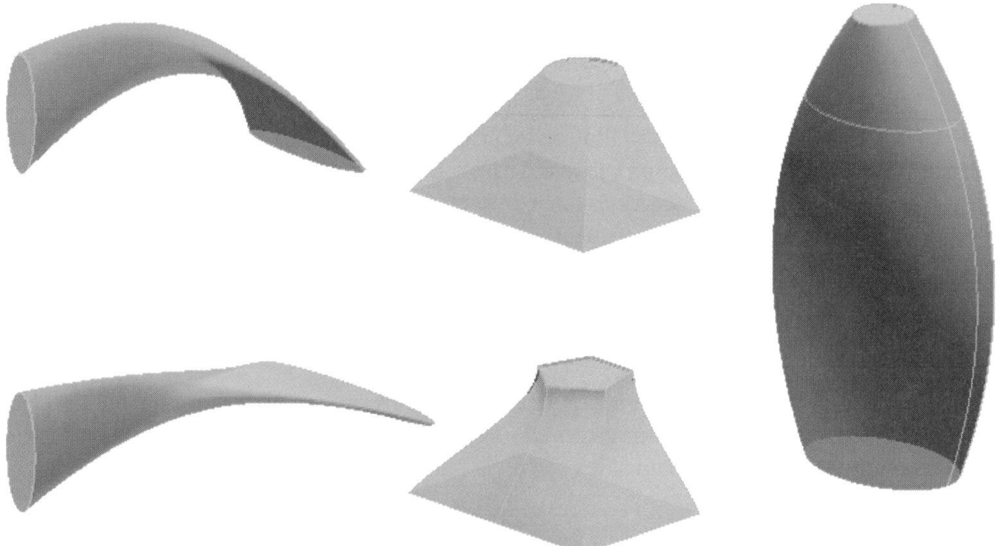

Figure 5-57 Examples of shapes that can be achieved with the LOFT operation

Using the **Cross sections only** option opens the **Loft Settings** dialog box (Figure 5-58). Here you can choose from four different methods to control the behavior of the lofted 3D object at the cross sections:

- **Ruled**
- **Smooth Fit**

Figure 5-58 The Loft Settings dialog box

- **Normal to the Start, End, Start and End**, or **All cross sections**
- Using **Draft angles** for start and end cross sections

The difference between **Ruled** and **Smooth Fit** methods of creating a lofted 3D object is noticeable only when lofting more than two cross sections (Figure 5-59).

Creating a loft 3D object **Normal to:** specific cross sections forces the lofted geometry to protrude perpendicular to the specified cross sections (Figure 5-60).

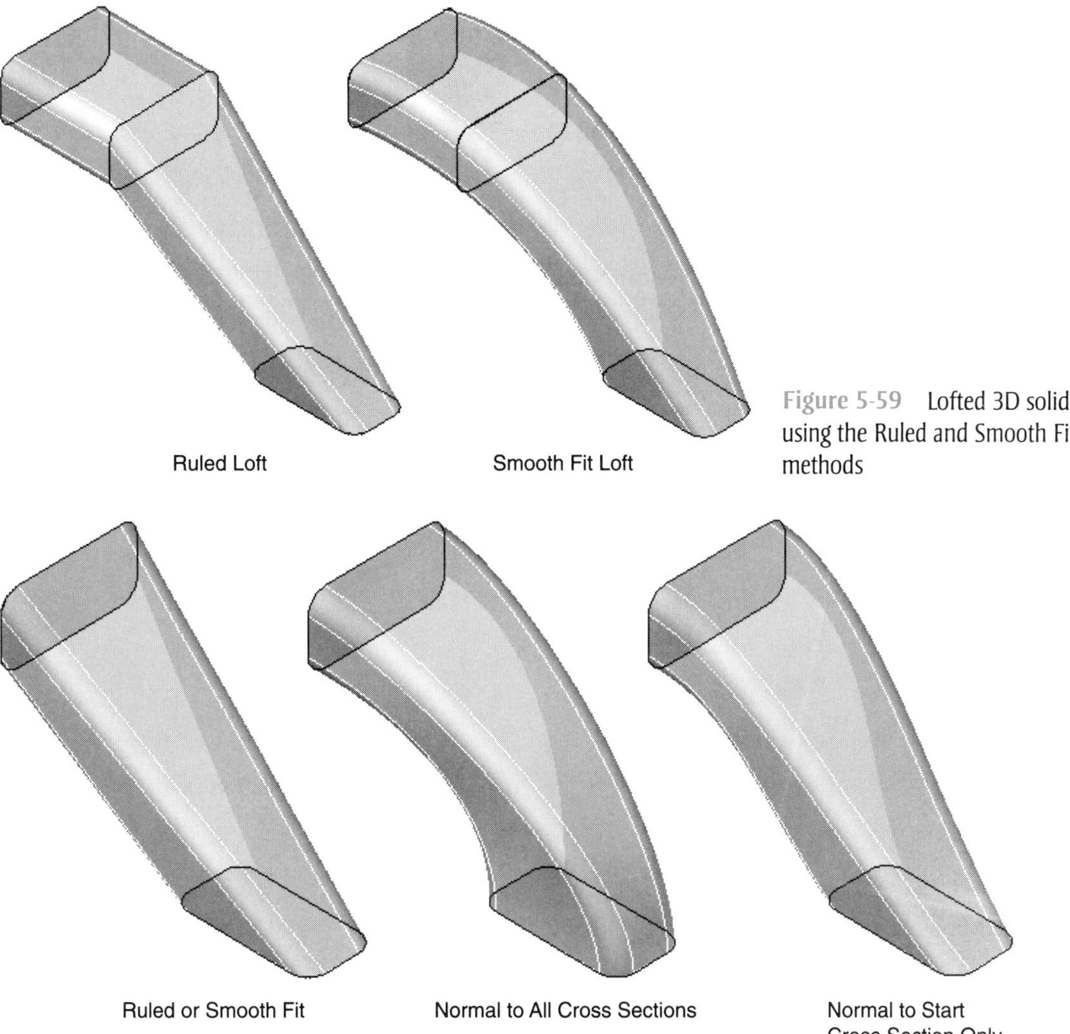

Figure 5-59 Lofted 3D solids using the Ruled and Smooth Fit methods

Figure 5-60 Lofted 3D solids using the Normal to: specific cross sections option

The **Draft angles** setting allows you to control the angle between the lofted geometry and the start or end cross sections. Angles over 90° tilt the surfaces of the lofted geometry inward, whereas angles from 90° to 0° tilt the surfaces of the lofted geometry outward. Specifying both **Draft angles** as 0° enables you to create 3D solids without sharp edges (Figure 5-61). The **magnitude** value controls the relative distance that the lofted geometry is drafted from the specified cross section.

You can loft between cross sections that have different numbers of segments. Using cross sections with an equal number of edges whenever possible, however, will allow you to obtain smoother lofted 3D solids and surfaces. For example, a 3D solid lofted between a circle and an ellipse provides a smoother result than the one created between a circle and a rectangle because both the circle and ellipse cross sections contain a single segment (Figure 5-62). A loft operation between a rectangle and a triangle, on the other hand, might give you odd results (Figure 5-63). To prevent odd results, you can add another segment to the cross sections by creating a simple chamfer or fillet in one of the vertices.

Using the **Path** or **Guides** options allows you to use a different approach to create lofted 3D objects. The settings or geometric conditions you specify when using the **Cross sections only**

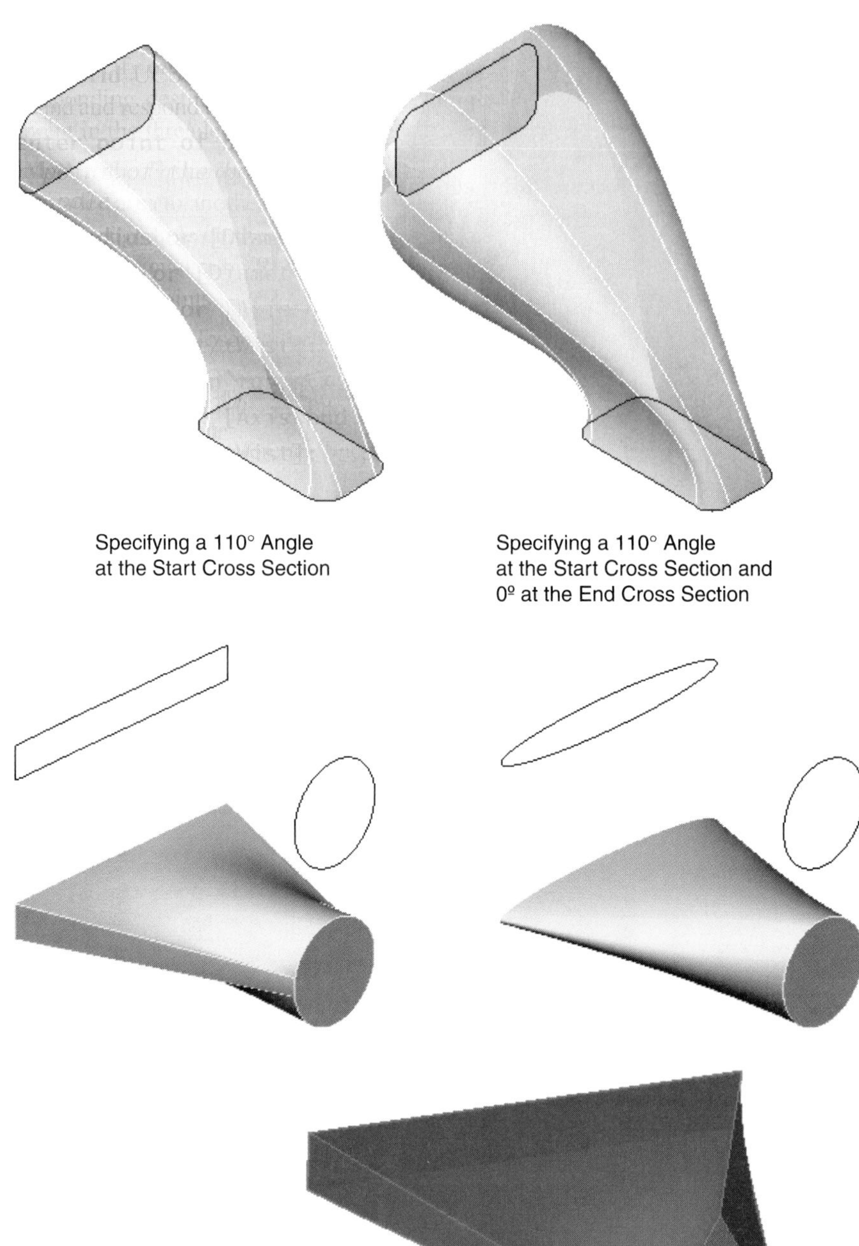

Specifying a 110° Angle
at the Start Cross Section
Specifying a 110° Angle
at the Start Cross Section and
0º at the End Cross Section

Figure 5-61 Lofted 3D solids using Draft angles

Figure 5-62 Using cross sections with an equal number of segments is beneficial for the smoothness of the resulting 3D solid

Figure 5-63 A lofted 3D solid between a rectangle and a triangle

option do not apply with the **Path** or **Guides** options. The **Path** option requires you to specify a single curve, which takes control over the centerline of the lofted 3D object between the cross sections. Using **Guides,** on the other hand, gives you the freedom of controlling specific areas on the surface of the lofted 3D object. Areas that are not guided will behave as a smooth-fit loft (Figure 5-64).

The **Path** curve must intersect the planes of all cross sections. The best results are obtained when it starts and ends on the center of the cross sections or close to it. Cross sections take priority over the path when using more than two cross sections; the path then tries to pull the loft centerline toward it in places having no cross sections. **Guides** must intersect the curve of each cross section, making the surface of the lofted 3D object follow them at their specific locations. When the cross section curves are made of several segments, guides are best used by placing their endpoints at the vertices of the curve of the cross section (Figure 5-65). In general, open continuously tangent and continuously curved wire objects such as lines, arcs, polylines, elliptical arcs, splines and spline-fit polylines, and 3D polylines behave very well when used as paths or guides. Helixes can be used only as paths.

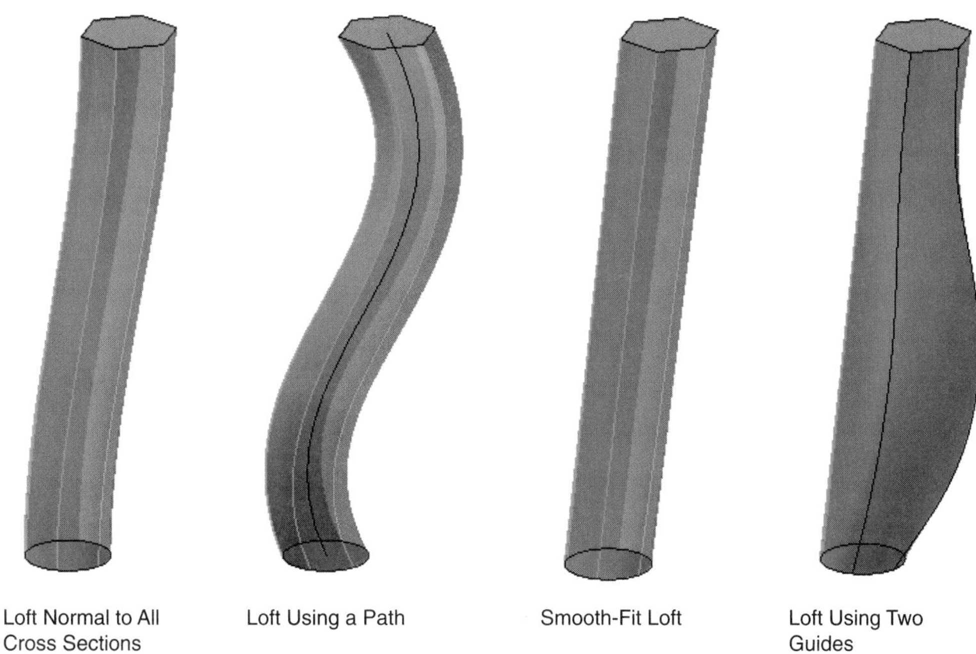

Figure 5-64 Lofted 3D solids using the Path or Guides options compared with the Cross sections only construction

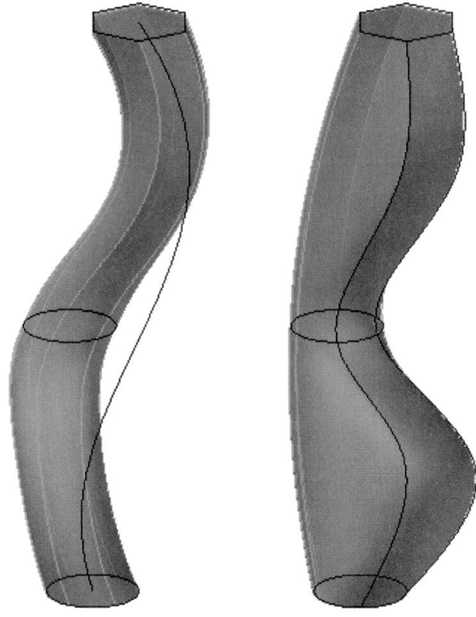

Figure 5-65 The Path must intersect all cross section planes, whereas Guides are required to intersect each cross section

Exercise 5-7: Using the LOFT Command

1. **OPEN** the drawing ***Exercise 5-7*** from the CD. It contains the six curves shown in Figure 5-66.
2. **SAVE** the drawing **AS *Exercise 5-7 solved.***
3. Set the **DELOBJ** system variable to **0**.
4. Invoke the **LOFT** command and respond to the prompts as follows.

   Select cross sections in lofting order: *Select the four closed curves in order from left to right.*

   Select cross sections in lofting order: ↵ *(To end the selection)*

   Enter an option [Guides/Path/Cross-sections only] <Cross-sections only>: *g* ↵

   Select guide curves: *Select the two open curves in any order.*

   Select guide curves: ↵ *(To end the selection)*

5. With **ORTHO** mode on, **MOVE** the lofted 3D solid **5″** along the positive direction of the *Y*-axis.
6. **ERASE** the two objects that you previously selected as guides.
7. Set the **DELOBJ** system variable to **1**.
8. Invoke the **LOFT** command and respond to the prompts as follows.

   Select cross sections in lofting order: *Select the four closed curves in the same order.*

   Select cross sections in lofting order: ↵ *(To end the selection)*

   Enter an option [Guides/Path/Cross sections only] <Cross sections only>: *(To open the* ***Loft Settings*** *dialog box)*
9. In the **Loft Settings** dialog box, select **Normal to:** and select **All cross sections** from its drop-down list. Click **OK** to close the dialog box.
10. Select the **Realistic** visual style.
11. Invoke the **3DORBIT** command to inspect the difference between a guided loft and a loft that is normal to all cross sections. The two lofted 3D solids should look like Figure 5-67.
12. **SAVE** the drawing.

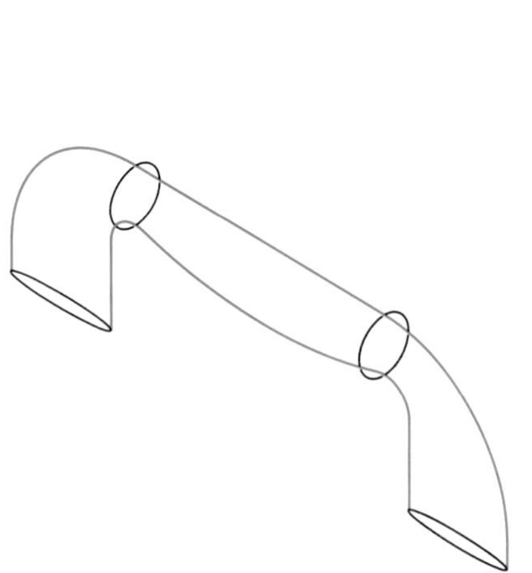

Figure 5-66 Object contained in the drawing file

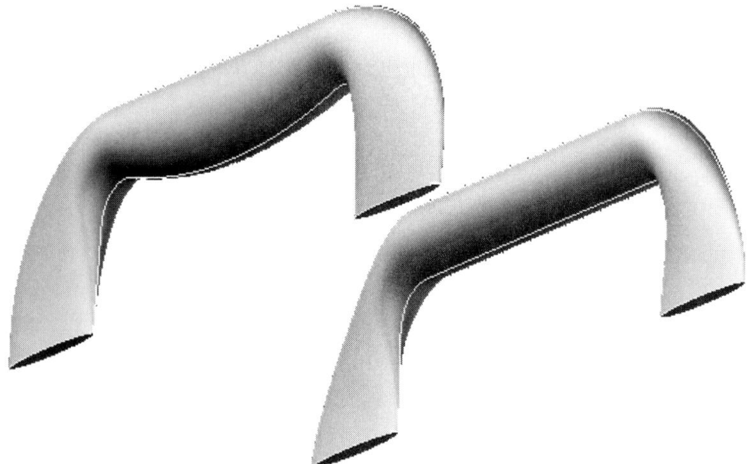

Figure 5-67 Two different results: a guided loft, and a loft that is normal to all cross sections

As a 3D CAD designer, you will analyze different procedures to ensure the creation of products that meet specific customer needs while achieving the desired aesthetics. The different types of loft operations are widely used to develop many of the modern free-form design shapes represented by 3D solids and surfaces. A complete understanding and demonstrated knowledge of these design tools and their concepts gives users an advantageous skill that is an extraordinary asset for many organizations.

POLYSOLID	
Modeling Toolbar	
Ribbon 3D Modeling panel	
Pull-down Menu	Draw/ Modeling/ Polysolid
Command Line	polysolid

Other Commands Used to Create 3D Solids and Surfaces—

The POLYSOLID Command

The **POLYSOLID** command creates a 3D solid of the **Sweep** type with a rectangular cross section that is swept along a segmented path defined by specifying a set of points. Each path segment can be straight or in the form of an arc. The base of the 3D solid is placed parallel to the current *XY* plane. The default height and width of the rectangular cross section are **4.00** and **0.25** units, respectively (Figure 5-68).

The different options you can use and the settings you can change in the **POLYSOLID** command are shown in its shortcut menu (Figure 5-69).

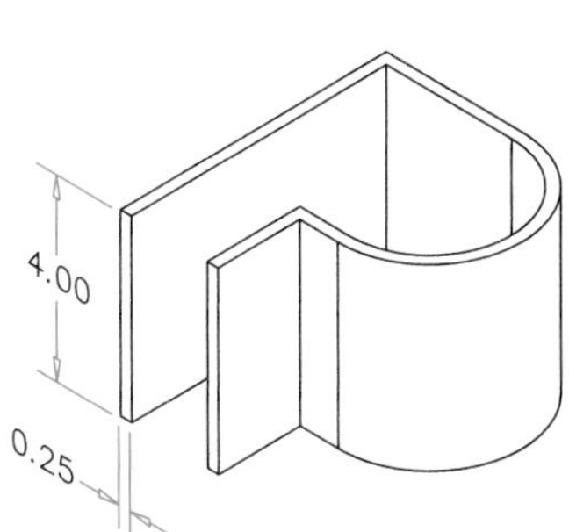

Figure 5-68 A 3D solid of the Sweep type created with the POLYSOLID command using the default Height and Width values

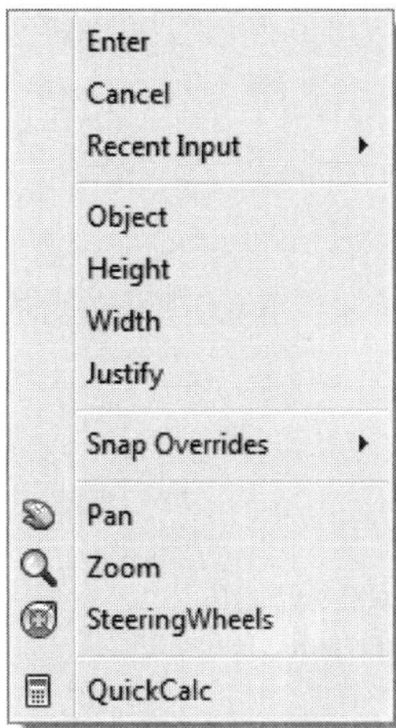

Figure 5-69 The POLYSOLID command shortcut menu

The **Height** and **Width** options allow you to change the dimensions of the rectangular cross section of the 3D solid. (You can do so only before specifying the first point.) The **Justify** option controls how the width of the rectangular cross section is justified or located with respect to specified points (Figure 5-70).

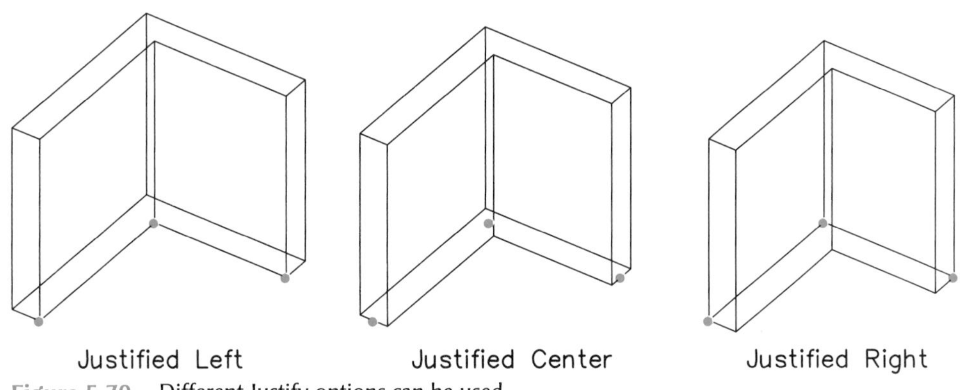

Figure 5-70 Different Justify options can be used

By using the **Object** option, you can convert lines, arcs, polylines, and circles into 3D solids. You can convert only one object at a time. The object must lie on the current UCS, so that the cross section of the 3D solid created is the one previously specified.

The CONVTOSOLID Command

CONVTOSOLID	
Ribbon Solid Editing panel	
Pull-down Menu	Modify/ 3D Operation/Convtosolid
Command Line	convtosolid

The **CONVTOSOLID** command converts specific objects into 3D solids. Only the following objects can be converted by this operation (Figure 5-71):

- Thickened polylines with uniform width
- Thickened closed polylines with **0** width
- Thickened circles

Multiple objects can be selected with this operation, either before or after invoking the command. The **DELOBJ** system variable controls whether the selected objects are kept or deleted. Thickened polylines with uniform width must lie on the current UCS in order to be properly converted to 3D solids.

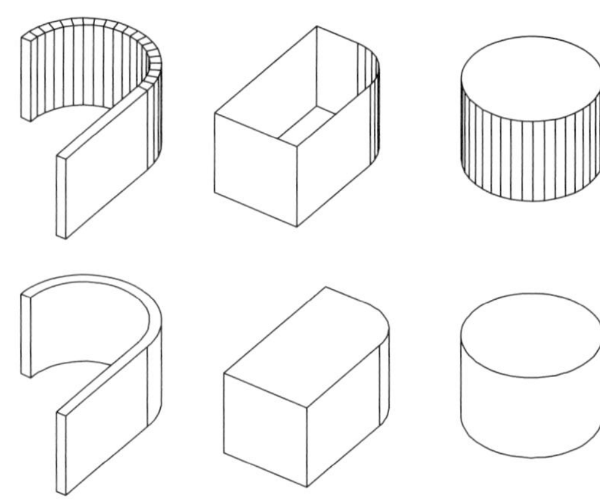

Figure 5-71 Objects (above) converted to 3D solids (below) with the CONVTOSOLID command

CONVTOSURFACE	
Ribbon Solid Editing panel	
Pull-down Menu	Modify/ 3D Operation/ Convtosurface
Command Line	convtosurface

The CONVTOSURFACE Command

The **CONVTOSURFACE** command converts surface-type objects into surfaces. Depending on the type of object selected, the conversion can generate planar surfaces or single-curvature surfaces.

In general, the objects selected must define a delimited surface. Planar objects such as circles, ellipses, closed polylines, regions, 2D solids, and planar 3D faces are converted to planar surfaces (Figure 5-72). The type of surface created with these objects is Planar.

Thickened objects, which are used to represent surfaces with a single curvature such as lines, arcs, circles, and polylines, are converted into single-curvature surfaces (Figure 5-73). The type of surface created with these objects is Extrusions.

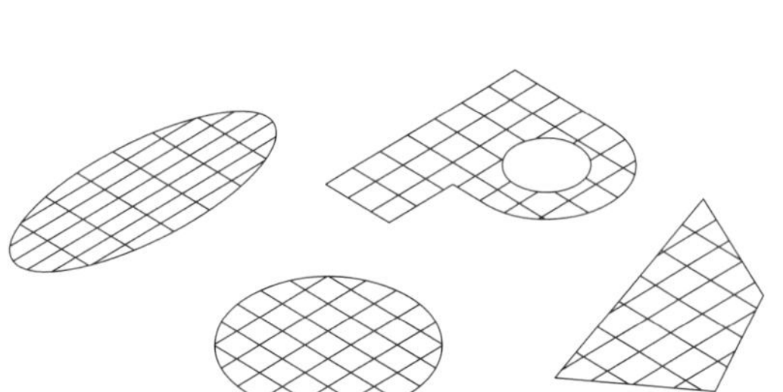

Figure 5-72 Closed planar objects can be converted to surfaces using the CONVTOSURFACE command

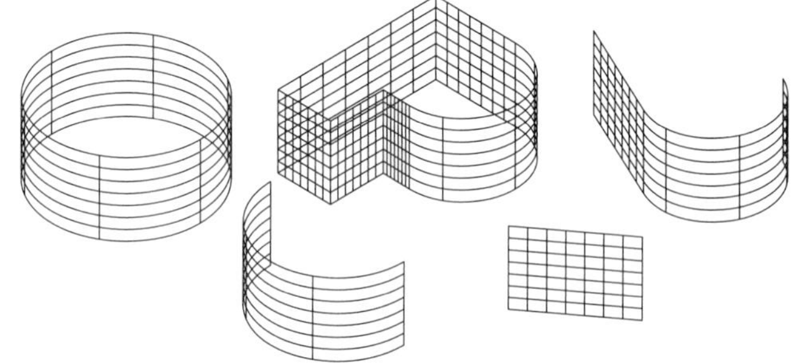

Figure 5-73 Thickened objects can be converted to surfaces using the CONVTOSURFACE command

As with the **CONVTOSOLID** command, more than one object can be selected with this operation, either before or after invoking the command. The **DELOBJ** system variable controls whether the selected objects are kept or deleted.

PLANESURF	
Modeling Toolbar	
Ribbon 3D Modeling panel	
Pull-down Menu	Draw/ Modeling/ Planesurf
Command Line	planesurf

The PLANESURF Command

The **PLANESURF** command creates planar surfaces. By default, a rectangular planar surface is created by specifying two of its corner points. Alternatively, you can use the **Object** options and select planar objects such as circles, ellipses, closed polylines, regions, 2D solids, and planar 3D faces and convert them into planar surfaces. The thickness of the objects is ignored with this operation.

Surfaces created with the **PLANESURF** command by specifying two corner points are projected onto the current *XY* plane.

The THICKEN Command

The **THICKEN** command creates 3D solids by thickening surfaces, both planar and nonplanar. You can control the side to which the surfaces are thickened by specifying a positive or a negative value (Figure 5-74).

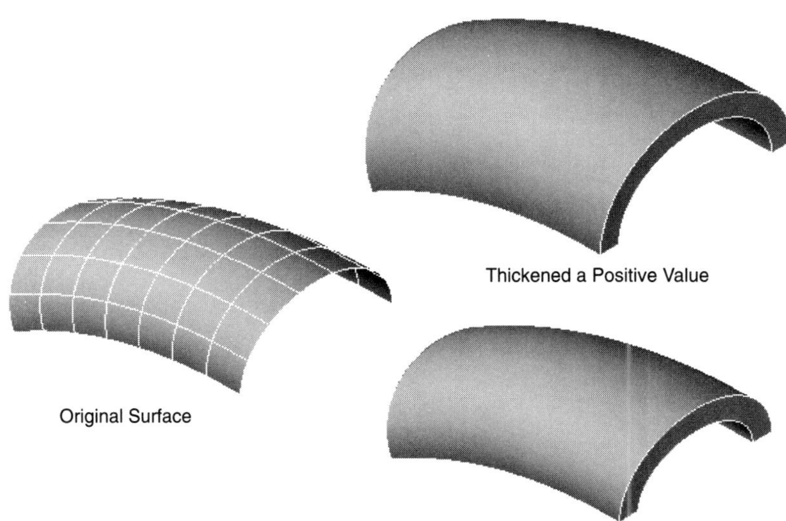

Figure 5-74 Using the THICKEN command, you can turn surfaces into 3D solids; the value sign determines which side the surface thickens to

THICKEN	
Ribbon Solid Editing panel	
Pull-down Menu	Modify/ 3D Operation/ Thicken
Command Line	thicken

OTHER OPERATIONS WITH 3D SOLIDS

OBTAINING COMPOSITE 3D SOLIDS WITH THE UNION, SUBTRACT, AND INTERSECT BOOLEAN OPERATIONS

Boolean operations can be performed only with regions or 3D solids. In the previous chapter, you learned details about using Boolean operations with regions. Here you will learn how to use Boolean operations with 3D solids.

One of the most important tasks in the development of a 3D model represented with 3D solids is to combine several elemental 3D solids into a single one, commonly known as a ***composite 3D solid***.

3D solids can be combined by using the same Boolean operations as the ones used to combine regions:

composite 3D solids: 3D solids obtained by combining 3D solids using one of the three Boolean operations: UNION, SUBTRACT, or INTERSECT.

- **UNION**
- **SUBTRACT**
- **INTERSECT**

While regions must be located in a common plane, 3D solids can be located anywhere in the 3D space. Although they are used similarly to regions and 3D solids, Boolean operations cannot be performed between 3D solids and regions.

UNION creates a 3D solid by joining any number of 3D solids. The resulting volume will be the sum of all the volumes that are not common.

SUBTRACT creates a 3D solid by subtracting a 3D solid or a group of 3D solids from another 3D solid or group of 3D solids. When subtracting 3D solids, you must consider the selection of two groups of 3D solids:

- First Group: 3D solids to subtract from
- Second Group: 3D solids to subtract

When more than one 3D solid is selected from the first group, the operation between them is automatically considered to be a **UNION** operation.

The **INTERSECT** operation creates a 3D solid from the unique common volume among a group of 3D solids.

The 3D solid that results from a Boolean operation depends on the relative location of the two 3D solids or groups of 3D solids interacting with each other. Figure 5-75 shows the three possible situations for each particular operation:

- The two 3D solids have no volume in common.
- One of the 3D solids is completely contained inside the other 3D solid.*
- One of the 3D solids is partially contained inside the other 3D solid.*

	BEFORE THE OPERATION	RESULT	COMMENTS
UNION			EVEN WHEN THE TWO SOLIDS SHARE NO VOLUME, THEY ARE JOINED AS A SINGLE SOLID THAT IS MADE OF TWO PIECES.
			THE RESULTING SOLID IS THE SAME AS THE BIGGER ONE. THE SMALL SOLID IS CONTAINED INSIDE THE BIGGER SOLID, NOT PROVIDING ANY NEW VOLUME TO IT.
			RESULTS IN A NEW SOLID. EACH SOLID PROVIDES A CERTAIN NEW VOLUME.
SUBTRACT	OBJECT TO SUBTRACT FROM (1ST GROUP); OBJECT TO SUBTRACT (2ND GROUP)		BECAUSE NO VOLUME IS SHARED, THE SOLID TO BE SUBTRACTED SIMPLY DISAPPEARS WITHOUT AFFECTING THE MAIN SOLID.
	OBJECT TO SUBTRACT (2ND GROUP); OBJECT TO SUBTRACT FROM (1ST GROUP)		A HOLE IS MADE THROUGH THE MAIN SOLID.
	OBJECT TO SUBTRACT FROM (1ST GROUP); OBJECT TO SUBTRACT (2ND GROUP)		THE SHARED VOLUME IS SUBTRACTED FROM THE MAIN SOLID.
INTERSECT			BECAUSE NO VOLUME IS SHARED, THE RESULT IS A NULL SOLID.
			THE SHARED VOLUME IS THAT OF THE SMALL SOLID. ITS ENTIRE VOLUME IS PRECISELY THE VOLUME SHARED.
			THE RESULTING SOLID IS THE UNIQUE COMMON VOLUME SHARED BY THE TWO SOLIDS.

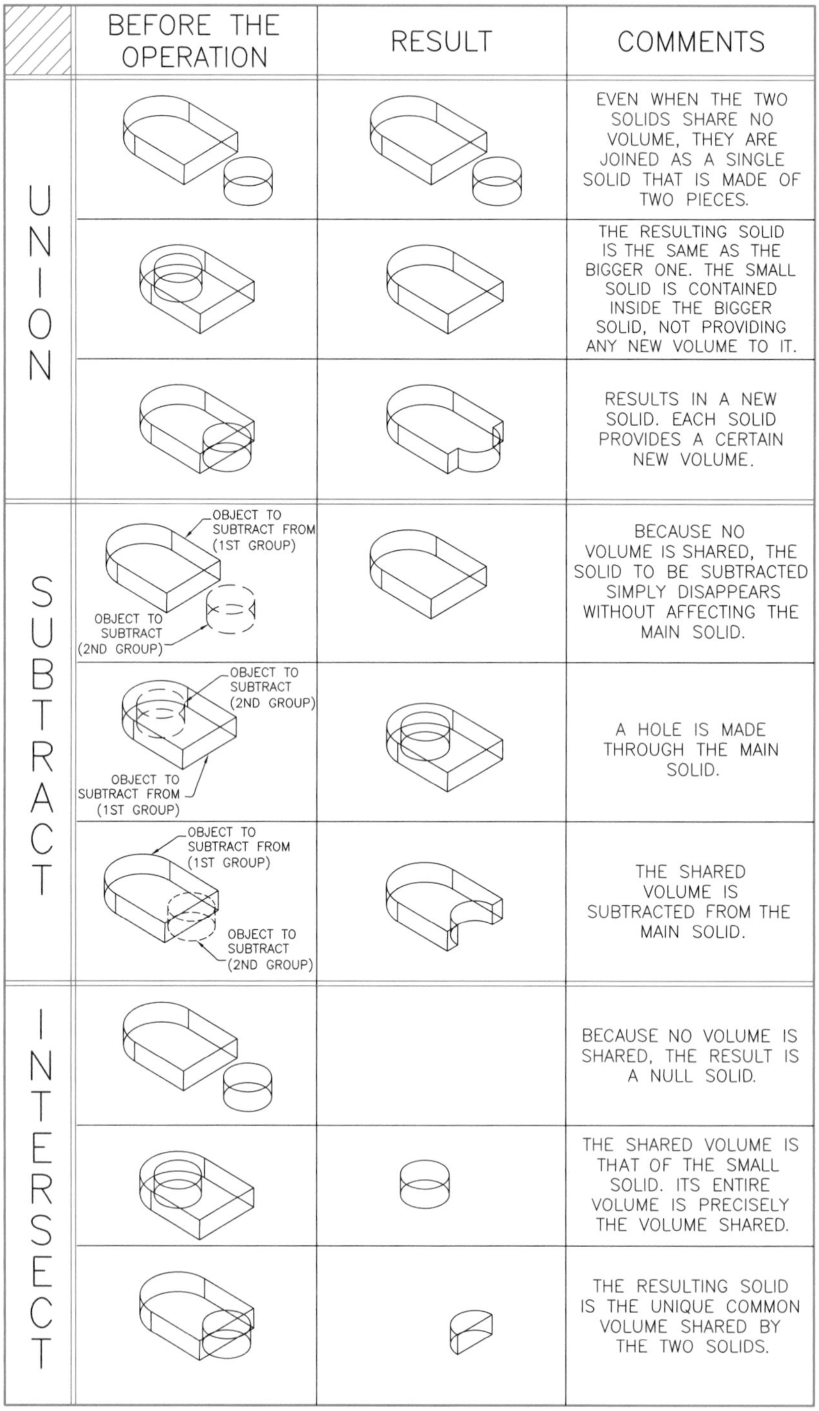

Figure 5-75 The three possible situations and results for each Boolean operation with 3D solids

* For the **SUBTRACT** command, the 3D solid shown in hidden lines is the one to be subtracted.

Exercise 5-8: Using Boolean Operations

In this exercise you will develop the same 3D model that you created in Tutorial 3-1: The Bracket Wireframe. This time you will make it a 3D solid model. The object's views and dimensions are shown in Figure 5-76. You will use these dimensions throughout the exercise to create the shapes, as well as the values for the height of the extrusion.

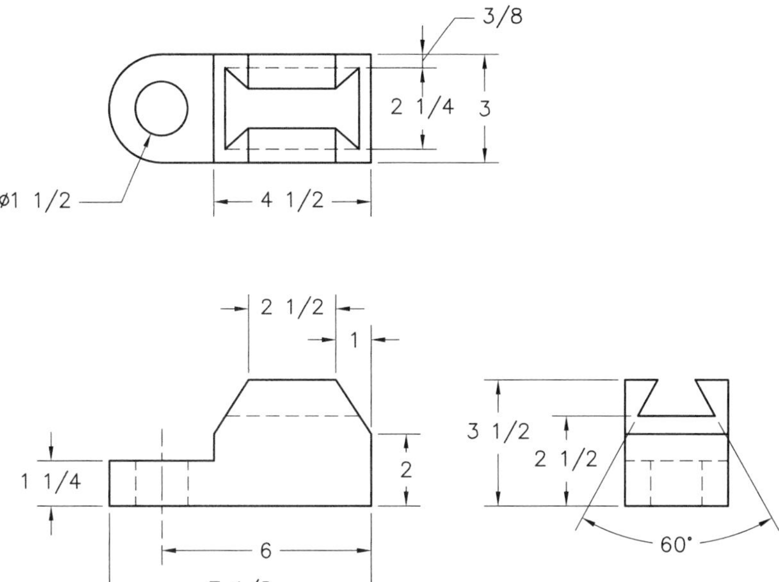

Figure 5-76 Dimensions to create the 3D solid model

Figure 5-77 shows two different approaches to starting the 3D model. The one on the right requires an extra step compared to the one on the left. The resulting shape, however, is closer to the final 3D model.

1. Start a **NEW** drawing.
2. **SAVE** the drawing **AS *Exercise 5-8.***
3. Set the **DISPSILH** system variable to **1** and the **ISOLINES** system variable to **0**.
4. Select the **SW Isometric** viewing point.

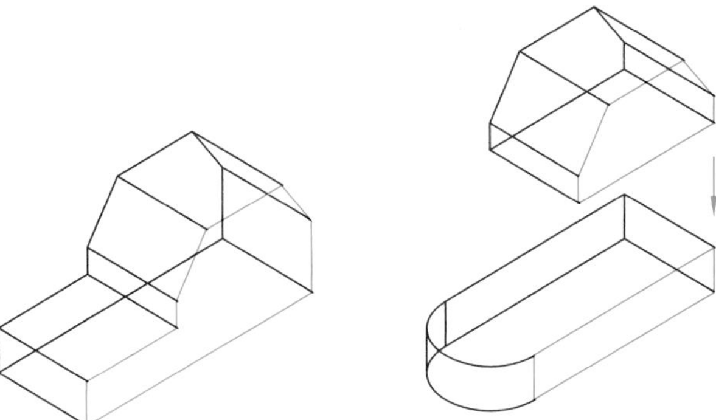

Figure 5-77 Two different approaches to starting the 3D model

5. Draw the profile shown in Figure 5-78.
6. Convert the profile to a closed polyline or a region.
7. **EXTRUDE** the profile. Refer to the drawing at the beginning of the exercise to find the value of the extrusion height (Figure 5-79).
8. Select the **Front** UCS and draw the profile highlighted in Figure 5-80 anywhere in the 3D space.
9. **EXTRUDE** the profile as required.

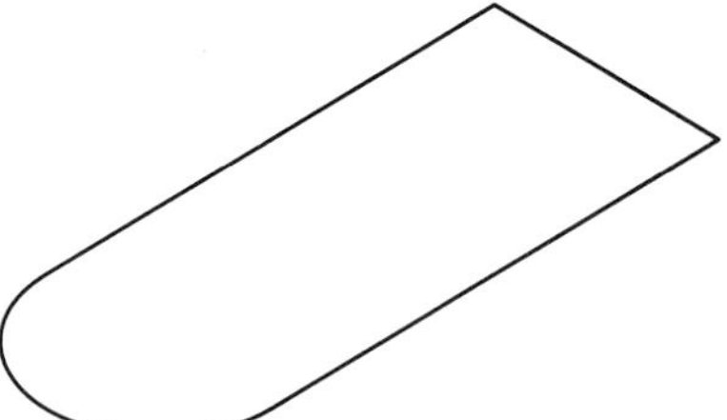

Figure 5-78 The first profile

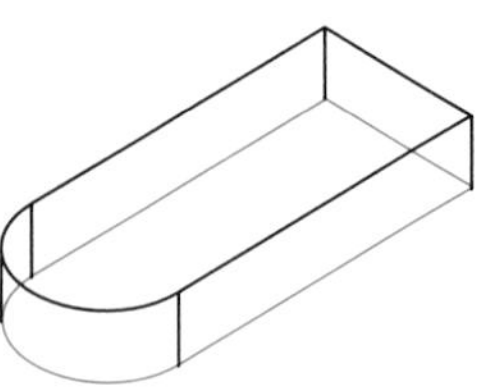

Figure 5-79 The profile extruded

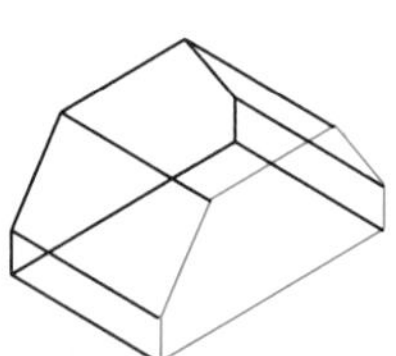

Figure 5-80 A second profile extruded

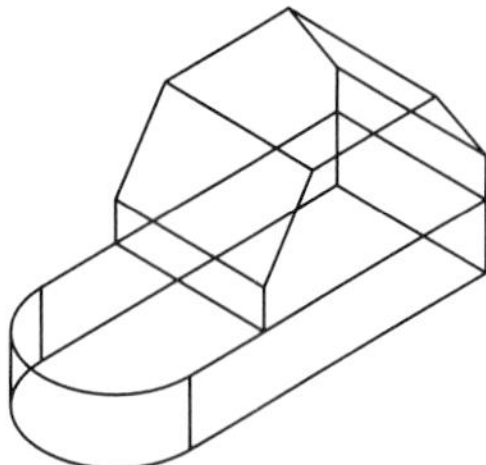

Figure 5-81 The two extruded 3D solids in their corresponding places

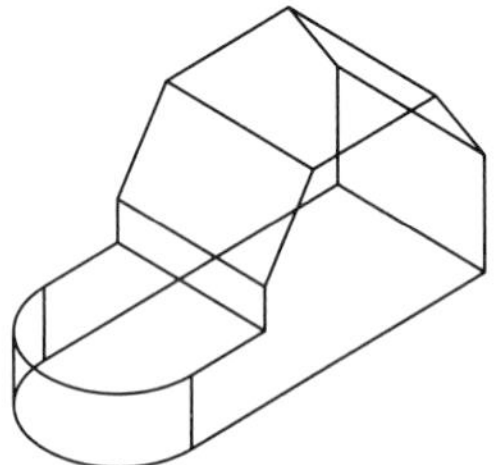

Figure 5-82 A single 3D solid is obtained after the UNION operation

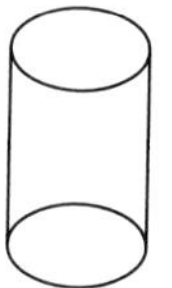

Figure 5-83 A cylinder 3D solid

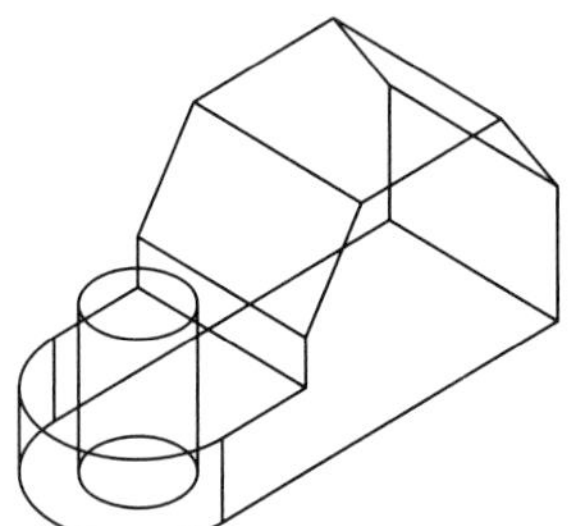

Figure 5-84 A cylinder 3D solid moved concentric with the cylindrical face

10. Snapping to the endpoints, **MOVE** the last 3D solid to the first 3D solid so it is located as shown in Figure 5-81.
11. Invoke the **UNION** command. When prompted, select both 3D solids and press **<Enter>** to end the command. The 3D model should look now like Figure 5-82.
12. Select the **Top** UCS.
13. Create a 3D solid in the shape of a cylinder (Figure 5-83). Its diameter should be the same as that of the hole. Make it **2 1/2″** high. For this operation you can either use the **CYLINDER** command or **EXTRUDE** a circle.
14. **MOVE** the cylinder from its bottom center point to the center point of the arc at the bottom of the main body (Figure 5-84).
15. Select the **Left** UCS.
16. Using the dimensions from the 2D drawing at the beginning of the exercise, create the profile highlighted in Figure 5-85 and **EXTRUDE** it **5″**.
17. **MOVE** the new 3D solid from the midpoint of its top right edge to the midpoint of the top right edge of the main 3D solid (Figure 5-86).
18. Make sure the **UCSORTHO** system variable is set to **1**. Select the **Front** view.
19. With **ORTHO** mode on, **MOVE** the last 3D solid **1″** to the right (Figure 5-88).
20. Invoke the **SUBTRACT** command and respond to the prompts as follows:

```
Select solids and regions to subtract from...
Select objects: Select the main solid.
Select objects: ↵ (To end the selection)
```

So far, you have created the main body of the model. The rest of the work will simply be to create and subtract the 3D solids that will give the 3D model its final shape.

Note:

The last 3D solid does not go all the way through the main 3D solid (Figure 5-87).

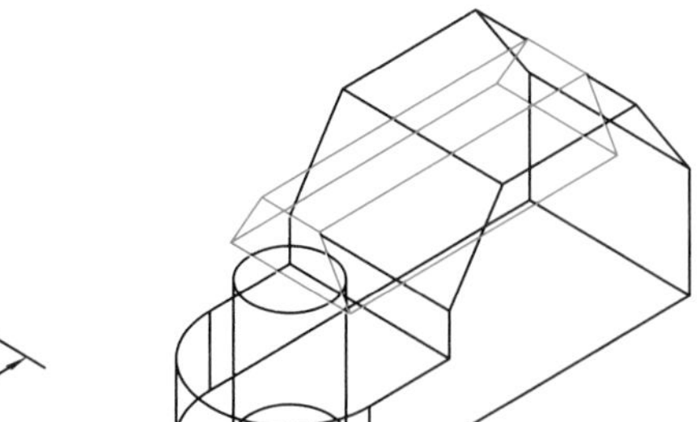

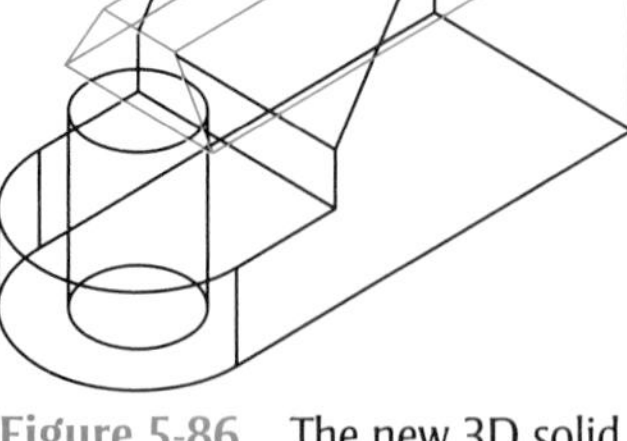

Figure 5-85 Create the 3D solid shown

Figure 5-86 The new 3D solid moved toward the main 3D solid

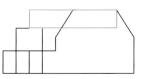

Figure 5-87 The front view

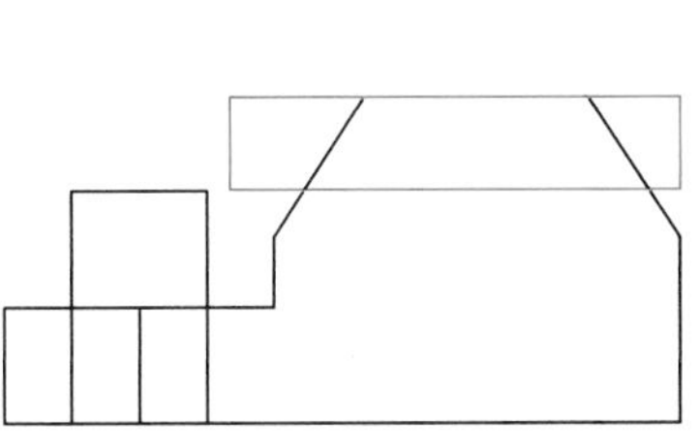

Figure 5-88 The new 3D solid is moved toward the right

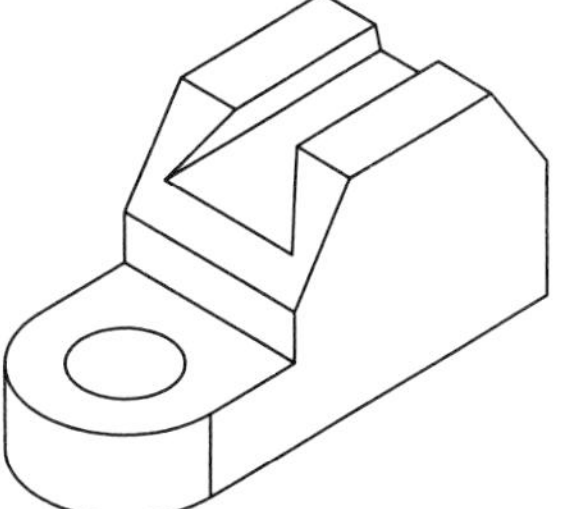

Figure 5-89 The resulting 3D solid after the SUBTRACT operation

Select solids and regions to subtract...
Select objects: *Select the cylinder solid.*
Select objects: *Select the small solid on top.*
Select objects: *(To end the selection)*

21. Select the **SW Isometric** viewing point.
22. Invoke the **HIDE** command. The 3D solid should look like Figure 5-89.
23. **SAVE** the drawing.

Using the 3D Solids History to Modify Composite 3D Solids

AutoCAD allows you to modify a composite 3D solid. You can do this by modifying the original 3D solids that were used to create the composite 3D solid.

You can display the original 3D solids of a composite 3D solid, if their ***history*** is set to **Record,** by holding down the **<Ctrl>** key. Hovering the pickbox pointer over them allows you to select them.

history: Original 3D solids involved in the Boolean operations of a composite 3D solid.

The **History** and **Show History** settings of the composite 3D solids can be controlled individually on each 3D solid through the **Properties** palette under **Solid History** (Figure 5-90). They can also be globally controlled using the **SOLIDHIST** and **SHOWHIST** system variables.

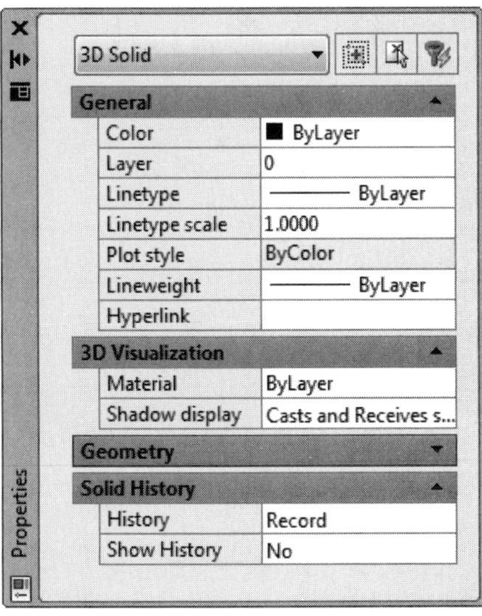

Figure 5-90 The History and Show History settings can be controlled in the Properties palette

The **SOLIDHIST** system variable determines whether the history for a new 3D solid is set to **Record** (**1**) or is not (**0**). The history of a composite 3D solid, however, is determined by the history of its original 3D solids rather than by the **SOLIDHIST** system variable. Only composite 3D solids combined through the Boolean operations with at least one of the original 3D solid's history set to **Record** can show the history of their original 3D solids.

It is more convenient to leave the **SOLIDHIST** system variable set at **Record** in order to retain the history of any new 3D solid created, which is the variable's default value. You can always change this property individually, prior to performing the Boolean operation.

The **SHOWHIST** system variable controls whether or not the original 3D solids or the history is shown in a drawing. It uses the following settings:

- **0** sets the **Show History** property to **No** for all solids. You cannot use the **Properties** palette to show the original 3D solids of individual composite 3D solids.
- **1** allows you to control the **Show History** property individually through the **Properties** palette.
- **2** displays the history of all solids. You cannot use the **Properties** palette to control the display of the original 3D solids of individual composite 3D solids. You need a **REGEN** operation to show the history.

It is more convenient to leave the **SHOWHIST** system variable to **1**, its default value. This enables you to control the **Show History** property individually through the **Properties** palette.

Showing the history of a composite 3D solid might be confusing if you continue performing Boolean operations with it. You can choose when to stop recording the history of a composite 3D solid by changing its status to **None** in the **Properties** palette. You can also erase the history of any 3D solid by using the **BREP** command, which turns objects into a basic representation only.

The history of a composite 3D solid is automatically erased by performing post operations such as **SLICE** or by performing editing operations with the **SOLIDEDIT** command.

FOR MORE DETAILS See Chapter 6 for more details about performing editing operations with the **SOLIDEDIT** command.

Exercise 5-9: Modifying a Composite 3D Solid by Modifying Its Original 3D Solids

1. **OPEN** the drawing ***Exercise 5-9*** from the CD.
2. **SAVE** the drawing **AS *Exercise 5-9 solved.***
3. Set both the **SOLIDHIST** and **SHOWHIST** system variables to **1**, if they are not already set. Access these settings by entering the name of each in the command line.
4. Invoke the **SUBTRACT** command, and subtract the cylinder from the box.
5. Select the **Realistic** visual style.
6. Select the composite 3D solid. Right-click in the drawing area and select **Properties** from the shortcut menu.
7. In the **Properties** palette, under **Solid History,** change the value of **Show History** to **Yes** (Figure 5-91).
8. Press the <**Esc**> key to unselect the composite 3D solid. The 3D model should look like Figure 5-92.

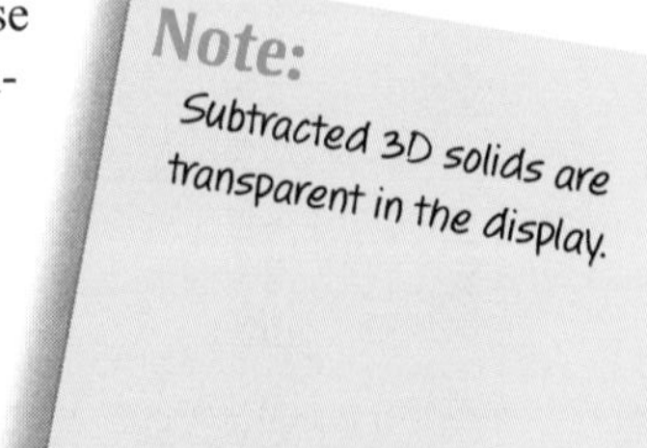

Note:
Subtracted 3D solids are transparent in the display.

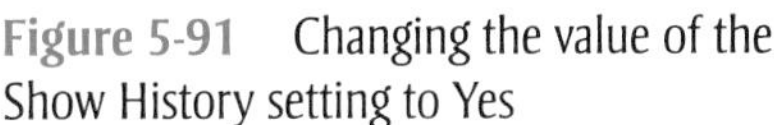

Figure 5-91 Changing the value of the Show History setting to Yes

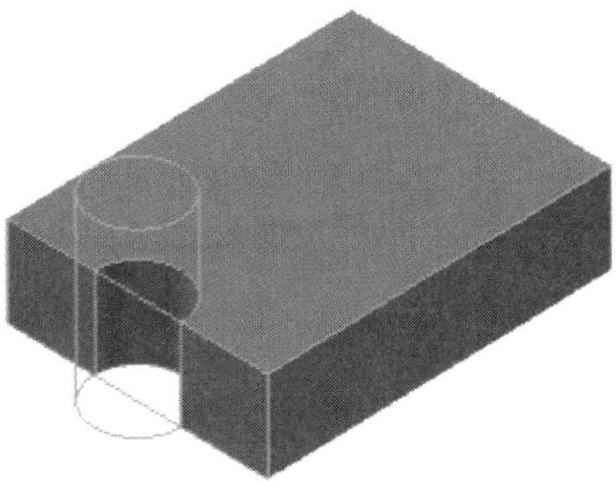

Figure 5-92 The composite 3D solid showing its history

9. Holding down the **<Ctrl>** key, select the original cylinder 3D solid that was used to create the hole (Figure 5-93).
10. Invoke the **MOVE** command. When prompted for the base point, click anywhere in the drawing area and start moving the pointer to see the hole move interactively.
11. Enter **@1.5,2,0** as the second point.
12. Select the composite 3D solid again and change the value of **Show History** to **No.** Change the **History** setting to **None.**
13. Press the **<Esc>** key to unselect the composite 3D solid. The 3D model should look like Figure 5-94.
14. **SAVE** the drawing.

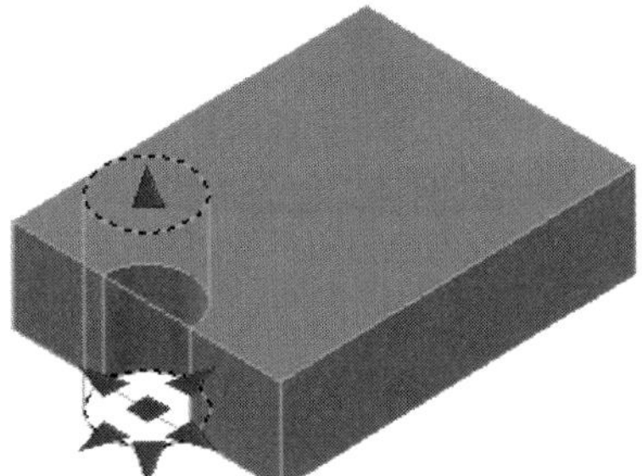

Figure 5-93 3D solid history object selected independently of the composite solid

Figure 5-94 3D solid history object is relocated to modify the composite solid

Converting 2D Drawings into 3D Models

The 3D model you developed in Exercise 5-8 could have been solved in another way: by using the **INTERSECT** command rather than joining and subtracting 3D solids. This method provides an easy and more efficient way to proceed, especially when the drawing views already exist as a CAD file. This is one of the procedures that can be used to generate 3D models more efficiently from the input of a 2D drawing. As you will see, no special tools are required to achieve these results.

Exercise 5-10: Converting 2D Drawings into 3D Models

In this exercise you will develop the model you created in Exercise 5-9 one more time. This time, however, you will use the existing drawing's views.

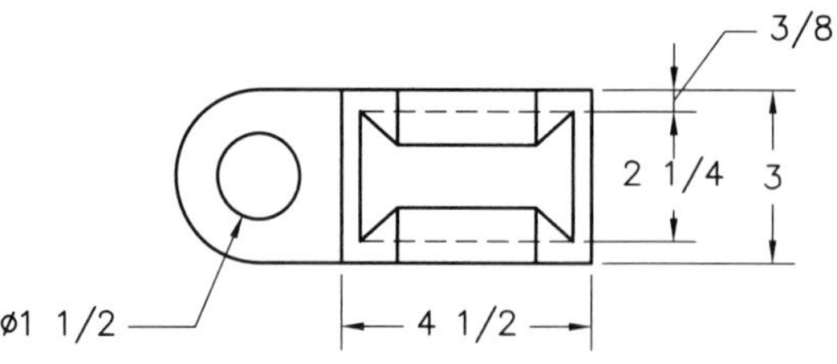

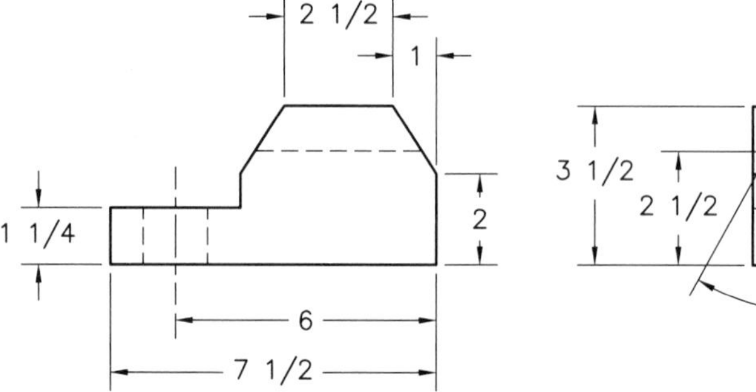

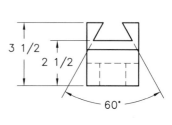

Figure 5-95 Objects contained in the drawing file

Suppose you need to convert the 2D drawing shown in Figure 5-95 into a 3D model. Your first task is to clean up the drawing views, leaving only the objects that define the outer profiles and islands. These objects will be used to create the regions that will be extended and finally intersected.

Note:

The top view region will remain in the same position. The other two views will be rotated and moved to the plane they belong to in 3D space.

1. **OPEN** the drawing ***Exercise 5-10*** from the CD, and **SAVE** it on your computer as ***Exercise 5-10 Solved.***
2. **ERASE** any unnecessary objects to clean up the drawing views. The drawing should look like Figure 5-96 after it is cleaned up.
3. Invoke the **REGION** command. Using a selection window, select all the objects to convert them into regions. The command prompt should advise you of the four regions created.

   `4 loops extracted.`

   `4 Regions created.`
4. Zoom into the objects representing the top view and **SUBTRACT** the circular regions from the outer one to create a single region with a hole.
5. Select the **SW Isometric** viewing point.

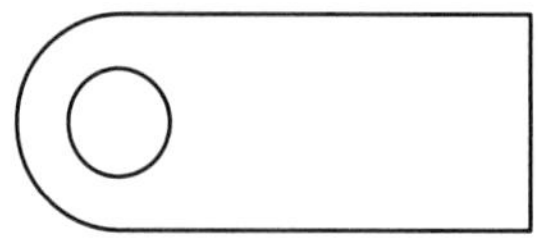

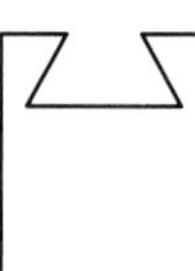

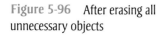

Figure 5-96 After erasing all unnecessary objects

6. Select the **Left** UCS.
7. **ROTATE** both the region representing the front view and the region representing the side view **–90°**. When prompted for the base point, specify any endpoint along the bottom line of the front view region. The drawing should look like Figure 5-97.
8. **MOVE** the region representing the front view from its right lower endpoint to the corresponding endpoint on the region representing the top view (Figure 5-98).
9. Select the **Top** UCS. **ROTATE** the region representing the side view 90°. Use any point on the region as a base point (Figure 5-99).

Note:

The three regions now have to be extruded a distance that goes farther than the model space with a 0° taper angle.

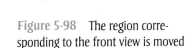

Figure 5-97 The regions corresponding to the front and the side views are rotated

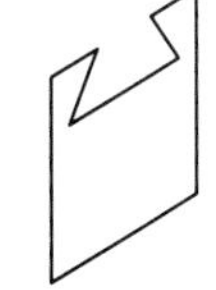

Figure 5-98 The region corresponding to the front view is moved

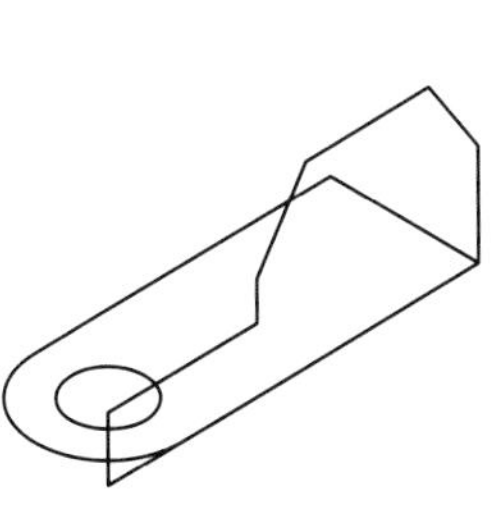

Figure 5-99 The region corresponding to the front view is rotated

10. **MOVE** the region representing the side view from its lower right endpoint to the corresponding endpoint on the other two regions (Figure 5-100).
11. With the **Top** UCS still current, **EXTRUDE** the top region **4** units.
12. **EXTRUDE** the region representing the front view **−3.5** units.
13. **EXTRUDE** the region representing the side view **−8** units (Figure 5-101).
14. Invoke the **INTERSECT** command and, when prompted, select the three 3D solids. Then press **<Enter>** to finish the operation.
15. Invoke the **HIDE** command. The 3D model should look like Figure 5-102.
16. **SAVE** the drawing.

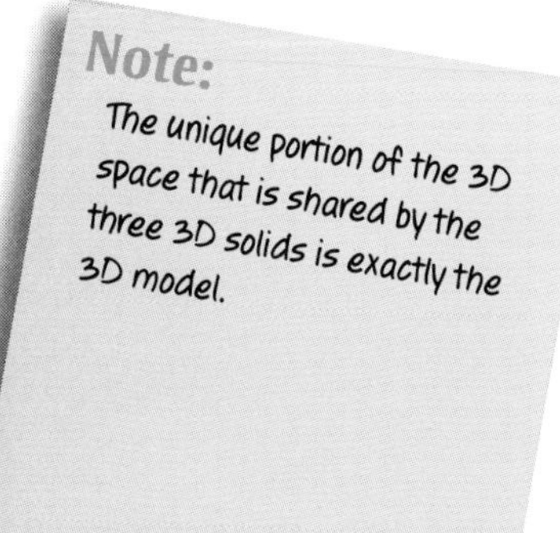

Note:
The unique portion of the 3D space that is shared by the three 3D solids is exactly the 3D model.

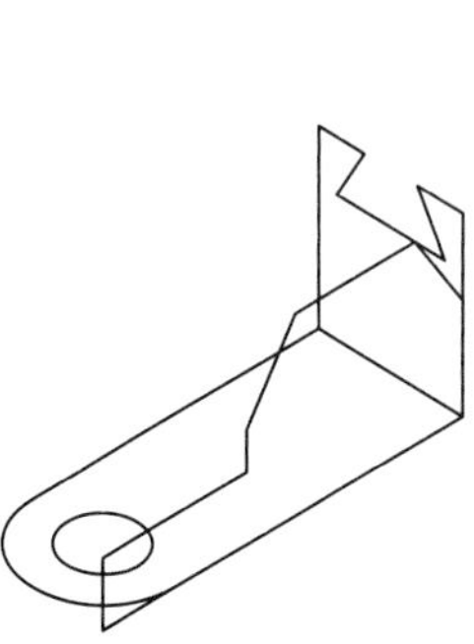

Figure 5-100 The region corresponding to the front view is moved

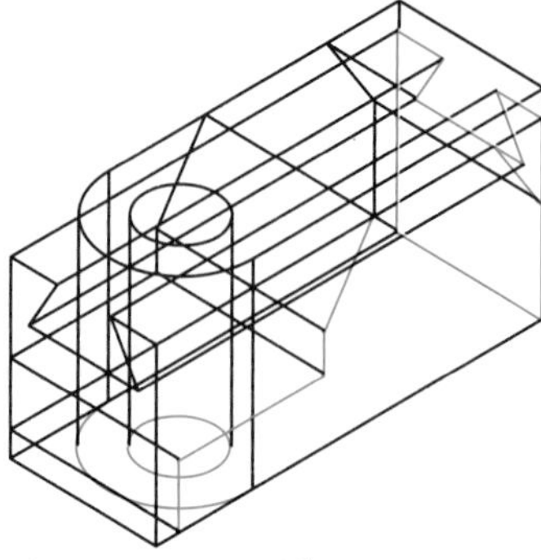

Figure 5-101 All regions are extruded so that the volumes meet in the 3D space

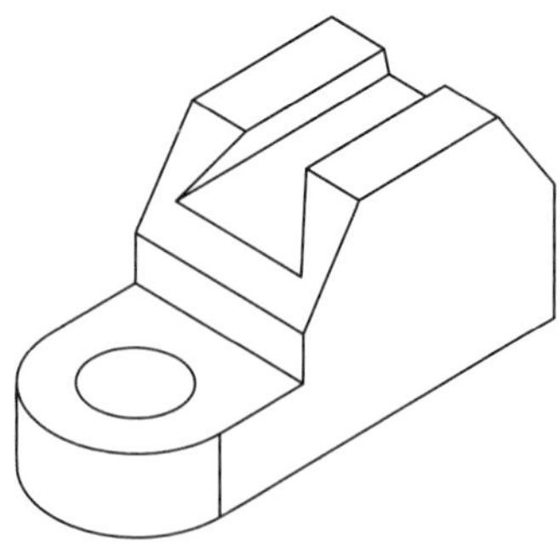

Figure 5-102 The resulting 3D solid after the INTERSECT operation

THE INTERFERE COMMAND

The **INTERFERE** command has a certain similitude to the **INTERSECT** command. The **INTERFERE** command can, however, check for interference or shared volume between 3D solids without deleting the original 3D solids. The command can also create new 3D solids whose shape is the same as the interfering volume.

Depending on how you respond to the command prompts, the command can perform two different tasks:

- Check interference and create new 3D solids from each interfering pair in a set of 3D solids
- Check interference and create interfering 3D solids between two sets of 3D solids

Note:

The **Nested selection** option enables you to select individual 3D solid objects that are nested in blocks and external references.

The command prompts you to select two sets of 3D solids. You can choose not to select a second set of 3D solids by pressing **<Enter>** when prompted to do so. Pressing **<Enter>** will initiate the interference checking process between the objects selected in the first and only group. The visual style and the color of the objects will change automatically according to those specified in the **Interference Settings** dialog box (Figure 5-103), which you can open by selecting the **Settings** option while selecting the first set of objects:

```
Select first set of objects or [Nested selection/Settings]:
```

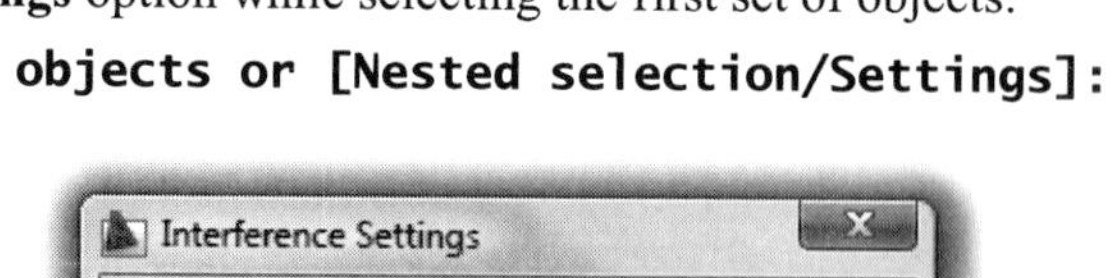

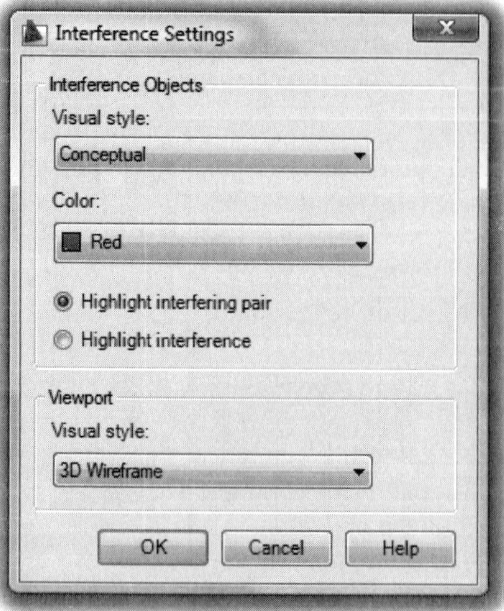

Figure 5-103 The Interference Settings dialog box

The **Interference Checking** dialog box is also displayed as soon as the selection process is finished. Figure 5-104 shows a set of three interfering 3D solids. Their corresponding **Interference Checking** dialog box is also displayed. Each 3D solid shares its volume with the other two, so in this particular case, three interference pairs are found.

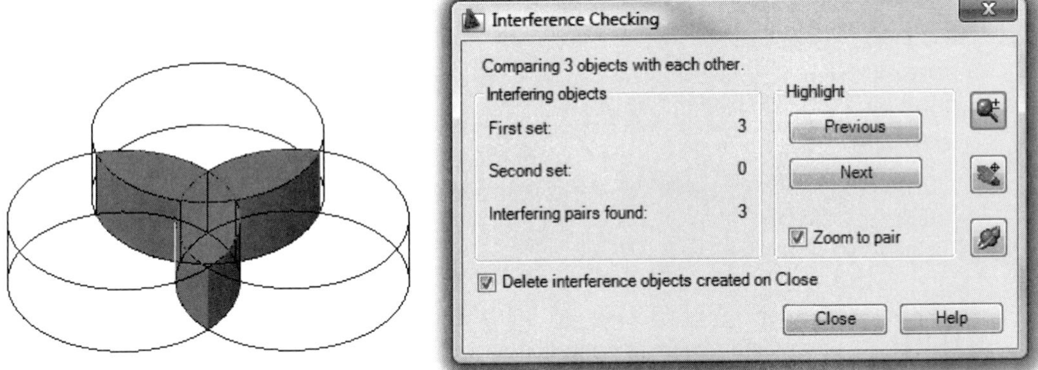

Figure 5-104 A set of three interfering 3D Solids with the corresponding Interference checking dialog box displayed

During the interference testing process, you can **Zoom, Pan,** and **Orbit** around the objects only by using the viewing tool buttons in the **Interference Checking** dialog box. When you are finished using a particular viewing tool, pressing the **<Esc>** key will take you back to the dialog box.

The **Next** and **Previous** buttons will cycle through each interfering pair, highlighting and zooming into it (Figure 5-105).

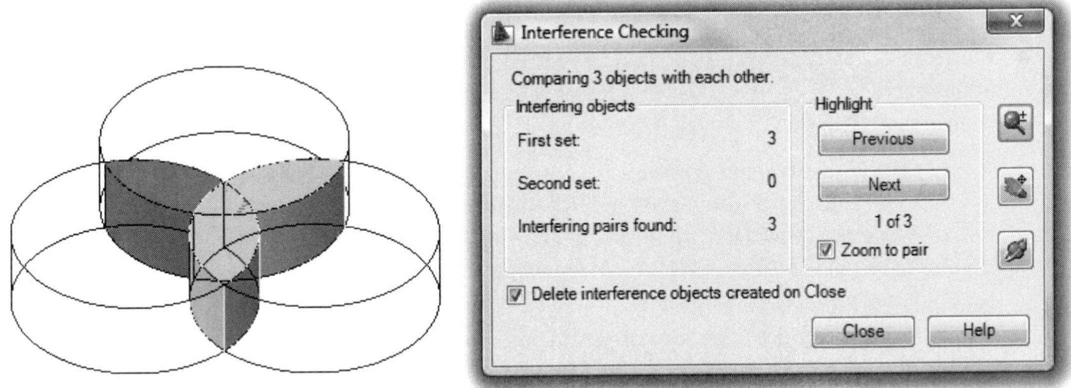

Figure 5-105 Clicking the Next and Previous buttons cycles through each interfering pair

You can create new 3D solids from each interfering pair in a set of 3D solids by clearing the **Delete interference objects created on Close** checkbox. Figure 5-106 shows the three new separated individual 3D solids that can be obtained with this operation after you close the **Interference Checking** dialog box.

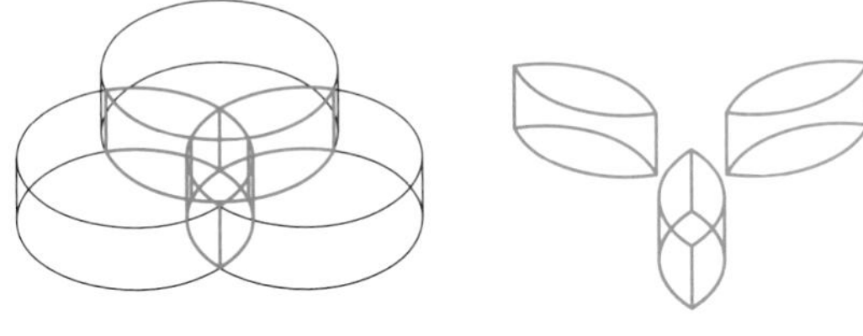

Figure 5-106 New 3D solids can be created from each interfering pair

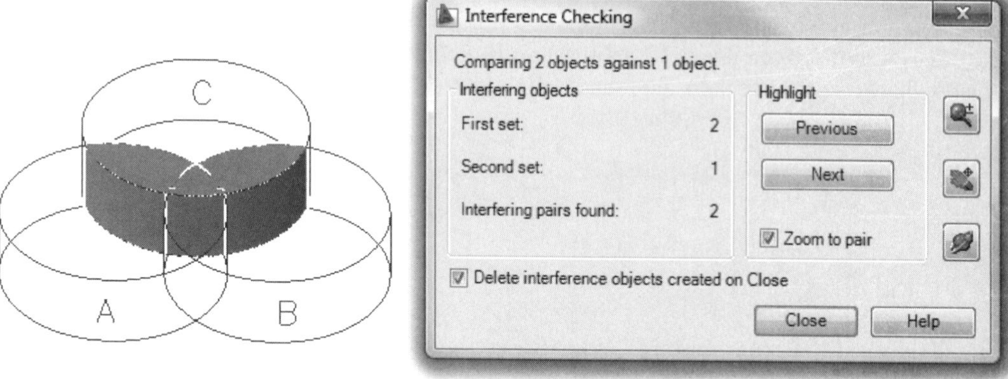

Figure 5-107 Checking for interference between two sets of 3D solids

When you enter the two sets of 3D solids, the **INTERFERE** command checks for interference only between 3D solids of two different sets. Interference between 3D solids of the same group is ignored. Figure 5-107 shows two sets of 3D solids. The first set consists of 3D solids **A** and **B**. The second set is composed only of the 3D solid **C**. When these two independent sets of 3D solids interfere with each other, only two interferences are found and two 3D solids are generated.

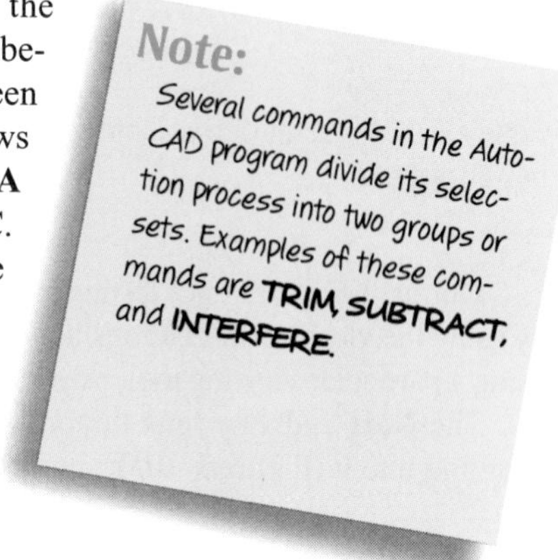

Note:
Several commands in the AutoCAD program divide its selection process into two groups or sets. Examples of these commands are TRIM, SUBTRACT, and INTERFERE.

As with the **Interference Checking** dialog box for objects within the same group, you can create new 3D solids from each interfering pair found between the two sets of objects by clearing the **Delete interference objects created on Close** checkbox.

Exercise 5-11: Using the INTERFERE Command

In this exercise you will use the **INTERFERE** command to detect parts that do not fit properly in an assembly design.

INTERFERE	
Ribbon Solid Editing Panel	
Pull-down Menu	Modify/ 3D Operation/Interference
Command Line	interfere

1. **OPEN** the drawing ***Exercise 5-11*** from the CD. It contains the assembly of several 3D solids: five hardware pieces and two other parts (Figure 5-108).
2. **SAVE** the drawing **AS *Exercise 5-11 solved.***
3. Invoke the **INTERFERE** command using one of the methods shown in the grid. Respond to the prompts as follows:

   Select first set of objects or [Nested selection/Settings]: *Using a selection window, select all the 3D solids.*

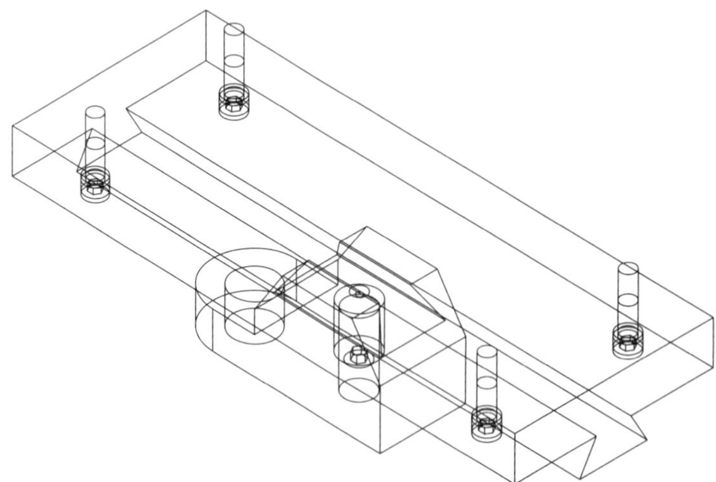

Figure 5-108 Objects contained in the drawing file

Select first set of objects or [Nested selection/Settings]: ↵ *(To end the selection of the first set)*

Select second set of objects or [Nested selection/checK first set] <checK>: ↵ *(Here a second set is not considered. The command checks for interference within the first set only.)*

4. Five **Interfering pairs found:** is shown in the **Interference Checking** dialog box (Figure 5-109). Click on the **Next** and **Previous** buttons to navigate through each of the interfering pairs.

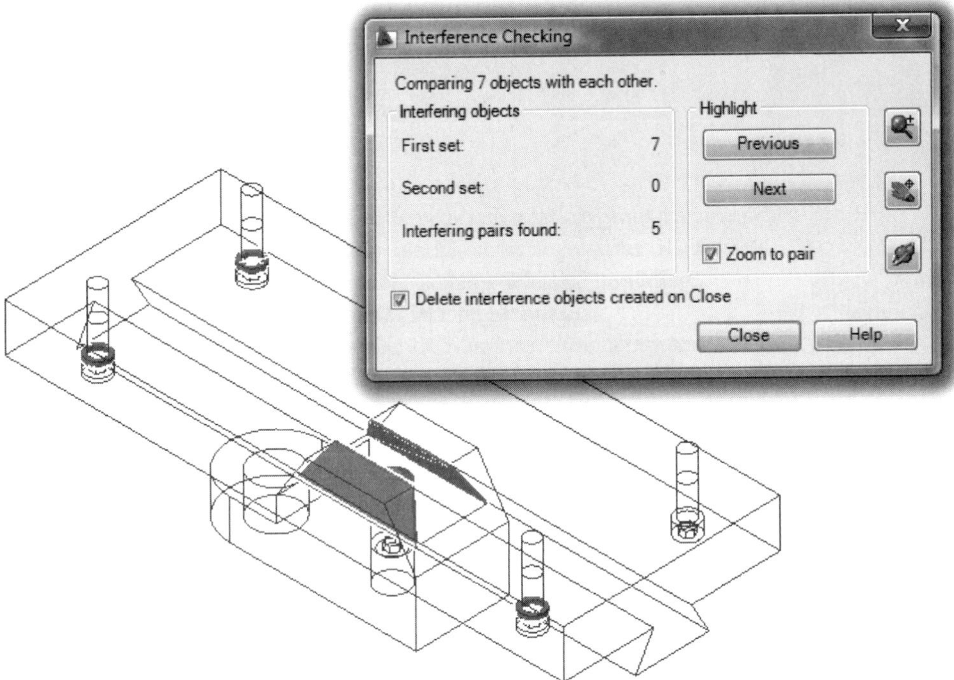

Figure 5-109 The interference checking scenario within a group of objects

5. Click on the **Close** button to close the **Interference Checking** dialog box.
6. Now let's find out how many of the hardware pieces interfere with the other two parts. Invoke the **INTERFERE** command again, and respond to the prompts as follows:

Select first set of objects or [Nested selection/Settings]: *Select the five bolts.*

Select first set of objects or [Nested selection/Settings]: ↵ *(To end the selection of the first set)*

Select second set of objects or [Nested selection/checK first set] <checK>: *Select the other two 3D solids.*

Select second set of objects or [Nested selection/checK first set] <checK>: ↵ *(To end the selection of the second set)*

7. Four **Interfering pairs found:** is shown in the **Interference Checking** dialog box after comparing the two main objects with any hardware (Figure 5-110). Click on the **Next** and **Previous** buttons to navigate through each of the interfering pairs. Then close the dialog box.
8. **SAVE** the drawing.

Note:

The **INTERFERE** command is a useful tool for detecting parts that may not fit properly, causing a mechanism to function incorrectly. In large assemblies you can use the **Highlight pair** setting to detect which pair of 3D solids is causing the interference. This allows you to correct design errors before production.

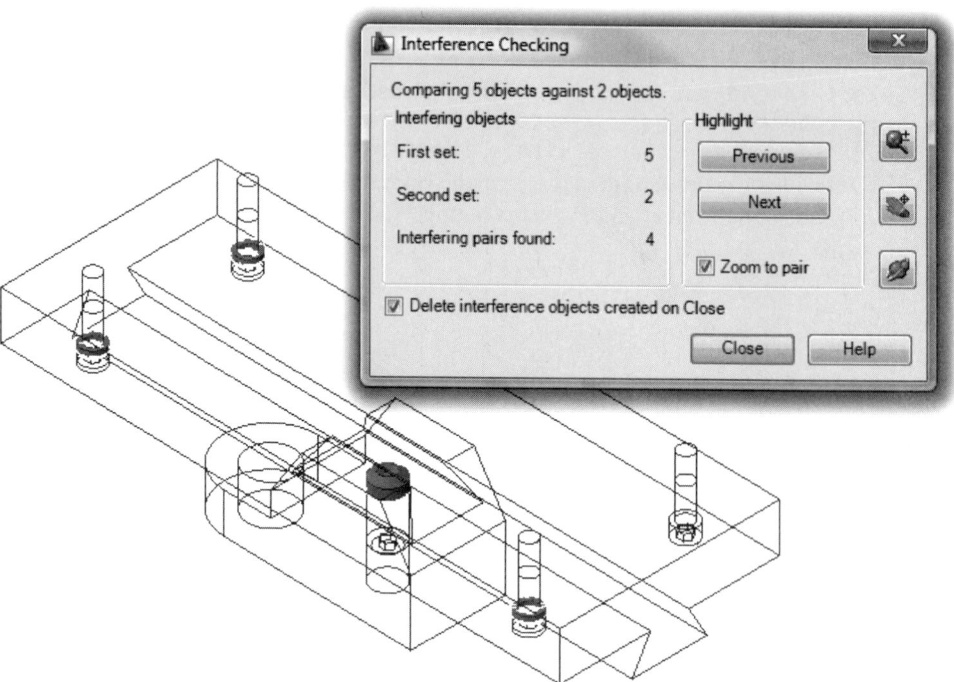

Figure 5-110 The interference checking scenario between two groups of objects

Determining possible failures is one of the most important tasks in the design of tools, engines, machines, and other mechanical devices. Therefore, the professional team in charge must make sure that components fit properly within mechanisms and assemblies in their different positions. The **INTERFERE** operation can incorporate an advanced method to perform this task accurately using 3D models. A complete knowledge and practical understanding of the **INTERFERE** operation and its applications gives 3D users a powerful tool. This skill can help many companies and organizations further enhance and understand design processes.

Slicing 3D Solids with the SLICE Command

Many other tools are used jointly with Boolean operations to enable you to obtain a 3D solid's final shape in less time. The **SLICE** command is one of the most useful of these tools.

imaginary slicing plane: Imaginary plane with which 3D solid objects are cut.

With the **SLICE** command, a 3D solid or group of 3D solids can be cut by an ***imaginary slicing plane*** or by a surface. Figure 5-111 shows the different options in the command's shortcut menu. Besides the **Surface** option, all other options are dedicated to defining the imaginary slicing plane.

You can slice a 3D solid according to the shape of the surface, creating faces on the 3D solid that have the same shape as the surface used to slice it (Figure 5-112). The surface must completely cross the 3D solid for the operation to proceed.

Using an imaginary slicing plane will create a flat cut through the 3D solids. The imaginary slicing plane can be defined by using one of the following options:

Perpendicular to the current *XY* plane: This is the default option. It activates itself when you specify the start point after completing the selection process. This option defines the imaginary slicing plane perpendicular to the current *XY* plane by specifying the start and second points (Figure 5-113). When you specify the second point, only the *X* and *Y* coordinates are read, and the Object Snap is projected onto the *XY* plane. This method is very useful when slicing 3D solids in an orthogonal view.

3points: With this option, the imaginary slicing plane is defined by specifying three different noncollinear points (Figure 5-114). This method substitutes for the default method if you press the **<Enter>** key before specifying any point.

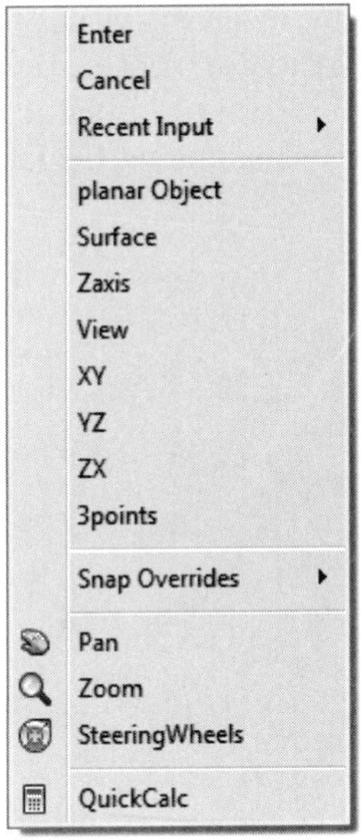

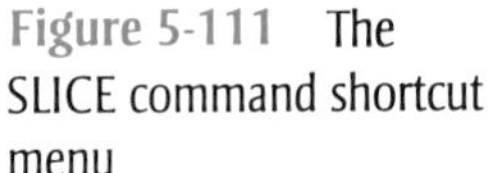
Figure 5-111 The SLICE command shortcut menu

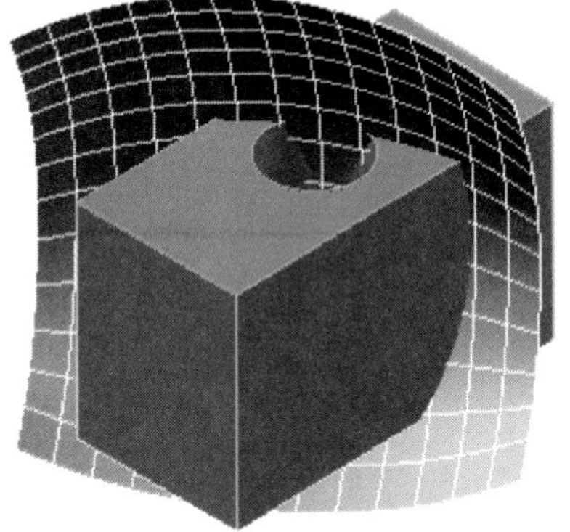

Figure 5-112 3D solids can be sliced by a surface

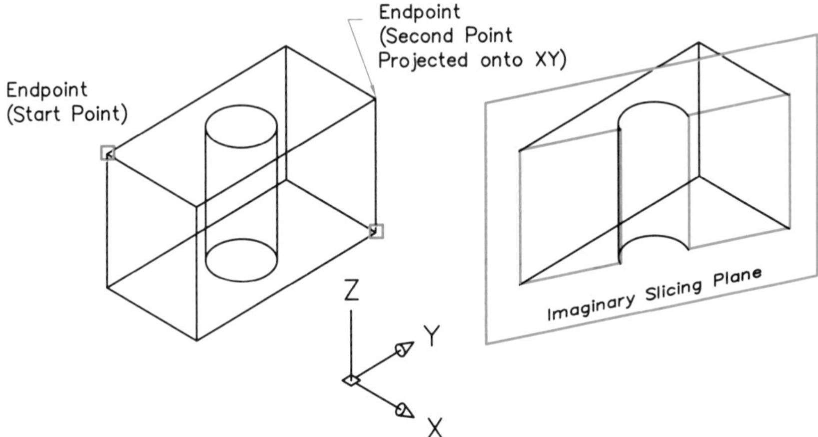

Figure 5-113 Slicing a 3D solid with an imaginary slicing plane defined perpendicular to the current XY plane

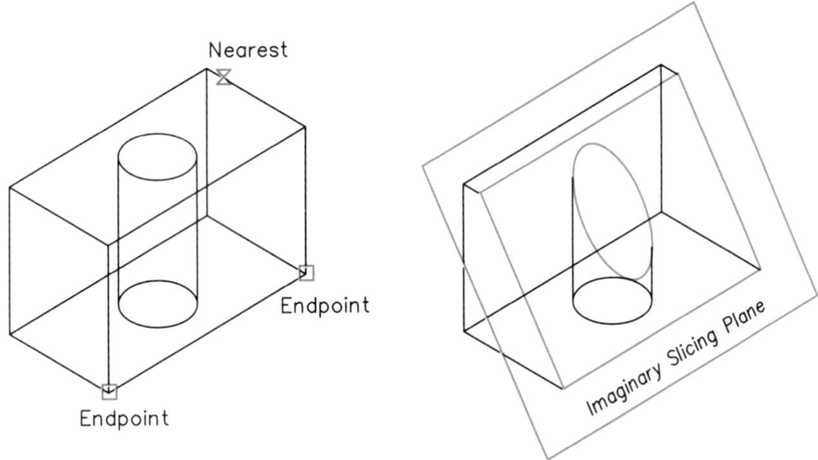

Figure 5-114 Slicing a 3D solid with an imaginary slicing plane defined by three points

***XY*, *YZ*, and *ZX*:** When you specify one of these options, the imaginary slicing plane aligns parallel to the specified plane of the current UCS. An additional point is also required to specify where the plane will go through. Figure 5-115 shows a 3D solid that has been sliced parallel to the *YZ* plane and is going through the midpoint of the top left edge.

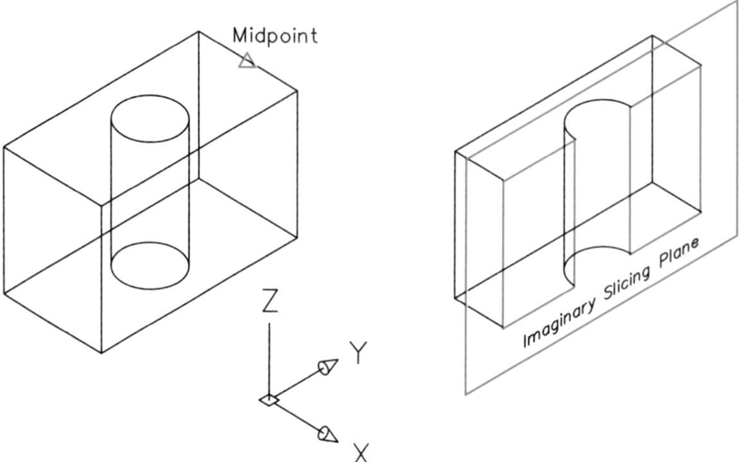

Figure 5-115 Slicing a 3D solid with an imaginary slicing plane defined parallel to one of the planes of the current UCS

Planar object: This option aligns the imaginary slicing plane with the plane to which a specific object belongs. Figure 5-116 shows an imaginary slicing plane aligned with the selected polyline. This option works for objects that are considered 2D objects and that belong to the *XY* plane of a specific UCS. Valid objects are circles, ellipses, arcs, planar splines, and polylines.

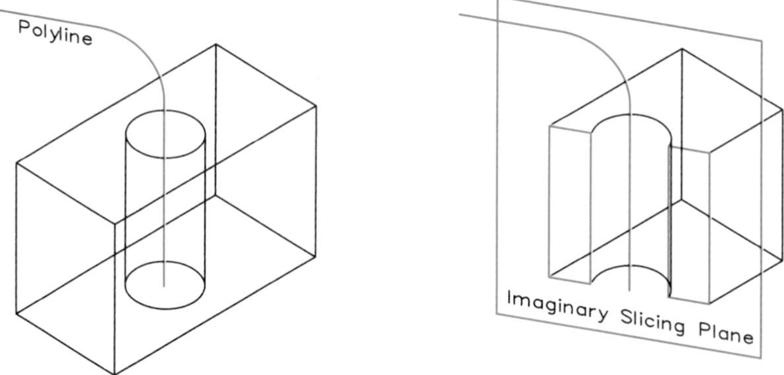

Figure 5-116 Slicing a 3D solid with an imaginary slicing plane defined by a planar curve (object

View: This method defines the imaginary slicing plane parallel to the viewing plane, which is your monitor screen. An additional point is also required to specify where the plane will go through (Figure 5-117).

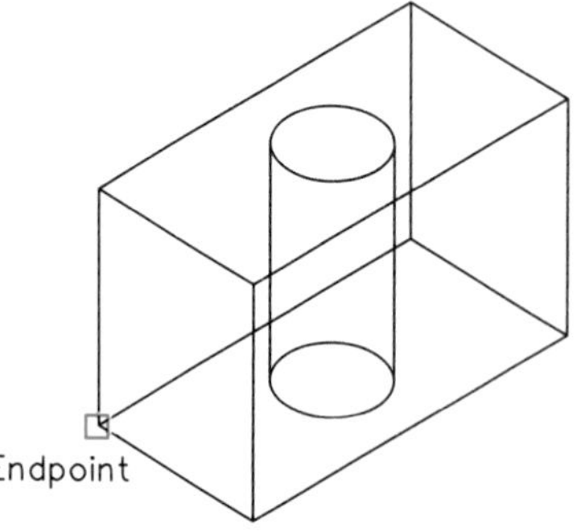

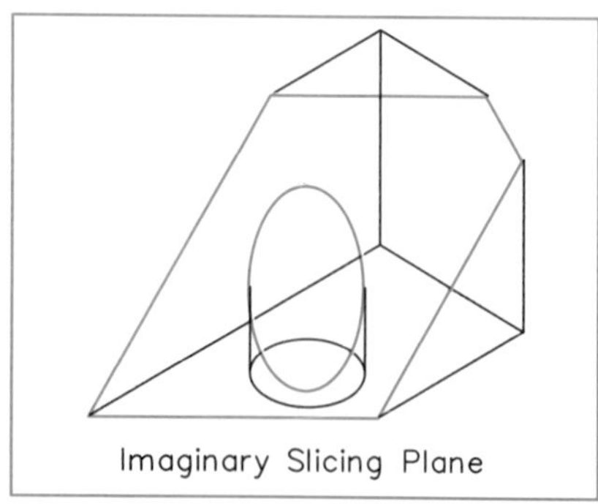

Figure 5-117 Slicing a 3D solid with an imaginary slicing plane defined parallel to the viewing plane

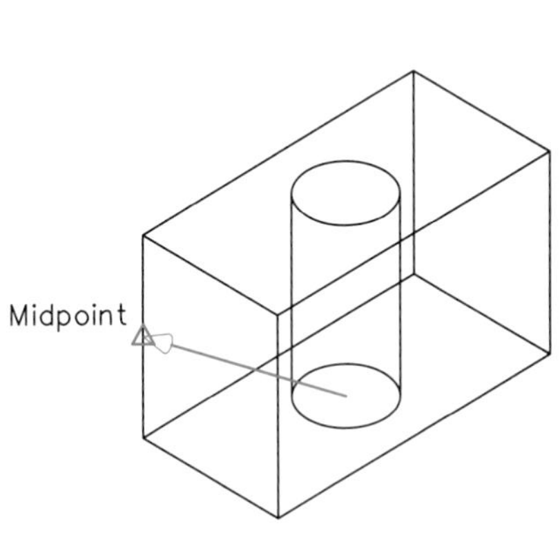
Midpoint

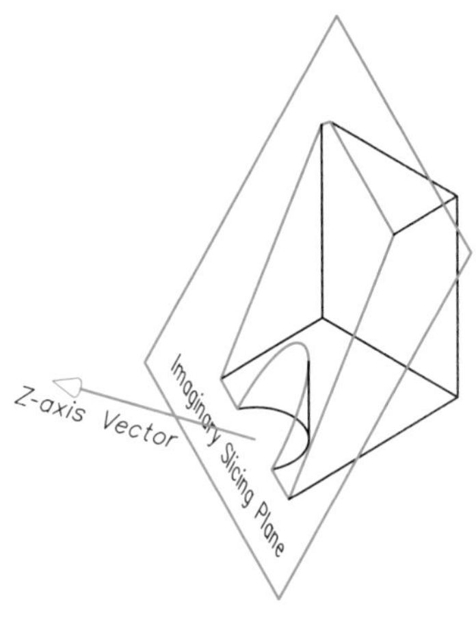
Z-axis Vector
Imaginary Slicing Plane

Figure 5-118 Slicing a 3D solid with an imaginary slicing plane defined perpendicular to a *Z*-axis vector

***Z*-axis:** With this option the imaginary slicing plane is aligned perpendicular to a vector between the two points specified and going through the first point specified (Figure 5-118).

After selecting the solids, and specifying an imaginary slicing plane or a surface, you must specify which portion to keep. You can keep only one of the two portions by specifying a point on the desired side, or you can keep both sides by pressing **<Enter>.**

Exercise 5-12: Using the SLICE Command

1. **OPEN** either ***Exercise 5-8*** or ***Exercise 5-10 solved.***
2. **SAVE** the drawing **AS *Exercise 5-12.***
3. Invoke the **SLICE** command to split the 3D solid. Respond to the prompts as follows:

Select objects to slice: *Select the 3D solid.*
Select objects to slice: ↵ *(To end the selection)*
Specify start point of slicing plane or [planar Object/Surface/Zaxis/View/XY/YZ/ZX/3points] <3points>: ↵ *(To use the 3 points option)*
Specify first point on plane: *Snap to any of the three endpoints indicated in* Figure 5-119.
Specify second point on plane: *Snap to any other indicated endpoint.*
Specify third point on plane: *Snap to the third endpoint.*
Specify a point on desired side or [keep Both sides] <Both>: ↵ *(To keep both sides)*

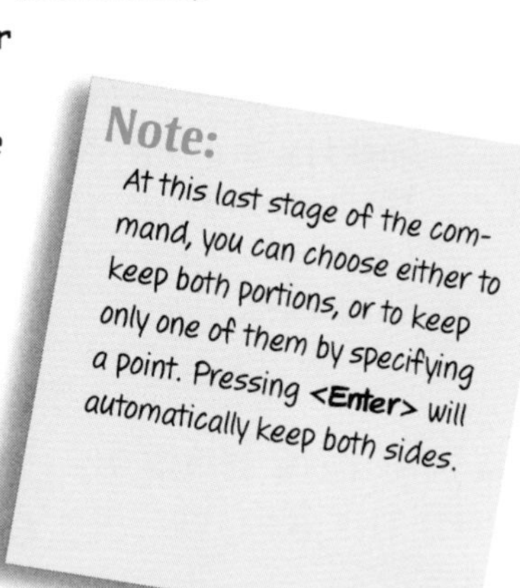
Note:
At this last stage of the command, you can choose either to keep both portions, or to keep only one of them by specifying a point. Pressing <Enter> will automatically keep both sides.

SLICE	
Ribbon Solid Editing Panel	
Pull-down Menu	Modify/ 3D Operation/ Slice
Command Line	slice

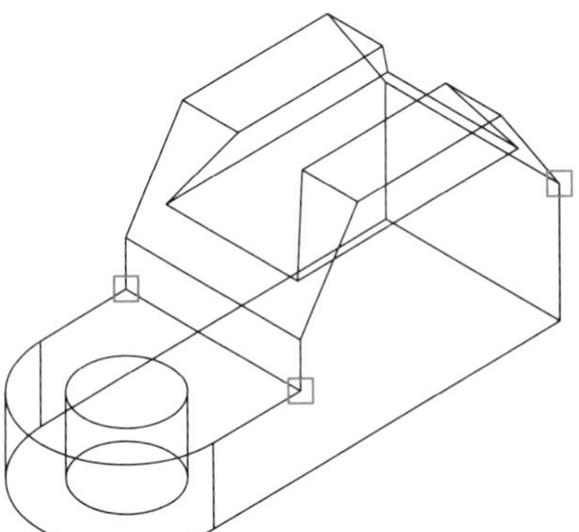

Figure 5-119 Points used to specify the imaginary slicing plane

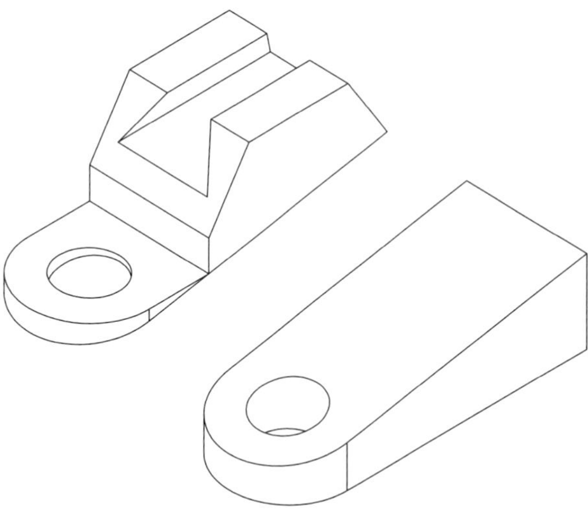

Figure 5-120 The sliced 3D solid after it is split

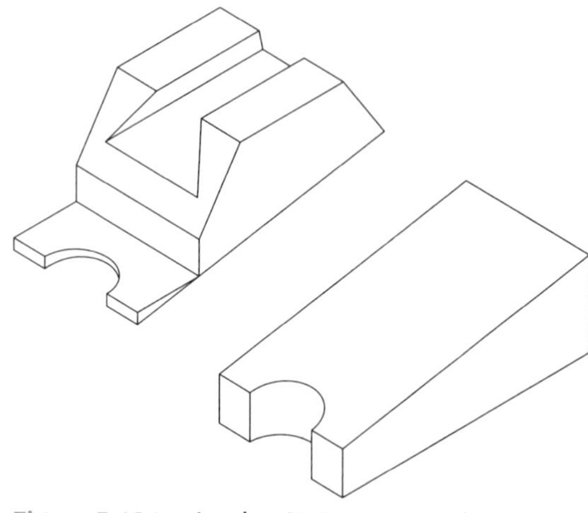

Figure 5-121 Another SLICE operation (after choosing to keep only one side)

Figure 5-122 The SECTION command shortcut menu

4. Select the **Top** UCS.
5. With the **ORTHO** mode activated, **MOVE** the upper 3D solid **5″** along the positive direction of the *Y* axis.
6. Invoke the **HIDE** command. The split 3D solid should look like Figure 5-120.
7. Invoke the **SLICE** command again and respond to the prompts as follows:

   Select objects to slice: *Select the two 3D solids.*

   Select objects to slice: ↵ *(To end the selection)*

   Specify start point of slicing plane or [planar Object/Surface/Zaxis/View/XY/YZ/ZX/3points] <3points>: *yz* ↵

   Specify a point on the YZ-plane <0,0,0>: *Snap to any of the center points on the cylindrical holes.*

   Specify a point on desired side or [keep Both sides] <Both>: *Snap to any point on the right portion of the solids to leave only the portions shown in* Figure 5-121.
8. **SAVE** the drawing.

Extracting Regions from 3D Solids with the SECTION Command

Sometimes it is necessary to extract precise geometry from existing 3D solids in order to use them in other 3D operations or simply to inspect internal details. The **SECTION** command can assist you with this task. It can be invoked only through the command line.

With the **SECTION** command you define an imaginary plane, just as you do with the **SLICE** command. Other than defining it as perpendicular to the current *XY* plane, all other methods apply.

The results obtained with these two commands, however, are different. The **SLICE** command divides 3D solids into two portions, whereas the **SECTION** command extracts only regions from them. The regions obtained are exactly the cross section that results after the 3D solid is intersected by the ***imaginary sectioning plane***.

imaginary sectioning plane: Imaginary plane that defines a section through 3D solids as it crosses these objects.

The methods used with the **SECTION** command to specify the imaginary sectioning plane are the same as those used to specify the imaginary slicing plane with the **SLICE** command. See the command's options shortcut menu in Figure 5-122.

The operation extracts a region even if the imaginary sectioning plane is specified flush with a planar face on a 3D solid (Figure 5-123).

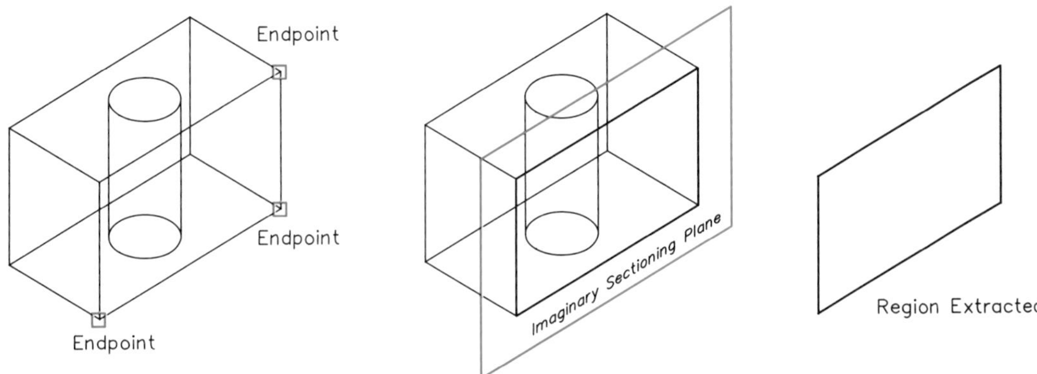

Figure 5-123 Specifying the imaginary sectioning plane flush with a planar face also extracts a region

Exercise 5-13: Using the SECTION Command

1. **OPEN** either ***Exercise 5-8*** or ***Exercise 5-10 solved.***
2. **SAVE** the drawing **AS *Exercise 5-13.***
3. Invoke the **SECTION** command by typing its name in the command line. Respond to the prompts as follows:

   Select objects: *Select the 3D solid.*

   Select objects: ↵ *(To end the selection)*

   Specify first point on Section plane by [Object/Zaxis/View/XY/YZ/ZX/3points] <3points>: *Snap to any of the three endpoints indicated in Figure 5-124.*

   Specify second point on plane: *Snap to any other indicated endpoint.*

   Specify third point on plane: *Snap to the third endpoint.*
4. Select the **Top** UCS.
5. With the **ORTHO** mode activated, **MOVE** the extracted region **6″** along the positive direction of the *Y*-axis. The 3D model should look like Figure 5-125.

Note:
Depending on the shape of the 3D solid and the place where the imaginary sectioning plane goes through, you will obtain simple and composite regions. In the example above, you created a composite region made of an external profile with an elliptical hole. You can modify the regions obtained, as you will do in this exercise.

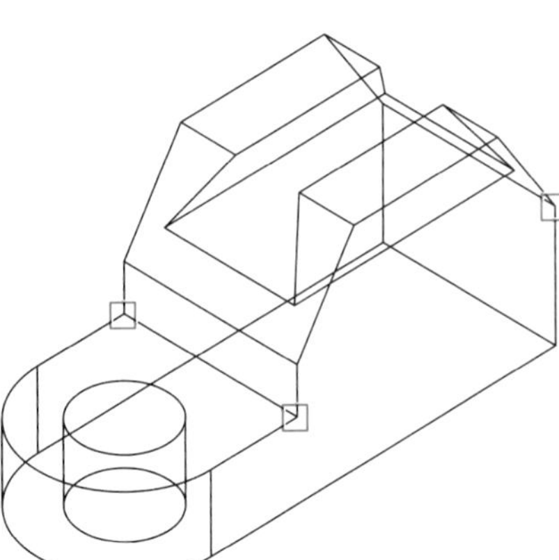

Figure 5-124 Points used to specify the imaginary sectioning plane

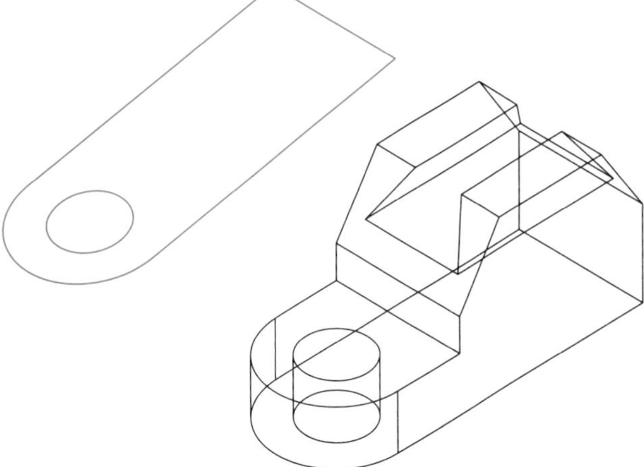

Figure 5-125 The extracted region after it is moved away

6. Select the **Top** UCS.
7. **EXPLODE** the region extracted.
8. **ERASE** the elliptical hole.
9. Invoke the **REGION** command and select the remaining objects. A new region without a hole is created, as shown in Figure 5-126.
10. Invoke the **SECTION** command again and respond to the prompts as follows:

    Select objects: *Select the solid.*

    Select objects: ↵ *(To end the selection)*

    Specify first point on Section plane by [Object/Zaxis/View/XY/YZ/ZX/3points] <3points>: *xy* ↵

    Specify a point on the XY-plane <0,0,0>: *Snap to the midpoint shown in* Figure 5-127.
11. **MOVE** the extracted region **6″** along the negative direction of the *Y*-axis. The 3D model should look like Figure 5-128.
12. **EXPLODE** the new composite region to separate it into two individual regions.
13. **SAVE** the drawing.

Note:
In this case, the region extracted is made of two regions combined. By exploding regions with this characteristic, you can separate the composite regions into individual ones.

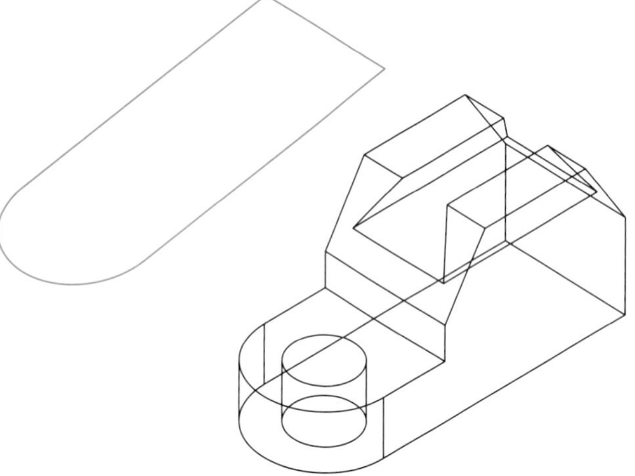

Figure 5-126 The extracted region can be used to generate other objects, such as the new region without the hole

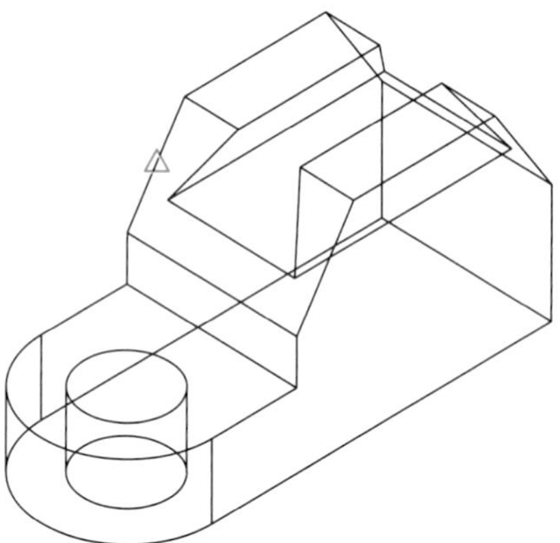

Figure 5-127 Point used to specify the imaginary sectioning plane parallel to the XY plane

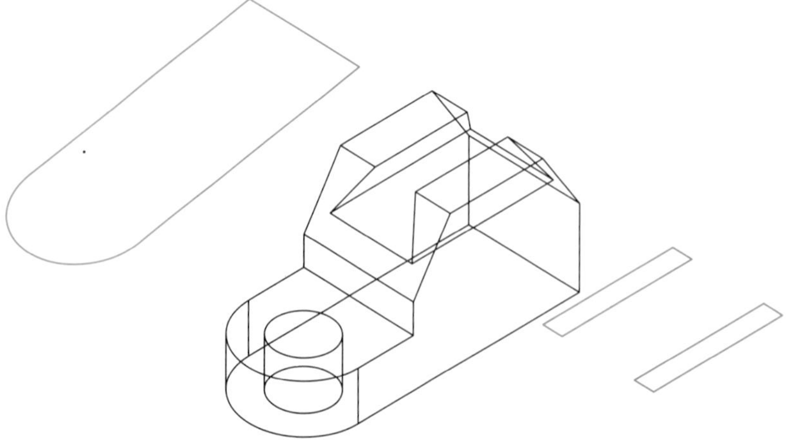

Figure 5-128 The extracted region after it is moved away

CREATING FILLETS AND CHAMFERS ON 3D SOLIDS

Most of the commands that belong to the **Modify** group of commands such as **COPY, MOVE, ROTATE,** and **ERASE,** to mention some, do not deviate from their ordinary process, regardless of the type of objects selected.

FILLET and **CHAMFER** commands, however, are a special case. Even though they also belong to the **Modify** group of commands, they work differently when the object selected is a 3D solid. If you select an edge of a 3D solid after invoking one of these two commands, the command deviates from its normal procedure.

The FILLET Command

In its standard 2D mode, the **FILLET** command prompts you to specify the two objects to be filleted (Figure 5-129). Picking on the edge of a 3D solid, on the other hand, provides enough information for the command to proceed. The command substitutes each selected edge with another face that is tangent to the two faces sharing that edge (Figure 5-130).

The **Chain** option of this command is available only after an edge of a 3D solid is selected. It enables you to select a group of edges that are continuously tangent, rather than selecting them one by one (Figure 5-131). You can switch back to the selection of individual edges at any time if needed.

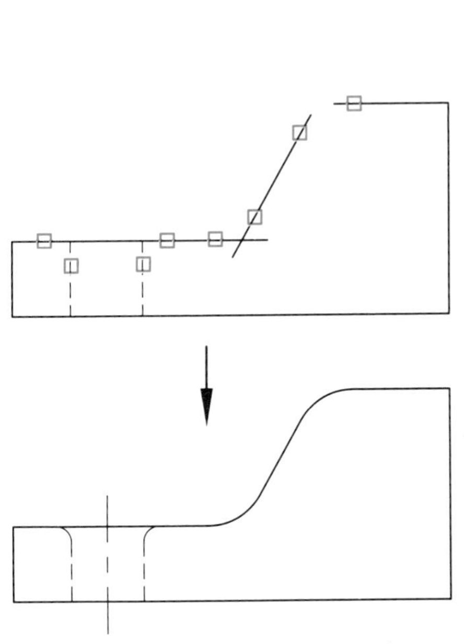
Figure 5-129 The FILLET command as used in a 2D operation

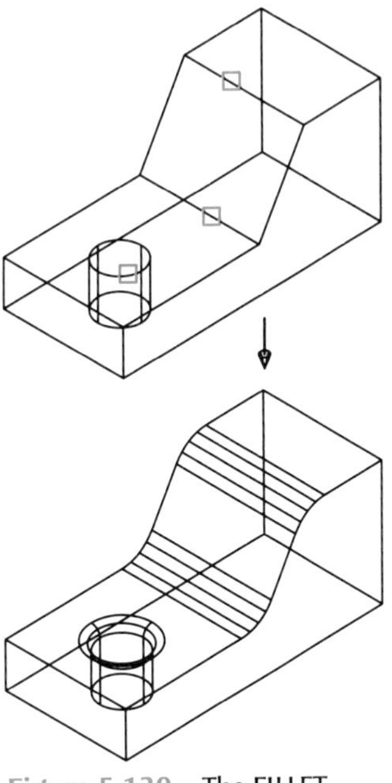
Figure 5-130 The FILLET command is used in a 3D operation by selecting the edge to be filleted

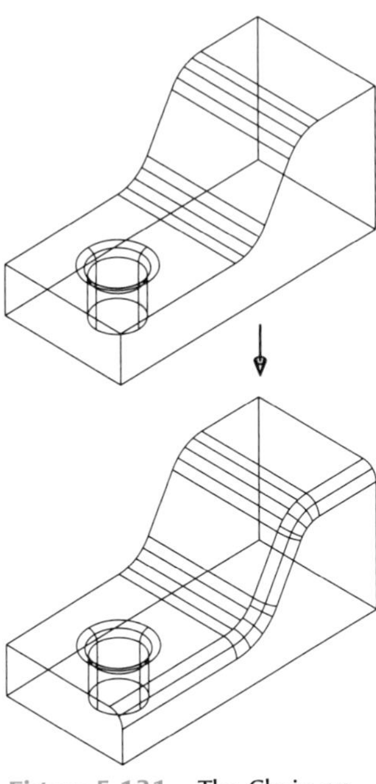
Figure 5-131 The Chain option of the FILLET command allows the selection of a group of continuously tangent edges

When creating fillets on three or more edges that converge on a common vertex, AutoCAD creates an additional blended face (Figure 5-132). This feature is possible only if performed within the same operation.

Another important aspect of the **FILLET** command is that you can change the **Radius** value within the same operation, prior to selecting any particular edge. In this case, a more complex blended face is created (Figure 5-133).

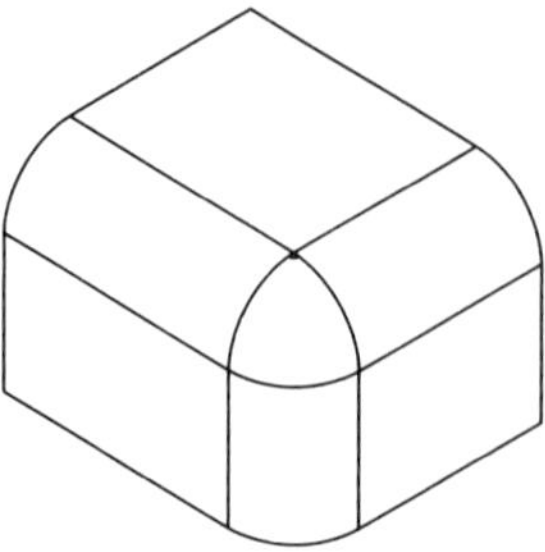
Figure 5-132 Fillets created on three converging edges

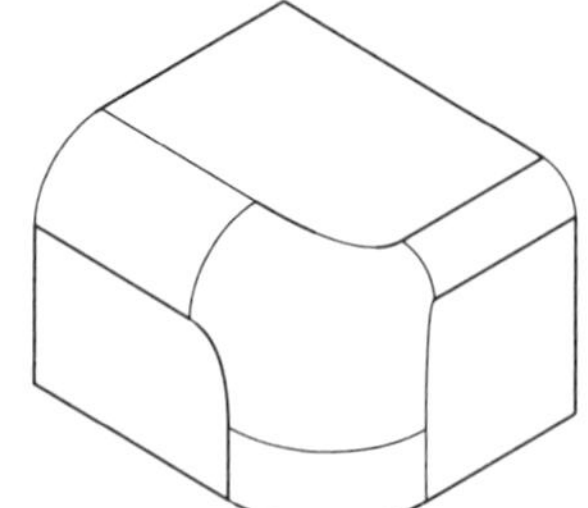
Figure 5-133 Fillets created on three converging edges using different Radius values

Exercise 5-14: Using the FILLET Command on 3D Solids

1. **OPEN** either ***Exercise 5-8*** or ***Exercise 5-10 solved***.
2. **SAVE** the drawing **AS *Exercise 5-14.***
3. Invoke the **FILLET** command and respond to the prompts as follows:

   Select first object or [Undo/Polyline/Radius/Trim/Multiple]: *Select the straight edge shown in* Figure 5-134.

   Enter fillet radius: *0.25* ↵

   Select an edge or [Chain/Radius]: *r* ↵

   Enter fillet radius <0.2500>: *0.125* ↵

   Select an edge or [Chain/Radius]: *Select the circular edge.*

   Select an edge or [Chain/Radius]: ↵ *(To end the selection)*
4. Invoke the **HIDE** command. The 3D model should look like Figure 5-135.

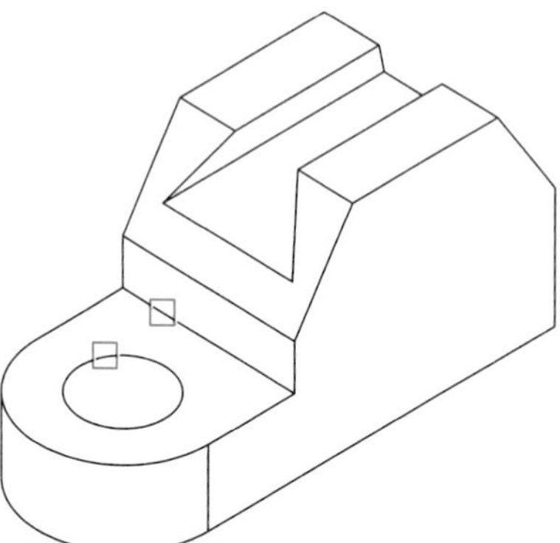
Figure 5-134 Edges to select

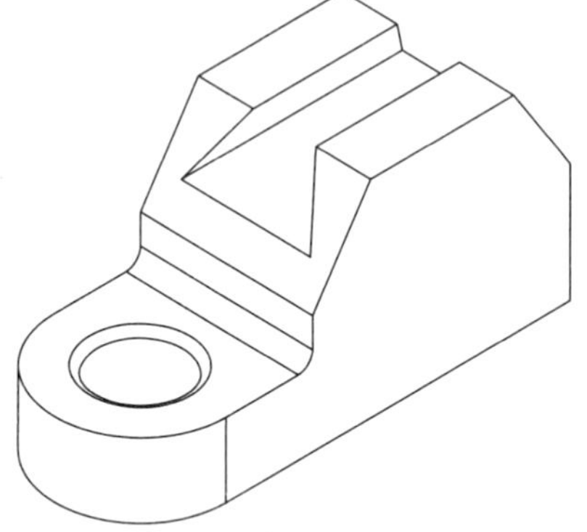
Figure 5-135 The 3D solid after the FILLET operation

5. Invoke the **REGEN** command.
6. Invoke the **FILLET** command again and respond to the prompts as follows:

   Current settings: Mode = TRIM, Radius = 0.1250

   Select first object or [Undo/Polyline/Radius/Trim/Multiple]: *Select either of the two straight edges shown in* Figure 5-136.

   Enter fillet radius <0.1250>: *0.25* ↵

   Select an edge or [Chain/Radius]: *c* ↵

   Select an edge chain or [Edge/Radius]: *Select the other straight edge.*

   Select an edge chain or [Edge/Radius]: ↵ *(To end the selection)*
7. Select the **Realistic** visual style. The 3D model should look like Figure 5-137.
8. **SAVE** the drawing.

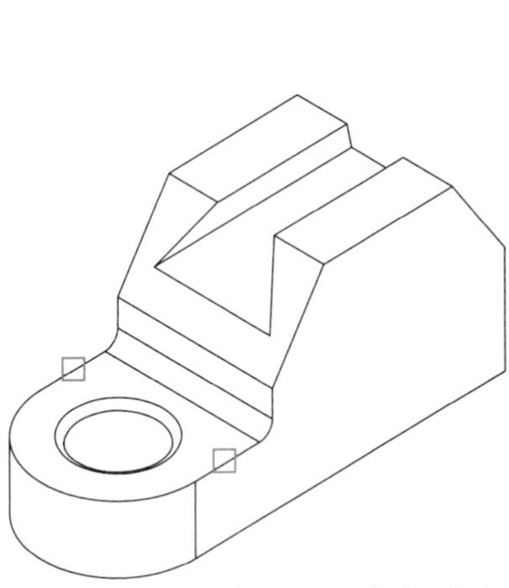

Figure 5-136 Places to pick the chain of edges

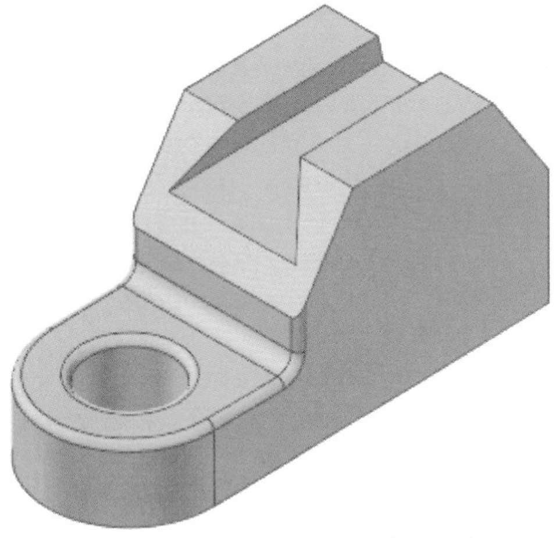

Figure 5-137 A shaded view of the resulting 3D solid

The CHAMFER Command

In 2D usage, the **CHAMFER** command creates an inclined line between two lines or polyline objects coexisting on a common plane. Such a line is typically used to represent a beveled edge. When used on 3D solids, the command creates an actual beveled edge, substituting the selected sharp edge with a chamfered face between the two adjacent faces, depending on the geometry (Figure 5-138).

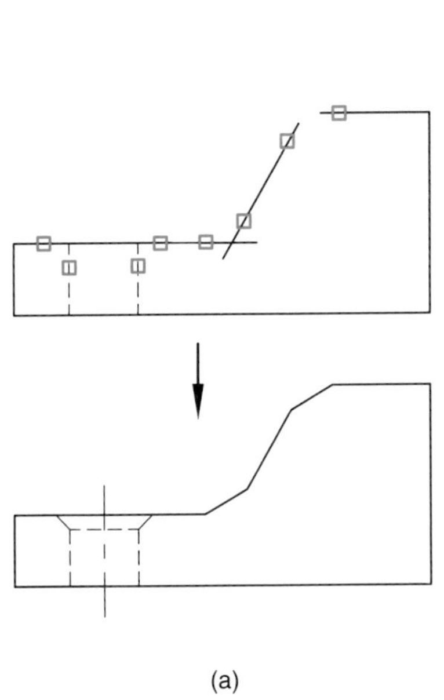

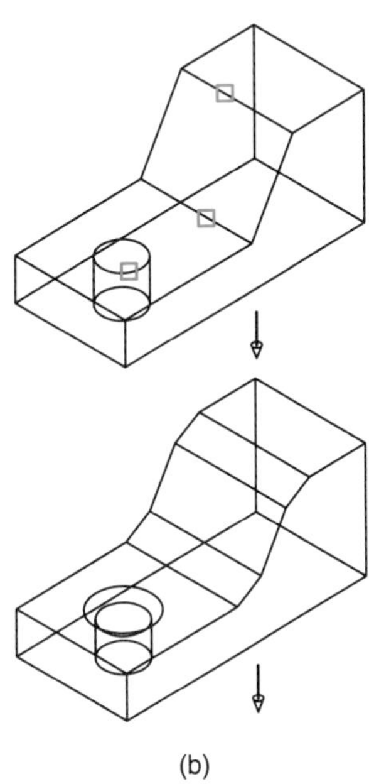

Figure 5-138 Comparison of the CHAMFER command as a 2D (a) and a 3D (b) operation

The selection process of this command differs quite a bit from that of the **FILLET** command. In each operation, you can select only edges that belong to a common face, which must be specified first. The AutoCAD program requires a face to be selected because the face establishes the base surface chamfer distance. In other words, the first chamfer distance is measured on this face from the edge to the inside of the 3D solid. The two options available are:

- Picking edges individually
- Selecting the entire **Loop**

The last option will include all the edges of the specified face. Selecting the entire **Loop** of a face will fail to chamfer if the edges pertaining to the **Loop** are not all either interior or exterior edges. The **Loop** of none of the three faces highlighted in Figure 5-139 can be selected because they include both types of edges.

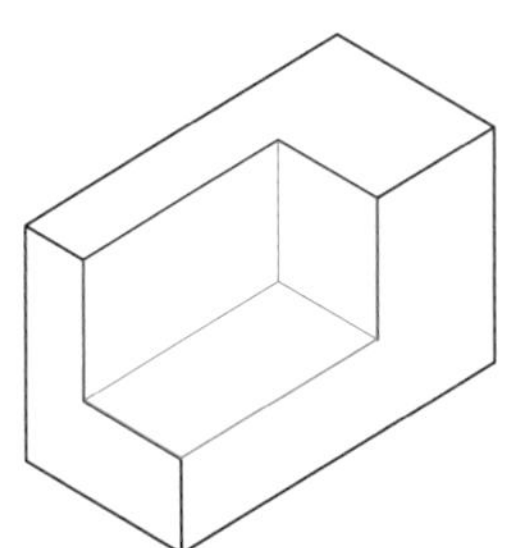

Figure 5-139 The Loop cannot be selected for any of the three faces highlighted

Exercise 5-15: Chamfering the Edges of 3D Solids

1. **OPEN** either ***Exercise 5-8*** or ***Exercise 5-10 solved.***
2. **SAVE** the drawing **AS *Exercise 5-15.***
3. Invoke the **CHAMFER** command and respond to the prompts as follows:

   Select first line or [Undo/Polyline/Distance/Angle/Trim/mEthod/Multiple]: *Select the straight edge shown in* Figure 5-140.

   Base surface selection...

   Enter surface selection option [Next/OK (current)] <OK>: *n* ↵ *(To select the face highlighted in* Figure 5-141*)*

   Enter surface selection option [Next/OK (current)] <OK>: ↵ *(To accept the selection, once the correct face is selected)*

   Specify base surface chamfer distance <0.5000>: *0.25* ↵

   Specify other surface chamfer distance <0.5000>: *0.25* ↵

   Select an edge or [Loop]: *Select the straight and the circular edges shown in* Figure 5-142.

   Select an edge or [Loop]: ↵ *(To end the command and create the chamfers)*

Note: By selecting a solid's edge, the command digresses to base surface selection. In this mode, you can specify one of the two faces adjacent to the selected edge.

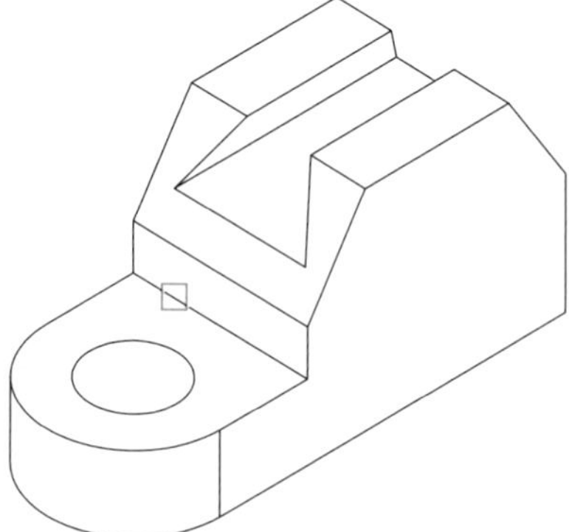

Figure 5-140 Edge selected to specify the base surface

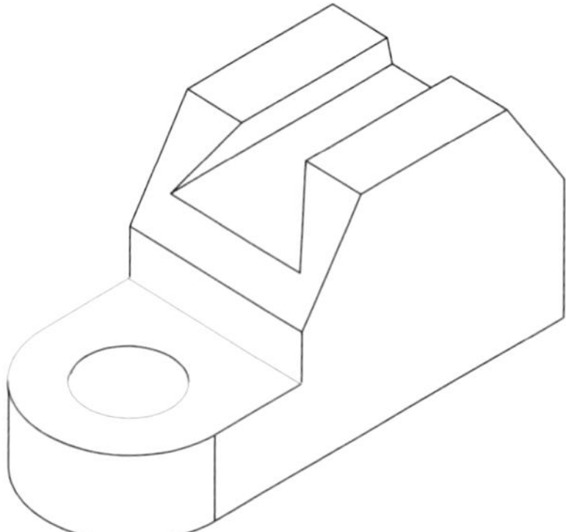

Figure 5-141 Face to be selected

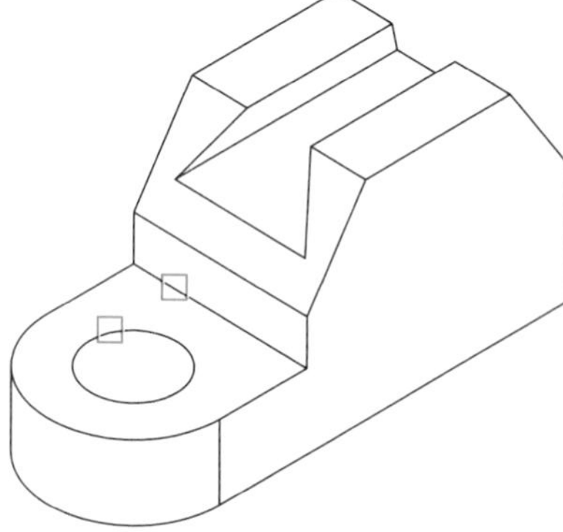

Figure 5-142 Edges to be selected from the face specified

4. Invoke the **HIDE** command. The 3D solid should look like Figure 5-143.
5. Invoke the **REGEN** command.
6. Invoke the **CHAMFER** command again and respond to the prompts as follows:

   Select first line or [Undo/Polyline/Distance/Angle/Trim/mEthod/Multiple]: *Select the edge shown in* Figure 5-144.

   Base surface selection...

   Enter surface selection option [Next/OK (current)] <OK>: *Select the bottom face, choosing* **Next** *if necessary. Press* ↵ *when you are finished.*

   Specify base surface chamfer distance <0.1250>: *0.5* ↵

   Specify other surface chamfer distance <0.1250>: *0.5* ↵

   Select an edge or [Loop]: *l* ↵

   Select an edge or [Loop]: *Select the same edge again, or any other edge on the selected face.*

   Select an edge or [Loop]: ↵ *(To end the command and create the chamfer)*

7. Invoke the **3DORBIT** command to inspect the chamfer around the loop. The 3D solid should look like Figure 5-145 after you invoke the **HIDE** command.
8. **SAVE** the drawing.

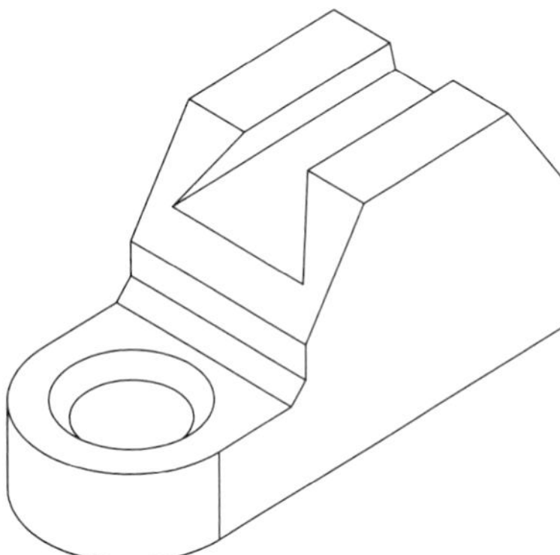

Figure 5-143 The 3D solid after the CHAMFER operation

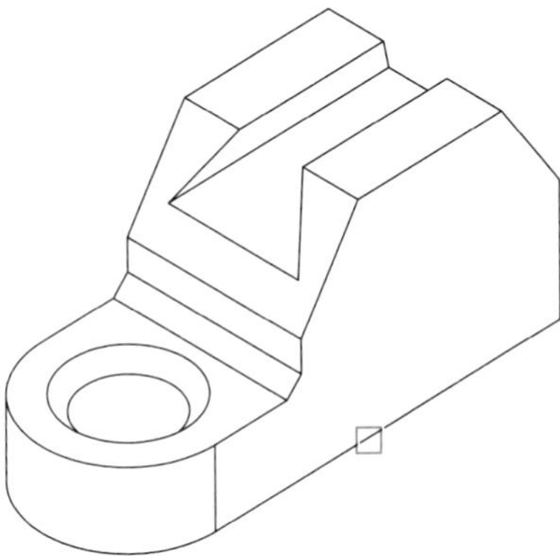

Figure 5-144 Edge to be selected

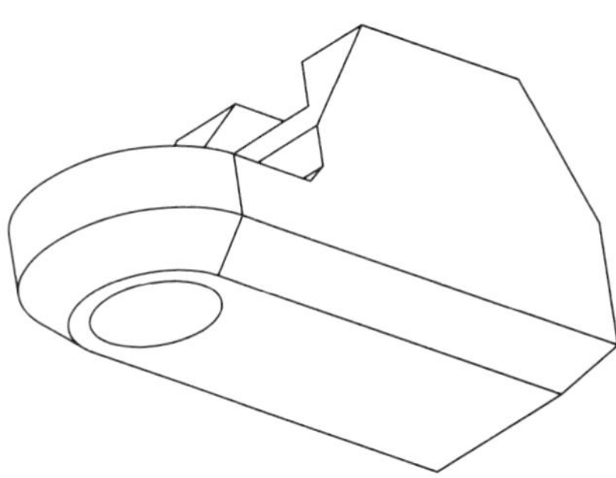

Figure 5-145 The 3D solid after the CHAMFER operation using the Loop option

Creating 3D Assembly Models

There are no special tools or commands in AutoCAD specifically related to assembly models. Parametric CAD programs, such as Autodesk® Inventor™, include tools specifically designed to be used with assemblies and allow you to establish and modify the relationships between different 3D objects. This type of program even uses a different type of file to perform assembly tasks.

With AutoCAD, assemblies can be created using the same file that you normally use to create 2D drawings and 3D models. This reduces the job to simply gathering all the 3D objects together inside the same drawing file and placing them in the right locations. You could also create all the 3D objects in the same drawing file if the resulting file size is not too large for your computer. Once all the necessary objects are together, all you need to do is to put them in the correct locations and make sure they are properly aligned.

Well-known commands such as **MOVE, COPY, ROTATE, MIRROR,** and so on, are the ones mainly used for assembly tasks. The **ALIGN** command, which is not so popular in 2D work, is the most useful one here. Additionally, you can take advantage of specialized commands such as **3DARRAY, MIRROR3D,** and **ROTATE3D** in 3D operations.

A single 3D solid object can better represent a complete object. Therefore, this type of object is more convenient to use in assemblies than any other type of 3D object.

FOR MORE DETAILS See Chapter 3 for specific information about the usage of the **Modify** group of commands in a 3D environment, as well as the specialized commands used in 3D operations.

Exercise 5-16: An Assembly of 3D Solids

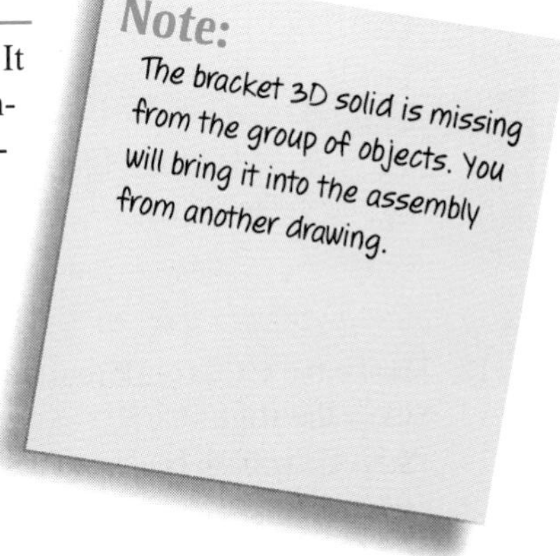
Note:
The bracket 3D solid is missing from the group of objects. You will bring it into the assembly from another drawing.

Student Files

1. **OPEN** the drawing ***Exercise 5-16*** from the CD. It contains a group of 3D solids disarranged throughout the 3D space. These objects will be used to create the assembly shown in Figure 5-146.
2. **SAVE** the drawing **AS *Exercise 5-16 solved.***
3. **OPEN** either ***Exercise 5-8*** or ***Exercise 5-10 solved.***
4. In the drawing that contains the bracket 3D solid, select the **SW Isometric** viewing point and the **Top** UCS.
5. Invoke the **COPYCLIP** (copy to clipboard) command and select the bracket.

6. **CLOSE** the drawing that contains the bracket. Select **No** when prompted to **SAVE** the changes.
7. Go back into ***Exercise 5-16 solved*** and make sure the **SW Isometric** viewing point and the **World** UCS are current.
8. Invoke the **PASTECLIP** (paste from the clipboard) command and specify an insertion point by clicking anywhere in the 3D space (Figure 5-147).

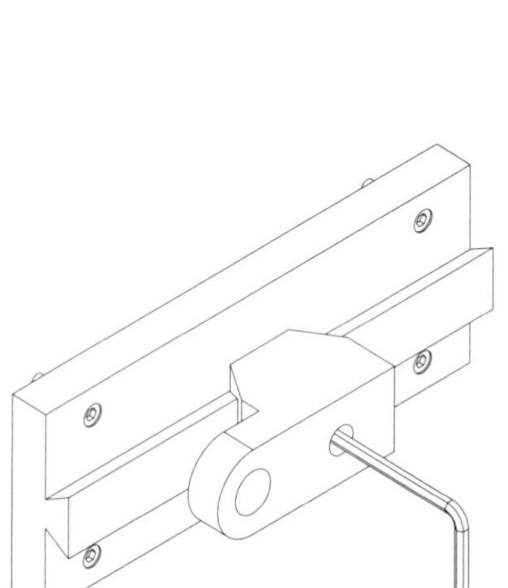

Figure 5-146 The completed assembly

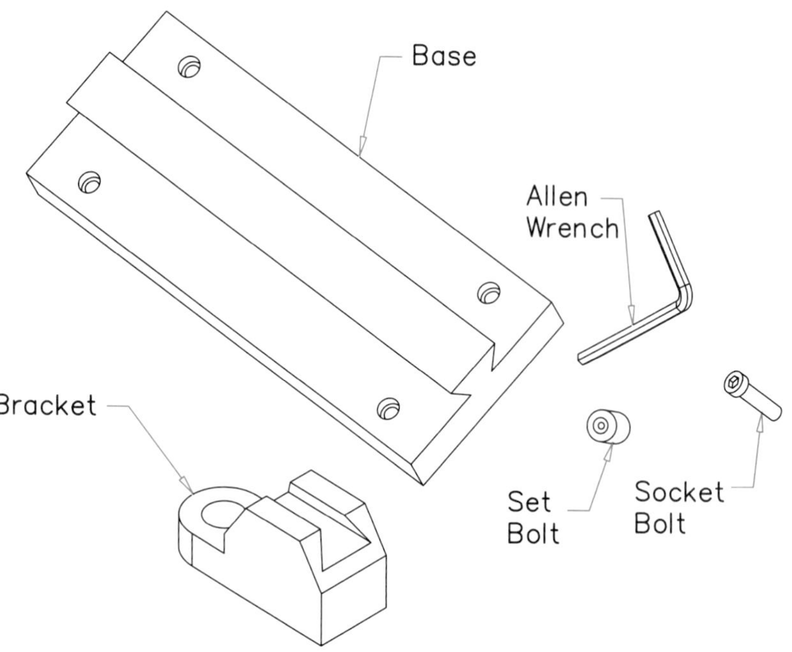

Figure 5-147 After pasting the bracket near the other components

9. Invoke the **ROTATE** command. When prompted, snap to any point on the bracket, and enter **90** as the rotation angle.
10. Select the Bracket and invoke the **ROTATE3D** command. Use the option that defines the axis aligned with the *Y*-axis. When prompted, snap to any point on the bracket and enter **−90** as the rotation angle (Figure 5-148).
11. Use the **Face** option of the **UCS** command to align the *XY* plane with one of the faces on the base. When prompted, select the highlighted face, picking it around the area shown in Figure 5-149. Press **<Enter>** to accept the face. The new UCS should align its *XY* plane as shown.

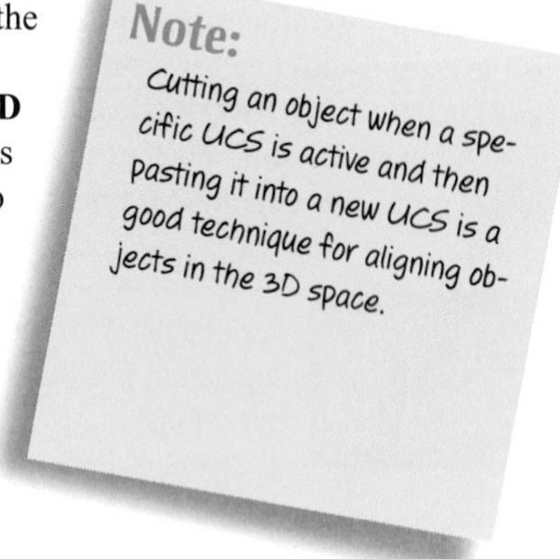

Note:
Cutting an object when a specific UCS is active and then pasting it into a new UCS is a good technique for aligning objects in the 3D space.

FOR MORE DETAILS See Chapter 1 for further information about the different options used to modify the UCS.

12. Invoke the **CUTCLIP** (cut to clipboard) command and select the base.
13. Select the **Right** UCS.
14. **PASTE** the base back into the drawing area, anywhere in the 3D space.

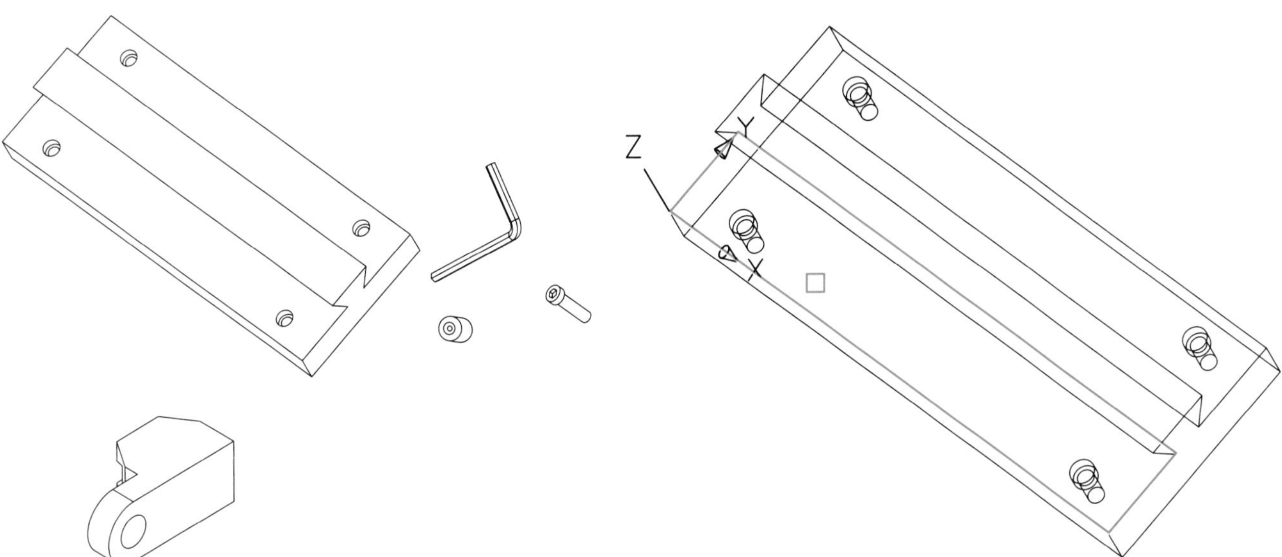

Figure 5-148 After rotating the bracket

Figure 5-149 The UCS is aligned with the selected face

15. **MOVE** the base closer to the other 3D solids. The 3D assembly model should look like Figure 5-150.
16. **MOVE** the socket bolt close to one of the holes on the base.
17. Make sure the **DUCS** mode is turned off and invoke the **3DALIGN** command. When prompted, select the socket bolt. Figure 5-151 shows the order in which you must select the four center points to locate the socket bolt properly: 1 and 2 are the two source points, while 3 and 4 are the destination points. The result should look like Figure 5-152.

On certain occasions having the **DUCS** (Dynamic UCS) mode on might interfere with the specification of the points. It is a good idea to turn this setting off for this particular operation.

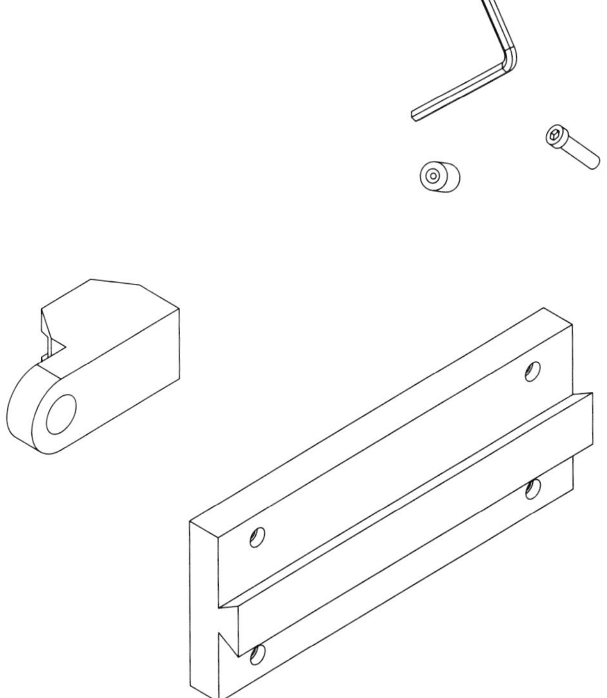

Figure 5-150 The base is moved closer to the other objects

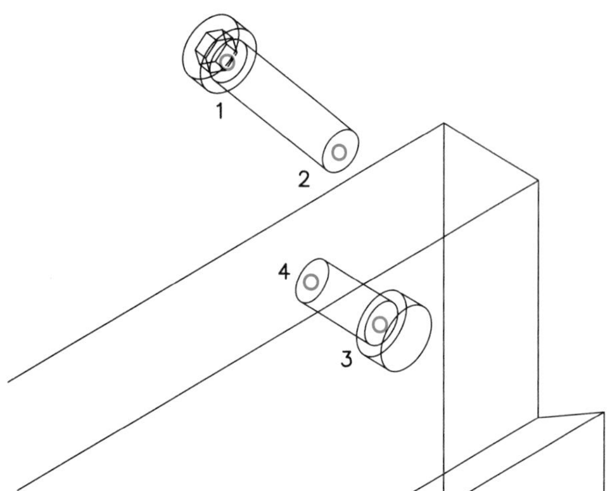

Figure 5-151 The order in which the points to align the bolt with its hole must be specified

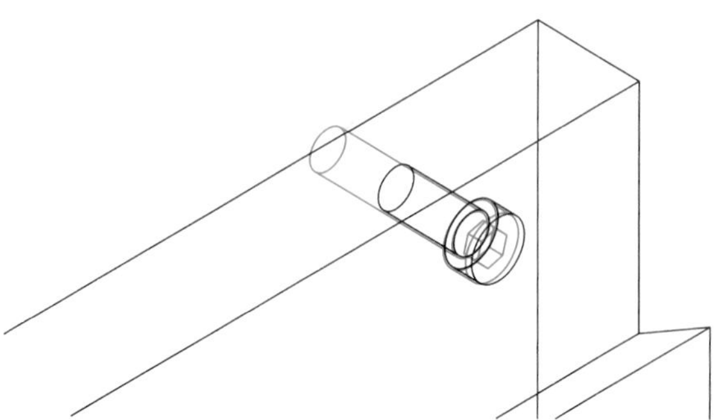

Figure 5-152 After the bolt is aligned

18. Select the **Right** view.
19. **MIRROR** the socket bolt, as you would normally do in a 2D operation, to place mirrored copies of the socket bolt in each of the three remaining holes (Figure 5-153).
20. Select the **SW Isometric** viewing point.
21. **ZOOM** into the bracket and create a hole through it, as specified in Figure 5-154.
22. **MOVE** the leftmost end of the Allen wrench close to the set screw.
23. Invoke the **3DALIGN** command. When prompted, **ZOOM** in as needed and select the Allen wrench. Follow Figure 5-155 for the order in which you should snap to the six endpoints: 1, 2, and 3 are the three source points, while 4, 5, and 6 are the three destination points.

> **Note:**
> Remember to press **<Enter>** after specifying all the points that define the source plane, as well as after specifying all the points that define the destination plane.

One of the approaches used to create a circular hole in a 3D solid is to place a circle in the correct location, **EXTRUDE** it long enough so it goes through the 3D solid, and **SUBTRACT** it from the 3D solid.

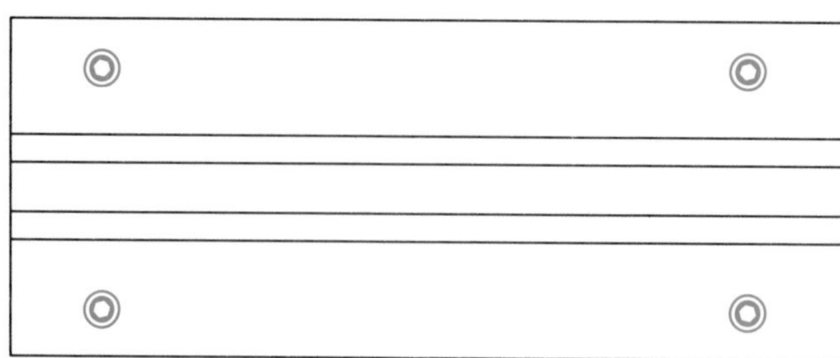

Figure 5-153 The three other bolts are obtained with MIRROR operations

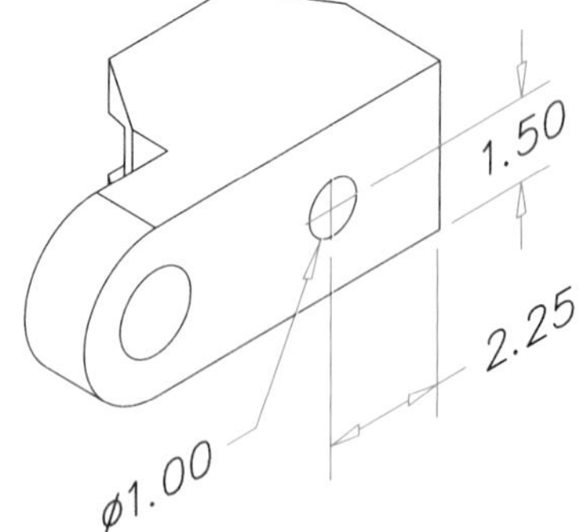

Figure 5-154 Dimensions for the hole

24. **MOVE** the socket screw and the Allen wrench together so the socket screw is close to the hole you opened on the bracket (Figure 5-156).
25. Invoke the **3DALIGN** command to align both the socket bolt and the Allen wrench with the hole of the bracket, as shown in Figure 5-157. Select the two center points on the socket bolt as the source points, and the two center points on the bracket hole as the destination points.

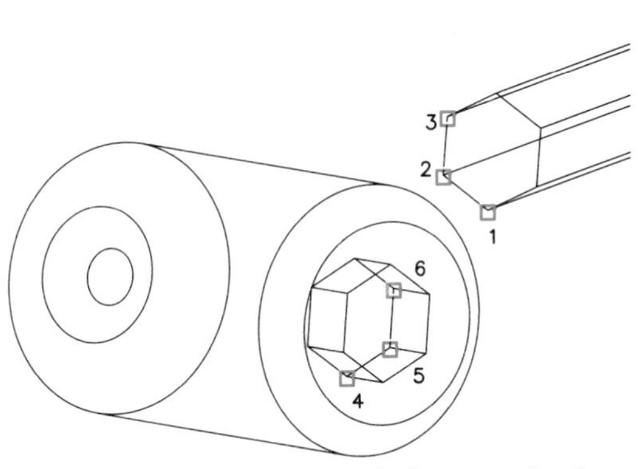

Figure 5-155 Order to specify the points for the 3DALIGN operation

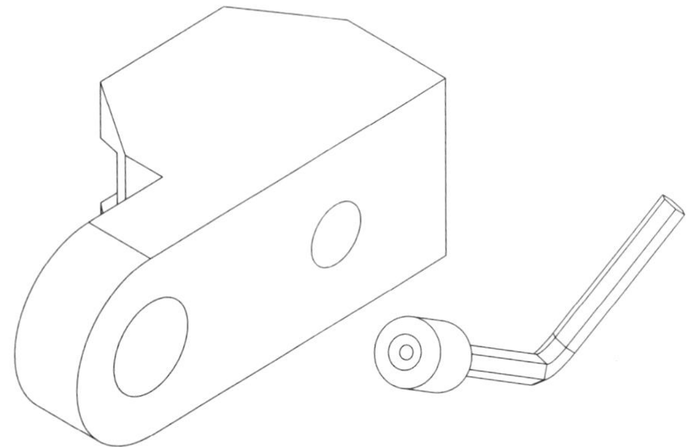
Figure 5-156 Objects moved closer to the base

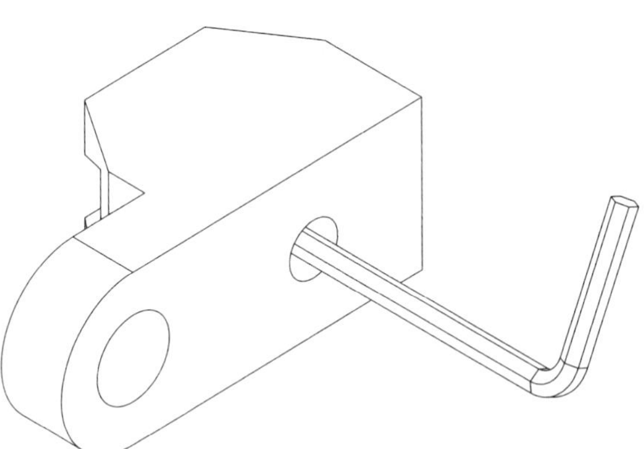
Figure 5-157 After aligning the objects with the hole on the bracket

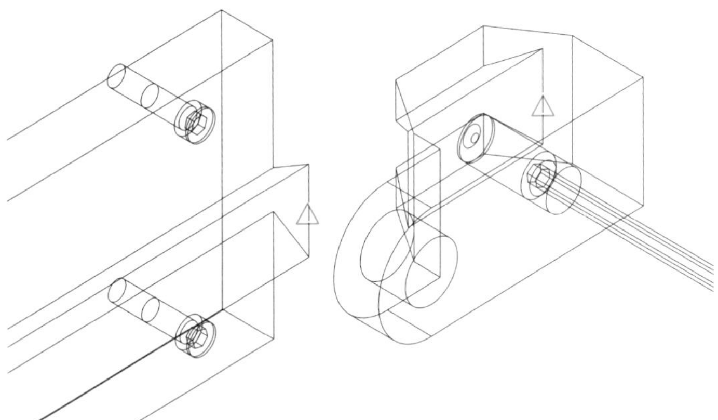
Figure 5-158 Points to be specified in the MOVE operation

26. **MOVE** the bracket together with the socket screw and the Allen wrench from the midpoint on the edge of the bracket to the midpoint on the edge of the base, as shown in Figure 5-158.
27. Once again, **MOVE** the previous 3D solids orthogonally along the base guide to locate them close to the middle of the base. The 3D assembly model should look like Figure 5-159.
28. **SAVE** the drawing.
29. On your own, try rotating the Allen wrench along with the set screw so that the bent end of the Allen wrench is aligned exactly downward.

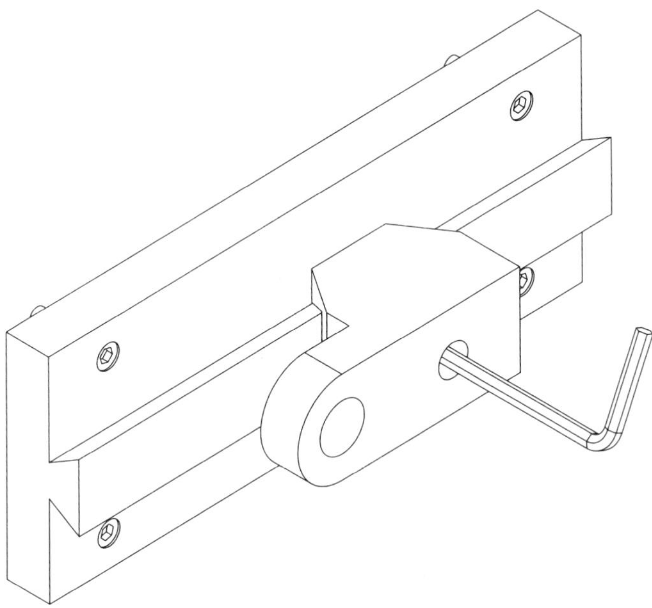
Figure 5-159 The final arrangement, after the objects are moved orthogonally toward the middle of the base

Summary

After reading this chapter, you should have learned the commands needed to create 3D solid primitives, as well as many other powerful tools related to the creation of 3D solids and surfaces such as **EXTRUDE, REVOLVE, SWEEP,** and **LOFT.** In addition, the Boolean operations with 3D solids, along with the many other operations you learned, will assist you in the development of very sophisticated 3D models. You have also learned how the **FILLET** and **CHAMFER** commands have a very specific use in these types of objects.

The many exercises contained in this chapter have given you the practice required to start using the tools contained in this chapter. They also have introduced you to the different approaches and uses for which 3D solids and surfaces are considered to be appropriate.

You have learned the techniques used to develop 3D assembly models in a practical way, as well as the methods needed to find possible failures caused by improper fitting of components, using the **INTERFERENCE** command.

Chapter Test Questions

Multiple Choice

1. Which system variable controls the display of silhouettes on curved faces?
   a. **FACETRES**
   b. **DISPSILH**
   c. **ISOLINES**
   d. None of the above
2. Which of the following is not a method used to develop an extruded object?
   a. Following a path
   b. Perpendicular to its plane
   c. Between two cross sections
   d. In a specified direction
3. Which of the following objects will create a surface if an **EXTRUDE** operation is performed with it?
   a. A circle
   b. An open non-self-intersecting polyline
   c. A region
   d. A closed non-self-intersecting polyline
4. Which of the following options cannot be used to define the axis of rotation of the **REVOLVE** command?
   a. Two points
   b. The *X*-axis of the current UCS
   c. The *XY* plane of the current UCS
   d. The *Z*-axis of the current UCS
5. Which of the following can be controlled on the swept objects in a **SWEEP** operation?
   a. Location of the base point
   b. Scaling
   c. Twisting
   d. All of the above
6. Which of the following enables you to control the behavior of very specific areas on the surfaces of lofted 3D objects?
   a. Using a path
   b. Using draft angles
   c. Using guides
   d. None of the above
7. Two concentric cylinders of different diameters that have their bases in the same plane and have the same height are combined using an **INTERSECT** operation. What will the resulting object be?
   a. A pipe
   b. The smaller cylinder
   c. The bigger cylinder
   d. No object
8. Many of the commands used to create 3D objects require that a plane be defined in the 3D space. Which of the following is an appropriate way to define such a plane?
   a. Specify three noncollinear points
   b. Specify the parallelism with respect to another plane and a point
   c. Specify a point and the direction of a vector perpendicular to it
   d. All of the above
9. Suppose that when using the **SLICE** command, you define the imaginary slicing plane as parallel to the *ZX* plane. Which of the following points cannot be used to specify the portion of the 3D solid to keep?
   a. A point on the *ZX* plane
   b. A point on the slicing plane
   c. A point on the *YZ* plane
   d. None of the above can be used
10. Which of the following commands changes its procedure and its prompts when the selected object is a 3D solid?
   a. **MOVE**
   b. **SCALE**
   c. **ROTATE**
   d. **FILLET**

Matching

Column A

a. **SECTION**
b. **DELOBJ**
c. **ISOLINES**
d. **SLICE**
e. **LOFT**
f. **DISPSILH**
g. **FACETRES**
h. **INTERSECT**
i. **SWEEP**
j. **INTERFERE**

Column B

1. Operation in which objects are passed through a curve
2. Command used to cut the 3D solid into two pieces
3. Operation that connects cross sections in a smooth transition
4. One of the Boolean operation commands
5. Command used to extract regions from a 3D solid
6. Controls the deletion of objects selected after the operation
7. Controls the number of contour lines
8. Command used to check interference between 3D solids
9. Turns an object's silhouettes on or off
10. Controls the number of facets per curved face

True or False

1. True or False: By properly specifying the parameters on the command prompt, you can create a frustum cone with an elliptical base, using the **CONE** command.
2. True or False: The **REVOLVE** command can create a 3D solid of revolution by turning a closed planar object around any imaginary axis that is not perpendicular to the object's plane.
3. True or False: The extrusion of a planar object always occurs perpendicular to the object's plane when a path or direction is not specified.
4. True or False: When more than one object is swept and a base point is not specified, its default location with respect to the sweep path is in the center of the first object selected.
5. True or False: The **INTERFERE** command can use either one or two sets of 3D solids to find the interferences existing within a group of 3D solids or between 3D solids from two different groups.
6. True or False: The imaginary slicing plane is the plane with which a 3D solid or group of 3D solids is cut through when using the **SLICE** command.
7. True or False: A 3D solid object can be sliced only by an imaginary plane.
8. True or False: The **Chain** option of the **FILLET** command allows you to automatically select a group of continuous edges, regardless of whether or not these edges are tangent.
9. True or False: The **THICKEN** command converts surfaces and regions into 3D solids by thickening them.
10. True or False: After showing the history of a composite 3D solid, you can **DELETE** one of the original 3D solids that was previously involved in a Boolean operation.

Chapter Tutorials

Tutorial 5-1: A Plastic Part Design

general

A common characteristic of plastic parts is that all the surfaces along the ejection direction need to be tapered. That way, the part can easily be ejected from the mold cavity without being damaged.

In this tutorial, you will develop a plastic staple that is used to secure electrical wires to walls.

1. Open a **NEW** drawing, through the **File** drop-down menu using **Imperial** units.
2. **SAVE** the drawing **AS** ***Tutorial 5-1***.
3. Draw the 2D profile shown in Figure 5-160. Turn the profile into either a region or a polyline.
4. Set the **DISPSILH** system variable to **1** and the **ISOLINES** system variable to **0**.
5. Set the **FACETRES** system variable to **6**.

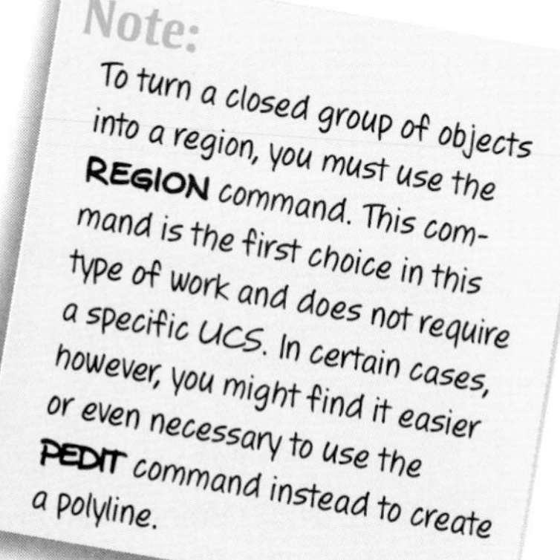

Note:
To turn a closed group of objects into a region, you must use the REGION command. This command is the first choice in this type of work and does not require a specific UCS. In certain cases, however, you might find it easier or even necessary to use the PEDIT command instead to create a polyline.

6. Select the **SE Isometric** viewpoint.
7. **EXTRUDE** the profile **−0.375″** (down) using a **Taper angle** of **2** (Figure 5-161).
8. While in the WCS, draw two circles on top of the face. Draw the circles concentric with the arc edges and specify **0.094″** as the diameter (Figure 5-162).

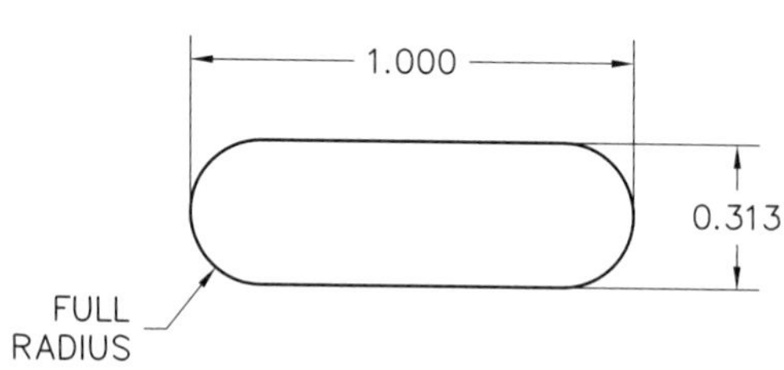

Figure 5-160 Profile dimensions

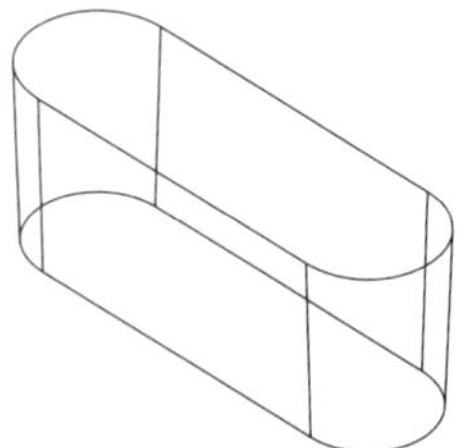
Figure 5-161 After a tapered EXTRUSION operation

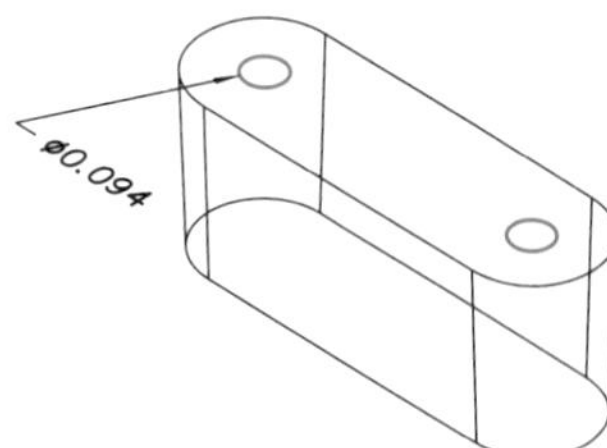

Figure 5-162 Two concentric circles on the top face

9. **EXTRUDE** the circles **−0.375″** (down) using a **Taper angle** of **2**. This operation will create two thin cones.
10. **SUBTRACT** the two thin cones from the main 3D solid (Figure 5-163).
11. Draw another two circles (**0.188″** diameter) concentric with the two arcs on the top face.
12. **EXTRUDE** the circles **−0.032″** (down) using a **Taper angle** of **2**.
13. **SUBTRACT** the two new 3D solids from the main one. The 3D model of the plastic part now should look like Figure 5-164 after you invoke the **HIDE** command.
14. Invoke the **REGEN** command.
15. Select the **Front** UCS.
16. Draw the 2D profile shown in Figure 5-165. Use the **Ttr (Tan tan radius)** option of the **CIRCLE** command to generate the arc.
17. Convert the profile into a region.
18. **EXTRUDE** the profile **1″** in any direction.
19. Draw a **LINE** at the bottom face from midpoint to midpoint (Figure 5-166).

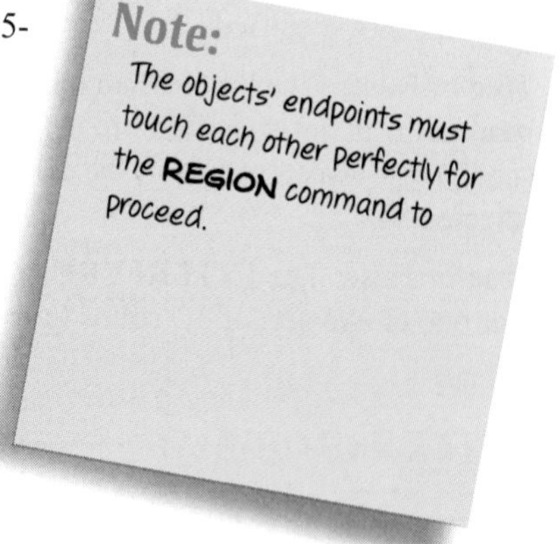

Note:
The objects' endpoints must touch each other perfectly for the REGION command to proceed.

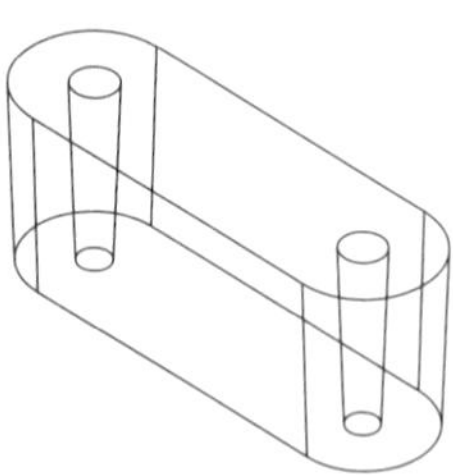
Figure 5-163 Holes created by subtracting the cones

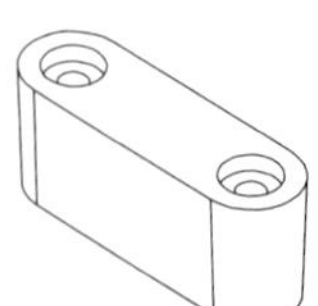
Figure 5-164 Recess created by subtracting the two new cones

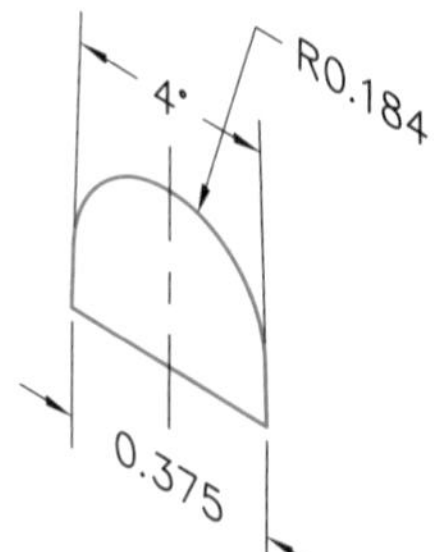

Figure 5-165 2D profile to be drawn

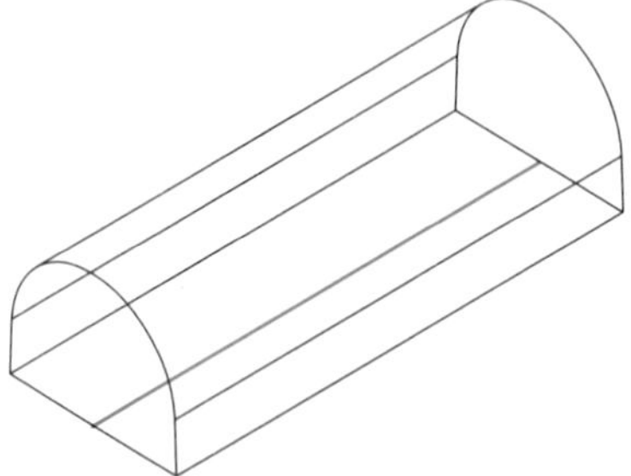
Figure 5-166 Extruded profile

20. **MOVE** the new 3D solid from the midpoint of the line to the midpoint of the straight edge at the bottom of the main 3D solid, as shown in Figure 5-167.

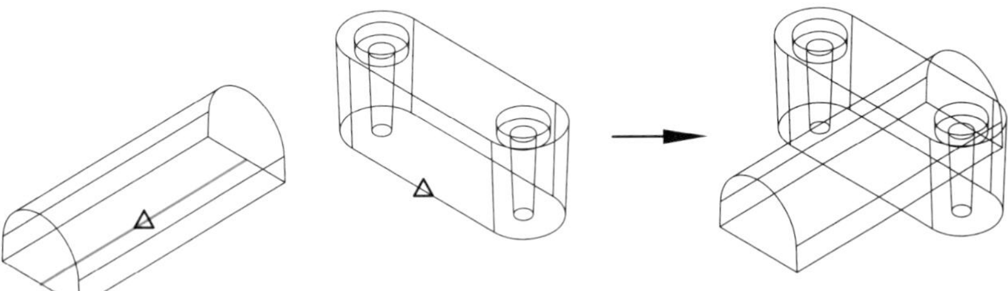

Figure 5-167 3D solid moved to the correct location

21. **ERASE** the line after the operation.
22. **SUBTRACT** the 3D solid that you just moved from the main 3D solid.
23. The 3D model should look like Figure 5-168 after you invoke the **HIDE** command.
24. **SAVE** your drawing.

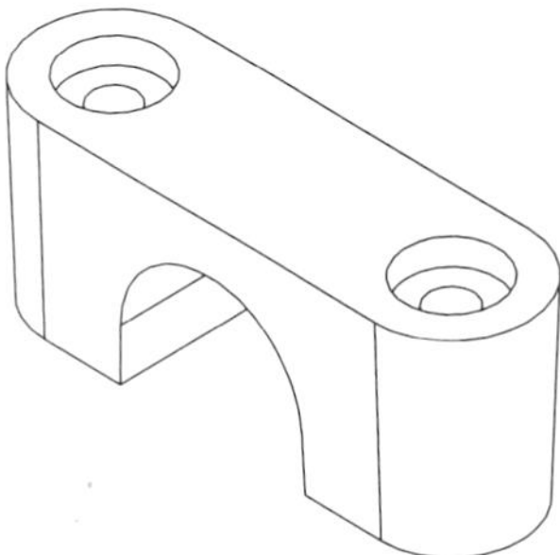

Figure 5-168 Final 3D solid model

Tutorial 5-2: A Plastic Injection Mold Cavity

Designing the cavity is probably the hardest task in the entire design of an injection mold. The solid modeling tools presented in this chapter enable you to obtain an extremely accurate mold cavity using a very simple procedure.

To start the job, you need to either re-create the 3D solid object of the part or obtain it from the designer of the plastic part. Quite often, the person in charge of the mold design is not the one in charge of designing the actual plastic part.

Note: The only purpose of this tutorial is to demonstrate the use of 3D operations in AutoCAD. It should not be considered as a tutorial specifically dedicated to the design of plastic injection molds.

1. **OPEN** ***Tutorial 5-1*** and **SAVE** it **AS** ***Tutorial 5-2***.
2. Select the **World** UCS and **ZOOM** out.
3. Invoke the **BOX** command and create the 3D solid block next to the 3D model of the plastic part, as shown in Figure 5-169. Follow the command prompts to enter the information.
4. Because of the shrinkage that occurs with plastic material when it cools inside the mold, the mold's cavity must be larger than the actual part by the shrinkage percentage recommended by the raw plastic provider. In our case we will use 7%. For AutoCAD, that simply translates into scaling the object up 7%. Invoke the **SCALE** command, and enlarge the plastic part 3D solid. Enter **1.07** when prompted for the scale factor. For the base point you can just snap to any point on the 3D solid.
5. **MOVE** the enlarged plastic part 3D solid to the proper place inside the solid block. To start, move the enlarged plastic part from the midpoint of the rightmost top straight edge to the midpoint of the leftmost vertical edge on the solid block.
6. Select the **Top** view. The 3D model should look like Figure 5-170.
7. Make sure the **OTRACK, OSNAP,** and **ORTHO** modes are turned on in the status bar. Also, make sure that the **Midpoint** and **Center** object snaps are selected in the **Drafting Settings** dialog box (Figure 5-171); the status bar shows in two possible modes: the icon and the text buttons. You can switch between these two modes right-checking on the bar.

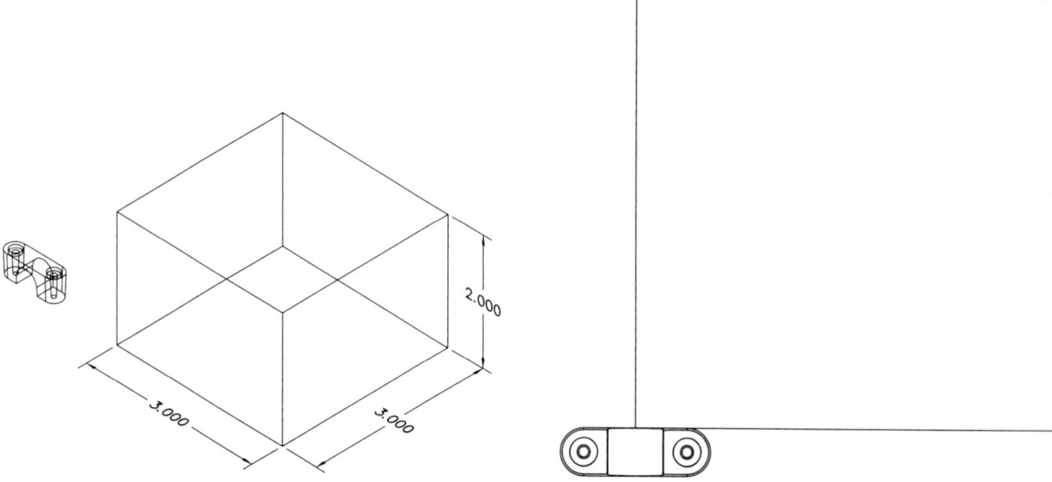

Figure 5-169 Dimensions for the box

Figure 5-170 Top view after moving the enlarged plastic part

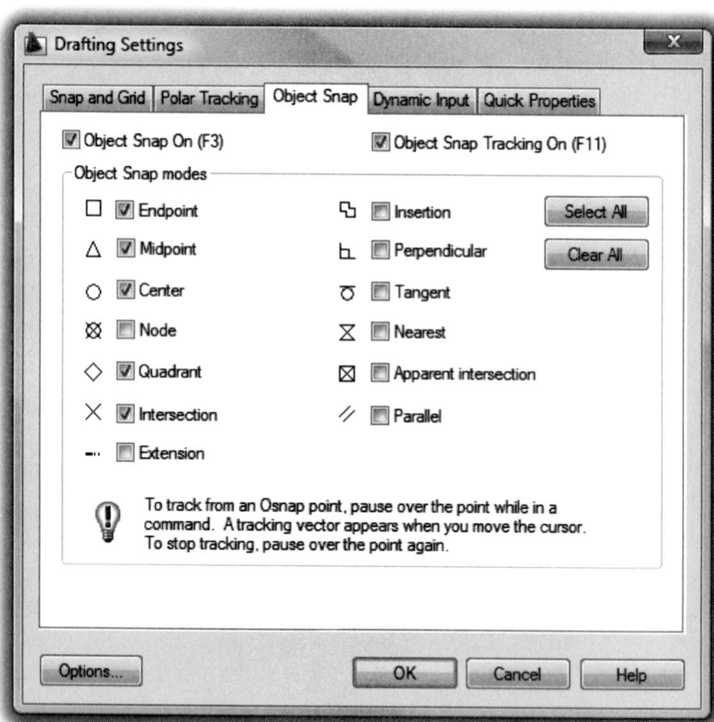

Figure 5-171 The Drafting Settings dialog box

8. Using **AutoTrack, MOVE** the enlarged plastic part along the *Y*-axis so it is centered with the block (Figure 5-172).

FOR MORE DETAILS	See Chapter 1 for more information on using the tracking methods.

9. Select the **SE Isometric** viewpoint.
10. **MOVE** the enlarged plastic part one more time from endpoint 1 to midpoint 2, as shown in Figure 5-173.

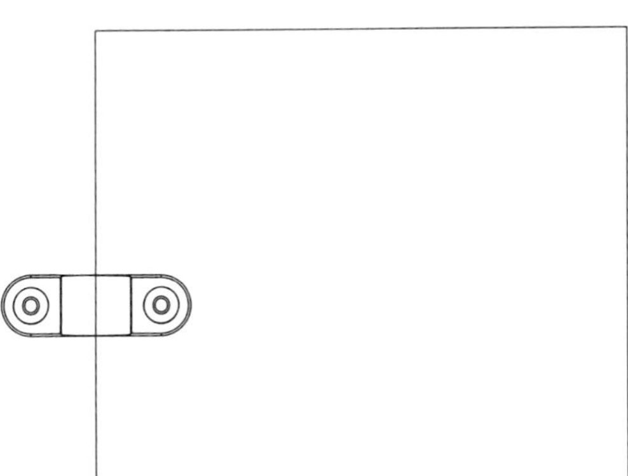

Figure 5-172 A MOVE operation using tracking techniques

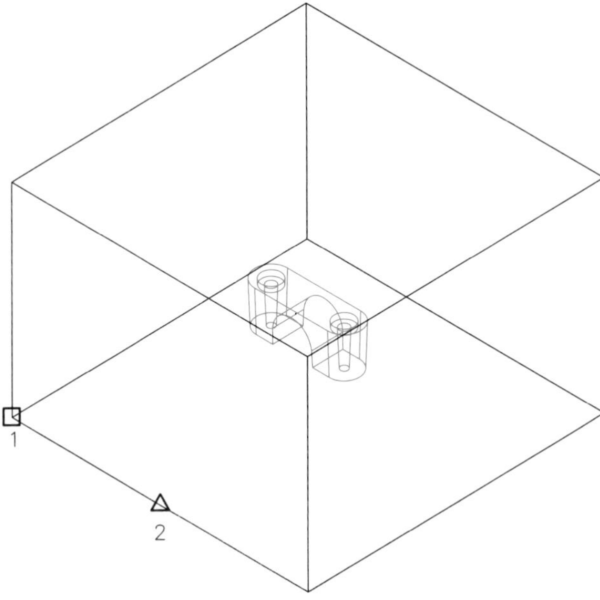

Figure 5-173 Another MOVE operation to center the object in the 3D solid box

11. Once the part is properly located, **SUBTRACT** the enlarged plastic volume from the solid block in order to create the cavity.
12. Invoke the **SLICE** command to divide the solid block into a top and a bottom block. Press **<Enter>** to use the **3point** option. Define the imaginary slicing plane by specifying a midpoint on three of the four vertical edges.
13. With **ORTHO** mode on, **MOVE** the top block **2″** up along the *Z*-axis.
14. Invoke the **3D ORBIT** command to get a clearer view of the model (Figure 5-174).
15. **ZOOM** into the cavity on the bottom block.
16. Select the **Realistic** visual style to obtain a clearer view (Figure 5-175). The two pins belong to the top half of the block, so they have to be removed from the bottom half.
17. Select the **2D Wireframe** visual style and the **Front** UCS.
18. Invoke the **SLICE** command to slice the bottom block. Use the **ZX** option to specify a cutting plane parallel to this plane. When prompted, snap to any point on either of the two bottom

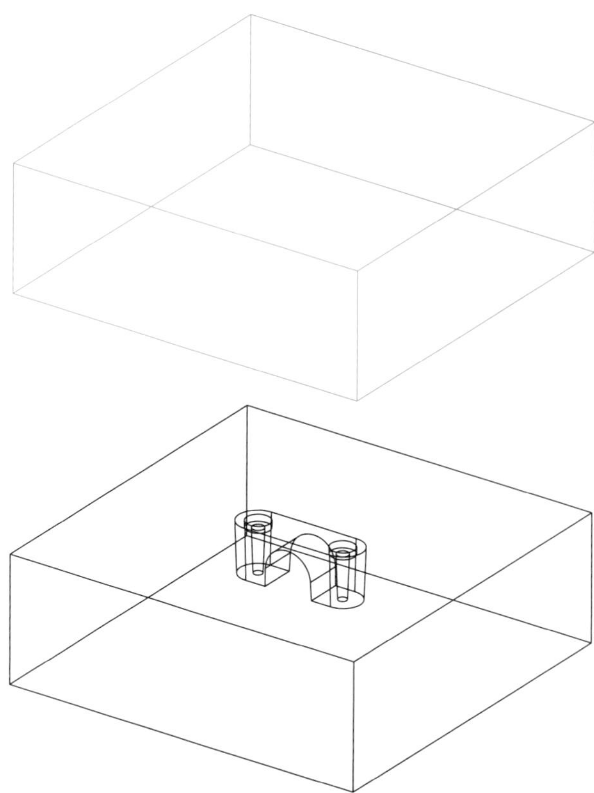

Figure 5-174 The 3D solid box is sliced and separated into two blocks

Figure 5-175 A shaded close view of the cavity

faces of the cavity, highlighted in Figure 5-176. Choose to **keep Both sides.**

19. Invoke the **SEPARATE** command to detach the two pins from the top block. After selecting the 3D solid, just press the **<Enter>** key until you exit all the prompts.

FOR MORE DETAILS To find more specific information about using the **SEPARATE** command, see Chapter 6.

20. The two pins should now be independent 3D solids. With **ORTHO** mode on, **MOVE** the pins **2″** up to place them flush with the bottom surface of the top block (Figure 5-177).

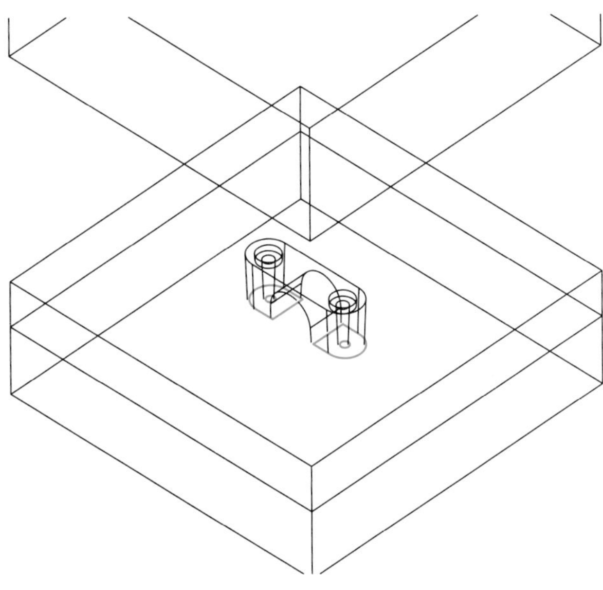

Figure 5-176 The bottom block is sliced

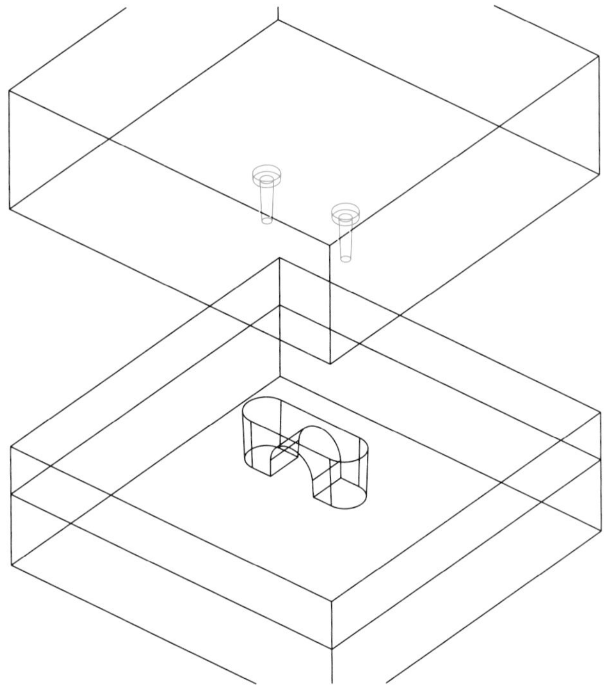

Figure 5-177 The separated pins are moved to the upper block

21. With the **UNION** command, join the two portions of the bottom block to combine it into a single 3D solid, now without the two pins. Invoke the **UNION** command again to join the two pins with the bottom block.
22. Select the **WCS**, and set a different **Color** as current. Draw the two circles highlighted in Figure 5-178. Use the pin geometry to specify the center and the radius of the circles.
23. **EXTRUDE** the two circles **−0.050″** (down) using a **Taper angle** of **2**.
24. **COPY** the two new 3D solids **2″** orthogonally down (Figure 5-179).
25. With the **UNION** command, join the two small cones on top with the top block.

Note:

Due to mold design strategies, when the mold is in a closed position, the two pins need to pass the bottom surface and penetrate a short length into the cavity.

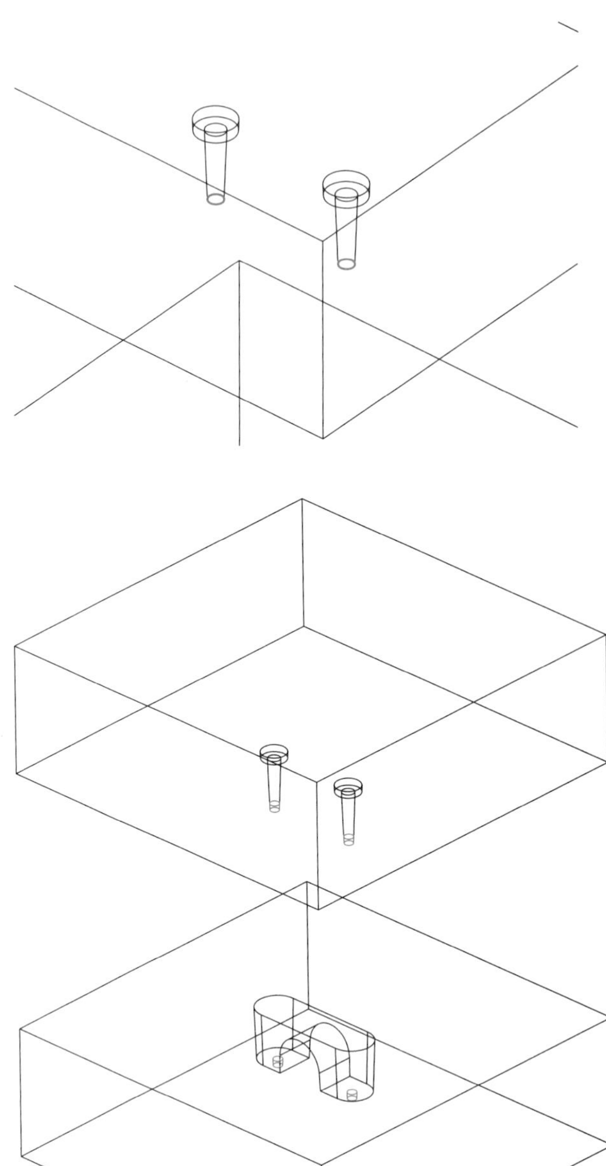

Figure 5-178 The two highlighted circles are created

Figure 5-179 The extruded 3D solids are copied to the bottom block

26. Using the **SUBTRACT** command, remove the two small cones at the bottom from the bottom half of the block (Figure 5-180).
27. Let's create an opening in the mold through which the melted plastic will run. With the **World** UCS still selected, draw the two circles shown in Figure 5-181 in the middle of the top and bottom faces of the top block.
28. Invoke the **LOFT** command. When prompted, select the two circles, selecting the bigger one first. Press **<Enter>** after completing the selection to open the **Loft Settings** dialog box.
29. Select **Draft angles**, and specify a start angle of **135**. Click **OK** to close the **Loft Settings** dialog box.
30. **SUBTRACT** the lofted 3D solid from the upper half of the block.
31. **MOVE** the top block **2″** down orthogonally along the *Z*-axis.
32. Select the **Top** view.

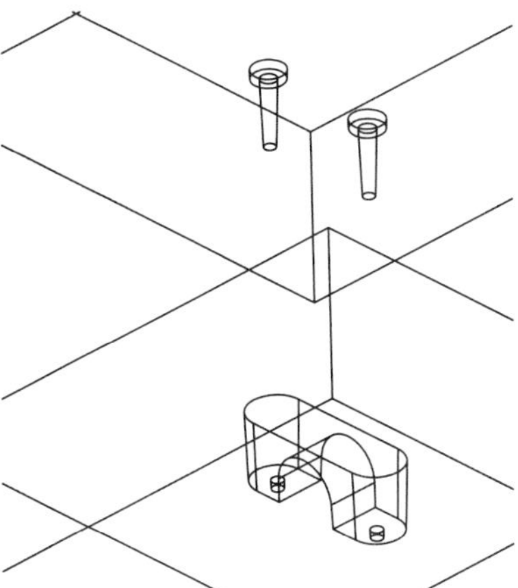

Figure 5-180 All 3D solids are subtracted

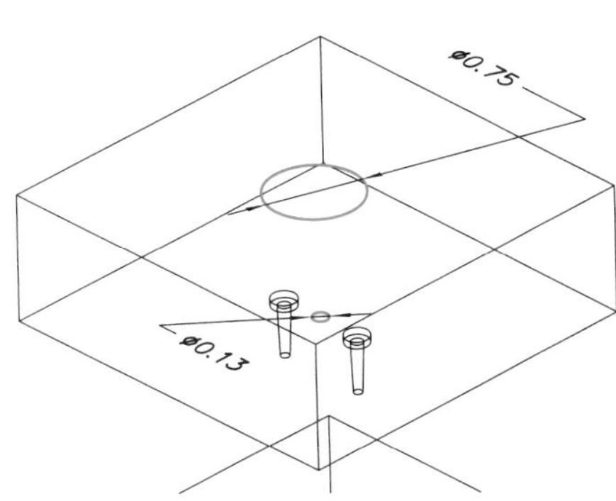

Figure 5-181 Dimensions for the circles

33. Invoke the **SLICE** command. When prompted, select the two halves of the block and press **<Enter>** to end the selection.
34. For the start point of the slicing plane, snap to the midpoint of one of the lower edges parallel to the *Y*-axis. For the second point, snap to the midpoint of the opposite edge. Click on any point located above the imaginary line between the two specified points to make this portion the one to keep.
35. Assign a different **Color** for each block.
36. Select the **Realistic** visual style. The 3D model should look like Figure 5-182 from the **SW Isometric** viewing point.
37. **SAVE** the drawing.

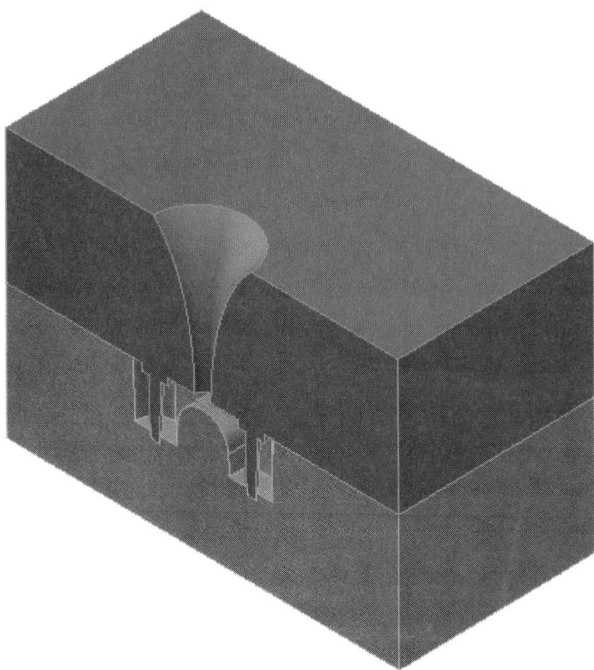

Figure 5-182 A shaded section view of the mold cavities closed

Tutorial 5-3: The Spiral Stair

In this tutorial you will add a 5′-diameter spiral stair to the interior of a building. Its partial model (Figure 5-183) has already been created for you.

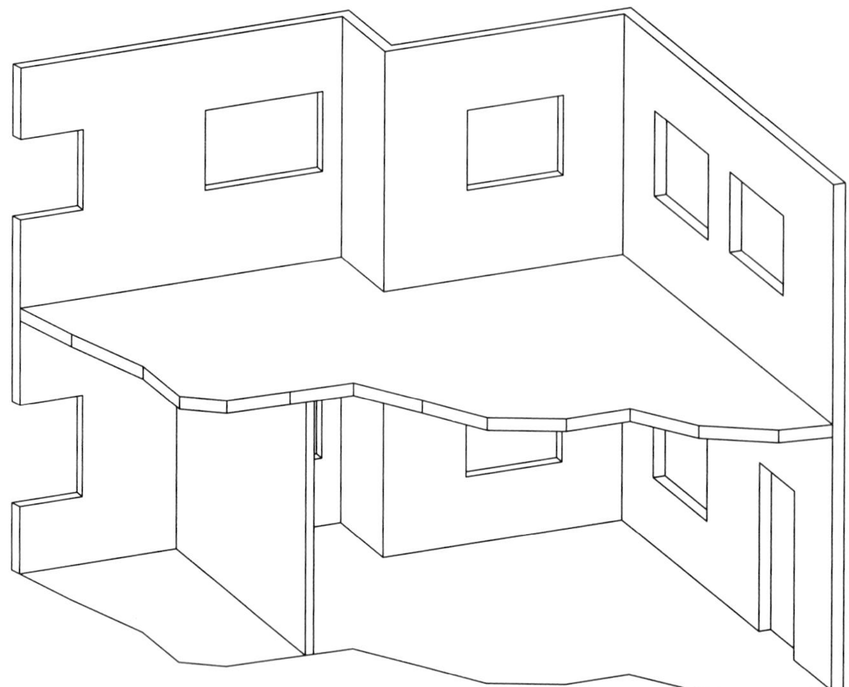

Figure 5-183 Partial model of a building contained in the drawing file

You will start the project by installing the stair pole. Then you will add the treads, the posts, and the handrail. You will also need to modify the top slab and add the railing on the second floor.

During this project you will not be asked to use the **3DORBIT** or the **HIDE** command. You should constantly use these commands, however, to obtain a clearer view.

1. **OPEN** ***Tutorial 5-3*** from the CD and **SAVE** it **AS** ***Tutorial 5-3 solved*** on your computer
2. Draw the two circles (**4″** diameter and **2′-8″** radius), as shown in Figure 5-184.

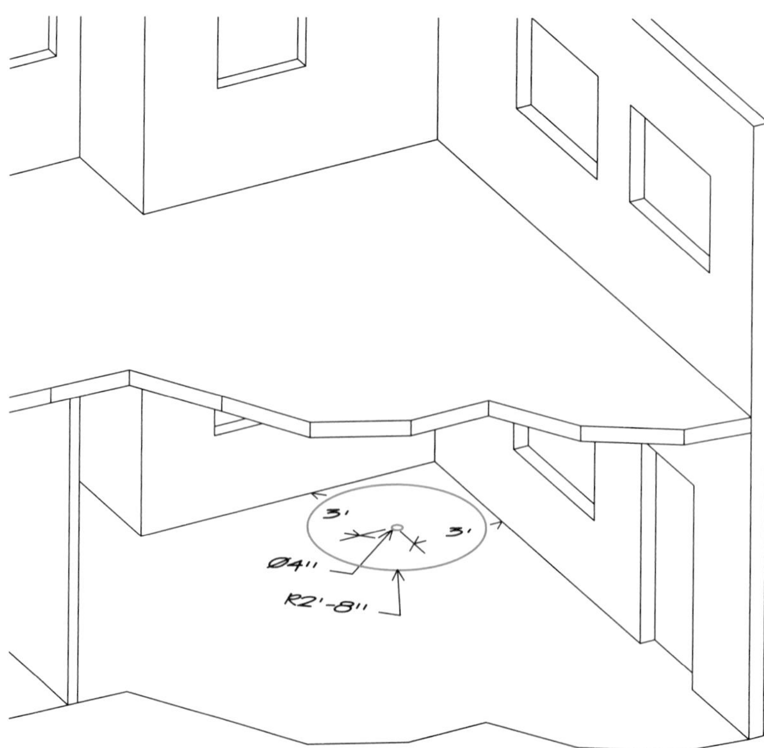

Figure 5-184 Dimensions and location of the circles

3. **EXTRUDE** the two circles **126″** upward.
4. **SUBTRACT** the bigger cylinder from the top slab (Figure 5-185).

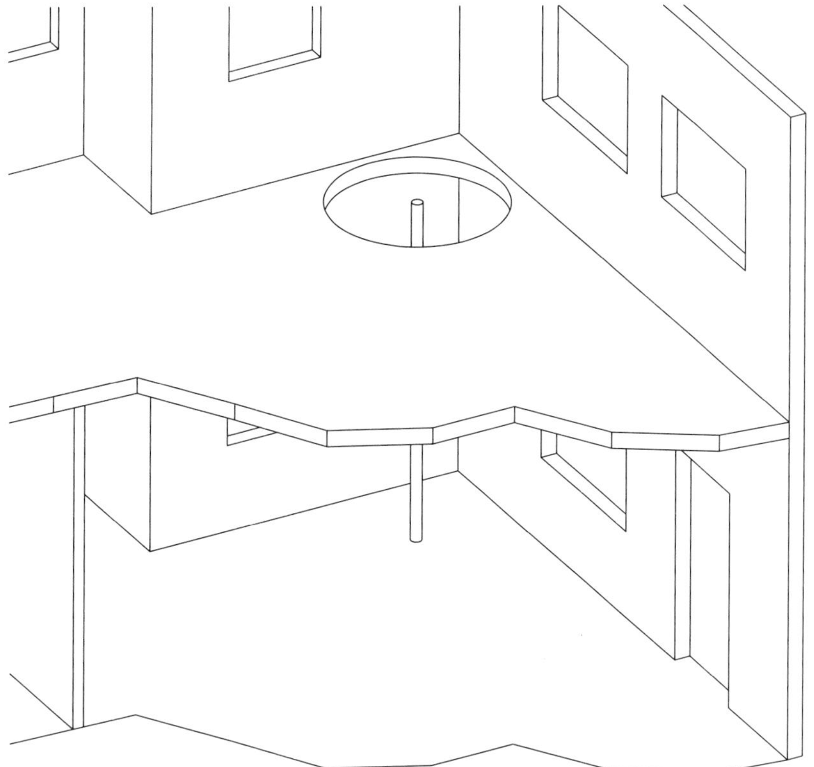

Figure 5-185 Hole opened in the slab by subtracting the cylinder and the stair pole

5. To create the tread, select the **Top** view. Then draw the profile and the circle shown in Figure 5-186 to the right of the 3D model.

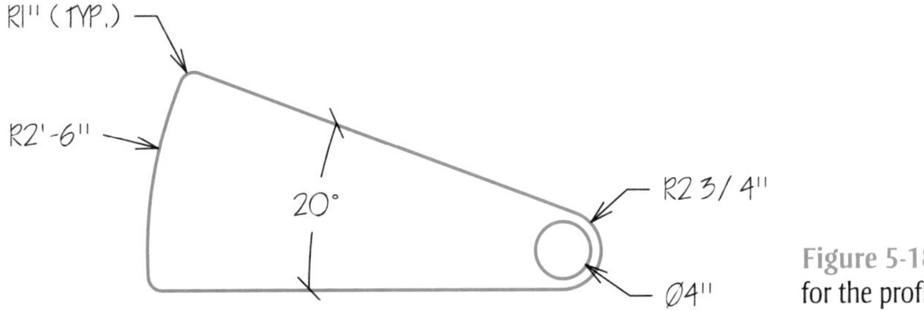

Figure 5-186 Dimensions for the profile

6. Select the **SE Isometric** viewing point and **ZOOM** into the objects you just drew.
7. Using the **REGION** command, convert the objects into two regions. Afterward **EXTRUDE** both regions **1″**.
8. **SUBTRACT** the cylinder from the outer 3D solid to create a hole. The resulting 3D solid should look like Figure 5-187 with the **Realistic** visual style selected.
9. To finish the tread, you will place a piece of pipe on the bottom face. Select the **2D Wireframe** visual style. Draw the two circles in the bottom face of the tread, as shown in Figure 5-188.
10. Invoke the **REGION** command and turn the two circles into two regions. **SUBTRACT** the small circular region from the bigger one.

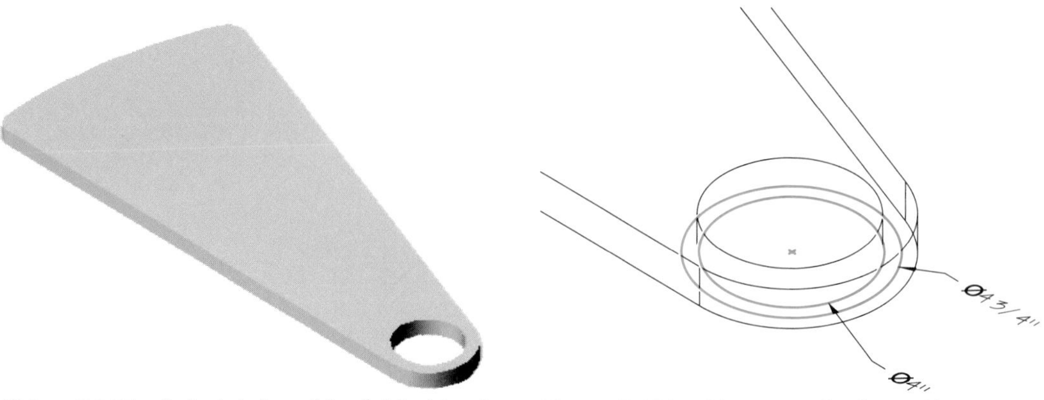

Figure 5-187 A shaded view of the finished tread

Figure 5-188 Dimensions for the profile

11. **EXTRUDE** the resulting regions **−6″** downward. The tread with the pipe should look like Figure 5-189 with the **Realistic** visual style selected.

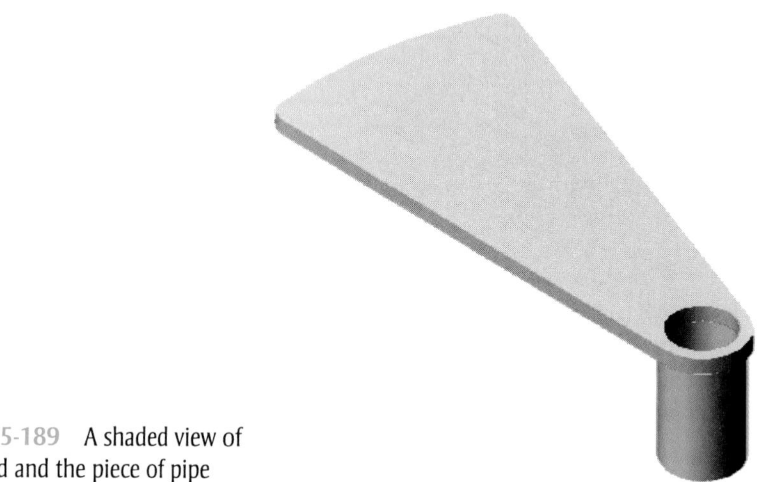

Figure 5-189 A shaded view of the tread and the piece of pipe

12. **MOVE** the two 3D solids (the tread with the tube) from the upper center point of the hole to the top center point of the pole.
13. **MOVE** the tread with the tube **7″** orthogonally along the negative direction of the *Z*-axis.
14. **COPY** the two 3D solids (the tread with the tube) **7″** down. The 3D model should look like Figure 5-190.

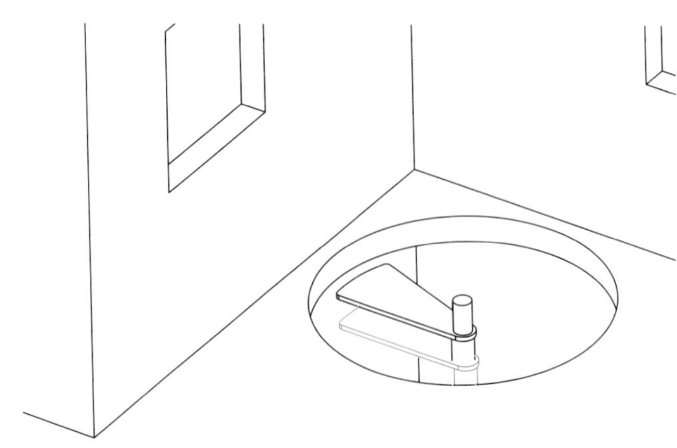

Figure 5-190 The first tread in place is copied down

15. Invoke the **ROTATE3D** command to rotate the copied tread. When prompted for the first point on the axis, specify the top-most center point on the pole. Specify another center point below it as the second point on the axis. Enter **28** for the rotation angle (Figure 5-191).

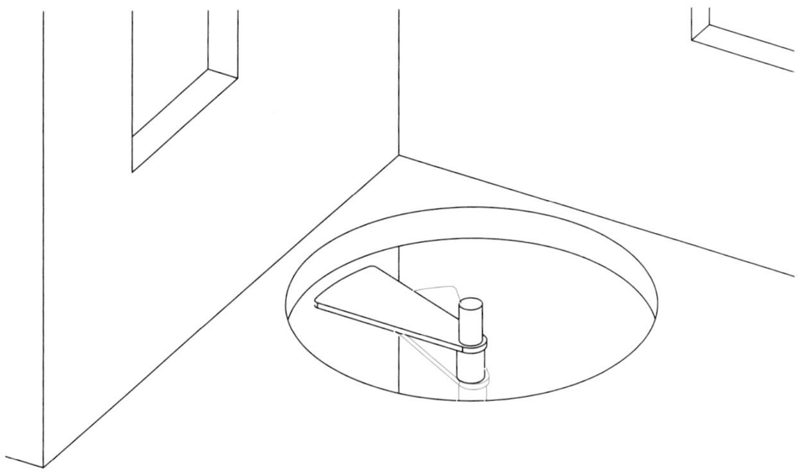

Figure 5-191 After rotating the copied tread

16. Repeat the last two steps until the tube of the last tread reaches the floor surface.
17. At this point, it is convenient to hide the walls and the top slab. To do so, create two new layers, named **Wall** and **Slab.** Specify different colors for them if you wish. Then assign each layer to the corresponding objects, and Freeze the two layers. The 3D model should look like Figure 5-192.

Note:
Next, you will draw the stair handrail. To create this 3D object you will perform a **SWEEP** operation along a helical path.

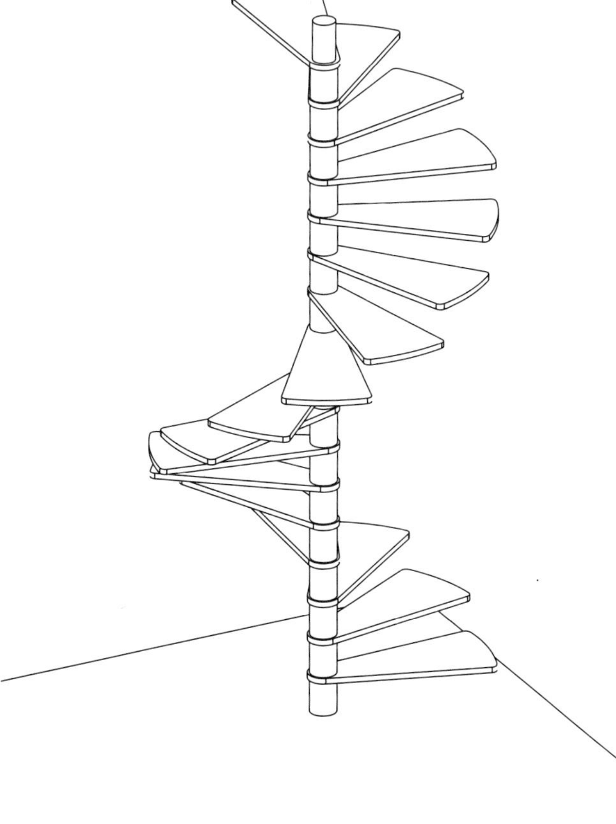

Figure 5-192 All the treads and pipes are created and located in the correct place

18. **COPY** one of the tubes on top of the last step also.
19. Make sure the **World** UCS is current and invoke the **HELIX** command and respond to the prompts as follows:

    Specify center point of base: *Snap to the center point of the bottom circular edge of the pole.*
    Specify base radius or [Diameter]: *29* ↵
    Specify top radius or [Diameter]: *29* ↵
    Specify helix height or [Axis endpoint/Turns/turn Height/tWist]: *h* ↵
    Specify distance between turns: *90* ↵
    Specify helix height or [Axis endpoint/Turns/turn Height/tWist]: *t* ↵
    Enter number of turns: *2* ↵

20. Invoke the **HIDE** command. The resulting helix should look like Figure 5-193.
21. Invoke the **REGEN** command and create a cylinder with a diameter of **3″** and a height of **50″**. Place the center point of its base on the endpoint of the helix (Figure 5-194).

Note:
The **Turn Height** is the key element needed to create the helix correctly. This value is obtained by analyzing a common point between two contiguous treads. From one point to another, the helix path must rotate 28° while rising 7″. This means that a complete turn (360°) will rise 360 × 7/28 = 90″ height. Two complete turns will create a helix long enough to reach the last tread. The handrail will be cut to fit in place later.

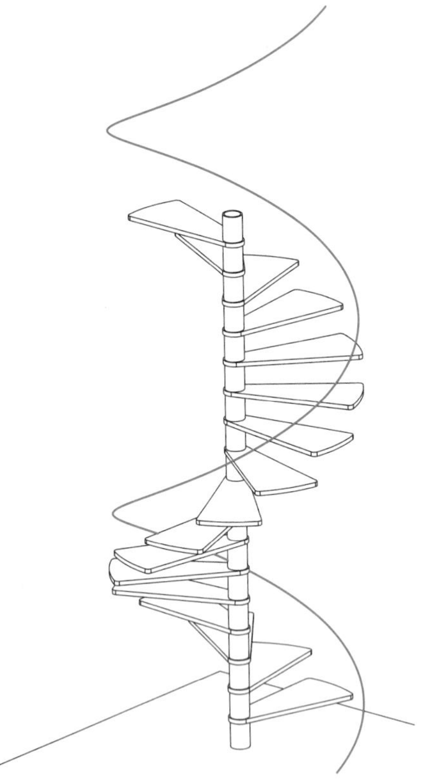

Figure 5-193 The resulting helix

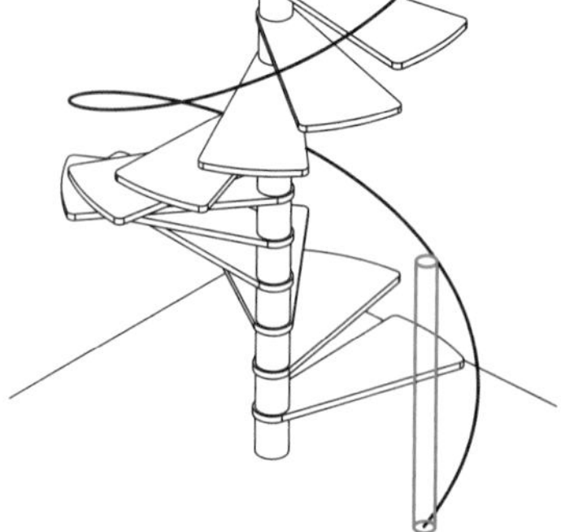
Figure 5-194 A cylinder is created

22. Draw a circle **1 ½″** in diameter next to the base of the cylinder.
23. Invoke the **SWEEP** command and sweep the circle along the helix.
24. **ERASE** the helix. The 3D model should look like Figure 5-195.
25. Select the **SE Isometric** viewing point.
26. With **ORTHO** mode on, **COPY** the 3″ cylinder **6″** orthogonally in the negative direction of the *Z*-axis.
27. **SUBTRACT** the copied cylinder from the swept handrail (Figure 5-196).

28. **ROTATE** the swept handrail and the **3″**-diameter cylinder (post) **66°** around any center point along the central pole.
29. **MOVE** the swept handrail **47″** orthogonally toward the positive direction of the Z-axis (Figure 5-197).

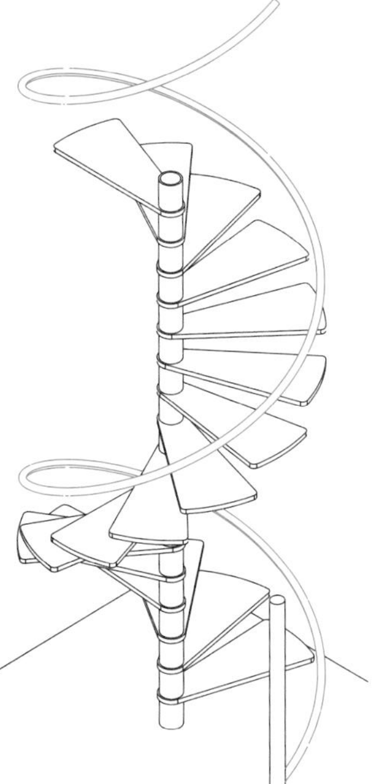

Figure 5-195 The swept handrail

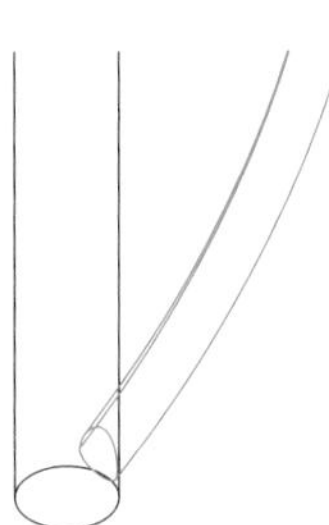

Figure 5-196 Trimming the handrail with a SUBTRACT operation

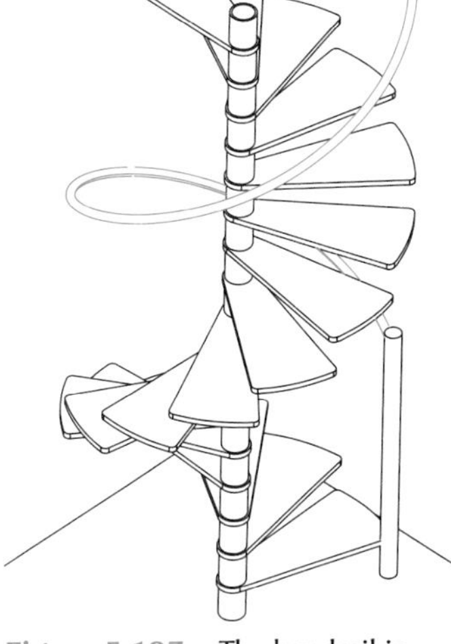

Figure 5-197 The handrail is moved up

30. Draw three **1″**-diameter circles on the top face of the topmost tread, as shown in Figure 5-198.
31. **EXTRUDE** the three circles up **60″** to create three round posts.
32. Duplicate the swept handrail by creating a **COPY** in place. You can do so by snapping to the same point when specifying the base point and second point.
33. **SUBTRACT** one of the spiral railings from the three round posts.
34. Invoke the **Separate** option of the **SOLIDEDIT** command to separate the now-combined 3D solid into six independent 3D solid objects. When prompted, simply select the combined posts. Press <**Esc**> to end the operation.

Note:

If you subtract from more than one 3D solid when performing a **SUBTRACT** operation, these 3D solids are automatically combined as if you were first performing a **UNION** operation with them.

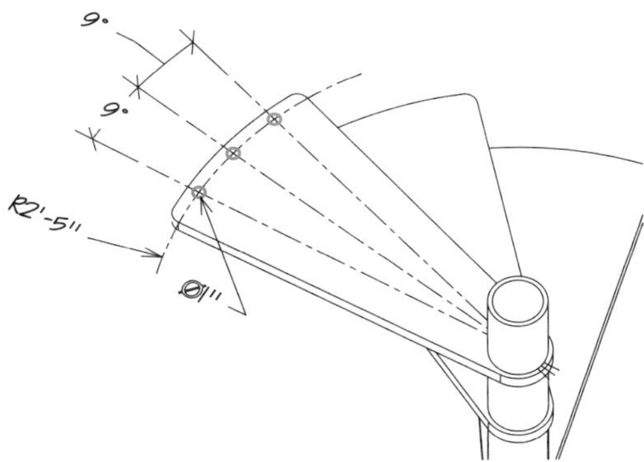

Figure 5-198 Dimensions to locate the circles in the top tread

SEPARATE	
Solid Editing Toolbar	
Ribbon Solid Editing panel	
Pull-down Menu	Modify/Solid Editing/Separate
Command Line	solidedit ← b ← p

FOR MORE DETAILS

See Chapter 6 for more information about the **SEPARATE** operation.

35. **ERASE** the three remaining portions of the posts above the railing. The 3D model should look like Figure 5-199.
36. Select the **Top** UCS if it is not set current.
37. **COPY** the three posts **7″** orthogonally down in the direction of the *Z*-axis.
38. Invoke the **ROTATE** command. Rotate the three new posts, copied **−28°** around any center point of the center post or pole of the stair. Use the **3D Orbit** tool as needed. The 3D model should look like Figure 5-200.

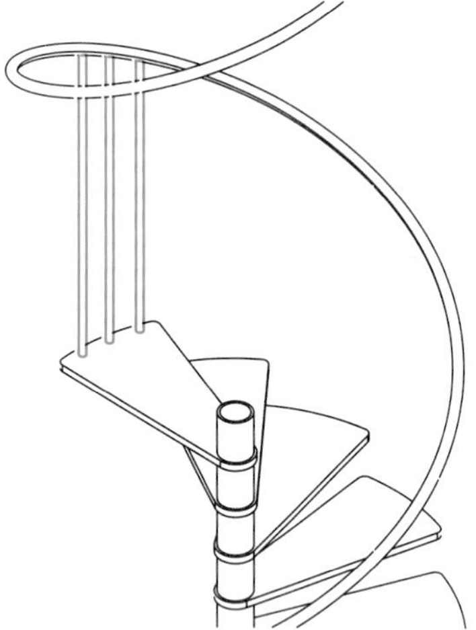

Figure 5-199 Trimming the three posts with a SUBTRACT operation

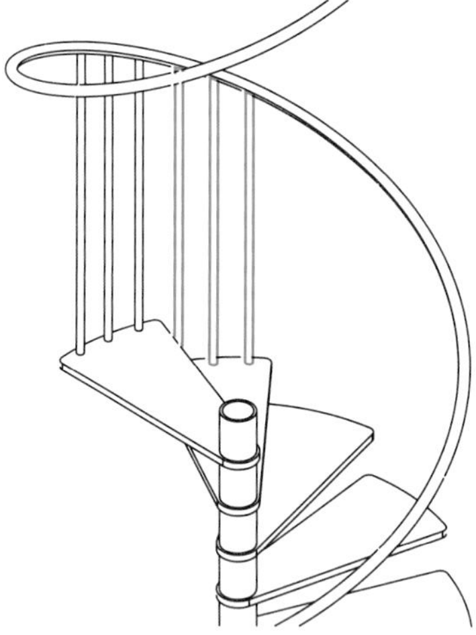

Figure 5-200 The three posts copied to the next tread

39. Repeat the previous two steps until you have placed three posts on all of the treads. Use the **3DORBIT** command as needed. When you are finished, the 3D model should look like Figure 5-201.

Selecting the **Realistic** visual style before placing the three posts on the treads will give you a better understanding of the operation.

40. Thaw the **Wall** and **Slab** layers.
41. Now, you will create the top board. Select the **Top** view. In an empty spot, draw the objects shown in Figure 5-202.
42. When you are finished, convert the objects into two regions (the outer profile and the circular region).
43. **SUBTRACT** the circular region from the outer profile to create a hole in it.
44. Select the **SW Isometric** viewing point and **EXTRUDE** the resulting region **1″**.
45. **MOVE** the top board to the stair so it sits on top of the last cylinder you placed (Figure 5-203).

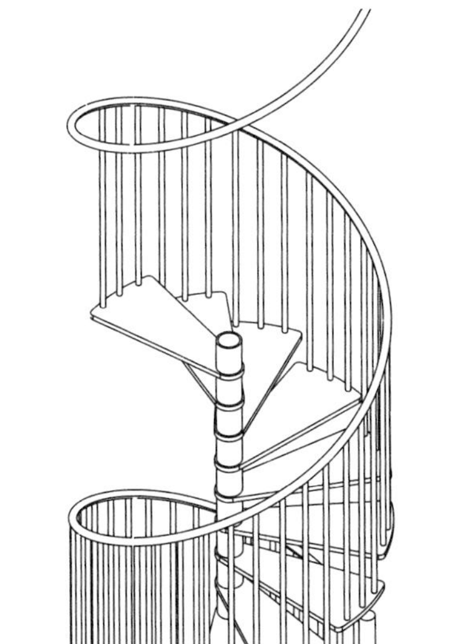

Figure 5-201 After placing the three posts on all the treads

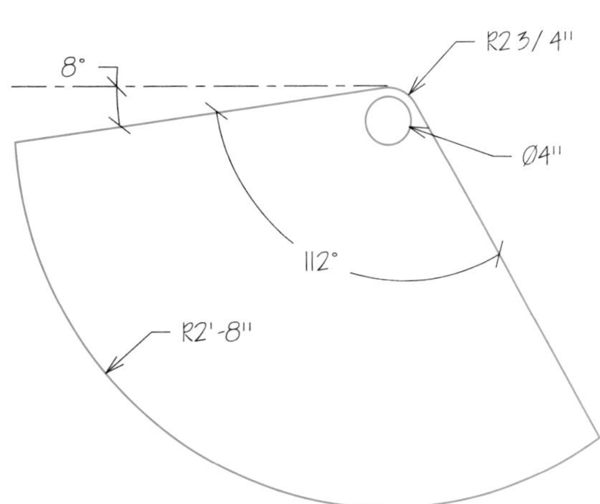

Figure 5-202 The top board profile

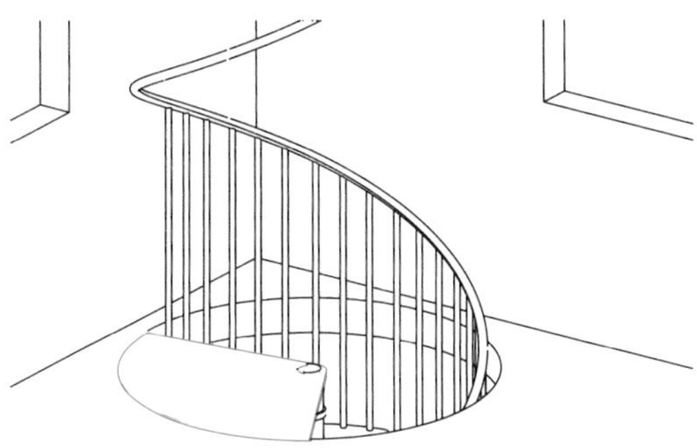

Figure 5-203 The top board moved to its location

46. Draw the four **3″**-diameter circles, as shown in Figure 5-204. The centerlines shown going through two of the circles should be parallel to the edges of the top board.

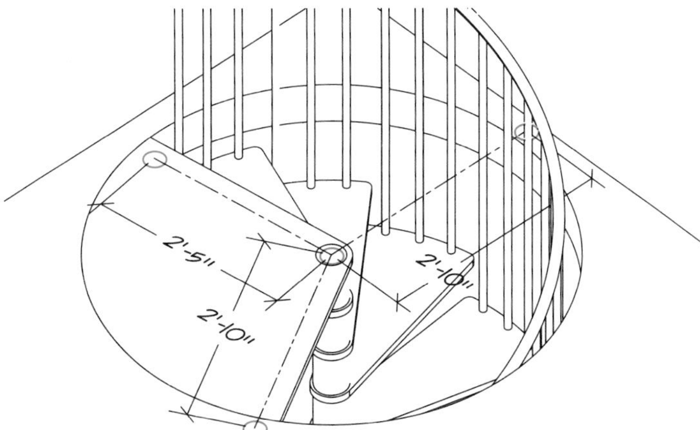

Figure 5-204 Dimensions to locate the three circles highlighted

You can align the UCS with the edge of the board in order to copy the circle parallel to it.

47. **EXTRUDE** the four circles up **42″** to create the four posts.
48. Create an in-place **COPY** of the **3″** post that connects to the handrail in order to duplicate it.
49. **SUBTRACT** one of the duplicate posts from the swept handrail.
50. Invoke the **SEPARATE** command to make the two portions of the handrail independent.
51. **ERASE** the remaining portion of the handrail (Figure 5-205).

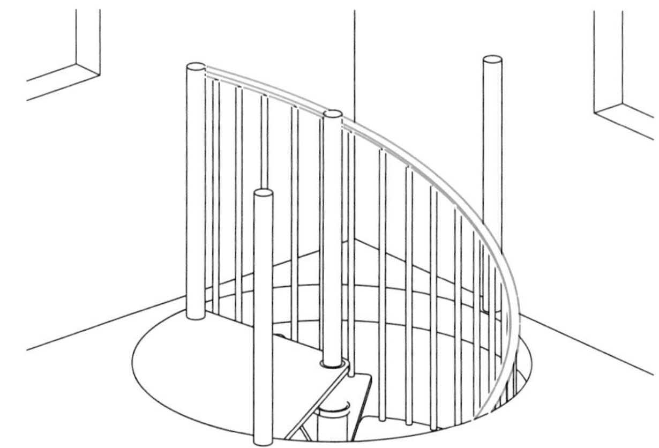

Figure 5-205 Trimming the handrail with a SUBTRACT operation

52. Use the **CYLINDER** command to create a **1½″**-diameter cylinder. Locate the center point of the base in one of the center points on the circular top edge of the posts. Use the **Axis endpoint** option and select the center point on the circular top edge of the other post (Figure 5-206).
53. Draw the arc shown in Figure 5-207 using the **Center, Start, End** method. Center it on the stair between the center points of the top circular edges of the posts.
54. Draw a **1½″**-diameter circle close to the arc.
55. **SWEEP** the circle along the arc.

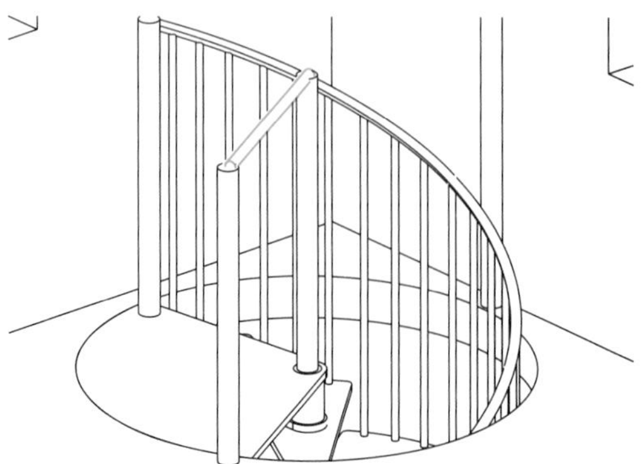

Figure 5-206 Adding a straight cylindrical handrail

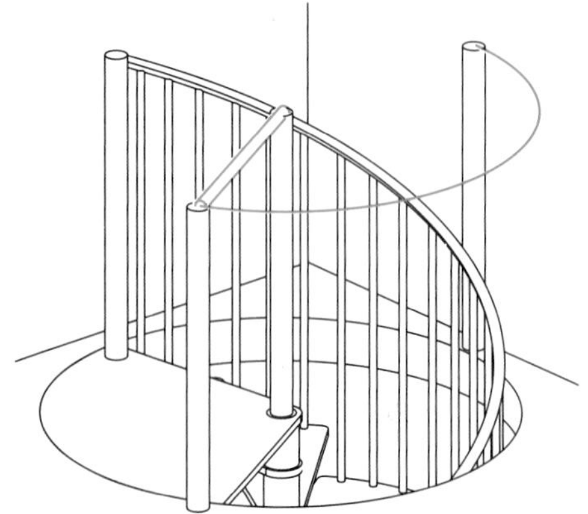

Figure 5-207 Arc created in place

56. **MOVE** the last cylinder created and the swept 3D solid **1″** down orthogonally, along the negative direction of the *Z*-axis (Figure 5-208).
57. **MOVE** the arc **42″** down orthogonally.
58. Invoke the **DDPTYPE** command and select the point style shown in Figure 5-209. Click **OK** to close the **Point Style** window.

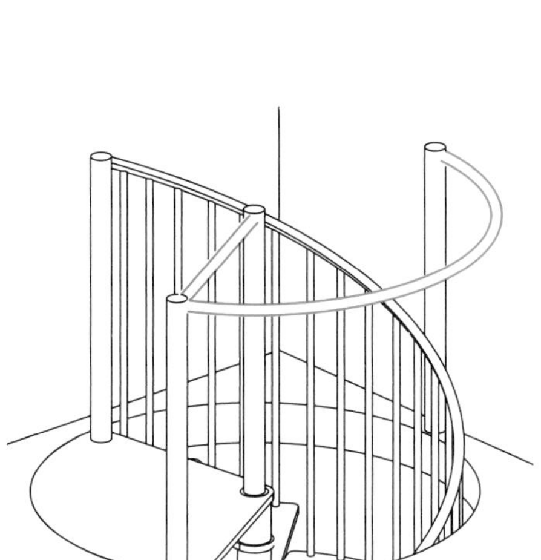

Figure 5-208 The handrail swept along the arc

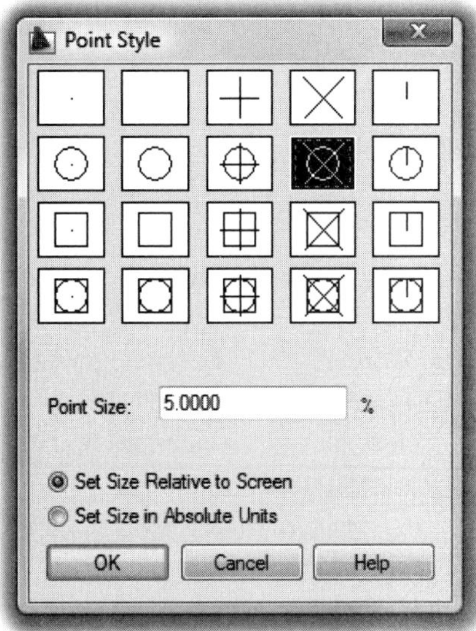

Figure 5-209 The Point Style window

59. Draw a polyline between the center points of the bottom edges of the posts located in the middle of the stair and the post receiving the two handrails.
60. Invoke the **DIVIDE** command. Select the polyline when prompted and divide it into **7** segments. Points are placed to indicate the divisions. Repeat the operation and divide the arc into **17** segments. The results of these operations are shown in Figure 5-210.

Note:
To create the remaining posts that connect to the handrails, follow the next steps.

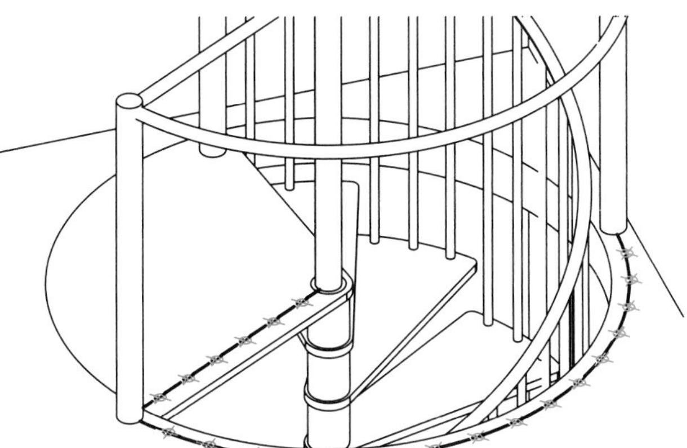

Figure 5-210 Points placed by the DIVIDE command

61. Create a cylinder **1″** in diameter and **41″** in length, placing the base's center point on any of the point entities.
62. **COPY** the cylinder from the center point of its base to each of the other points.
63. Create a duplicate of the handrail with the **COPY** command.
64. **SUBTRACT** the copy of the handrail from all the **1″**-diameter posts on the second floor.

Note:
You can set the Object Snap to snap only to nodes (points) in the **Drafting Settings** dialog box to make this operation easier.

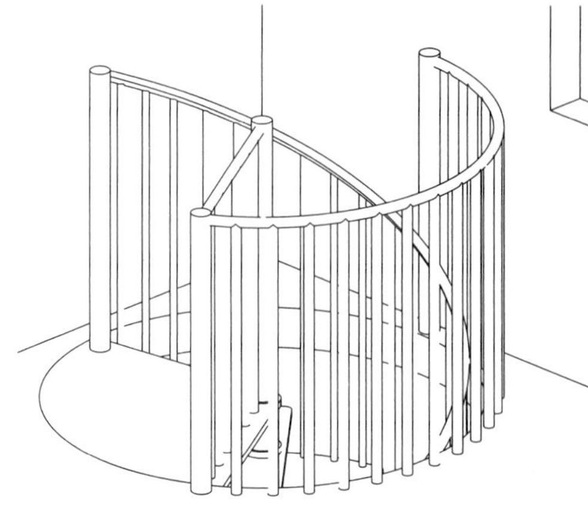

Figure 5-211 The finished top of the stairs

65. **ERASE** the arc, the polyline, and all the points. The top of the stairs should look like Figure 5-211.
66. Set the **PERSPECTIVE** system variable to **1** to select a perspective view.
67. Change the color of the elements of the stairs as you wish.
68. Invoke the **3DORBIT** to select a different viewing point.
69. Select the **Realistic** visual style. The 3D model should look like Figure 5-212.
70. **SAVE** the drawing.

Figure 5-212 A shaded perspective view of the spiral staircase

Tutorial 5-4: Design of a Valve in Metric Units

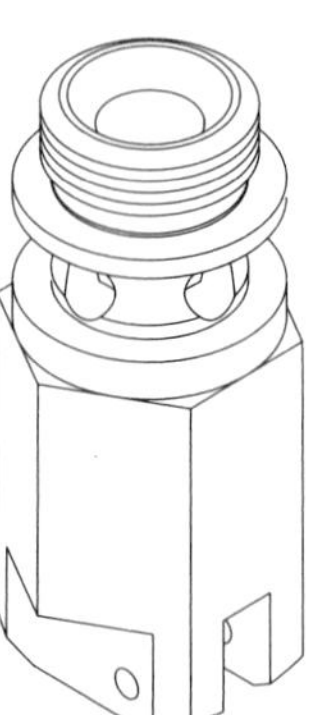

Figure 5-213 This valve will be developed in metric units

In this tutorial, you will develop the main part of a valve shown in Figure 5-213. This type of component is typically manufactured out of a hexagonal bar using lathe, mill, and drill operations. Pay special

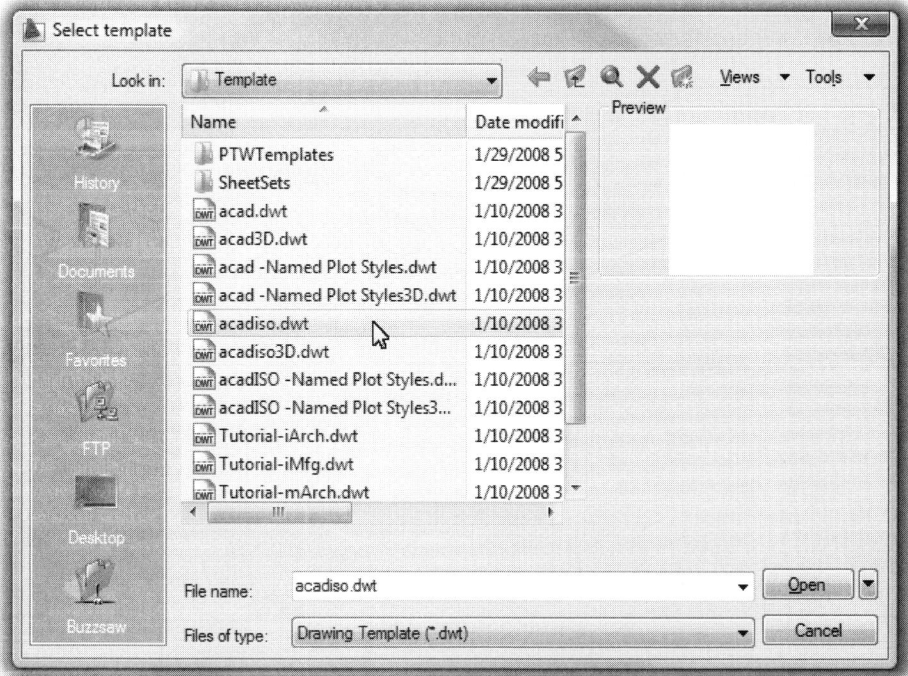

Figure 5-214 The Create New Drawing dialog box

attention to the procedure by which the 3D solid model is developed. It has been prepared in a way that can be compared to the actual manufacturing process of the part.

This tutorial has also been prepared in metric units. This will give you practice in using the International Standards Organization (ISO) system of measurement.

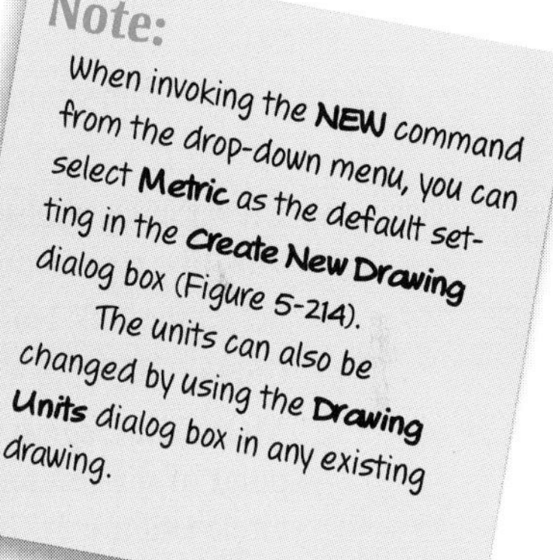

Note:
When invoking the NEW command from the drop-down menu, you can select Metric as the default setting in the Create New Drawing dialog box (Figure 5-214).
The units can also be changed by using the Drawing Units dialog box in any existing drawing.

1. Start a **NEW** drawing, using the **acadiso** template (Figure 5-214).
2. Change the **DISPSILH** system variable to **1**. Change the **ISOLINES** system variable to **0**. Change the value of the **FACETRES** system variable to **5**.
3. **SAVE** the drawing and specify ***Tutorial 5-4*** as the file name.
4. To start the 3D model, draw a **25**-mm-diameter circle and a six-sided **POLYGON** circumscribed in it (Figure 5-215).
5. Select the **SW Isometric** viewing point.
6. **EXTRUDE** the polyline up **60** mm (Figure 5-216).
7. Select the **Front** view. The **Front** UCS should be activated automatically.
8. Draw the profile shown in Figure 5-217 next to the 3D solid.

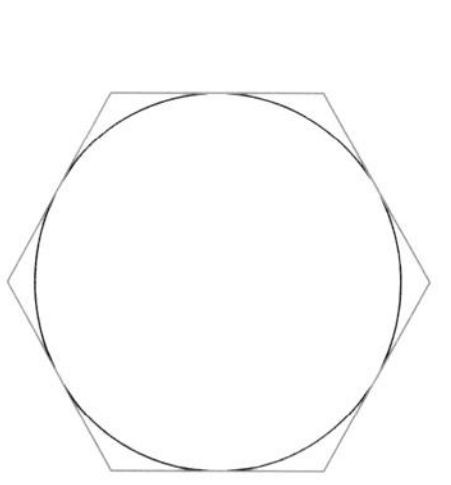

Figure 5-215 A circle with a circumscribed polygon

Figure 5-216 The extruded polygon

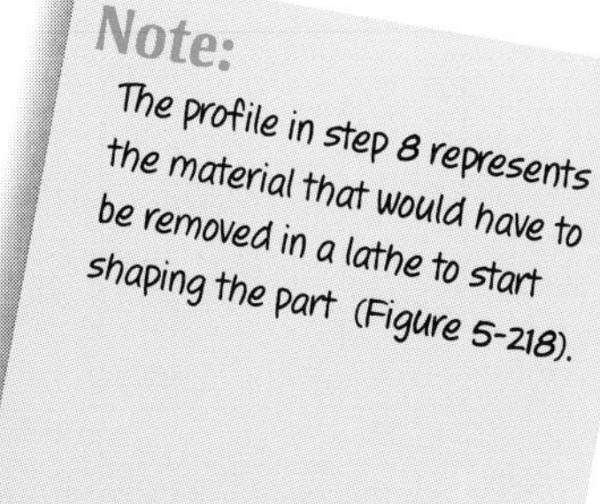

Note:
The profile in step 8 represents the material that would have to be removed in a lathe to start shaping the part (Figure 5-218).

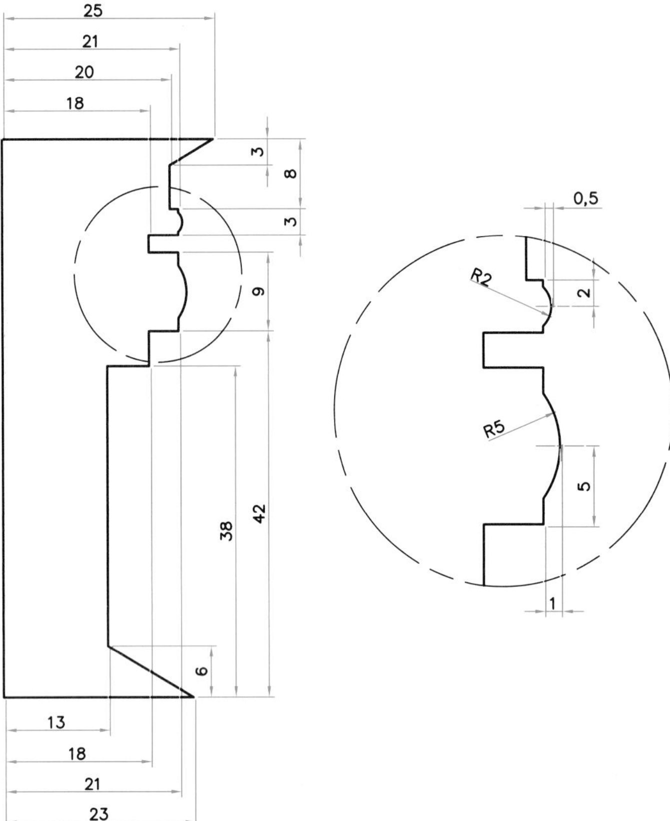

Figure 5-217 Dimensions for the profile

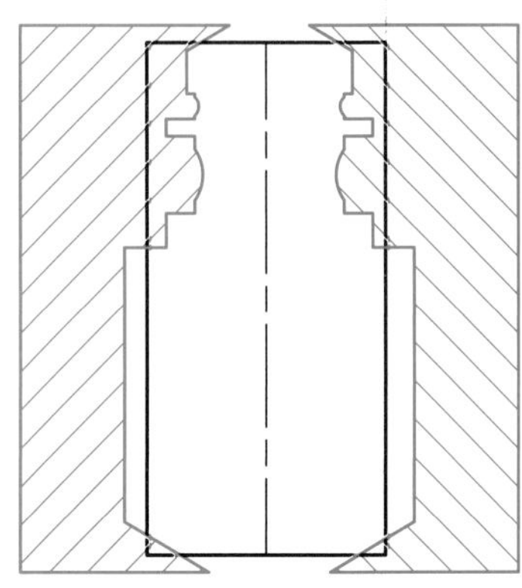
Figure 5-218 The profile shape is the section of the volume that will be removed from the 3D solid

9. Draw the highlighted reference line, as shown in Figure 5-219. This line represents the main axis of the object.
10. Select the **SW Isometric** viewing point.
11. Convert the objects into a region.
12. **MOVE** the region and the reference line from the bottom endpoint of the reference line to the center point of the reference circle (Figure 5-220).
13. **REVOLVE** the region, using the top and bottom endpoints of the reference line to specify the start and end points of the

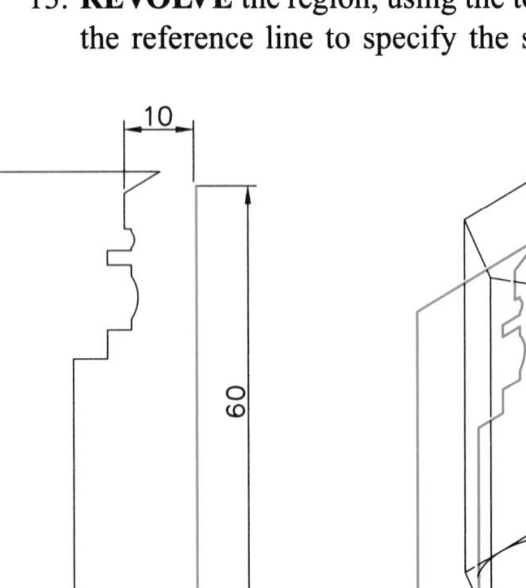

Figure 5-219 Dimensions for the reference line

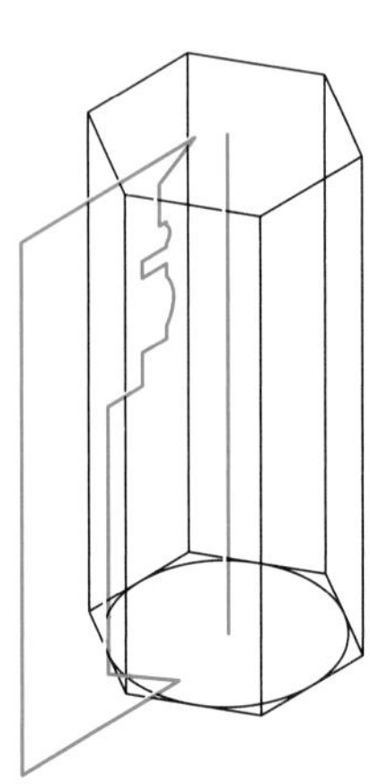
Figure 5-220 The region and the reference line are moved to the extruded bar

axis of revolution. Accept **360** as the angle of revolution (Figure 5-221).

14. **SUBTRACT** the revolved 3D solid from the extruded hexagonal bar.
15. **ERASE** both the reference line and the reference circle.
16. Invoke the **HIDE** command to check the new shape of the 3D solid. The result should look like Figure 5-222.

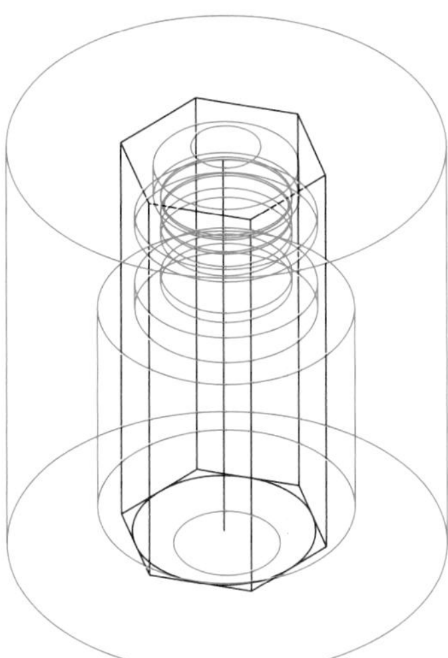

Figure 5-221 The profile is revolved, generating a revolved 3D solid

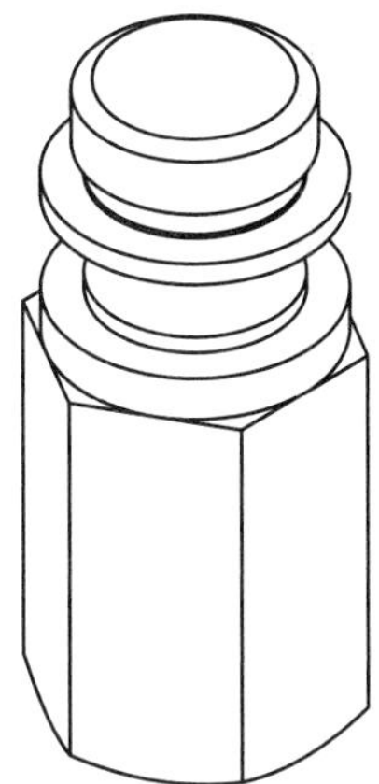

Figure 5-222 The 3D solid model is shaped by subtracting the revolved 3D solid

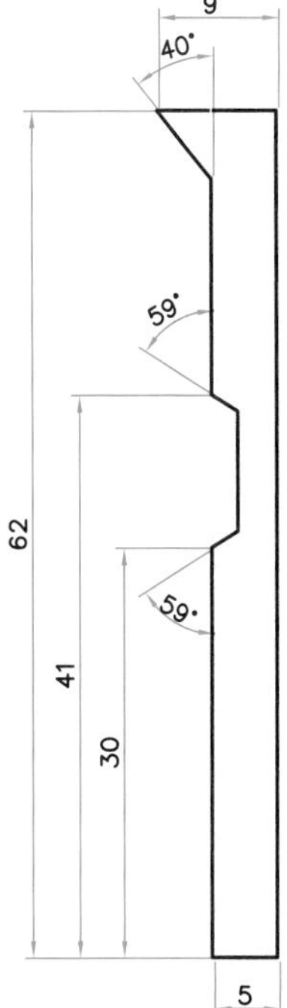

Figure 5-223 Dimensions for the profile

17. Select the **Front** view and draw the profile shown in Figure 5-223. This second profile will be used to create the 3D solid that will remove the material in the center of the object.
18. Select the **SW Isometric** viewing point.
19. Convert the profile into a region.
20. **MOVE** the region from its rightmost bottom endpoint to the center point of the bottom face (Figure 5-224).
21. **REVOLVE** the region **360°**, using any two center points on the 3D solid hexagonal bar to specify the start and end points of the axis of revolution.
22. **SUBTRACT** the new 3D solid from the hexagonal bar. The volume is removed from the part (Figure 5-225).
23. Select the **Front** view.
24. Draw the profile shown in Figure 5-226.
25. Select the **SW Isometric** viewing point.
26. Convert the profile into a region and then **EXTRUDE** the region **40** mm.
27. Draw a reference line diagonally on the top face, as shown in Figure 5-227, with the hidden lines removed.
28. **MOVE** the extruded 3D solid from the midpoint of the reference line to the center point of the bottom of the 3D solid.

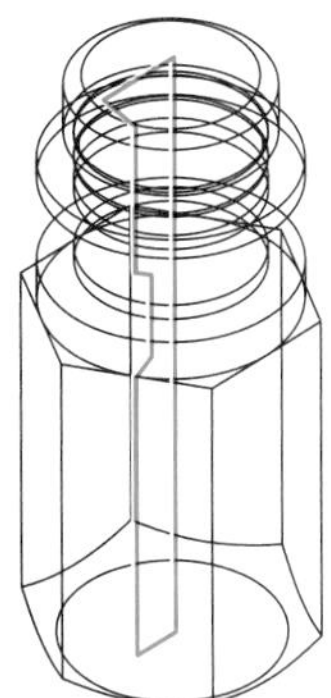

Figure 5-224 The region is moved to the 3D solid

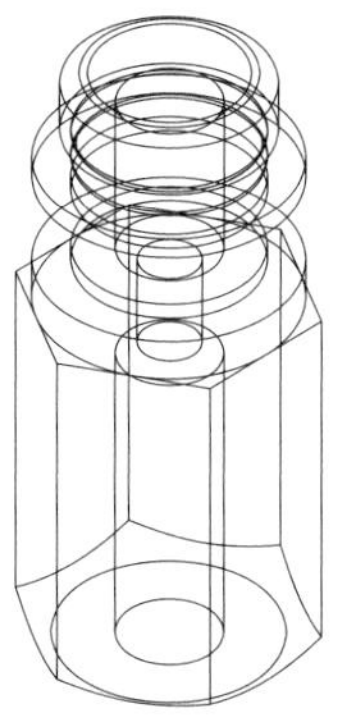

Figure 5-225 The region is revolved and subtracted from the 3D solid, shaping the inside cavity

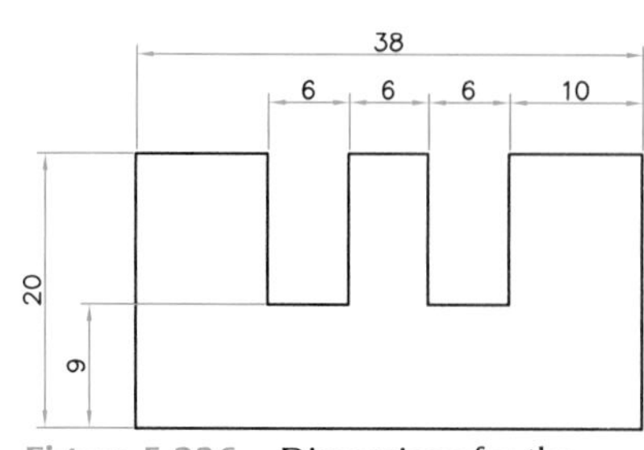

Figure 5-226 Dimensions for the profile

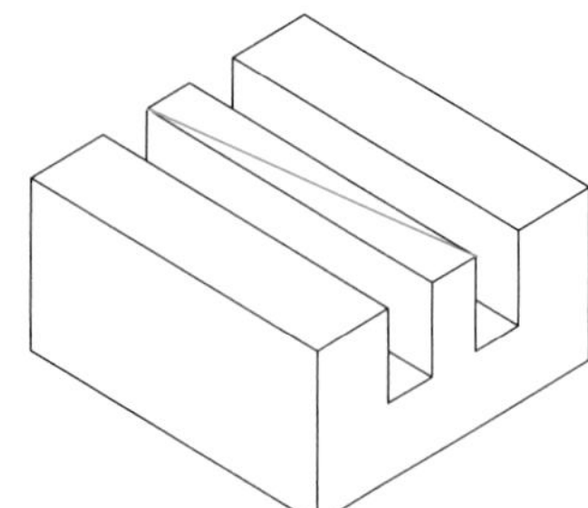

Figure 5-227 The extruded profile

29. **ERASE** the reference line.
30. With **ORTHO** mode on, **MOVE** the extruded 3D solid again **11** mm upward.
31. **SUBTRACT** the 3D solid from the hexagonal bar. The 3D solid model should now look like Figure 5-228.
32. Make sure the **Front** UCS is the current one and draw a **6**-mm-diameter circle with its center located on the topmost center point of the 3D solid. Figure 5-229 shows the result with the occulted lines removed.
33. **EXTRUDE** the circle **−20** mm.

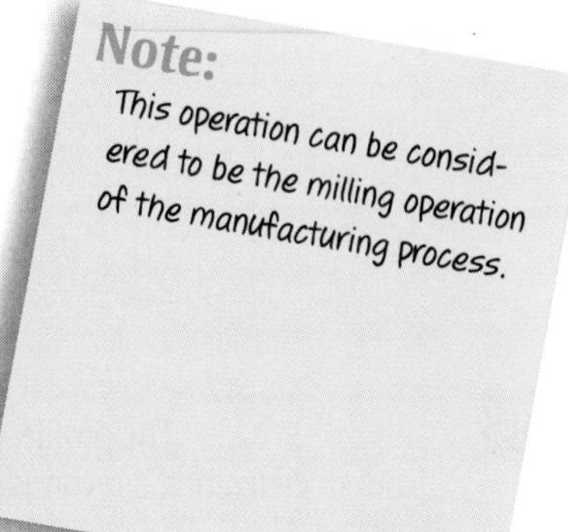

Note:
This operation can be considered to be the milling operation of the manufacturing process.

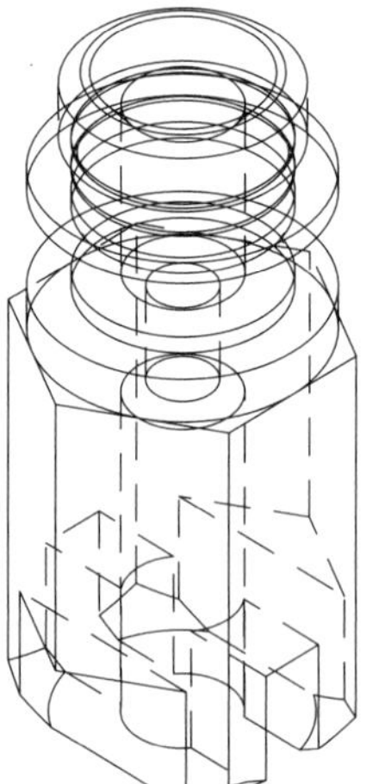

Figure 5-228 The new extruded 3D solid is subtracted from the 3D solid model

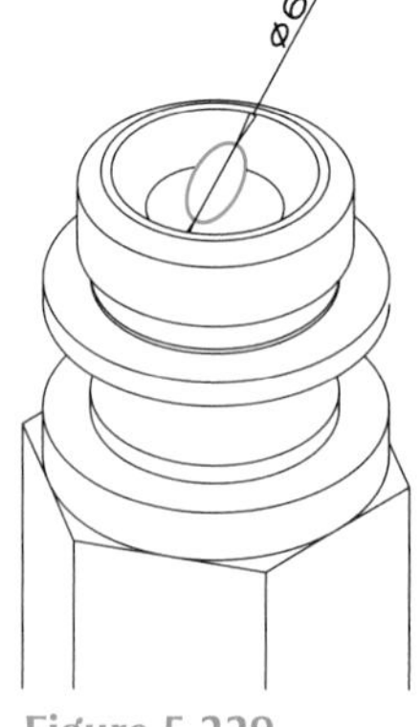

Figure 5-229 Dimensions and location of the circle

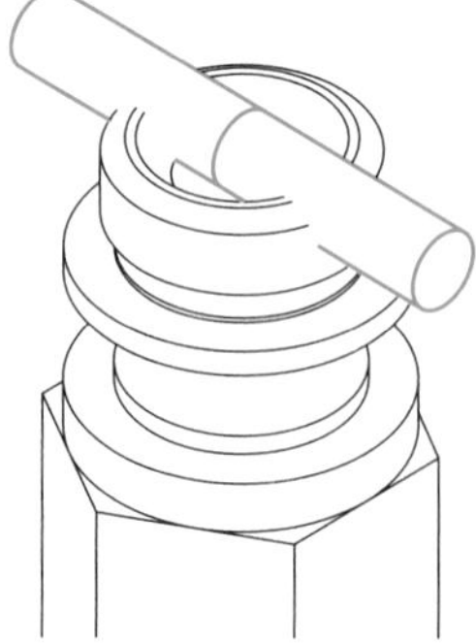

Figure 5-230 The two cylinders next to each other

34. **COPY** the cylinder from the center point of its front face to the center point of its back face (Figure 5-230).
35. **COPY** the two cylinders in the same place in order to duplicate them.

TIP You **COPY** a 3D solid over to duplicate it by simply specifying both the base point and the second point as the same.

36. Select the **Top** UCS.
37. **ROTATE** one of the duplicate cylinders **90°**. The result should look like Figure 5-231.
38. Select the **Left** UCS.
39. Use the **CYLINDER** command to create a **3**-mm-diameter cylinder. Select the midpoint of the bottom leftmost edge when prompted for the center point of the base of the cylinder and enter **–30** for the height (Figure 5-232).
40. **MOVE** the last cylinder up **4** mm orthogonally, then move it **6** mm along the positive direction of the *X*-axis (Figure 5-233).
41. **MOVE** the **(4)** cylinders on top **15.5** mm down orthogonally.
42. **SUBTRACT** the **(5)** cylinders from the 3D solid model.
43. Invoke the **HIDE** command. The 3D model should look like Figure 5-234.

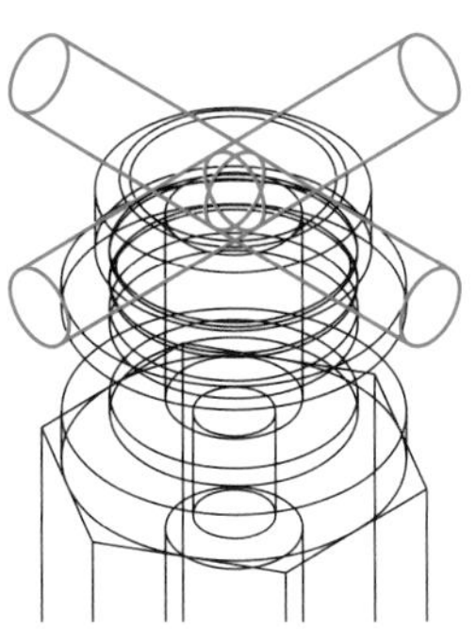

Figure 5-231 The four cylinders intersecting the 3D solid model

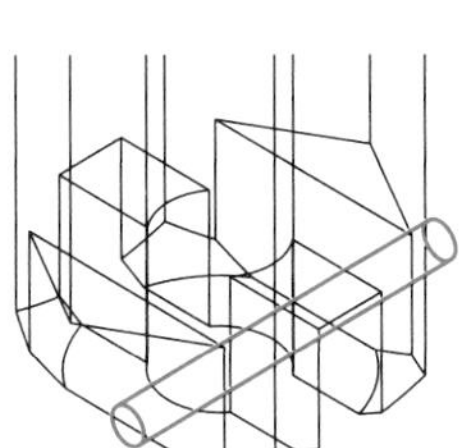

Figure 5-232 A new cylinder based on the bottom midpoint

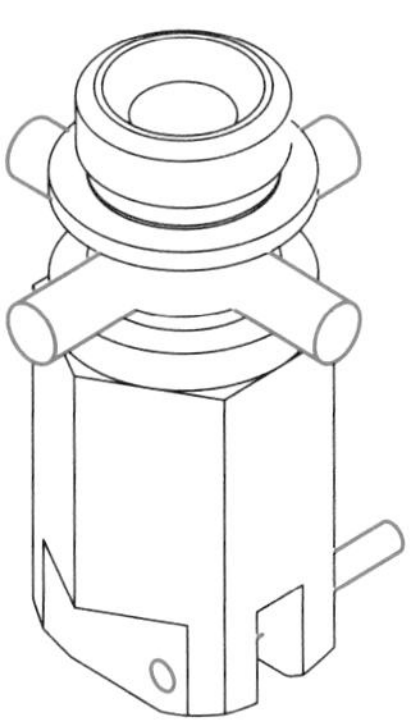

Figure 5-233 After moving the new cylinder

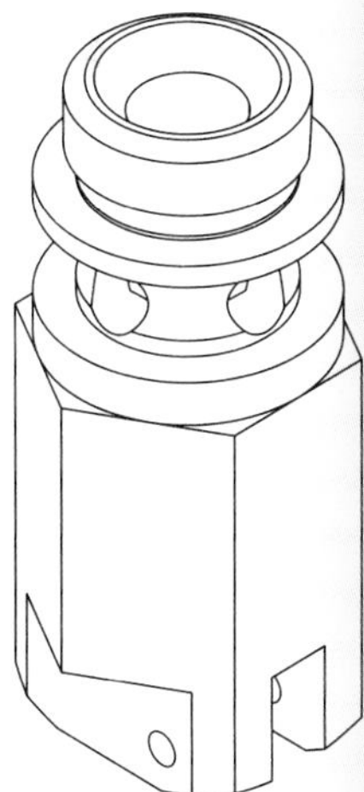

Figure 5-234 All cylinders are subtracted to generate the holes

44. To create the threads effect, you will simply create a set of triangular rings and subtract them from the 3D solid. Select the **Front** view and draw the profile shown in Figure 5-235.
45. Convert the profile into a region.
46. **MOVE** the region from the topmost left endpoint to the topmost right quadrant point on the 3D solid. The result should look like Figure 5-236.
47. Select the **SW Isometric** viewing point.
48. **REVOLVE** the region **360°**. Snap to the two topmost center points of the 3D solid to specify the axis of revolution.
49. **SUBTRACT** the threads from the 3D solid model.
50. **ZOOM** out to see the entire 3D model.
51. Select the **Realistic** visual style. The 3D model should look like Figure 5-237.
52. **SAVE** the drawing.

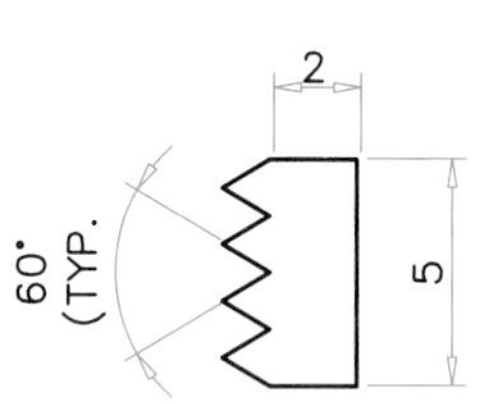

Figure 5-235 Dimensions for the thread profile

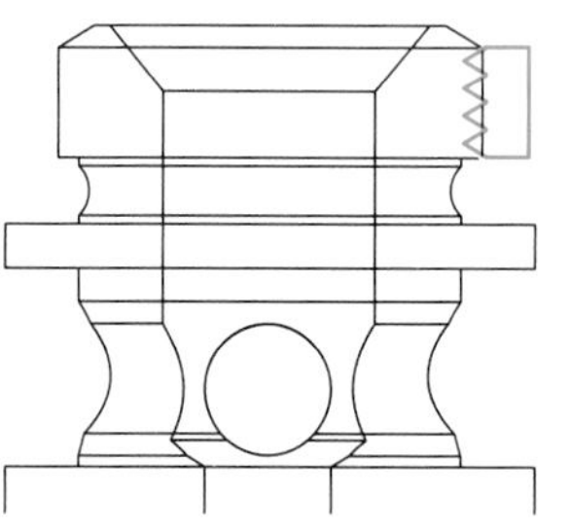
Figure 5-236 Thread profile moved to the 3D solid model

Figure 5-237 Shaded view of the final 3D model

Chapter Projects

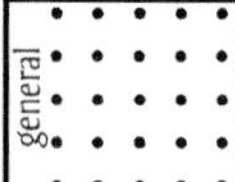

Project 5-1: Modeling a 3D Solid Part

Create the 3D solid model shown in Figure 5-238. Place the **6 × 4** face on the *XY* plane of the **World** UCS.

Hints for the Project

Create a 3D solid box, and then **SUBTRACT** two cylinders to open the holes. Finally, create a surface and slice the 3D solid with it to obtain the top shape.

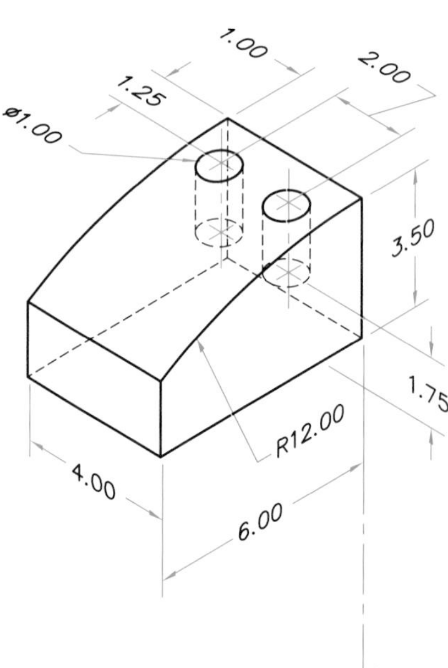

Figure 5-238 Dimensions for the solid part

Project 5-2: Designing a Turning Bracket

Start a **NEW** drawing in metric units and create the 3D solid model shown in Figure 5-239, as it is viewed from the **SW Isometric** viewing point on the left. Obtain the dimensions in millimeters from the 2D drawing in Figure 5-240. Save the drawing as ***Project 5-2.***

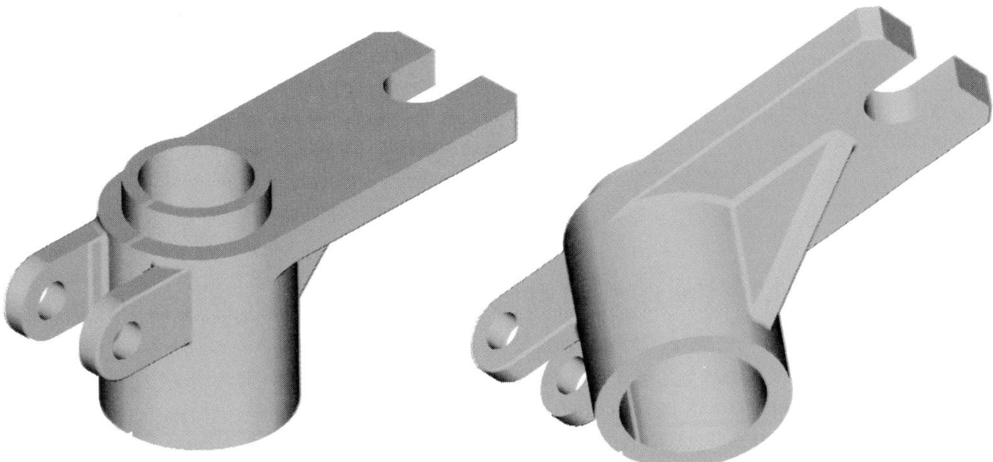

Figure 5-239 Shaded views of the final 3D model

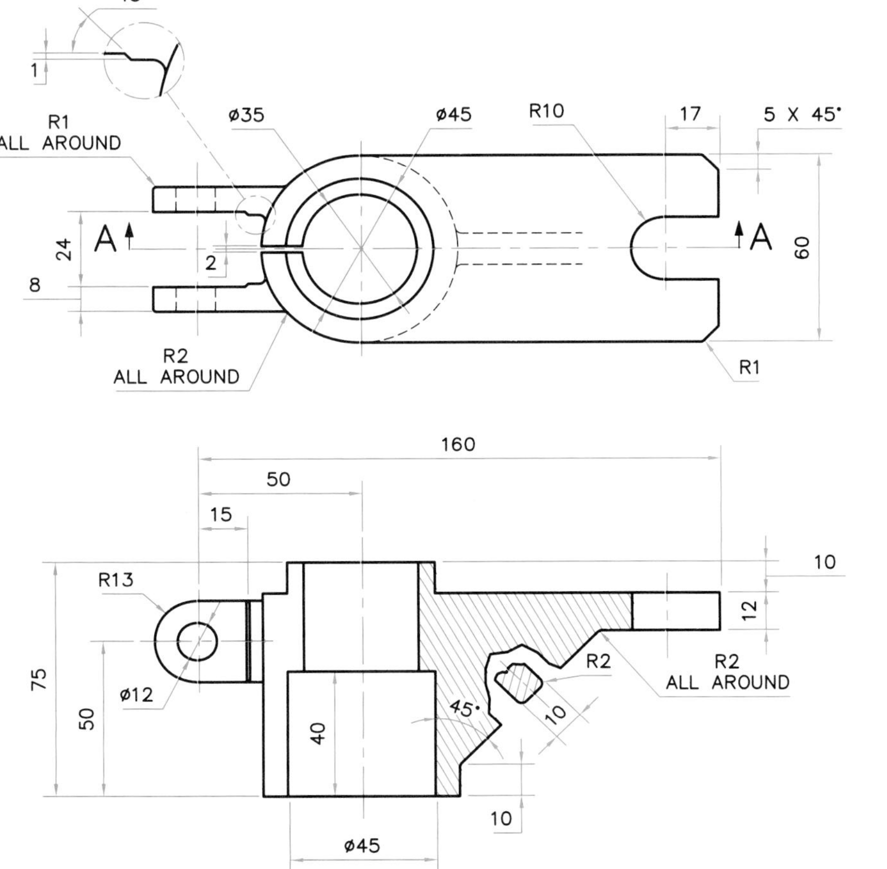

Figure 5-240 Dimensions for the turning bracket

Hints for the Project

Do not perform any filleting operation until all other faces of the 3D solid have been generated.

The order in which the fillets are created is important to achieve smooth, round edges. When creating corner fillets, first create the fillets that eliminate the sharp turns for other chain fillets, as shown in the example in Figure 5-241.

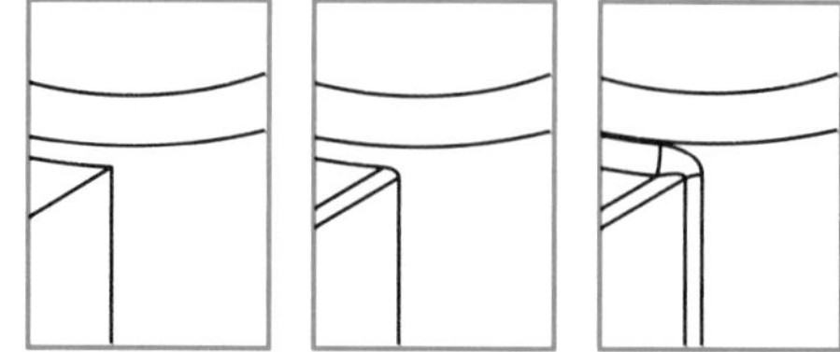

Figure 5-241 Hints for the FILLET operation

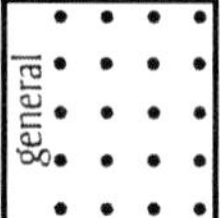

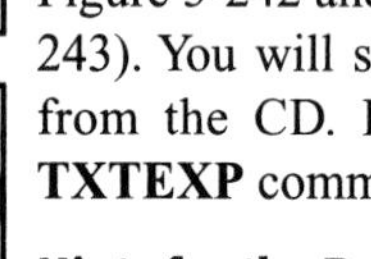

Project 5-3: Designing the 3D-CAD Emblem

In this project you will create a 3D emblem like the one shown in Figure 5-242 and place it in the door at the proper location (Figure 5-243). You will start the project by opening the drawing ***Project 5-3*** from the CD. It contains text that has been exploded with the **TXTEXP** command, and a section of a wall with a door.

Hints for the Project

The entire emblem can be a single 3D solid. The center of the exploded text can be found by creating four individual polylines. This will allow you to center the plate that will then be joined to the extruded text.

Note:

The **TXTEXP** command belongs to the group of Express Tools, which is installed only if you selected a **Full** installation of the AutoCAD software. The **TXTEXP** command explodes text into closed or open polylines, depending on the font of the selected text.

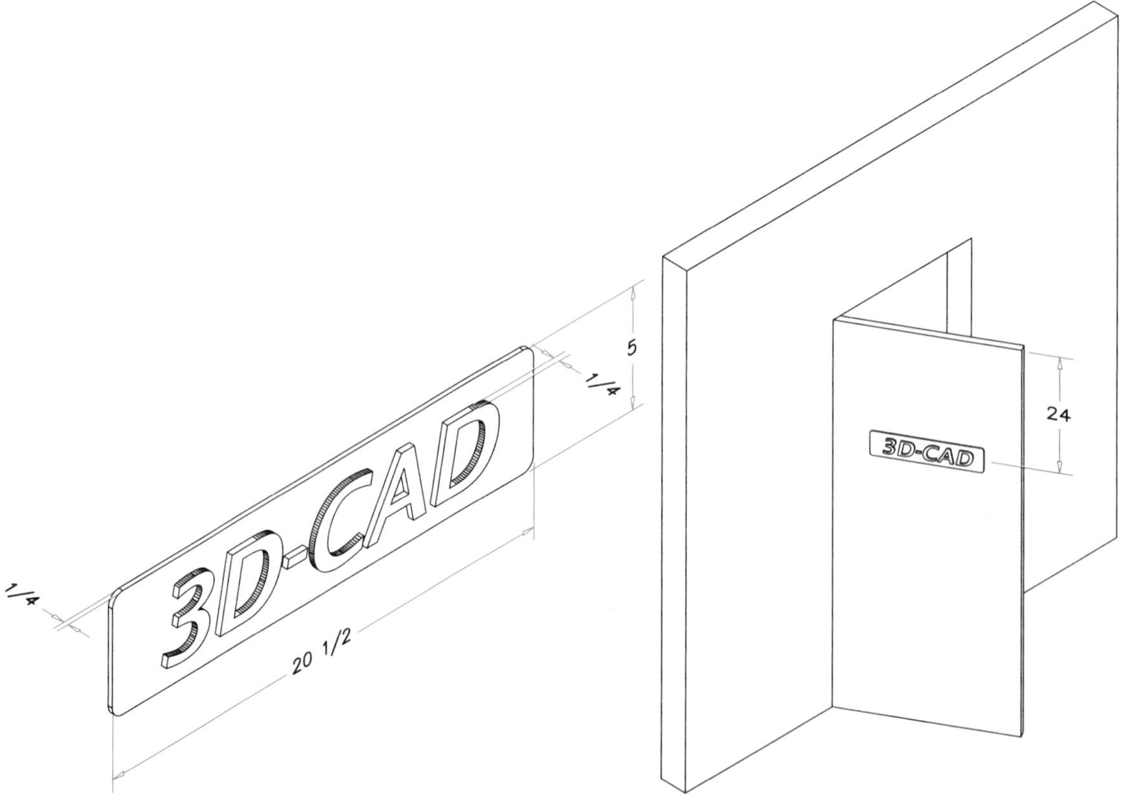

Figure 5-242 Dimensions for the emblem

Figure 5-243 Location of the emblem

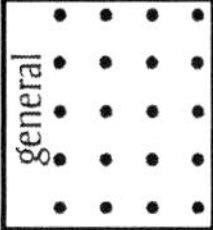

Project 5-4: 3D Solid Objects

Create the 3D solid models of the objects you previously created in Project 3-1, Project 3-2, and Project 3-3.

Hints for the Project

You can use some of the wireframe objects to create the 3D solids.

Project 5-5: Creating a Bolt 3D Model with Real Thread

OPEN the drawing ***Project 5-5*** from the CD. It contains the objects shown in Figure 5-244. You will use these objects to create the 3D model of the bolt with real thread shown in Figure 5-245.

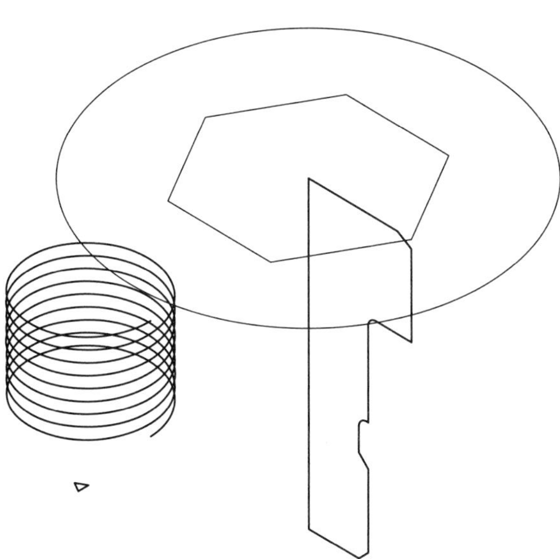

Figure 5-244 Objects contained in the drawing file

Figure 5-245 A shaded view of the final 3D model shows the bolt with a real thread

Hints for the Project

To create the thread, you can use the **Base point** option of the **SWEEP** command, and snap to the midpoint of the edge that is parallel to the *Y*-axis (Figure 5-246).

The hexagonal head can be created by subtracting a 3D solid having a hole of the same shape.

Figure 5-246 Hints for the SWEEP operation

Project 5-6: Creating the 3D Model of a Faucet

Using the knowledge you have acquired from this chapter, create the 3D model of the faucet shown in Figure 5-247. The dimensions of the object are shown in Figure 5-248.

Hints for the Project

The shape of the objects can be easily created with a **LOFT** operation following a centerline path. You can use some of the cross sections given as well as other sections to control the geometry of the 3D solid.

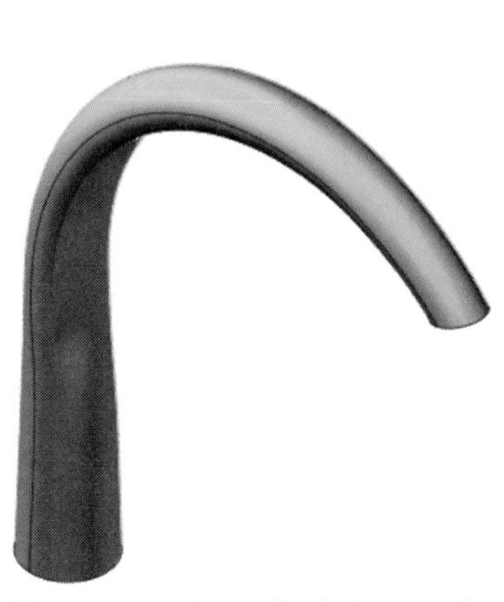

Figure 5-247 A shaded view of the faucet 3D model

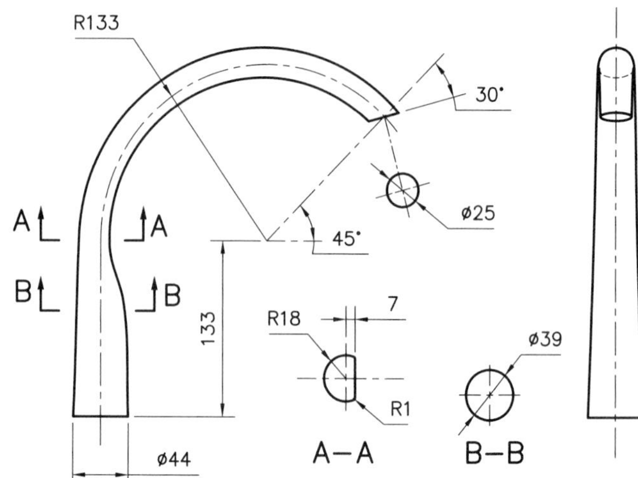

Figure 5-248 Dimensions for the cross sections and the path

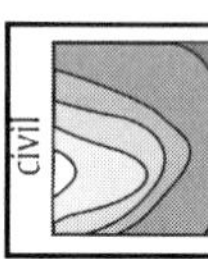

Project 5-7: Precast Concrete Form #1

Create the 3D model of the concrete cast shown in Figure 5-249. The dimensions of the object are shown in Figure 5-250. **SAVE** the drawing as ***Project 5-7.***

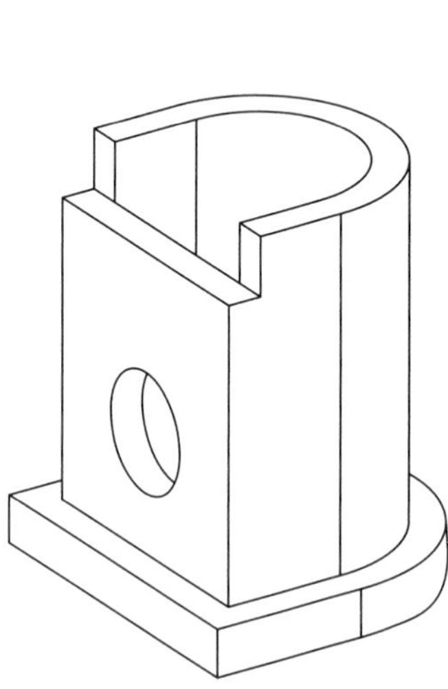

Figure 5-249 3D view of precast concrete form #1

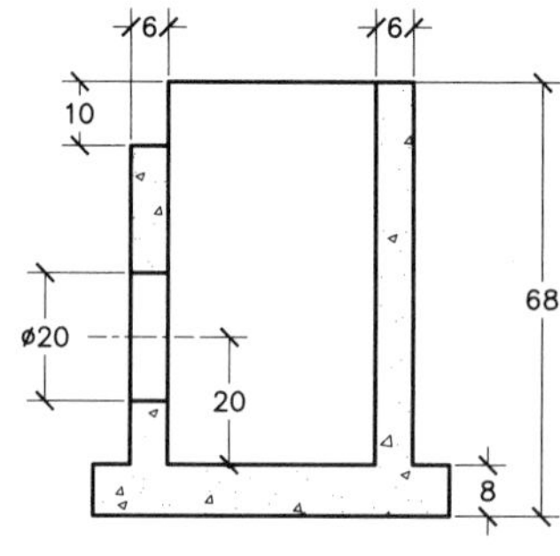

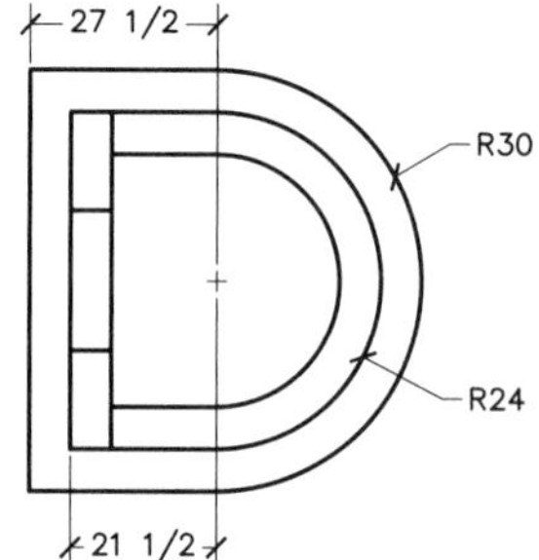

Figure 5-250 Dimensions of precast concrete form #1

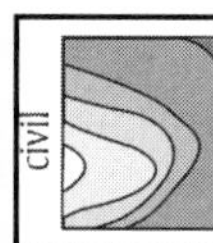

Project 5-8: Precast Concrete Form #2

Create a 3D solid to represent the concrete cast of the curb edge shown in Figure 5-251. The dimensions of the cross sections at the ends and the center provide enough information to develop the 3D object. Make the object **10′** long. Save the drawing as ***Project 5-8.***

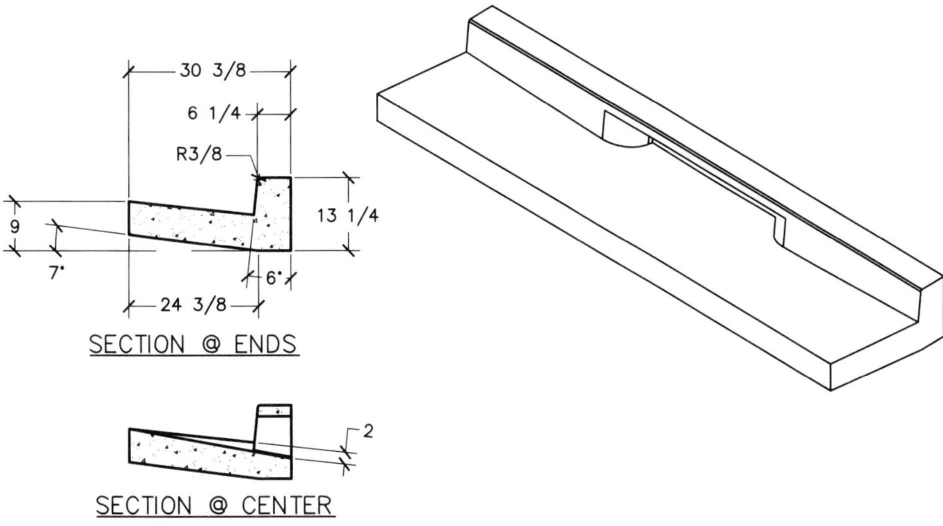

Figure 5-251 3D view and cross sections of precast concrete form #2

Hints for the Project

You can start by creating an extruded 3D solid, and then slice the object into several pieces to eliminate the one that would create the inlet. You can perform a **SLICE** operation using a surface to create the slope into the inlet (Figure 5-252). The **FILLET** operation can be performed at the end using a **6″** radius.

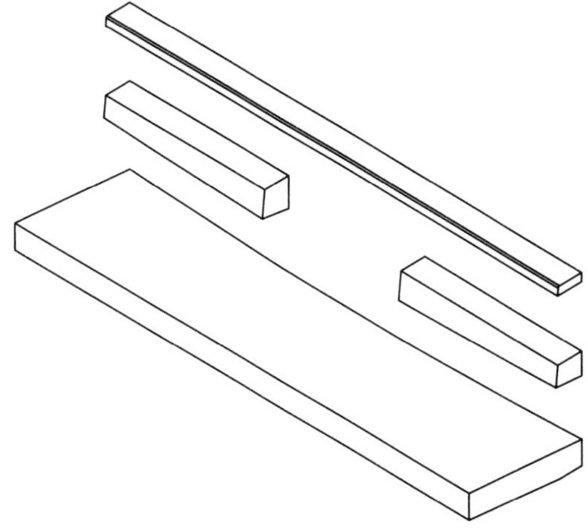

Figure 5-252 The individual 3D solids created with SLICE operations, shown as an exploded view as a hint on how to develop the 3D model

Project 5-9: Finding Interferences Between Components of the Spiral Staircase

Some of the components of the spiral staircase developed in Tutorial 5-3 interfere with each other. Find and eliminate these interferences.

Hints for the Project

You can use the **INTERFERE** command first to find any existing interferences. After you have found the interferences, you can eliminate them by giving the objects the correct shape. You can create duplicate in-place copies of the objects with which the components interfere and then **SUBTRACT** them.

Editing 3D Solids and Surfaces

6

Chapter Objectives

- Become familiar with the **SOLIDEDIT** command and its family of tools.
- Understand and control the process of selecting faces within a **SOLIDEDIT** operation.
- Modify a 3D solid's geometry by editing its edges.
- Modify a 3D solid's geometry by editing its faces.
- Modify a 3D solid's geometry by editing its body.
- Emphasize the use of the **Shell** operation.
- Extract geometry from the 3D solids for use in further operations.
- Understand the different types of 3D solids and surfaces.
- Use grips to edit 3D solids and surfaces.
- Modify composite 3D solids by modifying the history of their original 3D solids.

INTRODUCTION

About Editing 3D Solids

The activities of design and prototyping have much to do with constant modifications until the final product is defined. The more tools you have to make these changes, the less likely you will have to restart your 3D model from scratch. The 3D solids editing tools or options contained in the **SOLIDEDIT** command are very helpful in this regard.

The 3D solids editing tools, however, can be used not only to make changes on 3D solid objects but also to achieve specific shapes in the design process. As you will learn in this chapter, without these important and handy tools, you could not create many shapes of 3D models, at least in a simple manner.

Because of the way in which they proceed, many of the 3D solids editing tools are similar to the **Modify** group tools used in 2D.

Using the **SOLIDEDIT** command is not the only way to edit 3D solids. Depending on the type of 3D solid, the value of its geometric characteristics can also be modified through the **Properties** palette. In addition, many other editing capabilities that employ grips, including the manipulation of subobjects, mean that 3D solids have become flexible objects. Modifications made to a composite 3D solid, studied in the previous chapter, by using the original 3D solids recorded in its history can also be considered part of the editing capabilities of this type of object. The new surfaces have similar editing capabilities.

THE SOLIDEDIT COMMAND

OVERVIEW OF THE SOLIDEDIT COMMAND

SOLIDEDIT is a general command that contains a wide range of tools that can be used to perform certain modifications on 3D solid objects. It erases the history of the 3D solid, as mentioned in the previous chapter.

Each tool of the **SOLIDEDIT** command is organized according to its category in one of three groups of options: **Face, Edge,** or **Body.** Figure 6-1 shows the shortcut menu with the options of the **SOLIDEDIT** command, and the shortcut menus with the options of each group.

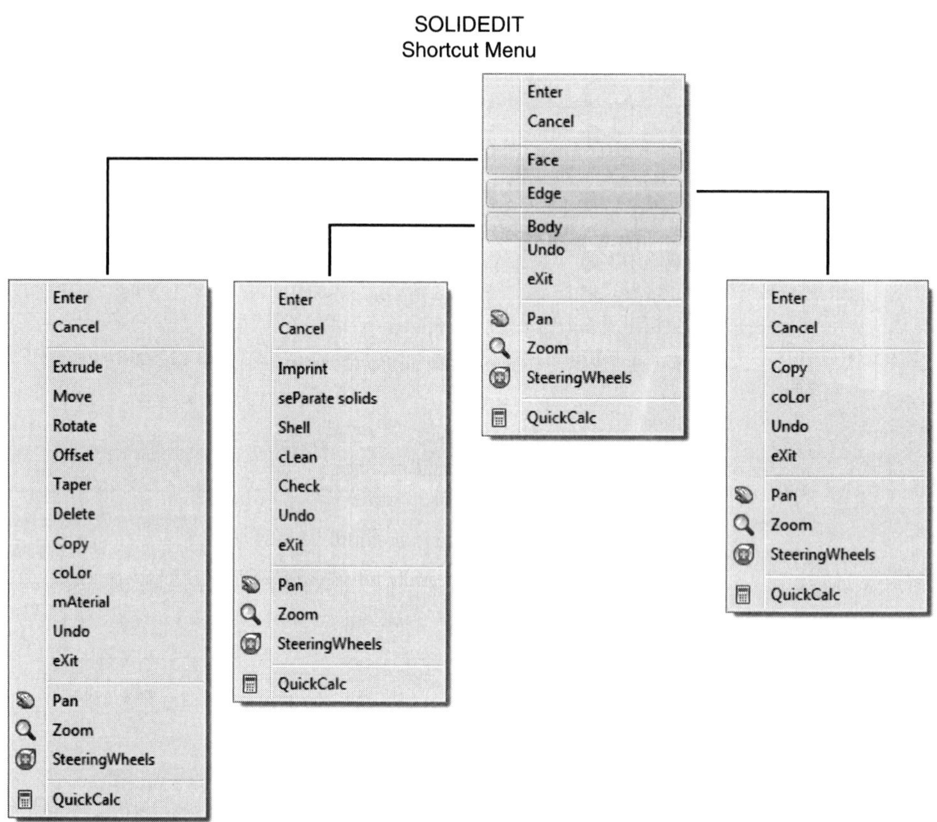

Figure 6-1 The SOLIDEDIT command and its subcategory shortcut menus

Accessing a particular **SOLIDEDIT** tool requires first invoking the command, then selecting the group and the particular option within this group. Accessing each individual tool from the **Solid Editing** panel of the **Ribbon**, however, is as simple as invoking any other command (Figure 6-2).

FACE EDITING TOOLS

The tools within this group are used to perform operations on the faces of 3D solids. Editing a face in most cases modifies the shape of the 3D solid as well. Because face editing tools use specific faces of a 3D solid, you can select faces only from a particular 3D solid in each operation.

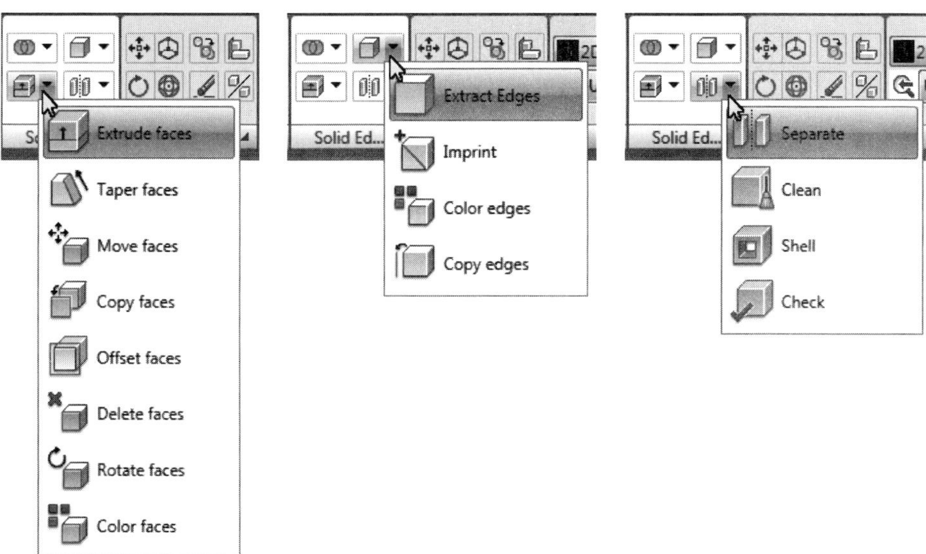

Figure 6-2 Location of the SOLIDEDIT tools in the toolbar and the pull-down menus

Selecting the Faces

As with all other tools or commands that modify objects, the face editing tools involve a selection process. The selection process of this group of tools prompts you to select specific faces of 3D solids instead of entire objects, as with most other commands.

Selecting faces differs quite a bit from the standard method of selecting objects. Regardless of which face editing tool has been invoked, the following methods will enable you to select faces properly when you are prompted:

1. **Picking an Edge:** An edge of a 3D solid is the border of any two adjacent faces. Because AutoCAD cannot distinguish between one face and another, picking an edge will automatically include the selection of both adjacent faces [Figure 6-3(a)]. If you want to remove one of these two faces, you can pick any edge of the face you want to remove while holding down the **<Shift>** key [Figure 6-3(b)].

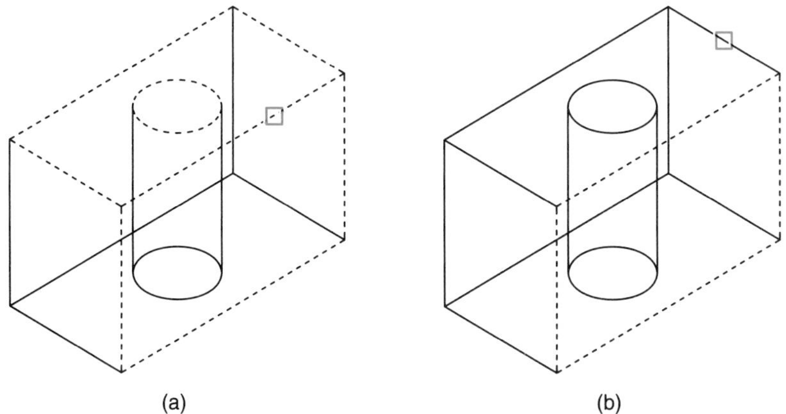

Figure 6-3 Picking an edge selects both adjacent faces (a). Faces are deselected when you hold down the <Shift> key (b)

2. **Picking a Face:** Picking inside the face contour is the easiest way to select a face. To understand the face selection process, you must realize that regardless of what face of a 3D solid you are looking at, there is always at least one other face behind it.

Clicking inside the face contour selects the face closer to you. A second click in the same place will select the face behind it, a third click the face behind the second, and so on (Figure 6-4).

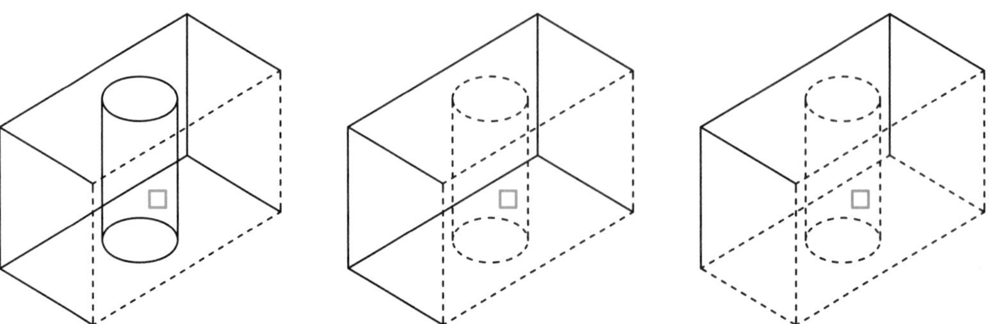

Figure 6-4 Picking on the same spot continuously selects the faces behind it

To remove faces from the selection, you must hold down the **<Shift>** key and click one of the edges of the face you want to remove. If you click any place other than an edge, including outside the 3D solid, while holding the **<Shift>** key down, you will remove the faces in the opposite order of their previous selection (Figure 6-5).

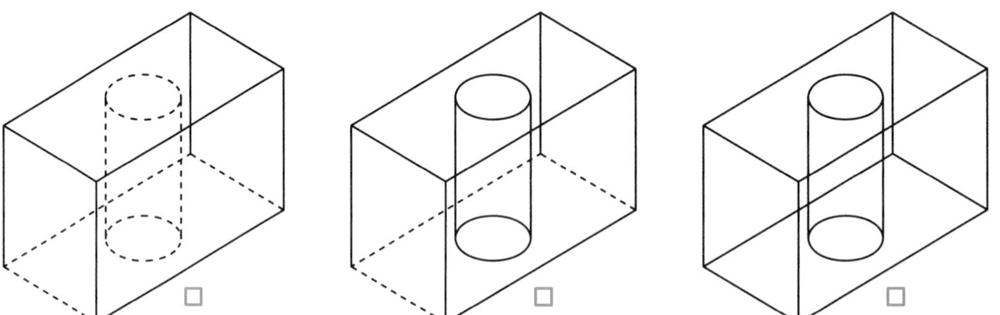

Figure 6-5 Holding down the <Shift> key while clicking on the same spot continuously deselects the faces in the same order

3. **Using the Command's Options:** After you make your first selection, you can ease the selection process by using the options available at the command prompt:

`Select faces or [Undo/Remove/ALL]:`

`all ↵ will select every face of the solid.`

`r ↵ will save you from having to hold the` ***<Shift>*** *`key when removing a face.`*

After selecting **Remove**, the options available in the command prompt change to:

`Remove faces or [Undo/Add/ALL]:`

This allows you to switch back to the **Add** mode.

4. **Picking a Silhouette or an Isoline:** You can use one of these methods when the **DISPSILH** system variable is on, or when the **ISOLINES** system variable is set at a value other than **0**. Isolines and silhouettes are not real entities; they are there only to represent curved faces. Picking an isoline or a silhouette will select only the curved face related to it. This is the most effective way of selecting curved faces, especially the interior ones (Figure 6-6).

5. **Using Selection Tools:** Additionally, you can select faces by entering the aliases **C, F,** and **CP** followed by **<Enter>**. This will activate one of the following selection tools,

Crossing/Fence/CPolygon, in the same order. These are the only standard selection methods that can be used. Any other selection method, such as **Window, Previous, or Last,** will not work.

Combining different selection methods is also possible at any time. The **PICKADD** system variable, which determines whether the **<Shift>** key is used to **Remove** or to **Add** objects, is ignored in the selection of faces.

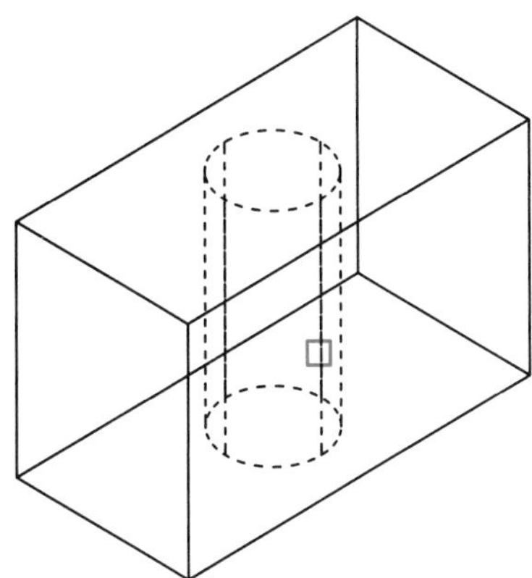

Figure 6-6 Picking an isoline or a silhouette selects only the curved face to which it belongs

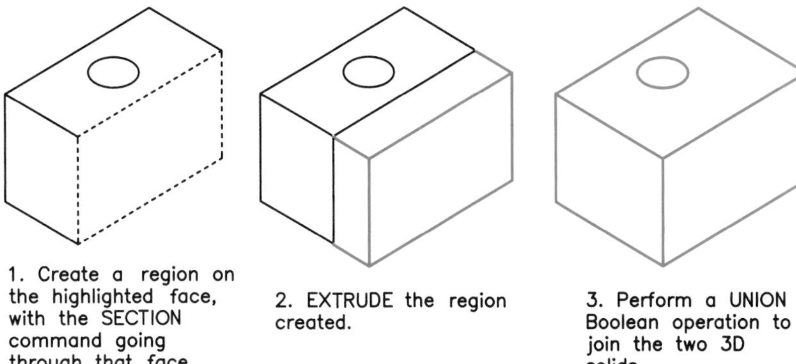

1. Create a region on the highlighted face, with the SECTION command going through that face.
2. EXTRUDE the region created.
3. Perform a UNION Boolean operation to join the two 3D solids.

Figure 6-7 Increasing one of the distances can take three steps using operations studied up to this point

Extrude Faces

EXTRUDE FACES	
Solid Editing Toolbar	
Ribbon Solid Editing panel	
Pull-down Menu	Modify/ Solids Editing/ Extrude faces
Command Line	solidedit ↵ f ↵ e

Figure 6-7 shows the steps you would perform to increase the size of a 3D solid in a particular direction, using the tools you have learned so far.

TIP To avoid any possible confusion, be aware that the **Extrude Faces** icon is exactly like the **EXTRUDE** command icon.

The **Extrude faces** tool, on the other hand, reduces this work to one single step by extruding the face directly. You can use this tool to protrude planar faces just as you would extrude a shape. As with the **EXTRUDE** command, you can perform the following three extrusion operations in one of two directions, outside or inside the 3D solid (Figure 6-8):

- Perpendicular to the planar face
- Perpendicular to the planar face with a taper angle
- Following a path

Move Faces

MOVE FACES	
Solid Editing Toolbar	
Ribbon Solid Editing panel	
Pull-down Menu	Modify/ Solids Editing/ Move faces
Command Line	solidedit ↵ f ↵ m

Just like the **MOVE** command is used in 2D, the **Move faces** tool can be used when working with 3D solids to move selected faces from one point to another without changing the orientation and topology of the selected faces. Faces surrounding the moved face(s), however, can be modified with the operation to accommodate the new location of the moved face(s).

Depending on the situation in which the tool is used, different results can be obtained. This tool makes it easy to move a hole or any other internal face(s) from one point to another, and even remove it from the 3D solid. In Figure 6-9, the face representing the hole in the original 3D solid

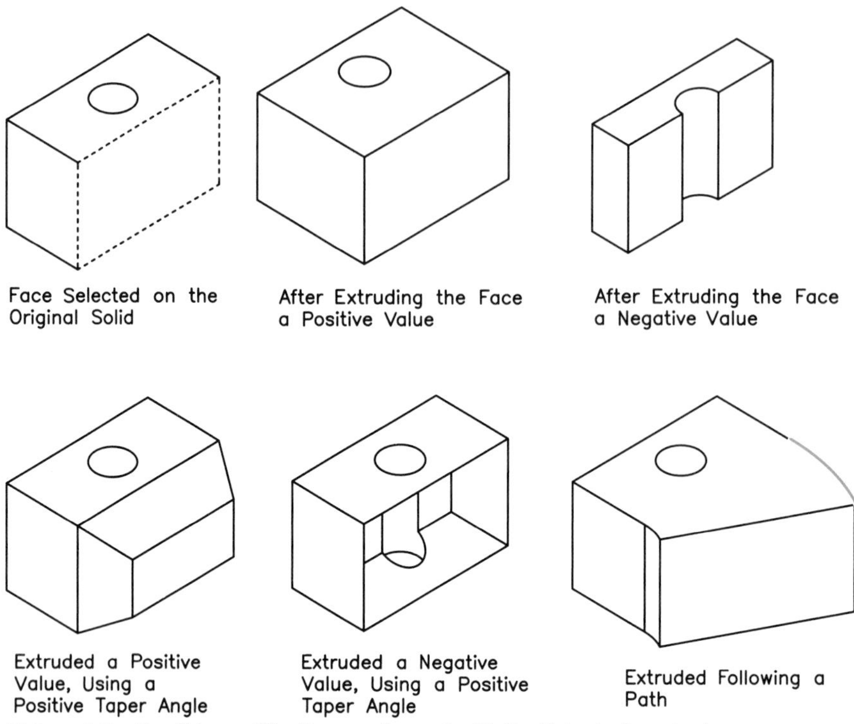

Figure 6-8 Possible modifications performed with the Extrude faces tool

has been moved from one point to another in three different operations. In the first operation, the face was moved from point 1 to point 2; in the second operation, it was moved from point 1 to point 3; and in the third operation, from point 1 to point 4. In the last operation, the face is simply lost because it is moved to a point outside the 3D solid's body.

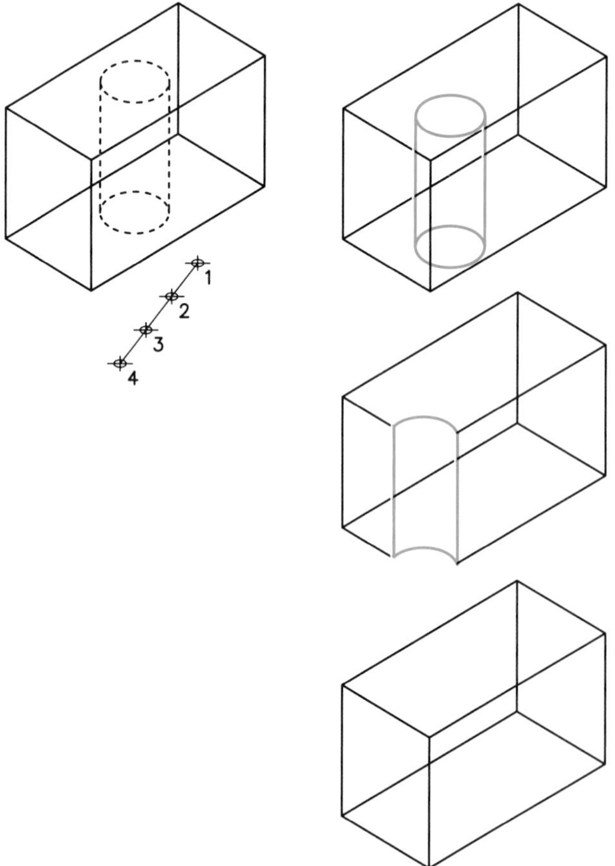

Figure 6-9 Moving a cylindrical hole using the Move faces tool can lead to different results

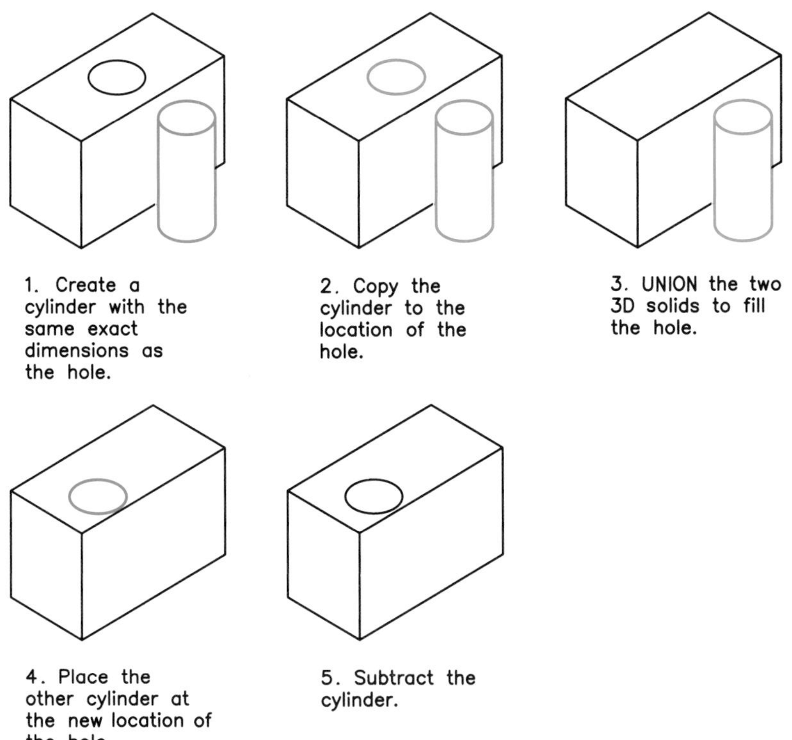

1. Create a cylinder with the same exact dimensions as the hole.
2. Copy the cylinder to the location of the hole.
3. UNION the two 3D solids to fill the hole.
4. Place the other cylinder at the new location of the hole.
5. Subtract the cylinder.

Figure 6-10 Without using the Move faces tool, moving a hole to a different location would result in a long list of steps

Without the use of the **Move faces** tool, the operation we previously described would result in a long list of steps (Figure 6-10).

Moved faces are automatically extended or trimmed in their new locations by the adjacent faces. This maintains the integrity of the 3D solid. In Figure 6-11, the two blind holes were moved parallel to the *X*-axis from point 1 to point 2. Their cylindrical faces then were trimmed due to the geometry condition of the top face.

An outer face that is moved also is extended or trimmed according to the adjacent faces that were not moved. For example, moving the selected face in Figure 6-12 from point 1 to point 2 will also modify all faces connected with it.

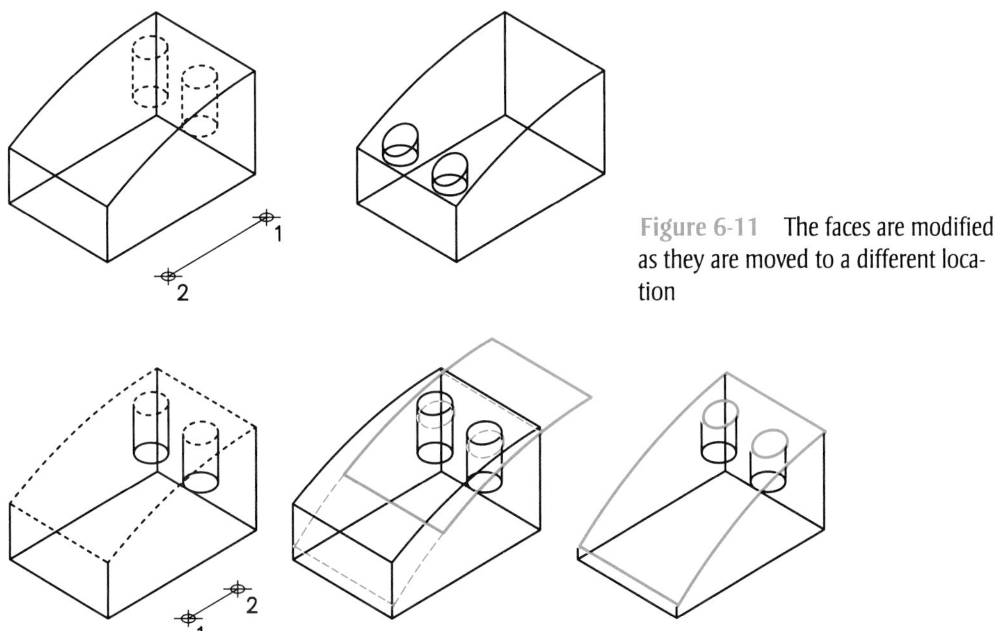

Figure 6-11 The faces are modified as they are moved to a different location

Figure 6-12 A visual approach to understand the Move faces operation

To better understand the **Move faces** and **Extrude faces** tools, let's look at some of their differences and similarities:

1. Extruding the left face a positive distance (from point 1 to point 2) protrudes the face of the solid [Figure 6-13(a)]. Moving the same face from point 2 to point 1 also modifies all faces around it in order to preserve their geometric relationship [Figure 6-13(b)].

2. The **Extrude faces** and **Move faces** operations will achieve the same result when they are performed inside the 3D solid, as long as the taper angle of the **Extrude faces** operation is 0. This occurs regardless of whether or not the operation interferes with another face inside it [Figure 6-14(a)].

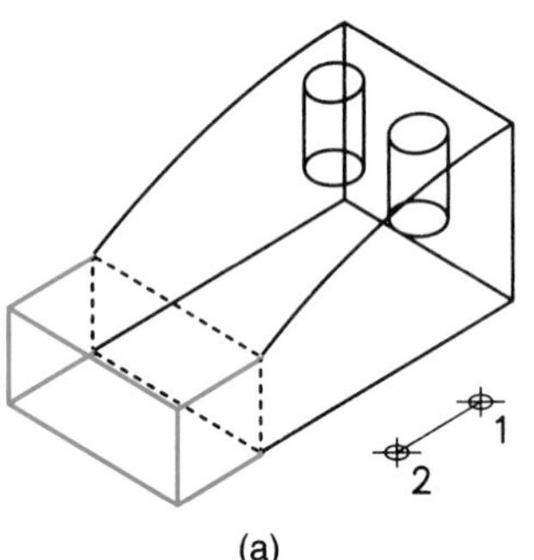

(a)

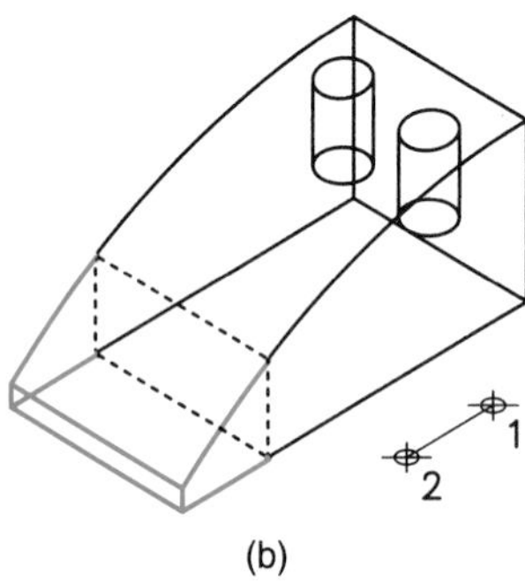

(b)

Figure 6-13 Difference between extruding (a) and moving (b) a single face the same distance

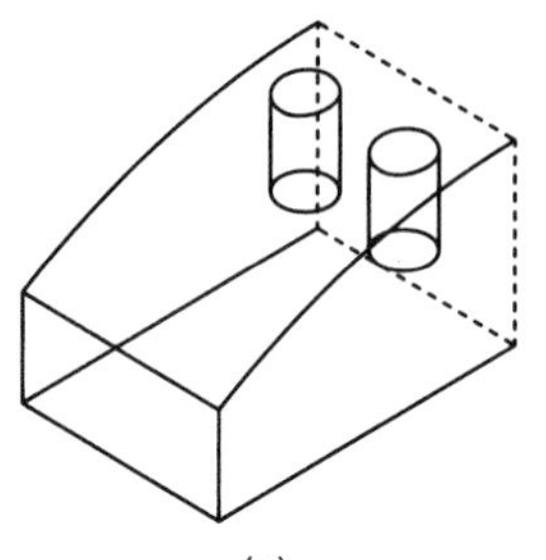

(a)

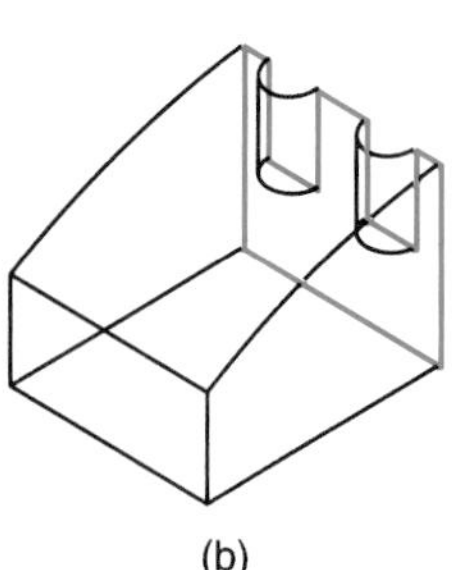

(b)

Figure 6-14 A face can be extruded or moved even if it encounters other faces in its new location

3. Extruding the left and front faces at the same time by a positive value protrudes each face individually. Moving these same two faces from point 1 to point 2 deforms the solid differently, so that the geometric relationship is maintained. In this case, the face parallel to the X-axis would move a distance of ΔY, while the face parallel to the Y-axis would move a distance of ΔX (Figure 6-15).

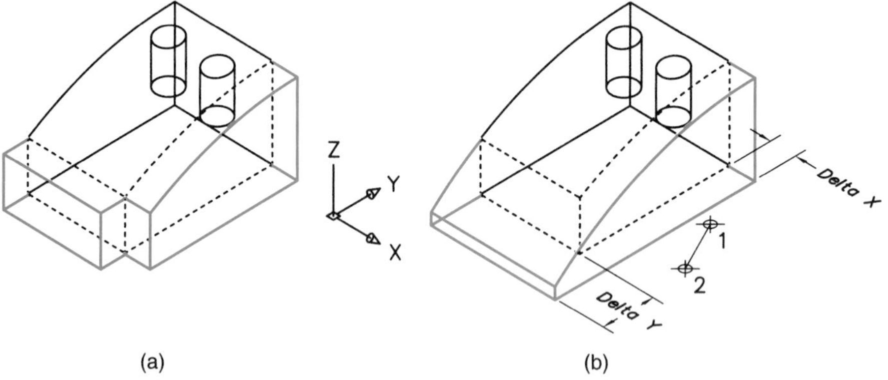

Figure 6-15 More than one face is extruded with the same value (a). When multiple faces are moved from one point to another, the faces are displaced according to the coordinate deltas (b)

OFFSET FACES	
Solid Editing Toolbar	
Ribbon Solid Editing panel	
Pull-down Menu	Modify/ Solids Editing/ Offset faces
Command Line	solidedit ↵ f ↵ o

Offset Faces

Like the **OFFSET** command in 2D work, the **Offset faces** tool modifies the solid by relocating the selected face(s) a certain distance parallel to the previous original location. A positive offset distance value will offset the face(s) outside the solid, increasing its size; a negative distance will reduce the size of the solid, offsetting the face(s) inward (Figure 6-16).

The **Offset faces** tool is very useful when performing tasks such as increasing or decreasing the size of an internal face, like the slotted hole on Figure 6-17. If, however, you were to perform

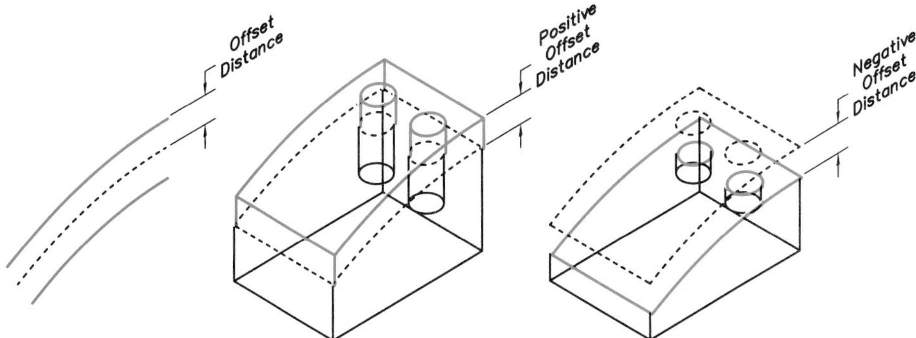

Figure 6-16 The faces can be offset outward and inward using the Offset faces tool

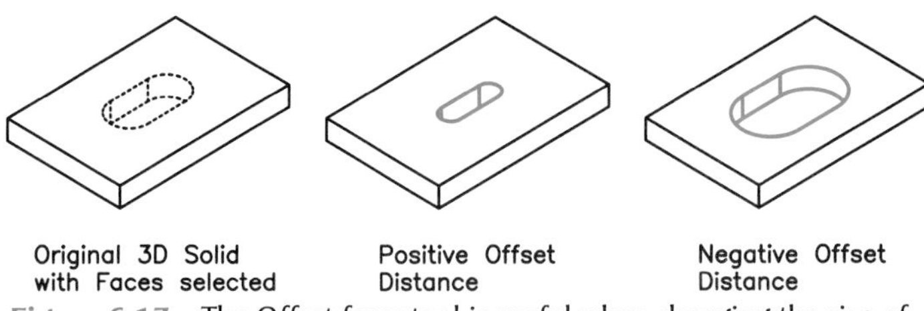

Figure 6-17 The Offset faces tool is useful when changing the size of a hole

this task using Boolean operations, it would take many more steps, especially if you were to reduce the size of the slotted hole.

As with the **Move faces** tool, if more than one face is selected, the offset faces blend to maintain the topology of the adjacent faces. The difference in the results obtained using these two tools arises basically from the way in which the displacement distance is considered.

The **Move faces** tool uses distances independently, which depend on the orientation of the face and the delta component of an axis normal to it [Figure 6-18(a)]. The **Offset faces** tool, on the other hand, uses the same specified distance to displace all selected faces [Figure 6-18(b)].

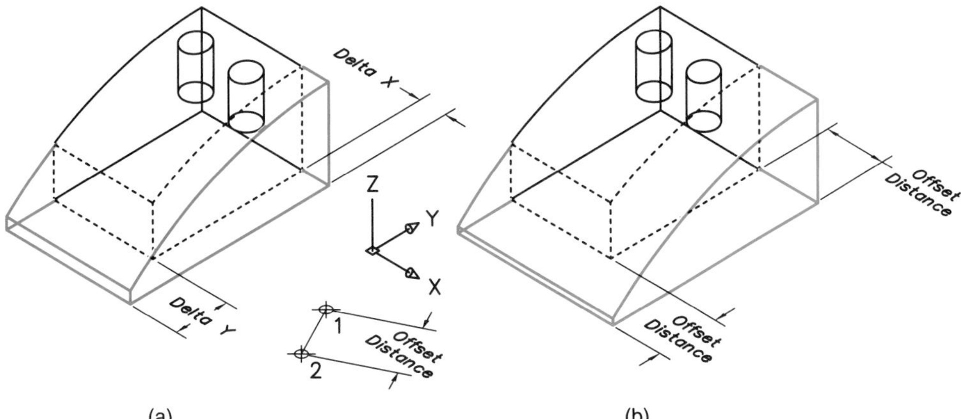

Figure 6-18 Unlike the Move faces operation (a), Offset faces displaces the faces an equal distance (b)

DELETE FACES	
Solid Editing Toolbar	
Ribbon Solid Editing panel	
Pull-down Menu	Modify/ Solids Editing/ Delete faces
Command Line	solidedit ↵ f ↵ d

Delete Faces

You can use this tool to delete one or more faces on a solid, filling in the gap or empty volume between the removed face and its adjacent faces.

Holes, fillets, and chamfers have faces that usually can be removed easily by this operation. Figure 6-19(a) shows the original 3D solid before the **Delete faces** operations. The same 3D solid is then shown in Figure 6-19(b) after the following faces have been deleted:

- The two faces created with the **CHAMFER** operation at the bottom
- The two faces created with the **FILLET** operation on top
- The two cylindrical faces representing the blind holes
- The leftmost face

The AutoCAD® program might find that certain face(s) cannot be filled due to geometric conditions. In these cases the tool will not proceed, and the following message will be displayed:

```
Modeling Operation Error:
Gap cannot be filled.
```

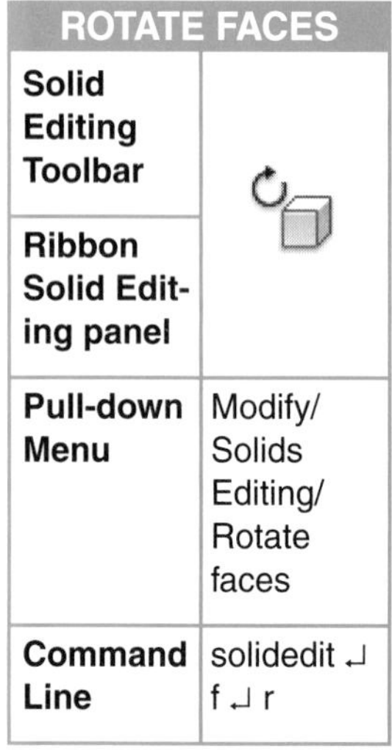

ROTATE FACES	
Solid Editing Toolbar	
Ribbon Solid Editing panel	
Pull-down Menu	Modify/ Solids Editing/ Rotate faces
Command Line	solidedit ↵ f ↵ r

Rotate Faces

With this tool, you can rotate selected faces a specified angle around an imaginary axis of rotation, keeping the relationship with the adjacent faces.

The following are the options of the **Rotate faces** tool:

2points: Even though the **2points** option does not appear in its shortcut menu (Figure 6-20), it is available as the default. This option is the method most commonly used to rotate faces. Specifying a point will automatically activate this option. You will then be prompted to specify a second point. These two points define the imaginary axis of rotation through which the faces are to rotate.

> **FOR MORE DETAILS** The positive rotation can be determined by pointing the thumb of your right hand from the first to the second point and curling the rest of the fingers, as the right-hand rule indicates. See Chapter 1 for further information.

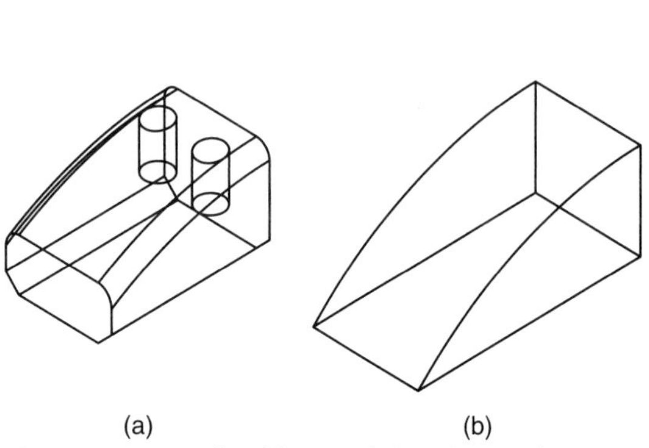

Figure 6-19 Holes, fillets, and chamfers can be removed easily by deleting their faces

Figure 6-20 The ROTATE3D command operation and the Rotate faces shortcut menus

Axis by Object: This option differs from the **Object** option of the **ROTATE3D** command. Depending on the type of object, the AutoCAD program has three interpretations:

1. A line is used directly as the imaginary axis of rotation.
2. For circles, ellipses, and arcs, the imaginary axis of rotation is considered to be perpendicular to the plane that contains the object and goes through its center.
3. The start and end points of polylines, 3D polylines, and splines are extracted and used by AutoCAD to establish the axis of rotation.

View: This method aligns the axis of rotation perpendicular to the viewing plane, that is, perpendicular to the monitor screen. You will be prompted to specify a point to locate the axis.

Xaxis / Yaxis / Zaxis: These three options instruct the AutoCAD program to align the axis of rotation parallel to an axis of the current UCS, as specified. You will then be asked for a point to locate where it will go through.

In Figure 6-21 the cylindrical hole was rotated 90° around an imaginary axis that goes through the center of the other cylindrical hole. The face is redefined in its new location.

Similarly, if the top curved face is rotated 30° around an imaginary axis that goes from the midpoint of the left bottom edge to the midpoint of the right bottom edge (Figure 6-22), the solid modifies all adjacent faces to maintain the 3D solid's integrity.

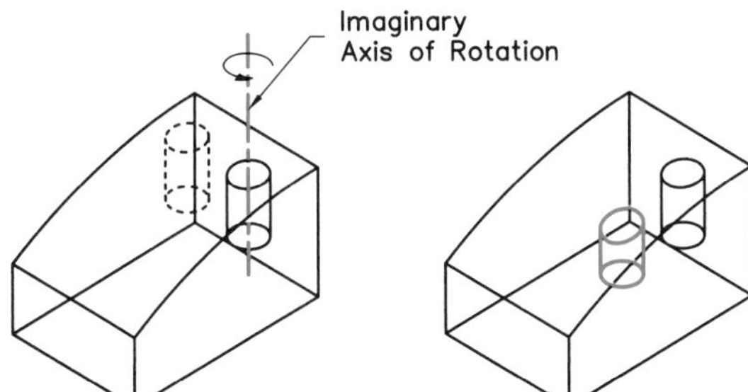

Figure 6-21 The selected face is rotated about the indicated imaginary axis

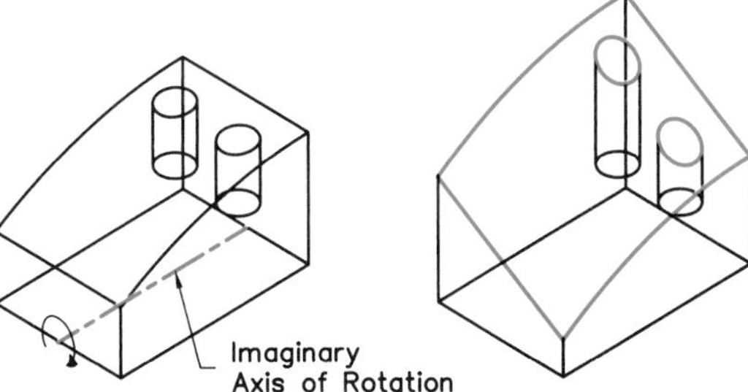

Figure 6-22 The top face is rotated about the indicated imaginary axis

As with the **Move faces** operation, a **Rotate faces** operation will proceed even if the selected face(s) moves outside the 3D solid's body. If because of the rotation, the face falls completely outside the 3D solid, it will be deleted (Figure 6-23).

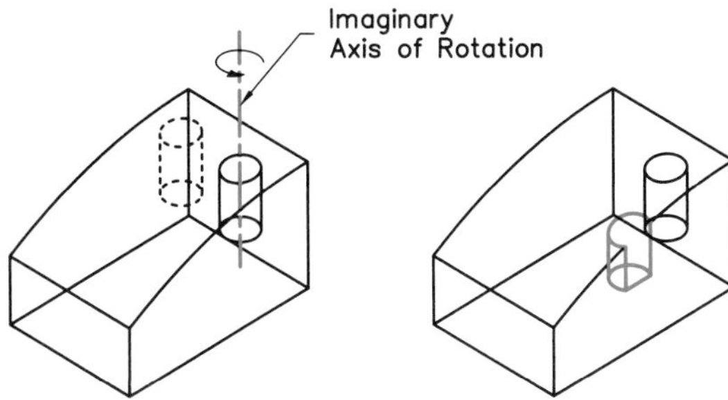

Figure 6-23 A face can be rotated farther than the limits of the 3D solid

TAPER FACES	
Solid Editing Toolbar	
Ribbon Solid Editing panel	
Pull-down Menu	Modify/ Solids Editing/ Taper faces
Command Line	solidedit ↵ f ↵ t

Taper Faces

With this tool, the faces are tapered at a certain angle. Tapering planar faces will cause them to incline. Tapering cylindrical faces will turn them into conical faces. Faces that are not planar or cylindrical cannot be tapered.

As you have learned, the **EXTRUDE** command enables you to create 3D solids in which all faces parallel to the extrusion direction are tapered at the same angle. The end of the extrusion at which the original shape was located keeps its dimensions, while the dimensions of the other end are affected by the taper angle.

With the **Taper faces** tool, you can taper planar and cylindrical faces of a 3D solid individually. You establish two necessary aspects of the face tapering operation by specifying two points:

tapering midplane: The cross section in the 3D solid that does not change its original dimensions when the Taper faces operation is performed.

1. The point through which the ***tapering midplane*** will go. AutoCAD refers to this point as the *base point.*
2. A second point that determines the direction of the **tapering vector,** which aligns the **tapering midplane** perpendicular to it. AutoCAD refers to this vector as the *axis of tapering.*

Figure 6-24 shows the modified 3D solid that results from tapering three of its faces, locating the base point on the midpoint of a vertical edge, and placing the second point on the top vertex of the same edge. This aligns the tapering midplane parallel to the bottom and top faces.

Try to keep the tapering midplane perpendicular to the extrusion direction. That way, you can avoid dealing with complicated combinations of angular displacements.

Internal faces such as holes are easy to taper as well. For cylindrical or conical faces, the tapering vector should be aligned with the centerline (Figure 6-25).

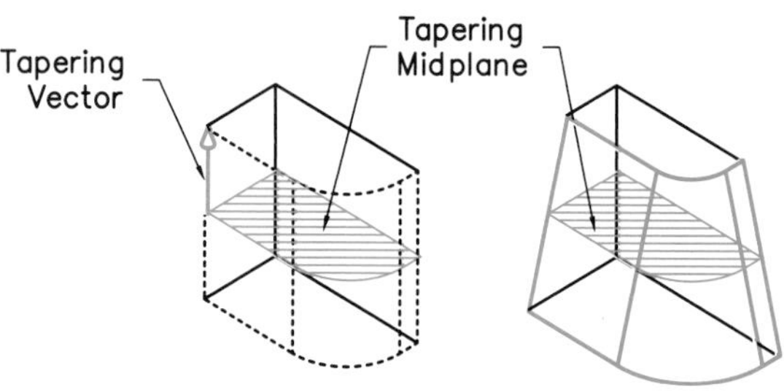

Figure 6-24 The tapering midplane defines the section of the 3D solids that remains unchanged with the Taper faces operation

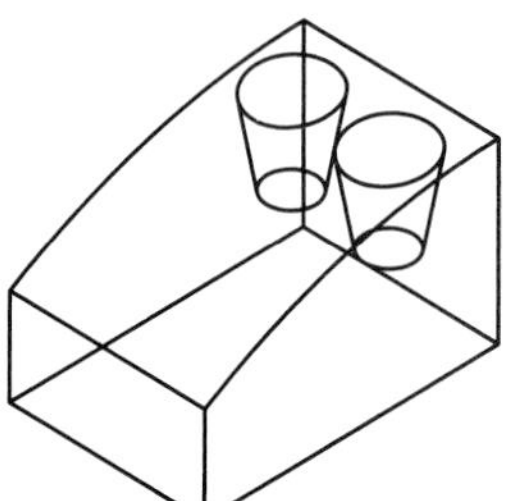

Figure 6-25 When tapering a cylindrical or conical face, the tapering vector should be aligned with its centerline

COPY FACES	
Solid Editing Toolbar	
Ribbon Solid Editing panel	
Pull-down Menu	Modify/ Solids Editing/ Copy faces
Command Line	solidedit ↵ f ↵ c

Copy Faces

This tool allows you to extract faces from a 3D solid to any location. Planar faces are extracted from a 3D solid as regions; nonplanar faces are extracted as surfaces.

Regions are typically copied for use in another 3D operation. For instance, let's assume that the bottom face of the 3D solid in Figure 6-26(a) needs to be modified so that it has the same exact curvature as the top face in Figure 6-26(d). This operation can be performed quickly by creating a copy of the front face down, for example, from point 1 to point 2 [Figure 6-26(b)] and then extruding the extracted region as shown in Figure 6-26(c) to create a new 3D solid. A third and final step would be to **SUBTRACT** the new 3D solid from the original one.

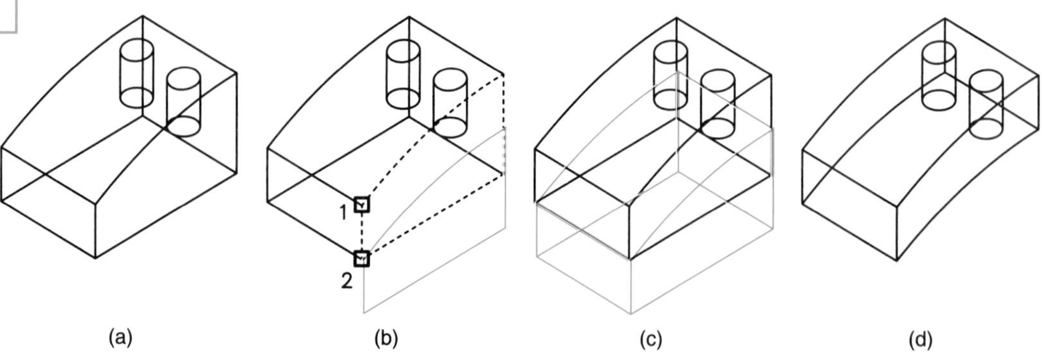

Figure 6-26 The new faces obtained with the Copy faces tool can be used to generate further modifications in the 3D solid

Color Faces

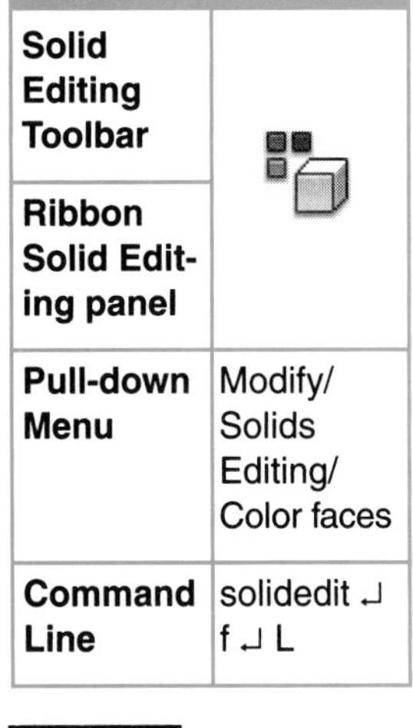

COLOR FACES	
Solid Editing Toolbar	
Ribbon Solid Editing panel	
Pull-down Menu	Modify/ Solids Editing/ Color faces
Command Line	solidedit ↵ f ↵ L

The **Color faces** tool enables you to change the color of individual faces on a 3D solid. Usually, the purpose of such a task is either to achieve a certain artistic look or to improve clarity when modeling.

There are two more aspects you need to know about the colors of solids:

1. Changing the **Color** property of a solid will turn all of its faces to this color.
2. The color of new faces generated by a slice or a Boolean operation will be affected by both the current color and the object's color.

Exercise 6-1: Using the Face Editing Tools

1. **OPEN** either the finished drawing ***Project 5-1***, or ***Exercise 6-1*** from the CD in case you did not finish it.
2. **SAVE** the drawing **AS *Exercise 6-1 solved.***
3. Select the **SE Isometric** viewing point and the **Top** UCS.
4. Use the **Extrude faces** tool to protrude the front face of the 3D solid shown in Figure 6-27(a). After the operation, the results should look like Figure 6-27(b). Invoke the **Extrude faces** option of the **SOLIDEDIT** command and respond to the prompts as follows:

   Select faces or [Undo/Remove/ALL]:
   Select the face as shown in Figure 6-27(a).

   Select faces or [Undo/Remove/ALL]:
   ↵ *(To end the selection)*

   Specify height of extrusion or [Path]: *1* ↵

   Specify angle of taper for extrusion: *0* ↵

   Enter a face editing option
   [Extrude/Move/Rotate/Offset/Taper/Delete/Copy/coLor/mAterial/ Undo/eXit] <eXit>: *<Esc> (To exit the command)*

Note:
This 3D solid should have been created in one of the projects of the previous chapter. If you don't have this model, take a few minutes to re-create it.

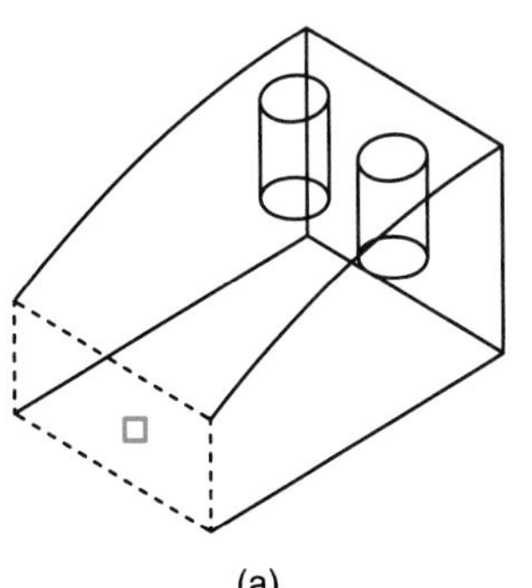

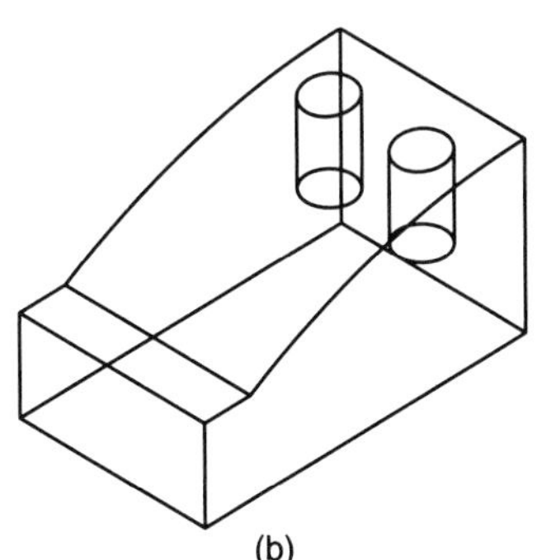

Figure 6-27 Face to select (a) and the modified 3D solid (b) after the Extrude faces operation

5. Invoke the **Move faces** option of the **SOLIDEDIT** command to relocate the two holes. After the operation, the 3D solid should look like Figure 6-28(a). Respond to the prompts as follows:

   Select faces or [Undo/Remove/ALL]:
   Select the two cylindrical faces of the holes.

   Select faces or [Undo/Remove/ALL]: ↵
   (To end the selection)

   Specify a base point or displacement:
   Specify endpoint 1 [Figure 6-28(b)].

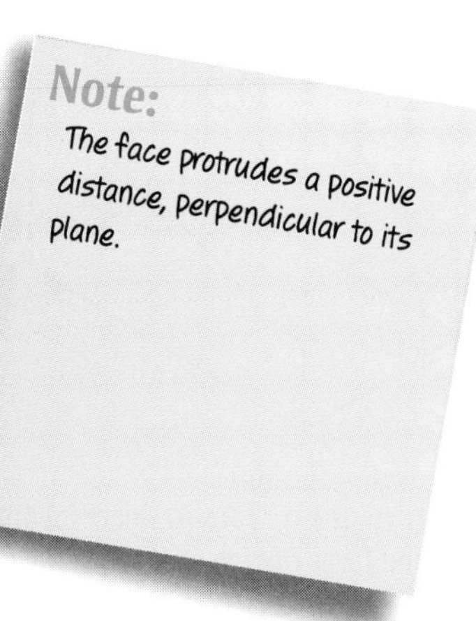
Note:
The face protrudes a positive distance, perpendicular to its plane.

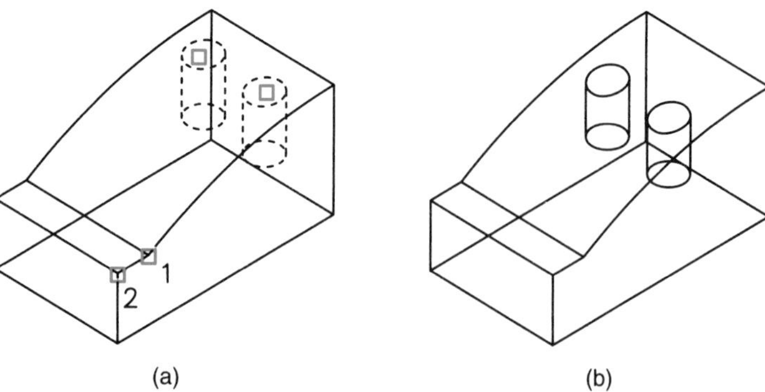

(a) (b)

Figure 6-28 Faces to select and points used to specify the displacement;(a); the modified 3D solid after the Move faces operation (b)

Specify a second point of displacement: *Specify endpoint 2.*

Enter a face editing option

[Extrude/Move/Rotate/Offset/Taper/Delete/Copy/coLor/mAterial/Undo/eXit] <eXit>: *<Esc> (To exit the command)*

6. Modify the size of one of the holes. After the operation, the 3D solid should look like Figure 6-29(b). Invoke the **Offset faces** option of the **SOLIDEDIT** command and respond to the prompts as follows:

 Select faces or [Undo/Remove/ALL]: *Select the cylindrical face shown in* Figure 6-29.

 Select faces or [Undo/Remove/ALL]: ↵ *(To end the selection)*

 Specify the offset distance: *−1/4* ↵

 Enter a face editing option

 [Extrude/Move/Rotate/Offset/Taper/Delete/Copy/coLor/mAterial/Undo/eXit] <eXit>: *<Esc> (To exit the command)*

7. Select the **Top** UCS.
8. Rotate one of the holes of the 3D solid. After the operation the results should look like

Note:
The two holes moved the distance measured between the two points. The cylindrical faces adjust to the new geometric conditions.

Note:
The selected face enlarges by offsetting the specified distance, adapting its shape to the new geometric conditions.

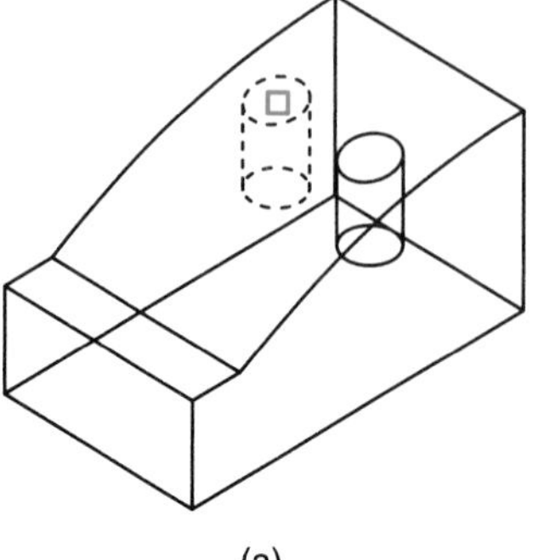

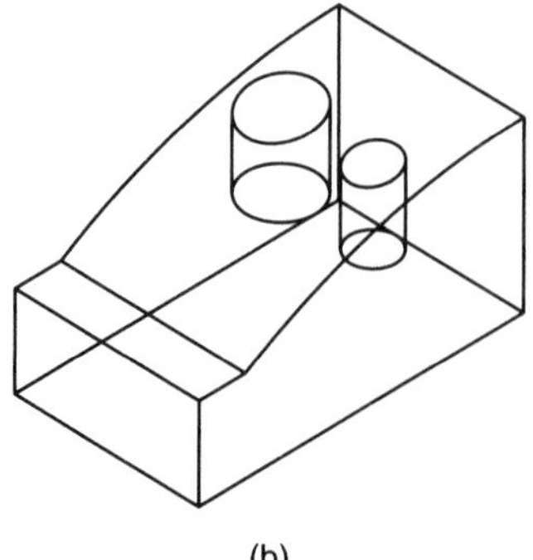

(a) (b)

Figure 6-29 Face to select (a) and the modified 3D solid (b) after the Offset faces operation

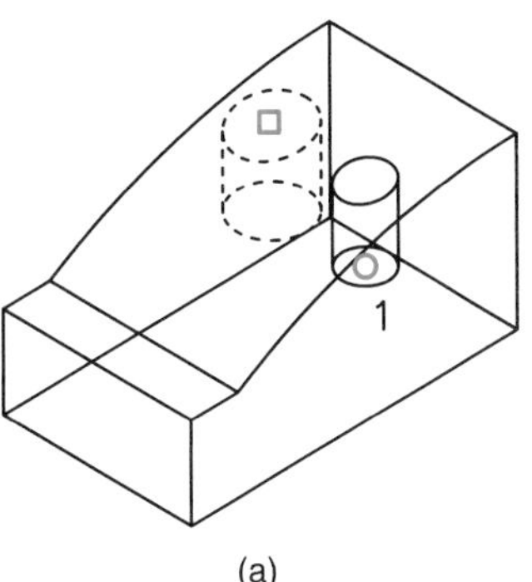

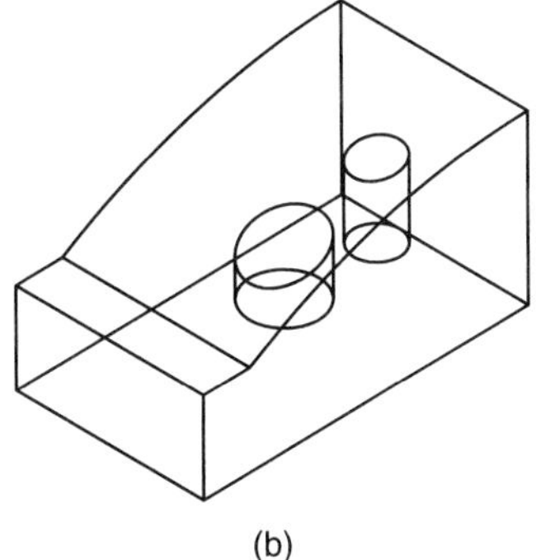

Figure 6-30 Face to select and point used to specify the axis of rotation;(a); the modified 3D solid after the Rotate faces operation (b)

Figure 6-30(b). Invoke the **Rotate faces** option of the **SOLIDEDIT** command and respond to the prompts as follows:

Select faces or [Undo/Remove/ALL]: *Select the cylindrical face of the larger hole [Figure 6-30(a)].*

Select faces or [Undo/Remove/ALL]: ↵ *(To end the selection)*

Specify an axis point or [Axis by object/View/Xaxis/Yaxis/Zaxis] <2points>: *z* ↵

Specify the origin of the rotation <0,0,0>: *Specify center point 1.*

Specify a rotation angle or [Reference]: *90* ↵

Enter a face editing option [Extrude/Move/Rotate/Offset/Taper/Delete/Copy/coLor/mAterial/Undo/eXit] <eXit>: *<Esc> (To exit the command)*

Note:
The selected face rotates around an imaginary axis parallel to the Z-axis and going through endpoint 1. The face changes to adapt its shape to the new geometrical conditions.

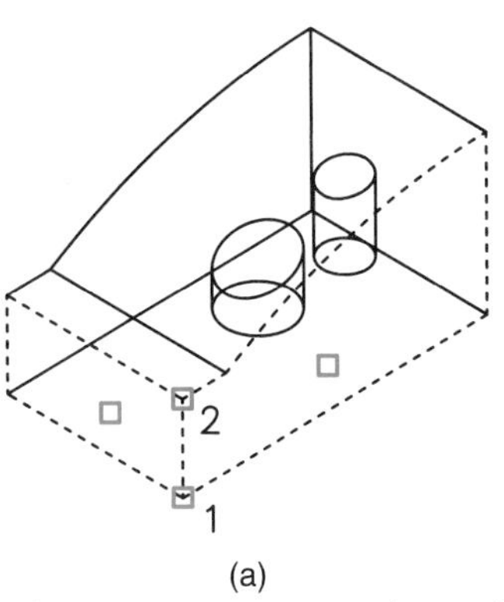

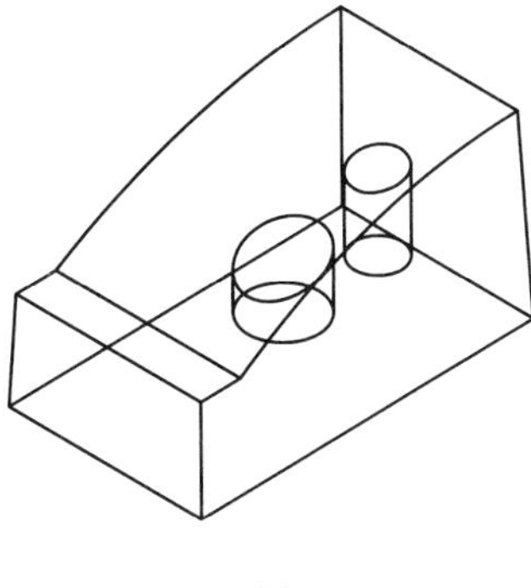

Figure 6-31 Faces to select and points used to specify the axis of tapering (a); the modified 3D solid after the Taper faces operation (b)

9. Use the **Taper faces** option of the **SOLIDEDIT** command to modify the faces of the 3D solid so it looks like Figure 6-31(b). Respond to the prompts as follows:

Select faces or [Undo/Remove/ALL]: *Select the two faces shown in* Figure 6-31(a).

Select faces or [Undo/Remove/ALL]: ↵ *(To end the selection)*

Specify the base point: *Specify endpoint 1.*

Specify another point along the axis of tapering: *Specify endpoint 2.*

Specify the taper angle: *5* ↵

Enter a face editing option

[Extrude/Move/Rotate/Offset/Taper/Delete/Copy/coLor/mAterial/Undo/eXit] <eXit>: *<Esc> (To exit the command)*

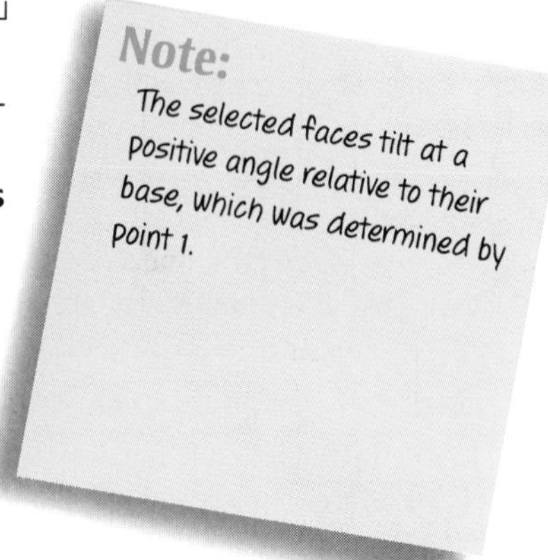
Note:
The selected faces tilt at a positive angle relative to their base, which was determined by point 1.

10. Select the **Front** UCS.
11. Using the **Taper faces** option of the **SOLIDEDIT** command, taper the cylindrical face of one of the holes, turning it into a conical face. After the operation, the 3D solid should look like Figure 6-32(b). Respond to the prompts as follows:

    Select faces or [Undo/Remove/ALL]: *Select the cylindrical face of the hole as shown in* Figure 6-32(a).

    Select faces or [Undo/Remove/ALL]: ↵ *(To end the selection)*

    Specify the base point: *Specify center point 1.*

    Specify another point along the axis of tapering: *With the ORTHO mode activated, move the cursor up to specify any point aligned vertically with point 1.*

    Specify the taper angle: *5* ↵

    Enter a face editing option

    [Extrude/Move/Rotate/Offset/Taper/Delete/Copy/coLor/mAterial/Undo/eXit] <eXit>: *<Esc> (To exit the command)*

12. Select the different orthographic views and invoke the **3DORBIT** command to inspect the modifications on the 3D solid.
13. **SAVE** the drawing.

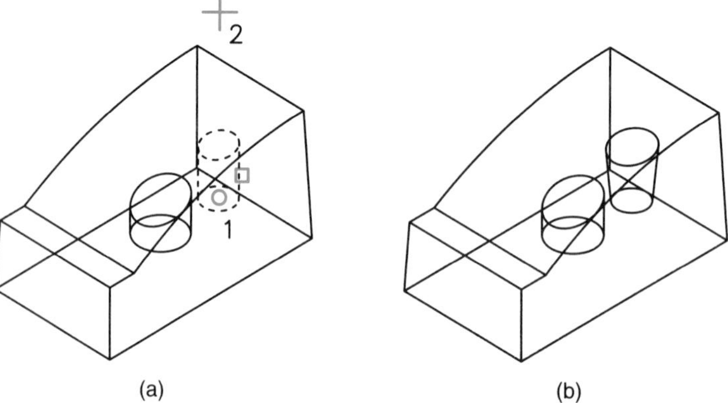
2
1
(a)
(b)

Figure 6-32 Face to select and points used to specify the axis of tapering (a); the modified 3D solid after the Taper faces operation (b)

Edge Editing Tools

The edge editing group has fewer tools to modify 3D solids. In fact, no geometric modification is performed on a 3D solid by using this group of tools. Edge editing is limited to extracting the edges or changing their color. As with the face editing tools, only one 3D solid can be used at a time.

Copy Edges

This tool allows you to extract one or more edges of a solid. The objects generated with this tool are lines, arcs, circles, ellipses, and splines.

This tool can save you a good amount of time whether the new extracted edge is used as an extrusion path, or for any other use. An alternative way of extracting edges is to copy the face with the **Copy faces** tool, and then explode the extracted face.

The **Copy edges** tool is also very helpful for other operations. An example is when you need to subtract material from a 3D solid that is swept along one of its edges.

Figure 6-33 shows the process where first the edge is copied over in the same place. (This step can be achieved by specifying the base point and the second point of displacement as the same point.) Next, a cross section is swept along the extracted path. Then the left face of the new 3D solid is extended using the **Offset faces** tool, just to make sure it goes completely through the main 3D solid. Finally, the new 3D solid is subtracted from the main one.

COPY EDGES	
Solid Editing Toolbar	
Ribbon Solid Editing panel	
Pull-down Menu	Modify/ Solids Editing/ Copy edges
Command Line	solidedit ↵ e ↵ c

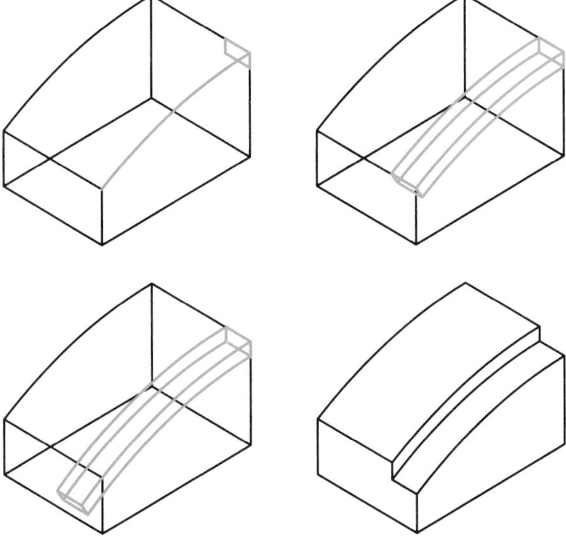

Figure 6-33 The new edges obtained with the Copy edges tool can be used to generate further modifications in the 3D solid

Color Edges

This tool changes the color of the specified edges. Its purpose is mainly to improve clarity when modeling. The color of an edge might change automatically after certain operations are performed, depending on the color currently in use, or the color of the solids interrelating in Boolean operations. In addition, changing the **Color** property of an entire solid will also affect the color of a specific edge.

COLOR EDGES	
Solid Editing Toolbar	
Ribbon Solid Editing panel	
Pull-down Menu	Modify/ Solids Editing/ Color edges
Command Line	solidedit ↵ e ↵ L

Body Editing Tools

In general, this group contains tools that enable you to perform operations that modify the entire 3D solid. By using these operations you can perform such important modifications to 3D solids as creating a shell or splitting its faces.

Imprint

This tool adds temporary edges to the faces of a 3D solid. It does so by finding the intersections of the solid's faces with another object that passes through the solid or is placed inside it.

Objects that can be imprinted are:

- Wireframe-type objects: arcs, circles, lines, polylines, 3D polylines, ellipses, and splines
- Surface-type objects: regions and surfaces
- 3D solids

IMPRINT	
Solid Editing Toolbar	
Ribbon Solid Editing panel	
Pull-down Menu	Modify/ Solids Editing/ Imprint
Command Line	solidedit ↵ b ↵ i

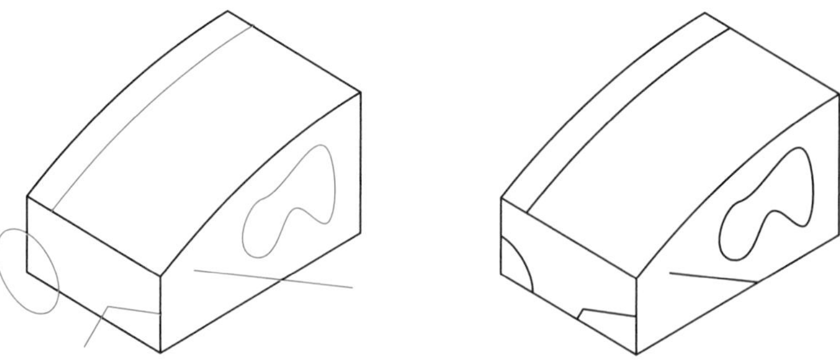

Figure 6-34 Wireframe objects coincident with the face of the 3D solid are imprinted as edges

For a wireframe-type object to be imprinted, it must be placed on a specific face of the 3D solid (Figure 6-34).

If a wireframe-type object intersects a face of the 3D solid face [Figure 6-35(a)], it will simply be imprinted as a point [Figure 6-35(b)].

Surface-type objects can either be placed on a solid's face or intersect it. After the operation, the intersecting edges of regions and surfaces are imprinted on the 3D solid's faces (Figure 6-36).

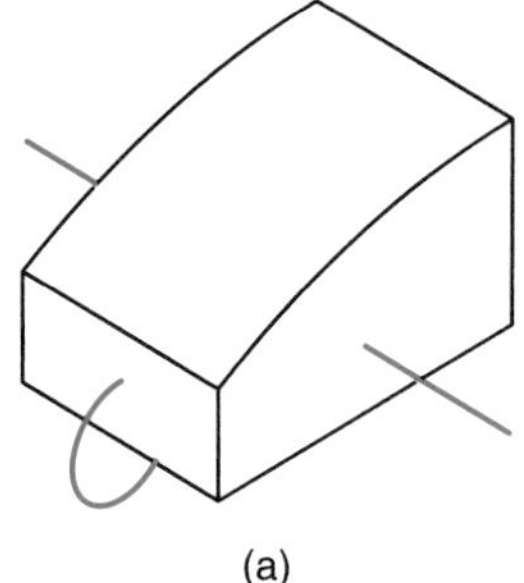

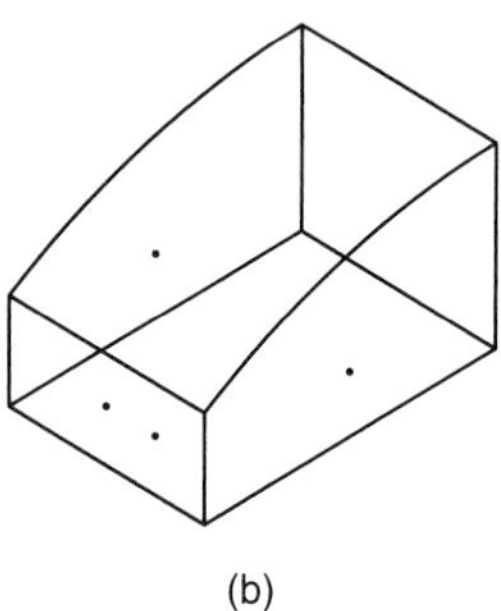

Figure 6-35 Wireframe objects intersecting the face (a) of the 3D solid are imprinted as points (b)

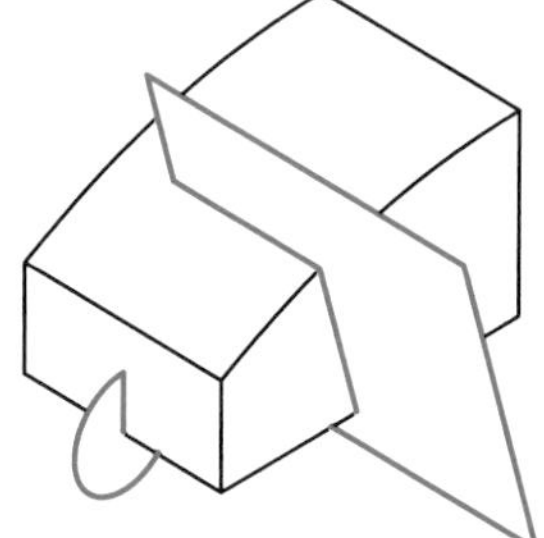

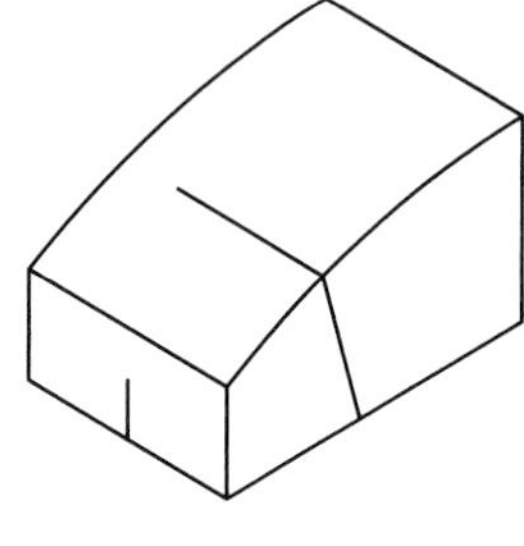

Figure 6-36 Surface-type objects intersecting the face of the 3D solid are imprinted as edges on the 3D solid's faces

A 3D solid object imprints an edge on a 3D solid for each intersection found between the faces of the objects (Figure 6-37).

Depending on the type of object imprinted, there are three types of impressions: points, nonsplitting edges, and splitting edges (Figure 6-38).

Split faces can be selected individually for purposes of performing some face editing operations. Edges imprinted on a 3D solid are automatically eliminated by performing most of the editing operations.

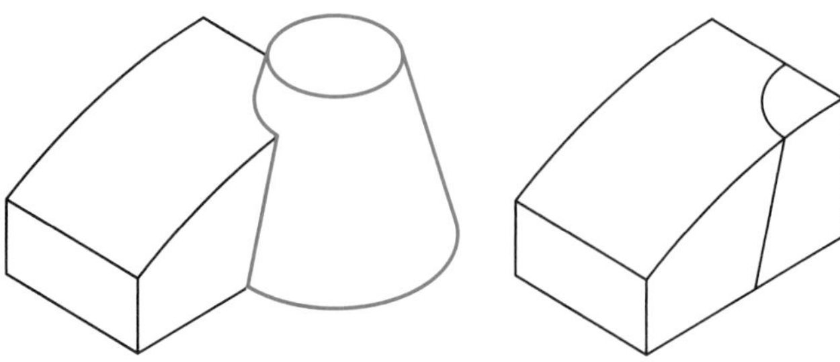

Figure 6-37 3D solids can also imprint their intersecting edges on the faces of other 3D solids

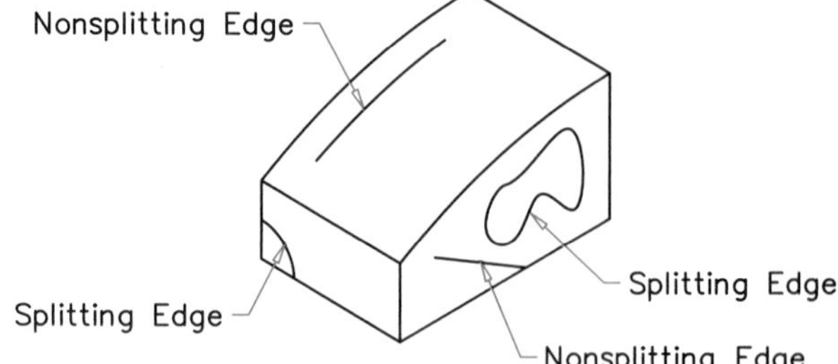

Figure 6-38 Imprinted edges can either split a face or not

Exercise 6-2: Splitting Faces with the Imprint Tool to Perform Further Face Editing Operations

1. **OPEN** either the finished drawing ***Project 5-1*** or ***Exercise 6-1*** from the CD, in case you did not finish ***Project 5-1.***
2. **SAVE** the drawing **AS *Exercise 6-2.***

3. Select the **SE Isometric** viewing point.
4. Select the **Right** UCS.
5. Use the **Copy edges** option of the **SOLIDEDIT** command to copy the selected edge, as indicated in Figure 6-39.
6. Use the **RECTANGLE** command to draw the rectangle in the face of the 3D solid, also as shown in Figure 6-39.

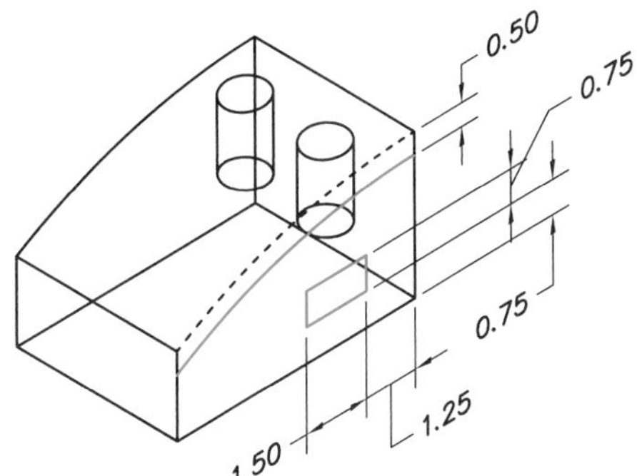

Figure 6-39 Edge to be copied and objects to be drawn on the 3D solid's face

7. Invoke the **Imprint** tool to imprint the arc and the polyline on the 3D solid's face. Respond to the prompts as follows:

   `Select a 3D solid:` *`Select the original solid.`*

   `Select an object to imprint:` *`Select the arc.`*

   `Delete the source object [Yes/No] <N>:` *`y`* ↵

   `Select an object to imprint:` *`Select the rectangle.`*

   `Delete the source object [Yes/No] <N>:` *`y`* ↵

   `Select an object to imprint:` *`<Esc> (To exit the command)`*

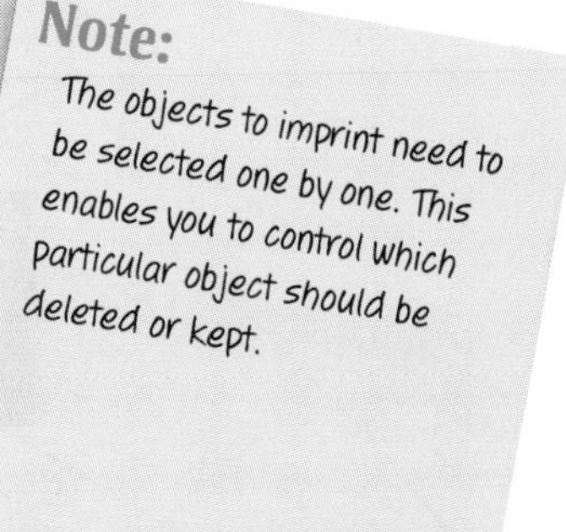

Note:
The objects to imprint need to be selected one by one. This enables you to control which particular object should be deleted or kept.

8. Select the **Extrude faces** option of the **SOLIDEDIT** command. When prompted, select the top portion of the face split by the arc and specify **−1**. The face is depressed 1″ after the operation (Figure 6-40).
9. Select the **Taper faces** option of the **SOLIDEDIT** command and click on the split face delimited by the imprinted rectangle (Figure 6-41). Specify midpoint **1** as the base point, and midpoint **2** as the other point along the axis of tapering. Enter −**20** for the taper angle. After the operation, the 3D solid should look like Figure 6-42.
10. With the **Rotate faces** option of the **SOLIDEDIT** command select the face shown in Figure 6-43. Select endpoints 1 and 2 for the axis of rotation. Enter **45** as the rotation angle. After the operation, the 3D solid should look like Figure 6-44.
11. With the **Right** UCS still current, invoke the **Move faces** option of the **SOLIDEDIT** command and select the four faces of the wedge (Figure 6-45). Move the selected faces orthogonally **0.76″** downward. After the operation, the 3D solid should look like Figure 6-46.
12. **SAVE** the drawing.

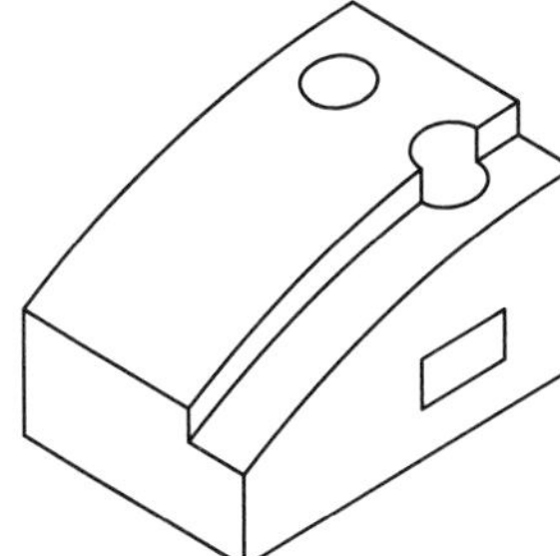

Figure 6-40 After extruding the split face

CLEAN	
Solid Editing Toolbar	
Ribbon Solid Editing panel	
Pull-down Menu	Modify/ Solids Editing/ Clean
Command Line	solidedit ↵ b ↵ L

Clean

In reality, imprinted edges do not make much sense geometrically. The **Clean** tool deletes all redundant edges and edges that have been imprinted but not used. This leaves only those that have become actual edges after a face editing operation.

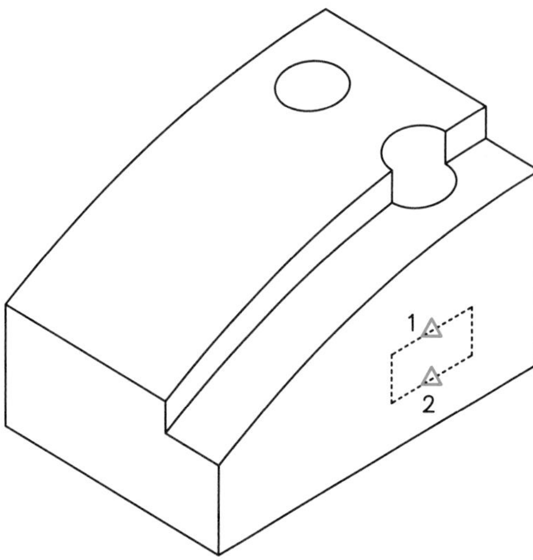

Figure 6-41 Order to specify the axis of tapering in the Taper faces operation

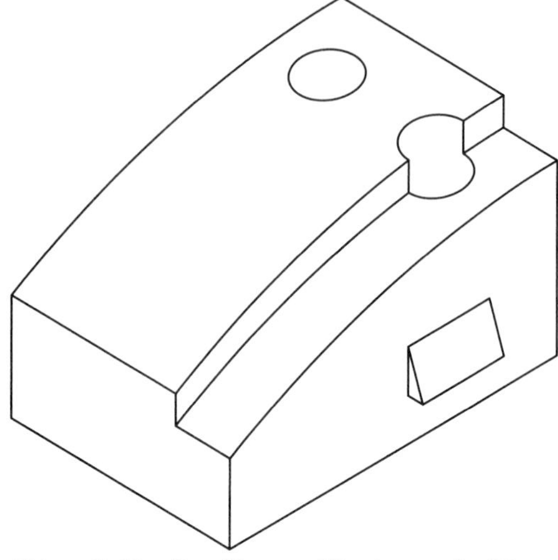

Figure 6-42 Resulting modification on the 3D solid

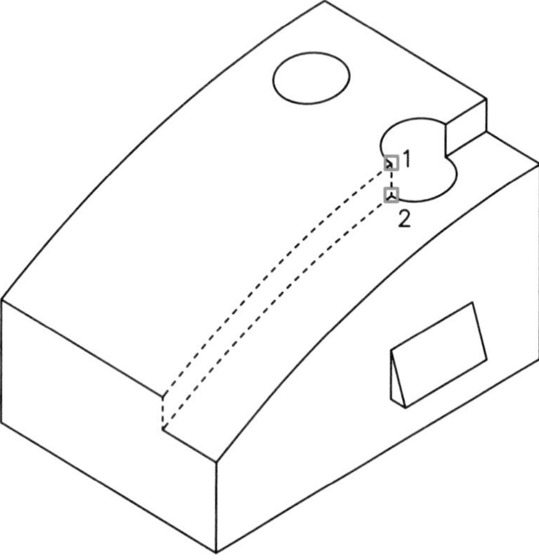

Figure 6-43 Order to specify the axis of rotation in the Rotate faces operation

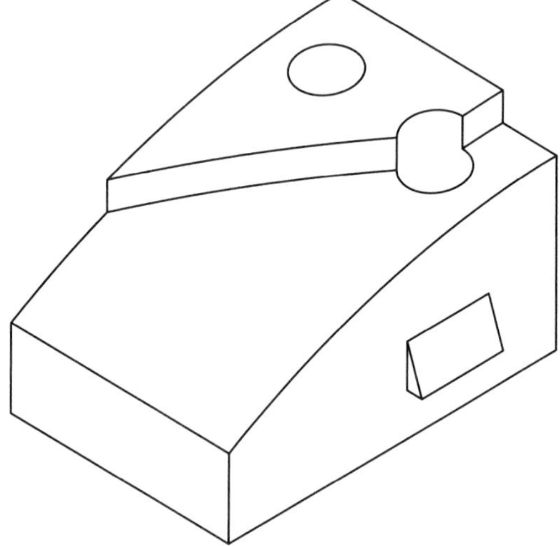

Figure 6-44 Resulting modification on the 3D solid

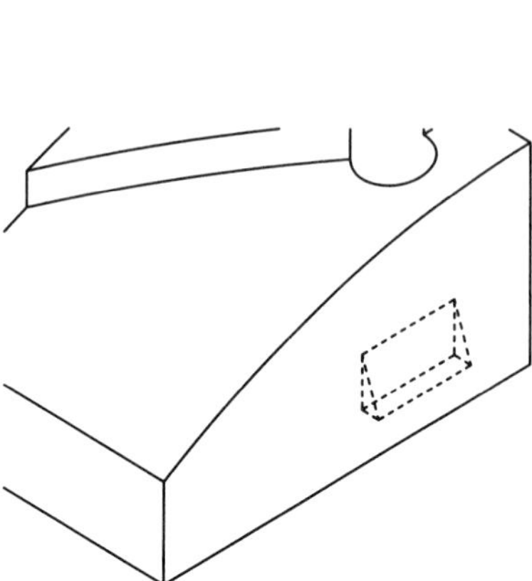

Figure 6-45 Faces to be selected

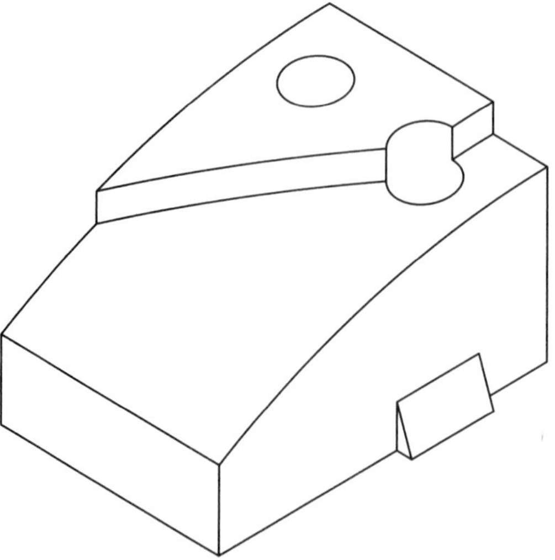

Figure 6-46 Resulting modification on the 3D solid after completing the Move faces operation

Separate

SEPARATE	
Solid Editing Toolbar	
Ribbon Solid Editing panel	
Pull-down Menu	Modify/ Solids Editing/ Separate
Command Line	solidedit ↵ b ↵ p

On certain occasions, you would prefer that separate 3D solids be integrated. But there are many other cases in which they need to be separated. The **Separate** tool separates 3D solids that are made up of more than one isolated piece.

Typically, a 3D solid is made up of a single piece. Some 3D solids, however, are made up of several independent pieces. Two common operations that may result in a 3D solid made up of more than one piece are:

- A **UNION** Boolean operation of two or more 3D solids that do not share any common volume.
- A **SLICE** operation through an imaginary plane that causes the remaining portion of the 3D solid to be made up of more than one piece (Figure 6-47).

Figure 6-47 3D solid can be made up of more than one piece after a SLICE operation

Shell

SHELL	
Solid Editing Toolbar	
Ribbon Solid Editing panel	
Pull-down Menu	Modify/ Solids Editing/ Shell
Command Line	solidedit ↵ b ↵ s

This is probably the most complex tool of the body editing group. It transforms a 3D solid into a shell-type 3D solid by removing its inside volume, leaving only a solid skin layer of a thickness specified by you. The barrel in Figure 6-48 has been modeled by shelling the solid on its left.

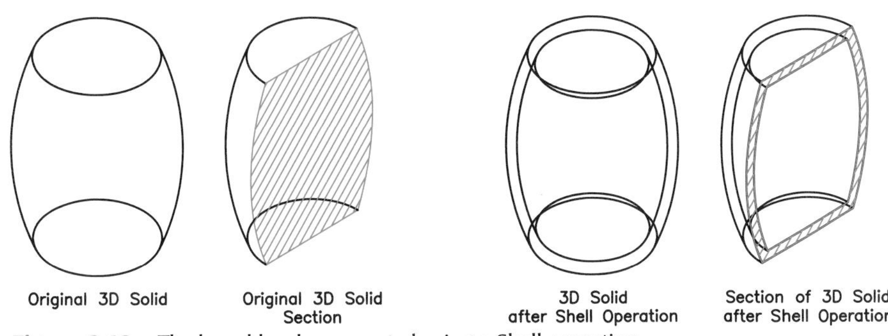

Figure 6-48 The barrel has been created using a Shell operation

Shelling will occur inside the solid's faces if the specified thickness is a positive value. If the thickness is specified as a negative value, then the shelling will occur outside the solid; in this case, the original faces of the solid will become the inside of the shell (Figure 6-49).

Despite the fact that the **Shell** tool belongs to the body editing group, it involves a face selection process. When the tool is first invoked, all of the 3D solid's faces are selected automatically. Thereafter, each face can be individually removed or added to the selection.

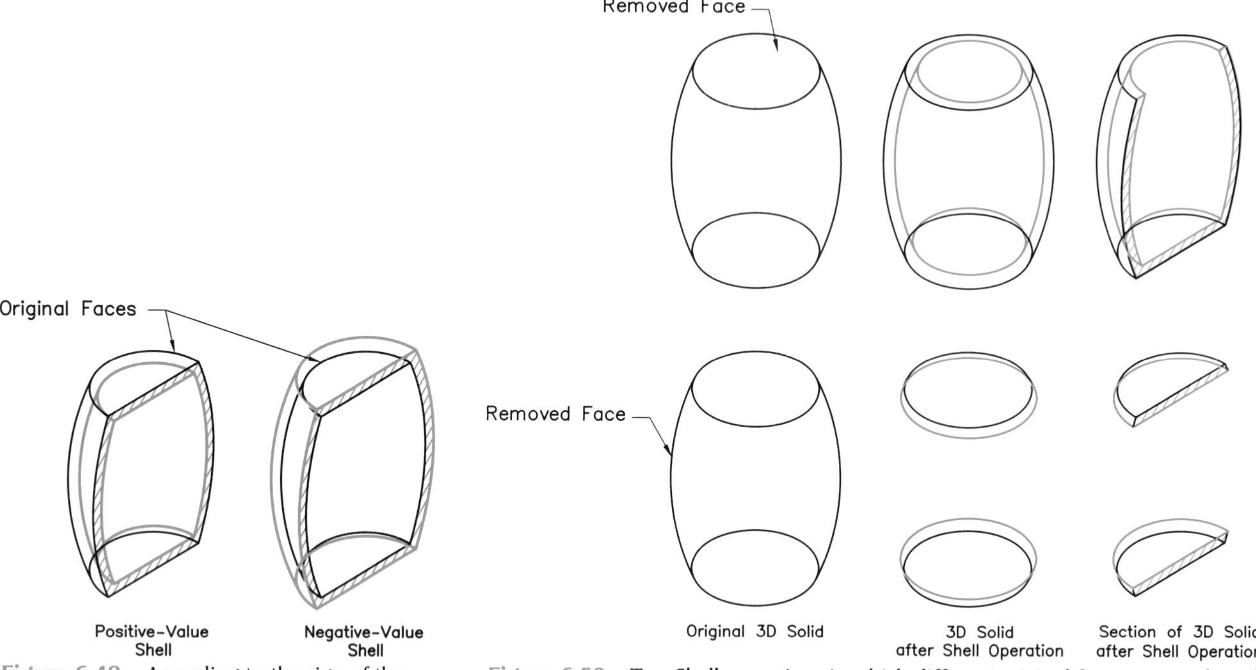

Figure 6-49 According to the sign of the value specified, the shell can occur inside or outside the 3D solid

Figure 6-50 Two Shell operations in which different original faces are unselected

After the selection process is completed, the unselected faces will disappear, creating an opening on the solid (Figure 6-50). Controlling the selection process is the key to success with the **Shell** tool.

Exercise 6-3: Using the Shell Tool

In this exercise you will perform a **Shell** operation on the 3D solid you have been using for the exercises in this chapter. Pay special attention during the selection process to remove only the bottom face.

1. **OPEN** the finished drawing ***Exercise 6-2.***
2. **SAVE** the drawing **AS *Exercise 6-3.***
3. Select the **SW Isometric** viewing point.
4. Invoke the **Shell** option of the **SOLIDEDIT** command and respond to the prompts as follows:

   Select a 3D solid: *Select the solid by picking any of its edges.*

   Remove faces or [Undo/Add/ALL]: *Select the edge shown in* Figure 6-51.

   Remove faces or [Undo/Add/ALL]: *a* ↵

   Select faces or [Undo/Remove/ALL]: *Select the right face by clicking on it as shown in* Figure 6-52.

   Select faces or [Undo/Remove/ALL]: ↵ *(To end the face selection process)*

   Enter the shell offset distance: *.125* ↵

   Enter a body editing option

   [Imprint/seParate solids/Shell/cLean/Check/Undo/eXit] <eXit>: *<Esc> (To exit the command)*

Note:
By default, all the faces are selected with this tool when you select the 3D solid. From that time on, it is not necessary to hold down the **<Shift>** key to unselect a face because the operation will actually prompt you to select faces for removal.

Note:
Two faces were removed automatically by selecting the edge. The front face should not have been removed, so you will add it back to the selection.

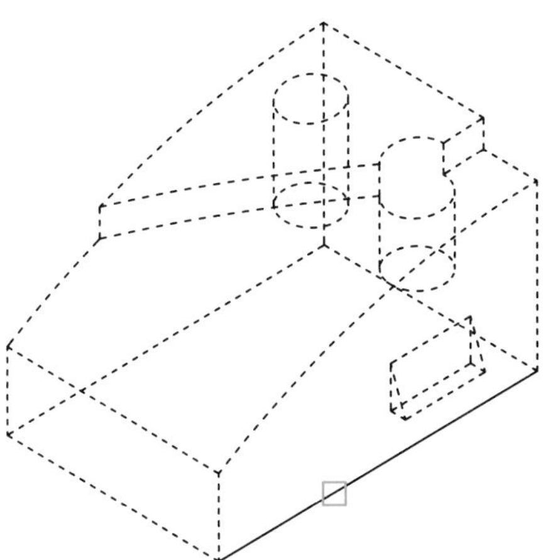

Figure 6-51 Picking the Edge shown will remove two faces

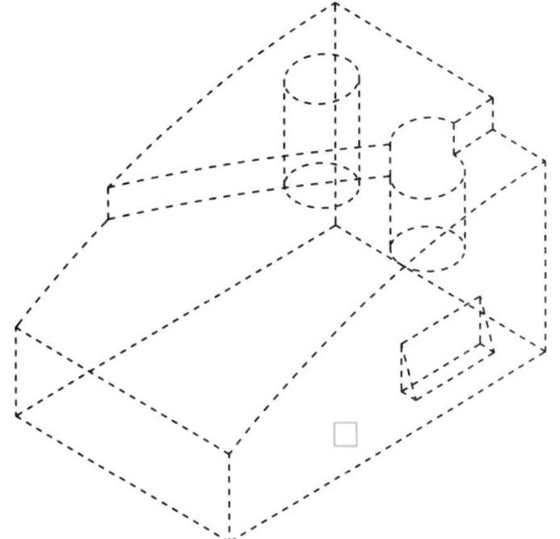

Figure 6-52 Adding one of the two faces removed

5. Select the **Realistic** visual style and invoke the **3DFORBIT** command to inspect the 3D solid with the volume removed. The results should look like Figure 6-53 from two different viewing points.
6. **SAVE** the drawing.

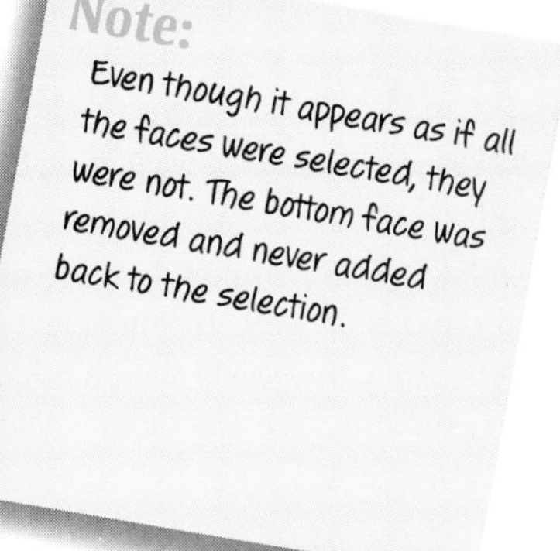

Note:
Even though it appears as if all the faces were selected, they were not. The bottom face was removed and never added back to the selection.

Plastic parts are typically developed as shell-type objects. They consist of thin walls that interconnect, forming the most dissimilar shapes and contours. The **Shell** operation is an excellent application for the design of plastic parts because it allows you to empty the volume of 3D solids, creating shell-type objects with constant wall thickness. Proficiency in the use of this particular tool can be seen as a potential benefit for organizations involved with this widespread manufacturing process.

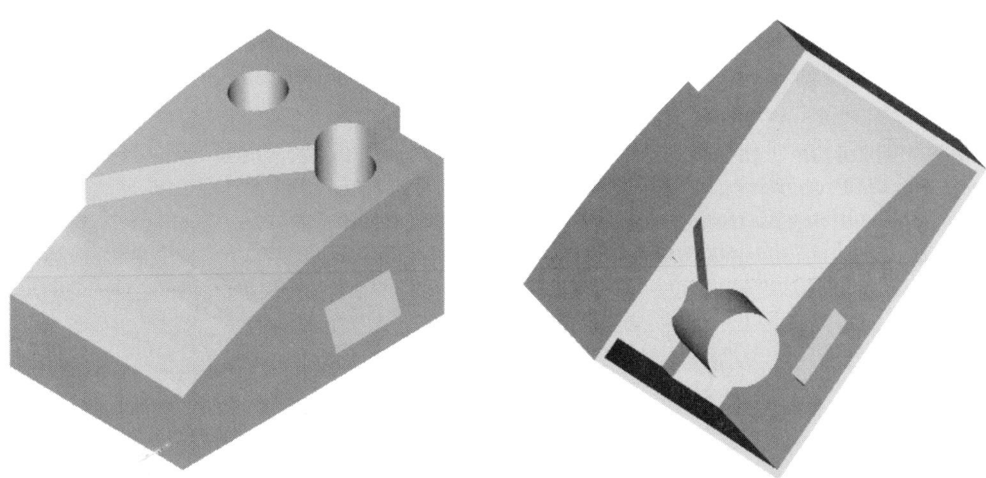

Figure 6-53 Different shaded views of the final 3D model

CHECK	
Solid Editing Toolbar	
Ribbon Solid Editing panel	
Pull-down Menu	Modify/ Solids Editing/ Check
Command Line	solidedit ↵ b ↵ c

Check

The AutoCAD software uses a technology named ***ShapeManager*** to generate 3D solids. A complex 3D solid could become an invalid ShapeManager solid after a certain operation. If this happens, you

ShapeManager: Modeler or engine used by AutoCAD to change the form and appearance of 3D solids.

will not be able to perform any more edit operations on it. A way to confirm if a 3D solid has become an invalid ShapeManager solid is by invoking the **Check** tool.

Even though face editing operations are not permitted on invalid ShapeManager solids, many operations can still be performed:

- Boolean operations
- Body and edge editing operations
- **SLICE** and **SECTION** commands
- Any standard operation (**ERASE, MOVE, COPY,** etc.)

The **SOLIDCHECK** system variable is related to the **Check** tool. When activated (**1**), which is its default status, it automatically determines whether or not the operation created a valid ShapeManager solid. **SOLIDCHECK** should not be turned off.

OTHER EDITING OPERATIONS WITH 3D SOLIDS

EXTRACTING THE EDGES OF 3D OBJECTS WITH THE XEDGES COMMAND

XEDGES	
Ribbon Solid Editing panel	
Pull-down Menu	Modify/ 3D Operation/ Extract Edges
Command Line	xedges

The **XEDGES** command can be used to extract edges not only from 3D solids but from surfaces and regions as well. If you select the entire object, this command will extract every one of its edges. You can specify which edges to extract by holding down the **<Ctrl>** key and picking the edges directly, or by using any selection tool such as windows and crossing windows.

EDITING ORIGINAL TYPES OF 3D SOLIDS AND SURFACES THROUGH THE PROPERTIES PALETTE

AutoCAD gives a unique, distinctive name to original 3D solids and surfaces according to the operation from which they originated. This name is shown as the **type** of 3D solid or surface, for example:

- Cylinder 3D solid type
- Extrusion 3D solid type
- Sweep-type surface
- Loft with cross section only surface type

You can find out the type of 3D solid or surface of an object through the AutoCAD text window by invoking the **LIST** command. You can also obtain such information from the **Geometry** section in the **Properties** palette (Figure 6-54).

The **Geometry** section of the **Properties** palette contains specific geometric properties about original 3D solids and surfaces. Some of these properties can be modified directly in the **Properties** palette, allowing you to edit the 3D object without invoking any command. Each section of the **Properties** palette can be folded or unfolded by clicking on its double arrow.

In all, there are 13 types of 3D solids and six types of surfaces. Each of the seven types of 3D solid primitives is generated with its own command. The **EXTRUDE, REVOLVE, SWEEP,** and **LOFT** commands generate their own type of 3D solid or surface as well. As you learned in the previous chapter, the **LOFT** command in particular generates three different types of 3D objects, depending on the method used. The **EXTRUDE** command generates a swept 3D object when using the **Path** option.

3D solids that have lost their history due to a postediting operation, as well as those turned into basic representations using the **BREP** command, are not listed as any particular type of 3D solid. Their geometric properties cannot be changed through the **Properties** palette.

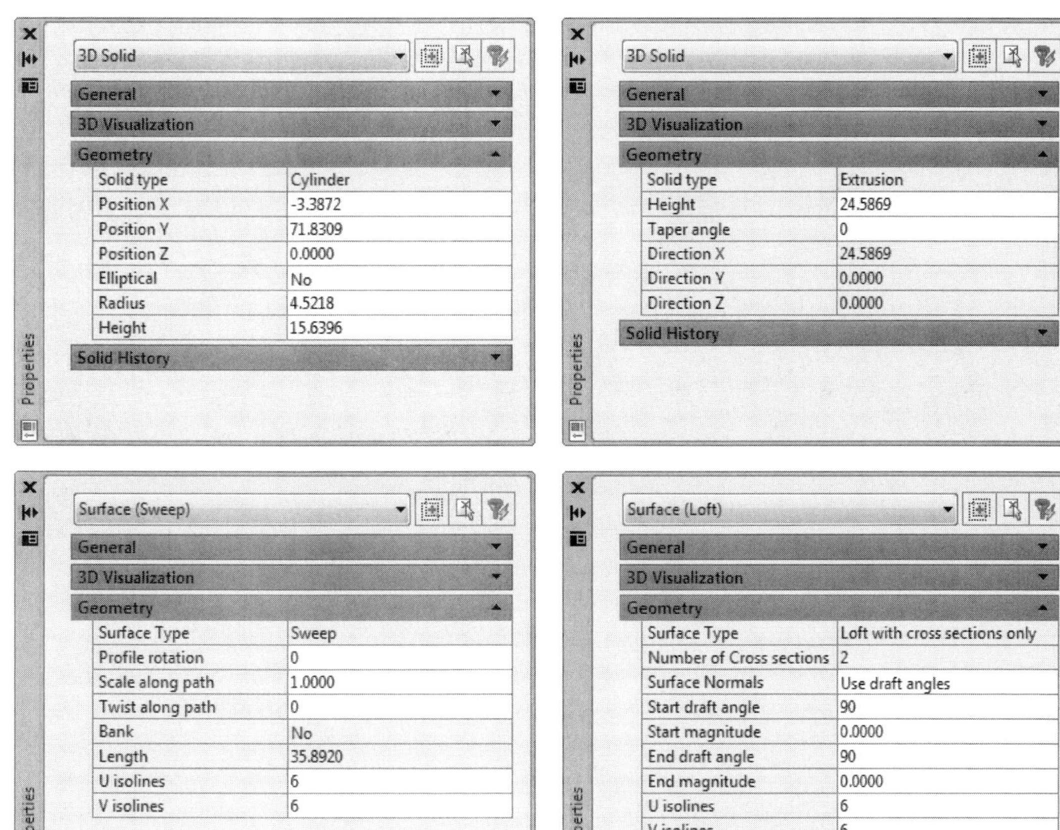

Figure 6-54 The Properties palette provides information about the type of 3D solid or surface selected

Exercise 6-4: Editing Original 3D Solids Through the Properties Palette

1. Start a **NEW** drawing in **Imperial** units.
2. **SAVE** the drawing **AS** ***Exercise 6-4***.
3. Select the **SE Isometric** viewpoint.
4. Select the **Realistic** Visual Style.
5. Turn on the **Grid** (<**F7**>).
6. Set the **FACETRES** system variable to **6**.
7. Select the **Green** color in the **Properties** toolbar.
8. Invoke the **CONE** command and create a **Cone** type of 3D Solid. Specify the center point, radius, and height by clicking anywhere in the drawing area while visualizing the object being developed.
9. Select the 3D Solid and open the **Properties** palette. Under **Geometry,** change the following properties (Figure 6-55):
   - **Base radius:** 2.5
   - **Top radius:** 1
   - **Height:** 3
10. **EXPLODE** the cone.
11. **ERASE** the conical surface.
12. **EXPLODE** the top and bottom regions.
13. Invoke the **LOFT** command and create a **Loft with cross sections only** 3D solid. Select the two circles as the cross sections. Finally, accept the **Smooth Fit** surface control in the **Loft Settings** dialog box and click **OK** to close it.
14. Select the 3D solid and open the **Properties** palette if you have previously closed it. Under **Geometry,** change the **Surface Normals** to **Use draft angles.**

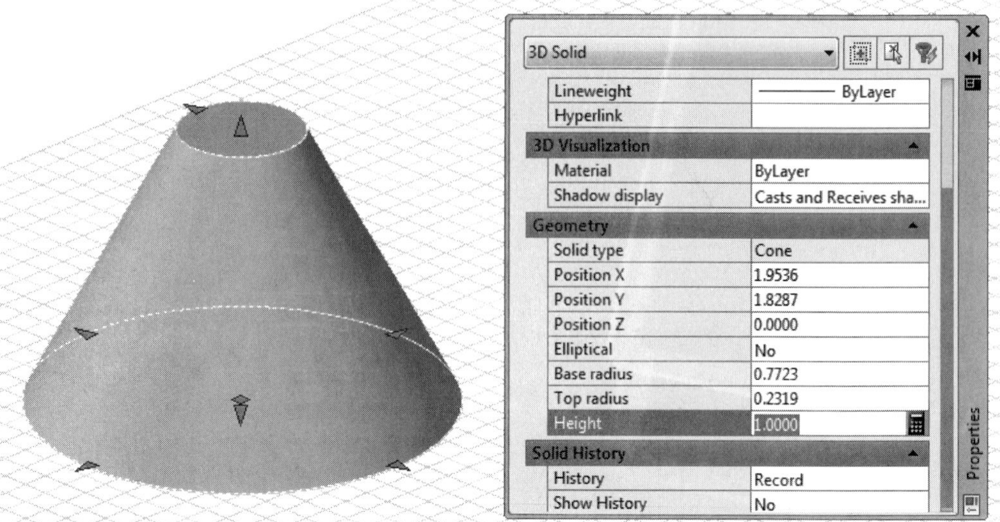

Figure 6-55 Modifying a cone-shaped 3D solid through the Properties palette

15. Set both the **Start draft angle** and **End draft angle** to **60**. The 3D model should look like Figure 6-56.
16. **SAVE** the drawing.

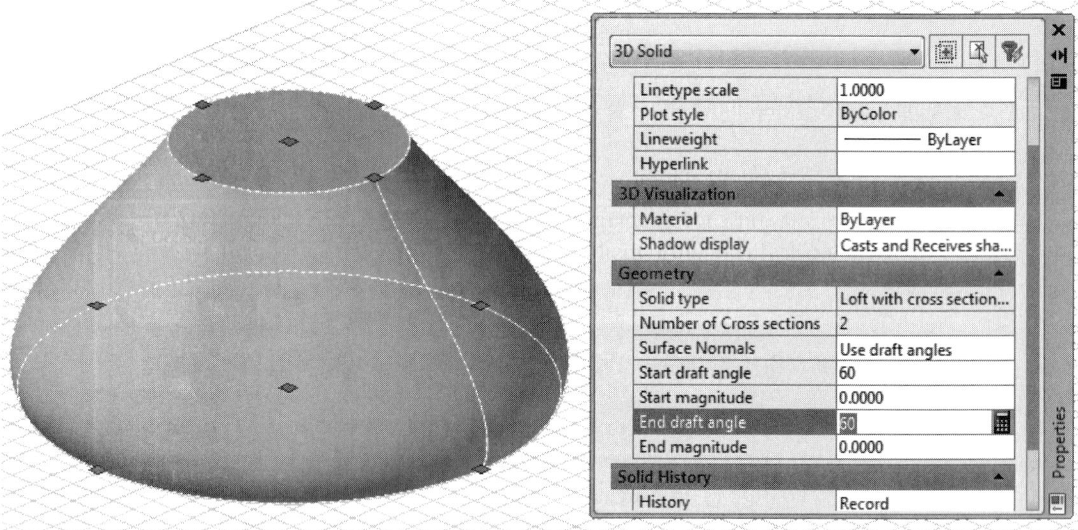

Figure 6-56 Modifying a Loft with cross sections only type of 3D solid through the Properties palette

Editing Composite 3D Solids Through the Properties Palette

Composites are not displayed under any particular type of 3D solid. Their geometric properties cannot be changed through the **Properties** palette either. However, the geometric properties of original 3D solids that are involved in the Boolean operation of a composite 3D solid whose **History** is set to **Record** can be changed in the **Properties** palette (Figure 6-57).

The original 3D solids of a composite 3D solid are selected by holding down the **<Ctrl>** key before making the selection. Only original 3D solids defined as a particular type display their geometric properties. Other composite 3D solids and basic representation 3D solids that were used to obtain the composite 3D solid will not display any geometric properties.

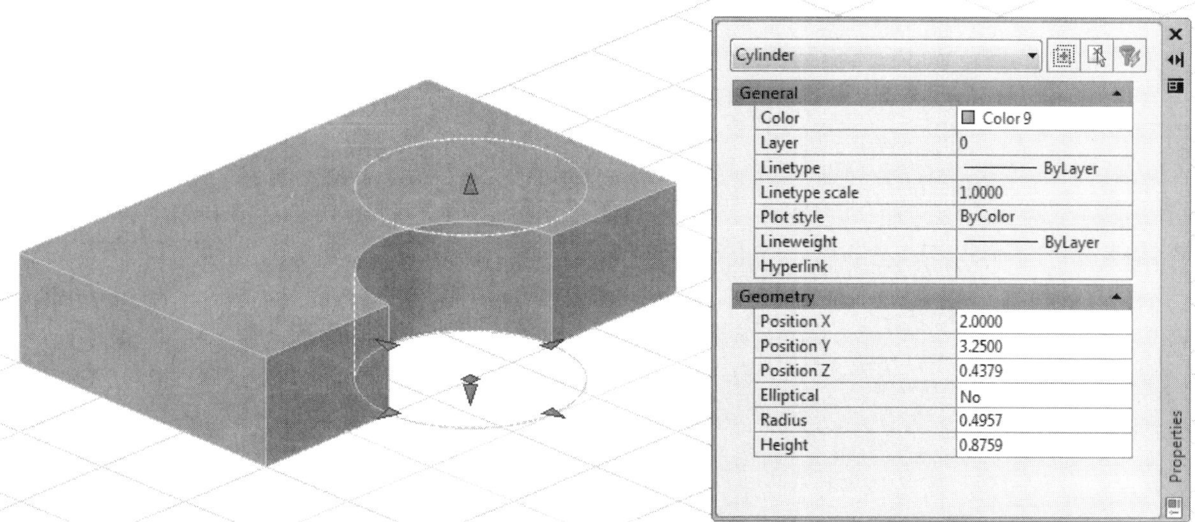

Figure 6-57 The properties of the original 3D solids that make up a composite 3D solid can be changed in the Properties palette

Using the Grips to Edit 3D Solids and Surfaces

Grips allow you to easily edit original 3D solids and surfaces. The number and location of grips depend on the type of 3D object selected, regardless of its shape. Figure 6-58 shows four identical shapes of different types of 3D solids. The grips show differently from one solid to another. Figure 6-59 shows a similar situation for three types of surfaces.

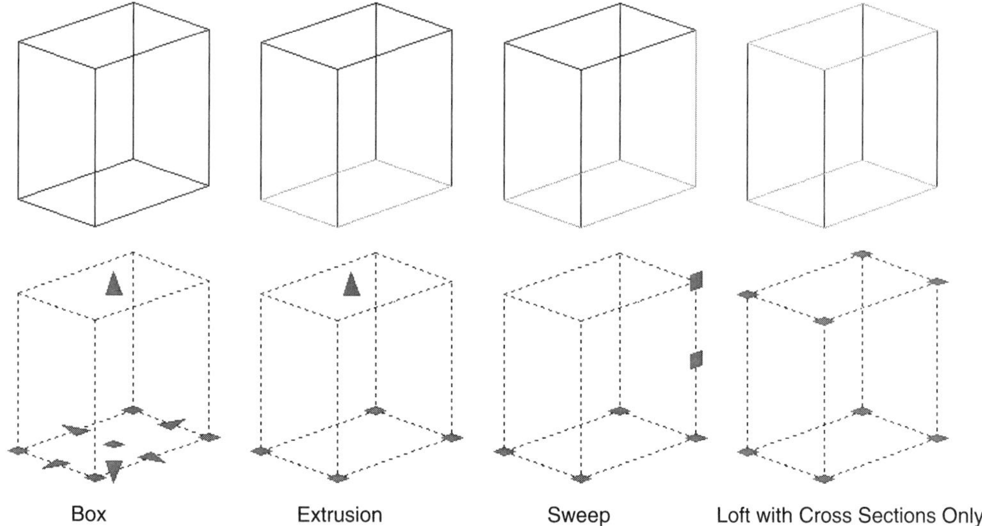

Figure 6-58 Different grips are shown for different types of 3D solids

Triangular or directional grips control the length of the 3D solid in a specific direction. These grips are used by all the primitive types and the **Extrusion** type of 3D solids. For example, selecting the directional grips located in the bottom of a box will modify the 3D solid in this specific direction (Figure 6-60).

The standard square grips located in vertices can be used to deform a 3D solid or surface depending on its type and the source object used to obtain it. For example, selecting any standard grip located on the vertex of a box-type 3D solid box can deform two of its dimensions (Figure 6-61).

The grips located on the vertices of an **Extrusion** type 3D solid can be used to deform the 3D solid only if the profile used was a closed polyline (Figure 6-62). If the 3D solid was created from a region or a surface, however, you will not be able to deform it using the standard grips.

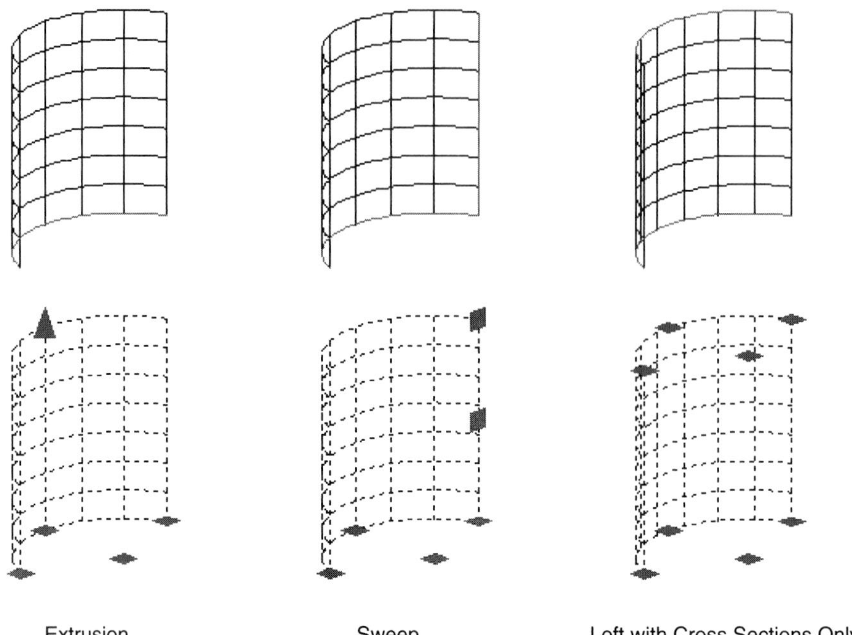

Figure 6-59 Different grips are shown for different types of surfaces

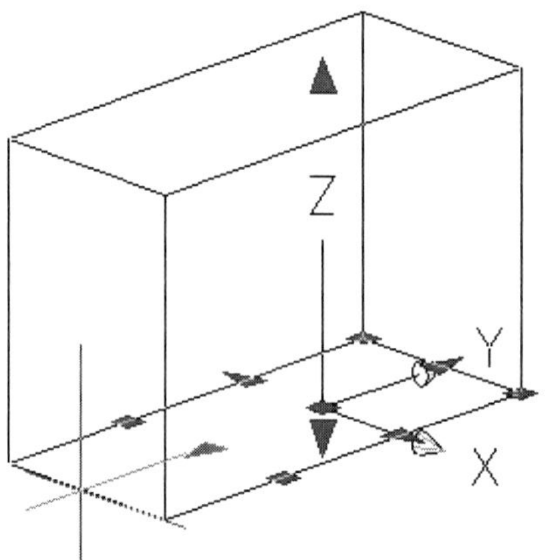

Figure 6-60 When triangular or directional grips are pulled, the 3D solid changes its size in the direction in which it is pulled

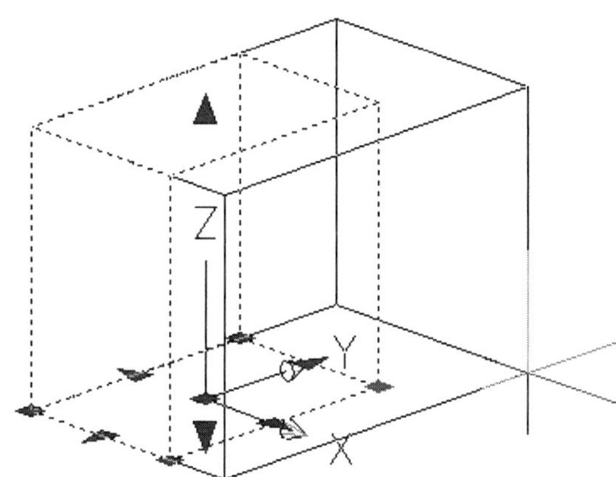

Figure 6-61 When a standard grip of a box-type 3D solid is pulled, it is deformed in two directions

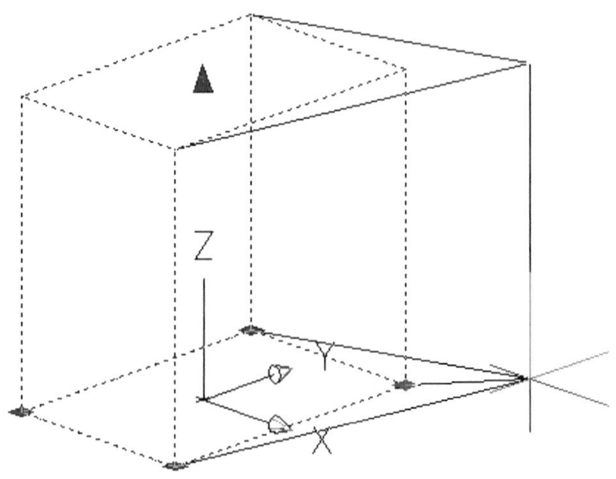

Figure 6-62 When a standard grip of an extruded-type 3D solid is pulled, the object is deformed differently from the box

Selecting the grips of swept-type 3D solids and surfaces enables you to modify both the profile and the sweep path control grips. Modifying the sweep path control grips also affects the plane in which the profile was placed in order to maintain its perpendicularity (Figure 6-63).

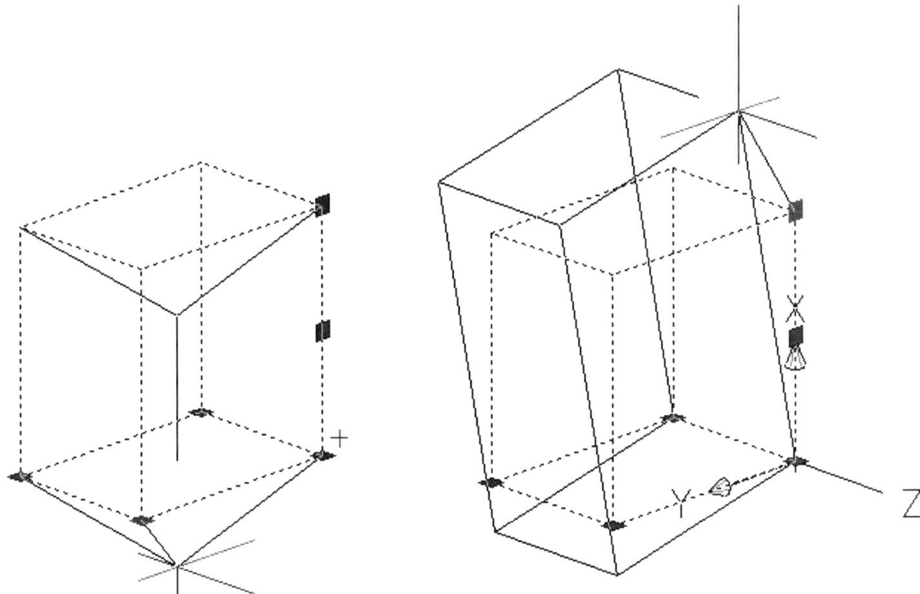

Figure 6-63 Different modifications can be made by pulling the grips of swept-type 3D solids

Loft with cross sections only and **Loft with path**–type 3D objects can be deformed by selecting the control grips of any of the cross sections' profiles, as well as the path (Figure 6-64). **Loft with guide curves**–type 3D objects cannot be deformed using standard grips.

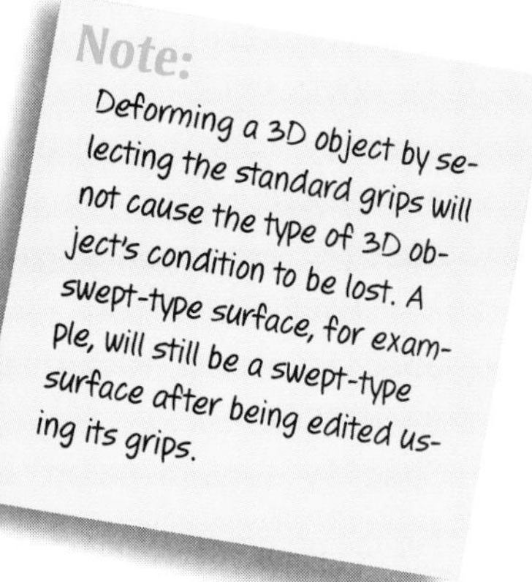

Note:
Deforming a 3D object by selecting the standard grips will not cause the type of 3D object's condition to be lost. A swept-type surface, for example, will still be a swept-type surface after being edited using its grips.

Composite 3D solids, as well as other 3D solids that have lost their history due to a postediting operation or through the **BREP** command, will show only the base control grip when they are selected (Figure 6-65).

You can, however, select and modify the grips of the original 3D solids of a composite 3D solid by holding down the **<Ctrl>** key before making the selection (Figure 6-66).

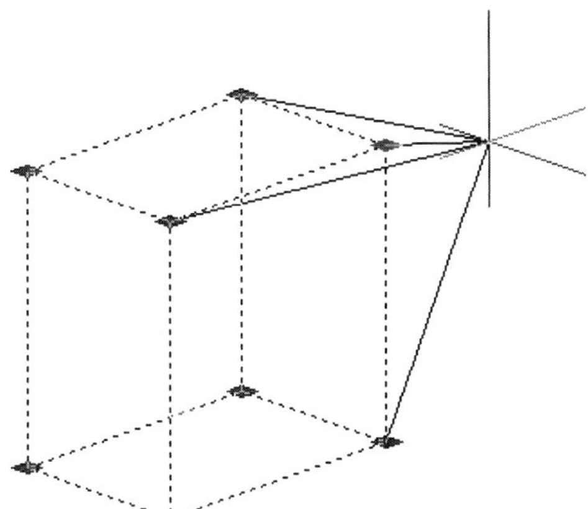

Figure 6-64 The cross sections of lofted 3D solids can be deformed by pulling the grips

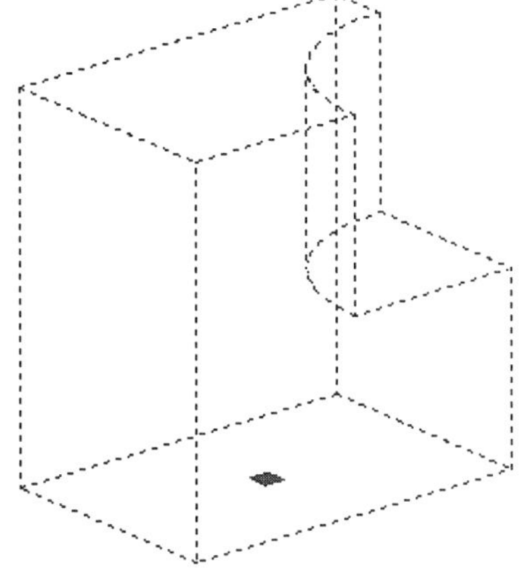

Figure 6-65 Only the positional grip shows up in a basic representation 3D solid

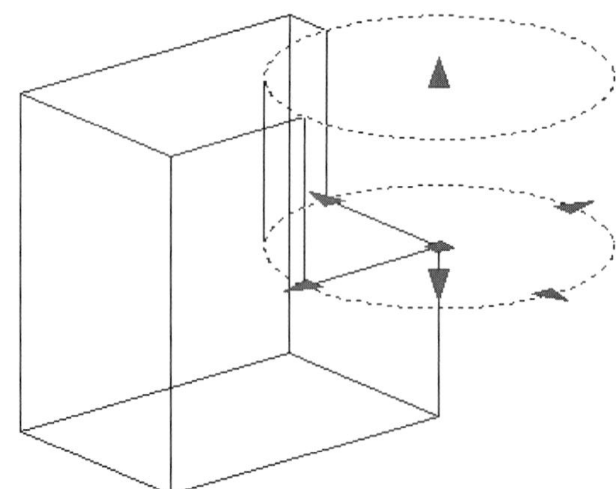

Figure 6-66 The original 3D solids of a selected composite

As with wire-type objects, you can cycle through the grip editing routine. This allows you to perform one of the following five operations:

- **Stretch**
- **Move**
- **Rotate**
- **Scale**
- **Mirror**

To move on to the next operation, you must press the <**Space**> key.

```
** STRETCH **
Specify stretch point or [Base point/Copy/Undo/eXit]:
** MOVE **
Specify move point or [Base point/Copy/Undo/eXit]:
** ROTATE **
Specify rotation angle or [Base point/Copy/Undo/Reference/eXit]:
** SCALE **
Specify scale factor or [Base point/Copy/Undo/Reference/eXit]:
** MIRROR **
Specify second point or [Base point/Copy/Undo/eXit]:
```

For the primitives type of 3D solids, these operations are available only when selecting the base control grip.

Exercise 6-5: Editing the Original 3D Solid of a Composite 3D Solid by Using the Grips

1. **OPEN** the drawing ***Exercise 6-5*** from the CD. It contains a simple composite 3D solid.
2. **SAVE** the drawing as ***Exercise 6-5 solved.***
3. Holding down the <**Ctrl**> key, click on one of the arc edges (Figure 6-67) to select the original 3D solid cylinder.

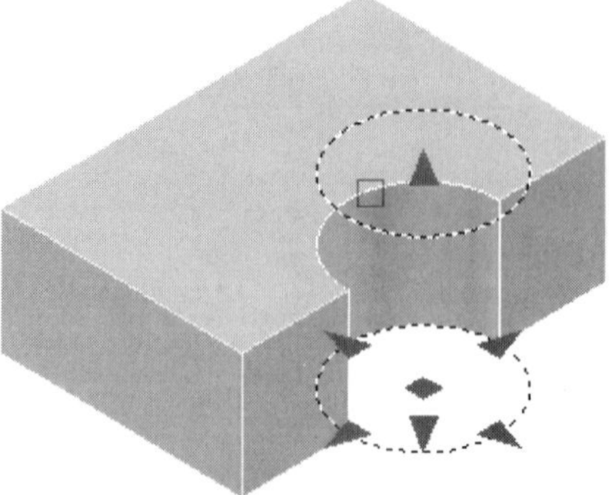

Figure 6-67 The original cylinder of a composite 3D solid is selected

4. Select the arrow grip shown in Figure 6-68. With the **ORTHO** mode on, move the pointer toward the arrow direction and enter **0.5** in the command line to increase the radius of the cylinder by 0.5″.
5. Press the **<Esc>** key to clear the grips.
6. **SAVE** the drawing.

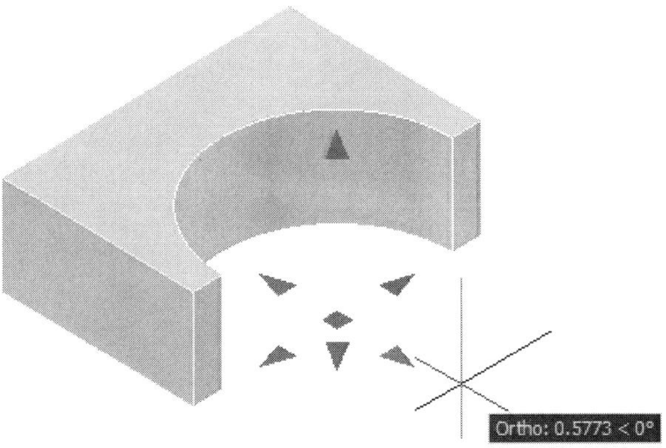

Figure 6-68 The original cylinder is modified by pulling one of its grips; as a result, the composite 3D solid is modified

EDITING 3D SOLIDS BY MODIFYING THE SUBOBJECTS

Subobjects are elements of an inferior order that are part of a 3D solid. Original 3D solids combined into a composite 3D solid can be considered to be subobjects as well. The term *subobjects,* however, more often refers to the elements forming part of any type of 3D solid, including basic representation solids. Faces, edges, and vertices are all subobjects of 3D solids.

subobject: Any face, edge, or vertex of a 3D solid. The original 3D solids of a composite 3D solid can be considered as subobjects as well.

You can select subobjects by holding down the **<Ctrl>** key, which is the same procedure used to select original 3D solids of a composite 3D solid. Figure 6-69 shows the three types of subobject selected, each on a different 3D solid.

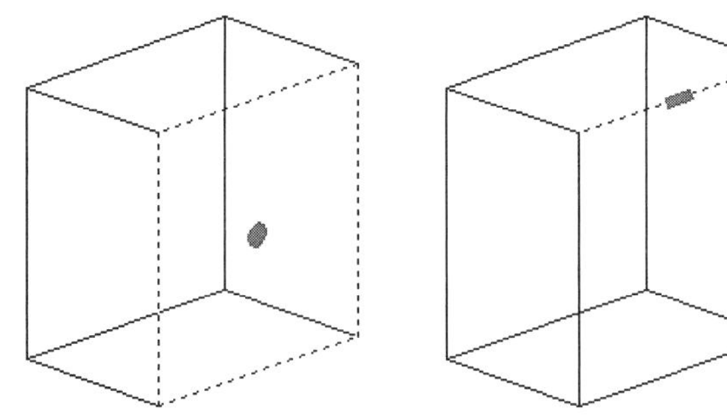

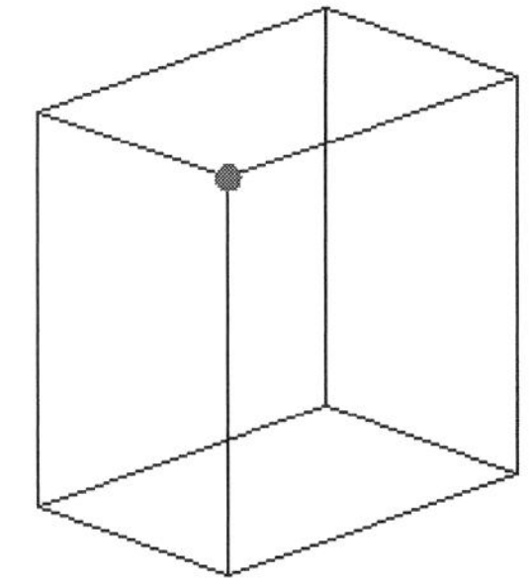

Figure 6-69 The three types of subobjects and their typical grips

You can simultaneously select multiple subobjects from different 3D solids, using any selection method such as windows and crossing windows (Figure 6-70).

After selecting the subobject, you can either select its grip to relocate it, or invoke the standard **MOVE, ROTATE,** and **SCALE** commands to deform the 3D object. For example, scaling down the selected face in Figure 6-71(a), based on the endpoint shown, will deform a box into the 3D solid shown in Figure 6-71(b).

As another example, moving down the selected edge in Figure 6-72(a) will deform the box into the 3D solid shown in Figure 6-72(b).

Selecting a 3D solid's subobjects creates an infinite number of editing possibilities. You can combine faces, edges, and vertices in the same operation.

Note:

Deforming a 3D object by using the subobjects will cause the information on the type of 3D object to be lost, turning the object into a basic representation 3D solid.

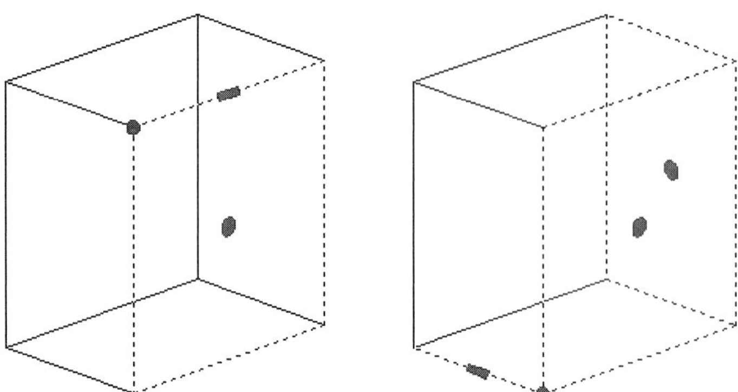

Figure 6-70 Several subobjects selected

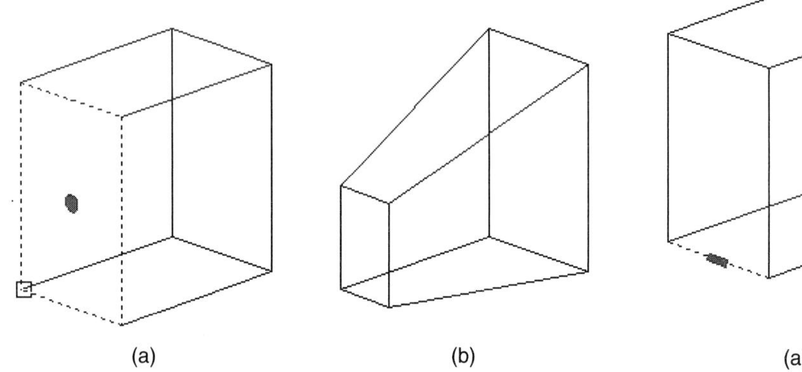

Figure 6-71 A selected face subobject (a); after it is scaled down with its base on the selected endpoint (b)

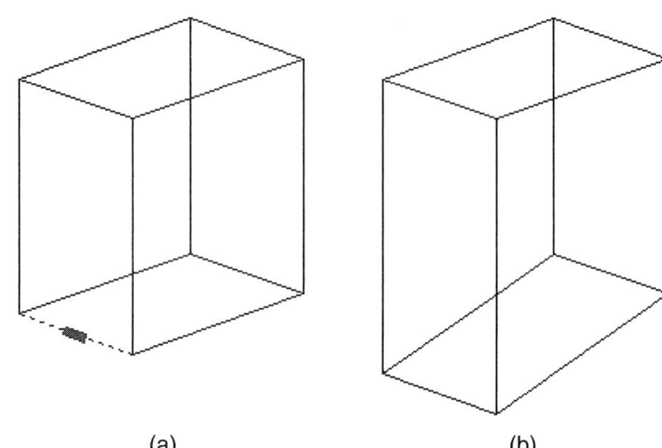

Figure 6-72 A selected edge subobject (a); after it is moved down (b)

Exercise 6-6: Editing the Original 3D Solid of a Composite 3D Solid by Using the Grips

1. **OPEN** the drawing ***Exercise 6-5*** from the CD. It contains a simple composite 3D solid.
2. **SAVE** the drawing as ***Exercise 6-6.***
3. Invoke the **BREP** command by entering its name in the command line, or change the **History** property to **None** in the **Properties** palette. This will erase the history of the 3D solid.
4. Holding down the **<Ctrl>** key, click on the cylindrical face to select this subobject (Figure 6-73).
5. Invoke the **MOVE** command, and click anywhere to specify the base point. With the **ORTHO** mode activated, move the pointer toward the negative direction of the *Y*-axis and enter **0.5** in the command line (Figure 6-74).
6. Select the **2D Wireframe** visual style.
7. Practice deforming the 3D solid by selecting vertex and edge subobjects.
8. **SAVE** the drawing.

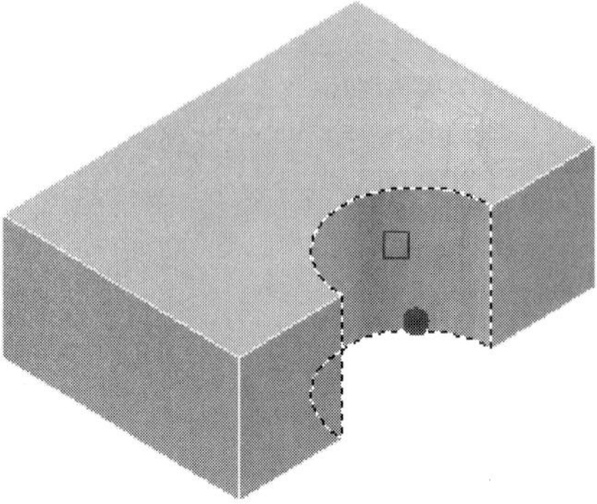

Figure 6-73 A selected face subobject

Figure 6-74 3D solid modified by moving the face subobject

Summary

Just like 2D drawings, 3D models frequently need to be changed. Regardless of the nature of the revision, the changes need to be made somehow.

Throughout this chapter you have learned the use of tools that modify the geometry of 3D solids. The knowledge acquired here should allow you to perform many of these changes. It is not always easy, however, to make major modifications on 3D solids. Sometimes starting from scratch is the best solution.

Besides the editing operations performed with the **SOLIDEDIT** command, as well as the use of grips and subobjects with 3D solids, you have also learned particular tools, such as the **Shell** tool, that are used to obtain specific geometric shapes. The **Shell** operation is a key operation in the design of objects with thin walls, such as plastic parts. Other tools will allow you to extract geometry that can be used in other operations (e.g., **Copy Faces, Copy Edges,** and the **XEDGES** command).

You have also learned how to split the faces of 3D solids with the **Imprint** tool. After you become familiar with this new tool as well as the others presented in this chapter, you should be able to create a greater number of different 3D solid shapes in less time.

Chapter Test Questions

Multiple Choice

1. Which of the following is not one of the categorized groups of tools contained in the **SOLIDEDIT** command?
   a. Vertex
   b. Edge
   c. Face
   d. Body
2. When selecting faces within the **SOLIDEDIT** command, which of the following actions will be accepted by AutoCAD?
   a. Picking a face
   b. Picking an edge
   c. Picking a silhouette
   d. All of the above
3. If you had to change the location of a hole through a board-shaped 3D solid, which of the following operations could you not use?
   a. Subobject editing
   b. Grip editing
   c. **Taper faces**
   d. **Move faces**
4. If you had to modify the length of a slot through a board-shaped 3D solid, which of the following operations could you use?
   a. **Copy faces**
   b. **Offset faces**
   c. **Move faces**
   d. **Rotate faces**
5. A cylindrical face of a 3D solid having a radius of 1.25 is edited using the **Offset faces** tool. If the offset distance specified is **–0.25,** what will the final radius of the edited face be?
   a. 1.50
   b. 1.25
   c. 1.00
   d. None of the above
6. With the **Rotate faces** operation, which of the following options is not available to define the imaginary axis of rotation?
   a. Selecting an object
   b. Selecting an edge
   c. Specifying two points
   d. The viewing plane
7. Which of the following operations could not be used to transform a 3D solid cone into a cylinder?
   a. Changing the geometry in the **Properties** palette
   b. **Rotate faces**
   c. Grip editing
   d. **Taper faces**
8. Which of the following objects could not be imprinted on the face of a 3D solid?
   a. Polyline
   b. 3D solid
   c. Spline
   d. Polygon mesh
9. The tools of the **SOLIDEDIT** command will not allow you to change the color of which of the following elements of 3D solids?
   a. The edges
   b. The faces
   c. The entire body
   d. All of the above
10. Which of the following is not a valid type of 3D object?
    a. Swept 3D solid
    b. **Loft with cross sections only** surface
    c. Cone surface
    d. 3D solid cylinder

Matching

Column A	Column B
a. **Shell**	1. Faces, edges, and vertices of 3D solids
b. **Separate**	2. Causes the faces of 3D solids to incline
c. **XEDGES**	3. Moves the faces of a 3D solid
d. **Move faces**	4. Extracts the 3D solid faces as surfaces and regions
e. **Imprint**	5. Relocates the faces parallel to their original location
f. **Extrude faces**	6. Makes the isolated pieces of 3D solids independent
g. **Copy faces**	7. Removes the inside volume of a 3D solid
h. **Offset faces**	8. Extracts edges from a 3D solid
i. **Subobjects**	9. Protrudes planar faces of a 3D solid
j. **Taper faces**	10. Adds temporary edges to a 3D solid's faces

True or False

1. True or False: Inside the **SOLIDEDIT** command, you can apply the same methods to select faces of a 3D solid as those used to select objects with the **ERASE** command.
2. True or False: Inside the **SOLIDEDIT** command, if all the faces of a 3D solid have been selected, picking an edge while holding the **<Shift>** key down will always remove two faces from the selection.
3. True or False: The **Extrude faces** operation can be performed with both planar and nonplanar faces of 3D solids.
4. True or False: The direction of the tapering vector aligns the tapering plane perpendicular to it.
5. True or False: The **Separate** tool is used to remove any holes, chamfers, and fillets from a 3D solid.
6. True or False: Of all the edges imprinted on a 3D solid, the only ones that are really useful for editing operations are the ones that reach the edges of the faces, causing them to split.
7. True or False: The **Clean** tool removes only the temporary imprinted edges that do not split any of the 3D solid's faces.
8. True or False: Selecting the grips enables you to modify the path stored on a swept surface.
9. True or False: The **BREP** command erases the history of 3D solids, turning them into basic representation 3D solids.
10. True or False: You cannot select the subobjects of a composite 3D solid that has been turned into a basic representation 3D solid.

Chapter Tutorials

Tutorial 6-1: The Enclosure of a Light Fixture

1. Start the project by opening a **NEW** drawing using **Imperial** units.
2. **SAVE** the drawing **AS *Tutorial 6-1.***
3. Set the **DISPSILH** system variable to **1**.
4. Set the **ISOLINES** system variable to **0**.
5. Set the **FACETRES** system variable to **6**.
6. Select the **SE Isometric** viewing point.
7. Select the **Right** UCS.
8. Draw a **4″**-diameter circle anywhere.
9. **EXTRUDE** the circle **–6″**. Specify 5° as the angle of taper by using the corresponding option.
10. Select the **Top** view.
11. Using the **RECTANGLE** command, draw the polyline highlighted in Figure 6-75. Place it as indicated.
12. **MIRROR** the rectangle symmetrically to the other side of the cone.

From an orthographic view you can use the quadrants or the center points to mirror objects around the axis of cones and cylinders.

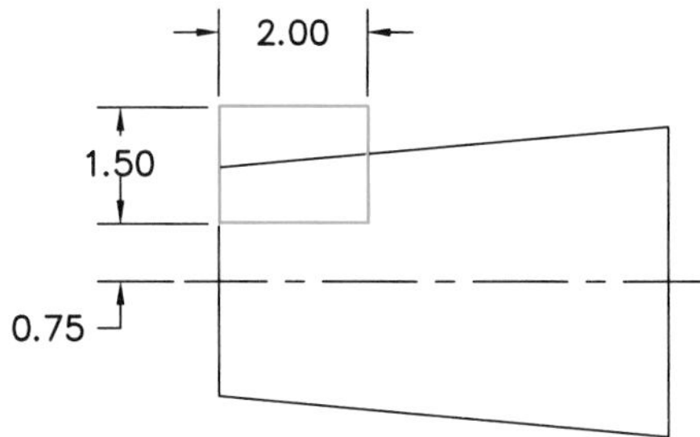

Figure 6-75 Dimensions for the rectangle

Note:

*Because you drew the first rectangle in the **Top** orthogonal view, the location of the rectangles with respect to the cone in the Y-axis of the **Front** view is uncertain.*

13. Select the **Front** view.
14. **MOVE** the two rectangles down orthogonally so that all their points are below the cone (Figure 6-76).
15. **EXTRUDE** the two rectangles a positive height value, large enough to go over the top of the cone (Figure 6-77).

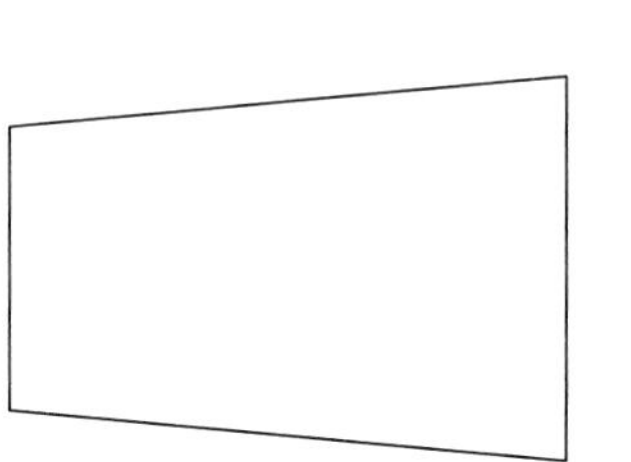

Figure 6-76 After the rectangles are moved

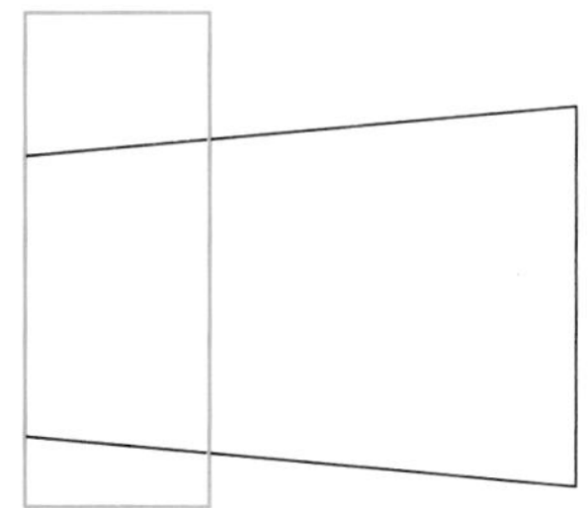

Figure 6-77 After the rectangles are extruded

A good approach here to specifying a distance without knowing the specific value is to click on any two points in the drawing area.

16. **SUBTRACT** the two new 3D solids from the cone.
17. Select the **SW Isometric** viewing point.
18. Invoke the **Rotate faces** option of the **SOLIDEDIT** command. Select the face highlighted in Figure 6-78. Specify the points for the axis of rotation by snapping to the endpoints indicated. Enter **30** for the rotation angle.
19. Repeat the same operation to rotate the corresponding face on the other side **30°**.
20. Select the **Top** view. The 3D model should look like Figure 6-79.
21. Select the **SW Isometric** viewing point.
22. After selecting the proper UCS, draw the three **1″**-diameter circles on the faces of the 3D solid, as shown highlighted in Figure 6-80.

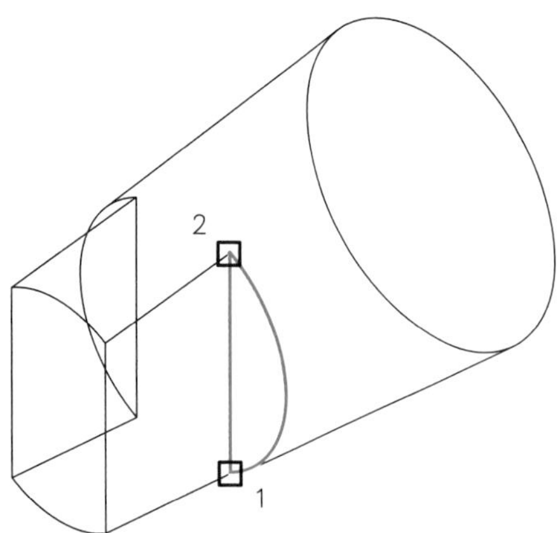

Figure 6-78 Face to select and points specified to define the axis of rotation

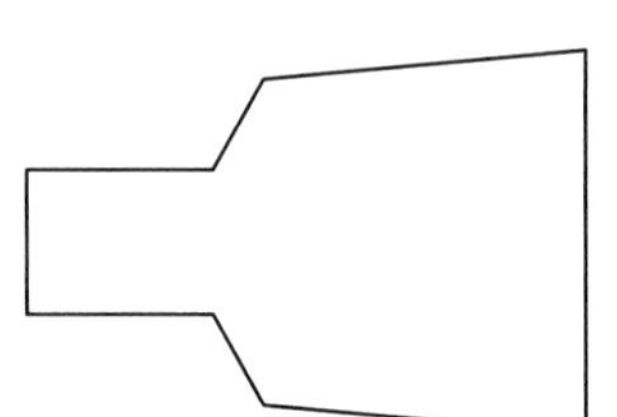

Figure 6-79 A top view of the 3D model

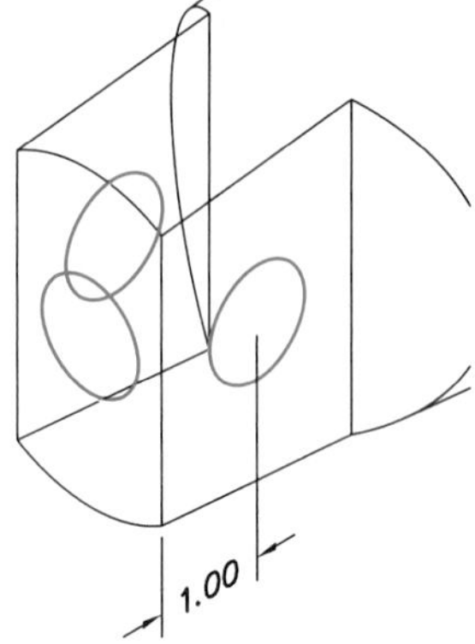

Figure 6-80 Circles to be imprinted

TIP

Selecting the **Top** view will reveal whether the three circles are correctly placed on top of the planar faces.

23. Invoke the **Imprint** body editing tool, and imprint all three circles on the faces of the 3D solid. Select **Yes** when prompted to delete the source objects.
24. Invoke the **Extrude faces** tool, and select the three circular faces split by the **Imprint** operation. Protrude the three faces **0.375″** and accept **0** as the angle of taper (Figure 6-81).

TIP

To select faces located in the back, you can either use the **3D Orbit** tool within the command and pick the face directly, or you can select two faces by picking a common edge and then remove the one that is not needed.

25. Select the **SW Isometric** viewing point.
26. **SLICE** the 3D solid in half, keeping only the bottom half (Figure 6-82).
27. With the **Copy faces** tool of the **SOLIDEDIT** command, copy the face highlighted in Figure 6-83 over in the same place.

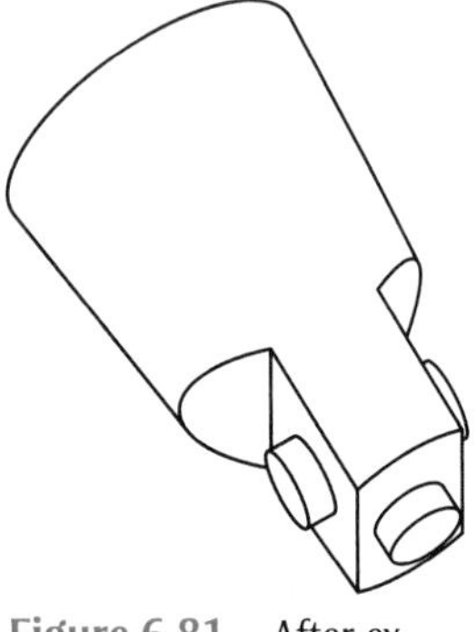

Figure 6-81 After extruding the split faces

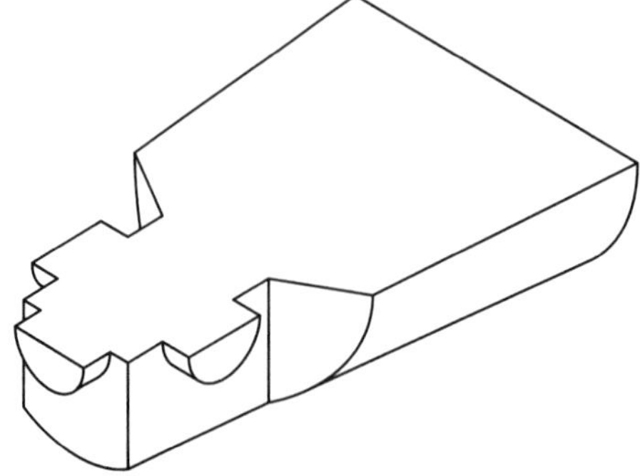

Figure 6-82 The 3D solid sliced in half

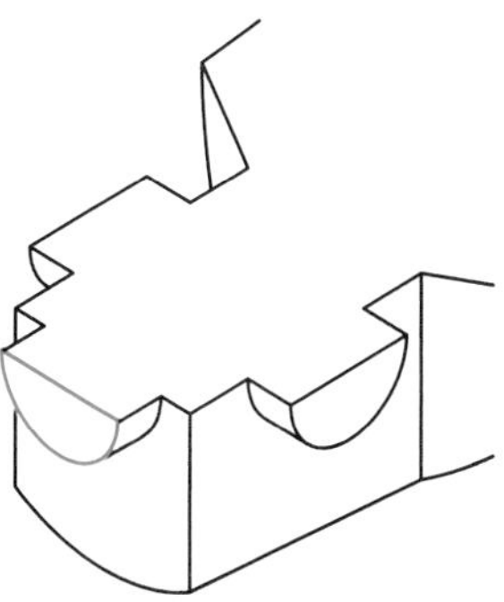

Figure 6-83 The face copied in place

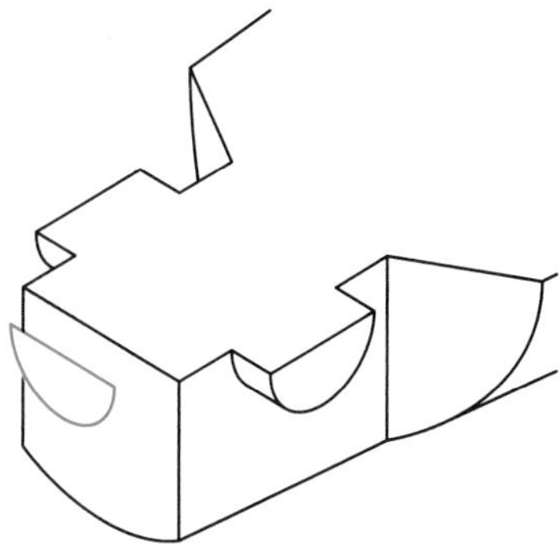

Figure 6-84 After deleting the half cylinder in the back

28. Invoke the **Delete faces** tool to delete the half cylinder in the back (Figure 6-84).

Remember, to copy a face over, specify the base point and the second point in the same place.

To delete the half cylinder, only two faces of the 3D solid should be selected for the operation: the face you just copied over and the cylindrical face.

29. Invoke the **Taper faces** tool of the **SOLIDEDIT** command. Incline the three highlighted faces, and specify the axis of tapering by snapping to the two endpoints shown in Figure 6-85. Specify **10** when prompted for the taper angle.

Because the three vertical faces are located one next to the other, they can be selected by picking the two shared edges.

30. After you invoke the **HIDE** command, the 3D solid should look like Figure 6-86.

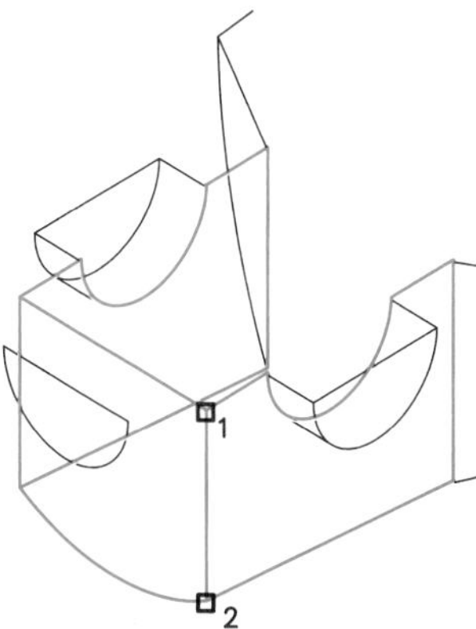

Figure 6-85 Faces selected and points specified to define the axis of tapering

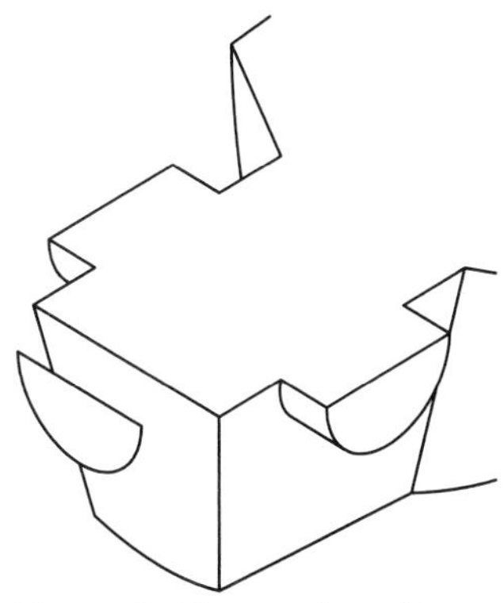

Figure 6-86 Resulting shape after the Taper faces operation

31. Select the **Front** view.
32. **EXTRUDE** the region extracted previously **–0.5,** with **0** as the angle of taper (Figure 6-87).

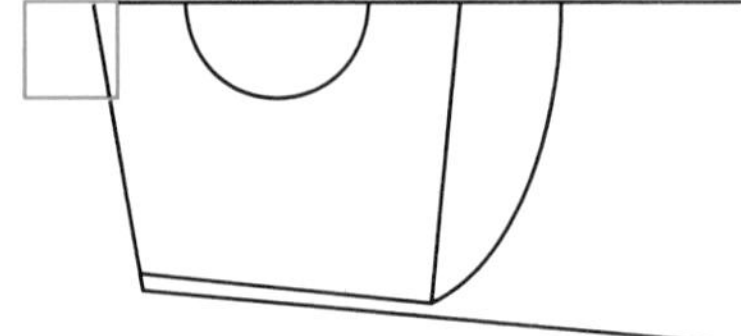

Figure 6-87 The region extruded toward the 3D solid

33. Join the two 3D solids with the **UNION** command.
34. Select the **SW Isometric** viewing point.
35. **FILLET** the four individual highlighted edges (Figure 6-88). Specify **0.125** as the **Radius** value.
36. **FILLET** the **Chain** of highlighted edges (Figure 6-89) using the previous **Radius** value.

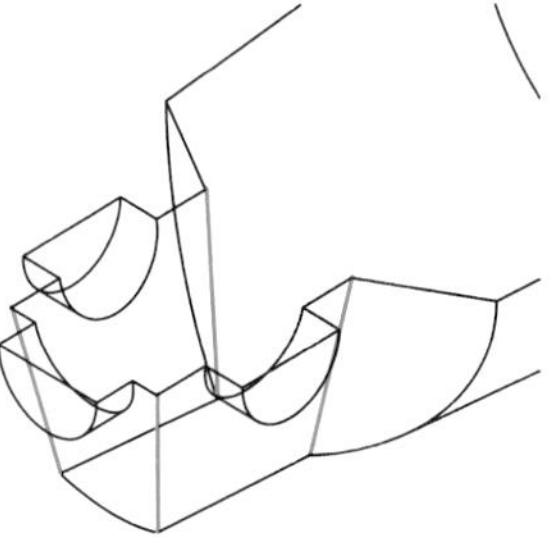

Figure 6-88 Edges to be selected for the FILLET operation

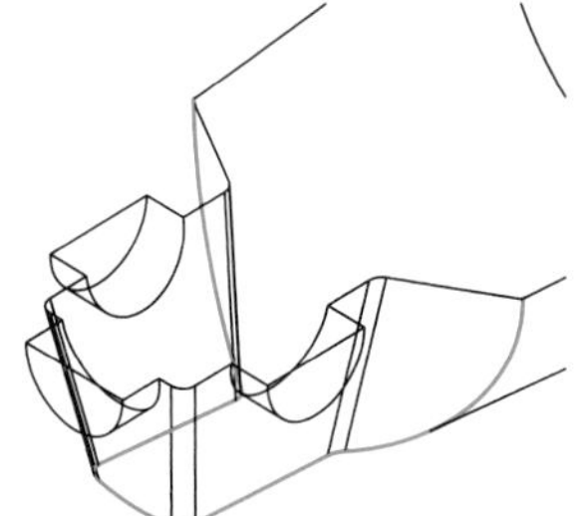

Figure 6-89 Chain of edges to be selected for a second FILLET operation

37. Invoke the **Offset faces** editing tool and select the two faces highlighted in Figure 6-90. Specify an offset distance of **–0.25** to shorten the length of the two half cylinders by 0.25″.
38. Invoke the **Shell** tool of the **SOLIDEDIT** command. When prompted, select the 3D solid, picking it on any of its edges. Pick the four highlighted edges in Figure 6-91 to remove the corresponding faces from the selection. Finally, press **<Enter>** to end the selection, and enter **0.09** as the shell offset distance.
39. Select the **Realistic** visual style.

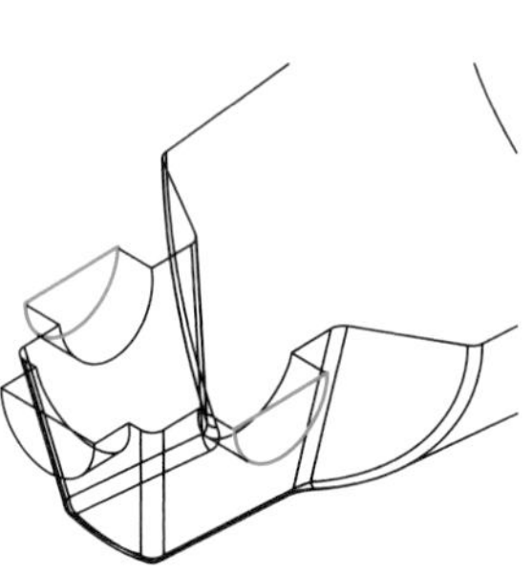

Figure 6-90 Faces to select for the Offset faces operation

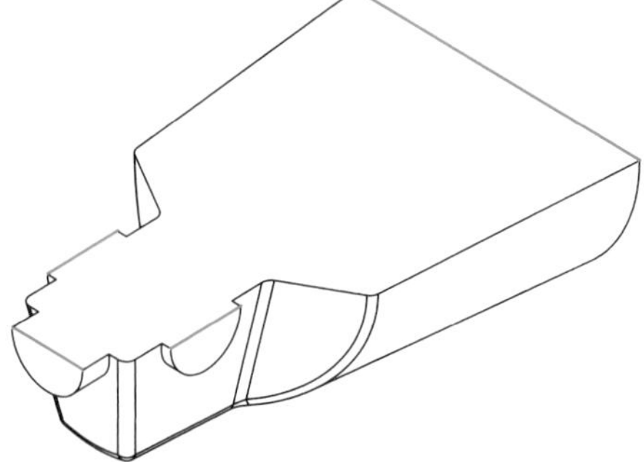

Figure 6-91 Edges where the 3D solid can be picked for the Shell operation; they will be picked to remove faces as well

40. Invoke the **3DORBIT** command to inspect the 3D solid (Figure 6-92).

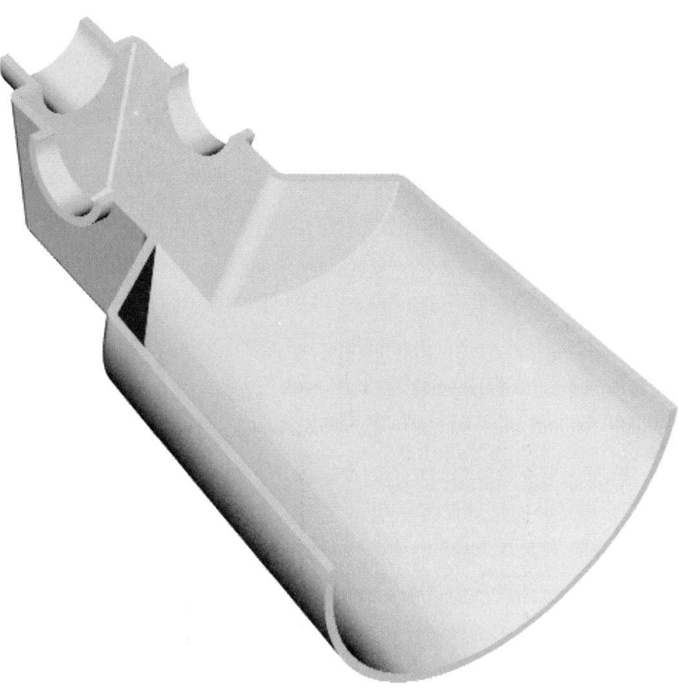

Figure 6-92 A shaded view of the resulting Shell operation

41. Invoke the **MIRROR3D** command. When prompted, select the 3D solid and specify any three points on the top face.
42. Invoke the **UNION** command to join the two 3D solids. The 3D model should look like Figure 6-93.
43. **SAVE** your drawing.

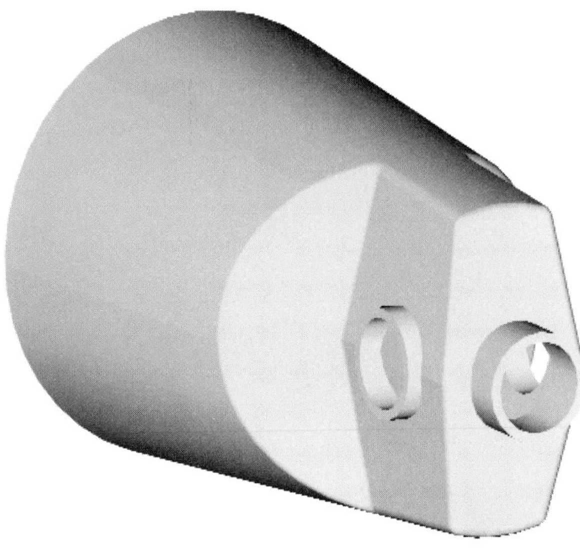

Figure 6-93 The 3D model after joining the two mirrored halves

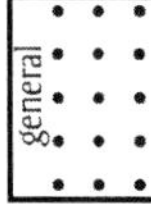

Tutorial 6-2: Revising Plastic Part Design

You have received a fax from one of your customers that informs you of several required changes on a product that you are designing. The customer has used a printout of the 3D view to write some comments for you (Figure 6-94).

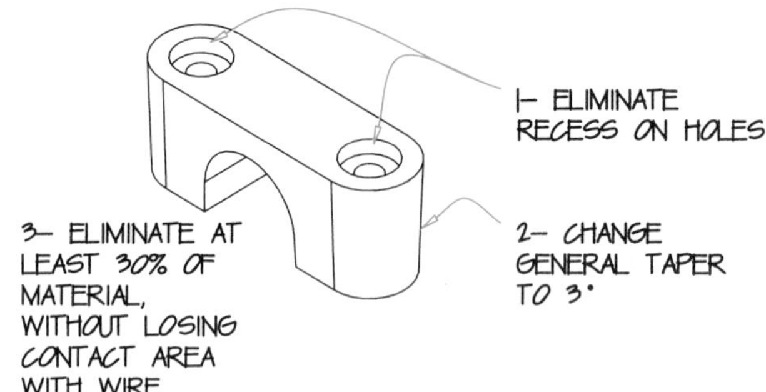
1– ELIMINATE RECESS ON HOLES
2– CHANGE GENERAL TAPER TO 3°
3– ELIMINATE AT LEAST 30% OF MATERIAL, WITHOUT LOSING CONTACT AREA WITH WIRE

Figure 6-94 Revision request received from a customer via fax

1. **OPEN** the finished ***Tutorial 5-1.***
2. **SAVE** the drawing **AS *Tutorial 6-2.***
3. Select the **SE Isometric** viewing point.
4. Let's start with comment 1. Invoke the **Delete faces** tool and, when prompted, select the four faces that are related to the two recessed holes. Select the surfaces by picking the two edges highlighted in Figure 6-95. Finish the operation by pressing **<Enter>** and then **<Esc>.**

Note:

To take care of the taper angle, you need to divide the process into three parts. This is because the two vertical flat faces of the middle tunnel through which the wire will run need to be tapered as well. These faces, however, do not start at the same height as the other vertical faces. The interior conical faces also need to be tapered, in the opposite direction.

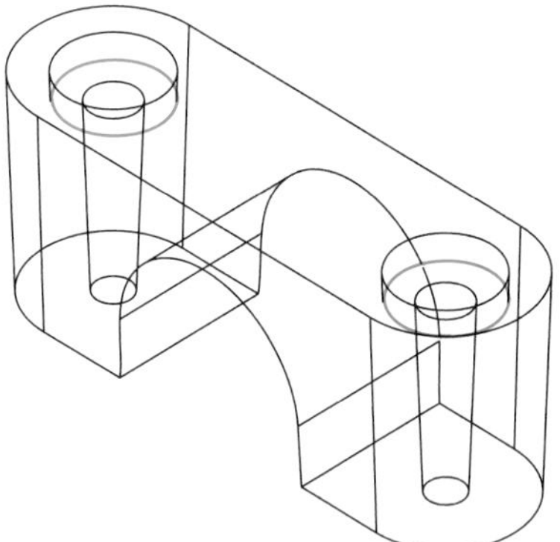

Figure 6-95 Edges to be selected

Note:

If you taper the vertical faces inside the tunnel, the plane of tapering will not move with the operation, regardless of where you locate it. This will cause the tangency between the planar face and the cylindrical face to be lost (Figure 6-97).

5. Invoke the **Taper faces** option of the **SOLIDEDIT** command. When prompted, select the four outer vertical faces by picking the two edges highlighted in Figure 6-96. Specify the axis of tapering by snapping to the two center points in the order shown. Enter **1** for the taper angle.

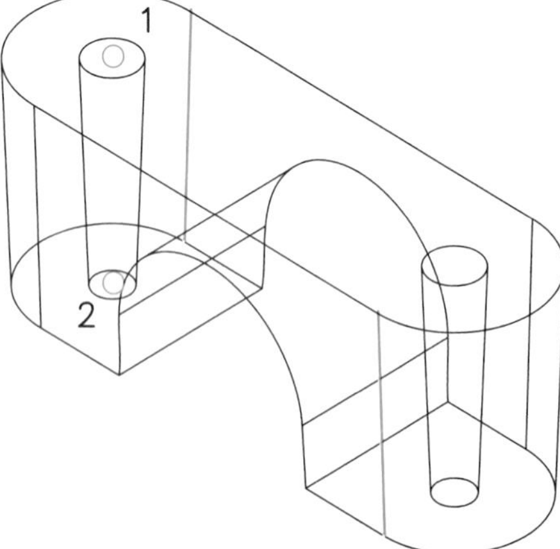
1
2

Figure 6-96 Edges to pick when selecting the faces and points to specify the axis of tapering

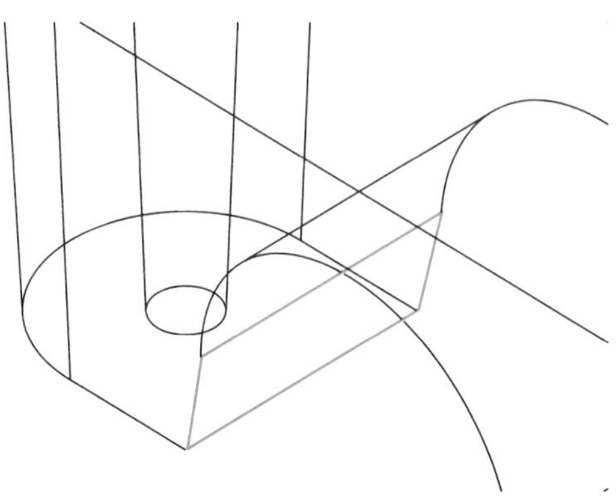

Figure 6-97 Tapering the highlighted face will lose the tangency with the cylindrical face

6. Invoke the **Rotate faces** option of the **SOLIDEDIT** command. When prompted, select the face inside the tunnel highlighted in Figure 6-98. Specify the axis of rotation by snapping to the two center points of the cylindrical face of the tunnel in the order shown. Enter **1** for the rotation angle.
7. Repeat the previous step for the other vertical face in the tunnel. Consider using the right-hand rule to determine which point to snap to first for a positive rotation angle.
8. Select the **Front** view.
9. Create an angular dimension to check whether the **Rotate faces** operation was successful or not. It should read **6°** (Figure 6-99).
10. **DELETE** the angular dimension.
11. Select the **SE Isometric** viewing point.
12. Invoke the **Taper faces** tool and, when prompted, select the two conical faces by picking a silhouette line on each face. Specify the axis of tapering by snapping to the bottom and top center points on either of these two faces. Select first the one at the bottom. Enter **1** for the taper angle.
13. Invoke the **MASSPROP** command. When prompted, select the 3D solid and press **<Enter>**.
14. Select the **Front** UCS.
15. Invoke the **Move faces** option of the **SOLIDEDIT** command. When prompted, select the two conical faces highlighted on Figure 6-100. Move them orthogonally **0.0469″** along the negative direction of the *X*-axis.

Before trying to provide a solution for comment 3, we must find out the current volume of the 3D solid so we can compare it with the new volume after certain modifications.

Note:

After invoking the **MASSPROP** command, you can read that the actual volume of the 3D solid is **0.0706** cubic inch.

TIP When performing face editing operations with small values, you can determine whether the operation is performed correctly by looking at the display when pressing **<Enter>**.

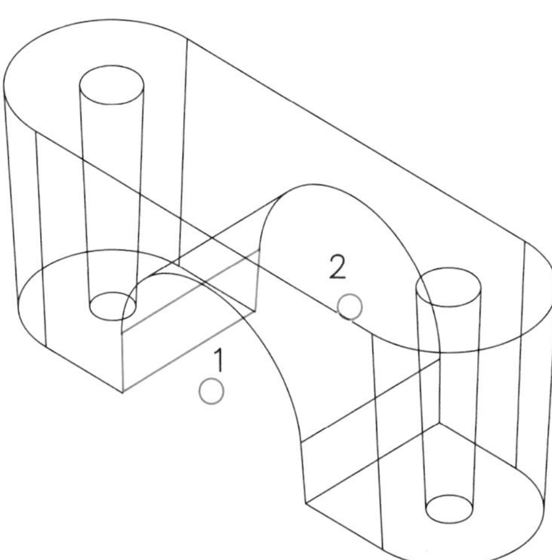

Figure 6-98 Face to select and points used to specify the axis of rotation

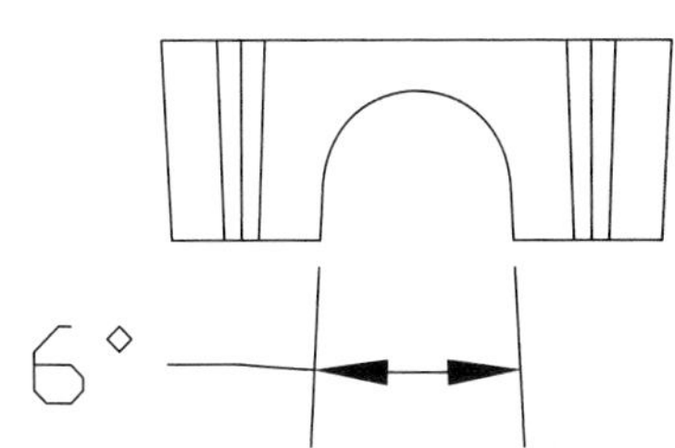

Figure 6-99 Checking the result of the operation

MASSPROP	
Inquiry Toolbar	
Ribbon Inquiry Editing panel	
Pull-down Menu	Tools/ Inquiry/ Region/ Mass Properties
Command Line	massprop

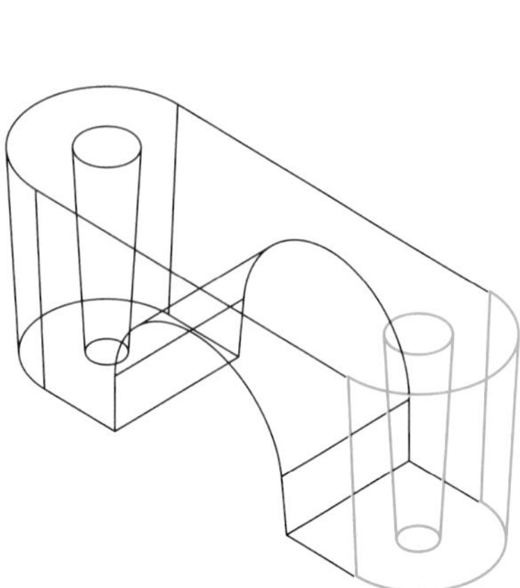

Figure 6-100 Faces to select for the Move faces operation

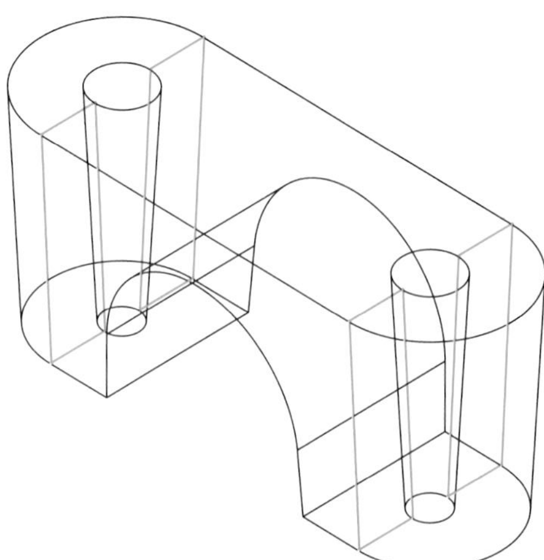

Figure 6-101 After splitting the 3D solid in three pieces

16. Repeat another **MOVE** operation, selecting the conical faces on the other side of the 3D solid. Move the faces **0.0469″** along the positive direction of the *XY*-axis.
17. Using the **SLICE** command, cut the 3D solid into three pieces by defining the imaginary slicing planes parallel to the *YZ* plane and going through one of the center points of each conical hole (Figure 6-101).
18. Invoke the **Offset faces** option of the **SOLIDEDIT** command. Offset each of the end conical faces **–0.0469″**.
19. With the **UNION** operation, join the three 3D solids again. The 3D model should look like Figure 6-102.
20. Invoke the **Taper faces** option of the **SOLIDEDIT** command. When prompted, select the four faces highlighted in Figure 6-103. Specify the axis of tapering by snapping to the two center points in the order shown. Enter **3** as the angle of taper.

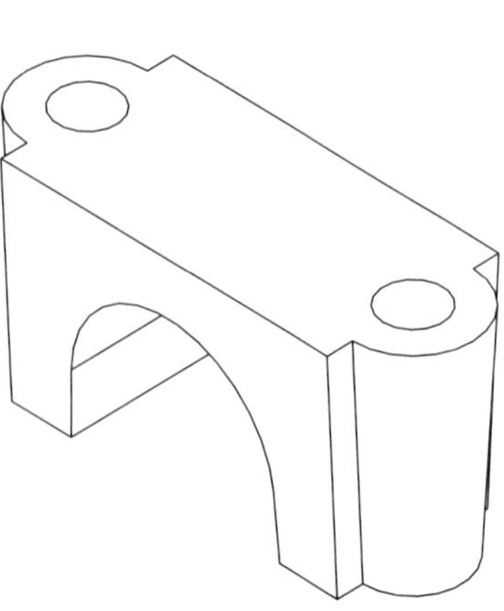

Figure 6-102 After offsetting the extreme faces and performing the UNION operation

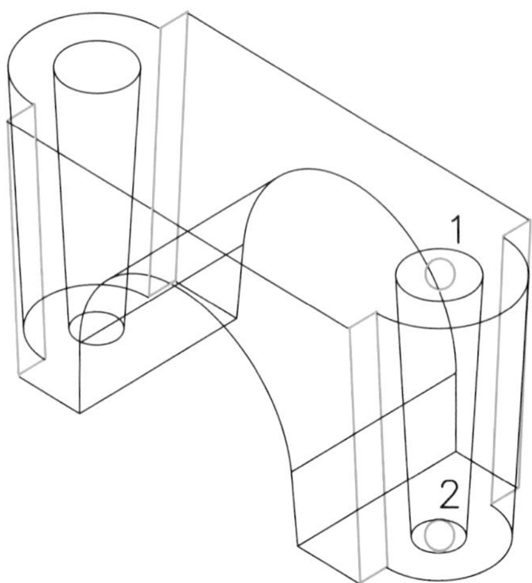

Figure 6-103 Faces to select and points used to specify the axis of tapering

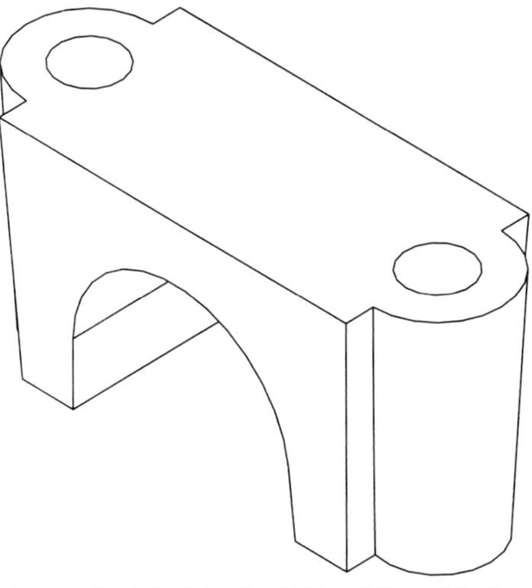

Figure 6-104 The final 3D solid model after it is modified

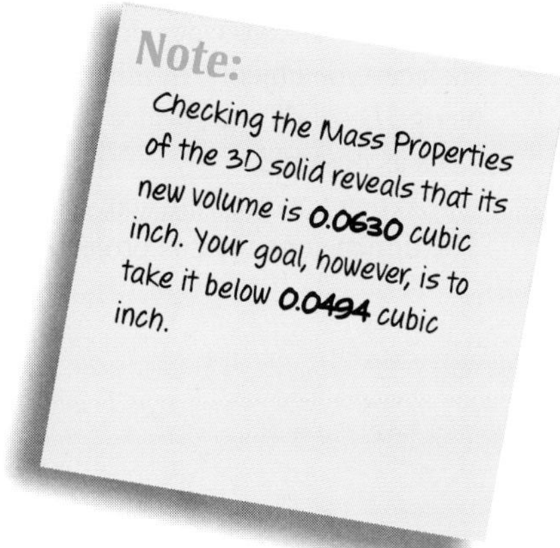

Note:
Checking the Mass Properties of the 3D solid reveals that its new volume is 0.0630 cubic inch. Your goal, however, is to take it below 0.0494 cubic inch.

21. Check the volume of the 3D solid again. This time, its value is **0.0460** cubic inch, which achieves your goal. The final 3D solid should look like Figure 6-104 after you hide the lines.
22. **SAVE** your drawing.

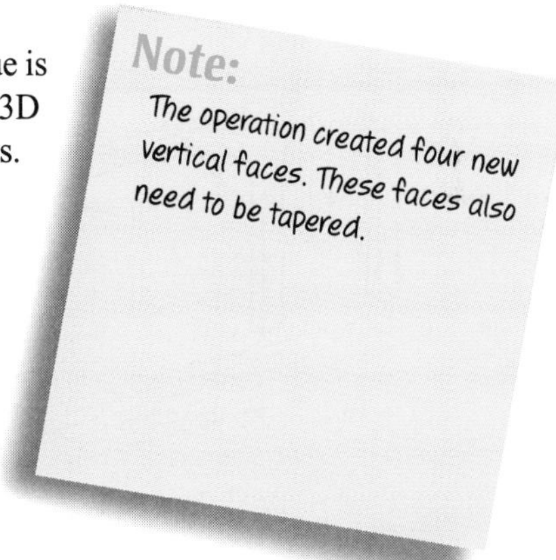

Note:
The operation created four new vertical faces. These faces also need to be tapered.

Most design time is usually dedicated to performing necessary adjustments, corrections, and other changes. This task can certainly be complicated in 3D models. The proper use of procedures and techniques, however, as exemplified in this tutorial can become an important asset. Understanding and applying these tools in the design process shows your ability to efficiently interact with customers in achieving specific objectives.

Chapter Projects

Project 6-1: Enhanced Machining Instruction

A part goes though several stages when it is manufactured. One of these is the machining process. You may create very precise drawings, but giving good instructions to the operators is key to achieving the expected results. If you have an existing 3D model, you can give it different uses that will serve as a visual instruction for operators.

Open the drawing ***Project 5-2*** and change the color of all the faces. You may use any two colors you like. One color will be applied on any surface that requires machining. The other color will be applied to all other surfaces.

Hints for the Project

Faces that require machining have no rounded edge. You can change the color of the entire 3D model first, and then apply the color used for the other types of faces.

Project 6-2: Solid Model of the Community Recreational Hall

In ***Project 4-4*** you developed a community recreational hall using surface-type objects. In this project you will develop the same model using 3D solids and surface objects. Use as many of the solids editing tools as possible.

When you are finished, the building will look like Figure 6-105. The dimensions for this project are shown in Figure 6-106.

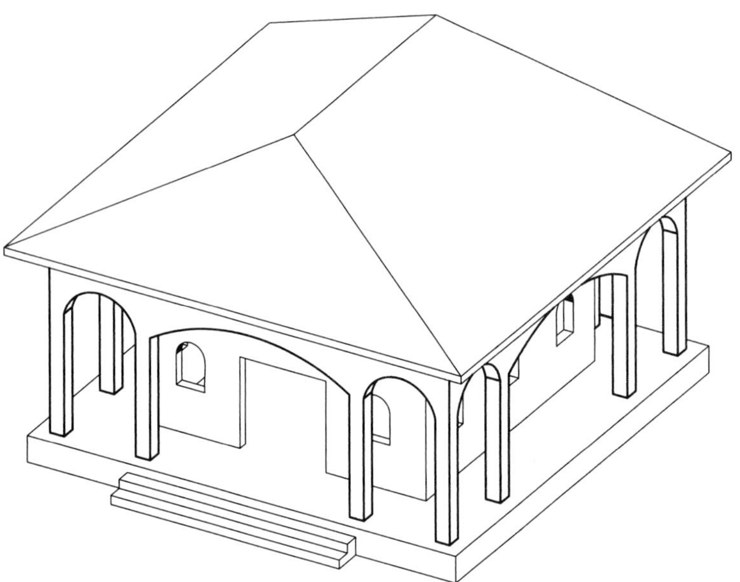

Figure 6-105 The completed 3D model of the community recreational hall

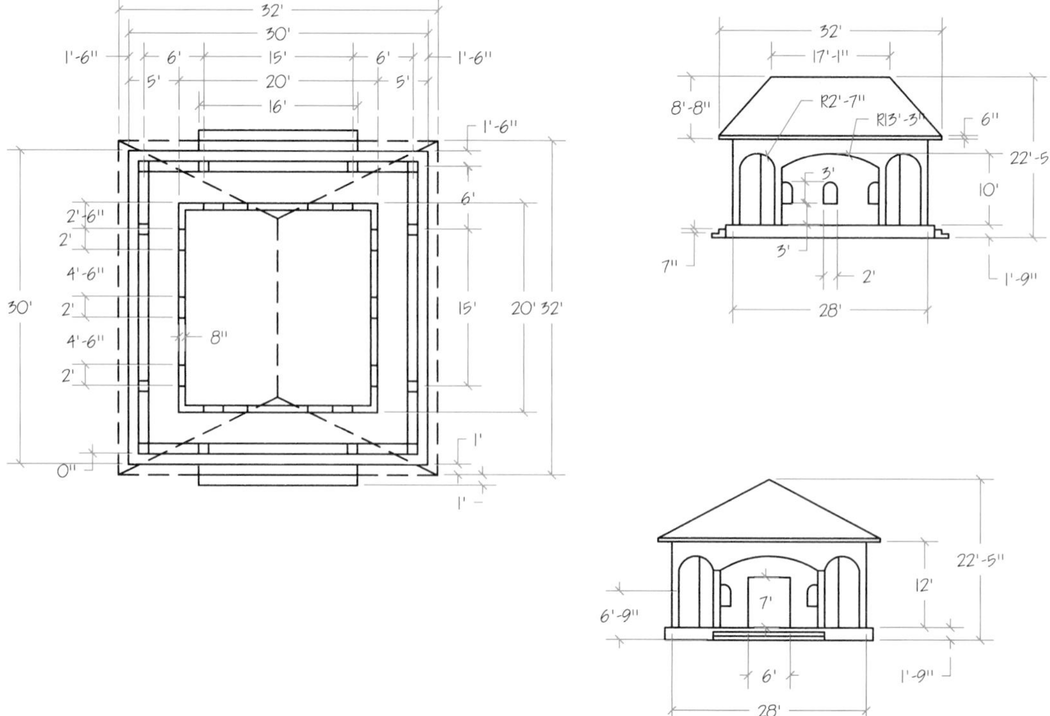

Figure 6-106 Dimensions for the community recreational hall

Hints for the Project

Because the purpose of this project is to use the solids editing tools, you will not use the Boolean operations. To create the openings in the walls, you can imprint 2D objects and then extrude the split faces. To create the roof as a single piece, you can create a block, and then split and taper all the vertical faces one by one.

Project 6-3: Finishing the Light Fixture

In this project you will finish the 3D model of the light fixture. The main part or enclosure was created in ***Tutorial 6-1***.

This project will become an assembly after you put the other three components in their proper place. When you are finished, rotate the light fixture enclosure **20**° downward. The finished project will look like Figure 6-107.

It is recommended that you create the rest of the components in a separate file. This will allow your computer to process less information, and therefore work faster.

Hints for the Project

The dimensions for the rest of the components are shown in Figure 6-108. The revolved component can be produced easily by using the **Shell** body editing tool.

Figure 6-107 The completed 3D model of the light fixture

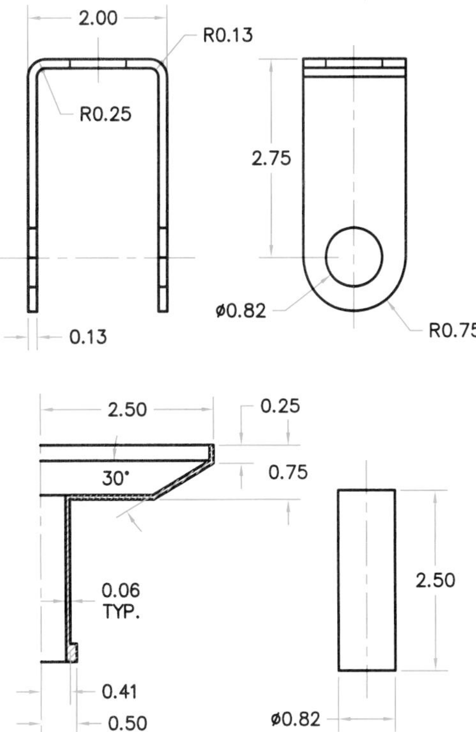

Figure 6-108 Dimensions for the components of the light fixture

Advanced Tutorials

7

Chapter Objectives

- Strengthen the knowledge you have acquired throughout previous chapters.
- Learn advanced approaches to quickly achieve complex 3D models.
- Walk through a real design process using 3D solid modeling.
- Put together the most-used tasks in a single project.
- Practice the manipulation of the UCS and the viewing system.
- Learn how to take advantage of the most commonly used solids editing tools.
- Evaluate different practical approaches that can be performed with 3D solids.
- Practice the different operations applied in the development of 3D assembly models.

Introduction

In this chapter you will go through the design process of a real product: a bench vise. In this detailed tutorial project, which starts from scratch, you will practice many of the tools learned in the previous chapters.

You will be able to achieve the final result by following the steps. You should not discard the possibility, however, of trying different approaches you could use at any step. There are always multiple possible solutions for almost every task in 3D modeling.

You can activate any visual style at any time. You can also invoke the **HIDE** or the **3DORBIT** command at any time. Using these tools will give you a clearer understanding of the operation you have just performed. Just remember to go back to the original viewing point and UCS so that the results reflect the assumed settings for the next step. Not having the correct settings for the viewing point and the UCS might end in an unexpected outcome.

Unless your 3D model has many parts, you don't need to use different layers for the modeling stage of a 3D project. Using different colors for different objects, however, is very helpful, especially for distinguishing which edge belongs to each object. Like any other object, 3D solids are created with the current color. Boolean operations affect the color of individual faces as well, depending on the color of the interacting objects.

Modeling the Main Body

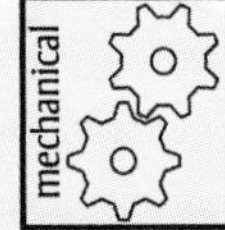

You start the development of a 3D solid by creating one or more original 3D solids. These are then combined by performing several Boolean operations. Then other post-operations are performed to achieve the main geometry. Fillets, chamfers, and holes are performed at the end of the modeling process.

It is not necessary to place any dimensions, centerlines, or any other annotation. Their only purpose is to help you follow the instructions.

1. Start a **NEW** drawing using **Imperial** units. Select the **acad** template to do so.
2. **SAVE** it **AS** ***Main Body.***
3. Set or check the value of the following system variables as specified:
   - **DISPSILH** to **1**.
   - **ISOLINES** to **0**.
   - **FACETRES** to **9**.
   - **VIEWRES** to **4000**.
   - **UCSORTHO** to **1**.
   - **UCSFOLLOW** to **0**.
4. Select the **Front** view.
5. Draw the objects shown in Figure 7-1 anywhere in the 3D space.
6. Invoke the **REGION** command and create a region from the objects.

TIP

Remember, the objects must touch each other at their endpoints to form a closed profile. Otherwise, they will not become a region.

7. Select the **Right** view.
8. Draw the objects shown in Figure 7-2.

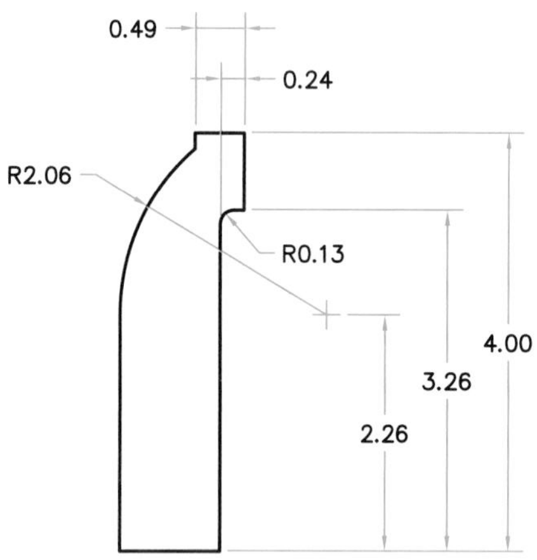

Figure 7-1 Profile dimensions

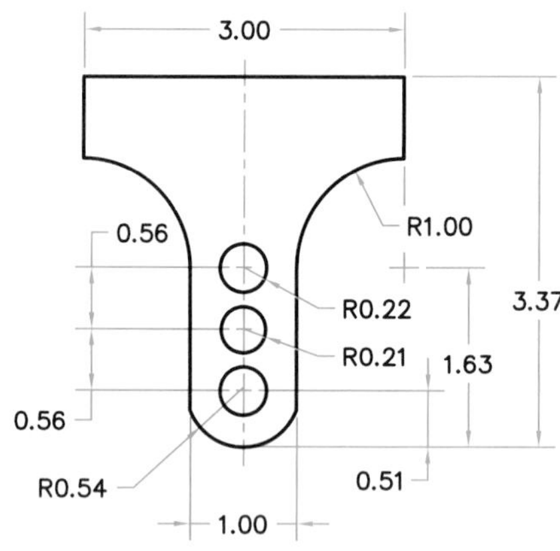

Figure 7-2 Profile dimensions

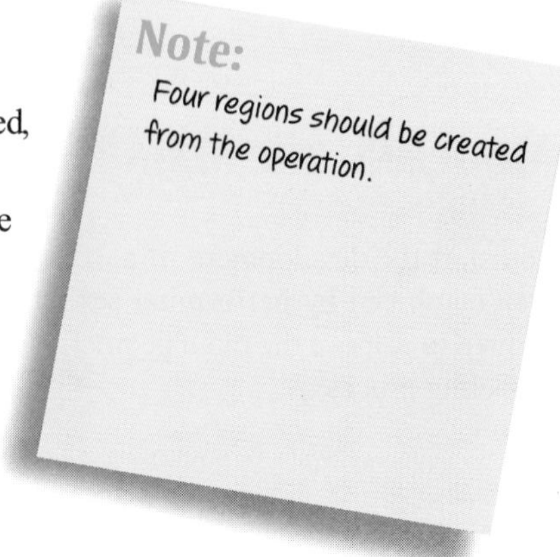

Note:
Four regions should be created from the operation.

9. Invoke the **REGION** command and, when prompted, select all the objects.
10. **SUBTRACT** the three circular regions from the main region.
11. Select the **Conceptual** visual style. If the operation was successfully performed, the shaded view should look like Figure 7-3.
12. Select the **2D Wireframe** visual style and the **SE Isometric** viewing point.

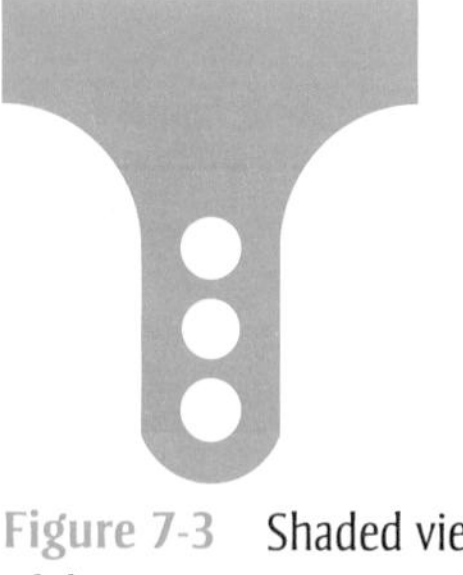

Figure 7-3 Shaded view of the composite region

13. **MOVE** one of the regions from one of its endpoints to the endpoint of the other region created (Figure 7-4).
14. With the **Right** UCS still current, **EXTRUDE** the profile on your left **–3.00** units and the one on your right **–1.50** units. Specify **0** as the angle of taper for both extrusions.
15. Invoke the **INTERSECT** command and select both 3D solids (Figure 7-5). The results with the occulted lines removed are shown on the right side of the figure.

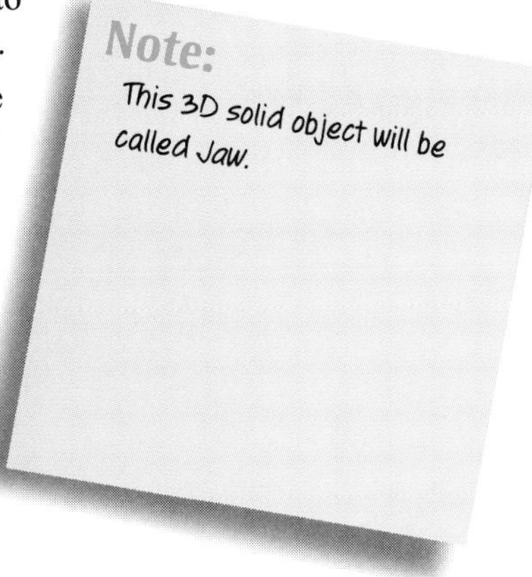
Note:
This 3D solid object will be called Jaw.

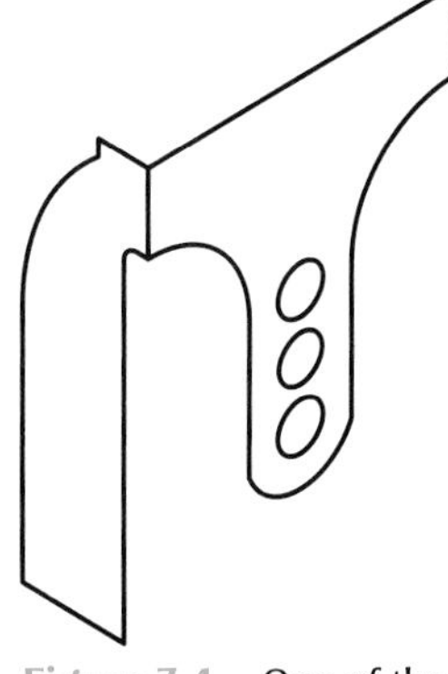
Figure 7-4 One of the regions is moved to the other region

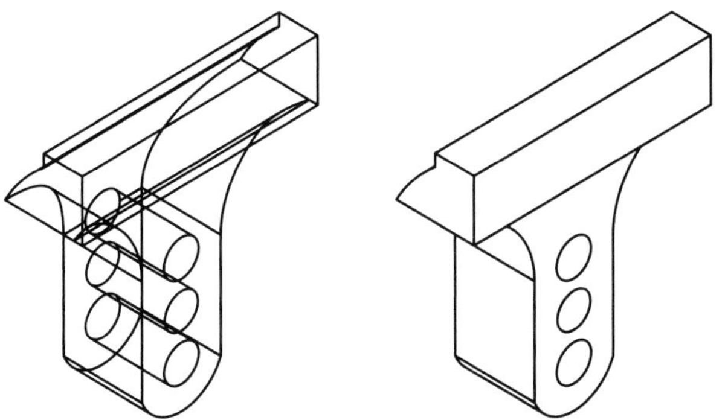
Figure 7-5 The 3D solid resulting from the INTERSECT operation

16. Select the **Right** UCS.
17. Create the region shown in Figure 7-6.
18. Select the **Front** UCS and create the region shown in Figure 7-7.
19. Select the **Front** UCS. Turn **ORTHO** mode off and **MOVE** the last region created from its top-left corner to the top-right corner of the other region. After the operation, your model should look like Figure 7-8.
20. Select the **Top** UCS and then create the region shown in Figure 7-10.

Note:
Due to the fillet radius in that particular corner, there is not a physical point to snap to. You can find the snap point by using the **AutoTrack** tools. In that case, you leave a blip mark on both endpoints, and then look for the intersection of the two orthogonal tracking traces (Figure 7-9). If you wish, you can move the region using a procedure other than the AutoTrack tools. Just make sure the region is placed in the proper location.

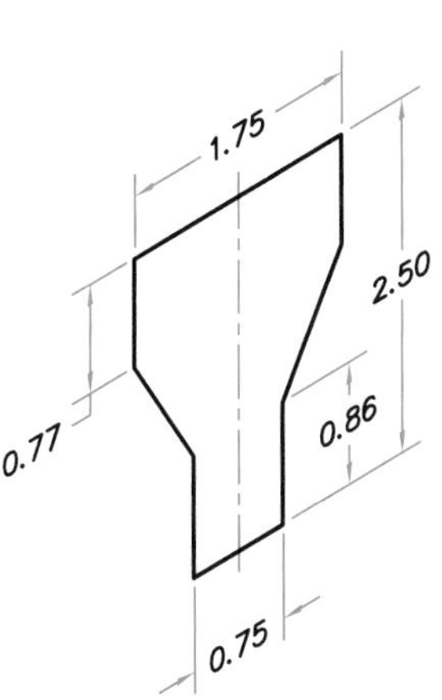

Figure 7-6 Profile dimensions

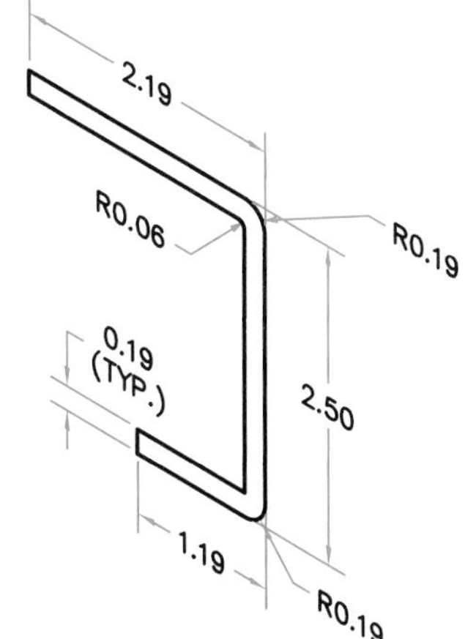

Figure 7-7 Profile dimensions

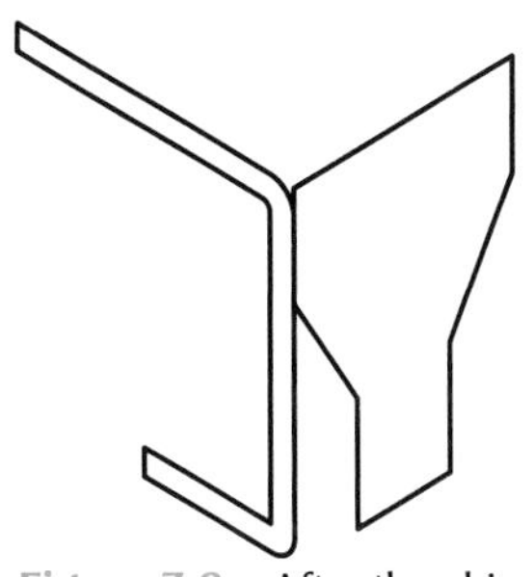
Figure 7-8 After the object is moved

FOR MORE DETAILS You can find more information about the **AutoTrack** tools in Chapter 1.

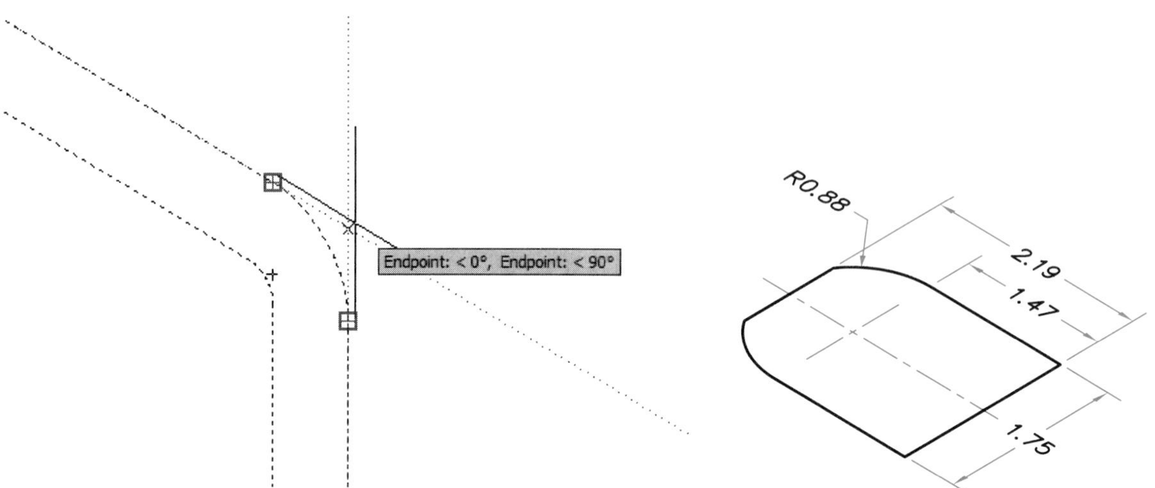

Figure 7-9 The destination point must be selected by using tracking techniques

Figure 7-10 Profile dimensions

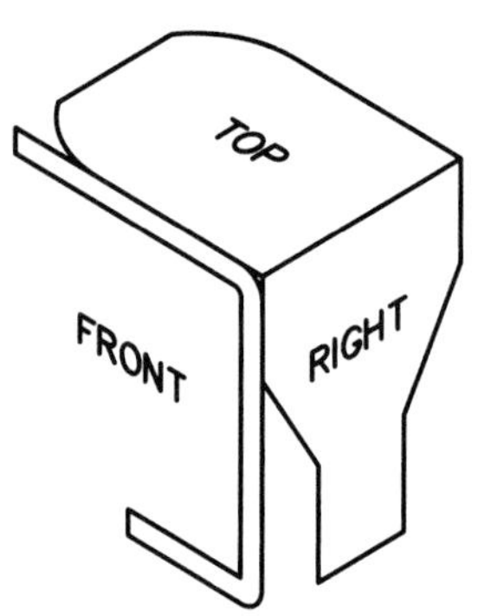

Figure 7-11 The last region is moved

21. **MOVE** the last region so that the three regions meet at the endpoint (Figure 7-11).
22. Make sure the **Top** UCS is still current and **EXTRUDE** the three regions individually. Specify the height of extrusion for each region as follows:
    - Region parallel to the front plane: **–1.75**
    - Region parallel to the right plane: **–2.5**
    - Region parallel to the top plane: **–2.5**
23. **INTERSECT** these three 3D solids. The results should look like Figure 7-12.
24. Next, you will combine the *Jaw* and the *Clamp*. Draw the line, shown highlighted in Figure 7-13, between the two endpoints of the *Jaw*.

Note: We will refer to this 3D solid as a *Clamp*.

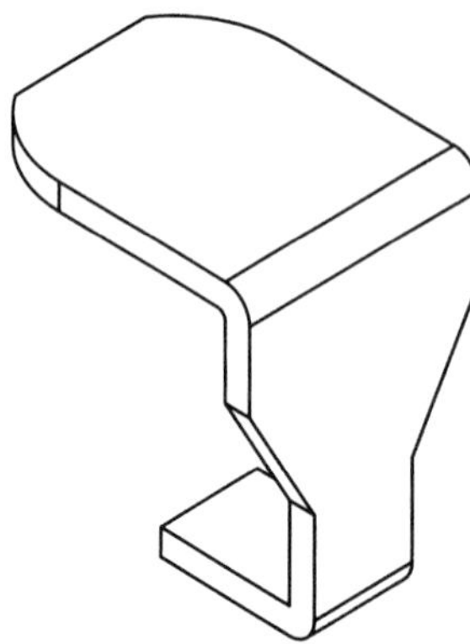

Figure 7-12 The 3D solid resulting from the INTERSECT operation

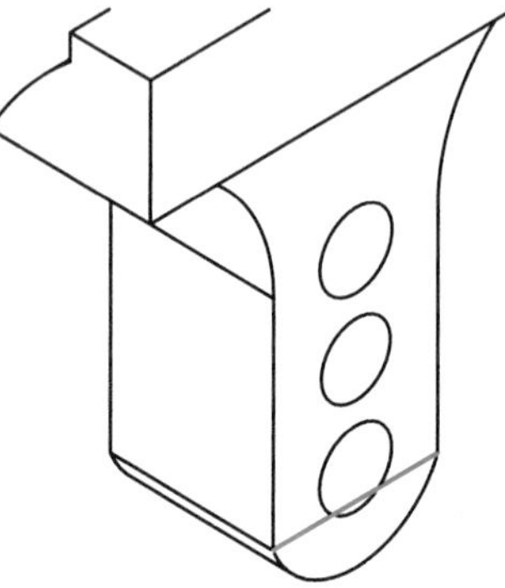

Figure 7-13 The highlighted line will be used as a reference

25. **MOVE** the *Clamp* from the midpoint of the tangent edge to the midpoint of the line you just created on the *Jaw*, as shown in Figure 7-14, with the hidden lines removed on the right.
26. **ERASE** the line you drew on the previous step.
27. **Top** should still be the current UCS. **MOVE** the *Jaw* **0.81** unit along the positive *X*-axis direction (Figure 7-15).

Note:
It is a good practice to intersect 3D solids throughout a design process. Such an operation avoids many other unnecessary steps, which saves time. If you are transforming a 2D drawing into a 3D model, it is also a good approach because you can get the profiles out of the drawing views.

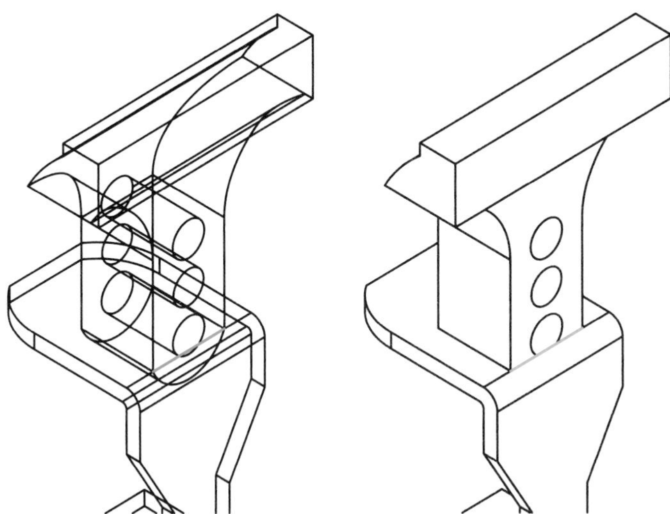

Figure 7-14 After moving the Clamp and erasing the line

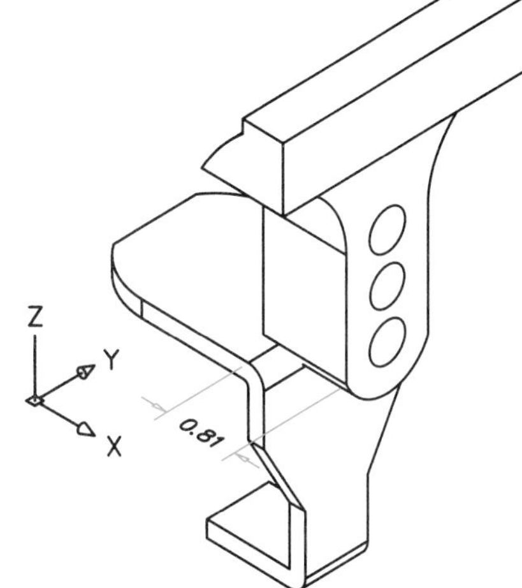

Figure 7-15 The Clamp moved again to its final location

28. Select the **Front** orthographic view (Figure 7-16).
29. **COPY** over the *Clamp* to create a duplicate of this object in the same place. Respond to the prompts as follows:

Select objects: *Select the Clamp portion.*

Select objects: ↵ *(To end the selection)*

Specify base point or [Displacement] <Displacement>: *0,0,0* ↵

Specify second point or <use first point as displacement>: *0,0,0* ↵

Specify second point or [Exit/Undo] <Exit>: ↵ *(To exit the command)*

Note:
Your next goal is to eliminate the portion of the Jaw that is interfering with the Clamp. The next few steps describe one of the possible approaches that can be used.

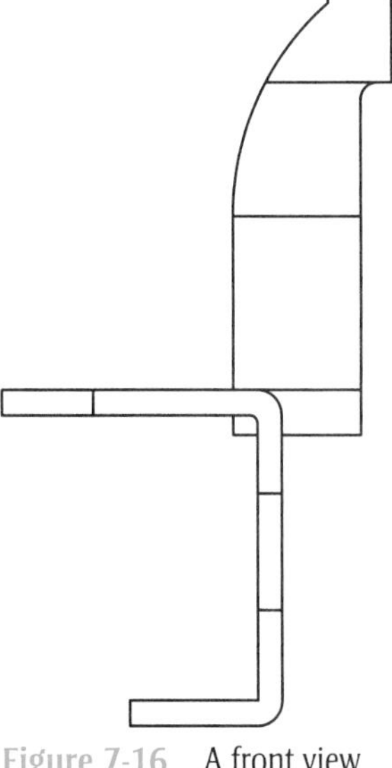

Figure 7-16 A front view of the 3D model

Avoid snapping to points in an orthogonal view. You cannot tell for sure whether you are snapping to the closest point or to the ones behind it.

30. **SUBTRACT** one of the two *Clamps* from the *Jaw*.

TIP: Select the *Clamp* by picking it directly instead of using a window or a crossing window. Using either of these two selection tools will cause both clamps to be selected, when only one should be selected.

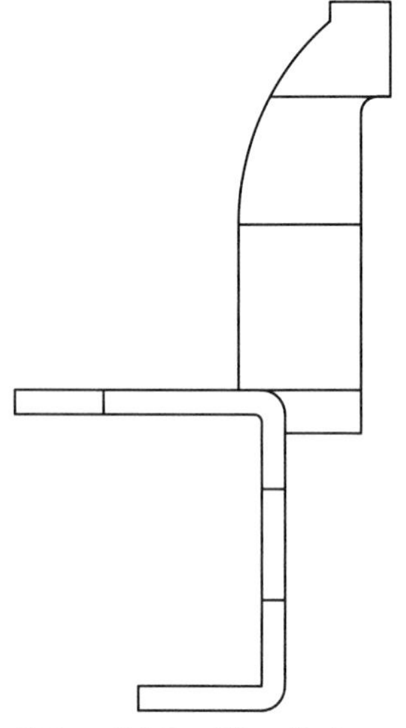

Figure 7-17 After eliminating the portion inside the Clamp

31. Use the **SEPARATE** command to disintegrate the 3D solid into two individual ones.
32. **ERASE** the smaller 3D solid located in the inside corner of the *Clamp*. After this, the 3D model should look like Figure 7-17.
33. With the **UNION** command, combine the *Clamp* and the *Jaw*. We will call this new 3D solid *Main Body*.
34. Select the **Right** view and create the region shown in Figure 7-18.
35. Select the **SE Isometric** viewing point.

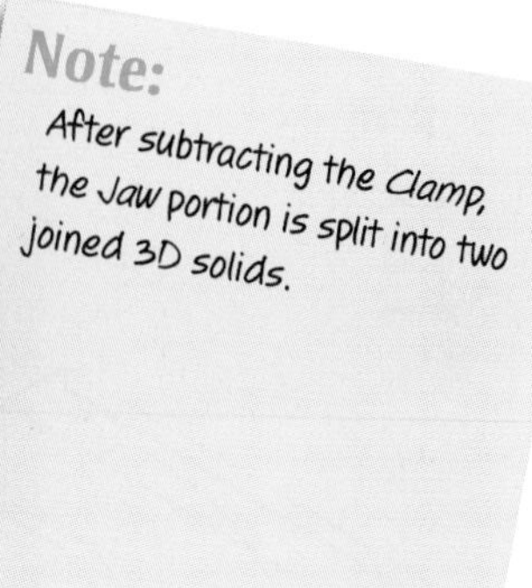

Note: After subtracting the Clamp, the Jaw portion is split into two joined 3D solids.

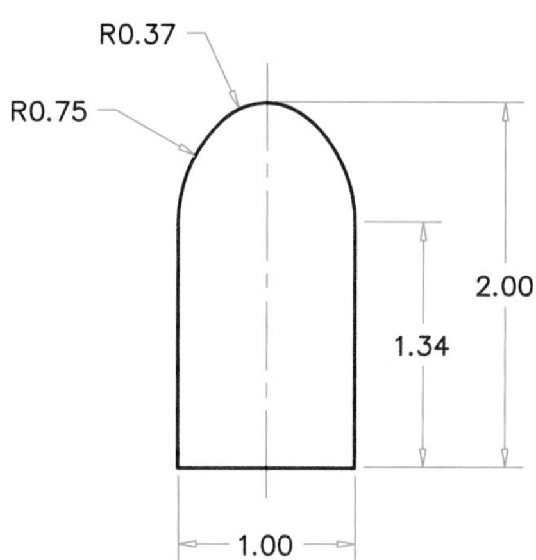

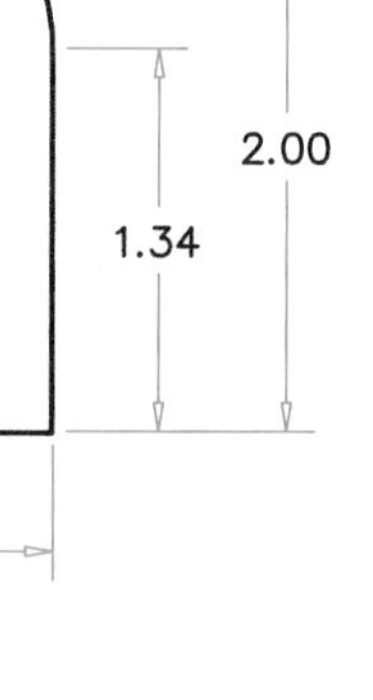

Figure 7-18 Profile dimensions

36. Invoke the **SECTION** command by entering its name in the command line and create a region on the *Main Body* parallel to the current *YZ* plane and going through the rightmost quadrant point of the upper circular edge highlighted in Figure 7-19.
37. Select the **Front** view.
38. Create the region shown in Figure 7-20.
39. Select the **SE Isometric** viewing point.
40. **MOVE** the region extracted with the **SECTION** command to the highlighted region shown in Figure 7-21, so that the two indicated endpoints meet.

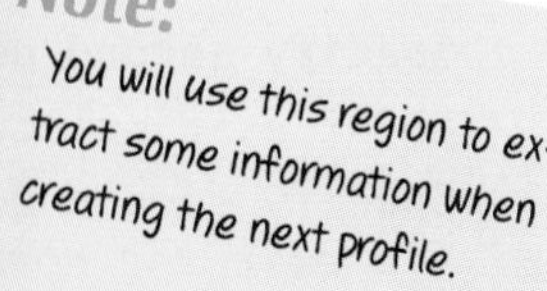

Note: You will use this region to extract some information when creating the next profile.

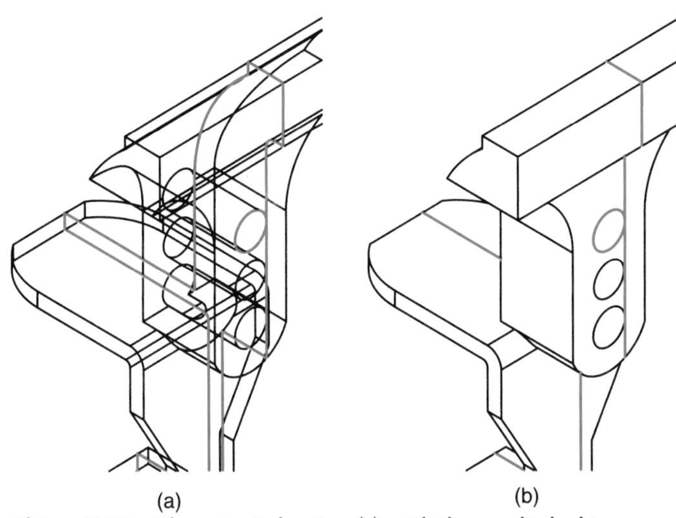

Figure 7-19 The extracted region (a); with the occulted edges removed (b)

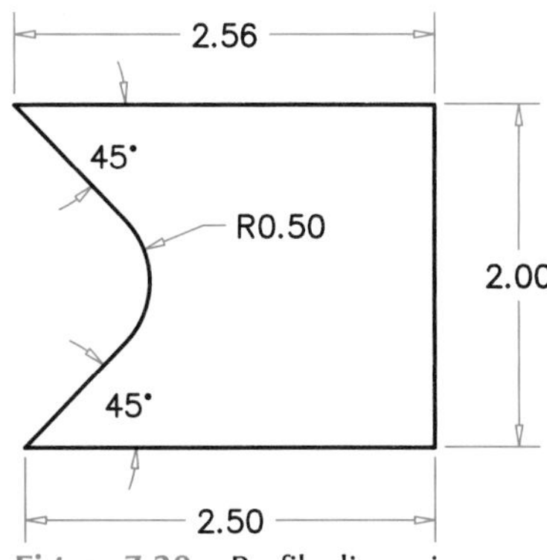

Figure 7-20 Profile dimensions

41. Obtain the region shown in Figure 7-22 by subtracting the two regions with the **SUBTRACT** command.
42. **MOVE** one of the regions from its endpoint to the other region (Figure 7-23).
43. Select the **Top** UCS.
44. With **ORTHO** mode activated, **MOVE** the region on the right **0.5″** along the positive *X*-axis (Figure 7-24).
45. **EXTRUDE** the region on the right **–3.00** units, and the one on the left **–1.00** unit. Specify **0** as the angle of taper for both extrusions.

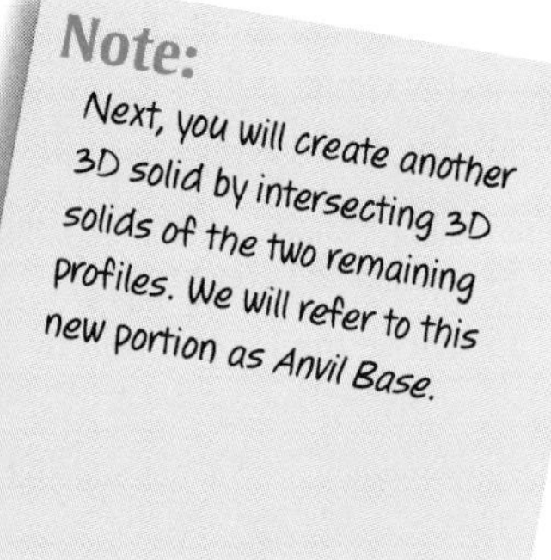

Note:
Next, you will create another 3D solid by intersecting 3D solids of the two remaining profiles. We will refer to this new portion as Anvil Base.

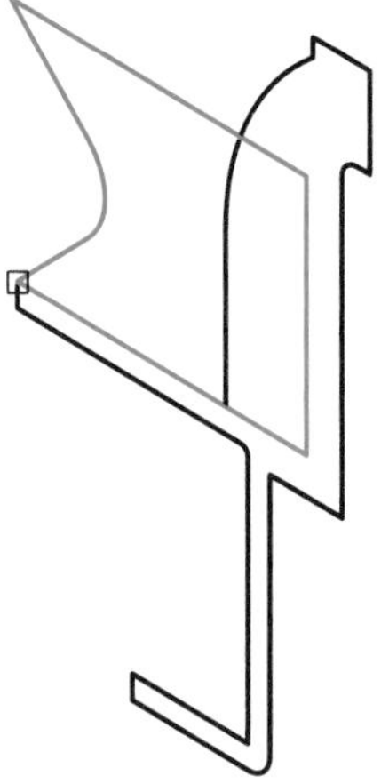
Figure 7-21 Point to be specified in the MOVE operation

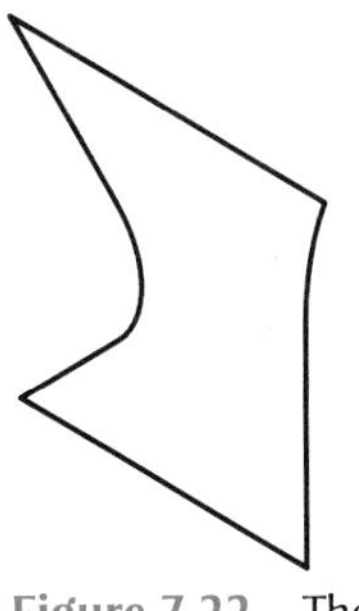
Figure 7-22 The resulting composite region after the SUBTRACT operation

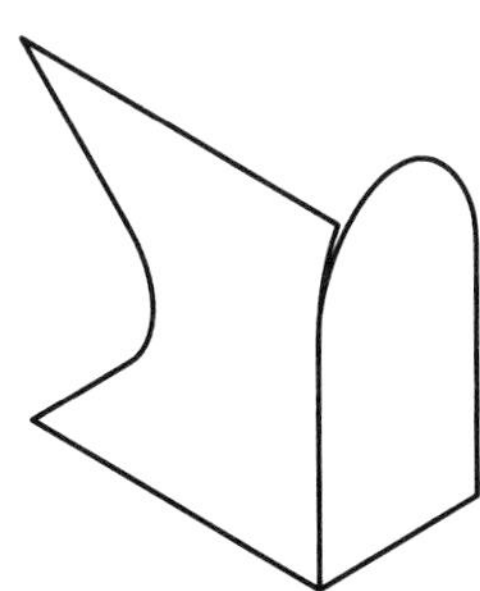
Figure 7-23 The region is moved to the other region

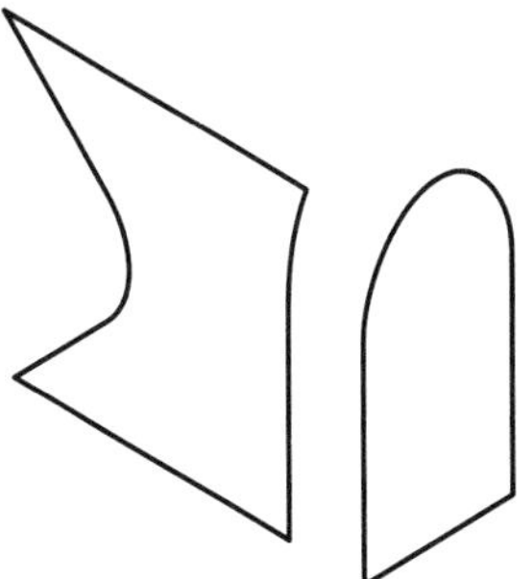
Figure 7-24 The region is moved away

46. With the **INTERSECT** command, create the new 3D solid shown in Figure 7-25. The 3D solid is shown with the hidden lines removed on the right side of the figure.
47. Invoke the **3DORBIT** command and rotate the viewing point to see the left side of the 3D models.

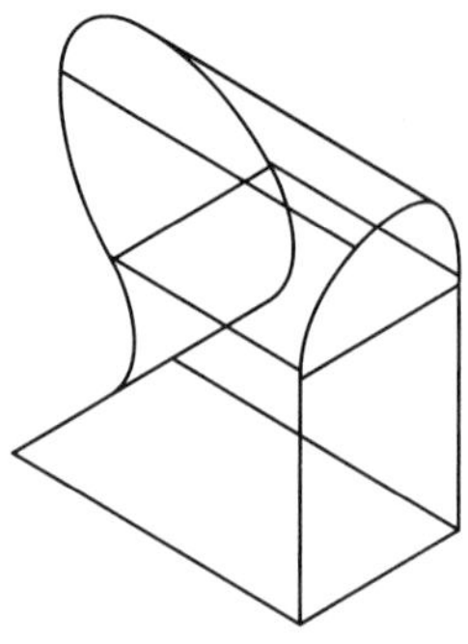
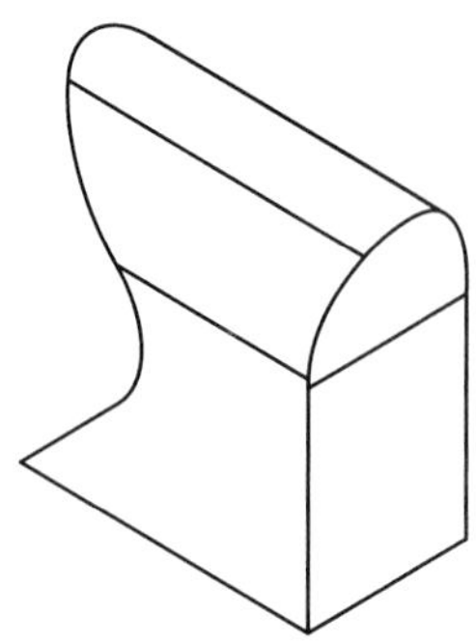

Figure 7-25 The 3D solid resulting from the INTERSECT operation

48. **MOVE** the *Anvil Base* to the *Main Body.* Snap to the endpoints to find the proper location (Figure 7-26).
49. With the **UNION** command, join the *Anvil Base* and the *Main Body*.
50. Select the **SE Isometric** viewing point.
51. Make sure the **Top** UCS is current.
52. Use the **SECTION** command to create a region that is parallel to the *YZ* plane and goes through any of the center points indicated in Figure 7-27.
53. **MOVE** the region to any empty place in the 3D space.
54. Select the **Right** view.
55. Move the UCS origin to any point on the extracted region.

Note:

In the following steps you will create the Anvil 3D solid and incorporate it into the Main Body with a smooth transition. In order to do that, you will extract a section and use its geometry to create the new profile tangent to it.

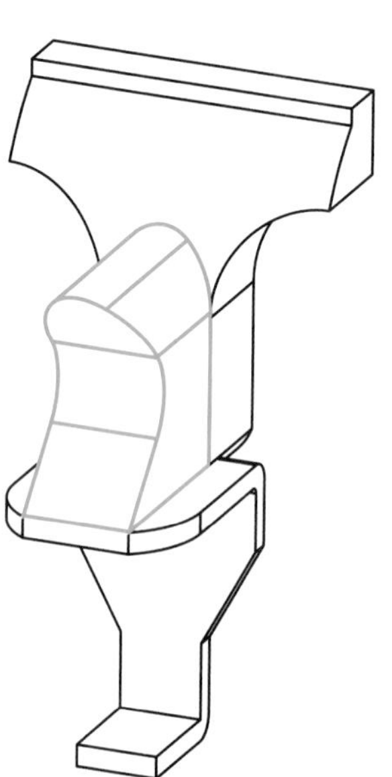

Figure 7-26 The Anvil Base is moved to the Main Body

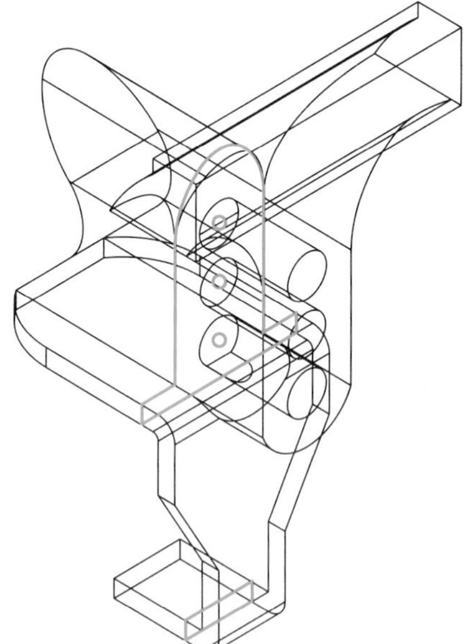

Figure 7-27 The resulting region

FOR MORE DETAILS

To find further information concerning UCS modifications, see Chapter 1.

56. **EXPLODE** the extracted region two times to separate the object into lines and arcs.
57. Create the profile shown in Figure 7-28 using the objects obtained by exploding the region.

Note: Because the region we are working with is composed of two individual areas, we will perform two **EXPLODE** operations. The first **EXPLODE** operation will separate the two regions. The second one will decompose the single region into 2D objects.

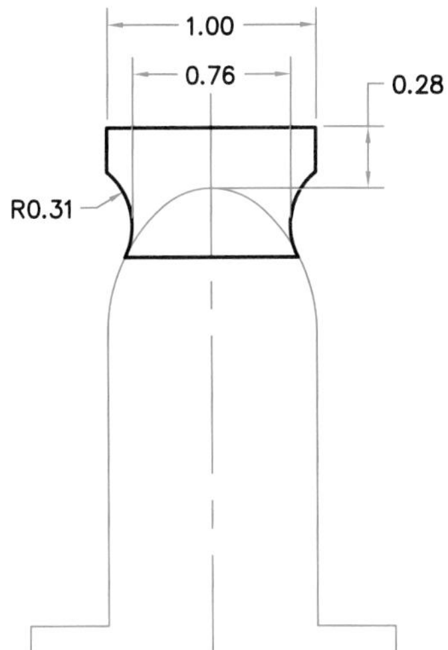

Figure 7-28 Profile dimensions

TIP You can obtain the arc by creating a circle tangent to the reference arc and tangent to another vertical reference line separated 0.76/2 from the symmetry line.

58. Select the **SE Isometric** viewing point.
59. Convert the new objects into a region.
60. **MOVE** the region from the midpoint of the extracted section to the midpoint of the *Main Body* (Figure 7-29).
61. **ERASE** the remaining objects from the exploded region.

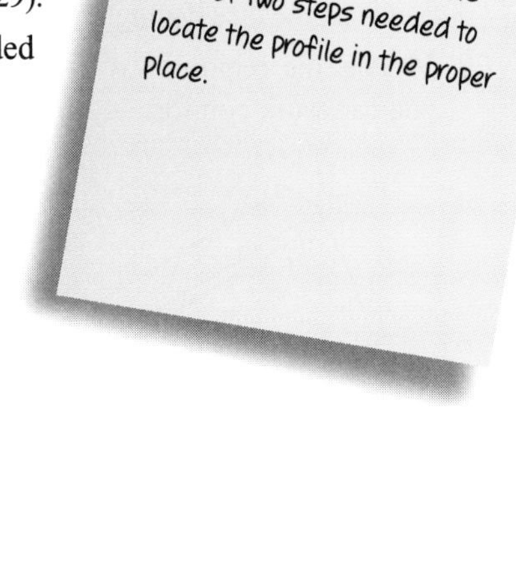

Note: This **MOVE** operation is the first of two steps needed to locate the profile in the proper place.

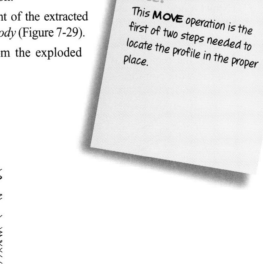

Figure 7-29 Points to perform the MOVE operation

TIP Keeping the model free of unnecessary objects is an important factor in avoiding errors and confusion.

62. Select the **Front** orthographic view.
63. With **ORTHO** mode activated, draw a **2.36″** polyline horizontally from the endpoint, as shown in Figure 7-30.
64. With **ORTHO** and **OTRACK** modes activated, **MOVE** the region from its top endpoint to align it vertically with the polyline's endpoint (Figure 7-31).
65. **ERASE** the polyline.
66. **EXTRUDE** the region **1.5** units (Figure 7-32).

Note:
Using the tracking tool to move the region guarantees that the region will only move in the X-axis direction, regardless of whether the two points specified have different Z coordinates.

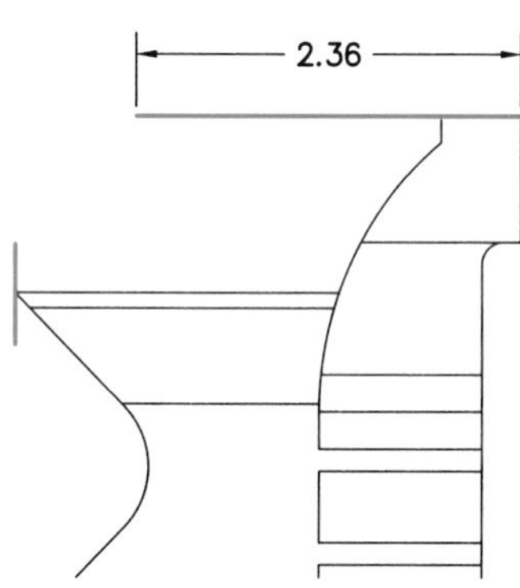

Figure 7-30 After the polyline is placed

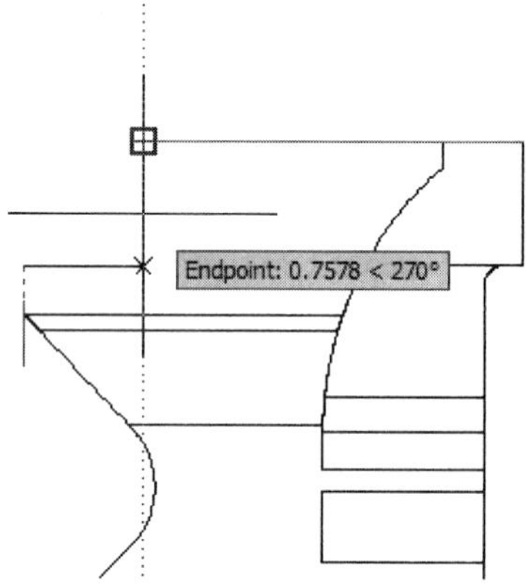

Figure 7-31 The region is moved to align it with the polyline

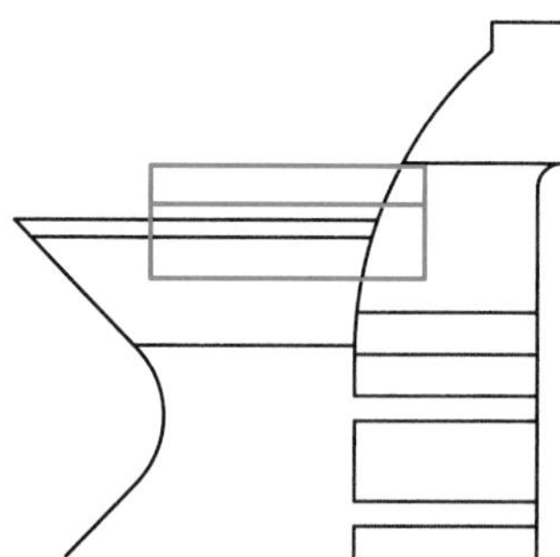

Figure 7-32 After extruding the region

67. With the **UNION** command, integrate the *Anvil* solid with the *Main Body*.
68. Select the **Isometric SW** viewing point (Figure 7-33).
69. Extract a new region using the **3 points** option of the **SECTION** command. Specify any three noncollinear points on the face highlighted on Figure 7-34.
70. **MOVE** the region away from the *Main Body* so you can work comfortably.

Note:
Next, you will cut off the volume inside the *Anvil Base* to clean up the path through which the bolt and the cylindrical guides will go. We will refer to this new 3D solid as *Cavity*.

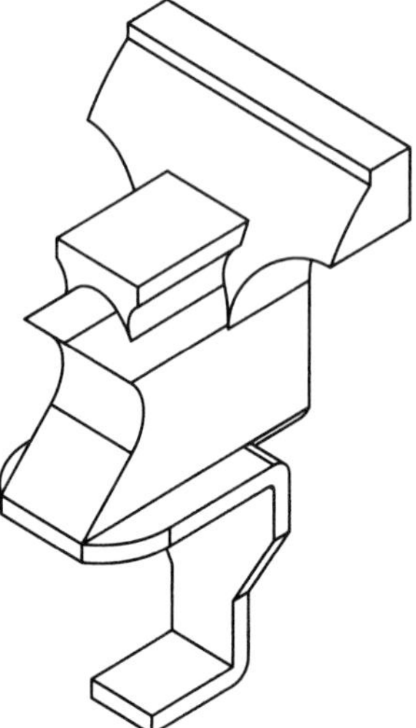

Figure 7-33 The 3D solid resulting from the UNION operation

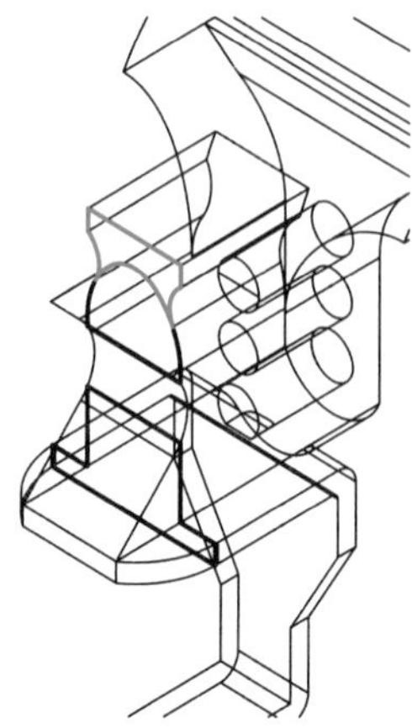

Figure 7-34 Face to specify the three points of the SECTION command

71. Select the **Left** view.
72. Move the UCS origin to any point on the extracted region.
73. Use the extracted region as a reference to draw the objects shown in Figure 7-35.
74. Convert the objects into a region.
75. Select the **Isometric SW** viewing point.
76. **EXTRUDE** the region **2.5** units to create the *Cavity*.
77. **MOVE** the *Cavity* from the midpoint of the region to the same point on the *Main Body* (Figure 7-36).
78. **ERASE** the region that you used as reference.
79. Select the **Front** view.
80. **MOVE** the *Cavity* orthogonally to the right so that the right planar face aligns vertically with the inside flat face of the *Clamp*.

Note:
Extracting regions and working on top of them clarifies the job and reduces the chance of making mistakes.

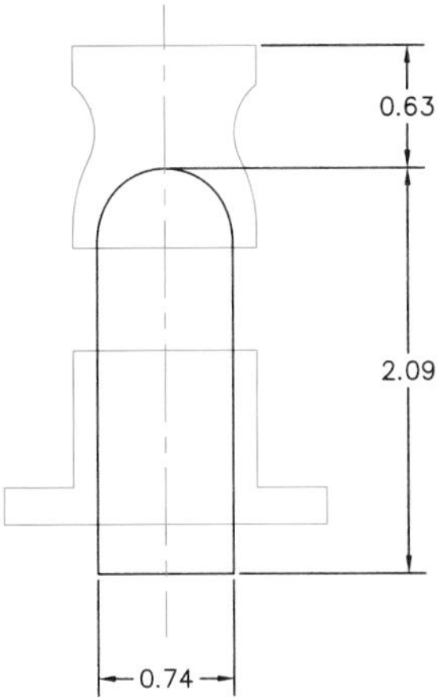

Figure 7-35 New profile created using the extracted region

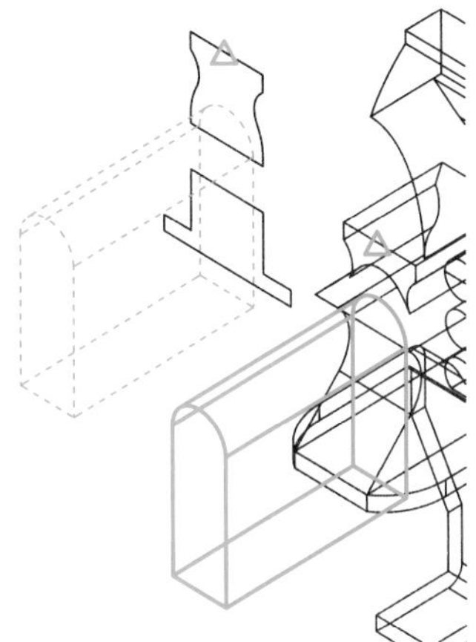
Figure 7-36 Points to specify in the MOVE operation

TIP
You can use the **AutoTrack** tool to find the second point of displacement to make sure that the object moves only in the direction of the *X*-axis Figure 7-37).

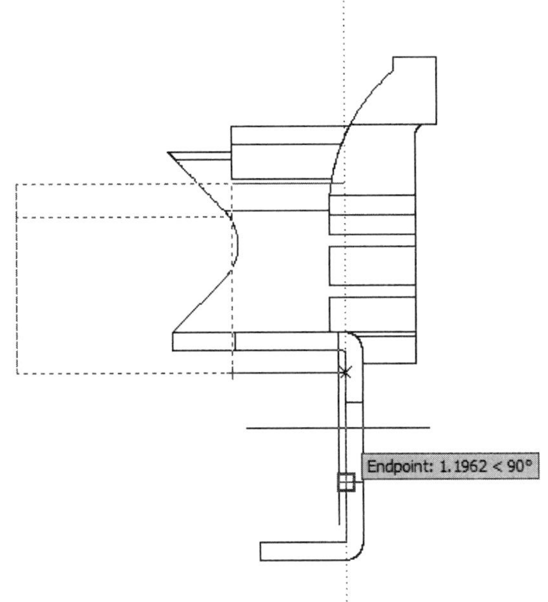

Figure 7-37 The Cavity moved using tracking methods

81. **SUBTRACT** the *Cavity* from the *Main Body*.
82. Select the **3D Hidden** visual style and inspect the 3D model with the **3DORBIT** command (Figure 7-38).
83. Select the **SE Isometric** viewing point.
84. Select the **Right** UCS.
85. Use the **Copy edges** option of the **SOLIDEDIT** command to copy the circular edge of the hole with the defect at the same place. Specify the base point and the second point of displacement as the same point.

By carefully inspecting the 3D model, you can see that the lower hole is not completely cylindrical. If a region were extracted along the center of the 3D solid, it would reveal such a defect (Figure 7-39).

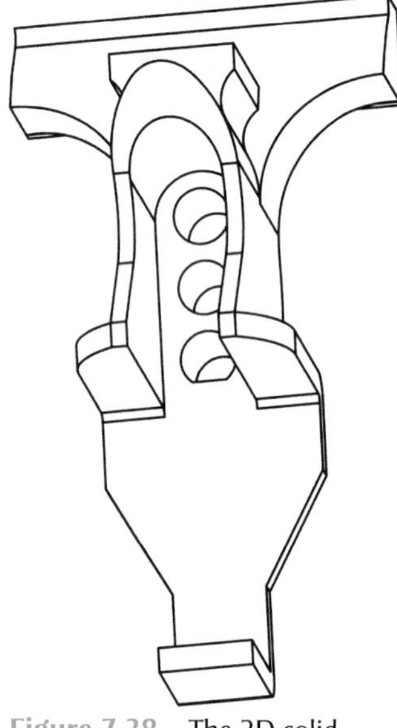

Figure 7-38 The 3D solid resulting from the SUBTRACT operation

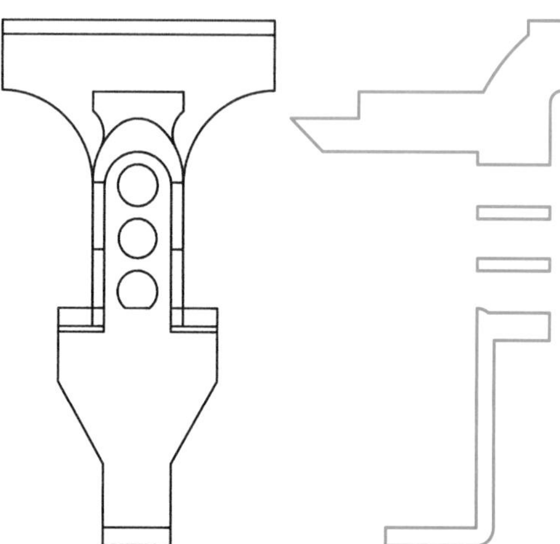

Figure 7-39 Inspecting the 3D model

86. **EXTRUDE** the new circle **–1.5** units (Figure 7-40).

TIP

The selection of the copied edge can easily be made using a selection window.

87. **SUBTRACT** the cylinder from the *Main Body* to correct the defect of the hole.
88. Select the **Top** UCS.
89. Invoke the **CYLINDER** command. Specify the midpoint of the highlighted edge for the center of the cylinder. Snap to the endpoint of the same edge to specify the radius. Specify **–0.66** for the height (Figure 7-41).
90. With the **UNION** command, join the cylinder with the *Main Body.*
91. Create a second cylinder with a radius of **0.21″** and a height of **1″**. Place its center concentric with the bottom circular edge of the previous cylinder.
92. **SUBTRACT** the second cylinder from the *Main Body* (Figure 7-42).

Note:

A rib is needed to give more stiffness to the Clamp portion. You will create the rib by sweeping a profile along a path.

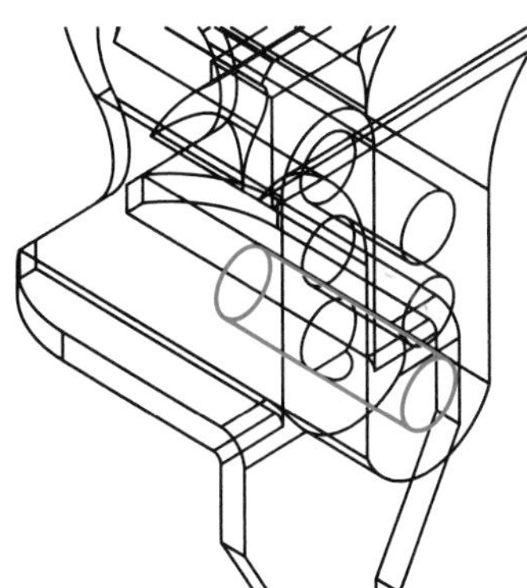

Figure 7-40 The circle extruded

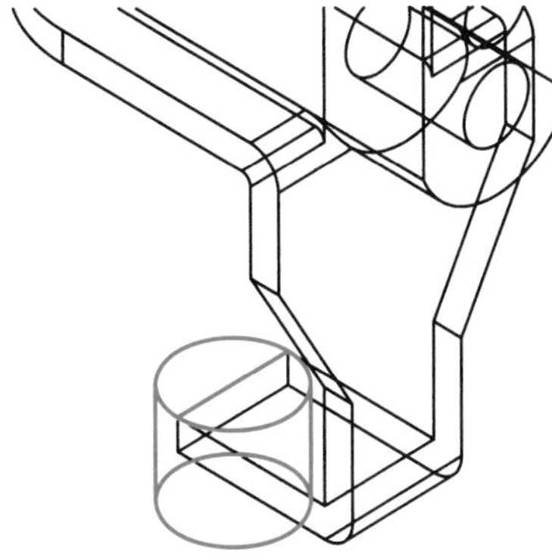

Figure 7-41 A cylinder created in place

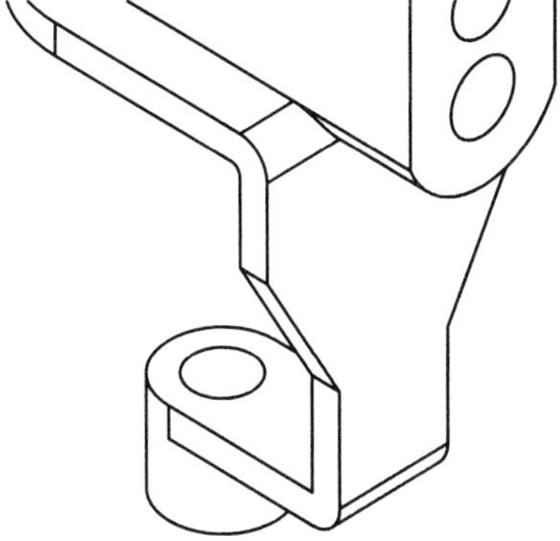

Figure 7-42 A hole created by subtracting a second cylinder

93. Select the **Front** view.
94. Draw the curve shown in Figure 7-43 as a single polyline.

If necessary, use the **PEDIT** command to join the segments. Remember that all the objects to be joined need to lie in the same plane and such plane must be parallel to the current UCS. Start by drawing a circle concentric with the right angle edge, and create the rest of the geometry using the circle as reference.

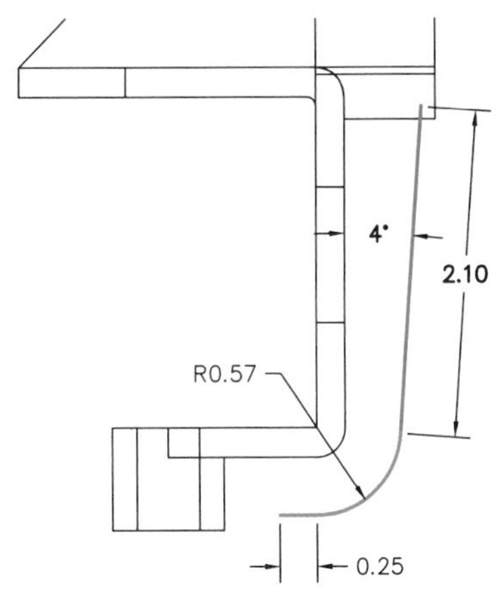

Figure 7-43 Curve dimensions

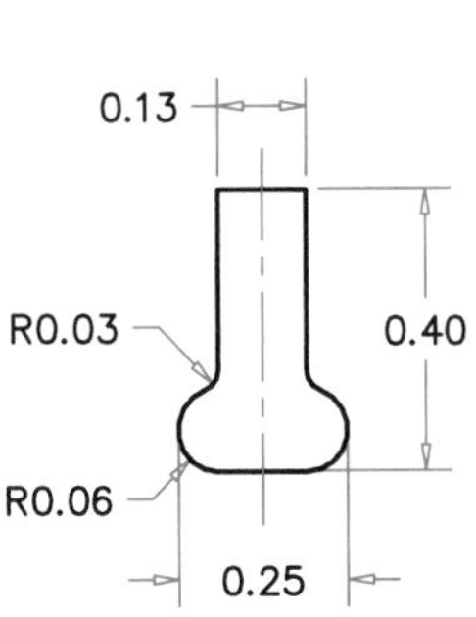

Figure 7-44 Profile dimensions

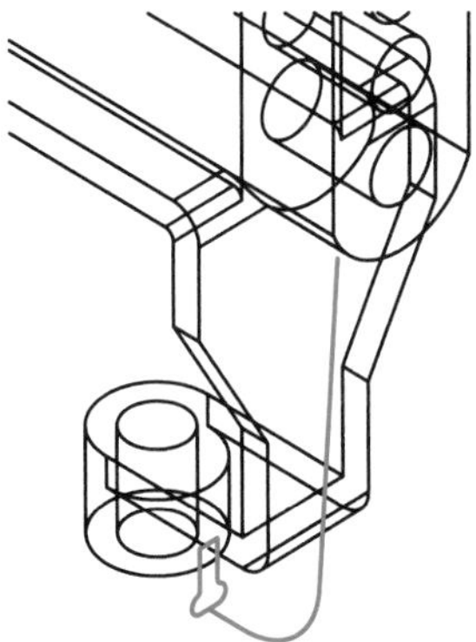

Figure 7-45 The profile is moved to the curve

95. Draw the region shown in Figure 7-44. This will be the cross section of the rib.
96. Select the **SE Isometric** viewing point.
97. **MOVE** the region from its bottom midpoint to the endpoint of the polyline (Figure 7-45).
98. **SWEEP** the region along the polyline.
99. **ERASE** the polyline used as the sweep path (Figure 7-46).
100. Select the **Top** view (Figure 7-47).
101. **MOVE** the rib orthogonally along the *Y*-axis to center it with the *Main Body*. You can do this either by

Note:

Because you created the extrusion path in an orthogonal view without knowing its Z-axis location, the swept rib will not be centered with the Main Body. Your next step will be to relocate and modify the rib before joining it with the Main Body.

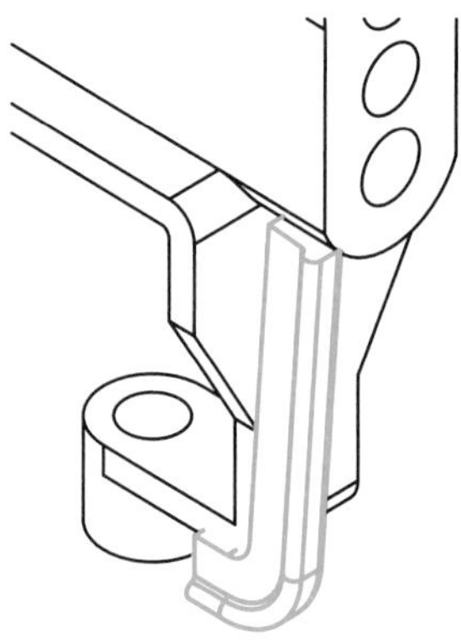
Figure 7-46 After sweeping the profile

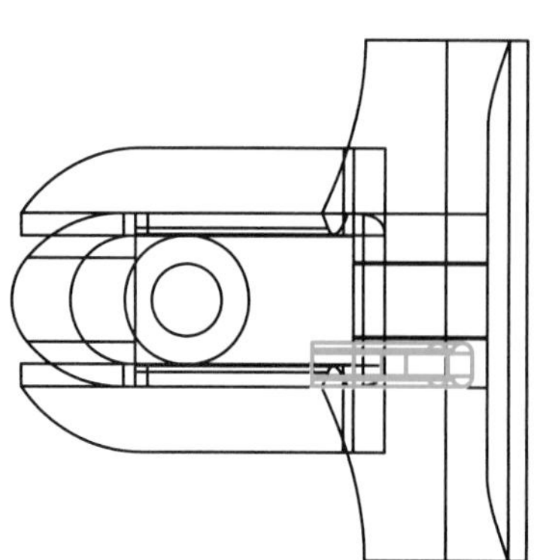
Figure 7-47 A Top view

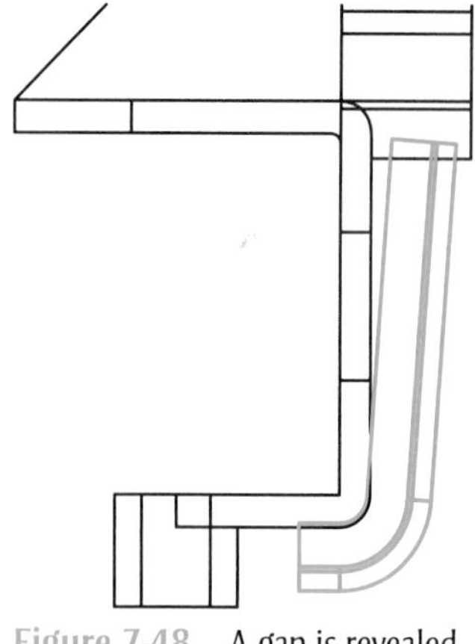
Figure 7-48 A gap is revealed in a Front view

tracking points or by using the point filters. Use the point filters this time. To do so, respond to the prompts as follows:

Select objects: *Select the rib.*

Select objects: ↵ *(To end the selection)*

Specify base point or displacement: *Specify any midpoint located at the center of the rib.*

Specify second point of displacement or <use first point as displacement>: ***.y*** ↵

Of: *Specify any midpoint located at the center of the Main Body.*

(need XZ): *With ORTHO mode activated, move the pointer over the Main Body. Click anywhere in the drawing area while the cursor trace is aligned with the Y-axis.*

> **Note:**
> As shown in Figure 7-48, there is a gap between the rib and the Main Body. This happened because of the 4° angle of the polyline used as the path. This gap will have to be filled before joining the 3D solids.

102. Select the **Front** view.
103. With the **CHECK** command, determine whether or not the rib is a valid ShapeManager solid. After you finish the selection, the AutoCAD® program responds with the following message:

This object is a valid ShapeManager solid.

Enter a body editing option

[Imprint/seParate solids/Shell/cLean/Check/Undo/eXit] <eXit>: *Press <Esc> to exit the command.*

> **Note:**
> The prompted message indicates that face editing operations can be performed on the rib.

104. Select the **SW Isometric** viewing point.
105. With **ORTHO** mode activated, **MOVE** the rib orthogonally down **2″**. This will make it easier to specify the points in the next operation.
106. Invoke the **Rotate faces** option of the **SOLIDEDIT** command and respond to the prompts as follows:

Select faces or [Undo/Remove]: *Select the face highlighted in* Figure 7-49.

Select faces or [Undo/Remove/ALL]: ↵ *(To end the selection)*

Specify an axis point or [Axis by object/View/Xaxis/Yaxis/Zaxis] <2points>: *Specify the center point of the leftmost arc edge.*

Specify the second point on the rotation axis: *Specify the other center point.*

Specify a rotation angle or [Reference]: *4* ↵

Enter a face editing option [Extrude/Move/Rotate/Offset/Taper/Delete/Copy/coLor/mAterial/Undo/eXit] <eXit>: *Press <Esc> to exit the command.*

There is another gap to be filled before joining the rib to the Main Body. You will extend the left portion of the rib so that it reaches the cylinder without getting into the hole.

107. Select the **Front** view.
108. **MOVE** the rib orthogonally back up the same **2″** (Figure 7-50).
109. Invoke the **Move faces** option of the **SOLIDEDIT** command and respond to the prompts as follows:

Select faces or [Undo/Remove]: *Select the face by clicking on the edge shown in* Figure 7-51.

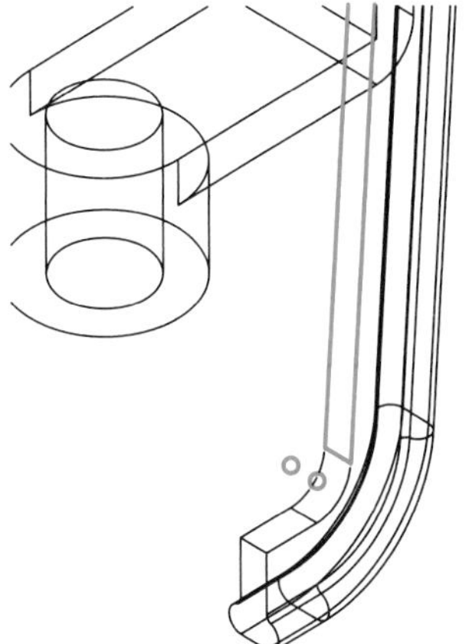

Figure 7-49 Face to be selected and points to be specified

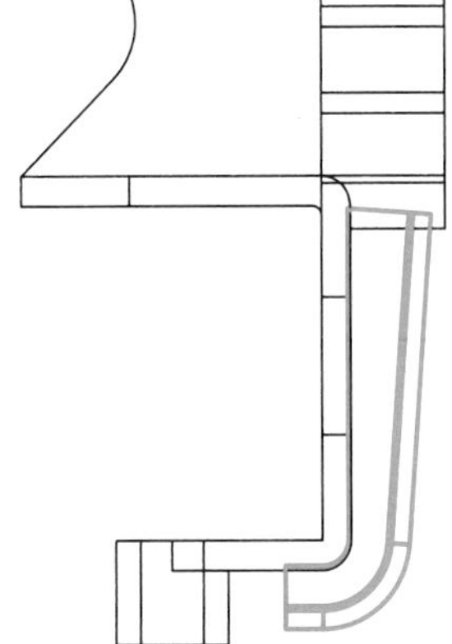

Figure 7-50 The corrected rib

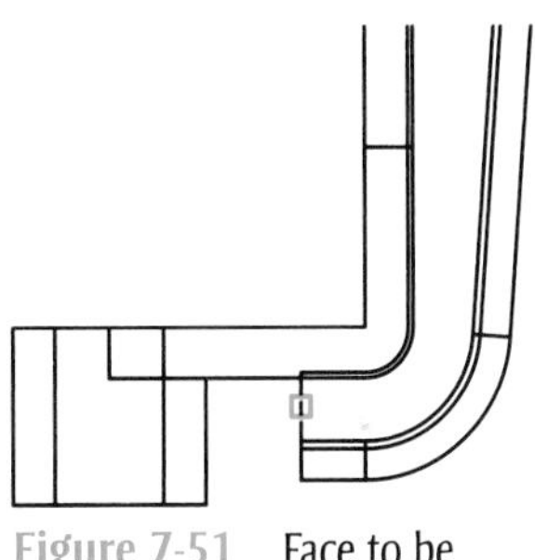

Figure 7-51 Face to be selected

Select faces or [Undo/Remove/ALL]: ↵ *(To end the selection)*

Specify a base point or displacement: *Click anywhere in an empty space on the drawing area.*

Specify a second point of displacement: *0.5* ↵ *(While ORTHO is activated and the pointer shows a direction to your left, that is, using the direct distance entry method)*

Note:

You will add two small pieces to the Main Body. We will call these pieces Tube Teeth. To make it simple, you will start by cutting a section through the model.

110. Invoke the **UNION** command to join the rib and the *Main Solid* (Figure 7-52).
111. Select the **SW Isometric** viewing point.
112. Invoke the **SECTION** command. Specify **XY** as the method to obtain the sectioning plane. Specify any center or midpoint that goes through the middle of the model.
113. With **ORTHO** activated, **MOVE** the new extracted region **2″** along the positive *X*-axis (Figure 7-53).
114. Select the **Front** view.
115. Change the UCS origin to any point in the extracted region.

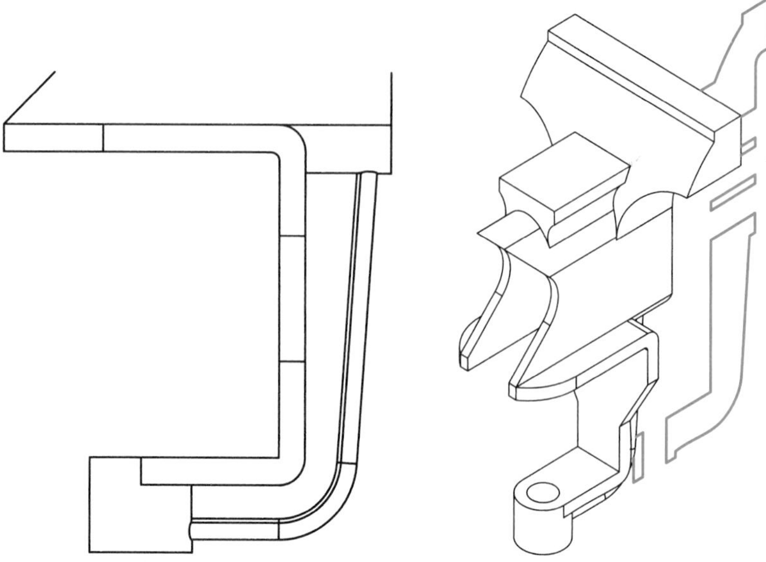

Figure 7-52 The 3D solid resulting from the UNION operation

Figure 7-53 The extracted region is moved away

116. **ZOOM** in to the top part of the extracted region and using the extracted region as reference, create the region shown in Figure 7-54.
117. With **ORTHO** activated, **MOVE** the new region **2″** back along the negative *X*-axis.
118. **ERASE** the extracted region.
119. **EXTRUDE** the region **0.13** unit.
120. Select the **SE Isometric** viewing point.
121. Invoke the **Taper faces** option of the **SOLIDEDIT** command and respond to the prompts as follows:

    Select faces or [Undo/Remove]: *Select only the highlighted face shown in* Figure 7-55.

    Select faces or [Undo/Remove/ALL]: ↵ *(To end the selection)*

    Specify the base point: *Specify endpoint 1.*

    Specify another point along the axis of tapering: *Specify perpendicular point 2.*

    Specify the taper angle: *-15* ↵

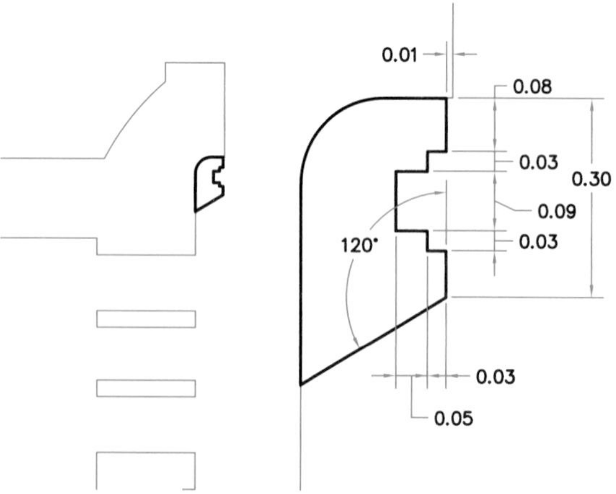

Figure 7-54 Profile based on the region and its dimensions

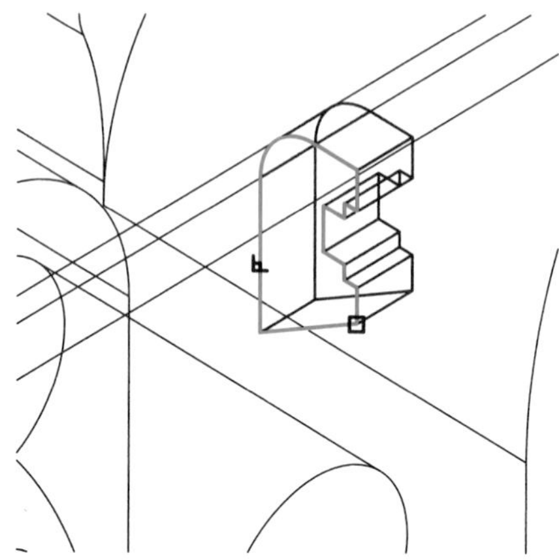

Figure 7-55 Face to be selected and points to be specified in the Taper faces operations

Enter a face editing option:
[Extrude/Move/Rotate/Offset/Taper/Delete/Copy/coLor/mAterial/Undo/ eXit] <eXit>: *Press <Esc> to exit the command.*

122. Select the **NE Isometric** view.
123. Invoke the **Taper faces** option of the **SOLIDEDIT** command again. Repeat exactly the same process to taper the face located at the other side of the *Tube Tooth*.
124. Select the **Top** viewing point.
125. With **ORTHO** mode activated, **MOVE** the *Tube Tooth* **0.38″** along the negative *Y*-axis.
126. **MIRROR** the *Tube Tooth* by using two midpoints or any other point aligned with the center of the model to define the mirror line (Figure 7-56).
127. Join the two *Tube Teeth* to the *Main Body* with the **UNION** command.
128. Select the **SW Isometric** view.
129. Invoke the **FILLET** command and respond to the prompts as follows:

Note:
The model is almost complete. Now you will add some fillets and chamfers as the final touches.

Select first object or [Polyline/ Radius/Trim]: *Select one of the two edges highlighted in* Figure 7-57.
Enter fillet radius <0.5000>: *0.13* ↵
Select an edge or [Chain/Radius]: *Select the second highlighted edge.*
Select an edge or [Chain/Radius]: ↵ *(To end the selection)*

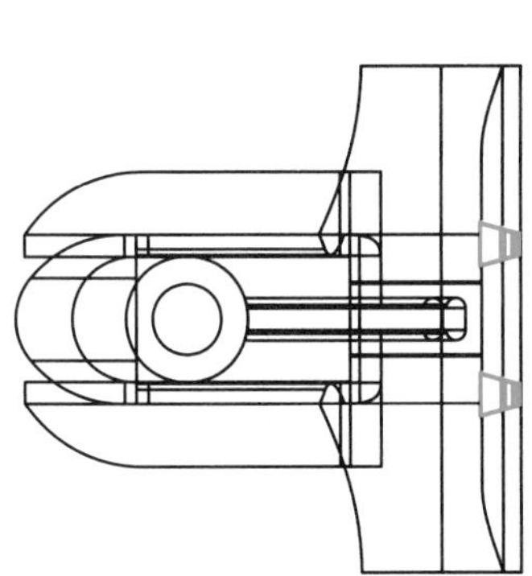
Figure 7-56 The mirrored copy of the Tube Tooth

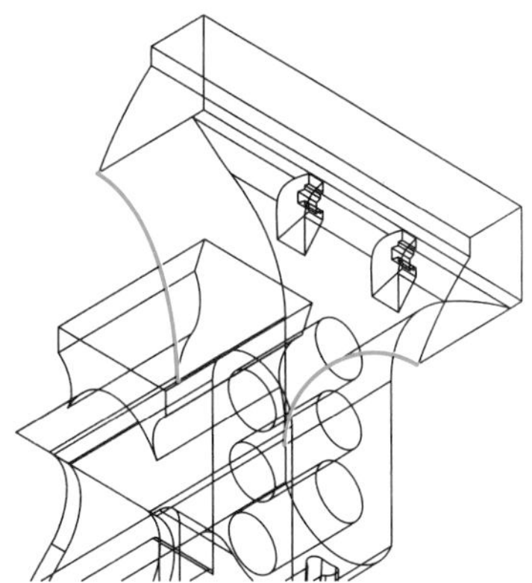
Figure 7-57 Edges to be filleted

130. Change the viewing point with the **3D Orbit** tool to see inside the *Cavity*.
131. **FILLET** the group of continuous edges highlighted in Figure 7-58. Use the **Chain** option and respond to the prompts as follows:

Select first object or [Polyline/Radius/Trim]: *Select any edge of the group.*
Enter fillet radius <0.1300>: ↵ *0.03* ↵
Select an edge or [Chain/Radius]: *c* ↵
Select an edge chain or [Edge/Radius]: *Select another edge of the group.*
Select an edge chain or [Edge/Radius]: ↵ *(To end the selection)*

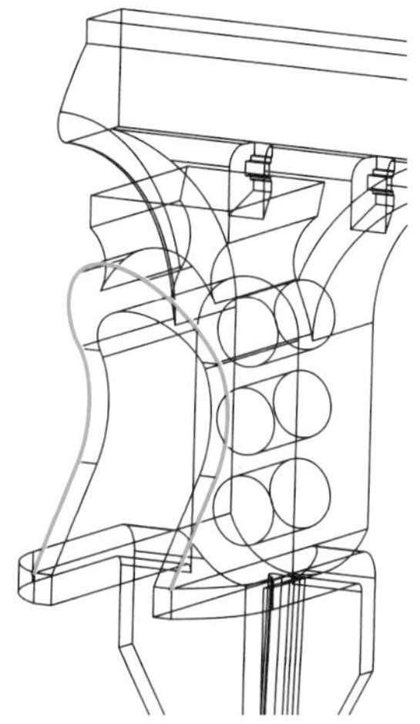
Figure 7-58 Chain of edges to be filleted

132. Select the **SE Isometric** viewing point.
133. **FILLET** the two chains of edges highlighted in Figure 7-59, using a radius of **0.03″**.
134. **FILLET** the edges highlighted in Figure 7-60, using the same fillet radius of **0.03″**. The AutoCAD program will recognize all the edges that are continuous by using the **Chain** option, making the selection easier.

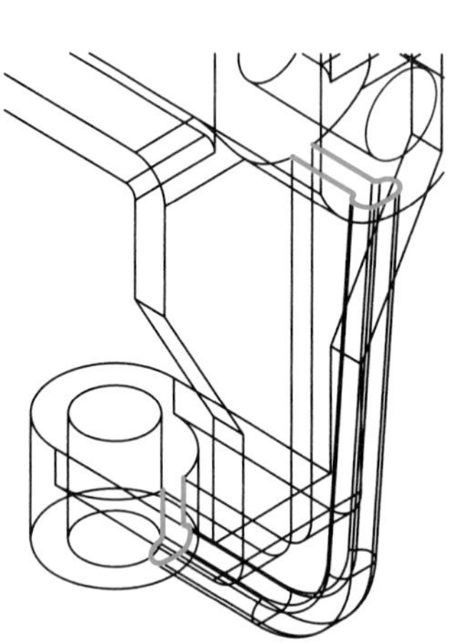

Figure 7-59 Chain of edges to be filleted

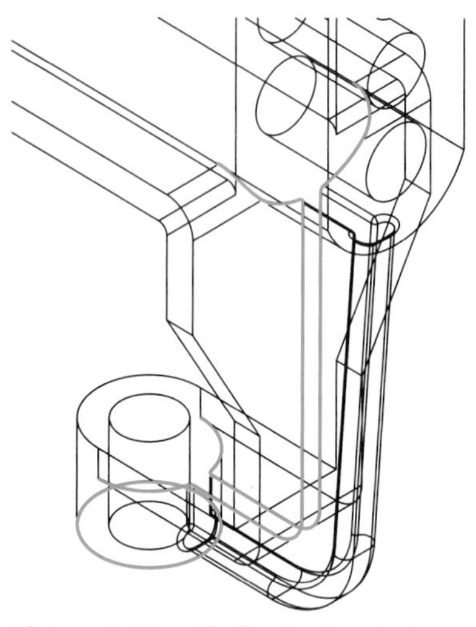

Figure 7-60 Chain of edges to be filleted

135. Using a radius value of **0.31″**, **FILLET** the four edges highlighted in Figure 7-61.
136. Invoke the **CHAMFER** command and respond to the prompts as follows:

Select first line or [Polyline/Distance/Angle/Trim/Method]: *Select any edge belonging to the face highlighted in* Figure 7-62.

Base surface selection...

Enter surface selection option

[Next/OK (current)] <OK>: *n* ↵ *(In case the selected face is not the highlighted one)*

Enter surface selection option [Next/OK (current)] <OK>: ↵ *(To end the selection)*

Note:
Next, you will create chamfers on the circular edges of all the holes, using the value of **0.02** for the two chamfer distances. Remember, unlike with the **FILLET** command, the edges selected in the **CHAMFER** command must belong to a common previously defined face.

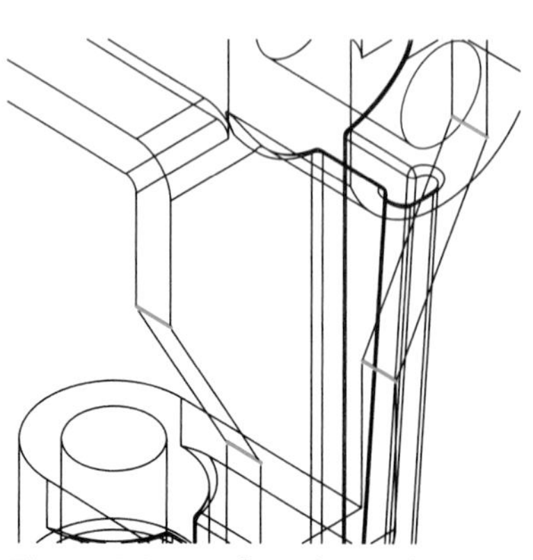

Figure 7-61 Other edges to be filleted

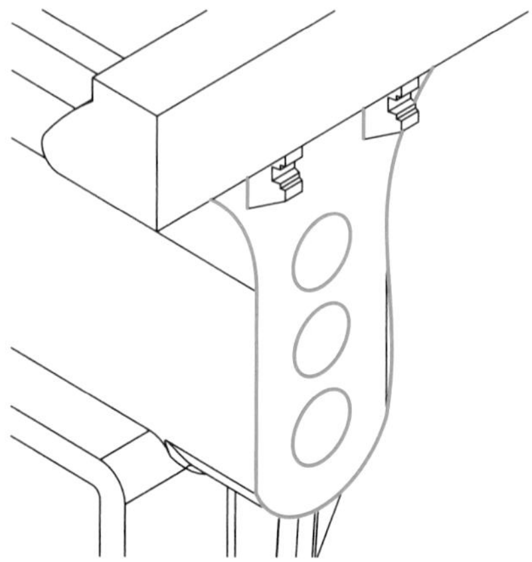

Figure 7-62 Face to be selected for the CHAMFER operation

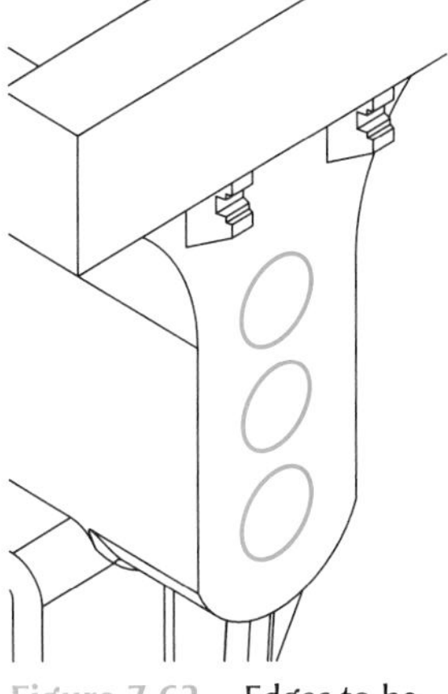
Figure 7-63 Edges to be chamfered

Specify base surface chamfer distance: *0.02* ↵

Specify other surface chamfer distance: *0.02* ↵

Select an edge or [Loop]: *Select the three circular edges highlighted in* Figure 7-63.

Select an edge or [Loop]: ↵ *(To end the selection)*

137. Select the **SW Isometric** viewing point.
138. Create the other chamfers highlighted in Figure 7-64. Use the same chamfer distances as with the previous one.
139. Select the **SE Isometric** viewing point.
140. Select the **Top** UCS.
141. Draw the polyline shown in Figure 7-65 between the two center points of the highlighted arc edges.

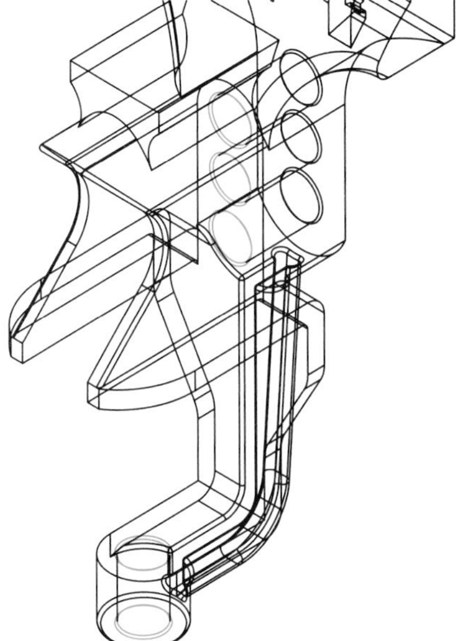
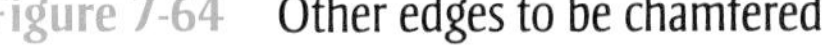
Figure 7-64 Other edges to be chamfered

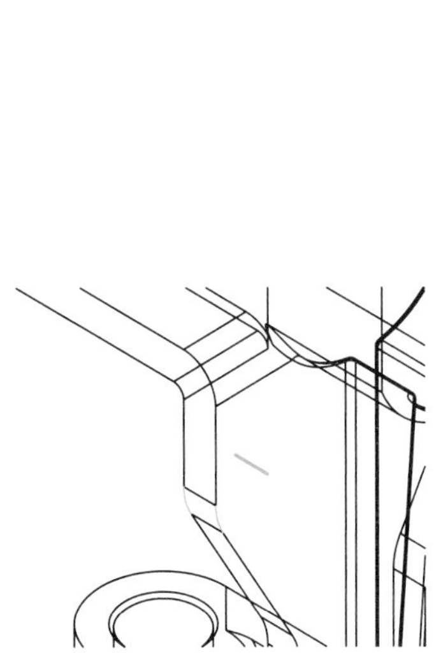
Figure 7-65 Polyline placed

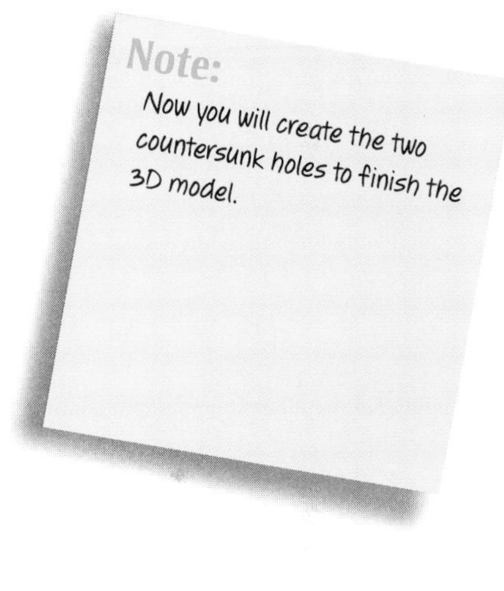
Note:
Now you will create the two countersunk holes to finish the 3D model.

142. Based on the polyline, create the region shown in Figure 7-66.
143. **REVOLVE** the region. Use two endpoints of the polyline to define the axis of revolution (Figure 7-67).

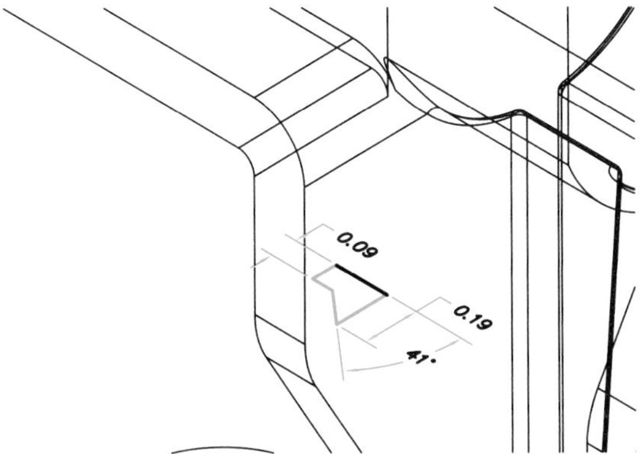
0.09
0.19
41°
Figure 7-66 Profile dimensions

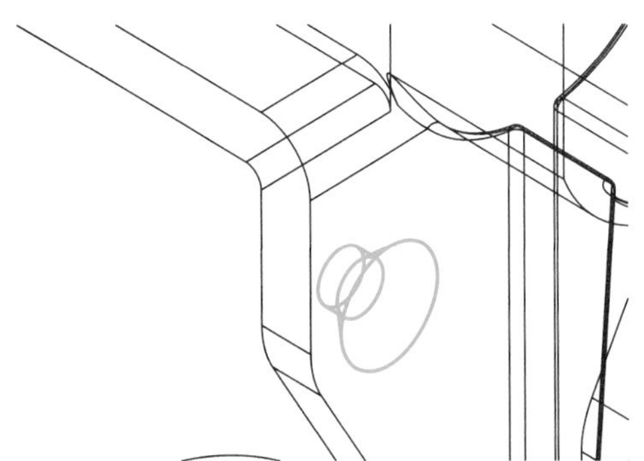
Figure 7-67 The revolved 3D solid

144. Invoke the **MIRROR3D** command. After you select the countersunk hole, specify any three of the many points that can define an imaginary plane going through the center of the 3D solid (Figure 7-68).
145. **SUBTRACT** the two countersunk holes from the *Main Body*.
146. After you invoke the **HIDE** command, the completed 3D model of the *Main Body* should look like Figure 7-69.
147. **SAVE** the drawing.

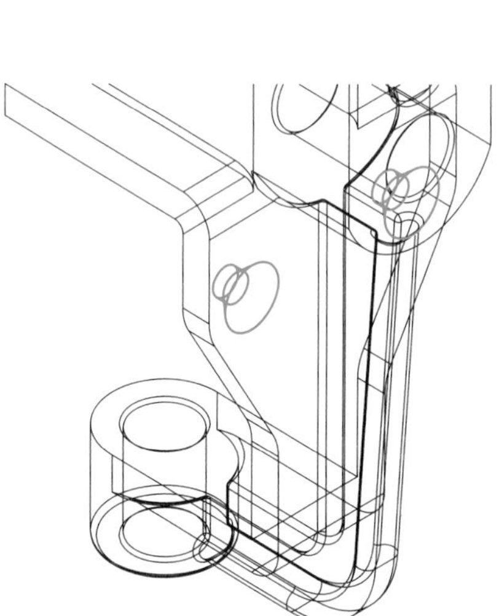

Figure 7-68 A mirrored copy of the revolved 3D solid

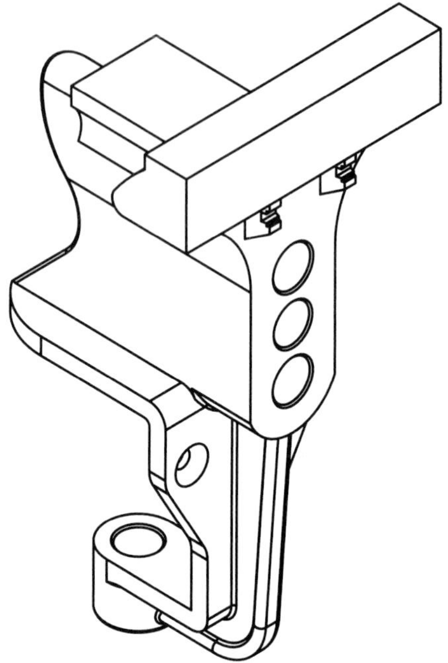

Figure 7-69 The finished 3D model of the Main Body

MODELING THE MOVING JAW

The second 3D model you will create will be named *Moving Jaw*. Because much of this model is exactly like the *Main Body*, you will simply modify a copy of this file. Using this approach will save you a good amount of design time.

1. **OPEN** the ***Main Body*** drawing.
2. **SAVE** it **AS *Moving Body***.
3. Select the **SW Isometric** viewing point.
4. Select the **Top** UCS.
5. Use the **SECTION** command to create the two regions shown in Figure 7-70. Their geometry will be used as a reference.
   - The first region will be parallel to the *ZX* plane, going through any point located at the center of the 3D solid.
   - The second one will be parallel to the *YZ* plane. Locate any point through which the highlighted region could go.
6. **MOVE** both regions anywhere outside the 3D solid.
7. Select the **Front** UCS.
8. Create the region shown in Figure 7-71, using the points or objects of the extracted regions as reference. Dimensions are given only for the geometry that is not yet defined.

TIP: To use the region's objects, **EXPLODE** the region as many times as needed. You can also leave the region intact and use only its points to place new objects. A circle can be drawn coradial with the arc to find the tangent point with the line.

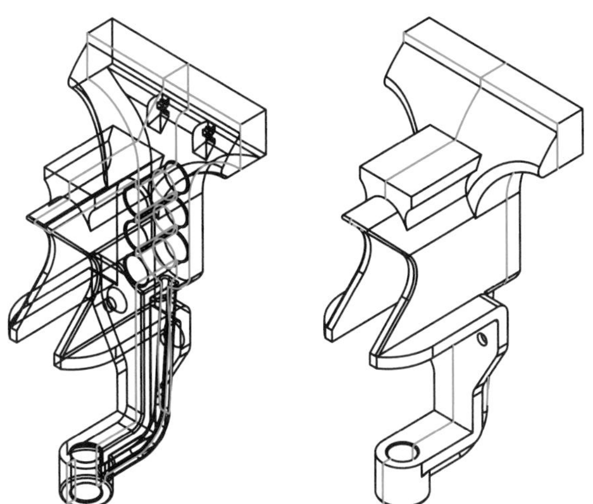

Figure 7-70 Two sections extracted, shown with the hidden lines removed at right

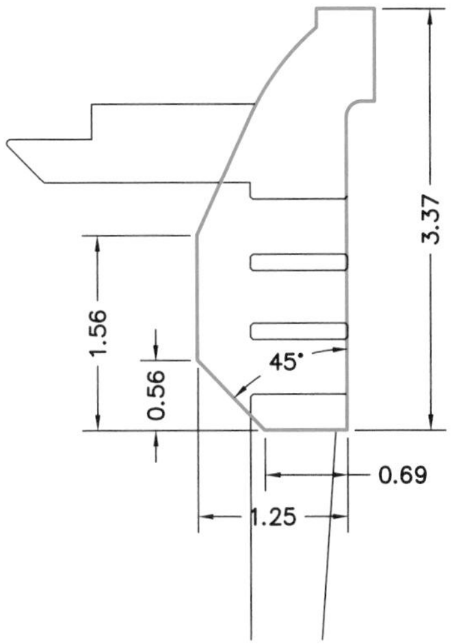

Figure 7-71 Profile created based on one of the extracted regions

9. **ERASE** the old region (or the remaining objects, if it was exploded) to keep the drawing clean.
10. Select the **Left** view.
11. Follow the same procedure to create the region shown in Figure 7-72, using the other region extracted.
12. **ERASE** any remaining objects around the region, as well as the three circles inside it.
13. Select the **SW Isometric** viewing point.
14. **MOVE** one of the regions to the other region, as shown in Figure 7-73.

Note: Because all the objects you need are already contained in the second region, you will not need any new dimensions. This time you might prefer to **EXPLODE** the region and use its objects. Basically, all you have to do is **DELETE** one of the arcs at the bottom and **EXTEND** the other arc to the line.

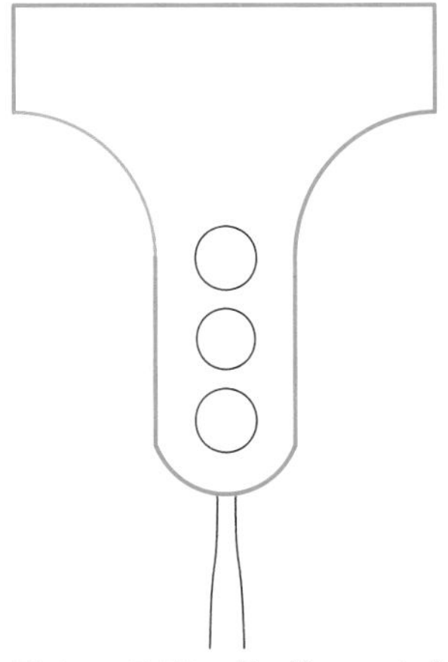

Figure 7-72 Profile created using the other extracted regions

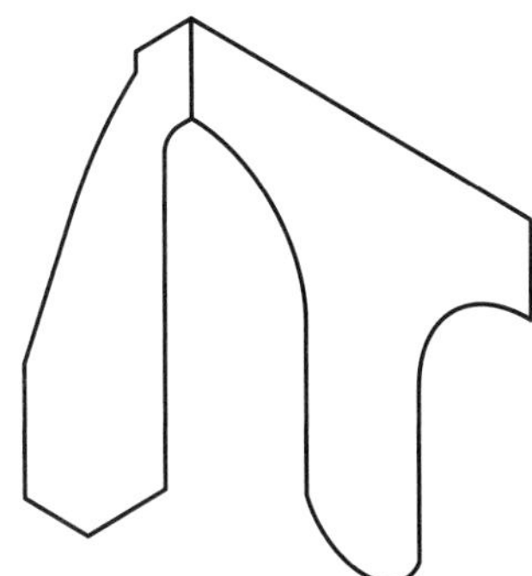

Figure 7-73 Regions placed together

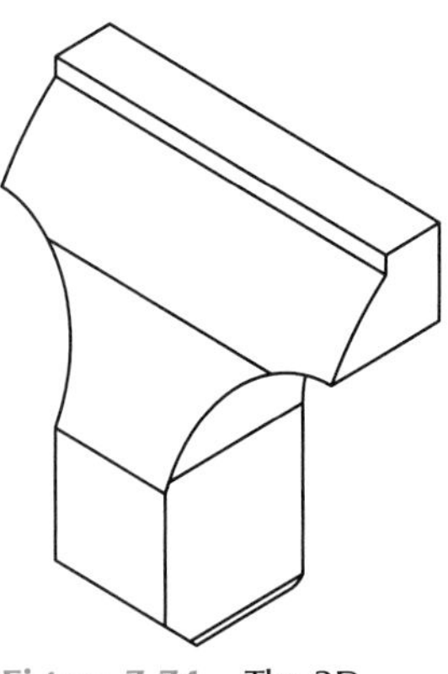
Figure 7-74 The 3D solid resulting from the INTERSECT operation

15. Make sure the **Left** UCS is current.
16. **EXTRUDE** the region that is on your right **2″** , and the one on your left **3″**.
17. **INTERSECT** the two 3D solids (Figure 7-74).
18. With the **SECTION** command, extract the same region on the *Main Body* you extracted before (Figure 7-75). Because the **Left** UCS is current, you can perform the operation parallel to the *XY* plane.
19. **MOVE** the region extracted to the *Moving Jaw*. Snap to the endpoints indicated in Figure 7-76 to place it correctly.
20. Select the **SE Isometric** viewing point.
21. Select the **Right** UCS.
22. Draw three circles concentric with the region's circular holes. Use the dimensions shown in Figure 7-77.

> **Note:**
> Now, you will create the three holes in the Moving Jaw piece. The most accurate way to make the holes concentric with the ones on the Main Body is by using the existing reference geometry.

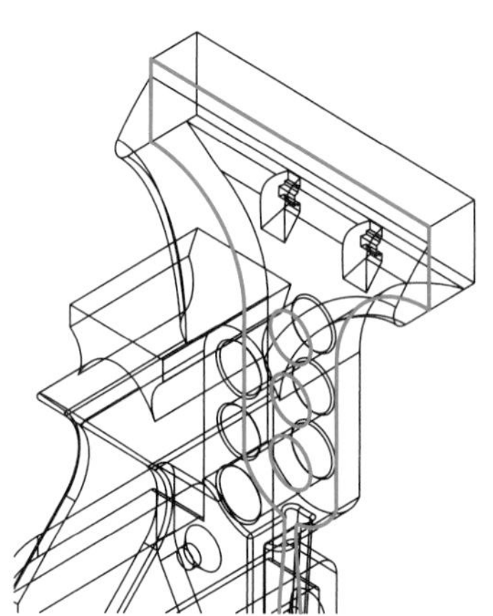
Figure 7-75 An extracted region

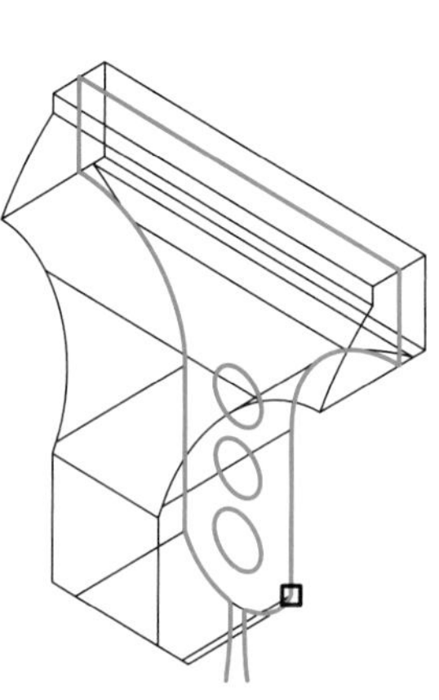
Figure 7-76 The region moved to the Moving Jaw using the point shown

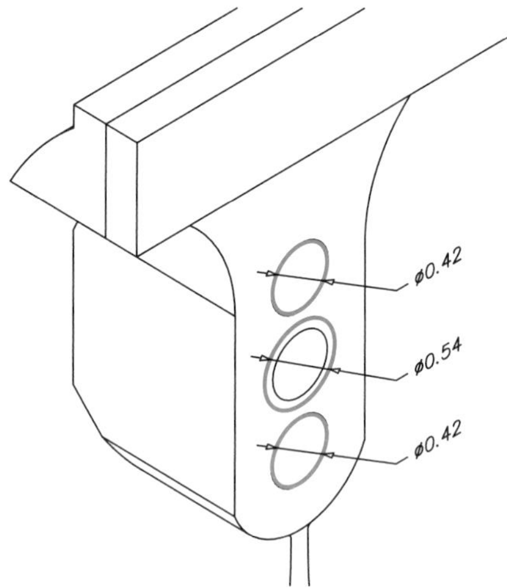

Figure 7-77 Circles created based on the reference region

23. **ERASE** the extracted region you used as a reference.
24. **EXTRUDE** the three circles, using the following heights:
    - **–2″** for the middle circle
    - **–0.75″** for the top and bottom circle
25. **SUBTRACT** the resulting three cylinders from the *Moving Jaw*. Your drawing should look like Figure 7-78.
26. Select the **Front** UCS.
27. Use the **SECTION** command to create a region on the *Main Body,* parallel to the *XY* plane and going through the center of the 3D solid (Figure 7-79).
28. **MOVE** the region out of the 3D solid.
29. Move the UCS origin to any point on the extracted region.

> **Note:**
> Next, you will extract the Tube Teeth from the Main Body, which is the only portion you need to add to the Moving Jaw. After this, you will no longer need the Main Body 3D solid.

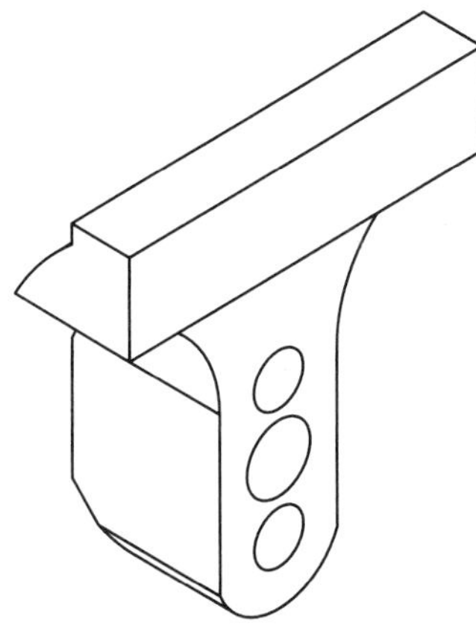

Figure 7-78 The three cylinders subtracted

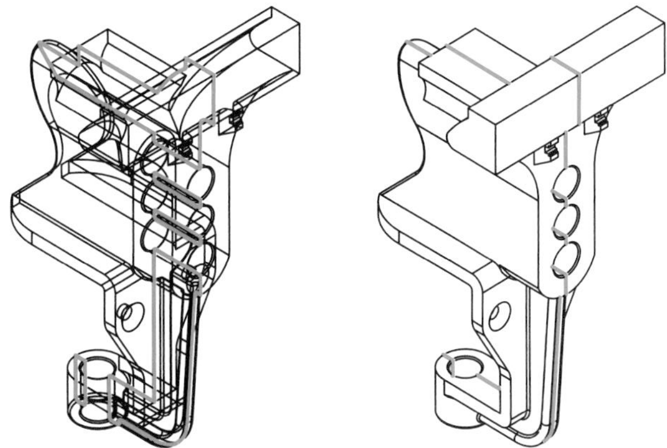

Figure 7-79 Another region extracted from the Main Body

30. Create the region shown in Figure 7-80. **EXPLODE** the extracted region to use its objects, if needed.
31. Select the **NW Isometric** viewing point.
32. **MOVE** the created region from the endpoint of the region to the endpoint of the *Main Body,* as shown in Figure 7-81.
33. **ERASE** the extracted region or its remaining objects.

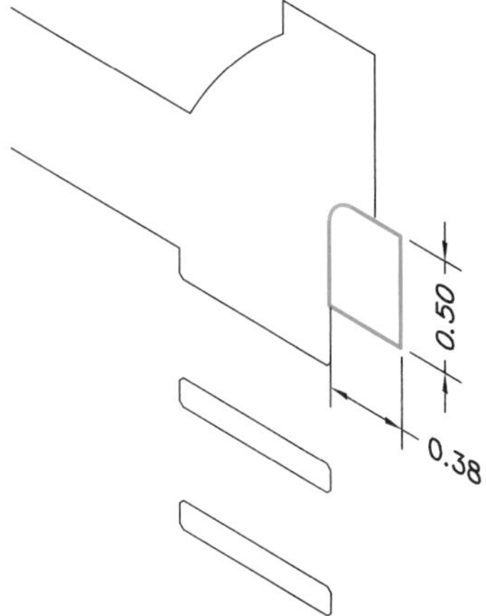

Figure 7-80 Profile to be created

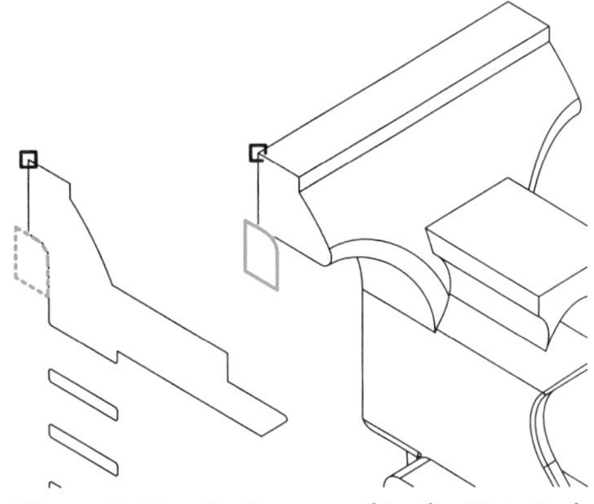

Figure 7-81 Region moved to the Main Body

You can change the viewing point by using the **3DORBIT** command, if needed, to make the selection of the objects easier.

34. Select the **SE Isometric** viewing point.
35. Select the **Front** UCS.
36. **EXTRUDE** the region **3″** (Figure 7-82).
37. Invoke the **Copy edges** option of the **SOLIDEDIT** command. When prompted, select the edge shown in Figure 7-83. Specify any point for both the base and the second point to copy the edge in the same place.
38. **INTERSECT** the *Main Body* and the extruded 3D solid. The resulting 3D solid and the extracted edge are shown in Figure 7-84.

Note:

Before you intersect these two 3D solids, you must leave a reference point. This is because the *Main Body* will disappear after the operation.

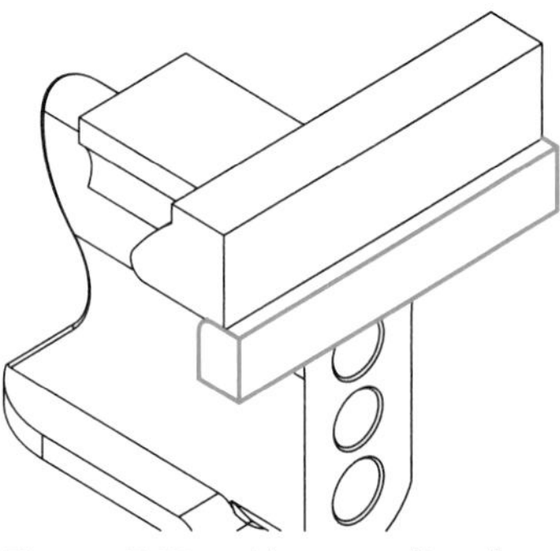

Figure 7-82 After extruding the region

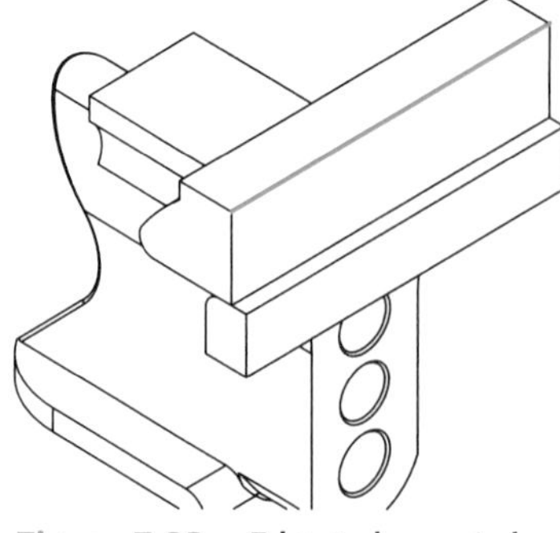

Figure 7-83 Edge to be copied

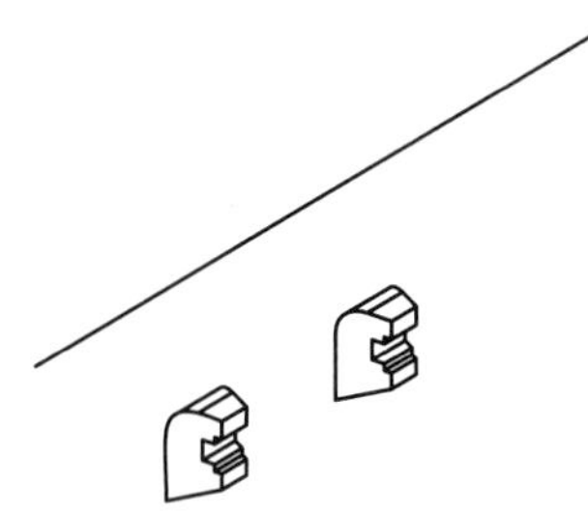

Figure 7-84 The 3D solid resulting from the INTERSECT operation

39. **MOVE** the resulting 3D solid from the endpoint of the reference edge to the corresponding endpoint of the *Moving Jaw* piece (Figure 7-85).
40. After you have placed the solid in the right position, perform a **UNION** operation to join the two 3D solids.
41. **ERASE** the reference line.
42. Invoke the **3DORBIT** command to get a viewpoint similar to the one shown in Figure 7-86. **FILLET** the highlighted edges, using a **Radius** value of **0.5″**.
43. **FILLET** the chain of edges shown in Figure 7-87, using a **Radius** value of **0.13″**.

TIP Sometimes the complexity of the geometry makes the chain of edges appear to be continuously tangent when it is not. In this case, you can select the next chain of edges manually.

TIP Selecting a cylindrical face for the **CHAMFER** operation allows you to select both of its circular edges.

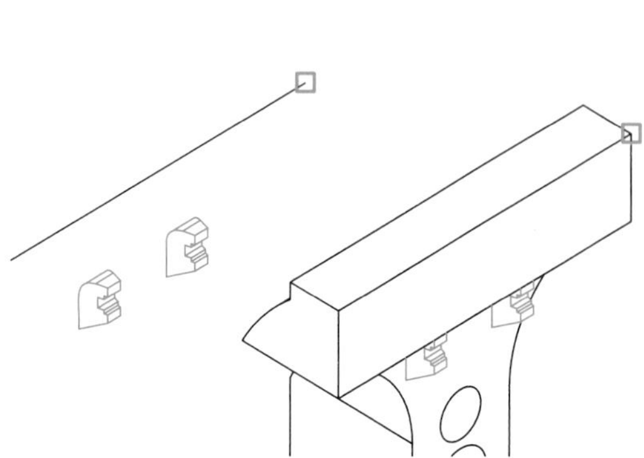

Figure 7-85 Points to be specified in the MOVE operation

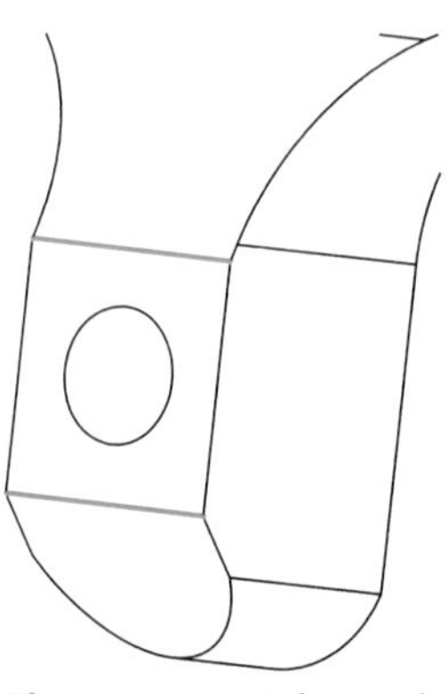

Figure 7-86 Edges to be filleted

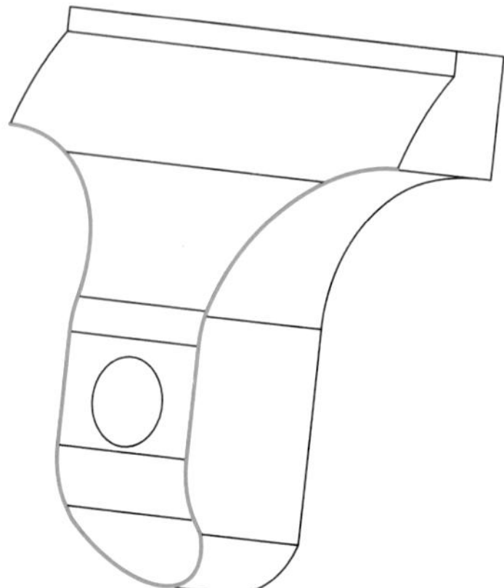

Figure 7-87 Chain of edges to be filleted

44. **CHAMFER** the six circular edges of the holes. Use **0.02** for both chamfer distances. The result is shown in Figure 7-88.
45. **SAVE** your drawing.

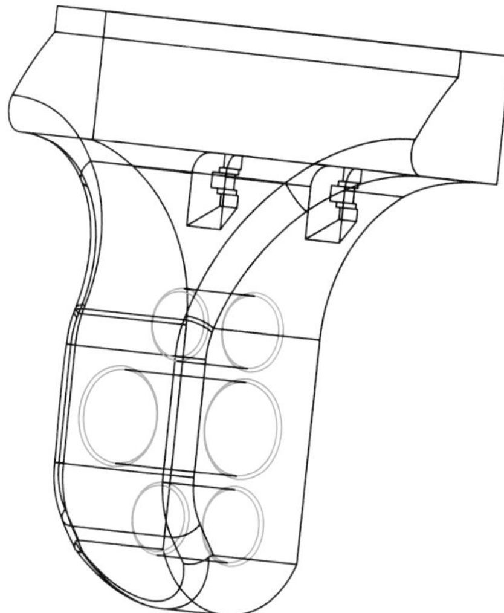

Figure 7-88 Edges are chamfered

A key element in the design of components with complex shapes is efficiency. As you have learned so far in this tutorial, you must not discard any geometry contained in other 3D models before starting from scratch. The use of this technique and other similar ones demonstrates a complete understanding of the procedures used to generate competent 3D models, while showing a commitment to efficiency and productiveness.

MODELING THE MISCELLANEOUS COMPONENTS

In this part of the project, you will create the remaining 3D solids needed for the bench vise assembly. These 3D solids can all be created in the same drawing file. You will also modify the *Main Body* and the *Moving Jaw* to allow installation of the *Aluminum Blocks*.

1. Start a **NEW** drawing using the **acad** template.
2. **SAVE** it **AS** ***Miscellaneous***.
3. Set or check the values of the following system variables as specified:
   - **DISPSILH** to **1**.
   - **ISOLINES** to **0**.
   - **FACETRES** to **9**.
   - **VIEWRES** to **2000**.
   - **UCSORTHO** to **1**.
   - **UCSFOLLOW** to **0**.
4. Next, you will create the *Main Bolt* and the *Fastening Bolt* 3D solids. Without changing the viewing point or the UCS, create the two regions shown in Figure 7-89.

Note:

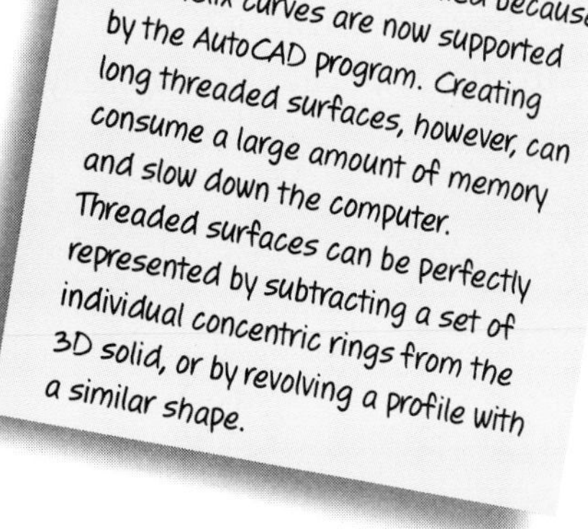

Real threads can be created because true helix curves are now supported by the AutoCAD program. Creating long threaded surfaces, however, can consume a large amount of memory and slow down the computer.
Threaded surfaces can be perfectly represented by subtracting a set of individual concentric rings from the 3D solid, or by revolving a profile with a similar shape.

TIP

A region will not be created unless the objects you select form a perfectly closed contour.

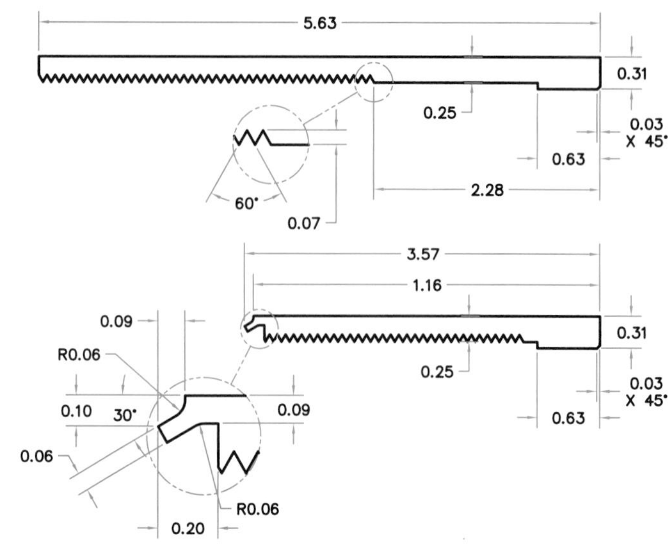

Figure 7-89 Dimensions of the profiles

5. **REVOLVE** each region around its highlighted edge, specifying any two points on it. Accept **360** as the angle of revolution for both operations (Figure 7-90).

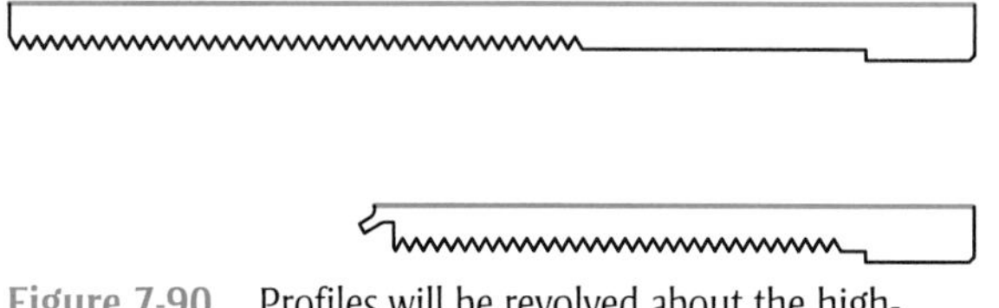

Figure 7-90 Profiles will be revolved about the highlighted axis

6. Draw the three circles shown in Figure 7-91. When prompted to specify the center point of the circles, snap to the center points of the circular edges as indicated.
7. With **ORTHO** mode activated, **MOVE** the circles to the left according to the distances shown in Figure 7-92.
8. Select the **SE Isometric** viewing point.
9. Select the **Right** UCS.
10. **MOVE** the circles orthogonally down **1″**.

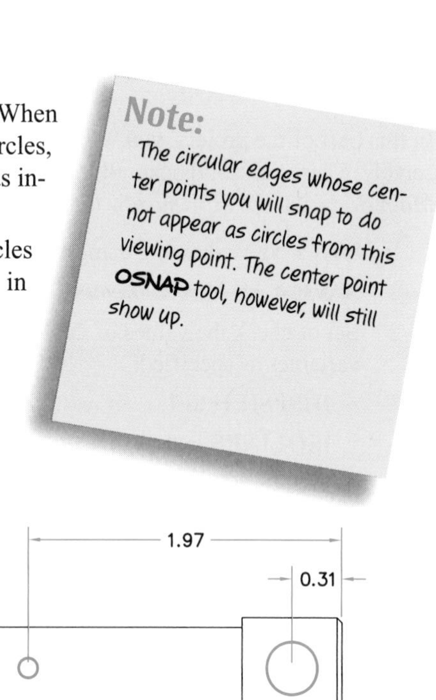

Note:
The circular edges whose center points you will snap to do not appear as circles from this viewing point. The center point OSNAP tool, however, will still show up.

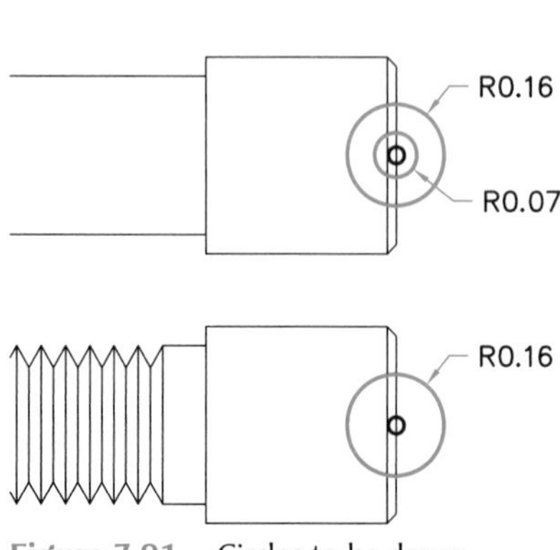

Figure 7-91 Circles to be drawn

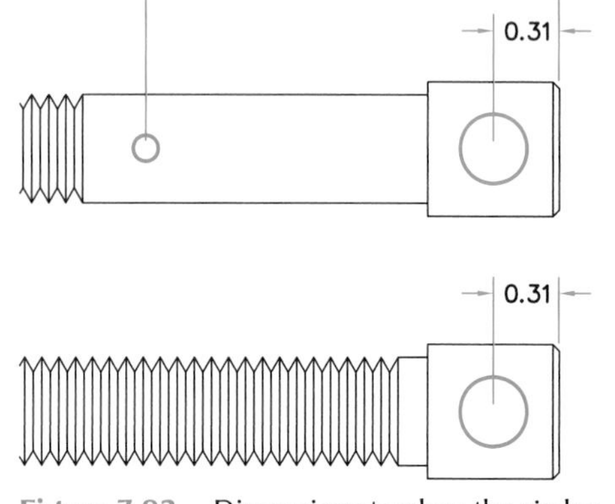

Figure 7-92 Dimensions to place the circles

11. **EXTRUDE** the circles **2″** (Figure 7-93).
12. Perform two **SUBTRACT** operations to create the holes in the *Main Bolt* and the *Fastening Bolt* individually (Figure 7-94).

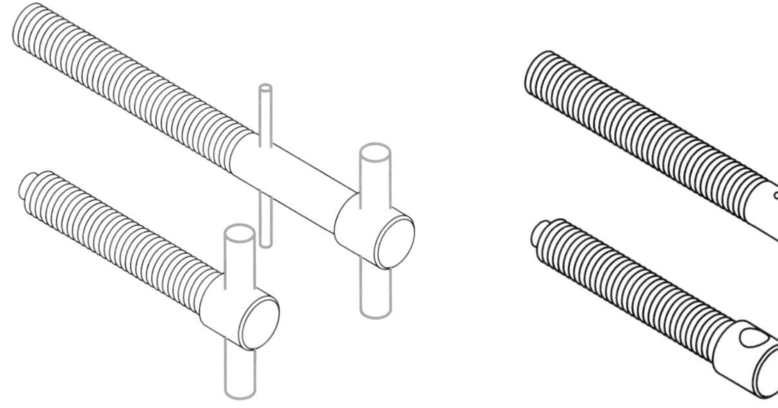

Figure 7-93 Extruded circles

Figure 7-94 The holes resulting from the SUBTRACT operation

13. With the **CYLINDER** command, create the cylinder shown in Figure 7-95.
14. **CHAMFER** both circular edges of the 3D solid cylinder. Specify both chamfer distances as **0.03″** (Figure 7-96). We will refer to the 3D solid you have just completed as *Guide.*
15. In an empty place, create a 3D solid sphere with a radius of **0.19**.
16. With **ORTHO** mode activated, **COPY** the sphere **3.25″** along the *X*-axis (Figure 7-97).

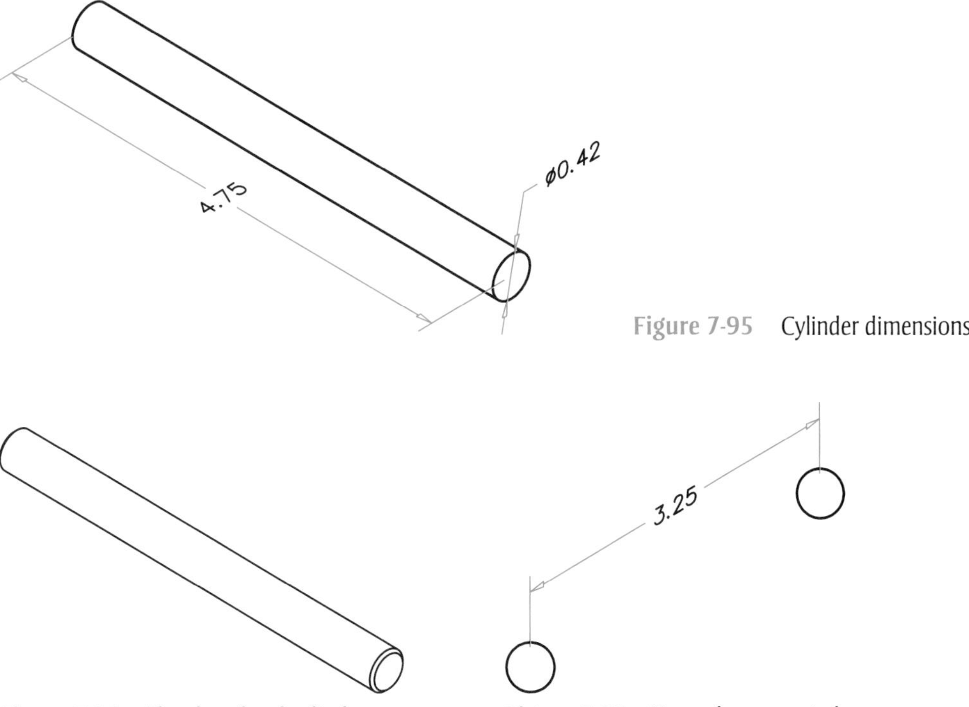

Figure 7-95 Cylinder dimensions

Figure 7-96 The chamfered cylinder

Figure 7-97 Two spheres created

17. Invoke the **CYLINDER** command and respond to the prompts as follows:

    Specify center point of base or [3P/2P/Ttr/Elliptical]: *Snap to the sphere's center point.*

    Specify base radius or [Diameter]: *0.13* ↵

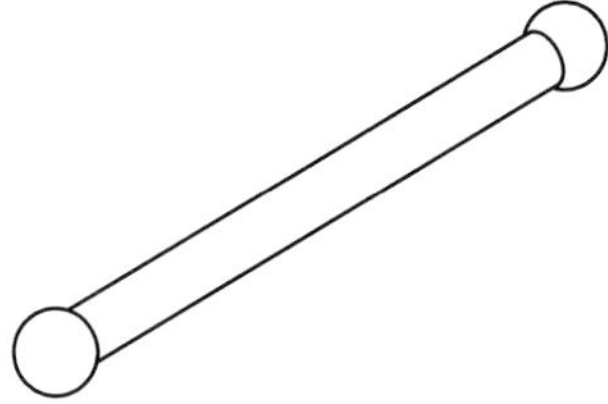

Figure 7-98 The 3D solid resulting from the UNION operation

Specify height or [2Point/Axis endpoint]: *a* ↵

Specify axis endpoint: *Snap to the center point of other sphere.*

18. Perform a **UNION** operation to join the cylinder and the two spheres. You have now completed the *Handle* (Figure 7-98).
19. Select the **Right** view.
20. Create the two regions and the two lines (centerlines) shown in Figure 7-99, anywhere in the 3D space.

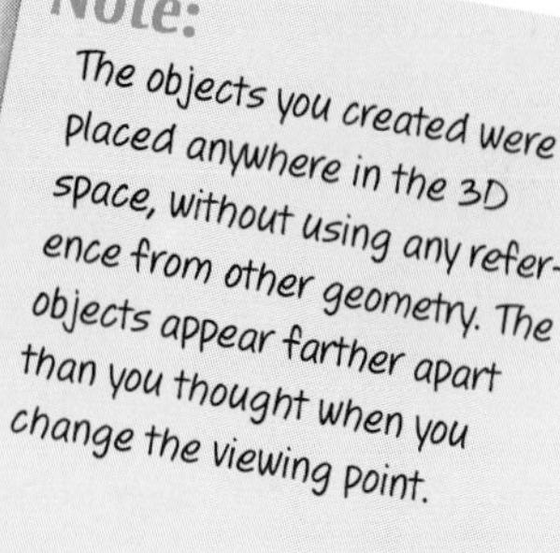

Note: The objects you created were placed anywhere in the 3D space, without using any reference from other geometry. The objects appear farther apart than you thought when you change the viewing point.

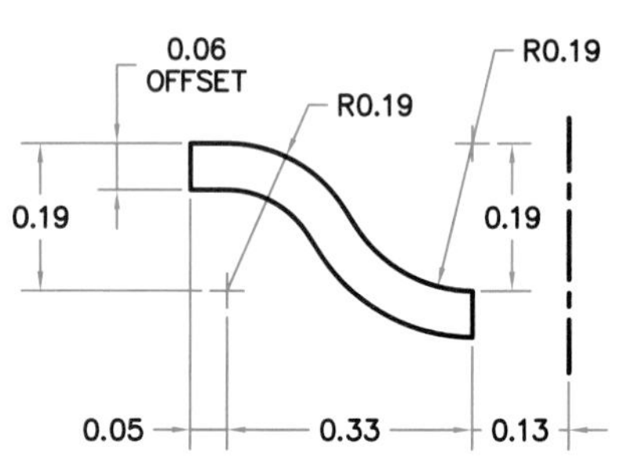

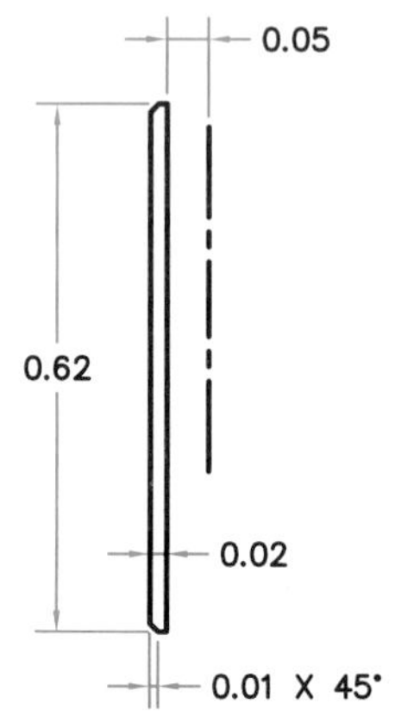

Figure 7-99 Dimensions of the profiles

21. **REVOLVE** each region individually **360°**. Use the endpoints of the centerlines to specify the axes of rotation.
22. **ERASE** the two centerlines. You nave just completed the *Pressing Plate* and the *Pin*.
23. **MOVE** the *Pressing Plate* and the *Pin* from their center points to the center point of the left spherical face of the *Handle*. Then move them orthogonally **2″** to the right (Figure 7-100).

TIP Place the objects in a known location relative to other objects. This helps to keep them close together in the infinite 3D space, regardless of the current viewing point.

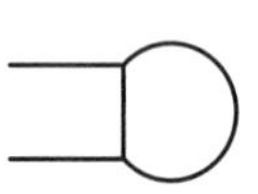

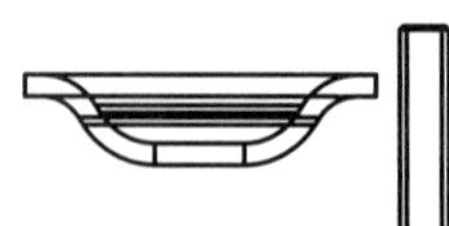

Figure 7-100 After the MOVE operation

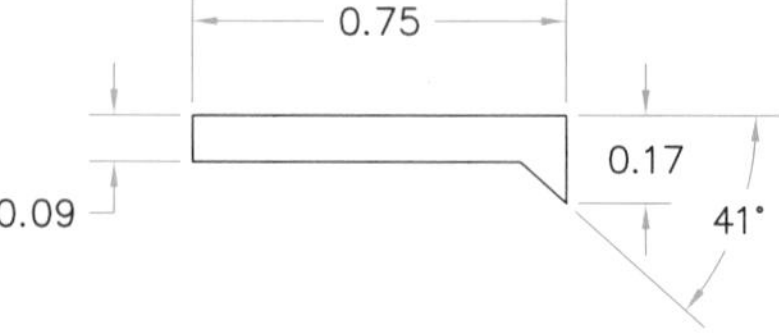

Figure 7-101 Profile dimensions

24. Create the region shown in Figure 7-101.
25. **REVOLVE** the region **360°** around any two points on the longer line. This 3D solid will be named *Screw*.
26. **MOVE** the new *Screw* from any point on it to the center point of the spherical face of the *Handle*. Then **MOVE** it orthogonally **1″** down (Figure 7-102).
27. Select the **SE Isometric** viewing point.
28. Select the **Top** UCS.

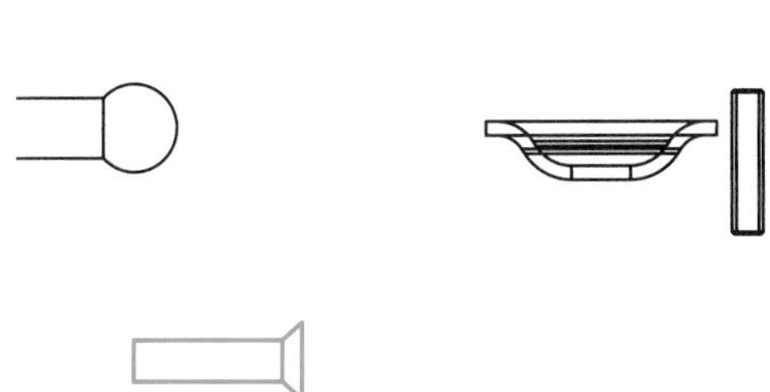

Figure 7-102 After the MOVE operation

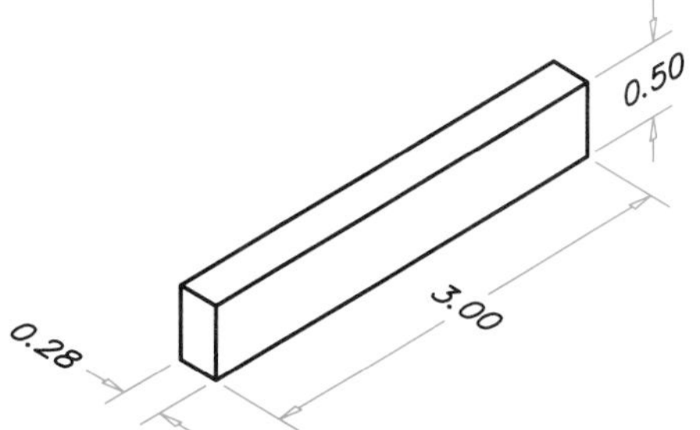

Figure 7-103 The box dimensions

29. Create a box with the dimensions shown in Figure 7-103.
30. **ROTATE** the *Screw* **–90°**. Specify any point on it as the base point. From the current viewing point, the *Screw* should look like Figure 7-104.
31. **COPY** the *Screw* from its rightmost center point to the midpoint of the vertical edge, as shown in Figure 7-105 with the hidden lines removed.
32. With **ORTHO** mode activated, **MOVE** the copy of the *Screw* **0.50″** along the positive *Y*-axis.
33. Use the **MIRROR3D** command to create another mirrored copy, as shown in Figure 7-106. Use three of the four midpoints of the box's longer edges to specify the points on the mirror plane.

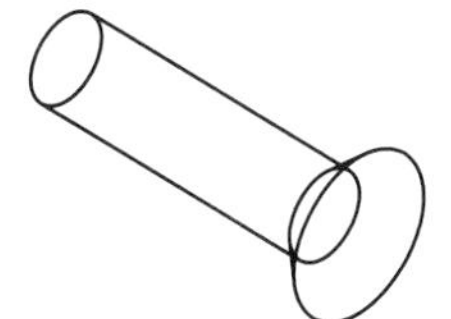

Figure 7-104 After rotating the Screw

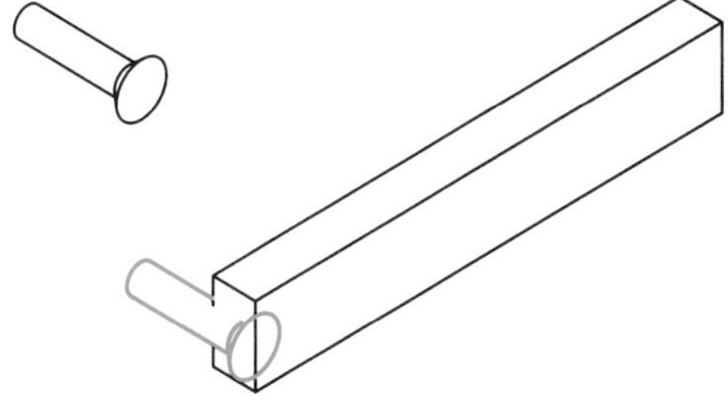

Figure 7-105 A copy of the Screw placed on the edge of the box

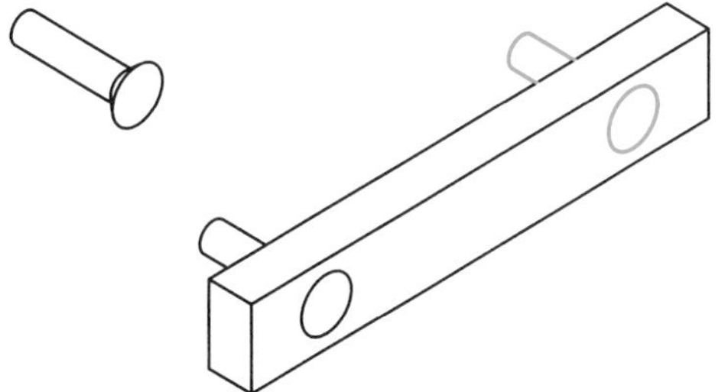

Figure 7-106 The two screws after the MIRROR operation

34. **SUBTRACT** the two *Screws* from the box to create the countersunk holes (Figure 7-107). This 3D solid will be called *Aluminum Block.*
35. Select the **Right** UCS.
36. **ZOOM** into the *Screw* and draw a vertical line between the two quadrant points of the circular face.
37. **OFFSET** the line **0.015″** to both sides.
38. **DELETE** the original line.
39. Invoke the **Imprint** body option of the **SOLIDEDIT** command and imprint the two lines in the face of the *Screw* (Figure 7-108). Respond **Yes**, when prompted, to delete the source objects.

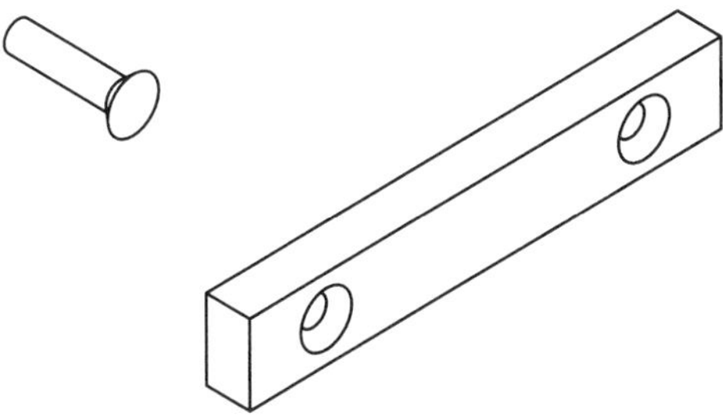

Figure 7-107 Holes created by subtracting the Screws

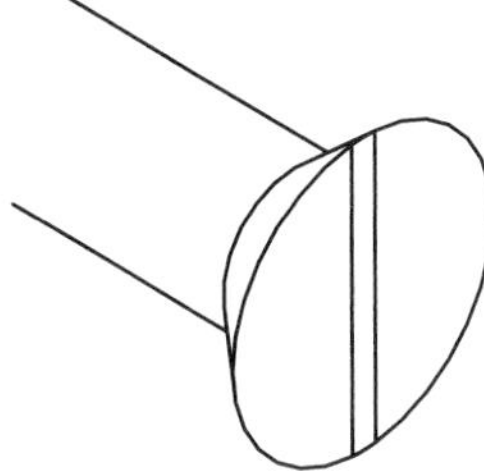

Figure 7-108 The two lines imprinted

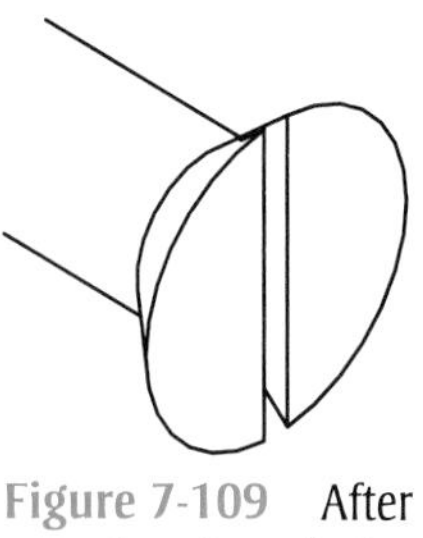

Figure 7-109 After extruding the split face inward

40. Invoke the **Extrude faces** option of the **SOLIDEDIT** command. Select only the split face, which represents the *Screw* slot, at the center. Specify **–0.03** as the height of the extrusion, and **0** as the angle of taper. The *Screw* with the slot should look like Figure 7-109.
41. Select the **Top** UCS.
42. **MOVE** the 3D solids around so they appear to be closer from this particular viewing point (Figure 7-110). The objects do not need to have the same arrangement in your drawing.
43. **SAVE** the drawing.

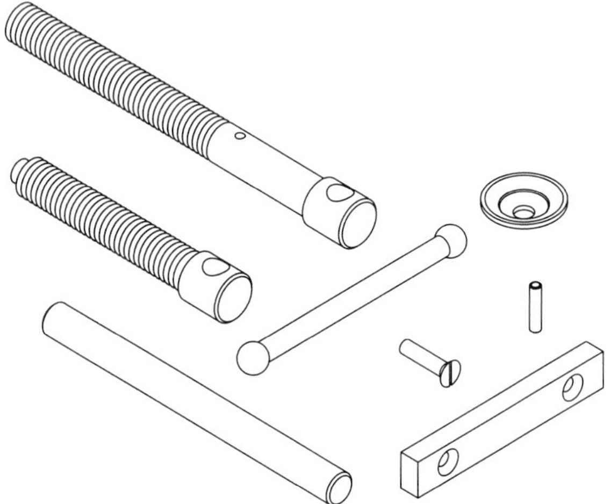

Figure 7-110 All of the miscellaneous components

CREATING THE BENCH VISE ASSEMBLY

Now that you have created all the 3D solids, you are ready to assemble them. The approach is very simple. First, you will gather all the 3D solids in the same file. Then you will place each one in the right location in the 3D space so that the relationships among all the parts make the assembly functional.

For this task, it is important that you select a different color for each 3D solid to make the operations easier. You can choose any colors you want.

1. **OPEN** the file ***Main Body***.
2. **SAVE** the file **AS** ***Bench-Vise***.
3. Select the **SE Isometric** viewing point.
4. Select the **Top** UCS.
5. **OPEN** the file ***Miscellaneous***.
6. Select the **Top** UCS.
7. Invoke the **COPYCLIP** (copy to clipboard) command. When prompted, select all the 3D solids contained in the file and press **<Enter>** to end the selection.
8. **CLOSE** the file ***Miscellaneous***.
9. Back in the file ***Bench-Vise***, invoke the **PASTECLIP** (paste from clipboard) command. When prompted, click anywhere close to the *Main Body*.
10. Repeat the same procedure to insert the *Moving Jaw* 3D solid into the ***Bench-Vise*** drawing file. Remember to change the UCS to **Top** before copying the 3D solid to the clipboard.
11. Turn the **OTRACK** mode off.
12. Invoke the **ALIGN** command and, when prompted, select the *Moving Jaw*. You will specify each of the three pairs of points one by one. For example, the first source point will be

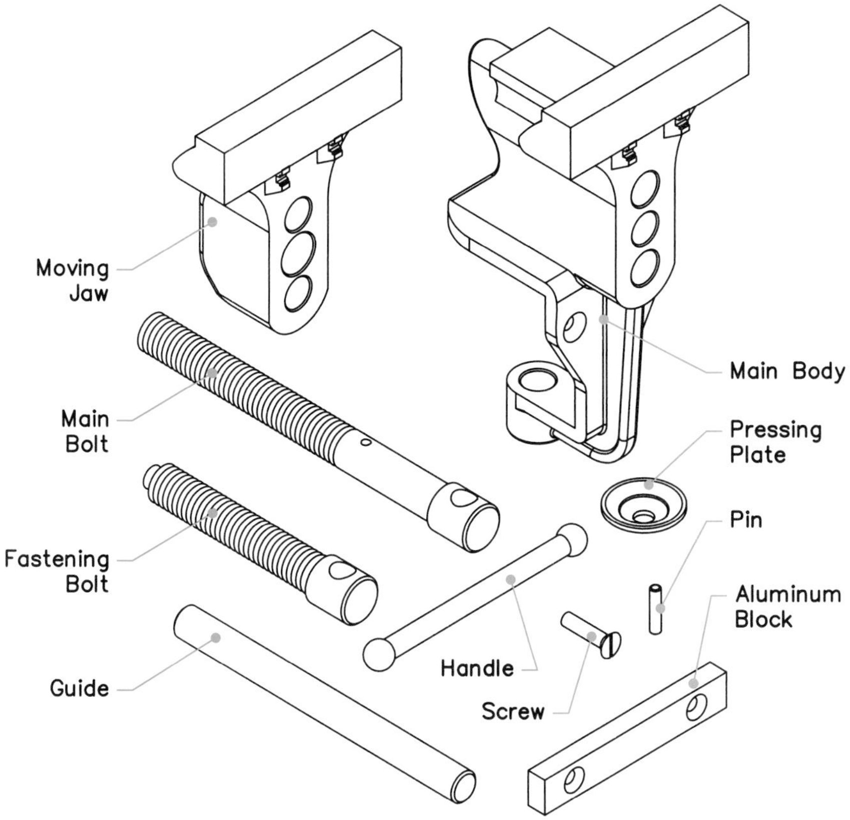

Figure 7-111 All of the bench vise components

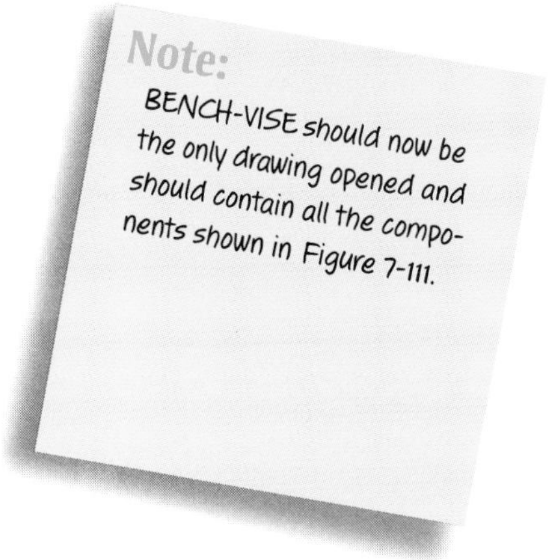

Note:
BENCH-VISE should now be the only drawing opened and should contain all the components shown in Figure 7-111.

endpoint 1, and the first destination point will be its corresponding endpoint, shown by the arrow (Figure 7-112).

13. With **ORTHO** mode activated, **MOVE** the *Moving Jaw* **1″** along the positive *X*-axis to open up the two jaws (Figure 7-113).
14. **ROTATE** the *Fastening Bolt* **90°**. Select any point on it as the base point.
15. With **ORTHO** mode off, **MOVE** the *Pressing Plate* closer to the *Fastening Bolt.*

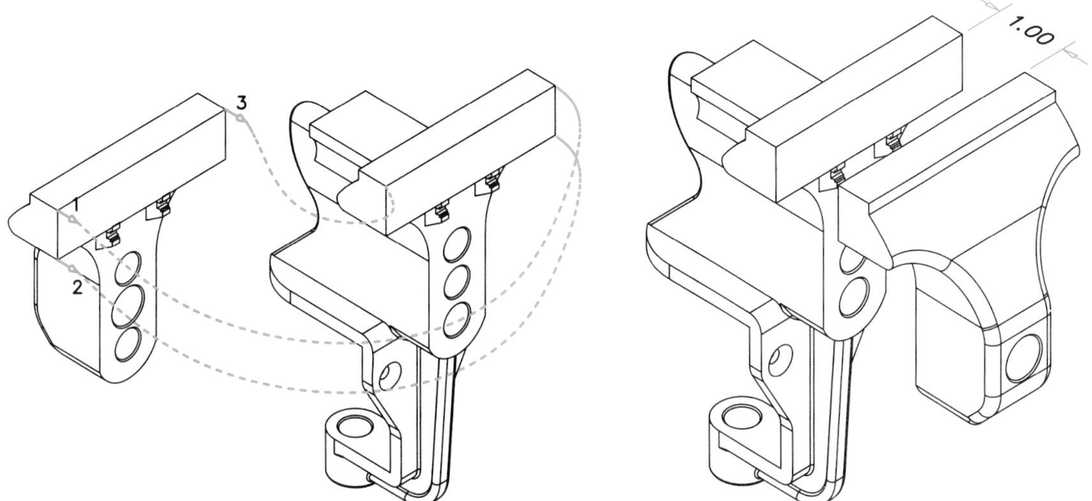

Figure 7-112 The order in which to specify the points for the ALIGN operation

Figure 7-113 The Moving Jaw moved away

16. Invoke the **3DALIGN** command to align the *Fastening Bolt* with the *Pressing Plate*. You will specify only two source center points, and then press **<Enter>** to specify the two corresponding destination center points (Figure 7-114). Center point 2 can be any center point in the threaded portion.
17. **MOVE** the *Fastening Bolt* and the *Pressing Plate* together from any center point on the threaded area to another center point on the vertical hole of the *Main Body* (Figure 7-115). The through hole on the *Fastening Bolt* should end up being aligned parallel to the *Y*-axis. Otherwise, invoke the **ROTATE** command and rotate the *Fastening Bolt* **90°** around any of its center points.
18. **MOVE** the *Pin* closer to the *Main Bolt*.
19. Using the **SECTION** command, extract a region through the *Main Bolt* parallel to the *XY* plane going through the middle of the 3D solid.
20. On the *Pin,* draw a reference line from the center point of the top face to the bottommost center point.
21. **MOVE** the *Pin* from the midpoint of the reference line to the center point of the circular edge of the region (Figure 7-116). **ZOOM** in as needed.

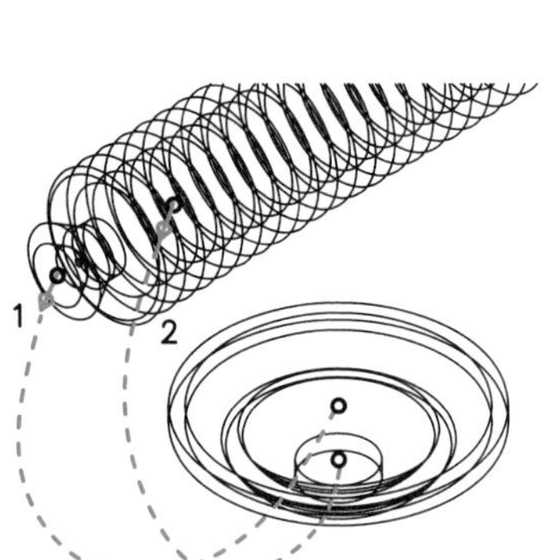

Figure 7-114 The order in which the points must be specified for the 3DALIGN operation

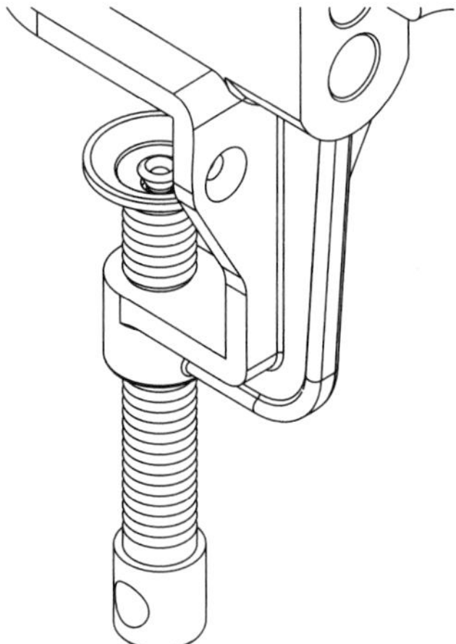

Figure 7-115 After moving the Fastening Bolt and the Pressing Plate

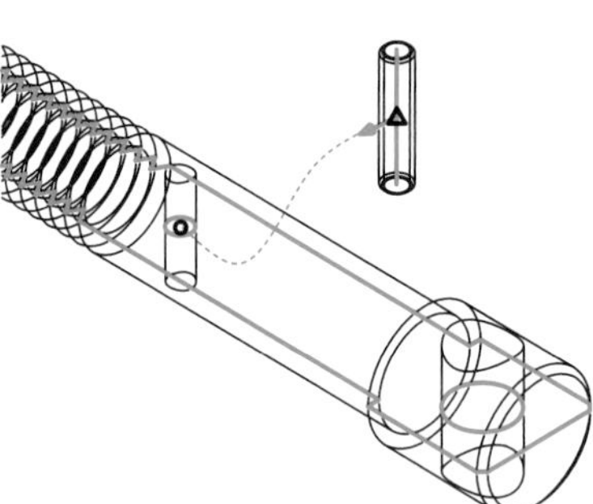

Figure 7-116 Points to specify in the MOVE operation

22. **ERASE** both the extracted region and the line.
23. **MOVE** the *Main Bolt* along with the *Pin* from the center point of the *Main Bolt* to the center point of the *Main Body's* middle horizontal hole. Both center points are shown in Figure 7-117.

To avoid selecting the center point at the end of the chamfer instead of the one on the planar face, select the center point OSNAP tool directly, and click the proper circular edge.

24. **MOVE** the *Guide* from its rightmost center point to the end of one of the two holes on the *Moving Jaw*.
25. **COPY** the *Guide* to the other hole as well. The assembly should look like Figure 7-118.
26. Make sure the **Top** UCS is current.
27. With the **SECTION** command, extract a region from the *Fastening Bolt,* parallel to the *ZX* plane and going through any of the center points along the 3D solid.
28. **MOVE** the *Handle* from the center point of the leftmost circular edge to the center point of the region's hole.

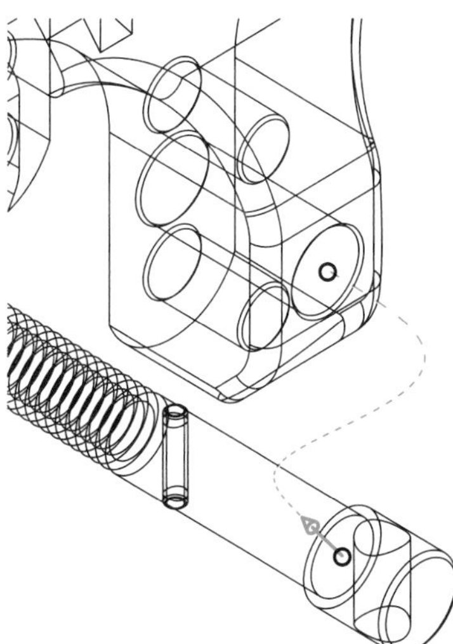
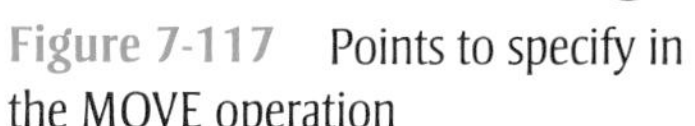

Figure 7-117 Points to specify in the MOVE operation

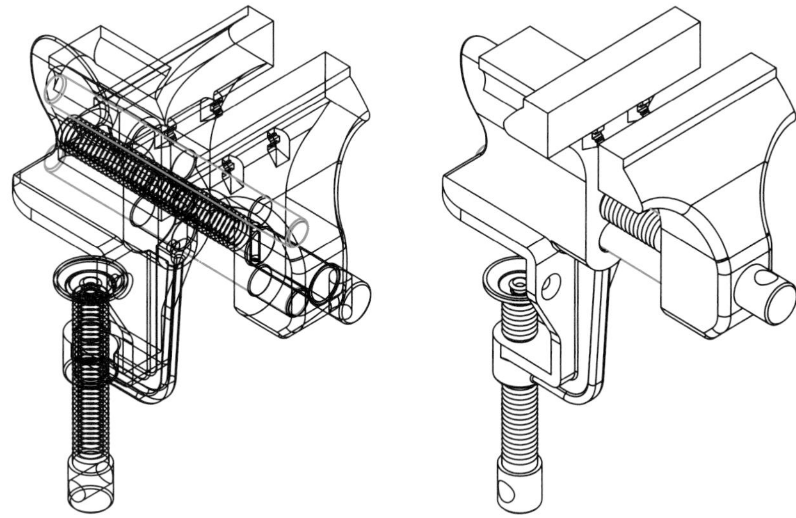

Figure 7-118 The Guide copied to the other location

29. With **ORTHO** mode activated, **MOVE** the *Handle* **1.5″** orthogonally along the negative *Y*-axis (Figure 7-119).
30. **ERASE** the extracted region.
31. **COPY** the *Handle* close to the *Main Bolt* hole.
32. Invoke the **ROTATE3D** command to rotate the copied *Handle* **90°**. Define the axis of rotation parallel to the *X*-axis and going through any point on it.
33. On the *Main Bolt,* extract a region with the **SECTION** command, parallel to the *XY* plane, going through any of the center points along the 3D solid.
34. **MOVE** the new *Handle* from the center point of the top circular edge to the center point of the hole on the region.
35. **ERASE** the extracted region.
36. Select the **Front** UCS.
37. With **ORTHO** mode activated, **MOVE** the new *Handle* **0.3″** along the negative *Y*-axis (Figure 7-120).

Note:

Because the hole on the Fastening Bolt did not have any circular edges, you had to create additional geometry to snap to it.

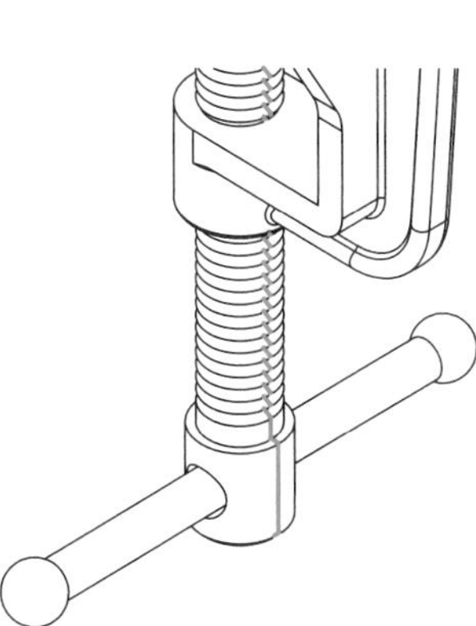

Figure 7-119 The handle placed in its location

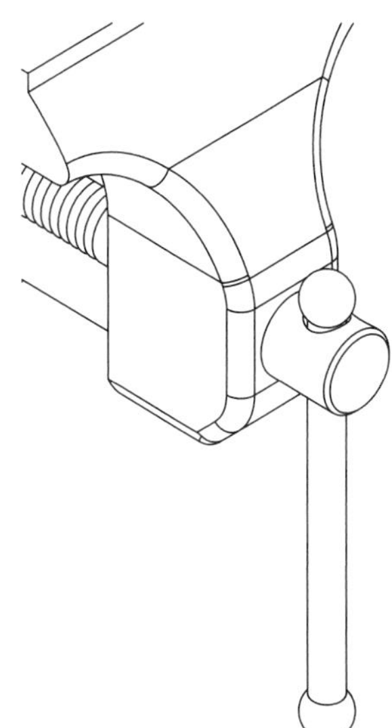

Figure 7-120 The second handle placed in its location

38. Invoke the **3DORBIT** command to obtain a view close to the one shown in Figure 7-121 (with the hidden lines removed).
39. Use the **RECTANGLE** command to draw a **0.25 × 0.50** rectangle anywhere in the 3D space.
40. **EXTRUDE** the rectangle **4″**.
41. **MOVE** the new 3D solid to the endpoint of the *Main Body*. Then **COPY** the 3D solid to the endpoint of the *Moving Jaw*. The result is shown in Figure 7-122.
42. With two independent **SUBTRACT** operations, subtract one of the 3D solids from the *Main Body* and the other one from the *Moving Jaw* (Figure 7-123).

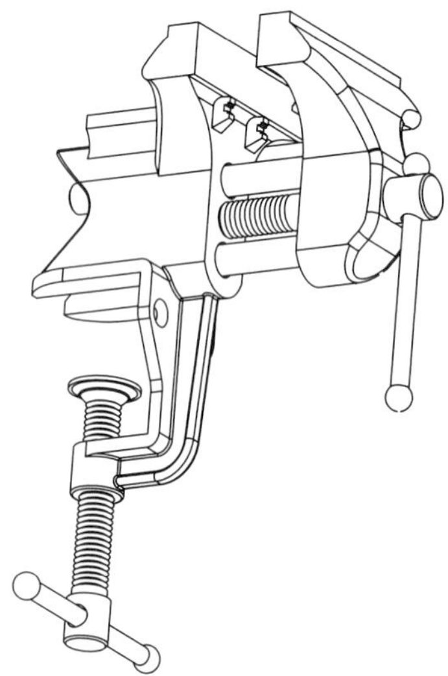

Figure 7-121 The assembly with the hidden lines removed

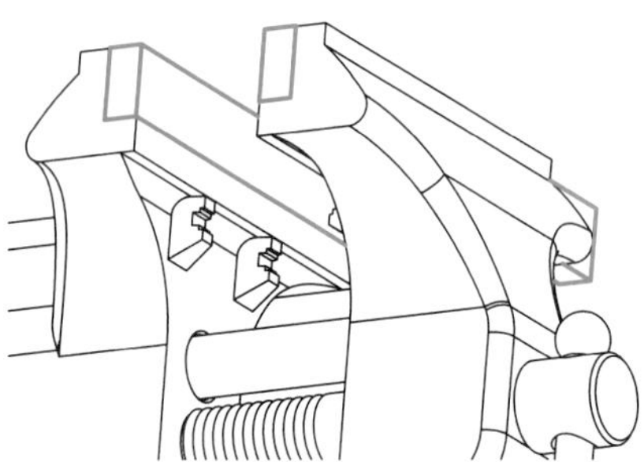

Figure 7-122 The 3D solids shaped as boxes after being moved and copied

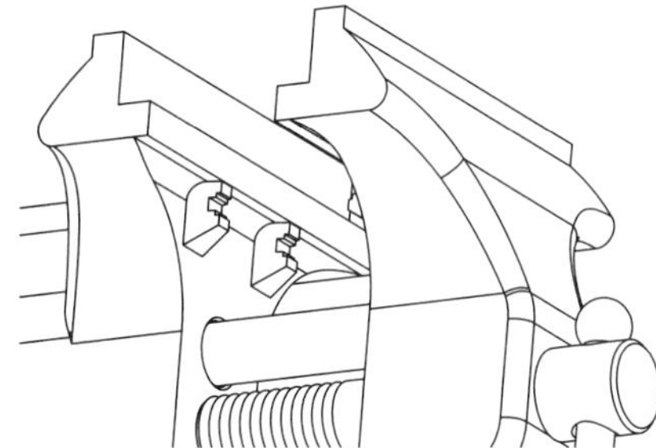

Figure 7-123 After subtracting the 3D solids

43. **MOVE** the *Aluminum Block* to the *Main Body*. Snap to the corresponding endpoints to place the *Aluminum Block* as shown in Figure 7-124.
44. Draw the highlighted reference line between the two endpoints as shown in Figure 7-125.
45. Use the **YZ** option of the **MIRROR3D** command to create a mirrored copy of the *Aluminum Block* on the *Moving Jaw*. Specify the midpoint of the line when prompted to specify the point on the *YZ* plane.
46. **ERASE** the reference line.
47. Invoke the **Copy edges** editing tool to copy the four circular edges highlighted in Figure 7-126, each in its own place.

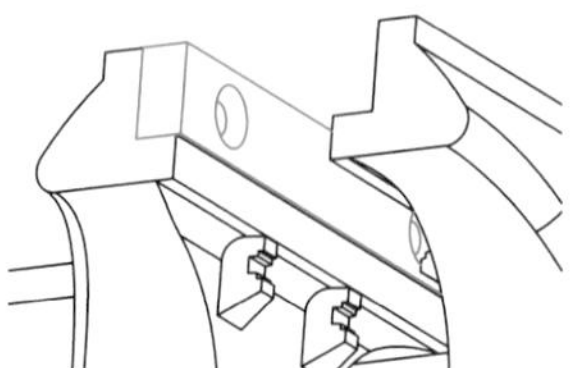

Figure 7-124 The Aluminum Block moved to the Main Body

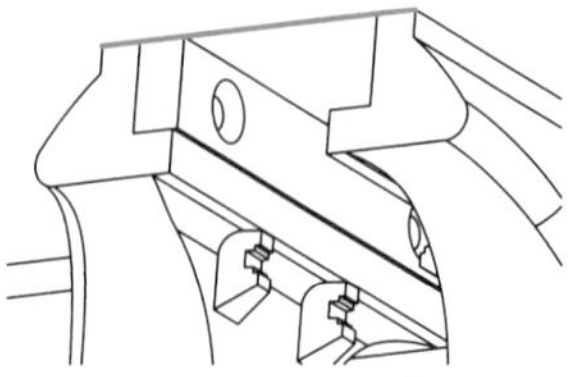

Figure 7-125 A reference line is placed

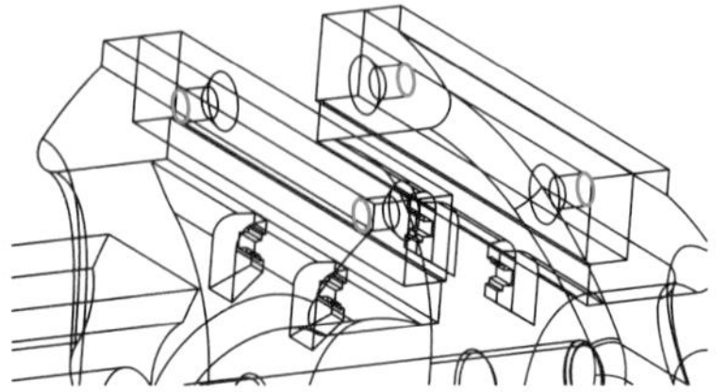

Figure 7-126 Edges are copied in place in both Aluminum Blocks

TIP

You can copy an object in its own place by specifying the base and the destination points as the same point. The editing tool operations work on only one 3D solid at a time.

48. **EXTRUDE** the two extracted circles on the *Main Body* **−0.19″** and the two extracted circles on the *Moving Jaw,* **0.19″**.
49. **SUBTRACT** the two cylinders from the *Main Body*. In a separate operation, **SUBTRACT** the two cylinders from the *Moving Jaw*.
50. Select the **World** UCS.
51. Invoke the **BLOCK** command to open the **Block Definition** dialog box. Type **Screw** under the **Name** field. Click on the **Select objects** button and select the *Screw*. Click on the **Pick point** button and snap to the center point of the circular edge between the cylindrical body and the head of the screw. Make sure **Convert to block** is selected, and click **OK** to close the dialog box.

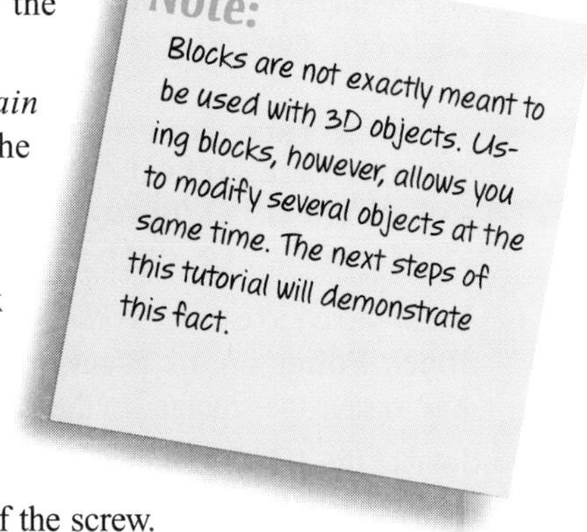

Note:
Blocks are not exactly meant to be used with 3D objects. Using blocks, however, allows you to modify several objects at the same time. The next steps of this tutorial will demonstrate this fact.

52. Select the *Screw* block, and then select its insertion point grid to move it to the first countersunk hole on the *Main Body.* Snap to the center point of the corresponding edge on the hole (Figure 7-127).
53. **COPY** the *Screw* block a few inches away from the *Main Body.*
54. **ROTATE** the new *Screw* block **180°**, using any point on it as the base point (Figure 7-128).
55. Select the copied *Screw* block, then select its insertion point grid to move it to the corresponding center point on the first countersunk hole of the *Moving Jaw.*
56. **COPY** both *Screw* blocks into the other holes of the *Aluminum Blocks* (Figure 7-129).
57. Select the **Front** view (Figure 7-130).
58. Use the **3D Orbit** tool to change the viewpoint to a viewpoint close to the one you had before.
59. Select the **World** UCS.
60. Double-click on any of the *Screw* blocks. Click **OK** in the **Edit Block Definition** dialog box. The screen changes to the **Block Editor** mode.
61. Invoke the **Move faces** editing tool and respond to the prompts as follows:

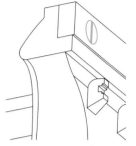

Figure 7-127 The Screw block is placed in the hole

Note:

As you can see, the screws we are using are too long for our product. Because they all have the same block definition, editing one of them will change the others. Using blocks is a very helpful way of organizing the job in case you ever need to change large numbers of the same part in the 3D assembly.

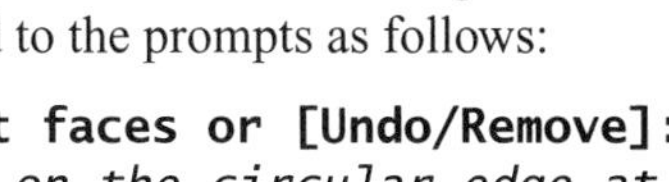

Select faces or [Undo/Remove]: *Click on the circular edge at the left (seen as a line from this viewing point).*

Select faces or [Undo/Remove/ALL]: ↵ *(To end the selection)*

Specify a base point or displacement: *Click anywhere in the drawing area.*

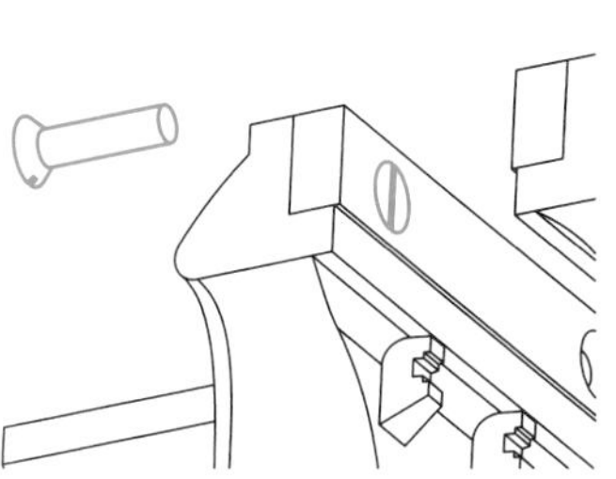

Figure 7-128 The new Screw after it is rotated

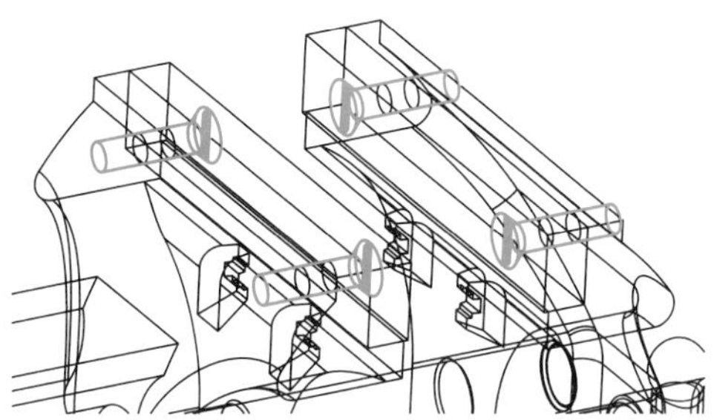

Figure 7-129 The four screws are placed

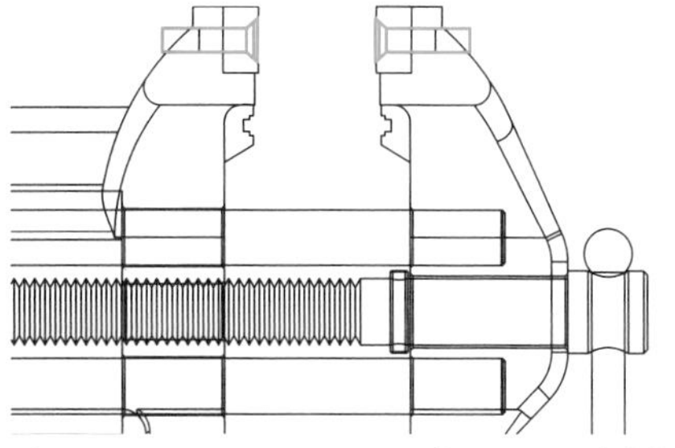

Figure 7-130 Inspecting the 3D model from the front view

Specify a second point of displacement: *With ORTHO mode activated, move the pointer toward the right and enter 0.31* ↵

Enter a face editing option [Extrude/Move/Rotate/Offset/Taper/Delete/Copy/coLor/mAterial/Undo/eXit] <eXit>: *Press* ***<Esc>*** *to exit the command.*

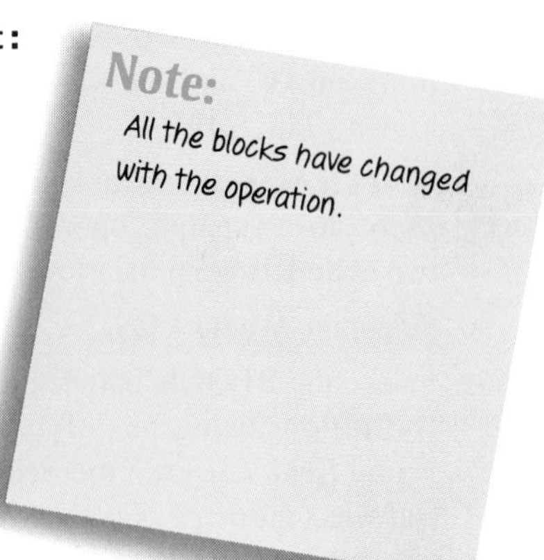

Note:
All the blocks have changed with the operation.

62. Press **<Esc>** to exit the command. Click on **Close Block Editor** on the **Block** toolbar, and select **Yes** to save the changes to the *Screw.*
63. Invoke the **HIDE** command. The 3D assembly model should look like Figure 7-131.
64. **SAVE** your drawing.

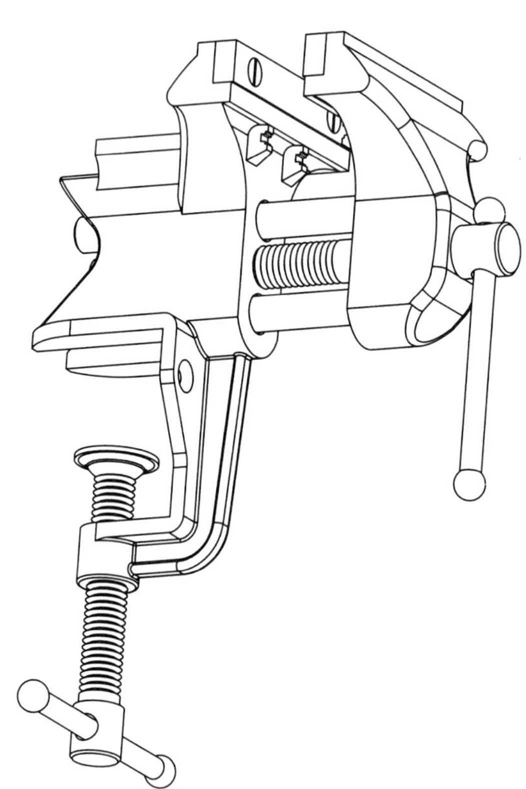

Figure 7-131 The final bench vise assembly

SUMMARY

The extensive tutorials in this chapter have given you the opportunity to use most of the operations learned in previous chapters. You have also learned some of the practical approaches that can be employed in a real design process to reduce the development time of 3D solid models and assemblies.

By comparing the 3D models developed in this tutorial with the 3D models developed in Chapter 2, you can measure your improvement in 3D modeling in general. You should also now be able to understand more clearly the specific operations performed in this chapter as well.

Generating Drawings and DWF Files

8

Chapter Objectives

- Learn to obtain accurate 2D and 3D sections using section objects.
- Use the **FLATSHOT** command to obtain quick projections of the drawing views.
- Learn to place dimensions throughout the 3D space.
- Generate exploded 3D views.
- Understand and manage the AutoCAD® program's paper space, and know the differences between paper space and model space.
- Generate and manipulate viewports, and be able to set view scales the correct way.
- Learn and practice the tools used to generate drawing views automatically from 3D models.
- Know the engineering information that can be obtained from 3D models.
- Learn to create DWF files of both 3D models and 2D drawings.

INTRODUCTION

Different Uses of the 3D Models

After you have finished the 3D model, you can use it to perform several other tasks, such as generating 2D drawings, obtaining rapid prototypes, rendering, publishing, and obtaining physical properties. Obtaining 2D drawings is probably the most important and common task. This chapter will take you through different techniques and processes that will allow you to generate quick and very precise drawings from 3D models.

The AutoCAD program allows you to create projected drawing views in both model space and paper space. In model space you can perform such tasks by using the following commands:

- **SECTIONPLANE**
- **FLATSHOT**

More automated ways of performing such tasks can be performed in paper space. Two different processes involving specific commands can be used:

- Simple views generation (**SOLPROF**)
- Automatic views generation (**SOLVIEW** and **SOLDRAW**)

Regardless of whether the orthogonal views are created in model space or paper space the final preparation of the document should always be completed in the layouts, or paper space.

A REVIEW OF PAPER SPACE

DEFINITION OF PAPER SPACE

As you know, the model space mode is an infinite 3D space where you create both 2D and 3D models. The objects are represented in model space with real dimensions as they would appear in real life.

The paper space mode is the infinite 2D plane where you prepare the technical documents of the objects contained in model space. The drawing views are scaled according to the relative proportions between the objects and the sheet of paper used. You can look at the paper space only from the Top view.

WORKING WITH LAYOUTS

You can switch to paper space mode by simply clicking on the tabs named **Layout1** and **Layout2** located at the lower left corner of the drawing area; you can then go back to model space by clicking the **Model** tab next to them. See Figure 8-1(a). Clicking the **MODEL** button on the status bar

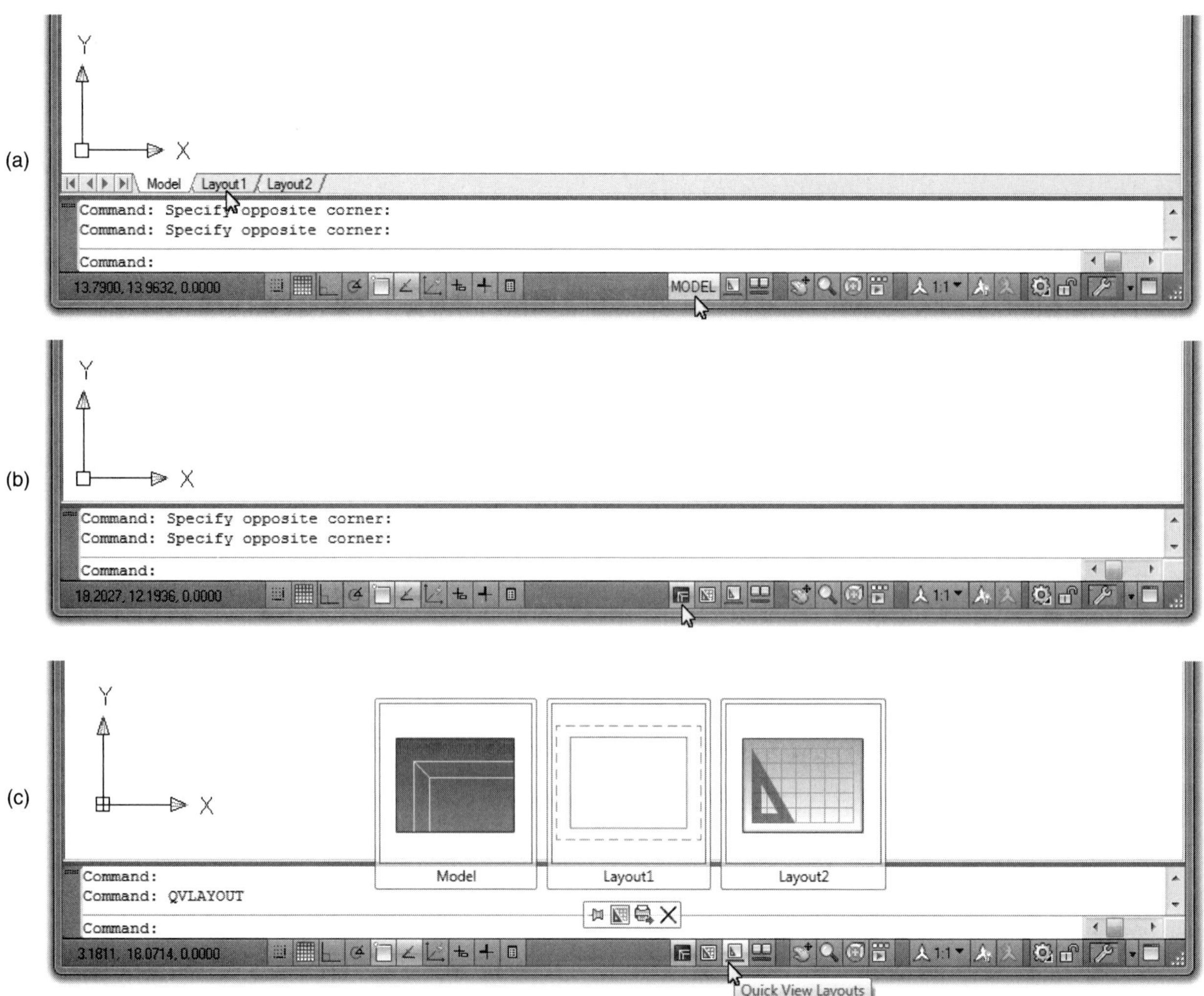

Figure 8-1 Accessing the paper space and model space modes through (a) the tabs and the status bar, and (b) the status bar. (c) Using the Quick View Layouts

will switch to the paper space as well; to completely switch back to the model space, you will have to click on the **Model** tab. The displaying of such tabs is controlled by the **Display Layout and Model Tabs** in the **Options** dialog box (Figure 8-2).

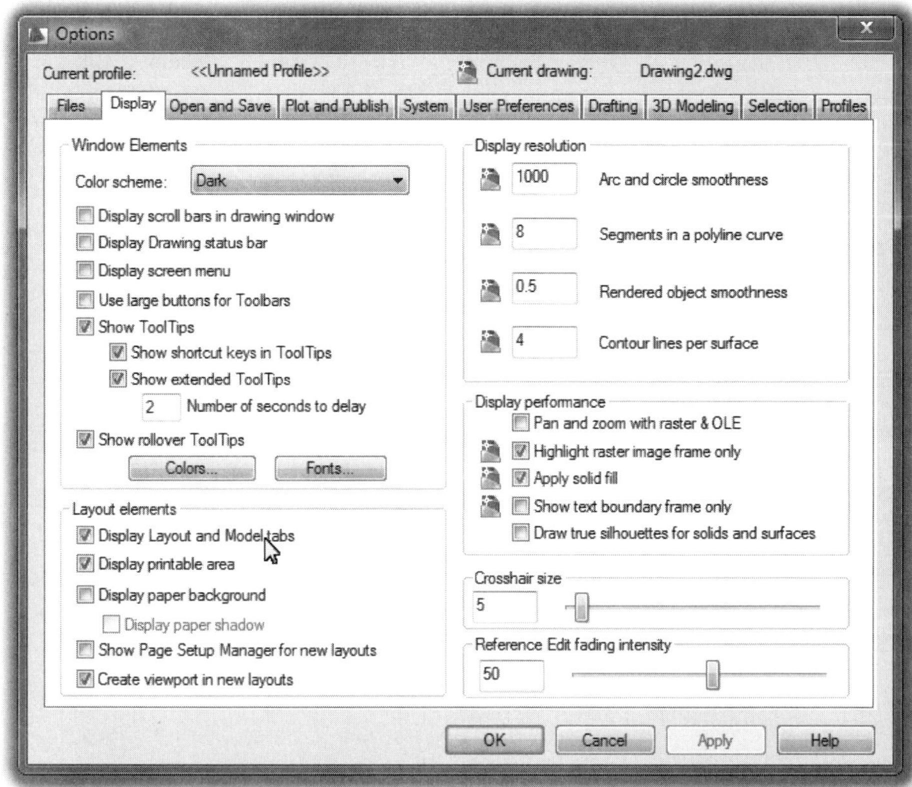

Figure 8-2 The Display tab of the Options dialog box allows you to select and unselect the Display Layout and Model tabs

When the **Display Layout and Model Tabs** option is not selected, you can use the buttons that appear one next to the other in the status bar to switch between model space and paper space [Figure 8-1(b)]. It is probably more convenient not to display the tabs because it gives you some more space for the drawing area. Whichever the case, you also click on the **Quick View Layout** button to display a thumbnail image of each layout as well and the model space. You can click on the images to access the particular tab [Figure 8-1(c)]. Layout images are displayed differently, depending on whether you have accessed the layout or not.

If the **Show Page Setup Manager for new layouts** is enabled in the **Options** dialog box, the **Page Setup Manager** dialog box will open automatically the first time you enter any layout. After you close it, you can see the paper space elements (Figure 8-3). You can place any object throughout the infinite plane (the gray area); however, only the objects located inside the printable area of the sheet will be plotted. Notice the different look of the UCS icon in the paper space mode.

Right-clicking a Layout tab exposes a shortcut menu containing a group of tools [Figure 8-4(a)]. In this shortcut menu, you can **Rename** or **Delete** a layout. You can also **Move or Copy** the layout, or create a **New layout** from scratch. You can bring a layout from a specific drawing by using the **From template ...** option as well. A similar shortcut menu shows up by right-clicking the **Quick View Layout** button on the status bar [see Figure 8-4(b)].

To properly prepare a layout or page for printing and publishing, you must specify the settings that control the following aspects:

- Page setup
- Viewports
- Objects placed directly on the paper, such as the title block

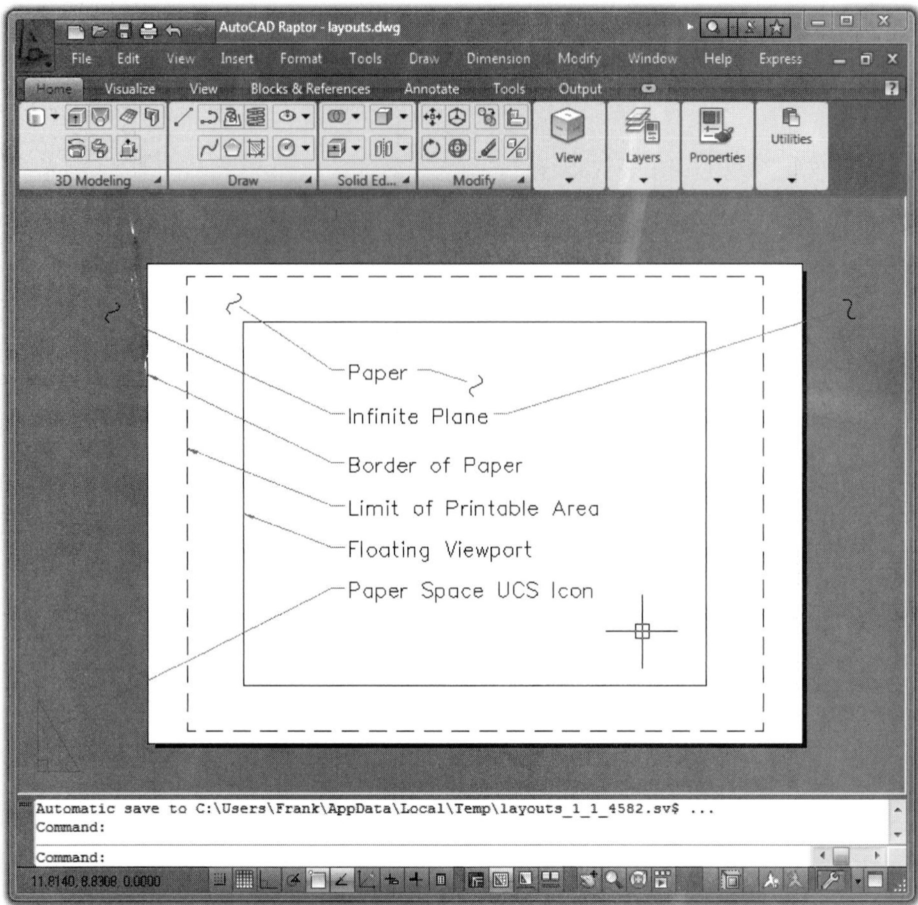

Figure 8-3 The paper space elements

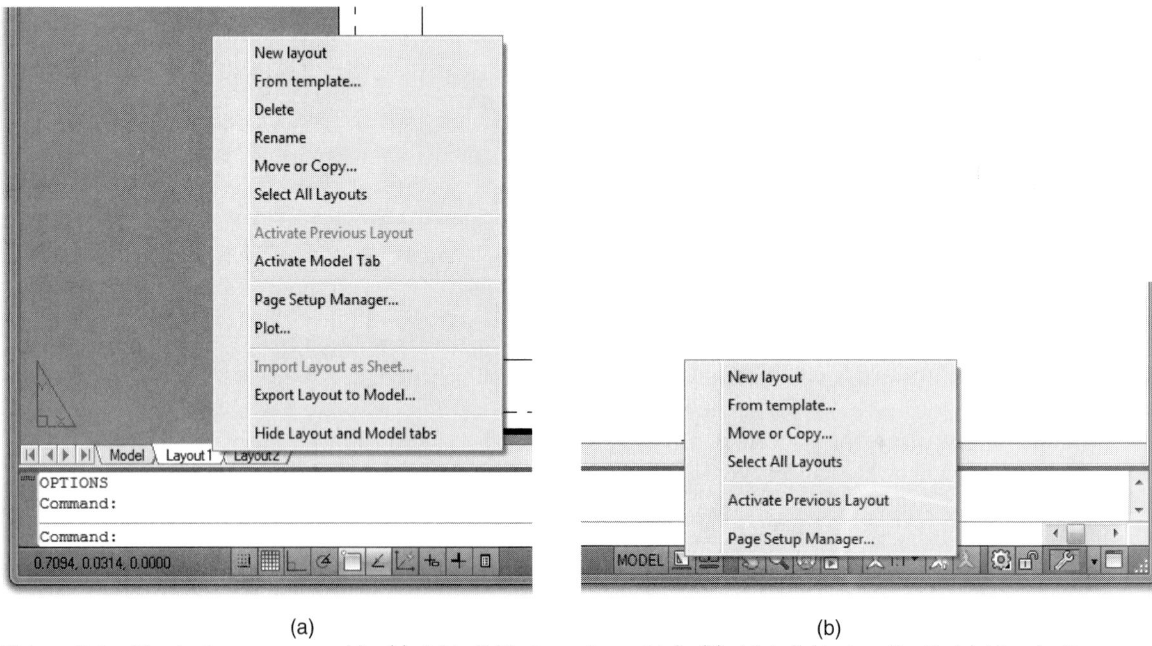

Figure 8-4 Shortcut menu exposed by (a) right-clicking on a Layout tab; (b) right-clicking on the Quick View button on the status bar

The Page Setup Manager

You open the **Page Setup Manager** dialog box (Figure 8-5) by invoking the **PAGESETUP** command. It can be accessed through the **Layouts** shortcut menu, the **File** pull-down menu, or the **Layouts** toolbar (Figure 8-6).

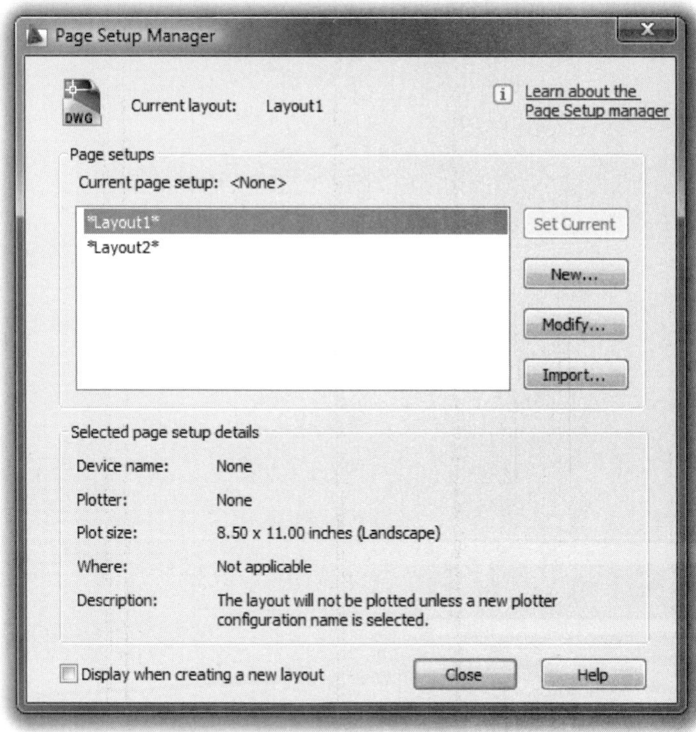

Figure 8-5 The Page Setup Manager dialog box

Figure 8-6 The Layouts toolbar

The **Page Setup Manager** gives you a report on the page setup details of the current layout. In essence, you can modify the page setup of the layouts directly by clicking the **Modify . . .** button, or you can apply a named page setup previously created such as the one named *My Page Setup* shown in Figure 8-7. You apply a named page setup by clicking the **Set Current** button. Doing so will override the current settings of the layout page setup.

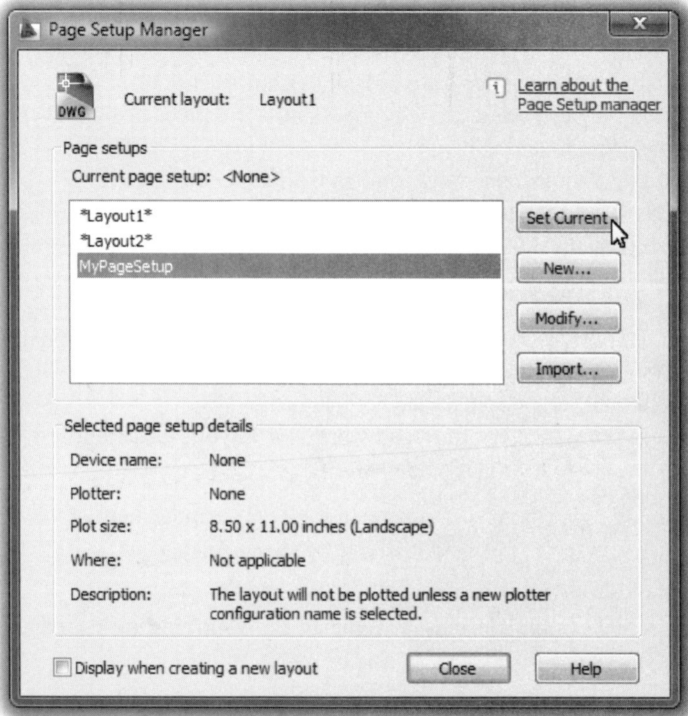

Figure 8-7 Using a named page setup in the Page Setup Manager dialog box

In either case, the **Page Setup** dialog box is opened. It is similar to the **Plot** dialog box. The main difference is that clicking **OK** will not send the drawing to the plotter, but will apply and store any settings for future plots in this particular layout (Figure 8-8).

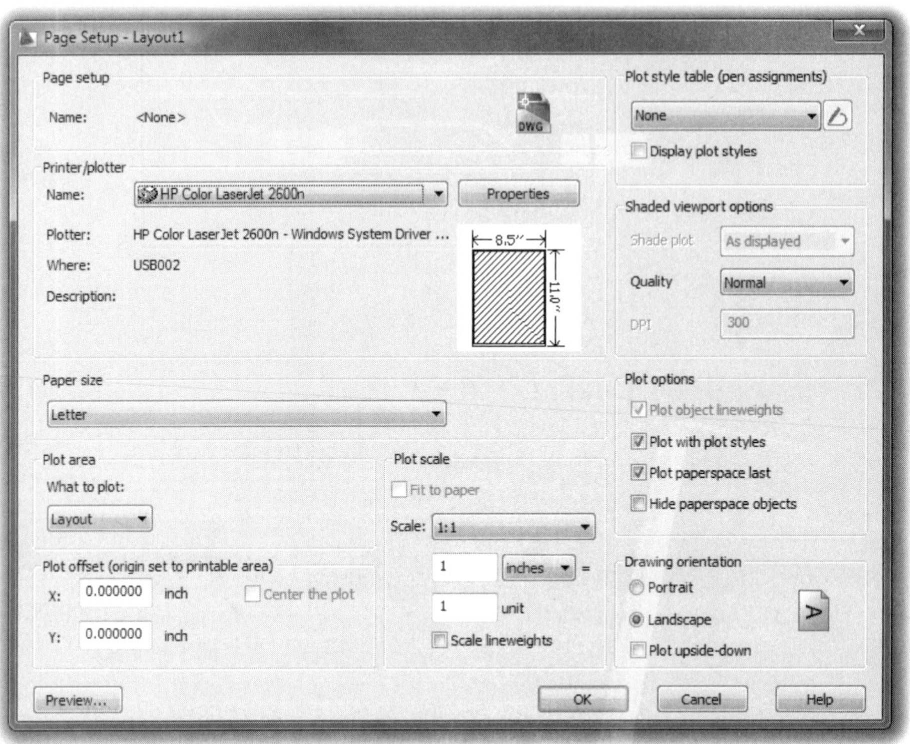

Figure 8-8 The Page Setup dialog box

FLOATING VIEWPORTS

The paper space mode can be conceived of as an infinite plane covering the entire model space. Through this infinite plane you can see the object existing in the model space by turning an area transparent. This is made possible by placing a paper space viewport, also known as a ***floating viewport***.

floating viewport: A viewport entity created in paper space, through which you can display any view of the objects contained in the model space.

The model space viewports studied in Chapter 1 are not entities, but partitions of the drawing area. Paper space viewports, on the other hand, are specific AutoCAD entities that allow you to see the model space from any viewpoint and with any zoom factor. Floating viewports can be modified by different settings and operations, including some in the **Properties** palette.

The **VPORTS** command opens the **Viewports** dialog box where you can create a specific arrangement of viewports in a specified area. In the **Viewports** dialog box, you can automatically generate a set of viewports that show the different views of the 3D model by selecting the **3D** option **Setup** (Figure 8-9).

Other operations to create and modify viewports are contained in the **Viewports** panel on the **Ribbon**. Additionally, other operations regarding the viewports can be accessed from the shortcut menu that displays by right-clicking on a selected viewport (Figure 8-10).

The **Viewports** toolbar should be used every time you work in a **Layout** tab. From left to right, the tools allow you to perform the following operations:

- Display the **Viewports** dialog box, where you can create a specific arrangement of viewports in a specified area
- Create a single rectangular viewport
- Create a polygonal viewport made of straight and arc segments, similar to creating a polyline.
- Convert closed objects such as circles, ellipses, polylines, and regions into viewports
- Clip an existing viewport with a polygonal shape, or delete a viewport's clipping
- Use the viewport scale drop-down list to set a specific view scale on the active viewport.

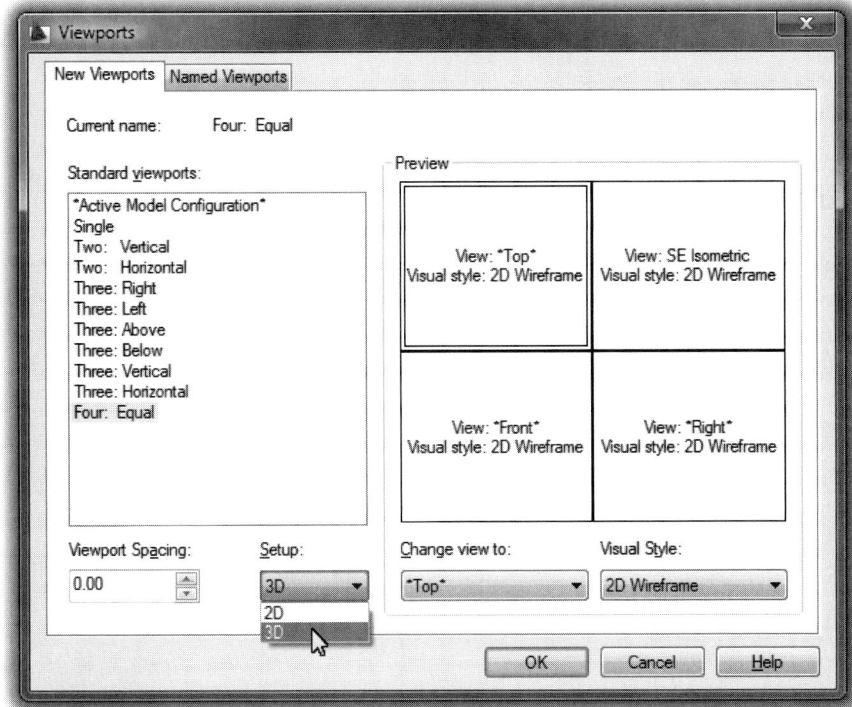

Figure 8-9 The Viewports dialog box

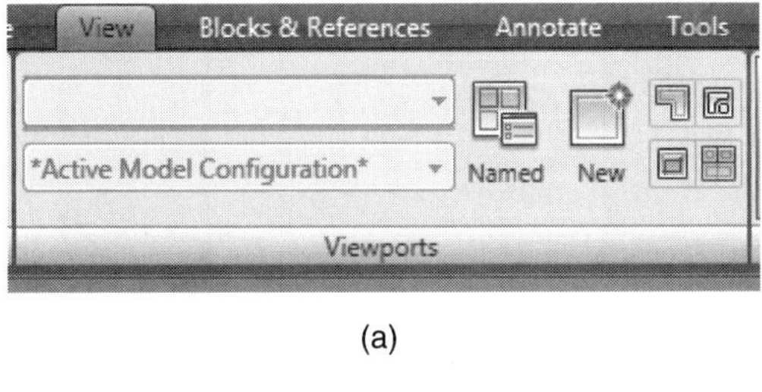

(a)

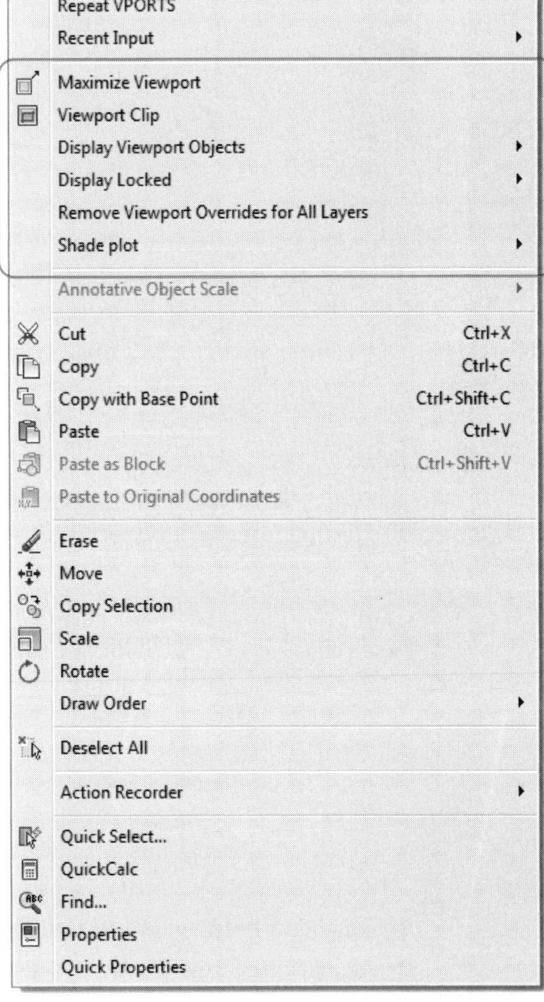

(b)

Figure 8-10 (a) The Viewports panel of the Ribbon; (b) a special shortcut menu is displayed by right-clicking while a viewport is selected

The viewport's shortcut menu also allows you to specify settings for the selected viewports. You can **Lock** the view scale or set a specific type of **Shade** in each viewport, among other operations.

You can place floating viewports anywhere in the paper space. A viewport can overlap another viewport, or it can be located completely inside it. In any case, only the part of a viewport located inside the printable area of the paper will be plotted.

A floating viewport can also be modified using commands such as **ERASE**, **SCALE**, **MOVE**, and **COPY**. The most important property of a viewport, however, is that it enables you to activate or deactivate the model space seen through it.

When a viewport is activated (Figure 8-11), the contour of the viewport changes to a thicker line. Any object existing in model space can be selected and modified; even new objects can be placed in the model space though this window. **ZOOM** and **PAN** operations through an activated viewport make it possible to obtain the drawing views with specific scales.

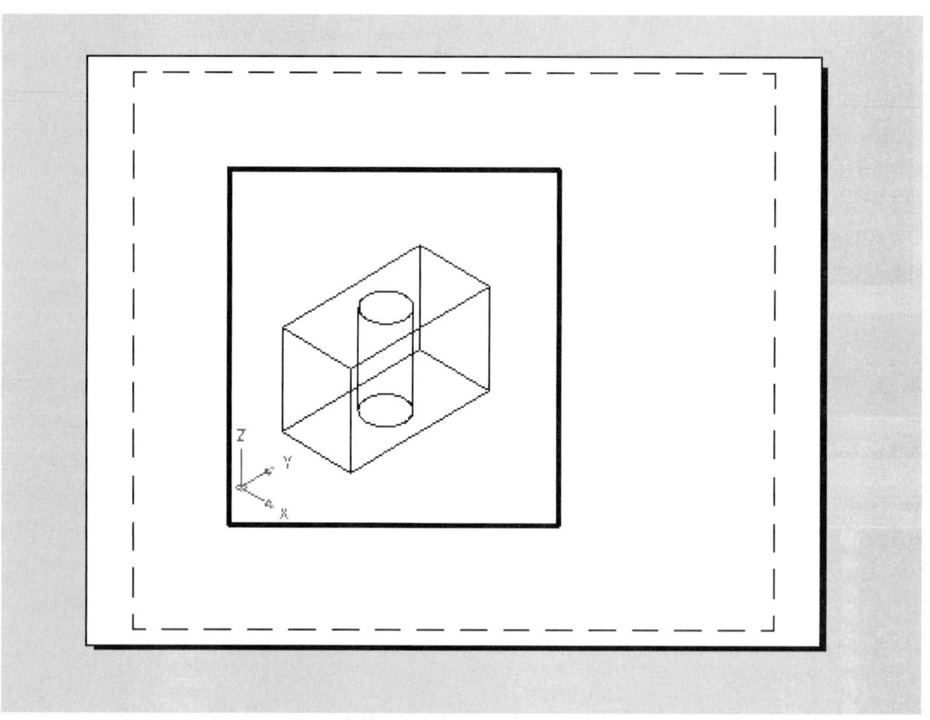

Figure 8-11 An activated viewport

When a viewport is deactivated (Figure 8-12), you can work only in the 2D infinite plane. Any object created will not appear when you switch to model space. You also cannot select or modify any object located in the model space.

To activate or deactivate a floating viewport, you can perform one of the following operations:

- Command line: . . . . . mspace ↵ (to activate)
  pspace ↵ (to deactivate)
- Mouse double-click: . . . . . Inside a viewport (to activate)
  Outside a viewport (to deactivate)
- Status button[*]: . . . . . Click **PAPER** button (to activate)
  Click **MODEL** button (to deactivate)

Viewports can also be maximized, and then minimized back, by performing one of the following operations:

- Invoking the **VPMAX** and **VPMIN** commands
- Double-clicking on the viewport contour

Note:
Only one viewport can be activated at a time. To activate another viewport, you can just click inside it, or you can press the <**Ctrl**> and <**R**> keys to cycle through the viewports.

[*]Only when the **Layout** and **Model** tabs are enabled.

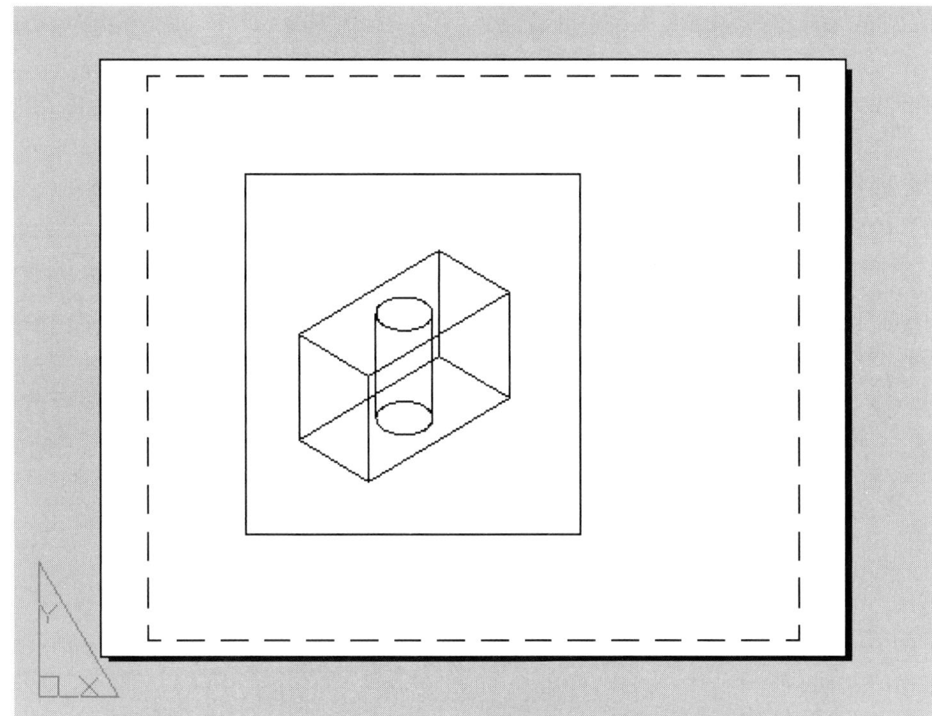

Figure 8-12 A deactivated viewport

- Using the **Maximize Viewport** button in the status bar
- Selecting **Maximize Viewport** on the shortcut menu, after selecting the viewport

Using Layers in Paper Space

In paper space, layers have two important additional properties that are not available in model space:

- Frozen/thawed in the currently active viewport
- Frozen/thawed in a new viewport

The first property enables you to show only a specific group of layers through each particular viewport. The second function, when turned on, helps you set the group of layers that will not automatically be shown on a new viewport. As you will see later, these properties are self-activated in the operations that generate the drawing views and, like any other property of layers, can be changed at any time. Other properties of the layers, such as **Color**, **Linetype**, and **Lineweight**, can be controlled in each viewport individually while the viewport is activated, or for the paper space in general with no viewport activated. Take a look at the **Current VP Freeze** and **New VP Freeze** columns in the **Layer Properties Manager** dialog box in Figure 8-13.

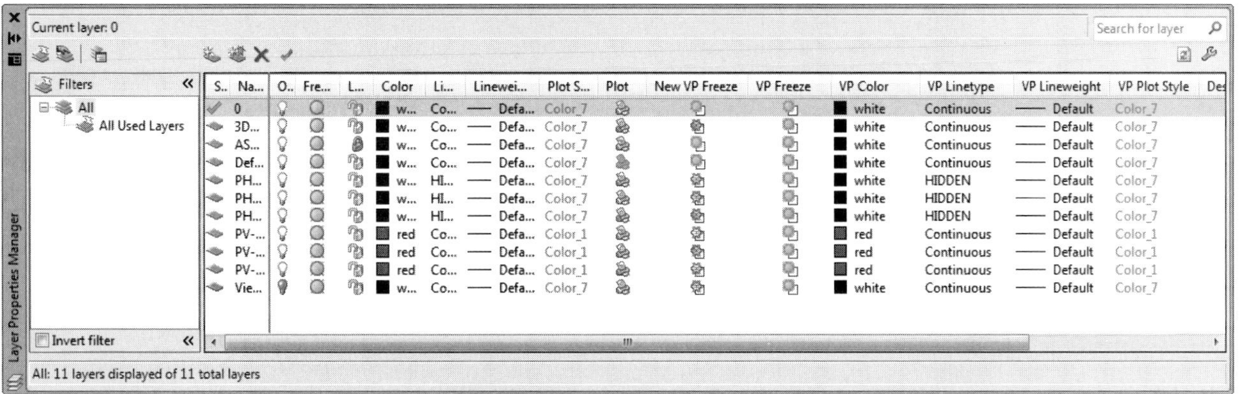

Figure 8-13 The Layer Properties Manager dialog box

USING THE PLOT STYLE TABLE EDITOR

The plot styles are individual files that AutoCAD uses to store information about printing preferences. There are two different types of plot styles files:

- Color-dependent plot style files (*.ctb*)
- Named plot style files (*.stb*)

The type of file used to manage the plot style is established the moment you create a new drawing. It depends on the option selected in the **Default plot style behavior for new drawings** section in the **Plot Style Table Settings** dialog box (Figure 8-14). This dialog box is accessed by clicking the **Plot Style Table Settings . . .** button in the **Plot and Publish** tab of the **Options** dialog box (Figure 8-15).

Figure 8-14 The Plot Style Table Settings dialog box

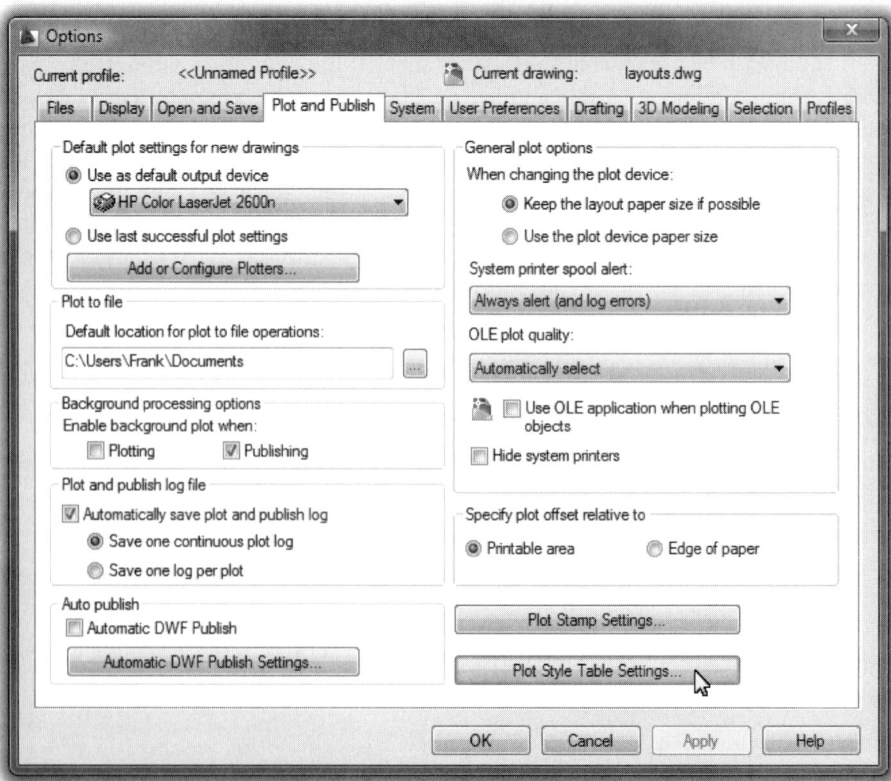

Figure 8-15 The Plot and Publish tab of the Options dialog box contains the Plot Style Table Settings . . . button

Color-dependent plot styles are the default when the AutoCAD software is first installed. Many users find these styles easier to use and to visualize because you know how an object will be plotted by looking at its color. Other users prefer using named plot styles. These plot styles can be assigned to the objects independently of their color, either by changing this property on the object directly or through the object's layer. Regardless of which method you use, the final purpose is the same. We will use color-dependent plot styles for the exercises in the book.

A new *.ctb* file can be created by selecting **New . . .** from the drop-down list of *.ctb* files located in the **Plot** dialog box (Figure 8-16). This will take you through a short process, where you can select **Start from scratch** in the **Begin** screen, and then easily continue with the rest of the process.

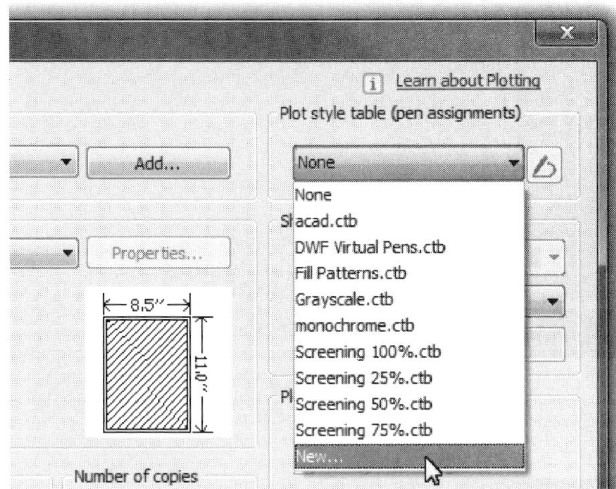

Figure 8-16 The drop-down list of .ctb files located in the Plot dialog box

After you create the *.ctb* files, you can edit them or edit files that already exist. The **Edit . . .** button, located to the right of the drop-down list (Figure 8-17), opens the **Plot Style Table Editor** for the specific file in use (Figure 8-18).

In the **Plot Style Table Editor**, you can change the properties of the colors so that they are plotted with specific characteristics. Of all these properties, three are sufficiently important to consider:

- **Color:** You can set a specific color to be plotted in any other color. Usually, you will assign each color to be plotted in black or in its own color.
- **Screening:** The value of this property can be decreased from 100% to 1% to obtain faded or grayed tones. It is very helpful when plotting heavy hatches or when trying to save some ink in a plot for review.
- **Lineweight:** This is really the most important property because it controls the line thickness for each particular color.

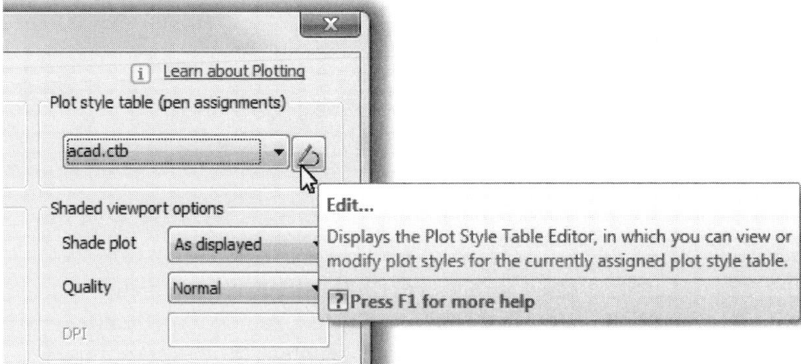

Figure 8-17 The Edit . . . button located to the right of the drop-down list in the Plot dialog box

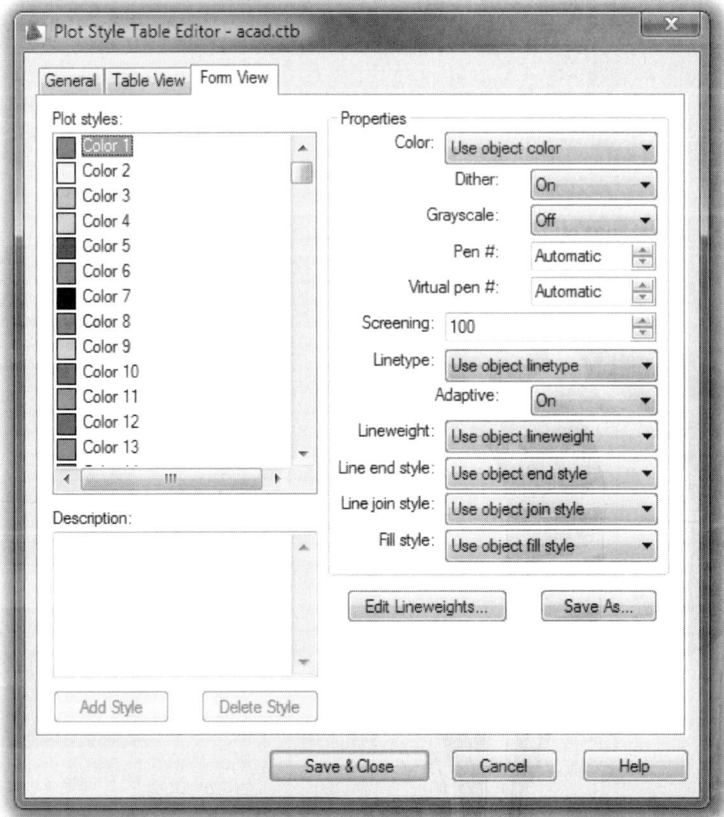

Figure 8-18 The Plot Style Table Editor dialog box

Specific line thickness values are used for the different drafting standards (ANSI, ISO, etc.), but most companies and draftpersons use their own thickness values to accommodate their unique needs, commonly within the following values:

Visible lines	0.3 to 0.6 mm (0.012 to 0.024″)
Hidden lines	0.15 to 0.3 mm (0.006 to 0.012″)
Dimensions, centerlines, break lines, and hatches	0.05 to 0.15 mm (0.002 to 0.006″)
Texts and annotations	0.2 to 0.4 mm (0.008 to 0.016″)
Titles and section lines	0.5 to 1.4 mm (0.197 to 0.055″)

GENERATING DRAWING VIEWS IN MODEL SPACE

Creating 2D and 3D Sections Using Section Objects

section object: An AutoCAD entity that allows you to temporarily slice 3D objects and create 2D and 3D sections from them.

A ***section object*** is an AutoCAD entity created with the **SECTIONPLANE** command. You can use section objects to perform multiple tasks. Their main use is to create live sectioning of 3D solids, surfaces, and regions, allowing you to see the interior geometry of the 3D solids (Figure 8-19). Additionally, you can generate 2D and 3D sections from the sliced objects.

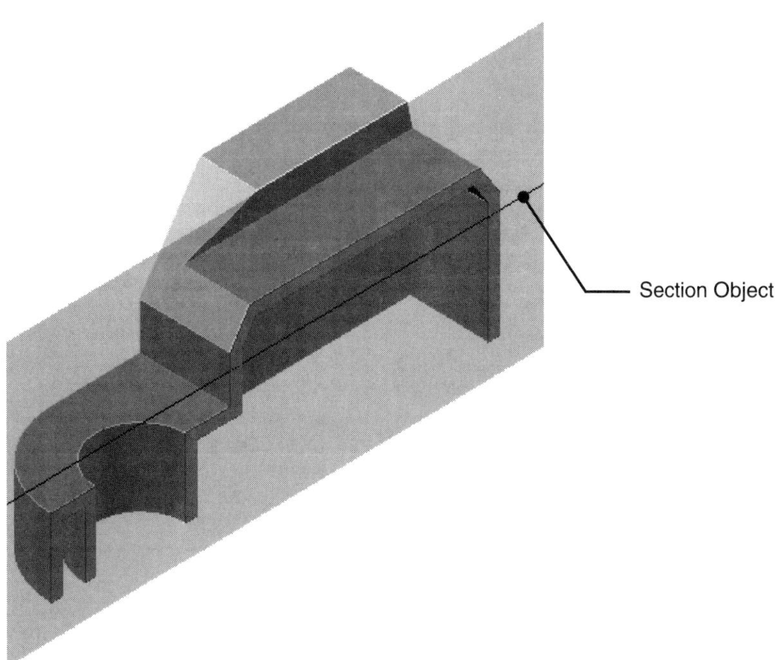

Figure 8-19 A section object with live sectioning enabled

As with any other entity, you can modify section objects using operations such as **MOVE**, **ROTATE**, **COPY**, **ERASE** and **MIRROR** (Figure 8-20). You can also assign a section object a layer and turn the layer off without canceling the sectioning effect (Figure 8-21).

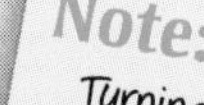

Note: Turning off a layer that has been previously assigned to a section object simply hides the section object. The objects continue to be sectioned by the section object. Freezing the layer, on the other hand, not only hides the section object, but also cancels its slicing effect.

When you invoke the **SECTIONPLANE** command, you can use one of four methods to create the section object. Two of the methods are implicit in the same first prompt. The other two can be optionally selected:

```
Select face or any point to locate
section line or [Draw section/Ortho-
graphic]:
```

1. **Selecting a Planar Face:** This method places a section object on the planar face of the 3D solid. The face is selected by clicking on it.

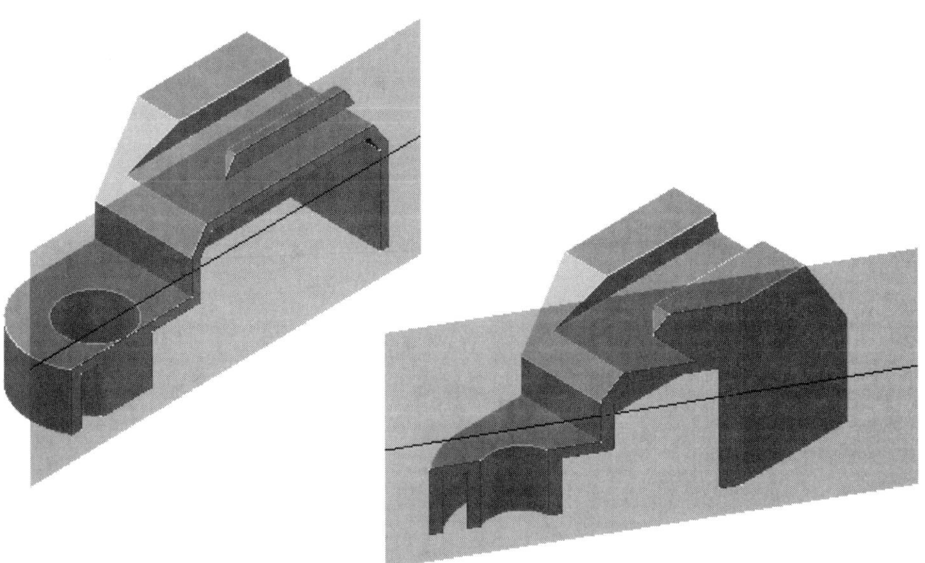

Figure 8-20 A section object can be moved, rotated, and more

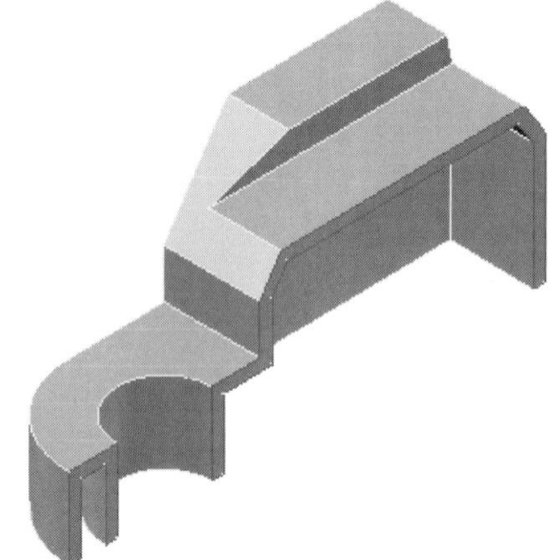

Figure 8-21 The layer assigned to a section object can be turned off without affecting its sectioning effect

2. **Specifying Two Points:** If the first click does not find a planar face, it is considered to be the first point of the section line, and then a second, or through, point is required to create the section object. The slicing plane is created perpendicular to the current *XY* plane.
3. **Draw Section:** This option allows you to specify a set of points that define the segments of a jogged section object. Each segment of the section object defines a plane perpendicular to the current *XY* plane.
4. **Orthographic:** This method places a section object on the selected orthographic plane in the middle of the 3D object.

After you create a section object, you can change its appearance by selecting another type of slicing object. You can do so by clicking on the big down arrow that is revealed after the section object is selected [Figure 8-22(a)].

- **Section Plane:** The section object behaves as a plane that extends infinitely in all directions [Figure 8-22(a)].

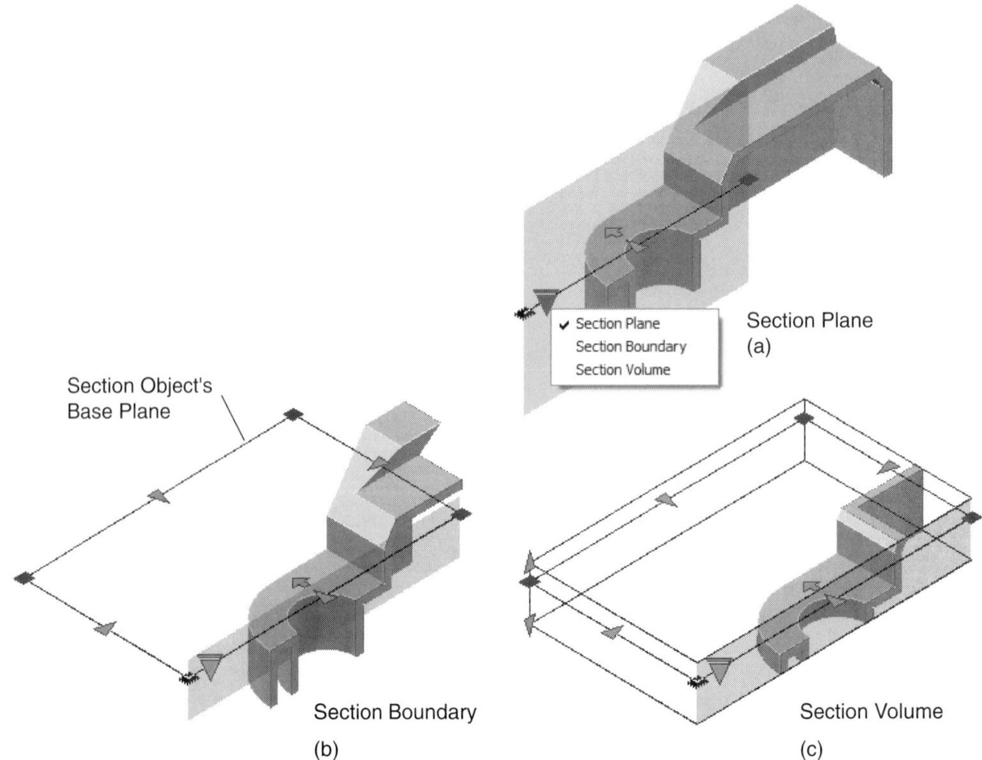

Figure 8-22 A section object can be manifested in three different ways

- **Section Boundary:** The section object behaves as a boundary delimited in length and width by its corners, extending infinitely high in both directions [Figure 8-22(b)].
- **Section Volume:** The section object behaves as a box, enclosing a volume delimited in length, width, and height by its vertices [Figure 8-22(c)].

You can manipulate the available grips of a selected section object depending on its type. Figure 8-23 shows the uses of the different grips.

Right-clicking in the drawing area while a section object is selected displays a special section in the shortcut menu that contains other settings and tools (Figure 8-24).

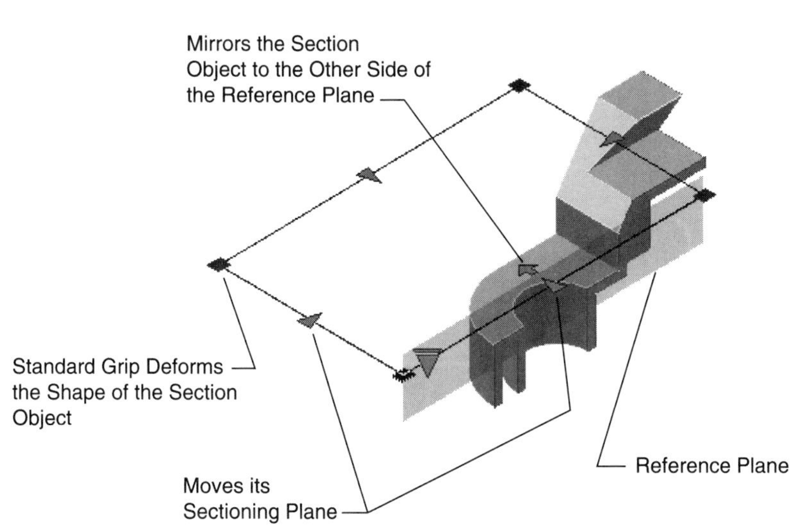

Figure 8-23 Uses of the different grips of the section object

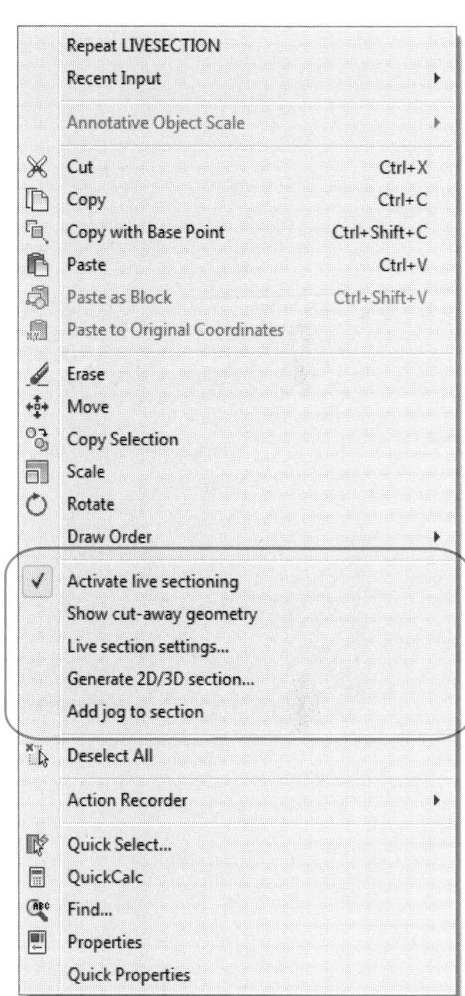

Figure 8-24 A special section in the shortcut menu is displayed by right-clicking the drawing area while a section object is selected

In this section of the shortcut menu you can perform the following tasks:

- Activate or deactivate the live sectioning
- Show or hide the sliced portion of the 3D objects in a different color
- Modify the section object by adding a step or jog
- Open the **Generate Section/Elevation** dialog box to generate 2D or 3D sections (Figure 8-25).
- Open the **Section Settings** dialog box to modify settings affecting **Live Section**, as well as the creation of 2D and 3D sections with the section object (Figure 8-26).

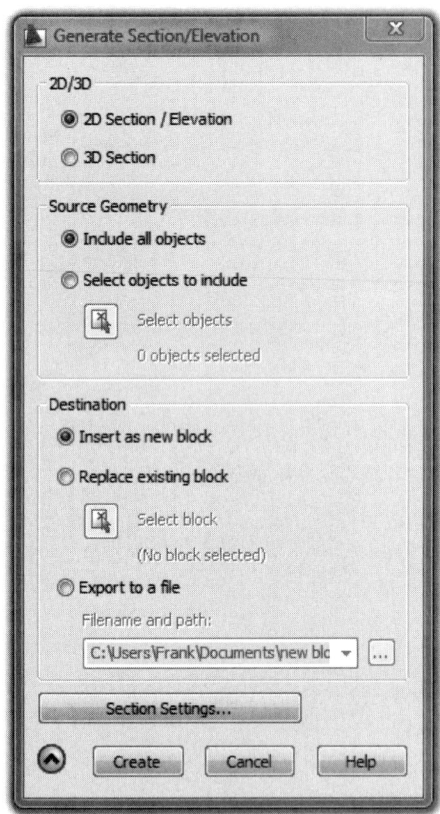

Figure 8-25 The Generate Section/Elevation dialog box

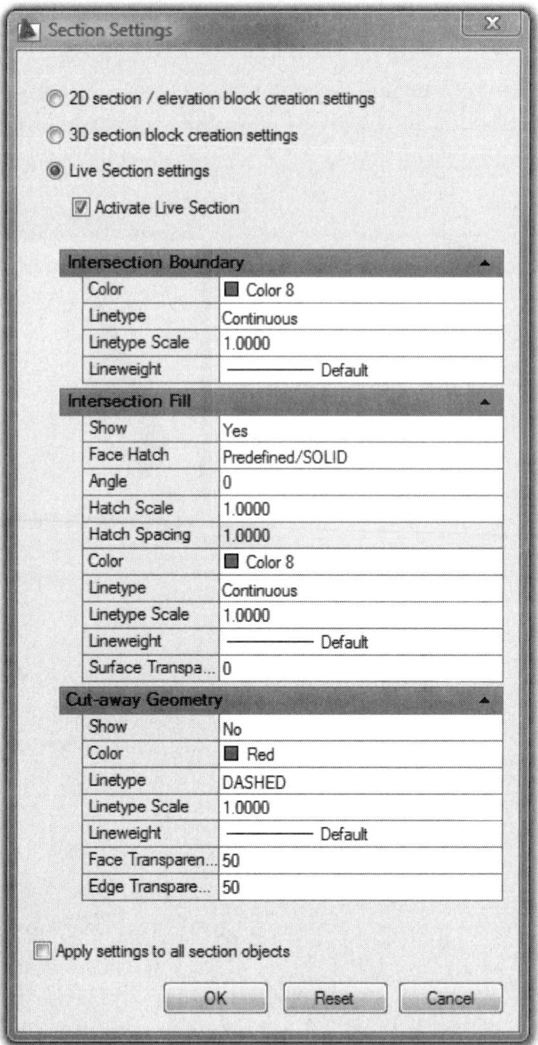

Figure 8-26 The Section Settings dialog box

The **Properties** palette also contains a special section where you can control other properties of the section object. These properties include the section object's **Name**, **Color**, and **Plane Transparency** (Figure 8-27).

Live sectioning can be activated or deactivated, allowing you to inspect inside the 3D objects whenever needed. 2D section and 3D section operations are used to extract geometry from the 3D objects whether or not live sectioning is enabled.

> **Note:**
> Section objects created by specifying two points or using the **Draw section** option are initially placed with **Activate live sectioning** disabled. This setting can be modified by invoking the **LIVESECTION** command, through the section objects shortcut menu, or through the **Properties** palette.

The geometry is extracted as block entities through the **Generate Section/Elevation** dialog box. You can choose to select specific objects under **Source Geometry**. You can also choose to replace existing block definitions or to save blocks as separate drawing files under **Destination**. Clicking the **Create** button closes the **Generate Section/Elevation** dialog box and takes you through a series of prompts. Here you can specify different scale factors along the three axes, as well as the rotation of the block generated.

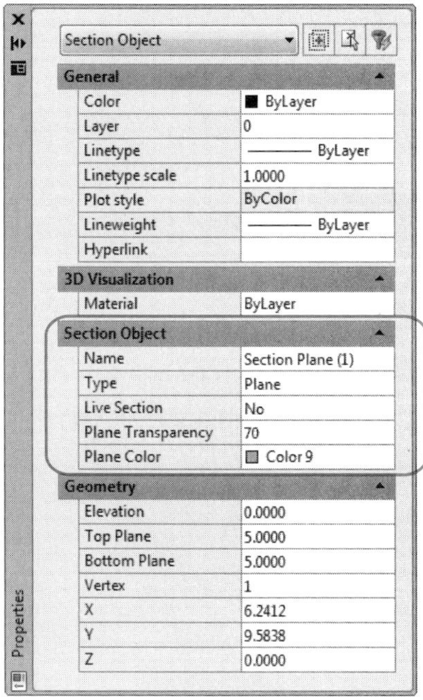

Figure 8-27 Section objects can be modified through the Properties palette

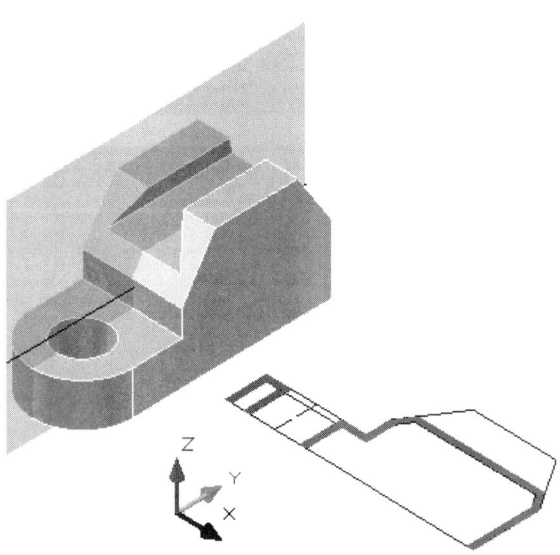

Figure 8-28 A section view generated when a section object goes through the object

2D section blocks are placed in the current *XY* plane. If the section object cuts the 3D object, a section view is generated (Figure 8-28).

On the other hand, if the section object does not cut the 3D object and is located in front of it, a projected view is generated (Figure 8-29). You cannot, however, create projected views with different linetypes for hidden and visible edges in the same 2D section block. As you will learn later, other operations enable you to create projected views in a more effective way.

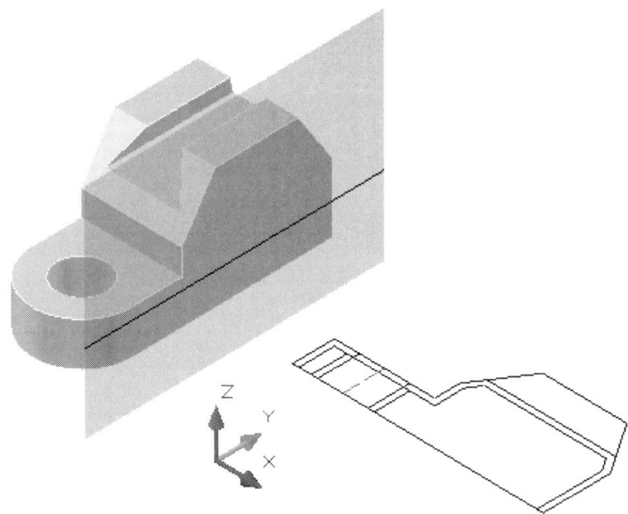

Figure 8-29 A projected view generated when a section object does not go through the object

One of the most important uses of section objects is creating jogged 2D sections. This procedure is the only one that allows you to obtain this type of drawing view (Figure 8-30).

3D section blocks maintain the orientation of the sectioned objects (Figure 8-31). When a 3D section block is exploded, it ungroups into a sliced copy of the 3D object, a hatch, and its boundary objects (Figure 8-32).

By adding jogs to the section object, you can create 3D section blocks slicing the 3D objects virtually anywhere (Figure 8-33).

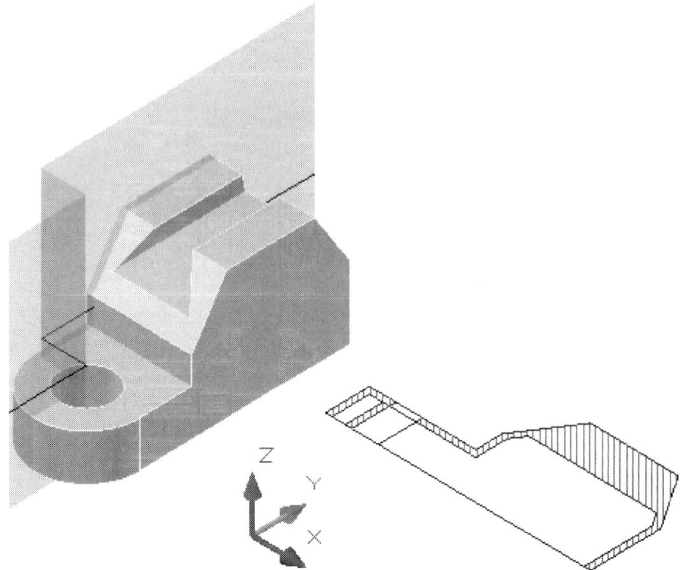

Figure 8-30 A section object containing jogs can be used to generate jogged section views

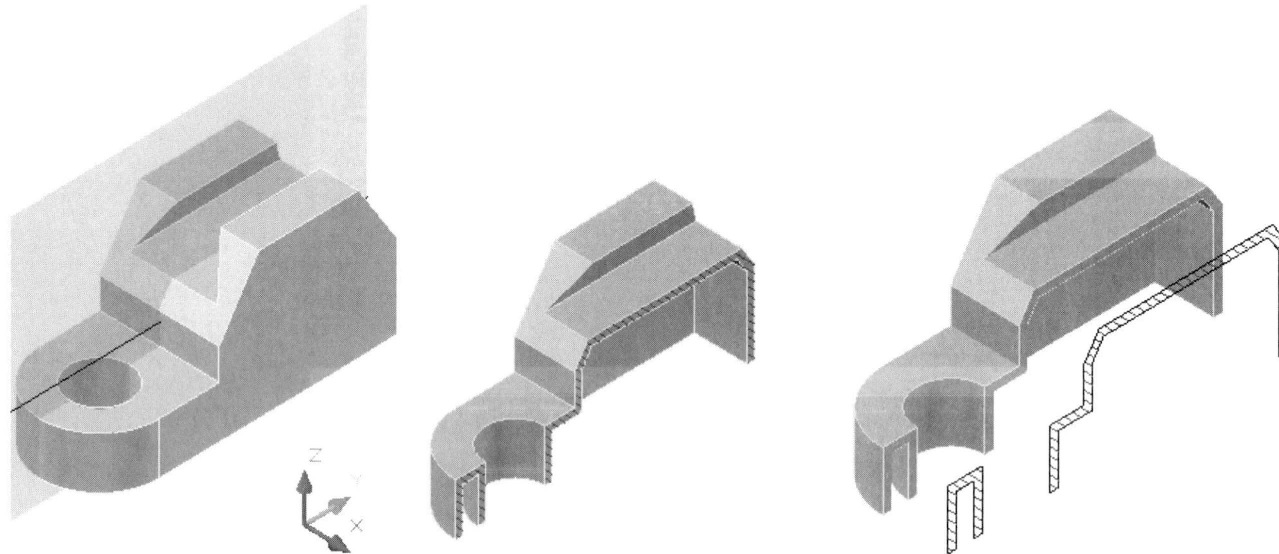

Figure 8-31 A 3D section block obtained with a section object

Figure 8-32 A 3D section block is composed of a 3D solid, a hatch, and its boundary objects

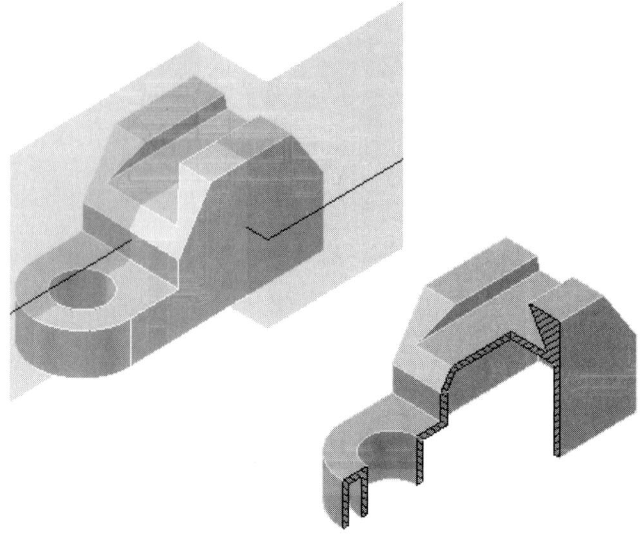

Figure 8-33 A 3D section block obtained with a jogged section object

Exercise 8-1: Using Section Objects

1. **OPEN** ***Exercise 8-1*** from the CD.
2. **SAVE** it **AS** ***Exercise 8-1 solved***.
3. Invoke the **SECTIONPLANE** command and respond to the prompts as follows:

   `Select face or any point to locate section line or [Draw section/Orthographic]:` *`Click to the left and over the 3D solid`* `(Figure 8-34).`

   `Specify through point:` *`With ORTHO mode activated, click to the right of the 3D solid so that the section object crosses it.`*

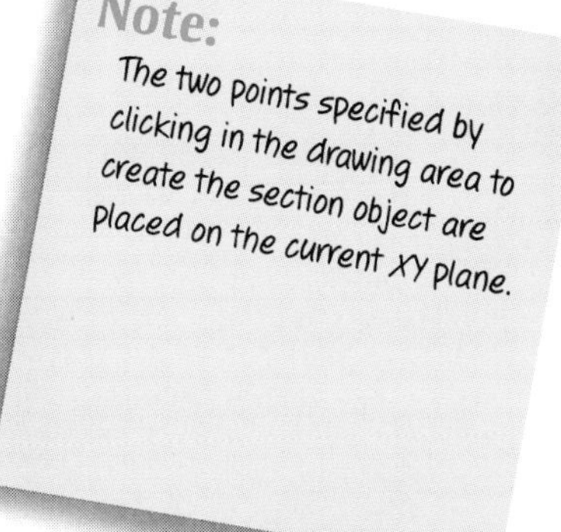

Note:
The two points specified by clicking in the drawing area to create the section object are placed on the current XY plane.

SECTIONPLANE	
Ribbon: Solid Editing panel	
Pull-down Menu	Draw/ Modeling/ Section Object
Command Line	section-plane

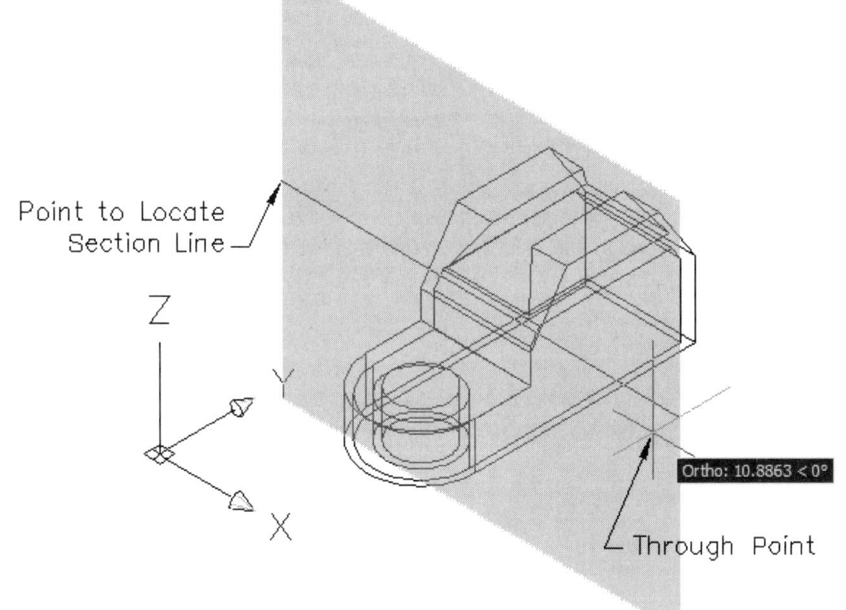

Figure 8-34 Points to be specified in the SECTIONPLANE command

4. Select the **Realistic** visual style.
5. Select the section object by clicking its plane and open the **Properties** palette.
6. In the **Properties** palette (Figure 8-35), change the **Plane Color** property to **Red**.
7. While the section object is still selected, right-click in the drawing area and select **Activate live sectioning** to turn this feature on.
8. Press **<Esc>** to unselect the section object. The sectioned 3D object should look more or less like Figure 8-36.
9. Select the section object again and right-click in the drawing area. Select **Generate 2D/3D section . . .** from the shortcut menu.
10. In the **Generate Section/Elevation** dialog box, select **2D Section/Elevation** and click on the **Section Settings . . .** button.
11. In the **Section Settings** window, make sure **2D section/elevation block creation settings** is selected and scroll down to **the Cut-away Geometry** settings. Set both **Show** and **Hidden Line** to **No** (Figure 8-37).

> **Note:**
> Because the points of the section object were not specified in an exact location, your section object might end up located in a different place.

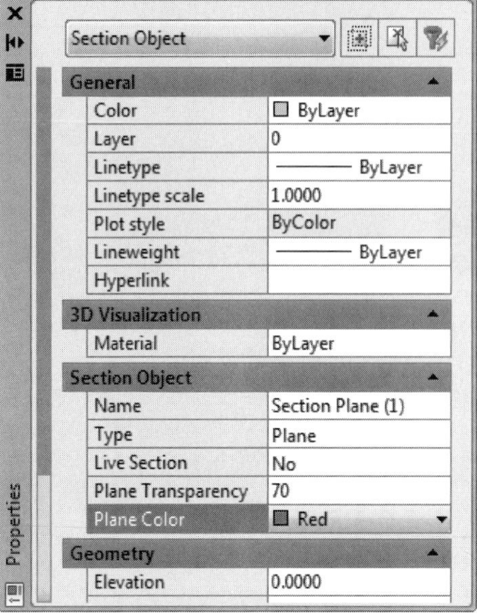

Figure 8-35 The Properties palette

Figure 8-36 After activating live sectioning

12. Scroll to the **Background Lines** settings and set **Hidden Lines** to **No**.
13. Scroll to the **Intersection Fill** settings and change the **Face Hatch** to **Select hatch pattern type . . .** (Figure 8-38). In the **Hatch Pattern Type** dialog box, select **ANSI131** (Figure 8-39) and click **OK** to close the dialog box. Click **OK** to close the **Section Settings** dialog box also.

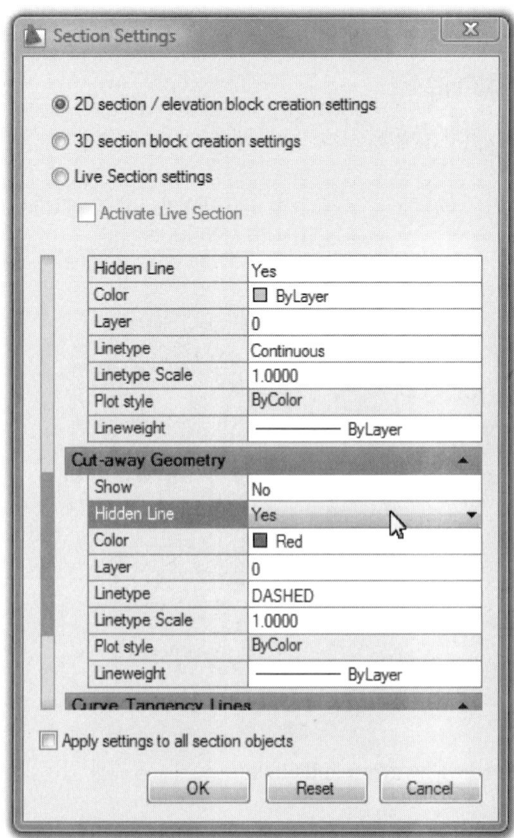

Figure 8-37 Specifying settings in the Section Settings dialog box

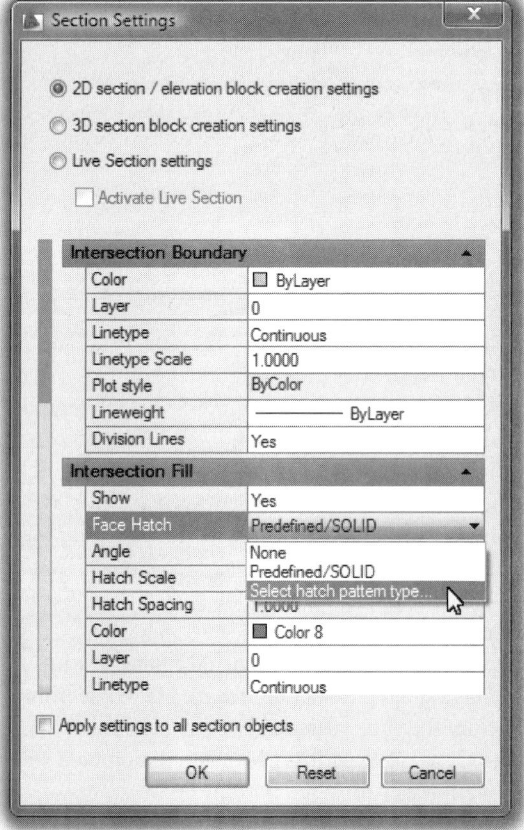

Figure 8-38 Specifying settings in the Section Settings dialog box

14. Back in the **Generate Section/Elevation** dialog box, click the **Create** button.
15. Click anywhere in the drawing area to specify an insertion point. Respond by pressing **<Enter>** to all other prompts. The 2D section created should look like Figure 8-40.

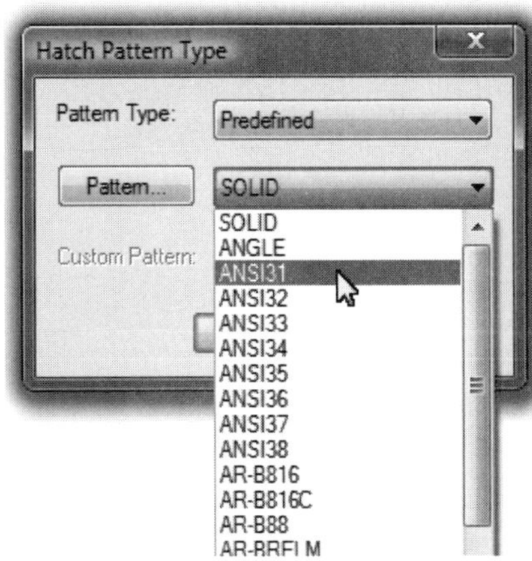

Figure 8-39 The Hatch Pattern Type dialog box

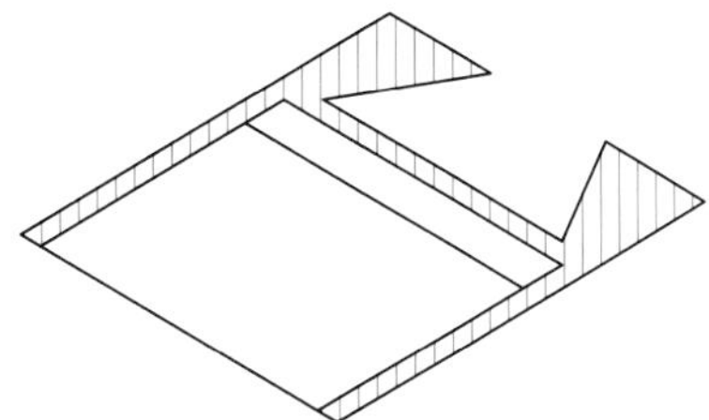

Figure 8-40 The resulting 2D section

16. Select the **Top** view and select the section object again.
17. With **ORTHO** mode activated, pull the grips located at the endpoints of the section object to get them closer to the 3D object (Figure 8-41).

Only one of the two endpoint grips can actually be used to stretch the section object.

18. Select the triangular grip located in the middle of the section object and stretch it downward. Try placing the section object close to the location shown in Figure 8-42.

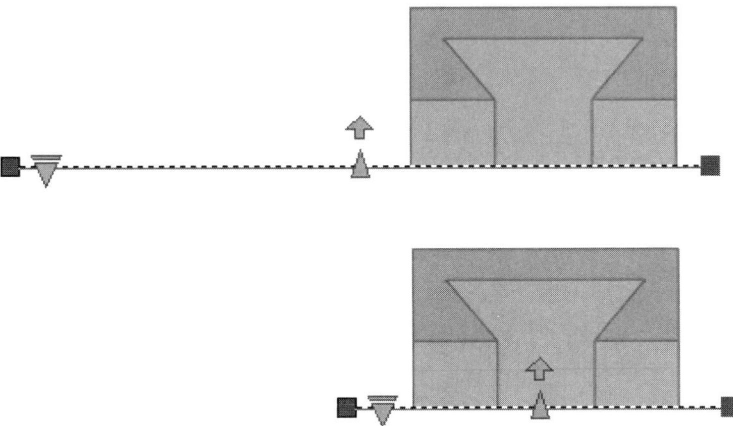

Figure 8-41 Using the grips to adjust the section object

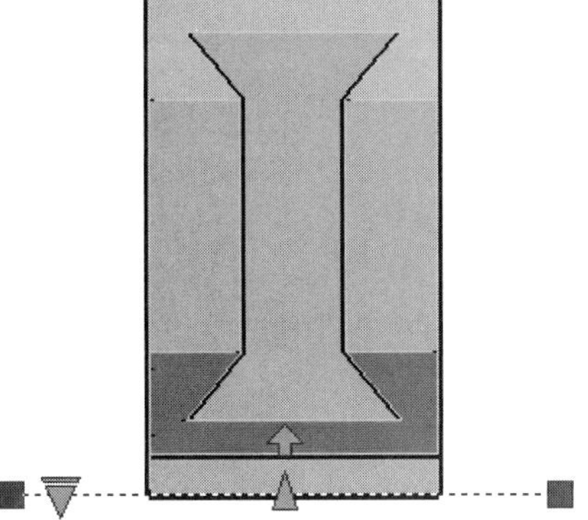

Figure 8-42 Using the grips to move the section object

19. Select the **SE Isometric** viewing point.
20. Select the section object and right-click in the drawing area. Deselect **Activate live sectioning** in the shortcut menu to turn the sectioning effect off.
21. Invoke the **MOVE** command and move the section object from its midpoint to the center point of the bottom circular edge on the hole.
22. Turn **Activate live sectioning** on.

23. Invoke the **ROTATE** command and rotate the section object around its midpoint **90°** (Figure 8-43).
24. Select the section object and right-click to select **Add jog to section** from the shortcut menu. When prompted to specify a point, click on any point on the section object.
25. Select the **Top** view.
26. Select the section object and turn **Activate live sectioning** off.
27. Following in order the three operations shown in Figure 8-44, readjust the jogged section object.
28. Select the **SE Isometric** viewing point.
29. Select the section object and right-click in the drawing area. Select **Generate 2D/3D section . . .** from the shortcut menu.

Note:
The object snap automatically overrides to the nearest point when adding a jog. This allows you to actually specify a point on the section object.

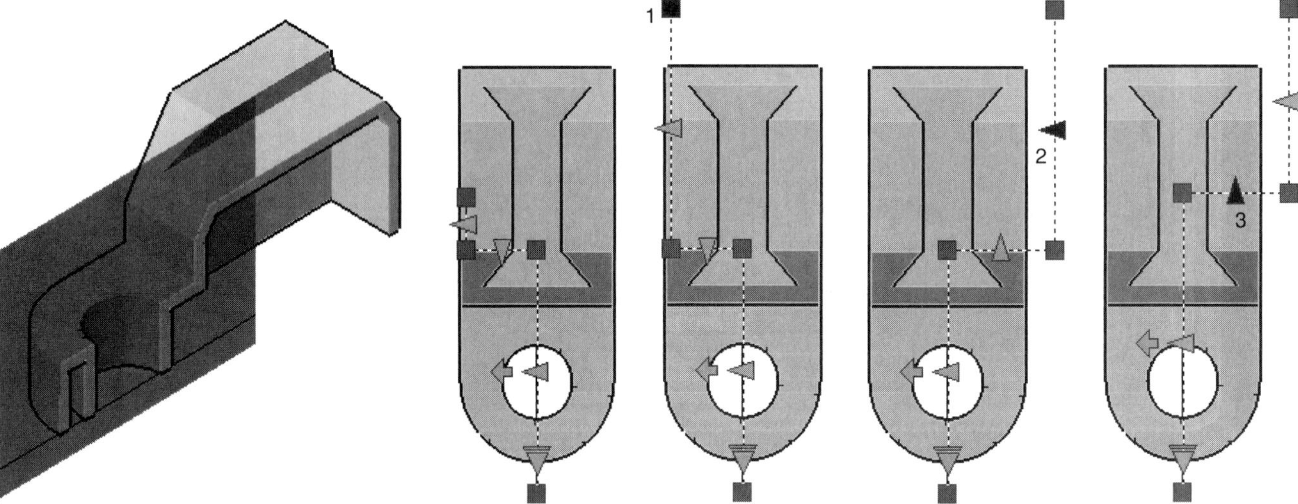

Figure 8-43 The isometric view

Figure 8-44 Procedure to adjust the jogged section object from the top view

30. In the **Generate Section/Elevation** dialog box, select **3D Section** and click on the **Section Settings . . .** button. Under **Intersection Fill**, set the **Face Hatch** as **Predefined/ANSI131**, similar to what you did previously for the 2D section. When finished, close the **Section Settings** window by clicking **OK**.
31. Under **Destination**, select **Export to a file,** and click on the browse button (**. . .**).
32. In the **Browse for Drawing File** dialog box, type **Exercise 8-2** as the **File name**, and look for the folder where you have the other drawings. Click the **Save** button to close the dialog box. Then go back into the **Generate Section/Elevation** dialog box and click the **Create** button to generate the file.
33. Select the section object and turn **Activate live sectioning** on. Press <**Esc**> to unselect the section object.
34. Select the section object once again. Click on the arrowlike grid located inside the cylindrical hole (Figure 8-45). This action will switch the sectioned side.
35. Unselect the section object and invoke the **3DORBIT** command to inspect the other side of the 3D model (Figure 8-46).
36. **SAVE** the drawing.

Note:
Unlike 3D sections created inside the same drawing, 3D sections exported as independent drawing files are not generated as blocks.

Note:
Using jogged section objects can produce effects similar to these obtained using boundary section objects.

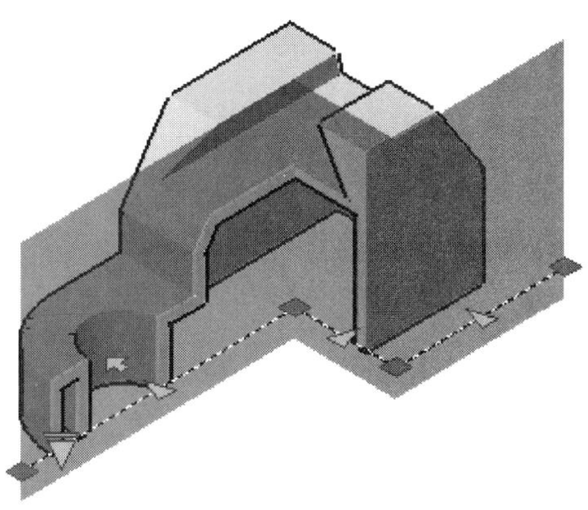

Figure 8-45 After activating live sectioning

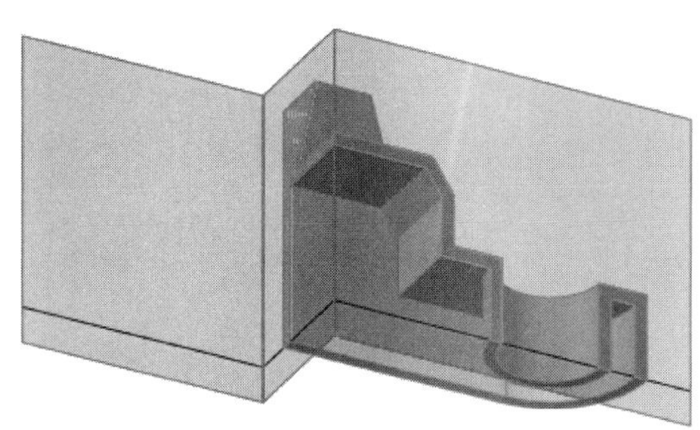

Figure 8-46 Inspecting the opposite side of the sectioned object

Creating Views Using the FLATSHOT Command

The **FLATSHOT** command allows you to create projected views in a very simple way: It generates a block by projecting the current view onto the current *XY* plane. Any existing 3D solid, surface, or region is included in the projected block.

For example, if you select the **Right** view, the *XY* plane automatically aligns with the **Right** plane. Thus, the projected block will correspond to the **Right** view and will be placed in the **Right** plane, which is where the current *XY* plane is.

Just as with the **SECTIONPLANE** command, you can specify different scale factors along the three axes in the **FLATSHOT** command. You can also select the rotation of the block generated.

Unlike the **SECTIONPLANE** command, **FLATSHOT** enables you to control the behavior of obscured lines. Many drawings contain standard projected views and sections, in which case you can use both commands jointly.

Exercise 8-2: Creating 2D Drawing Views in Paper Space Using the FLATSHOT and the SECTIONPLANE Commands

1. **OPEN** the file ***Exercise 8-2*** from the CD.
2. **SAVE** it **AS** ***Exercise 8-2 solved***.
3. Select the **Top** view.
4. Invoke the **FLATSHOT** command to open the **Flatshot** dialog box.
5. Under **Obscured lines**, select the **HIDDEN** linetype and select the color **Green**. Make sure that **Show** is checked and click the **Create** button (Figure 8-47).

FLATSHOT	
Ribbon: Solid Editing panel	
Command Line	flatshot

To select the **HIDDEN** linetype, you must first load from the **Select Linetype** dialog box. You open this box by selecting **Other . . .** from the **Linetype** drop-down list.

6. Click in any empty spot of the drawing area to specify the insertion point. Respond by pressing **<Enter>** to all other prompts. The projected block created should look like Figure 8-48.
7. Select the **Front** view.
8. Invoke the **FLATSHOT** command and click the **Create** button in the **Flatshot** dialog box.
9. As in the previous projection, click anywhere in the drawing area to specify the insertion point. Press **<Enter>** to accept all other prompts (Figure 8-49).
10. Select the **SE Isometric** viewing point.
11. Right-click in the drawing area and select **Cut** from the shortcut menu. When prompted, select the block projected onto the Front plane and press **<Enter>** to end the selection.
12. Select the **World** UCS.

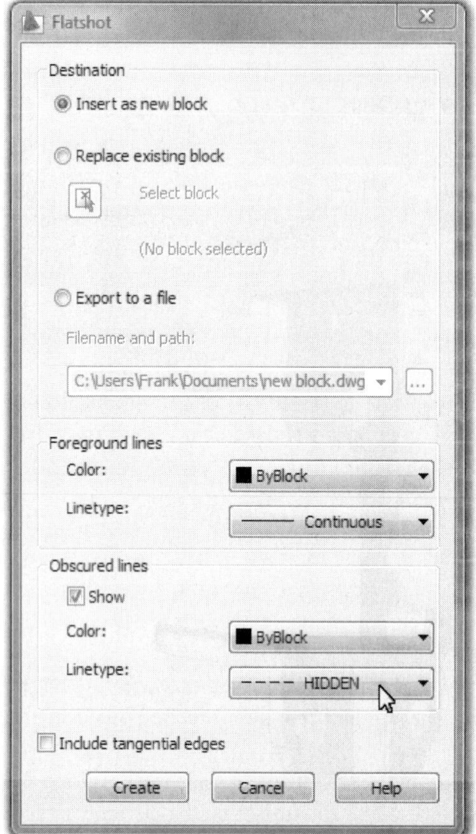

Figure 8-47 The Flatshot dialog box

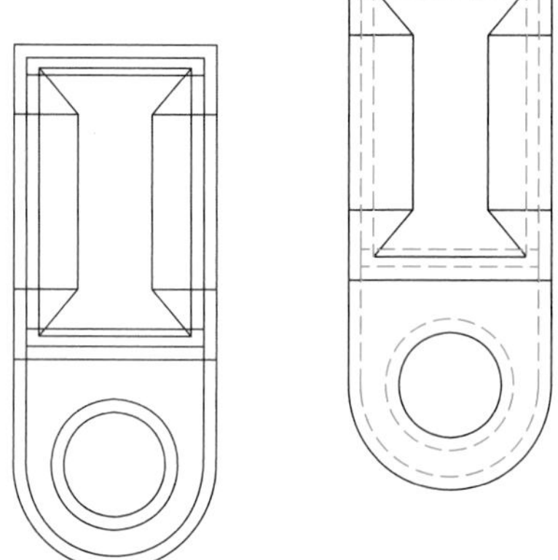

Figure 8-48 A projected block created with the FLATSHOT operation

13. Right-click in the drawing area to select **Paste** from the shortcut menu. Click in an empty spot to insert the block from the clipboard (Figure 8-50).

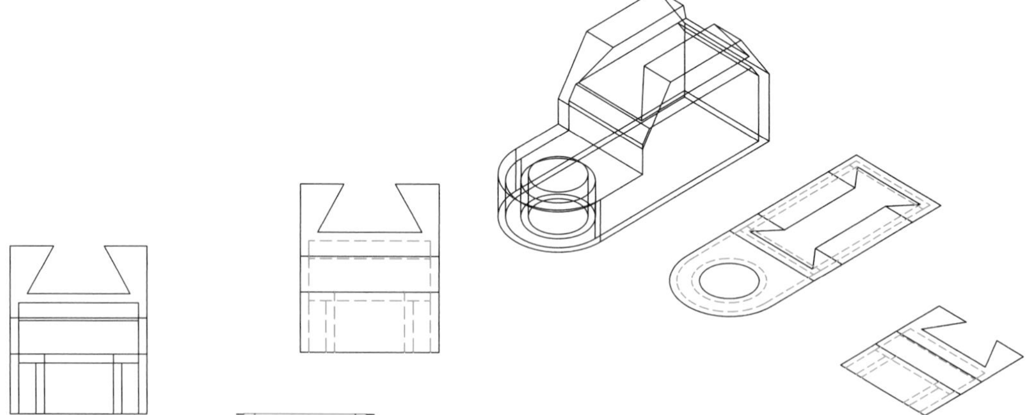

Figure 8-49 The front-projected block created with the FLATSHOT operation

Figure 8-50 The front-projected block pasted in the XY plane of the WCS

14. Invoke the **FLATSHOT** command. In the **Flatshot** dialog box, uncheck the **Show** checkbox under **Obscured lines** and click the **Create** button.
15. Click anywhere in the drawing area and press **<Enter>** to accept all other prompts (Figure 8-51).
16. Invoke the **SECTIONPLANE** command and respond to the prompts as follows:

```
Select face or any point to locate section line or [Draw section/
Orthographic]: o ↵
```

Align section to: [Front/bAck/Top/Bottom/ Left/Right] Top: *r* ↵

17. Select the section object created and right-click to select **Generate 2D/3D section . . .** from the shortcut menu.
18. In the **Section Settings** palette, make the following changes:
    - Under **Intersection Fill**, set the **Face Hatch** as **Predefined/ANSI131**.
    - Under **Background Lines**, set **Hidden Line** to **No**.
    - Under **Cut-away Geometry**, set both **Show** and **Hidden Lines** to **No**.
    - Under **Curve Tangency Lines**, set **Show** to **No**.

Note:
A section object with **Life sectioning** activated is placed in the middle of the 3D solid.

19. Click **OK** to close the **Section Settings** dialog box.
20. Click **Create** to generate the section block. Click anywhere in the drawing area to specify an insertion point. Respond by pressing **<Enter>** to all other prompts.
21. **ERASE** the section object.
22. Select the **Top** view. The objects should look like Figure 8-52 in your own arrangement.

Figure 8-51 The isometric-projected block created with the FLATSHOT operation

Figure 8-52 All drawing views seen from the Top view

23. **ROTATE** the block projected onto the Top plane **–90°** about any point on it.
24. **MOVE** the projected blocks to space them out, if needed (Figure 8-53).
25. Click the **Layout1** tab to switch to paper space.
26. Right-click on top of the **Layout1** tab and select **From template ...**
27. In the **Select Template From File** dialog box, look for the file **TB-Imperial.dwt** on the CD. Select the file and click the **Open** button.
28. In the **Insert Layout(s)** dialog box, select **ANSI A (11 × 8.5)** and click **OK** (Figure 8-54).

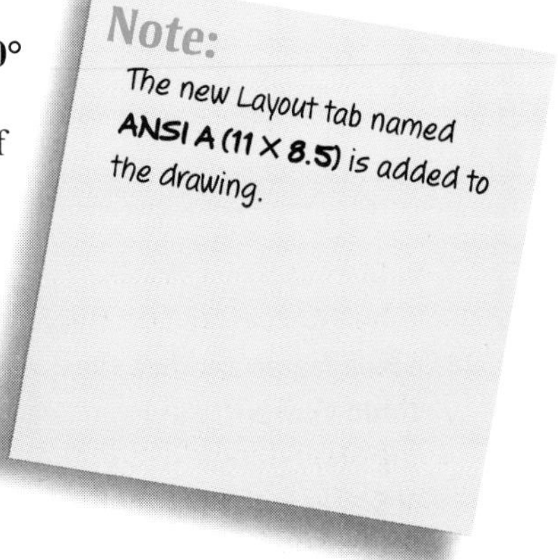

Note:
The new Layout tab named ANSI A (11 × 8.5) is added to the drawing.

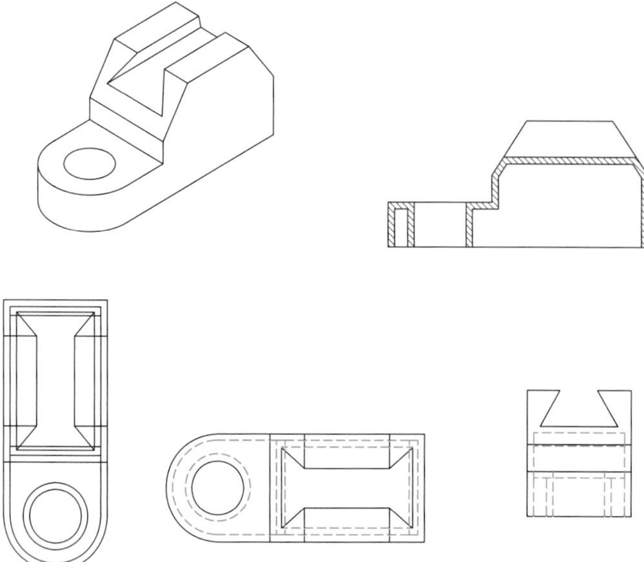

Figure 8-53 The drawing views after they are relocated

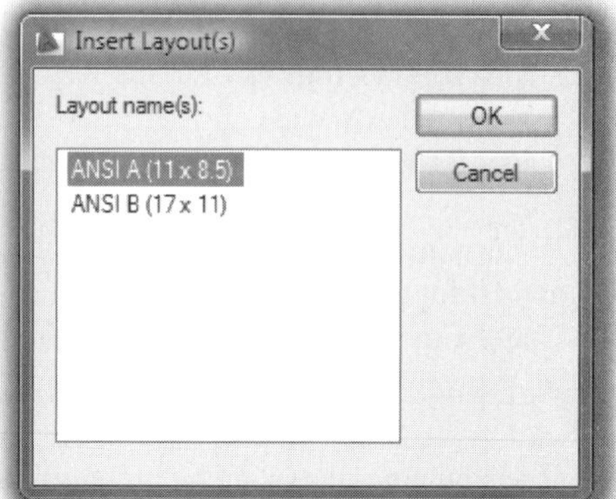

Figure 8-54 The Insert Layout(s) dialog box

29. Click the **ANSI A (11 × 8.5)** Layout tab. It contains a title block and a page already prepared with no viewports.
30. Invoke the **VPORTS** command to open the **Viewports** dialog box. In the **New Viewports** tab select **Four: Equal**, select **2D** under **Setup**, and click **OK**. When prompted for the first and opposite corners, click two points diagonally inside the title block, to place the four viewports. (Figure 8-55).
31. Double-click inside the top-right viewport to activate it.
32. **ZOOM** and **PAN** to center the block containing the **Top** view in the viewport.
33. Locate the **Viewport** toolbar and select the scale **1:2** from its drop-down list window (Figure 8-56).

Note:

The cut-and-paste procedure you used allowed you to locate all the blocks containing the drawing views in the same plane. This procedure allowed you to use the same viewing point in every viewport. You could have avoided the cutting-and-pasting process, however, by using a different approach: You could have changed the viewing point through the active viewport so the viewing plane is located parallel to the plane containing the projected block. For example, to show the block projected onto the front plane, you could select the Front orthographic view through the viewport.

TIP When a viewport is active, any **ZOOM** operation, including the ones with the mouse wheel, will cause the view to zoom in and out. This will affect the current scale.

34. Click inside another viewport to make it active. Repeat the same procedure with the other three viewports to locate each corresponding view. When you are finished, the 2D drawing should look like Figure 8-57. The isometric view does not need to be shown to any specific scale.

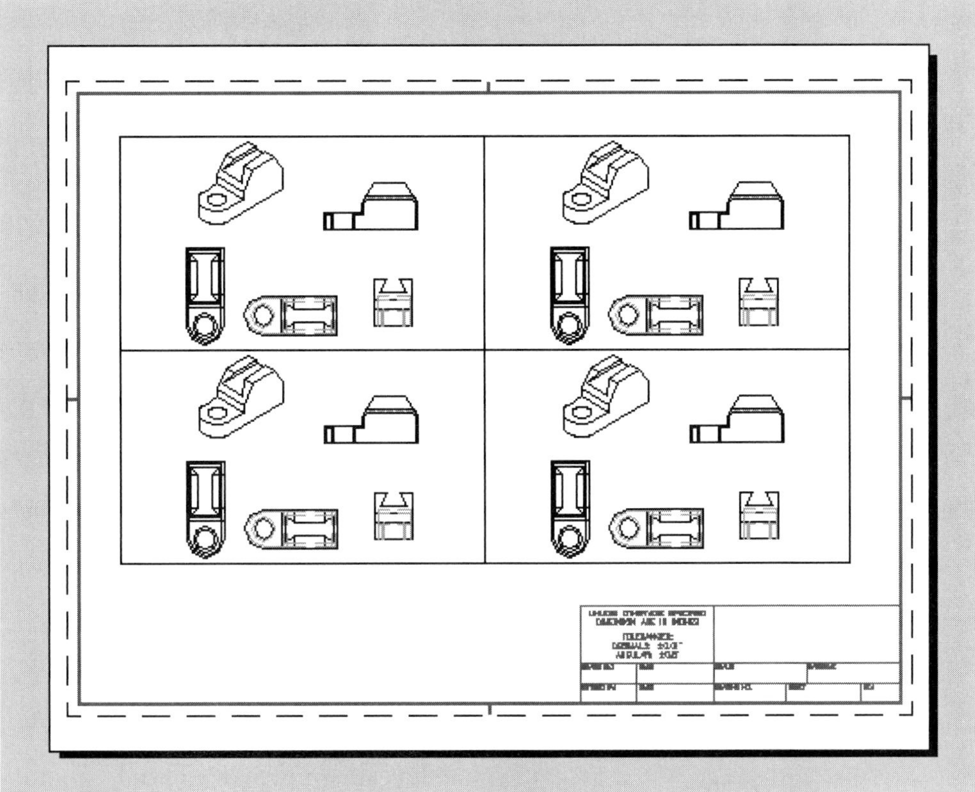

Figure 8-55 Four viewports are created

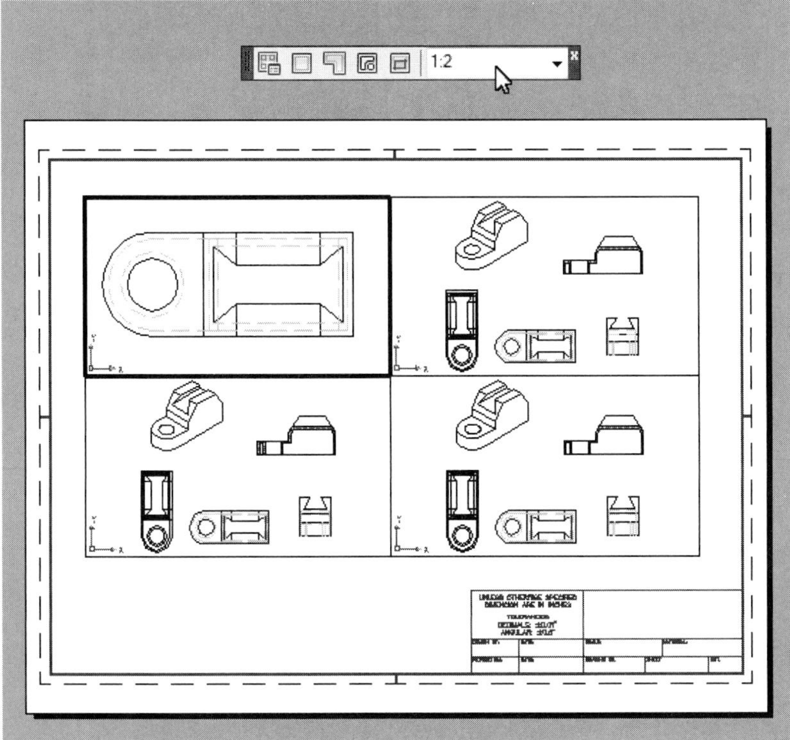

Figure 8-56 After adjusting the scale and the view in the top-left viewport

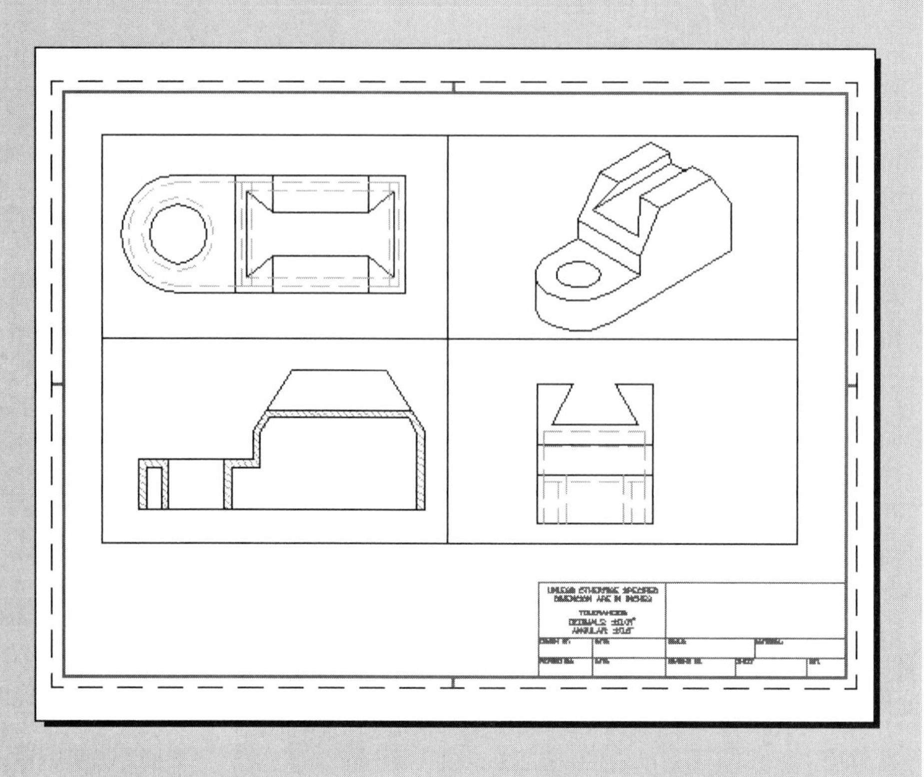

Figure 8-57 After adjusting all viewports

35. Double-click outside the viewports to deactivate them, or return to paper mode.
36. **MOVE** the viewport containing the top projected block from a point on the block to a point on the block of the viewport below (Figure 8-58).
37. With **ORTHO** mode activated, **MOVE** the viewport back up, maintaining the vertical alignment (Figure 8-59).
38. Repeat the same procedure to align the viewport showing the right view.
39. Select all viewports and set the **Display locked** property to **Yes** in the **Properties** palette (Figure 8-60).
40. Create a new layer named ***VP***. Assign the layer to all viewport objects, and then turn it off. This will hide all the viewport objects (Figure 8-61).
41. Place the dimensions on top of the paper. When you are finished, the drawing will look like Figure 8-62.
42. Open the **Page Setup** dialog box for the current Layout. Select your printing device and the **monochrome.ctb** plot style. Close the dialog box by clicking **OK**.
43. Invoke the **PREVIEW** command and **PLOT** the drawing.
44. **SAVE** the drawing.

Note:
In this procedure, the drawing views are not aligned. You can align them by using the **Align** option of the **MVSETUP** command, or by simply moving the viewports around. Anyhow, it is not the viewports that need to be aligned, but rather the drawing views.

Note:
You can place the dimensions either inside the model space or on top of the paper space. AutoCAD corrects the measurement scale factor when placing dimensions on views that are not scaled 1 : 1.

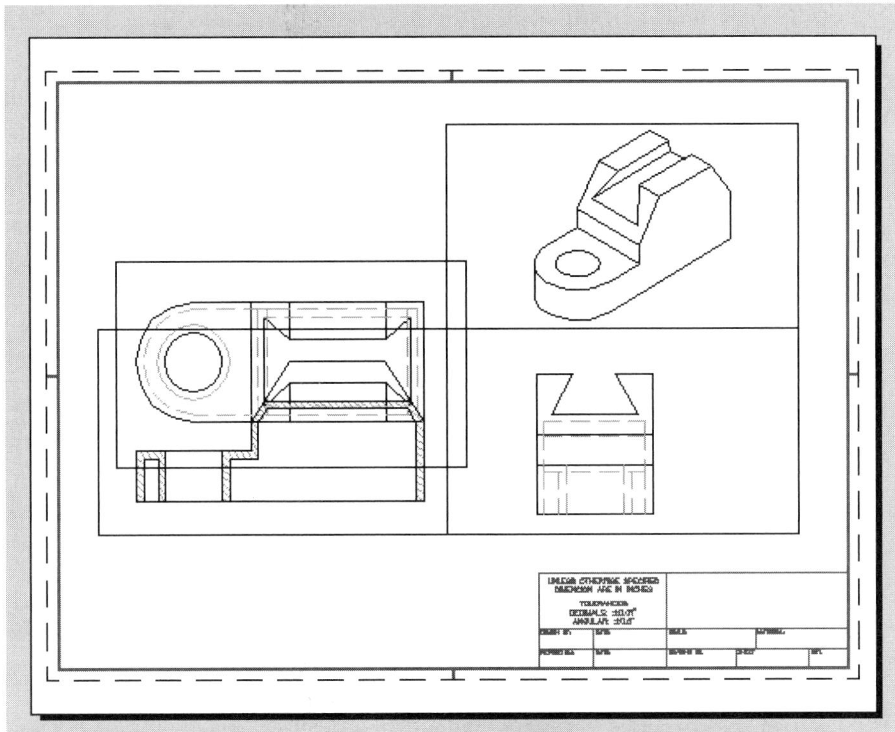

Figure 8-58 The viewport is moved, snapping to points on the objects located in the model space

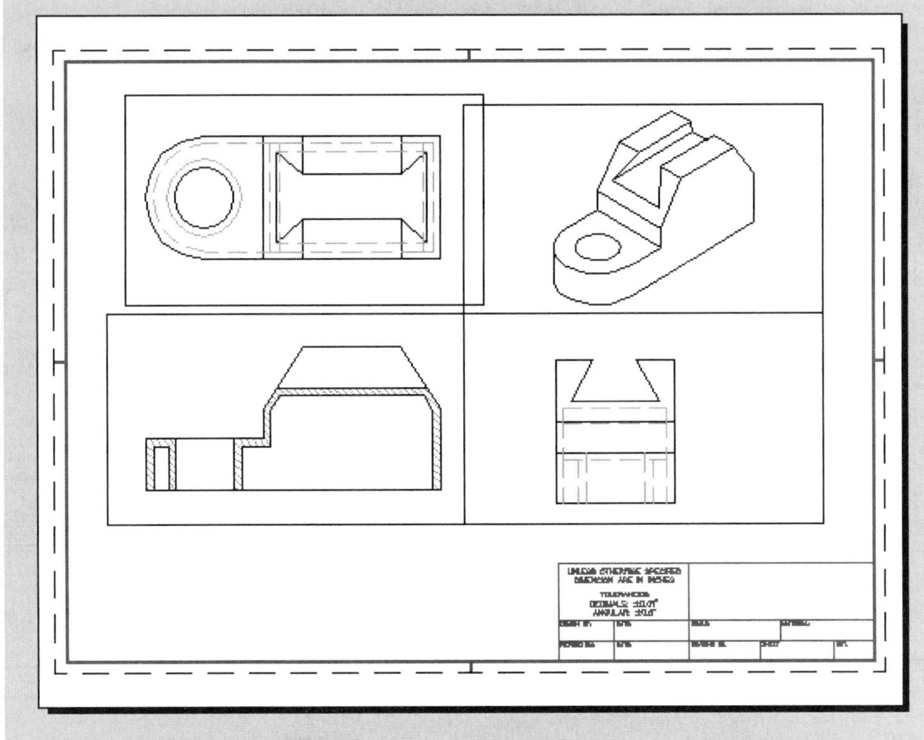

Figure 8-59 The viewport is moved back upward orthogonally

Placing Dimensions in the 3D Space

An elaborate drawing document that includes all the views and drafting standards often is not necessary. Instead, you can provide a quick isometric view with the proper dimensions, which might enable others to understand the drawing better. Using isometric views of 3D sections will enhance technical documents even more by enabling you to provide details and dimensions of the inside geometry.

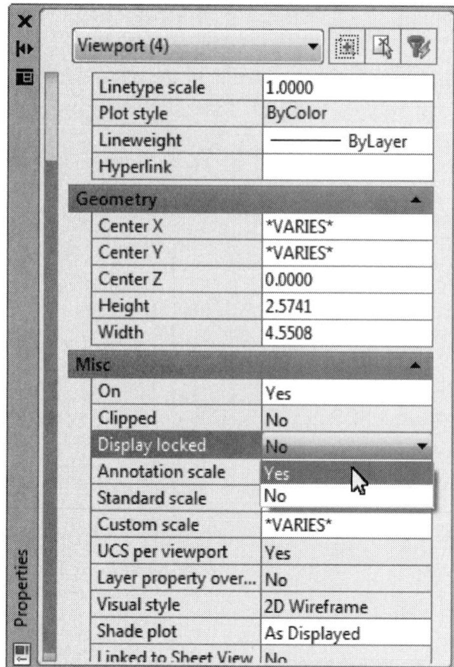

Figure 8-60 The Properties palette

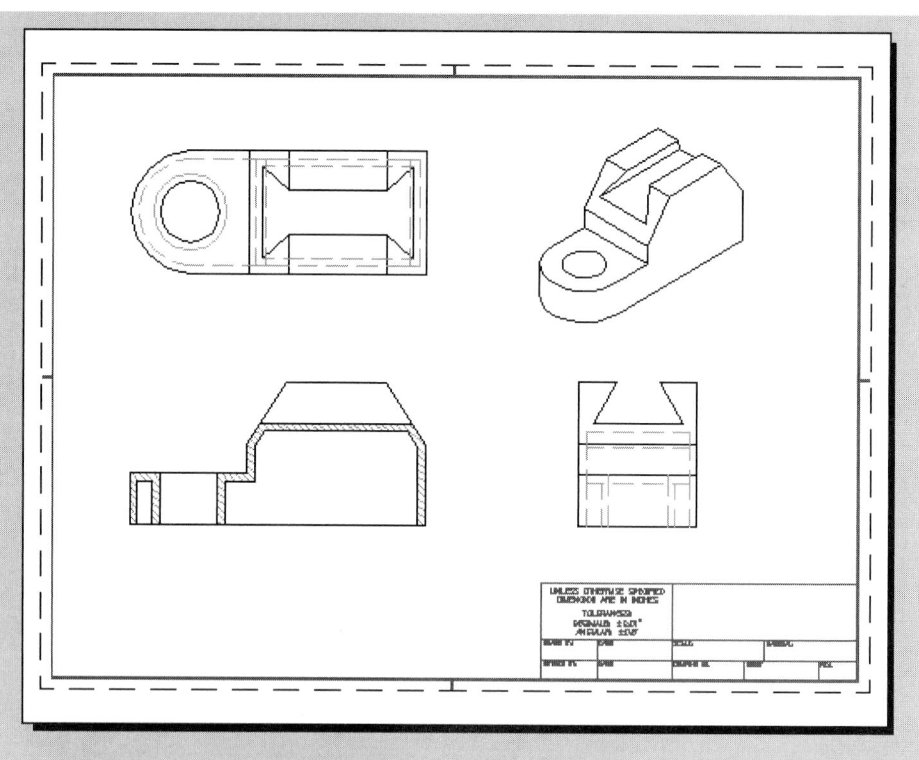

Figure 8-61 After turning the viewport's assigned layer off

Figure 8-63 shows a dimensioned isometric view (a) versus the standard drawing views displayed on the right (b).

Placing dimensions on 3D objects is really simple. Because the dimensions are always placed in the current *XY* plane, the UCS must be aligned beforehand with the face where the dimensions are to be placed.

When you place a dimension in the 3D space, the control grips at the origin of the extension lines are located at the points you specify. The rest of the dimension, however, is always placed in the current *XY* plane. In an orthographic view, this effect is not noticeable and the

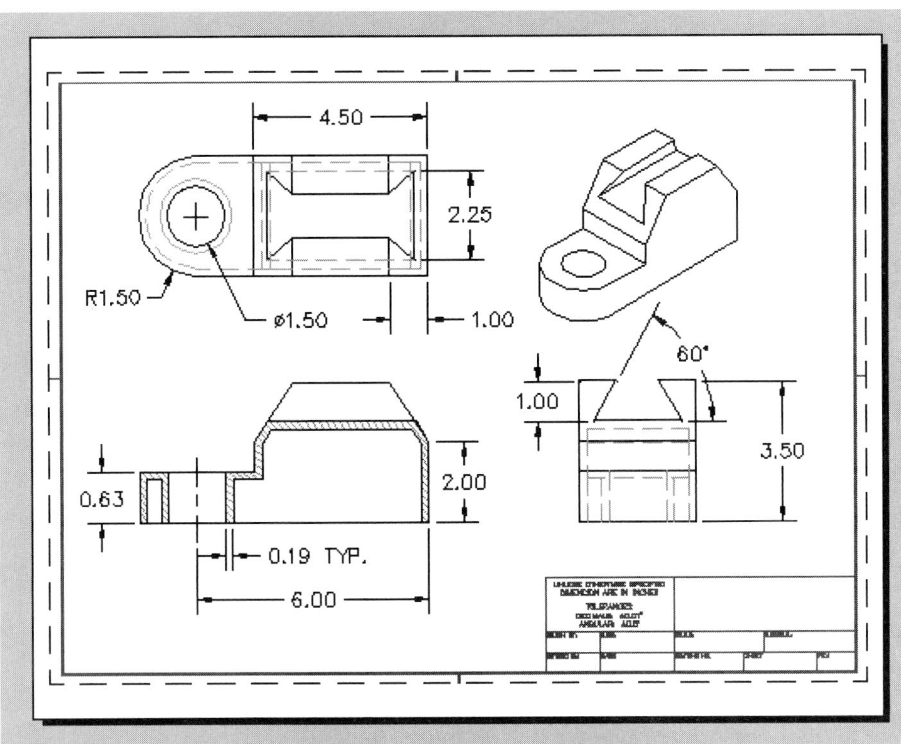

Figure 8-62 Dimensions placed in paper space

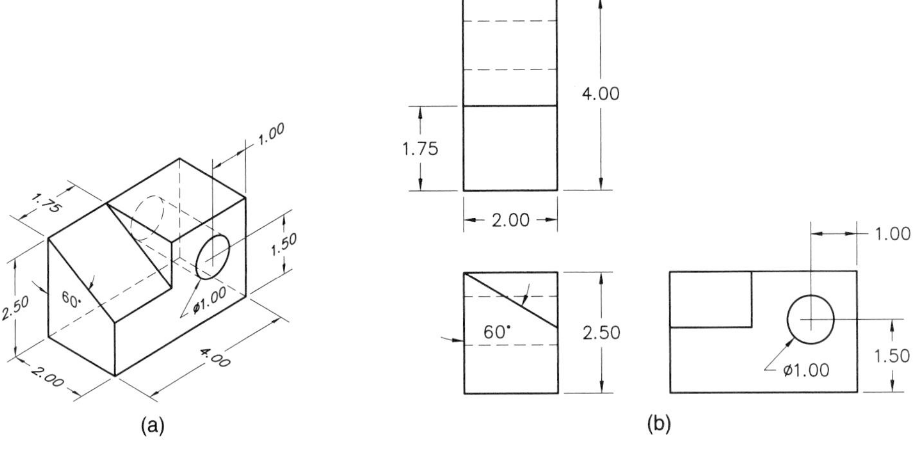

Figure 8-63 A dimensioned isometric view (a) can be used instead of the standard drawing views (b)

dimension appears to be completely contained in a plane. But from a nonorthographic viewing point, the dimension must be placed using the correct UCS to look right. Figure 8-64 shows the difference between placing a dimension in the 3D space using the incorrect and the correct UCS.

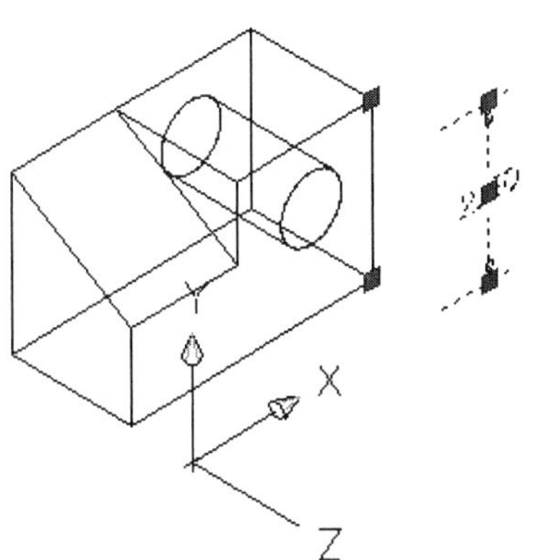

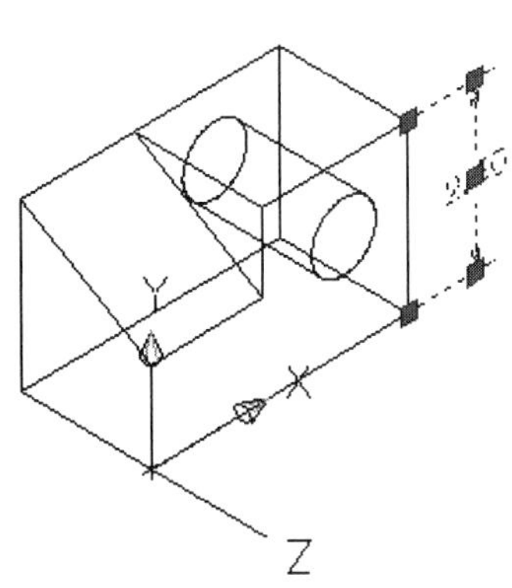

Figure 8-64 The UCS must be properly aligned before placing a dimension in the 3D space

Exercise 8-3: Placing Dimensions in the 3D Space and Setting up the Page in Paper Space

1. **OPEN** the file ***Exercise 8-3*** you saved in **Exercise 8-1** by creating a 3D section. You can also open this file from the CD in case you did not complete the exercise.
2. **SAVE** the drawing **AS *Exercise 8-3 solved***.
3. Select the **SE Isometric** viewing point.
4. Open the **Visual Styles Manager** palette. Select the **2D Wireframe** visual style by clicking on its sample image and make the following changes (Figure 8-65):
   - Set **Contour lines** to **0**
   - Set **Draw true silhouettes** to **Yes**
   - Set **Solid smoothness** to **8**
5. Close the **Visual Styles Manager** palette and invoke the **REGEN** command.
6. Set the UCS icon to show up at its origin, rather than at the lower-left corner of the display. You can do so by checking the **Origin** option in the **View** drop-down menu, as shown in Figure 8-66.

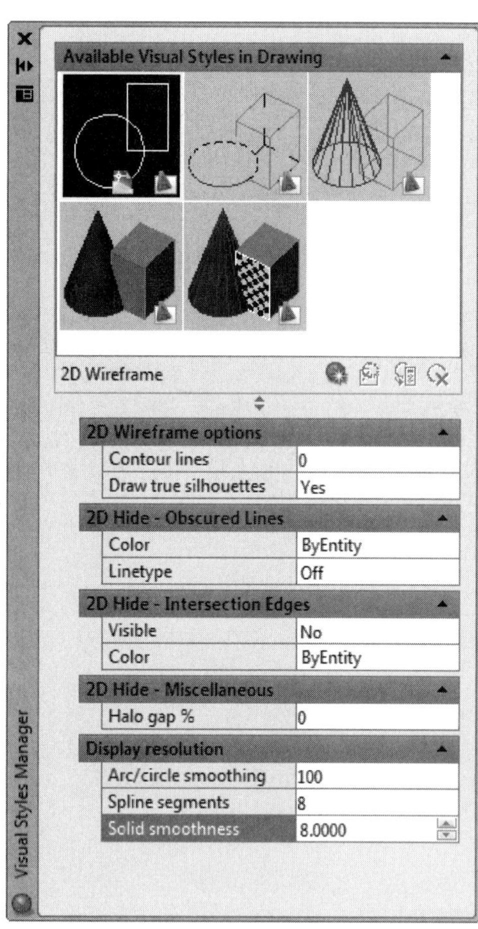

Figure 8-65 The Visual Styles Manager palette

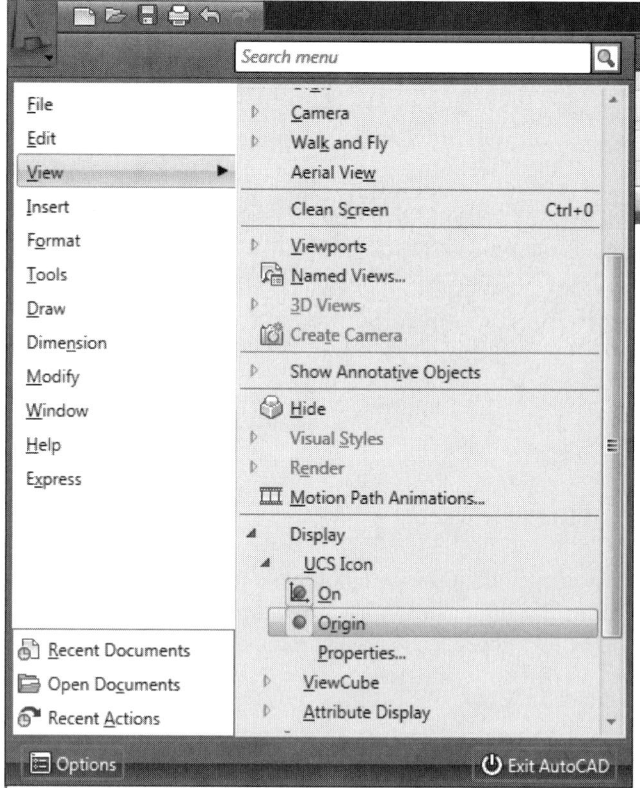

Figure 8-66 Accessing the UCS icon's Origin option from the View enhanced drop-down menu

7. Open the **Dimension Style Manager**. Click on the **Modify** button and set the **Precision** to two places in the **Primary Units** tab. Change other settings, such as the **Text Style** and **Colors**, to your liking. When finished, close the **Dimension Style Manager** dialog box.
8. Place the dimensions shown in Figure 8-67.

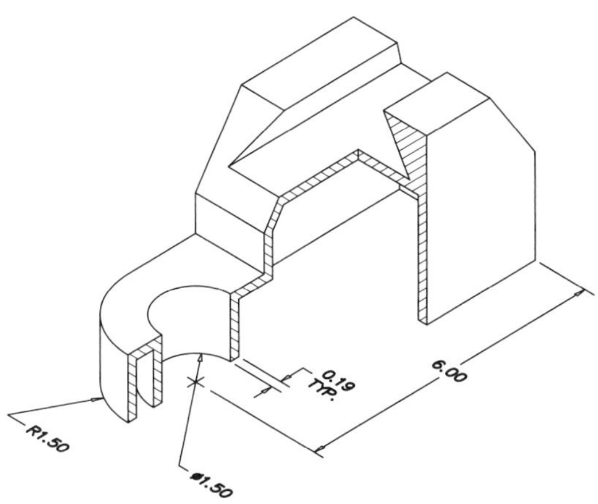

Figure 8-67 First dimensions placed

9. Select the **Right** UCS.
10. Place the UCS origin at the endpoint shown in Figure 8-68.
11. Place the dimensions shown in Figure 8-69.
12. Relocate the UCS origin to any point on the opposite face and place the dimensions shown in Figure 8-70.
13. Continue changing and relocating the UCS to place the rest of the dimensions. When you are finished, the dimensioned 3D section should look like Figure 8-71. Use the **3D Orbit** tool, if needed.

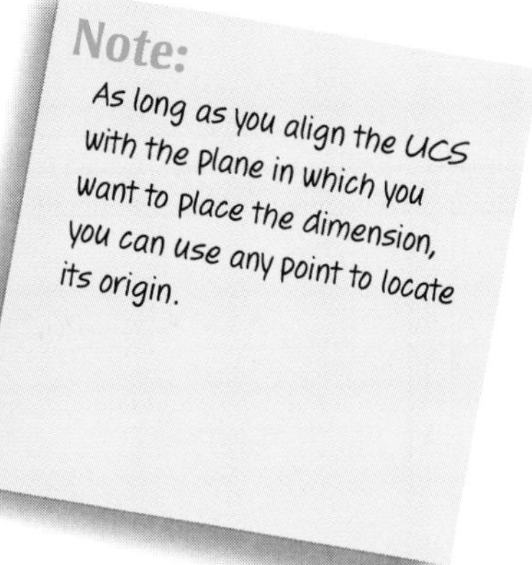

Note:
As long as you align the UCS with the plane in which you want to place the dimension, you can use any point to locate its origin.

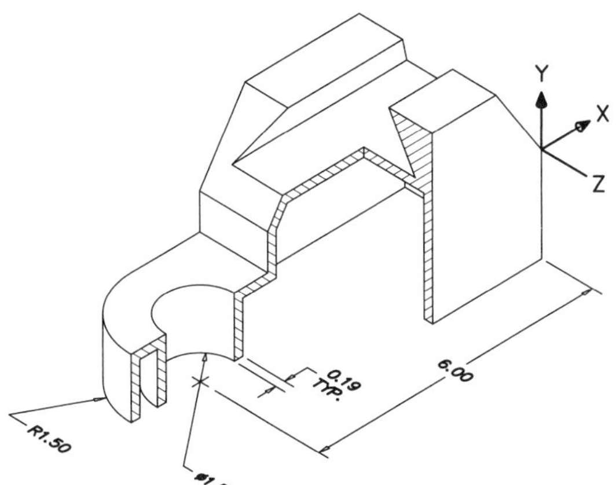

Figure 8-68 The UCS is relocated

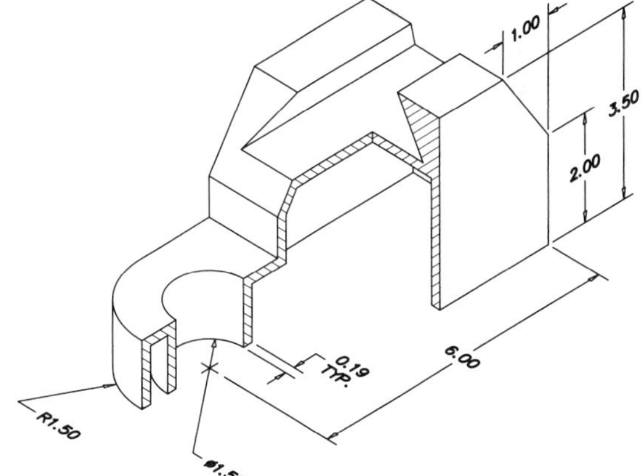

Figure 8-69 Other dimensions added in the new UCS

14. Click the **Layout1** tab to switch to paper space.
15. **OPEN** the file ***TB-Imperial*** from the CD. It contains a title block drawn in the layout (Figure 8-72).

16. Right-click in the drawing area and select **Copy** from the shortcut menu. This will invoke the **COPYCLIP** command. When prompted, select all the objects forming the title block by using a selection window. Press **<Enter>** to end the selection.
17. **CLOSE the *TB-Imperial*** drawing file.
18. Once you are back in ***Exercise 8-2***, right-click in the drawing area and select **Paste** from the shortcut menu. Specify a point that approximately centers the title block on the paper (Figure 8-73).
19. Right-click on top of the **Layout1** tab and select **Page Setup Manager . . . .**

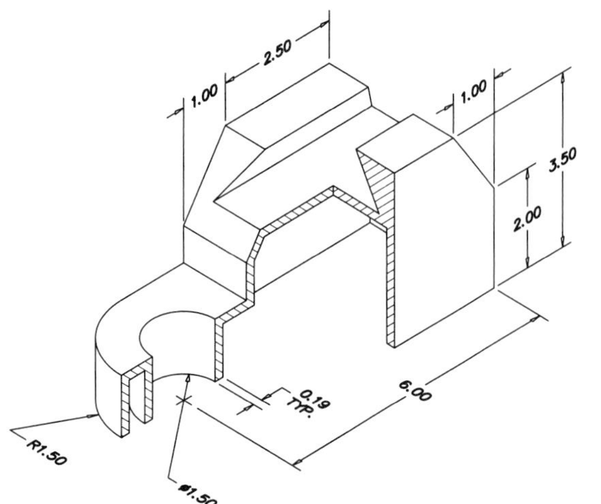

Figure 8-70 More dimensions added after changing the UCS

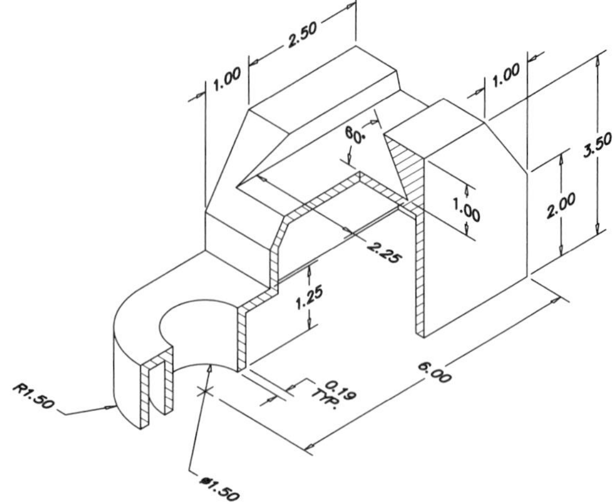

Figure 8-71 After placing all the dimensions

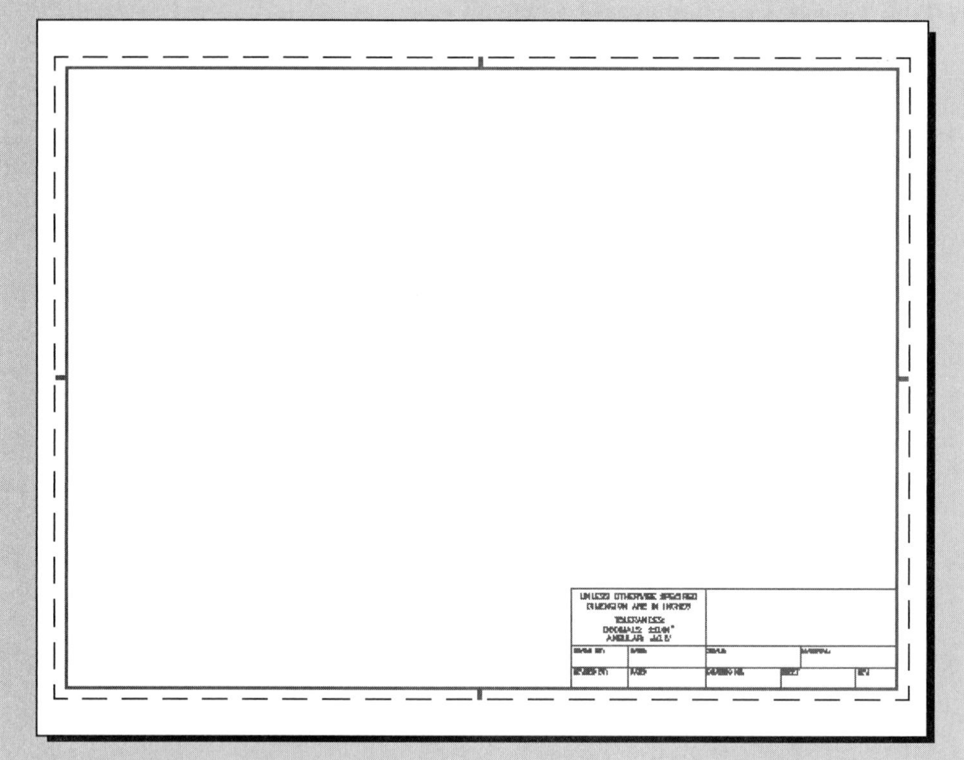

Figure 8-72 Title block contained in the drawing file

20. **Click on the Modify . . .** button to open the **Page Setup – Layout1** dialog box. Make the following changes:
    - Under **Printer/Plotter**, select your device.
    - Under **Plot style table**, select **monochrome.ctb**.
    - Under **Paper size**, select **Letter** or **8.50 × 11.00**.
    - Under **Drawing orientation**, select **Landscape**.
    - Under **Plot area**, select **Window**. When prompted to specify the first corner, select one of the corners in the main rectangle. Then select the diagonally opposite one.
    - Under **Plot offset**, check the **Center the plot** checkbox.
    - Make sure the **Scale** reads **1:1**. Click **OK** to close the **Page Setup – Layout1** dialog box.
21. Close the **Page Setup Manager** dialog box. The title block should now be perfectly centered on the paper (Figure 8-74).

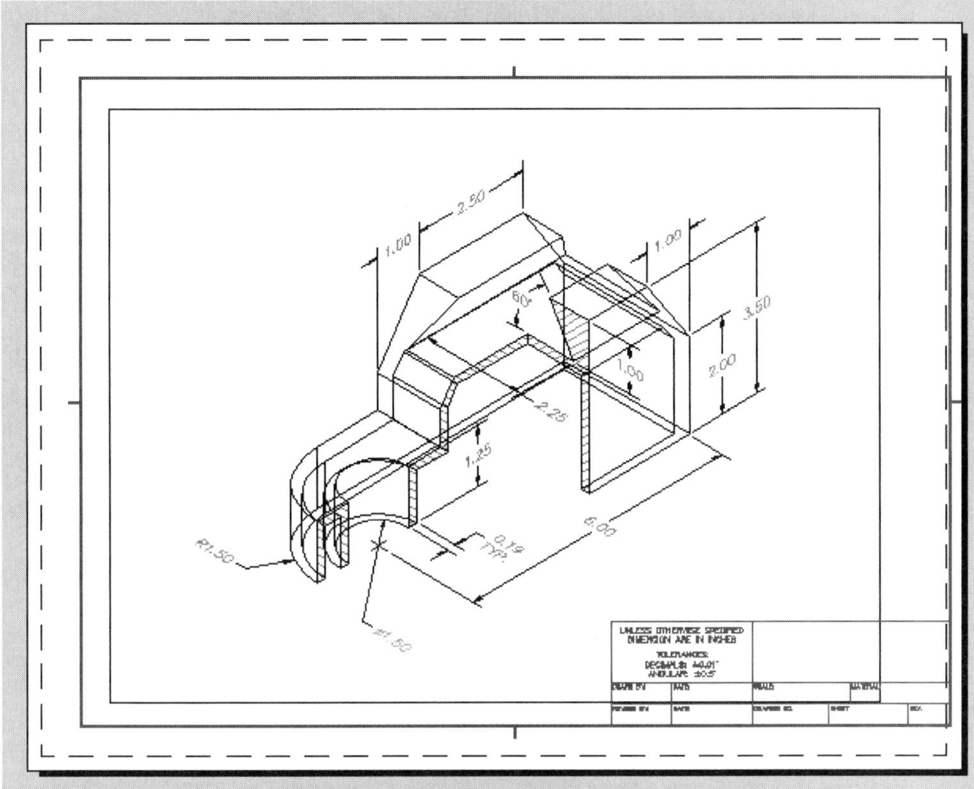

Figure 8-73 Title block pasted into Layout1

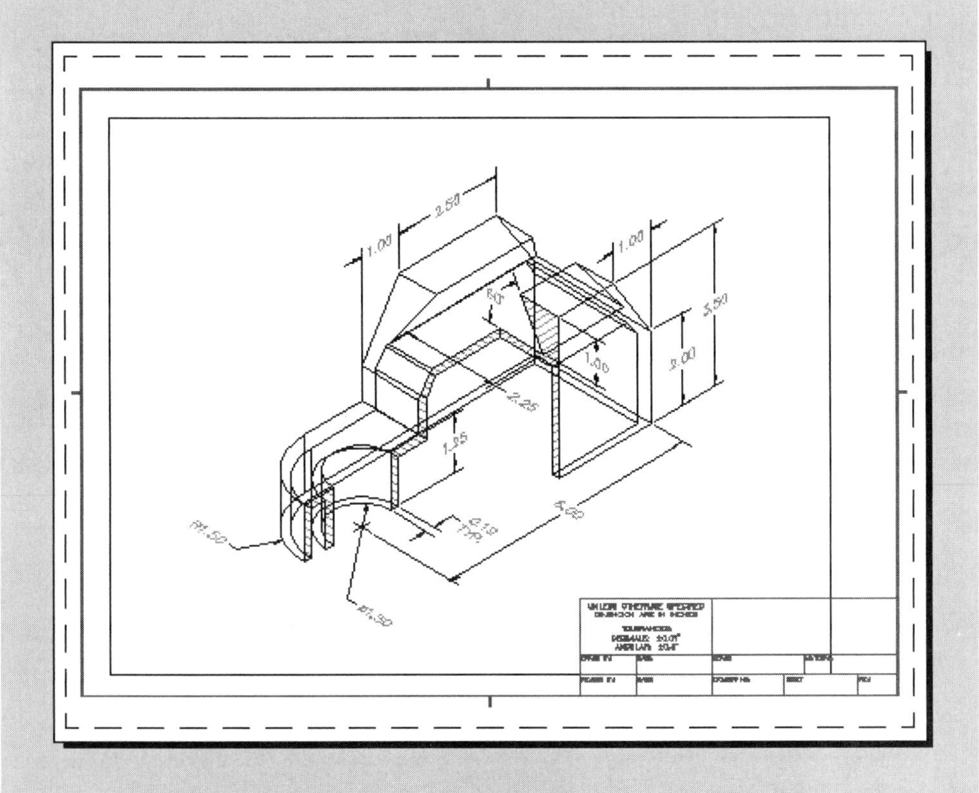

Figure 8-74 The title block is perfectly centered on the paper

PREVIEW	
Standard Toolbar	
Pull-down Menu	File/Plot Preview
Command Line	preview

22. Open the **Layer Properties Manager** and create a new layer named *VIEWPORT.* Change its color to **Green**, and click on its **Plotter** icon to prevent it from being plotted. Click **OK** to close the **Layer Properties Manager** dialog box.
23. Apply the *VIEWPORT* layer to the viewport.
24. Double-click inside the viewport to make it active. **ZOOM** and **PAN** with the mouse wheel to set the isometric view to a proper size and location.
25. Double-click outside the viewport to deactivate it.
26. Select the viewport and right-click to display the shortcut menu. Set **Display Locked** to **Yes** and **Shade plot** to **Hidden**.
27. Invoke the **PREVIEW** command. It should look like Figure 8-75.
28. **PLOT** the drawing and then **SAVE** it.

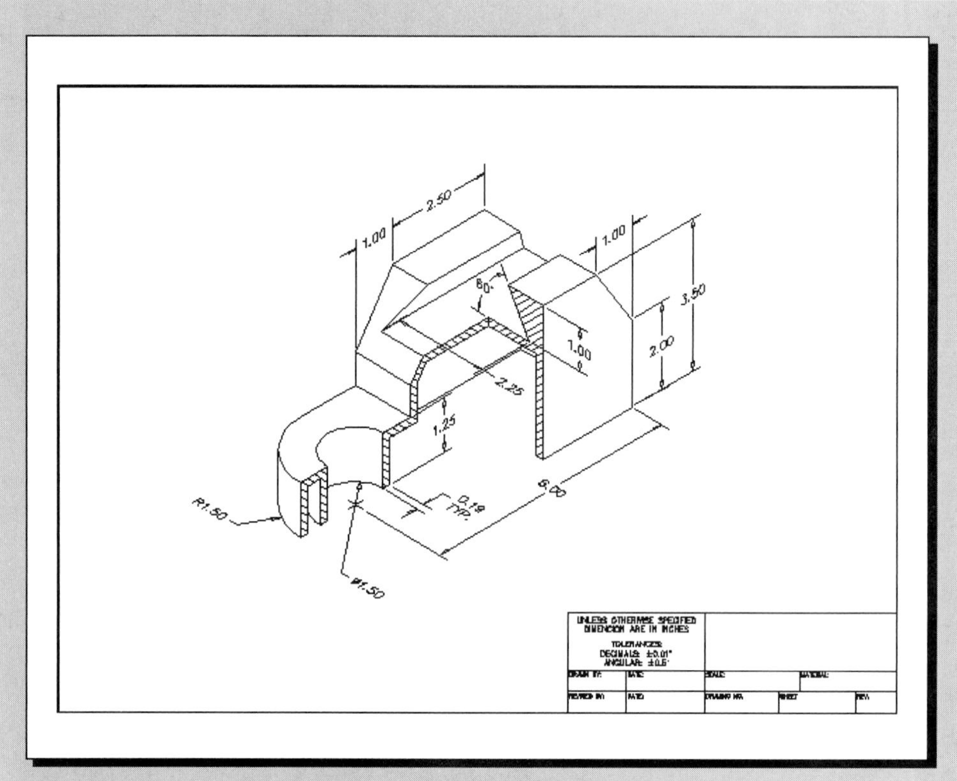

Figure 8-75 The plot preview

EXPLODED ASSEMBLY DRAWINGS

Exploded 3D isometric views are commonly used for assembly instruction, product presentation, and many other purposes. They not only clearly demonstrate how to put the parts together but also provide a professional way to present a product design.

The AutoCAD program does not possess any special tools to produce assemblies or exploded views. To create exploded views, simply space the 3D objects that form the assembly out in strategic directions and then place centerlines to show the assembling traces.

Exercise 8-4: Creating Exploded Drawing Views

1. **OPEN** the drawing ***Exercise 8-4*** from the CD. It contains the assembly of several 3D solids.
2. **SAVE** the drawing **AS *Exercise 8-4 solved*.**
3. Select the view named **Exploded View** from the drop-down list located in the **View** panel of the **Ribbon** (Figure 8-76).
4. Invoke the **HIDE** command. The 3D model should look like Figure 8-77.

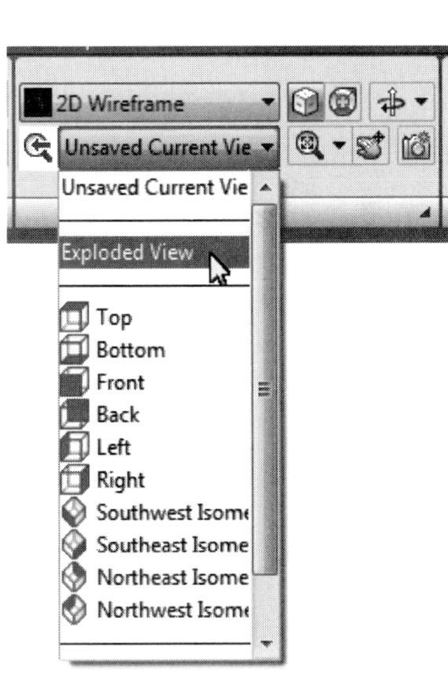

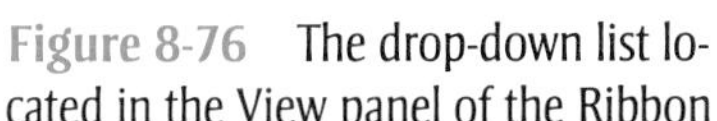

Figure 8-76 The drop-down list located in the View panel of the Ribbon

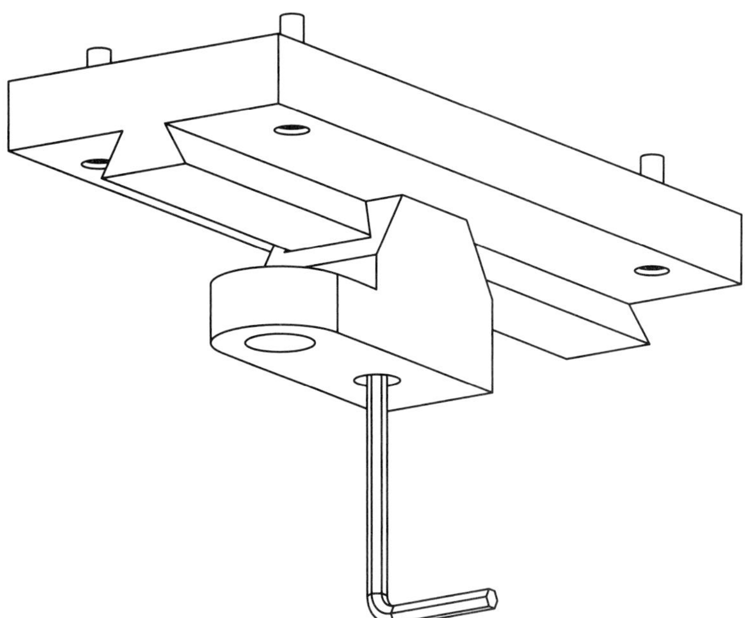

Figure 8-77 Assembly contained in the drawing file

5. Invoke the **REGEN** command. Select the **Front** UCS.
6. **MOVE** the wrench and the set screw orthogonally down **4″**.
7. **MOVE** the wrench orthogonally down **2″**.
8. Invoke the **HIDE** command. The 3D model should look like Figure 8-78.
9. **MOVE** the wrench, the set screw, and the bracket **20″** along the positive *X*-axis.
10. **MOVE** the four socket head screws **6.5″** along the negative *Y*-axis. The 3D model should look like Figure 8-79.

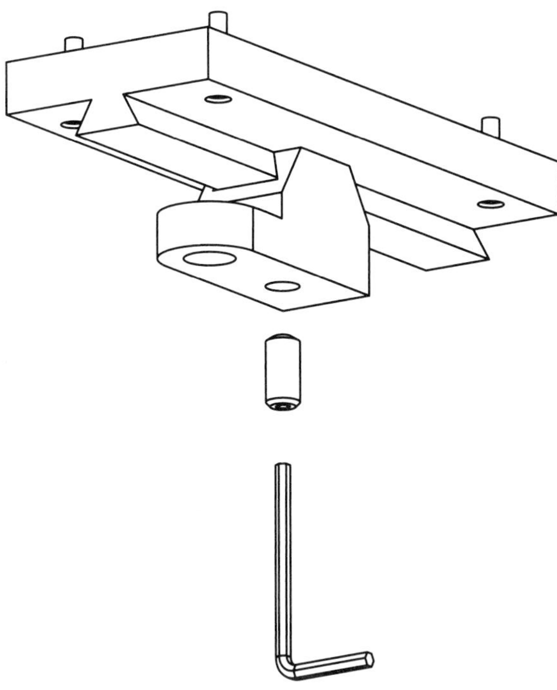

Figure 8-78 The wrench is moved orthogonally down

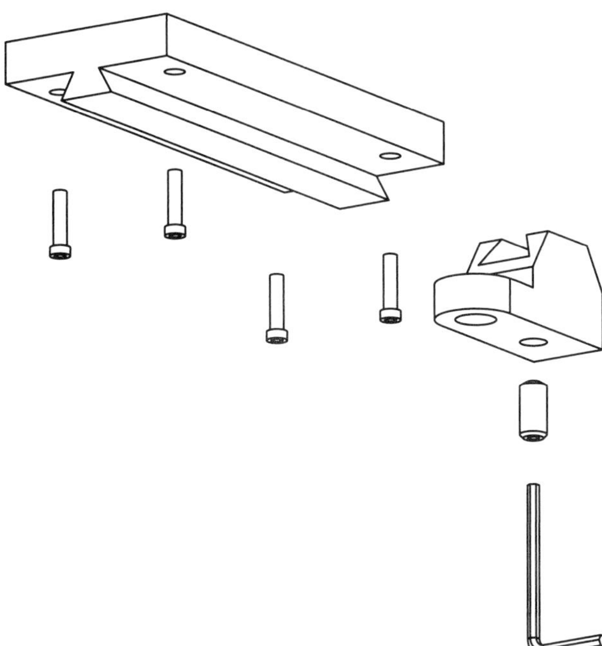

Figure 8-79 The four socket screws are moved orthogonally down

11. First, load the **Center** linetype into the drawing and then set it current in the drop-down list on the **Properties** toolbar. The next object created will have this property.
12. Draw all the highlighted polylines shown in Figure 8-80. Snap to center points to locate all the polylines properly. For the polyline that shows the dovetail connection, just draw a short line going from the midpoint of the bottom edge in the direction of the *X*-axis.

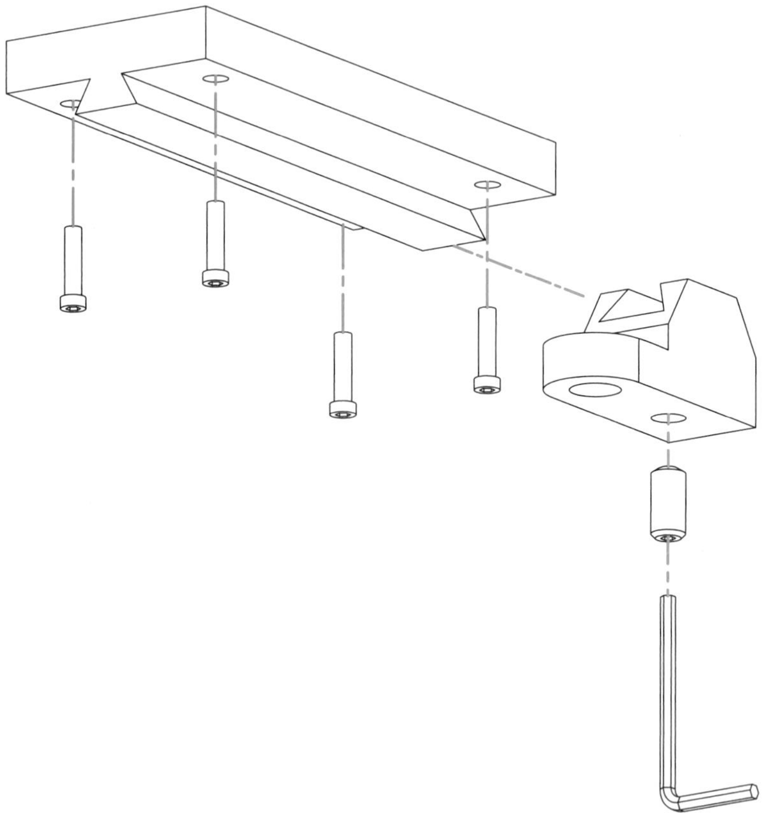

Figure 8-80 After placing the assembly trails.

13. Click the **Layout1** tab to switch to paper space. It contains the same title block as in the previous exercise.
14. Double-click inside the viewport to make it active.
15. Select the view named **Exploded View** from the drop-down list located in the **View** toolbar, as you did in step 3.
16. **ZOOM** and **PAN** with the mouse wheel to set the view to the proper size.
17. Double-click outside the viewport to deactivate it.
18. Select the viewport and right-click to display the shortcut menu. Set **Display Locked** to **Yes.** Display the shortcut menu again and set the **Shade plot** to **Hidden**.
19. Invoke the **PREVIEW** command. The result should look like Figure 8-81.
20. **PLOT** the drawing and then **SAVE** it.

3D exploded assembly drawings are very important technical documents. They constitute a strong bridge for communicating special instructions in the fabrication process. Products that require end-user assembly are better accepted when you provide quality exploded assembly drawings to accompany them. Whether you use these techniques in your current job position or in your own business, perfecting this skill will enable you to provide technical documents with a higher level of professionalism.

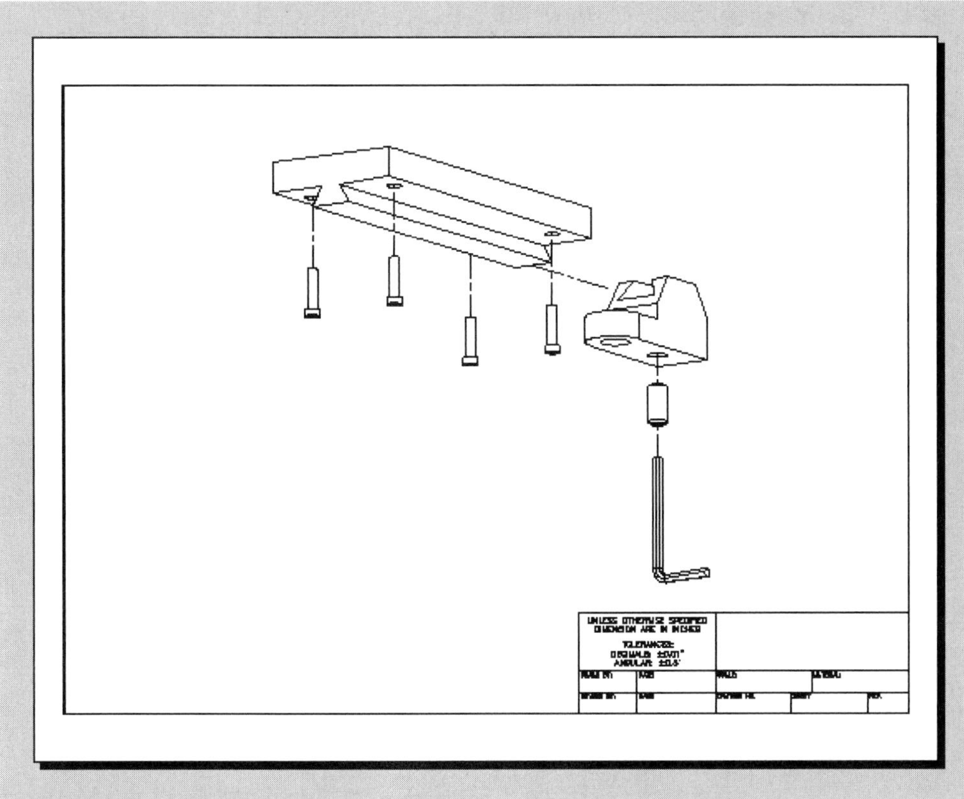

Figure 8-81 The plot preview

CREATING DRAWING VIEWS IN PAPER SPACE

CREATING VIEWS IN PAPER SPACE WITH THE SOLPROF COMMAND–

The **SOLPROF** command enables you to extract the profile (edges and silhouettes) of the 3D solids you select, according to the viewing point on the viewport. This command can be invoked only from paper space and requires you to select the 3D solids through an active viewport.

This command generates either one or two anonymous blocks (blocks that cannot be inserted or edited).

By answering **Yes** or **No** to the command's prompts, you can alter three different aspects of the results:

1. You can create a single block or create separate blocks for the visible lines and the hidden or occulted lines. This option also creates either a single layer or two layers, one for each block.
2. You can create blocks that contain the profile projected onto a plane that is parallel to the current viewing plane and goes though the origin, or you can extract the edges and create blocks as 3D wireframes.
3. You may choose to include the tangential edges in the blocks or not.

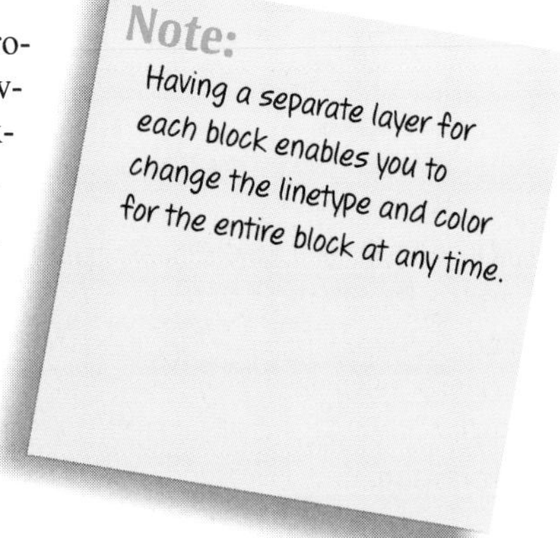

Note:
Having a separate layer for each block enables you to change the linetype and color for the entire block at any time.

For example, responding **Yes** to these three questions creates two projected blocks without including the tangential edges: one for the visible edges and silhouettes, and another one for the occulted edges and silhouettes. Each block will have its own layer assigned to it.

Exercise 8-5: Generating the Drawing Views in Paper Space Using the SOLPROF Command

1. **OPEN** either ***Exercise 5-8*** or ***Exercise 5-10*** as completed in Chapter 5.
2. **SAVE** it **AS** ***Exercise 8-5***.
3. Select the **SW Isometric** viewpoint.
4. Select the **World** UCS.
5. Make sure all the checkboxes concerning **Layout elements** in the **Display** tab of the **Options** dialog box are checked (Figure 8-82). Click **OK** to close the dialog box.
6. Click on the **Layout1** tab. Click the **Close** button to close the **Page Setup Manager** dialog box. The paper should be displayed with a single viewport that shows the current view in the model space (Figure 8-83).
7. **ERASE** the viewport. Without the viewport, you will see only an empty paper.
8. Invoke the **VPORTS** command to open the **Viewports** dialog box (Figure 8-84). In the **New Viewports** tab, select **Four: Equal** from the list. Select **3D** under **Setup**, and specify a value of **0.5** for the **Viewport Spacing**. Click **OK** to close the dialog box. When prompted for the first and opposite corners, click two points diagonally where the four viewports can fit. When you are finished, the layout should look like Figure 8-85.
9. Double-click inside the viewport located on the top left. It becomes activated as shown in Figure 8-86.
10. Locate the **Viewport** toolbar (Figure 8-87). The scale drop-down list of the **Viewport** toolbar shows the actual scale factor for the current active viewport.
11. Click on the drop-down list arrow and select the scale **1:2** (Figure 8-88).
12. Click inside any other viewport to make it active and change its scale factor to the **1:2** scale. Repeat the same procedure for the two other viewports containing orthographic

Note: The **Page Setup** dialog box is automatically opened the first time you enter a layout whenever the **Show Page Setup Manager for new layouts** option is enabled.

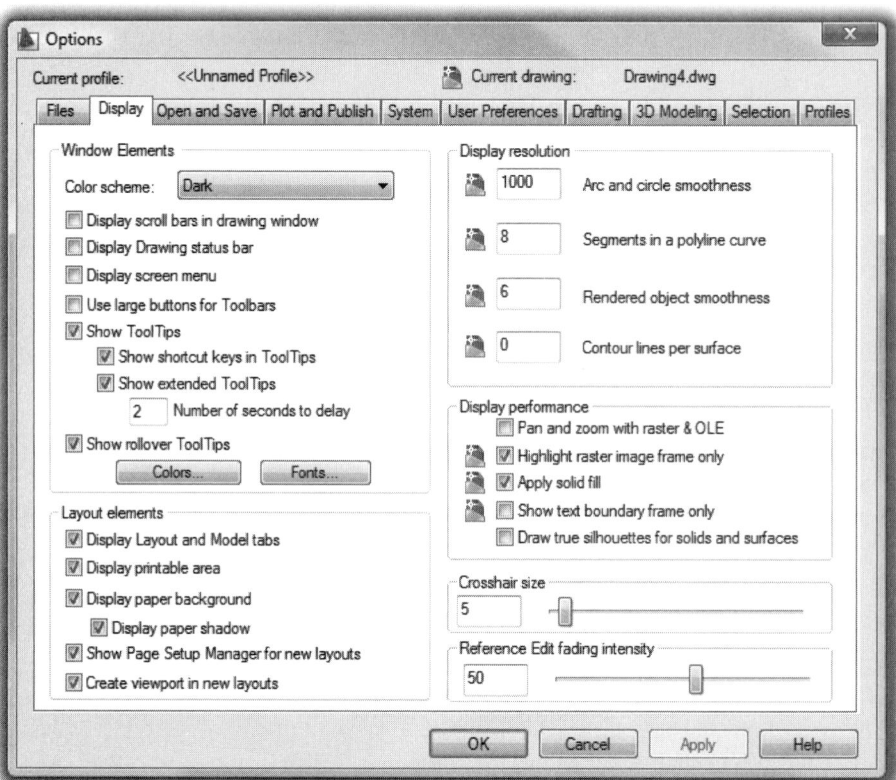

Figure 8-82 Layout elements settings located in the Display tab of the Options dialog box

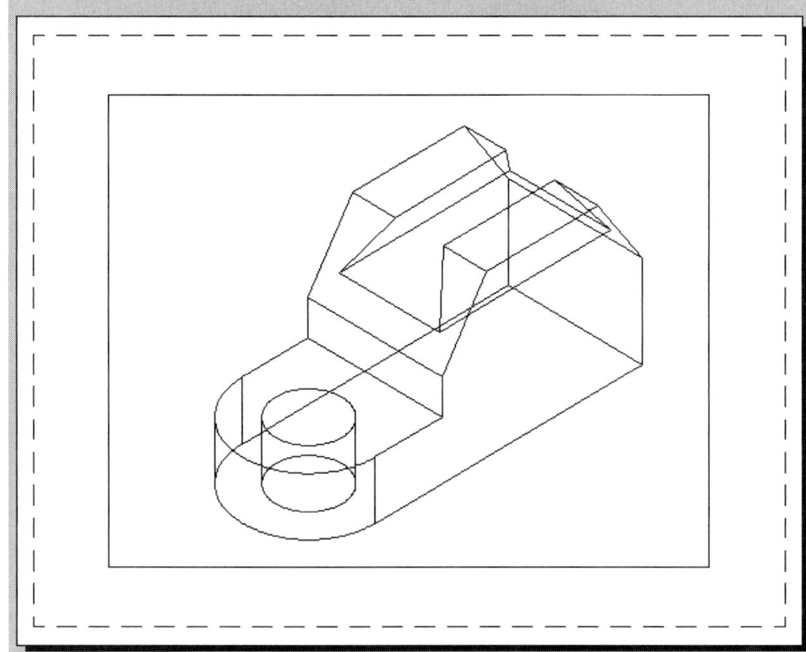

Figure 8-83 Default viewport when entering a layout

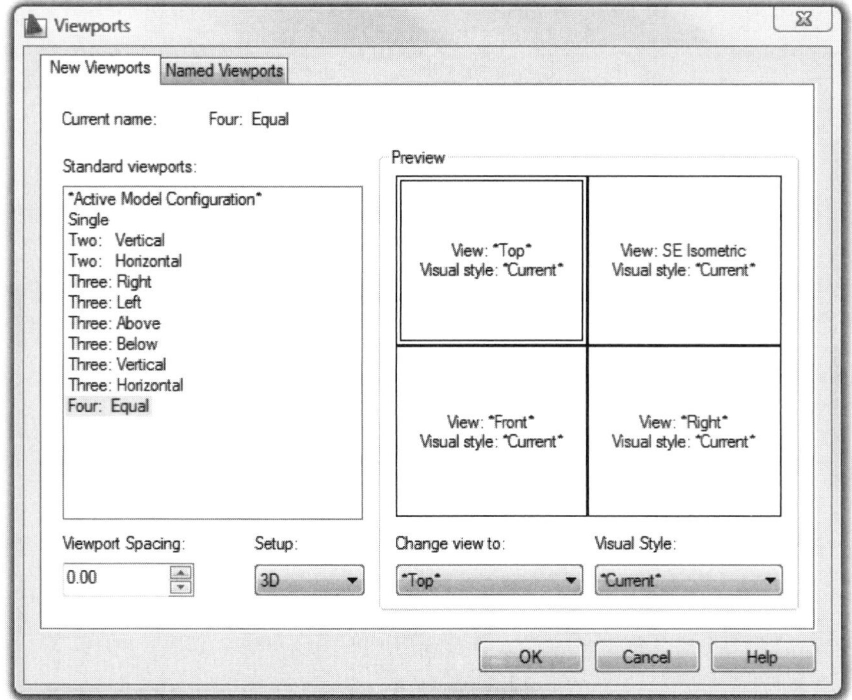

Figure 8-84 The Viewports dialog box

views. If needed, **PAN** the view inside the viewport containing the isometric view to show it entirely.

13. When you are finished, double-click on any area outside the viewports or click the **MODEL** button in the status bar. The scaled viewports should look like Figure 8-89.

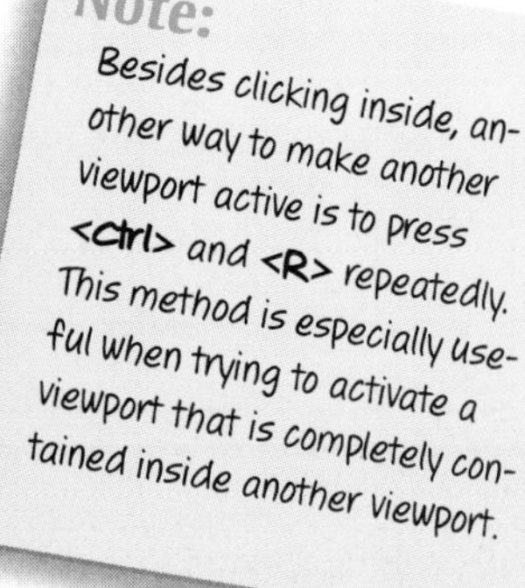

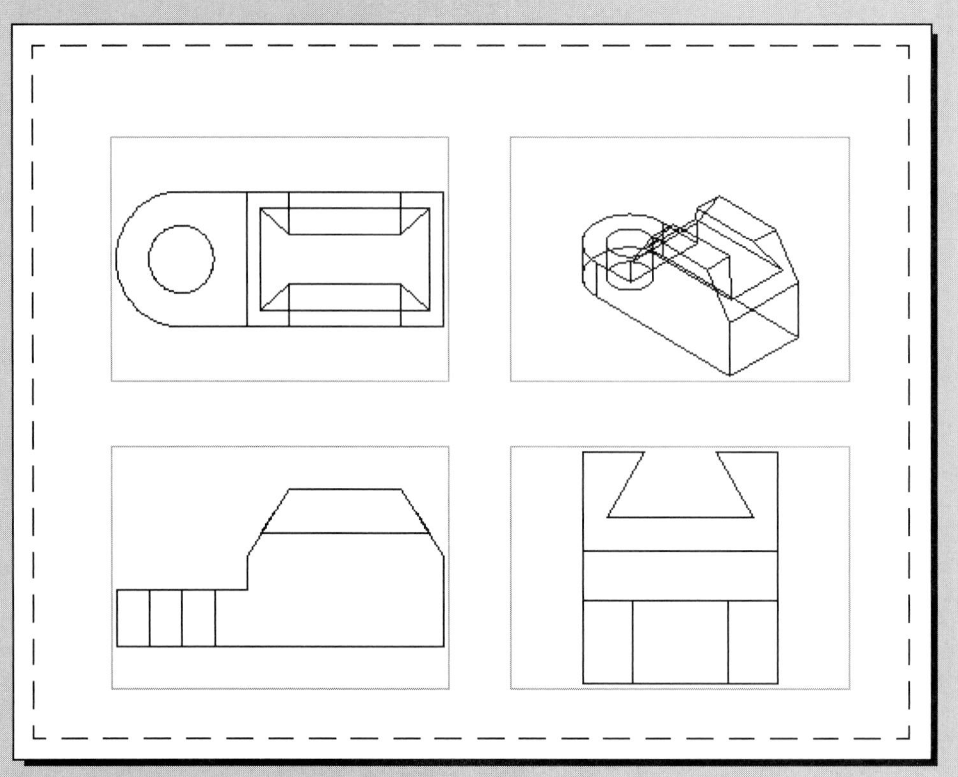

Figure 8-85 The resulting viewport arrangement

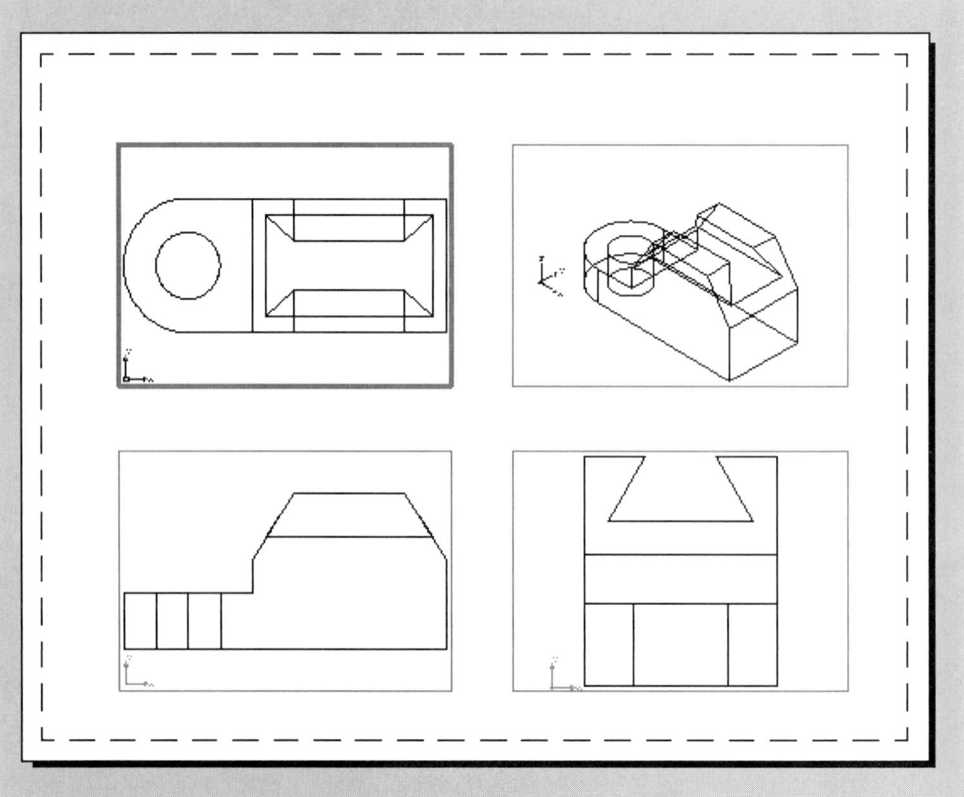

Figure 8-86 The top-left viewport is activated

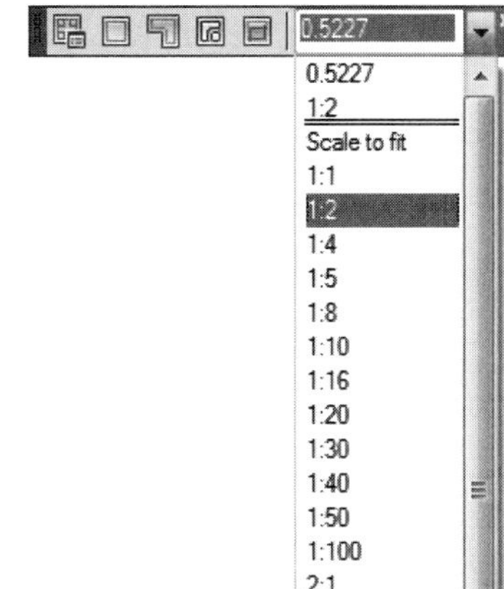

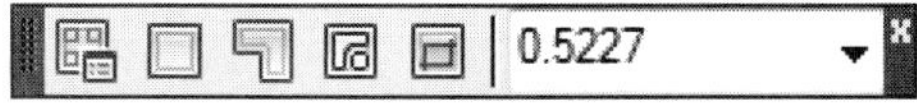

Figure 8-87 The Viewports toolbar

Figure 8-88 The scale drop-down list in the Viewports toolbar

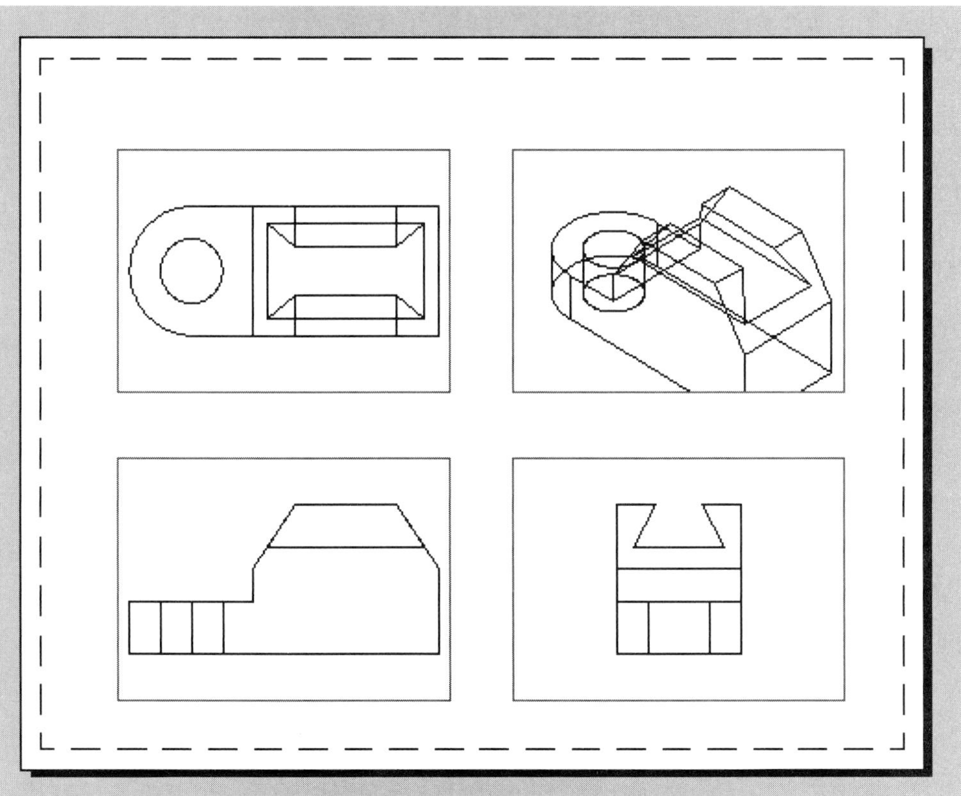

Figure 8-89 After setting the scale of the viewports

Depending on the size of the viewport, the 3D solid may or may not fit inside it. If the 3D solid does not fit, you can select the viewport object by clicking on it, and stretch it by grabbing its grips. This operation will not change the scale factor.

14. Double-click again inside the viewport that contains the **SE Isometric** view to make it active. Select the **SW Isometric** view. The view updates to the new viewing point (Figure 8-90).

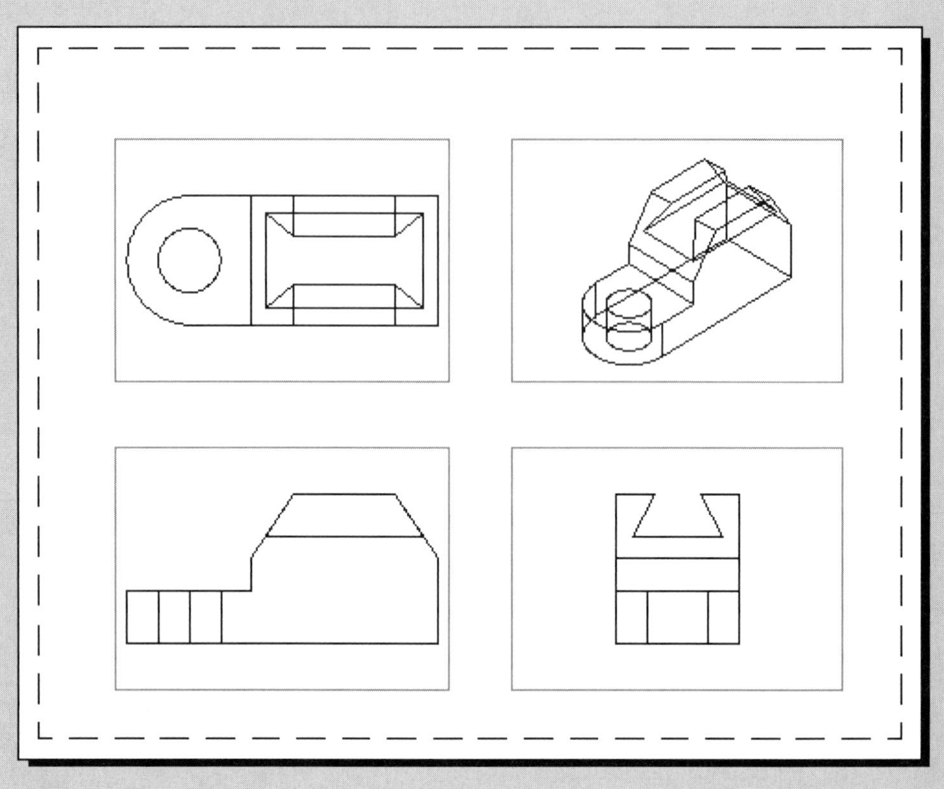

Figure 8-90 Changing the viewing point through a viewport

15. Double-click outside the viewports to deactivate any one that is active. Select the four viewports and right-click to show the shortcut menu. Select **Yes** for the **Display Locked** option.
16. **Double-click** inside the top-left viewport to activate it.
17. Invoke the **SOLPROF** command and respond to the prompts as follows:

    Select objects: *Select the 3D solid through the active viewport.*

    Select objects: ↵ *(To end the selection)*

    Display hidden profile lines on separate layer? [Yes/No] <Y>: ↵ *(To accept the default)*

    Project profile lines onto a plane? [Yes/No] <Y>: ↵ *(To accept the default)*

    Delete tangential edges? [Yes/No] <Y>: ↵ *(To accept the default)*
18. Activate one by one the three remaining viewports, except the one containing the isometric view, and invoke the **SOLPROF** command to create the projected profiles. Respond **Yes** to all the prompts for each viewport.
19. Double-click outside the viewports to deactivate any one that is activated.

Note:

When you create several viewports using one of the viewport configurations, the views are automatically aligned with each other. Such alignment, however, can be noticed only between viewports whose views are related, and whose scale factor is the same. For example, if you create two viewports using the **Two: Horizontal** configuration, and you show the Top and Front views on the viewports, the views should end up aligned after selecting the same scale.

This advantageous characteristic can save you the time required to align the views manually. You can lose this alignment, however, by performing operations that displace the center of the view, such as **PAN**, **ZOOM WINDOW**, or using the mouse wheel while a viewport is active.

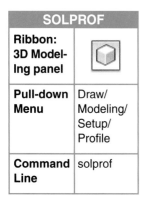

SOLPROF	
Ribbon: 3D Modeling panel	
Pull-down Menu	Draw/ Modeling/ Setup/ Profile
Command Line	solprof

20. Switch to model space by clicking on the **Model** tab.
21. Switch back to paper space by clicking on the **Layout1** tab.
22. Invoke the **VPMAX** command by double-clicking on the bottom-left viewport's border.
23. Invoke the **3DORBIT** command and rotate the viewpoint (Figure 8-91).
24. Right-click and select **Minimize Viewport** to go back to **Layout1**.
25. Load the **HIDDEN** linetype into the drawing.
26. Open the **Layer Properties Manager** dialog box. Create two new layers named *Viewport* and *3DSolid*.
27. Select all the **PH-** layers. Change their linetype to **HIDDEN**. Give these layers a color different from that of the **PV-** layers. See Figure 8-92 as a guide. Click **OK** to close the **Layer Properties Manager** dialog box.

Note:
Any modification you perform in the model space will be shown through the viewports. There are three ways to access the model space.
1. Click the **Model** tab to go back into the model space.
2. Through an active viewport, you can use the **3D Orbit** tool and do any modification. This is not recommended, however, because all the settings regarding scale as well as the alignment will be lost, regardless of whether or not the viewport is locked.
3. Maximize a viewport.

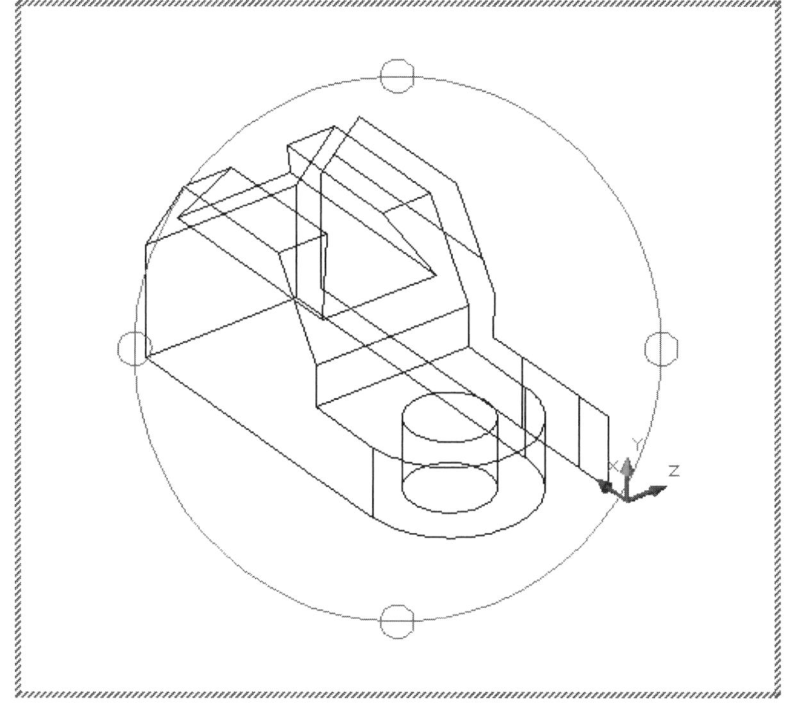

Figure 8-91 Using the 3D Orbit tool through a maximized viewport

Note:
In model space, you will see the different projected blocks created through each viewport for the selected 3D solid.

Note:
The advantage of using the maximized viewing mode is that you will see only the layers that are thawed in this particular viewport. In addition, the scale and alignment of the viewport remain unchanged.

TIP
The **HIDDEN** linetype can be loaded directly from the **Layers Properties Manager** window.

28. Maximize the viewport that shows the Top view.
29. Invoke the **3DORBIT** command to change the viewing point.
30. Assign the *3DSolid* layer to the 3D solid object. In the drop-down **Layer Control** window located in the **Layers** panel of the **Ribbon**, **Freeze** the *3DSolid* layer for the current viewport (third icon) (Figure 8-93). Click **OK** to close the warning.

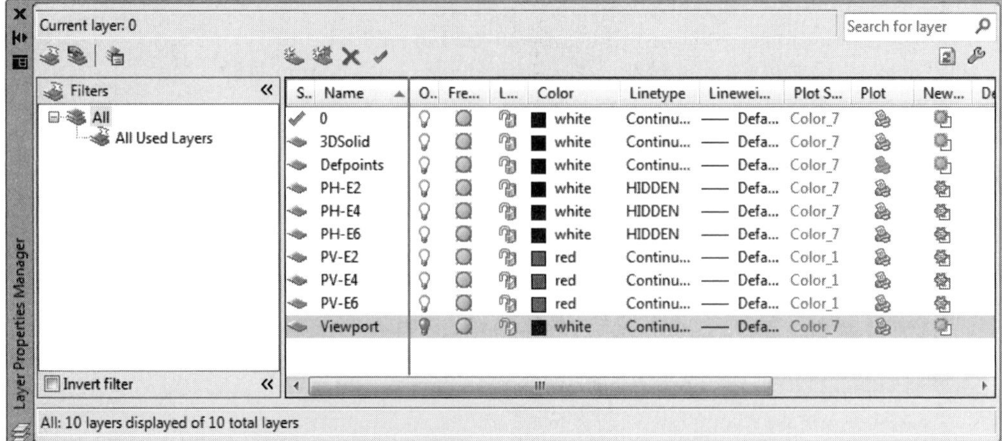

Figure 8-92 List of layers contained in the Layer Properties Manager dialog box

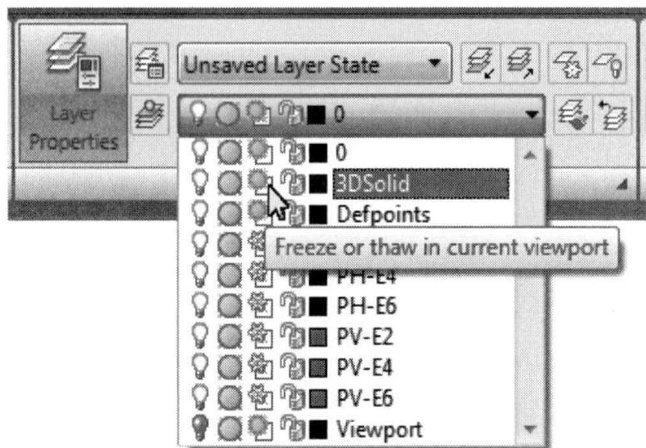

Figure 8-93 The Layer Control drop-down list located on the Layers panel of the Ribbon

31. Right-click and select **Minimize Viewport** to go back to **Layout1.**
32. Activate one by one the viewports containing the Front and Right views to **Freeze** the *3DSolid* layer in each one. After deactivating the last active viewport, the 2D drawing should look like Figure 8-94.
33. Set the **LTSCALE** system variable to **0.5**.
34. Select the viewport that contains the isometric view. Right-click in the drawing area to display the shortcut menu and set **Shade plot** to **Hidden**.
35. Select the four viewports and change their layer to the *Viewport* layer.
36. **MOVE** all the viewports up to make some room for a title block.

Note:

The six new layers that start with **PV-** and **PH-** have been created automatically. They separate the visible and hidden projected blocks for each viewport. The digits following the dash stand for the viewport's handle ID, which can be obtained by invoking the **LIST** command after selecting the specific viewport.

At this point, if you need to **MOVE** the viewports around, you should move two at a time in an orthogonal direction to avoid losing the alignment between the views.

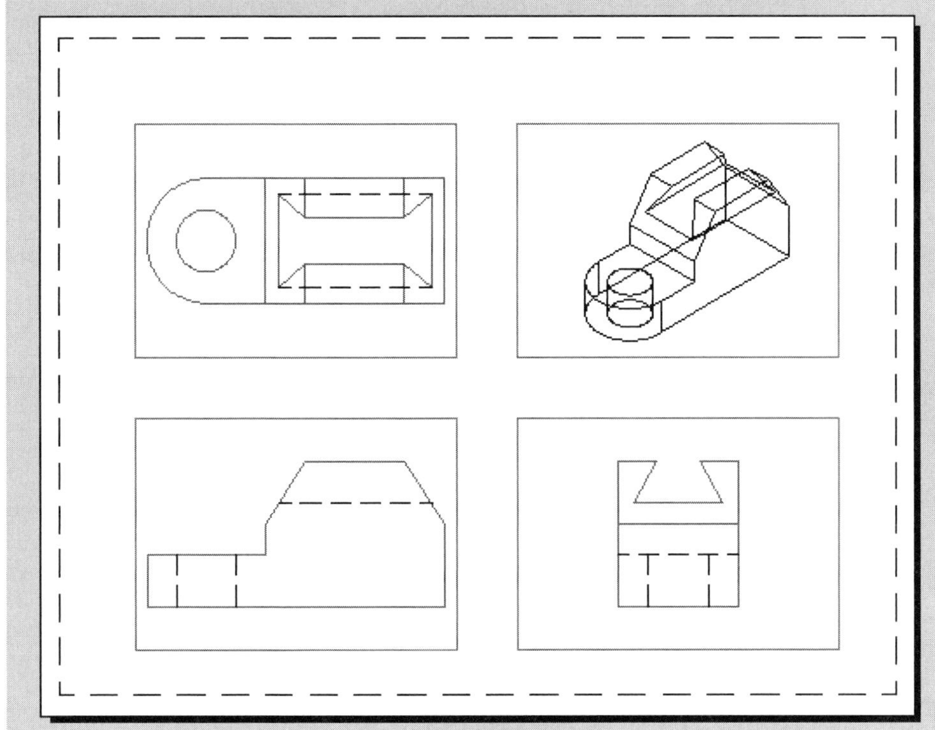

Figure 8-94 The viewports showing the projected objects

37. In the **Layer control** drop-down window, turn the *Viewport* layer off. The drawing should look like Figure 8-95.
38. This time you will create a simple title block yourself. Draw the objects shown in Figure 8-96 anywhere in the gray area to represent the title block.

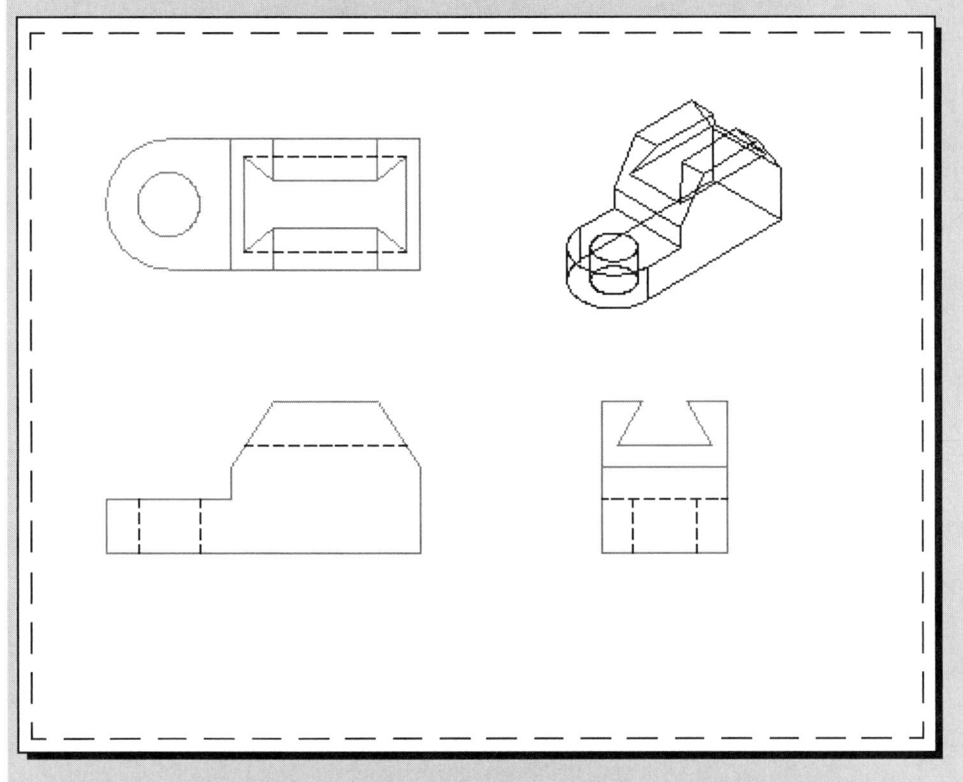

Figure 8-95 After turning the Viewport layer off

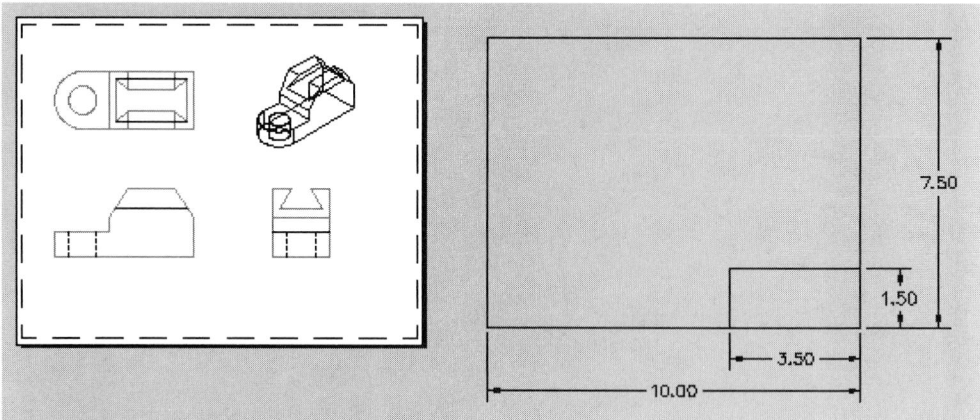

Figure 8-96 A representative title block created in paper space

39. With **ORTHO** mode off, **MOVE** the title block into the drawing sheet so that all the drawing views fit well inside it. Do not be concerned about centering the title block with the paper, but rather center it with the drawing views (Figure 8-97).

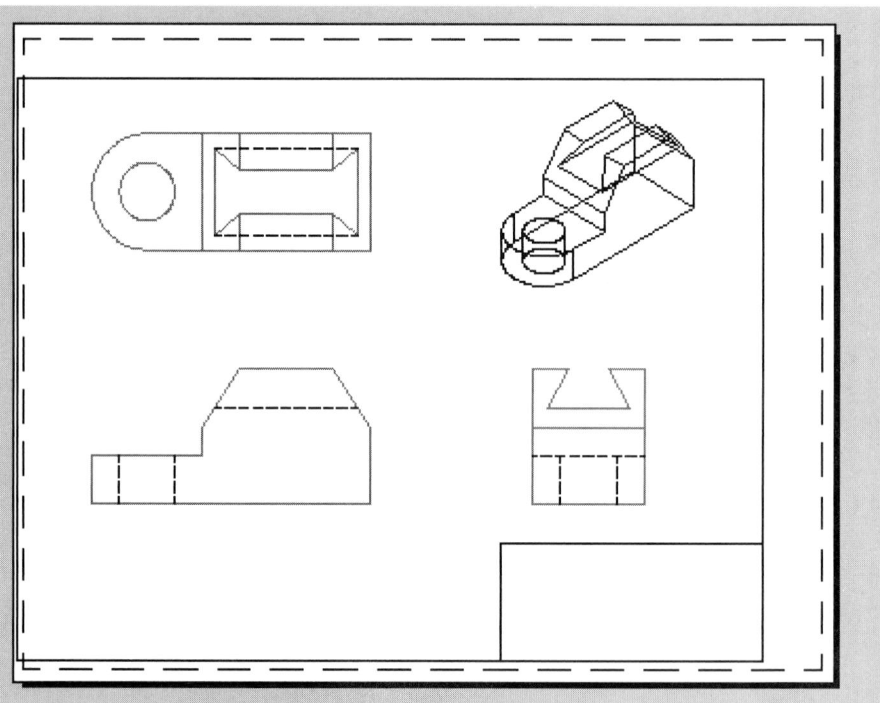

Figure 8-97 The title block moved to the paper area

40. Point to the **Layout1** tab and right-click on it. Select **Page Setup Manager. . . .** On the **Page Setup Manager** dialog box, select ***Layout1*** and click the **Modify . . .** button.
    - Under **Printer/Plotter**, select your printing device, or any virtual printer if you do not have one installed.
    - Select **monochrome.ctb** from the **Plot Style table** drop-down list.
    - Select **8.5 × 11″** or **Letter** for **Paper size**.
    - Select **Landscape** for **Drawing orientation**.
    - Select **1:1** for **Plot scale**
    - Under the plot area, select the **Window** button and specify the two diagonal corners on the border of the title block by snapping to its endpoints. When you return to the dialog box, check the **Center the plot** box (Figure 8-98).
    - Click **OK** to close the **Page Setup** dialog box. Close the **Page Setup Manager** dialog box. The drawing should look like Figure 8-99.

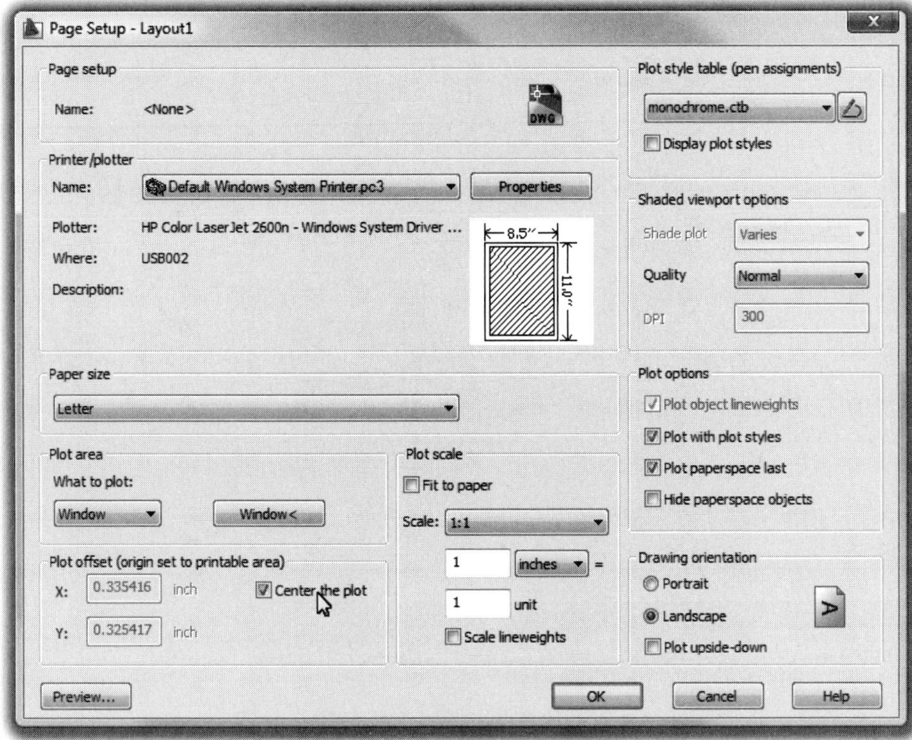

Figure 8-98 The Page Setup dialog box

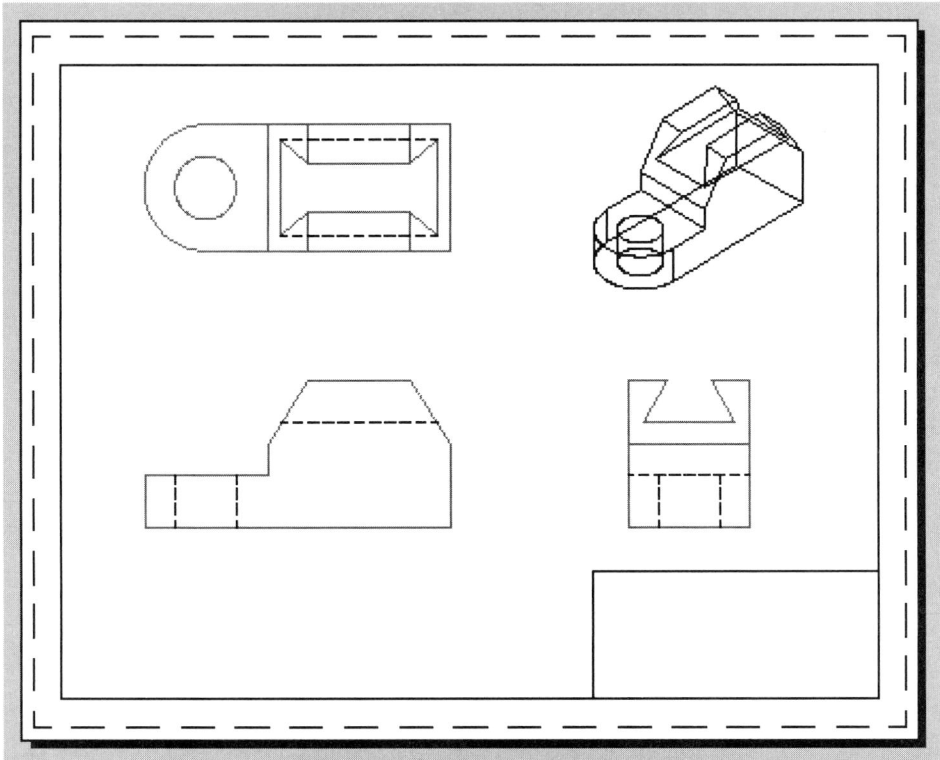

Figure 8-99 After centering the title block in the paper area

41. Place dimensions and centerlines. Figure 8-100 shows the **Plot Preview** that appears just before you send the plot to the printer.
42. **SAVE** the drawing.

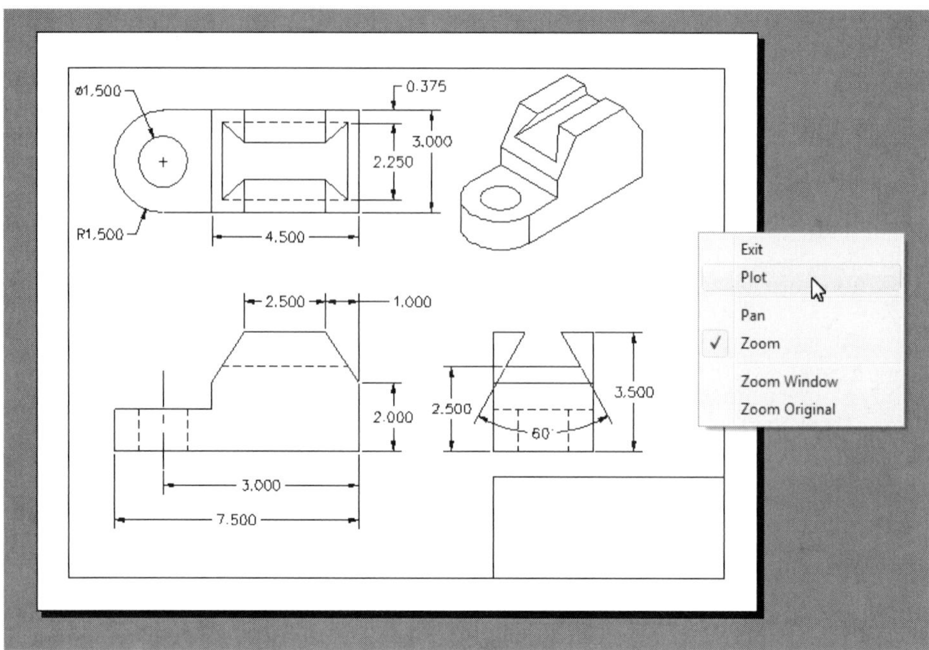

Figure 8-100 The plot preview after placing the dimensions

Creating Views and Sections with the SOLVIEW and SOLDRAW Commands

The AutoCAD program provides many tools to generate drawing views in both paper space and model space. These tools can be combined to accomplish specific tasks. In this topic, you will learn the most sophisticated way to obtain drawing views in paper space: using the **SOLVIEW** and **SOLDRAW** commands jointly.

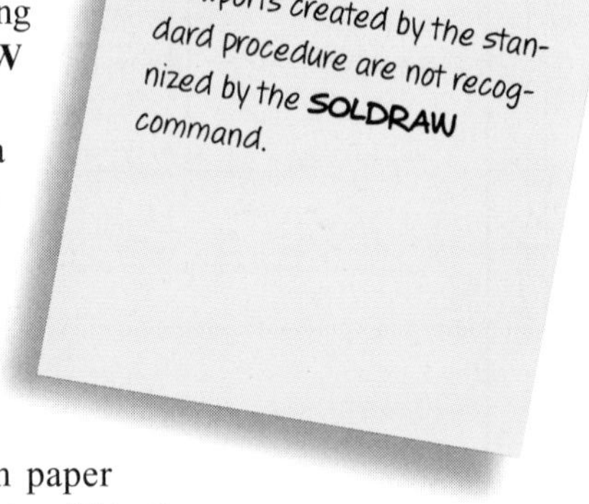

Note:
Viewports created by the standard procedure are not recognized by the SOLDRAW command.

This pair of commands works together in a prepare–resolve process. The **SOLVIEW** command creates a special type of floating viewport, which is then resolved and processed with the **SOLDRAW** command. The **SOLDRAW** command generates the view projections according to the type of view, using different layers for visible, hidden, and hatch objects.

The **SOLVIEW** command can be invoked only in paper space. It allows you to create one or more special viewports within the same operation. For each viewport, you can specify the type of view it will contain. Depending on the option selected, you can create viewports that contain the following views:

UCS: Parallel to the *XY* plane of the **Current**, **World**, or any **Named** UCS. This is the only option you can use to specify the first viewport (Figure 8-101).

TIP

Using the **Front** or the **Top** UCS is the best choice for creating the first view with the **SOLDRAW** command. This view can be used as the Top or Plan view, and to place any other view relative to it.

Ortho: Creates the corresponding FRONT, BACK, RIGHT, or LEFT orthographic projection of any other view specified, always perpendicular to it. Figure 8-102 shows the four

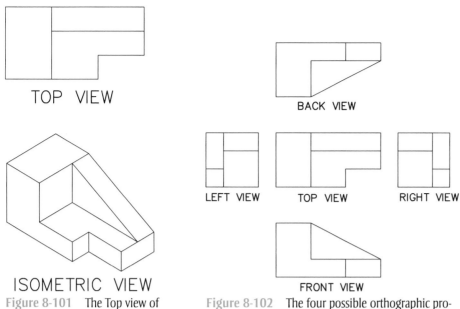

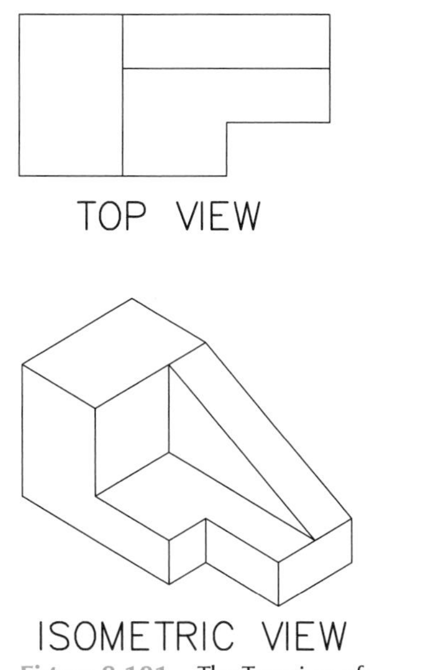

Figure 8-101 The Top view of the object shown in the isometric view can be the first view generated

Figure 8-102 The four possible orthographic projections relative to the Top view

possible orthographic projections of the Top view after it has been resolved with the **SOLDRAW** command.

You can create orthographic projections from other orthographic views to obtain different alignments.

Auxiliary: Perpendicular to the specified view as viewed from a plane you specify with two points. Figure 8-103 shows an auxiliary view after it has been resolved with the **SOLDRAW** command. The dotted lines are added for illustration purposes.

Section: Creates section views perpendicular to the specified view through a plane you specify with two points. Figure 8-104 shows a section view after it has been resolved with the **SOLDRAW** command. The dotted lines are added for illustration purposes.

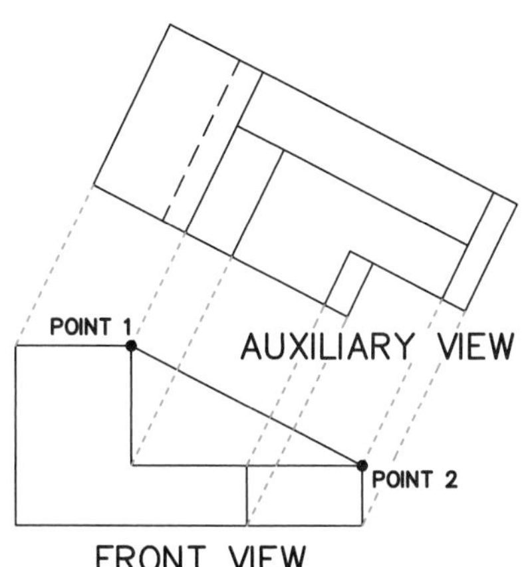

Figure 8-103 An auxiliary view relative to the Front view

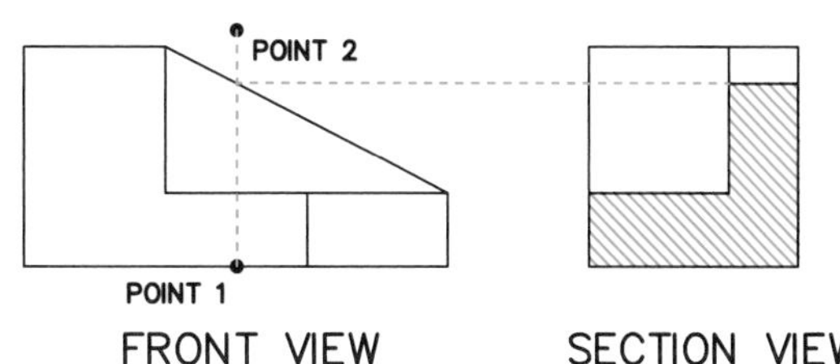

Figure 8-104 A section view relative to the Front view

The first special viewport generated with the **SOLVIEW** command requires you to respond to a set of prompts, which include requests for the following information:

1. Type of view (UCS only)
2. Scale
3. Center point
4. Two diagonal points to locate the viewport's corners
5. Name

> **Note:**
> You must enter all the required information; otherwise, the AutoCAD program will create a regular floating viewport.

For any subsequent viewport you must specify additional information, depending on the type of view created. For example, you must specify the first and second points of an inclined plane for an auxiliary view.

The **SOLVIEW** operation creates the following set of layers along with each viewport:

- *Name*-DIM
- *Name*-HAT (only for section views)
- *Name*-HID
- *Name*-VIS

The last three layers are automatically assigned to the objects by the **SOLDRAW** operation. The -DIM layer can be assigned to dimensions or used at your convenience.

Exercise 8-6: Generating Drawing Views and Sections in Paper Space Using the SOLVIEW and SOLDRAW Commands

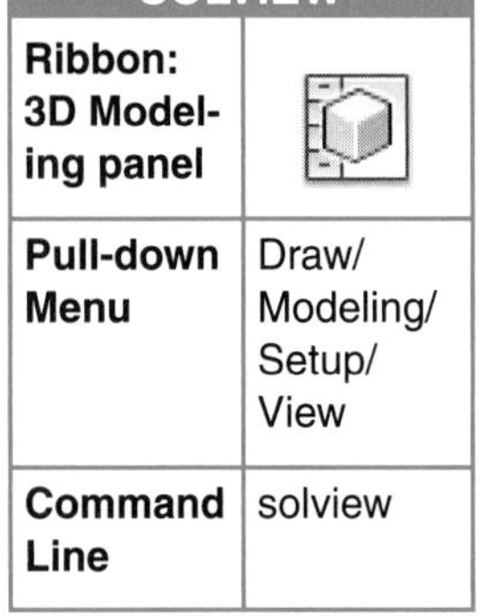

SOLVIEW	
Ribbon: 3D Modeling panel	
Pull-down Menu	Draw/ Modeling/ Setup/ View
Command Line	solview

You will use the same 3D solid object as in a previous exercise. Thus you will be able to focus on the operations used in this procedure, and compare both methods efficiently.

> **Note:**
> A temporary active viewport that covers the entire sheet is created. You will reduce its size in the next step.

1. **OPEN** either ***Exercise 5-8*** or ***Exercise 5-10*** as completed in Chapter 5.
2. **SAVE** it **AS *Exercise 8-6***.
3. Select the **SW Isometric** viewpoint.
4. Select the **World** UCS.
5. Click on the **Layout1** tab to switch to paper space. Close the **Page Setup** dialog box if it opens automatically.
6. **DELETE** the viewport that the AutoCAD program automatically creates for you to completely clear the paper.
7. Invoke the **SOLVIEW** command. Respond to the prompts as follows:

   Enter an option [Ucs/Ortho/Auxiliary/ Section]: u

   Enter an option [Named/World/?/Current] <Current>: ↵ *(To accept the current UCS (World))*

   Enter view scale <1.0000>: *0.5* ↵ *(For a 1:2 scale)*

   Specify view center: *Click in the upper-left side of the paper* (Figure 8-105).

   Specify view center <specify viewport>: *Click inside the viewport to relocate its center. You can click as many times as needed. When you are finished, press* ***<Enter>****.*

   Specify first corner of viewport: *Click to the left and over the view.*

   Specify opposite corner of viewport: *Click to the right and below the view* (Figure 8-106).

   Enter view name: *TopView* ↵

> **Note:**
> Entering the view name is the end of the cycle for the first view. Pressing **<Enter>** now will exit the command. You will continue with a second cycle to create a section view.

Figure 8-105 First point to be specified in the SOLVIEW operation

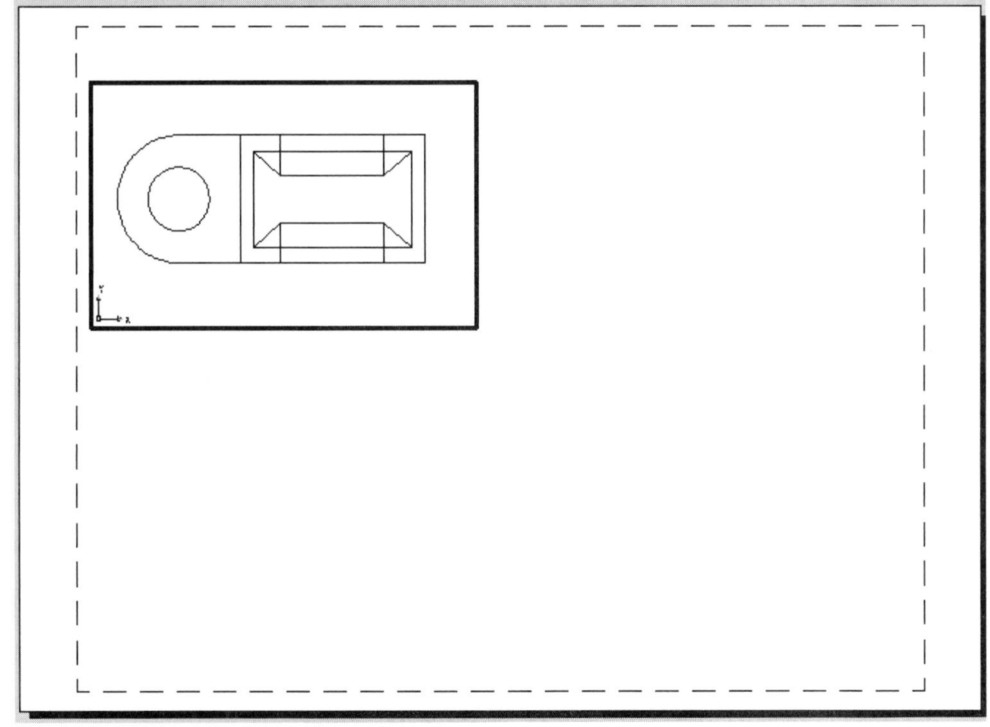

Figure 8-106 After specifying the viewport's two corners

Enter an option [Ucs/Ortho/Auxiliary/Section]: *S* ↵
Specify first point of cutting plane: *Snap to the center point shown in* Figure 8-107*.*

The AutoCAD program turns the object snap off at this stage of the command. You must select the **Center point** snap tool directly.

Specify second point of cutting plane: *Snap to the midpoint.*
Specify side to view from: *Click on any empty place inside the viewport and below the 3D model.*
Enter view scale <0.5000>: ↵ *(To accept the value)*

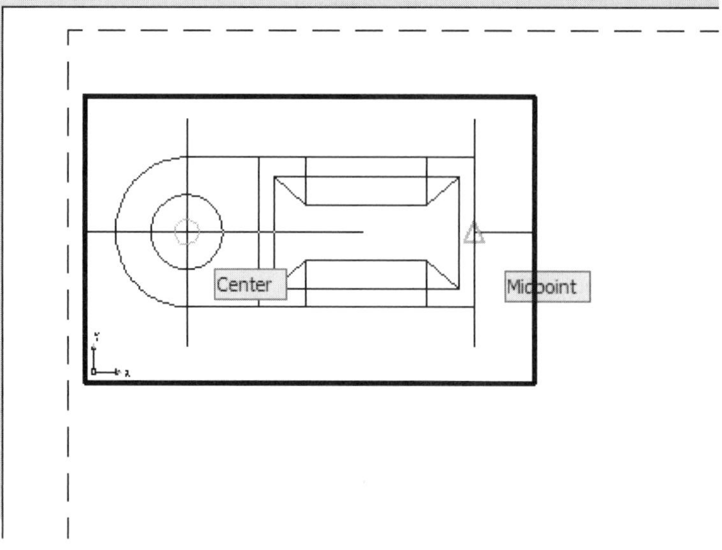

Figure 8-107 Points to be specified for the section view

Specify view center: *Click below the viewport to locate the new view.*

Specify view center <specify viewport>: *Click to relocate the view center as many times as needed. When you are finished, press* ***<Enter>****.*

Specify first corner of viewport: *Click to the left and over the new view.*

Specify opposite corner of viewport: *Click to the right and below the new view* (Figure 8-108).

Enter view name: *SectionView* ↵

Note:
Entering the view name is the end of the second cycle for the second view. You will continue with a third cycle to create an orthographic view.

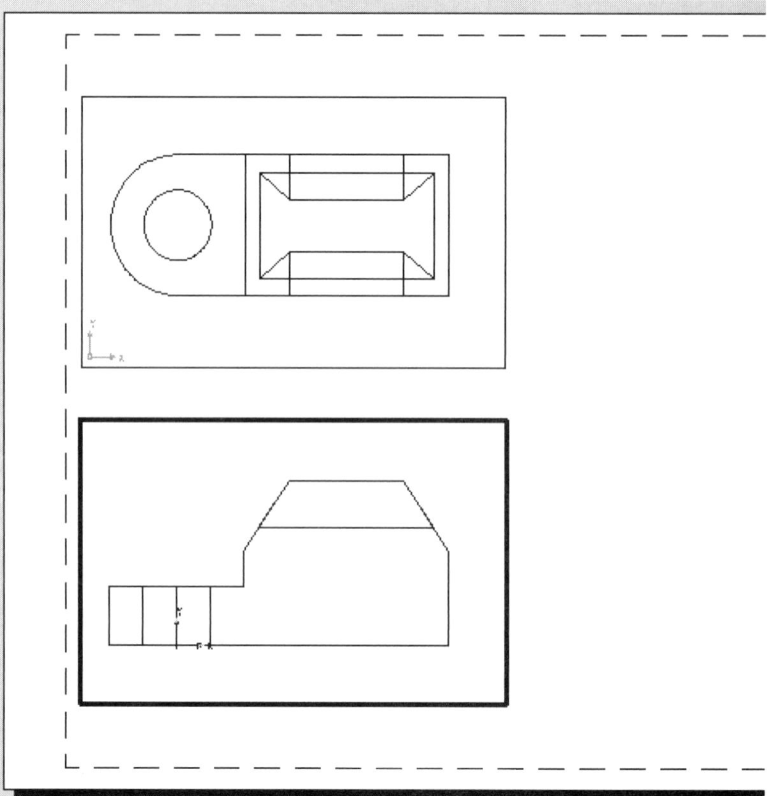

Figure 8-108 After completing the section view

Enter an option [Ucs/Ortho/Auxiliary/Section]: *o ↵*

Specify side of viewport to project: *Snap to the midpoint of the right border of the viewport that contains the Front view.*

Specify view center: *Click to the right of the viewport.*

Specify view center <specify viewport>: *Click to relocate the view center as many times as needed. When you are finished, press* **<Enter>**.

Specify first corner of viewport: *Click to the left and over the new view.*

Specify opposite corner of viewport: *Click to the right and below the new view.*

Enter view name: *RightView ↵*

Enter an option [Ucs/Ortho/Auxiliary/Section]: *↵(To exit the command) The drawing views should look like* Figure 8-109.

Note:

For the **Ortho** option, the AutoCAD program turns on the midpoint object snap only.

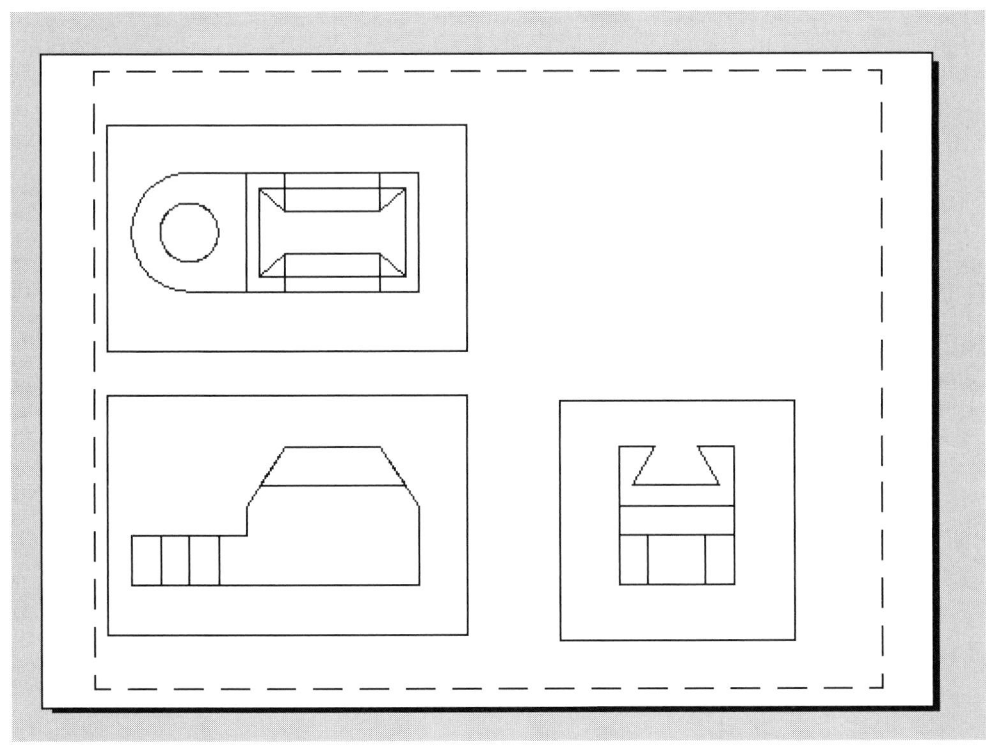

Figure 8-109 The viewport containing the Front view is created

8. Invoke the **SOLDRAW** command. When prompted, select the three viewports and press **<Enter>** to end the selection. The AutoCAD program processes the projected objects and assigns the corresponding layers (Figure 8-110).
9. Open the **Layer Properties Manager** dialog box and perform the following operations:
   - Create a new layer named *3DSolid* (Figure 8-111).
   - Select all the **-VIS** layers and change their color to any other one.
   - Select all the **-HID** layers and change their linetype to **HIDDEN**. (This linetype can be loaded from the **Layer Properties Manager** directly.)

Note:

The AutoCAD program creates a set of layers for each of the views. The section view generates an additional layer for the hatch entity. An additional layer named VPORTS is also created and assigned to the viewports.

SOLDRAW	
Ribbon: 3D Modeling panel	
Pull-down Menu	Draw/ Modeling/ Setup/ Drawing
Command Line	soldraw

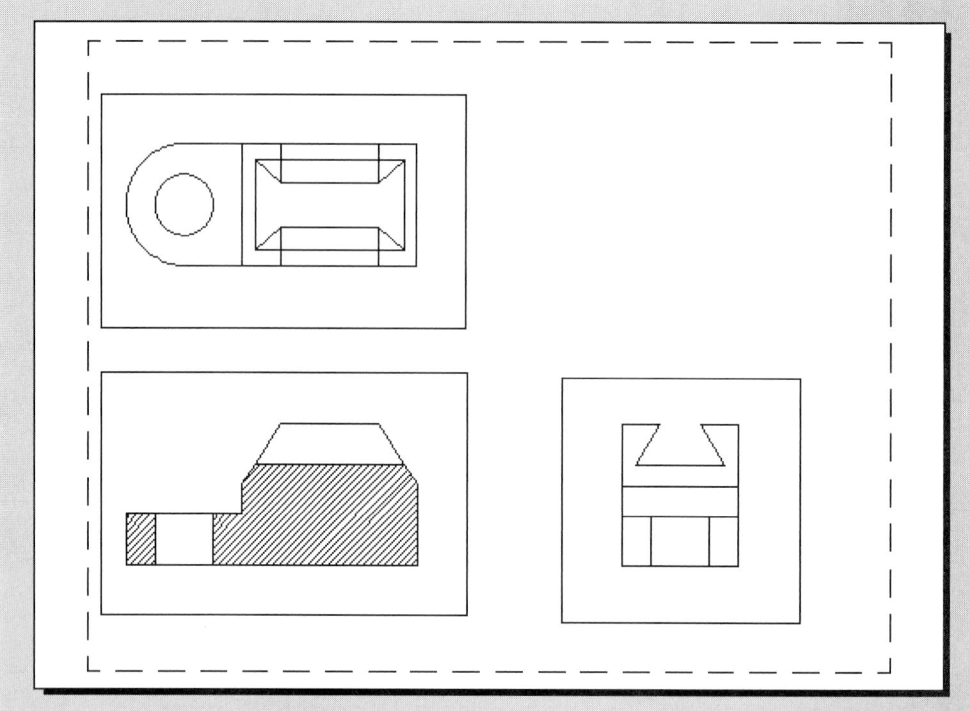

Figure 8-110 The viewports are resolved with the SOLDRAW operation

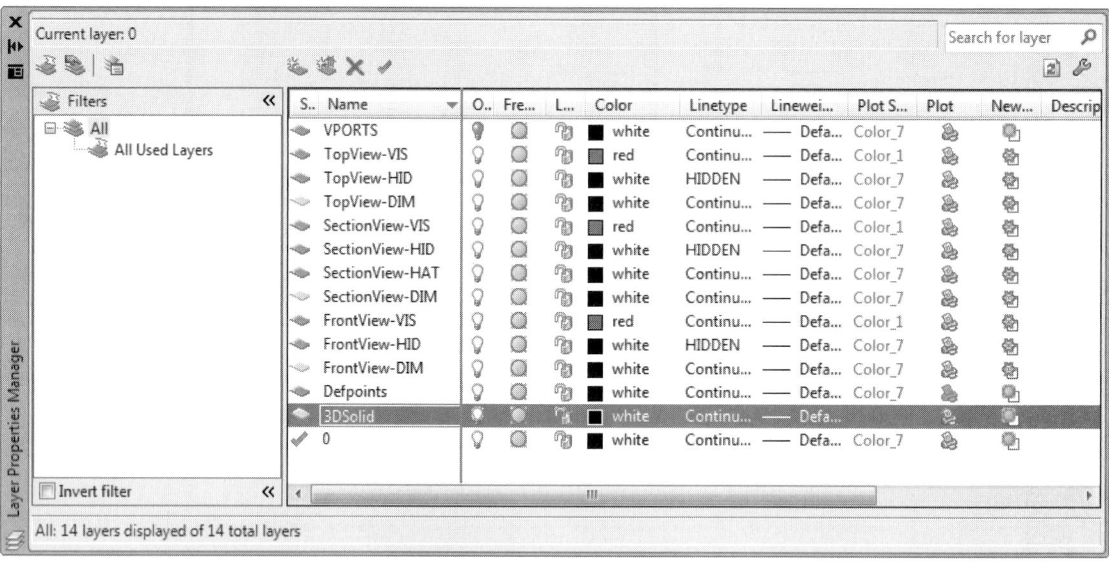

Figure 8-111 The Layer Properties Manager dialog box

10. Change the **LTSCALE** system variable to **0.5**.
11. Select the three viewports and right-click in the drawing area to display the shortcut menu. Set their **Display Lock** property to **Yes**.
12. **MOVE** the viewports up to make room for a title block. If needed, continue moving the views orthogonally without losing the alignment between them.
13. Draw the objects shown in Figure 8-112 anywhere in the gray area to represent the title block.
14. Turn **ORTHO** mode off and **MOVE** the title block to the paper so that all the drawing views fit inside.
15. Double-click on the border of the viewport that contains the section view to maximize it.

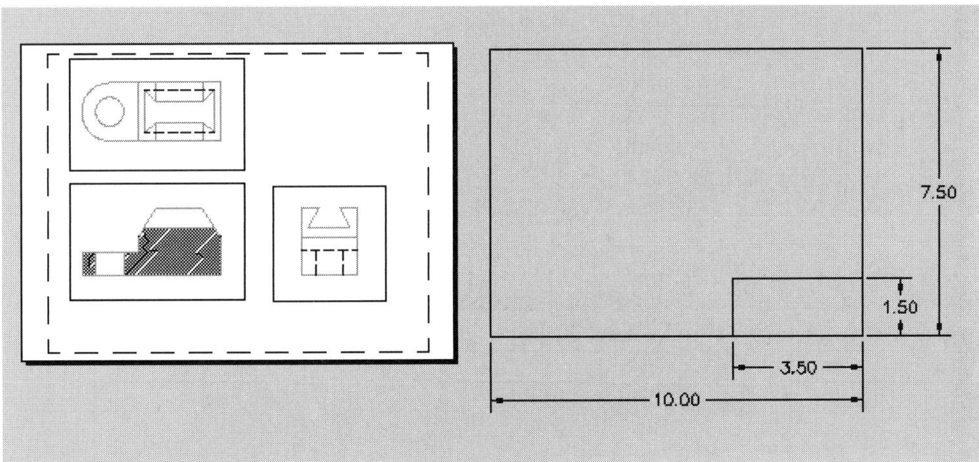

Figure 8-112 A representative title block drawn in the gray area

16. Double-click on the hatch to open the **Hatch Edit** dialog box. Set its scale to **2** and click **OK** to close the dialog box.
17. Right-click in the drawing area and select **Minimize Viewport** from the shortcut menu.
18. Select the three viewports. Look at the **Layer control** drop-down window to make sure the *VPORTS* layer is assigned to them.
19. In the **Layer control** drop-down window, set the **0 Layer** as current and then turn the *VPORTS* layer off. The drawing should look like Figure 8-113.

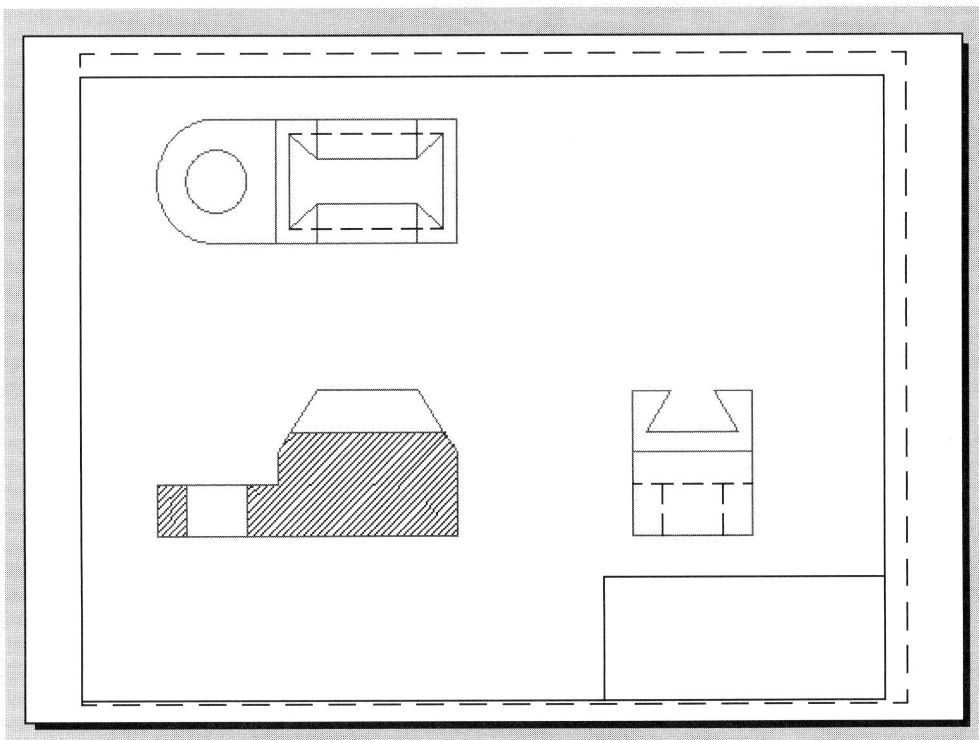

Figure 8-113 After turning the VPORTS layer off

20. Right-click on the **Layout1** tab to access the **Page Setup Manager** dialog box. Select ***Layout1*** and click the **Modify . . .** button.
    - Under **Printer/Plotter**, make a selection, or select any virtual printer if you do not have one installed.
    - Select **monochrome.ctb** for the **Plot Style table**.

- Select **8.5 × 11″** or **Letter** for **Paper size**.
- Select **Landscape** for **Drawing orientation**.
- Select **1:1** for **Plot scale**.
- Under the plot area, select the **Window** button and specify the two diagonal corners of the title block by snapping to its endpoints. After you return to the dialog box, check the **Center the plot** box.
- Click **OK** to close the **Page Setup** dialog box. The drawing should look like Figure 8-114.

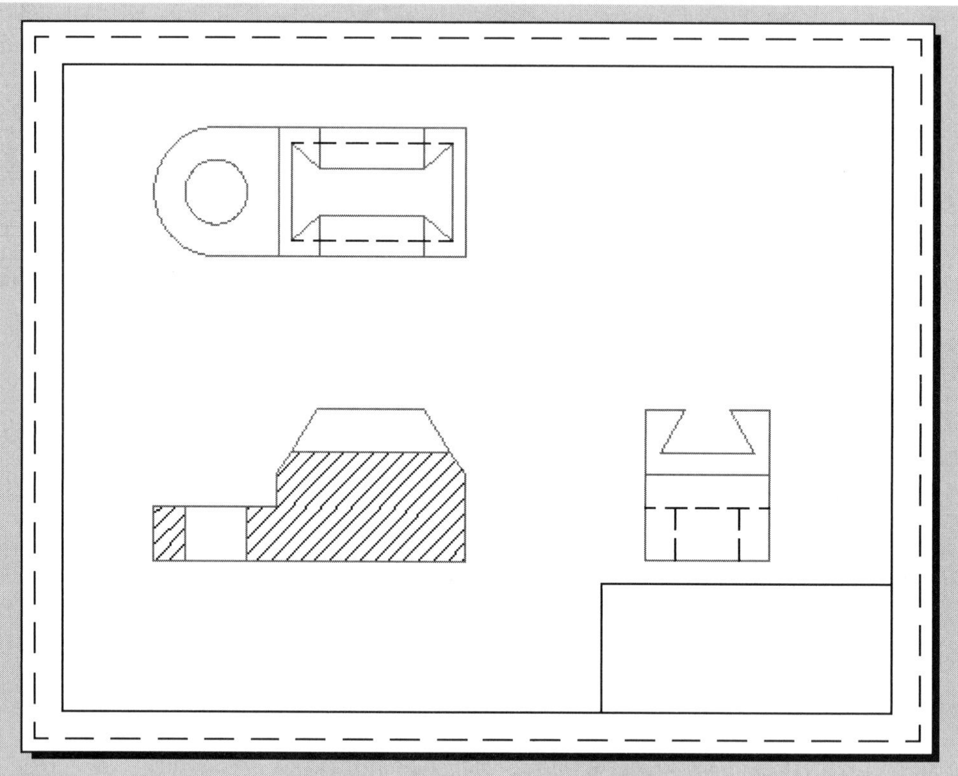

Figure 8-114 After setting up the page

21. Create a new viewport in the upper-right corner of the paper, using the **–VPORTS** command.
22. Double-click inside the new viewport to activate it.
23. Select the **SW Isometric** viewing point.
24. Double-click outside the paper to deactivate the viewport.

TIP

You do not necessarily need to create the 3D views by using one of the automated ways of creating views, nor do you have to project them onto a plane.

25. Select the new viewport, and right-click in the drawing area and set the **Shade plot** to **Hidden** from the shortcut menu. Display the shortcut menu again and set the **Display Locked** property to **Yes**.
26. Assign the *VPORTS* layer to the new viewport.
27. Place dimensions and centerlines. Figure 8-115 shows the **Plot Preview** that appears just before you send the plot to the printer.
28. **SAVE** the drawing.

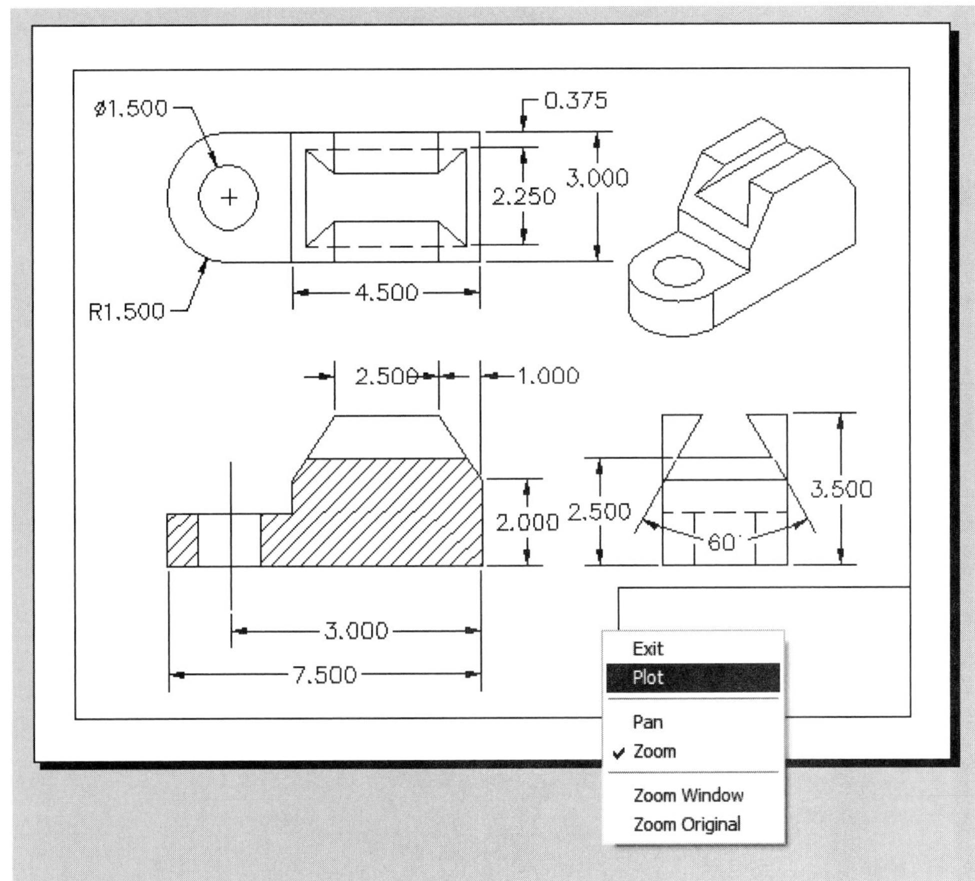

Figure 8-115 The plot preview right before it is sent to the printer

The preparation of engineering drawings for complex objects using the traditional 2D methods demands a high level of experience and concentration to avoid mistakes. Generating 2D drawings from an existing 3D model, on the other hand, not only is a faster approach, but also guarantees reliable accuracy. Your proper use of the techniques and procedures related to this important task along with your ability to generate 3D models will demonstrate special skills in the production of technical documents.

PUBLISHING AND PROTOTYPING

CREATING DWF FILES USING THE PUBLISH AND 3DDWF COMMANDS

With the AutoCAD software, you can create DWFx (Design Web Format; the "x" stands for the DWFx ePlot [XPS compatible plotter used]) files that contain different 3D models and layouts. DWFx files open with the Autodesk® Design Review software, which is free and can be downloaded from the Autodesk® website. The Autodesk® Design Review software is also included with the standard installation of the AutoCAD software.

Creating DWFx files allows you to communicate your ideas and projects to people who do not use AutoCAD. Such files allow them to observe, analyze, and plot your 3D models and 2D drawings using the Autodesk® Design Review software (Figure 8-116).

The **PUBLISH** command enables you to create DWFx files that include the model space and the layout content of several DWG files. The layouts can be included only as 2D drawings. You can choose, however, whether the model space content is included as a 2D drawing or a 3D model. Invoking the **PUBLISH** command opens the **Publish** dialog box (Figure 8-117).

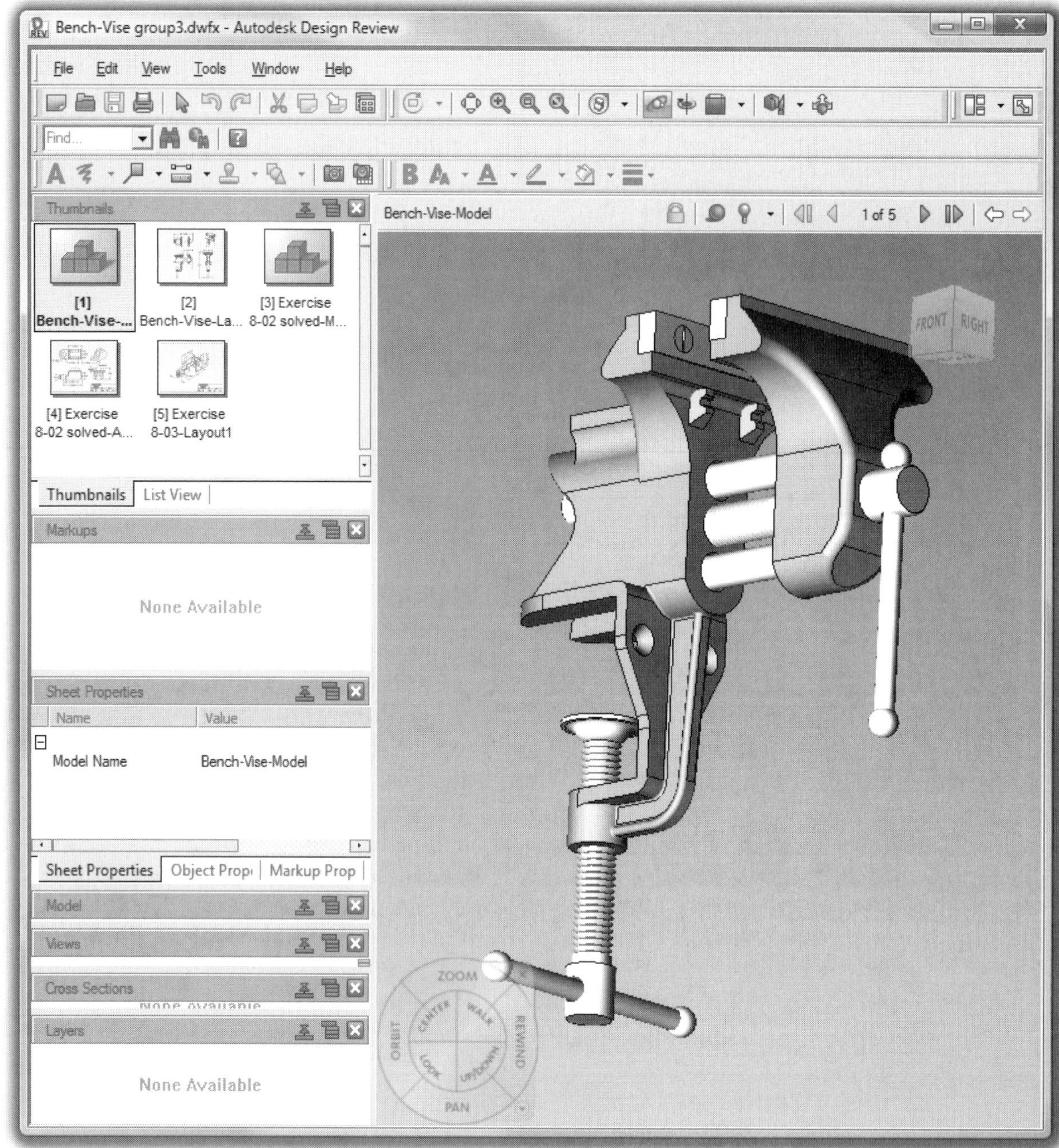

Figure 8-116 The Autodesk® Design Review window

By default, the models and layouts of all the DWG files opened are included as individual sheets to publish. You can remove any selected sheet by clicking the **Remove Sheets** button or by pressing the **<Delete>** key. You can also bring in another DWG file by clicking the **Add Sheets** button. You can click the **Page Setup/3D DWF** drop-down list of one of the model sheets to specify whether the content in the model space will be included as a 2D drawing or a 3D model (Figure 8-118). This flexibility allows you to generate DWFx files that contain both 2D drawings and 3D models. It is more convenient, however, to generate DWF files that contain a single 3D model that is independent from all the 2D drawing sheets.

Note:
To initialize a particular layout sheet, you must first open the **Page Setup Manager** or the **Plot** dialog box at least once inside this particular layout. You would perform the same procedure to initialize a model space sheet.

Clicking on the **Publish Options . . .** button will open the **Publish Options** palette, where you can modify other details about the DWF file. For example, you can

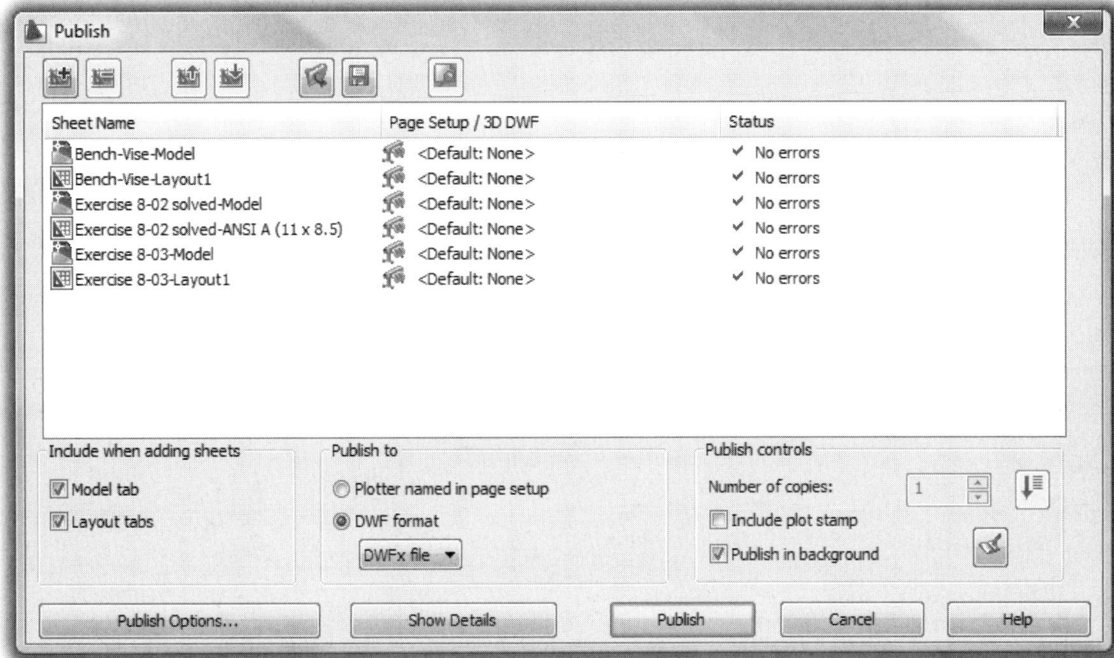

Figure 8-117 The Publish dialog box

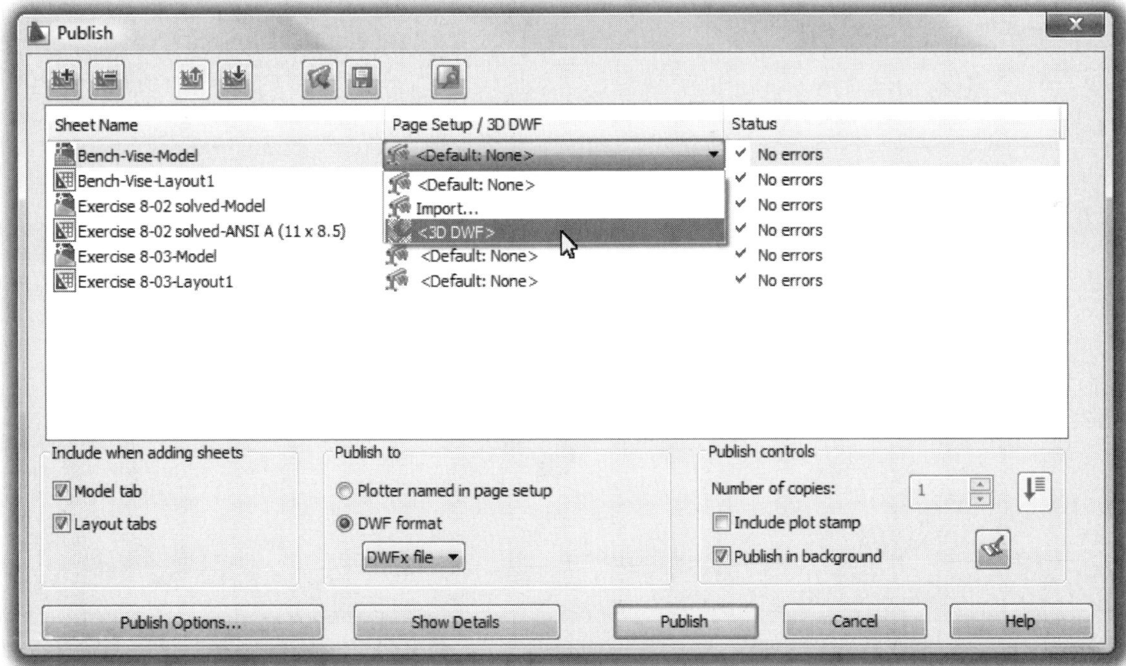

Figure 8-118 The Page Setup/3D DWF drop-down list in the Publish dialog box

set up a **Password** so that your file can be seen only by those whom you authorize (Figure 8-119). The default **Location** or path where the DWF file will be saved is also changed in the **Publish Options** palette. Clicking on the **Publish** button will start the process by which the DWF file is generated.

On the other hand, the **3DDWF** and the **EXPORT** commands are used only to generate 3D DWF files of the model space content of a particular drawing file. Invoking these two commands opens the **Export 3D DWF** and the **Export Data** dialog boxes, respectively, where you can select a **Name** and **Path** for the 3D DWF files (Figures 8-120 and 8-121). In the **Export Data** dialog box, you must select **3D DWF (*.dwf)** as the file type.

The advantage of using the **3DDWF** and the **EXPORT** commands is that you can select specific objects in the model space to be included in the **3D DWF** file. You do so by selecting the

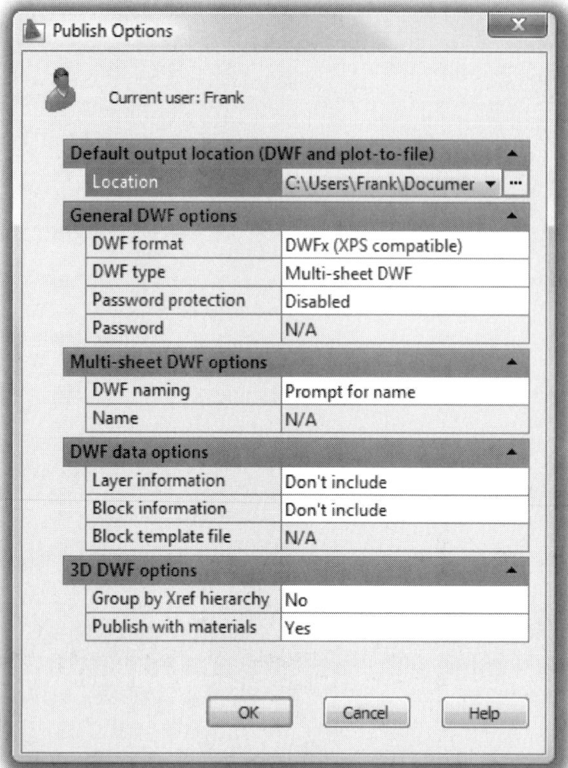

Figure 8-119 The Publish Options palette

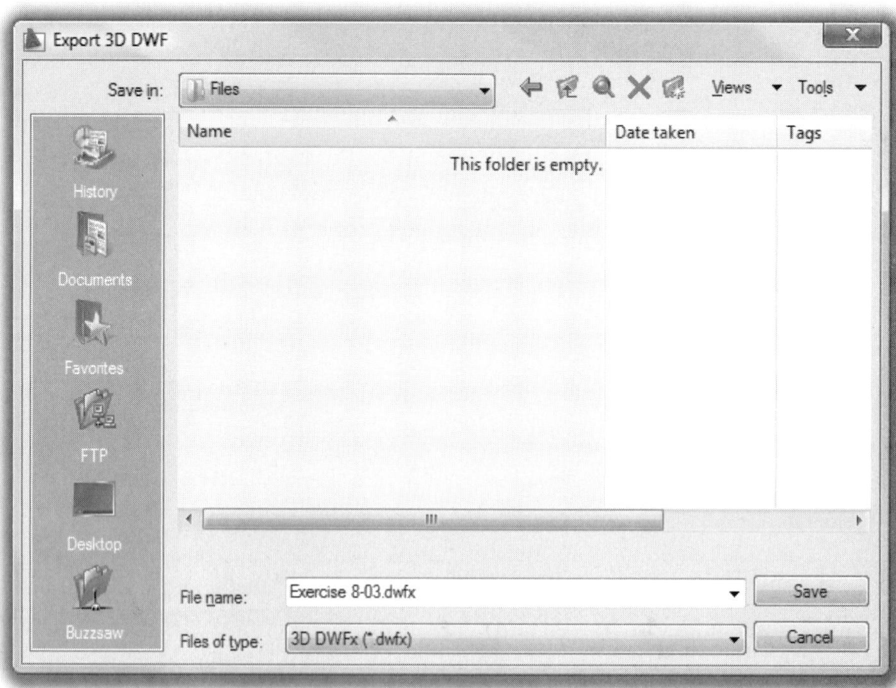

Figure 8-120 The Export 3D DWF dialog box

Selected model space objects option in the **3D DWF Publish** dialog box and then clicking the **Select Objects** button. You can also specify whether the objects will be shown with the material applied by checking the **Publish with Materials** option.

FOR MORE DETAILS	See Chapter 9 for more information about applying materials.

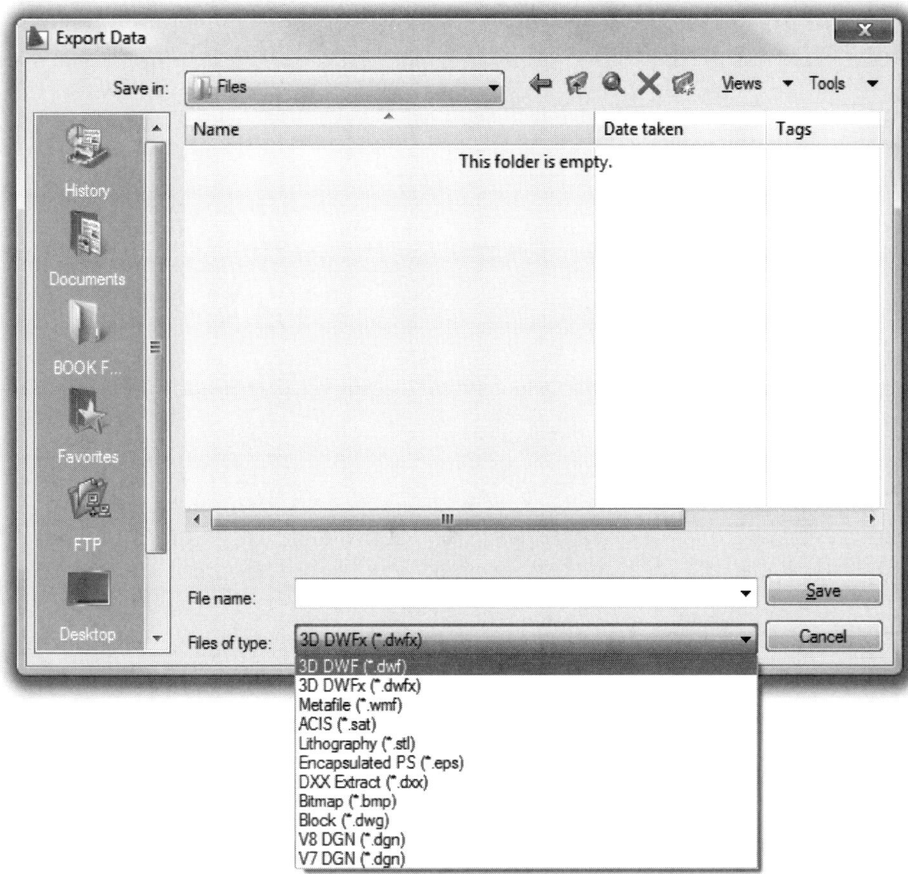

Figure 8-121 3D DWF (*.dwf) must be selected in the Export Data dialog box

You open the **3D DWF Publish** dialog box by selecting **Options . . .** from the **Tools** drop-down menu in either the **Export 3D DWF** or the **Export Data** dialog box (Figure 8-122).

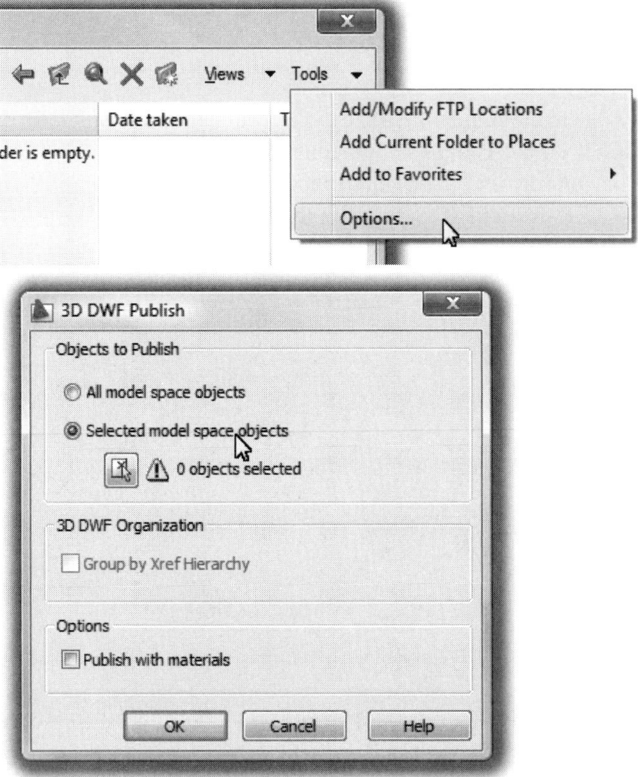

Figure 8-122 The 3D DWF Publish dialog box; accessing Options . . . from the Tools drop-down menu

The **3DDWFPREC** system variable controls the smoothness of the 3D objects included in the DWF file. The value of this variable can be set between **2** and **6**. Higher values result in a better quality, but they also increase the file size (Figure 8-123). The **DISPSILH** system variable also affects the generation of DWF files. When **DISPSILH** is turned on (**1**), the 3D content of DWF files is generated showing the **Facets** edges. Including the 3D model objects in the DWF files as 2D content will have the opposite effect.

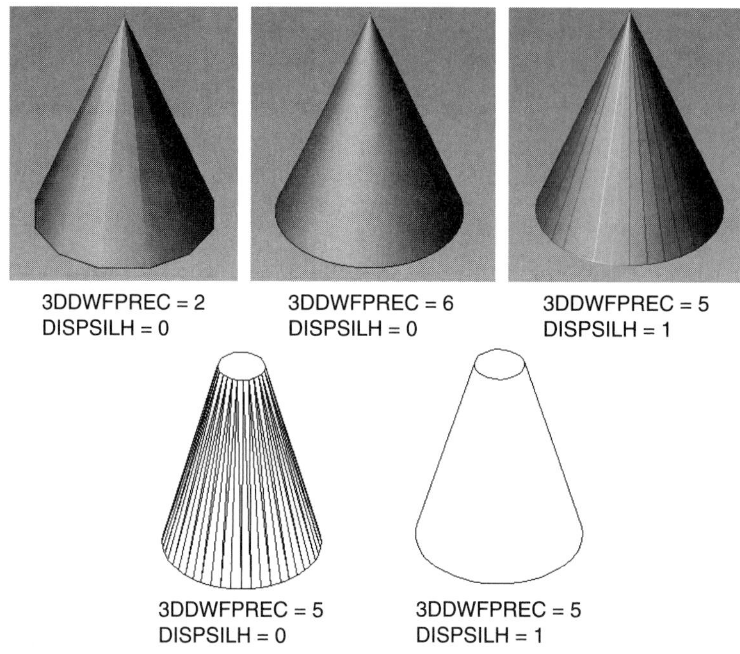

Figure 8-123 The 3DDWFPREC system variable controls the smoothness of the DWF objects

Exercise 8-7: Creating DWF Files That Contain Multiple 2D Drawings Using the PUBLISH Command

1. **CLOSE** any drawing you might have opened.
2. **OPEN** the following drawings:
   - ***Bench-Vise*** from Chapter 7
   - ***Exercise 8-2 solved***
   - ***Exercise 8-3 solved***
3. Switch to the ***Bench-Vise*** file though the thumbnail previews displayed by clicking on the **Quick View Drawings** button on the status bar (Figure 8-124).
4. Click on **Layout1** to switch to paper space. Close the **Page Setup Manager** if it opens up.
5. **ERASE** the default viewport in the layout.

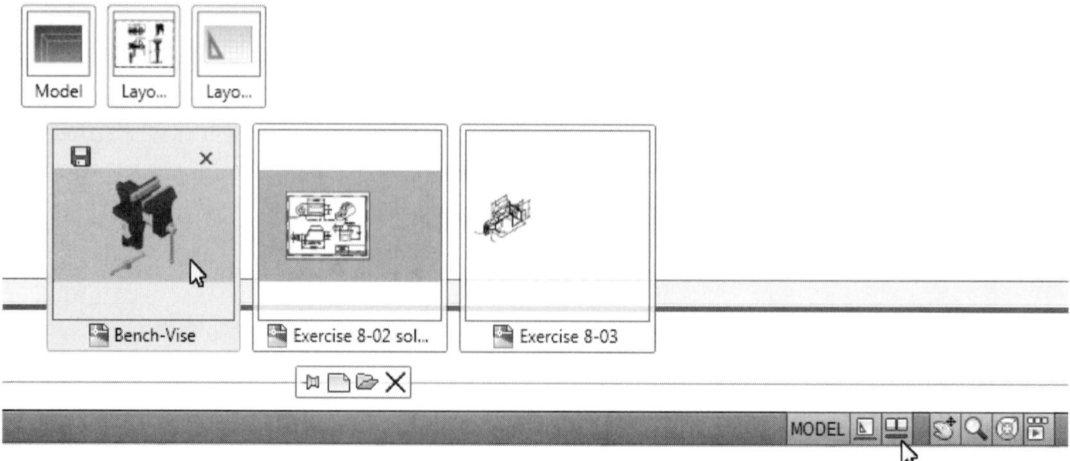

Figure 8-124 Switching to the Bench-Vise by clicking its thumbnail icon; these icons are displayed on the Quick View Drawings button on the status bar

6. Invoke the **VPORTS** command and create four equal viewports using a **3D** setup. Define the viewport spacing as **0**. When prompted, specify two points diagonally close to the corners of the paper. The layout should look like Figure 8-125.

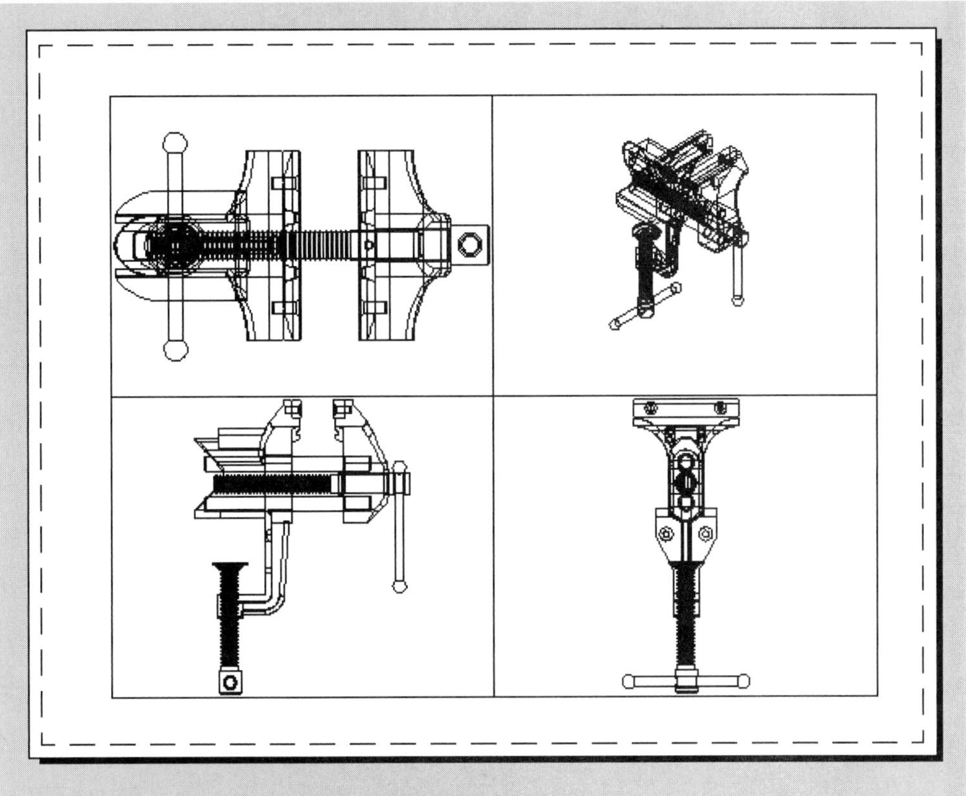

Figure 8-125 The initial 3D setup of the four viewports

7. Double-click inside one of the viewports that show an orthographic view. Set the scale to **1:2** in the **Viewports** toolbar drop-down list.

TIP

Avoid making any **ZOOM** or **PAN** operations, especially with the wheel mouse, while a viewport is active to keep the views correctly aligned.

8. Activate the other two viewports that contain orthographic views to set the same scale factor. When you are finished, double-click outside the viewports to get back to paper space.
9. Select all the viewports to expose their grips. Then select common grips and stretch the viewports so the drawing views are shown in their entirety. **MOVE** the viewports around without losing the alignment, and separate them if necessary. The views' layout should look like Figure 8-126.
10. Select all the viewports. Set the **Shade Plot** to **Hidden** through the shortcut menu or in the **Properties** palette.
11. Create a new layer, apply it to the viewports, and turn it off to hide the viewports.
12. Open the **Page Setup** window for Layout1. Select **monochrome.ctb** as the plot style and close the **Page Setup** window.
13. Place the main dimensions in the orthographic views (Figure 8-127).
14. In the ***Bench-Vise*** drawing file, click the **Model** tab to switch to model space. Right-click on the **Model** tab and select **Page Setup Manager. . . .** Click **Modify . . .** to open the **Page Setup – Model** dialog box.

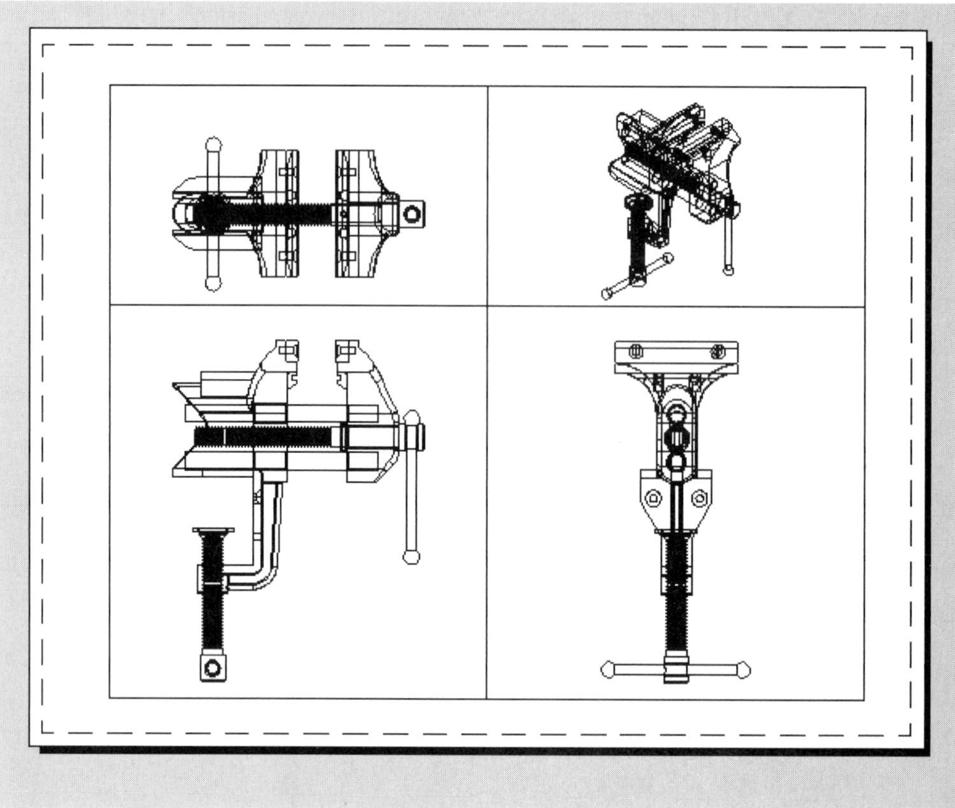

Figure 8-126 After the viewports are adjusted

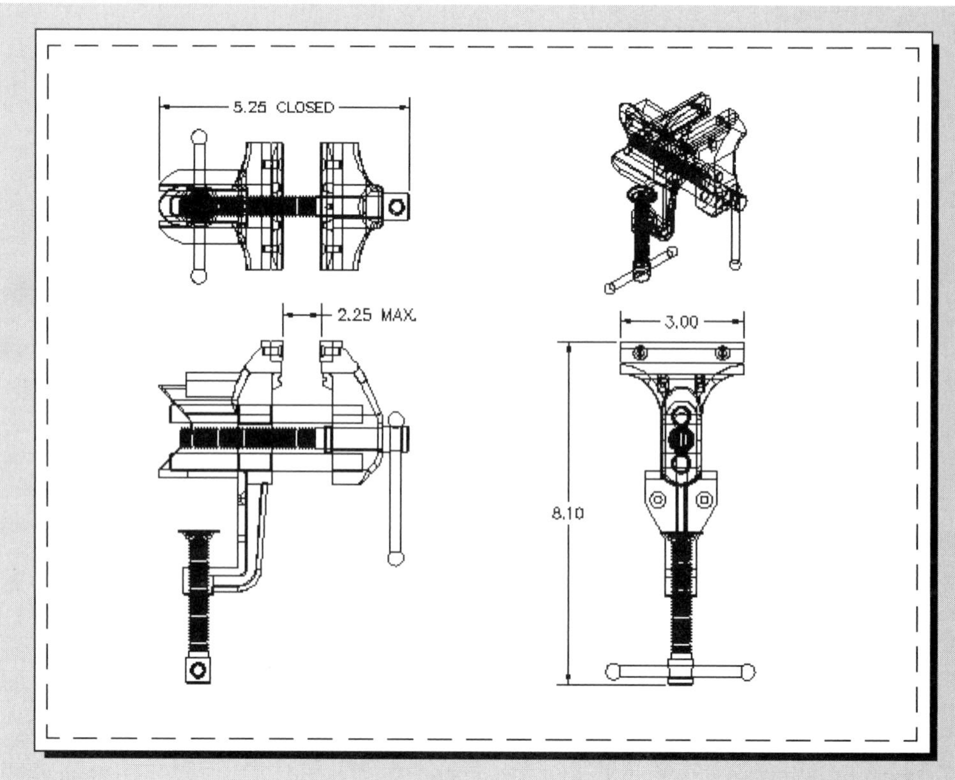

Figure 8-127 Main dimensions placed in the orthographic views

15. Select a plotter, and select **monochrome.ctb** as the plot style. Under **Plot scale**, check **Fit to paper**. Under **Plot area**, select **Window** and click on the **Window** button. When prompted, specify two points that enclose the 3D model in the drawing area.
16. Under **Shaded viewport options**, select the **Hidden** shade plot. Close the **Page Setup – Model** window by clicking **OK**. Close the **Page Setup Manager . . .** dialog box as well.
17. Repeat the previous three steps in the ***Exercise 8-3 solved*** drawing file to define aspects of the published sheet for the model space content.
18. Set the **3DDWFPREC** system variable to **4** and the **DISPSILH** system variable to **1** in each drawing file.
19. **SAVE** each drawing file.
20. Invoke the **PUBLISH** command from any of the three drawing files. In the **Publish** dialog box, select **DWF file** under **Publish to** and remove the following sheets:

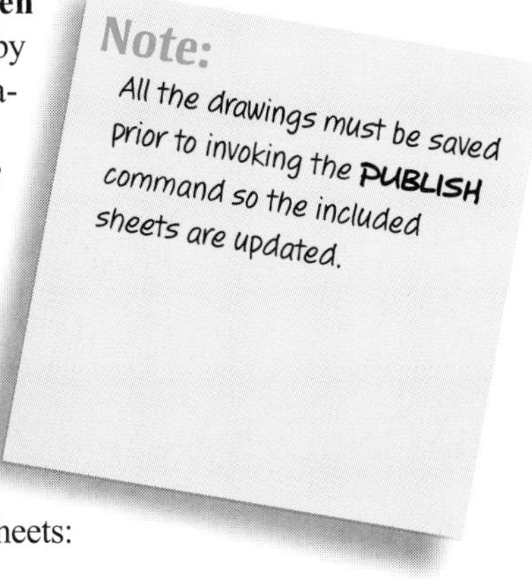

Note:
All the drawings must be saved prior to invoking the PUBLISH command so the included sheets are updated.

- **Bench-Vise-Layout2**
- **Exercise 8-2 solved-Model**
- **Exercise 8-2 solved-Layout1**
- **Exercise 8-2 solved-Layout2**
- **Exercise 8-3-solved-Layout2**

PUBLISH	
Standard Toolbar	
Ribbon: Publish panel	
Pull-down Menu	File/ Publish...
Command Line	publish

To remove a sheet you can either use the **Remove Sheet** button, or right-click on the sheet and select **Remove.** You can also select the sheet and press **<Delete>**. To select multiple sheets, press and hold **<Ctrl>**.

21. After you remove the sheets, the **Publish** dialog box should contain only the sheets shown in Figure 8-128. Click the **Publish Options . . .** button to open the **Publish Options** dialog box. Under **General DWF options** make sure that **DWF type** is set to **Multi-sheet DWF** (Figure 8-129). Click **OK** to close the **Publish Options** dialog box.

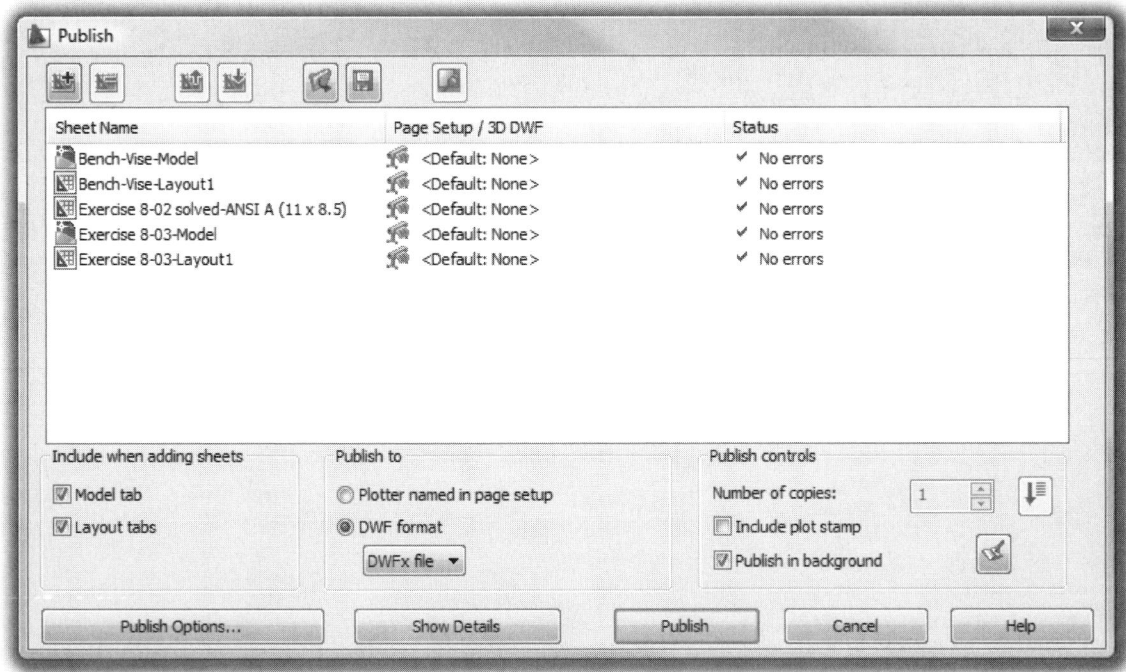

Figure 8-128 These sheets should be contained in the Publish dialog box

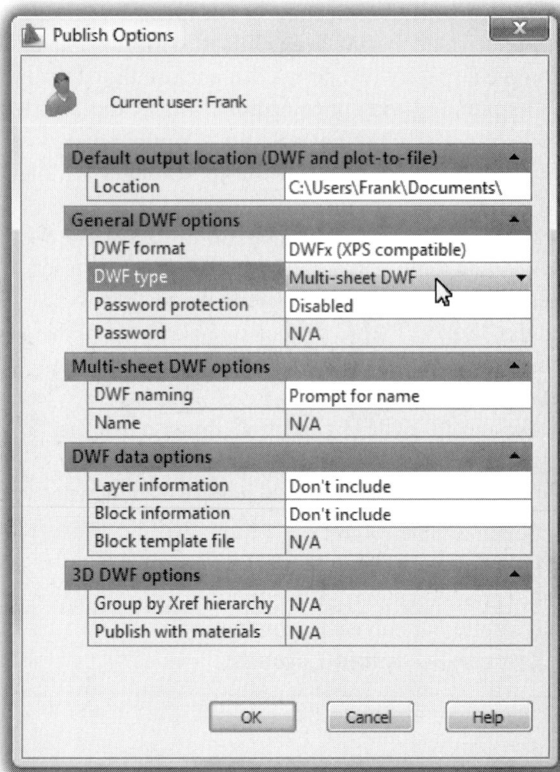

Figure 8-129 The Publish Options dialog box

22. Click the **Publish** button. In the **Select DWF File** dialog box, look for where you have other exercise drawing files, and type **My Projects** as the file name. Click the **Select** button to generate the DWF file. Click **No** to close the **Save Sheet List** dialog box in case it opens up.
23. Wait a few minutes and open Windows Explorer. Look for the DWF file you just created. Right-click on the file and select **Open** with the **Autodesk DWF Application** if you are using Windows XP®, or select the file and choose **Open–Autodesk DWF Application** from the top **Ribbon** if you are using Windows Vista® (Figure 8-130).

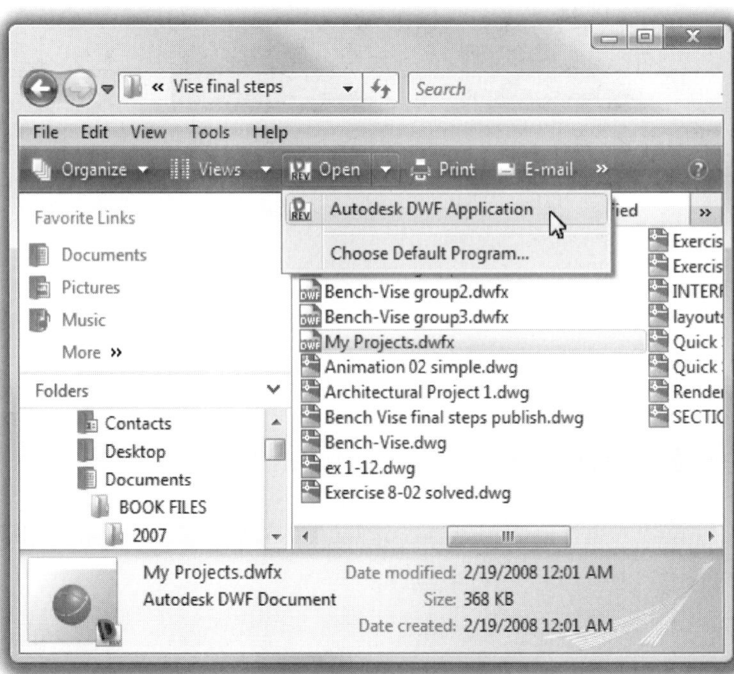

Figure 8-130 Opening the DWF file with Autodesk DWF Application from Windows Explorer

TIP The **Plot/Publish** animated icon in the lower right corner of the AutoCAD display will indicate when the publishing job has been completed.

24. The **Contents** window of the **Autodesk DWF Viewer** should contain five thumbnail icons (Figure 8-131). Click on each thumbnail icon to view its content.

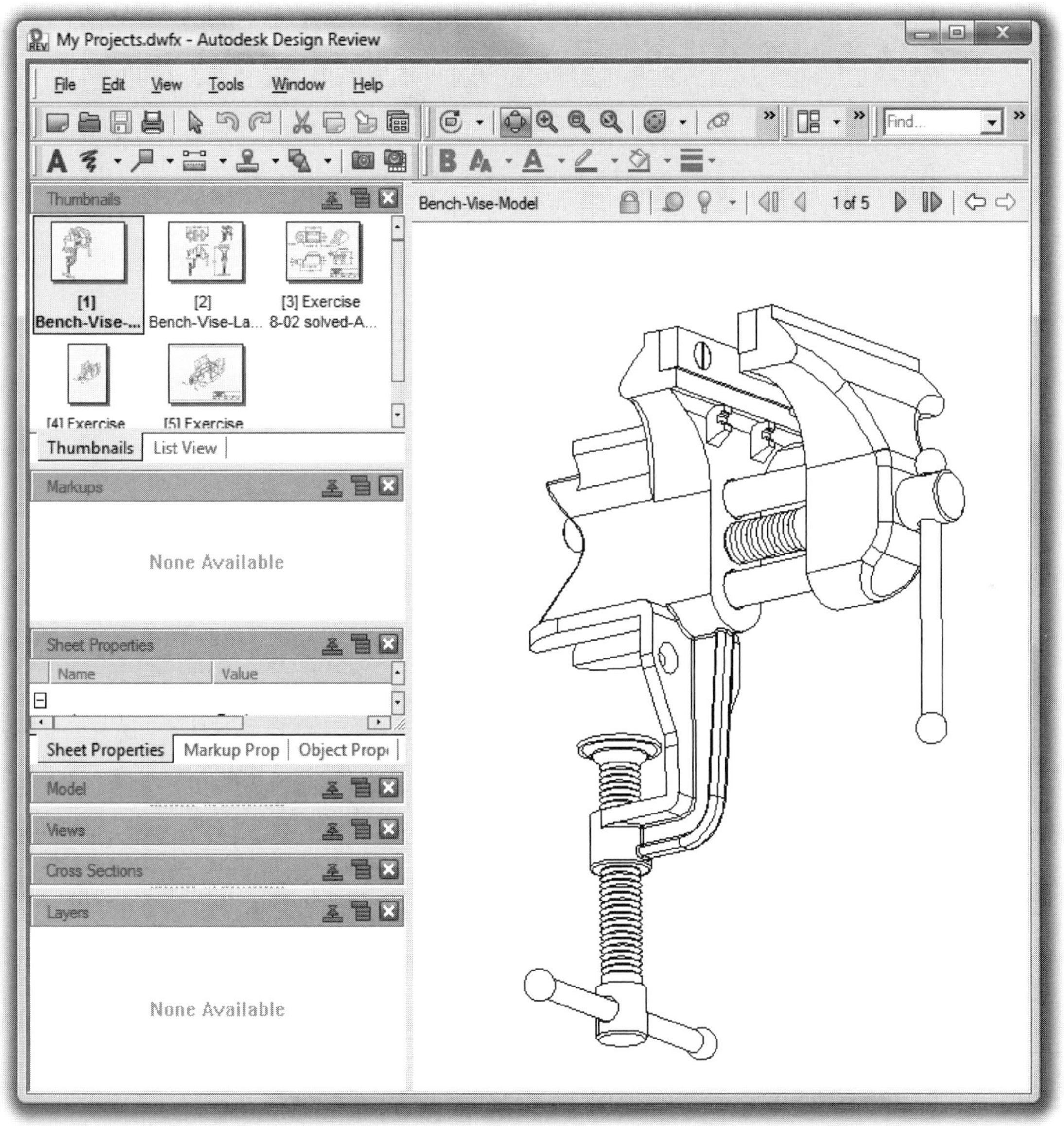

Figure 8-131 The Autodesk DWF Viewer window

3DDWF	
Standard Toolbar	
Command Line	3ddwf

Exercise 8-8: Creating DWF Files of 3D Objects Using the 3DDWF Command

1. **OPEN** the ***Bench-Vise*** drawing from Chapter 7 if it is closed.
2. Click on the **Model** tab to switch to model space.
3. Set the **3DWDFPREC** system variable to **5**, the **DISPSILH** variable to **0**, and the **ISOLINES** variable to **4**.

4. Invoke the **REGEN** command and **SAVE** the drawing.
5. Invoke the **3DDWF** command to open the **Export 3D DWF** dialog box. Type **Main Body Subassembly** as the file name and look for the location where you saved the DWF file in the previous exercise (Figure 8-132).

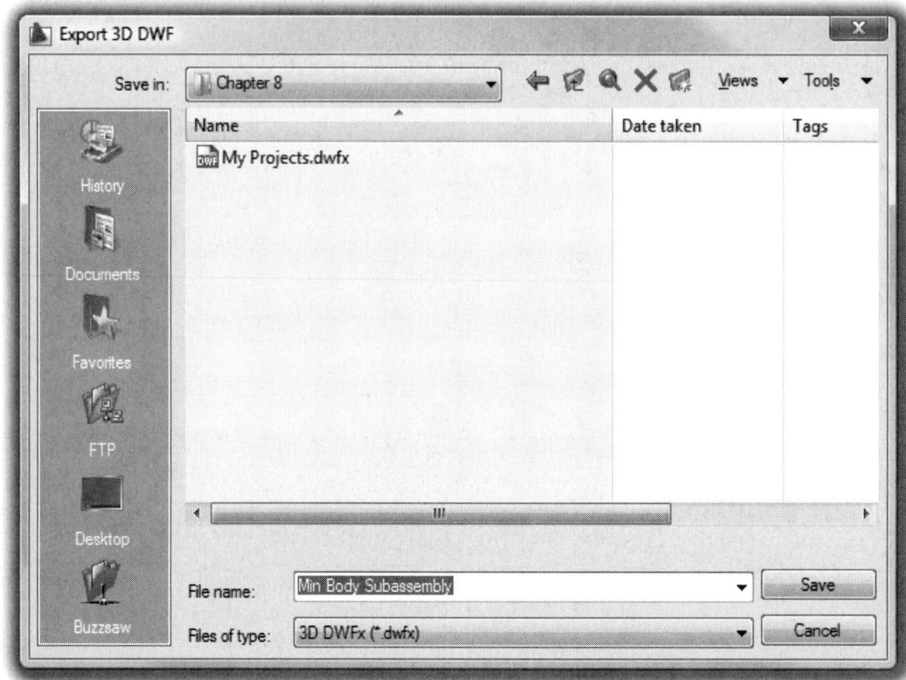

Figure 8-132 The Export 3D DWF dialog box

6. In the **Export 3D DWF** dialog box, click on **Tools/Options . . .** to open the **3D DWF Publish** dialog box. Under **Objects to Publish** select **Selected model space objects** and click the button located right below this setting (Figure 8-133).

Figure 8-133 The 3D DWF Publish dialog box

7. When prompted, select the *Main Body* and the other six components associated with it, including the two *Screws*. When you are finished, press **<Enter>** to return to the **3D DWF Publish** dialog box, and click **OK** to close it.
8. Click the **Save** button to start the process.
9. Click **Yes** to the inquiry: **Would you like to view it now**?
10. This will open the **Main Body Subassembly.dwf** file in the **Autodesk Design Review** application (Figure 8-134).
11. In the **Autodesk Design Review** window, click on the flyout button next to the 3D orbiting tools and select **Front Top Right** (Figure 8-135).

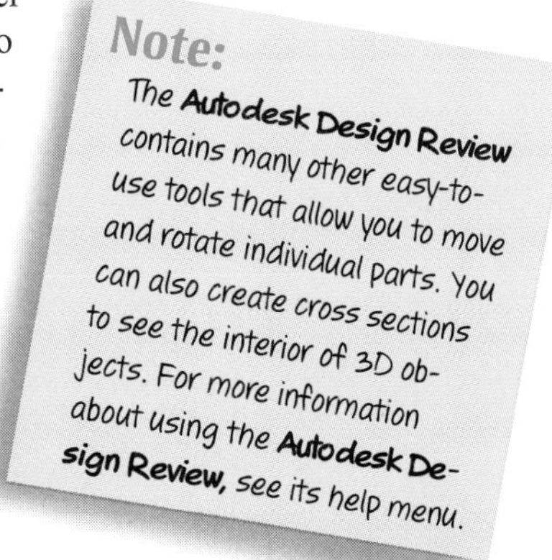

Note:
The **Autodesk Design Review** contains many other easy-to-use tools that allow you to move and rotate individual parts. You can also create cross sections to see the interior of 3D objects. For more information about using the **Autodesk Design Review**, see its help menu.

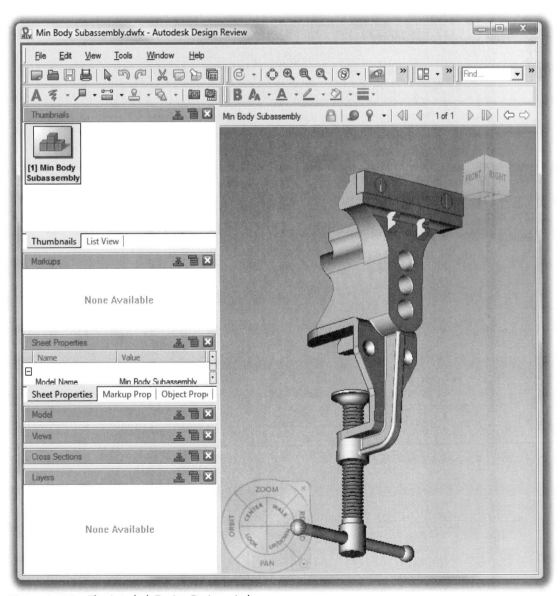

Figure 8-134 The Autodesk Design Review window

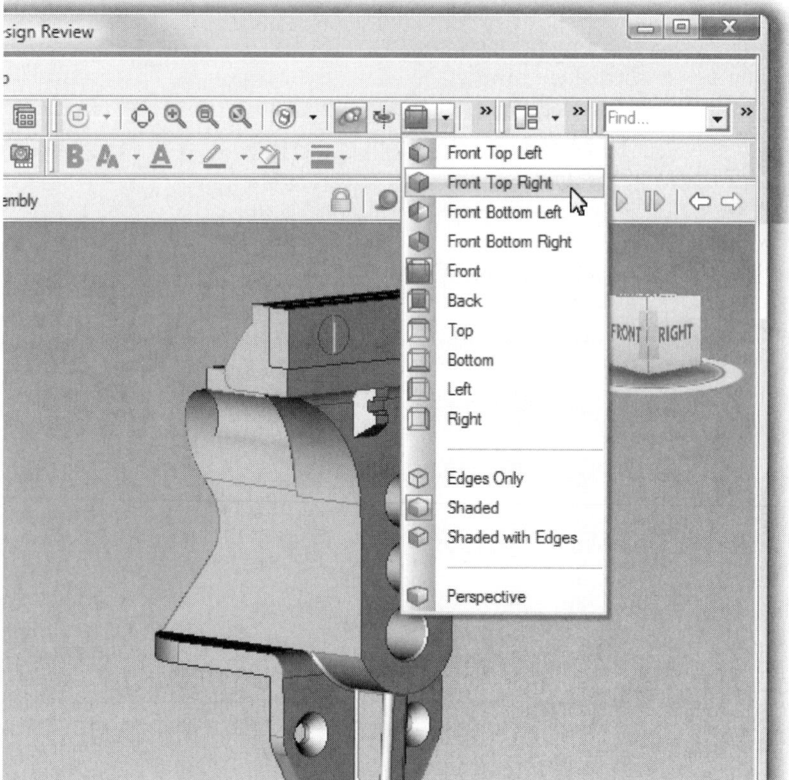

Figure 8-135 Selecting the Front Top Right option in the Autodesk Design Review window

12. Right-click on the viewing area and click on the **Select** tool at the very top of the shortcut menu. Select the *Main Body.* Right-click again and select **Transparent** from the shortcut menu. The 3D model should look like Figure 8-136.

Rapid Prototyping

Rapid prototyping is a modern process of creating prototypes. Rapid prototyping employs different technologies such as *stereolithography* (SLA), *selective laser sintering* (SLS), *fused deposition modeling* (FDM), *3D printing,* and *PolyJet.* Selecting the appropriate technology depends on factors such as accuracy, strength, smoothness, and cost.

Stereolithography is one of the most cost-effective technologies commonly used to obtain rapid prototypes. In this process, a computer program extracts a set of parallel cross sections every 0.008″ to 0.004″ throughout the 3D model. A laser beam then re-creates the entire area covered by the cross sections on the surface of a liquid resin, solidifying it. A platform carries the solidified layer and submerges it to a depth equal to the distance between the cross sections, allowing more liquid resin to set on top of the solidified layer. Next, the laser beam solidifies the second layer of liquid, adhering it to the first layer. When the last layer is solidified, the platform moves all the way up and the process is completed.

The promptness, accuracy, and cost effectiveness of rapid prototyping technologies have made it increasingly accepted. Many companies even allow you to upload the **STL** file, obtain an instant electronic quote, and order the service.

You can use the **EXPORT** or the **STLOUT** command to create **STL** files from a 3D solid and request a rapid prototype via the Internet. **STL** files must be created from a single 3D solid that lies in the positive octant; that is, the *X, Y,* and *Z* coordinates must be positive for any point of the 3D solid.

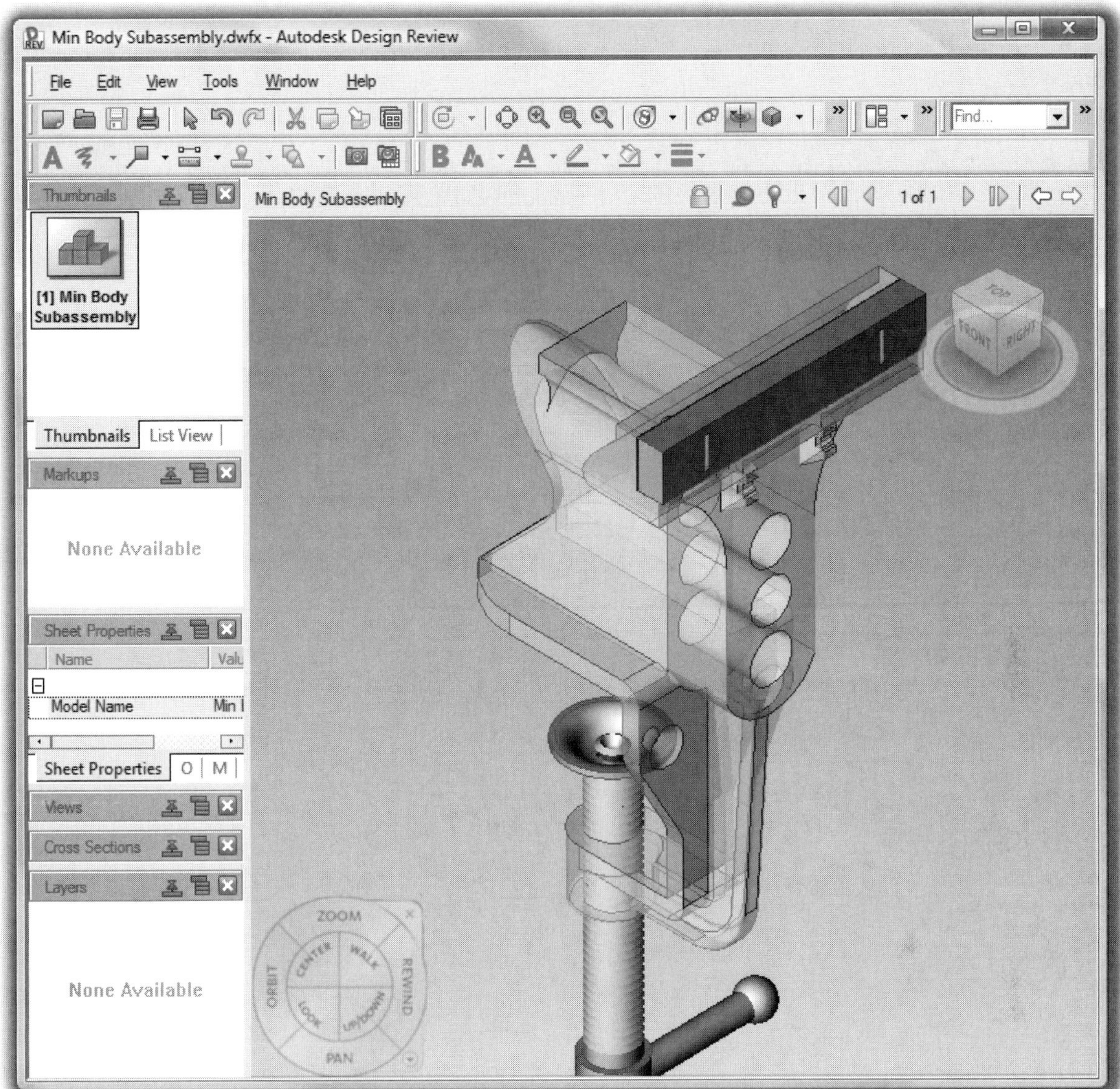

Figure 8-136 Using the Transparent mode to view the objects in the Autodesk Design Review window

The cost of a rapid prototype depends mostly on the 3D solid's volume. You can use the **MASSPROP** command to obtain not only the volume, but also other engineering information of a 3D solid or a region, such as the centroid and the moment of inertia.

SUMMARY

Even the most expert drafters and designers sometimes make mistakes when they undertake the projecting of drawing views of complex objects. After going through this chapter, you should have learned something very important: Anyone able to create a 3D model does not have to worry much about creating drawing views that contain errors.

As you have also learned, the AutoCAD program contains several procedures from which you can automatically obtain professional drawing views that are free of errors. You can use the technique that best suits your type of work, or you might prefer to use several of them together.

In this chapter you reviewed the paper space concept and set up the viewports to create 2D drawings the correct way. You also learned how to create the increasingly accepted DWF files using different procedures, which can expand your design communication efforts without any limitations.

Chapter Test Questions

Multiple Choice

1. Right-clicking on a paper space tab exposes a shortcut menu. Which of the following is not part of this menu list?
   a. **Viewports**
   b. **Rename**
   c. **Page Setup Manager . . .**
   d. **New layout**
2. Which of the following operations cannot be performed by clicking on the icons of the **Viewports** toolbar?
   a. Convert objects to viewport
   b. Specify a hidden shade plot
   c. Create a single rectangular viewport
   d. Set the scale on an active viewport
3. Which of the following properties of viewports must be changed to avoid losing the scale and alignment of the views by mistake?
   a. Layer
   b. Display locked
   c. Shade plot
   d. Maximize
4. Which of the following options cannot be used to create a section object?
   a. Orthographic
   b. Specifying two points
   c. Normal to a vector
   d. Selecting a planar face
5. Which of the following operations cannot be selected through the section object's shortcut menu?
   a. Change the type of section object
   b. Activate live sectioning
   c. Change the section object settings
   d. Create 2D/3D sections
6. Placing dimensions on top of a 3D object is a practical way of providing technical information. What is the most important consideration when performing this task?
   a. Changing the layers
   b. Selecting an orthographic view
   c. Relocating the UCS
   d. Rotating the object in the 3D space
7. Which of the following is impossible to obtain with the **SOLPROF** command?
   a. A block containing both the projected visible and hidden lines
   b. A block containing only the projected visible lines
   c. A section view of the 3D solid
   d. A 3D wireframe
8. Which of the following is necessary to obtain an STL file?
   a. No points of the 3D solid can have negative *X*, *Y*, or *Z* coordinates.
   b. The hidden lines must be turned off.
   c. Only one 3D solid must exist in the drawing.
9. Which of the following views cannot be created with the **SOLVIEW** command after a first viewport is created?
   a. Orthographic
   b. Auxiliary
   c. Isometric
   d. Section
10. Which of the following mass properties of a 3D solid cannot be obtained with the **MASSPRO** command?
    a. Volume
    b. Moment of inertia
    c. Surface area
    d. Bounding box

Matching

Column A	Column B
a. **SOLDRAW**	1. Extracts the profile of the selected 3D solids
b. Paper space	2. Temporarily slices 3D objects and creates sections
c. **SOLVIEW**	3. Generates profiles and sections of the views
d. **PUBLISH**	4. An infinite 2D space
e. Floating viewports	5. Generates DWF files of selected 3D objects
f. **VPMAX**	6. Creates views projected onto the current *XY* plane
g. **SOLPROF**	7. Objects that allow you to see the model space through them
h. **FLATSHOT**	8. Generates DWF files of 3D models and 2D drawings
i. **3DDWF**	9. Maximizes a viewport
j. Section object	10. Creates a special type of viewport

True or False

1. True or False: It is not possible to view the same objects in model space through two viewports that are each placed in a different Layout tab.
2. True or False: When used in paper space, layers have an additional function: You can freeze them in each viewport independently.
3. True or False: You can **MOVE** or **COPY** a viewport to another place by snapping not only to a point on it, but also to any point of the objects that are seen though them.
4. True or False: Double-clicking inside a viewport will maximize it.
5. True or False: You can achieve similar results by either adding a jog to an existing section object or using the **Draw section** option of the **SECTIONPLANE** command.
6. True or False: With the **FLATSHOT** command you can quickly obtain projected views that use different properties for visible and occulted lines.
7. True or False: To create exploded assembly drawings, you must use special tools and settings exclusively dedicated to this task.
8. True or False: With the **SOLPROF** command, you can only obtain the projections of orthographic and isometric views.
9. True or False: The **SOLDRAW** command allows you to resolve any floating viewport in a layout.
10. True or False: Using the **3DDWF** command, you can create DWF files of both 2D drawings and 3D models.

Chapter Tutorials

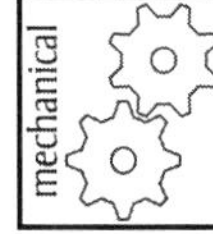

Tutorial 8-1: Generating the Drawing of the Sofa Table Model

In this tutorial you will generate the drawing of the *Sofa Table* 3D model, created in Chapter 2. The projected drawing views will be generated using the **SOLPROF** command.

1. **OPEN** ***SofaTable***.
2. **SAVE** the drawing **AS** ***Tutorial 8-1***.
3. Select the **SE Isometric** viewing point and the **2D Wireframe** visual style.
4. Click on the **Layout1** tab to switch to paper space and close the **Page Setup Manager** window in case it opens.
5. **ERASE** the viewport.
6. Invoke the **VPORTS** command. In the **Viewports** dialog box, select **Three-Right** under **Standard viewports:**. Under **Viewport Spacing:** specify **1**. Under **Setup:** select **3D** (Figure 8-137). Click on the **OK** button to close the dialog box. When prompted, specify two points diagonally inside the paper. The layout should look like Figure 8-138.
7. Double-click inside the top-left viewport to activate it. Locate the **Viewports** toolbar and select the scale **1″ = 1′-0″** from the drop-down list (Figure 8-139).

Do not use the mouse wheel at this moment to perform **ZOOM** or **PAN** operations. Doing so will cause the Top and Front drawing views to lose their alignment.

8. Repeat the operation for the viewports containing the Front view using the same scale.
9. Click inside the viewport that contains the Isometric view to make it active. Invoke the **3DORBIT** command to slightly change the viewing point. Do not use the mouse wheel. After these changes, the drawing should look like Figure 8-140.

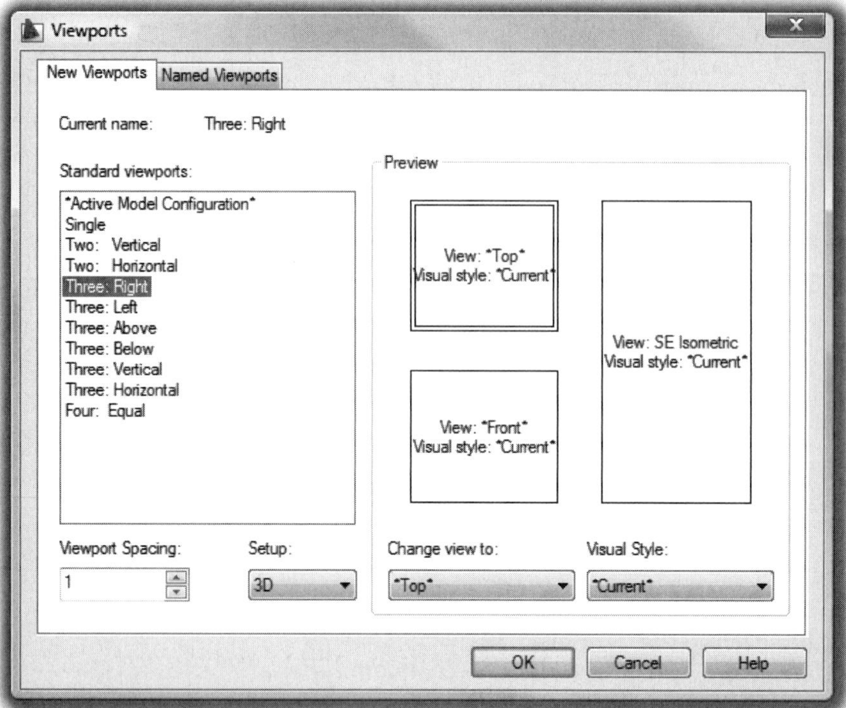

Figure 8-137 The Viewports dialog box

10. Double-click outside the viewports to deactivate whichever viewport is active. Select the three viewports and double-click on any of them to open the **Properties** palette. Under **Misc**, set the **Displayed locked** value to **Yes**.

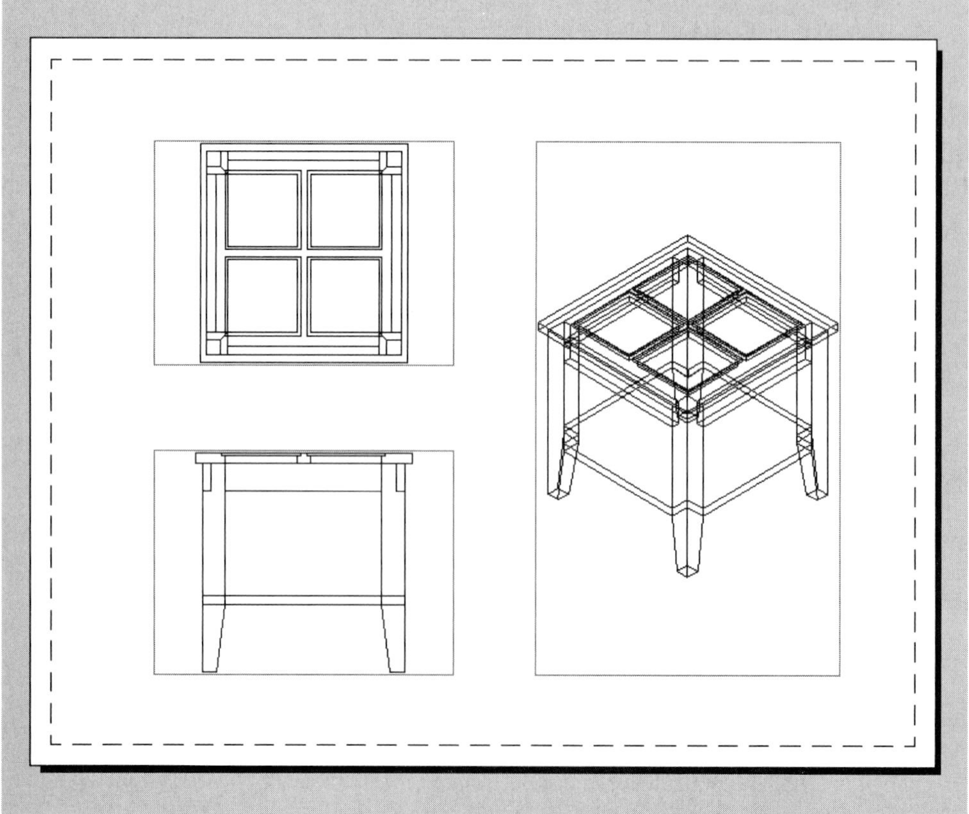

Figure 8-138 The resulting viewport arrangement in the layout

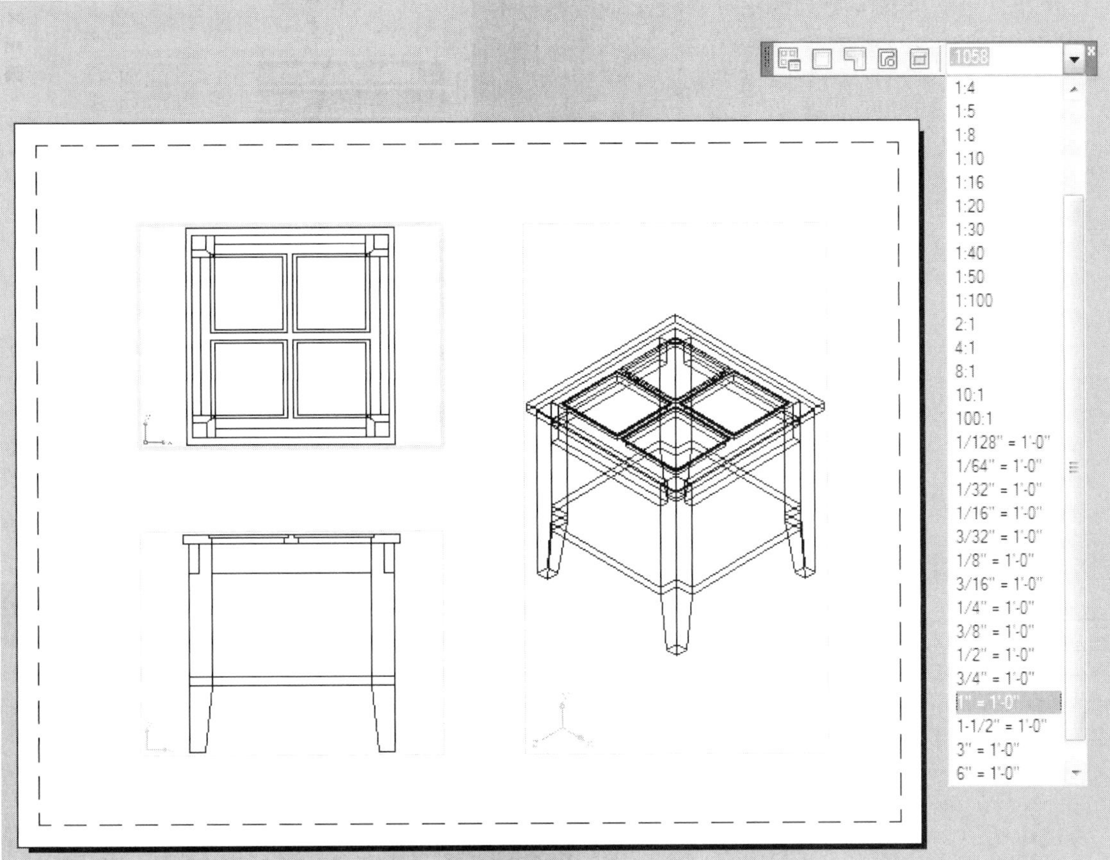

Figure 8-139 The scale drop-down list in the Viewports toolbar

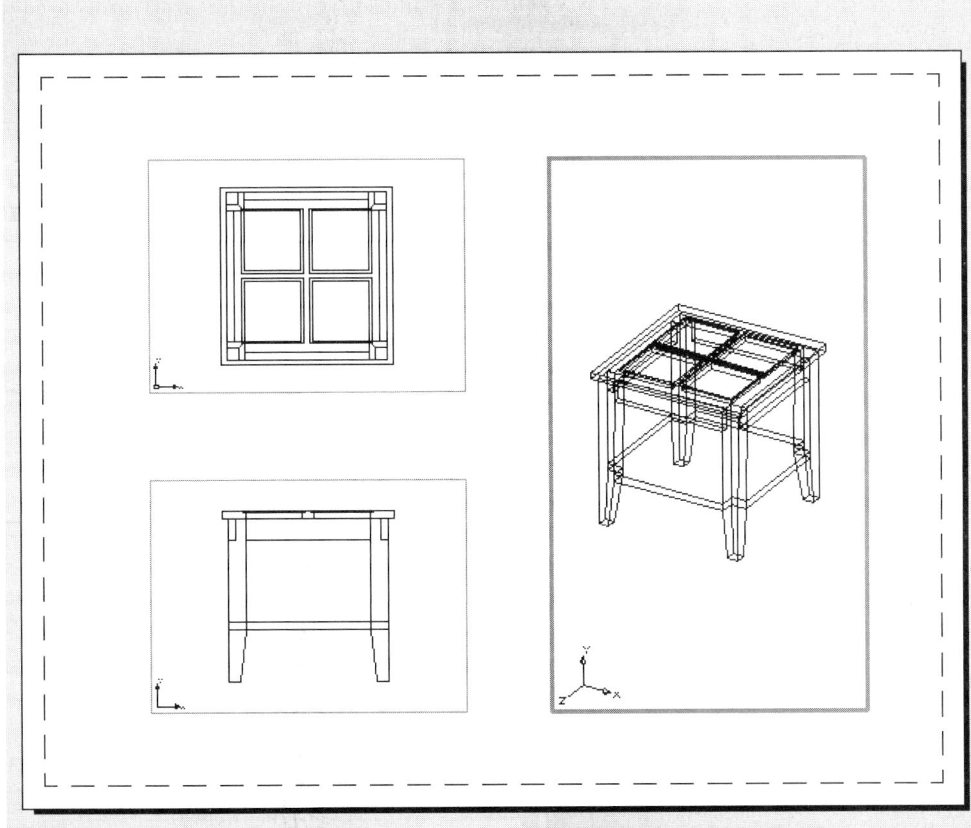

Figure 8-140 Changing the viewing point in a viewport

11. Holding the <**Shift**> key down, deselect the two viewports that contain the orthographic views, leaving only the viewport that contains the selected 3D view. In the **Properties** palette, change the **Shade plot** value to **Hidden** for this viewport (Figure 8-141).

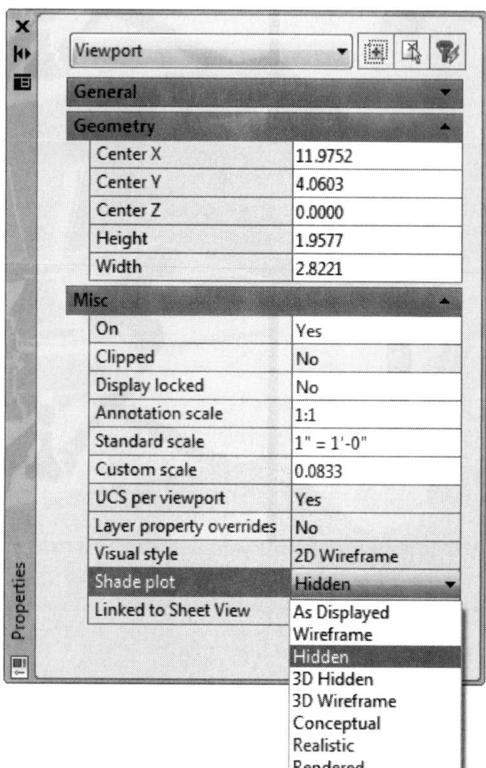

Figure 8-141 Setting the Shade plot for the viewports with the Properties palette

12. Load the **HIDDEN** linetype into the drawing.
13. Double-click inside the viewport that contains the Top view to make it active.
14. Invoke the **SOLPROF** command and respond to the prompts as follows:

    Select objects: *Using a selection window, select all the 3D solids inside the active viewport.*

    Select objects: ↵ *(To end the selection)*

    Display hidden profile lines on separate layer? [Yes/No] <Y>: ↵ *(To accept the default)*

    Project profile lines onto a plane? [Yes/No] <Y>: ↵ *(To accept the default)*

    Delete tangential edges? [Yes/No] <Y>: ↵ *(To accept the default)*

15. Click inside the viewport that contains the Front view to make it active.
16. Invoke the **SOLPROF** command and respond to the prompts the same way you did with the previous viewport.

Note:

The **SOLPROF** command automatically generates new layers for both viewports, creating separate blocks for the hidden and the visible edges. The layers generated for the hidden edges are automatically set with the HIDDEN linetype if the HIDDEN linetype was previously loaded into the drawing.

17. Open the **Layer Properties Manager** and change the color of the two layers that were automatically assigned to the visible lines (PV-) to **Blue**. Change the color of the two layers that were automatically assigned to the hidden lines (PH-) to **Red**. Click **OK** to close the dialog box (Figure 8-142).

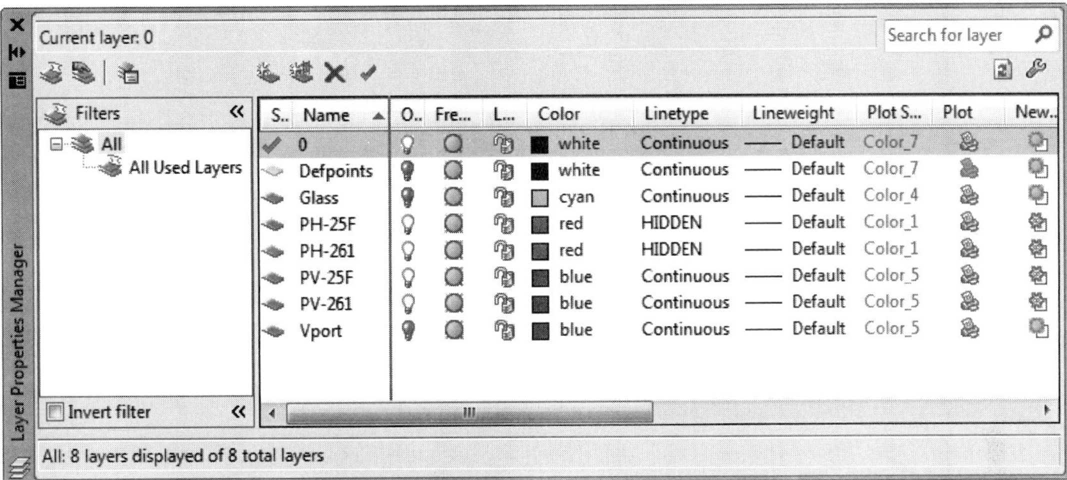

Figure 8-142 The Layers Properties dialog box after changing the Color property

18. Double-click inside the viewport that contains the Top view to make it active. Locate the **Layers** drop-down list on the **Layers** panel of the **Ribbon**. Click on the third icon of **Layer 0**. This will freeze this layer in the active viewport (Figure 8-143). Repeat the same operation for the viewport that contains the Front view.

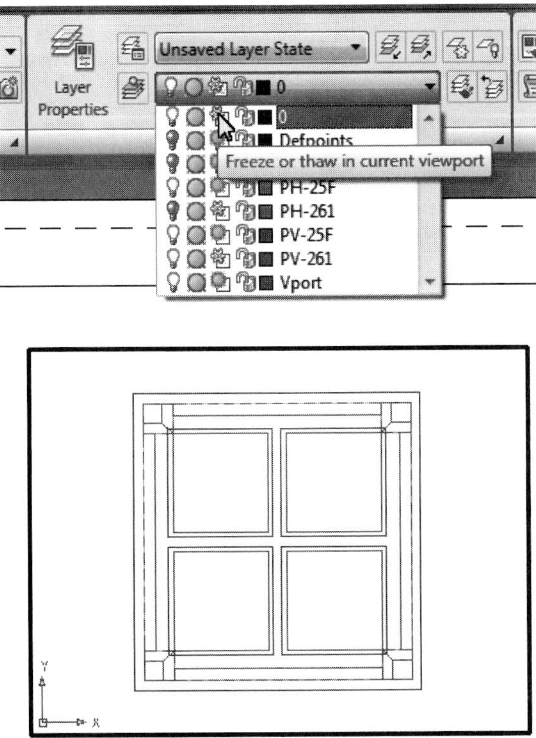

Figure 8-143 Freezing a layer in the active viewport

19. Double-click outside the viewports to return to paper space.
20. Set the **LTSCALE** system variable to **0.3**.
21. Create a new layer and give it any name. Select the three viewports, assign them the new layer, and then turn the layer off. The drawing should look like Figure 8-144.

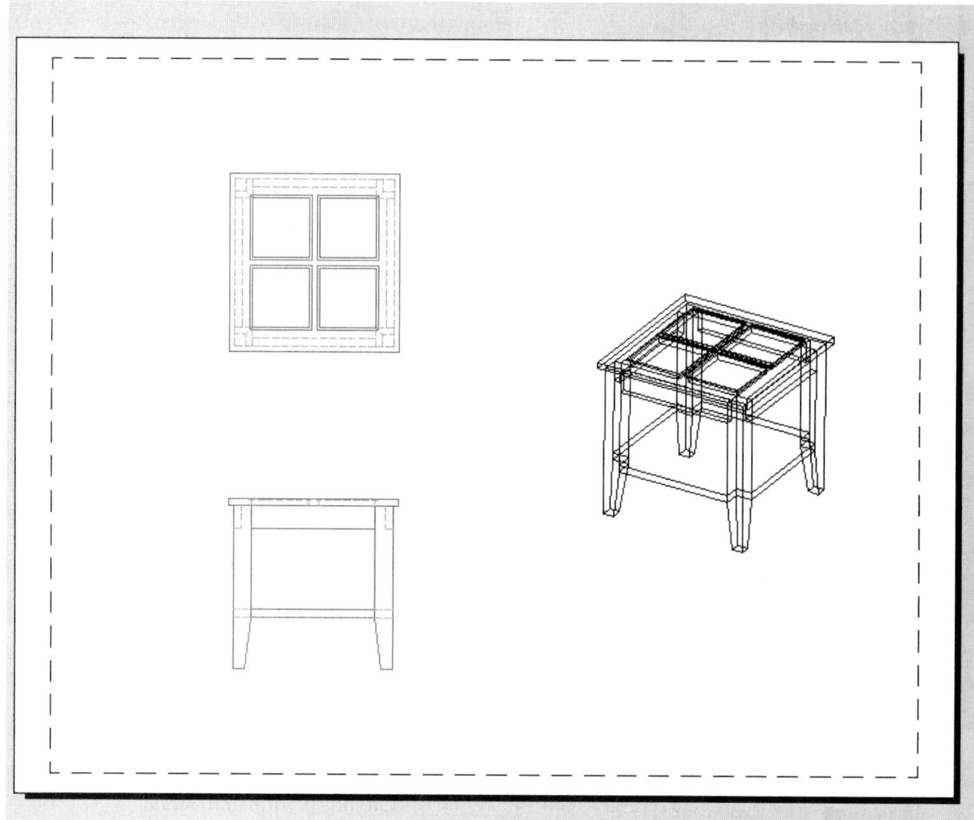

Figure 8-144 After turning the viewport's assigned layer off

22. Place some dimensions in the orthographic views on top of the paper.
23. Create a simple title block on your own, or use one from another drawing.
24. Open the **Page Setup** dialog box for **Layout1** and specify the plot device, plot style, and so on. Center the title block on the paper by specifying a **Window** as the plot area, centered with the plot.
25. **PLOT** your drawing. It should look like the one shown in Figure 8-145.
26. **SAVE** the drawing.

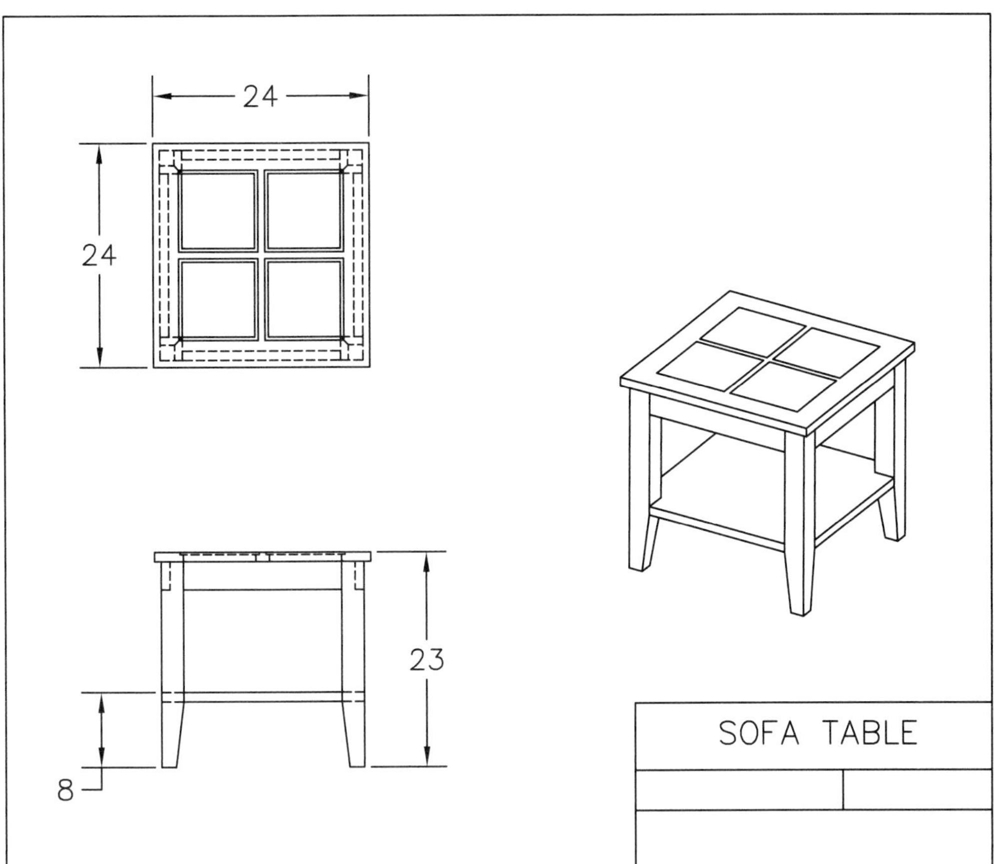

Figure 8-145 The final drawing document with dimensions

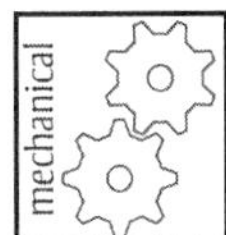

Tutorial 8-2: The Drawing of the Main Body

In this tutorial you will generate the drawing of the *Main Body* 3D model, created in Chapter 7. The projected drawing views will be created using the **SOLVIEW** and the **SOLDRAW** commands.

For this tutorial, you will now create a **Pen Style Table** file to specify the **Lineweight** values for the colors shown in the following chart.

Color	Lineweight	Use in Drawing
White (7)	0.35 mm	Visible edges
Cyan (4)	0.15 mm	Hidden edges
Yellow (2)	0.20 mm	Dimension text Notes
Red (1)	0.10 mm	Dimension lines Centerlines Hatches Small texts
Magenta (6)	0.50 mm	Section lines Titles

1. **OPEN** the ***Main Body*** drawing.
2. **SAVE** it **AS** ***Tutorial 8-2***.
3. Open the **Plot** dialog box. Select **New . . .** from the **Plot style table (pen assignment)** drop-down list to create a new **.ctb** file.
4. In the **Begin** step, select **Start from scratch** and click **Next**. Name the file **MyColorStyle** and click **Next**.
5. In the **Finish** step, check only **Use this plot style for the current drawing** and click **Finish**.
6. Make sure that **MyColorStyle.ctb** appears as the current **Plot style table** and click on the **Edit** button to change the properties of the colors that you will use.
7. In the **From View** tab of the **Plot Style Table Editor,** select all the colors under **Plot styles** and change their **Color** to **Black** under **Properties.** To select all the colors, select the first one, then scroll to the last color and select it while holding the **<Shift>** key down. After setting the plot color, perform the following individual changes:
   - Select **Color 1** and change its **Lineweight** property to **0.1000 mm.**
   - Select **Color 2** and change its **Lineweight** property to **0.2000 mm.**
   - Select **Color 4** and change its **Lineweight** property to **0.1500 mm**.
   - Select **Color 6** and change its **Lineweight** property to **0.5000 mm**.
   - Select **Color 7** and change its **Lineweight** property to **0.3500 mm**.
8. Click the **Save & Close** button to return to the **Plot** dialog box.
9. Click on the **Colors . . .** button located in the **Display** tab of the **Options** dialog box to open the **Drawing Window Colors** dialog box.
10. Under **Context,** select **Sheet/layout**. Under **Interface element**, select **Uniform Background**. Under **Color**, select **Black** (Figure 8-146).
11. Click **Apply & Close** to close the **Drawing Window Colors** dialog box. Click **OK** to close the **Options** dialog box.
12. Open the **Layer Properties Manager** and create a new layer named **3D Model**. Select the **Green** color for the new layer. Close the **Layer Properties Manager** and assign the layer **3D Model** to the 3D solid. Set the **Color** property of the 3D solid as **ByLayer**.
13. Make sure **UCSORTHO** is set to **1** and select the **Top** view.
14. Click on the **Layout1** tab to switch to paper space.
15. Depending on the options settings, the **Page Setup Manager** may or may not open automatically the first time you access **Layout1**. If the **Page Setup Manager** does not open, right-click on the **Layout1** tab to open it from the shortcut menu.
16. Select **Layout1** and click the **Modify . . .** button to enter the **Page Setup** dialog box. Select your printing device from the list and select **MyColorStyle.ctb** as the plot style. Click **OK** to close the dialog box. Close the **Page Setup Manager** window.

Note:
The set of colors that you will use with this tutorial makes a better contrast with a black display background. Next, you will change the background color of the paper in the **Options** dialog box.

Note:
When you change the background color, it will be shown in any other drawing you open. You can always change the background color to white again. You can also restore the default colors by clicking the **Restore** button on the **Drawing Window Colors** dialog box after you finish this tutorial.

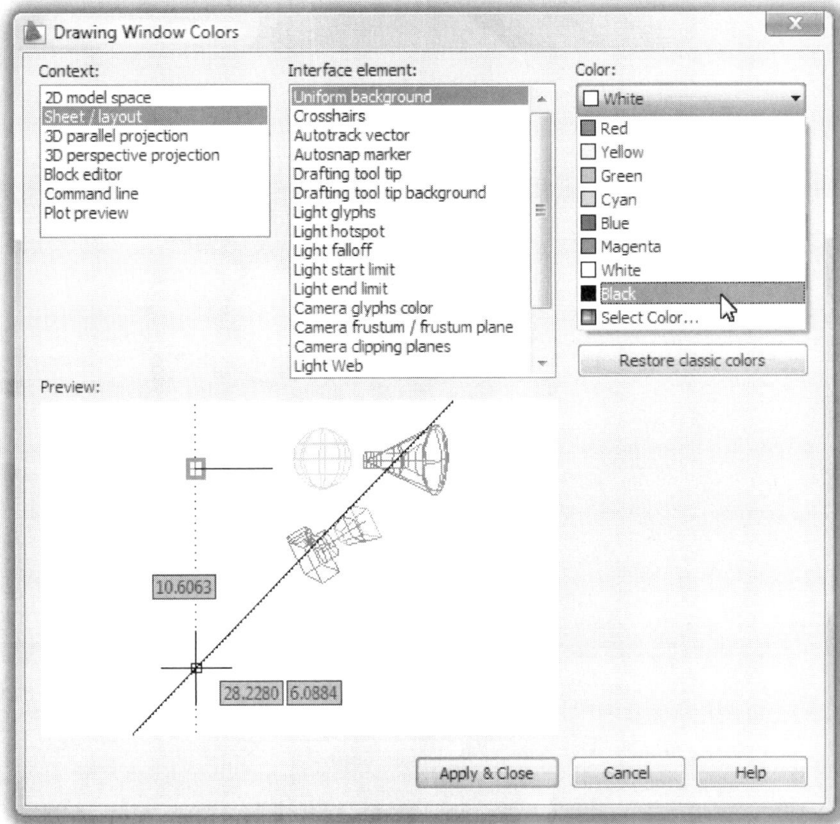

Figure 8-146 The Drawing Window Colors dialog box

17. **DELETE** the viewport that the AutoCAD program automatically creates to clean up the sheet of paper.
18. Invoke the **SOLVIEW** command and respond to the prompts as follows:

Enter an option [Ucs/Ortho/Auxiliary/Section]: *u* ↵

Enter an option [Named/World/?/Current] <Current>: ↵ *(To accept the current UCS World))*

Enter view scale <1.0000>: *0.5* ↵ *(For a 1:2 scale)*

If you are not sure about which scale you can use so that all the views fit properly in the specific paper size, just specify any scale value, trying to make your best guess. It can later be changed in the **Scale** drop-down list of the **Viewports** toolbar.

Specify view center: *Click in the lower-left side of the sheet.*

Specify view center <specify viewport>: *Click to relocate the view center as many times as needed. When finished, press* **<Enter>**.

Specify first corner of viewport: *Click to the left and over the view.*

Specify opposite corner of viewport: *Click to the right and below the view* (Figure 8-147).

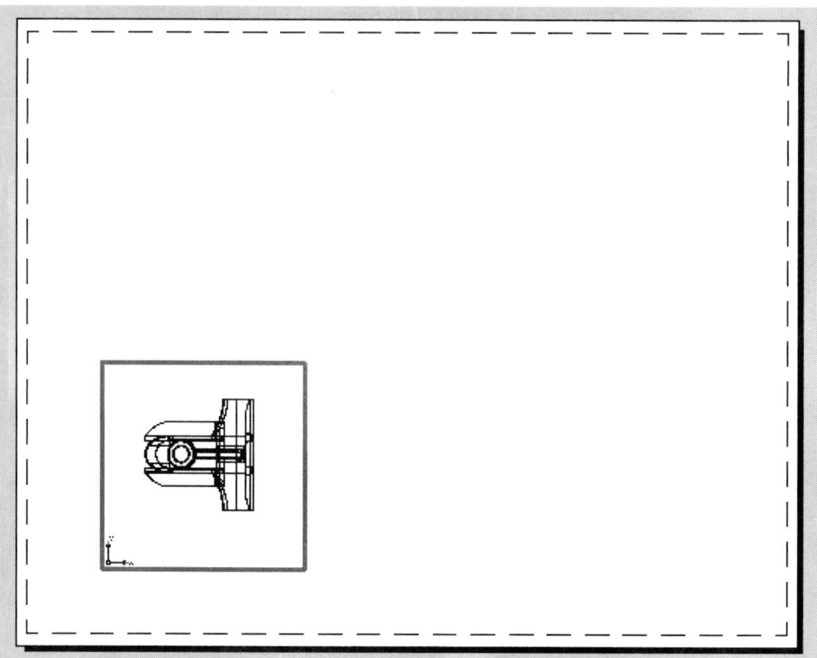

Figure 8-147 After completing the first viewport with the SOLVIEW operation

TIP

Do not use the mouse wheel during the entire process of the **SOLVIEW** command. Zooming with the mouse wheel will alter the view scale. Then, when you reset the scale to the correct factor, the alignment of the drawing view with respect to the other view will be lost. To achieve the alignment again, you will have to move the views manually.

Enter view name: *TopView* ↵

Enter an option [Ucs/Ortho/Auxiliary/Section]: *s* ↵

Specify first point of cutting plane: *Select the midpoint on the left;* see Figure 8-148.

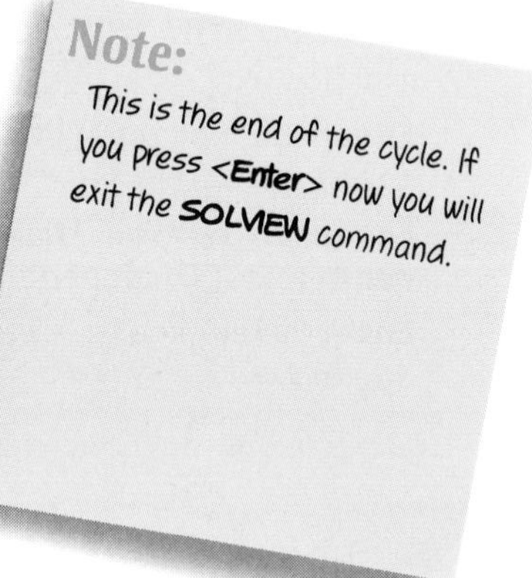
Note:
This is the end of the cycle. If you press <Enter> now you will exit the SOLVIEW command.

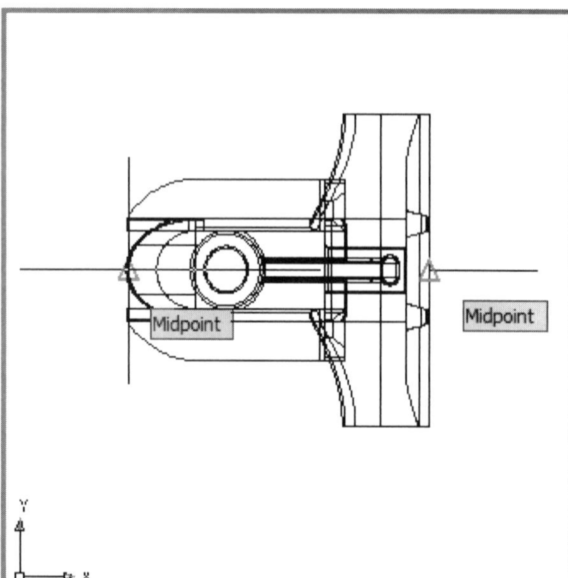
Midpoint
Midpoint
Y
X

Figure 8-148 Points to be specified for the section view

Because the AutoCAD program turns OSNAP mode off at this stage of the command, you must specify the midpoint snap by selecting this object snap directly.

Specify second point of cutting plane: *Specify the midpoint on the right.*

Specify side to view from: *Click on an empty place inside the viewport and below the 3D model.*

Note:

The two points in Figure 8-148 establish the location of the sectioning plane.

Enter view scale <0.5000>: ↵ *(To accept the value)*

Specify view center: *Specify a point by clicking above the Top view.*

Specify view center <specify viewport>: *Click to relocate the view center as many times as needed. When finished, press* ***<Enter>***.

Specify first corner of viewport: *Click to the left and over the new view.*

Specify opposite corner of viewport: *Click to the right and below the new view. The drawing views should look like* Figure 8-149.

Enter view name: *SectionA* ↵

Enter an option [Ucs/Ortho/Auxiliary/Section]: *o* ↵ *(To create a third view, using the orthographic option)*

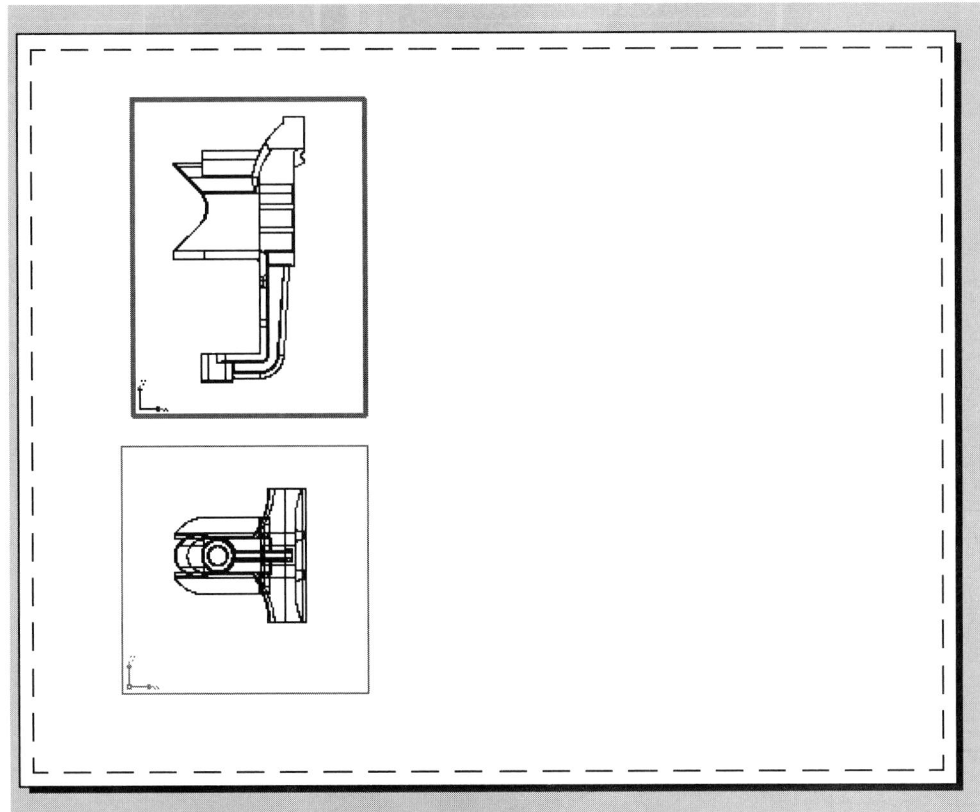

Figure 8-149 After completing the section view

Specify side of viewport to project: *Snap to the midpoint of the right border of the viewport that contains the "SectionA" view.*

Specify view center: *Specify a point by clicking to the right of the "SectionA" view.*

Specify view center <specify viewport>: *Click to relocate the view center as many times as needed. When finished, press* **<Enter>**.

Specify first corner of viewport: *Click to the left and over the new view.*

Specify opposite corner of viewport: *Click to the right and below the new view. The drawing views should look like* Figure 8-150.

Enter view name: *SideView* ↵

Enter an option [Ucs/Ortho/Auxiliary/Section]: ↵ *(To exit the command)*

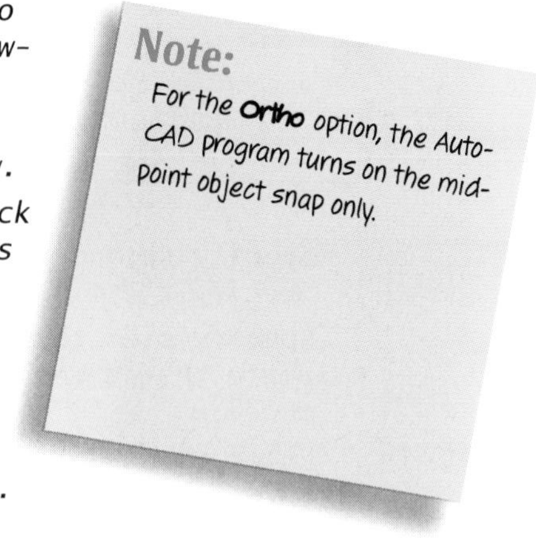

Note:
For the Ortho option, the AutoCAD program turns on the midpoint object snap only.

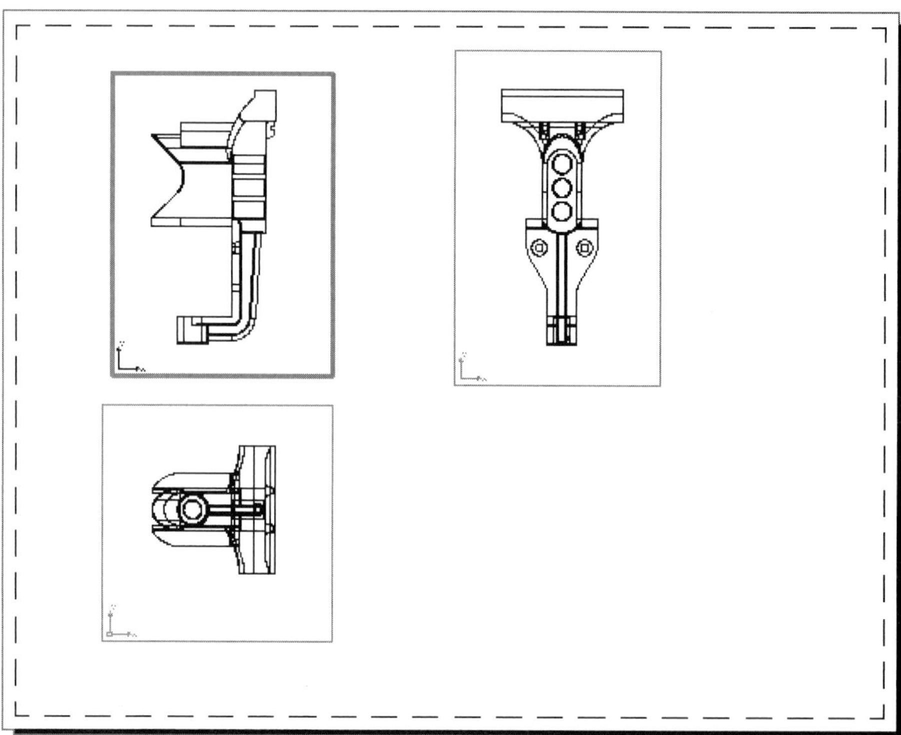

Figure 8-150 After completing the third view

19. Open the **Layer Manager** dialog box. As you can see, the AutoCAD program has created a set of layers for each view. You will change some properties of these layers before using the **SOLDRAW** command. Use Figure 8-151 along with the information below.
    - Change the color of layers ending with **-HID** to **Cyan** (4).
    - Change the color of layers ending with **-DIM** and **-HAT** to **Red** (1).
    - The color of layers ending with **-VIS** should stay as **White** (7).
    - Change the linetype of layers ending with **-HID** to **HIDDEN**.

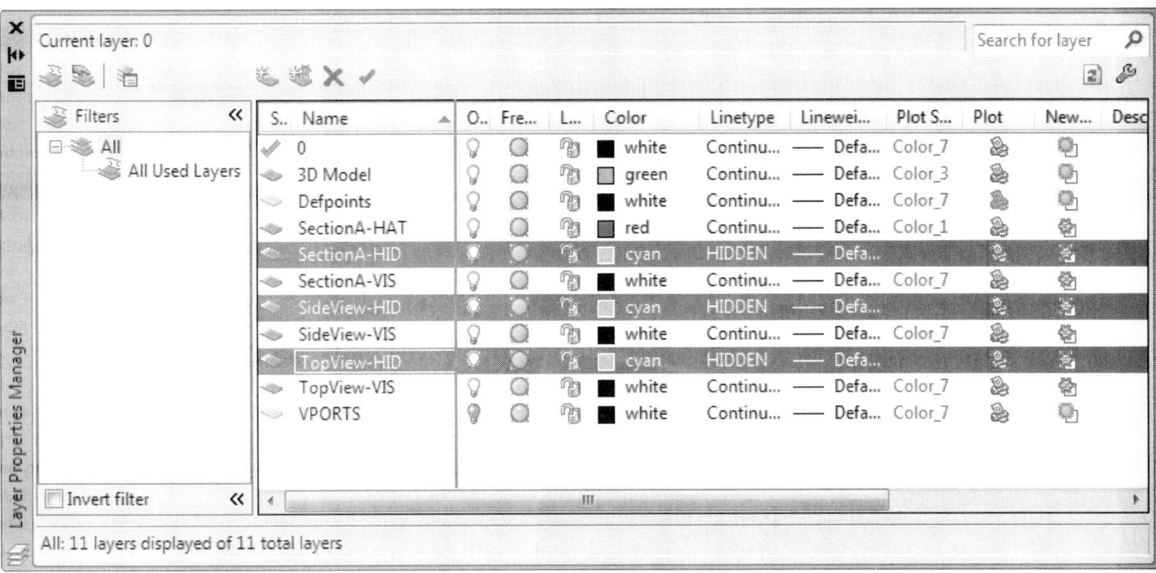

Figure 8-151 The Layer Manager dialog box

TIP

To use the **HIDDEN** linetype, you must first load it to the drawing. You can do so directly from the **Layer Properties Manager**.

20. Set the **LTSCALE** system variable to **0.4**.
21. Invoke the **SOLDRAW** command. When prompted, select the three viewports and press **<Enter>** to end the selection.
22. Select the three viewports and assign them the layer *VPORT*.
23. With the viewports still selected, right-click on the drawing area and set the **Display locked** attribute to **Yes** in the shortcut menu.
24. With ORTHO mode activated, **MOVE** the viewports around to a desired location without losing their alignment.
25. Set **Layer 0** as current and turn the *VPORTS* layer off to hide the viewports.
26. Open the **Dimension Style Manager** dialog box and click on **New . . .** to create a new dimension style. Under **New Style Name:** type **Mechanical Style** and then click **Continue**. In the **Modify Dimension Style** dialog box, change the following parameters:
    - Click the **Text** tab. Click the **. . .** button near **Text Style** to open the **Text Style** dialog box. Select **romans.shx** from the **Fonts** drop-down list and click **Apply.** Click **Close** to return to the **Modify Dimension Style** dialog box. Under **Text Alignment** select **Aligned with dimension line**.
    - Click the **Lines** tab. Change both the **Dimension lines** and the **Extension lines** to **Red** (1).
    - Click the **Primary Units** tab and set the **Precision** to two decimal places (0.00).
    - Click the **Fit** tab and set the overall scale value to **0.45** under **Scale for dimension features**. Click **OK** to close the **Modify Dimension Style** dialog box.

Note:

The AutoCAD program processes the projected objects and assigns layers accordingly in each viewport with the **SOLDRAW** operation.

- In the **Dimension Style Manager** click on **New . . .** again while **Mechanical Style** is selected. Select **Radius dimensions** under **Use for:**. Click **Continue** to open the **Modify Dimension Style** dialog box. Click the **Text** tab and select **Horizontal** under **Text Alignment.** Click **OK** to return to the **Dimension Style Manager** dialog box.
- Repeat the previous operation to create substyles for **Diameter dimension** and **Angular dimension**.
- Before closing the **Dimension Style Manager**, set **Mechanical Style** as the current style by selecting it and then clicking on the **Set Current** button.

27. Create a new viewport in the lower-right corner of the paper using the **VPORTS** command or the icon on the **Viewports** toolbar.
28. Double-click inside the new viewport to activate it.
29. Select the **SW Isometric** viewing point.
30. **ZOOM** in or out to set a proper scale factor (not necessarily a standard scale factor).
31. Double-click outside the paper to deactivate the active viewport.
32. Select the viewport you just created and right-click in the paper area. Set the **Display Locked** attribute to **Yes** from the shortcut menu. Expose the same shortcut menu again and set the **Shade plot** to **Hidden**.
33. Change the layer of the new viewport to the *VPORT* Layer. Click **OK** to close the warning message, if it is displayed.

34. Open the ***TB-Imperial*** drawing from the CD.
35. Copy the entire title block located in the **ANSI A (11 × 8.5)** layout to the clipboard using the **COPYCLIP** command. **CLOSE** the drawing without saving it.
36. Go back to **Layout1** of ***Tutorial 8-2***. Right-click in the paper area and select **Paste as Block** from the shortcut menu. When prompted, specify a point anywhere. Then **MOVE** the block so that all the views fit inside. The drawing should look like Figure 8-152.
37. Right-click on the **Layout1** tab to access the **Page Setup** dialog box for this layout through the **Page Setup Manager** window.
38. In the **Page Setup** dialog box, select **Window** under **Plot area**. When prompted, specify the two diagonal corners by snapping to the endpoints on the title block.
39. In the **Page setup** dialog box, check the **enter the plot** checkbox. Make sure the scale is **1:1** and click **OK** to close the dialog box.
40. Set **Layer 0** as current and add some dimensions to the drawing views.
41. **EXPLODE** the title block and fill in the fields using *Text* or *Mtext* objects.

You can still move the viewport around, if needed, by turning its layer on first. When you move a viewport that contains dimensions, you should move the dimensions along with the viewport.

42. Create the **Detail I** view. Figure 8-153 shows the finished document after it has been printed.

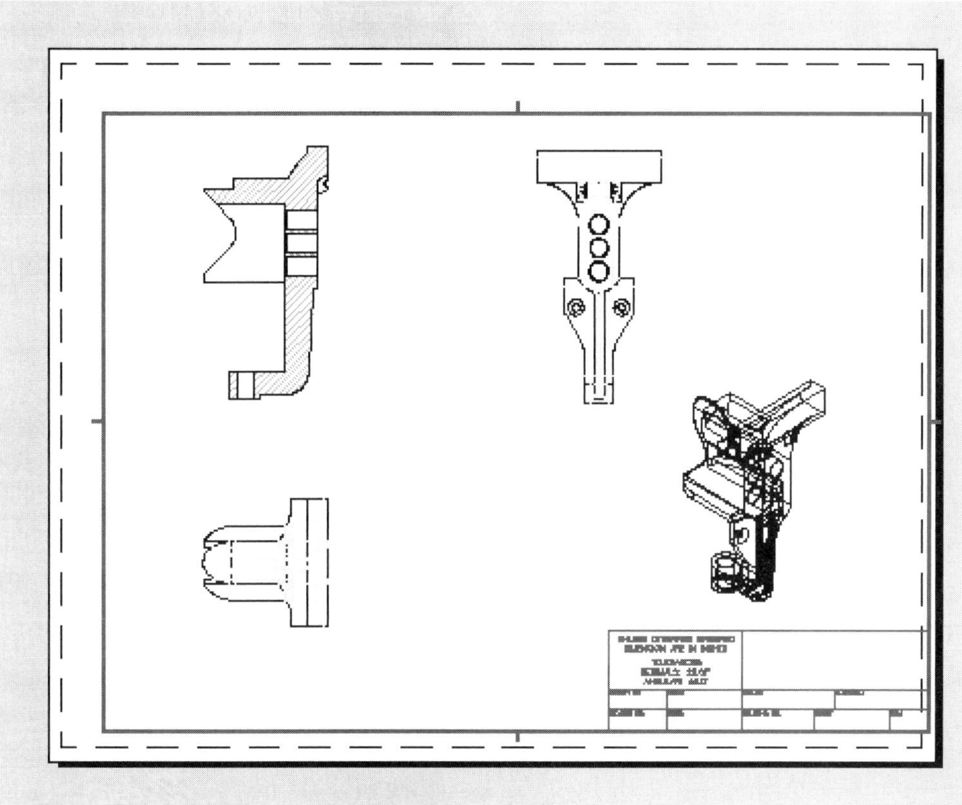

Figure 8-152 After pasting the title block in the layout

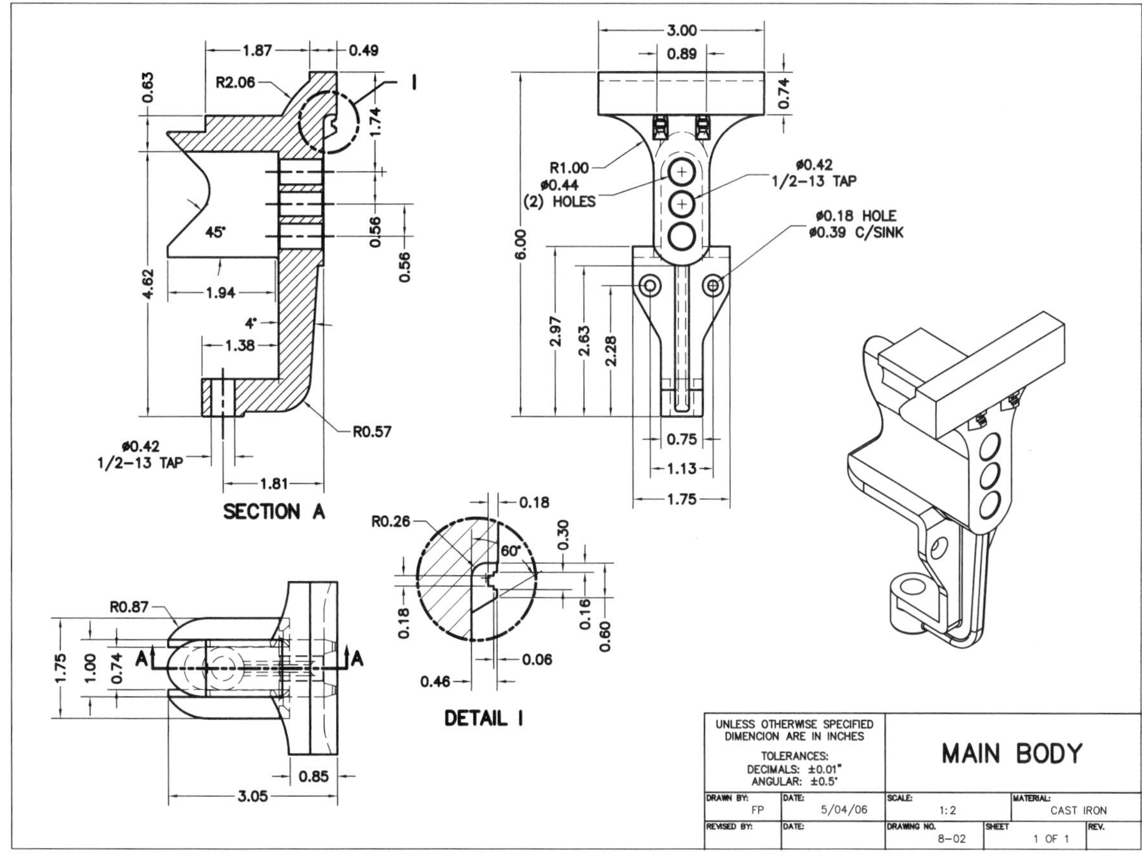

Figure 8-153 The final drawing document with dimensions

You can create a detail view by drawing a circle in the drawing area and then converting it into a viewport. You can then activate the viewport and freeze the layers you do not need. The scale of the viewport that contains the detail view is typically two, four, or eight times bigger than the scale of the view you are magnifying.

43. **SAVE** the drawing.
44. Create a **DWF** file of this layout only using the **PUBLISH** command.

Tutorial 8-3: A 3D Exploded View of the Bench Vise

1. **OPEN** the ***Bench-Vise*** drawing file as it was finished in Chapter 7.
2. **SAVE** the drawing **AS *Tutorial 8-3***.
3. Select the **Isometric SE** viewing point.
4. Select the **Front** UCS.
5. With ORTHO mode on, **MOVE** the following nine components **3.5″** along the positive *X*-axis (Figure 8-154).
   - the two *Guides*
   - the *Moving Jaw*
   - the *Aluminum Block* located on the *Moving Jaw*
   - the two *Screws* located on the *Moving Jaw*
   - the *Main Bolt*
   - the *Pin*
   - the *Handle* located on the *Main Bolt*

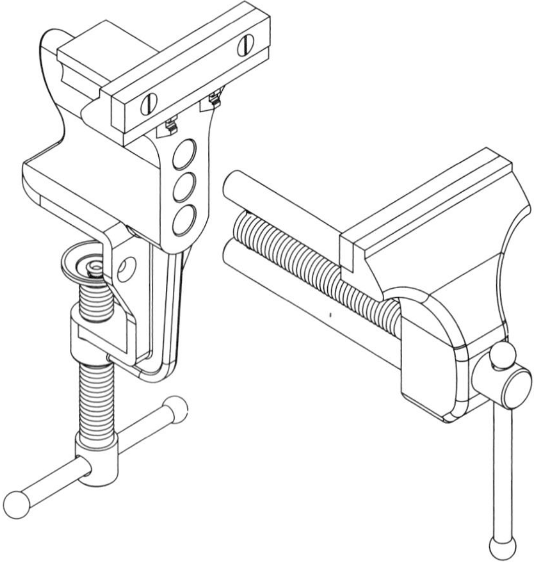

Figure 8-154 The first set of components is moved

6. **MOVE** the following seven components **3″** along the positive *X*-axis (Figure 8-155).
   - the *Moving Jaw*
   - the *Aluminum Block* located on the *Moving Jaw*

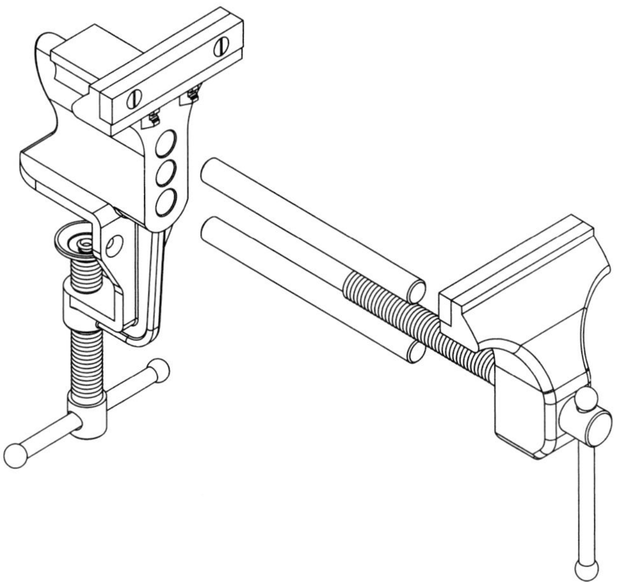

Figure 8-155 The second set of components is moved

- the two *Screws* located on the *Moving Jaw*
- the *Main Bolt*
- the *Pin*
- the *Handle* located on the *Main Bolt*

7. **MOVE** the following three components, **6″** along the positive *X*-axis (Figure 8-156).
    - the *Main Bolt*
    - the *Pin*
    - the *Handle* located on the *Main Bolt*
8. **MOVE** the *Pin* **1.5″** along the negative *Y*-axis.

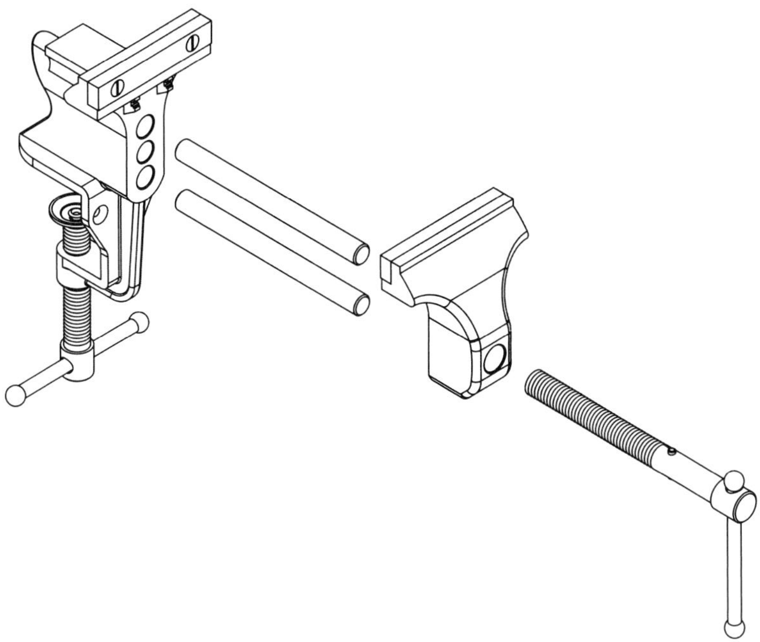

Figure 8-156 The third set of components is moved

9. **Move** the following three components **3″** along the negative *Y*-axis.
   - the *Fastening Bolt*
   - the *Pressing Plate*
   - the *Handle* located on the *Fastening Bolt*
10. **MOVE** the *Fastening Bolt* and its *Handle* **1″** along the negative *Y*-axis (Figure 8-157).

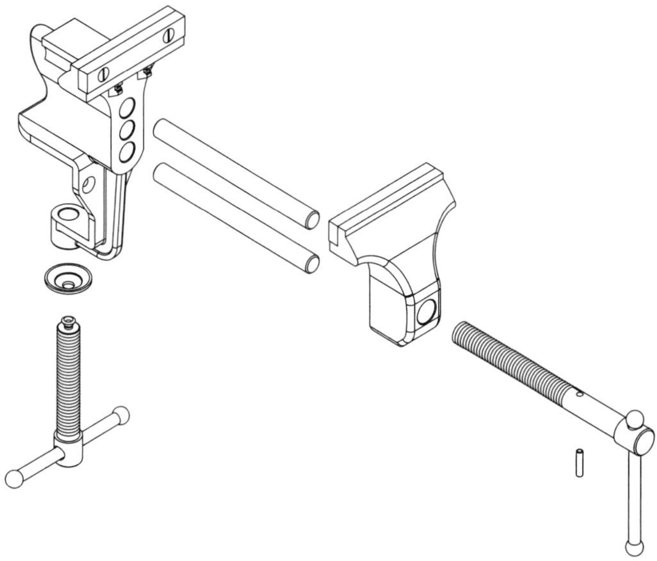

Figure 8-157 The fourth set of components is moved

11. **MOVE** the *Aluminum Block* located on the *Moving Jaw* and its two *Screws* **1″** along the negative *X*-axis.
12. **MOVE** the two *Screws* you just moved **1″** along the negative *X*-axis (Figure 8-158).

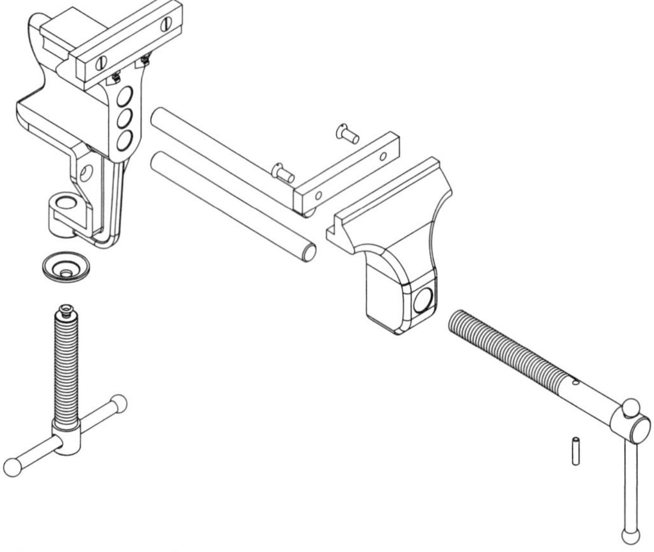

Figure 8-158 The two screws are moved

13. **MOVE** the *Aluminum Block* located on the *Main Body* and its two *Screws* **1″** along the positive *X*-axis.

14. **MOVE** the two *Screws* you just moved **1″** along the positive *X*-axis as well (Figure 8-159).

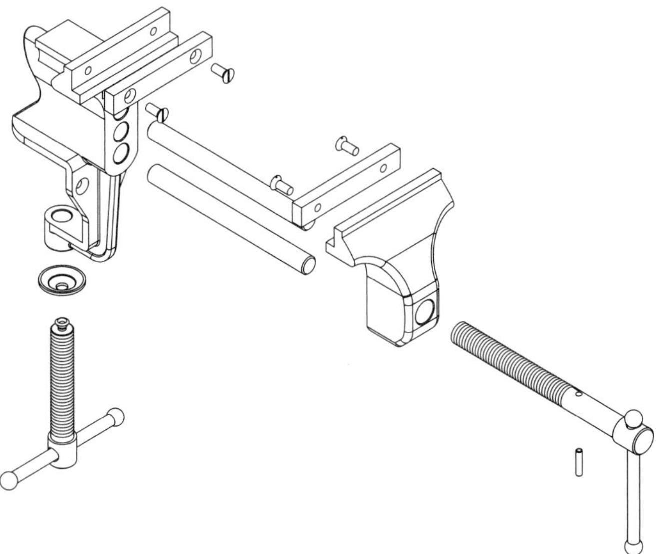

Figure 8-159 The other two screws are moved

15. Set center points as the only Object Snap mode active in the **Object Snap** tab of the **Drafting Settings** dialog box (Figure 8-160).

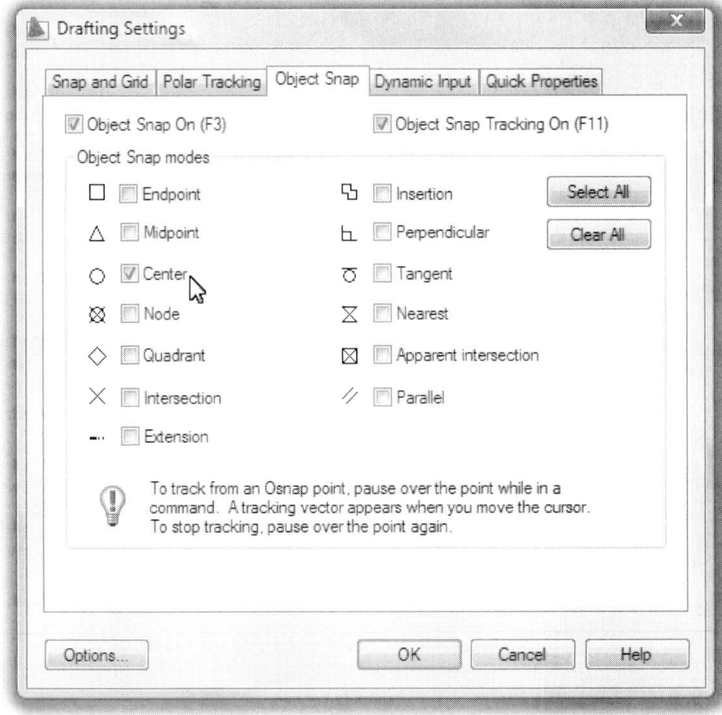

Figure 8-160 The Drafting Settings dialog box

16. Using a different color, draw nine polylines to show the assembly traces. Snap to the farthermost center points to place the polylines.
17. Set the **LTSCALE** system variable to **0.4**.
18. Load the **CENTER** linetype into the drawing and change the **Linetype** of the polylines to **CENTER**. The 3D model should look now like Figure 8-161.

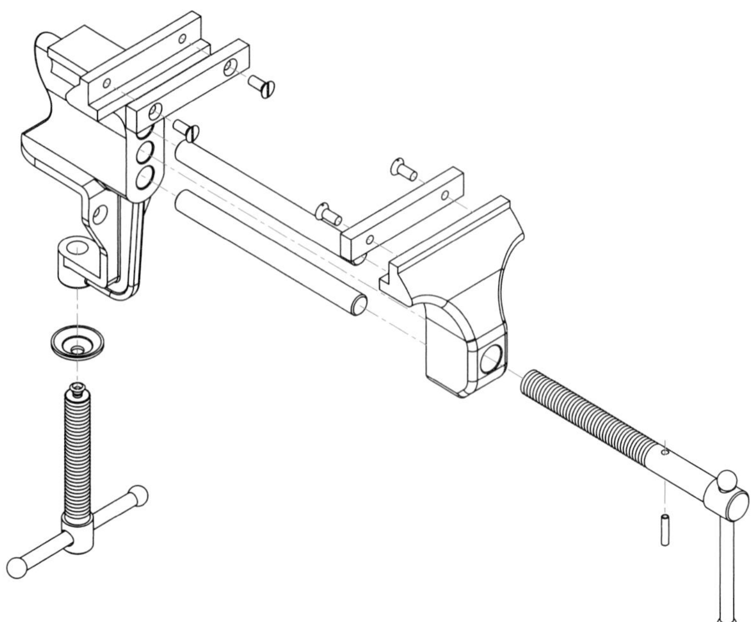

Figure 8-161 The completed 3D model

19. Select the **World** UCS.
20. **MOVE** all the objects from the bottom circular edge of the *Fastening Bolt* to the origin **0,0,0**.
21. **MOVE** all the objects again from any base point to the relative destination point @**4,4,0**.

Note:

You have just generated the **STL** file of the Main Body. This file can be used to request an instant quote and a rapid prototyping service via the Internet. The rapid prototype would look like Figure 8-162 if the service requested was a stereolithography process.

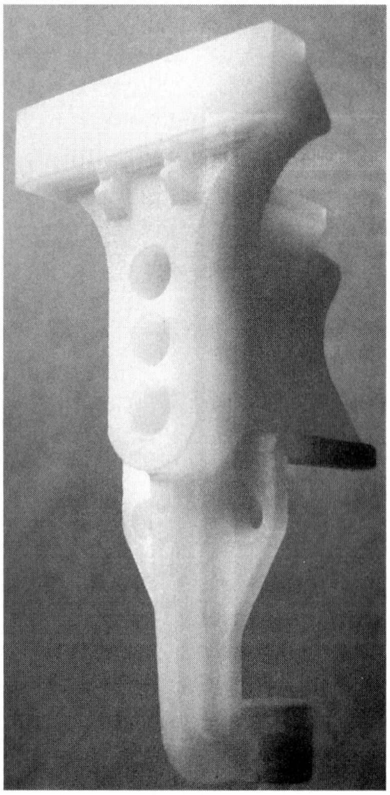

Figure 8-162 Rapid prototype of the Main Body generated by the stereolithography process

22. Double-click the mouse wheel in the drawing area to fit the objects in the display.
23. Invoke the **EXPORT** command through the **File** drop-down menu.
24. In the **Export data** dialog box, select **Lithography (*.stl)** as the file type. Type **Main Body** for the file name and select the folder in which you want the file to be saved.
25. Click **Save** to create the STL file. When prompted, select the *Main Body* and press **<Enter>**.
26. **OPEN** the file ***TB-Imperial*** and click on the **ANSI B (17 × 11)** layout.
27. Invoke the **COPYCLIP** command by right-clicking in the drawing area and selecting **Copy** from the shortcut menu. When prompted, select all the objects and press **<Enter>** to finish the command.
28. **CLOSE** the file ***TB-Imperial***.
29. Go back to the ***Tutorial 8-8*** file and click on the **Layout2** tab to switch to paper space. Close the **Page Setup Manager** window if necessary and **ERASE** the existing default viewport.
30. **PASTE** the objects from the clipboard into **Layout2**. Specify any point as the insertion point by clicking on the drawing area.
31. Access the **Page Setup - Layout2** dialog box through the **Page Setup Manager** window. Select your plotter device and select the **monochrome.ctb** plot style table. Select the **ANSI expand B (17.00 × 11.00 Inches)** paper (Figure 8-163).

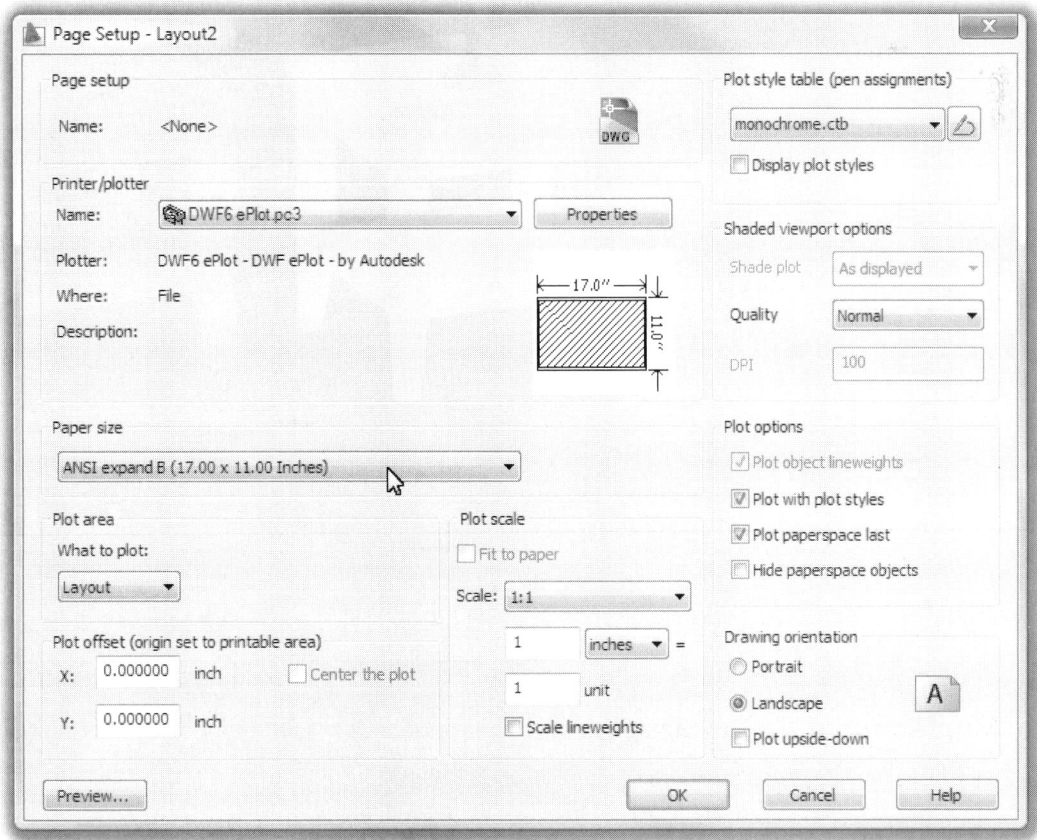

Figure 8-163 The Page Setup dialog box for Layout2

32. Select **Window** under the plot area and specify two diagonal endpoints on the title block's main rectangle. Return to the **Page Setup** dialog box and select the **Center the plot** checkbox. Close the **Page Setup** and the **Page Setup manager . . .** dialog boxes.
33. Create a new viewport that encloses the entire paper.

TIP When you need a single viewport, create it outside the printable area to prevent its border from being plotted.

34. Activate the viewport. **ZOOM** and **PAN** with the mouse wheel to obtain a desired view.
35. Turn on the **Display Locked** property of the viewport, and change its **Shade plot** to **Hidden**. Access these settings through the **Properties** palette or through the shortcut menu.
36. **PLOT** the drawing. After being plotted, the drawing should look like Figure 8-164.
37. **SAVE** your drawing.

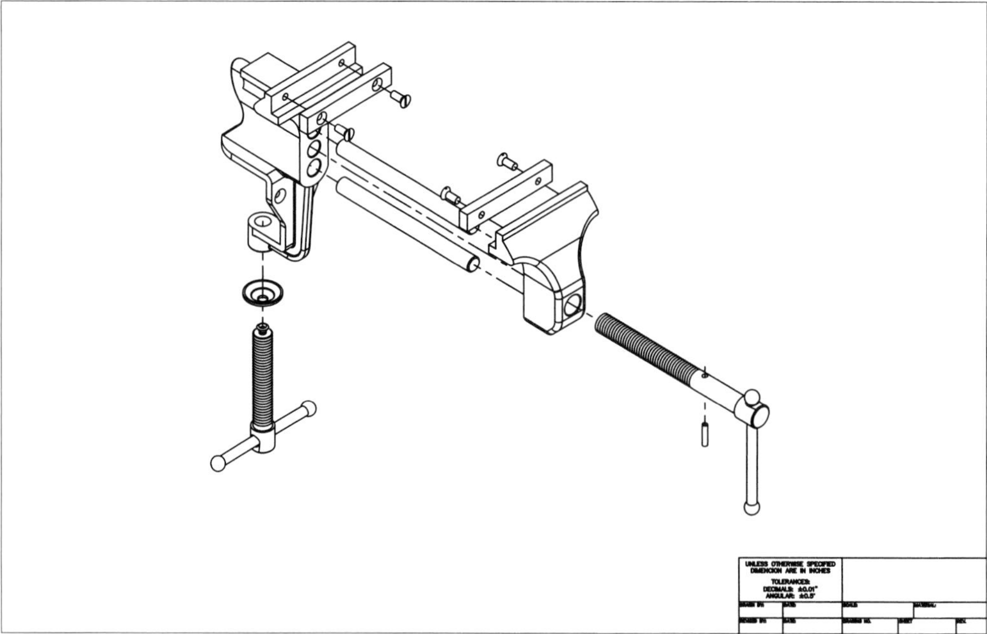

Figure 8-164 The completed drawing

Chapter Projects

Project 8-1: Isometric Drawing of a Valve with Dimensions in the 3D Space

OPEN the drawing ***Tutorial 5-4*** that you developed in Chapter 5 and **SAVE** it **AS** ***Project 8-1***. With the **FLATSHOT** command, obtain the top, front, and side orthographic views. Use a section object to generate the 3D section shown in Figure 8-165.

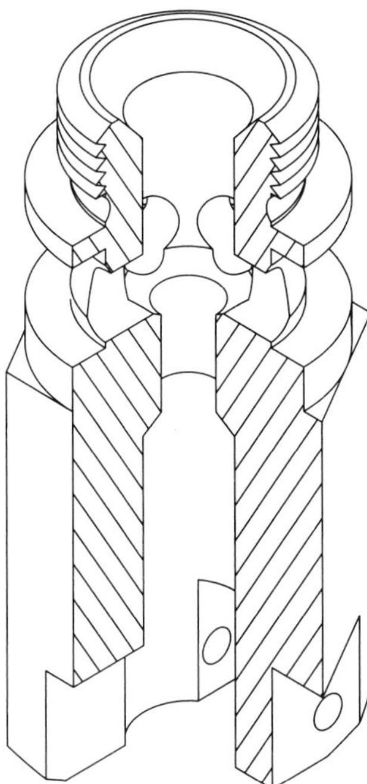

Figure 8-165 3D section to be generated using a section object

Use the three orthographic views and an Isometric view in which you show the 3D section to generate the 2D drawing in **Layout1**. Use one of the title blocks contained in the layouts of the ***TB-Metric*** drawing included in the CD.

Project 8-2: Documentation for the Construction of a Spiral Stair

OPEN the finished ***Tutorial 5-3*** and **SAVE** it **AS** ***Project 8-2***.

Use the **SOLPROF** command to obtain the drawing views of the spiral stair. Then place the most important dimensions to provide sufficient information for others to build it.

Hints for the Project

Because you will need to provide not only the installation document but also specific details for the stairsteps, posts, and other components, it might be useful to create several layers that you can freeze and thaw in specific viewports of the paper space tabs.

In the installation document, you must include the distances from the walls, the starting orientation of the first step, and the relative location of the next steps. You also must provide information about the vertical distance between the steps as well as any other information you consider important. Do not forget to include a 3D perspective view as part of your documentation.

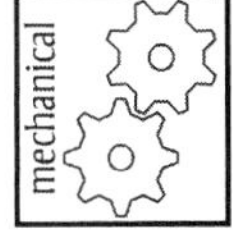

Project 8-3: Creating a Drawing of the Turning Bracket

OPEN the finished ***Project 5-2*** and **SAVE** it **AS** ***Project 8-3***.

Using the **SOLVIEW** and **SOLDRAW** commands jointly, create the drawing document of the turning bracket. Include a section view to place the interior dimensions of the part.

Hints for the Project

Refer to ***Project 5-2*** for tips on which dimensions to place as well as on how to create section cuts and detail views.

Project 8-4: Extracting Elevations of the Community Recreational Hall 3D Solid Model

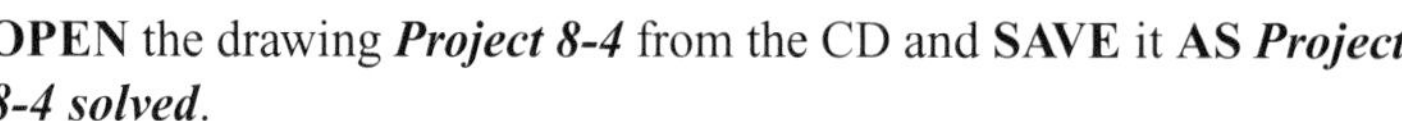

OPEN the drawing ***Project 8-4*** from the CD and **SAVE** it **AS *Project 8-4 solved*.**

Select a top view of the 3D solid model of the community recreational hall and create the two elevations and two sections shown in Figure 8-166.

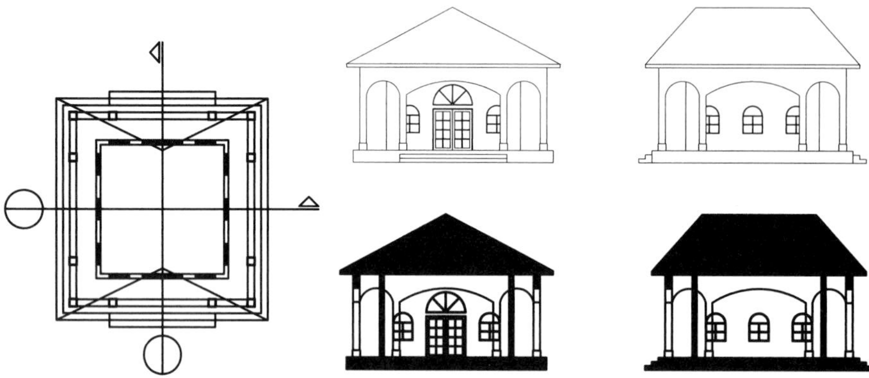

Figure 8-166 Elevations and sections to be developed

Hints for the Project

Use the **FLATSHOT** command to create the elevations and the **SECTIONPLANE** command to create the sections.

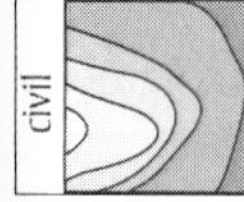

Project 8-5: Curve Inlet System Installation Instructions

Open the finished drawing ***Project 5-7*** and save it as ***Project 8-5***. Then open the drawing ***Project 5-8*** and **Copy** the curve 3D model to insert it into ***Project 8-5***. After you place it in the correct location, the assembly should look like Figure 8-167.

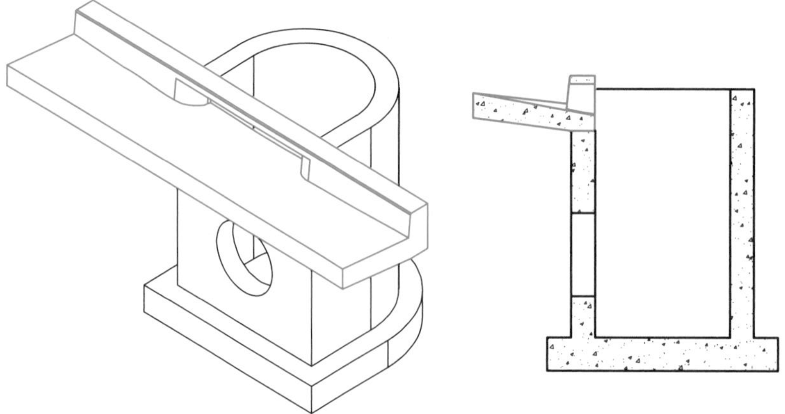

Figure 8-167 A 3D and a section view of the two precast concrete forms in place

Add a sidewalk and create a manhole as shown in Figure 8-168. Use the **SECTIONPLANE** command to create a 3D section in which the objects are sliced as shown in Figure 8-169. Place dimensions on the objects through the 3D space.

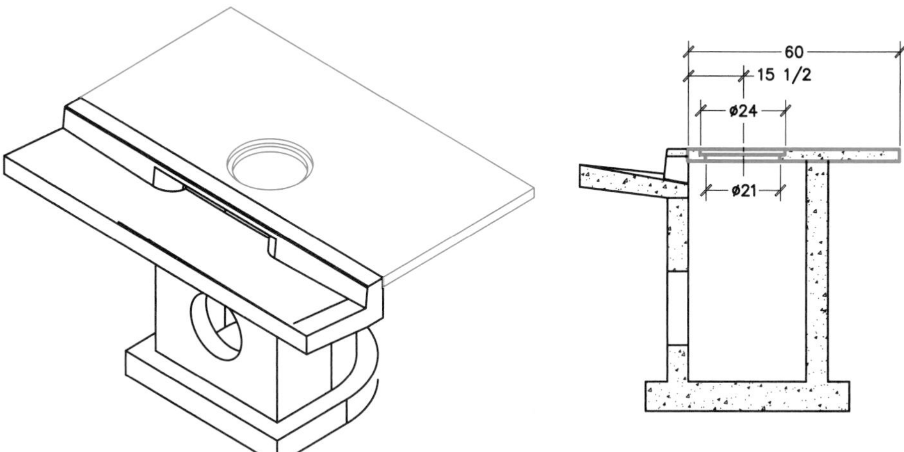

Figure 8-168 Instructions for the sidewalk and the manhole

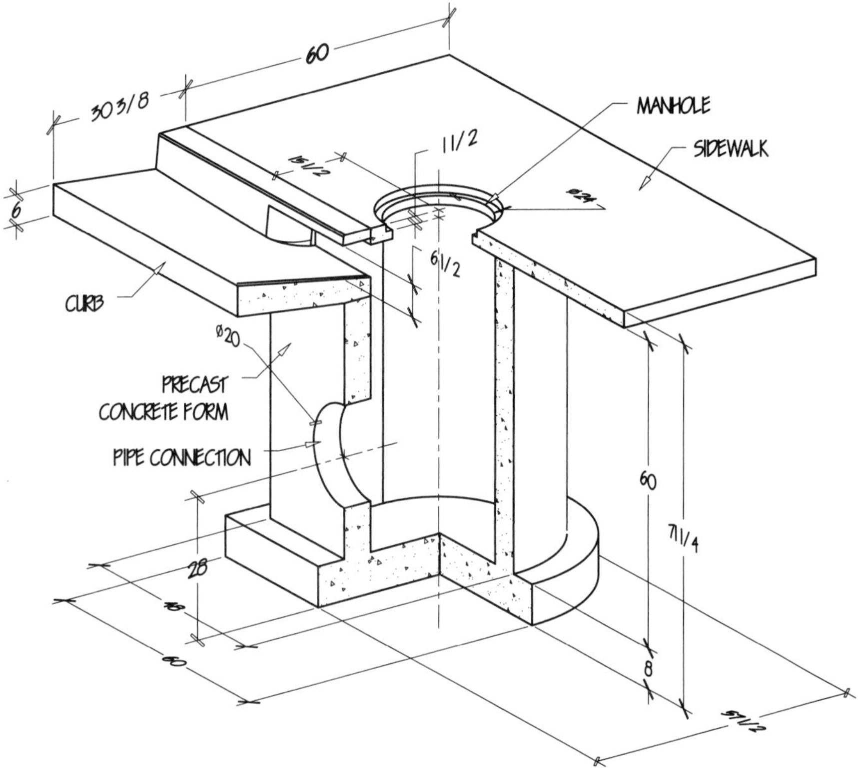

Figure 8-169 The sectioned 3D view with dimensions and annotations

Rendering and Other Presentations

9

Chapter Objectives

- Use the Render Presets
- Learn how to obtain and save a rendered image
- Understand the use of lighting within the AutoCAD® program
- Create and modify the different types of lights
- Use existing materials from the tool palettes
- Create new materials using the materials templates
- Apply materials and textures to 3D objects
- Learn to create special effects such as transparency and reflection
- Learn to create materials containing bitmaps
- Create effects in 3D models using the visual styles
- Create computer animations that record 3D navigation operations
- Create computer animations using motion paths

INTRODUCTION

DEFINITION OF RENDERING

In CAD, *rendering* is the act of generating an image from a 3D model. The AutoCAD® program can render the following types of objects:

- 3D solids
- Surfaces
- Polygon meshes
- Regions
- 3D faces
- Thickened objects

Whether used for publicity purposes, or just to obtain a clearer idea of your design, rendering plays a necessary artistic role in the 3D modeling. In the past, this work was labor intensive because real artists had to touch up pictures of the product by hand to produce the proper images for catalogs. With the **Render** process you can create excellent quality images, which can then be used to illustrate catalogs or any other type of document. The commands and settings are in the **Light, Material,** and **Render** control panels of the **Ribbon.** The **Render** toolbar, and the **View/Render** drop-down menu provide access to these tools and settings as well (Figure 9-1).

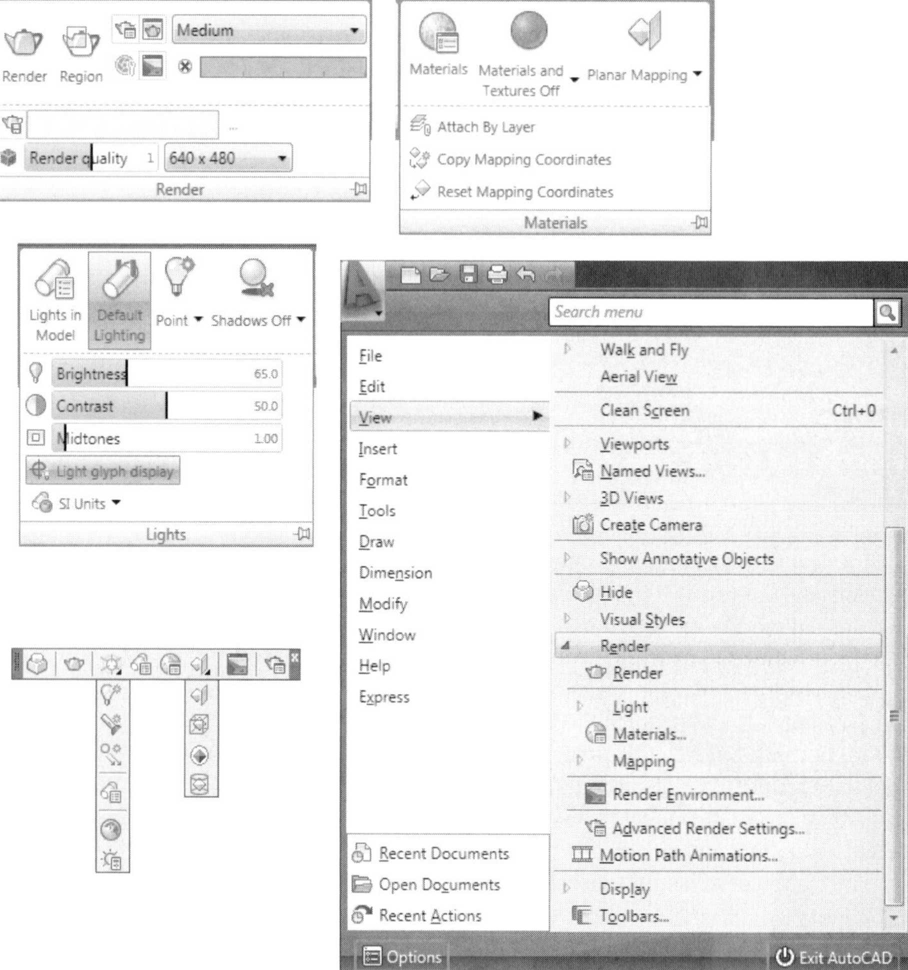

Figure 9-1 The different locations of the Render commands and tools

System Variables Affecting the Smoothness of Rendered Objects

Before getting into the group of tools specifically related to the **Render** process, you should know that certain system variables studied earlier can improve the smoothness of rendered images. The **FACETRES** system variable, for example, controls the smoothness of the nonplanar faces of 3D solids and nonplanar surfaces. Increasing its value will improve the quality of the rendered images (Figure 9-2).

You can control the smoothness of polygon meshes by increasing the mesh density with the **SURFTAB1** and **SURFTAB2** system variables. The **SURFU** and **SURFV** variables control the

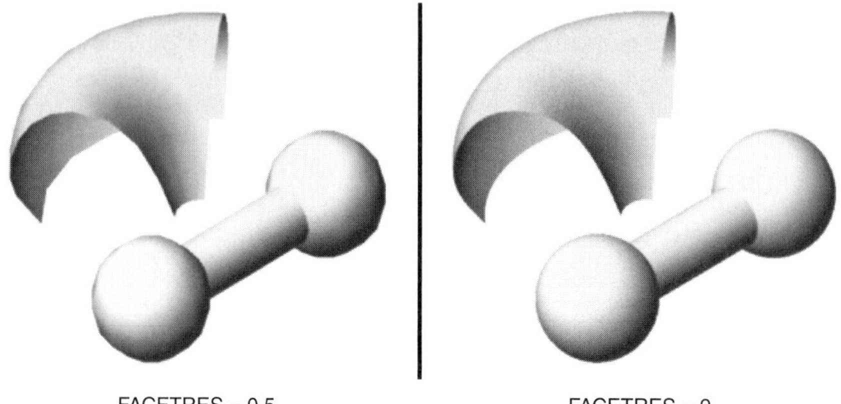

Figure 9-2 Increasing the value of the FACETRES system variable improves the smoothness of the non-planar faces of 3D solids and surfaces

smoothness of polygon meshes that have been transformed by the **Smooth surface** operation of the **PEDIT** command. The **SPLINESEGS** system variable controls the smoothness of thickened objects.

THE BASICS OF RENDERING

OBTAINING A SIMPLE RENDERED IMAGE

Obtaining a rendered image is as simple as pressing a button. Simply invoking the **RENDER** command will generate a rendered image using the current Render Preset. Figure 9-3 shows the most basic rendered image in which no special elements have been used. Alternatively you can invoke the **RENDERCROP** command and specify a crop window to render instead of rendering the entire screen. Its icon is located next to the **RENDER** command icon in the **Render** control panel on the **Ribbon.**

RENDERCROP	
Ribbon: Render Panel	
Command Line	rendercrop

Figure 9-3 A basic rendered image without using any special elements

Using other **Render** elements such as lights, shadows, materials, and textures can improve the quality of your rendered images. Controlling settings regarding lighting effect and quality of the surfaces can also give you more realistic images (Figure 9-4).

As you will learn later, the number of settings involved in the **Render** process is extremely large and to study every single one in depth could take a very long time. Experimenting with too many settings will probably cause you to spend an excessive amount of time trying to find the best image possible.

Still, the rendering process requires a lot of patience because trial and error in most cases is what will lead you to obtain the desired results. You can simplify the work substantially without sacrificing quality, however, by concentrating on the most important settings concerning the following aspects:

- Preparing the model
- Creating lights and specifying the shadows cast
- Creating and applying materials and textures
- Adjust mapping of materials using image files
- Selecting one of the Render Presets supplied with the program
- Defining a few other aspects such as destination and output size
- Creating the rendered image

Figure 9-4 A rendered image in which elements and settings regarding this type of output have been used

RPREF	
Render Toolbar	
Ribbon: Render panel	
Pull-down Menu	View/ Render/ Advanced Settings...
Command Line	rpref

RENDER	
Render Toolbar	
Ribbon: Render panel	
Pull-down Menu	View/ Render/ Render
Command Line	render

Exercise 9-1: Creating a Basic Rendered Image

1. **OPEN** ***Exercise 9-1*** from the CD.
2. **SAVE** the drawing **AS** ***Exercise 9-1 solved.***
3. Select **Render View** from the **Views** drop-down list located in the **Views** toolbar or in the **3D Navigate** control panel. This named view has been previously created to allow you to quickly change the viewing point to the one stored with it.
4. Open the **Viewports** dialog box. Select the **2D** setup and the **Two: Horizontal** to divide the display into two viewports that show the same view.
5. If needed, **ZOOM** into the corner of the room where furniture is located, in both viewports. Try to obtain a similar zoom factor for both viewports.

TIP By using the **Scale** option of the **ZOOM** command, you can obtain the exact same zoom factor in two viewports by specifying the same scale factor in both viewports. For this exercise you can use a value between **1/7** and **1/9.**

6. Select **Medium** from the **Render Presets** drop-down list located in the **Render** panel of the **Ribbon** (Figure 9-5).
7. Invoke the **RPREF** command to open the **Advanced Render Settings** palette (Figure 9-6). Under **Render Context,** select **Viewport** as the **Destination.**
8. Click inside the bottom viewport to make it the active one.
9. Invoke the **RENDER** command using one of the methods shown in the grid.
10. Click inside the other viewport to make it the active one and select the **Realistic** visual style.
11. Select **No edges** from the **Edge** control flyout button located in the **Visual Style** control panel of the **Ribbon** (Figure 9-7). The two viewports should look like Figure 9-8.
12. **SAVE** the drawing.

Note: Even though certain visual styles are also considered to be rendered images, the simplest rendered image obtained with a render process is of a superior quality. One reason is that the **Render** process uses different types of filters to eliminate the aliasing effect that makes the edges and silhouettes appear to be jagged or stepped.

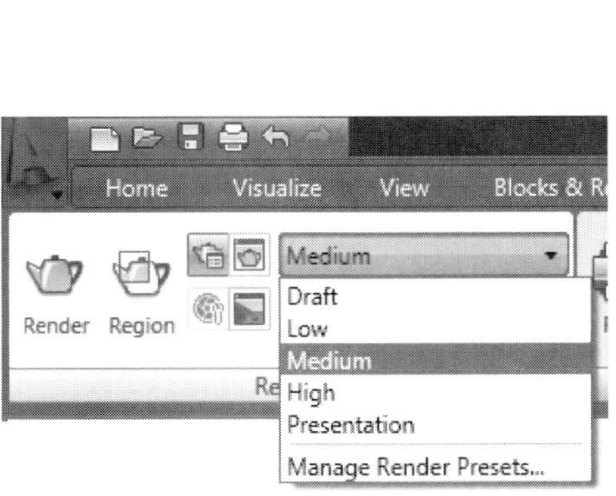

Figure 9-5

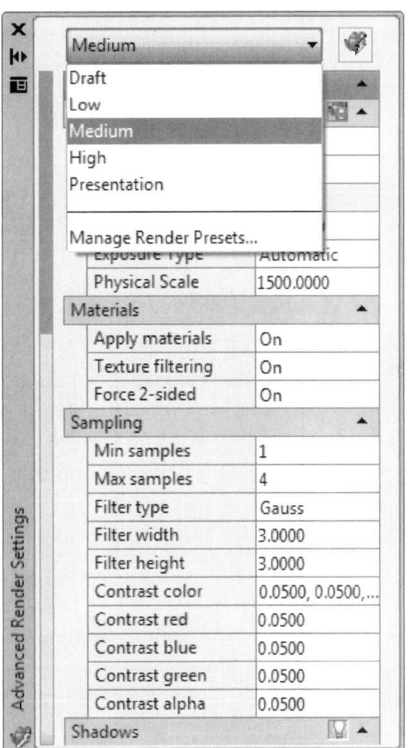

Figure 9-6 The Advanced Render Settings palette

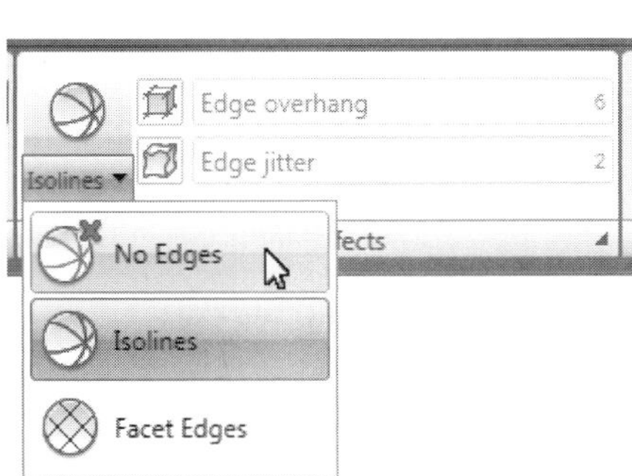

Figure 9-7 The Edge control flyout button located in the Edge Effects panel of the Ribbon

Figure 9-8 Comparison between a modified visual style (above) and a basic rendered image (below)

Realistic rendered images have a wide range of important uses, from providing visualized and conceived ideas to creating marketing images for catalogs. Demonstrated ability in producing rendered images increases job opportunities in organizations that value and require this skill.

Using Render Presets

Render Preset: A named collection of settings controlling the quality of the rendered image generated with the **RENDER** command.

A ***Render Preset*** is a named collection of settings that control the quality of the rendered image. You can use one of the **Standard Render Presets** (**Draft, Low, Medium, High,** and **Presentation**) that come with the AutoCAD program, or use your own **Custom Render Presets** from the **Render Presets** drop-down list. You can access this list from the **Render** panel of the **Ribbon** (Figure 9-9), or in the **Advanced Render Settings** palette (Figure 9-10), which opens when you invoke the **RPREF** command.

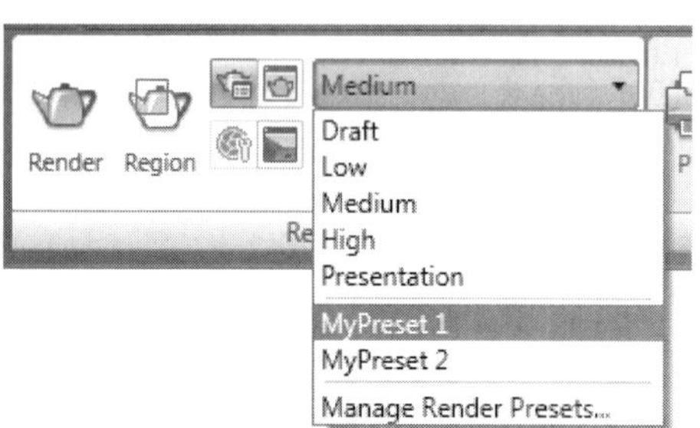

Figure 9-9 The Render Presets drop-down list located in the Render panel of the Ribbon

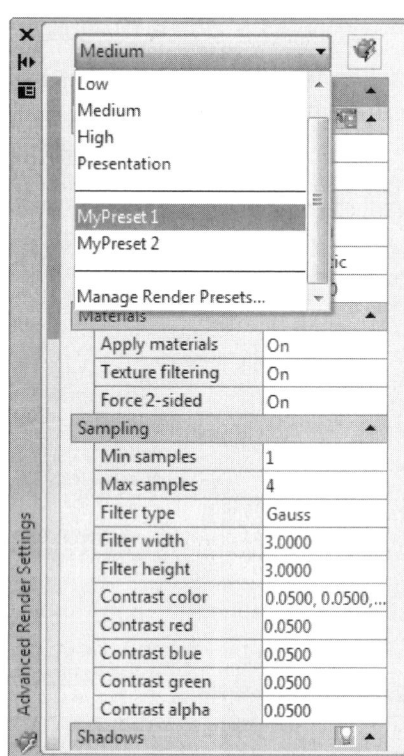

Figure 9-10 The Render Presets drop-down list located in the Advanced Render Settings palette

The **Render Presets Manager** dialog box (Figure 9-11) is the third way of accessing and setting one of the Render Presets current. The **Render Presets Manager** opens when you invoke the **RENDERPRESETS** command, or select **Manage Render Presets...** from the **Render Presets** drop-down list in the **Render** panel of the **Ribbon**. The **Render Presets Manager** dialog box is where you create **Custom Render Presets.** Clicking the **Create Copy** button will open the **Copy Render Preset** dialog box in which you can specify a name. You can create custom Render Presets by copying the current settings, or by copying any other selected Render Preset.

Each of the five **Standard Render Presets** contains specific rendering settings that, when used as a whole, enable you to obtain rendered images of different degrees of quality. Using the **Standard Render Presets** is a great way to start creating rendered images.

You can make temporary changes to the selected Render Preset in the **Advanced Render Preset** palette. An asterisk is added in front of the name of the Render Preset warning you of its nonoriginal condition (Figure 9-12).

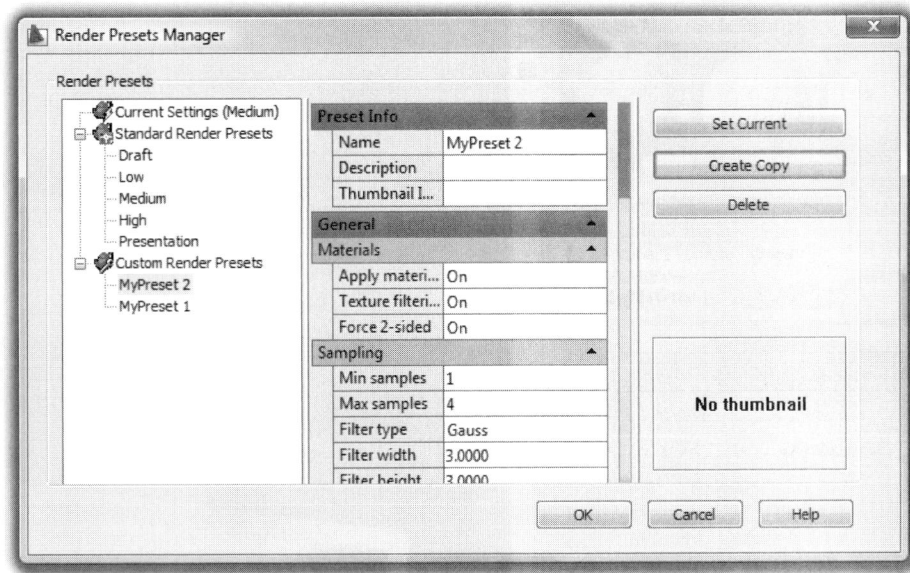

Figure 9-11 The Render Presets Manager dialog box

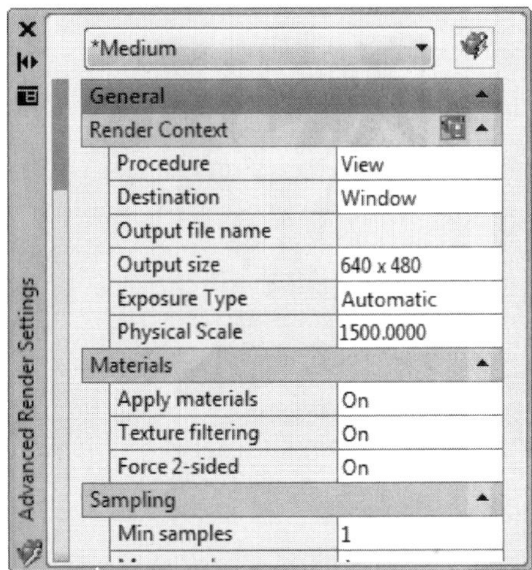

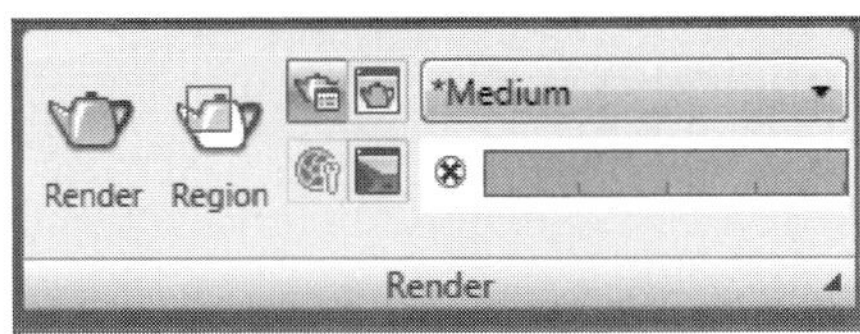

Figure 9-12 Both the Advanced Render Settings palette and the Render panel indicate that the Render Preset has been modified

The **Standard Render Presets** cannot be permanently modified. The **Custom Render Presets,** however, can be modified permanently in the **Render Presets Manager**. To make the changes permanent, you have to click on the **Set Current** button while the render preset is selected (Figure 9-13).

THE RENDER CONTEXT

Render Context is a group of settings that determine the procedure used to input the render information as well as the type of output you will obtain. This is the only group of settings that is not stored with the Render Presets; rather, it is stored in the **Render Context** with the drawing (Figure 9-14).

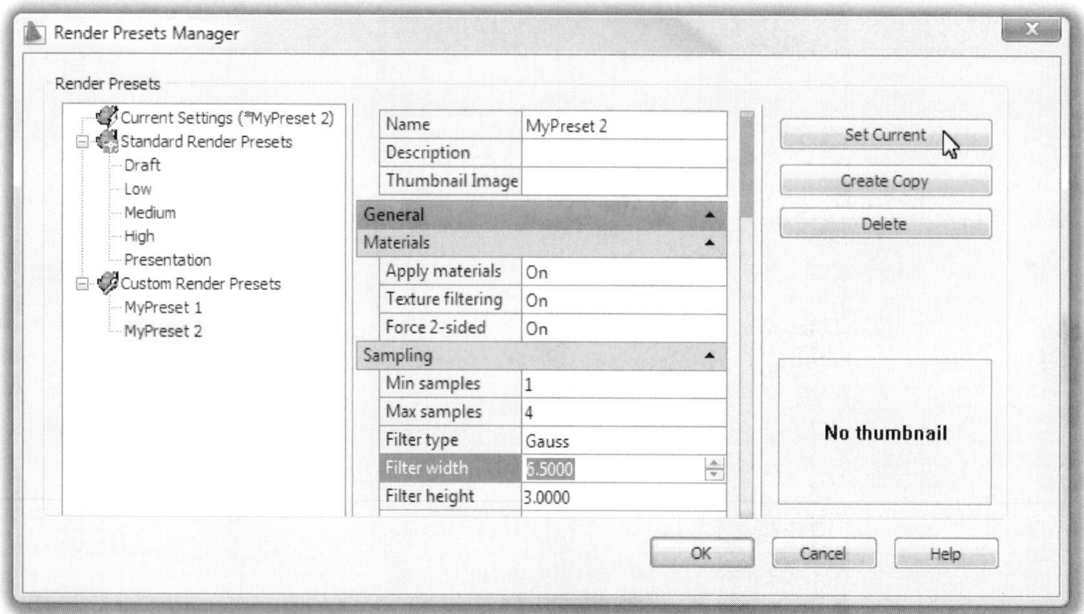

Figure 9-13 The changes made to the Custom Render Presets are not permanent until you click on the Set Current button

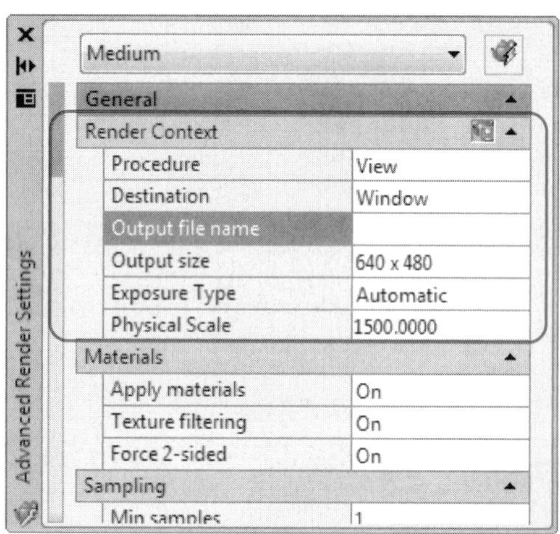

Figure 9-14 Render Context tools located in the Advanced Render Settings palette

Rendering Procedure

The **Rendering Procedure** setting allows you to change the way the AutoCAD program proceeds immediately after you invoke the **RENDER** command. The options are as follows:

View: This is the default procedure. When selected, it causes the entire view in the active viewport to be rendered.

Selected: This procedure enables you to select the objects that will be rendered.

Crop: This procedure allows you to render only a cropped window by specifying two points.

The rendering process takes a certain amount of time to produce the rendered image. The rendered area as well as the number of objects and their complexity are two important factors that, along with other render settings, determine the amount of time required. By using both the **Selected** and the **Crop** rendering procedures, you can reduce the time of the rendering process. The **Selected** procedure is particularly useful when testing the effects of a new material applied on a particular object because it does not require you to render the entire screen.

Rendering Destination

The **Destination** determines the type of output for the rendered image. The **Viewport** destination generates the rendered image in the currently active viewport. Using several viewports allows you to visually compare the effects before and after applying a specific setting.

When the **Window** destination is selected, invoking the **RENDER** command opens the **Render** window (Figure 9-15), where the rendered image is generated. As you generate other rendered images from the current model, they are added to the list in the **History** pane. This allows you to temporarily store the different rendered images that you have generated without having to save them.

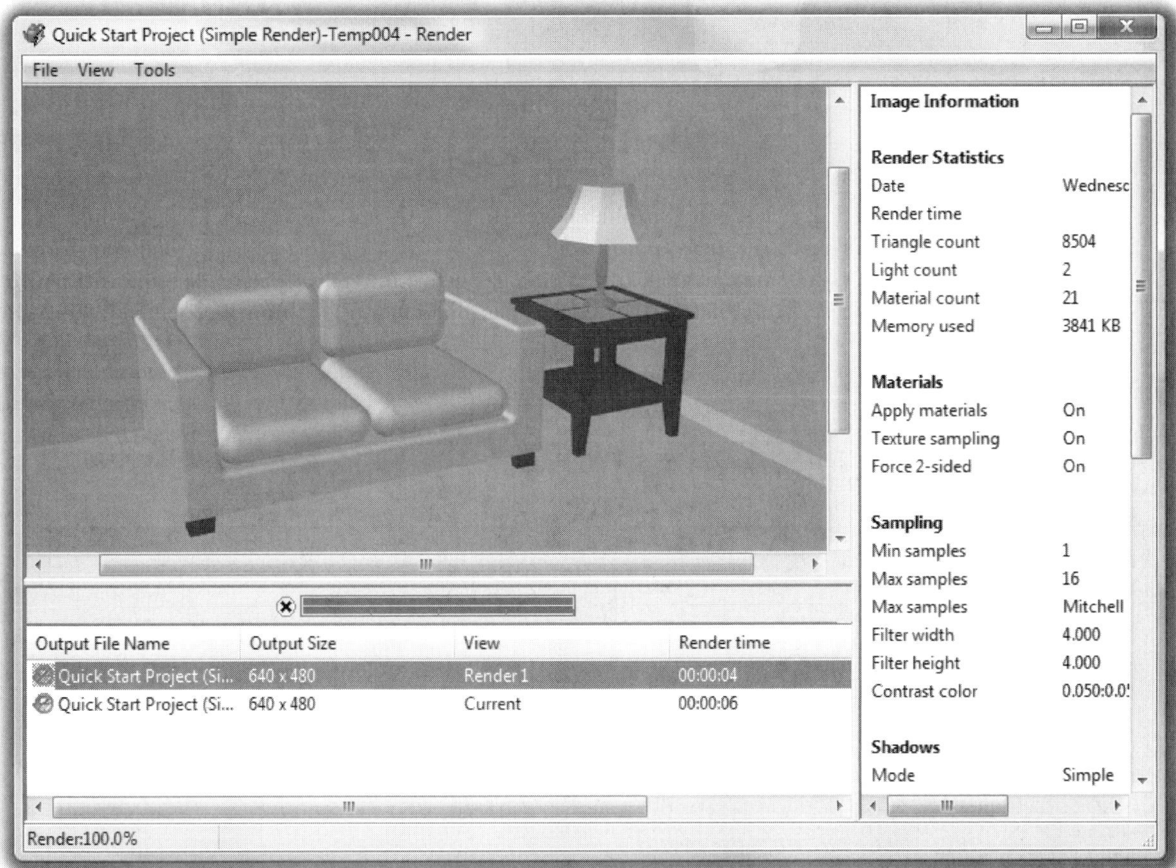

Figure 9-15 The Render window

In the **Render** window you can perform the following operations (to access some of the operations you must right-click on the temporary image file):

- **ZOOM** and **PAN**
- Obtain information
- Save a file
- Delete a file regardless of whether it is saved or not
- Purge a file from the history list without deleting it, if it has been saved previously

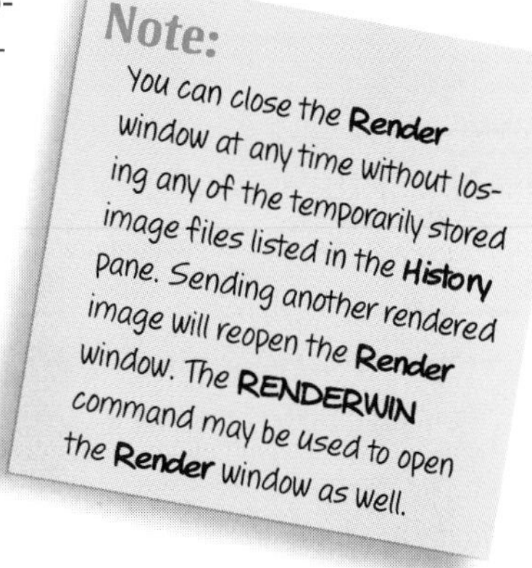

RENDERWIN	
Ribbon: Render panel	
Command Line	renderwin

Saving a Rendered Image

You can use one of the following three procedures to save a rendered image:

- Save a temporary image file from the history list in the **Render** window.
- Render directly to a specified file when rendering to the **Render** window.

- Save an image previously rendered to a viewport by using the **SAVEIMG** command.

As previously mentioned, you can save one of the temporary image files from the history list in the **Render** window; however, you can also choose to send a rendered image directly to a file when rendering to the **Render** window. This lists the file in the history instead of making it a temporary file. To do so, you must first enable this type of output in the **Render** panel of the **Ribbon** (Figure 9-16) and then click the browse **(...)** button to open the **Render Output File** dialog box (Figure 9-17), where you must specify the location, name, and type of file (BMP, PXC, TGA, TIF, JPEG, JPG, and PNG).

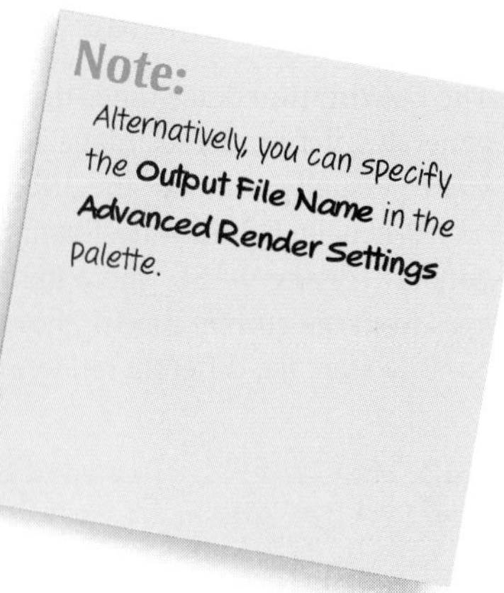

Note:
Alternatively, you can specify the Output File Name in the Advanced Render Settings Palette.

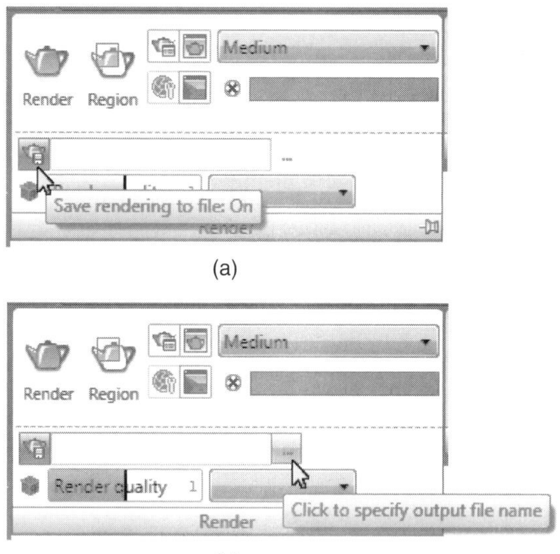

Figure 9-16 (a) Enabling to save the file and (b) clicking the browse button to specify the location

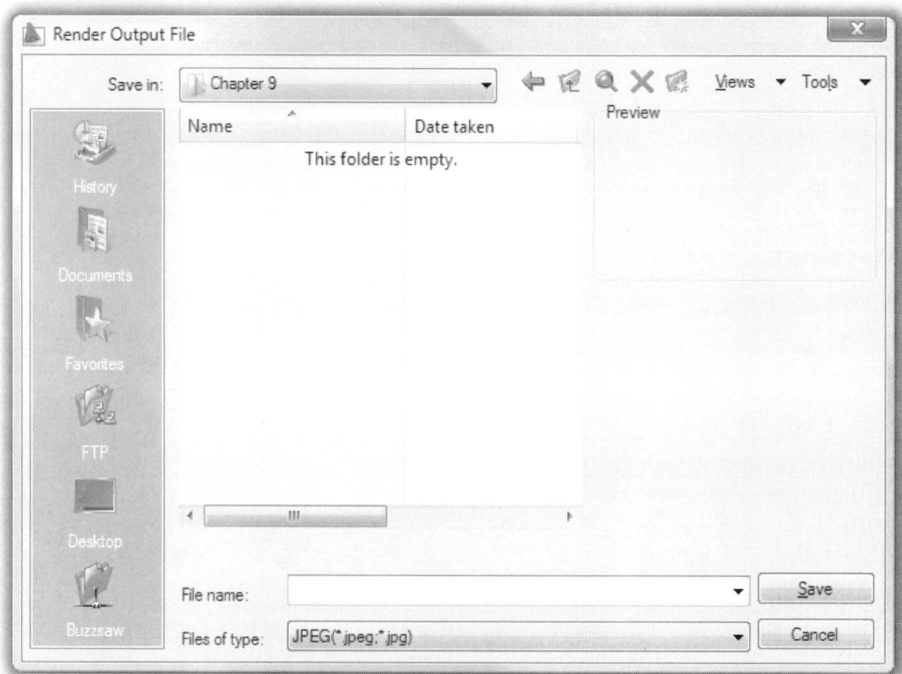

Figure 9-17 The Render Output File dialog box

After you specify all the required information, clicking the **Save** button on the **Render Output File** dialog box will bring up another dialog box where you can select specific color and other imaging options depending on the type of file selected. Figure 9-18 shows the **Options** dialog box for three different image file formats.

You can also control the **Output Size** in pixels or the resolution of the rendered image in the **Advanced Render Settings** palette or in the **Render** control panel of the **Ribbon**. You can select one of four standard sizes from the **Output Size** drop-down list, which are based on a 4:3 aspect ratio, or select **Specify Output Size** to define your own size in the **Output Size** dialog box (Figure 9-19). Unlocking the **Image Aspect** will allow you to use a different ratio.

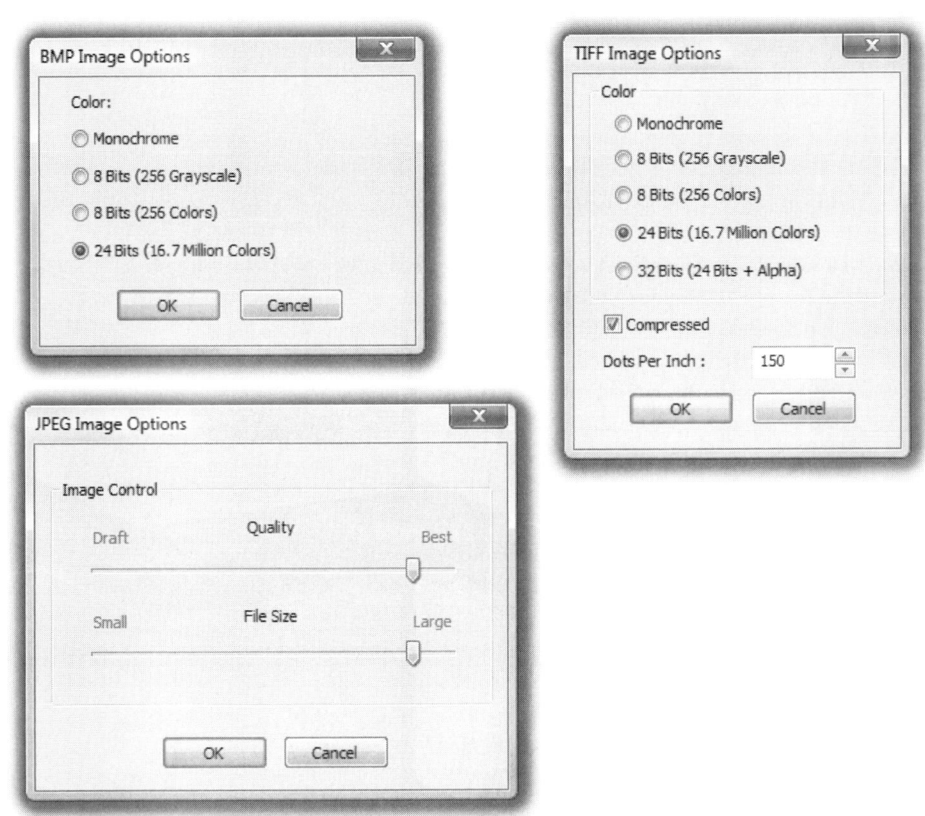

Figure 9-18 Options dialog box for three different image file formats

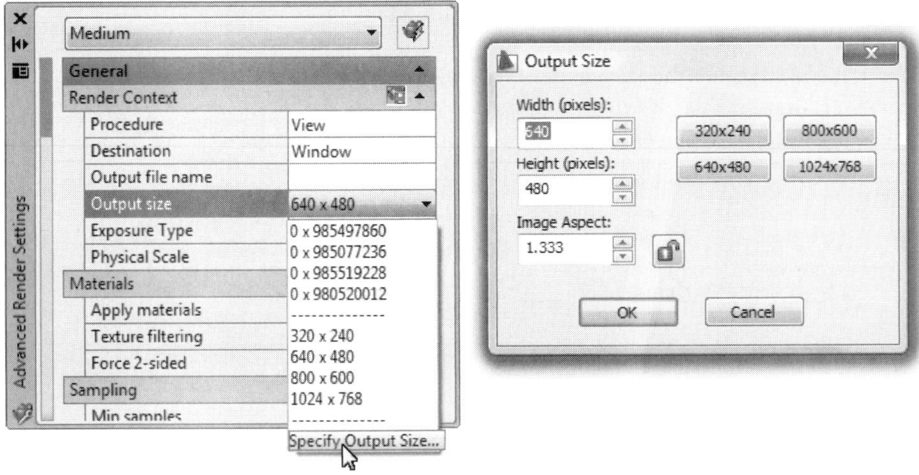

Figure 9-19 The Output Size dialog box

SAVEIMG	
Pull-down Menu	Tools/ Display Image/ Save...
Command Line	saveimg

When the file is sent to the viewport, on the other hand, it is not saved automatically, regardless of whether **Save rendering to file** is enabled or not. You can save the rendered image from a viewport only by using the **SAVEIMG** command. The output size is not as specified in the **Output Size** drop-down list either; it is controlled by the size of the viewport itself.

Exposure Type

This allows you to set the tone operator to either **Automatic** or **Logarithmic.** These two settings indicate that the tone operator used will either match the current viewport tone operator or will use a logarithmic exposure control. Owing to its direct relation to the light effect, this setting will also be discussed in the **Creating Illumination Effects** section in this chapter.

Exercise 9-2: Saving Rendered Images

1. **OPEN** ***Exercise 9-1.***
2. **SAVE** it **AS** ***Exercise 9-2.***
3. Invoke the **RPREF** command to open the **Advance Render Settings** palette. Under **Render Context,** select **Window** as the **Destination**. When finished, close the palette.
4. Select **Render View** from the **Views** drop-down list located in the **Views** toolbar or in the **3D Navigate** control panel.
5. Invoke the **RENDER** command.
6. In the **Render** panel of the **Ribbon**, enable saving the rendering to an image file directly. You can do so by clicking on the button shown highlighted (On) in Figure 9-20.
7. Click the browse **(...)** button to open the **Render Output File** dialog box. Select the location where you want to save the image file. Select the **TIF(*.tif)** file type and type in **FurnitureRenderA** as the file name.
8. Click the **Save** button. Click **OK** to close the **TIFF Image Options** dialog box and accept the defaults.
9. Invoke the **RENDER** command.
10. In the **Render** window, select the ***Exercise 9-2-Temp000*** temporary file from the history list. Select **Save** from the **File** drop-down menu to open the **Render Output File** dialog box. Select the same location as for the other image file, select the same type of file, and type **FurnitureRenderB** as the file name.
11. Click the **Save** button. Click **OK** to close the **TIFF Image Options** dialog box and accept the defaults.
12. Use Windows Explorer to browse for the image files in the location you specified. Right-click on one of the files and select **Open With** to use the image file using your favorite imaging program.
13. **SAVE** the drawing.

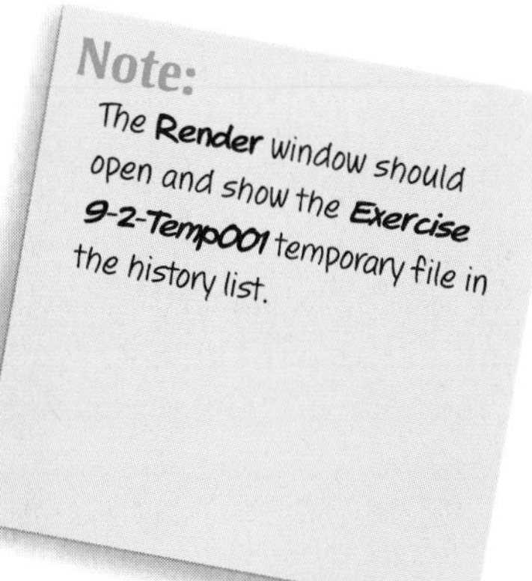

Note:
The **Render** window should open and show the **Exercise 9-2-Temp001** temporary file in the history list.

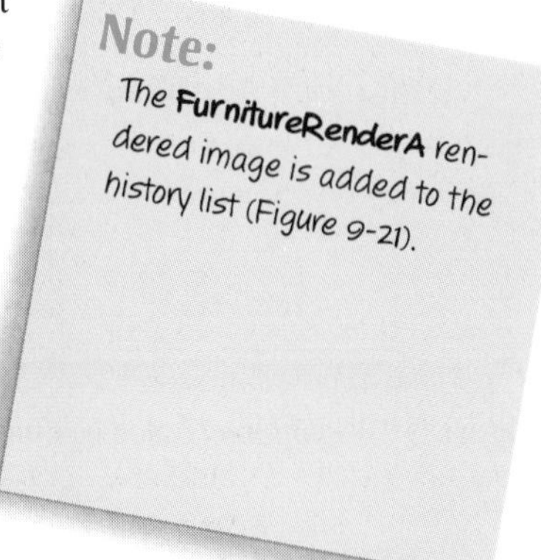

Note:
The **FurnitureRenderA** rendered image is added to the history list (Figure 9-21).

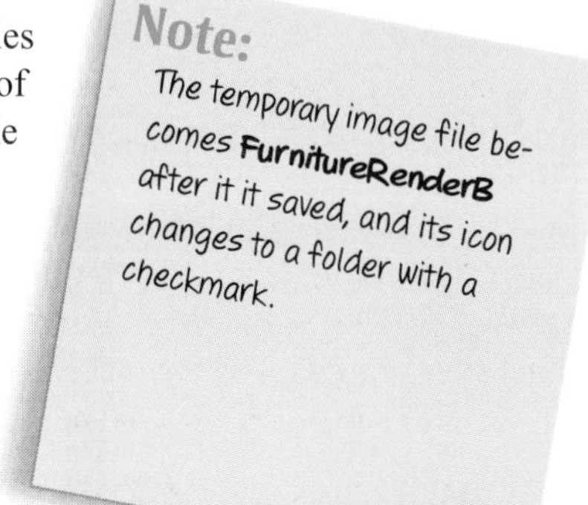

Note:
The temporary image file becomes **FurnitureRenderB** after it saved, and its icon changes to a folder with a checkmark.

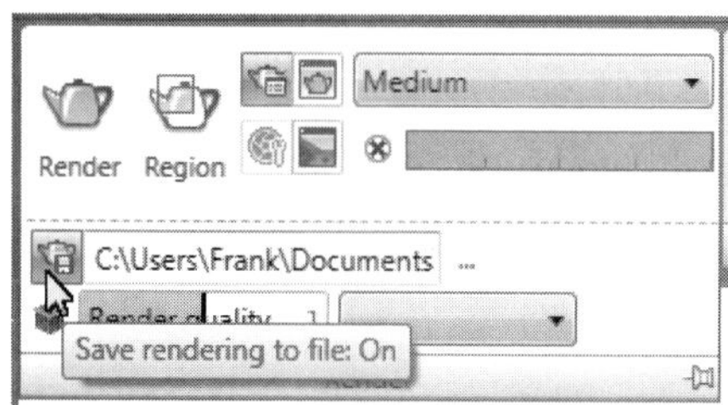

Figure 9-20 Clicking on the button indicated allows rendering to an image file directly

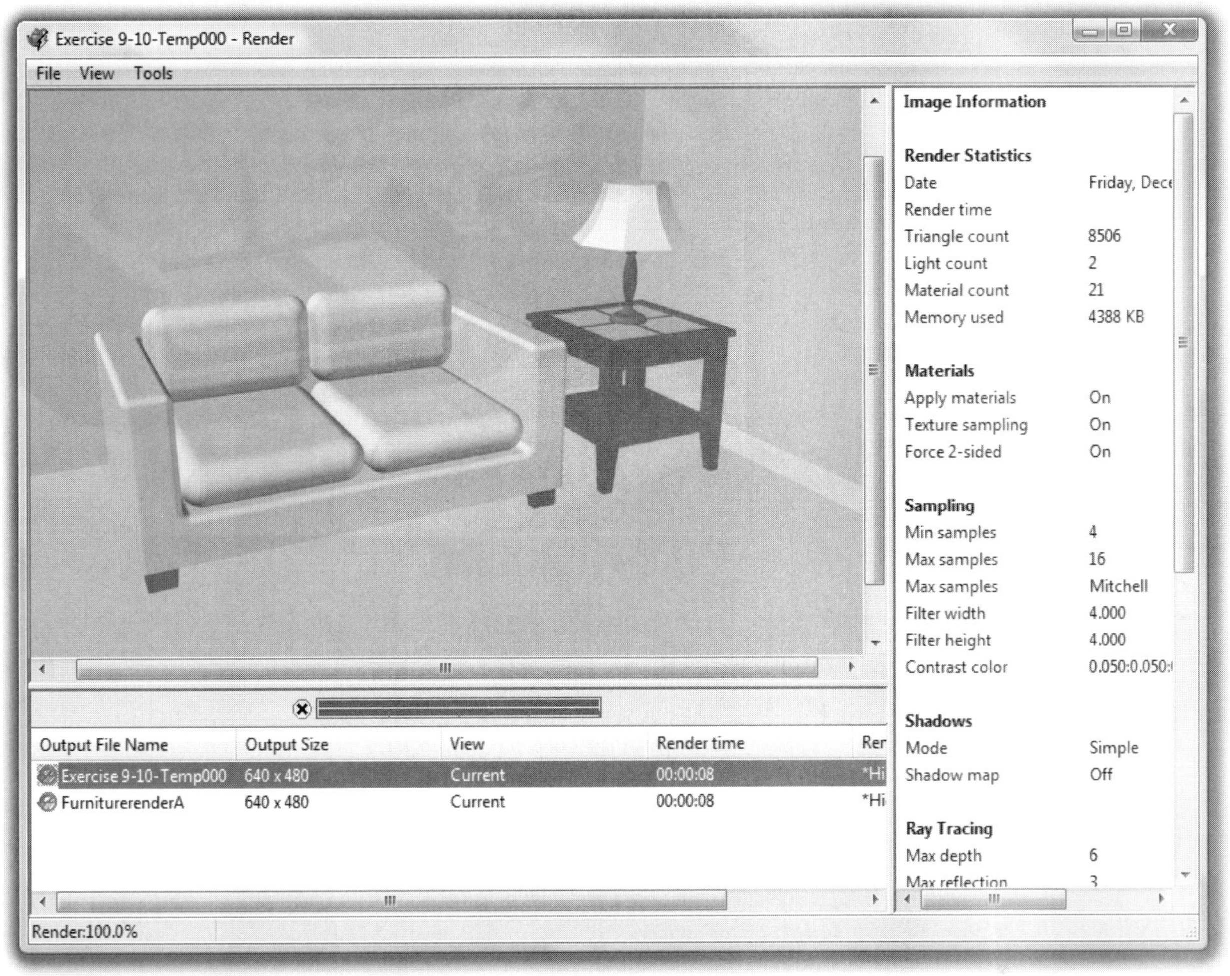

Figure 9-21 The Render window. Two items are contained in the render history list

USING BACKGROUND AND FOG ENVIRONMENT

When rendering a scene such as the corner of the living room shown in the previous illustrations, you can cover the entire viewport by placing walls, floors, and other relatively large 3D objects. This allows you to control the total area of the rendered image.

When creating a rendered image of an isolated 3D object, you need not use other 3D objects to cover the entire viewport. You can achieve this purpose by simply changing the background environment associated with a named view.

> **Note:**
> The Sun & Sky type of background is available only when Photometric lighting is enabled, that is, when the **LIGHTINGUNITS** is set to 1 or 2.

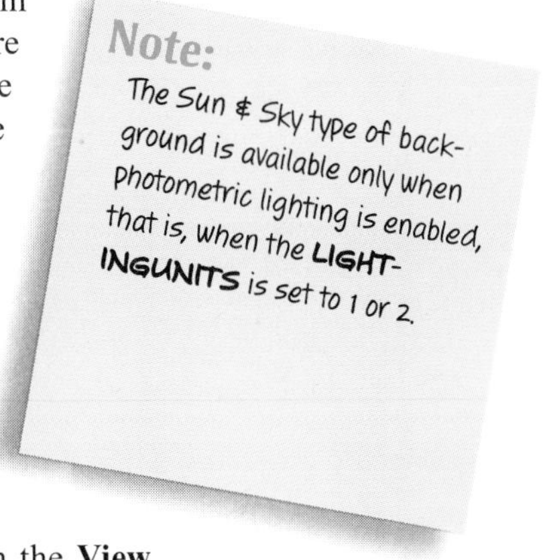

Backgrounds are always associated with a defined Model View. The type of background can be specified in the **New View** dialog box (Figure 9-22), which opens when you click on the **New...** button in the **View Manager** dialog box, or it can be specified afterward in the **View Manager** dialog box for the selected Model View (Figure 9-23). Either way you can choose from one of the following types of backgrounds:

- Solid
- Gradient
- Image
- Sun & Sky

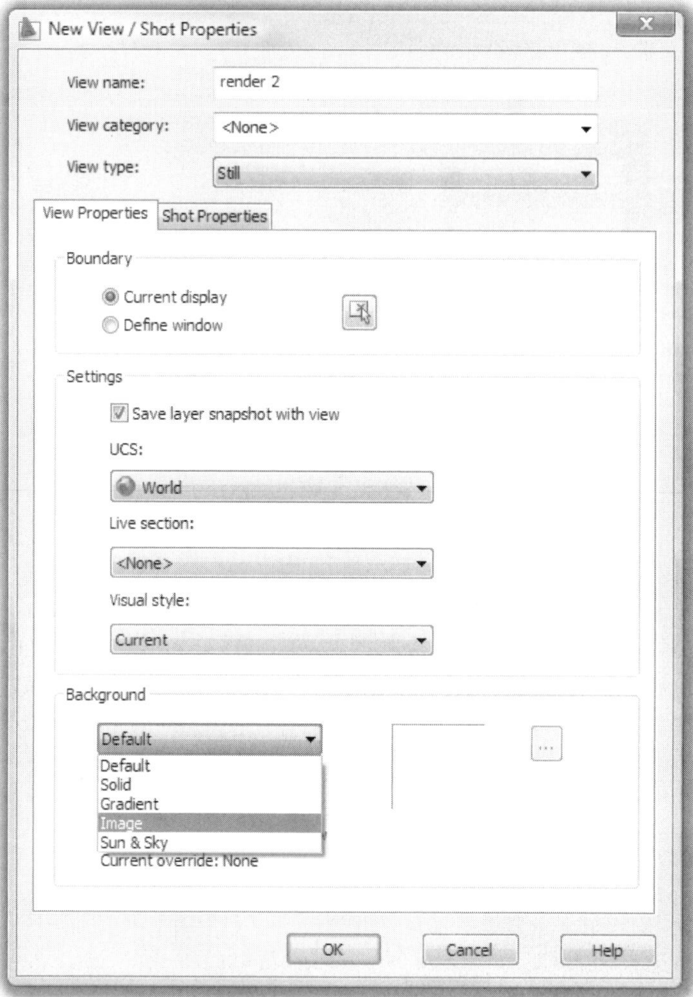

Figure 9-22 Selecting the type of background in the New View dialog box

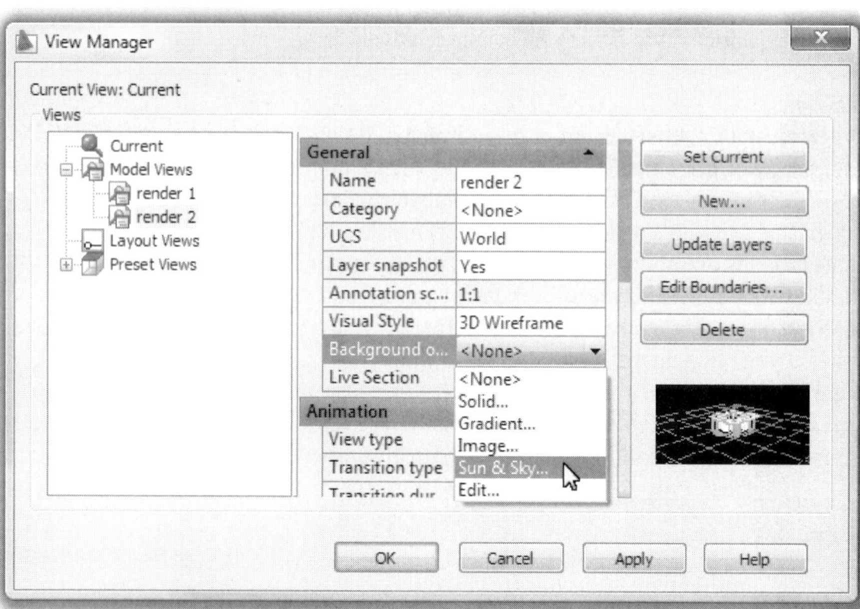

Figure 9-23 Selecting the type of background for a defined Model View in the View Manager dialog box

FOR MORE DETAILS See the Photometric Light section for more detail.

The **Solid** background override allows you to define a flat or single-color background. Clicking on the **Color:** window will open the **Select Color** window, where you can specify a color (Figure 9-24).

Gradient generates a two- or three-color gradient background. Each band color can be specified individually (Figure 9-25). You can specify a two-color gradient background by unselecting the **Three color** checkbox. You can also specify a **Rotation:** between –90° and 90°.

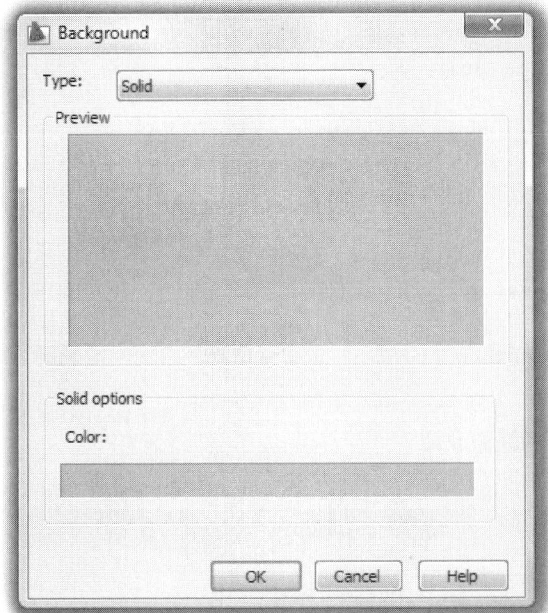

Figure 9-24 The Background dialog box for the Solid type

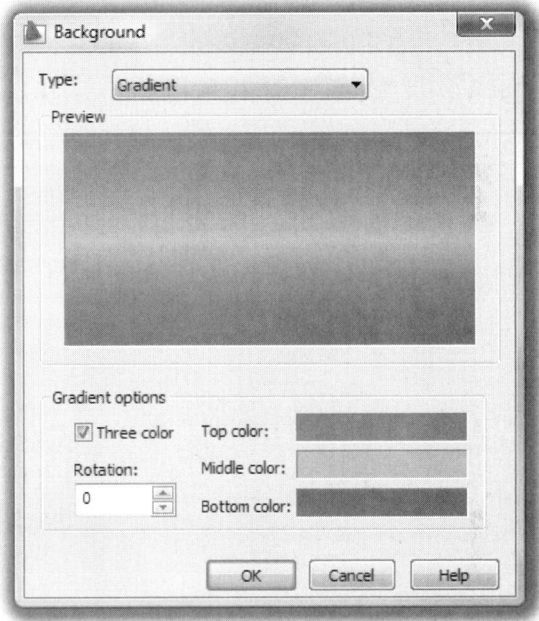

Figure 9-25 The Background dialog box for the Gradient type

Image enables you to browse and select an image file to be used as background (Figure 9-26). Clicking the **Adjust Image...** button opens the **Adjust Background Image** dialog box, where you can select one of three image positions (**Center, Stretch,** or **Tile**) (Figure 9-27). If you select the **Center** or **Tile** position, you can offset or scale the image to make specific adjustments. Keeping the **Maintain aspect ratio when scaling** option checked will prevent image distortion. Figure 9-28 shows examples of the three different types of background.

Sun & Sky is a more complex type of background. Selecting this background opens the **Adjust Sun & Sky Background** dialog box, where you can interactively adjust the many properties that define the simulated appearance of the sky and the sun (Figure 9-29). These properties are picked from the current settings of the Sun Properties.

FOR MORE DETAILS See The Sun Light section for more detail on the Sun Properties.

Figure 9-26 The Background dialog box for the Image type

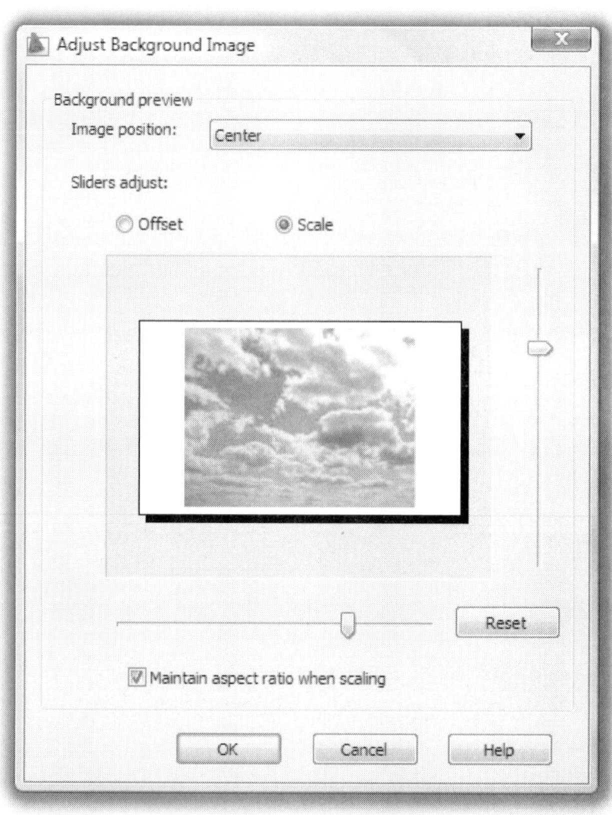

Figure 9-27 The Adjust Background Image dialog box

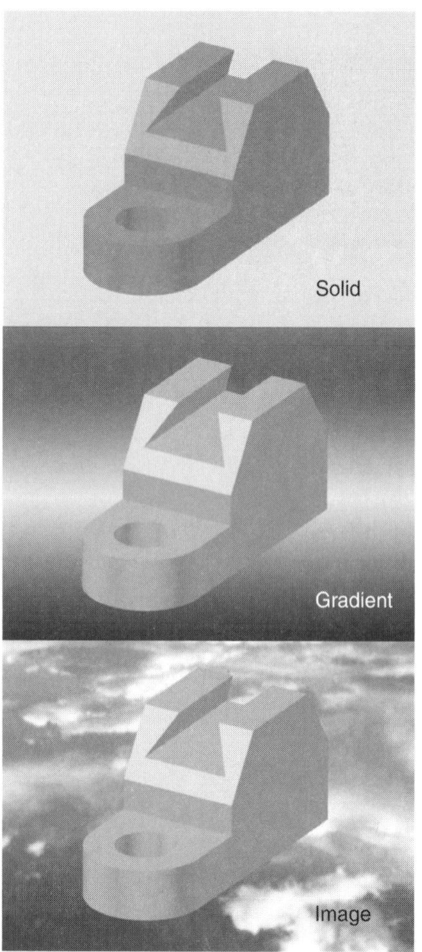

Figure 9-28 The three simple types of background

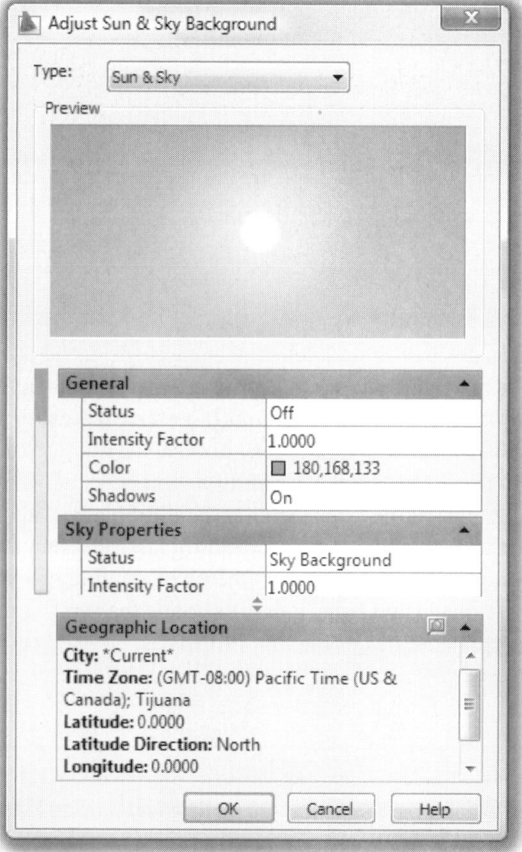

Figure 9-29 The Adjust Sun & Sky Background dialog box

RENDERENVIRONMENT	
Render Toolbar	
Pull-down Menu	View/ Render/ Render Environ-ment...
Command	Fog

The sky display can also be controlled in the **Sun** panel of the **Ribbon** (Figure 9-30); through its flyout button, you can choose among the following three settings:

- **Sky off**
- **Sky background**
- **Sky background and illumination**

The background is shown with the rendered image. But it is also shown when any visual style is selected (except **2D Wireframe**). You can turn the background off in a visual style individually through the **Visual Styles Manager** palette (Figure 9-31).

Another environmental effect can be created using the **FOG** command. When you invoke it, the **Render Environment** dialog box is displayed (Figure 9-32). In this dialog box you can turn

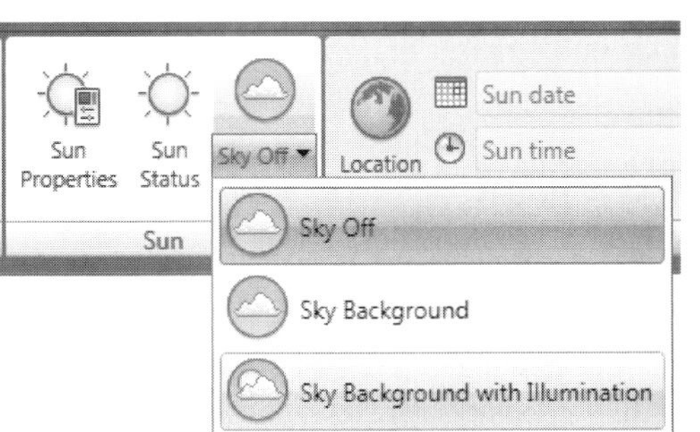

Figure 9-30 The Sky control flyout button, located in the Sun panel of the Ribbon

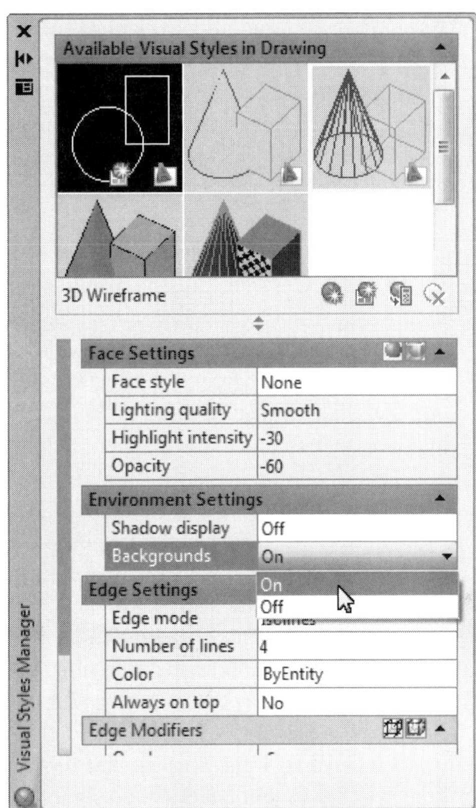

Figure 9-31 The background can be turned off through the Visual Styles Manager palette

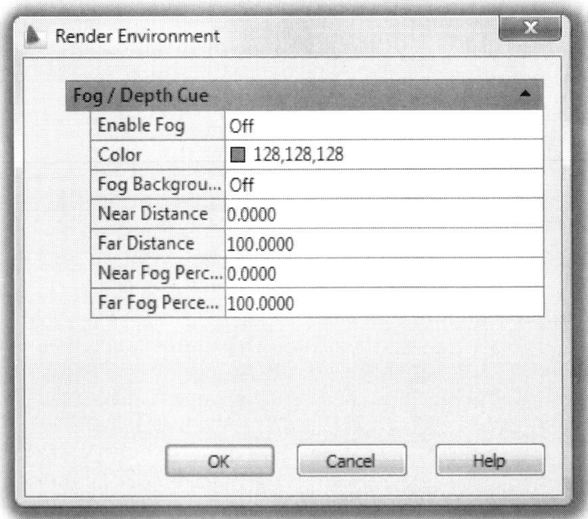

Figure 9-32 The Render Environment dialog box

the fog effect on and off. You can also set the distance from the camera at which the fog effect starts (**Near Distance**) and the distance from the camera at which the fog ends (**Far Distance**). By changing the **Near Fog Percentage** and **Far Fog Percentage**, you can control the intensity of the fog effect. Typically, the fog effect is higher at farther distances than at closer distances.

CREATING ILLUMINATION EFFECTS

OPTICAL PRINCIPLES OF LIGHT AND ITS PHOTOMETRIC QUANTITIES

Illumination is what allows us to see all objects around us. If there were no light, objects would not be visible at all, nor would their color, brightness, or any other properties. Shadows would not exist either.

Light is a very complex phenomenon, and its behavior is studied in optical physics. In essence, light is a form of energy that emanates or radiates from a source object in moving particles called *photons*. Depending on the medium through which the light travels and the type of light source, the energy of light, or its intensity, tends to decrease or attenuate as it gets farther from the object emitting it.

For materials of a certain transparency, light rays are divided into two portions when they reach an object's surface (incident rays). The rays reflected from the surface are called *reflected rays*. Those that penetrate the surface and get inside the object are called *refracted rays* (Figure 9-33). The angle between the incident rays and the surface normal is the same as the angle between the normal and the reflected rays. The refracted rays, on the other hand, change direction when they enter into another medium due to the differences in speed at which the rays travel in the two mediums.

How much of the light is reflected or refracted varies depending on the specific material properties of the object, as well as the angle of incidence of the light rays.

In the AutoCAD program you can create light sources that follow the same optical principles as real light sources. Using and combining different light sources enables you to control the illumination of the surfaces of 3D objects, which produces an infinite number of visual effects.

Light is a complex phenomenon. The simple inclusion of another 3D object may alter the illumination effect on preexisting objects. The intensity with which the surfaces are illuminated depends on how perpendicular they are to the light rays. The more perpendicular, the higher the illumination (Figure 9-34).

Photometry is the science that determines how the brightness of light is measured, as it is perceived by the human eye. Measurable values of light intensity, such as luminous intensity, luminous flux, and illuminance, are among the most important measured quantities in photometry.

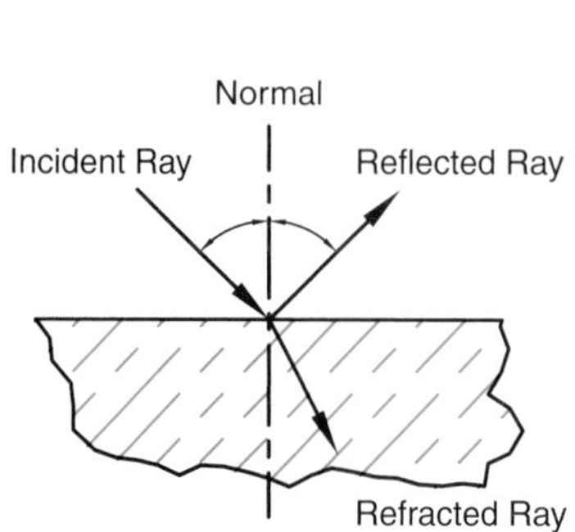

Figure 9-33 Optical behavior of light rays striking a surface

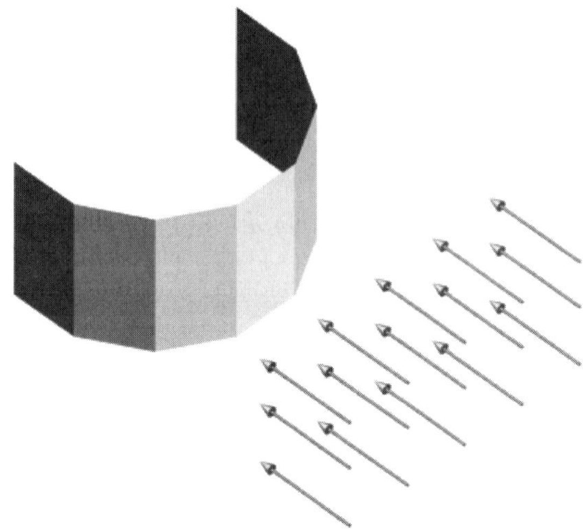

Figure 9-34 Illumination effect increases as faces are located more perpendicular to the light rays

This diversification of measured quantities is due to the complexity of the illumination phenomenon itself, but all the quantities represent how bright and intense the light is.

Luminous intensity is a measurement of the power of the light emitted by a light source in a particular direction. For both systems, the customary and the International System of Units (SI), its value is measured in candelas (cd).

Luminous flux is a measurement of the total power of light emitted by a light source. For example, a 100-watt (W) incandescent lightbulb emits about 1,700 lumens (lm), which is its unit of measurement for both the customary and the SI systems. Manufacturers of lightbulbs and lamps usually specify this quantity for their products. From its value, one can tell how efficient a bulb is; for example, both a 60-W incandescent bulb and a 15-W compact fluorescent bulb emit approximately 900 lumens.

Illuminance measures the luminous flux arriving at a surface per unit area. This is the only one with different units. It is specified in lux in the SI system and in foot-candles in the customary system. One foot-candle is equal to 10.76 lux.

Creating Lights in AutoCAD

Default Lighting

There are two different ways of illuminating the 3D model: using the ***default lighting*** or using user-created lights.

Default lighting provides light to the 3D model using two distant light sources. This illumination enables you to produce rendered images using a basic lighting setting, as well as to distinguish the faces in a rendered visual style.

You can make the default lighting use only one distant light source instead of two in a specific viewport by changing the **DEFAULTLIGHTINGTYPE** system variable value from the default **1** to **0.** Figure 9-35 shows the effect of changing this value on a rendered image that uses the default lighting.

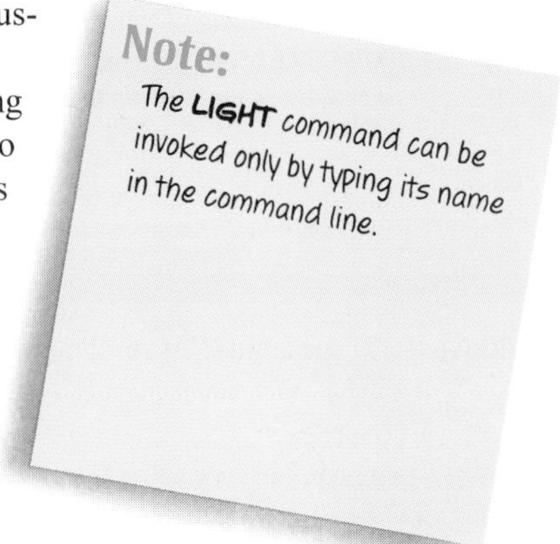
Note:
The LIGHT command can be invoked only by typing its name in the command line.

default lighting: The default illumination provided by the AutoCAD program. It uses two distant light sources that follow the view direction.

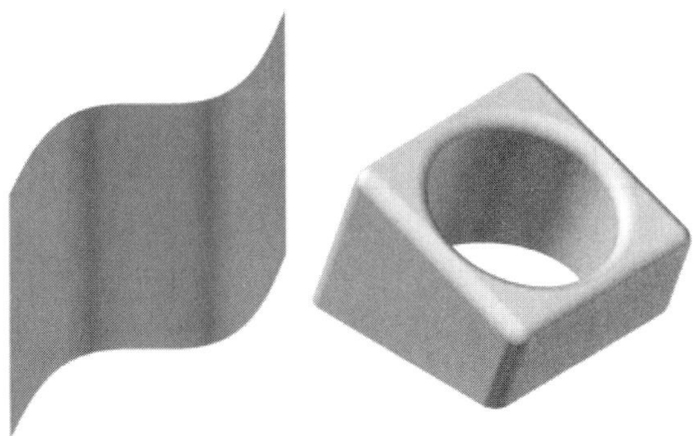

DEFAULTLIGHTINGTYPE = 1

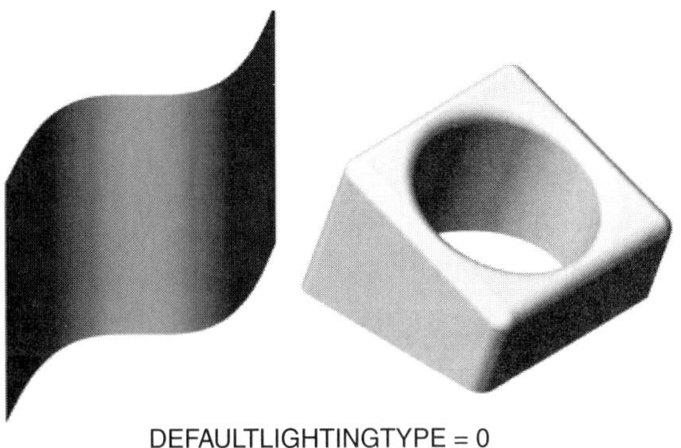

DEFAULTLIGHTINGTYPE = 0

Figure 9-35 The DEFAULTLIGHTINGTYPE system variable determines whether the default lighting uses two (above) or one distant light

Figure 9-36 The LIGHT command shortcut menu

Using the default lighting in rendered images gives very limited control over the illumination effects of the 3D model. You can create user-created lights (**Point** lights, **Spot** lights, **Web** lights, and **Distant** lights) by invoking the **LIGHT** command. Figure 9-36 shows these options within the command's shortcut menu.

User-created lights and the default lighting cannot be used at the same time. You can make AutoCAD turn off the default light automatically when user-created lights are added or turned on; this will reset the value of the **DEFAULTLIGHTING** system variable to **0.** All you have to do is select the choice that turns the default lighting off in the warning message that AutoCAD displays. This happens only when the **DEFAULTLIGHTING** system variable is set to **1** when you add a new light (Figure 9-37).

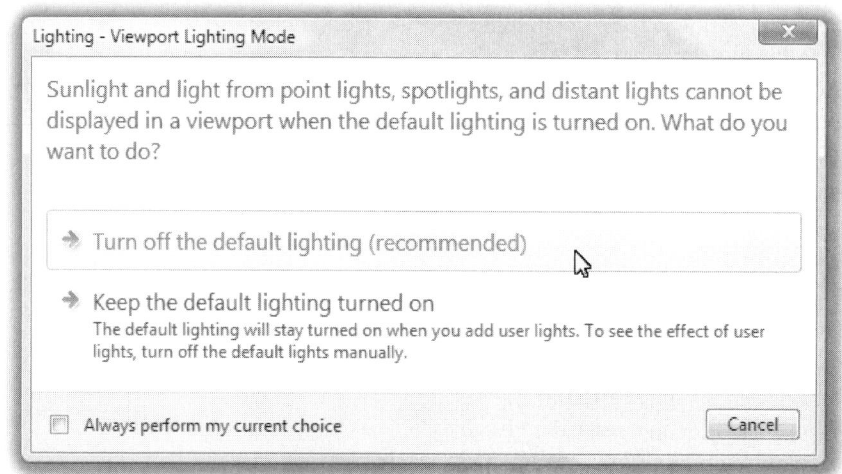

Figure 9-37 The AutoCAD program's warning

Photometric Lights

AutoCAD allows you to use and manipulate photometric properties of the lights in order to illuminate your scenes for more realistic rendered images. This allows you to use light sources with known real values of intensity, such as a 75-W incandescent bulb or a 32-W fluorescent lamp.

In order to use the **Photometric properties** of the lights, Figure 9-38(a), the **LIGHTINGUNITS** system variable must be set to **1** to **2.** When its value is set to **0,** the photometric properties are not enabled. The only difference between setting this value to 1 or 2 is that AutoCAD uses different units of measurement for the illuminance—lux or foot-candle, respectively. You can set the **LIGHTINGUNITS** system variables in the **Lights** panel of the **Ribbon** [Figure 9-38(b)].

When the photometric lighting is enabled, the **LOGEXPBRIGHTNESS** system variable is also enabled to control the global brightness level of the drawing. You can also change the value of this system variable in the **Adjust Rendered Exposure** dialog box (Figure 9-39) by changing the **Brightness** value. Other illumination effects such as **Contrast** and **Mid tones** also can be adjusted in this dialog box. However, the most important feature of the **Adjust Rendered Exposure** dialog box is that you can interactively preview a sample of the future rendered image, which can save render processing time. You open the **Adjust Rendered Exposure** dialog box by invoking the **RENDEREXPOSURE** command by entering its name in the command prompt.

Any light (distant, spot, point, and web) can be adjusted using the photometric properties. Distant lights, however, may result in overexposure when the photometric properties are enabled, providing an unwanted result. AutoCAD displays the warning shown in Figure 9-40 if it intends to use distant lights when photometric properties are enabled.

From the **Tool Palettes,** you can access the **Photometric Lights** group of palettes, which contain many common lights used in real applications (Figure 9-41). Its type of light, color, and photometric characteristics are set to simulate the effects of the real light sources they represent.

(a)

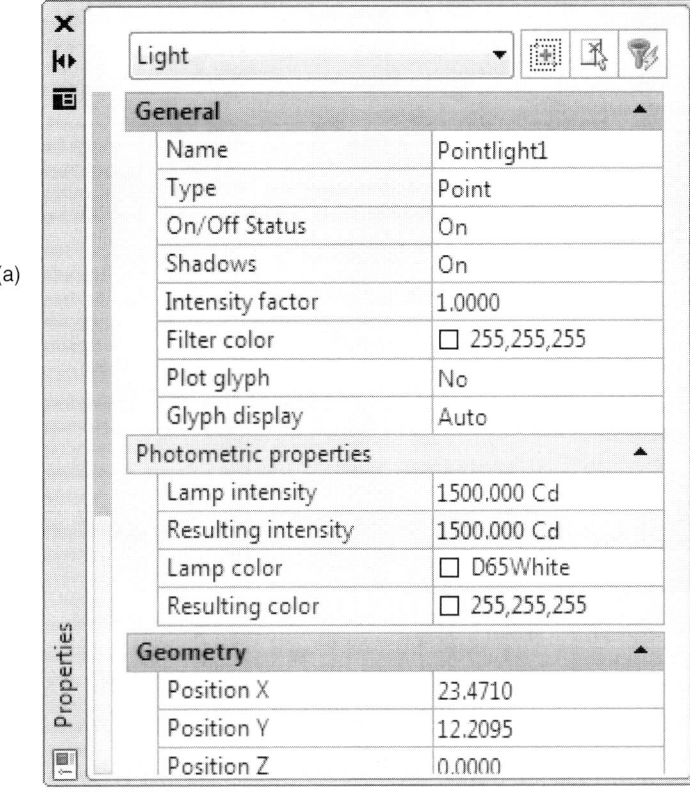

(b)

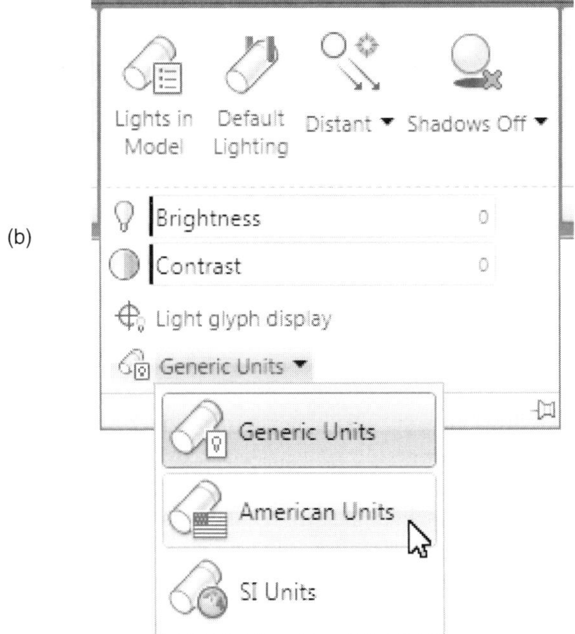

Figure 9-38 (a) The Photometric properties located in the Properties palette and (b) the LIGHTINGUNITS system variable in the Lights panel of the Ribbon

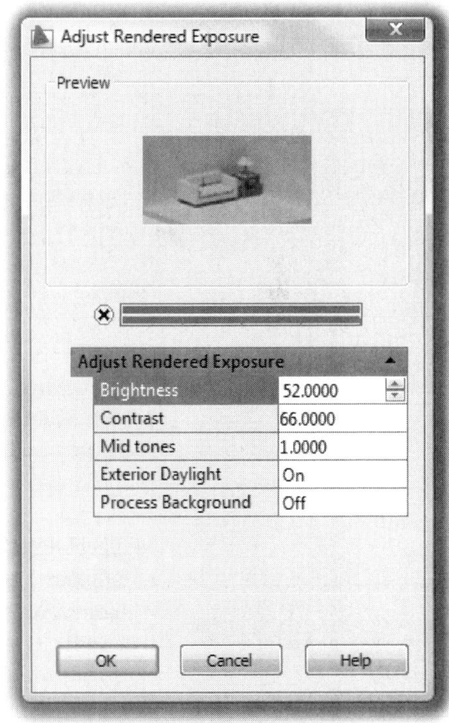

Figure 9-39 Adjust Rendered Exposure dialog box

Distant Lights

Similar to daylight, a distant light emits parallel light rays that travel from infinity in the direction specified. Distant light reaches any object with the same intensity regardless of its location or relative distance. This type of light has no specific location, so no object can be located behind it.

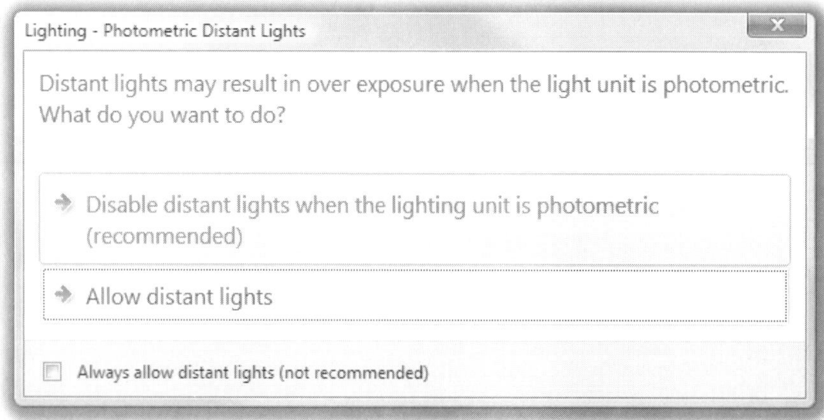

Figure 9-40 Photometric distant light warning

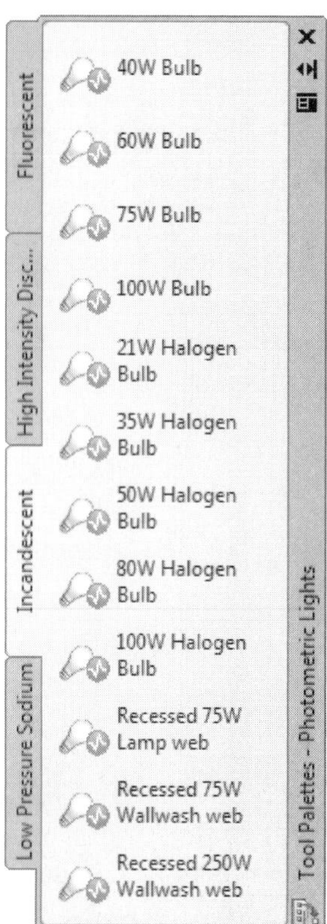

Figure 9-41 The Photometric Lights group of Tool Palettes

DISTANTLIGHT	
Render Toolbar	
Ribbon: Lights panel	
Pull-down Menu	View/ Render/ Light/New Distant Light
Command Line	distantlight

LIGHTLIST	
Render Toolbar	
Ribbon: Lights panel	
Pull-down Menu	View/ Render/ Light/Light List...
Command Line	lightlist

To create a distant light, you can invoke either the **LIGHT** or the **DISTANTLIGHT** commands. In either case, you must define a vector direction by providing coordinate values or use the **Specify** option to specify two points:

Specify vector direction or [Specify] <0.0000,-0.0100,1.0000>:

The coordinates of the vector direction can be entered only through the command line. The direction is defined from the origin (0,0,0) to the specified coordinates. The **Specify** option enables you to specify two points using your pointing device: the direction from and the direction to.

Using a distant light allows you to control with precision the direction from which the light rays strike the objects' surfaces. It can also generate shadows whenever this setting is enabled. Figure 9-42 compares the lighting effect of a distant light with that of the AutoCAD program's default lighting.

Shadows, along with other properties, can be specified through the command line the moment the distant light is created. Figure 9-43 shows the command's options in its shortcut menu.

You can also change more easily the properties of a distant light after it has been created by accessing them in the **Properties** palette (Figure 9-44). Unlike point lights and spot lights, distant lights do not generate a glyph in 3D because they have no specific location. To access the properties of a distant light, you must select it from the **Lights in Model** palette (Figure 9-45), which opens when you invoke the **LIGHTLIST** command.

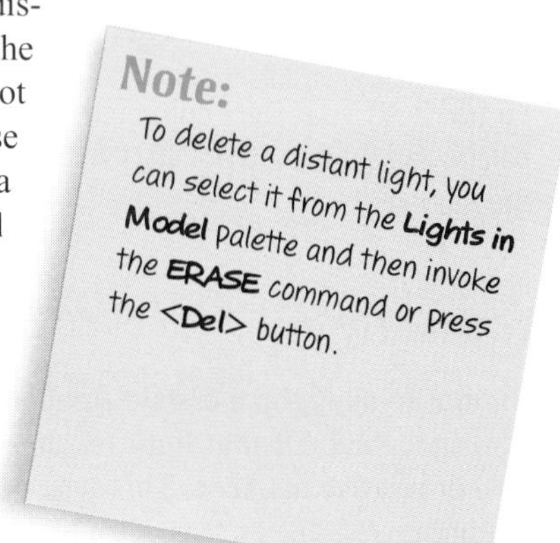

Note:
To delete a distant light, you can select it from the Lights in Model palette and then invoke the ERASE command or press the <Del> button.

In the **Properties** palette, you can change the **Name** of the distant light, turn its **Status** on and off, and change its **Intensity factor** and **Color.** You can also control whether a particular light will cast **Shadows** or not; when this property is on, you can set specific details about the way the shadows are cast.

Figure 9-42 Default lighting (above) versus using a distant light (below)

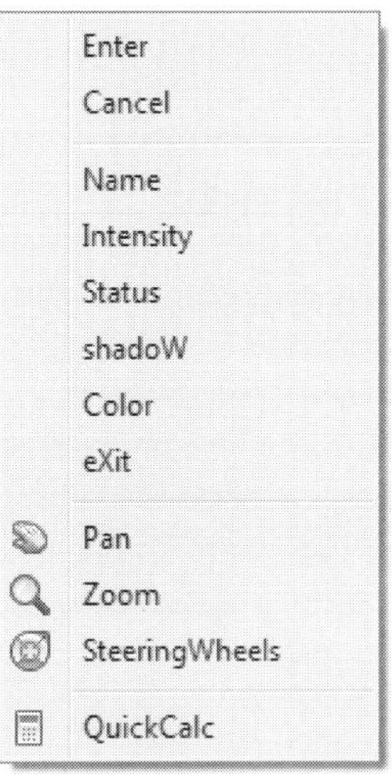

Figure 9-43 The DISTANTLIGHT command shortcut menu

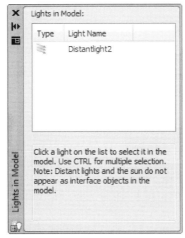

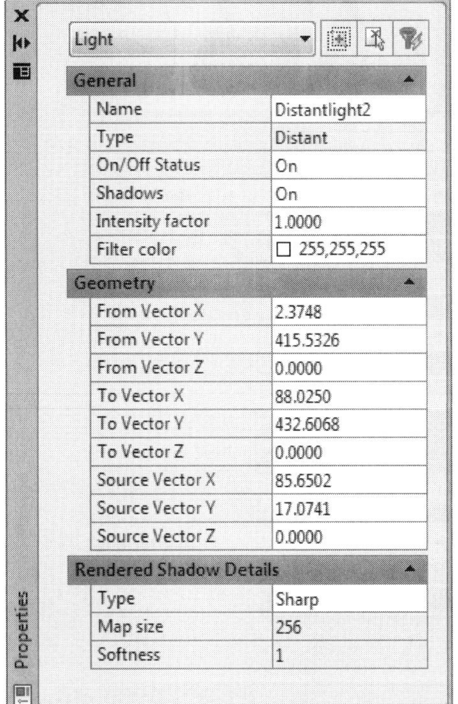

Figure 9-44 The Properties palette provides access to the Distant Light settings

Lights in Model:

Type	Light Name
	Distantlight2

Click a light on the list to select it in the model. Use CTRL for multiple selection. Note: Distant lights and the sun do not appear as interface objects in the model.

Lights in Model

Figure 9-45 The Lights in Model palette

In general, lights can cast either ray-traced or map shadows. The main difference between these types of shadows is the way in which the area close to the border of the shadow is generated.

Ray-traced shadows are generated when an object blocks the light rays' traces in their path from a light source, and are more accurate than map shadows. They can generate high-quality shadows with a sharp, well-defined outline, and can transmit color from objects using materials of a certain transparency. Because they do not use a bitmap to be generated, no further adjustment has to be made to their resolution. Ray-traced shadows are the default type of shadow for any light source and are listed in the **Properties** palette as the **Sharp** type.

FOR MORE DETAILS For more information about using a material and its transparency properties, see the section on using materials and textures in this chapter.

Selecting the **Soft** type of shadows in the **Properties** palette enables you to cast map shadows with a specific light. They cannot transmit color from objects that use transparent materials; however, they are the only way to generate shadows with soft edges. Figure 9-46 shows the difference between these shadows and the ray-traced shadows discussed above. You can adjust the **Map size** or resolution of the bitmap to improve the quality of the shadow. The **Softness** property is a measure of how much sharpness the shadow's contour loses.

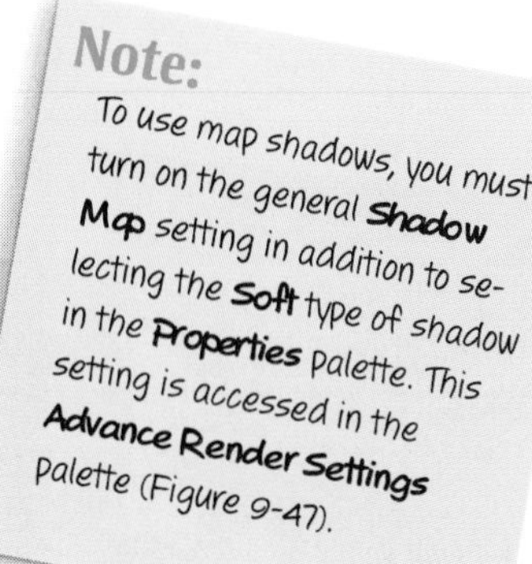

Note:
To use map shadows, you must turn on the general **Shadow Map** setting in addition to selecting the **Soft** type of shadow in the **Properties** palette. This setting is accessed in the **Advance Render Settings** palette (Figure 9-47).

Figure 9-46 Difference between Sharp (Ray traced), shown above, and Soft (Mapped) shadow, shown below

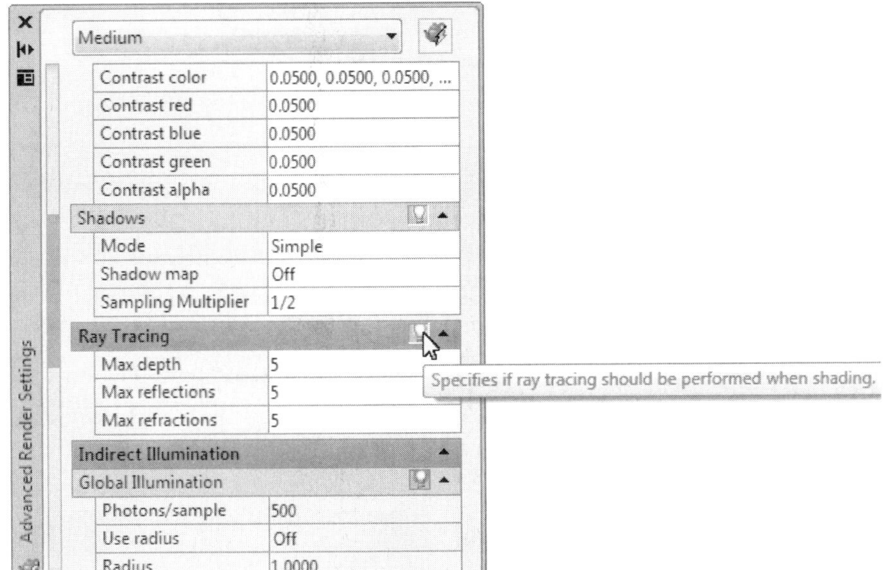

Figure 9-47 The Advanced Render Settings palette

In addition to controlling the effect of shadows for each light, you can also control their effect in each object by changing the **Shadow display** property in the **Properties** palette (Figure 9-48). By default, all objects are created with the property of casting and receiving shadows; however, you can change this property to **Casts shadows, Receives shadows,** or **Ignores shadows** for any object that can be rendered. Figure 9-49 shows the effect caused on the rendered image by modifying this property in the lamp base of the 3D model.

Point Lights

Similar to an incandescent lightbulb, a point light emits light beams from the source in all directions in the 3D space (Figure 9-50). Unlike a distant light, a point light has a specific location and generates a glyph, which allows you not only to select the light but also to perform operations such as **MOVE, ROTATE, COPY,** and **ERASE.**

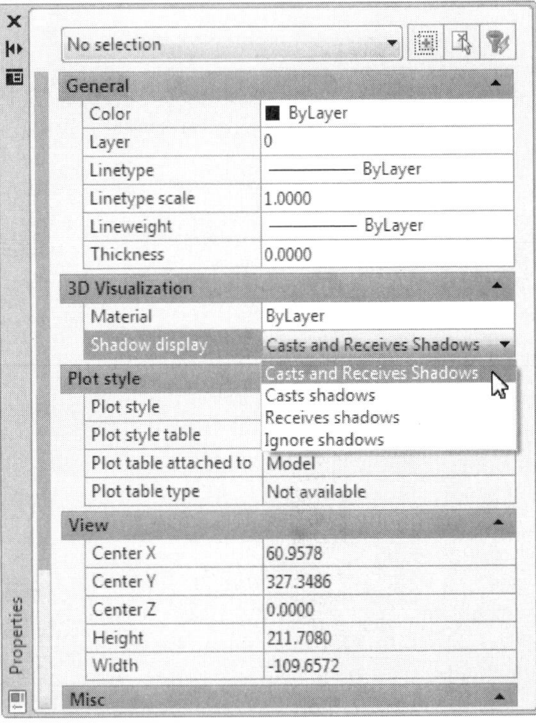

Figure 9-48 The Shadow display property in the Properties palette

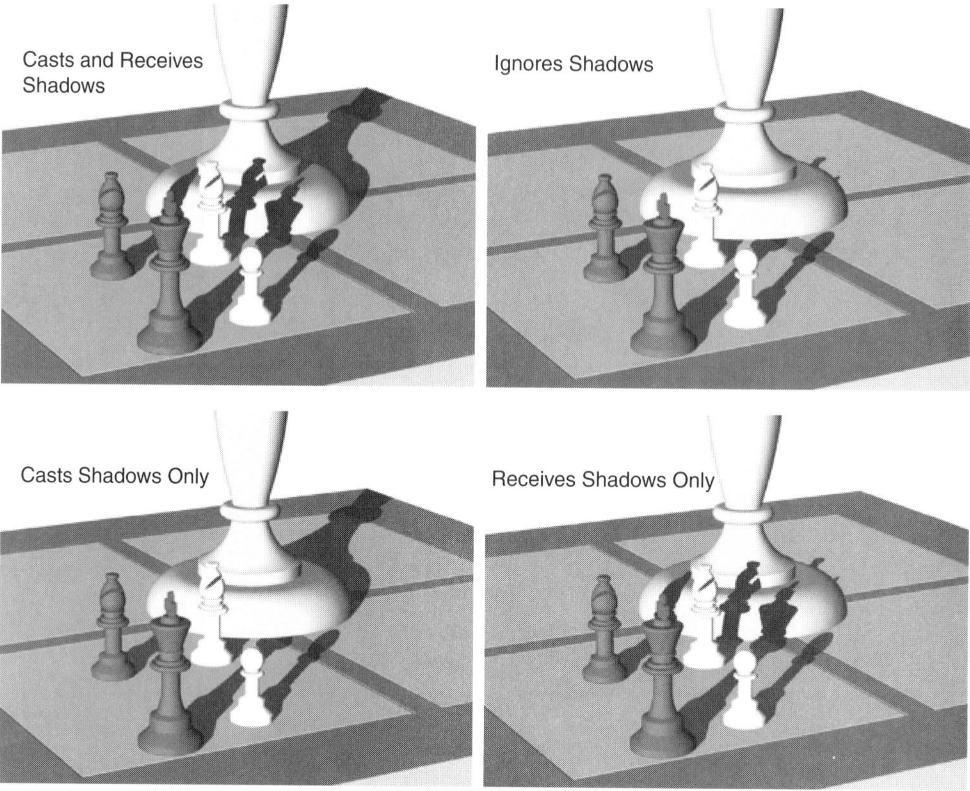

Figure 9-49 The four Shadow display options applied to the lamp base

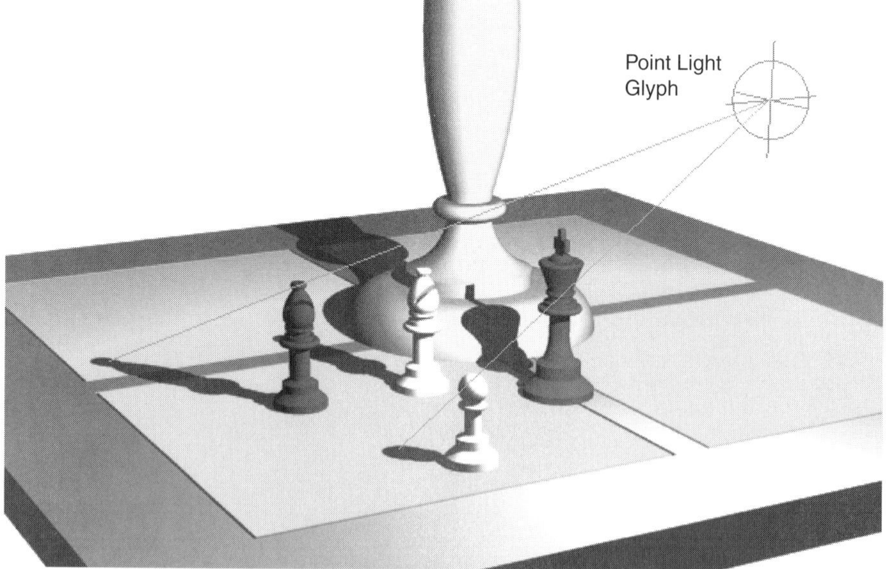

Figure 9-50 A point light emits light in all directions

POINTLIGHT	
Render Toolbar	
Ribbon: Lights panel	
Pull-down Menu:	View/ Render/ Light/New Point Light
Command Line	pointlight

The size and color of the glyph for point and spot lights can be controlled through the **Light Glyph Appearance** dialog box (Figure 9-51) which can be accessed by clicking on the **Lights Glyph Settings...** button located in the **Drafting** tab of the **Options** dialog box (Figure 9-52). You can turn off or on all the glyphs in the drawing by clicking the corresponding button in the **Lights** panel of the **Ribbon** (Figure 9-53).

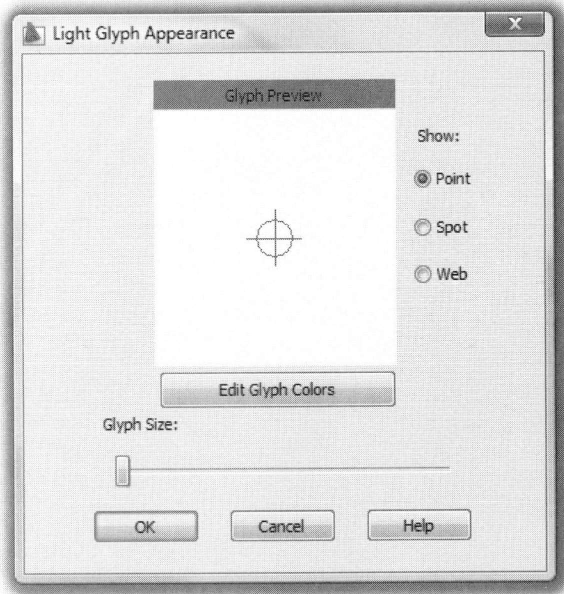

Figure 9-51 The Light Glyph Appearance dialog box

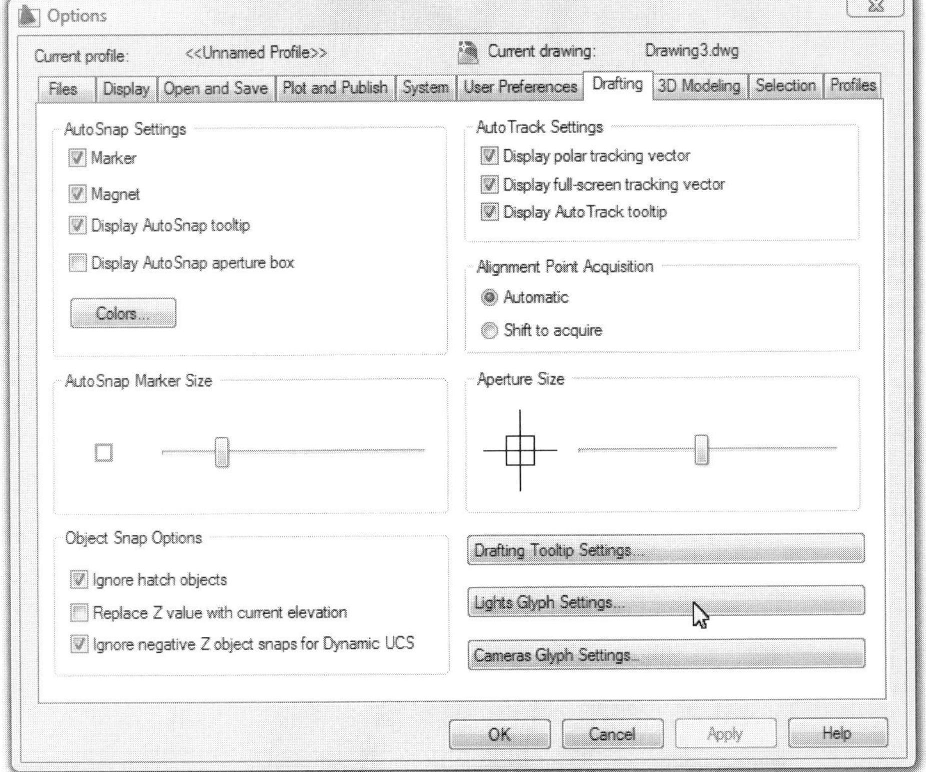

Figure 9-52 The Lights Glyph Settings... button is located in the Drafting tab of the Options dialog box

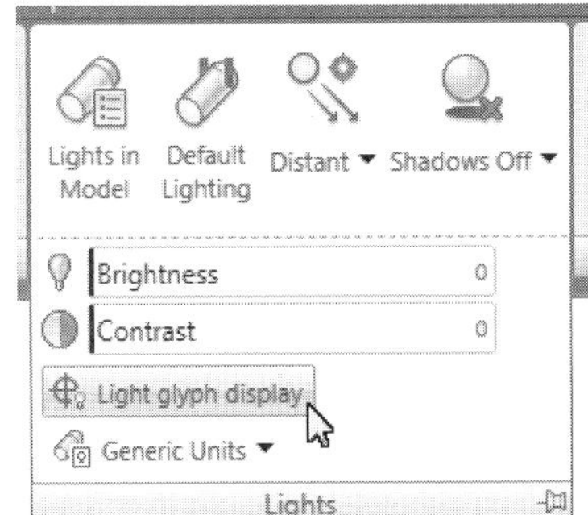

Figure 9-53 The indicated button in the Lights panel of the Ribbon turns the light glyph off or on

To create a point light, you can invoke the **LIGHT** or the **POINTLIGHT** command. After specifying the location, you can modify the settings for shadows and other properties. Figure 9-54(a) shows the command's options in its shortcut menu when the photometric properties are not enabled. When the photometric properties are enabled, the shortcut menu also includes an option for these properties [Figure 9-54(b)].

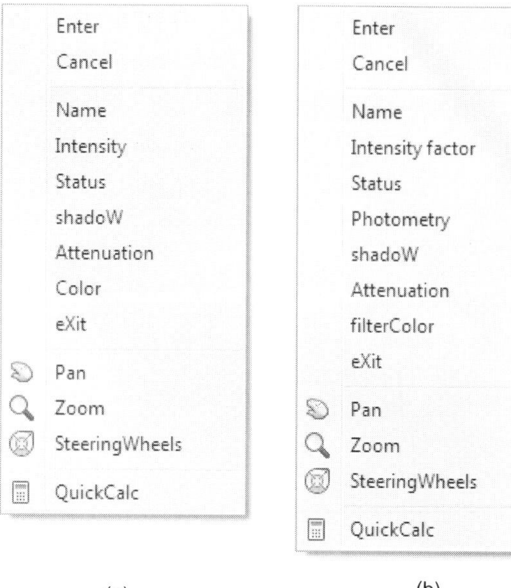

Figure 9-54 The POINTLIGHT command shortcut menus with and without Photometric Properties enabled

As with distant lights, you can access these settings for point lights much more easily in the **Properties** palette (Figure 9-55), which can contain the photometric properties if they are enabled. You can select a point light to see its properties either by selecting its glyph or by selecting the light from the list in the **Lights in Model** palette.

Note:
You can control the settings for shadows in the same manner as you can with the distance lights.

In the **Properties** palette, you can change the **Name** of the point light. You can turn its **Status** on and off, change its **Intensity factor,** and change its **Color.**

Unlike distant lights, which are considered to always have the same intensity throughout the 3D space, the intensity of point and spot lights can diminish proportionally as their distance from the object increases. (This phenomenon is known as ***attenuation.***) As a result, objects that appear farther from the light source will appear less illuminated.

attenuation: Proportional reduction of light intensity over distance.

Under the **Type** of attenuation in the **Properties** palette, you can set **Point** and **Spot** lights to have no attenuation by selecting **None**. By selecting **Inverse Linear** or **Inverse Square** you specify two different relationships between intensity and the distance.

Note:
When **Inverse Square** attenuation is selected, the intensity decreases much faster than with inverse linear attenuation as the distance increases. Usually, the use of attenuation requires higher values of intensity.

Where P_1 is the location of the light, P_2 is the location of the object, and D is the distance between P_1 and P_2, the inverse linear attenuation can be expressed by:

$$\text{Intensity @ } P_2 = \text{Intensity @ } P_1 / D$$

and the inverse square attenuation can be expressed by:

$$\text{Intensity @ } P_2 = \text{Intensity @ } P_1 / D^2$$

The **Start limit offset** and **End limit offset** properties specify the distances from the source at which the light starts and ends, respectively. No light is cast beyond the end limit; this allows you to prevent certain objects from being illuminated by a specific light. Enabling the **Use limits** property allows you to control these two distances either by accessing the **Properties** palette or by pulling the glyph's grips (Figure 9-56).

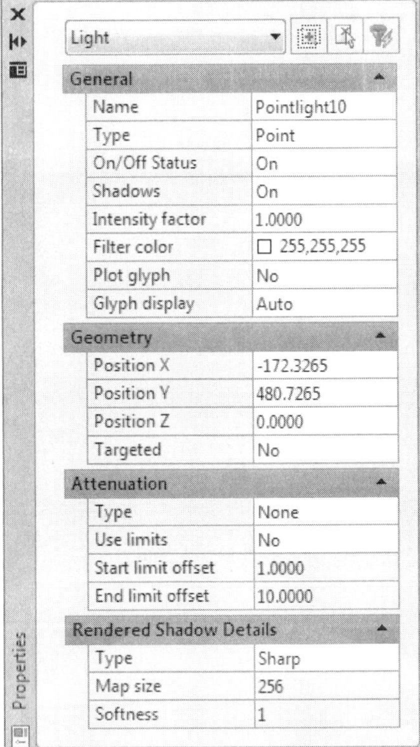

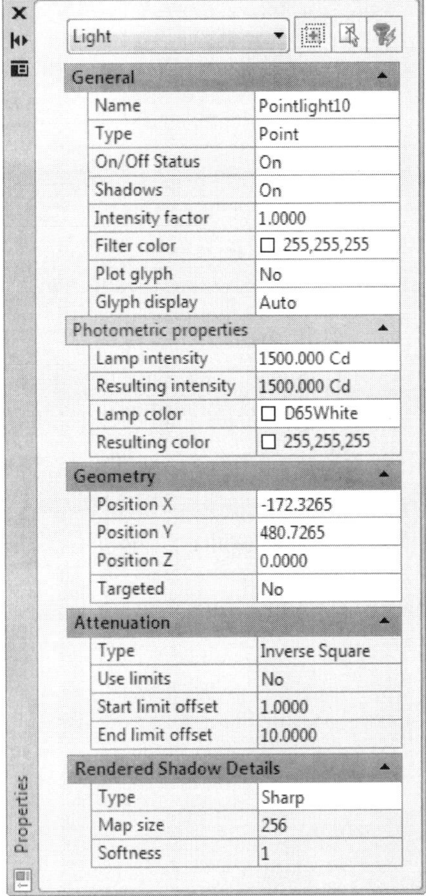

Figure 9-55 The Properties palette provides access to the Point Light settings; the photometric properties are available when LIGHTINGUNITS is set to 1 or 2

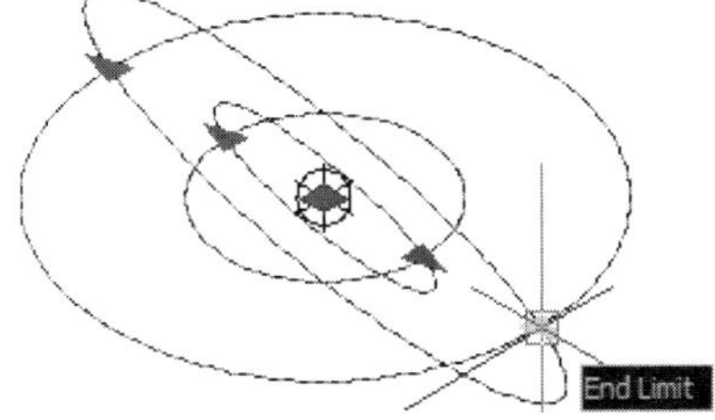

Figure 9-56 The point light grips can be used to modify the Start limit offset and End limit offset values

When photometric lighting is enabled, that is, when **LIGHTINGUNITS** is set to **1** or **2**, the attenuation properties have no effect on the light. Photometric lights are defined by real values, including their own attenuation values.

You can control the intensity of photometric lights by changing the **Intensity factor** value on the **Properties** palette, just like you do with standard light. The **Lamp intensity** property, located under **Photometric properties,** is a better choice to set the intensity because it allows you to set real values; the **Lamp color** property allows you to select predetermined natural colors. Clicking on the buttons located inside the value fields of these two properties opens the **Lamp Intensity** and the **Lamp Color** dialog boxes, respectively; see Figure 9-57. In the **Lamp Intensity** dialog box, you can control the intensity of the light by specifying a value of **Intensity, Flux,** or **Illuminance.** In the **Lamp Color** dialog box, you can select from a group of standard colors such as Fluorescent, Incandescent, Xenon, Halogen, and so on.

Note:

Changing the **Intensity Factor** in the dialog box or in the **Properties** palette multiplies the photometric value.

Photometric lighting provides a more realistic illumination effect. Figure 9-58 shows the same point light with the standard lighting (top) and photometric lighting (bottom).

Spot Lights

Spot lights are probably the most common type of light used in rendered images. Resembling an actual spotlight or a flashlight, this type of light emits its light beams from the source in the form

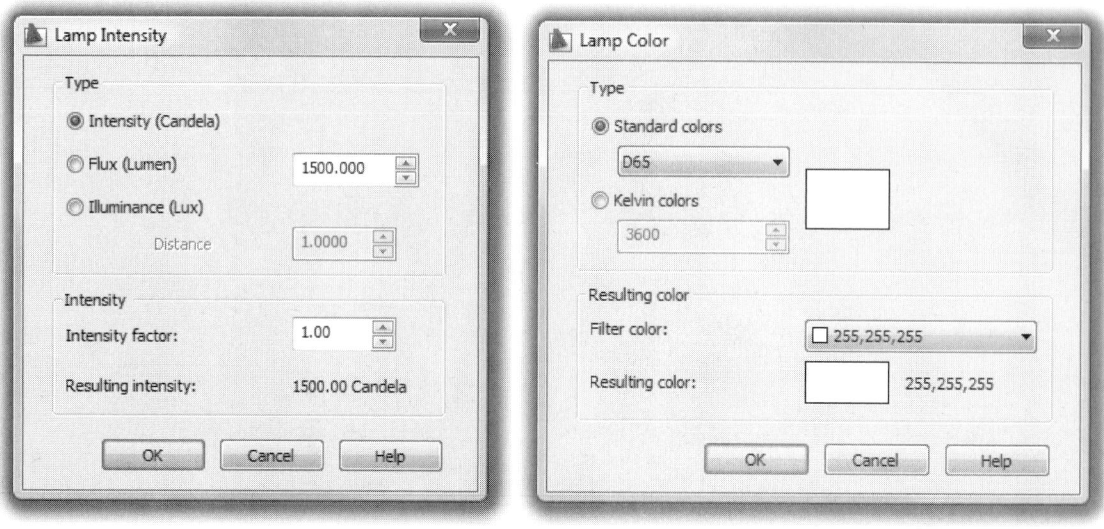

Figure 9-57 The Lamp Intensity and Lamp Color dialog boxes

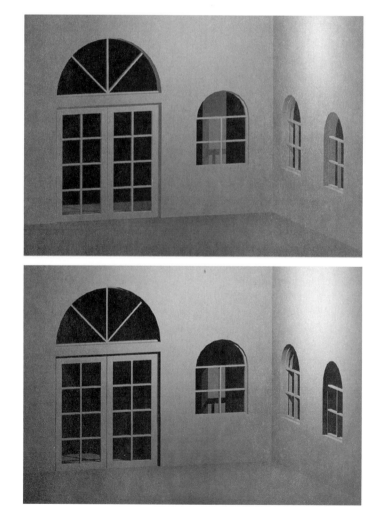

Figure 9-58 Ilumination effect created with a standard point light (top), and using photometric lighting (bottom)

Figure 9-59 Spot lights emit light in the form of a cone

SPOTLIGHT	
Render Toolbar	
Ribbon: Lights panel	
Pull-down Menu	View/ Render/ Light/New Spotlight
Command Line	spotlight

of a cone (Figure 9-59). A spot light requires you to specify not only a source location but also a direction because you will be prompted to specify the target. This type of light also generates a glyph, which allows you to select it, perform operations such as **MOVE** and **ROTATE**, and modify some of its properties by pulling its grips.

To create a spot light, you can invoke the **LIGHT** or the **SPOTLIGHT** command. Alternatively, you can create a spot light using the **FREESPOT** command or the **Freespot** option of the **LIGHT** command. With these two options, you will not be prompted to specify a target, and the spot light will be automatically aligned with the *Z*-axis of the current UCS. The only difference between Spot lights and Freespot lights is that Freespot light does not have a specified target. Spot lights can be turned into Freespot (and vice versa) by changing the **Targeted** property in the **Properties** palette.

As with the other two types of light, you can specify the settings for the shadows and other properties after specifying the light's location and direction. Figure 9-60 shows the command's options in its shortcut menu. The **Properties** palette, as mentioned previously, gives you easier access to the same properties after the spot light has been created (Figure 9-61).

Hotspot angle and ***falloff angle*** are two new properties, inherent only to this type of light. Figure 9-62 shows the effect caused on the rendered image when different **Falloff** angle values are set in a spot light.

The cone of light emitted by a spot light is composed of two main conical volumes, each with different characteristics. An inner cone, called the *hotspot*, concentrates the light, without reducing its intensity as it gets farther from the cone's centerline. The outer conical volume surrounding the inner cone, called *falloff*, diminishes the light's intensity to zero as it gets farther from the centerline (Figure 9-63). The hotspot and falloff angles control how much the cones of light open. The value of the falloff angle cannot be set below that of the hotspot angle.

Note:
The settings for shadows and attenuation, as well as for start and end limit offset, are controlled in the same manner as with point lights.

Note:
The photometric properties of spot lights are controlled in the same manner as with point lights.

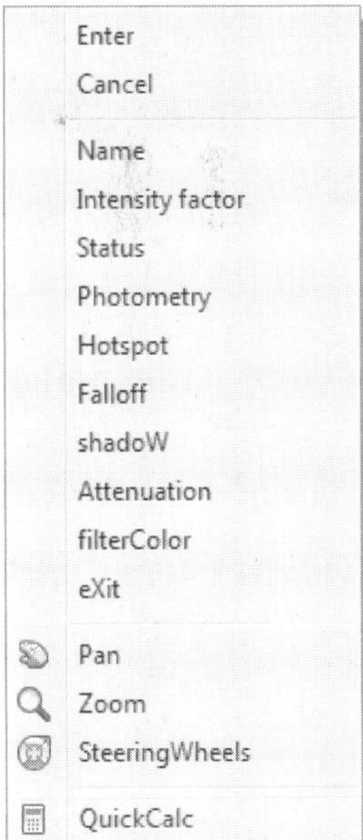

Figure 9-60 The SPOTLIGHT command shortcut menu

hotspot angle and falloff angle: The angles of the inner and outer cones defining the characteristics of the light rays emitted by a spot light.

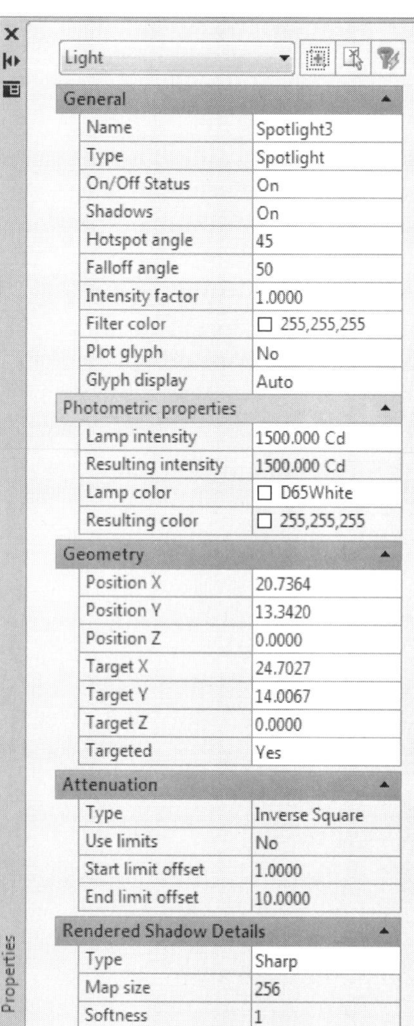

Figure 9-61 The Properties palette provides access to the Spotlight settings

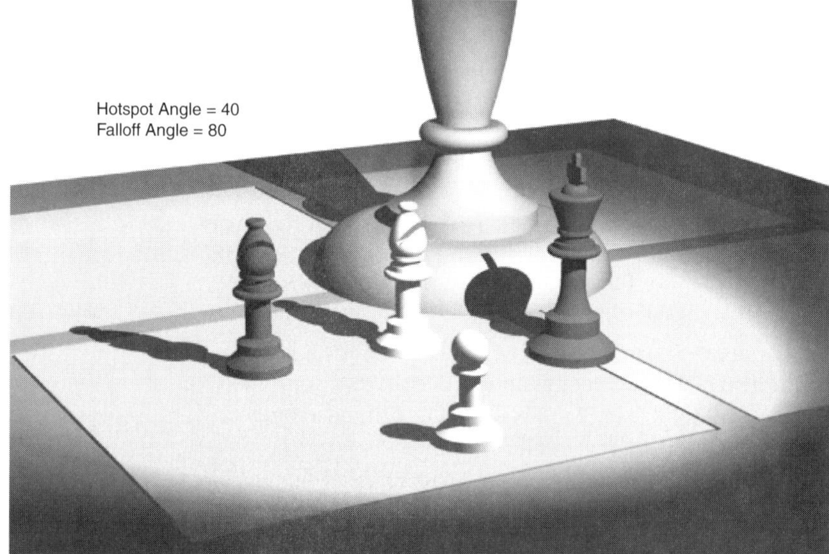

Figure 9-62 Effect of using different Falloff angle values in a spot light

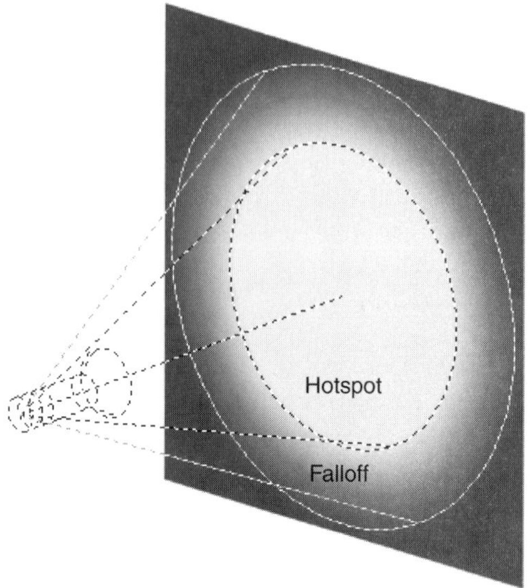

Figure 9-63 Differentiation of areas illuminated by the Hotspot and the Falloff light zones

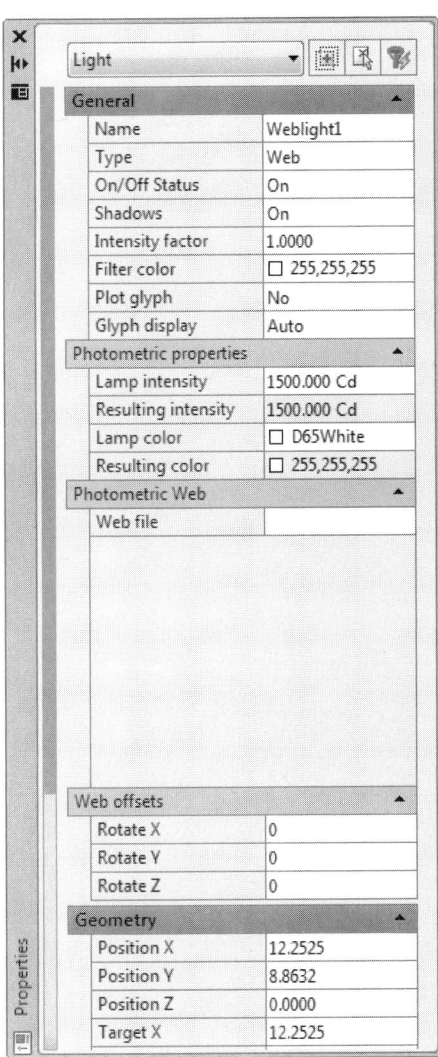

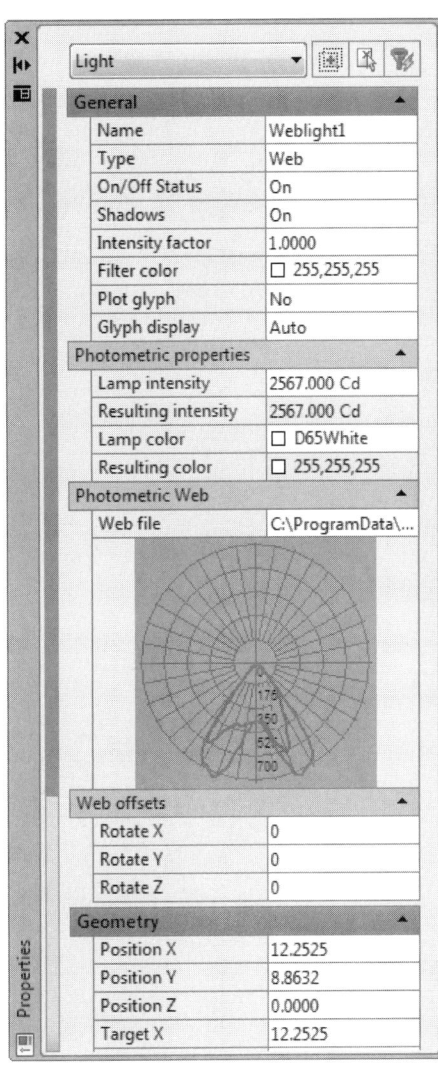

Figure 9-64 Properties palettes showing an isotropic and an anisotropic photometric web light

Web Lights

When the photometric properties are enabled, web lights offer a detailed 3D distribution of the intensity of the light emanating from the light source in all directions. When a web light is originally created, it provides an isotropic distribution of the light, which is represented as a sphere-shaped web. The effect of an isotropic web light is the same as the point light. The main purpose of a web light, however, is to show an anisotropic (nonuniform) light distribution. To do so, you must select one of the web files provided with the AutoCAD program. Figure 9-64 shows the **Properties** palette with the original Web light on the left and with an anisotropic light distribution to the right.

Web files are created by using data provided by manufacturers of light and light fixtures. Depending on the web file you select, the light glyph will change to represent the photometric web according to its 3D light distribution.

Web lights are created by invoking either the **WEBLIGHT** or **FREEWEB** command, or you can also use the **LIGHT** command and select either of these options. Either of these commands can be invoked by entering its name in the command prompt. As with spot lights, Web lights are different from Freeweb lights because the Freeweb lights have no target location.

By using web lights, you can create more realistic illuminated scenes than with spot or point lights. Walls can be given a unique washed effect as they are hit with this type of photometric light (Figure 9-65).

Point, web, and spot lights can be transformed into one another by changing the **Type** property (Figure 9-66).

Figure 9-65 The illumination effects of an anisotropic Web light

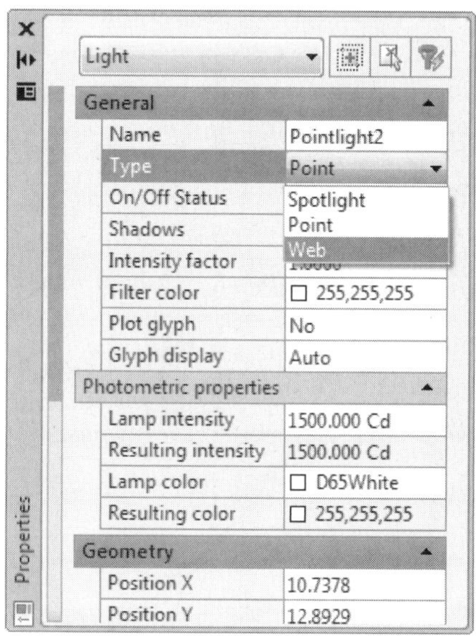

Figure 9-66 Point, Web, and Spot lights can be transformed into one another through the Properties palette

The Sun Light

The sun light behaves like any other distant light. It emits parallel light rays that travel from infinity in a specific direction, reaching any object with the same intensity. This special kind of distant light can be used to simulate the effect of the sunlight on your 3D model. Thus, it should be used for exterior environments only.

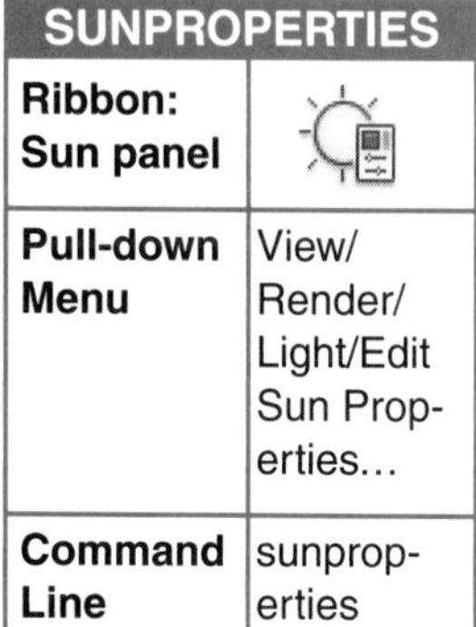

SUNPROPERTIES	
Ribbon: Sun panel	
Pull-down Menu	View/ Render/ Light/Edit Sun Properties...
Command Line	sunproperties

Like other distant lights, the sun does not place a glyph on the 3D model. It is not listed in the **Lights in Model** palette either. The properties of the sun are accessed in a special palette named **Sun Properties** rather than in the **Properties** palette (Figure 9-67). The **Sun Properties** palette is opened by invoking the **SUNPROPERTIES** command.

As with any other light, you can change the sun light's **Status** (on/off), **Intensity, Color,** and the effect of the shadows caused by its light rays. What really makes this particular light unique is the way in which its direction is specified. Simulating the presence of the real sun, the direction of the sun light is specified by its geographic location, the date, and the time of day rather than by an arbitrary vector direction.

The date and time can be changed in the **Sun Properties** palette. The **Geographic Location** dialog box allows you to determine the **Latitude** and **Longitude** of the sun light's direction by

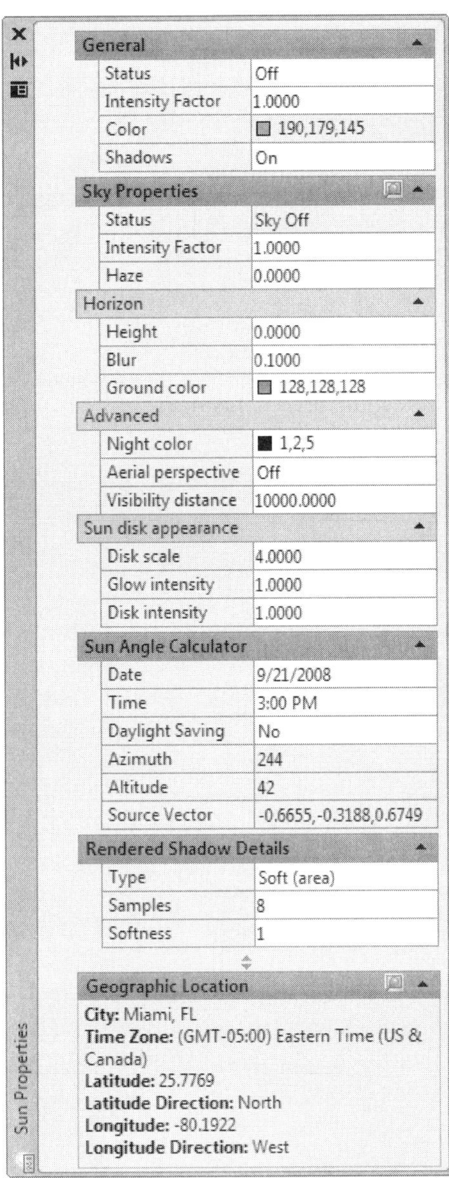

Figure 9-67 The Sun Properties palette

specifying its values directly (if you know such information) [Figure 9-68(a)]. Clicking on the **Use Map...** button opens the **Location Picker** dialog box, where you can easily select a location [Figure 9-68(b)]. You can open the **Geographic Location** dialog box by invoking the **GEOGRAPHICLOCATION** command or by clicking the button on the **Geographic Location** pane.

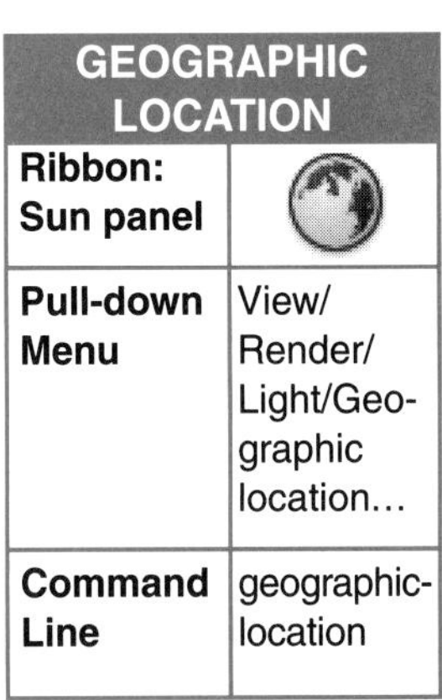

GEOGRAPHIC LOCATION	
Ribbon: Sun panel	
Pull-down Menu	View/ Render/ Light/Geo-graphic location...
Command Line	geographic-location

Under **Sun Angle Calculator** located in the **Properties** palette, you can control the direction in which the sun's light strikes the earth based on a particular geographic location. By modifying the **Date** and **Time,** you can change the incidence of the sun's light rays on your 3D model. The incidence is controlled by the **Azimuth** and **Altitude** angle settings. The **Azimuth** represents the angular position along the horizon. The **Azimuth** angle when the sun's light comes from the north (*Y*-axis) is zero, and its value is between 180° (clockwise) and –180° (counterclockwise). The **Altitude** represents the inclination of the horizon. Its values fall between –90° and 90° (Figure 9-69). Under **Sky Properties,** you can adjust the appearance of the sky and the sun.

Exercise 9-3: Placing User-Created Lights

1. **OPEN** ***Exercise 9-2.***
2. **SAVE** it **AS** ***Exercise 9-3.***
3. Invoke the **RPREF** command to open the **Advanced Render Settings** palette. Under **Render Context,** select **Viewport** as the **Destination.**

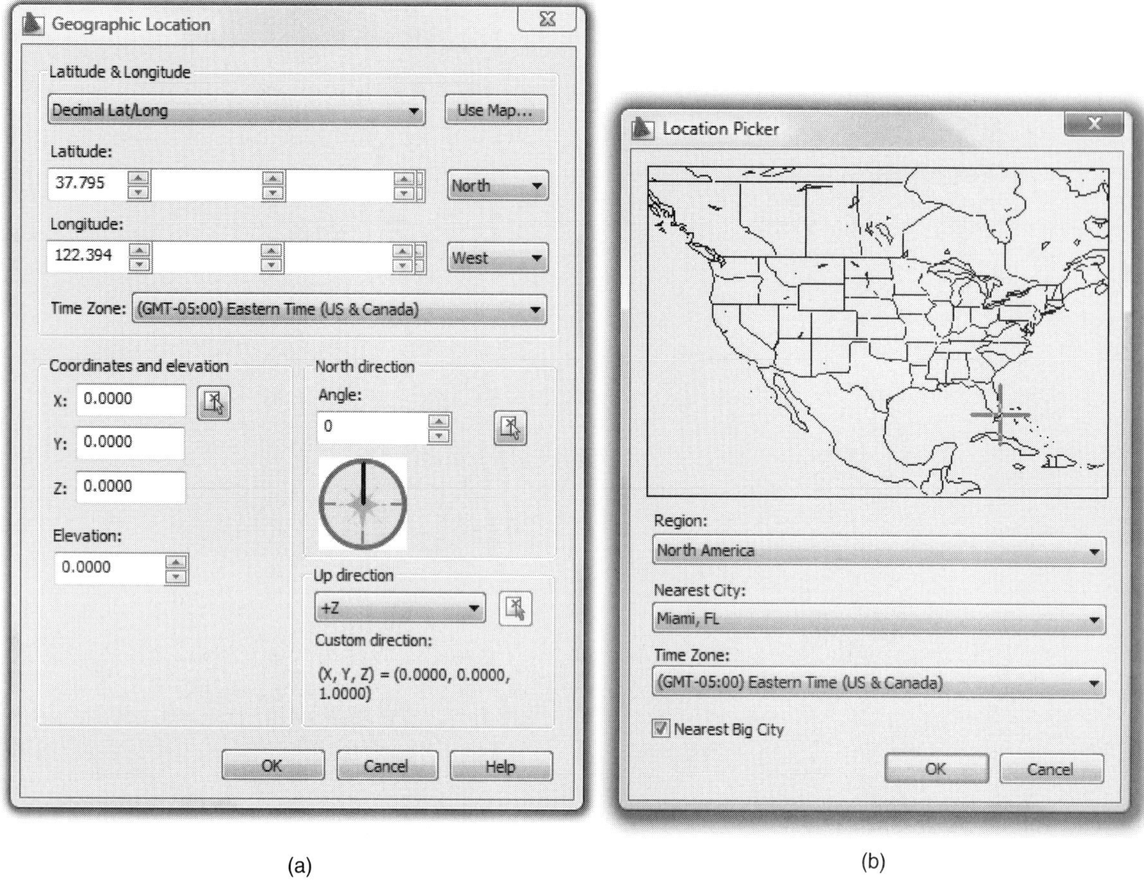

Figure 9-68 (a) The Geographic Location dialog box and (b) the Location Picker dialog box

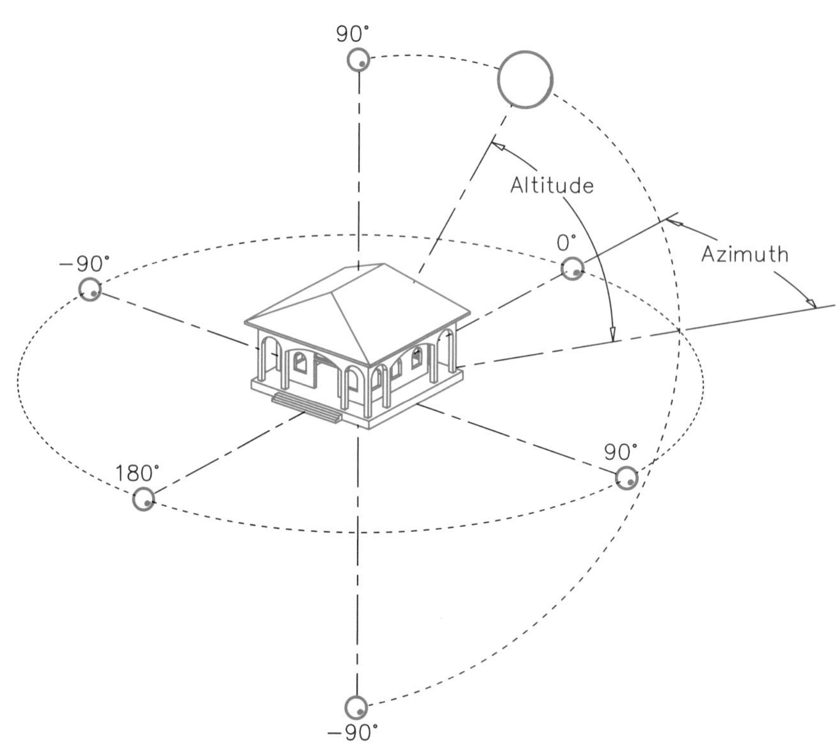

Figure 9-69 The azimuth and altitude angles

4. Make sure the **LIGHTINGUNITS** system variable is set to **2** and invoke the **LIGHT** command by typing its name in the command line.
5. Respond **Yes** to the **Viewport Lighting Mode** warning, and then enter **P** to specify a point light.
6. When prompted to specify the source location, snap to the top endpoint of the reference line located over the lamp base (Figure 9-70). Press **<Enter>** to end the command.
7. Select **Render View** from the **Views** drop-down list located in the **Views** toolbar or in the **3D Navigate** control panel.
8. Invoke the **RENDER** command. The rendered image should look like Figure 9-71.

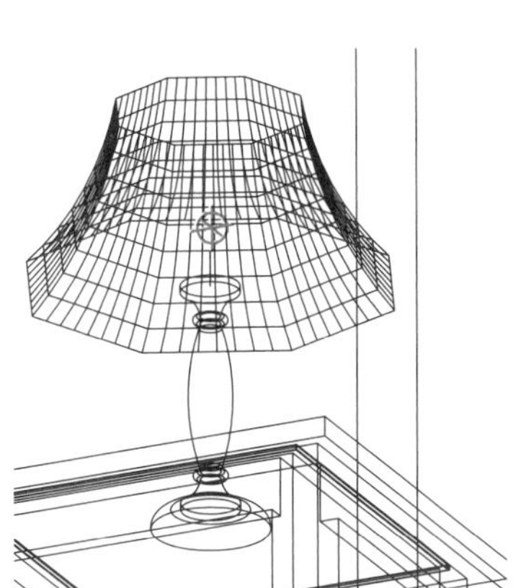

Figure 9-70 Location of the point light

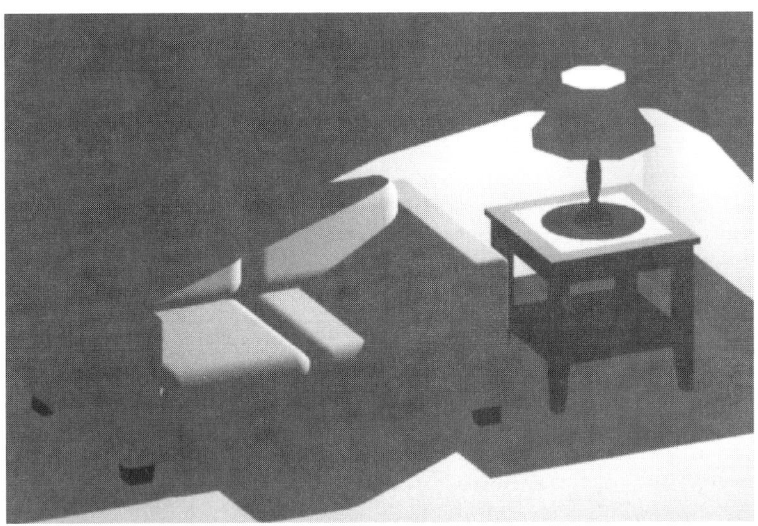

Figure 9-71 The resulting rendered image

Using the **Medium** render preset should work OK with most computers. You can experiment with lower or higher levels of quality based on the properties of your equipment and the video adapter you have installed.

9. Invoke the **REGEN** command to regenerate the display.
10. Draw the line shown in Figure 9-72 between the two endpoints on the top of the walls.
11. Invoke the **WEBLIGHT** command by entering its full name in the command prompt. When prompted to specify a source location, snap to the midpoint of the line you just drew.
12. Snap to any point on the left front corner of the table top to specify the target location. Press **<Enter>** to end the command.
13. Invoke the **LIGHTLIST** command by clicking its icon in the **Light** panel of the **Ribbon.** This will open the **Lights in Model** palette.
14. Open the **Properties** palette.

Note:

You can add some general illumination to the 3D model by using a direct light coming from the top.

When working with lights, it is a good idea to anchor both the **Lights in Model** and the **Properties** palettes, one below the other, on the right of the AutoCAD window (Figure 9-73).

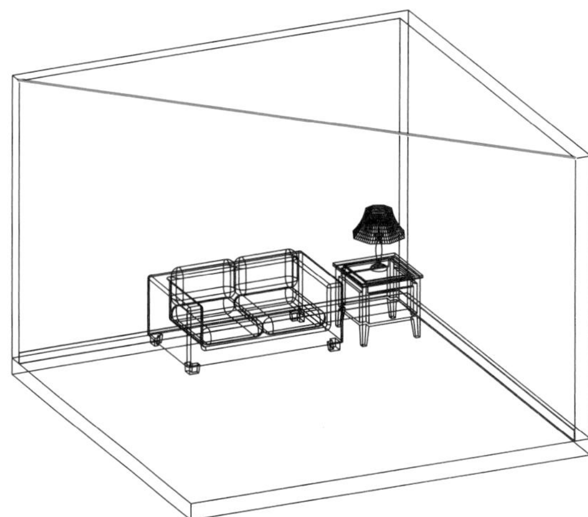

Figure 9-72 Reference line

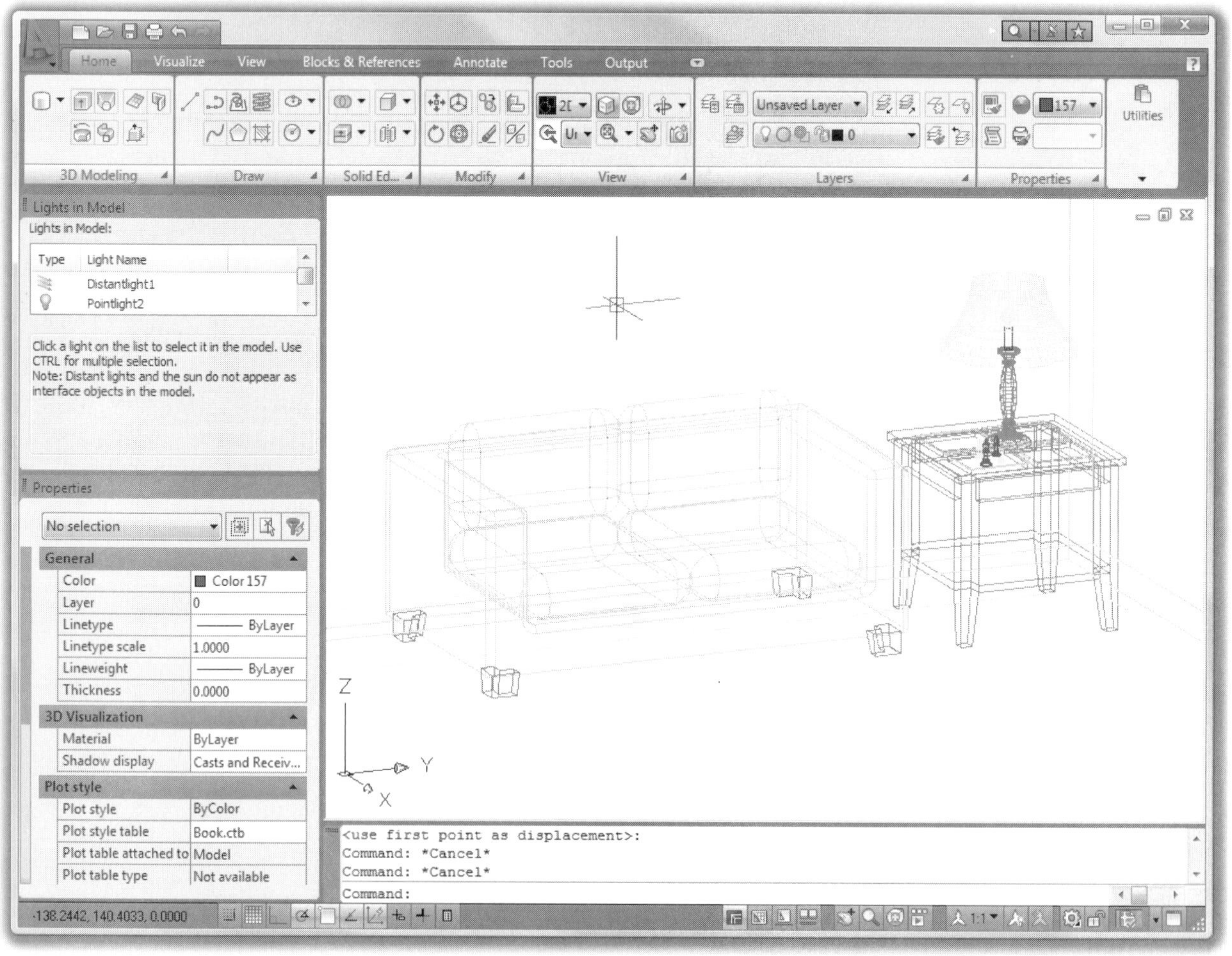

Figure 9-73 When working with lights, the Lights in Model and the Properties palettes can be anchored to the right for easier access

15. Select **Weblight2** from the **Lights in Model** palette to access its properties.
16. In the **Properties** palette, turn its **Shadows** property OFF. Under **Photometric properties,** set the **Lamp Intensity** to **800 Cd.**
17. Select **Render View** from the **Views** drop-down list located in the **Views** toolbar or in the **3D Navigate** panel.

18. Invoke the **RENDER** command. The rendered image should look like Figure 9-74.
19. Invoke the **REGEN** command to regenerate the display.
20. Invoke the **SPOTLIGHT** command by clicking on its icon in the **Light** panel of the **Ribbon**. When prompted to specify a source location, snap to the midpoint of the line you drew on top of the walls. Snap to the midpoint of the bottom front edge of the sofa for the target location.
21. Select the point light from the **Lights in Model** palette, and change its **Lamp Intensity** to **95 Cd** in the **Properties** palette.
22. Press the <**Esc**> key to unselect the point light. Then select the spot light by picking its glyph. In the **Properties** palette, change its **Lamp Intensity** to **800 Cd** and its **Falloff angle** value to **75.**
23. Select **Render View** from the **Views** drop-down list located in the **Views** toolbar or in the **3D Navigate** control panel.
24. Invoke the **RENDER** command. The rendered image should look like Figure 9-75.
25. Select **Weblight2** and change the Web file that controls the 3D anisotropic distribution of light. Experiment with different choices on your own.
26. **SAVE** the drawing.

Note:
Changing the **Lamp Intensity** of the web light and canceling its **Shadows** will cause this light to provide a soft general illumination to the 3D model without creating a mixture of shadows.

Figure 9-74 The resulting rendered image

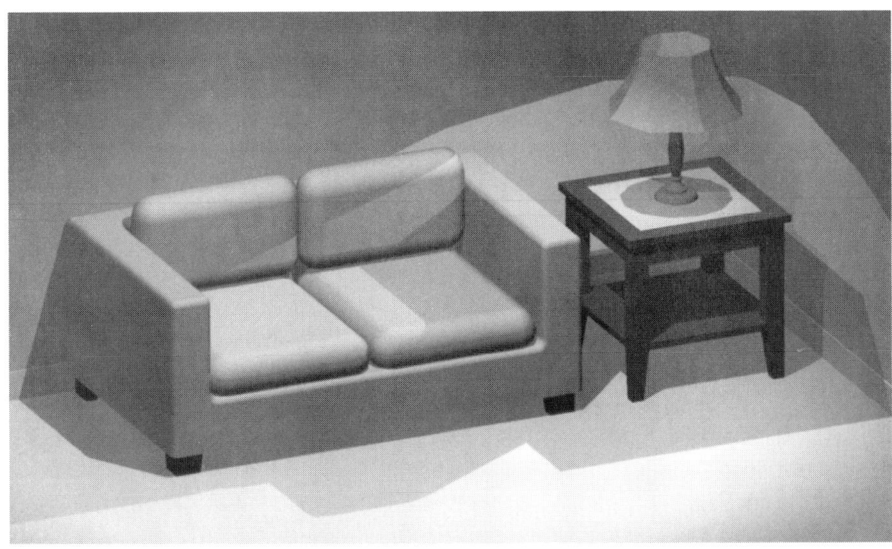

Figure 9-75 The resulting rendered image after the specified settings are changed

MATERIALS AND TEXTURES

PURPOSE OF USING MATERIALS

Materials are used to provide properties such as shininess, translucency, and texture to the 3D objects in the model so they look like real objects when rendered. By applying materials you can simulate almost any property of the real-world objects. Similar to a layer, **Material** is a property inherent only to objects that can be rendered. The **Material** property can be handled in the **Properties** palette.

MATERIALS	
Render Toolbar	
Ribbon: Materials panel	
Pull-down Menu	View/ Render/ Materi-als...
Command Line	materials

USING MATERIALS FROM THE TOOL PALETTES

Materials are created and stored in the **Materials** palette, which you can display by invoking the **MATERIALS** command. The top window (**Available Materials in Drawing**) displays sample images of any material available in the current drawing. Any new drawing starts off with a material named *Global*. This is the material we have been using throughout the exercises. The name of the selected material's icon is displayed in the drop-down list window below the icon's window. Also, hovering the mouse pointer over the icon displays a tooltip with the material's name (Figure 9-76).

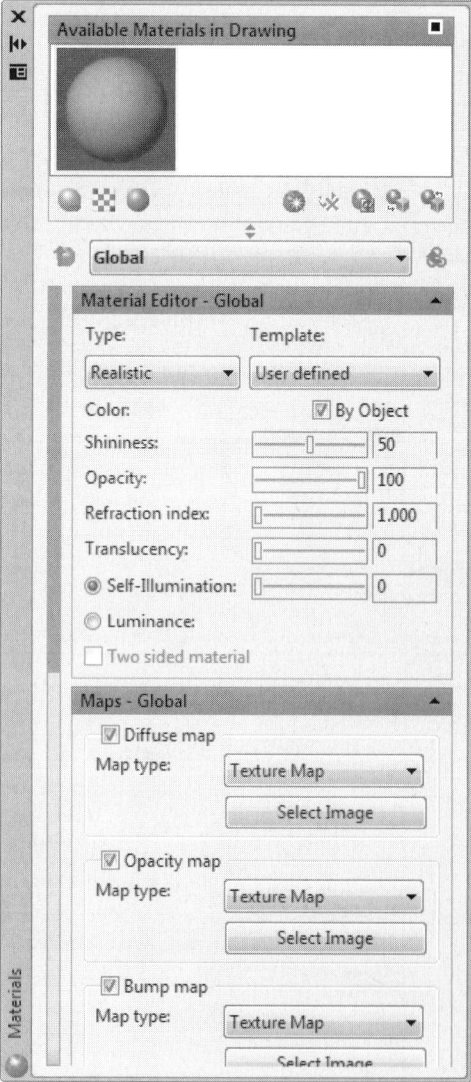

Figure 9-76 In the Materials palette, the tooltip description allows you to know the material's name

You can add other materials into the drawing either by creating them or by importing from the many materials stored by categorized palettes in the **Materials** and **Materials Library** groups of palettes. As you learned in a previous chapter, right-clicking on the vertical ribbon of the **Tool Palettes** shows a shortcut menu from which you can select one of the defined groups of palettes (Figure 9-77). You can select **Add to Current Drawing** from the shortcut menu that is displayed after you right-click on a particular material's icon (Figure 9-78). The sample image of the material added to the drawing is displayed in the **Materials** palette immediately. Alternatively, you can select **Copy** from the shortcut menu in the **Materials** palette and then right-click inside the sample images area in the **Materials** palette and select **Paste** (Figure 9-79). As with many other properties, pasting an AutoCAD object that has been copied to the clipboard from another drawing will also bring in any material that has been applied to that object.

In the reverse of this process, you can add any new material you create to a palette. You do this by selecting **Export to Active Tool Palette** or by dragging and dropping the material into the active palette directly.

Applying the Materials

After the materials are available in the drawing, you can apply them to the objects just as you assign a **Color** or a **Linetype** property. There are several methods you can use to do so. The **Materials** palette is probably the most frequently used. After you select the desired material, click on the **Apply Material** button, which is the second button from the right below the icon's pane. Double-clicking the material's icon will also activate this task. Then, you will be prompted to select the objects.

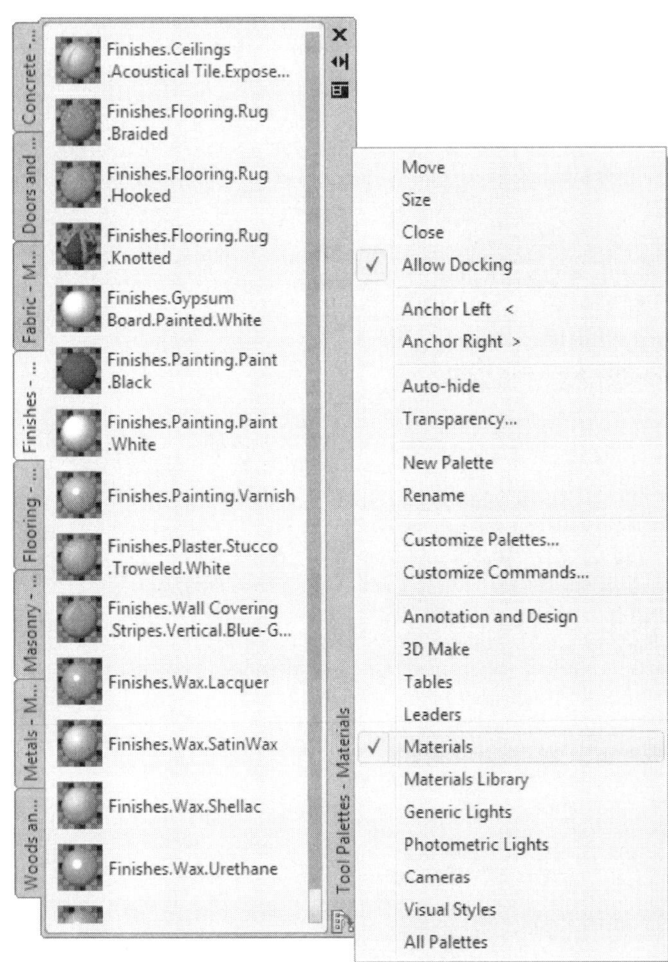

Figure 9-77 The Materials group of palettes can be selected in the Tool Palettes main shortcut menu

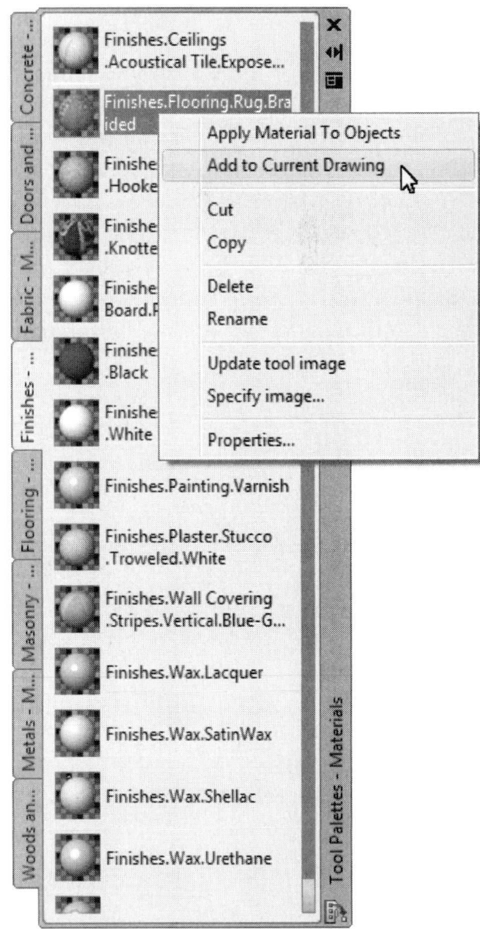

Figure 9-78 Shortcut menu displayed after right-clicking on a particular material in the Tool Palettes

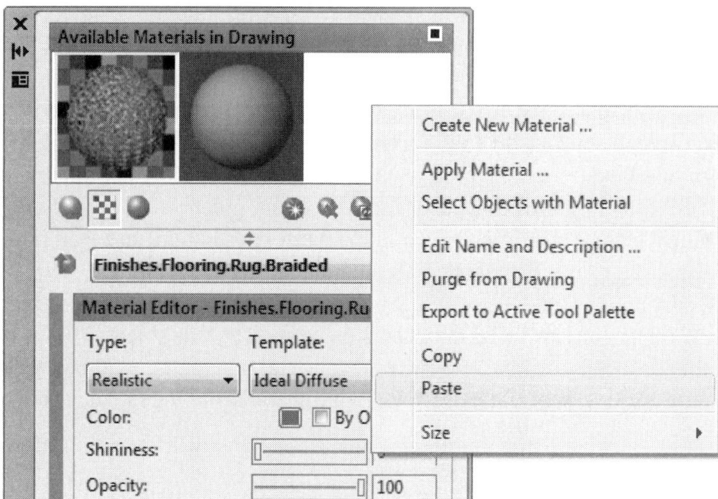

Figure 9-79 Shortcut menu displayed in the Materials palette

Because **Material** is another property of objects, you can also use the **Properties** palette to change the material for selected objects (Figure 9-80). Objects that can be rendered are the only ones that possess this property.

Another way of applying a material is by linking it to a specific layer. Invoking the **MATERIALATTACH** command will display the **Material Attachment Options** dialog box, allowing you to drag a material from the list on the left and drop it over the layer. This creates a linkage similarly to linking a linetype to a layer (Figure 9-81). The **Delete** button detaches the material from the layer. The **MATERIALATTACH** command can by invoked only through the command line.

Materials are shown after the rendered image is processed. You can also display them by selecting the **Realistic** visual style, which is the only predefined visual style for which, by default, materials are enabled (Figure 9-82).

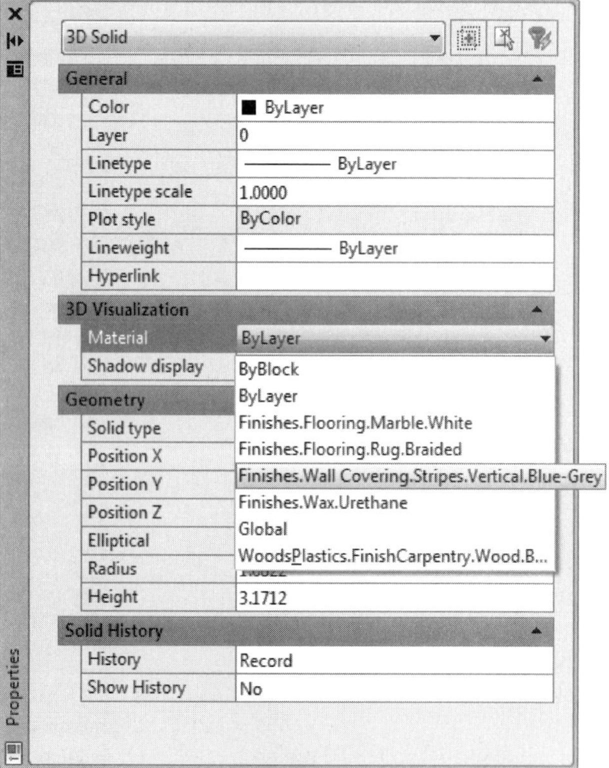

Figure 9-80 The Properties palette allows you to change the material for selected objects

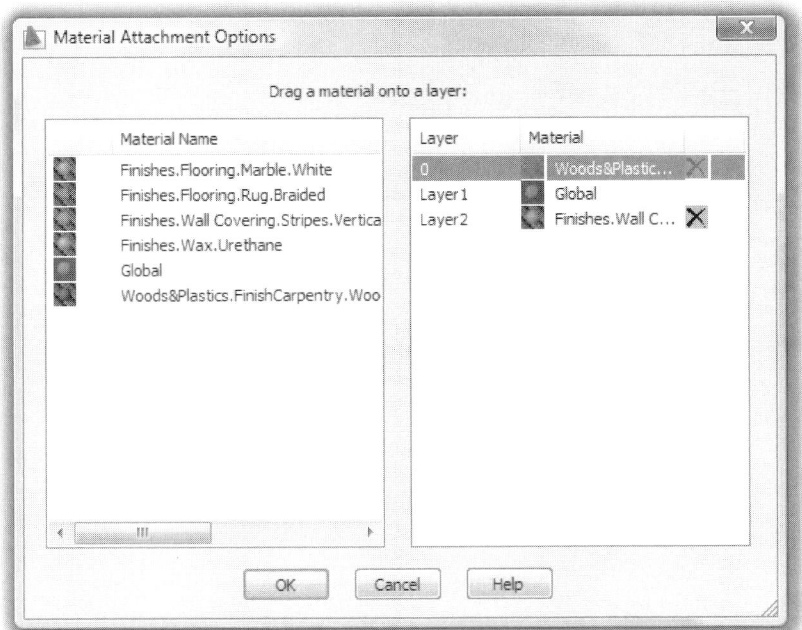

Figure 9-81 The Material Attachment Options dialog box

Figure 9-82 Materials can be shown in both the rendered image and the Conceptual visual style

Creating New Materials and Textures

You can create a material by copying and modifying one of the materials existing in the current drawing. For example, a material named *Green Marble* would be copied as *Copy of Green Marble* in the sample images area. Then you can right-click on its sample image and select **Edit Name and Description...** to open the **Edit Name and Description** dialog box and change the material's name (Figure 9-83). You can also create a new material from scratch by clicking the corresponding button in the **Materials** palette. The **Create New Material** dialog box allows you to specify a name for the new material (Figure 9-84).

You can change the swatch geometry that is used to represent each material's sample image to a box, a cylinder, or a sphere by clicking the corresponding flyout button shown in Figure 9-85. A second flyout button allows you to change the illumination effect of the sample

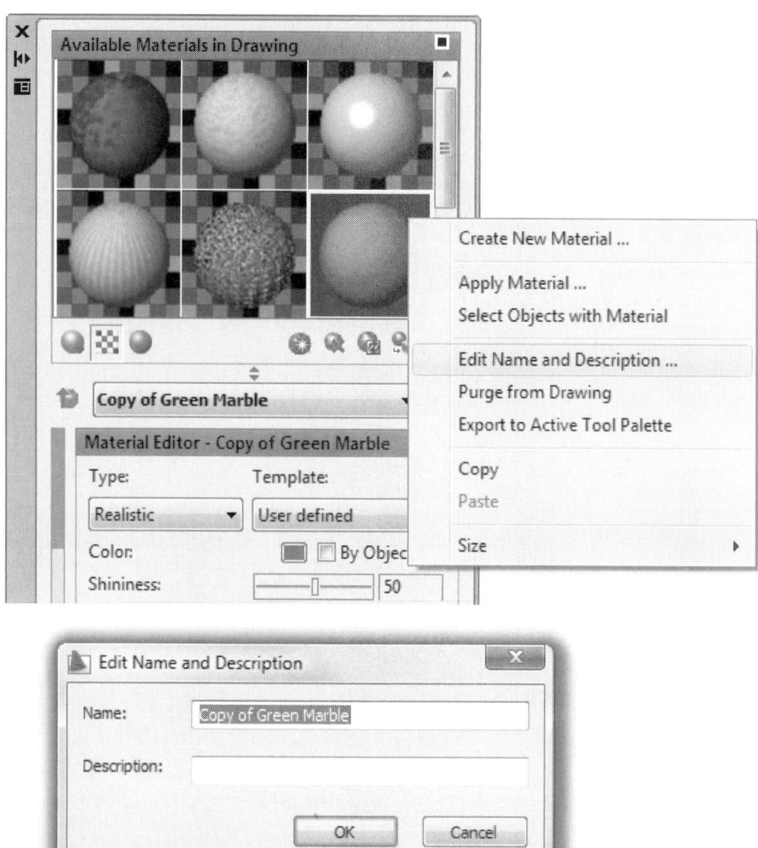

Figure 9-83 The Edit Name and Description dialog box and the action that displays it

Figure 9-84 The Create New Material dialog box and the action that displays it

Figure 9-85 The Swatch Geometry and the Preview Swatch Lighting Model for the sample image can be changed in the flyout buttons

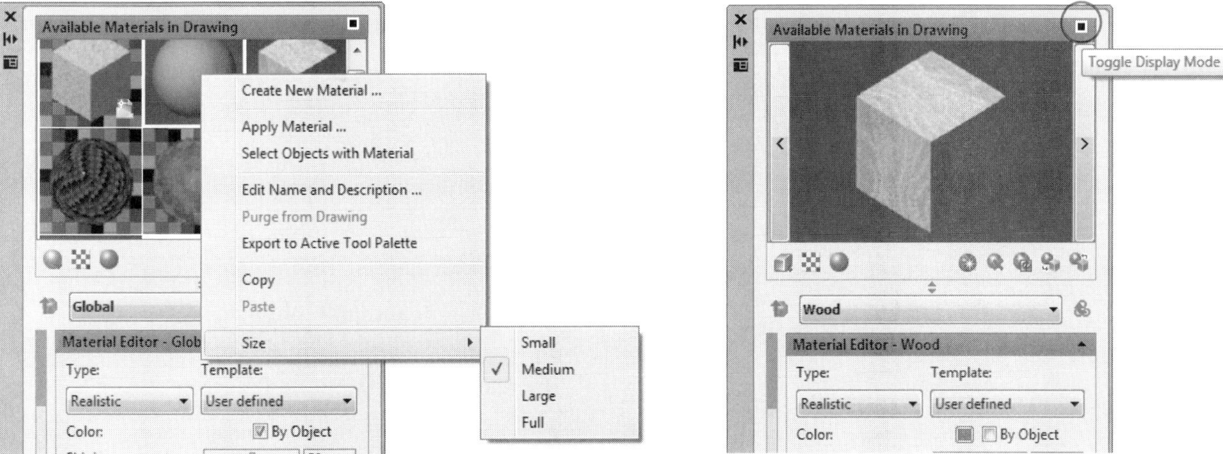

Figure 9-86 The size of the sample image can be changed or toggled to full size

image. You can also specify whether a material sample image uses a checkered underlay by clicking the button next to it. This allows you to determine how transparent the material is. You can also change the size of the sample images through the shortcut menu, or toggle the display mode to full size (Figure 9-86).

Specific properties for each particular material are controlled in the **Material Editor** area. The number of properties and initial settings for any material are first determined by *type* of material and the ***template*** it uses. New materials created from scratch always use the **Realistic** type. You can choose among four types of materials: **Realistic, Realistic Metal, Advanced,** and **Advanced Metal** (Figure 9-87). If you select the **Realistic** and **Realistic Metal** types of materials, you can also select one of the templates; by simply changing a material's template you can make a very close approach to the final material you intend to achieve. You change the material's template by selecting one from the drop-down list, after the material is selected (Figure 9-88).

template: Predefined collection of specific properties and property settings that gives a material a specific appearance.

The **Advanced** and **Advanced Metal** type of materials allow you to create special effects on materials. Selecting the **Advanced** type of material turns on all possible properties, thus allowing you to create materials with any characteristics. The **User defined** template of the **Realistic** type of materials is a simpler general version in which the reflection map as well as some of the colors' settings are not available. **Advanced Metal** and **Realistic Metal** types of materials turn off properties related to transparency, which are not supposed to belong to metals (Figure 9-89 and Figure 9-90).

Figure 9-87 You can choose from one of four types of materials

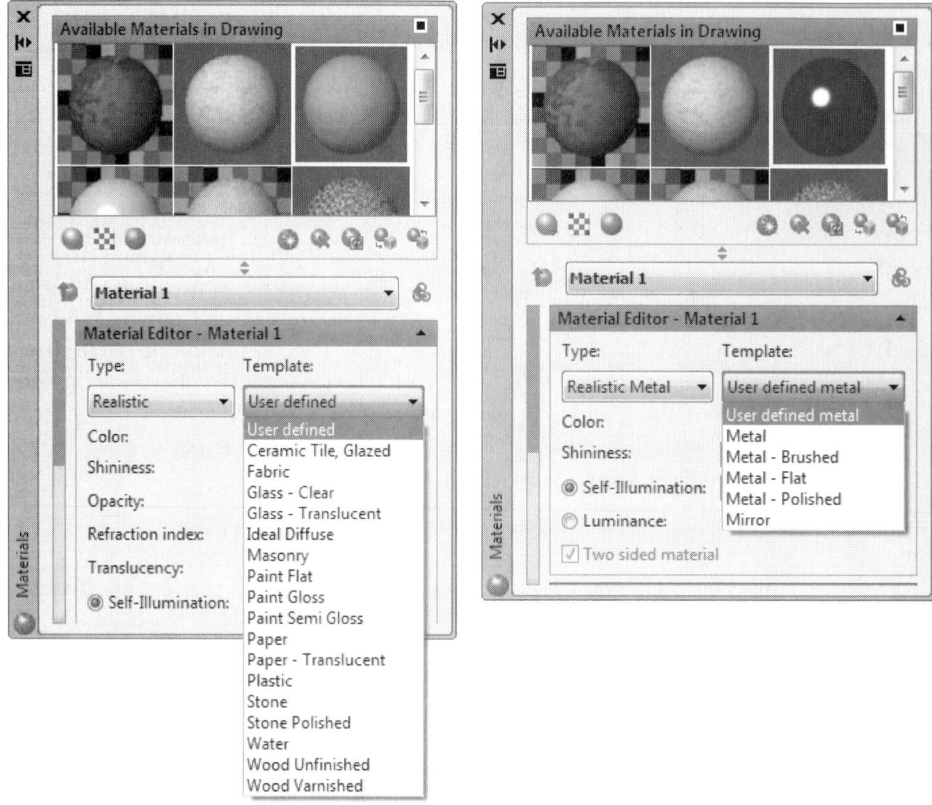

Figure 9-88 Templates available for the Realistic and Realistic Metal types of materials

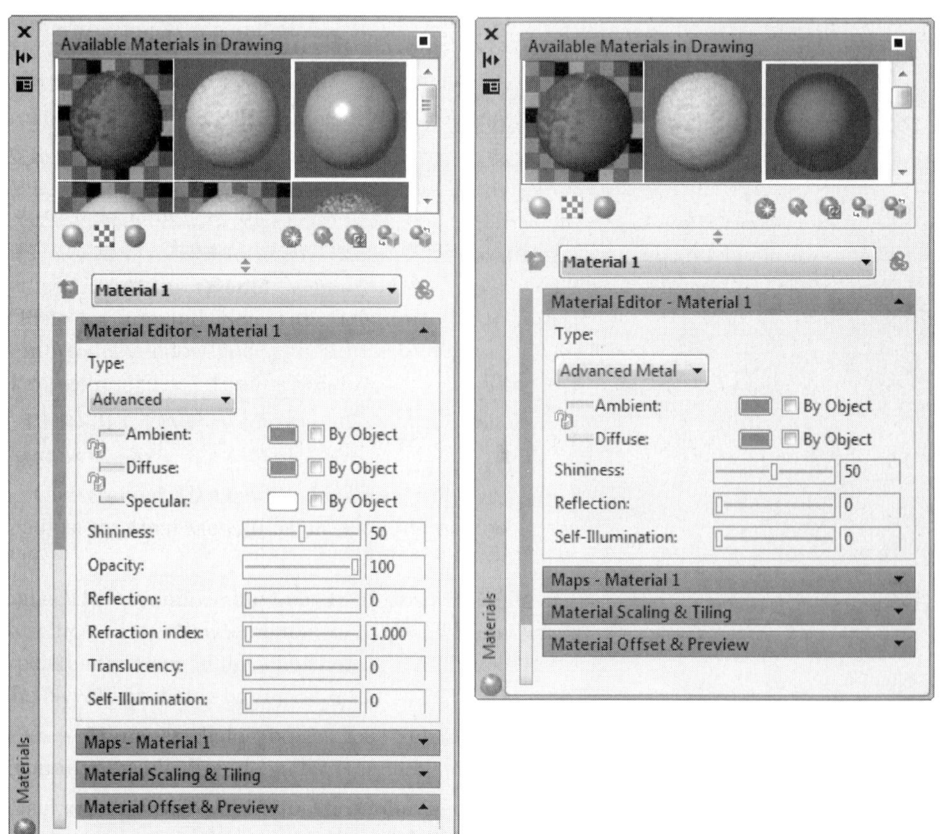

Figure 9-89 Properties available for the Advanced and Advanced Metal templates

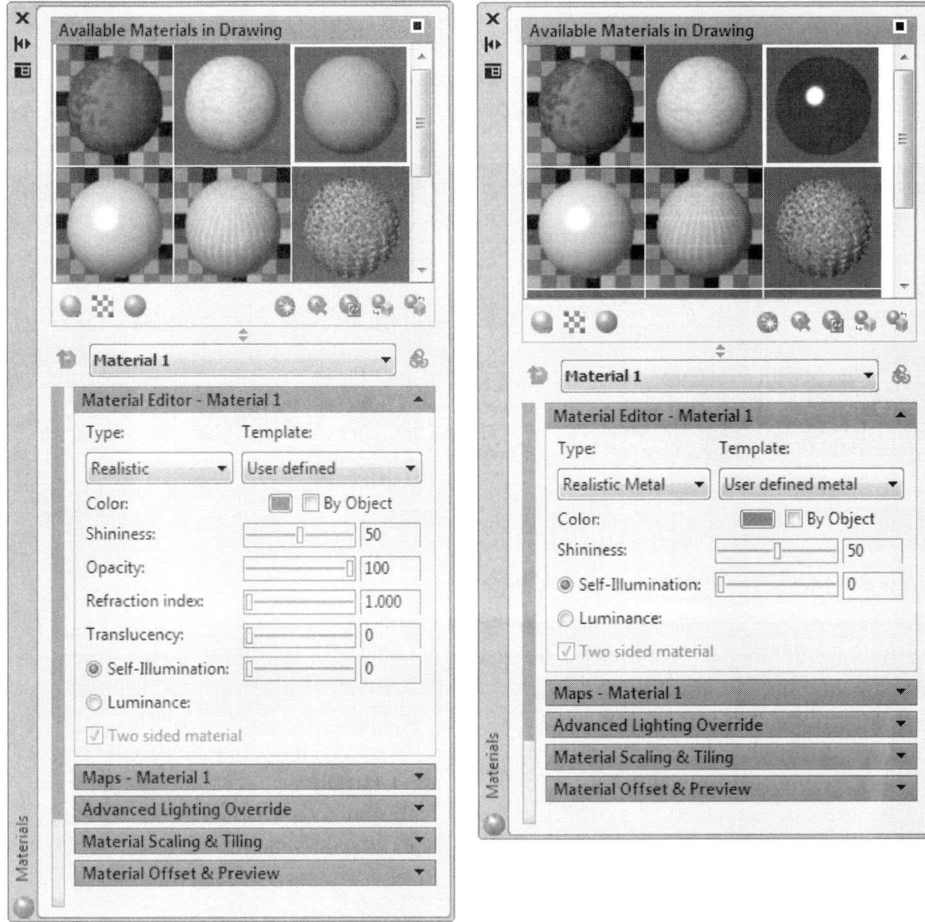

Figure 9-90 Properties available for the Realistic and Realistic Metal templates

Material's Colors

In general, you can control the effects of colors on a material using three options. **Diffuse** controls the general or main color of the material. You can use the same object's color by selecting the **By object** checkbox or specify another color independently. This is the most noticeable color. **Specular** controls the color of the areas that are more illuminated. **Ambient** sets the general ambient tone that is given to the main color. This is the least noticeable color effect.

The effects of all three colors can be controlled only when the **Advanced** type of material is used. By clicking on the **Lock** button, you can link either the **Specular** or the **Ambient** color to the **Diffuse** color. You can even link both and let the **Diffuse** color control all the color aspects Figure 9-91. When the **Diffuse** and **Specular** colors are not linked, however, the surfaces appear to be shinier (Figure 9-92).

Controlling the Illumination Effects on the Object's Surfaces

The following properties affect in one way or another the effects of the incidence of light on materials:

- Shininess
- Refraction index
- Translucency
- Self-illumination

Shininess defines how reflective the material is. Using higher **Shininess** values accentuates the areas highlighted by the illumination, making them look smaller and with a more defined

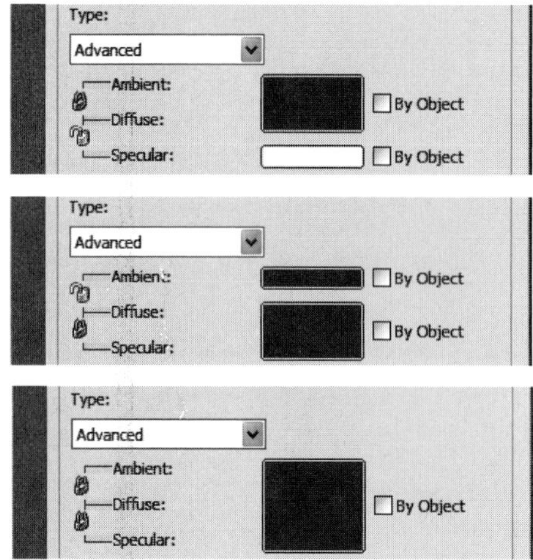

Figure 9-91 Possible linkage between the different materials' colors

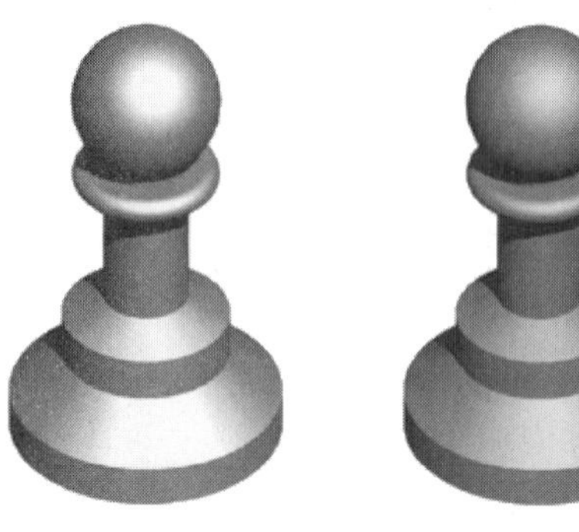

Figure 9-92 Effects of linking the diffuse and specular colors

presence of the **Specular** color (Figure 9-93). High values of this property should be used in materials that will be applied to objects with smooth surfaces.

Refraction index refers to the ratio of the velocity of light in a vacuum to its velocity in a specified medium. Refraction is a property inherent only to materials that are not opaque because it refers to the portion of the light that goes into the objects. As the refraction index increases, light rays are bent more inside the objects, causing other objects seen through them to appear distorted (Figure 9-94). Materials with certain transparency or smaller opacity can properly show the different levels of refraction.

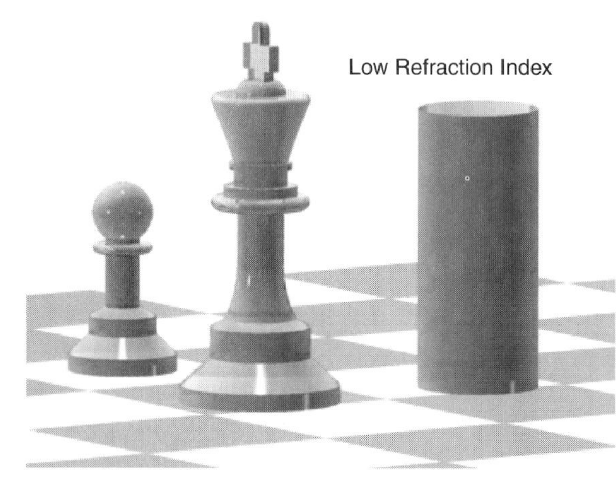

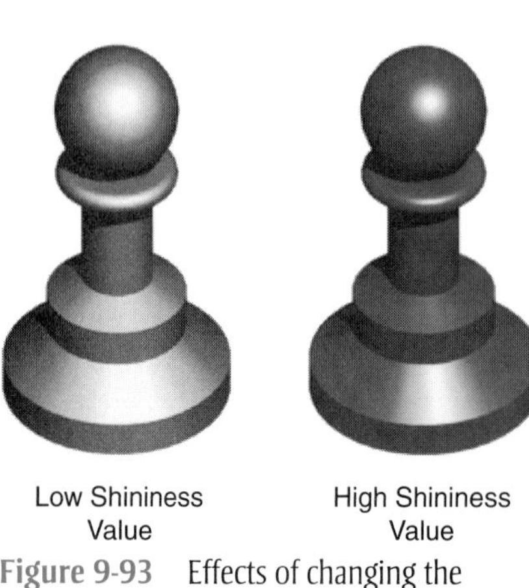

Figure 9-93 Effects of changing the Shininess value in a material

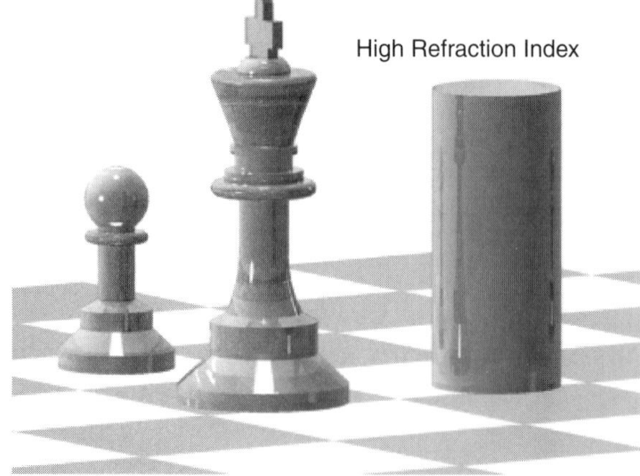

Figure 9-94 Effects of changing the Refraction index value in a material

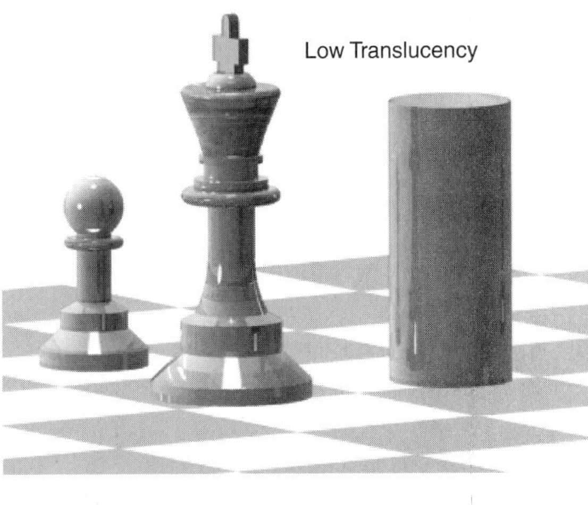

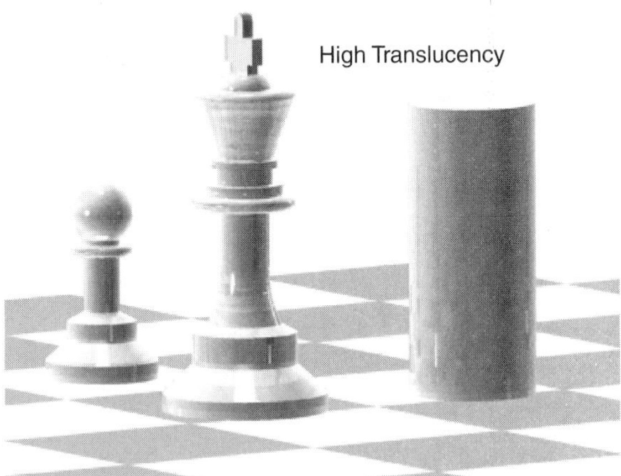

Figure 9-95 Effects of changing the Translucency value in a material

Figure 9-96 Effects of changing the Self-illumination value in a material

Translucency is a measurement of how much light enters and diffuses inside nonopaque objects (Figure 9-95).

The **Self-illumination** property controls brightness as well. Objects with self-illumination appear to be emitting light. Too high a value of self-illumination may cause the object not to be discernible (Figure 9-96). By selecting **Luminance,** you can specify photometric values for these properties.

Diffuse Maps

Other effects such as texture, roughness, reflection, and even transparency can be accurately defined by using an existing bitmap file. Valid formats are TGA, BMP, PNG, JFIF, TIFF, GIF, and PCX. You can use a bitmap file for the following four properties:

- **Diffuse maps**
- **Opacity**
- **Reflection**
- **Bump maps**

A diffuse map is the map most frequently used in a material. You can use the **Texture Map** option and attach a bitmap file or use one of the internal map types (**Checker, Marble, Noise, Speckle, Tiles, Waves,** or **Wood**) (Figure 9-97). Then you can apply the material with texture to cover the surfaces of the objects. You can also set the slide button on an intermediate value to allow the **Diffuse** color to blend with the bitmap file. When the slide button is completely to the right, the **Diffuse** color has no effect.

The main purpose of using a texture map is to create effects that can be represented by patterns of bitmaps, such as floor tiles, bricks, wallpapers, wood finishes, and metal finishes. You could even use a texture map to apply a specific color. The appearance achieved depends on the bitmap you use. The AutoCAD program comes with several images that you can use for this

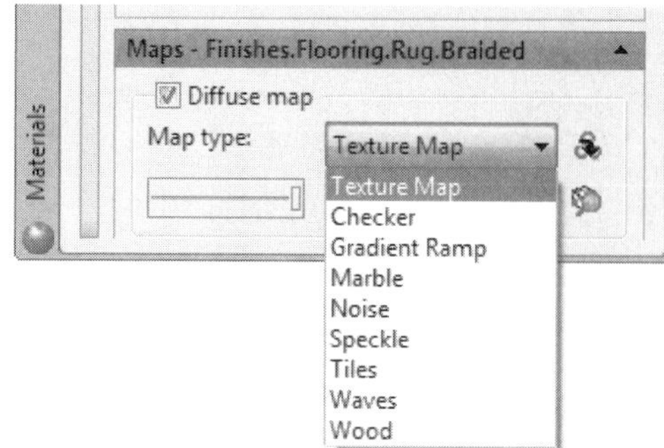

Figure 9-97 The Diffuse map drop-down menu in the MATERIALS palette

purpose. Other bitmaps can be purchased on the Internet, or you can simply take a picture with a digital camera of the spot you want to bring into your rendered image. Figure 9-98 shows some examples of effects you can achieve by using texture maps. Because you can stretch a single bitmap over a surface, you can also create effects such as wall pictures or labels.

To select a bitmap, you must click the **Select Image** button on the **Materials** palette to open the **Select Image File** dialog box (Figure 9-99), which allows you to browse, preview, and select

Figure 9-98 Four samples applied to the tabletop using texture maps

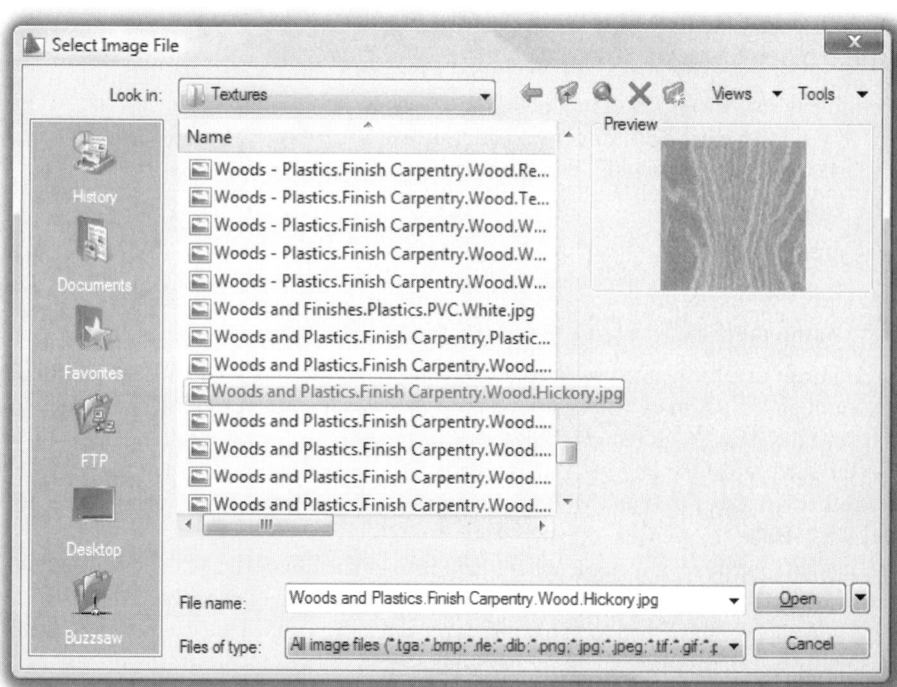

Figure 9-99 The Select Image File dialog box

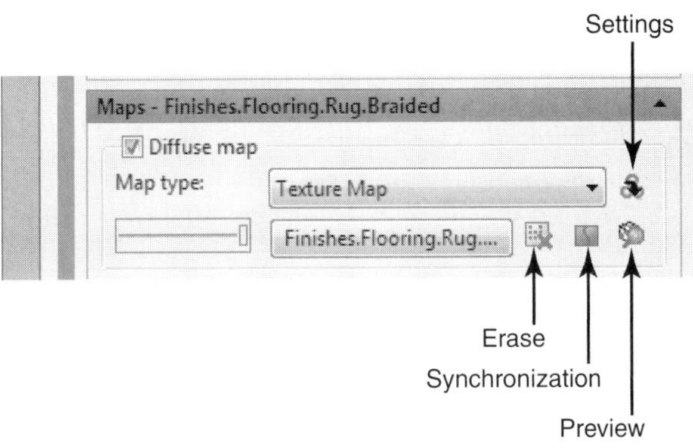

Figure 9-100 Four new buttons and the slide bar appear after specifying a map

the bitmap. After you select the file or choose one of the internal map types, the **Select Image** button changes to the name of the file and four new buttons, along with the slide bar, appear next to it (Figure 9-100).

The **Erase** button allows you to delete the current map information from the material. The next button controls whether or not the map is synchronized with the material. When the synchronization is enabled, changes in the setting of the map will affect the maps used in the material. When the synchronization is disabled, any changes in the setting of the map will affect only the current map; an AutoCAD warning is displayed to let you know this (Figure 9-101). Clicking the third button will open the corresponding **Map Preview** window (Figure 9-102). You can leave this window opened while the **Materials** palette is opened and check the **Auto Update** checkbox to visualize any changes you make to the particular map.

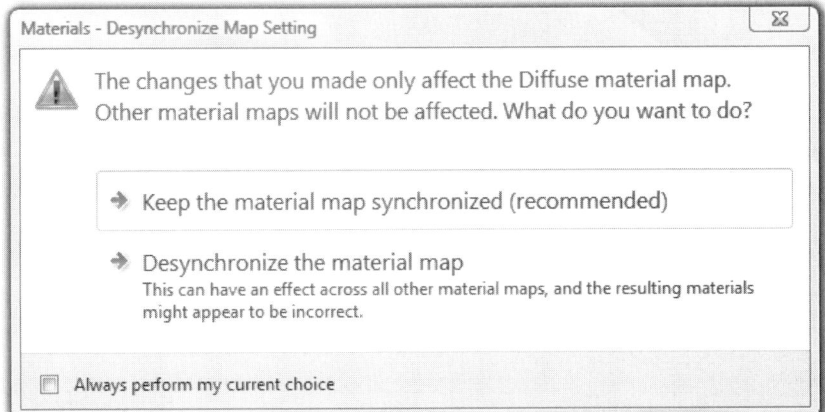

Figure 9-101 AutoCAD warning about the map desynchronization

Figure 9-102 The Diffuse Map Preview

The **Map Settings** button causes the entire **Materials** palette to switch from the **Material Editor** to the **Map Editor,** displaying the settings for this particular map instead of the settings of the material (Figure 9-103). You can switch from one map to another map at any time, or even back to the material's editor, through the drop-down list located below the sample images pane (Figure 9-104). You can control the same type of settings for the top-level material and for each map in particular. These settings are equally arranged in two panes: **Scaling & Tiling** and **Offset & Preview.**

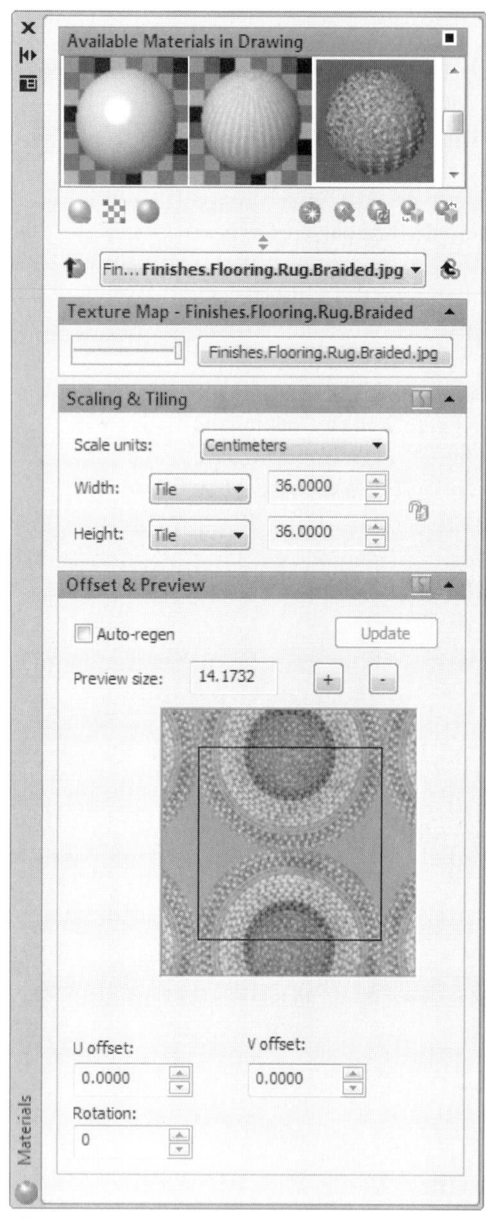

Figure 9-103 The Map Editor

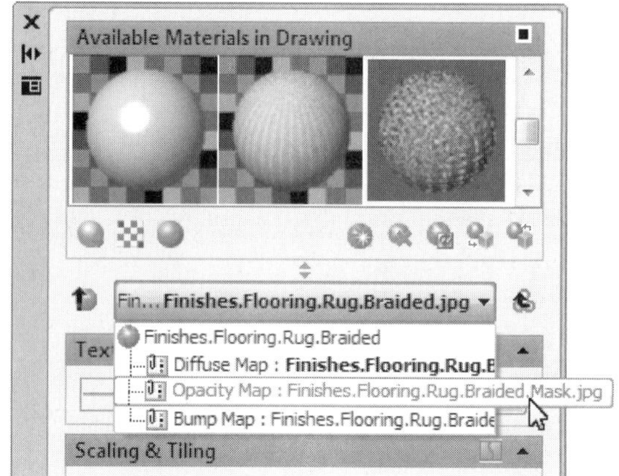

Figure 9-104 The drop-down list allows easy access to the other maps and to the top-level material

After specifying the proper **Scale units,** the first thing you should do is select a proper **Preview size.** For example, the piece of lumber shown in Figure 9-105 would require a **Preview** size of around 8 × 8 units. Because you are using real **Scale units,** the preview shows how the bitmap is actually tiled in an area using a fixed scale or real-world scale. The size of the preview does not affect the mapping. You can then change the scale in the *U* and *V* directions independently in the **U Tile:** and **V Tile:** text boxes or by moving the slice buttons. Clicking on the lock icon will lock the U and V proportion. You can also specify the behavior of the tiling effect in the *U* and *V* directions independently (**None, Tile,** or **Mirror**). After you adjust the **Scale** to the new **Preview size,** the bitmap is easily mapped on the rendered image (Figure 9-106). You can also offset the image to locate a different area inside the 8 × 8 square, either inside the **U offset:** and **V offset:** text boxes, or

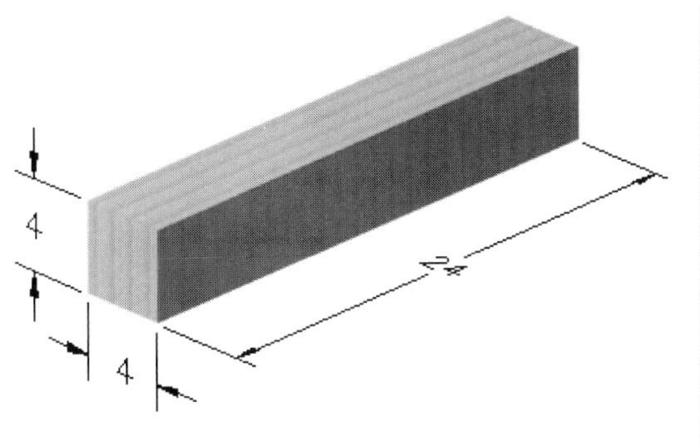

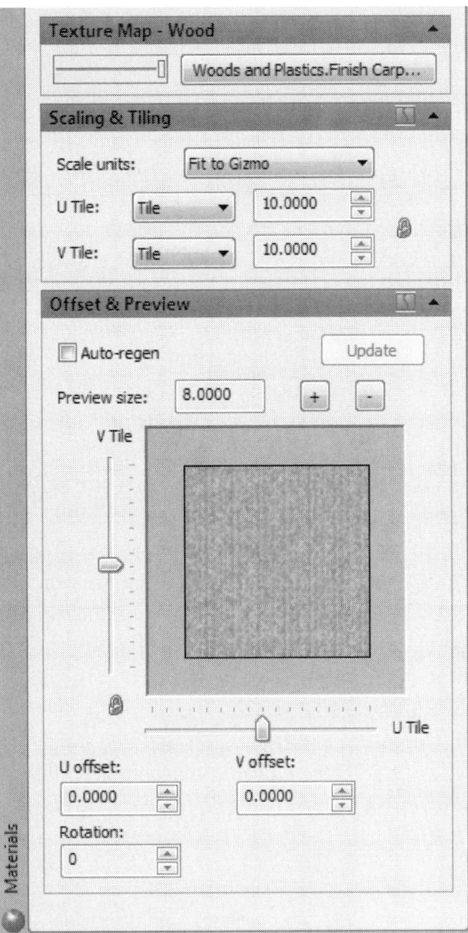

Figure 9-105 When using a particular Scale unit, the Preview size must be set correspondingly to the object size

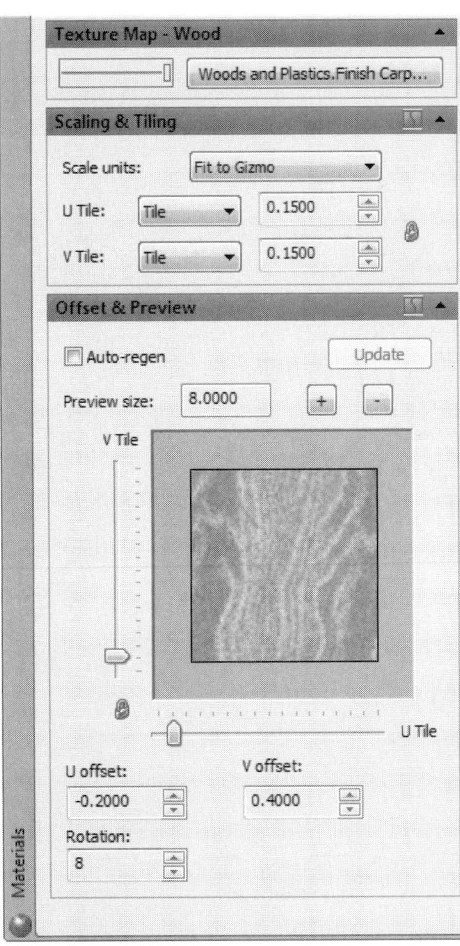

Figure 9-106 Result of adjusting the scale to the new preview size

by clicking and dragging inside the preview image. Specifying a rotation is also possible. You can do so by using the **Rotation:** text box, or right-click and drag inside the preview image.

When you use the **Fit to Gizmo** option under the **Scale units,** the square in the preview represents the tile that must be stretched to fit each face of the object. Setting this option as **1** will represent how the image will look in each face, which is more convenient. For this option, selecting the **Tile** options provides you with U × V number of tiled images to cover the faces. This option is especially useful for representing a defined pattern such as a chessboard. In Figure 9-107 an original image of 2 × 2 squares is used four times to fit the board (a region). When the **Tile** value of **U** and **V** is set to **1,** a single image will be stretched to cover a face. Pictures and other single images can be obtained with this option (Figure 9-108).

Note:
UV is a coordinate system that is used as a reference to define the bitmap's distances in two perpendicular directions, similar to the XY coordinate system. The UV coordinate system, however, is completely independent of the XY coordinate system. It moves and rotates with the bitmap.

Besides the texture map created with image files, you can also use the other type of preset maps (**Checker, Marble, Noise, Speckle, Tiles, Waves,** and **Wood**). If you select any of these maps, clicking the **Map Settings** button displays the editor of this particular map inside the **Materials palette,** where you can adjust its appearance. Figure 9-109 shows, for instance, the **Wood** map editor. Each type of map is defined by its particular specific properties. As with texture maps, you can create a blended effect by using the **Slice** button. Particularly for the wood type of maps, the **Radial noise** and **Axial noise** control the randomness of the grain pattern along and across, respectively. The **Grain thickness** value determines how thick the wood rings are.

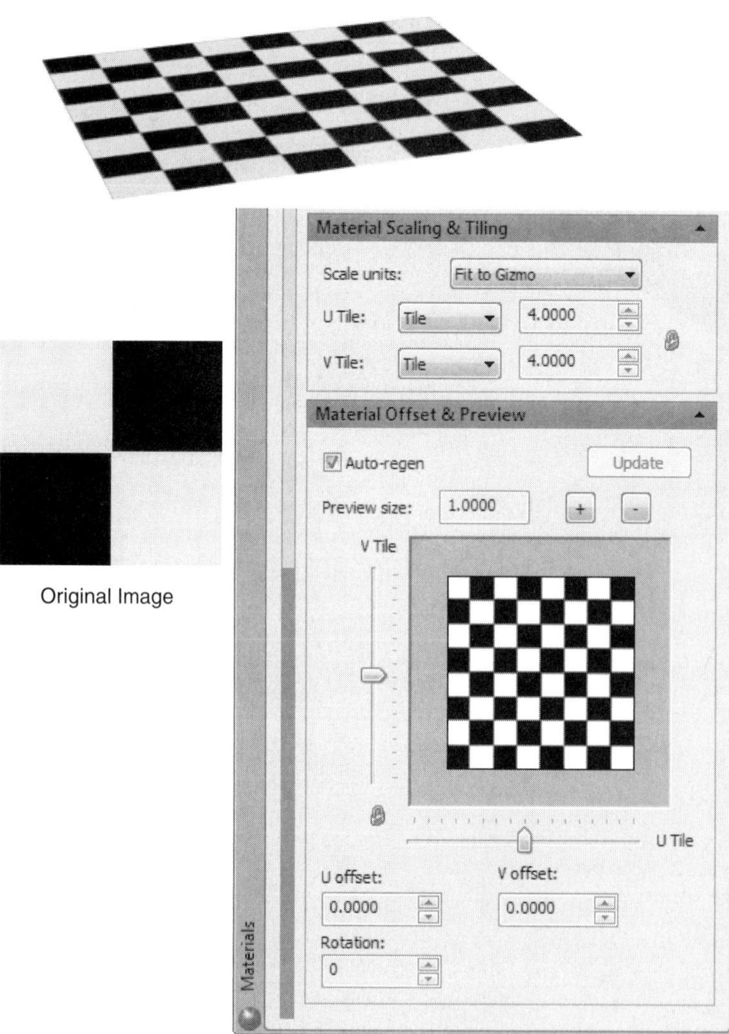

Figure 9-107 The original image of 2 × 2 squares is repeated four times to fit the board

Figure 9-108 Pictures can be created with this option

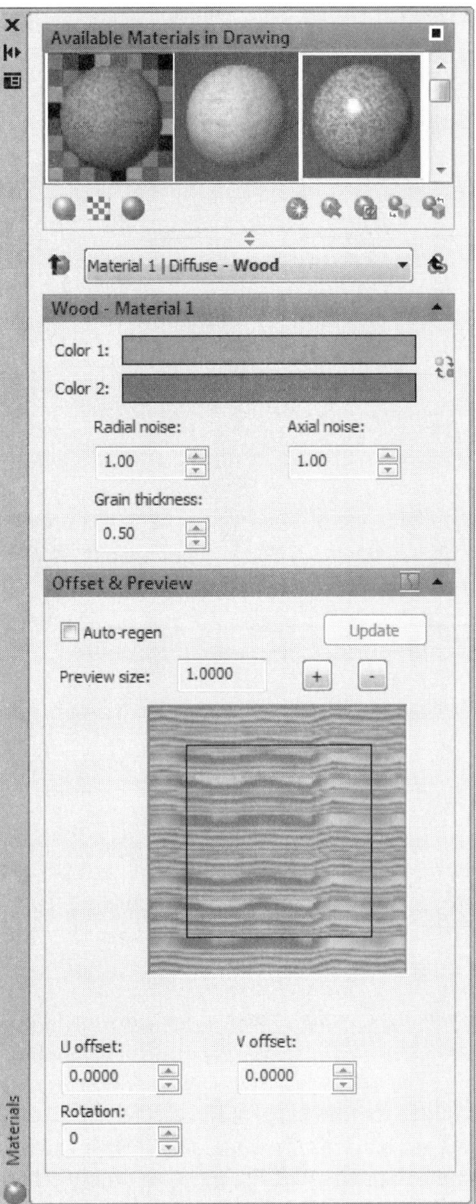

Figure 9-109 The editor of the Wood diffuse map in the **Materials** palette

Opacity Maps

Opacity is a property that mostly affects the transparency effect on materials; it can help you accomplish two important functions. First, it determines how transparent a material is without using a bitmap file. The lower the value of the opacity, the more transparent will be the objects to which you apply the materials. The slide button is always present for **Realistic** and **Advanced** types of materials, to enable you to adjust their value at all times.

Second, **Opacity** enables you to assign different values of transparency to different areas on the same face. To achieve this effect, you must use a bitmap file. Images containing black-and-white areas are ideal for opacity purposes because black areas make the surface fully transparent and white areas make them fully opaque. Any other color would provide an intermediate opacity, depending on its grayscale value.

The bitmaps used to create opacity maps are selected and adjusted the same way as the bitmaps for texture maps. Unlike with texture maps, however, the **Diffuse** color is always present because the opacity map does not provide any color to the material.

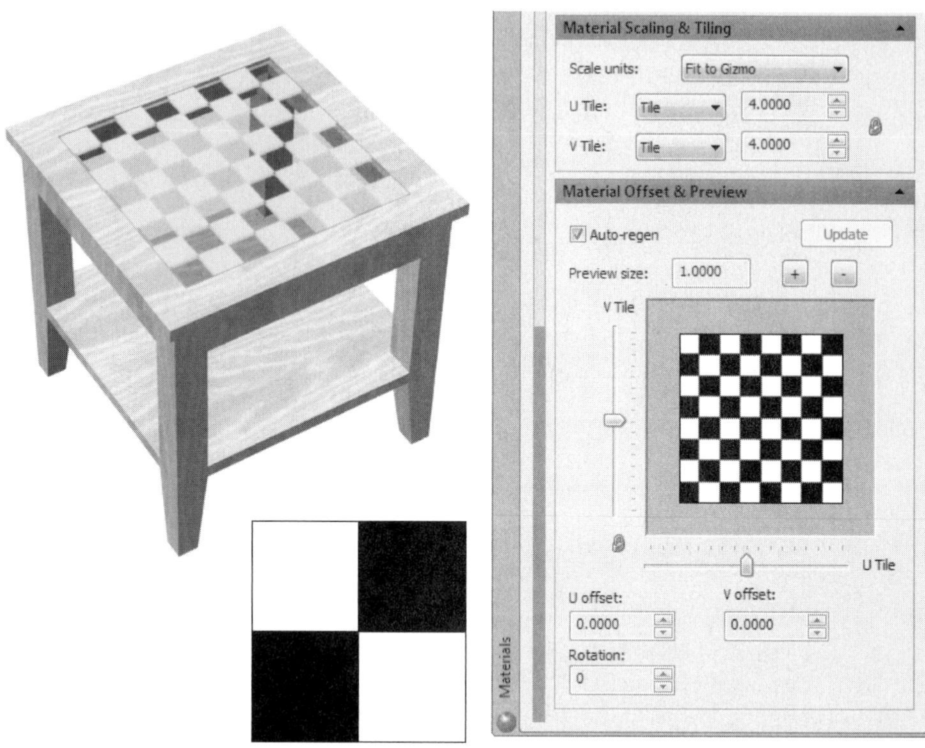

Figure 9-110 The tabletop can be given the effect of having an engraved chessboard by using an opacity map

For example, by using an opacity map, you can give a tabletop the effect of being a pane of glass with a chessboard engraved on it (Figure 9-110). Another suitable use can be to create the effect of windows without really having them modeled.

Creating Landscapes

By using a texture map and its equivalent opacity map together, you can simulate the presence of other objects such as plants or people (Figure 9-111).

This effect is easily achieved; however, you must obtain or prepare the image files that correspond to both types of maps. The image to be attached to the texture map must contain the object in a black background. The corresponding image file to attach as the opacity map must be the same exact file with the shape of the object cropped (Figure 9-112).

Figure 9-111 Landscape objects can be simulated by using a texture map and its equivalent opacity map together

Figure 9-112 A texture map and its corresponding opacity map

You must create a new material using the **Advanced** template, then attach each image file to its corresponding type of map. You must set the same **Bitmap Scale** for both images in the **Adjust Bitmap** dialog box. Because the image should be stretched one time onto the 3D object, you should set the **Scale units** as **Fit to Gizmo** and set **U Tile** and **V Tile** both to **1** (Figure 9-113).

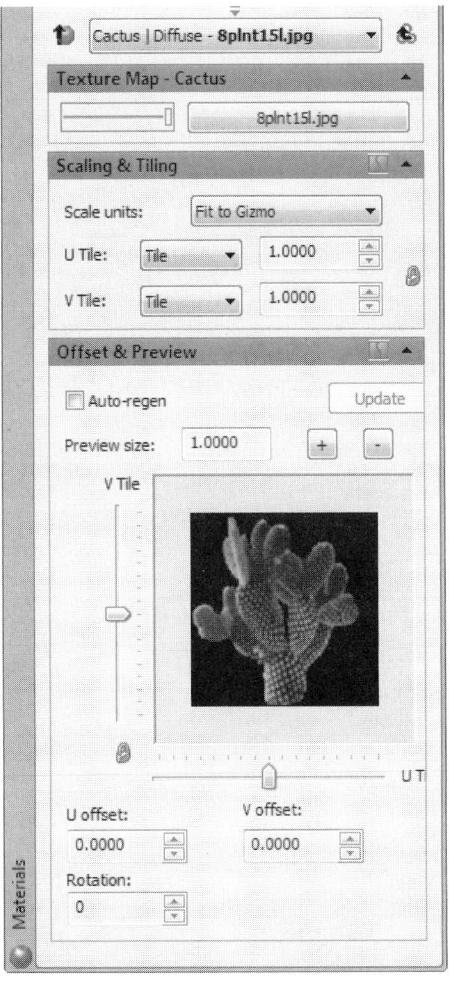

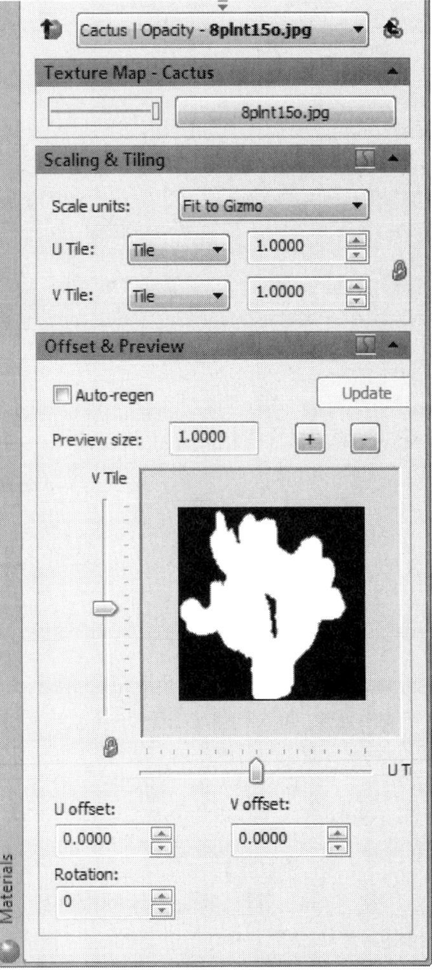

Figure 9-113 In the texture editors of both the Diffuse and Opacity maps, the Scale units must be set to Fit to Gizmo among other settings

The 3D object to which you apply the material for landscape purposes must be properly oriented to make the image appear as real as possible. If you need the landscape object to cast shadows, you can use very thin, extruded 3D solids or a surface like the one shown in Figure 9-114. You

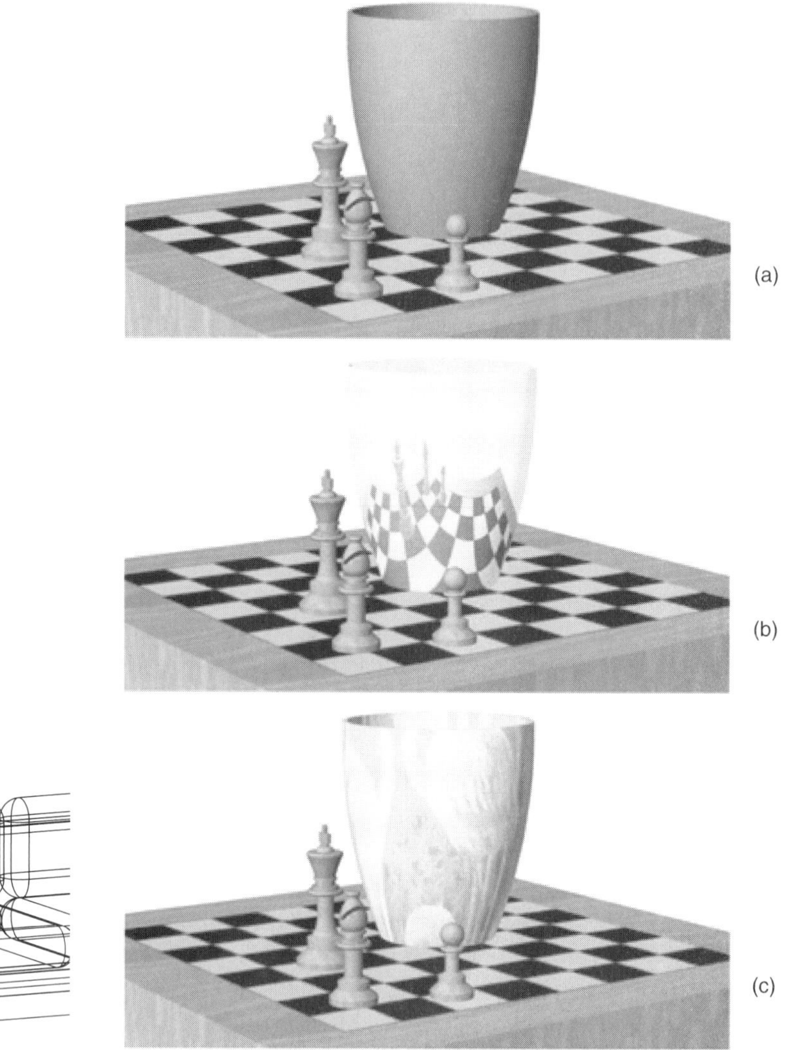

Figure 9-115 Effects of the Reflection property on a material: (a) no reflection; (b) reflection of its own environment; and (c) reflection of an attached image file

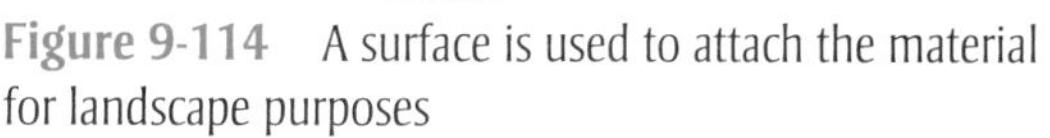

Figure 9-114 A surface is used to attach the material for landscape purposes

can use a simple imaging application such as Paint to prepare the image files. You can also use more sophisticated software, such as Adobe Photoshop®.

Reflection Maps

The **Reflection** property is available only for materials that use the **Advanced** and **Advanced Metal** templates. As with the **Opacity** property, you can use the **Reflection** property to control two effects. Without using a bitmap file, moving the slide button determines how reflective a material is.

Reflective objects normally reflect their own environment, which consists of the other objects around them. By using an image file with shiny materials, however, you can make the objects with this material attached reflect that image file instead of other objects. Figure 9-115(a) shows the rendered image with no **Reflection** property specified. In Figure 9-115(b), the rendered image shows the reflection of the object in its own environment. In Figure 9-115(c), the object reflects an attached bitmap instead.

Note:
The colors contained in a bitmap file used as a bump map do not affect the diffuse color of the material. Higher differences in their grayscale values, however, enhance the bumping effect.

Bump Maps

A bump map creates an embossed 3D texture in surfaces, giving them an appearance that is closer to that of the real objects. A bump map requires an image file to be selected. One example in which a bump map makes an outstanding difference is in brick and masonry walls (Figure 9-116). When used on wood, a bump map creates an antique or aged effect (Figure 9-117). Excellent results are usually achieved when the same bitmap file is used for both the texture map and the bump map.

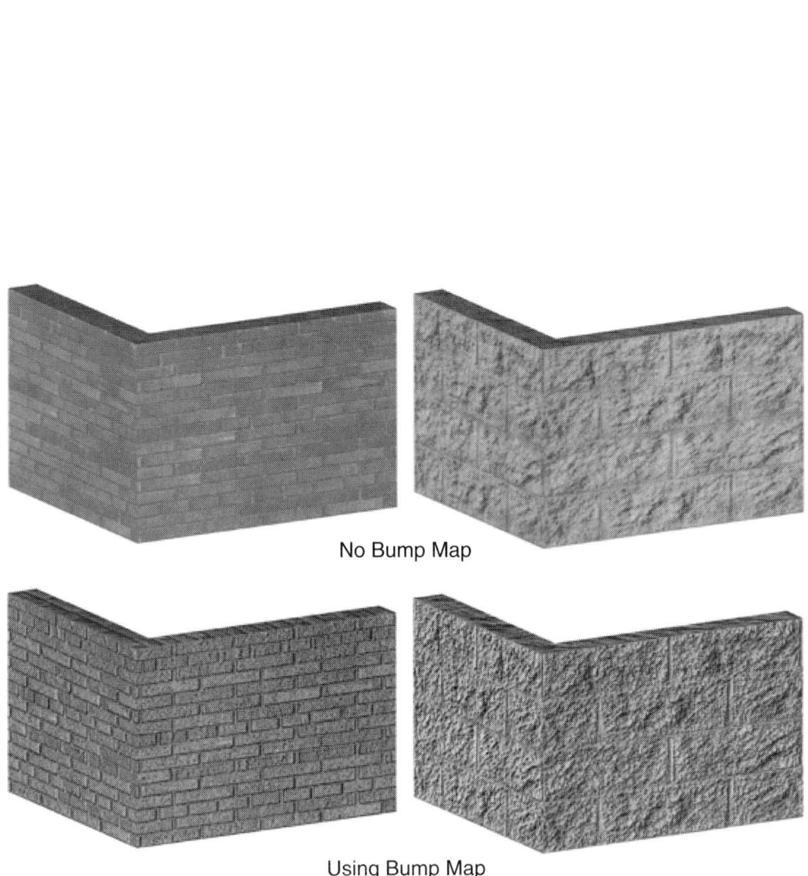

Figure 9-116 Rendered image of a masonry wall with and without bump maps

Figure 9-117 Rendered image with and without bump maps attached to the woodlike material

Exercise 9-4: Using Materials

1. **OPEN** ***Exercise 9-3.***
2. **SAVE** it **AS** ***Exercise 9-4.***
3. Invoke the **MATERIALS** command to display the **Materials** palette.
4. Invoke the **TOOLPALETTES** command to open the **Tool Palettes.** Right-click on its blue ribbon and select the **Materials** group of palettes from the shortcut menu.
5. Click on the **Flooring** tab. Right-click on the **Finishes. Flooring.Marble.White** material sample icon and select **Add to Current Drawing** (Figure 9-118).
6. Close the **Tool Palettes.** The new material sample should show up in the **Materials** palette.

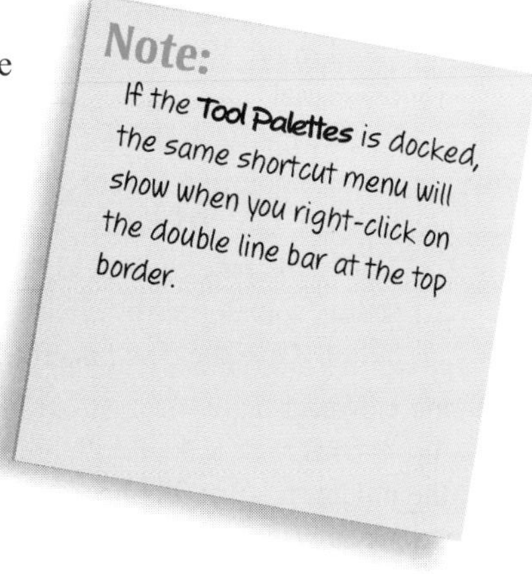

Note:
If the **Tool Palettes** is docked, the same shortcut menu will show when you right-click on the double line bar at the top border.

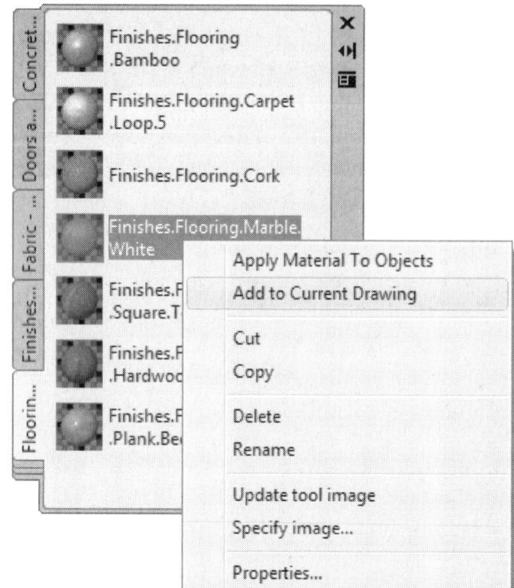

Figure 9-118 Selecting Add to Current Drawing from the shortcut menu

7. Select the material you just brought into the drawing. Right-click on its sample image, and select **Edit Name and Description.** In the **Edit Name and Description** dialog box, change its name to **Marble Floor** and then click **OK.**
8. While the **Marble Floor** material is still selected, click on the swatch geometry flyout button and select the box as the sample image. Click on the checkered underlay button to turn the checkered underlay off.
9. Click the **Diffuse:** color box and select color **9** from the **Index Color** tab. Make sure the **By Object** checkbox is cleared. Scroll down to **Scaling & Tiling** and set both **U Tile** and **V Tile** to 4. Under **Scale units,** select **Fit to Gizmo.**
10. Click the **Apply material** button and select the 3D solid that represents the floor. Press **<Enter>** to end the selection.

Note:
The selected material shows a thick yellow outline around its sample image.

TIP You can find information about any tool by placing the pointer over it and reading its brief description inside the **Description** box, located at the bottom of the palette.

11. Select **Render View** from the **Views** drop-down list located in the **Views** toolbar or in the **3D Navigate** control panel.
12. Invoke the **RENDER** command. The rendered image should look like Figure 9-119.
13. Invoke the **REGEN** command and open the **Materials** palette in case you have closed it. Create four new materials by clicking on the **New Material** button. Give the new materials the following names:
    - Wood
    - Brass
    - Glass
    - Canvas

Note:
The rendered image can be created underneath the Materials palette. It is more convenient, however, to close or dock the Materials palette before invoking the RENDER command.

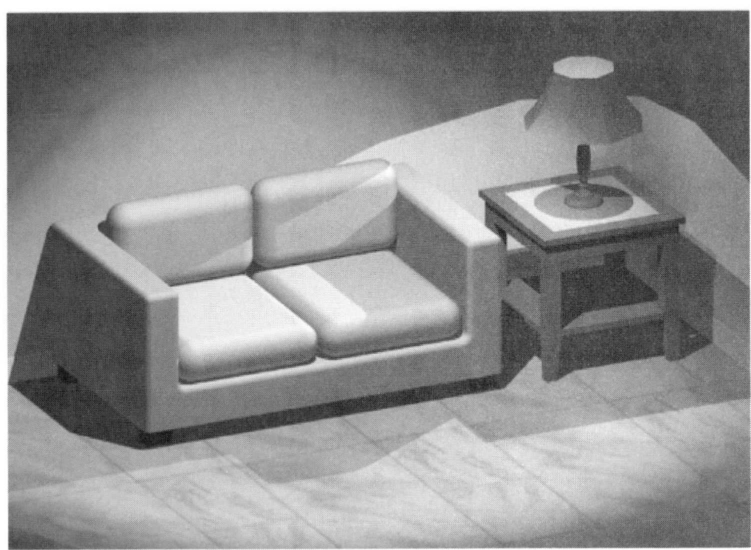

Figure 9-119 The resulting rendered image

14. Select the **Wood** material. Under **Diffuse map,** make sure **Texture Map** is selected from the drop-down list under **Map type** and click on the **Select Image** button. In the **Select Image File** dialog box, select the JPEG file named **Woods and Plastics.Finish Carpentry.Wood.Hickory** from the AutoCAD program's **Template** folder.

The AutoCAD program should automatically open the **Textures** folder containing the **Textures** bitmaps. If you are not taken to the **Textures** folder, you must manually browse to locate it. Because you do not want to spend time trying to locate this folder manually, you can find it using other procedures. One of them is performing a **Search** operation through Windows Explorer. Another fast way of locating this folder is as described below.

Close the **Select Image File** dialog box and open the **Options** dialog box. **Copy** the path corresponding to **Texture Maps Search Path** from the **Files** tab of the **Options** dialog box (Figure 9-120). The **Options** dialog box can be closed afterward.

Open the **Select Image File** dialog box again through the **Materials** palette, and simply **Paste** the path in the **File name:** box. After clicking the **Open** button, you should be taken to the **Textures** folder.

15. From the main drop-down list located under the material sample images, select **Diffuse Map: Woods and Plastics.Finish Carpentry.Wood.Hickory.jpg** to access the **Texture Map** editor for the **Diffuse Map** (Figure 9-121). Under the **Scaling & Tiling** section, set the **Scale units** as **None,** and set both **U Tile** and **V Tile** to **0.05.** Go back to the main material window by selecting **Wood** from the main drop-down list.
16. While the **Wood** material is still selected, select the box as **Swatch Geometry.** Click the **Apply Material** button and apply it to the 3D solid that represents the table base.
17. Click the **Indicate Materials in use** button to obtain information about which materials have been applied so far.

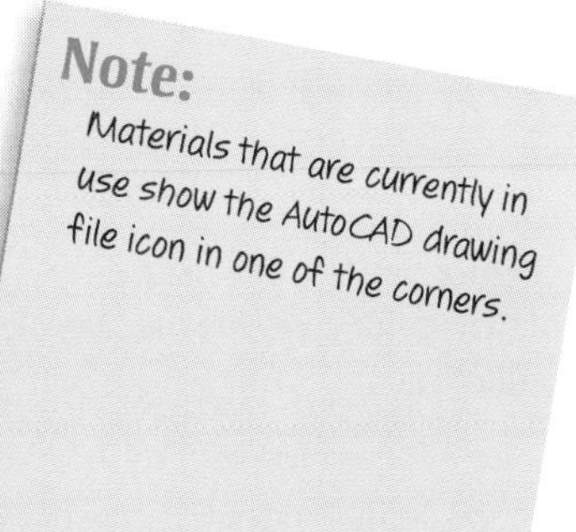

Note:
Materials that are currently in use show the AutoCAD drawing file icon in one of the corners.

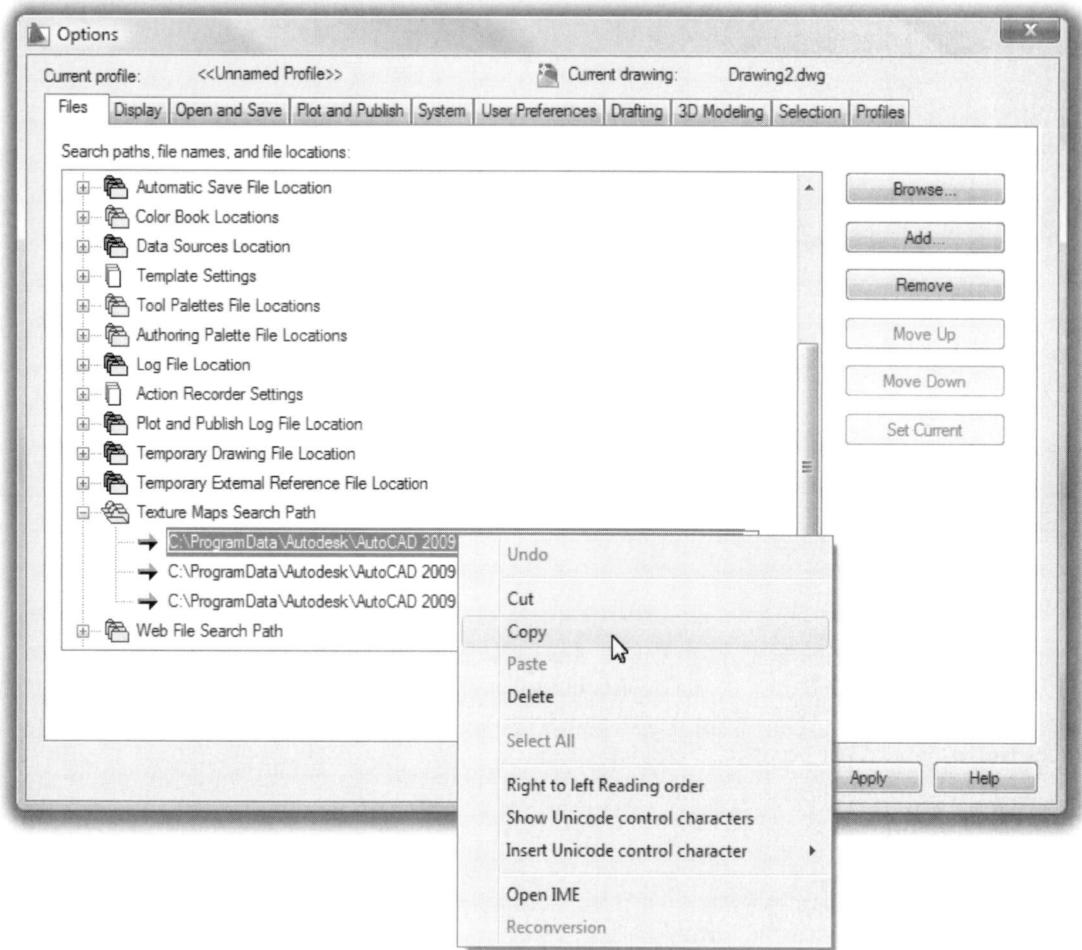

Figure 9-120 The Texture Maps Search Path can be obtained from the Files tab of the Options dialog box

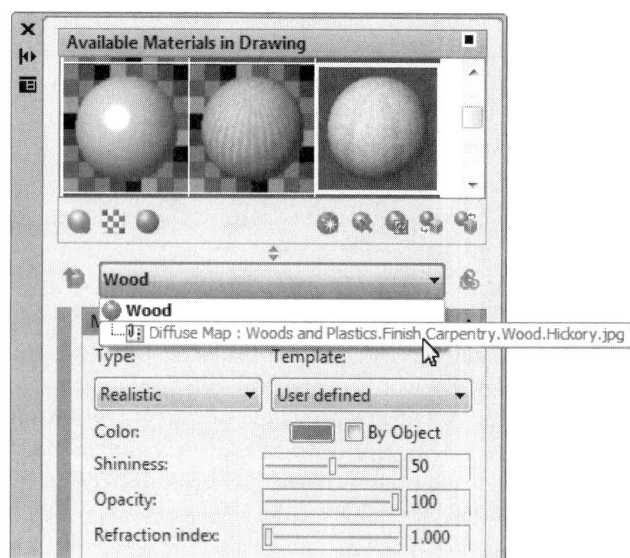

Figure 9-121 The main drop-down list for accessing the Map Editor

18. Select the **Brass** material. Select **Realistic Metal** as the type of material, and then select **Metal-Polished** as the template. Check the **By Object** option to use it as the **Diffuse** color.
19. With the **Brass** material still selected, click the **Checkered Underground** button. Apply this material to the 3D solid that represents the lamp base.

Figure 9-122 The sample images after clicking the Checkered Underground button

20. Click the **Indicate Materials in use** button. The sample images on the **Materials** palette should look like Figure 9-122.
21. Select the **Glass** material and click the **Checkered Underground** button.
22. Select the **By Object** option as the **Diffuse** color.
23. Move the **Shininess** slide button all the way to the right.
24. Move the **Refraction index** slide button to a value close to **2.00** or enter this value directly in the box.
25. Move the **Opacity** slide button to a value around **15.**
26. Apply this material to the 3D solid that represents the tabletop. **ZOOM** in as necessary and select the object by picking its edge.
27. Invoke the **RENDERCROP** command. When prompted, specify a window around the table to see how the new materials look so far (Figure 9-123).
28. Invoke the **REGEN** command. Select the **Canvas** material from the **Materials** palette and change its template to **Fabric.**
29. Select the **By Object** option as the **Diffuse** color.
30. Move the **Self-Illumination** slide button to a value around **20.**
31. Move the **Opacity** slide button to a value around **80.**
32. Apply this material to the eight polygon meshes that represent the lamp top.
33. Select **Render View** from the **Views** drop-down list located in the **Views** toolbar or in the **3D Navigate** control panel.
34. Invoke the **RENDER** command. The rendered image should look like (Figure 9-124).

Figure 9-123 The resulting cropped rendered image

Figure 9-124 The resulting rendered image

35. Invoke the **REGEN** command. You will now create some reflection effects on the rendered image.
36. Select the **Marble Floor** material in the **Materials** palette and change its type of material to **Advanced.**
37. Set all three colors to be **By Object.**
38. Move the **Shininess** slide button to a value around **50.**
39. Move the **Reflection** slide button to a value around **26.**
40. Select the view named **Render View** from the drop-down menu in the **View** toolbar.
41. Invoke the **RENDER** command. The rendered image should look like Figure 9-125.
42. Invoke the **REGEN** command.
43. Select the **Right** UCS.
44. Using the **RECTANGLE** command, create a **20** × **28** rectangle. **EXTRUDE** the rectangle **1** unit.

Figure 9-125 The resulting rendered image after changing the specified settings

45. **MOVE** the extruded 3D solid flush with the inside face of the wall, just above the sofa and centered with it (Figure 9-126).

TIP You can relocate the extruded 3D solid using several **MOVE** operations, and select orthogonal views if necessary. Using **AutoTrack** might also be helpful.

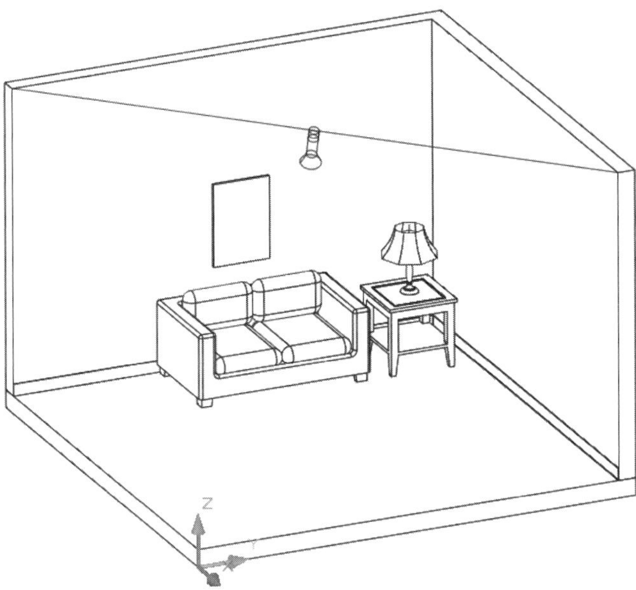

Figure 9-126 After placing the extruded rectangle

46. Create a new material and name it **Picture.** Select the box **Geometry Swatch** for this material.
47. Click the **Diffuse:** color box and select color **254** from the **Index Color** tab. Leave the **By Object** checkbox unchecked.
48. Using Windows Explorer, **Copy** the ***Flamingos*** image file from the CD and **Paste** it into the AutoCAD **Textures** folder, or into any other folder whose path you can remember.
49. Under **Diffuse map,** make sure **Texture Map** is selected from the drop-down list and click the **Select Image** button. Select the ***Flamingos*** image file from the location where you placed it. If you prefer, you can use any other picture.

Note:

Remember that selecting an image file from a path different from that of the **Textures** folder will cause the AutoCAD program to search in this other folder the next time. So you will again have to relocate the **Textures** folder yourself. You can also create a backup copy of the entire **Textures** folder to another location and use it as your bitmap working folder. Then you can add, delete, or rename any file you want.

50. Scroll down and select **Fit to Gizmo.** Set **U Tile** and **V Tile** both to **1.**
51. Apply the **Picture** material to the new 3D solid.
52. Select the view named **Render View** from the drop-down list on the **View** toolbar.
53. Set the **PERSPECTIVE** system variable to **1** by clicking the **Perspective Projection** icon in the **3D Navigate** panel of the **Ribbon.** This operation automatically switches to the **3D Wireframe** visual style, displaying a perspective view of the 3D model.
54. **ZOOM** and **PAN** as necessary. Invoke the **RENDER** command. The rendered image should look like Figure 9-127.
55. **SAVE** the drawing.

Figure 9-127 The final rendered image

ADJUSTING MATERIALS' MAPS ON OBJECTS

MATERIALMAP	
Render Toolbar	
Ribbon: Materials panel	
Pull-down Menu	View/ Render/ Mapping/ ...
Command Line	mate-rialmap

In addition to adjusting bitmaps for a specific material, you can also adjust the orientation at which an applied material is mapped to a specific object. This is achieved using the **MATERIALMAP** command. The primary use of this command is to change the method of wrapping the object with the material applied, so that its maps are properly shown. You can choose among **Box, Planar, Spherical,** and **Cylindrical** methods, as shown in the shortcut menu of the **MATERIALMAP** command (Figure 9-128). Although the 3D objects may not necessarily have the same shapes, there is always one that closely represents an object's overall look. Selecting this shape will improve the display of the material on the objects and faces in the rendered image. You can also use this tool to create specific effects.

Planar mapping maps the image onto the object as if were projected in a single direction. Faces located more perpendicular to the projection display the image more clearly. This type of mapping is better applied on planar objects, especially regions.

Box mapping is the default mapping method when the materials are applied. It adjusts the mapping of the image as if it were projected onto the object perpendicularly from the six different faces of a box-shaped solid.

Cylindrical mapping maps the image as if it were projected onto the object perpendicularly from the cylindrical face of a cylinder-shaped solid. The image is wrapped only horizontally around the object.

Spherical mapping maps the image as if it were projected onto the object perpendicularly from the spherical face enclosing the object. As a result, the image is distorted both horizontally and vertically, with maximum compression at the two poles.

Selecting which mapping method to use depends on the shape of the object. But it is a good idea to try other choices as well (Figure 9-129).

As you try the different mapping methods, you will need to adjust the *UV* coordinate system used as a reference to define the bitmap. The scale at which the image is mapped onto the objects

Enter
Cancel

Box
Planar
Spherical
Cylindrical
copY mapping to
Reset mapping

Pan
Zoom
SteeringWheels

QuickCalc

Figure 9-128 The MATERIALMAP command shortcut menu

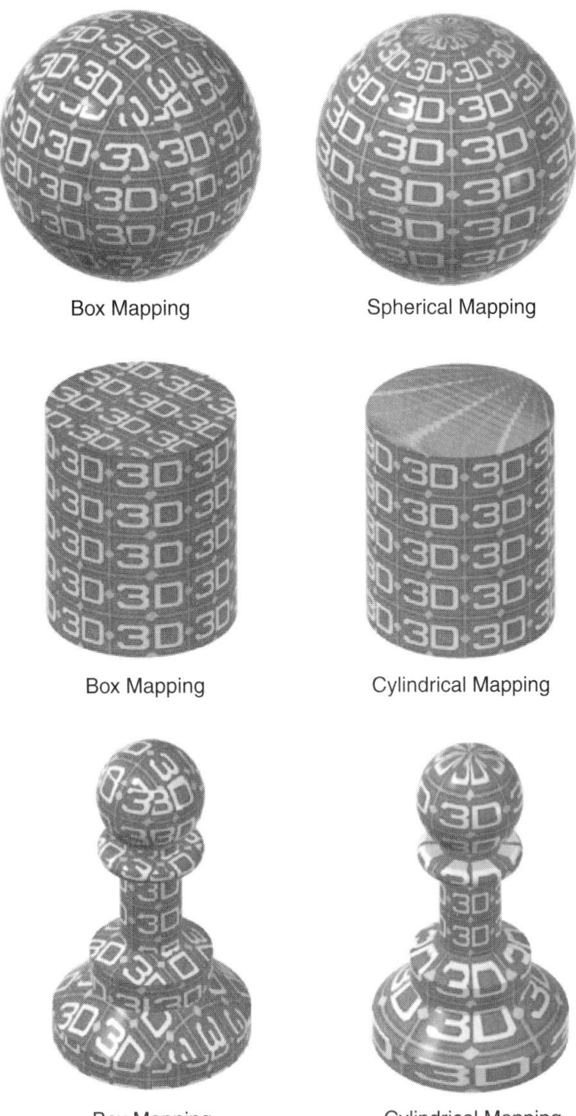

Figure 9-129 Comparison of using different mapping methods on objects with different shapes

is affected by differences in how it projects on the faces. The *UV* coordinate system is adjusted in the **Adjust Bitmap** dialog box, which is accessed through the **Materials** palette.

You can make other adjustments by using the mapping grip tool that is displayed when a mapping method is applied to the object, along with an object that represents the type of mapping and its corresponding grips (Figure 9-130). You can switch between the move and rotate mapping grip tools for each mapping method.

The move mapping grip tool allows you to move the *UV* coordinates along one of the three axes or within one of the three planes (Figure 9-131). Clicking the corresponding element will constrain the movement to it. To constrain movement within a plane, you must click one of the squares between the axes. The rotate mapping grip tool allows you to rotate the *UV* coordinates in the direction of the selected ring (Figure 9-132). In addition to using the mapping grip tools, you can use the grips displayed on the objects that represent the type of mapping to perform other adjustments. Pulling a particular grip will stretch the image in this direction.

Among its options, the **MATERIALMAP** command allows you to **Reset** the mapping coordinates as well as to **Copy** mapping coordinates from one object to another. All the operations related to this command can be easily accessed through the **Materials** panel on the **Ribbon** (Figure 9-133).

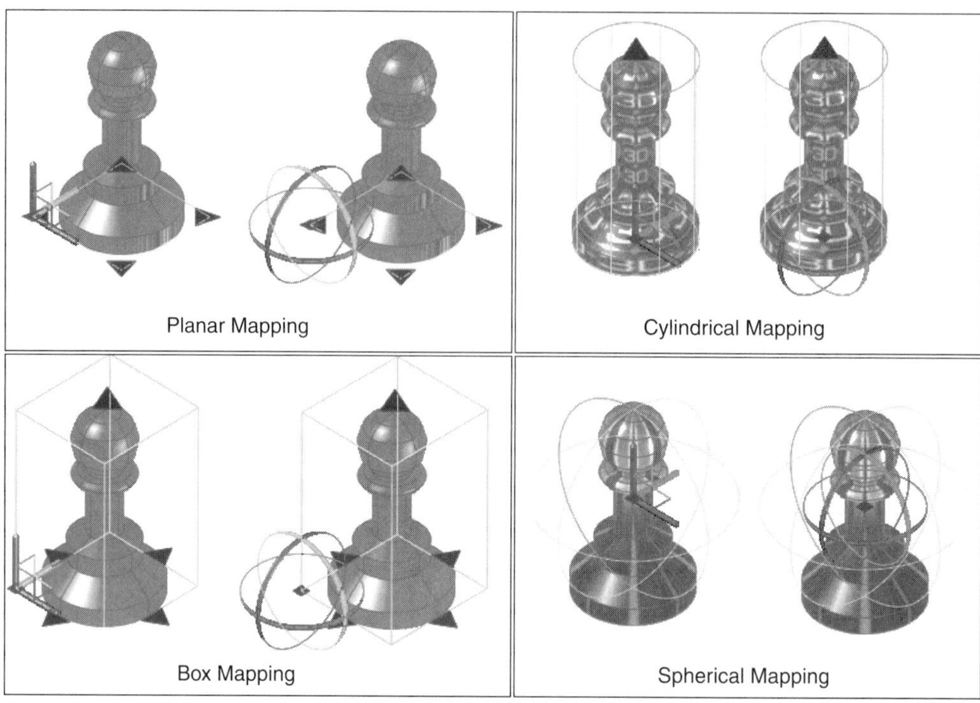

Figure 9-130 The move and rotate mapping grip tools displayed with each mapping method

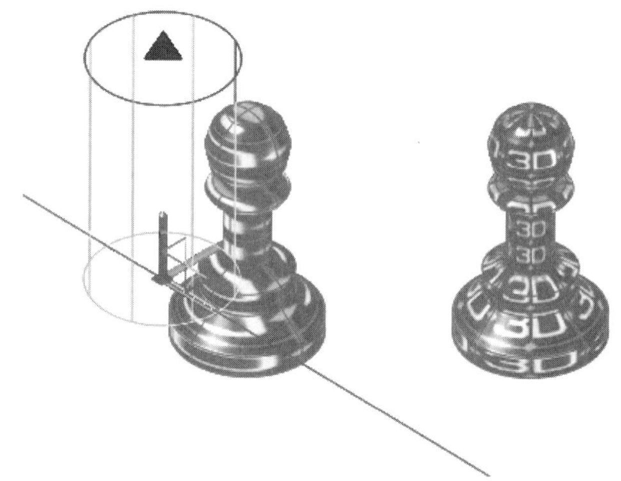

Figure 9-131 Effects of using the move mapping grip tool on the material's mapping

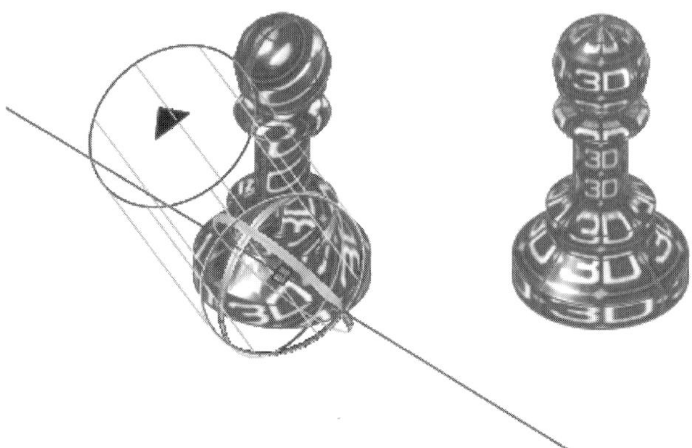

Figure 9-132 Effects of using the rotate mapping grip tool on the material's mapping

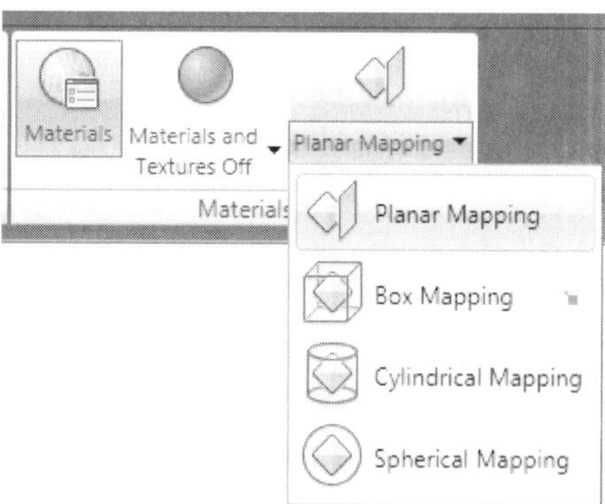

Figure 9-133 The Materials Mapping flyout icons located in the Materials panel on the Ribbon

ADVANCED USE OF VISUAL STYLES

CREATING AND MODIFYING VISUAL STYLES

In Chapter 1 you learned about the AutoCAD program's predefined visual styles. If you are using rendered visual styles (**Realistic** or **Conceptual**) to assist in the development of a 3D model, the predefined visual styles offer plenty of options. Visual styles can also be used, however, to create artistic representations of a 3D model (Figure 9-134).

Figure 9-134 Visual styles can be used to create pictorial illustrations

You can create and modify visual styles through the **Visual Styles Manager** palette. The sample images allow you to know which visual style is currently being used when you place a special icon on it. For instance, Figure 9-135 shows the five predefined visual styles; by looking at the sample images you can see that the **2D Wireframe** is currently in use. The predefined visual styles always show the AutoCAD's program icon on them.

To create a new visual style, you can perform one of the following operations:

- Right-click on a sample image and select **Copy.** Then right-click on an empty space of the panel and select **Paste.** You can also use a drag-and-drop operation while holding down the **<Ctrl>** key.
- Click on the **Create New Visual Style** button.

Clicking on the **Create New Visual Style** button will open the **Edit Name and Description** dialog box (Figure 9-136), where you can specify a name for the visual style. Right-clicking on any existing visual style and selecting **Edit Name and Description...** also will allow you to rename an existing visual style.

As with materials, you can export your own visual style to the **Tool Palettes** by clicking the corresponding button (the third button, going from left to right). This way you can make it available for other drawings (Figure 9-137).

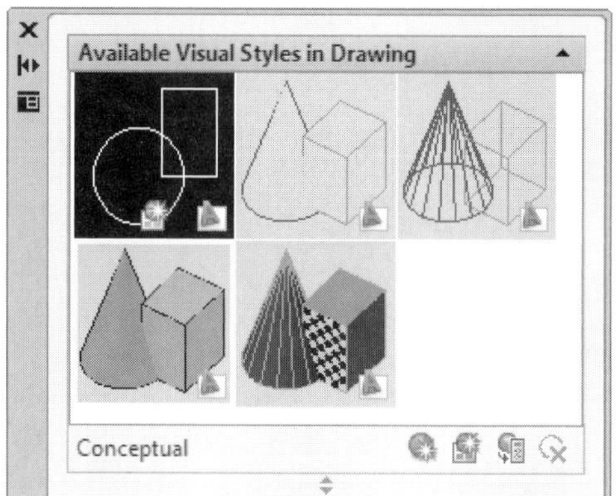

Figure 9-135 The five predefined visual styles

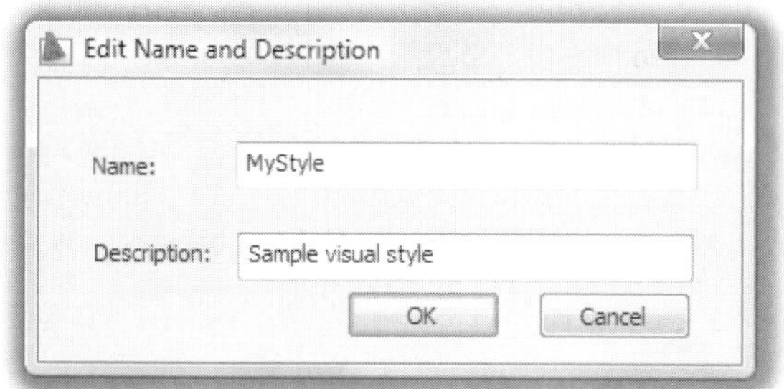

Figure 9-136 The Edit Name and Description dialog box

The settings that control the effects of a visual style are organized into three groups:

- Face settings
- Environment settings
- Edge settings

Face Settings

Face settings enable you to control visual properties that affect the display of faces. The **Face style** is the most important property because it defines whether the visual style displays as rendered or as a wireframe (Figure 9-138). **None** displays a wireframe 3D model. **Real** and **Warm-Cool** face styles display the 3D model rendered. **Real** uses dark and light colors, whereas **Warm-Cool** uses warm and cool colors.

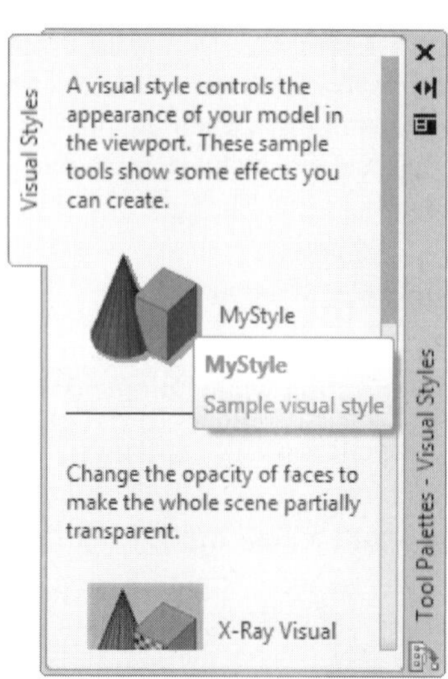

Figure 9-137 A visual style exported to the tool palettes

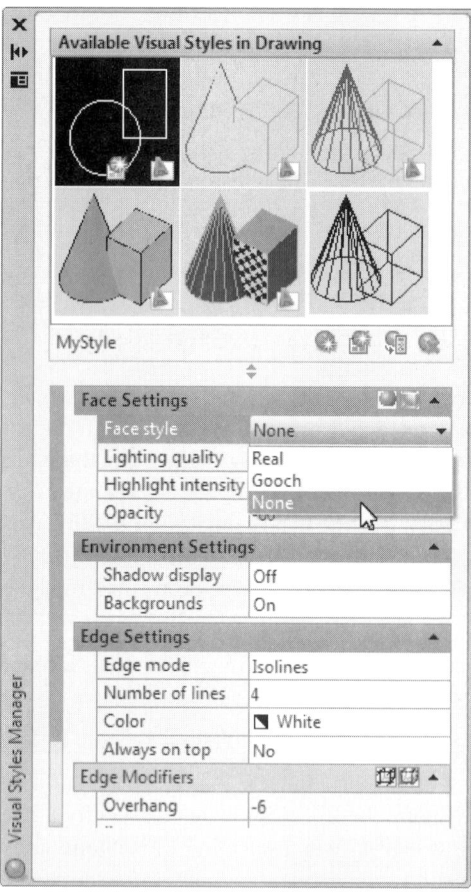

Figure 9-138 The Face style drop-down list in the Visual Styles Manager dialog box

When **Real** or **Warm-Cool** face styles are selected, you can also select one of four face color modes (**Normal, Desaturate, Tint,** and **Monochrome**) (Figure 9-139). The last three color modes are a degradation of the **Normal** color mode, just as with many digital cameras. **Desaturate** simply softens or makes faint the color. Both **Tint** and **Monochrome** modes use the **Tint Color** specified below the **Face color mode** setting. **Tint** displays the objects in tones of the **Tint Color,** depending on how dark or light its normal color is. **Monochrome,** on the other hand, displays the 3D model in the **Tint Color** itself, affected only by the incidence of light. You can combine the **Real** and **Warm-Cool** styles with any of the face color modes and create eight different effects.

When the **Normal** color mode is selected, you can also choose to display the **Materials** or the **Materials and textures.** Any property that is defined by a bitmap attached to the material will not be displayed unless you select the **Materials and textures** mode.

Environment Settings

This group of settings controls the behavior of the shadows and the background. If the 3D model has any user-created lights, you can choose to turn off the default lighting and use the user-created lights. This will be noticeable only when one of the rendered face styles, **Real** or **Warm-Cool,** is selected.

You can use one of four modes for shadows: **Full shadows with ground plane, Full Shadows, Ground shadow,** and **Off** (Figure 9-140).

The **Ground shadow** is independent of any user-created lights. Its effect is as if the rays of a distant light were illuminating the objects in the direction of the negative *Z*-axis of the WCS (Figure 9-141). By default, the plane receiving the **Ground shadow** is located in the *XY* plane of the WCS. You can move this plane up or down parallel to it by changing the value of the **SHADOWPLANELOCATION** system variable. **Full shadows**, on the other hand, shows the shadows of any user-created light that is turned on (Figure 9-142). You can display both ground and full shadows by selecting **Full shadows with ground plane.**

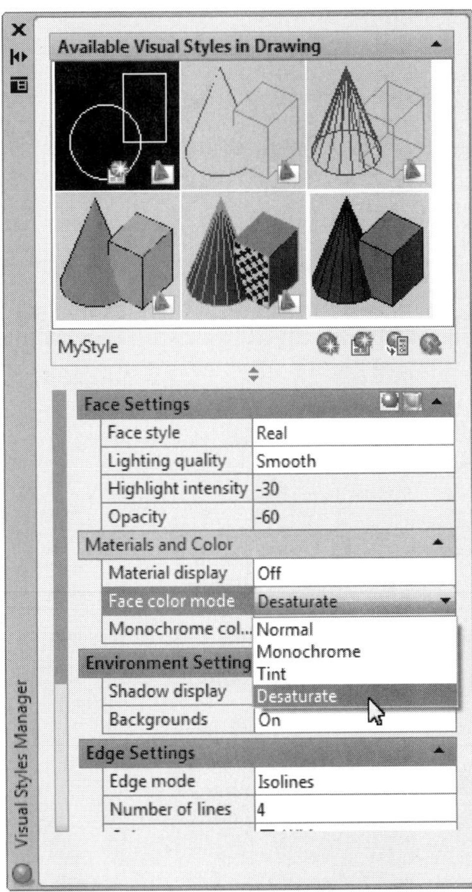

Figure 9-139 The Face color mode drop-down list in the Visual Styles Manager dialog box

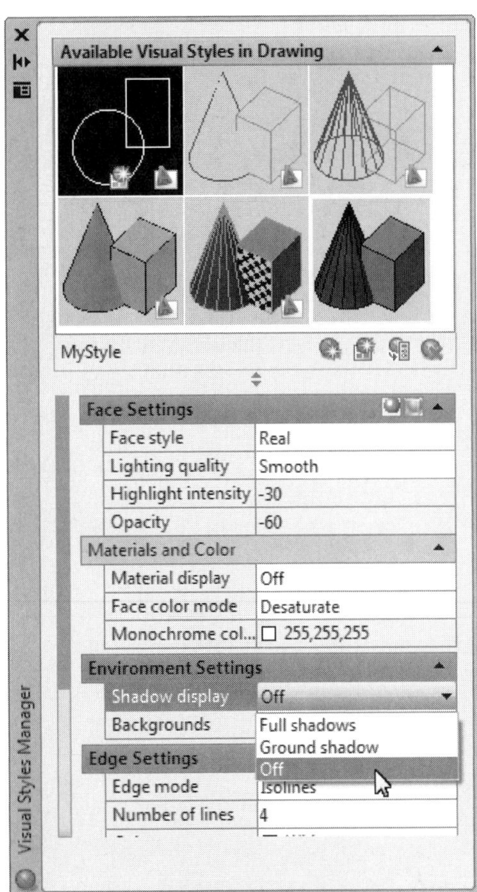

Figure 9-140 The Shadow display drop-down list in the Visual Styles Manager dialog box

Figure 9-141 Visual style using Ground shadow

Figure 9-142 Visual style using Full shadows

If you have specified a background with the **Background** dialog box, the **Background** setting determines whether it is turned on or off for a particular visual style.

Edge Settings

This group of settings controls the behavior of edges and silhouettes. In general, you can select one of three modes to display the edges: **Facet Edges, Isolines,** or **None** (Figure 9-143).

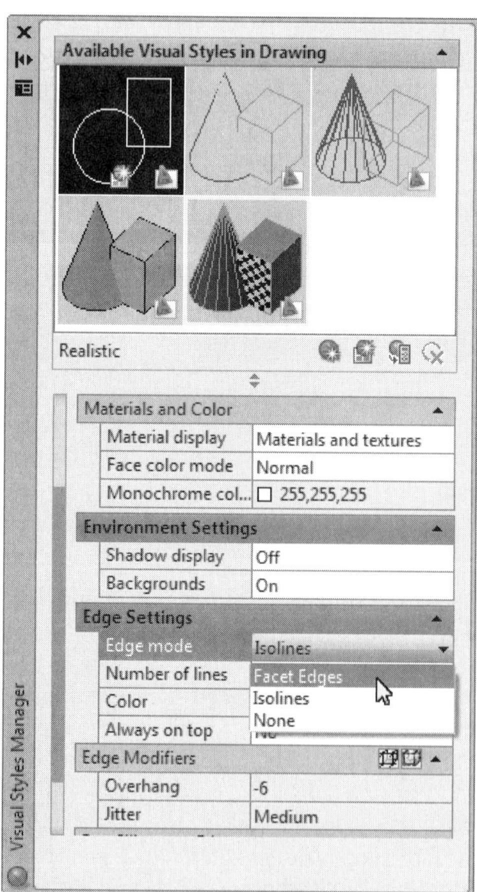

Figure 9-143 The Edge mode drop-down list in the Visual Styles Manager dialog box

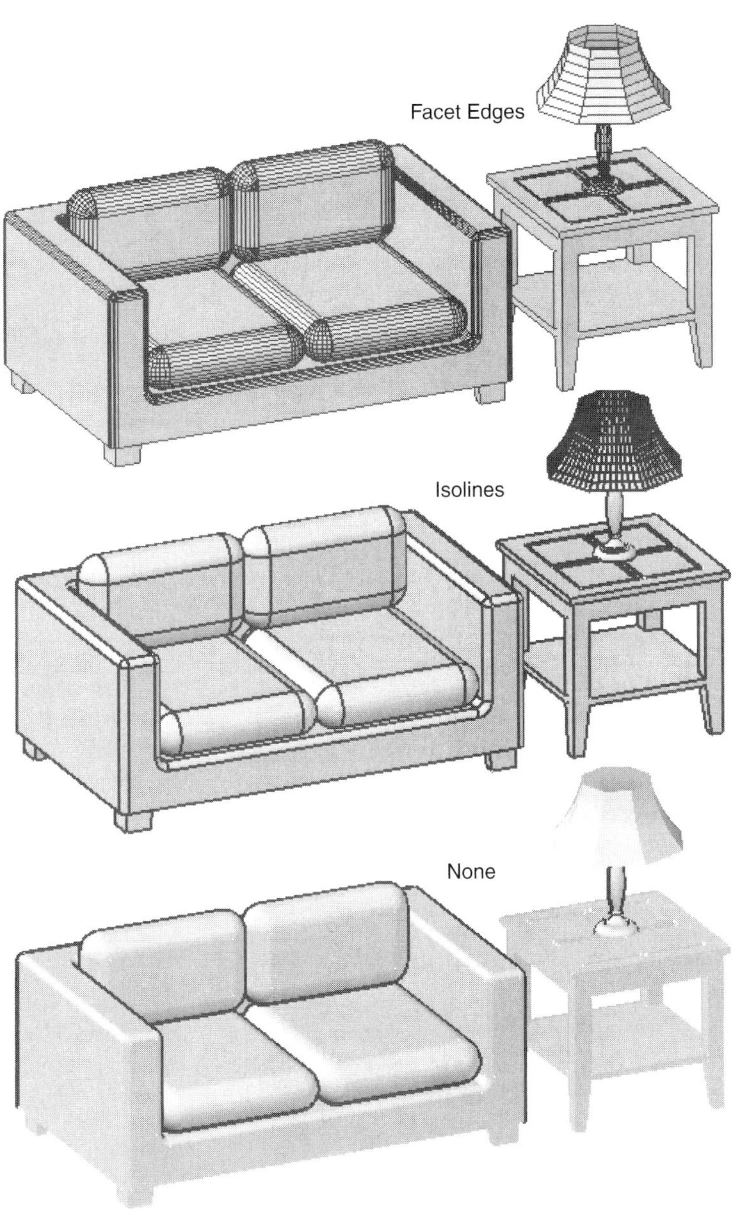

Figure 9-144 Effect of selecting the Edge mode settings

None mode displays only the silhouette of the 3D objects. **Isolines** displays all the edges, including the tangential edges. **Facet Edges** displays all the edges and borders of the facets (Figure 9-144). You can control the **Width** and **Color** of the edges displayed in a particular mode. Because these settings cannot be changed in the **None** mode, you must change them prior to switching to this mode.

Depending on the particular viewing point, each edge of a 3D model can become one of the following types:

- **Fast Silhouette Edges**
- **Obscured Edges**
- **Intersection Edges**

Regardless of the current edges mode, you can control each category of edges independently. For example, turning on the **Fast Silhouette Edges** display mode will display the edges in a different way by delimiting the contours of the shaded areas (Figure 9-145).

Under **Edge Modifiers** you can control two other special visual effects for the edges in general: **Overhang, Jitter, Crease angle,** and **Halo gap %.** All edge modifiers are available in the **Facet Edges** mode. In the **Isolines** mode, however, only the **Overhang** and **Jitter** effects can be used.

The **Overhang** and **Jitter** effects give the impression of a drawing sketched by hand, which can be used to create accented presentations for both 3D models and 2D drawings (Figure 9-146).

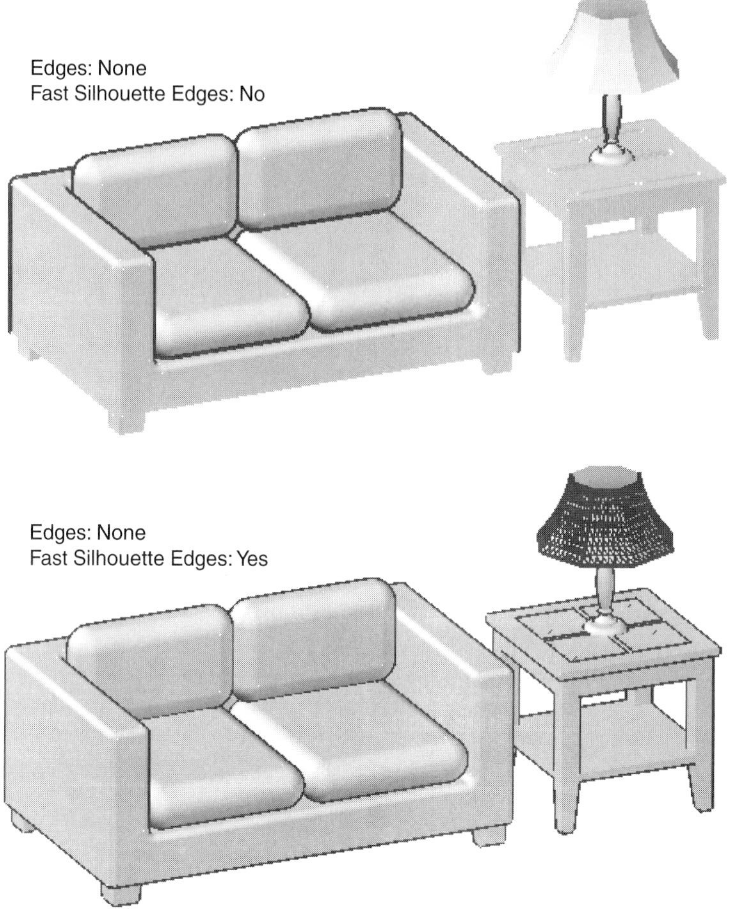

Figure 9-145 Effect of turning Fast Silhouette Edges on and off

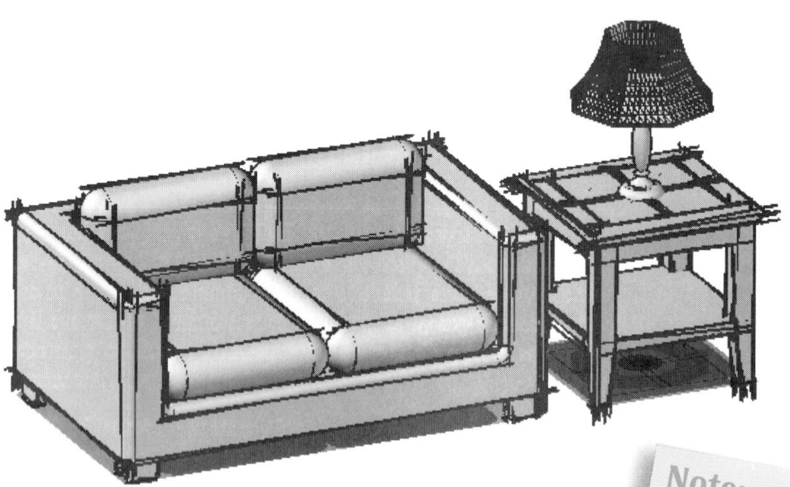

Figure 9-146 Effect of altering the Overhang and Jitter settings

To turn these effects on or off on a particular visual style, you must click on the buttons shown in Figure 9-147. **Crease angle** sets the maximum angle between two adjacent facets up to which its edges are not shown. As this value increases, fewer facet edges will be displayed. **Halo gap %** sets the gap displayed when an object is hidden by another object.

Note:

All the visual style settings can also be controlled from the **Visual Style** panel in the **Ribbon**. This is especially helpful when you need to create quick effects. You must be aware, however, that these changes will not be stored in any particular visual style; selecting another visual style will reset any changes.

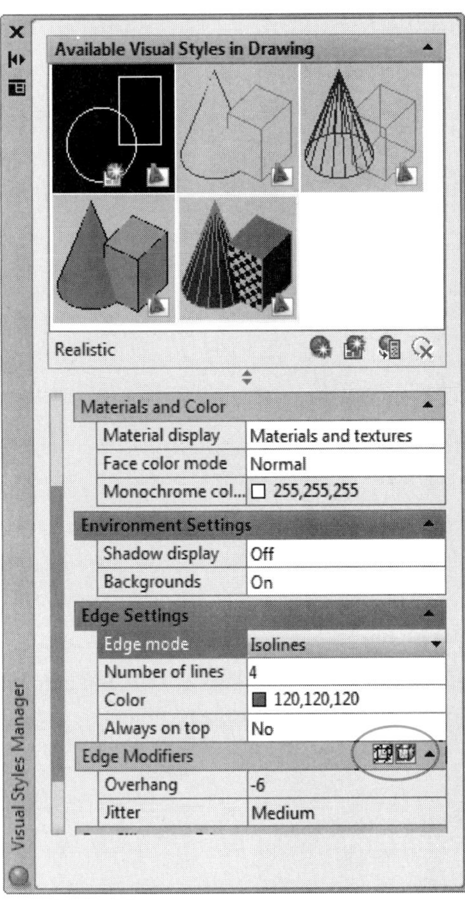

Figure 9-147 Buttons that control whether the Overhang and Jitter are turned on or off on a visual style

CREATING ANIMATIONS

DEFINING COMPUTER ANIMATION

A computer ***animation*** generates and records successive positions of a 3D model, or frames, to create a video file that, when replayed, gives an illusion of movement. With the AutoCAD program, you can record, preview, and save an animation using one of two procedures:

- Using the **Animations** panel in the **Ribbon**
- Using the **Motion Path Animation** dialog box, displayed with the **ANIPATH** command

animation: A video file created by recording successive positions of the 3D model, giving the impression of movement when replayed.

Recording a 3D Navigation Scene

The display of a 3D model is defined by a default camera located between the viewer and the target. As you know, the viewing direction is always perpendicular to the viewing plane and defined by a vector from the camera position to the camera target. You can read and modify the camera and target locations in the **View** panel on the **Ribbon** (Figure 9-148).

Every time you **ZOOM, PAN,** or perform a **3D Orbit** operation, you change the location of the camera position and the camera target. Other operations such as **Adjust Distance** or **Swivel** modify either one or the other. The continuous change of these locations is precisely the meaning of *3D navigation,* which includes any of the following operations:

- **3DORBIT** (Constrained Orbit)
- **3DFORBIT** (Free Orbit)
- **3DCORBIT** (Continuous Orbit)

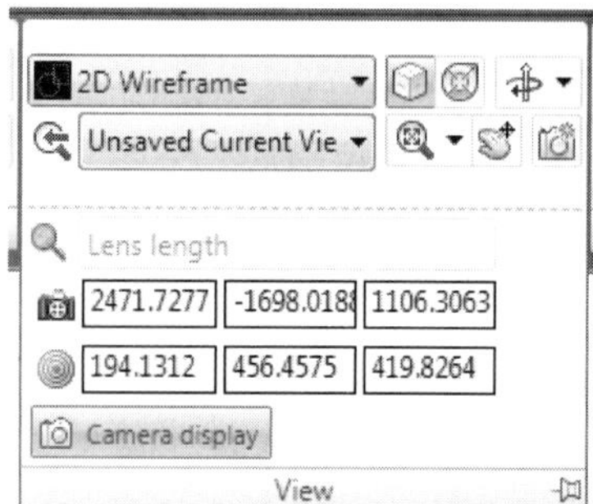

Figure 9-148 The actual coordinates of the camera and the target are displayed in the View panel of the Ribbon

- **3DSWIVEL** (Swivel)
- **3DDISTANCE** (Adjust Distance)
- **3DWALK** (Walk)
- **3DFLY** (Fly)
- **3DZOOM** (Zoom)
- **3DPAN** (Pan)

All 3D navigation commands can be found in the **3D Navigation** toolbar (Figure 9-149). After you invoke any of these commands, you can switch between them by simply pressing a number key between **1** and **9,** or you can right-click to select a mode from the shortcut menu (Figure 9-150). For example, after you invoke the **3DZOOM** command, pressing the key activates the **3DFORBIT** operation.

Figure 9-149 The 3D Navigation toolbar

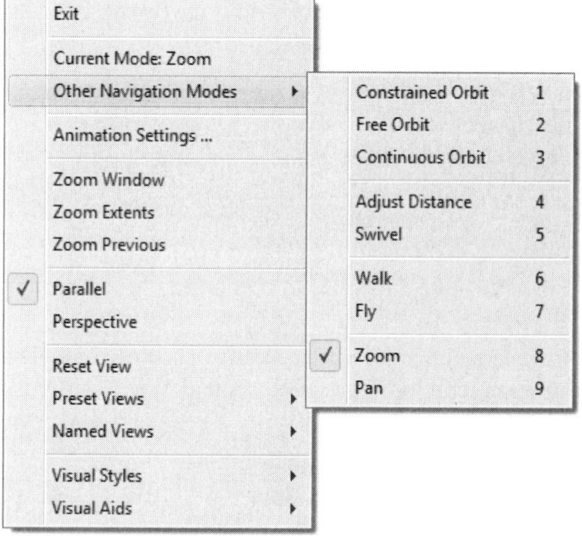

Figure 9-150 The 3D Navigation shortcut menu

The **Record** button in the **Animations** panel on the **Ribbon** becomes available when any of the 3D navigation operations are activated (Figure 9-151). Whenever the recording mode is available, you can simply press the **Record** button to start recording the 3D navigation operations that you perform.

TIP During a recording, you should switch between the 3D navigation modes only by pressing the corresponding number key or through the shortcut menu. The transition time is reduced greatly, however, when you use the number keys.

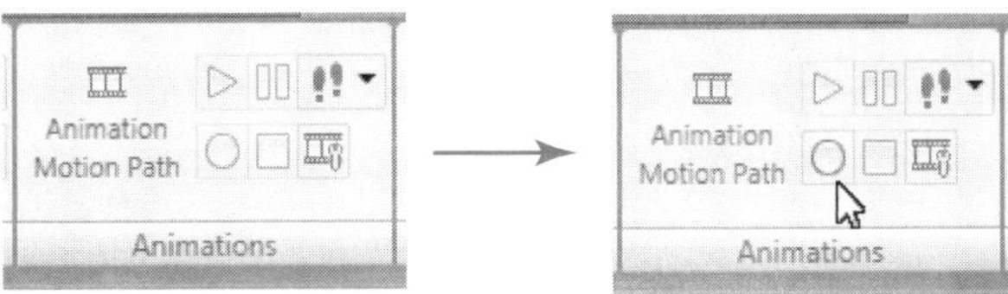

Figure 9-151 The Record and playback buttons in the Animations panel on the Ribbon

Anytime after you start recording, you can click the **Pause** button to temporarily stop recording. The **Play** button turns green as soon as you start the recording process. Pressing this button will also stop the recording and open the **Animation Preview** window (Figure 9-152). In the **Animation Preview** window, you can replay the animation. Press its **Record** button to continue recording, or click the **Save** button to create a video file. You can also move the slide button to view a specific frame of the animation. Closing the **Animation Preview** window will return you to the 3D navigation modes, where you can perform the same operations. The recording is discarded by exiting the 3D navigation mode.

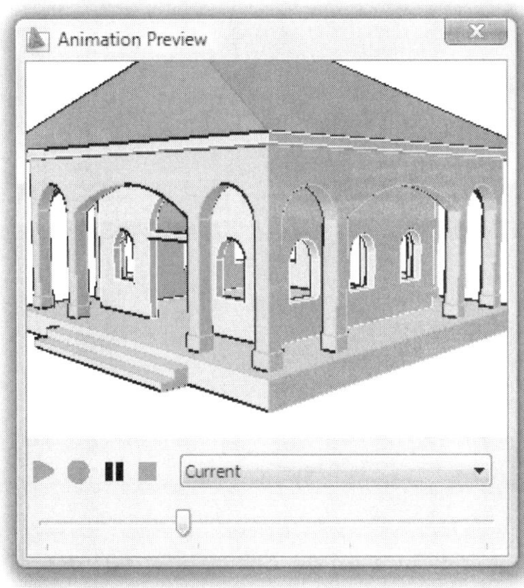

Figure 9-152 The Animation Preview window

Before recording and saving your first animation, you should check the settings located in the **Animation Settings** dialog box (Figure 9-153). This box is displayed when you press the **Animation Settings** button in the **Animations** panel on the **Ribbon**.

You can select one of the visual styles from the list and one of the digital video formats supported for the video file output. AVI, MPG, and WMV files can be played in Windows Media Player, whereas MOV files can be played with the QuickTime player. The **Resolution** setting affects the size and quality of the video file. **Frame rate** controls the number of frames or pictures used per second; you can set this value between 1 and 60.

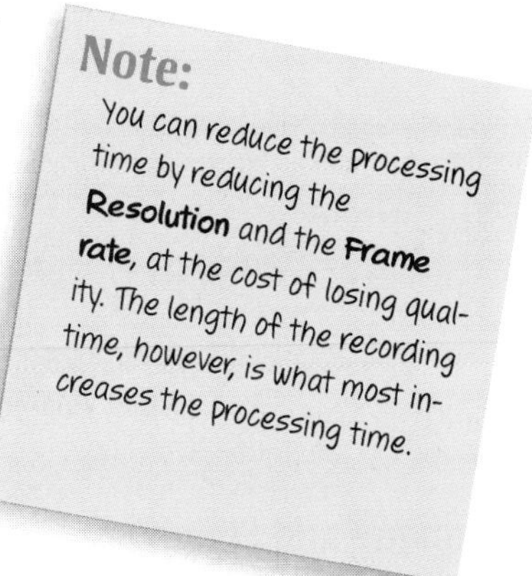
Note: You can reduce the processing time by reducing the **Resolution** and the **Frame rate**, at the cost of losing quality. The length of the recording time, however, is what most increases the processing time.

Clicking the **Save** button in the **Animation Preview** window will open the **Save As** dialog box, where you can specify a location and a name for the video file (Figure 9-154). The **Animation Settings** dialog box can also be accessed from this window by clicking the **Animation settings...** button. After you click **Save,** the process of creating the video starts to run and the **Creating Video** window is displayed (Figure 9-155).

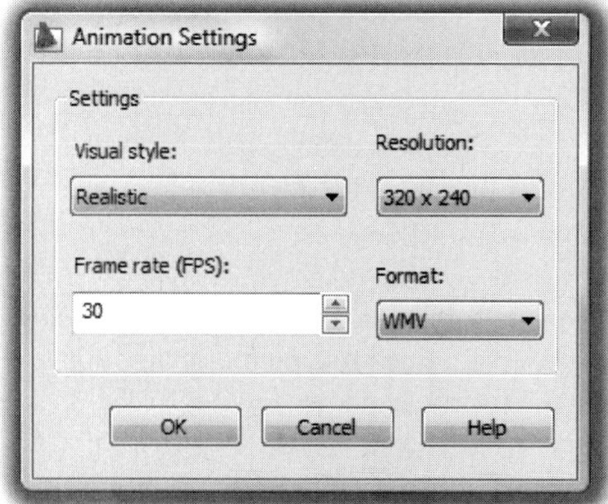

Figure 9-153 The Animation Settings dialog box

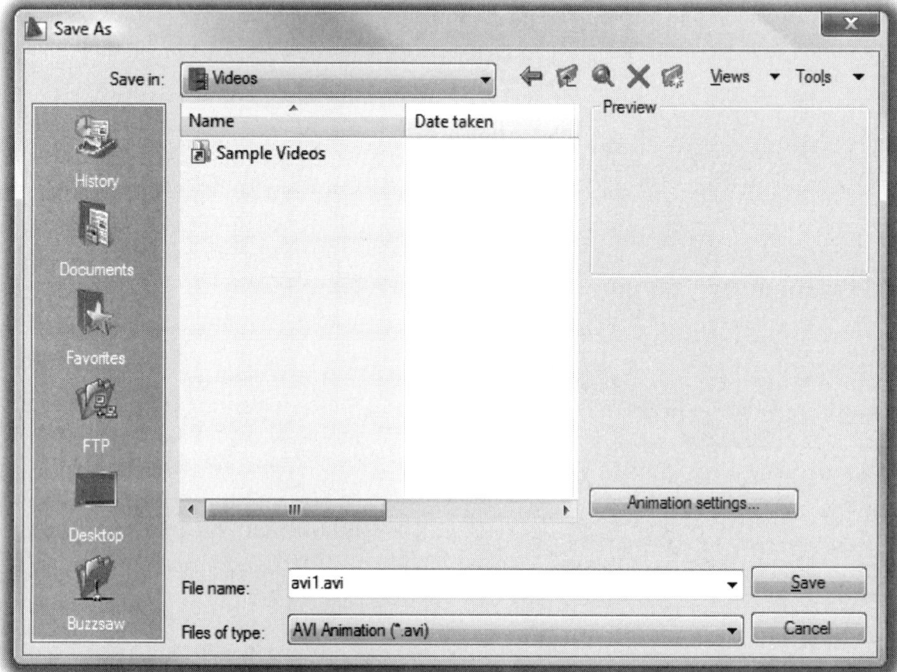

Figure 9-154 The Save As dialog box

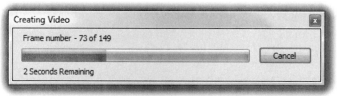

Figure 9-155 The Creating Video window

3DWALK	
3D Navigation Toolbar	
Ribbon: Animations panel	
Pull-down Menu	View/ Walk and Fly/Walk
Command Line	3dwalk

Walking and Flying Through the 3D Model

The **Walk** and **Fly** modes are special 3D navigation modes that allow you to go through the model and turn around, as if you were playing a video game. These modes are available only in a perspective view.

When you switch to the **Walk** or **Fly** modes from another navigation mode, or invoke the **3DWALK** or **3DFLY** commands, special navigation instructions for these two modes are displayed in the help search window (Figure 9-156). After expanding it, this menu shows you how

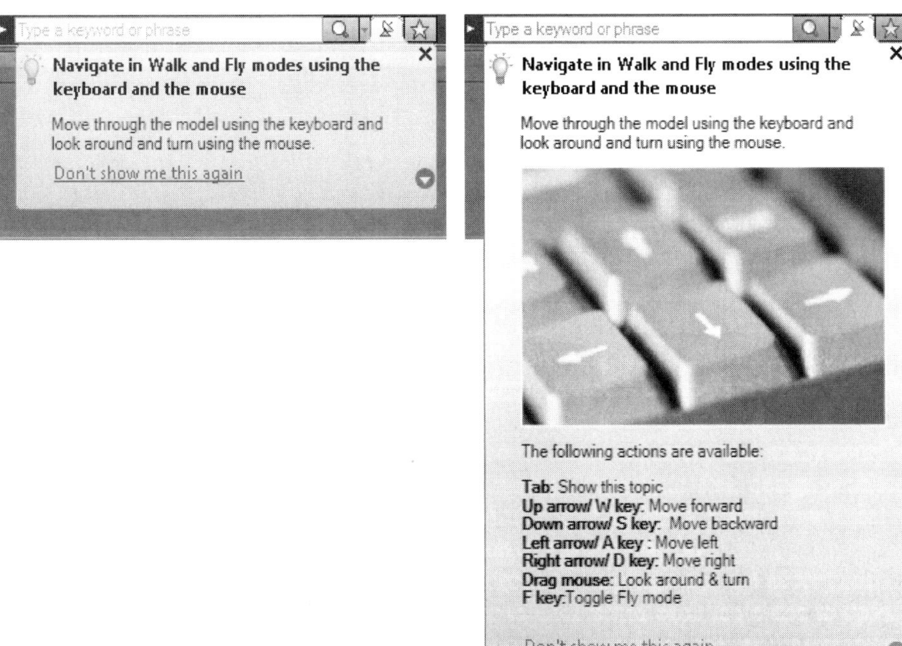

Figure 9-156 The 3D Walk and Fly navigation instructions

3DFLY	
3D Navigation Toolbar	
Ribbon: Animations panel	
Pull-down Menu	View/ Walk and Fly/Fly
Command Line	3dfly

to use the keys and the mouse to move throughout the 3D model. You can make these instructions show up again by pressing the <Tab> key after it closes. You can toggle between **Walk** and **Fly** modes by pressing the corresponding number or the <F> key. The **Position Locator** window also opens in these navigation modes, displaying the top view of the 3D model (Figure 9-157). You can drag the position or the target indicator to relocate the view. You can also drag both indicators at the same time by clicking in an intermediate location.

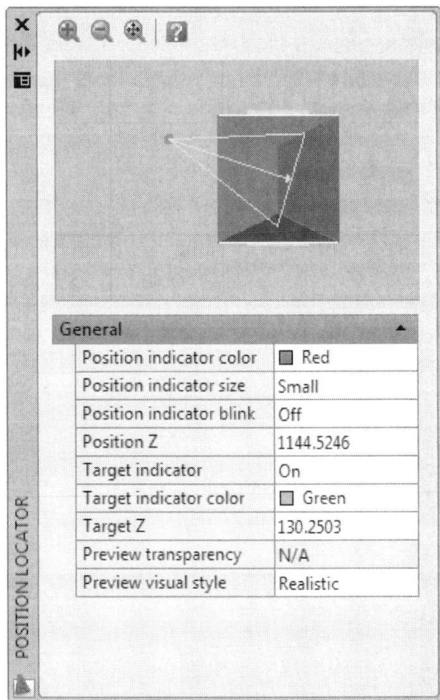

Figure 9-157 The Position Locator window

In the **Walk** mode, the camera position moves parallel to the *XY* plane of the WCS at the fixed distance of **5′** above it, regardless of the direction toward which the camera aims. The height of the camera target does not change either unless you drag the left mouse button, even when moving to the sides. Using this mode gives the impression that a person is carrying the camera or that you are actually walking though the 3D model. When the **Walk** mode is activated, the view automatically aligns itself to show the 3D model with the proper verticality and direction to simulate walking over the *XY* plane of the WCS (Figure 9-158).

Original Viewing Point

Viewing Point Before Starting the Walkthrough

Figure 9-158 The view aligns itself when the Walk mode is activated

The **Fly** mode, on the other hand, does not restrict the camera position to any height, allowing you to move in any direction. In this mode, moving forward makes the camera fly from the camera position to the camera target. Even though the locations of the camera position and the camera target change, the direction does not change when you move forward or backward, unless you drag the mouse or move to the sides.

When either of these two modes is active, the shortcut menu displayed with a right-click provides access to the **Walk and Fly Settings** dialog box (Figure 9-159). In this dialog box, among other settings, you can change the speed at which the camera walks or flies through the model either by changing the distance between the steps (**Step size**) or by changing the number of **Steps per second.**

Note:
In the **Walk** and **Fly** 3D navigation modes, you can create walk-through and fly-through animations by using the same recording procedures that you use with any other 3D navigation mode.

motion paths: User-created routes through which the camera, the target, or both gradually move while the camera keeps its focus on the target.

ANIPATH	
Ribbon: Animations panel	
Pull-down Menu	View/ Motion Path Animations...
Command Line	anipath

Recording Predefined Motion Path Scenes

You have previously learned to create animations in which the camera is directly controlled by the user operations. Using ***motion paths*** enables you to create animations in which the camera position and camera target gradually change their location according to a predefined **Path** or **Point.** These elements are defined in the **Motion Path Animation** dialog box (Figure 9-160), which opens when you invoke the **ANIPATH** command.

As with standard animations, you can control the video's format and resolution, as well as the visual style use. Because the animation is not created by user operations, you must also define its

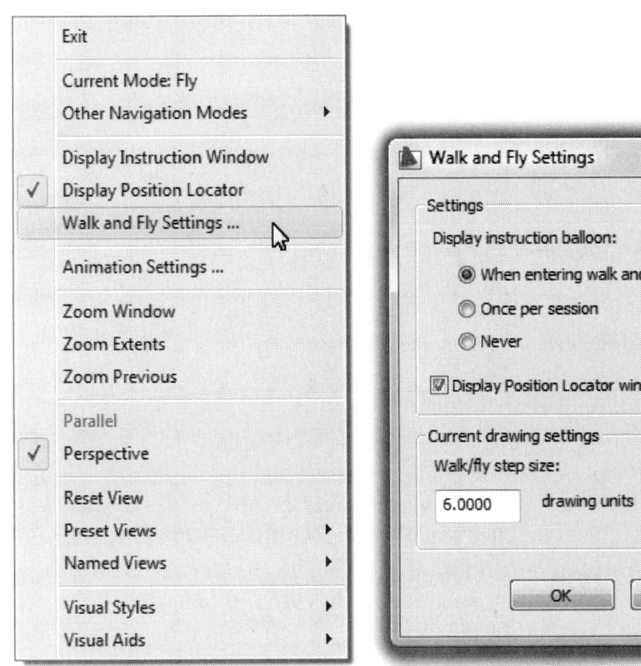

Figure 9-159 The shortcut displayed when the 3D Walk and Fly navigation modes are activated and the Walk and Fly Settings dialog box

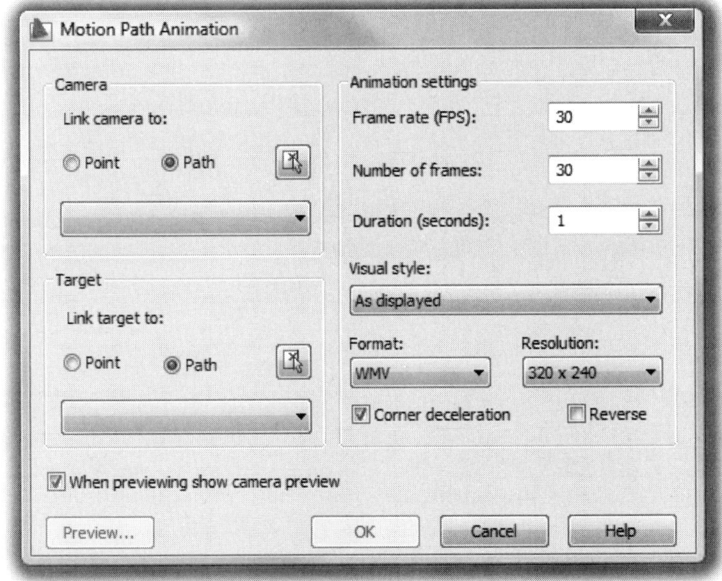

Figure 9-160 The Motion Path Animation dialog box

Duration. The total **Number of frames** is equal to the **Frame rate** times the **Duration.** After you set a **Frame rate,** you can specify either the **Number of frames** or the **Duration** (in seconds). The other value is automatically recalculated.

You can specify a point by snapping to the geometry of the 3D model. To define a path, select one of the following objects, previously created:

- Line
- Arc
- Ellipse (entire or trimmed)
- Circle
- Polyline
- 3D Polyline

You can specify a path for the camera and another one for the target, or you can combine a point with a path. In any case, you should try to keep this combination simple to achieve reasonable results. For example, making the camera move along a line whose midpoint is close to the target, defined as a *point,* can create the effect of approaching and leaving the target. Using two parallel lines, one for the camera and the other for the target, can simulate a straight walk-through or fly-through, depending on the location of the parallel lines.

Note:
You cannot select a point for both the camera and the target because this combination will cause no movement at all.

By selecting **Corner deceleration,** you can make the camera move more slowly when it reaches a corner of a path. Selecting **Reverse** makes the animation travel through the path in the opposite direction.

After you have specified everything, you can click the **Preview** button to open the **Animation Preview** window and watch the animation preview. You can also move the slide button to view a specific frame of the animation. After you close the **Animation Preview** window, you can click the **OK** button in the **Motion Path Animation** dialog box to save the video file.

Figure 9-161 shows the 3D model from which an animation has been recorded. It uses an arc as the motion path for the camera and a point for the target, as well as several positions of the camera along its motion path. The corresponding frame images of the video obtained are shown in Figure 9-162.

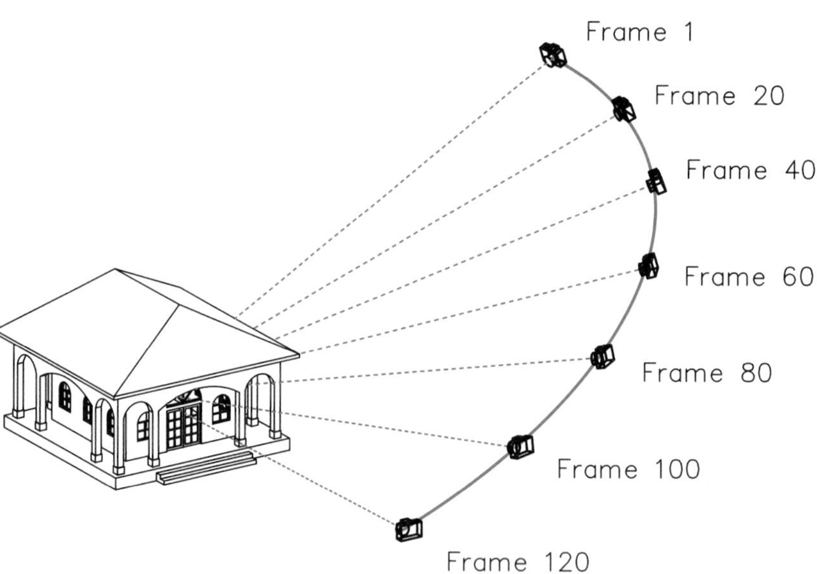

Figure 9-161 Position of the camera for different frame intervals as it moves along the motion path

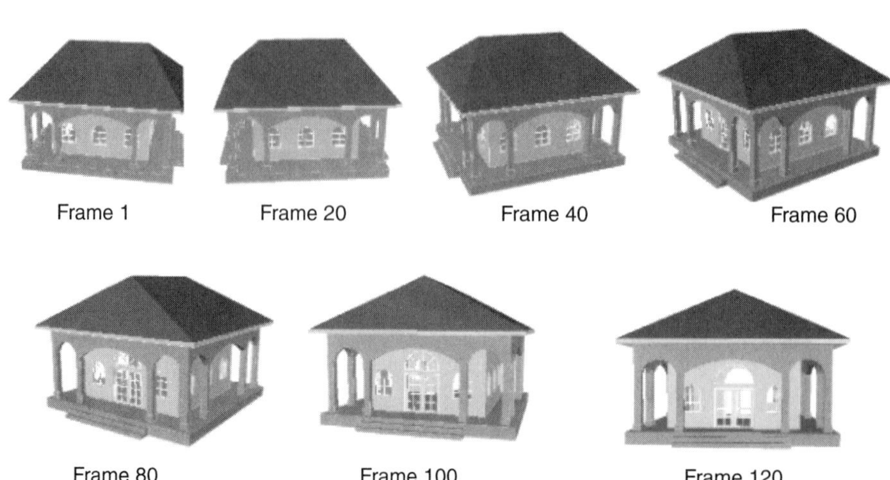

Figure 9-162 The corresponding image for each frame recorded

Exercise 9-5: Animations—Recording 3D Navigation Operations

1. **OPEN** ***Exercise 9-5*** from the CD.
2. **SAVE** it **AS** ***Exercise 9-5 solved.***
3. Select the **Realistic** visual style.
4. Locate the **Animations** panel on the **Ribbon.**
5. Using the mouse wheel button, perform a **PAN** operation to center the 3D model in the display. Do not change the zoom factor.

   Next, you will record a scene in which you zoom into the 3D model by using a single smooth action. Click at the lower area of the screen and drag the pointer straight up slowly, just passing the middle of the screen. Then press <1> to start the **Constrained Orbit.** Without delay, click in the leftmost side of the screen about the middle and drag the pointer horizontally all the way to the right, at an intermediate speed. Between 12 and 16 seconds should elapse from the moment you click the **Record** button to the moment you click the **Play** button.
6. Invoke the **3DZOOM** command by typing the command in the command prompt window.
7. Click the **Record** button and without delay perform the operation you planned.
8. When finished, press the **Play** button. This operation stops the recording and opens the **Animation Preview** window.
9. Wait until the **Animation Preview** finishes playing, then click the black square button to save the video file (Figure 9-163).

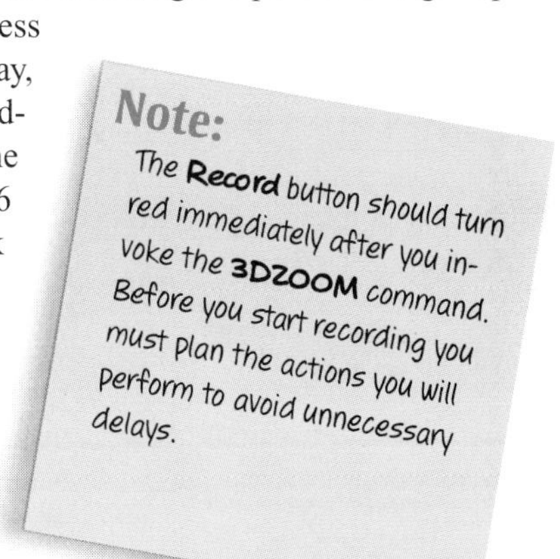

Note:
The Record button should turn red immediately after you invoke the 3DZOOM command. Before you start recording you must plan the actions you will perform to avoid unnecessary delays.

Figure 9-163 The Animation Preview window

10. In the **Save As** dialog box, click the **Animation settings...** button to open the **Animation Settings** dialog box.
11. Select the **AVI** format and click **OK** to close the **Animation Settings** dialog box.
12. In the **Save As** dialog box, select a location for the video file and type **Hall-Navigation** as the file name. Click **Save** to close the dialog box and start the **Creating Video** process.
13. **SAVE** the drawing.
14. Use Windows Explorer to browse for the **Hall-Navigation** video file. Right-click on it, and select **Play.** It should open in Windows Media Player.

Exercise 9-6: Animations—Recording a Walk-through Operation

1. **OPEN *Exercise 9-5 solved.***
2. **SAVE** the drawing **AS *Exercise 9-6.***
3. Open the **Walk and Fly Settings** dialog box by invoking the **WALKFLYSETTINGS** command; the icon is located in the **Animations** panel on the **Ribbon.**
4. In the **Walk and Fly Settings** dialog box, set the **Step size** to **30** and the **Steps per second** to **3** [Figure 9-164(a)]. In the **View** panel of the **Ribbon,** set the **Z** coordinate of the **Camera Position** to **60** and press **<Enter>** [Figure 9-164 (b)].

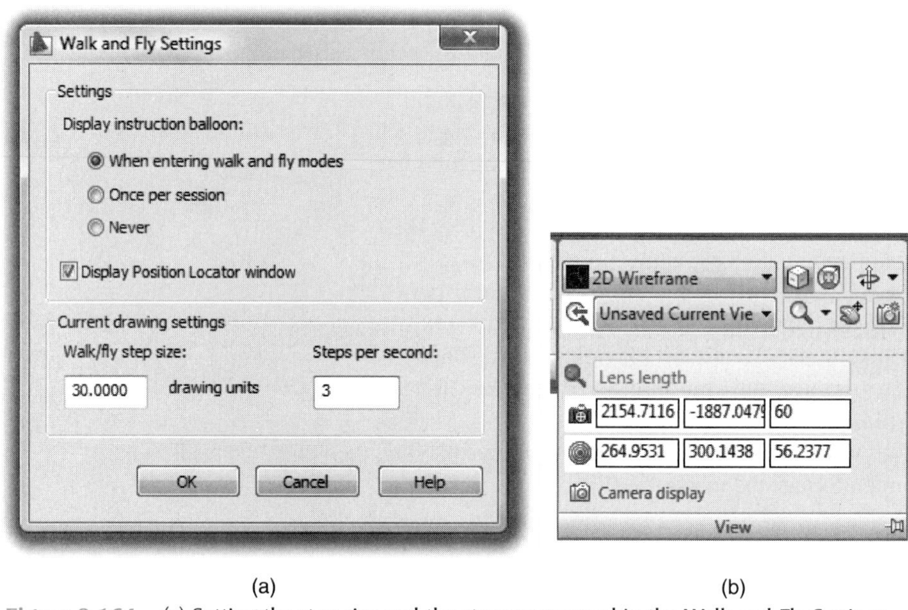

Figure 9-164 (a) Setting the step size and the steps per second in the Walk and Fly Settings dialog box; (b) setting the *Z* coordinate of the camera position

5. Select the **Front** view.
6. Set the **PERSPECTIVE** system variable to **1** by entering its name in the command prompt window.
7. Click on the corresponding icon in the **3D Navigation** toolbar to invoke the **3DDISTANCE** command. Click and drag downward in the drawing area to see the 3D model farther. Press **<Esc>** to exit the command.
8. Click on the corresponding icon in the **Animations** panel to invoke the **3DWALK** command.
9. Close the **Walk and Fly—Change to Perspective View** warning by clicking the **Change** button.
10. Click the **X** button to close the **Position Locator** window.
11. Press the **<Up arrow>** key repeatedly or keep it pressed by intervals to approach the 3D model.
12. After you have gone through the 3D model, press the **<Down arrow>** key repeatedly to move out of the 3D model.
13. With the **3DWALK** command still active, click the **Record** button and repeat the same **Walk** operation. Enter the building, go through it, and then go back outside.
14. Immediately click the **Play** button to stop recording.
15. After the animation preview finishes playing, click the **Save** button.
16. Click the **Animation Settings...** button and select the **AVI** format in the **Animation Settings** dialog box.
17. Select a location for the video file and type **Hall-Walkthrough** in the **File name** field. Click **Save** to close the dialog box and start the **Create Video** process.

18. Continue performing **3D Walk** operations. Click and drag the left button to direct the camera up and down; drag it right and left to change the walk direction. At the same time use the arrow keys to walk forward, backward, or right and left.
19. Press the **<F>** key to switch to **Fly** mode. Click and drag the left button to change the direction in which the camera will fly forward. At the same time use the arrow keys to fly forward, backward, or right and left.
20. When finished, right-click in the drawing area and select **Exit.**
21. Select the **Parallel Projection** by setting the **PERSPECTIVE** system variable to 0; enter its name in the command prompt window to do so.
22. Select the **SE Isometric** viewing point.
23. **SAVE** the drawing.
24. Using Windows Explorer, browse for the ***Hall-Walkthrough*** video file, right-click on it, and select **Play** to watch the animation.

Exercise 9-7: Recording a Motion Path Animation

1. **OPEN** ***Exercise 9-5 solved.***
2. **SAVE** the drawing **AS** ***Exercise 9-7.***
3. Select the **2D Wireframe** visual style.
4. Invoke the **3DORBIT** command to slightly change the viewing point.
5. Using a color that can be seen easily, draw the polyline highlighted in Figure 9-165. Snap to the three points shown.

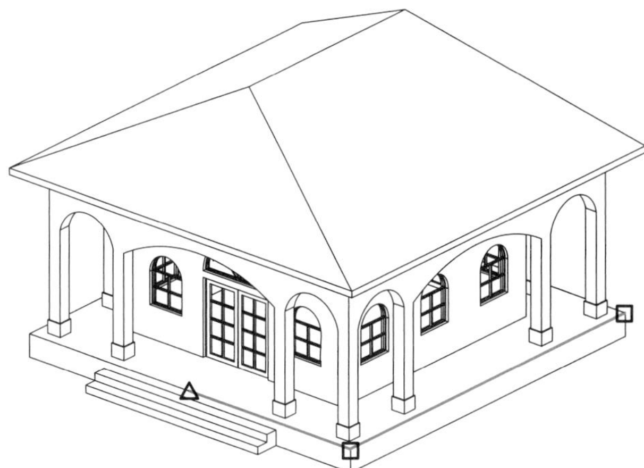

Figure 9-165 Points to specify when creating the polyline

6. Offset the polyline outward **300″**.
7. With **ORTHO** mode on, **MOVE** the inner polyline 80″ and the outer polyline **120″** along the positive direction of the *Z*-axis.
8. Select the outer polyline and stretch the grip on its rightmost endpoint **300″** along the negative *Y*-axis. The two polylines should look like Figure 9-166.

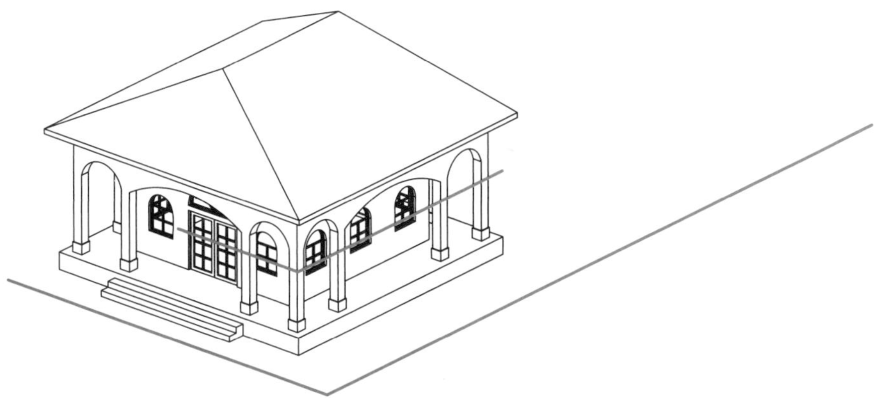

Figure 9-166 After stretching the polyline

9. Select the **Realistic** visual style.
10. Invoke the **ANIPATH** command to display the **Motion Path Animation** dialog box.
11. Under **Camera,** select **Path** and click the **Select Path** button. Select the outer polyline.
12. In the **Path Name** dialog box, type ***Outer Polyline*** in the name field and click **OK.**
13. Under **Target,** select **Path** and click the **Select Path** button. Select the inner polyline.
14. In the **Path Name** dialog box, type ***Inner Polyline*** as the name and click **OK.**
15. Set the **Duration** to **6** seconds and change the format to **AVI** (Figure 9-167). The **Number of frames** setting should automatically change to **180.**

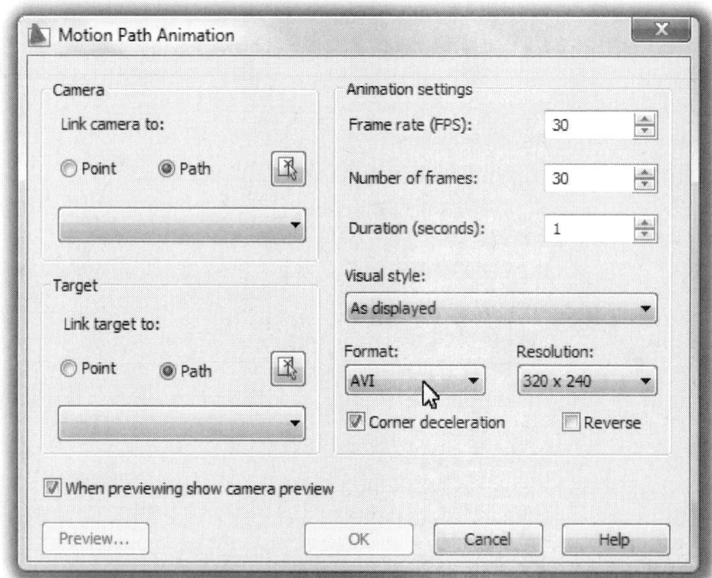

Figure 9-167 The Motion Path Animation dialog box

16. Click the **Preview** button to open the **Animation Preview** window.
17. After the preview stops, close the **Animation Preview** window.
18. In the **Motion Path Animation** dialog box, click **OK** to open the **Save As** dialog box.
19. Select a location for the video file and type **Hall-Motion Path** as the file name. Click **Save** to close the dialog box and start the **Creating Video** process.
20. **SAVE** the drawing.
21. Use Windows Explorer to browse for the ***Hall-Motion Path*** video file, right-click on it, and select **Play** to watch the animation.

Creating View Sequences with ShowMotion

With the ShowMotion tools, you can create animations that use different types of shots and transitions between them. It is a very simple tool to use, and you can use it to create professional presentations of the 3D models in model space or the drawings views in paper space.

Every time you create a new View in the **View Manager,** you are basically creating a new shot. The types of shots that can be created are **Still, Cinematic,** and **Recorded Walk** (Figure 9-168). You are required to enter a View or shot name; giving the shot a View Category allows you to define groups of shots that can later be played back together.

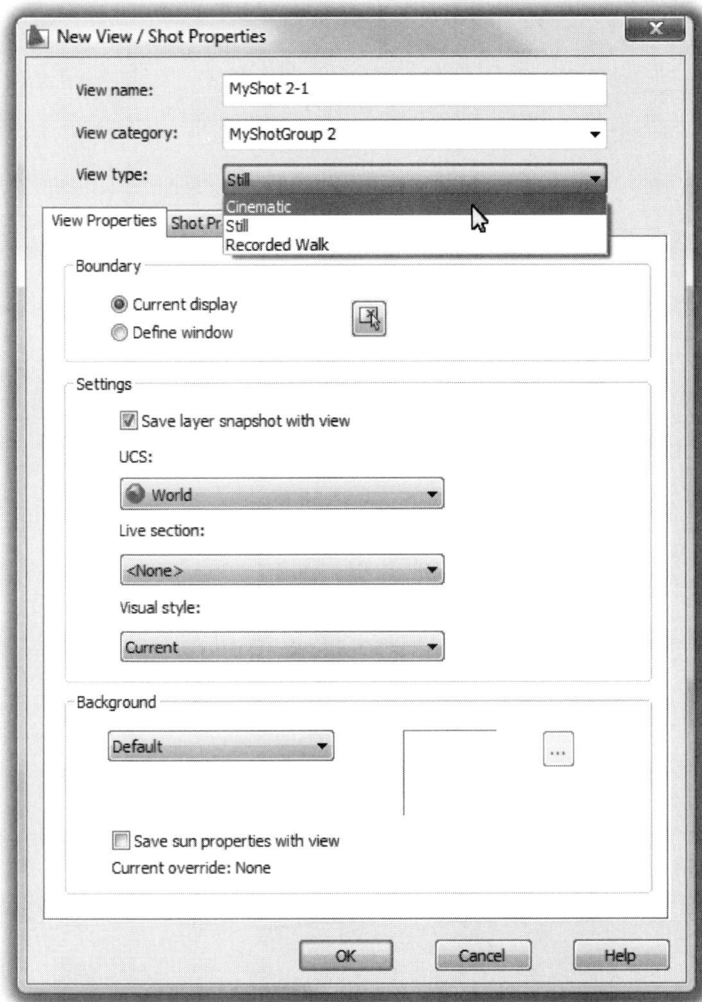

Figure 9-168 The New View/Shot Properties dialog box

In the **Shot Properties** tab, you can specify different parameters related to the behavior of this particular shot (Figure 9-169). You can select among eight different types of movements for the model space Views: Zoom In, Zoom Out, Track Left, Track Right, Crank Up, Crank Down, Look, and Orbit. For paper space Views, you can use only the Pan + Zoom type of movement. You can also set how long the shot movement will last by specifying the duration. Settings concerning the transition can also be specified here.

You can play back entire group of categories or single shots throughout the thumbnail views displayed at the bottom center of the AutoCAD window. Such thumbnails along with the controls are displayed by invoking **NAVESMOTION** command. This command can be easily invoked using the icon located in the status bar. Let's say, for example, you have created four new views or shots; MyShot 1-1 and MyShot 1-2 under the category of MyShotGroup 1, and MyShot 2-1 and MyShot 2-2 under the category of MyShotGroup 2. Once the **NAVESMOTION** command is invoked, hovering the mouse pointer over one of the categories will show you a snapshot of all the shots contained on it (Figure 9-170). You can then click inside the category you want to play. Hovering the mouse pointer over one of the shots changes the thumbnail images of the shots for the particular corresponding category to a larger scale (Figure 9-171). Clicking inside one of these shots will cause it to playback by itself. You can use the ShowMotion controls to play back the shot or sequence of shots repeatedly in the form of a loop.

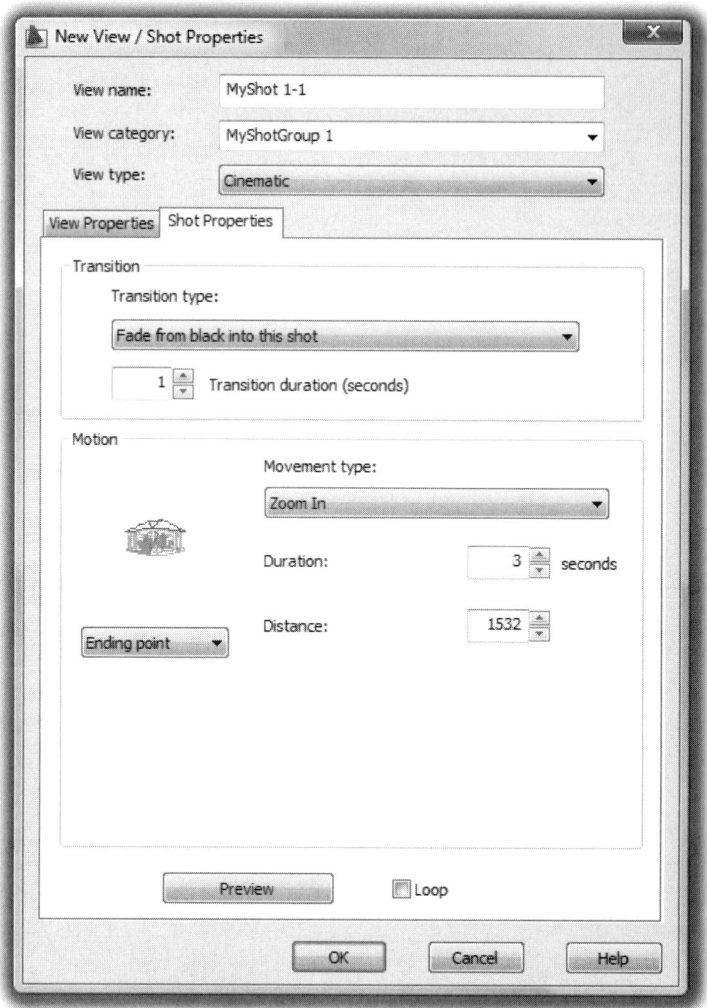

Figure 9-169 The Shot Properties tab of the New View/Shot Properties dialog box

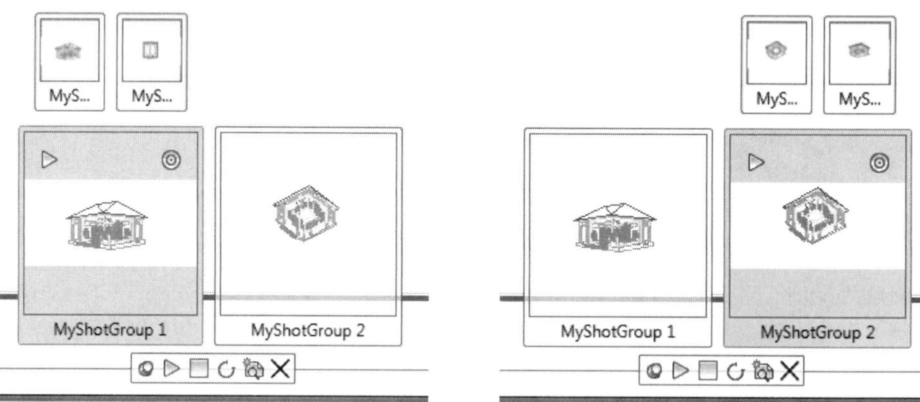

Figure 9-170 The ShowMotion thumbnails focusing on the category for playback

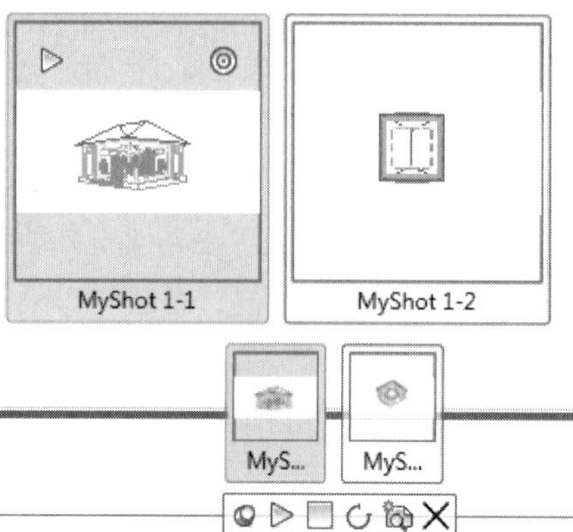

Figure 9-171 The ShowMotion thumbnails focusing on the shots of a particular category for playback individually

Creating animations is a beneficial skill for many technical disciplines, especially architecture. Although animations are not a standard type of presentation yet, firms that have a strategic modernization policy have discovered the outstanding benefits that this particular skill can bring to their organizations.

SUMMARY

After completing this chapter you should be able to create illumination effects on a 3D model by placing and modifying the different types of lights. You should also be able to create different types of materials effects, using bitmaps to make the 3D objects resemble how they look in the real world.

All these skills should enable you to generate professional-quality rendered images. Such illustrations can be used to enhance the presentation of your designs or ideas.

Most render effects are defined by attaching and adjusting bitmap files. You can use the image files contained in AutoCAD's **Textures** folder. But you can also create your own bitmap files by taking digital pictures of real objects. Most of the pictures will not even have to be edited.

Along with rendered images, you can also develop artistic illustrations by creating new visual styles. You can modify many settings that affect faces and edges to suit your presentation goal.

By creating animations, you can also generate video files for presentation purposes. Using motion paths will enable you to create very sophisticated video presentations for concept products and 3D architectural models.

CHAPTER TEST QUESTIONS

Multiple Choice

1. In which of the following cases is it impossible to create a rendered image from the 3D model?
   a. The 3D object has no material applied.
   b. The 3D model consists of a wireframe only.
   c. The 3D model contains no lights.
   d. The background has not been defined.
2. Which of the following cannot be used as a render procedure in the **Advanced Render Settings** palette?
   a. View
   b. Crop
   c. Fence
   d. Selected
3. For which of the following types of lights must you define both a location and a direction?
   a. Spot light
   b. Sun light
   c. Point light
   d. Direct light
4. Shadows are one of the key elements you need to control in a rendered image. In which of the following is it impossible to set aspects that specifically affect the way shadows are displayed?
   a. 3D objects
   b. Viewport
   c. Lights
   d. Render presets
5. Which of the following can be used to attach a material to a 3D object?
   a. Layers
   b. **Properties** palette
   c. **Materials** palette
   d. All of the above
6. Which of the following properties is the one that most affects the transparency effect on objects?
   a. Shininess
   b. Opacity
   c. Reflection
   d. Refraction index
7. When the **Walk** 3D navigation mode is activated, pressing the <**Up arrow**> key will make the camera:
   a. Move forward parallel to the *XY* plane
   b. Zoom into the 3D model
   c. Move in a direction toward the target
   d. None of the above
8. To create a material that, when applied to the 3D objects, displays specific areas of its surfaces as translucent after the rendering process, you must use a(n):
   a. Opacity map
   b. Reflection map
   c. Bump map
   d. Texture map
9. You can create animations in which:
   a. Only the camera moves
   b. Both the camera and the target move
   c. Only the target moves
   d. All of the above

Matching

Column A		Column B	
a.	**MATERIALATTACH**	1.	Creates motion path animations
b.	Bump map	2.	One of the 3D navigation modes
c.	Render Presets	3.	Opens the **Render** window
d.	**RENDERCROP**	4.	One of the face color modes in the visual styles
e.	Attenuation	5.	Creates an embossed 3D texture in the surfaces
f.	Desaturate	6.	Renders a selected crop window
g.	**RENDERWIN**	7.	Opens the **Advanced Render** palette
h.	**RPREF**	8.	Links a material to a specific layer
i.	Fly	9.	A named collection of render settings
j.	**ANIPATH**	10.	Diminishing of light intensity over distance

True or False

1. True or False: A Render Preset is a list of the last rendered images obtained from the current 3D model.
2. True or False: Any of the three lights (direct, spot, and point) can be directly selected by picking its glyph.
3. True or False: The angular difference between the hotspot and the falloff angle determines how big the transitional zone is between the fully lighted and the dark zones.
4. True or False: A material template is a predefined collection of settings that gives a material a specific appearance.
5. True or False: To use a material that you have created in a previous drawing, you can use the **Tool Palettes** as the bridge, or copy and paste an object carrying the material.
6. True or False: Woodlike materials can by created either by using a bitmap that looks like wood, or by using one of the two internally defined textures.
7. True or False: When working with the **Advanced** visual style settings, selecting the **Tint** color mode for the faces enhances the colors over the **Normal** color mode.
8. True or False: After activating the **3D Orbit** tool, you can switch to the **Walk** 3D navigation mode by pressing the number **6.**
9. True or False: You can create an animation that shows a 3D object moving and rotating throughout the 3D space to align itself with a stationary object.
10. True or False: It is not possible to define a point for both the camera and the target when creating a motion path animation.

Chapter Tutorials

Tutorial 9-1: The Bench-Vise Final Presentation

1. **OPEN** the ***Bench-Vise*** drawing created in Chapter 7.
2. **SAVE** the drawing **AS *Tutorial 9-1.***
3. Select the **Top** UCS.
4. Select the **SE Isometric** viewing point.
5. Use the **PAN** command to make some room and create the **12 × 12 × 1** board using the **BOX** command (Figure 9-172).
6. Select the **Front** view.
7. **MOVE** the board so that its top and right faces are placed flush with the faces of the *Main Body* (Figure 9-173).
8. Using **AutoTrack, MOVE** the *Pressing Plate,* the *Fastening Bolt,* and the *Handle* orthogonally up or down so that the top of the *Pressing Plate* is placed flush with the bottom face of the board (Figure 9-174).

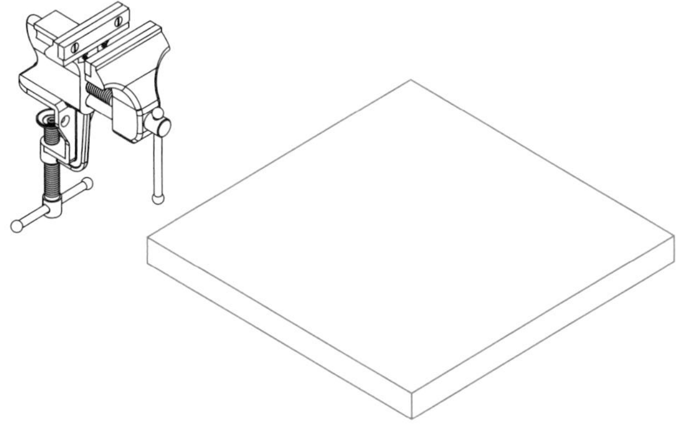

Figure 9-172 After placing the 12 × 12 × 1 board

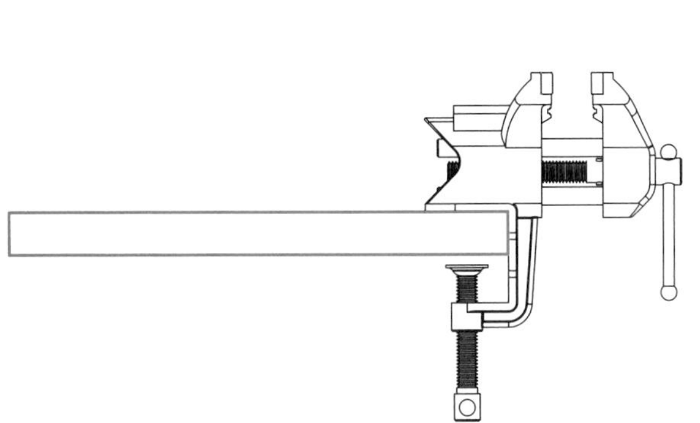

Figure 9-173 Front view after moving the board

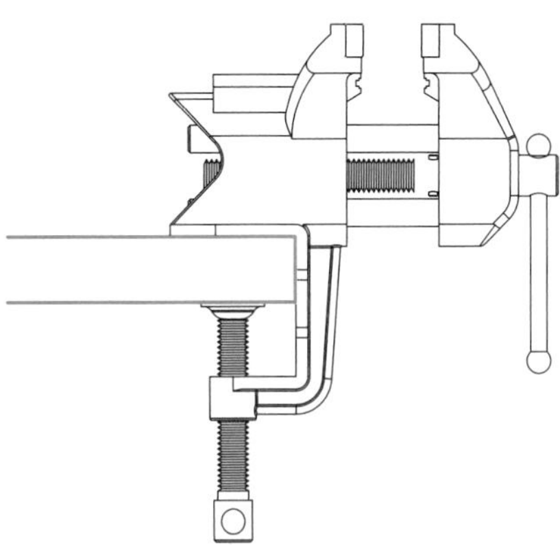

Figure 9-174 The pressing plate and the other objects are placed flush with the bottom of the board

9. Select the **Top** view.
10. Using a tracking method, **MOVE** the board orthogonally in the negative *Y*-axis direction (down) to center it with the *Bench-Vise* (Figure 9-175).

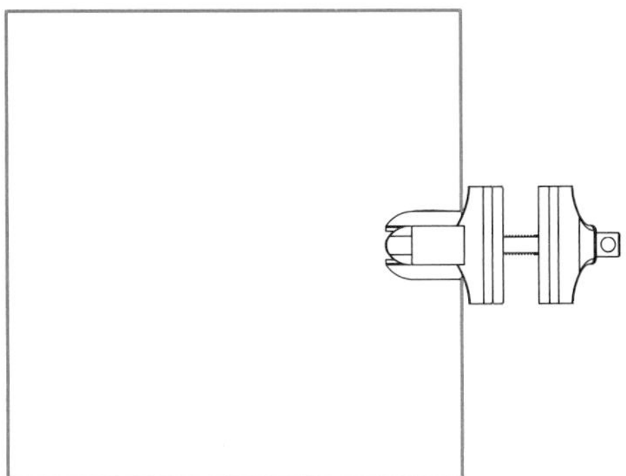

Figure 9-175 The board is centered with the bench vise

11. Select the **SE Isometric** viewing point.
12. Invoke the **MATERIALS** command to open the **Materials** palette.
13. Dock the **Materials** palette to the left of the AutoCAD window.
14. Click on the corresponding button to create a new material. Name it **board-mat.**

15. Select the **board-mat** material and select **Box** as the **Swatch Geometry** of the sample image.
16. Under **Diffuse map,** make sure **Texture map** appears in the drop-down list and click on the **Select Image** button to open the **Select Image File** dialog box.
17. Search for the **Textures** folder and select the image file named **Woods and Plastics.Finish Carpentry. Wood.Cherry.** Click the **Open** button to close the dialog box and insert the file.

FOR MORE DETAILS If you have trouble finding the **Textures** folder, refer to ***Exercise 9-4*** for tips on how to search for it.

18. Click on the **Settings** button to display only the map settings inside the **Materials** palette. Under **Scaling and Tiling**, set the units to **Fit to Gizmo**. Click the lock icon to link the **U Tile** and the **V Tile** values and specify a value of **0.250** for them (Figure 9-176). Click the **Home** button to go one level up to the material settings.

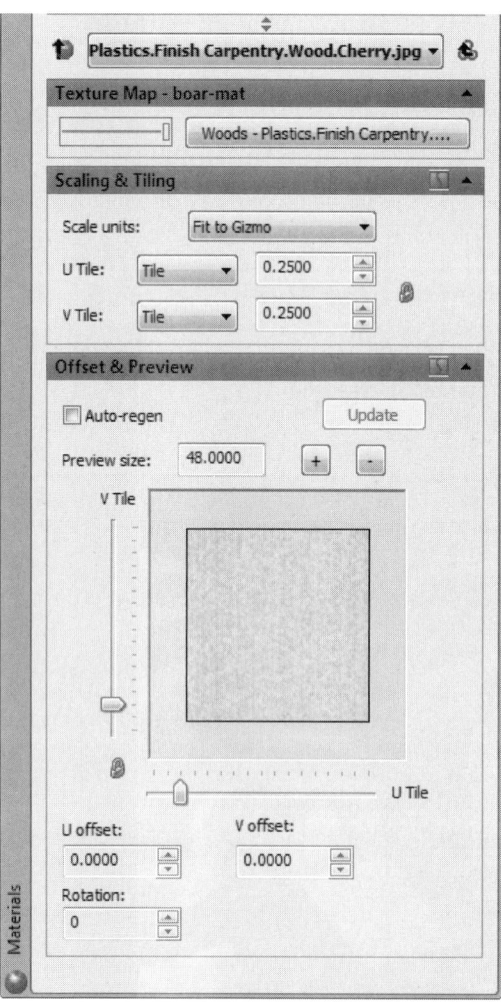

Figure 9-176 The controls for adjusting the Texture bitmap in the Material palette

19. Under **Material Offset and Preview,** set the preview size to 1 and click the **Update** button. Click the **Apply Material** button. Select the board and press **<Enter>** to end the selection.

20. Create three more materials and name them **Steel, Cast Iron,** and **Alum.**
21. Select the **Steel** material sample image and turn on the **Checkered Underlay.** Select the **Realistic Metal** type, and then select the **Metal - Polished** template. Click the **Diffuse** color box and select color **253** from the **Index Color** tab. Click **OK** to close the **Select Color** window.
22. Apply this material to all the components of the *Bench-Vise,* except the *Main Body,* the *Moving Jaw,* and the two *Aluminum Blocks*. Use Figure 9-177 as a reference catalog for the components.

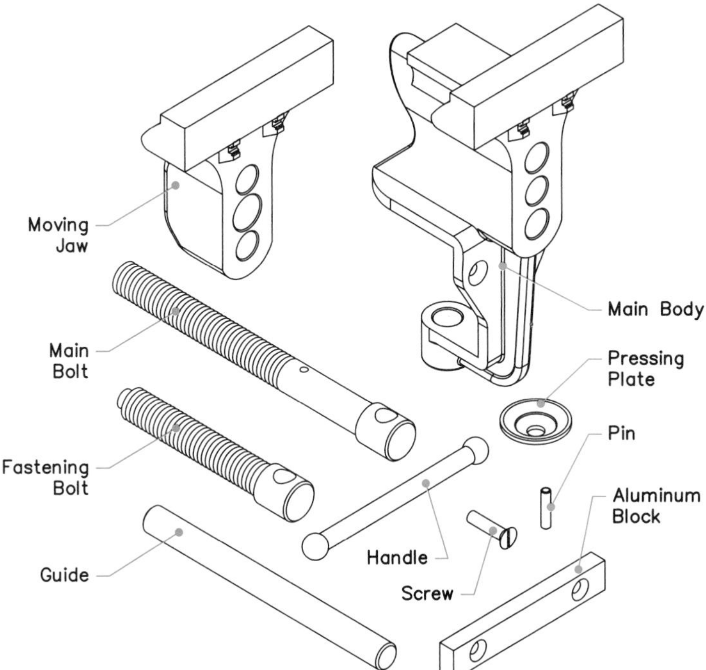

Figure 9-177 Component reference catalog

TIP When you apply the material, you can select all the components using a selection window. Then you can use the **Remove Material** button to remove the selected material from the excluded components.

23. Select the **Alum** material and select the **Realistic** type for it. Click the **Diffuse** color box and select color **254** from the **Index Color** tab. Click **OK** to close the **Select Color** window.
24. Apply this material to the two *Aluminum Blocks*.
25. Select the **Cast Iron** material, select the **Realistic** type, then select the **Paint Flat** template. Click the **Diffuse** color box, and select color **147** from the **Index Color** tab. Click **OK** to close the **Select Color** window.
26. Set its **Shininess** value to **0.**
27. Scroll to **Bump Map** and click its **Select Image** button. Select the file **Metals.Ornamental Metals.Bronze. Satin.bump** from the **Bump** folder that is located inside the **Templates** folder.
28. Set the **Bump Map** slide button to a value between **100** and **150.**

29. Apply this material to the *Main Body* and the *Moving Jaw*.
30. Use the **3D Orbit** tool to select a view close to the one shown in Figure 9-178 and draw a line that runs from the endpoint of the board to the relative point **@6,2,10** (shown highlighted in the figure).
31. Invoke the **SPOTLIGHT** command. Click **Yes** to close the warning if it shows up. When prompted for the *source location,* snap to the top endpoint of the line. Snap to the top edge's midpoint on the furthermost *Aluminum Block* when prompted for the *target location*. Press **<Enter>** to end the command. The **Spotlight** glyph should be placed as shown in Figure 9-179, pointing in the direction indicated.

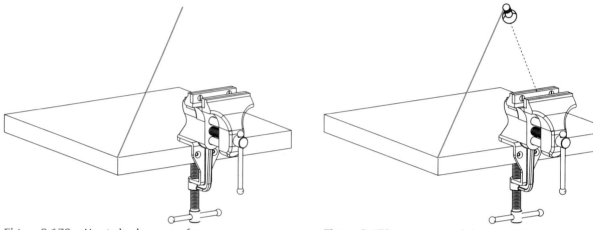

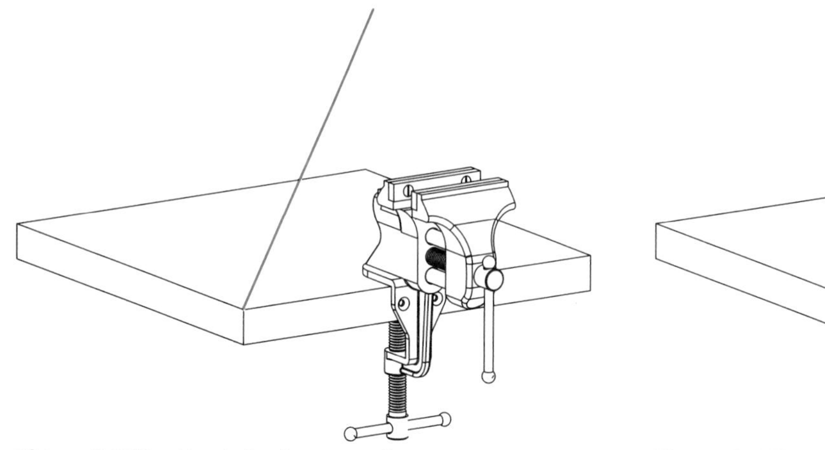

Figure 9-178 Line to be drawn as reference

Figure 9-179 Location and direction of the spot light

32. Select the **Spot** light and set its **Intensity factor** to **0.80** in the **Properties** palette.
33. Invoke the **DISTANTLIGHT** command. Click in an empty spot to specify the direction from, and then click on any point orthogonally below to specify the direction to. This will make the **Distant** light illuminate the 3D model in the negative *Z*-axis direction. Press **<Enter>** to end the command.
34. Open the **Lights in Model** window by invoking the **LIGHTLIST** command. Select the **Distantlight** from the **Lights in Model** window, and set its **Intensity factor** to **0.30** in the **Properties** palette. Turn its **Shadows** property off.
35. Set the **PERSPECTIVE** system variable to **1** to set the view in perspective mode.
36. Use the **Constrained 3D Orbit** and any other 3D navigation tool to adjust the final view to create the presentation of the *Bench-Vise*.
37. Invoke the **VIEW** command to open the **View Manager** dialog box. Click on the **New...** button. In the **New View** dialog box, type **Render View** in the **View name** field. Click **OK** to close the **New View** dialog box.
38. In the **View Manager** dialog box, select **Solid...** from the **Background override** drop-down list (Figure 9-180).
39. In the **Background** window, click on the **Color** box to open the **Select Color** dialog box. Select the color **255,255,255** in the **True Color** tab by moving the slide button all the way up. Click

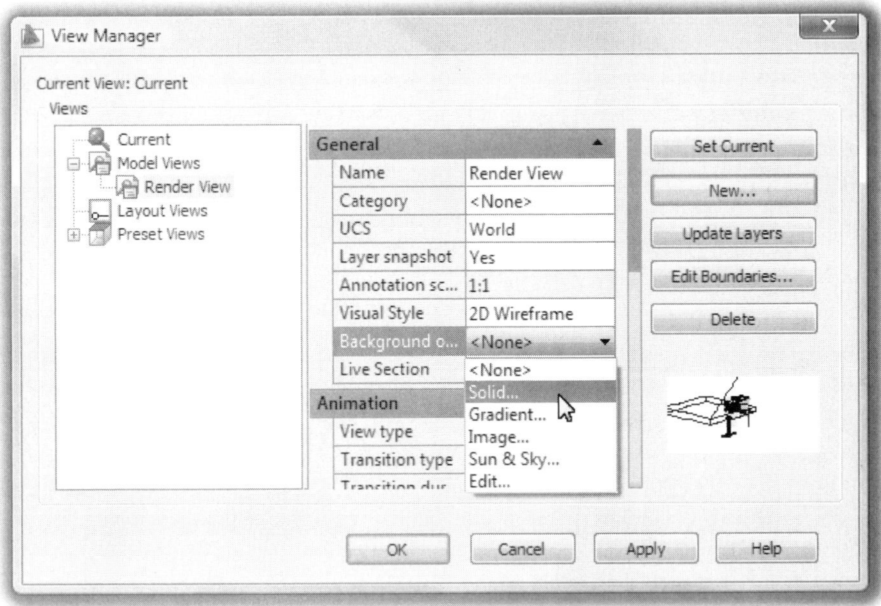

Figure 9-180 The View Manager dialog box

OK to close the **Select Color** dialog box, the **Background** window, and finally the **View Manager** dialog box.

40. Invoke the **RPREF** command to open the **Advanced Render Settings** palette. Select **View** under **Rendering Procedure** and **Viewport** under **Destination.**
41. Select **Render View** from the drop-down list located in the **View** toolbar or in the **3D Navigate** control panel.
42. Invoke the **RENDER** command. After the image is processed, it should look similar to the one in Figure 9-181.
43. **SAVE** the drawing.
44. Press the <**PrtScrn**> key to copy your entire screen to the clipboard. You can now open any imaging application such as Paint, paste the image from the clipboard, crop it, and save it for further uses or editing. This is another simple procedure for saving an image file.

Note:
To use the background you specified previously, you must select the **Named View** associated with it.

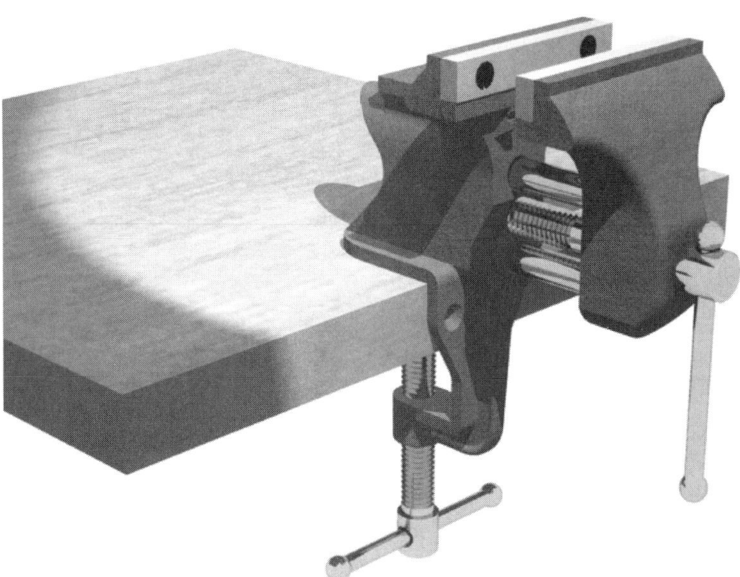

Figure 9-181 Final rendered image

Tutorial 9-2: Creating a Landscape Object

1. **OPEN** ***Exercise 9-5*** from the CD.
2. **SAVE** it **AS** ***Tutorial 9-2.***
3. Select the **SE Isometric** viewing point.
4. Select the **World** UCS.
5. Using the **3DORBIT** command, select a viewpoint similar to the one in Figure 9-182.

Figure 9-182 View to be selected with the 3DOrbit command

6. Open the **Materials** palette and create a new material. Name it *Palm.* Select the **Advanced** type for the **Palm** material. Turn **On** the **Checkered Underlay.**
7. Link the material's three colors so that only one **Color** box is shown by clicking the two **Lock** icons.
8. Move the **Shininess** slide button all the way to the right. Move the **Reflection** slide button located at the bottom all the way to the right (Figure 9-183).
9. Using Windows Explorer, **Copy** the image files **8tree14l** and **8tree14o** from the CD and **Paste** them into another folder in your computer.
10. Under **Diffuse map,** select **Texture Map** from the drop-down list and click the **Select Image** button. In the **Select Image File** dialog box, select the **8tree141** image file from the location where you previously copied it. Click **Open** to insert the file.
11. Under **Opacity** click the **Select Image** button and insert **8tree14o.**
12. Under **Diffuse map,** click the button located next to the button with the image file name. In the **Adjust Bitmap** dialog box, set both **U Tile** and **V Tile** to **1.** Under **Bitmap Scale,** select **Fit to Gizmo** and select **None** for the tiling option from the drop-down list for both tiles. Close the **Adjust Bitmap** dialog box by clicking the **Close** button.
13. Click the **Adjust scale...** button located under **Opacity.** In the **Adjust Bitmap** dialog box, repeat exactly the same settings you set for the diffuse map.
14. Select the **Front** UCS.
15. Using the **RECTANGLE** command, draw the **230** × **288** rectangle and **MOVE** it to the endpoint as shown in Figure 9-184.
16. Select the **World** UCS.
17. **ROTATE** the rectangle around the lower-left endpoint **30°.**

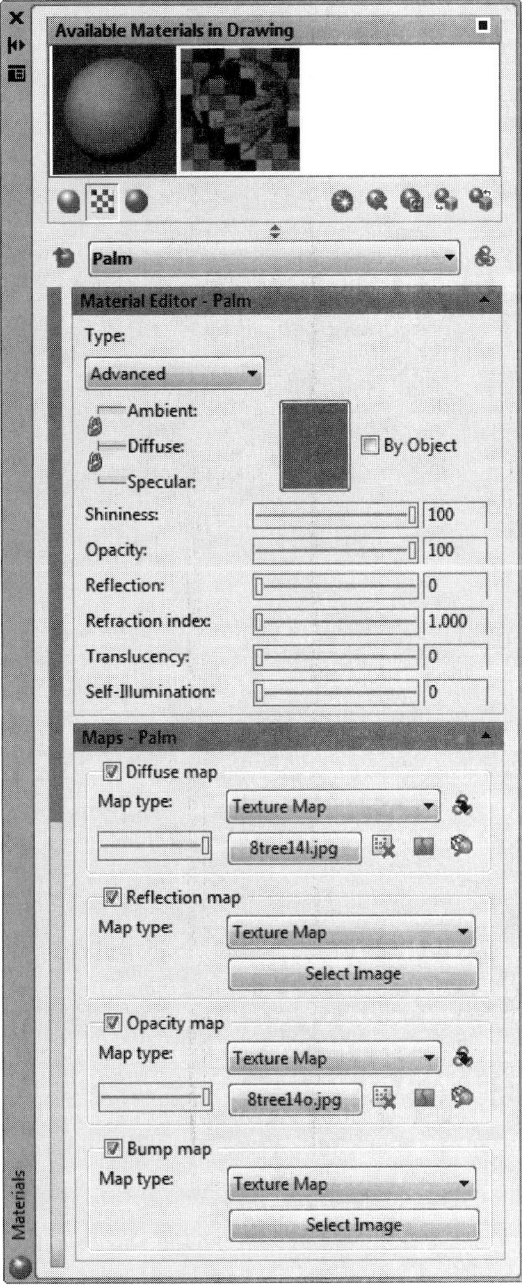

Figure 9-183 Settings to be specified in the Materials palette

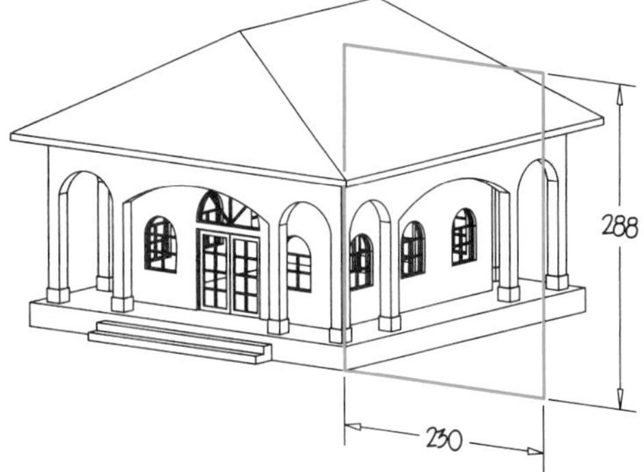

Figure 9-184 Dimensions and location used to create the rectangle

18. Place a copy of the rectangle on the midpoint of the same edge and **Scale** it down a factor of **0.75** based on its lower-left endpoint (Figure 9-185).

Figure 9-185 After scaling down the copy of the rectangle

19. **Extrude** the rectangles to the new 3D solids.
20. In the **Materials** palette, select the **Palm** material and apply it to the two 3D solids.
21. Select the **Global** material and set its **Diffuse** color **By Object.**
22. Set the **PERSPECTIVE** system variable to **1** to display a perspective view.
23. Open the **Advanced Render Settings** palette. Select **View** under **Rendering Procedure** and **Viewport** under **Destination.**
24. Open the **View Manager** dialog box. Click on the **New...** button and create a view named *Corner View.* Click **OK** to close the **New View** dialog box.
25. In the **View Manager** dialog box, select **Solid...** from the **Background override** drop-down list. Click the **Color** box In the **Background** window and select the color **255,255,255** in the **True Color** tab by moving the slide button all the way up. Click **OK** to close the **Select Color** dialog box, the **Background** window, and the **View Manager** dialog box.
26. Select **Corner View** from the drop-down list located in the **View** toolbar or in the **3D Navigate** panel.
27. Invoke the **RENDER** command. After you complete the render process, the image should look similar to the one in Figure 9-186.
28. **SAVE** the drawing.

Figure 9-186 The rendered image reveals the landscape objects

Chapter Projects

Project 9-1: Enhancing the Hall with the Landscape Objects

OPEN the drawing ***Tutorial 9-2*** and **SAVE** it **AS** ***Project 9-1.*** Enhance the rendered image by applying materials with texture to represent a tiled roof and textured walls.

Use the Sun light to create shadow effects. Create a thin 3D solid flush with the building base, big enough to receive the shadows of

Figure 9-187 The final enhanced render image

other objects in the 3D model. When finished, the rendered image should look similar to Figure 9-187.

Project 9-2: Presentation Image of the Spiral Stair

OPEN the finished drawing ***Tutorial 5-3 solved*** and **SAVE** it **AS** ***Project 9-2.*** Create a rendered image of the 3D model.

Hints for the Project

Create a material with texture that represents finished wood and apply it to the treads. Create a material that looks like shiny stainless steel and apply it to the posts and railing. For the floor, use shiny marble with the quality of reflection so that it creates a soft mirror image. Select other colors for the 3D objects around the stairs. Place some lights to illuminate the model. When finished, the rendered image should look similar to Figure 9-188.

Figure 9-188 Rendered image of a portion of the spiral stair after adding materials and light

general

Project 9-3: Two Options for Representing a Chessboard

OPEN ***Exercise 9-1*** from the CD and copy the entire table into a new drawing. **SAVE** it **AS** ***Project 9-3.*** Create two different rendered images of the 3D model. In the first rendered image, make the tabletop

Figure 9-189 Two different render effects are achieved by modifying the properties of the materials

look like an opaque chessboard. In the second one, make the tabletop look like a pane of glass with an engraved chessboard. The results should be similar to the ones in Figure 9-189.

Project 9-4: The Bench-Vise Motion Path Animation

OPEN the ***Bench-Vise Presentation*** drawing you developed in **Tutorial 9-1** and **SAVE** it **AS** ***Project 9-4.*** Create several motion path animations, using the **Realistic** visual style to show the materials.

Hints for the Project

Use a path for the camera and a point for the target, and vice versa.

Drafting Standards and Practices

Appendix

A

The American National Standards Institute (ANSI) is a nonprofit organization whose membership includes private companies. ANSI supervises the development of standards in the United States and accredits standards developed by other organizations such as the American Society of Mechanical Engineers (ASME) and the American Society of Testing Materials (ASTM), among others, as well as government agencies and corporations.

ANSI is the U.S. standards body for the International Standards Organization (ISO). Standards bodies from other member countries along with major corporations form this organization in which worldwide standards are produced.

In the United States, drafting standards are published and set mainly by the American Society of Mechanical Engineers (ASME) and, more recently, by the International Standards Organization (ISO). For example, the ASME Y14.5M-1994 (sometimes referred to as ANSI/ASME Y14.5M-1994) controls geometric dimensioning and tolerancing standards for the United States, whereas ISO 8015 is the equivalent international standard that controls fundamental tolerancing principles.

Although the standards organizations endorse and recommend the resources and principles necessary for complete standardization, today engineering drafting practices are not followed equally by all companies. Because of the use of computers, following drafting standards is not enough to ensure proper standardization in engineering drawings. Additionally, CAD standards within the company need to be properly implemented and used. Whether a particular element is made to comply with rules and principles stated in the ASME and ISO drafting standards or with accepted industry practice, the following list can serve as a guideline for elements a company needs to consider when developing its CAD standards:

- Standard sheet sizes
- Drawing formats and title blocks
- Drawing views
- Standard drawing scales
- Line conventions
- Lettering

Standard Sheet Sizes

Sheet sizes and formats recommended in the United States for engineering drawings and documents are based on two ANSI/ASME standards:

- **Y14.1-1995,** Decimal Inch Drawing Sheet Size and Format
- **Y14.1M-1995,** Metric Drawing Sheet Size and Format

Inch drawing sheet sizes are based on the dimensions of the commercial letter size, also known as *ANSI A* (8.50 × 11.00) and metric drawing sheet sizes are based on the *ISO A4* size that has a width-height ratio of 1 to $\sqrt{2}$. Subsequent standard sizes are multiples of the ANSI A or ISO A4 size (Figure A-1). The relationship between the different sizes allows you to fold drawings into the base letter size or the A4 size for storage or correspondence, as well as avoid unnecessary waste by cutting sheets from rolls of paper. Table A-1 shows a complete list of paper sizes.

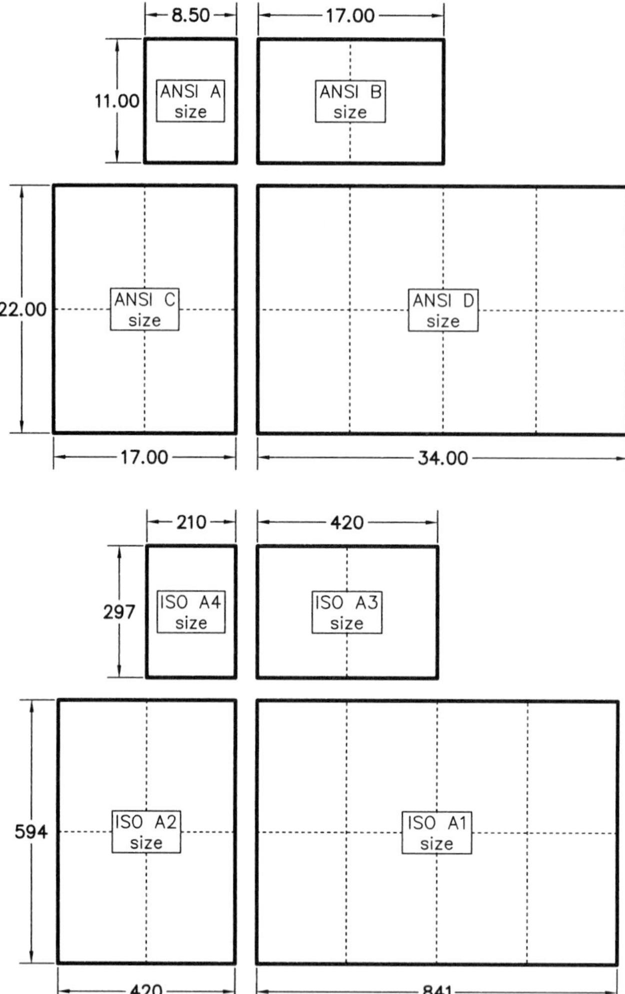

Figure A-1 ANSI and ISO paper sizes are obtained from multiples of the letter and A4 sizes, respectively

Table A-1 Standard of paper sizes in the landscape orientation.

ANSI Sheet Sizes (inches)	
A	8.50 X 11.00
B	11.00 X 17.00
C	17.00 X 22.00
D	22.00 X 34.00
E	34.00 X 44.00

ISO Sheet Sizes (mm)	
A4	210 X 297
A3	297 X 420
A2	420 X 594
A1	594 X 841
A0	841 X 1189

Selecting which sheet size to use in a drawing depends on several factors. One of these factors is the sizes supported by the device that will be used to print the document. Other factors such as document storage, amount of information contained, and company-specific practices might also influence the size used.

Drawing Formats and Title Blocks

A drawing format represents both the sheet size and the drawing border. The area inside the drawing border is the area of paper that actually will be occupied by the drawing (Figure A-2). Most printing devices can print only within a certain area. When you create a drawing format, the

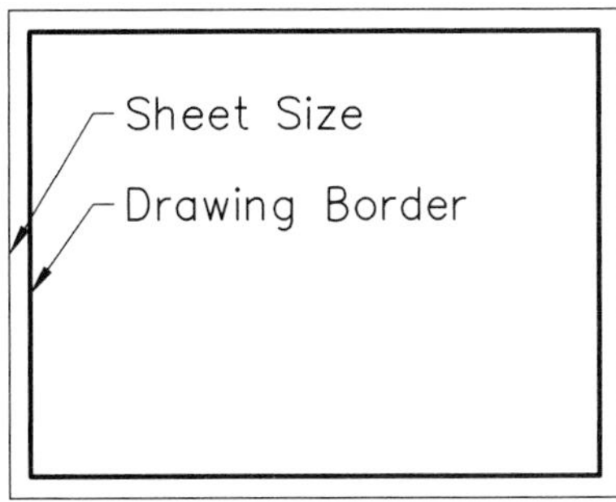

Figure A-2 A drawing format is made up of the paper area with the drawing border inside

rectangle representing the drawing border must be smaller than the dimensions of the printable area. This ensures that the entire drawing will be printed out. Whenever possible, the offset value should be 0.25 for the ANSI A size and 0.50 for the ANSI B and ANSI C sizes. Other sizes of paper can use higher values.

The title block is probably the least standardized element of the drawing. One of the most commonly used formats for both the title block and the revision block is shown in Figure A-3 (in the ANSI C size). The company's CAD standards should stipulate that the same title block and revision block be used for all sheet sizes. With the AutoCAD® program it is possible to create blocks that contain attributes. This object facilitates the entering of data in the title and revision blocks and ensures a better uniformity.

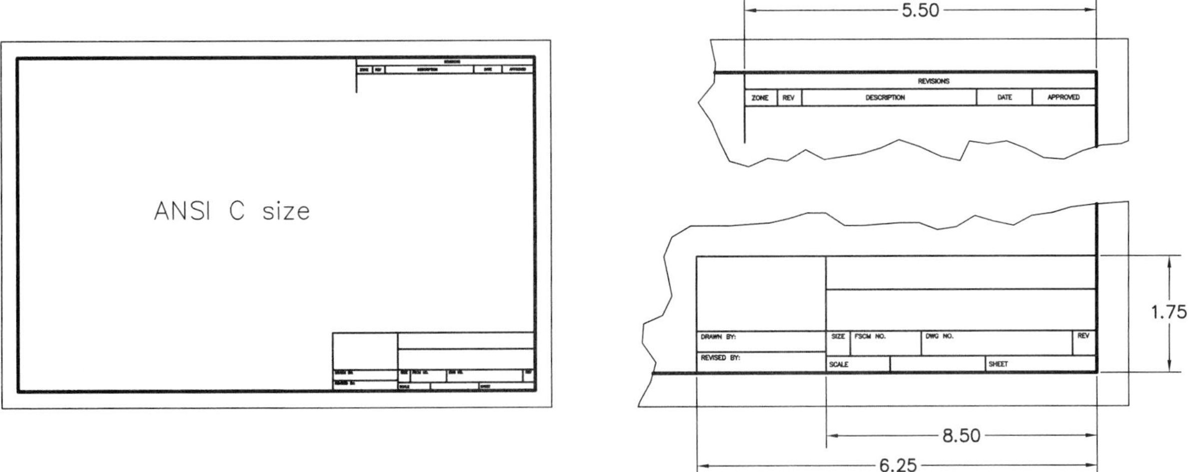

Figure A-3 One of the formats most commonly used for title blocks and revision blocks in mechanical drawings

Drawing Views

A drawing must contain as many views as needed to show most clearly the geometry of the objects and the possible ways of reproducing it. These views may include the three standard orthographic projected views, sections/elevations, auxiliary, details, or 3D views. There are two ways of showing the orthographic projected views; some engineering drawings show the corresponding symbol (Figure A-4):

- **Third Angle Projection:** The Front view is displayed at the lower left, the Top view is shown at the top, and the Right view is shown at the right. This method is primarily used in the United States and is based on the fact that the view you look at is placed on the same side as the one from which you are viewing it.
- **First Angle Projection:** The Front view is displayed at the upper left, the Top view is shown at the bottom, and the Right view is shown at the left. This method is primarily used for metric drawings and is based on the fact that the view you look at is placed on the side opposite from where you are viewing it.

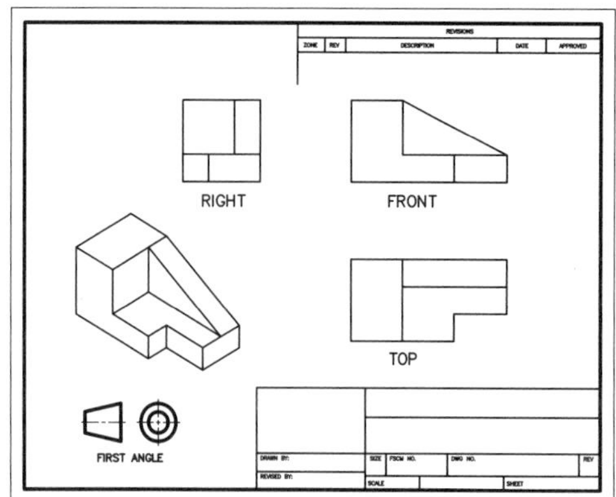

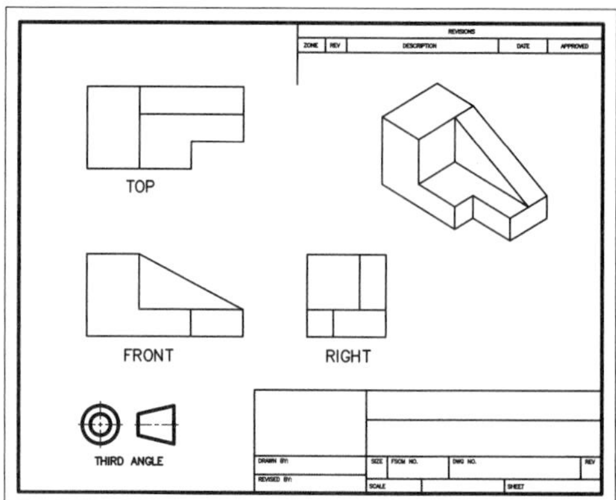

Figure A-4 The third and first angle projections are typically used to set up the drawing views in ANSI and ISO drawings, respectively

Standard Drawing Scales

A scale represents the ratio of the object's size in the drawing to its real size. The scale used to prepare a drawing is usually selected to achieve the best possible usage of the sheet's drawing area. A properly selected scale avoids excessive gathering of information or excessive waste of paper. Drawing scales are either full, reducing, or enlarging scales.

The scales of inch drawings are based on fractions of an inch, and can be denoted in two different ways: as a ratio (e.g., 1:4) for scales up to 1:8, or as an inch amount to a foot (e.g., 1/4″ = 1′-0″) for smaller scale ratios. Regardless of the type of notation used, a scale always reflects a ratio. For example, the scale 1:4 has a ratio of 1/4, which means that the object is reduced to one quarter of its original size in the drawing. The ratio of the scale 1/4″ = 1′-0″ is 1/48; an object shown at this scale is reduced to one forty-eighth of its original size. The inverse of the ratio is determined by finding how many times the inch amount fits into a foot. Because 1 inch has four quarters of an inch, then 1 foot has 4 × 12 = 48 quarters of an inch. The standard scales are shown in Table A-2 in their common notation, as well as the corresponding ratios.

Because objects need to have relatively large reductions in architectural drawings, the scales used are usually in the "inch amount to a foot" notation. Mechanical drawings, on the other hand, tend to use the ratio scales. Large machinery drawings, however, may require bigger scales.

The scales of metric drawings use only a ratio notation based on decimal places. The standard scales are shown below:

- Full: 1:1
- Enlargement: 2:1, 5:1, 10:1
- Reduction: 1:2, 1:5, 1:10, 1:50, 1:100; 1:200

Table A-2 ANSI standard drawing scales and their corresponding ratios.

Inch Scales		Ratio
Enlargement	Reduction	
8:1		8
4:1		4
2:1		2
1:1 (FULL)		1
	1:2	1/2
	1:4	1/4
	1:8	1/8
	1″ = 1′–0″	1/12
	3/4″ = 1′–0″	1/16
	1/2″ = 1′–0″	1/24
	1/4″ = 1′–0″	1/48
	1/8″ = 1′–0″	1/96
	1/16″ = 1′–0″	1/192

Knowing the ratio of the scale used is as important as selecting the proper scale. Properly implemented CAD standards should use the scale ratio values to determine the size of texts, dimensions, and symbols for the different scales.

Line Conventions

The ANSI/ASME Y14.2M-1992 standard establishes the line and lettering practices recommended for preparing engineering drawings. Lines should be shown in two different widths in printed engineering drawings:

- THICK: 0.6 mm (0.024″)
- THIN: 0.3 mm (0.012″)

The THICK width value is used for visible lines, cutting plane lines, viewing plane lines, and short break lines. The THIN width value is used for hidden lines, section (hatch) lines, centerlines, long break lines, phantom lines, and all the dimension lines (Figure A-5).

With the AutoCAD program you can control drawing line widths by using either color-dependent plot styles or named plot styles. A company's CAD standards can include a set of lineweights specified either by colors or by layers to obtain the proper line width. AutoCAD linetypes are defined according to standards in the *acad.lin* and *acadiso.lin* files. Figure A-6 shows the standard proportions of the most commonly used linetypes, based on a common segment. This illustration can be used as a guideline to determine the LTSCALE values, either globally or in particular objects. Drawings that use proper linetype proportions will look more professional and understandable.

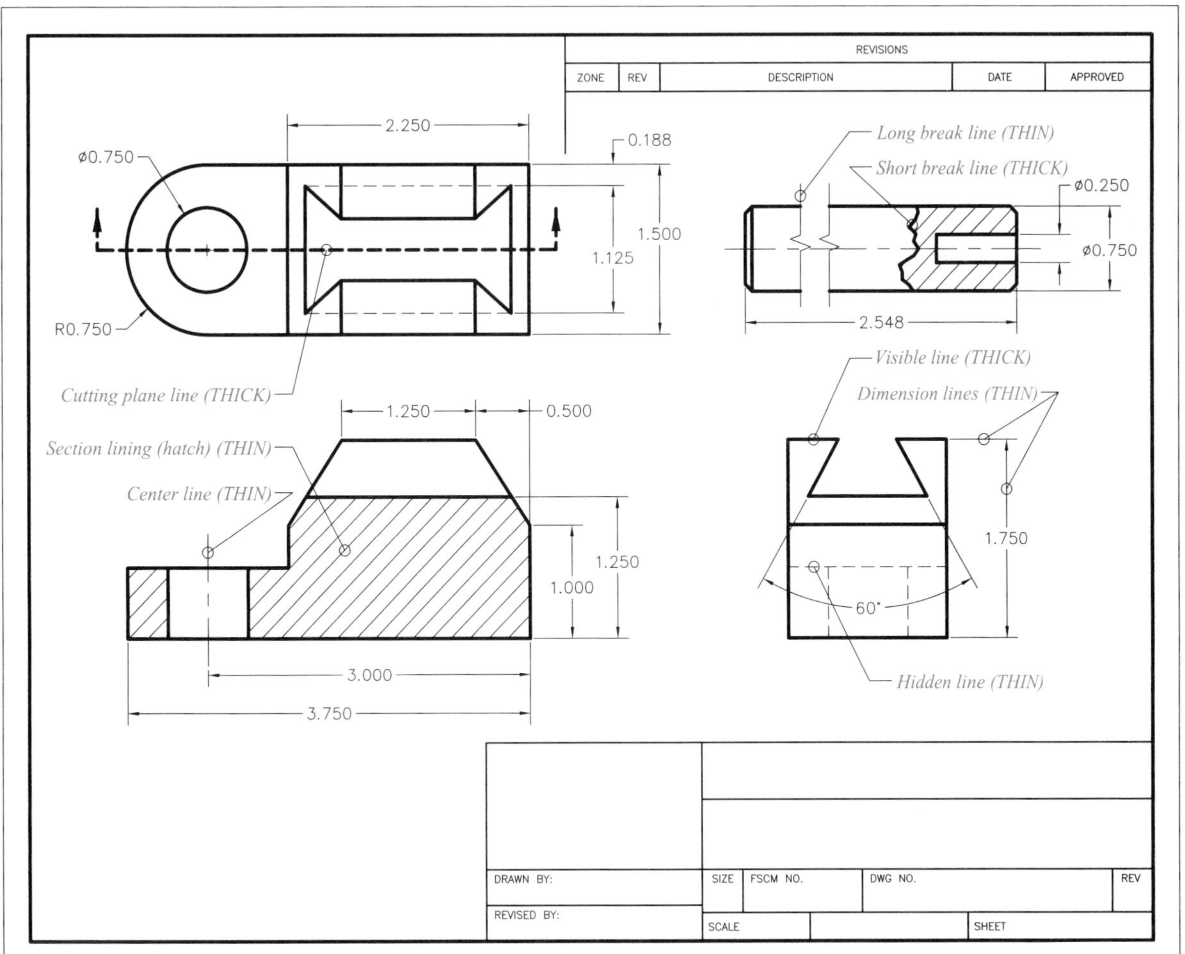

Figure A-5 Examples of ANSI standard line conventions

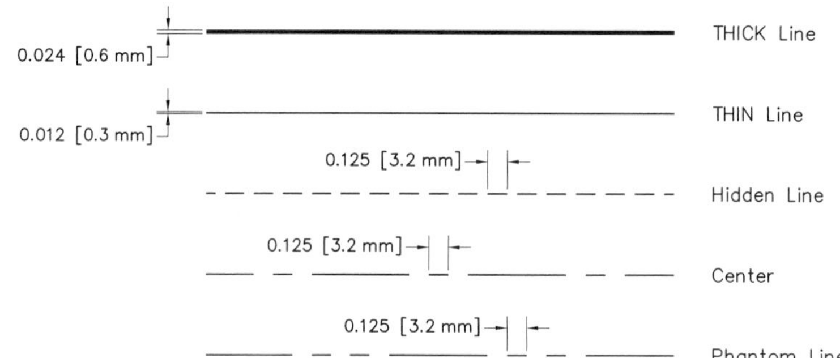

Figure A-6 Correct use of linetype proportions according to ANSI/ASME standards

The lining or hatching used to denote cross sections in drawings is also standardized. Figure A-7 shows the hatch symbols used for the most common materials.

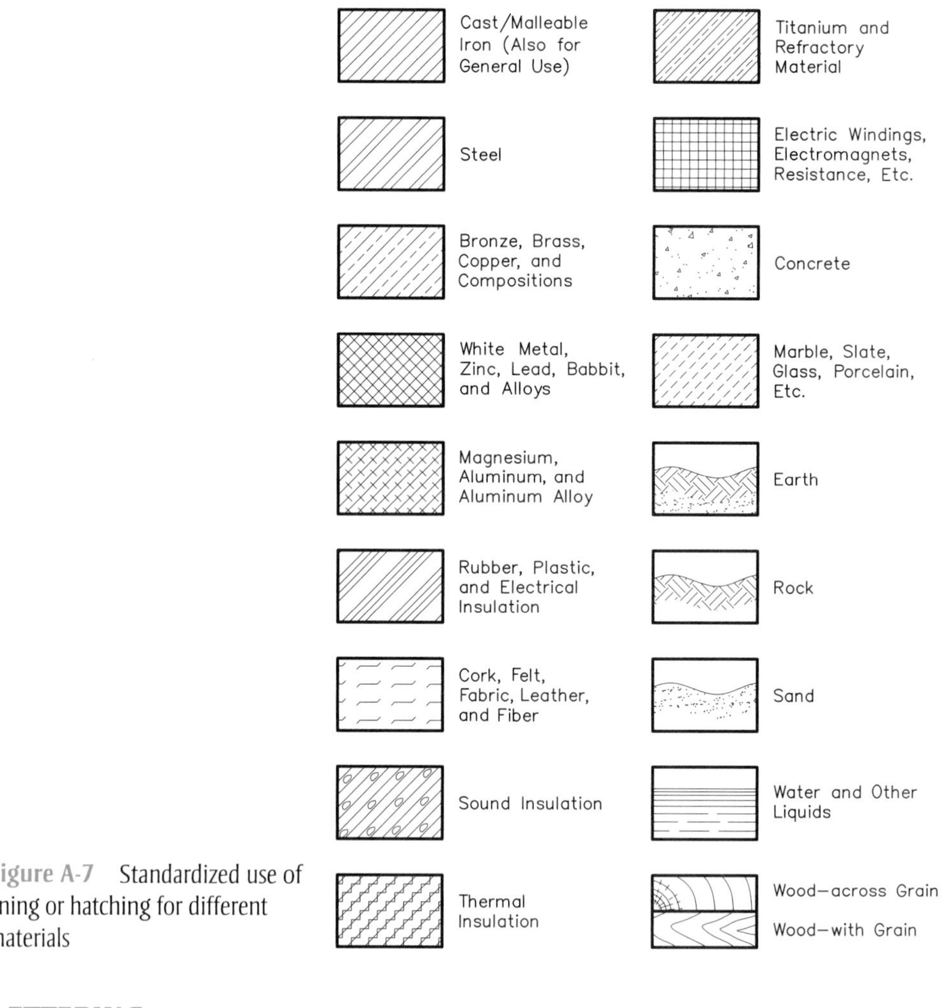

Figure A-7 Standardized use of lining or hatching for different materials

LETTERING

The consistency of lettering height in engineering drawings, regardless of the scale used and the nature of the object (dimension or text), is probably the most critical part of the standardization effort. The development of a company's CAD standards can also help accomplish this important task. A good starting point is to determine the exact letter size desired on the plotted/printed drawing. In inch drawings, the most common letter size for dimensions and notes in general is 1/8. This size of lettering is easily read by operators, and when reduced in copies for faxing, is still legible. A different size might also be used depending on specific needs. Because the scale ratios used in inch drawings are fractions, it is convenient to reduce or enlarge the size of the lettering by fractions as well (e.g., 1/16, 1/32, or 1/64).

A company's CAD standards should include text and dimension styles that can be used in a drawing depending on the scales used. This will provide control of the **Text Height** property in text entities and the overall scale for features of dimension entities (Figure A-8).

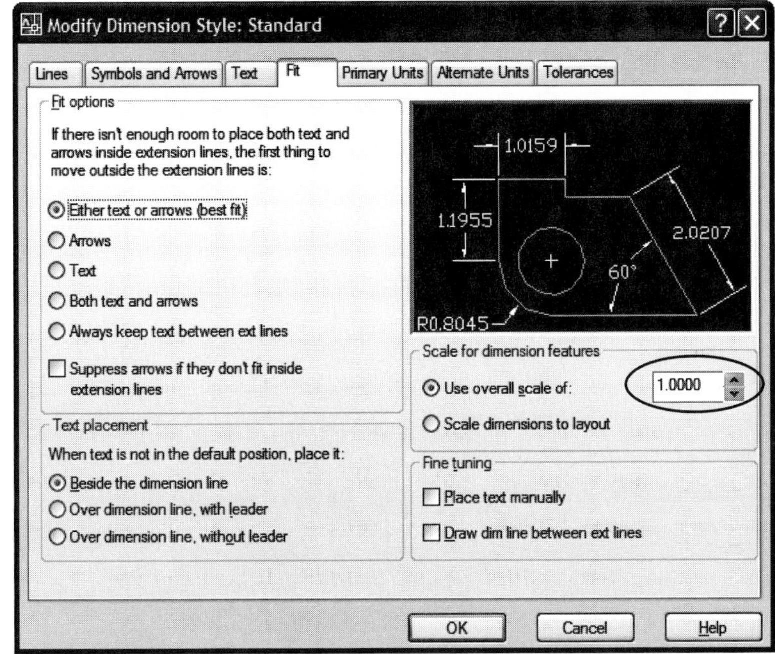

Figure A-8 Location of the overall scale window in the Modify Dimension Style: Standard dialog box

The text height used in a particular scale should be based on the inverse of the scale ratio:

$$\text{Text Height} = \text{Letter Size} \times \frac{1}{\text{Ratio}}$$

For dimensions, the overall scale used in a particular scale should be based on the inverse of the scale ratio and the actual text height used in the dimension style:

$$\text{Overall Scale} = \frac{\text{Letter Size}}{\text{Text Height (Dimension)}} \times \frac{1}{\text{Ratio}}$$

Table A-3 shows the text height and overall scale that you would have to use if the desired letter size is 1/8 and the text height in the dimension style is set to 1/8 as well. Modifying the text height in the dimension style requires modifying all other features in the dimensions to maintain their proportion. You can use the same approach with metric drawings when developing the company's CAD standards.

Table A-3 Text height and overall scale according to the scale ratio, based on 1/8″ printed letter height.

Inch Scales	Ratio	Text Height (inches)	Dimension Overall Scale (Using 1/8 Text Height)
8:1	8	1/64	1/8
4:1	4	1/32	1/4
2:1	2	1/16	1/2
1:1	1	1/8	1
1:2	1/2	1/4	2
1:4	1/4	1/2	4
1:8	1/8	1	8
1″ = 1′–0″	1/12	1 1/2	12
3/4″ = 1 –0″	1/16	2	16
1/2″ = 1′–0″	1/24	3	24
1/4″ = 1′–0″	1/48	6	48
1/8″ = 1′–0″	1/96	12	96
1/16″ = 1′–0″	1/192	24	192

Appendix B

COMMAND REFERENCE

The list below provides brief definitions of the AutoCAD® commands. You can find detailed explanation about some of these commands, especially the ones related to 3D work, in this text. For more details about other commands, you can use the AutoCAD program's **Help** menus.

3D	Creates polygon meshes and polyface meshes that look like 3D primitives such as boxes, cones, and spheres.
3DALIGN	Aligns objects with other objects in 2D and 3D.
3DARRAY	Creates both rectangular and polar 3D arrays.
3DCLIP	Opens the **Adjust Clipping Planes** window, allowing you to manipulate the clipping planes.
3DCONFIG	Provides 3D graphics system configuration settings.
3DCORBIT	Launches **3D Orbit** mode and allows you to set objects in continuous orbital movement.
3DDISTANCE	Starts the interactive 3D view and allows you to adjust the camera distance.
3DDWF	Creates a 3D DWF file from selected objects in the 3D model.
3DFACE	Creates a three- or four-sided 3D face object.
3DFLY	Starts the **Fly** 3D Navigation mode, allowing you to fly through the model in the viewing direction.
3DFORBIT	Launches **3D Orbit** mode and allows you to select any viewing point by freely orbiting around the objects.
3DMESH	Creates M-open and N-open polygon meshes.
3DMOVE	Displays the move grip tool in a 3D view and moves objects a specified distance in a specified direction.
3DORBIT	Launches **3D Orbit** mode constrained by the *Z*-axis.
3DORBITCTR	Allows you to specify a new center of rotation in **3D Orbit** view.
3DPAN	Starts the interactive 3D view and enables you to drag the view horizontally and vertically.
3DPOLY	Creates a 3D polyline through the 3D space.
3DROTATE	Allows you to rotate the selected objects around an imaginary axis parallel to the current *X*-, *Y*-, or *Z*-axis.
3DSIN	Imports a 3D Studio (*.3ds) file.
3DSWIVEL	Starts the interactive 3D view and allows you to change the target by swiveling the camera.
3DWALK	Starts the **Walk** 3D navigation mode, allowing you to walk through the model with the camera restrained to a distance above the *XY* plane of the WCS.

3DZOOM	Allows you to perform zoom operations in the current view.
ABOUT	Displays information about AutoCAD.
ACISIN	Imports the selected ACIS file containing 3D solids and regions.
ACISOUT	Exports selected 3D solids, surfaces, and regions to an ACIS file format.
ACTRECORD	Starts the **Action Recorder.**
ACTSTOP	Stops the **Action Recorder** and provides the option of saving the recorded actions to an action macro file.
ACTUSERINPUT	Inserts a request for user input into an action macro.
ACTUSERMESSAGE	Inserts a user message into an action macro.
ADCCLOSE	Closes the **DesignCenter** palette.
ADCENTER	Opens the **DesignCenter** palette.
ADCNAVIGATE	Opens the **DesignCenter** palette and allows you to specify a path.
ALIGN	Performs movements and rotations to align the selected objects from the base set of points to the specified destination set of points.
AMECONVERT	Converts AME solid models to AutoCAD 3D solid objects.
ANIPATH	Creates animations by moving the camera, the path, or both along a path predefined in a 3D model.
ANNORESET	Resets the location of all scale representations for an annotative object to that of the current scale representation.
ANNOUPDATE	Updates existing annotative objects to match the current properties of their styles.
APERTURE	Controls the size of the object snap target box.
APPLOAD	Loads and unloads applications and defines applications loaded in the Startup Suite.
ARC	Creates an arc.
ARCHIVE	Packages the current sheet set files to be archived.
AREA	Returns the area and perimeter of specified corners or selected object.
ARRAY	Creates rectangular and polar arrayed copies of selected objects.
ARX	Loads, unloads, and provides information about ObjectARX applications.
ATTACHURL	Attaches hyperlinks to objects or areas in a drawing.
ATTDEF	Creates an attribute definition.
ATTDISP	Controls global settings regarding the visibility of attributes in a drawing.
ATTEDIT	Changes attribute information.
ATTEXT	Extracts the data of the attribute information text associated with a block into a file.
ATTIPEDIT	Changes the textual content of an attribute within a block.
ATTREDEF	Redefines the attributes of a selected block.
ATTSYNC	Updates the block instances with the current attributes defined.
AUDIT	Checks for errors in a drawing and attempts to correct them.
AUTOPUBLISH	Publishes drawings to DWF or DWFx files automatically to the location specified.

BACKGROUND	Sets up the background for your view.
BACTION	Creates an action in a dynamic block definition inside the block editor.
BACTIONSET	Specifies the selected set of objects associated with an action in a dynamic block definition.
BACTIONTOOL	Adds an action to a dynamic block definition.
BASE	Sets the insertion base point for the current drawing.
BASSOCIATE	Associates an action with a parameter in a dynamic block definition.
BATTMAN	Edits attribute properties of a block definition.
BATTORDER	Specifies the order of attributes for a block.
BAUTHORPALETTE	Opens the block authoring palettes in the block editor.
BAUTHORPALETTECLOSE	Closes the block authoring palettes in the block editor.
BCLOSE	Closes the block editor.
BCYCLEORDER	Changes the cycling order of grips for a dynamic block reference.
BEDIT	Opens the **Edit Block Definition** dialog box and then the block editor.
BGRIPSET	Creates, deletes, or resets grips associated with a parameter.
BHATCH	Fills an enclosed area or selected objects with a hatch pattern or gradient fill.
BLIPMODE	Controls the display of temporary marker blips.
BLOCK	Creates a block definition from objects you select.
BLOCKICON	Generates preview images for blocks displayed in **DesignCenter.**
BLOOKUPTABLE	Displays or creates a lookup table for a dynamic block definition.
BMPOUT	Creates a BMP file from selected objects.
BOUNDARY	Creates regions or polylines from areas enclosed by other coplanar objects.
BOX	Creates a box-shaped 3D solid.
BPARAMETER	Adds a parameter with grips to a dynamic block definition.
BREAK	Breaks the selected curved object between two points or at a point.
BREP	Removes the history from 3D solids, turning them into basic representation 3D solids.
BROWSER	Launches the default web browser.
BSAVE	Saves the current block definition inside the block editor.
BSAVEAS	Saves a copy of the current block definition under a new name.
BVHIDE	Makes objects invisible in the current visibility state or in all visibility states in a dynamic block definition.
BVSHOW	Makes objects visible in the current visibility state or in all visibility states in a dynamic block definition.
BVSTATE	Creates, sets, or deletes a visibility state in a dynamic block.
CAL	Evaluates mathematical and geometric expressions.
CAMERA	Creates camera objects, saving a camera and target location as a named view.
CHAMFER	Bevels the edges of 3D objects or adds an inclined line between two other lines.

CHANGE	Changes the properties of selected objects.
CHECKSTANDARDS	Checks the current drawing for standards violations according to a Standards file.
CHPROP	Changes the properties of an object.
CHSPACE	Transfers objects from model space to paper space, or vice versa, through a floating viewport.
CIRCLE	Creates a circle.
CLASSICLAYER	Manages layer and layer properties.
CLEANSCREENOFF	Restores the display of toolbars and dockable windows (excluding the command line).
CLEANSCREENON	Clears the screen of toolbars and dockable windows (excluding the command line).
CLOSE	Closes the current drawing.
CLOSEALL	Closes all open drawings.
COLOR	Sets the color property for new objects.
COMMANDLINE	Displays the command line.
COMMANDLINEHIDE	Hides the command line.
COMPILE	Compiles shape files and PostScript font files into SHX files.
CONE	Creates a cone-shaped 3D solid with a circular or elliptical base.
CONVERT	Optimizes 2D polylines and associative hatches created in AutoCAD Release 13 or earlier.
CONVERTCTB	Converts a color-dependent plot style table (CTB) to a named plot style table (STB).
CONVERTOLDLIGHTS	Converts lights created in previous releases to lights in AutoCAD 2007 format.
CONVERTOLDMATERIALS	Converts materials created in previous releases to materials in AutoCAD 2007 format.
CONVERTPSTYLES	Converts the current drawing to either named or color-dependent plot styles.
CONVTOSOLID	Converts polylines and circles with thickness to 3D solids.
CONVTOSURFACE	Converts closed objects and open thickened objects to surfaces.
COPY	Creates copies of selected objects.
COPYBASE	Copies selected objects to the clipboard with a specified base point.
COPYCLIP	Copies selected objects or text in any window to the clipboard.
COPYHIST	Copies the history of the command line text to the clipboard.
COPYLINK	Copies the current view to the clipboard to be linked to other OLE applications.
COPYTOLAYER	Copies one or more objects to another layer.
CUI	Manages customization of workspaces, toolbars, menus, shortcut menus, and keyboard shortcuts.
CUIEXPORT	Exports customized settings.
CUIIMPORT	Imports customized settings.
CUILOAD	Loads a CUI file.
CUIUNLOAD	Unloads a CUI file.
CUSTOMIZE	Opens the **Customize** window to mange palettes and tool palette groups.
CUTCLIP	Copies objects to the clipboard, removing them from the drawing.
CYLINDER	Creates a cylinder-shaped 3D solid with a circular or elliptical base and top.

DATAEXTRACTION	Exports object property, block attribute, and drawing information to a data extraction table or to an external file and specifies a data link to an Excel spreadsheet.
DATALINK	Displays the **Data Link Manager** dialog box.
DATALINKUPDATE	Updates data to or from an established external data link.
DBCONNECT	Provides an interface to external database tables.
DBLIST	Lists database information for each object in the drawing.
DDEDIT	Allows editing of single-line text, dimension text, attribute definitions, and feature control frames.
DDPTYPE	Allows specifying of the display style and the size of point objects.
DDVPOINT	Changes the 3D viewing direction.
DELAY	Sets the delay time between operations within a script.
DETACHURL	Removes hyperlinks from selected objects.
DGNADJUST	Changes the display options of selected DGN underlays.
DGNATTACH	Attaches a DGN underlay to the current drawing.
DGNCLIP	Defines a clipping boundary for a selected DGN underlay.
DGNEXPORT	Creates one or more DGN files from the current drawing.
DGNIMPORT	Imports the data from a DGN file into a new DWG file.
DGNLAYERS	Controls the display of layers in a DGN underlay.
DGNMAPPING	Allows users to create and edit user-defined DGN mapping setups.
DIM and DIM1	Accesses **Dimensioning** mode.
DIMALIGNED	Creates an aligned linear dimension.
DIMANGULAR	Creates an angular dimension.
DIMARC	Creates an arc length dimension.
DIMBASELINE	Creates a linear, angular, or ordinate dimension with base on another dimension.
DIMBREAK	Breaks or restores dimension and extension lines where they cross other objects.
DIMCENTER	Adds a center mark or centerlines to circles and arcs.
DIMCONTINUE	Creates a linear, angular, or ordinate dimension from the second extension line of another dimension.
DIMDIAMETER	Creates a diameter dimension for the selected circle or arc.
DIMDISASSOCIATE	Removes associativity from selected dimensions.
DIMEDIT	Edits dimension text and extension lines on dimension objects.
DIMINSPECT	Adds or removes inspection information for a selected dimension.
DIMJOGGED	Creates jogged radius dimensions.
DIMJOGLINE	Adds or removes a jog line on a linear or aligned dimension.
DIMLINEAR	Creates linear dimensions.
DIMORDINATE	Creates ordinate point dimensions.
DIMOVERRIDE	Overrides dimensioning system variables.
DIMRADIUS	Creates radial dimensions for circles and arcs.
DIMREASSOCIATE	Associates selected dimensions to geometric objects.

DIMREGEN	Updates the locations of all associative dimensions.
DIMSPACE	Adjusts the spacing between linear dimensions or angular dimensions.
DIMSTYLE	Creates and modifies dimension styles.
DIMTEDIT	Moves and rotates dimension text.
DIST	Returns the distance, angle, and axis-specific distance between two points.
DISTANTLIGHT	Creates a distant light.
DIVIDE	Places evenly spaced point objects or blocks along wire-type objects.
DONUT	Draws filled circles and rings.
DRAGMODE	Controls the way dragged objects are displayed.
DRAWINGRECOVERY	Displays a list of drawing files that can be recovered in the event of program or system failure.
DRAWINGRECOVERYHIDE	Closes the **Drawing Recovery Manager.**
DRAWORDER	Changes the order in which coplanar objects are shown to ease their selection.
DSETTINGS	Opens the **Drafting Settings** dialog box to allow specify settings that affect object snap, tracking, and dynamic input.
DSVIEWER	Opens the **Aerial View** window.
DVIEW	Defines parallel projection or perspective views by using a camera and target.
DWFADJUST	Allows adjustment of a DWF underlay from the command line.
DWFATTACH	Attaches a DWF underlay to the current drawing.
DWFCLIP	Uses clipping boundaries to define a subregion of a DWF underlay.
DWFFORMAT	Sets the default DWF format to either DWF or DWFx for the following commands: **PUBLISH, 3DDWF,** and **EXPORT.**
DWFLAYERS	Controls the display of layers in a DWF or DWFx underlay.
DWGPROPS	Sets and displays the properties of the current drawing.
DXBIN	Imports DXB (drawing exchange binary) files.
EATTEDIT	Edits attributes contained in a block.
EATTEXT	Exports block attribute information to a table or to an external file.
EDGE	Changes the visibility of three-dimensional face edges.
EDGESURF	Creates a polygon mesh from four curves placed one next to the other, forming a closed loop.
ELEV	Sets elevation and thickness values of objects subsequently created.
ELLIPSE	Creates an ellipse or an elliptical arc.
ERASE	Removes selected objects from a drawing.
ETRANSMIT	Packages a set of files for Internet transmission.
EXPLODE	Breaks down a selected object into its immediate inferior objects, if any.
EXPORT	Saves objects to other file formats.
EXPORTLAYOUT	Exports all visible objects from the current layout to the model space of the new drawing.
EXPORTTOAUTOCAD	Creates a new DWG file with all AEC objects exploded.
EXTEND	Extends an object to meet the closest boundary object selected in its path.

EXTERNALREFERENCES	Displays the **External References** palette.
EXTERNALREFERENCESCLOSE	Closes the **External References** palette.
EXTRUDE	Creates an extruded 3D solid or surface by extruding a closed or open object, respectively.
FIELD	Creates a multiline text object with a field that can be updated automatically as the field value changes.
FILL	Controls the filling of objects such as hatches, 2D solids, and polylines with width.
FILLET	Rounds and fillets the edges of objects.
FILTER	Specifies the requirements that an object must meet to be included in a selection set.
FIND	Allows finding, replacing, selecting, or zooming to specified text.
FLATSHOT	Creates blocks by projecting all 3D objects onto the current *XY* plane.
FREEPOINT	Creates a target point light without a prompt for the target point.
FREESPOT	Creates a free spotlight, which is similar to a spotlight but without a specified target.
FREEWEB	Creates a free weblight, which is similar to a weblight but without a specified target.
GEOGRAPHICLOCATION	Allows you to set the latitude and longitude of a specific location.
GOTOURL	Opens the file or web page associated with the hyperlink attached to an object.
GRADIENT	Fills an enclosed area or selected object with a gradient fill.
GRAPHSCR	Switches from the text window to the drawing area.
GRID	Displays the grid in the current viewport.
GROUP	Creates and manages saved sets of objects called *groups*.
HATCH	Fills an enclosed area or selected objects with a hatch pattern, solid fill, or gradient fill.
HATCHEDIT	Modifies an existing hatch or fill.
HELIX	Creates a 2D or 3D spiral.
HELP	Displays **Help** menus to find specific information and solutions.
HIDE	Hides obscured lines of 3D objects.
HIDEPALETTES	Hides currently displayed palettes, including the command line.
HLSETTINGS	Opens the **Visual Styles Manager** to change the display properties of lines in a 2D wireframe.
HYPERLINK	Attaches a hyperlink to an object or modifies an existing hyperlink.
HYPERLINKOPTIONS	Controls the display of the hyperlink cursor, tooltips, and shortcut menu.
ID	Returns the coordinates of a location.
IMAGE	Manages images.
IMAGEADJUST	Controls the display of an image's brightness, contrast, and fade values.
IMAGEATTACH	Attaches a new image to the current drawing.
IMAGECLIP	Uses clipping boundaries to define a subregion of an image object.
IMAGEFRAME	Controls whether image frames are displayed and plotted.
IMAGEQUALITY	Controls the display quality of images.
IMPORT	Imports different file formats.

IMPRESSION	Gives a CAD drawing a hand-drawn look by exporting it for rendering in Autodesk Impression.
IMPRINT	Creates temporary edges, imprinted on the faces of a 3D solid.
INSERT	Brings a drawing or named block into the current drawing.
INSERTOBJ	Inserts a linked or embedded object.
INTERFERE	Checks for interferences or shared volume between 3D solids and creates new 3D solids from the interferences.
INTERSECT	Creates composite solids or regions from the intersection of two or more solids or coplanar regions.
ISOPLANE	Specifies the current isometric plane.
JOGSECTION	Adds a jogged segment to a section object.
JOIN	Joins objects to form a single, continuous object.
JPGOUT	Saves selected objects to a file in JPEG file format.
JUSTIFYTEXT	Changes the justification point of selected text objects without changing their locations.
LAYCUR	Changes the layer of selected objects to the current layer.
LAYDEL	Deletes the layer of a selected object together with all objects on the layer, and purges the layer from the drawing.
LAYER	Manages layers and layer properties.
LAYERCLOSE	Closes **Layer Properties Manager** dialog box.
LAYERP	Undoes the last change or set of changes made to layer settings.
LAYERPMODE	Controls whether changes made to the layers are being tracked or not.
LAYERSTATE	Saves, restores, and manages named layer states.
LAYFRZ	Freezes the layer of selected objects.
LAYISO	Isolates the layer of selected objects, turning off all other layers.
LAYLCK	Locks the layers of selected objects.
LAYMCH	Changes the layer of a selected object to match the destination layer.
LAYMCUR	Makes the layer of a selected object current.
LAYMRG	Merges selected layers onto a destination layer.
LAYOFF	Turns off the layer of the selected object.
LAYON	Turns on all layers.
LAYOUT	Creates and modifies drawing Layout tabs.
LAYOUTWIZARD	Creates a new Layout tab and specifies page and plot settings.
LAYTHW	Thaws all layers.
LAYTRANS	Changes a drawing's layers to layer standards you specify.
LAYULK	Unlocks the layer of a selected object.
LAYUNISO	Turns on (unisolates) layers that were turned off with the last **LAYISO** command.
LAYVPI	Isolates an object's layer to the current viewport.
LAYWALK	Dynamically displays layers in a drawing.
LEADER	Creates a leader line connected to an annotation.
LENGTHEN	Changes the length of objects.
LIGHT	Creates a light.
LIGHTLIST	Opens the **Lights in Model** palette to select and modify lights.
LIGHTLISTCLOSE	Closes the **Lights in Model** palette.

LIMITS	Sets and controls the limits of the grid display in the current **Model** or **Layout** tab.
LINE	Creates straight line segments.
LINETYPE	Loads, sets, and modifies linetypes.
LIST	Displays database information for selected objects.
LIVESECTION	Turns on live sectioning for a selected section object.
LOAD	Makes shapes available for use by the SHAPE command.
LOFT	Creates different lofted 3D solids or surfaces by connecting a set of two or more curves.
LOGFILEOFF	Closes the text window log file opened by **LOGFILEON.**
LOGFILEON	Writes the text window contents to a file.
LTSCALE	Sets the global linetype scale factor.
LWEIGHT	Manages the current **Lineweight** settings.
MARKUP	Displays the details of markups and allows you to change their status.
MARKUPCLOSE	Closes the **Markup Set Manager.**
MASSPROP	Calculates the mass properties of regions or 3D solids.
MATCHCELL	Matches the properties between two table cells.
MATCHPROP	Matches the properties of a specific object to other selected objects.
MATERIALATTACH	Attaches materials to objects by layer.
MATERIALMAP	Maps a material to selected objects.
MATERIALS	Manages, applies, and modifies materials in the **Materials** palette.
MATERIALSCLOSE	Closes the **Materials** palette.
MEASURE	Places point objects or blocks at measured intervals on a wire-type object.
MENU	Loads a customization file.
MINSERT	Inserts multiple instances of a block in a rectangular array.
MIRROR	Creates a mirror image copy of objects.
MIRROR3D	Creates a mirror image of objects around an imaginary plane.
MLEADER	Creates a multileader object.
MLEADERALIGN	Organizes selected multileaders along a specified line.
MLEADERCOLLECT	Organizes selected multileaders containing blocks as content into a group attached to a single leader line.
MLEADEREDIT	Adds leader lines to, or removes leader lines from, a multileader object.
MLEADERSTYLE	Creates and modifies multileader styles.
MLEDIT	Edits multiline intersections, breaks, and vertices.
MLINE	Creates multiple parallel lines.
MLSTYLE	Creates, modifies, and manages multiline styles.
MODEL	Switches from a Layout tab to the Model tab.
MOVE	Moves selected objects to a different location.
MREDO	Reverses the effects of several previous **UNDO** or **U** commands.
MSLIDE	Creates a slide file of the current model viewport or the current layout.
MSPACE	Switches from paper space to a model space viewport.
MTEDIT	Edits multiline text.

MTEXT	Creates multiline text objects.
MULTIPLE	Repeats the next command until canceled.
MVIEW	Creates and controls layout viewports.
MVSETUP	Sets up the specifications of a drawing.
NAVSMOTION	Displays the ShowMotion interface.
NAVSMOTIONCLOSE	Closes the ShowMotion interface.
NAVSWHEEL	Displays the SteeringWheels.
NAVVCUBE	Controls the visibility and display properties of the ViewCube.
NETLOAD	Loads a .NET application.
NEW	Creates a new drawing.
NEWSHEETSET	Creates a new sheet set.
NEWVIEW	Expedites the creation of a new view.
NEWSHOT	Creates a named view with motion that is played back when viewed with ShowMotion.
NEWVIEW	Creates a named view with no motion.
OBJECTSCALE	Adds or deletes supported scales for annotative objects.
OFFSET	Creates an object parallel or concentric to the selected object.
OLELINKS	Updates, changes, and cancels existing OLE links.
OLESCALE	Controls the size, scale, and other properties of a selected OLE object.
OOPS	Restores erased objects.
OPEN	Opens an existing drawing file.
OPENDWFMARKUP	Opens a DWF file that contains markups.
OPENSHEETSET	Opens a selected sheet set.
OPTIONS	Customizes the program settings.
ORTHO	Constrains cursor movement to the horizontal or vertical direction.
OSNAP	Sets running object snap modes.
PAGESETUP	Controls the page layout, plotting device, paper size, and other settings for each new layout.
PAN	Displaces the view in the current viewport.
PARTIALOAD	Loads additional geometry into a partially opened drawing.
PARTIALOPEN	Loads geometry and named objects from a selected view or layer into a drawing.
PASTEASHYPERLINK	Inserts data from the clipboard as a hyperlink.
PASTEBLOCK	Pastes copied objects as a block.
PASTECLIP	Pastes data contained in the clipboard.
PASTEORIG	Pastes a copied object in a new drawing using the coordinates from the original drawing.
PASTESPEC	Inserts data from the clipboard and controls the format of the data.
PCINWIZARD	Displays a wizard to import PCP and PC2 configuration file plot settings into the Model tab or current layout.
PEDIT	Edits polylines, 3D polylines, and polygon meshes.
PFACE	Creates a polyface mesh vertex by vertex.
PLAN	Changes the viewing plane to the current *XY* plane.
PLANESURF	Creates a planar surface.
PLINE	Creates a polyline object.
PLOT	Plots a drawing to a plotter, printer, or file with the specified settings.
PLOTSTAMP	Places a plot stamp on a specified corner of each drawing and logs it to a file.

PLOTSTYLE	Sets the current plot style for new objects or assigns a plot style to selected objects.
PLOTTERMANAGER	Displays the **Plotter Manager,** where you can add or edit a plotter configuration.
PNGOUT	Saves selected objects to a file in a Portable Network Graphics (PNG) format.
POINT	Creates a point object.
POINTLIGHT	Creates a point light.
POLYGON	Creates a closed polyline shaped as an equilateral polygon of *n* sides.
POLYSOLID	Creates a 3D polysolid.
PRESSPULL	Presses or pulls bounded areas to create or modify 3D solids.
PREVIEW	Shows the preview image of the printed document.
PROPERTIES	Opens the **Properties** palette to control properties of existing objects.
PROPERTIESCLOSE	Closes the **Properties** palette.
PSETUPIN	Imports a user-defined page setup into a new drawing layout.
PSPACE	Switches from a model space viewport to paper space.
PUBLISH	Publishes drawings to DWF or PDF files or plotters.
PUBLISHTOWEB	Creates HTML pages that include images of selected drawings.
PURGE	Removes unused named elements from the drawing, such as block definitions and layers.
PYRAMID	Creates a pyramid-shaped 3D solid.
QCCLOSE	Closes **QuickCalc.**
QDIM	Creates a dimension quickly.
QLEADER	Creates a leader and leader annotation.
QNEW	Starts a new drawing with the option of using a default drawing template file.
QSAVE	Saves the current drawing using the file format specified in the **Options** dialog box.
QSELECT	Creates a selection set based on filtering criteria.
QTEXT	Controls the display and plotting of text and attribute objects.
QUICKCALC	Opens the **QuickCalc** calculator.
QUICKCUI	Displays the **Customize User Interface** dialog box in a collapsed state.
QUIT	Exits the program.
QVDRAWING	Displays open drawings and layouts in a drawing in preview images.
QVDRAWINGCLOSE	Closes preview images of open drawings and layouts in a drawing.
QVLAYOUT	Displays preview images of model space and layouts in a drawing.
QVLAYOUTCLOSE	Closes preview images of model space and layouts in a drawing.
RAY	Creates lines extending to infinity in one direction.
RECOVER	Repairs a damaged drawing through the opening process.
RECOVERALL	Repairs a damaged drawing and xrefs.
RECTANG	Draws a rectangle-shaped polyline.
REDEFINE	Restores AutoCAD internal commands overridden by **UNDEFINE.**

REDO	Reverses the effects of previous **UNDO** or **U** commands.
REDRAW	Refreshes the display in the current viewport.
REDRAWALL	Refreshes the display in all viewports.
REFCLOSE	Saves back or discards changes made during in-place editing of a reference or a block.
REFEDIT	Allows the selection of an external reference or block reference for editing.
REFSET	Adds or removes objects from a working set during in-place editing of a reference or a block.
REGEN	Regenerates the entire drawing from the current viewport.
REGENALL	Regenerates the drawing and refreshes all viewports.
REGENAUTO	Controls automatic regeneration of a drawing.
REGION	Converts sets of objects that form planar loops into regions object.
REINIT	Reinitializes the digitizer, digitizer input/output port, and program parameters file.
RENAME	Changes the names of objects.
RENDER	Creates a rendered image of the 3D model using the current render settings.
RENDERCROP	Prompts you to specify the portion of the display to be rendered.
RENDERENVIRONMENT	Provides visual cues for the apparent distance of objects.
RENDEREXPOSURE	Provides settings to interactively adjust the global lighting for the most recent rendered output.
RENDERPRESETS	Specifies render presets, reusable rendering parameters, for rendering an image.
RENDERWIN	Displays the **Render** window if a rendered image has been processed in it.
RESETBLOCK	Resets one or more dynamic block references to the default values of the block definition.
RESUME	Continues an interrupted script.
REVCLOUD	Creates a polyline of sequential arcs to form a cloud shape.
REVOLVE	Creates revolved 3D solids or surfaces by revolving 2D objects around an imaginary axis.
REVSURF	Creates a revolved polygon mesh around a selected axis.
RIBBON	Opens the **Ribbon** window.
RIBBONCLOSE	Closes the **Ribbon** window.
ROTATE	Rotates objects around a base point.
ROTATE3D	Rotates objects around an imaginary axis defined anywhere in the 3D space.
RPREF	Allows access to advanced rendering settings in the **Render Settings** palette.
RPREFCLOSE	Closes the **Render Settings** palette if this palette is displayed.
RSCRIPT	Repeats a script file.
RULESURF	Creates a ruled polygon mesh between two curves.
SAVE	Saves the drawing under the current file name or a specified name.
SAVEAS	Saves a copy of the current drawing under a new file name.
SAVEIMG	Saves an image rendered in a viewport to a file.

SCALE	Enlarges or reduces selected objects proportionally in all directions from the base point.
SCALELISTEDIT	Controls the list of scales available for layout viewports, page layouts, and plotting.
SCALETEXT	Enlarges or reduces selected text objects without changing their locations.
SCRIPT	Executes a sequence of commands from a script file.
SECTION	Extracts regions from selected 3D solids by specifying an intersecting imaginary plane.
SECTIONPLANE	Creates a section object that acts as a cutting plane through a 3D object.
SECURITYOPTIONS	Controls security settings using the **Security Options** dialog box.
SELECT	Places selected objects in the **Previous** selection set.
SETBYLAYER	Sets which of the properties are to be overridden to ByLayer for selected objects.
SETIDROPHANDLER	Specifies the default type of i-drop content for the current Autodesk application.
SETVAR	Lists or changes the values of system variables.
SHADEMODE	Starts the **VSCURRENT** command.
SHAPE	Inserts a shape from a shape file that has been loaded using **LOAD.**
SHEETSET	Opens the **Sheet Set Manager.**
SHEETSETHIDE	Closes the **Sheet Set Manager.**
SHELL	Accesses operating system commands.
SHOWPALETTES	Restores the display of hidden palettes.
SIGVALIDATE	Displays information about the digital signature attached to a file.
SKETCH	Creates a series of freehand line segments.
SLICE	Slices 3D solids with an imaginary plane or a surface object.
SNAP	Restricts cursor movement to specified intervals.
SOLDRAW	Generates profiles and sections in viewports created with **SOLVIEW.**
SOLID	Creates solid-filled triangles and quadrilaterals.
SOLIDEDIT	General command to access the 3D solid editing tools.
SOLPROF	Creates profile images of 3D solids in paper space.
SOLVIEW	Creates special floating viewports containing orthographic, auxiliary, or section views of 3D solids.
SPACETRANS	Converts length values between model space and paper space.
SPELL	Checks spelling in a drawing.
SPHERE	Creates a sphere-shaped 3D solid.
SPLINE	Fits a smooth curve to a sequence of points within a specified tolerance.
SPLINEDIT	Edits a spline or spline-fit polyline.
SPOTLIGHT	Creates a spot light.
STANDARDS	Manages the association of standards files with drawings.
STATUS	Displays drawing statistics, modes, and extents.
STLOUT	Stores a solid in an ASCII or binary file.
STRETCH	Stretches portions of objects included in a crossing window.
STYLE	Creates, modifies, or sets named text styles.
STYLESMANAGER	Displays the **Plot Style Manager.**

SUBTRACT	Combines selected coplanar regions or 3D solids by subtraction.
SUNPROPERTIES	Opens the **Sun** window and sets the properties of the sun light.
SUNPROPERTIESCLOSE	Closes the **Sun** window.
SWEEP	Creates a swept 3D solid or surface by sweeping a closed or open curve along a path.
SYSWINDOWS	Arranges windows and icons when the application window is shared with external applications.
TABLE	Creates an empty table object in a drawing.
TABLEDIT	Edits text in a table cell.
TABLEEXPORT	Exports data from a table object in CSV file format.
TABLESTYLE	Defines a new table style.
TABLET	Calibrates, configures, and turns on and off an attached digitizing tablet.
TABSURF	Creates a tabulated polygon mesh from a path curve and a direction vector.
TARGETPOINT	Creates a target point light.
TASKBAR	Controls how drawings are displayed on the Windows taskbar.
TEXT	Creates a single-line text object.
TEXTSCR	Opens the text window.
TEXTTOFRONT	Brings text and dimensions in front of all other objects in the drawing.
THICKEN	Creates 3D solids by thickening selected surfaces.
TIFOUT	Saves selected objects to a file in TIFF file format.
TIME	Displays the date and time statistics of a drawing.
TINSERT	Inserts a block in a table cell.
TOLERANCE	Creates geometric tolerances.
TOOLBAR	Displays, hides, and customizes toolbars.
TOOLPALETTES	Opens the tool palettes.
TOOLPALETTESCLOSE	Closes the tool palettes.
TORUS	Creates a torus-shaped 3D solid.
TPNAVIGATE	Displays a specified tool palette or palette group.
TRACE	Creates solid lines.
TRANSPARENCY	Controls whether background pixels in an image are transparent or opaque.
TRAYSETTINGS	Controls the display of icons and notifications in the status bar tray.
TREESTAT	Displays information about the drawing's current spatial index.
TRIM	Trims objects at a cutting edge defined by other objects.
U	Reverses the most recent operation.
UCS	Manages user coordinate systems.
UCSICON	Controls the visibility and placement of the UCS icon.
UCSMAN	Manages user-defined coordinate systems.
UNDEFINE	Allows an application-defined command to override an internal command.
UNDO	Reverses the effect of commands.
UNION	Combines selected coplanar regions or 3D solids by addition.
UNITS	Controls coordinate and angle display formats and precision.
UPDATEFIELD	Manually updates fields in selected objects in the drawing.

UPDATETHUMBSNOW	Manually updates thumbnail previews for sheets, sheet views, and model space views in the **Sheet Set Manager.**
VBAIDE	Displays the **Visual Basic Editor.**
VBALOAD	Loads a global VBA project into the current work session.
VBAMAN	Loads, unloads, saves, creates, embeds, and extracts VBA projects.
VBARUN	Runs a VBA macro.
VBASTMT	Executes a VBA statement on the AutoCAD command line.
VBAUNLOAD	Unloads a global VBA project.
VIEW	Saves and restores named views, camera views, layout views, and preset views.
VIEWGO	Restores a named view.
VIEWPLAY	Plays the animation associated with a named view.
VIEWPLOTDETAILS	Displays information about completed plot and publish jobs.
VIEWRES	Sets the resolution for objects in the current viewport.
VISUALSTYLES	Creates and modifies visual styles and applies a visual style to a viewport.
VISUALSTYLESCLOSE	Closes the **Visual Styles Manager.**
VLISP	Displays the **Visual LISP** interactive development environment (IDE).
VPCLIP	Clips viewport objects and reshapes the viewport border.
VPLAYER	Sets layer visibility within viewports.
VPMAX	Maximizes the current layout viewport for editing.
VPMIN	Restores the current layout viewport.
VPOINT	Sets the viewing direction in the 3D space.
VPORTS	Creates multiple viewports in model space or paper space.
VSCURRENT	Sets the visual style in the current viewport.
VSLIDE	Displays an image slide file in the current viewport.
VSSAVE	Saves a visual style.
VTOPTIONS	Displays a change in view as a smooth transition.
WALKFLYSETTINGS	Allows the control of settings regarding the 3D **Walk** and 3D **Fly** navigation modes.
WBLOCK	Writes an object or a block to a new drawing file.
WEBLIGHT	Creates a web light.
WEDGE	Creates a wedge-shaped 3D solid with the sloped face tapering along the *X*-axis.
WHOHAS	Displays ownership information for opened drawing files.
WIPEOUT	Covers existing objects with a blank area.
WMFIN	Imports a Windows metafile.
WMFOPTS	Sets options for WMFIN.
WMFOUT	Saves objects to a Windows metafile.
WORKSPACE	Creates, modifies, and saves workspaces and makes a workspace current.
WSSAVE	Saves a workspace.
WSSETTINGS	Sets options for workspaces.
XATTACH	Attaches an external reference to the current drawing.
XBIND	Binds one or more definitions of named objects in an external reference (xref) to the current drawing.

XCLIP	Defines an xref or block clipping boundary and sets the front and back clipping planes.
XEDGES	Creates wireframe geometry by extracting edges from a 3D solid or surface.
XLINE	Creates an infinite line.
XOPEN	Opens a selected xref in a new window.
XPLODE	Breaks a compound object into its component objects.
XREF	Starts the **EXTERNALREFERENCES** command.
ZOOM	Makes objects appear closer or farther in the current viewport.

Appendix C

System Variables

Most of the system variables are controlled in different dialog boxes, palettes, and other windows. They can appear as checkboxes, slide buttons, radial buttons, drop-down lists, or text boxes. They can also be accessed through the command line, however.

The list below provides brief definitions of the AutoCAD® system variables. You can find detailed explanation about some variables in this text. For more details about other system variables, you can use the AutoCAD program's **Help** menus.

3DCONVERSIONMODE	Converts material and light definitions to the current product release.
3DDWFPREC	Controls the smoothness of the 3D objects included in a DWF file.
3DSELECTIONMODE	Controls the selection precedence of visually overlapping objects when using 3D visual styles.
ACADLSPASDOC	Controls the loading of the *acad.lsp* file into every drawing or into only the first drawing opened.
ACADPREFIX	Stores the directory path specified by the **ACAD** environment variable.
ACADVER	Stores the version number of the AutoCAD software.
ACISOUTVER	Controls the ACIS version of SAT files generated with the **ACISOUT** command.
ACTPATH	Specifies the additional paths to use when locating available action macros for playback.
ACTRECORDERSTATE	Specifies the current state of the **Action Recorder.**
ACTRECPATH	Specifies the path used to store new action macros.
ACTUI	Controls the behavior of the **Action Recorder** panel when you are recording and playing back macros.
ADCSTATE	Indicates whether **DesignCenter™** is open or closed.
AFLAGS	Sets options for attributes.
ANGBASE	Sets the base angle to 0 with respect to the current UCS.
ANGDIR	Sets the direction of positive angles.
ANNOALLVISIBLE	Hides or displays annotative objects that do not support the current annotation scale.
ANNOAUTOSCALE	Updates annotative objects to support the annotation scale when the annotation scale is changed.
ANNOTATIVEDWG	Specifies whether the drawing will behave as an annotative block when it is inserted into another drawing.
APBOX	Turns the display of the **AutoSnap™** aperture box on or off.
APERTURE	Controls the display size (in pixels) for the object snap target box.
APSTATE	Stores a value that indicates whether the **Block Authoring Palettes** window is open in the block editor.

AREA	Stores the last value of area calculated by the **AREA** command.
ATTDIA	Controls whether the **INSERT** command uses a dialog box for attribute value entry.
ATTIPE	Controls the display of the in-place editor used to create multiline attributes.
ATTMODE	Controls attribute display.
ATTMULTI	Controls whether multiline attributes can be created.
ATTREQ	Controls whether **INSERT** uses default attribute settings when inserting blocks.
AUDITCTL	Controls whether **AUDIT** creates an audit report file.
AUNITS	Sets units for angles.
AUPREC	Sets the number of decimal places for angular units.
AUTODWFPUBLISH	Controls whether DWF (Design Web Format) files are created automatically when you save or close drawing (DWG) files. The **AUTOPUBLISH** command controls additional options.
AUTOSNAP	Controls the display of the **AutoSnap™** marker, tooltip, and magnet.
BACKGROUNDPLOT	Controls whether background plotting is turned on or off.
BACKZ	Stores the back clipping plane offset (in drawing units) from the target plane for the current viewport.
BACTIONCOLOR	Sets the text color of actions in the block editor.
BDEPENDENCYHIGHLIGHT	Controls whether or not dependent objects are highlighted when editing a block in the block editor.
BGRIPOBJCOLOR	Sets the color of grips in the block editor.
BGRIPOBJSIZE	Sets the display size of custom grips in the block editor.
BINDTYPE	Controls how xref names are handled when binding or editing xrefs in place.
BLIPMODE	Controls whether marker blips are visible.
BLOCKEDITLOCK	Disallows opening of the block editor and editing of dynamic block definitions.
BLOCKEDITOR	Returns whether or not the block editor is open.
BPARAMETERCOLOR	Sets the color of parameters in the block editor.
BPARAMETERFONT	Sets the font used for parameters and actions in the block editor.
BPARAMETERSIZE	Sets the size of parameter text and features in the block editor.
BTMARKDISPLAY	Controls the display of value set markers for dynamic block references.
BVMODE	Controls the display of invisible objects in the block editor.
CALCINPUT	Controls whether or not mathematical expressions and global constants are evaluated in windows and dialog boxes.
CAMERADISPLAY	Turns the display of camera objects.
CAMERAHEIGHT	Specifies the default height for new camera objects.
CANNOSCALE	Sets the name of the current annotation scale for the current space.
CANNOSCALEVALUE	Returns the value of the current annotation scale.
CAPTURETHUMBNAILS	Specifies if and when thumbnails are captured for the **Rewind** tool.
CDATE	Reads calendar date and time.
CECOLOR	Sets the color of new objects.
CELTSCALE	Sets the current object linetype scaling factor.
CELTYPE	Sets the linetype of new objects.

CELWEIGHT	Sets the lineweight of new objects.
CENTERMT	Controls how grips stretch multiline text that is centered horizontally.
CHAMFERA	Sets the first chamfer distance when **CHAMMODE** is set to **0.**
CHAMFERB	Sets the second chamfer distance when **CHAMMODE** is set to **0.**
CHAMFERC	Sets the chamfer length when **CHAMMODE** is set to **1.**
CHAMFERD	Sets the chamfer angle when **CHAMMODE** is set to **1.**
CHAMMODE	Sets the input method for **CHAMFER.**
CIRCLERAD	Sets the default circle radius. A zero indicates no default.
CLAYER	Sets the current layer.
CLEANSCREENSTATE	Stores a value that indicates whether the clean screen state is on.
CLISTATE	Stores a value that indicates whether or not the command line is displayed.
CMATERIAL	Sets the material of new objects. Valid values are BYLAYER, BYBLOCK, and the name of a material in the drawing.
CMDACTIVE	Indicates whether an ordinary command, transparent command, script, or dialog box is active.
CMDDIA	Controls the display of dialog boxes for some commands.
CMDECHO	Controls whether prompts and input are echoed during the **AutoLISP** command function.
CMDINPUTHISTORYMAX	Sets the maximum number of previous input values that are stored for a prompt in a command.
CMDNAMES	Displays the names of the active and transparent commands.
CMLEADERSTYLE	Sets the name of the current multileader style.
CMLJUST	Specifies multiline justification.
CMLSCALE	Controls the overall width of a multiline.
CMLSTYLE	Sets the multiline style.
COMPASS	Controls the display of the 3D compass in the current viewport when the **3D Orbit** tool is activated.
COORDS	Controls the format and update frequency of coordinates on the status line.
COPYMODE	Controls whether the **COPY** command repeats automatically.
CPLOTSTYLE	Controls the current plot style for new objects.
CPROFILE	Displays the name of the current profile.
CROSSINGAREACOLOR	Controls the color of the selection area during crossing selection.
CSHADOW	Sets the shadow display property for a 3D object.
CTAB	Returns the name of the current (Model or Layout) tab in the drawing.
CTABLESTYLE	Sets the name of the current table style.
CURSORSIZE	Determines the size of the crosshairs.
CVPORT	Displays the identification number of the current viewport.
DATALINKNOTIFY	Controls the notification for updated or missing data links.
DATE	Stores the current date and time.
DBCSTATE	Stores the status of the **dbConnect Manager.**
DBLCLKEDIT	Controls the double-click editing behavior in the drawing area. Double-click actions can be customized using the **Customize User Interface** (CUI) editor.

DBMOD	Indicates the drawing modification status.
DCTCUST	Displays the path and file name of the current custom spelling dictionary.
DCTMAIN	Displays the file name of the current main spelling dictionary.
DEFAULTLIGHTING	Controls default lighting in the current viewport.
DEFAULTLIGHTINGTYPE	Specifies the type of default lighting.
DEFLPLSTYLE	Specifies the default plot style for layer 0.
DEFPLSTYLE	Specifies the default plot style for new objects.
DELOBJ	Controls whether objects used to create other objects are retained or deleted.
DEMANDLOAD	Specifies settings about loading certain applications.
DGNFRAME	Determines whether DGN underlay frames are visible or plotted in the current drawing.
DGNIMPORTMAX	Limits the number of elements that are translated when importing a DGN file. This limit prevents the program from running out of memory and suspending when importing large DGN files.
DGNMAPPINGPATH	Stores the location of the dgnsetups.ini file, where DGN mapping setups are stored.
DGNOSNAP	Controls object snapping for geometry in DGN underlays.
DIASTAT	Stores the exit method of the most recently used dialog box.
DIMADEC	Controls the precision for angular dimensions.
DIMALT	Controls the display of alternate units in dimensions.
DIMALTD	Controls the precision for alternate units.
DIMALTF	Controls the multiplier for alternate units.
DIMALTRND	Rounds off the alternate dimension units.
DIMALTTD	Sets the number of decimal places for the tolerance values in the alternate units of a dimension.
DIMALTTZ	Controls suppression of zeros in tolerance values.
DIMALTU	Sets the units format for alternate units of all secondary dimension styles except **Angular.**
DIMALTZ	Controls the suppression of zeros for alternate unit dimension values.
DIMANNO	Indicates whether the current dimension style is annotative.
DIMAPOST	Specifies a text prefix or suffix (or both) for the alternate dimension measurement.
DIMARCSYM	Controls display of the arc symbol in an arc length dimension.
DIMASSOC	Controls the associativity of dimension objects.
DIMASZ	Controls the size of arrowheads.
DIMATFIT	Determines how dimension text and arrows are arranged when there is not sufficient space for both.
DIMAUNIT	Sets the units format for angular dimensions.
DIMAZIN	Suppresses zeros for angular dimensions.
DIMBLK	Sets the arrowhead displayed.
DIMBLK1	Sets the arrowhead for the first end of the dimension line when **DIMSAH** is on.
DIMBLK2	Sets the arrowhead for the second end of the dimension line when **DIMSAH** is on.
DIMCEN	Controls placing center marks with the **DIMCENTER, DIMDIAMETER,** and **DIMRADIUS** commands.
DIMCLRD	Assigns colors to dimension lines, arrowheads, and dimension leader lines.

DIMCLRE	Assigns colors to the extension lines of the dimensions.
DIMCLRT	Assigns colors to dimension text.
DIMDEC	Sets the precision for the primary units of a dimension.
DIMDLE	Sets the distance the dimension line extends beyond the extension line when oblique strokes are drawn instead of arrowheads.
DIMDLI	Controls the spacing of the dimension lines in baseline dimensions.
DIMDSEP	Specifies a single-character decimal separator for decimal unit format.
DIMEXE	Specifies how far to extend the extension line beyond the dimension line.
DIMEXO	Specifies how far extension lines are offset from origin points.
DIMFRAC	Sets the fraction format for architectural or fractional unit formats.
DIMFXL	Sets the total length of the extension lines starting from the dimension line toward the dimension origin.
DIMFXLON	Controls whether extension lines are set to a fixed length.
DIMGAP	Sets the distance around the dimension text when the dimension line breaks to accommodate dimension text.
DIMJOGANG	Determines the angle of the transverse segment of the dimension line in a jogged radius dimension.
DIMJUST	Controls the horizontal positioning of dimension text.
DIMLDRBLK	Specifies the arrow type for leaders.
DIMLFAC	Sets a scale factor for linear dimension measurements.
DIMLIM	Generates dimension limits as the default text.
DIMLTEX1	Sets the linetype of the first extension line.
DIMLTEX2	Sets the linetype of the second extension line.
DIMLUNIT	Sets units for all dimension types except **Angular.**
DIMLWD	Assigns lineweight to dimension lines.
DIMLWE	Assigns lineweight to extension lines.
DIMPOST	Specifies a text prefix and suffix for the dimensions.
DIMRND	Rounds all dimension distances to the specified value.
DIMSAH	Controls the display of dimension line arrowheads.
DIMSCALE	Sets the overall scale factor for the dimension variables.
DIMSD1	Controls suppression of the first dimension line.
DIMSD2	Controls suppression of the second dimension line.
DIMSE1	Suppresses display of the first extension line.
DIMSE2	Suppresses display of the second extension line.
DIMSOXD	Suppresses arrowheads when they do not fit inside the extension lines.
DIMSTYLE	Stores the name of the current dimension style.
DIMTAD	Controls the vertical position of text in relation to the dimension line.
DIMTDEC	Sets the number of decimal places to display in tolerance values for the primary units in a dimension.
DIMTFAC	Specifies a scale factor for the text height of fractions and tolerance values relative to the dimension text.
DIMTFILL	Controls the background of dimension text.
DIMTFILLCLR	Sets the color for the text background in dimensions.
DIMTIH	Controls the position of dimension text inside the extension lines for all dimension types except **Ordinate.**
DIMTIX	Draws text between extension lines.
DIMTM	Sets the lower limit for the dimension tolerance when **DIMTOL** or **DIMLIM** is on.

DIMTMOVE	Sets dimension text movement rules.
DIMTOFL	Controls the placement of a dimension line between extension lines when the text is placed outside.
DIMTOH	Controls the position of dimension text outside extension lines.
DIMTOL	Displays tolerances in dimension text.
DIMTOLJ	Sets the vertical justification for tolerance values relative to the nominal dimension text.
DIMTP	Sets the upper limit for the dimension tolerance when **DIMTOL** or **DIMLIM** is on.
DIMTSZ	Specifies the size of oblique strokes drawn instead of dimension arrowheads.
DIMTVP	Controls the vertical position of dimension text in relation to the dimension line.
DIMTXSTY	Specifies the text style of the dimension.
DIMTXT	Specifies the height of dimension text, unless the current text style height is not zero.
DIMTZIN	Controls the suppression of zeros in tolerance values.
DIMUPT	Controls options for user-positioned text.
DIMZIN	Controls the suppression of zeros in the primary unit value.
DISPSILH	Controls whether or not the silhouette edges of nonplanar faces of a 3D solid are displayed in wireframe visual styles.
DISTANCE	Stores the distance computed by the DIST command.
DONUTID	Sets the default for the inside diameter of a donut.
DONUTOD	Sets the default for the outside diameter of a donut.
DRAGMODE	Controls the display of objects being dragged.
DRAGP1	Sets the regen-drag input sampling rate.
DRAGP2	Sets the fast-drag input sampling rate.
DRAGVS	Sets the visual style while creating 3D solid primitives.
DRAWORDERCTL	Controls the display order of overlapping objects.
DRSTATE	Returns the active status of the **Drawing Recovery** window.
DTEXTED	Specifies the user interface displayed for editing single-line text.
DWFFRAME	Determines whether the DWF underlay frame is visible.
DWFOSNAP	Determines whether object snapping is active for underlay geometry attached to DWF.
DWGCHECK	Checks drawings for potential problems when opening them.
DWGCODEPAGE	Stores the same value as **SYSCODEPAGE** (for compatibility reasons).
DWGNAME	Stores the name of the drawing entered by the user.
DWGPREFIX	Stores the drive/directory prefix for the drawing.
DWGTITLED	Indicates whether the current drawing has been named.
DXEVAL	Controls when data extraction tables are compared against the data source; if the data is not current, displays an update notification.
DYNDIGRIP	Controls the dynamic dimensions displayed during grip editing.
DYNDIVIS	Controls how many dynamic dimensions are displayed during grip editing.
DYNMODE	Turns **Dynamic Input** features on and off.
DYNPICOORDS	Sets whether pointer input uses relative or absolute format for coordinates.
DYNPIFORMAT	Sets whether pointer input uses polar or Cartesian format for coordinates.
DYNPIVIS	Controls when pointer input is displayed.

DYNPROMPT	Controls the display of prompts in **Dynamic Input** tooltips.
DYNTOOLTIPS	Controls which tooltips are affected by tooltip appearance settings.
EDGEMODE	Controls how the **TRIM** and **EXTEND** commands determine cutting and boundary edges.
ELEVATION	Stores the current plane parallel to the current *XY* plane in which new objects are created.
ENTERPRISEMENU	Stores the CUI file name and path.
ERRNO	Displays the number of the appropriate error code when an AutoLISP function call causes an error that the AutoCAD program detects.
ERSTATE	Determines whether the **External References** palette is inactive or active.
EXPERT	Controls the display of certain prompts.
EXPLMODE	Controls whether the **EXPLODE** command supports nonuniformly scaled blocks.
EXTMAX	Stores the upper-right coordinates of the drawing extents.
EXTMIN	Stores the lower-left coordinates of the drawing extents.
EXTNAMES	Sets the parameters for named object names stored in definition tables.
FACETRATIO	Controls the aspect ratio of faceting for cylindrical and conic solids.
FACETRES	Adjusts the smoothness of shaded and rendered objects and objects with hidden lines removed.
FIELDDISPLAY	Controls whether fields are displayed with a gray background.
FIELDEVAL	Controls how fields are updated.
FILEDIA	Suppresses display of file navigation dialog boxes.
FILLETRAD	Stores the current fillet radius.
FILLMODE	Specifies whether hatches and fills, two-dimensional solids, and wide polylines are filled in.
FONTALT	Specifies which alternative font is to be used when the specified font file cannot be located.
FONTMAP	Specifies the font mapping file to be used.
FRONTZ	Stores the front clipping plane offset from the target plane.
FULLOPEN	Indicates whether the current drawing is partially open.
FULLPLOTPATH	Controls whether the full path of the drawing file is sent to the plot spooler.
GEOLATLONGFORMAT	Controls the format of the latitude and longitude values in the **Geographic Location** dialog box, and the coordinate status bar in **Geographic** mode.
GEOMARKERVISIBILITY	Controls the visibility of geographic markers.
GRIDDISPLAY	Controls the display behavior and display limits of the grid.
GRIDMAJOR	Controls the frequency of major grid lines compared to minor grid lines.
GRIDMODE	Specifies whether the grid is turned on or off.
GRIDUNIT	Specifies the *X* and *Y* grid spacing for the current viewport.
GRIPBLOCK	Controls the assignment of grips in blocks.
GRIPCOLOR	Controls the color of exposed, unselected grips.
GRIPDYNCOLOR	Controls the color of custom grips for dynamic blocks.
GRIPHOT	Controls the color of selected grips.
GRIPHOVER	Controls the fill color of an exposed, unselected grip when the cursor hovers over it.

GRIPOBJLIMIT	Suppresses the display of grips when the selection exceeds the specified number of objects.
GRIPS	Controls the use of selection grips.
GRIPSIZE	Sets the size of the grip box in pixels.
GRIPTIPS	Controls the display of grip tips when the cursor hovers over grips on custom objects that support grip tips.
GTAUTO	Controls the display of grips when selecting objects prior to starting a command in a viewport set to a 3D visual style.
GTDEFAULT	Controls whether or not the **3DMOVE** and **3DROTATE** commands start automatically when the **MOVE** and **ROTATE** commands (respectively) are started in a 3D view.
GTLOCATION	Controls the initial location of grip tools when objects are selected prior to running the **3DMOVE** or **3DROTATE** commands.
HALOGAP	Specifies the gap that is displayed where an object is hidden by another object.
HANDLES	Reports whether object handles can be accessed by applications.
HIDEPRECISION	Controls the accuracy of hides and shades.
HIDETEXT	Specifies whether text objects are considered during a **HIDE** command.
HIGHLIGHT	Controls object highlighting.
HPANG	Specifies the hatch pattern angle.
HPASSOC	Controls whether hatch patterns and gradient fills are associative.
HPBOUND	Sets the object type created by the **BHATCH** and **BOUNDARY** commands.
HPDOUBLE	Specifies hatch pattern doubling for user-defined patterns.
HPDRAWORDER	Controls the draw order of hatches and fills.
HPGAPTOL	Allows setting a gap tolerance for open hatch boundaries.
HPINHERIT	Controls the origin of the resulting hatch when using the **Inherit Properties** option.
HPMAXLINES	Controls the maximum number of hatch lines that will generate.
HPNAME	Sets a default hatch pattern name.
HPOBJWARNING	Sets the number of hatch boundary objects that can be selected before displaying a warning message.
HPORIGIN	Allows changing a new hatch origin point for new hatch objects.
HPORIGINMODE	Controls how **HATCH** determines the default hatch origin point.
HPSCALE	Specifies the hatch pattern scale factor.
HPSEPARATE	Controls whether **HATCH** creates a single hatch object or separate hatch objects when filling several closed boundaries.
HPSPACE	Specifies the hatch pattern line spacing for user-defined simple patterns.
HYPERLINKBASE	Specifies the path used for all relative hyperlinks in a drawing.
IMAGEHLT	Controls how the raster image is highlighted.
IMPLIEDFACE	Controls whether or not implied faces are detected.
INDEXCTL	Controls whether layer and spatial indexes are created and saved in drawing files.

INETLOCATION	Stores the Internet location used by the **BROWSER** command and the **Browse the Web** dialog box.
INPUTHISTORYMODE	Controls the history display content and location.
INSBASE	Stores the insertion base point set by the **BASE** command.
INSNAME	Sets a default block name for the **INSERT** command.
INSUNITS	Specifies a value for automatic scaling of blocks, images, or xrefs inserted or attached to a drawing.
INSUNITSDEFSOURCE	Sets source content value when **INSUNITS** is set to **0.**
INSUNITSDEFTARGET	Sets target drawing value when **INSUNITS** is set to **0.**
INTELLIGENTUPDATE	Controls the graphics refresh rate.
INTERFERECOLOR	Sets the ACI color of interference objects.
INTERFEREOBJVS	Sets the visual style for interference objects.
INTERFEREVPVS	Specifies the visual style in the viewport during interference checking.
INTERSECTIONCOLOR	Specifies the color of intersection polylines.
INTERSECTIONDISPLAY	Sets the display of intersection polylines.
ISAVEBAK	Improves the speed of incremental saves, especially for large drawings.
ISAVEPERCENT	Controls the amount of wasted space tolerated in a drawing file.
ISOLINES	Specifies the number of contour lines per surface on objects.
LASTANGLE	Stores the end angle of the last arc entered relative to the *XY* plane of the current UCS.
LASTPOINT	Stores the last point entered.
LASTPROMPT	Stores the last string echoed to the command line.
LATITUDE	Specifies the latitude of the drawing model in decimal format.
LAYEREVAL	Controls when the **Unreconciled New Layer** filter list in the **Layer Properties Manager** dialog box is evaluated for new layers.
LAYEREVALCTL	Controls the overall unreconciled new layer filter list in the **Layer Properties Manager** dialog box, which is evaluated for new layers.
LAYERFILTERALERT	Deletes excessive layer filters to improve performance.
LAYERMANAGERSTATE	Returns value indicating whether the **Layer Properties Manager** dialog box is open or closed.
LAYERNOTIFY	Specifies when an alert displays for new layers that have not yet been reconciled.
LAYLOCKFADECTL	Controls the dimming for objects on locked layers.
LAYOUTREGENCTL	Specifies how the display list is updated in the Model and Layout tabs.
LEGACYCTRLPICK	Specifies the keys for selection cycling and the behavior for CTRL + left-click.
LENSLENGTH	Stores the lens length (in millimeters) used in perspective viewing mode.
LIGHTGLYPHDISPLAY	Controls whether light glyphs are displayed.
LIGHTINGUNITS	Controls whether generic or photometric lights are used, and indicates the current lighting units.
LIGHTLISTSTATE	Indicates the status of the **Lights in Model** palette window.
LIGHTSINBLOCKS	Controls whether lights contained in blocks are used when rendering.
LIMCHECK	Controls the creation of objects outside the grid limits.
LIMMAX	Stores the upper-right grid limits for the current space.
LIMMIN	Stores the lower-left grid limits for the current space.

LINEARBRIGHTNESS	Controls the global brightness level of the drawing in the standard lighting workflow.
LINEARCONTRAST	Controls the global contrast level of the drawing in the standard lighting workflow.
LOCALE	Displays a code that indicates the current locale.
LOCALROOTPREFIX	Stores the path to the folder where customizable files are located.
LOCKUI	Locks the position and size of toolbars and dockable windows.
LOFTANG1	Sets the draft angle at the first cross section in a loft operation.
LOFTANG2	Sets the draft angle at the last cross section in a loft operation.
LOFTMAG1	Sets the magnitude of the draft angle at the first cross section in a loft operation.
LOFTMAG2	Sets the magnitude of the draft angle at the last cross section in a loft operation.
LOFTNORMALS	Controls the normals of a lofted object where it passes through cross sections.
LOFTPARAM	Controls the shape of lofted 3D solids and surfaces.
LOGEXPBRIGHTNESS	Controls the global brightness level of the drawing when using photometric lighting.
LOGEXPCONTRAST	Controls the global contrast level of the drawing when using photometric lighting.
LOGEXPDAYLIGHT	Controls whether exterior daylight is used when using photometric lighting.
LOGEXPMIDTONES	Controls the global midtones level of the drawing when using photometric lighting.
LOGEXPHYSICALSCALE	Controls the relative brightness of self-illuminated materials in a photometric environment.
LOGFILEMODE	Specifies whether the text window content is written to a log file.
LOGFILENAME	Specifies the path and name of the text window log file.
LOGFILEPATH	Specifies the path for the text window log file.
LOGINNAME	Displays the user's name.
LONGITUDE	Specifies the longitude of the drawing model.
LTSCALE	Sets the global linetype scale factor.
LUNITS	Sets linear units.
LUPREC	Sets the precision displayed for all read-only linear units.
LWDEFAULT	Sets the value for the default lineweight.
LWDISPLAY	Controls whether or not the lineweight is displayed.
LWUNITS	Controls the units in which lineweights are displayed.
MATSTATE	Indicates whether the **Materials** window is open.
MAXACTVP	Sets the maximum number of viewports that can be active in a layout.
MAXSORT	Sets the maximum number of symbol and block names sorted by listing commands.
MBUTTONPAN	Controls the behavior of the wheel button of the pointing device.
MEASUREINIT	Controls the default units when a drawing is started from scratch.
MEASUREMENT	Controls whether the current drawing uses imperial or metric hatch pattern and linetype files.
MENUBAR	Controls the display of the menu bar.
MENUCTL	Controls the page switching of the screen menu.
MENUECHO	Sets menu echo and prompt control bits.
MENUNAME	Stores the customization file name and path.

MIRRTEXT	Controls whether or not texts are mirrored with the **MIRROR** command.
MLEADERSCALE	Sets the overall scale factor applied to multileader objects.
MODEMACRO	Displays a text string on the status line.
MSLTSCALE	Scales linetypes displayed on the model tab by the annotation scale.
MSMSTATE	Stores a value indicating whether or not the **Markup Set Manager** is open.
MSOLESCALE	Controls the size of an OLE object with text that is pasted into model space.
MTEXTED	Sets the application to use for editing multiline text objects.
MTEXTFIXED	Sets the display size and position of multiline text.
MTEXTTOOLBAR	Controls the display of the **Text Formatting** toolbar.
MTJIGSTRING	Sets the sample text displayed at the cursor when the **MTEXT** command is started.
MYDOCUMENTSPREFIX	Stores the full path to the My Documents folder.
NAVSWHEELMODE	Specifies the current mode of the SteeringWheel.
NAVSWHEELOPACITYBIG	Controls the opacity of the big SteeringWheels.
NAVSWHEELOPACITYMINI	Controls the opacity of the mini SteeringWheels.
NAVSWHEELSIZEBIG	Specifies the size of the big SteeringWheels.
NAVSWHEELSIZEMINI	Specifies the size of the mini SteeringWheels.
NAVVCUBEDISPLAY	Controls the display of the ViewCube for the current viewport when the 3D graphics system is active.
NAVVCUBELOCATION	Identifies the corner in a viewport where the ViewCube is displayed.
NAVVCUBEOPACITY	Controls the opacity of the ViewCube when it is inactive.
NAVVCUBEORIENT	Controls whether the ViewCube reflects the current UCS or WCS.
NAVVCUBESIZE	Specifies the size of the ViewCube.
NOMUTT	Suppresses the message display.
NORTHDIRECTION	Specifies the angle of the sun from north.
OBSCUREDCOLOR	Specifies the color of obscured lines.
OBSCUREDLTYPE	Specifies the linetype of obscured lines.
OFFSETDIST	Sets the default offset distance.
OFFSETGAPTYPE	Controls how potential gaps between segments are treated when closed polylines are offset.
OLEFRAME	Controls whether a frame is displayed and plotted on all OLE objects in the drawing.
OLEHIDE	Controls the display and plotting of OLE objects.
OLEQUALITY	Sets the default plot quality for OLE objects.
OLESTARTUP	Controls whether the source application of an embedded OLE object loads when plotting.
OPENPARTIAL	Controls whether a drawing can be worked on before it is fully open.
OPMSTATE	Stores a value indicating whether or not the **Properties** palette is open.
ORTHOMODE	Constrains cursor movement to the perpendicular.
OSMODE	Sets running object snaps.
OSNAPCOORD	Controls whether coordinates entered on the command line override object snap settings.
OSNAPNODELEGACY	Controls whether the **Node** object snap can be used to snap to multiline text objects.
OSNAPZ	Controls whether object snaps are automatically projected onto a plane parallel to the *XY* plane of the current UCS at the current elevation.

OSOPTIONS	Automatically suppresses object snaps on hatch objects and when using a dynamic UCS.
PALETTEOPAQUE	Controls whether windows can be made transparent.
PAPERUPDATE	Controls the display of a warning when printing a layout with paper size conflicts.
PDMODE	Controls how point objects are displayed.
PDSIZE	Sets the display size for point objects.
PEDITACCEPT	Suppresses display of the prompt when the selected object is not a polyline in **PEDIT.**
PELLIPSE	Controls the type of ellipse created with the **ELLIPSE** command.
PERIMETER	Stores the last perimeter value computed by the **AREA** or **LIST** commands.
PERSPECTIVE	Specifies whether the current viewport displays a perspective viewing mode.
PERSPECTIVECLIP	Determines the location of eyepoint clipping. The value determines where the eyepoint clipping occurs as a percentage.
PFACEVMAX	Sets the maximum number of vertices per face.
PICKADD	Controls whether the **<Shift>** key is used to add or remove objects from the selection.
PICKAUTO	Controls automatic windowing at the *Select Objects* prompt.
PICKBOX	Sets the object selection target height in pixels.
PICKDRAG	Controls the method of drawing a selection window.
PICKFIRST	Controls whether you select objects before or after you issue a command.
PICKSTYLE	Controls the use of group selection and associative hatch selection.
PLATFORM	Indicates which platform is in use.
PLINEGEN	Sets how linetype patterns are generated at the vertices of a 2D polyline.
PLINETYPE	Specifies whether optimized 2D polylines are used.
PLINEWID	Stores the default polyline width.
PLOTOFFSET	Controls whether the plot offset is relative to the printable area or to the edge of the paper.
PLOTROTMODE	Controls the orientation of plots.
PLQUIET	Controls the display of optional plot-related dialog boxes and nonfatal errors for scripts.
POLARADDANG	Contains user-defined polar angles.
POLARANG	Sets the polar angle increment.
POLARDIST	Sets the snap increment when the **SNAPTYPE** system variable is set to **1** (PolarSnap).
POLARMODE	Controls settings for polar and object snap tracking.
POLYSIDES	Sets the default number of sides for the **POLYGON** command.
POPUPS	Displays the status of the currently configured display driver.
PREVIEWEFFECT	Specifies the visual effect for previewing a selection of objects.
PREVIEWFILTER	Excludes specified object types from selection previewing.
PREVIEWTYPE	Specifies the view to use for the drawing thumbnail.
PRODUCT	Returns the product name.
PROGRAM	Returns the program name.
PROJECTNAME	Assigns a project name to the current drawing.
PROJMODE	Sets the current projection mode for trimming or extending.
PROXYGRAPHICS	Specifies whether images of proxy objects are saved in the drawing.

PROXYNOTICE	Displays a notice when a proxy is created.
PROXYSHOW	Controls the display of proxy objects in a drawing.
PROXYWEBSEARCH	Specifies how the program checks for object enablers.
PSLTSCALE	Controls paper space linetype scaling.
PSOLHEIGHT	Controls the default height for a swept 3D solid created with the **POLYSOLID** command.
PSOLWIDTH	Controls the default width for a swept 3D solid created with the **POLYSOLID** command.
PSTYLEMODE	Indicates whether the current drawing is in a **Color Dependent** or **Named Plot Style** mode.
PSTYLEPOLICY	Controls whether an object's color property is associated with its plot style.
PSVPSCALE	Sets the view scale factor for all newly created viewports.
PUBLISHALLSHEETS	Controls how the Publish dialog box list is populated when the **PUBLISH** command is invoked.
PUBLISHCOLLATE	Controls whether sheets are published as a single job.
PUBLISHHATCH	Controls whether hatch patterns published in DWF format (DWF file or DWFx file) are treated as a single object when they are opened in Autodesk Impression.
PUCSBASE	Stores the UCS that defines the origin and orientation of orthographic UCS settings in paper space only.
QCSTATE	Determines whether **QuickCalc** is active or not.
QPLOCATION	Sets the location mode of the **Quick Properties** panel.
QPMODE	Sets the on or off state of the **Quick Properties** panel.
QTEXTMODE	Controls how text is displayed.
QVDRAWINGPIN	Controls the default display state of preview images of drawings.
QVLAYOUTPIN	Controls the default display state of preview images of model space and layouts in a drawing.
RASTERDPI	Controls paper size and plot scaling when switching between dimensional and dimensionless output devices.
RASTERPERCENT	Sets the maximum percentage of available virtual memory that is allowed for plotting a raster image.
RASTERPREVIEW	Specifies whether BMP preview images are saved with the drawing.
RASTERTHRESHOLD	Specifies a raster threshold in megabytes. If the plotted raster image exceeds this threshold, the availability of system memory is checked.
RECOVERYMODE	Controls whether recovery information on a drawing is recorded after a system failure.
REFEDITNAME	Displays the name of the reference being edited.
REGENMODE	Controls automatic regeneration of the drawing.
RE-INIT	Reinitializes the digitizer, digitizer port, and *acad.pgp* file.
REMEMBERFOLDERS	Sets the default path displayed in standard file selection dialog boxes.
RENDERPREFSSTATE	Stores a value that indicates the status of the **Render Settings** palette.
RENDERUSERLIGHTS	Controls whether to override the setting for viewport lighting during rendering.
REPORTERROR	Controls whether an error report can be sent to Autodesk, Inc. if the program closes unexpectedly.
RIBBONSTATE	Indicates whether the **Ribbon** palette is open or closed.
ROAMABLEROOTPREFIX	Stores the path to the root folder where customizable files are installed.
ROLLOVERTIPS	Controls the display of object rollover tooltips in the application. The content in tooltips can be customized in the **Customize User Interface** (CUI) editor.

RTDISPLAY	Controls the display of raster images and OLE objects during **Realtime ZOOM** or **PAN.**
SAVEFIDELITY	Controls whether the drawing is saved with visual fidelity.
SAVEFILE	Stores the current automatic save file name.
SAVEFILEPATH	Specifies the path to the directory for all automatic save files.
SAVENAME	Stores the file name and path of the most recently saved drawing.
SAVETIME	Sets the automatic save interval in minutes.
SCREENBOXES	Stores the number of boxes in the screen menu area of the drawing area.
SCREENMODE	Indicates the state of the display.
SCREENSIZE	Stores the current viewport size in pixels.
SELECTIONANNODISPLAY	Controls whether alternate scale representations are temporarily displayed in a dimmed state when an annotative object is selected.
SELECTIONAREA	Controls the display of effects for selection areas.
SELECTIONAREAOPACITY	Controls the transparency of the window and crossing window selection boxes.
SELECTIONPREVIEW	Controls the display of selection previewing.
SETBYLAYERMODE	Controls which properties are selected for SETBYLAYER.
SHADEDGE	Controls the shading of edges in rendering.
SHADEDIF	Sets the ratio of diffuse reflective light to ambient light.
SHADOWPLANELOCATION	Controls the location of an invisible ground plane where shadows are cast.
SHORTCUTMENU	Controls whether **Default, Edit,** and **Command** mode shortcut menus are available in the drawing area.
SHOWHIST	Controls the **Show History** property for solids in a drawing.
SHOWLAYERUSAGE	Displays icons in the **Layer Properties Manager** that indicate whether layers are in use.
SHOWMOTIONPIN	Controls the default display state of the thumbnail shots.
SHPNAME	Sets a default shape name.
SIGWARN	Controls whether a warning is displayed when a file with an attached digital signature is opened.
SKETCHINC	Sets the record increment for the **SKETCH** command.
SKPOLY	Controls whether the **SKETCH** command generates lines or polylines.
SNAPANG	Sets the snap and grid rotation angle relative to the current UCS.
SNAPBASE	Sets the snap and grid origin point relative to the current UCS.
SNAPISOPAIR	Controls the isometric plane for the current viewport.
SNAPMODE	Turns the **Snap** mode on and off.
SNAPSTYL	Sets the snap style for the current viewport.
SNAPTYPE	Sets the type of snap for the current viewport.
SNAPUNIT	Sets the snap spacing for the current viewport.
SOLIDCHECK	Turns the solid validation on or off for the current session.
SOLIDHIST	Controls the **History** property setting for new and existing objects.
SORTENTS	Controls object sorting in support of draw order for several operations.
SPLFRAME	Controls the display of splines and spline-fit polylines.
SPLINESEGS	Sets the number of line segments for each spline-fit polyline.

SPLINETYPE	Sets the type of curve generated by the **Spline** option of the **PEDIT** command.
SSFOUND	Displays the sheet set path and the file name.
SSLOCATE	Locates and opens the sheet set associated with a drawing when it is opened.
SSMAUTOOPEN	Displays the **Sheet Set Manager** when a drawing associated with a sheet is opened.
SSMPOLLTIME	Controls the time interval between automatic refreshes of the status data in a sheet set.
SSMSHEETSTATUS	Controls how the status data in a sheet set is refreshed.
SSMSTATE	Returns the status of the **Sheet Set Manager** window.
STANDARDSVIOLATION	Specifies whether a user is notified of standards violations in the current drawing.
STARTUP	Controls whether the **Create New Drawing** dialog box is displayed when starting a new drawing.
STATUSBAR	Controls the display of the **Application and Drawing Status** toolbars.
STEPSIZE	Specifies the step size in the **Walk** 3D navigation mode.
STEPSPERSEC	Specifies the number of steps taken per second in the **Walk** 3D navigation mode.
SUNPROPERTIESSTATE	Indicates whether the **Sun Properties** window is open.
SUNSTATUS	Indicates whether the sun is casting light in the current viewport.
SURFTAB1	Sets the number of tabulations for the **RULESURF** and **TABSURF** commands.
SURFTAB2	Sets the polygon mesh density in the *N* direction for the **REVSURF** and **EDGESURF** commands.
SURFTYPE	Controls the type of surface that the polygon mesh is made to fit with the **PEDIT** command.
SURFU	Sets the faceted surface density for the **PEDIT** command's **Smooth** option in the *M* direction and the number of U isolines on surfaces.
SURFV	Sets the faceted surface density for the **PEDIT** command's **Smooth** option in the *N* direction and the number of V isolines on surfaces.
SYSCODEPAGE	Indicates the system code page.
TABLEINDICATOR	Controls the display of row numbers and column letters when the **In-Place Text Editor** is in use.
TABLETOOLBAR	Controls the display of the **Table** toolbar.
TABMODE	Controls the use of the tablet.
TARGET	Stores the location of the target point for the current viewport.
TBCUSTOMIZE	Controls whether toolbars can be customized.
TDCREATE	Stores the local time and date on which the drawing was created.
TDINDWG	Stores the total editing time.
TDUCREATE	Stores the universal time and date on which the drawing was created.
TDUPDATE	Stores the local time and date of the last update/save.
TDUSRTIMER	Stores the user-elapsed timer.
TDUUPDATE	Stores the universal time and date of the last update/save.
TEMPOVERRIDES	Turns temporary override keys on and off.
TEMPPREFIX	Contains the name of the directory configured for placement of temporary files.
TEXTEVAL	Controls how entered text strings are evaluated.
TEXTFILL	Controls the filling of TrueType fonts while plotting and rendering.

TEXTOUTPUTFILEFORMAT	Provides **Unicode** options for plot and text window log files.
TEXTQLTY	Controls the resolution tessellation fineness of text outlines for TrueType fonts while plotting and rendering.
TEXTSIZE	Sets the default height for new text objects drawn with the current text style.
TEXTSTYLE	Sets the name of the current text style.
THICKNESS	Sets the current 3D thickness.
THUMBSIZE	Specifies the maximum generated size for thumbnail previews in pixels.
TILEMODE	Makes the Model tab or the last Layout tab current.
TIMEZONE	Sets the time zone for the sun in the drawing.
TOOLTIPMERGE	Combines drafting tooltips into a single tooltip.
TOOLTIPS	Controls the display of tooltips.
TPSTATE	Determines whether or not the **Tool Palettes** window is active.
TRACEWID	Sets the default trace width.
TRACKPATH	Controls the display of polar and object snap tracking alignment paths.
TRAYICONS	Controls whether a tray is displayed on the status bar.
TRAYNOTIFY	Controls whether service notifications are displayed in the status bar tray.
TRAYTIMEOUT	Controls the length of time to display service notifications.
TREEDEPTH	Specifies the maximum depth.
TREEMAX	Limits memory consumption during drawing regeneration.
TRIMMODE	Controls whether selected edges for chamfers and fillets are trimmed.
TSPACEFAC	Controls the line spacing of the multiline text.
TSPACETYPE	Controls the type of line spacing used in multiline text.
TSTACKALIGN	Controls the vertical alignment of stacked text.
TSTACKSIZE	Controls the percentage of stacked text fraction height.
UCSAXISANG	Stores the default angle when rotating the UCS around the *X*-, *Y*-, or *Z*-axis.
UCSBASE	Stores the name of the UCS defining the origin and orientation of orthographic UCS settings.
UCSDETECT	Controls whether or not dynamic UCS acquisition is active.
UCSFOLLOW	Changes the current viewing plane to the *XY* plane of the selected UCS.
UCSICON	Controls the display of the UCS icon.
UCSNAME	Stores the name of the current coordinate system.
UCSORG	Stores the origin point of the current coordinate system.
UCSORTHO	Determines whether the related orthographic UCS is automatically restored when an orthographic view is selected.
UCSVIEW	Determines whether the current UCS is saved with a named view.
UCSVP	Determines whether the UCS in viewports remains fixed or changes to reflect the UCS of the current viewport.
UCSXDIR	Stores the *X* direction of the current UCS.
UCSYDIR	Stores the *Y* direction of the current UCS.
UNDOCTL	Returns the state of the **Auto**, **Control**, and **Group** options of the **UNDO** command.
UNDOMARKS	Stores the number of marks placed in the **UNDO** control stream by the **Mark** option.

UNITMODE	Controls the display format for units.
UPDATETHUMBNAIL	Controls the updating of thumbnail previews in the **Sheet Set Manager.**
USERI1-5	Provides storage and retrieval of integer values.
USERR1-5	Provides storage and retrieval of real numbers.
USERS1-5	Provides storage and retrieval of text string data.
VIEWCTR	Stores the center of view in the current viewport.
VIEWDIR	Stores the viewing direction in the current viewport.
VIEWMODE	Stores the view mode for the current viewport.
VIEWSIZE	Stores the height of the view displayed in the current viewport.
VIEWTWIST	Stores the view twist angle for the current viewport.
VISRETAIN	Controls the properties of xref-dependent layers.
VPLAYEROVERRIDES	Indicates if there are any layers with viewport (VP) property overrides for the current layout viewport.
VPLAYEROVERRIDESMODE	Controls whether layer property overrides associated with layout viewports are displayed and plotted.
VPMAXIMIZEDSTATE	Stores a value that indicates whether the viewport is maximized.
VSBACKGROUNDS	Controls whether backgrounds are displayed in the visual style applied to the current viewport.
VSEDGECOLOR	Sets the color of edges in the visual style of the current viewport.
VSEDGEJITTER	Controls the degree to which lines appear as though sketched with a pencil.
VSEDGEOVERHANG	Specifies the amount of edge overhang in pixels.
VSEDGES	Controls the types of edges that are displayed in the viewport.
VSEDGESMOOTH	Specifies the angle at which crease edges are displayed.
VSFACECOLORMODE	Controls how the color of faces is calculated.
VSFACEHIGHLIGHT	Controls the display of specular highlights on faces.
VSFACEOPACITY	Controls the transparency of faces in the current viewport.
VSFACESTYLE	Controls how faces are displayed in the current viewport.
VSHALOGAP	Sets the halo gap in the visual style applied to the current viewport.
VSHIDEPRECISION	Controls the accuracy of hides and shades in the visual style.
VSINTERSECTIONCOLOR	Specifies the color of intersection polylines in the visual style.
VSINTERSECTIONEDGES	Controls the display of intersection edges in the visual style.
VSINTERSECTIONLTYPE	Controls whether intersection lines are displayed, and also sets their linetype.
VSISOONTOP	Displays isolines on top of shaded objects in the visual style.
VSLIGHTINGQUALITY	Sets the lighting quality in the current viewport.
VSMATERIALMODE	Controls the display of materials in the current viewport.
VSMAX	Stores the upper-right corner of the current viewport's virtual screen.
VSMIN	Stores the lower-left corner of the current viewport's virtual screen.
VSMONOCOLOR	Sets the color for monochrome and tint display of faces in the visual style.
VSOBSCUREDCOLOR	Specifies the color of obscured lines in the visual style.
VSOBSCUREDEDGES	Controls whether obscured edges are displayed.

VSOBSCUREDLTYPE	Specifies the linetype of obscured lines in the visual style.
VSSHADOWS	Controls whether a visual style displays shadows.
VSSILHEDGES	Controls the display of silhouette curves of 3D solids in the visual style.
VSSILHWIDTH	Specifies the width in pixels of silhouette edges.
VSSTATE	Stores a value that indicates whether the **Visual Styles** palette is open.
VTDURATION	Sets the duration of a smooth view transition in milliseconds.
VTENABLE	Controls when smooth view transitions are used.
VTFPS	Sets the minimum speed of a smooth view transition in frames per second.
WHIPARC	Determines whether the display of circles and arcs is smooth.
WHIPTHREAD	Controls the use of an additional processor to improve the speed of operations that regenerate the drawing.
WINDOWAREACOLOR	Controls the color of the transparent selection area during window selection.
WMFBKGND	Controls the background display of objects inserted from a Windows metafile file format.
WMFFOREGND	Controls the assignment of the foreground color of objects inserted from a Windows metafile file format.
WORLDUCS	Indicates whether the UCS is the same as the WCS.
WORLDVIEW	Determines whether input to the **3DORBIT**, **DVIEW**, and **VPOINT** commands is relative to the WCS or to the current UCS.
WRITESTAT	Indicates whether a drawing file is read-only.
WSCURRENT	Returns the current workspace name in the command line interface and sets a workspace to current.
XCLIPFRAME	Controls the visibility of xref clipping boundaries.
XEDIT	Controls whether the current drawing can be edited in-place when referenced by another drawing.
XFADECTL	Controls the fading intensity percentage for references edited in-place.
XLOADCTL	Turns xref demand loading on and off.
XLOADPATH	Creates a path for storing temporary copies of demand-loaded xref files.
XREFCTL	Controls whether external reference log files are created.
XREFNOTIFY	Controls the notification for updated or missing xrefs.
XREFTYPE	Controls the default reference type when you attach or overlay an external reference.
ZOOMFACTOR	Controls the magnification increment value when the mouse wheel is rotated.
ZOOMWHEEL	Toggles the direction zoom operations when you scroll the mouse wheel.

GLOSSARY

3D Orbit: The most useful viewing tool for quickly selecting any viewing point. With this simple-to-use tool, you can look at the objects from virtually any point in the 3D space.

3D polyline: A curve placed in the 3D space that does not belong to a plane. It can contain only straight segments and cannot be filleted.

animation: A video file created by recording successive positions of the 3D model, giving the impression of movement when replayed.

attenuation: Proportional reduction of light intensity over distance. You can select three different attenuations for point lights and spot lights: **None, Inverse Linear,** and **Inverse Square**.

AutoTrack: A powerful drafting tool that allows you to find points or to align objects along specified directions named traces, instead of snapping directly to the objects. It is especially useful when placing 3D geometry in an orthogonal view, because the depth, or *Z* coordinate, is ignored.

Boolean operations: Union, subtract, and intersect operations that are performed on regions and 3D solids. The term is also used in algebra to define logical operations (AND, OR, XOR, and NOT), which resemble the operations performed with this group of tools in the AutoCAD® program.

camera: An object that encapsulates the geometric definitions of a particular view. A model view is created with each camera, which allows you to quickly change the viewing point as defined by the camera.

composite 3D solids: 3D solids obtained by combining 3D solids using one of the three Boolean operations UNION, SUBTRACT, or INTERSECT.

default lighting: The default illumination provided by the AutoCAD program. It uses two distant light sources that follow the view direction.

direct distance entry: A practical method of specifying the coordinates of the next point by entering a distance while the cursor indicates a specific known direction. Using this method, you simply enter **3** while the cursor points toward the positive *X*-axis, instead of having to enter **@0,3** or **@3>0**.

facets: Edges or subdivisions of a 3D solid's nonplanar faces and nonplanar surfaces, produced by internal calculations of the AutoCAD program.

floating viewport: A viewport entity created in paper space, through which you can display any view of the objects contained in the model space.

helix: 2D or 3D spiral curve that coils around an axis, gradually growing horizontally, vertically, or in both directions. 2D spiral curves grow only horizontally.

history: Original 3D solids involved in the Boolean operations of a composite 3D solid. A composite 3D solid can be modified by modifying its history.

hotspot angle and falloff angle: The angles of the inner and outer cones defining the characteristics of the light rays emitted by a spot light. The intensity of light inside the inner cone is always the same, whereas that inside the outer cone diminishes in intensity from the hotspot angle to the falloff angle.

imaginary axis of revolution: The vector, defined by specifying any two points, about which the objects are revolved. Its direction is defined from the first point to the second point.

imaginary axis of rotation: An imaginary vector defined by specifying two points, or a direction vector and a point, about which the objects are rotated. It is the equivalent of the point in a 2D rotation.

imaginary mirror plane: Imaginary plane about which the selected object is copied to the opposite side as a mirror image. It is the equivalent of the mirror line in a 2D mirror operation.

imaginary sectioning plane: Imaginary plane that defines a section through 3D solids as it crosses these objects. To define a plane in the 3D space it is necessary to specify one of the following: three points, another plane and a point, or a vector.

imaginary slicing plane: Imaginary plane with which 3D solid objects are cut. To define a plane in 3D space it is necessary to specify one of the following: three points, another plane and a point, or a vector.

isometric view: A 3D drawing view in which the three principal dimensions of the objects are aligned with three axes 120° apart as they project onto the viewing plane.

LOFT: Operation in which a set of open or closed objects are connected through a blended smooth transition, creating 3D solids and surfaces.

model view: A combination of geometric specifications that define a view plus additional elements such as UCS, layer snapshot, and visual style.

motion paths: User-created routes through which the camera, the target, or both gradually move while the camera keeps its focus on the target.

move grip tool: Editing tool that allows you to choose among six movements along one of the three axes and parallel to one of the three planes.

nonplanar curve: A curve placed throughout the 3D space that is not completely contained in a plane. Helixes are examples of nonplanar curves.

obscured lines: Edges or other objects that cannot be seen from the current viewing point because of their position relative to other objects. Obscured lines can be removed by invoking the **HIDE** command.

orthographic UCS: A particular type of reorientation of the WCS in which the *XY* plane aligns parallel to the imaginary orthographic viewing planes. The six orthographic UCS are predefined in the AutoCAD program, so you can quickly select them.

orthographic view: View in which objects are seen from a viewing point perpendicular to the orthographic imaginary planes. According to drafting standards, three orthographic views are used to describe the dimensions and shape of objects: Top, Front, and Right.

perspective view: View in which the 3D objects represented give the impression not only of height, width, and depth, but also of relative distance from the viewing point to the viewing target.

point filters: A method of entering a point by which the *X*, *Y*, and *Z* coordinates are given in separate stages using any combination. The different stages can contain information about a single coordinate or the combination of any two coordinates.

polygon mesh: Surface object composed of individual three- or four-sided polygons joined one with the other. The mesh is organized by an N × M matrix. A polygon mesh can be either open or closed in either of the two directions.

predefined visual styles: Predefined collections of settings, saved as visual styles, that control the display of edges and faces of 3D objects. There are five predefined visual styles: **2D Wireframe, 3D Hidden, 3D Wireframe, Conceptual**, and **Realistic**.

Render Preset: A named collection of settings controlling the quality of the rendered image generated with the **RENDER** command.

Ribbon: A special palette that provides a single, compact placement for the tools and commands needed for a particular workspace. The **Ribbon** is made of tabs and panels that are totally customizable.

right-hand rule: A method used to remember the unchangeable relationship between the three axes of the coordinate system and the positive rotation about them. It is based on placing the thumb, the index finger, and middle finger 90° from each other to determine the positive direction of any third axis, or curling all the fingers around the thumb to determine the positive rotation about any vector whose direction is known.

rotation grip tool: Editing tool that enables you to choose between three directions of rotation that are aligned with the axes of the current UCS.

section object: An AutoCAD entity that allows you to temporarily slice 3D objects and create 2D and 3D sections from them. Section objects are created with the **SECTIONPLANE** command.

ShapeManager: Modeler or engine used by the AutoCAD program to change the form and appearance of 3D solids. After each edit operation, the system checks whether the 3D solid is still a valid ShapeManager solid.

silhouette: Outline that defines the limit or profile of the curved faces of an object in the 3D space, causing it to look more real. Silhouettes are not physical edges.

spline: Nonplanar continuous curve that goes through a set of points specified anywhere in the 3D space. This object is created with the **SPLINE** command.

spline-fit polyline: Polylines and 3D polylines after they have been transformed by the **Spline** option of the **PEDIT** command. As the name implies, spline-fit polylines are not real splines, but approximations to them.

subobject: Any face, edge, or vertex of a 3D solid. The original 3D solids of a composite 3D solid can be considered to be subobjects as well. Subobjects are selected by holding down the <**Ctrl**> key.

SWEEP: Operation in which open or closed planar objects are passed through a curve, creating 3D solids and surfaces.

tapering midplane: The cross section in the 3D solid that does not change its original dimensions when the **Taper faces** operation is performed. In the argot of mold design, it is known as the *parting line*.

template: Predefined collection of specific properties and property settings that gives a material a specific appearance.

Tool Palettes: Customizable AutoCAD window that allows the user to organize tools and many other settings by palettes. You can add a tool by dragging objects into a palette. You can create a tool palette by right-clicking on the **Tool Palettes** title bar and selecting **New Palette**.

User Coordinate System (UCS): The WCS after it has been reoriented using one of many possible methods. In 3D operations it is essential to relocate the coordinate system throughout the 3D space in order to create the objects.

viewing point: The point in the 3D space that establishes the viewing direction of the user. The viewing direction is considered to be a vector from the viewing point to the origin of the coordinate system.

viewports: Areas into which the model space is divided. You can use existing viewport configurations or create new ones.

visual style: A collection of settings or modifiers that control the display of edges and shading of 3D objects. Visual styles can be created and modified in the **Visual Style Manager** palette.

workspaces: Specific arrangements of user interface elements, including their contents, properties, display status, and locations. Workspaces allow you to quickly switch between specific arrangements of menus, toolbars, and dockable windows, as well as many other settings previously specified.

World Coordinate System (WCS): The AutoCAD program's reference coordinate system, which serves as a reference for all other coordinate systems. This is the default coordinate system for any new drawing, and the one in which most 2D work is done.

Index